W9-AVJ-080

America Reads Seventh Edition

Patterns in Literature

America Reads Seventh Edition

Beginnings in Literature
Alan L. Madsen
Sarah Durand Wood
Philip M. Connors

Discoveries in Literature
Edmund J. Farrell
Ruth S. Cohen
L. Jane Christensen

Explorations in Literature
Ruth S. Cohen
Nancy C. Millett
Raymond J. Rodrigues

Patterns in Literature
Edmund J. Farrell
Ouida H. Clapp
Karen J. Kuehner

Traditions in Literature
James E. Miller, Jr.
Helen McDonnell
Russell J. Hogan

The United States in Literature
The Red Badge of Courage Edition
Three Long Stories Edition
James E. Miller, Jr.
Carlota Cárdenas de Dwyer
Kerry M. Wood

England in Literature
Macbeth Edition
Hamlet Edition
Helen McDonnell
John Pfordresher
Gladys V. Veidemanis

Testbooks

Guidebooks

America Reads Seventh Edition

Patterns in Literature

Edmund J. Farrell

Ouida H. Clapp

Karen J. Kuehner

Scott, Foresman and Company

Editorial Offices: Glenview, Illinois
Regional Offices: Sunnyvale, California
Tucker, Georgia
Glenview, Illinois
Oakland, New Jersey
Dallas, Texas

Edmund J. Farrell Professor, English Education, University of Texas, Austin. Formerly: Associate Executive Director, National Council of Teachers of English (NCTE); Chairman, English Department, James Lick High School, San Jose, California; Chairman, NCTE Commission on Literature; recipient, NCTE Distinguished Service Award.

Ouida H. Clapp Formerly Director of Language Arts for the public schools of Buffalo, New York. Co-Chair, Committee on American Literature and the American Multicultural Heritage, NCTE. Member, NCTE Advisory Board on Publications for Students. Editor, 1975–1977, NCTE *Classroom Practices in the Teaching of English*. Past President and Fellow, New York State English Council.

Karen J. Kuehner Teacher of English, Glenbrook South High School, Glenview, Illinois. Formerly teacher of English at Evanston Township High School, Evanston, Illinois. Teacher at Institute of Education, Shanghai, People's Republic of China, 1980–1981.

Cover: *Nantucket Harbor* (detail) crewel point used with special permission from Erica Wilson. From Erica Wilson Needleworks, 717 Madison Avenue, New York, NY 10021

Pronunciation key and dictionary entries are from *Scott, Foresman Advanced Dictionary* by E. L. Thorndike and Clarence L. Barnhart. Copyright © 1983 Scott, Foresman and Company.

ISBN: 0-673-27053-X

2345678910-VHJ-93929190898887

Table of Contents

Unit 1

The First Short Story Unit

Unit 2

Modern Drama

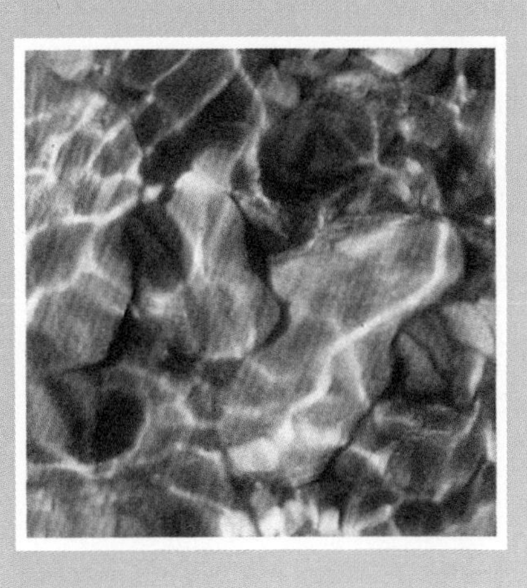

Unit 3

Poetry

Unit 4

Shakespearean Drama

Unit 5

The Second Short Story Unit

Unit 6

Greek Drama

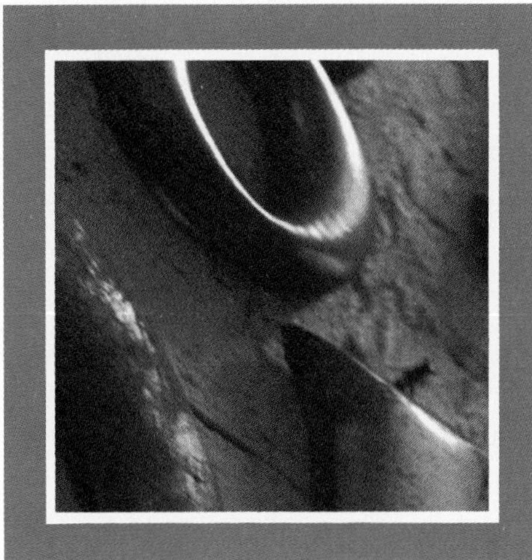

Unit 7

Prose Forms

Unit 8

The Novel

Handbook of Literary Terms

Composition Guide

Unit 1

The First Short Story Unit

See **POINT OF VIEW** Handbook of Literary Terms

A Death in the House

Clifford D. Simak

The doctor won't treat it, and later the town officials won't bury it. But Mose feels that the creature he's found deserves a decent burial—even if it doesn't look human.

Old Mose Abrams was out hunting cows when he found the alien. He didn't know it was an alien, but it was alive and it was in a lot of trouble and Old Mose, despite everything the neighbors said about him, was not the kind of man who could bear to leave a sick thing out there in the woods.

It was a horrid-looking thing, green and shiny, with some purple spots on it; and it was repulsive even twenty feet away. And it stank.

It had crawled, or tried to crawl, into a clump of hazel brush, but hadn't made it. The head part was in the brush and the rest lay out there naked in the open. Every now and then the parts that seemed to be arms and hands clawed feebly at the ground, trying to force itself deeper in the brush, but it was too weak; it never moved an inch.

It was groaning, too, but not too loud—just the kind of keening sound a lonesome wind might make around a wide, deep eave. But there was more in it than just the sound of winter wind; there was a frightened, desperate note that made the hair stand up on Old Mose's nape.

Old Mose stood there for quite a spell, making up his mind what he ought to do about it, and a while longer after that working up his courage, although most folks offhand would have said that he had plenty. But this was the sort of situation that took more than just ordinary screwed-up courage. It took a lot of foolhardiness.

But this was a wild, hurt thing and he couldn't leave it there, so he walked up to it and knelt down. It was pretty hard to look at, though there was a sort of fascination in its repulsiveness that was hard to figure out—as if it were so horrible that it dragged one to it. And it stank in a way that no one had ever smelled before.

Mose, however, was not finicky. In the neighborhood, he was not well known for fastidiousness. Ever since his wife had died almost ten years before, he had lived alone on his untidy farm, and the housekeeping that he did was the scandal of all the neighbor women. Once a year, if he got around to it, he sort of shoveled out the house; but the rest of the year he just let things accumulate.

So he wasn't as upset as some might have been with the way the creature smelled. But the sight of it upset him; and it took him quite a while before he could bring himself to touch it; and when he finally did, he was considerably surprised. He had been prepared for it to be either cold or slimy, or maybe even both. But it was neither. It was warm and hard and it had a

clean feel to it, and he was reminded of the way a green cornstalk would feel.

He slid his hand beneath the hurt thing and pulled it gently from the clump of hazel brush and turned it over so he could see its face. It hadn't any face. It had an enlargement at the top of it, like a flower on top of a stalk, although its body wasn't any stalk, and there was a fringe around this enlargement that wiggled like a can of worms; and it was then that Mose almost turned around and ran.

But he stuck it out.

He squatted there, staring at the no-face with the fringe of worms; and he got cold all over and his stomach doubled up on him and he was stiff with fright—and the fright got worse when it seemed to him that the keening of the thing was coming from the worms.

Mose was a stubborn man. One had to be stubborn to run a runty farm like this. Stubborn and insensitive in a lot of ways. But not insensitive, of course, to a thing in pain.

Finally he was able to pick it up and hold it in his arms and there was nothing to it, for it didn't weigh much. Less than a half-grown shoat, he figured.

He went up the woods path with it, heading back for home; and it seemed to him the smell of it was less. He was hardly scared at all and he was warm again and not cold all over.

For the thing was quieter now and keening just a little. And although he could not be sure of it, there were times when it seemed as if the thing were snuggling up to him, the way a scared and hungry baby will snuggle to any grown person that comes and picks it up.

Old Mose reached the buildings and he stood out in the yard a minute, wondering whether he should take it to the barn or house. The barn, of course, was the natural place for it, for it wasn't human—it wasn't even as close to human as a dog or cat or sick lamb would be.

He didn't hesitate too long, however. He took it into the house and laid it on what he called a bed, next to the kitchen stove. He got it straightened out all neat and orderly, pulled a dirty blanket over it, and then went to the stove and stirred up the fire until there was some flame.

Then he pulled up a chair beside the bed and had a good, hard, wondering look at this thing he had brought home. It had quieted down a lot and seemed more comfortable than it had out in the woods. He tucked the blanket snug around it with a tenderness that surprised himself. He wondered what he had that it might eat, and even if he knew, how he'd manage feeding it, for it seemed to have no mouth.

"But you don't need to worry none," he told it. "Now that I got you under a roof, you'll be all right. I don't know too much about it, but I'll take care of you the best I can."

By now it was getting on toward evening, and he looked out the window and saw that the cows he had been hunting had come home by themselves.

"I got to go get the milking done and the other chores," he told the thing lying on the bed, "but it won't take me long. I'll be right back."

Old Mose loaded up the stove so the kitchen would stay warm and he tucked the thing in once again, then got his milk pails and went down to the barn.

He fed the sheep and pigs and horses and he milked the cows. He hunted eggs and shut the chicken house. He pumped a tank of water.

Then he went back to the house.

It was dark now and he lit the oil lamp on the table, for he was against electricity. He'd refused to sign up when REA[1] had run out the line and a lot of the neighbors had gotten sore at him for being uncooperative. Not that he cared, of course.

He had a look at the thing upon the bed. It didn't seem to be any better, or any worse, for that matter. If it had been a sick lamb or an ail-

1. ***REA,*** Rural Electrification Administration.

ing calf, he would have known right off how it was getting on, but this thing was different. There was no way to tell.

He fixed himself some supper and ate it and wished he knew how to feed the thing. And he wished, too, that he knew how to help it. He'd got it under shelter and he had it warm, but was that right or wrong for something like this? He had no idea.

He wondered if he should try to get some help, then felt squeamish about asking help when he couldn't say exactly what had to be helped. But then he wondered how he would feel himself if he were in a far, strange country, all played out and sick, and no one to get him any help because they didn't know exactly what he was.

That made up his mind for him and he walked over to the phone. But should he call a doctor or a veterinarian? He decided to call the doctor because the thing was in the house. If it had been in the barn, he would have called the veterinarian.

He was on a rural line and the hearing wasn't good and he was halfway deaf, so he didn't use the phone too often. He had told himself at times it was nothing but another aggravation and there had been a dozen times he had threatened to have it taken out. But now he was glad he hadn't.

The operator got old Dr. Benson and they couldn't hear one another too well, but Mose finally made the doctor understand who was calling and that he needed him. The doctor said he'd come.

With some relief, Mose hung up the phone and was just standing there, not doing anything, when he was struck by the thought that there might be others of these things down there in the woods. He had no idea what they were or what they might be doing or where they might be going, but it was pretty evident that the one upon the bed was some sort of stranger from a very distant place. It stood to reason that there might be more than one of them, for far traveling was a lonely business and anyone—or anything—would like to have some company along.

He got the lantern down off the peg and lit it and went stumping out the door. The night was as black as a stack of cats and the lantern light was feeble, but that made not a bit of difference, for Mose knew this farm of his like the back of his hand.

He went down the path into the woods. It was a spooky place, but it took more than woods at night to spook Old Mose. At the place where he had found the thing, he looked around, pushing through the brush and holding the lantern high so he could see a bigger area, but he didn't find another one of them.

He did find something else, though—a sort of outsized birdcage made of metal latticework that had wrapped itself around an eight-inch hickory tree. He tried to pull it loose, but it was jammed so tight that he couldn't budge it.

He sighted back the way it must have come. He could see where it had plowed its way through the upper branches of the trees, and out beyond were stars, shining bleakly with the look of far away.

Mose had no doubt that the thing lying on his bed beside the kitchen stove had come in this birdcage contraption. He marveled some at that, but he didn't fret himself too much, for the whole thing was so unearthly that he knew he had little chance of figuring it out.

He walked back to the house. He scarcely had the lantern blown out and hung back on its peg when he heard a car drive up.

The doctor, when he came up to the door, became a little grumpy at seeing Old Mose standing there.

"You don't look sick to me," the doctor said. "Not sick enough to drag me clear out here at night."

"I ain't sick," said Mose.

"Well, then," said the doctor, more grumpily than ever, "what did you mean by phoning me?"

"I got someone who is sick," said Mose. "I

hope you can help him. I would have tried myself, but I don't know how to go about it.''

The doctor came inside and Mose shut the door behind him.

''You got something rotten in here?'' asked the doctor.

''No, it's just the way he smells. It was pretty bad at first, but I'm getting used to it by now.''

The doctor saw the thing lying on the bed and went over to it. Old Mose heard him sort of gasp and could see him standing there, very stiff and straight. Then he bent down and had a good look at the critter on the bed.

When he straightened up and turned around to Mose, the only thing that kept him from being downright angry was that he was so flabbergasted.

''Mose,'' he yelled, ''what *is* this?''

''I don't know,'' said Mose. ''I found it in the woods and it was hurt and wailing and I couldn't leave it there.''

''You think it's sick?''

''I know it is,'' said Mose. ''It needs help awful bad. I'm afraid it's dying.''

The doctor turned back to the bed again and pulled the blanket down, then went and got the lamp so that he could see. He looked the critter up and down, and he prodded it with a skittish finger, and he made the kind of mysterious clucking sound that only doctors make.

Then he pulled the blanket back over it again and took the lamp back to the table.

''Mose,'' he said, ''I can't do a thing for it.''

''But you're a doctor!''

''A human doctor, Mose. I don't know what this thing is, but it isn't human. I couldn't even guess what is wrong with it, if anything. And I wouldn't know what could be safely done for it even if I could diagnose its illness. I'm not even sure it's an animal. There are a lot of things about it that argue it's a plant.''

Then the doctor asked Mose straight out how he came to find it and Mose told him exactly how it happened. But he didn't tell him anything about the birdcage, for when he thought about it, it sounded so fantastic that he couldn't bring himself to tell it. Just finding the critter and having it here was bad enough, without throwing in the birdcage.

''I tell you what,'' the doctor said. ''You got something here that's outside all human knowledge. I doubt there's ever been a thing like this seen on Earth before. I have no idea what it is and I wouldn't try to guess. If I were you, I'd get in touch with the university up at Madison. There might be someone there who could get it figured out. Even if they couldn't they'd be interested. They'd want to study it.''

Mose went to the cupboard and got the cigar box almost full of silver dollars and paid the doctor. The doctor put the dollars in his pocket, joshing Mose about his eccentricity.

But Mose was stubborn about his silver dollars. ''Paper money don't seem legal, somehow,'' he declared. ''I like the feel of silver and the way it clinks. It's got authority.''

The doctor left; he didn't seem as upset as Mose had been afraid he might be. As soon as he was gone, Mose pulled up a chair and sat down beside the bed.

It wasn't right, he thought, that the thing should be so sick and no one to help—no one who knew any way to help it.

He sat in the chair and listened to the ticking of the clock, loud in the kitchen silence, and the crackling of the wood burning in the stove.

Looking at the thing lying on the bed, he had an almost fierce hope that it could get well again and stay with him. Now that its birdcage was all banged up, maybe there'd be nothing it could do but stay. And he hoped it would, for already the house felt less lonely.

Sitting in the chair between the stove and bed, Mose realized how lonely it had been. It had not been quite so bad until Towser died. He had tried to bring himself to get another dog, but he never had been able to. For there was no dog that would take the place of Towser and it had seemed unfaithful even to try. He could have gotten a cat, of course, but that would remind him too much of Molly; she had been very fond of cats, and until the time she died, there had always been two or three of them underfoot around the place.

But now he was alone. Alone with his farm and his stubbornness and his silver dollars. The doctor thought, like all the rest of them, that the only silver Mose had was in the cigar box in the cupboard. There wasn't one of them who knew about the old iron kettle piled plumb full of them, hidden underneath the floor boards of the living room. He chuckled at the thought of how he had them fooled. He'd give a lot to see his neighbors' faces if they could only know. But he was not the one to tell them. If they were to find it out, they'd have to find it out themselves.

He nodded in the chair and finally he slept, sitting upright, with his chin resting on his chest and his crossed arms wrapped around himself as if to keep him warm.

When he woke, in the dark before the dawn, with the lamp flickering on the table and the fire in the stove burning low, the alien had died.

There was no doubt of death. The thing was cold and rigid and the husk that was its body was rough and drying out—as a corn stalk in the field dries out, whipping in the wind once the growing has been ended.

Mose pulled the blanket up to cover it, and although this was early to do the chores, he went out by lantern light and got them done.

After breakfast, he heated water and washed his face and shaved; and it was the first time in years he'd shaved any day but Sunday. Then he put on his one good suit and slicked down his hair and got the old jalopy out of the machine shed and drove into town.

He hunted up Eb Dennison, the town clerk, who also was the secretary of the cemetery association.

"Eb," he said, "I want to buy a lot."

"But you've got a lot," protested Eb.

"That plot," said Mose, "is a family plot. There's just room for me and Molly."

"Well, then," asked Eb, "why another one? You have no other members of the family."

"I found someone in the woods," said Mose. "I took him home and he died last night. I plan to bury him."

"If you found a dead man in the woods," Eb warned him, "you better notify the coroner and sheriff."

"In time I may," said Mose, not intending to. "Now how about that plot?"

Washing his hands of the affair entirely, Eb sold him the plot.

Having bought his plot, Mose went to the undertaking establishment run by Albert Jones.

"Al," he said, "there's been a death out at the house. A stranger I found out in the woods. He doesn't seem to have anyone and I aim to take care of it."

"You got a death certificate?" asked Al, who subscribed to none of the niceties affected by most funeral-parlor operators.

"Well, no, I haven't."

"Was there a doctor in attendance?"

"Doc Benson came out last night."

"He should have made you out one. I'll give him a ring."

He phoned Dr. Benson and talked with him awhile and got red around the gills. He finally slammed down the phone and turned on Mose.

"I don't know what you're trying to pull off," he fumed, "but Doc tells me this thing of yours isn't even human. I don't take care of dogs or cats or——"

"This ain't no dog or cat."

"I don't care what it is. It's got to be human for me to handle it. And don't go trying to bury it in the cemetery, because it's against the law."

Considerably discouraged, Mose left the undertaking parlor and trudged slowly up the hill toward the town's one and only church.

He found the minister in his study working on a sermon. Mose sat down in a chair and fumbled his battered hat around and around in his work-scarred hands.

"Parson," he said, "I'll tell you the story from first to last," and he did. He added, "I don't know what it is. I guess no one else does, either. But it's dead and in need of decent burial and that's the least that I can do. I can't bury it in the cemetery, so I suppose I'll have to find a place for it on the farm. I wonder if you could bring yourself to come out and say a word or two."

The minister gave the matter some deep consideration.

"I'm sorry, Mose," he said at last. "I don't believe I can. I am not sure at all the church would approve of it."

"This thing may not be human," said Old Mose, "but it is one of God's critters."

The minister thought some more, and did some wondering out loud, but made up his mind finally that he couldn't do it.

So Mose went down the street to where his car was waiting and drove home, thinking about what heels some humans are.

Back at the farm again, he got a pick and shovel and went into the garden, and there, in one corner of it, he dug a grave. He went out to the machine shed to hunt up some boards to make the thing a casket, but it turned out that he had used the last of the lumber to patch up the hog pen.

Mose went to the house and dug around in a chest in one of the back rooms which had not been used for years, hunting for a sheet to use as a shroud, since there would be no casket. He couldn't find a sheet, but he did unearth an old white linen tablecloth. He figured that would do, so he took it to the kitchen.

He pulled back the blanket and looked at the critter lying there in death and a sort of lump came into his throat at the thought of it—how it had died so lonely and so far from home without a creature of its own to spend its final hours with. And naked, too, without a stitch of clothing and with no possessions, with not a thing to leave behind as a remembrance of itself.

He spread the tablecloth out on the floor beside the bed and lifted the thing and laid it on the cloth. As he laid it down, he saw the pocket in it—if it was a pocket—a sort of slitted flap in the center of what could be its chest. He ran his hand across the pocket area. There was a lump inside it. He crouched for a long moment beside the body, wondering what to do.

Finally he reached his fingers into the flap and took out the thing that bulged. It was a ball, a little bigger than a tennis ball, made of cloudy glass—or, at least, it looked like glass. He squatted there, staring at it, then took it to the window for a better look.

There was nothing strange at all about the ball. It was just a cloudy ball of glass and it had a rough, dead feel about it, just as the body had.

He shook his head, took the ball back and put it where he'd found it, and wrapped the body securely in the cloth. He carried it to the garden and put it in the grave. Standing solemnly at the head of the grave, he said a few short words and then shoveled in the dirt.

He had meant to make a mound above the grave and he had intended to put up a cross, but at the last he didn't do either one of these. There would be snoopers. The word would get around and they'd be coming out and hunting for the spot where he had buried this thing he had found out in the woods. So there must be no mound to mark the place and no cross as well. Perhaps it was for the best, he told himself, for what could he have carved or written on the cross?

By this time it was well past noon and he was getting hungry; but he didn't stop to eat, because there were other things to do. He went out into the pasture to catch Bess; and, hitching her to the stoneboat, went down into the woods.

He hitched her to the birdcage that was wrapped around the tree and she pulled it loose as pretty as you please. Then he loaded it on the stoneboat, hauled it up the hill, and stowed it in the back of the machine shed, in the far corner by the forge.

After that, he hitched Bess to the garden plow and gave the garden a cultivating that it didn't need, so it would be fresh dirt all over and no one could locate where he'd dug the grave.

He was just finishing the plowing when Sheriff Doyle drove up and got out of the car. The sheriff was a soft-spoken man, but he was no dawdler. He got right to the point.

"I hear," he said, "you found something in the woods."

"That I did," said Mose.

"I hear it died on you."

"Sheriff, you heard right."

"I'd like to see it, Mose."

"Can't. I buried it. And I ain't telling where."

"Mose," the sheriff said, "I don't want to make you trouble, but you did an illegal thing. You can't go finding people in the woods and just bury them when they up and die on you."

"You talk to Doc Benson?"

The sheriff nodded. "He said it wasn't any kind of thing he'd ever seen before. He said it wasn't human."

"Well, then," said Mose, "I guess that lets you out. If it wasn't human, there could be no crime against a person. And if it wasn't owned, there ain't any crime against property. There's been no one around to claim they owned the thing, is there?"

The sheriff rubbed his chin. "No, there hasn't. Maybe you're right. Where did you study law?"

"I never studied law. I never studied nothing. I just use common sense."

"Doc said something about the folks up at the university might want a look at it."

"I tell you, Sheriff," said Mose. "This thing came here from somewhere and it died. I don't know where it came from and I don't know what it was and I don't hanker none to know. To me it was just a living thing that needed help real bad. It was alive and it had its dignity and in death it deserved some respect. When the rest of you refused it decent burial, I did the best I could. And that is all there is to it."

"All right, Mose," the sheriff said, "if that's how you want it."

He turned around and stalked back to the car. Mose stood beside old Bess hitched to her plow and watched him drive away. He drove fast and reckless as if he might be angry.

Mose put the plow away and turned the horse back to the pasture; by now it was time to do chores again.

He got the chores all finished, made himself some supper and after supper sat beside the stove, listening to the ticking of the clock, loud in the silent house, and the crackle of the fire.

All night long the house was lonely.

The next afternoon, as Mose was plowing corn, a reporter came and walked up the row with him and talked with him when he came to the end of the row. Mose didn't like this reporter much. He was too flip and he asked some funny questions, so Mose clammed up and didn't tell him much.

A few days later, a man showed up from the university and showed him the story the reporter had gone back and written. The story made fun of Mose.

"I'm sorry," the professor said. "These newspapermen are unaccountable. I wouldn't worry too much about anything they write."

"I don't," Mose told him.

The man from the university asked a lot of questions and made quite a point about how important it was that he should see the body.

But Mose only shook his head. "It's at peace," he said. "I aim to leave it that way."

The man went away disgusted, but still quite dignified.

For several days there were people driving by and dropping in, the idly curious, and there were some neighbors Mose hadn't seen for months. But he gave them all short shrift and in a little while they left him alone and he went on with his farming and the house stayed lonely.

He thought again that maybe he should get a dog, but he thought of Towser and he couldn't do it.

One day, working in the garden, he found the plant that grew out of the grave. It was a funny-looking plant and his first impulse was to root it out.

But he didn't do it, for the plant intrigued him. It was a kind he'd never seen before and he decided he would let it grow, for a while at least, to see what kind it was. It was a bulky, fleshy plant, with heavy, dark green, curling leaves, and it reminded him in some ways of the skunk cabbage that burgeoned in the woods come spring.

There was another visitor, the queerest of the lot. He was a dark and intense man who said he was the president of a flying saucer club. He wanted to know if Mose had talked with the thing he'd found out in the woods and seemed terribly disappointed when Mose told him he hadn't. He wanted to know if Mose had found a vehicle the creature might have traveled in and Mose lied to him about it. He was afraid, the wild way the man was acting, that he might demand to search the place; and if he had, he'd likely have found the birdcage hidden in the machine shed back in the corner by the forge. But the man got to lecturing Mose about withholding vital information.

Finally Mose had taken all he could of it, so he stepped into the house and picked up the shotgun from behind the door. The president of the flying saucer club said good-by rather hastily and got out of there.

Farm life went on as usual, with the corn laid by and the haying started, and out in the garden the strange plant kept on growing and now was taking shape. Old Mose couldn't believe his eyes when he saw the sort of shape it took and he spent long evening hours just standing in the garden, watching it and wondering if his loneliness were playing tricks on him.

The morning came when he found the plant standing at the door and waiting for him. He should have been surprised, of course, but he really wasn't, for he had lived with it, watching it of eventide; and although he had not dared admit it even to himself, he had known what it was.

For here was the creature he'd found in the woods, no longer sick and keening, no longer close to death, but full of life and youth.

It was not entirely the same, though. He stood and looked at it and could see the differences—the little differences that might have been those between youth and age, or between a father and a son, or again the differences expressed in an evolutionary pattern.

"Good morning," said Mose, not feeling strange at all to be talking to the thing. "It's good to have you back."

The thing standing in the yard did not answer him. But that was not important; he had not expected that it would. The one important point was that he had something he could talk to.

"I'm going out to do the chores," said Mose. "You want to tag along?"

It tagged along with him and it watched him as he did the chores and he talked to it, which was a vast improvement over talking to himself.

At breakfast, he laid an extra plate for it and pulled up an extra chair, but it turned out the critter was not equipped to use a chair, for it wasn't hinged to sit.

Nor did it eat. That bothered Mose at first, for he was hospitable; but he told himself that a big, strong, strapping youngster like this one knew enough to take care of itself, and he probably didn't need to worry too much about how it got along.

After breakfast, he went out to the garden with the critter accompanying him, and sure enough, the plant was gone. There was a collapsed husk lying on the ground, the outer covering that had been the cradle of the creature now at his side.

Then he went to the machine shed. The creature saw the birdcage, rushed over to it, and looked it over minutely. Then it turned around to Mose and made a sort of pleading gesture.

Mose went over to it and laid his hands on one of the twisted bars and the critter stood beside him and laid its hands on, too, and they pulled together. It was no use. They could move the metal some, but not enough to pull it back in shape again.

They stood and looked at one another, although looking may not be the word, for the critter had no eyes to look with. It made some funny motions with its hands, but Mose couldn't understand. Then it lay down on the floor and showed him how the birdcage ribs were fastened to the base.

It took a while for Mose to understand how the fastening worked and he never did know exactly why it did. There wasn't actually any reason that it should work that way.

First you applied some pressure, just the right amount at the exact and correct angle, and the bar would move a little. Then you applied some more pressure, again the exact amount and at the proper angle, and the bar would move some more. You did this three times and the bar came loose, although there was, God knows, no reason why it should.

Mose started a fire in the forge and shoveled in some coal and worked the bellows while the critter watched. But when he picked up the bar to put it in the fire, the critter got between him and the forge and wouldn't let him near. Mose realized then he couldn't—or wasn't supposed to—heat the bar to straighten it and he never questioned the entire rightness of it. For, he told himself, this thing must surely know the proper way to do it.

So he took the bar over to the anvil and started hammering it back into shape again, cold, without the use of fire, while the critter tried to show him the shape that it should be. It took quite a while, but finally it was straightened out to the critter's satisfaction.

Mose figured they'd have themselves a time getting the bar back in place again, but it slipped on as slick as could be.

Then they took off another bar and this one went faster, now that Mose had the hang of it.

But it was hard and grueling labor. They worked all day and only straightened out five bars.

It took four solid days to get the bars on the birdcage hammered into shape and all the time the hay was waiting to be cut.

But it was all right with Mose. He had someone to talk to and the house had lost its loneliness.

When they got the bars back in place, the critter slipped into the cage and starting fooling with a dingus on the roof of it that looked like a complicated basket. Mose, watching, figured that the basket was some sort of control.

The critter was discouraged. It walked around the shed looking for something and seemed unable to find it. It came back to Mose and made its despairing, pleading gesture. Mose showed it iron and steel; he dug into a carton where he kept bolts and clamps and bushings and scraps of metal and other odds and ends, finding brass and copper and even some aluminum, but it wasn't any of these.

And Mose was glad—a bit ashamed for feeling glad, but glad all the same.

For it had been clear to him that when the birdcage was all ready, the critter would be leaving him. It had been impossible for Mose to stand in the way of the repair of the cage, or to refuse to help. But now that it apparently couldn't be, he found himself well pleased.

Now the critter would have to stay with him and he'd have someone to talk to and the house would not be lonely. It would be welcome, he told himself, to have folks again. The critter was almost as good a companion as Towser.

Next morning, while Mose was fixing breakfast, he reached up in the cupboard to get the box of oatmeal and his hand struck the cigar box. It came crashing to the floor. It fell over on its side and the lid came open; the dollars went free-wheeling all around the kitchen.

Out of the corner of his eye, Mose saw the critter leaping quickly in pursuit of one of them. It snatched it up and turned to Mose, with the coin held between its fingers, and a sort of thrumming noise was coming out of the nest of worms on top of it.

It bent and scooped up more of them and

cuddled them and danced a sort of jig, and Mose knew, with a sinking heart, that it had been silver the critter had been hunting.

So Mose got down on his hands and knees and helped the critter gather up all the dollars. They put them back into the cigar box and Mose picked up the box and gave it to the critter.

The critter took it and hefted it and had a disappointed look. Taking the box over to the table, it took the dollars out and stacked them in neat piles; and Mose could see it was very disappointed.

Perhaps, after all, Mose thought, it had not been silver the thing had been hunting for. Maybe it had made a mistake in thinking that the silver was some other kind of metal.

Mose got down the oatmeal and poured it into some water and put it on the stove. When it was cooked and the coffee was ready, he carried his breakfast to the table and sat down to eat.

The critter still was standing across the table from him, stacking and restacking the piles of silver dollars. And now it showed him, with a hand held above the stacks, that it needed more of them. This many stacks, it showed him, and each stack so high.

Mose sat stricken, with a spoon full of oatmeal halfway to his mouth. He thought of all those other dollars, the iron kettle packed with them, underneath the floor boards in the living room. And he couldn't do it; they were the only thing he had—except the critter now. And he could not give them up so the critter could go and leave him too.

He ate his bowl of oatmeal without tasting it and drank two cups of coffee. And all the time the critter stood there and showed him how much more it needed.

"I can't do it for you," Old Mose said. "I've done all you can expect of any living being. I found you in the woods and I gave you warmth and shelter. I tried to help you, and when I couldn't, at least I gave you a place to die in. I buried you and protected you from all those other people and I didn't pull you up when you started growing once again. Surely you can't expect me to keep on giving endlessly."

But it was no good. The critter could not hear him and he did not convince himself.

He got up from the table and walked into the living room with the critter trailing him. He loosened the floor boards and took out the kettle, and the critter, when it saw what was in the kettle, put its arms around itself and hugged in happiness.

They lugged the money out to the machine shed and Mose built a fire in the forge and put the kettle in the fire and started melting down that hard-saved money.

There were times he thought he couldn't finish the job, but he did.

The critter got the basket out of the birdcage and put it down beside the forge and dipped out the molten silver with an iron ladle and poured it here and there into the basket, shaping it in place with careful hammer taps.

It took a long time, for it was exacting work, but finally it was done and the silver almost gone. The critter lugged the basket back into the birdcage and fastened it in place.

It was almost evening now and Mose had to go and do the chores. He half expected the thing might haul out the birdcage and be gone when he came back to the house. And he tried to be sore at it for its selfishness—it had taken from him and had not tried to pay him back—it had not, so far as he could tell, even tried to thank him. But he made a poor job of being sore at it.

It was waiting for him when he came from the barn carrying two pails full of milk. It followed him inside the house and stood around and he tried to talk to it. But he didn't have the heart to do much talking. He could not forget that it would be leaving, and the pleasure of its present company was lost in his terror of the loneliness to come.

For now he didn't even have his money to help ward off the loneliness.

As he lay in bed that night, strange thoughts came creeping in upon him—the thought of an even greater loneliness than he had ever known upon this runty farm, the terrible, devastating loneliness of the empty wastes that lay between the stars, a driven loneliness while one hunted for a place or person that remained a misty thought one could not define, but which it was most important that one should find.

It was a strange thing for him to be thinking, and quite suddenly he knew it was no thought of his, but of this other that was in the room with him.

He tried to raise himself, he fought to raise himself, but he couldn't do it. He held his head up a moment, then fell back upon the pillow and went sound asleep.

Next morning, after Mose had eaten breakfast, the two of them went to the machine shed and dragged the birdcage out. It stood there, a weird alien thing, in the chill brightness of the dawn.

The critter walked up to it and started to slide between two of the bars, but when it was halfway through, it stepped out again and moved over to confront Old Mose.

"Good-by, friend," said Mose. "I'll miss you."

There was a strange stinging in his eyes.

The other held out its hand in farewell, and Mose took it and there was something in the hand he grasped, something round and smooth that was transferred from its hand to his.

The thing took its hand away and stepped quickly to the birdcage and slid between the bars. The hands reached for the basket, there was a sudden flicker, and the birdcage was no longer there.

Mose stood lonely in the barnyard, looking at the place where there was no birdcage and remembering what he had felt or thought—or been told?—the night before as he lay in bed.

Already the critter would be there, out between the stars, in that black and utter loneliness, hunting for a place or thing or person that no human mind could grasp.

Slowly Mose turned around to go back to the house, to get the pails and go down to the barn to get the milking done.

He remembered the object in his hand and lifted his still-clenched fist in front of him. He opened his fingers and the little crystal ball lay there in his palm—and it was exactly like the one he'd found in the slitted flap in the body he had buried in the garden. Except that one had been dead and cloudy and this one had the living glow of a distant-burning fire.

Looking at it, he had the strange feeling of a happiness and comfort such as he had seldom known before, as if there were many people with him and all of them were friends.

He closed his hand upon it and the happiness stayed on—and it was all wrong, for there was not a single reason that he should be happy. The critter finally had left him and his money was all gone and he had no friends, but still he kept on feeling good.

He put the ball into his pocket and stepped spryly for the house to get the milking pails. He pursed up his whiskered lips and began to whistle though it had been a long, long time since he had even thought to whistle.

Maybe he was happy, he told himself, because the critter had not left without stopping to take his hand and try to say good-by.

And a gift, no matter how worthless it might be, how cheap a trinket, still had a basic value in simple sentiment. It had been many years since anyone had bothered to give him a gift.

It was dark and lonely and unending in the depths of space with no Companion. It might be long before another was obtainable.

It perhaps was a foolish thing to do, but the old creature had been such a kind savage, so fumbling and so pitiful and eager to help. And one who travels far and fast must likewise travel light. There had been nothing else to give.

Discussion

1. (a) Whose thoughts are expressed in the last two paragraphs? **(b)** From these two paragraphs, what do we learn about the "critter" and about the gift Mose has been given?

2. Describe Mose's life as it was before the arrival of the alien. In this description consider how Mose lived, why he lived that way, and what his neighbors and the townspeople thought of him. Find examples from the story to support your description.

3. (a) Trace Mose's efforts as he seeks first to get medical help for and then to bury the creature. (Whom does he contact and how does each person respond to him?) **(b)** What do Mose's actions tell you about him?

Application
Point of View

1. Is the narrator a character or someone outside the story?

2. Who do we learn the most about in the story?

3. Does the narrator provide any commentary on the actions of the characters?

4. What is the point of view of the story?

Vocabulary
Idioms

Mose's speech and thoughts and the speech of some of his neighbors often contain idioms. An *idiom* is a phrase or expression whose meaning cannot be understood from the ordinary meanings of the words in it. Idioms occur in almost every language and—in any given language—they do not present problems for people who grew up speaking that language. Problems arise when a person begins to study another language and attempts to understand idioms by translating the literal meaning of each word in them. For example, suppose that Mose and the creature were able to talk in English but that the creature had only recently begun to learn the language. How would the alien interpret Mose's conclusion about "what heels some people are"?

Each sentence that follows contains an idiom found in the story. On your paper, write that idiom after the number of the sentence in which it appears. Be prepared to discuss both the literal and the idiomatic meaning of each expression.

1. When he refused to have electricity in his house, many of Mose's neighbors had gotten sore at him.

2. Mose clammed up when the reporter began to ask odd questions.

3. The town clerk washed his hands of the whole problem by selling Mose the plot in the cemetery.

4. Mose was terrified, and a part of him wanted to run away; but the creature was helpless and in pain, so Mose stuck it out.

5. The undertaker announced that he didn't care what Mose was trying to pull off.

Clifford Simak 1904–

While building a career as a reporter, columnist, and newspaper editor, Clifford Simak has also become one of the most highly respected writers of science fiction. In the course of his writing career, he has received almost every major award given to science-fiction writers in both the United States and in England.

See **SETTING** Handbook of Literary Terms

The Man to Send Rain Clouds

Leslie Silko

The family are Native Americans, with centuries-old customs and religious beliefs. The priest who has come to live among them brings his own centuries-old religion and customs.

One

They found him under a big cottonwood tree. His Levi jacket and pants were faded light blue so that he had been easy to find. The big cottonwood tree stood apart from a small grove of winterbare cottonwoods which grew in the wide, sandy arroyo.[1] He had been dead for a day or more, and the sheep had wandered and scattered up and down the arroyo. Leon and his brother-in-law, Ken, gathered the sheep and left them in the pen at the sheep camp before they returned to the cottonwood tree. Leon waited under the tree while Ken drove the truck through the deep sand to the edge of the arroyo. He squinted up at the sun and unzipped his jacket—it sure was hot for this time of year. But high and northwest the blue mountains were still deep in snow. Ken came sliding down the low, crumbling bank about fifty yards down, and he was bringing the red blanket.

Before they wrapped the old man, Leon took a piece of string out of his pocket and tied a small gray feather in the old man's long white hair. Ken gave him the paint. Across the brown wrinkled forehead he drew a streak of white, and along the high cheekbones he drew a strip of blue paint. He paused and watched Ken throw pinches of corn meal and pollen into the wind that fluttered the small gray feather. Then Leon painted with yellow under the old man's broad nose; and finally, when he had painted green across the chin, he smiled.

"Send us rain clouds, Grandfather." They laid the bundle in the back of the pickup and covered it with a heavy tarp before they started back to the pueblo.[2]

They turned off the highway onto the sandy pueblo road. Not long after they passed the store and post office they saw Father Paul's car coming toward them. When he recognized their faces he slowed his car and waved for them to stop. The young priest rolled down the car window.

"Did you find old Teofilo?" he asked loudly.

Leon stopped the truck. "Good morning, Father. We were just out to the sheep camp. Everything is O.K. now."

"Thank God for that. Teofilo is a very old man. You really shouldn't allow him to stay at the sheep camp alone."

"No, he won't do that any more now."

"Well, I'm glad you understand. I hope I'll be seeing you at Mass this week—we missed

---

1. ***arroyo*** (ə roi′ō). In the southern United States, the dry bed of a stream is called an *arroyo.*

2. ***pueblo*** (pweb′lō), an Indian village consisting of houses built of adobe and stone, usually with flat roofs and often several stories high.

you last Sunday. See if you can get old Teofilo to come with you." The priest smiled and waved at them as they drove away.

Two

Louise and Teresa were waiting. The table was set for lunch, and the coffee was boiling on the black iron stove. Leon looked at Louise and then at Teresa.

"We found him under a cottonwood tree in the big arroyo near sheep camp. I guess he sat down to rest in the shade and never got up again." Leon walked toward the old man's bed. The red plaid shawl had been shaken and spread carefully over the bed, and a new brown flannel shirt and pair of stiff new Levis were arranged neatly beside the pillow. Louise held the screen door open while Leon and Ken carried in the red blanket. He looked small and shriveled, and after they dressed him in the new shirt and pants he seemed more shrunken.

It was noontime now because the church bells rang the Angelus.[3] They ate the beans with hot bread, and nobody said anything until after Teresa poured the coffee.

Ken stood up and put on his jacket. "I'll see about the gravediggers. Only the top layer of soil is frozen. I think it can be ready before dark."

Leon nodded his head and finished his coffee. After Ken had been gone for a while, the neighbors and clanspeople came quietly to embrace Teofilo's family and to leave food on the table because the gravediggers would come to eat when they were finished.

Three

The sky in the west was full of pale-yellow light. Louise stood outside with her hands in the pockets of Leon's green army jacket that was too big for her. The funeral was over, and the old men had taken their candles and medicine bags[4] and were gone. She waited until the body was laid into the pickup before she said anything to Leon. She touched his arm, and he noticed that her hands were still dusty from the corn meal that she had sprinkled around the old man. When she spoke, Leon could not hear her.

"What did you say? I didn't hear you."

"I said that I had been thinking about something."

"About what?"

"About the priest sprinkling holy water for Grandpa. So he won't be thirsty."

Leon stared at the new moccasins that Teofilo had made for the ceremonial dances in the summer. They were nearly hidden by the red blanket. It was getting colder, and the wind pushed gray dust down the narrow pueblo road. The sun was approaching the long mesa where it disappeared during the winter. Louise stood there shivering and watching his face. Then he zipped up his jacket and opened the truck door. "I'll see if he's there."

Four

Ken stopped the pickup at the church, and Leon got out; and then Ken drove down the hill to the graveyard where people were waiting. Leon knocked at the old carved door with its symbols of the Lamb.[5] While he waited he looked up at the twin bells from the king of Spain with the last sunlight pouring around them in their tower.

The priest opened the door and smiled when he saw who it was. "Come in! What brings you here this evening?"

The priest walked toward the kitchen, and Leon stood with his cap in his hand, playing with the earflaps and examining the living room—the brown sofa, the green armchair, and the brass lamp that hung down from the ceiling by links of chain. The priest dragged a chair out of the kitchen and offered it to Leon.

"No thank you, Father. I only came to ask you if you would bring your holy water to the graveyard."

---

3. ***Angelus*** (an′jə ləs), prayer said by Roman Catholics in memory of Christ's assuming human form.

4. ***medicine bag,*** bag containing objects believed to provide power to protect or to heal.

5. ***Lamb,*** the Lamb of God, or Christ.

The priest turned away from Leon and looked out the window at the patio full of shadows and the dining-room windows of the nuns' cloister across the patio. The curtains were heavy, and the light from within faintly penetrated; it was impossible to see the nuns inside eating supper. "Why didn't you tell me he was dead? I could have brought the Last Rites[6] anyway."

Leon smiled. "It wasn't necessary, Father."

The priest stared down at his scuffed brown loafers and the worn hem of his cassock. "For a Christian burial it was necessary."

His voice was distant, and Leon thought that his blue eyes looked tired.

"It's O.K. Father, we just want him to have plenty of water."

The priest sank down into the green chair and picked up a glossy missionary magazine. He turned the colored pages full of lepers and pagans without looking at them.

"You know I can't do that, Leon. There should have been the Last Rites and a funeral Mass at the very least."

Leon put on his green cap and pulled the flaps down over his ears. "It's getting late, Father. I've got to go."

When Leon opened the door Father Paul stood up and said, "Wait." He left the room and came back wearing a long brown overcoat. He followed Leon out the door and across the dim churchyard to the adobe steps in front of the church. They both stooped to fit through the low adobe entrance. And when they started down the hill to the graveyard only half of the sun was visible above the mesa.

The priest approached the grave slowly, wondering how they had managed to dig into the frozen ground; and then he remembered that this was New Mexico, and saw the pile of cold loose sand beside the hole. The people stood close to each other with little clouds of steam puffing from their faces. The priest looked at them and saw a pile of jackets, gloves, and scarves in the yellow, dry tumbleweeds that grew in the graveyard. He looked at the red blanket, not sure that Teofilo was so small, wondering if it wasn't some perverse Indian trick—something they did in March to ensure a good harvest—wondering if maybe old Teofilo was actually at sheep camp corralling the sheep for the night. But there he was, facing into a cold dry wind and squinting at the last sunlight, ready to bury a red wool blanket while the faces of his parishioners were in shadow with the last warmth of the sun on their backs.

His fingers were stiff, and it took him a long time to twist the lid off the holy water. Drops of water fell on the red blanket and soaked into dark icy spots. He sprinkled the grave and the water disappeared almost before it touched the dim, cold sand; it reminded him of something—he tried to remember what it was, because he thought if he could remember he might understand this. He sprinkled more water; he shook the container until it was empty, and the water fell through the light from sundown like August rain that fell while the sun was still shining, almost evaporating before it touched the wilted squash flowers.

The wind pulled at the priest's brown Franciscan[7] robe and swirled away the corn meal and pollen that had been sprinkled on the blanket. They lowered the bundle into the ground, and they didn't bother to untie the stiff pieces of new rope that were tied around the ends of the blanket. The sun was gone, and over on the highway the eastbound lane was full of headlights. The priest walked away slowly. Leon watched him climb the hill, and when he had disappeared within the tall, thick walls, Leon turned to look up at the high blue mountains in the deep snow that reflected a faint red light from the west. He felt good because it was finished, and he was happy about the sprinkling of the holy water; now the old man could send them big thunderclouds for sure.

---

6. ***Last Rites,*** religious rites performed for a dying person or at a funeral.

7. ***Franciscan*** (fran sis′kən). The Franciscan religious order was founded in 1209 by Saint Francis of Assisi.

Discussion

1. Before he knows of the death, Father Paul tells Leon and Ken that Teofilo shouldn't stay alone at the sheep camp. **(a)** Why does the priest say this? **(b)** Why might Teofilo have wanted to work? **(c)** Why might his family have allowed him to do so? Give reasons for your opinions.

2. Find evidence in the story to suggest that the family knows Teofilo is dead before Ken and Leon go to look for him.

3. From the time the young men find Teofilo to the end of the burial service for him, there are a number of indications of the family's regard for the old man. Cite as many of these as you can find.

4. The attitude of the community toward Father Paul is a complex one. Describe this attitude, using examples from the story to support your opinion.

5. Father Paul's attitude toward the community is equally complex. **(a)** Why is he upset when Leon does tell him of Teofilo's death? (There is more than one reason.) **(b)** Why do you think he agrees to sprinkle the holy water?

Application

Setting

1. (a) Find the paragraph in "The Man to Send Rain Clouds" where the setting (the time and place in which the story occurs) is directly stated. **(b)** Who states this—the narrator or one of the characters?

2. Before it is stated directly, both the behavior of the characters and description by the narrator suggest setting. Skim the story to find three or four good examples of these suggestions to share with the class.

3. Could this story have taken place in any other setting? Explain.

Leslie Silko 1948–

Leslie Silko was born in Albuquerque and grew up at Laguna Pueblo, New Mexico. Silko states that although she is descended from several tribes of Native Americans, she considers Laguna the force that shaped her. In speaking of her roots, she calls Laguna Pueblo "everything I am as a writer and human being."

See **PLOT** Handbook of Literary Terms

The Most Dangerous Game

Richard Connell

"The world is made up of two classes—the hunters and the hunted. Luckily, you and I are hunters."

Off there to the right—somewhere—is a large island," said Whitney. "It's rather a mystery ——"

"What island is it?" Rainsford asked.

"The old charts call it 'Ship-Trap Island,' " Whitney replied. "A suggestive name, isn't it? Sailors have a curious dread of the place. I don't know why. Some superstition——"

"Can't see it," remarked Rainsford, trying to peer through the dank tropical night that was palpable as it pressed its thick, warm blackness in upon the yacht.

"You have good eyes," said Whitney, with a laugh, "and I've seen you pick off a moose moving in the brown fall bush at four hundred yards; but even you can't see four miles or so through a moonless Caribbean night."

"Nor four yards," admitted Rainsford. "Ugh! It's like moist black velvet."

"It will be light enough in Rio," promised Whitney. "We should make it in a few days. I hope the jaguar guns have come. We'll have some good hunting up the Amazon. Great sport, hunting."

"The best sport in the world," agreed Rainsford.

"For the hunter," amended Whitney. "Not for the jaguar."

"Don't talk rot, Whitney," said Rainsford. "You're a big-game hunter, not a philosopher. Who cares how a jaguar feels?"

"Perhaps the jaguar does," observed Whitney.

"Bah! They've no understanding."

"Even so, I rather think they understand one thing—fear. The fear of pain and the fear of death."

"Nonsense," laughed Rainsford. "This hot weather is making you soft, Whitney. Be a realist. The world is made up of two classes—the hunters and the hunted. Luckily, you and I are hunters. Do you think we've passed that island yet?"

"I can't tell in the dark. I hope so."

"Why?" asked Rainsford.

"The place has a reputation—a bad one. It's gotten into sailor lore, somehow. Didn't you notice that the crew's nerves seemed a bit jumpy today?"

"They were a bit strange, now you mention it. Even Captain Nielsen——"

"Yes, even that tough-minded old Swede, who'd go up to the devil himself and ask him for a light. All I could get out of him was: 'This place has an evil name among seafaring men, sir.' Then he said to me, very gravely: 'Don't you feel anything?'—as if the air about us was actually poisonous. Now, you mustn't laugh when I tell you this—I did feel something like a sudden chill.

"There was no breeze. The sea was as flat as a plate-glass window. We were drawing near the island then. What I felt was a—a mental chill; a sort of sudden dread."

"Pure imagination," said Rainsford. "One superstitious sailor can taint the whole ship's company with his fear."

"Maybe. But sometimes I think sailors have an extra sense that tells them when they are in danger. Sometimes I think evil is a tangible thing—with wave lengths, just as sound and light have. An evil place can, so to speak, broadcast vibrations of evil. Anyhow, I'm glad we're getting out of this zone. Well, I think I'll turn in now, Rainsford."

"I'm not sleepy," said Rainsford. "I'm going to smoke another pipe up on the afterdeck."

"Good night, then, Rainsford. See you at breakfast."

"Right. Good night, Whitney."

Rainsford, reclining in a steamer chair, indolently puffed on his favorite brier. The sensuous drowsiness of the night was on him. "It's so dark," he thought, "that I could sleep without closing my eyes; the night would be my eyelids——"

An abrupt sound startled him. Off to the right he had heard it, and his ears, expert in such matters, could not be mistaken. Again he heard the sound, and again. Somewhere, off in the blackness, someone had fired a gun three times.

Rainsford sprang up and moved quickly to the rail, mystified. He strained his eyes in the direction from which the reports had come, but it was like trying to see through a blanket. He leaped upon the rail and balanced himself there, to get greater elevation; his pipe, striking a rope, was knocked from his mouth. He lunged for it; a short, hoarse cry came from his lips as he realized he had reached too far and had lost his balance. The cry was pinched off short as the blood-warm waters of the Caribbean Sea closed over his head.

He struggled up to the surface and tried to cry out, but the wash from the speeding yacht made him gag and strangle. Desperately he struck out with strong strokes after the receding lights of the yacht, but he stopped before he had swum fifty feet. A certain cool-headedness had come to him; it was not the first time he had been in a tight place. There was a chance that his cries could be heard by someone aboard the yacht, but that chance was slender, and grew more slender as the yacht raced on. He wrestled himself out of some of his clothes, and shouted with all his power. The lights of the yacht became faint and ever-vanishing fireflies; then they were blotted out entirely by the night.

Rainsford remembered that the shots had come from the right; and doggedly he swam in that direction, swimming with slow, deliberate strokes, conserving his strength. For a seemingly endless time he fought the sea. He began to count his strokes; he could do possibly a hundred more and then——

Rainsford heard a sound. It came out of the darkness, a high, screaming sound, the sound of an animal in an extremity of anguish and terror.

He did not recognize the animal that made the sound; he did not try to; with fresh vitality he swam toward the sound. He heard it again; then it was cut short by another noise, crisp, staccato.

"Pistol shot," muttered Rainsford, swimming on.

Ten minutes of determined effort brought another sound to his ears—the most welcome he had ever heard—the muttering and growling of the sea breaking on a rocky shore. He was almost on the rocks before he saw them. With his remaining strength he dragged himself from the swirling waters. Jagged crags appeared to jut up into the opaqueness; he forced himself upward, hand over hand. Gasping, his hands raw, he reached a flat place at the top. Dense jungle came down to the very edge of the cliffs. What perils that tangle of trees and underbrush might hold for him did not concern Rainsford just then. All he knew was that he was safe from the sea, and that utter weariness was on him. He flung himself down and tumbled headlong into the deepest sleep of his life.

When he opened his eyes, he knew from the position of the sun that it was late in the afternoon. Sleep had given him new vigor; a sharp hunger was picking at him. He looked about him, almost cheerfully.

"Where there are pistol shots, there are men. Where there are men, there is food," he thought. But what kind of men, he wondered, in so forbidding a place? An unbroken front of snarled and ragged jungle fringed the shore. He saw no sign of a trail through the closely knit web of weeds and trees; it was easier to go along the shore, and he floundered along by the water. Not far from where he had landed, he stopped.

Some wounded thing, by the evidence a large animal, had thrashed about in the underbrush; the jungle weeds were crushed down and the moss was lacerated; one patch of weeds was stained crimson. A small, glittering object not far away caught Rainsford's eye and he picked it up. It was an empty cartridge.

"A twenty-two," he remarked. "That's odd. It must have been a fairly large animal, too. The hunter had his nerve with him to tackle it with a light gun. It's clear that the brute put up a fight. I suppose the first three shots I heard was when the hunter flushed his quarry[1] and wounded it. The last shot was when he trailed it here and finished it."

He examined the ground closely and found what he had hoped to find—the print of hunting boots. They pointed along the cliff in the direction he had been going. Eagerly he hurried along, now slipping on a rotten log or a loose stone, but making headway; night was beginning to settle down.

Bleak darkness was blacking out the sea and jungle when Rainsford sighted the lights. He came upon them as he turned a crook in the coastline, and his first thought was that he had come upon a village, for there were many lights. But as he forged along he saw to his great astonishment that all the lights were in one enormous building—a lofty structure with pointed towers plunging upward into the gloom. His eyes made out the shadowy outlines of a palatial château; it was set on a high bluff, and on three sides of it cliffs dived down to where the sea licked greedy lips in the shadows.

"Mirage," thought Rainsford. But it was no mirage, he found, when he opened the tall

---

1. ***flushed his quarry,*** drove the pursued animal out of its hiding place.

spiked iron gate. The stone steps were real enough; the massive door with a leering gargoyle for a knocker was real enough; yet about it all hung an air of unreality.

He lifted the knocker; and it creaked up stiffly, as if it had never before been used. He let it fall, and it startled him with its booming loudness. He thought he heard steps within; the door remained closed. Again Rainsford lifted the heavy knocker, and let it fall. The door opened suddenly, and Rainsford stood blinking in the river of glaring gold light that poured out. The first thing his eyes discerned was the largest man he had ever seen—a gigantic creature, solidly made and black-bearded almost to the waist. In his hand the man held a long-barreled revolver, and he was pointing it straight at Rainsford's heart. Out of the snarl of beard, two small eyes regarded Rainsford.

"Don't be alarmed," said Rainsford with a smile which he hoped was disarming. "I'm no robber. I fell off a yacht. My name is Sanger Rainsford of New York City."

The menacing look in the eyes did not change. The revolver pointed as rigidly as if the giant were a statue. He gave no sign that he understood Rainsford's words, or that he had even heard them. He was dressed in uniform, a black uniform trimmed with gray astrakhan.

"I'm Sanger Rainsford of New York," Rainsford began again. "I fell off a yacht. I am hungry."

The man's only answer was to raise with his thumb the hammer of his revolver. Then Rainsford saw the man's free hand go to his forehead in a military salute, and he saw him click his heels together and stand at attention. Another man was coming down the broad marble steps, an erect, slender man in evening clothes. He advanced to Rainsford and held out his hand.

In a cultivated voice marked by a slight accent that gave it added precision and deliberateness, he said: "It is a very great pleasure and honor to welcome Mr. Sanger Rainsford, the celebrated hunter, to my home."

Automatically Rainsford shook the man's hand.

"I've read your book about hunting snow leopards in Tibet, you see," explained the man. "I am General Zaroff."

Rainsford's first impression was that the man was singularly handsome; his second was that there was an original, almost bizarre quality about the general's face. He was a tall man past middle age, for his hair was a vivid white; but his thick eyebrows and pointed military mustache were as black as the night from which Rainsford had come. His eyes, too, were black and very bright. He had high cheekbones, a sharp-cut nose, a spare, dark face, the face of a man used to giving orders, the face of an aristocrat. Turning to the giant in uniform, the general made a sign. The giant put away his pistol, saluted, withdrew.

"Ivan is an incredibly strong fellow," remarked the general, "but he has the misfortune to be deaf and dumb. A simple fellow, but, I'm afraid, like all his race, a bit of a savage."

"Is he Russian?"

"He is a Cossack,"[2] said the general, and his smile showed red lips and pointed teeth. "So am I."

"Come," he said, "we shouldn't be chatting here. We can talk later. Now you want clothes, food, rest. You shall have them. This is a most restful spot."

Ivan had reappeared, and the general spoke to him with lips that moved but gave forth no sound.

"Follow Ivan, if you please, Mr. Rainsford," said the general. "I was about to have my dinner. I'll wait for you. You'll find that my clothes will fit you, I think."

It was to a huge, beam-ceilinged bedroom with a canopied bed big enough for six men that Rainsford followed the silent giant. Ivan laid out an evening suit, and Rainsford, as he put it on,

---

2. ***He is a Cossack*** (kos′ak). The Cossacks, who lived in southern Russia, were noted for their love of fighting and their excellent horsemanship.

noticed that it came from a London tailor who ordinarily cut and sewed for none below the rank of duke.

The dining room to which Ivan conducted him was in many ways remarkable. There was a medieval magnificence about it; it suggested a baronial hall of feudal times with its oaken panels, its high ceiling, its vast refectory table where twoscore men could sit down to eat. About the hall were mounted heads of many animals—lions, tigers, elephants, moose, bears; larger or more perfect specimens Rainsford had never seen. At the great table the general was sitting alone.

"You'll have a cocktail, Mr. Rainsford," he suggested. The cocktail was surpassingly good; and, Rainsford noted, the table appointments were of the finest—the linen, the crystal, the silver, the china.

They were eating borsch.[3] Half apologetically General Zaroff said: "We do our best to preserve the amenities of civilization here. Please forgive any lapses. We are well off the beaten track, you know."

Rainsford was finding the general a most thoughtful and affable host, a true cosmopolite. But there was one small trait of the general's that made Rainsford uncomfortable. Whenever he looked up from his plate he found the general studying him, appraising him narrowly.

"Perhaps," said General Zaroff, "you were surprised that I recognized your name. You see, I read all books on hunting published in English, French, and Russian. I have but one passion in my life, Mr. Rainsford, and that is the hunt."

"You have some wonderful heads here," said Rainsford as he ate a particularly well-cooked filet mignon. "That Cape buffalo is the largest I ever saw."

"Oh, that fellow. Yes, he was a monster."

"Did he charge you?"

"Hurled me against a tree," said the general. "Fractured my skull. But I got the brute."

"I've always thought," said Rainsford, "that the Cape buffalo is the most dangerous of all big game."

For a moment the general did not reply; he was smiling his curious red-lipped smile. Then he said slowly: "No. You are wrong, sir. The Cape buffalo is not the most dangerous big game." He sipped his wine. "Here in my preserve on this island," he said in the same slow tone, "I hunt more dangerous game."

Rainsford expressed his surprise. "Is there big game on this island?"

The general nodded. "The biggest."

"Really?"

"Oh, it isn't here naturally, of course. I have to stock the island."

"What have you imported, general?" Rainsford asked. "Tigers?"

The general smiled. "No," he said. "Hunting tigers ceased to interest me some years ago. I exhausted their possibilities, you see. No thrill left in tigers, no real danger. I live for danger, Mr. Rainsford."

The general took from his pocket a gold cigarette case and offered his guest a long black cigarette with a silver tip; it was perfumed and gave off a smell like incense.

"We will have some capital hunting, you and I," said the general. "I shall be most glad to have your society."

"But what game——" began Rainsford.

"I'll tell you," said the general. "You will be amused, I know. I think I may say, in all modesty, that I have done a rare thing. I have invented a new sensation. May I pour you another glass of port, Mr. Rainsford?"

"Thank you, general."

The general filled both glasses, and said: "God makes some men poets. Some He makes kings, some beggars. Me He made a hunter. My hand was made for the trigger, my father said. He was a very rich man with a quarter of a million acres in the Crimea,[4] and he was an ardent sportsman. When I was only five years old, he gave me a little gun to shoot sparrows with.

---

3. ***borsch*** (bôrsh), a rich red soup, colored with beet juice and served with sour cream.

4. ***the Crimea*** (krī mē′ə *or* kri mē′ə), a peninsula in southwestern Russia, jutting down into the Black Sea.

When I shot some of his prize turkeys with it, he did not punish me; he complimented me on my marksmanship. I killed my first bear when I was ten. My whole life has been one prolonged hunt. I went into the army—it was expected of noblemen's sons—and for a time commanded a division of Cossack cavalry, but my real interest was always the hunt. I have hunted every kind of game in every land. It would be impossible for me to tell you how many animals I have killed."

The general puffed at his cigarette.

"After the debacle in Russia[5] I left the country, for it was imprudent for an officer of the Czar to stay there. Many noble Russians lost everything. I, luckily, had invested heavily in American securities. Naturally, I continued to hunt—grizzlies in your Rockies, crocodiles in the Ganges,[6] rhinoceroses in East Africa. It was in Africa that the Cape buffalo hit me and laid me up for six months. As soon as I recovered I started for the Amazon to hunt jaguars, for I had heard they were unusually cunning. They weren't." The Cossack sighed. "I was bitterly disappointed. I was lying in my tent with a splitting headache one night when a terrible thought pushed its way into my mind. Hunting was beginning to bore me! And hunting, remember, had been my life. I have heard that in America businessmen often go to pieces when they give up the business that has been their life."

"Yes, that's so," said Rainsford.

The general smiled. "I had no wish to go to pieces," he said. "I must do something. Now, mine is an analytical mind, Mr. Rainsford. Doubtless that is why I enjoy the problems of the chase."

"No doubt, General Zaroff."

"So," continued the general, "I asked myself why the hunt no longer fascinated me. You are much younger than I am, Mr. Rainsford, and have not hunted as much; but perhaps you can guess the answer."

"What was it?"

"Simply this: hunting had ceased to be what you call 'a sporting proposition.' It had become too easy. I always got my quarry. Always. There is no greater bore than perfection."

The general lit a fresh cigarette.

"No animal had a chance with me any more. That is no boast; it is a mathematical certainty. The animal had nothing but his legs and his instinct. Instinct is no match for reason. When I thought of this it was a tragic moment for me, I can tell you."

Rainsford leaned across the table, absorbed in what his host was saying.

"It came to me as an inspiration what I must do," the general went on.

"And that was?"

The general smiled the quiet smile of one who has faced an obstacle and surmounted it with success. "I had to invent a new animal to hunt," he said.

"A new animal? You're joking."

"Not at all," said the general. "I never joke about hunting. I needed a new animal. I found one. So I bought this island, built this house, and here I do my hunting. The island is perfect for my purposes—there are jungles with a maze of trails in them, hills, swamps——"

"But the animal, General Zaroff?"

"Oh," said the general, "it supplies me with the most exciting hunting in the world. No other hunting compares with it for an instant. Every day I hunt, and I never grow bored now, for I have a quarry with which I can match my wits."

Rainsford's bewilderment showed in his face.

"I wanted the ideal animal to hunt," explained the general. "So I said: 'What are the attributes of an ideal quarry?' And the answer was, of course: 'It must have courage, cunning, and, above all, it must be able to reason.'"

"But no animal can reason," objected Rainsford.

5. ***the debacle*** (dā bä′kəl or di bak′əl) ***in Russia.*** In the Russian Revolution of 1917 the government of the Czar was overthrown, the property of the nobles confiscated, and most of the nobility driven into exile.
6. ***Ganges*** (gan′jēz), a river in India regarded by the Hindus as being sacred.

"My dear fellow," said the general, "there is one that can."

"But you can't mean——" gasped Rainsford.

"And why not?"

"I can't believe you are serious, General Zaroff. This is a grisly joke."

"Why should I not be serious? I am speaking of hunting."

"Hunting? Good heavens, General Zaroff, what you speak of is murder."

The general laughed with entire good nature. He regarded Rainsford quizzically. "I refuse to believe that so modern and civilized a young man as you seem to be harbors romantic ideas about the value of human life. Surely your experiences in the recent war——"

"Did not make me condone cold-blooded murder," finished Rainsford stiffy.

Laughter shook the general. "How extraordinarily droll you are!" he said. "One does not expect nowadays to find a young man of the educated class, even in America, with such a naïve, and, if I may say so, mid-Victorian point of view. Ah, well, I'll wager you'll forget your notions when you go hunting with me. You've a genuine new thrill in store for you, Mr. Rainsford."

"Thank you, I'm a hunter, not a murderer."

"Dear me," said the general, quite unruffled, "again that unpleasant word. But I think I can show you that your scruples are quite ill-founded."

"Yes?"

"Life is for the strong, to be lived by the strong, and, if needs be, taken by the strong. The weak of the world were put here to give the strong pleasure. I am strong. Why should I not use my gift? If I wish to hunt, why should I not? I hunt the scum of the earth—sailors from tramp ships—lascars,[7] blacks, Chinese, whites, mongrels—a thoroughbred horse or hound is worth more than a score of them."

"But they are men," said Rainsford hotly.

"Precisely," said the general. "That is why I use them. It gives me pleasure. They can reason, after a fashion. So they are dangerous."

"But where do you get them?"

The general's left eyelid fluttered down in a wink. "This island is called Ship-Trap," he answered. "Sometimes an angry god of the high seas sends them to me. Sometimes, when Providence is not so kind, I help Providence a bit. Come to the window with me."

Rainsford went to the window and looked out toward the sea.

"Watch! Out there!" exclaimed the general, pointing into the night. Rainsford's eyes saw only blackness, and then, as the general pressed a button, far out to sea Rainsford saw the flash of lights.

The general chuckled. "They indicate a channel," he said, "where there's none: giant rocks with razor edges crouch like a sea monster with wide-open jaws. They can crush a ship as easily as I crush this nut." He dropped a walnut on the hardwood floor and brought his heel grinding down on it. "Oh, yes," he said, casually, as if in answer to a question, "I have electricity. We try to be civilized here."

"Civilized? And you shoot down men?"

A trace of anger was in the general's black eyes, but it was there for only a second; then he said, in his most pleasant manner: "Dear me, what a righteous young man you are! I assure you I do not do the thing you suggest. That would be barbarous. I treat these visitors with every consideration. They get plenty of good food and exercise. They get into splendid physical condition. You shall see for yourself tomorrow."

"What do you mean?"

"We shall visit my training school," smiled the general. "It's in the cellar. I have about a dozen pupils down there now. They're from the Spanish bark *San Lucar* that had the bad luck to go on the rocks out there. A very inferior lot,

---

7. ***lascars*** (las′kərz), East Indian sailors.

I regret to say. Poor specimens and more accustomed to the deck than to the jungle."

He raised his hand, and Ivan brought thick Turkish coffee. Rainsford, with an effort, held his tongue in check.

"It's a game, you see," pursued the general blandly. "I suggest to one of them that we go hunting. I give him a supply of food and an excellent hunting knife. I give him three hours' start. I am to follow, armed only with a pistol of the smallest caliber and range. If my quarry eludes me for three whole days, he wins the game. If I find him"—the general smiled—"he loses."

"Suppose he refuses to be hunted?"

"Oh," said the general, "I give him his option, of course. He need not play that game if he doesn't wish to. If he does not wish to hunt, I turn him over to Ivan. Ivan once had the honor of serving as official knouter to the Great White Czar,[8] and he has his own ideas of sport. Invariably, Mr. Rainsford, invariably they choose the hunt."

"And if they win?"

The smile on the general's face widened. "To date I have not lost," he said.

Then he added, hastily: "I don't wish you to think me a braggart, Mr. Rainsford. Many of them afford only the most elementary sort of problem. Occasionally I strike a tartar.[9] One almost did win. I eventually had to use the dogs."

"The dogs?"

"This way, please. I'll show you."

The general steered Rainsford to a window. The lights from the windows sent a flickering illumination that made grotesque patterns on the courtyard below, and Rainsford could see moving about there a dozen or so huge black shapes; as they turned toward him, their eyes glittered greenly.

"A rather good lot, I think," observed the general. "They are let out at seven every night. If anyone should try to get into my house—or out of it—something extremely regrettable would occur to him." He hummed a snatch of a gay French song.

"And now," said the general, "I want to show you my new collection of heads. Will you come with me to the library?"

"I hope," said Rainsford, "that you will excuse me tonight, General Zaroff. I'm really not feeling at all well."

"Ah, indeed?" the general inquired solicitously. "Well, I suppose that's only natural after your long swim. You need a good, restful night's sleep. Tomorrow you'll feel like a new man, I'll wager. Then we'll hunt, eh? I've one rather promising prospect——"

Rainsford was hurrying from the room.

"Sorry you can't go with me tonight," called the general. "I expect rather fair sport—a big, strong black. He looks resourceful——. Well, good night, Mr. Rainsford; I hope you have a good night's rest."

The bed was good, and the pajamas of the softest silk, and he was tired in every fiber of his being; nevertheless, Rainsford could not quiet his brain with the opiate of sleep. He lay, eyes wide open. Once he thought he heard stealthy steps in the corridor outside his room. He sought to throw open the door; it would not open. He went to the window and looked out. His room was high up in one of the towers. The lights of the château were out now, and it was dark and silent, but there was a fragment of sallow moon, and by its wan light he could see, dimly, the courtyard; there, weaving in and out in the pattern of shadow, were black, noiseless forms; the hounds heard him at the window and looked up, expectantly, with their green eyes. Rainsford went back to the bed and lay down. By many methods he tried to put himself to sleep. He had achieved a doze when, just as morning began to come, he heard, far off in the jungle, the report of a pistol.

General Zaroff did not appear until lunch-

---

8. ***Ivan . . . knouter*** (nout′ər) ***to the Great White Czar*** (zär). During the reign of Alexander III (1881–1894), Ivan was the official flogger of those doomed to be lashed with a knout, a terrible whip made of plaited leather thongs and wire.
9. ***strike a tartar.*** The general means that sometimes he encounters a man who isn't easily manageable.

eon. He was dressed faultlessly in the tweeds of a country squire. He was solicitous about the state of Rainsford's health.

"As for me," sighed the general, "I do not feel so well. I am worried, Mr. Rainsford. Last night I detected traces of my old complaint."

To Rainsford's questioning glance the general said: "Ennui. Boredom."

Then, taking a second helping of crêpes suzette,[10] the general explained: "The hunting was not good last night. The fellow lost his head. He made a straight trail that offered no problems at all. That's the trouble with these sailors; they have dull brains to begin with, and they do not know how to get about in the woods. They do excessively stupid and obvious things. It's most annoying. Will you have another glass of wine, Mr. Rainsford?"

"General," said Rainsford firmly, "I wish to leave this island at once."

The general raised his eyebrows; he seemed hurt. "But, my dear fellow," he protested, "you've only just come. You've had no hunting——"

"I wish to go today," said Rainsford. He saw the dead black eyes of the general on him, studying him. General Zaroff's face suddenly brightened.

He filled Rainsford's glass from a dusty bottle.

"Tonight," said the general, "we will hunt—you and I."

Rainsford shook his head. "No, general," he said. "I will not hunt."

The general shrugged his shoulders and delicately ate a hothouse grape. "As you wish, my friend," he said. "The choice rests entirely with you. But may I not venture to suggest that you will find my idea of sport more diverting than Ivan's?"

He nodded toward the corner to where the giant stood, scowling, his thick arms crossed on his hogshead of a chest.

"You don't mean——" cried Rainsford.

"My dear fellow," said the general, "have I not told you I always mean what I say about hunting? This is really an inspiration. I drink to a foeman worthy of my steel—at last."

The general raised his glass, but Rainsford sat staring at him.

"You'll find this game worth playing," the general said enthusiastically. "Your brain against mine. Your woodcraft against mine. Your strength and stamina against mine. Outdoor chess! And the stake is not without value, eh?"

"And if I win——" began Rainsford huskily.

"I'll cheerfully acknowledge myself defeated if I do not find you by midnight of the third day," said General Zaroff. "My sloop will place you on the mainland near a town."

The general read what Rainsford was thinking.

"Oh, you can trust me," said the Cossack. "I will give you my word as a gentleman and a sportsman. Of course, you in turn must agree to say nothing of your visit here."

"I'll agree to nothing of the kind," said Rainsford.

"Oh," said the general, "in that case—but why discuss that now? Three days hence we can discuss it over a bottle of wine, unless——"

The general sipped his port.

Then a businesslike air animated him. "Ivan," he said to Rainsford, "will supply you with hunting clothes, food, a knife. I suggest you wear moccasins; they leave a poorer trail. I suggest, too, that you avoid the big swamp in the southeast corner of the island. We call it Death Swamp. There's quicksand there. One foolish fellow tried it. The deplorable part of it was that Lazarus followed him. You can imagine my feelings, Mr. Rainsford. I loved Lazarus; he was the finest hound in my pack. Well, I must beg you to excuse me now. I always take a siesta after lunch. You'll hardly have time for a nap, I fear. You'll want to start, no doubt. I shall not follow till dusk. Hunting at night is so

---

10. *crêpes suzette,* thin dessert pancakes, usually rolled, sometimes served with a flaming brandy sauce.

much more exciting, don't you think? *Au revoir,*[11] Mr. Rainsford, *au revoir.*"

General Zaroff, with a deep, courtly bow, strolled from the room. From another door came Ivan. Under one arm he carried khaki hunting clothes, a haversack of food, a leather sheath containing a long-bladed hunting knife; his right hand rested on a cocked revolver thrust in the crimson sash about his waist. . . .

Rainsford had fought his way through the bush for two hours. "I must keep my nerve. I must keep my nerve," he said through tight teeth.

He had not been entirely clear-headed when the château gates snapped shut behind him. His whole idea at first was to put distance between himself and General Zaroff; and, to this end, he had plunged along, spurred on by something very much like panic. Now he had got a grip on himself, had stopped, and was taking stock of himself and the situation.

He saw that straight flight was futile; inevitably it would bring him face to face with the sea. He was in a picture with a frame of water, and his operations, clearly, must take place within that frame.

"I'll give him a trail to follow," muttered Rainsford, and he struck off from the rude path he had been following into the trackless wilderness. He executed a series of intricate loops; he doubled on his trail again and again, recalling all the lore of the fox hunt, and all the dodges of the fox. Night found him leg-weary, with hands and face lashed by the branches, on a thickly wooded ridge. He knew it would be insane to blunder on through the dark, even if he had the strength. His need for rest was imperative and he thought: "I have played the fox, now I must play the cat of the fable."[12] A big tree with a thick trunk and outspread branches was nearby, and, taking care to leave not the slightest mark, he climbed up, and stretching out on one of the broad limbs, after a fashion, rested. Rest brought him new confidence and almost a feeling of security. Even so zealous a hunter as General Zaroff could not trace him there, he told himself; only the devil himself could follow that complicated trail through the jungle after dark. But, perhaps, the general was a devil——

An apprehensive night crawled slowly by like a wounded snake, and sleep did not visit Rainsford, although the silence of a dead world was on the jungle. Toward morning when a dingy gray was varnishing the sky, the cry of some startled bird focused Rainsford's attention in that direction. Something was coming through the bush, coming slowly, carefully, coming by the same winding way Rainsford had come. He flattened himself down on the limb, and through a screen of leaves almost as thick as tapestry, he watched. The thing that was approaching was a man.

It was General Zaroff. He made his way along with his eyes fixed in utmost concentration on the ground before him. He paused, almost beneath the tree, dropped to his knees and studied the ground. Rainsford's impulse was to hurl himself down like a panther, but he saw that the general's right hand held something metallic—a small automatic pistol.

The hunter shook his head several times, as if he were puzzled. Then he straightened up and took from his case one of his black cigarettes; its incense-like smoke floated up to Rainsford's nostrils.

Rainsford held his breath. The general's eyes had left the ground and were traveling inch by inch up the tree. Rainsford froze there, every muscle tensed for a spring. But the sharp eyes of the hunter stopped before they reached the limb where Rainsford lay; a smile spread over his brown face. Very deliberately he blew a smoke ring into the air; then he turned his back on the tree and walked carelessly away, back along the trail he had come. The swish of the underbrush against his hunting boots grew fainter and fainter.

---

11. ***Au revoir*** (ō rə vwär′), good-by; till I see you again. [French]
12. ***I have played the fox . . . cat of the fable.*** Rainsford means that he has used craft; now he must, like a cat at a mousehole, employ watchful waiting.

The pent-up air burst hotly from Rainsford's lungs. His first thought made him feel sick and numb. The general could follow a trail through the woods at night; he could follow an extremely difficult trail; he must have uncanny powers; only by the merest chance had the Cossack failed to see his quarry.

Rainsford's second thought was even more terrible. It sent a shudder of cold horror through his whole being. Why had the general smiled? Why had he turned back?

Rainsford did not want to believe what his reason told him was true, but the truth was as evident as the sun that by now had pushed through the morning mists. The general was playing with him! The general was saving him for another day's sport! The Cossack was the cat; *he* was the mouse. Then it was that Rainsford knew the full meaning of terror.

"I will not lose my nerve. I will not."

He slid down from the tree, and struck off again into the woods. His face was set and he forced the machinery of his mind to function. Three hundred yards from his hiding place he stopped where a huge dead tree leaned precariously on a smaller, living one. Throwing off his sack of food, Rainsford took his knife from its sheath and began to work with all his energy.

The job was finished at last, and he threw himself down behind a fallen log a hundred feet away. He did not have to wait long. The cat was coming again to play with the mouse.

Following the trail with the sureness of a bloodhound, came General Zaroff. Nothing escaped those searching black eyes, no crushed blade of grass, no bent twig, no mark, no matter how faint, in the moss. So intent was the Cossack on his stalking that he was upon the thing Rainsford had made before he saw it. His foot touched the protruding bough that was the trigger. Even as he touched it, the general sensed his danger and leaped back with the agility of an ape. But he was not quite quick enough; the dead tree, delicately adjusted to rest on the cut living one, crashed down and struck the general a glancing blow on the shoulder as it fell; but for his alertness, he must have been smashed beneath it. He staggered, but he did not fall; nor did he drop his revolver. He stood there, rubbing his injured shoulder; and Rainsford, with fear again gripping his heart, heard the general's mocking laugh ring through the jungle.

"Rainsford," called the general, "if you are within sound of my voice, as I suppose you are, let me congratulate you. Not many men know how to make a Malay man-catcher. Luckily for me I, too, have hunted in Malacca.[13] You are proving interesting, Mr. Rainsford. I am going now to have my wound dressed; it's only a slight one. But I shall be back. I shall be back."

When the general had gone, Rainsford took up his flight again. It was flight now, a desperate, hopeless flight that carried him on for some hours. Dusk came, then darkness, and still he pressed on. The ground grew softer under his moccasins; the vegetation grew ranker, denser; insects bit him savagely. Then, as he stepped forward, his foot sank into the ooze. He tried to wrench it back, but the muck sucked viciously at his foot as if it were a giant leech. With a violent effort, he tore his foot loose. He knew where he was now. Death Swamp and its quicksand.

His hands were tight closed as if his nerve were something tangible that someone in the darkness was trying to tear from his grip. The softness of the earth had given him an idea. He stepped back from the quicksand a dozen feet or so and, like some huge prehistoric beaver, he began to dig.

Rainsford had dug himself in in France when a second's delay meant death. That had been a pleasant pastime compared to his digging now. The pit grew deeper; when it was above his shoulders, he climbed out and from some hard saplings cut stakes and sharpened them to a fine point. These stakes he planted in the bottom of the pit with the points sticking up. With flying fingers he wove a rough carpet of weeds and

---

13. ***Malacca*** (mə lak′ə), an area in the southwestern part of the Malay Peninsula.

branches, and with it he covered the mouth of the pit. Then, wet with sweat and aching with tiredness, he crouched behind the stump of a lightning-charred tree.

He knew his pursuer was coming; he heard the padding sound of feet on the soft earth, and the night breeze brought him the perfume of the general's cigarette. It seemed to Rainsford that the general was coming with unusual swiftness; he was not feeling his way along, foot by foot. Rainsford, crouching there, could not see the general, nor could he see the pit. He lived a year in a minute. Then he felt an impulse to cry aloud with joy, for he heard the sharp crackle of the breaking branches as the cover of the pit gave way; he heard the sharp scream of pain as the pointed stakes found their mark. He leaped up from his place of concealment. Then he cowered back. Three feet from the pit a man was standing, with an electric torch in his hand.

"You've done well, Rainsford," the voice of the general called. "Your Burmese tiger pit[14] has claimed one of my best dogs. Again you score. I think, Mr. Rainsford, I'll see what you can do against my whole pack. I'm going home for a rest now. Thank you for a most amusing evening."

At daybreak Rainsford, lying near the swamp, was awakened by a sound that made him know that he had new things to learn about fear. It was a distant sound, faint and wavering; but he knew it. It was the baying of a pack of hounds.

Rainsford knew he could do one of two things. He could stay where he was and wait. That was suicide. He could flee. That was postponing the inevitable. For a moment he stood there, thinking. An idea that held a wild chance came to him, and, tightening his belt, he headed away from the swamp. The baying of the hounds drew nearer, then still nearer, nearer, ever nearer. On a ridge Rainsford climbed a tree. Down a watercourse, not a quarter of a mile away, he could see the bush moving. Straining his eyes, he saw the lean figure of General Zaroff; just ahead of him Rainsford made out another figure whose wide shoulders surged through the tall jungle weeds; it was the giant Ivan, and he seemed pulled forward by some unseen force; Rainsford knew that Ivan must be holding the pack in leash.

They would be on him any minute now. His mind worked frantically. He thought of a native trick he had learned in Uganda.[15] He slid down the tree. He caught hold of a springy young sapling and to it he fastened his hunting knife, with the blade pointing down the trail; with a bit of wild grapevine, he tied back the sapling. Then he ran for his life. The hounds raised their voices as they hit the fresh scent. Rainsford knew now how an animal at bay feels.

He had to stop to get his breath. The baying of the hounds stopped abruptly; and Rainsford's heart stopped, too. They must have reached the knife.

He shinned excitedly up a tree and looked back. His pursuers had stopped. But the hope that was in Rainsford's brain when he had climbed died, for he saw in the shallow valley that General Zaroff was still on his feet. But Ivan was not. The knife, driven by the recoil of the springing tree, had not wholly failed.

Rainsford had hardly tumbled to the ground when the pack took up the cry again.

"Nerve, nerve, nerve!" he panted, as he dashed along. A blue gap showed between the trees dead ahead. Ever nearer drew the hounds. Rainsford forced himself on toward that gap. He reached for it. It was the shore of the sea. Across a cove he could see the gloomy gray stone of the château. Twenty feet below him the sea rumbled and hissed. Rainsford hesitated. He heard the hounds. Then he leaped far out into the sea.

When the general and his pack reached the place by the sea, the Cossack stopped. For some minutes he stood regarding the blue-green expanse of water. He shrugged his shoulders.

---

14. ***Burmese*** (bėr′mēz) ***tiger pit,*** a deep pit covered by brush; used for trapping tigers in Burma.
15. ***Uganda*** (yü gan′də *or* ü gän′dä), formerly a British protectorate in eastern Africa, now an independent state.

Then he sat down, took a drink of brandy from a silver flask, lit a perfumed cigarette, and hummed a bit from *Madame Butterfly*.[16]

General Zaroff had an exceedingly good dinner in his great paneled dining hall that evening. With it he had a bottle of his rarest wine. Two slight annoyances kept him from perfect enjoyment. One was the thought that it would be difficult to replace Ivan; the other was that his quarry had escaped him; of course the American hadn't played the game—so thought the general as he tasted his after-dinner liqueur. In his library he read, to soothe himself, from the works of Marcus Aurelius.[17] At ten he went up to his bedroom. He was deliciously tired, he said to himself, as he locked himself in. There was a little moonlight; so, before turning on his light, he went to the window and looked down at the courtyard. He could see the great hounds, and he called: "Better luck another time," to them. Then he switched on the light.

A man, who had been hiding in the curtains of the bed, was standing there.

"Rainsford!" screamed the general. "How did you get here?"

"Swam," said Rainsford. "I found it quicker than walking through the jungle."

The general sucked in his breath and smiled. "I congratulate you," he said. "You have won the game."

Rainsford did not smile. "I am still a beast at bay," he said, in a low, hoarse voice. "Get ready, General Zaroff."

The general made one of his deepest bows. "I see," he said. "Splendid! One of us is to furnish a repast for the hounds. The other will sleep in this very excellent bed. On guard, Rainsford."

He had never slept in a better bed, Rainsford decided.

---

16. ***Madame Butterfly,*** a tragic opera by Puccini (pü chē′nē).
17. ***Marcus Aurelius*** (mär′kəs ô rē′li əs), a Roman emperor (A.D. 161–180) and famous philosopher.

Discussion

1. At the end of the story, what has happened to Zaroff? How do you know?

2. What do you think is the main purpose of the shipboard conversation between Rainsford and Whitney?

3. (a) As the action progresses, whose side are you on—Rainsford's or Zaroff's? **(b)** In what ways does taking sides increase suspense for readers?

4. (a) Do you think General Zaroff is a believable character? **(b)** Could anyone actually have his philosophy of hunting? Defend your answer.

5. Early in the story, Rainsford gives his philosophy of hunting. Do you think that events in the story have caused him to change his beliefs? Why or why not?

Application

Plot

1. What is the major conflict in the story?

2. What pattern of events grows from this conflict?

3. What is the climax of the story?

4. How is the conflict resolved?

Vocabulary

Context, Pronunciation Key

Each word in the list that follows might be used in describing a person. Fill the blank in each sentence with a word from the list. Use context (the other words and ideas in the sentence) as a guide in making your choice. Write the completed sentences on your paper.

mystified	ardent
menacing	imprudent
cultivated	uncanny

1. It would be ____ of us to leave work early; if the boss finds out, we probably would be fired.

2. They are such ____ football fans that they have attended every home game—regardless of weather—for the last nine years.

3. Zaroff's ____ voice was only one of the indications that he was an educated man who possessed highly refined tastes.

4. At first they were merely puzzled by her odd behavior, but when she began to speak words that made no sense at all, they were completely ____.

5. You do have the ____ ability to read my thoughts.

6. He uttered the threat with a ____ gesture that silenced those around him.

Now use your Glossary to determine the proper meanings and pronunciations of the following words. Then indicate on your paper with a "T" or an "F" whether the statements are true or false.

analytical	affable
solicitous	apprehensive

7. Both *apprehensive* and *analytical* have a primary accent on the third syllable.

8. *Affable* comes from the word *fable.*

9. The accented syllable in the word *solicitous* rhymes with *pick.*

10. An *apprehensive* person is fearful.

See **STEREOTYPE** Handbook of Literary Terms

Blues Ain't No Mockin Bird Toni Cade Bambara

It took too long for the photographer to get the point. Smiling, he handed the camera to Granddaddy . . .

The puddle had frozen over, and me and Cathy went stompin in it. The twins from next door, Tyrone and Terry, were swingin so high out of sight we forgot we were waitin our turn on the tire. Cathy jumped up and came down hard on her heels and started tap-dancin. And the frozen patch splinterin every which way underneath kinda spooky. "Looks like a plastic spider web," she said. "A sort of weird spider, I guess, with many mental problems." But really it looked like the crystal paperweight Granny kept in the parlor. She was on the back porch, Granny was, making the cakes drunk. The old ladle drippin rum into the Christmas tins, like it used to drip maple syrup into the pails when we lived in the Judson's woods, like it poured cider into the vats when we were on the Cooper place, like it used to scoop buttermilk and soft cheese when we lived at the dairy.

"Go tell that man we ain't a bunch of trees."

"Ma'am?"

"I said to tell that man to get away from here with that camera." Me and Cathy look over toward the meadow where the men with the station wagon'd been roamin around all mornin. The tall man with a huge camera lassoed to his shoulder was buzzin our way.

"They're makin movie pictures," yelled Tyrone, stiffenin his legs and twistin so the tire'd come down slow so they could see.

"They're makin movie pictures," sang out Terry.

"That boy don't never have anything original to say," say Cathy grown-up.

By the time the man with the camera had cut across our neighbor's yard, the twins were out of the trees swingin low and Granny was onto the steps, the screen door bammin soft and scratchy against her palms. "We thought we'd get a shot or two of the house and everything and then——"

"Good mornin," Granny cut him off. And smiled that smile.

"Good mornin," he said, head all down the way Bingo does when you yell at him about the bones on the kitchen floor. "Nice place you got here, aunty. We thought we'd take a——"

"Did you?" said Granny with her eyebrows. Cathy pulled up her socks and giggled.

"Nice things here," said the man, buzzin his camera over the yard. The pecan barrels, the sled, me and Cathy, the flowers, the printed stones along the driveway, the trees, the twins, the toolshed.

"I don't know about the thing, the it, and the stuff," said Granny, still talkin with her eyebrows. "Just people here is what I tend to consider."

Camera man stopped buzzin. Cathy giggled into her collar.

"Mornin, ladies," a new man said. He had come up behind us when we weren't lookin. "And gents," discoverin the twins givin him a nasty look. "We're filmin for the county," he said with a smile. "Mind if we shoot a bit around here?"

"I do indeed," said Granny with no smile. Smilin man was smilin up a storm. So was Cathy. But he didn't seem to have another word to say, so he and the camera man backed on out the yard, but you could hear the camera buzzin still. "Suppose you just shut that machine off," said Granny real low through her teeth, and took a step down off the porch and then another.

"Now, aunty," Camera said, pointin the thing straight at her.

"Your mama and I are not related."

Smilin man got his notebook out and a chewed-up pencil. "Listen," he said movin back into our yard, "we'd like to have a statement from you . . . for the film. We're filmin for the county, see. Part of the food stamp campaign. You know about the food stamps?"

Granny said nuthin.

"Maybe there's somethin you want to say for the film. I see you grow your own vegetables," he smiled real nice. "If more folks did that, see, there'd be no need——"

Granny wasn't sayin nuthin. So they backed on out, buzzin at our clothesline and the twins' bicycles, then back on down to the meadow. The twins were danglin in the tire, lookin at Granny. Me and Cathy were waitin, too, cause Granny always got somethin to say. She teaches steady with no letup. "I was on this bridge one time," she started off. "Was a crowd cause this man was goin to jump, you understand. And a minister was there and the police and some other folks. His woman was there, too."

"What was they doin?" asked Tyrone.

"Tryin to talk him out of it was what they was doin. The minister talkin about how it was a mortal sin, suicide. His woman takin bites out of her own hand and not even knowin it, so nervous and cryin and talkin fast."

"So what happened?" asked Tyrone.

"So here comes . . . this person . . . with a camera, takin pictures of the man and the minister and the woman. Takin pictures of the man in his misery about to jump, cause life so bad and people been messin with him so bad. This person takin up the whole roll of film practically. But savin a few, of course."

"Of course," said Cathy, hatin the person. Me standin there wonderin how Cathy knew it was "of course" when I didn't and it was *my* grandmother.

After a while Tyrone say, "Did he jump?"

"Yes, did he jump?" say Terry all eager.

And Granny just stared at the twins till their faces swallow up the eager and they don't even care any more about the man jumpin. Then she goes back onto the porch and lets the screen door go for itself. I'm lookin to Cathy to finish the story cause she knows Granny's whole story before me even. Like she knew how come we move so much and Cathy ain't but a third cousin we picked up on the way last Thanksgivin visitin. But she knew it was on account of people drivin Granny crazy till she'd get up in the night and start packin. Mumblin and packin and wakin everybody up sayin, "Let's get on away from here before I kill me somebody." Like people wouldn't pay her for things like they said they would. Or Mr. Judson bringin us boxes of old clothes and raggedy magazines. Or Mrs. Cooper comin in our kitchen and touchin everything and sayin how clean it all was. Granny goin crazy, and Granddaddy Cain pullin her off the people, sayin, "Now, now, Cora." But next day loadin up the truck, with rocks all in his jaw, madder than Granny in the first place.

"I read a story once," said Cathy soundin like Granny teacher. "About this lady Goldilocks who barged into a house that wasn't even hers. And not invited, you understand. Messed over the people's groceries and broke up the people's furniture. Had the nerve to sleep in the folks' bed."

"Then what happened?" asked Tyrone.

"What they do, the folks, when they come in to all this mess?"

"Did they make her pay for it?" asked Terry, makin a fist. "I'd've made her pay me."

I didn't even ask. I could see Cathy actress was very likely to just walk away and leave us in mystery about this story which I heard was about some bears.

"Did they throw her out?" asked Tyrone, like his father sounds when he's bein extra nasty-plus to the washinmachine man.

"Woulda," said Terry. "I woulda gone upside her head with my fist and——"

"You woulda done whatcha always do—go cry to Mama, you big baby," said Tyrone. So naturally Terry starts hittin on Tyrone, and next thing you know they tumblin out the tire and rollin on the ground. But Granny didn't say a thing or send the twins home or step out on the steps to tell us about how we can't afford to be fightin amongst ourselves. She didn't say nuthin. So I get into the tire to take my turn. And I could see her leanin up against the pantry table, starin at the cakes she was puttin up for the Christmas sale, mumblin real low and grumpy and holdin her forehead like it wanted to fall off and mess up the rum cakes.

Behind me I hear before I can see Granddaddy Cain comin through the woods in his field boots. Then I twist around to see the shiny black oilskin cuttin through what little left there was of yellows, reds, and oranges. His great white head not quite round cause of this bloody thing high on his shoulder, like he was wearin a cap on sideways. He takes the shortcut through the pecan grove, and the sound of twigs snappin overhead and underfoot travels clear and cold all the way up to us. And here comes Smilin and Camera up behind him like they was goin to do somethin. Folks like to go for him sometimes. Cathy say it's because he's so tall and quiet and like a king. And people just can't stand it. But Smilin and Camera don't hit him in the head or nuthin. They just buzz on him as he stalks by with the chicken hawk slung over his shoulder, squawkin, drippin red down the back of the oilskin. He passes the porch and stops a second for Granny to see he's caught the hawk at last, but she's just starin and mumblin, and not at the hawk. So he nails the bird to the toolshed door, the hammerin crackin through the eardrums. And the bird flappin himself to death and droolin down the door to paint the gravel in the driveway red, then brown, then black. And the two men movin up on tiptoe like they was invisible or we were blind, one.

"Get them persons out of my flower bed, Mister Cain," say Granny moanin real low like at a funeral.

"How come your grandmother calls her husband 'Mister Cain' all the time?" Tyrone whispers all loud and noisy and from the city and don't know no better. Like his mama, Miss Myrtle, tell us never mind the formality as if we had no better breeding than to call her Myrtle, plain. And then this awful thing—a giant hawk—come wailin up over the meadow, flyin low and tilted and screamin, zigzaggin through the pecan grove, breakin branches and hollerin, snappin past the clothesline, flyin every which way, flyin into things reckless with crazy.

"He's come to claim his mate," say Cathy fast, and ducks down. We all fall quick and flat into the gravel driveway, stones scrapin my face. I squinch my eyes open again at the hawk on the door, tryin to fly up out of her death like it was just a sack flown into by mistake. Her body holdin her there on that nail, though. The mate beatin the air overhead and clutchin for hair, for heads, for landin space.

The camera man duckin and bendin and runnin and fallin, jigglin the camera and scared. And Smilin jumpin up and down swipin at the huge bird, tryin to bring the hawk down with just his raggedy ole cap. Granddaddy Cain straight up and silent, watchin the circles of the hawk, then aimin the hammer off his wrist. The giant bird fallin, silent and slow. Then here comes Camera and Smilin all big and bad now that the awful screechin thing is on its back and broken, here they come. And Granddaddy Cain looks up at them like it was the first time noticin, but not payin them too much mind cause he's listenin, we all listenin, to that low groanin music comin from the porch. And we figure any minute, somethin in my back tells me any minute now, Granny gonna bust through that screen with somethin in her hand and murder on her mind. So Granddaddy say above the buzzin, but quiet, "Good day, gentlemen." Just like that. Like he'd invited them in to play cards and they'd stayed too long and all the sandwiches were gone and Reverend Webb was droppin by and it was time to go.

They didn't know what to do. But like Cathy say, folks can't stand Granddaddy tall and silent and like a king. They can't neither. The smile the men smilin is pullin the mouth back and showin the teeth. Lookin like the wolf man, both of them. Then Granddaddy holds his hand out—this huge hand I used to sit in when I was a baby and he'd carry me through the house to my mother like I was a gift on a tray. Like he used to on the trains. They called the other men just waiters. But they spoke of Granddaddy separate and said, The Waiter. And said he had engines in his feet and motors in his hands and couldn't no train throw him off and couldn't nobody turn him round. They were big enough for motors, his hands were. He held that one hand out all still and it gettin to be not at all a hand but a person in itself.

"He wants you to hand him the camera," Smilin whispers to Camera, tiltin his head to talk secret like they was in the jungle or somethin and come upon a native that don't speak the language. The men start untyin the straps, and they put the camera into that great hand speckled with the hawk's blood all black and crackly now. And the hand don't even drop with the weight, just the fingers move, curl up around the machine. But Granddaddy lookin straight at the men. They lookin at each other and everywhere but at Granddaddy's face.

"We filmin for the county, see," say Smilin. "We puttin together a movie for the food stamp program . . . filmin all around these parts. Uhh, filmin for the county."

"Can I have my camera back?" say the tall man with no machine on his shoulder, but still keepin it high like the camera was still there or needed to be. "Please, sir."

Then Granddaddy's other hand flies up like a sudden and gentle bird, slaps down fast on top of the camera and lifts off half like it was a calabash cut for sharing.

"Hey," Camera jumps forward. He gathers up the parts into his chest and everything unrollin and fallin all over. "Whatcha tryin to do? You'll ruin the film." He looks down into his chest of metal reels and things like he's protectin a kitten from the cold.

"You standin in the misses' flower bed," say Granddaddy. "This is our own place."

The two men look at him, then at each other, then back at the mess in the camera man's chest, and they just back off. One sayin over and over all the way down to the meadow, "Watch it, Bruno. Keep ya fingers off the film." Then Granddaddy picks up the hammer and jams it into the oilskin pocket, scrapes his boots, and goes into the house. And you can hear the squish of his boots headin through the house. And you can see the funny shadow he throws from the parlor window onto the ground by the stringbean patch. The hammer draggin the pocket of the oilskin out so Granddaddy looked even wider. Granny was hummin now—high, not low and grumbly. And she was doin the cakes again, you could smell the molasses from the rum.

"There's this story I'm goin to write one day," say Cathy dreamer. "About the proper use of the hammer."

"Can I be in it?" Tyrone say with his hand up like it was a matter of first come, first served.

"Perhaps," say Cathy, climbin onto the tire to pump us up. "If you there and ready."

Discussion

1. (a) From what point of view is the story told? **(b)** What mental image have you formed of the narrator? Is it a boy or a girl? Why have you drawn this conclusion? **(c)** What kind of person is the narrator? Use specific references from the story to support your answers.

2. What information does the author reveal to the reader in describing the many uses Granny has made of the ladle?

3. How does the narrator feel about Cathy? Explain.

4. (a) Describe Granny and Granddaddy. **(b)**

What does the narrator think of each grandparent? Use specific references from the story to support your answers.

5. How would you describe the relationship between Granny and Granddaddy? Support your description with examples from the story.

Application

Stereotype

1. What kinds of things aggravate Granny, give her the "blues"?

2. In what ways are the photographers' comments about the family's growing its own vegetables similar to those of the woman who came into the kitchen, touched everything, and said "how clean it all was"?

Composition

Living close to the grandparents, the child in "Blues Ain't No Mockin Bird" is in a position to anticipate what they will do or say under given circumstances. Their tones of voice and their facial expressions have particular meaning for the grandchild. When the child says that Granny "smiled that smile" or that Granny spoke "with her eyebrows," the image of the grandmother becomes clearer in your mind. When you hear Granny say, "Go tell that man we ain't a bunch of trees" and "Your mama and I are not related," your understanding of the character becomes even more clear.

Select someone you know—a friend, a relative, or a person whom you have frequent opportunity to observe closely—who is admirable or amusing or eccentric. Write a short character sketch of that person. In preparation, make a list of things such as a pet expression that the person uses frequently, some obsession that affects the person's outlook, or a particularly noticeable physical characteristic that seems to relate itself in some way to his or her behavior. Focus, as Toni Cade Bambara does, on an incident in which you observed this person, and use the incident to illustrate the distinctive traits. (See *Writing a Description,* page 667, in Composition Guide.)

Toni Cade Bambara 1939–

In explaining her title, "Blues Ain't No Mockin Bird," Bambara says that in an old Mississippi Delta song called "Blues Ain't No Mockin' Bird," singers like "Big Bill" Broonzy and "Mississippi John" Hurt used several layers of irony to criticize the attempts of ethnomusicologists [experts who study the music of ethnic groups] to interpret the "blues." She wants her readers to see that "outsiders, so-called experts" like the photographers in the story are mistaken in their definition of the black experience. Their vision is dim and limited. The legendary song of death that a mocking bird sings is limited to its seven-note scale; the "blues" in the black experience is a part of a constant and undying battle against trouble. The spirit of this fight is not defeatist or fatalistic; and for the family in "Blues Ain't No Mockin Bird," that fight ends in triumph.

Toni Cade Bambara has written essays, reviews, and short stories, which have appeared in textbooks and in such publications as *Black World,* the *Massachusetts Review,* and *Redbook.* She is also author of *Tales and Stories for Black Folks, Gorilla, My Love, The Salt Eaters* (1980), and *The Sea Birds Are Still Alive* (1982).

In 1981 Toni Cade Bambara was one of a group of writers chosen by the Before Columbus Foundation to receive that organization's second annual awards for "literary achievement by people of various ethnic backgrounds."

See **CHARACTERIZATION** Handbook of Literary Terms

Split Cherry Tree

Jesse Stuart

Dave is the only one of eleven children allowed to attend school. Now his father is calling that school "a bug school, a lizard school, a snake school."

"I don't mind staying after school," I says to Professor Herbert, "but I'd rather you'd whip me with a switch and let me go home early. Pa will whip me anyway for getting home two hours late."

"You are too big to whip," says Professor Herbert, "and I have to punish you for climbing up that cherry tree. You boys knew better than that! The other five boys have paid their dollar each. You have been the only one who has not helped pay for the tree. Can't you borrow a dollar?"

"I can't," I says. "I'll have to take the punishment. I wish it would be quicker punishment. I wouldn't mind."

Professor Herbert stood and looked at me. He was a big man. He wore a gray suit of clothes. The suit matched his gray hair.

"You don't know my father," I says to Professor Herbert. "He might be called a little old-fashioned. He makes us mind him until we're twenty-one years old. He believes: 'If you spare the rod, you spoil the child.' I'll never be able to make him understand about the cherry tree. I'm the first of my people to go to high school."

"You must take the punishment," says Professor Herbert. "You must stay two hours after school today and two hours after school tomorrow. I am allowing you twenty-five cents an hour. That is good money for a high school student. You can sweep the schoolhouse floor, wash the blackboards, and clean windows. I'll pay the dollar for you."

I couldn't ask Professor Herbert to loan me a dollar. He never offered to loan it to me. I had to stay and help the janitor and work out my fine at a quarter an hour.

I thought as I swept the floor: "What will Pa do to me? What lie can I tell him when I go home? Why did we ever climb that cherry tree and break it down for anyway? Why did we run crazy over the hills away from the crowd? Why did we do all of this! Six of us climbed up in a little cherry tree after one little lizard! Why did the tree split and fall with us? It should have been a stronger tree! Why did Eif[1] Crabtree just happen to be below us plowing and catch us in his cherry tree? Why wasn't he a better man than to charge us six dollars for the tree?"

It was six o'clock when I left the schoolhouse. I had six miles to walk home. It would be after seven when I got home. I had all my work to do when I got home. It took Pa and me both to do the work. Seven cows to milk. Nineteen head of cattle to feed, four mules, twenty-five hogs, firewood and stovewood to cut and

1. ***Eif*** (īf).

"Split Cherry Tree" by Jesse Stuart. Reprinted with permission of the Jesse Stuart Foundation, Eastern Kentucky University, Richmond, KY. (Slightly abridged.)

water to draw from the well. He would be doing it when I got home. He would be mad and wondering what was keeping me!

I hurried home. I would run under the dark leafless trees. I would walk fast uphill. I would run down the hill. The ground was freezing. I had to hurry. I had to run and reached the long ridge that led to our cow pasture. I ran along this ridge. The wind dried the sweat on my face. I ran across the pasture to the house.

I threw down my books in the chipyard, I ran to the barn to spread fodder on the ground for the cattle. I didn't take time to change my clean school clothes for my old work clothes. I ran out to the barn. I saw Pa spreading fodder on the ground to the cattle. That was my job. I ran up to the fence. I says: "Leave that for me Pa. I'll do it. I'm just a little late."

"I see you are," says Pa. He turned and looked at me. His eyes danced fire. "What in th' world has kept you so. Why ain't you been here to help me with this work? Make a gentleman out'n one boy in th' family and this is what you get! Send you to high school and you get too onery fer th' buzzards to smell!"

I never said anything. I didn't want to tell why I was late from school. Pa stopped scattering the bundles of fodder. He looked at me. He says: "Why are you gettin' in here this time o' night? You tell me or I'll take a hickory withe to you right here on th' spot."

I says: "I had to stay after school." I couldn't lie to Pa. He'd go to school and find out why I had to stay. If I lied to him it would be too bad for me.

"Why did you haf to stay atter school?" says Pa.

I says: "Our biology class went on a field trip today. Six of us boys broke down a cherry tree. We had to give a dollar apiece to pay for the tree. I didn't have the dollar. Professor Herbert is making me work out my dollar. He gives me twenty-five cents an hour. I had to stay in this afternoon. I'll have to stay in tomorrow afternoon!"

"Are you telling me th' truth?" says Pa.

"I'm telling you the truth," I says. "Go and see for yourself."

"That's just what I'll do in th' mornin'," says Pa. "Jist whose cherry tree did you break down?"

"Eif Crabtree's cherry tree!"

Pa says, "What was you doing clear out in Eif Crabtree's place? He lives four miles from th' County High School. Don't they teach you no books at that high school? Do they jist let you get out and gad over th' hillsides? If that's all they do I'll keep you at home, Dave. I've got work here fer you to do!"

"Pa," I says, "Spring is just getting here. We take a subject in school where we have to have bugs, snakes, flowers, lizards, frogs, and plants. It is Biology. It was a pretty day today. We went out to find a few of these. Six of us boys saw a lizard at the same time sunning on a cherry tree. We all went up the tree to get it. We broke the tree down. It split at the forks. Eif Crabtree was plowing down below us. He ran up the hill and got our names. The other boys gave their dollar apiece. I didn't have mine. Professor Herbert put mine in fòr me. I have to work it out at school."

"Poor man's son, huh," says Pa. "I'll attend to that myself in th' mornin'. I'll take keer o' 'im. He ain't from this county nohow. I'll go down there in th' mornin' and see 'im. Lettin' you leave your books and galavant all over th' hills. What kind of a school is it nohow! Didn't do that, my son, when I's a little shaver in school. All fared alike too."

"Pa please don't go down there," I says. "Just let me have fifty cents and pay the rest of my fine! I don't want you to go down there! I don't want you to start anything with Professor Herbert!"

"Ashamed of your old Pap are you, Dave," says Pa, "atter th' way I've worked to raise you! Tryin' to send you to school so you can make a better livin' than I've made.

"I'll straighten this thing out myself! I'll take keer o' Professor Herbert myself! He ain't got no right to keep you in and let the other boys

off jist because they've got th' money! I'm a poor man. A bullet will go in a Professor same as it will any man. It will go in a rich man same as it will a poor man. Now you get into this work before I take one o' these withes and cut the shirt off'n your back!"

I thought once I'd run through the woods above the barn just as hard as I could go. I thought I'd leave high school and home forever! Pa could not catch me! I'd get away! I couldn't go back to school with him. He'd have a gun and maybe he'd shoot Professor Herbert. It was hard to tell what he would do. I could tell Pa that school had changed in the hills from the way it was when he was a boy but he wouldn't understand. I could tell him we studied frogs, birds, snakes, lizards, flowers, insects. But Pa wouldn't understand. If I did run away from home it wouldn't matter to Pa. He would see Professor Herbert anyway. He would think that high school and Professor Herbert had run me away from home. There was no need to run away. I'd just have to stay, finish foddering the cattle, and go to school with Pa the next morning.

I would take a bundle of fodder, remove the hickory witheband from around it, and scatter it on rocks, clumps of greenbriars, and brush so the cattle wouldn't tramp it under their feet. I would lean it up against the oak trees and the rocks in the pasture just above our pigpen on the hill. The fodder was cold and frosty where it had set out in the stacks. I would carry bundles of the fodder from the stack until I had spread out a bundle for each steer. Pa went to the barn to feed the mules and throw corn in the pen to the hogs.

The moon shone bright in the cold March sky. I finished my work by moonlight. Professor Herbert really didn't know how much work I had to do at home. If he had known he would not have kept me after school. He would have loaned me a dollar to have paid my part on the cherry tree. He had never lived in the hills. He didn't know the way the hill boys had to work so that they could go to school. Now he was teaching in a County High School where all the boys who attended were from hill farms.

After I'd finished doing my work I went to the house and ate my supper. Pa and Mom had eaten. My supper was getting cold. I heard Pa and Mom talking in the front room. Pa was telling Mom about me staying after school.

"I had to do all th' milkin' tonight, chop th' wood myself. It's too hard on me atter I've turned ground all day. I'm goin' to take a day off tomorrow and see if I can't remedy things a little. I'll go down to that high school tomorrow. I won't be a very good scholar fer Professor Herbert nohow. He won't keep me in atter school. I'll take a different kind of lesson down there and make 'im acquainted with it."

"Now Luster," says Mom, "you jist stay away from there. Don't cause a lot o' trouble. You can be jailed fer a trick like that. You'll get th' Law atter you. You'll jist go down there and show off and plague your own boy Dave to death in front o' all th' scholars!"

"Plague or no plague," says Pa, "he don't take into consideration what all I haf to do here, does he? I'll show 'im it ain't right to keep one boy in and let the rest go scot-free. My boy is good as th' rest, ain't he? A bullet will make a hole in a schoolteacher same as it will anybody else. He can't do me that way and get by with it. I'll plug 'im first. I aim to go down there bright and early in the mornin' and get all this straight! I aim to see about bug larnin' and this runnin' all over God's creation huntin' snakes, lizards, and frogs. Ransackin' th' country and goin' through cherry orchards and breakin' th' trees down atter lizards! Old Eif Crabtree ought to a-poured th' hot lead to 'em instead o' chargin' six dollars fer th' tree! He ought to a-got old Herbert th' first one!"

I ate my supper. I slipped upstairs and lit the lamp. I tried to forget the whole thing. I studied plane geometry. Then I studied my biology lesson. I could hardly study for thinking about Pa. "He'll go to school with me in the morning. He'll take a gun for Professor Herbert! What will Professor Herbert think of me! I'll tell him when Pa leaves that I couldn't help it. But Pa might shoot him. I hate to go with Pa. Maybe he'll cool off about it tonight and not go in the morning."

Pa got up at four o'clock. He built a fire in the stove. Then he built a fire in the fireplace. He got Mom up to get breakfast. Then he got me up to help feed and milk. By the time we had our work done at the barn, Mom had breakfast ready for us. We ate our breakfast. Daylight came and we could see the bare oak trees covered white with frost. The hills were white with frost. A cold wind was blowing. The sky was clear. The sun would soon come out and melt the frost. The afternoon would be warm with sunshine and the frozen ground would thaw. There would be mud on the hills again. Muddy water would then run down the little ditches on the hills.

"Now Dave," says Pa. "Let's get ready fer school. I aim to go with you this mornin' and look into bug-larnin', frog-larnin', lizard- and snake-larnin', and breakin' down cherry trees! I don't like no sicha foolish way o' larnin' myself!"

Pa hadn't forgot. I'd have to take him to school with me. He would take me to school with him. We were going early. I was glad we were going early. If Pa pulled a gun on Professor Herbert there wouldn't be so many of my classmates there to see him.

I knew that Pa wouldn't be at home in the high school. He wore overalls, big boots, a blue shirt and a sheepskin coat and a slouched black hat gone to seed at the top. He put his gun in its holster. We started trudging toward the high school across the hill.

It was early when we got to the County High School. Professor Herbert had just got there. I just thought as we walked up the steps into the schoolhouse: "Maybe Pa will find out Professor Herbert is a good man. He just doesn't know him. Just like I felt toward the Lambert boys across the hill. I didn't like them until I'd seen them and talked to them. After I went to school with them and talked to them, I liked them and we were friends. It's a lot in knowing the other fellow."

"You're th' Professor here, ain't you?" says Pa.

"Yes," says Professor Herbert, "and you are Dave's father."

"Yes," says Pa, pulling out his gun and laying it on the seat in Professor Herbert's office. Professor Herbert's eyes got big behind his black-rimmed glasses when he saw Pa's gun. Color came into his pale cheeks.

"Jist a few things about this school I want to know," says Pa. "I'm tryin' to make a scholar out'n Dave. He's the only one out'n eleven youngins I've sent to high school. Here he comes in late and leaves me all th' work to do! He said you's all out bug huntin' yesterday and broke a cherry tree down. He had to stay two hours after school yesterday and work out money to pay on that cherry tree! Is that right?"

"Wwwwy," says Professor Herbert, "I guess it is."

He looked at Pa's gun.

"Well," says Pa, "this ain't no high school. It's a bug school, a lizard school, a snake school! It ain't no school nohow!"

"Why did you bring that gun," says Professor Herbert to Pa.

"You see that little hole," says Pa as he picked up the long blue forty-four and put his finger on the end of the barrel, "a bullet can come out'n that hole that will kill a schoolteacher same as it will kill any other man. It will kill a rich man same as a poor man. It will kill a man. But atter I come in and saw you, I know'd I wouldn't need it. This maul o' mine[2] could do you up in a few minutes."

Pa stood there, big, hard, brown-skinned, and mighty beside of Professor Herbert. I didn't know Pa was so much bigger and harder. I'd never seen Pa in a schoolhouse before. I'd seen Professor Herbert. He always looked big before to me. He didn't look big standing beside of Pa.

"I was only doing my duty," says Professor

2. ***this maul o' mine.*** Pa feels that he would need only his fist.

Herbert, "Mr. Sexton, and following the course of study the state provided us with."

"Course o' study," says Pa, "what study, bug study? Varmit study? Takin' youngins to th' woods. Boys and girls all out there together a-galavantin' in the brush and kickin' up their heels and their poor old Ma's and Pa's at home a-slavin' to keep 'em in school and give 'em a education! You know that's dangerous too puttin' a lot o' boys and girls out together like that!

Students are coming into the schoolhouse now.

Professor Herbert says: "Close the door, Dave, so others won't hear."

I walked over and closed the door. I was shaking like a leaf in the wind. I thought Pa was going to hit Professor Herbert every minute. He was doing all the talking. His face was getting red. The red color was coming through the brown weather-beaten skin on Pa's face.

"I was right with these students," says Professor Herbert. "I know what they got into and what they didn't. I didn't send one of the other teachers with them on this field trip. I went myself. Yes, I took the boys and girls together. Why not?"

"It jist don't look good to me," says Pa, "a-takin' all this swarm of youngins out to pilage th' whole deestrict. Breakin' down cherry trees. Keepin' boys in atter school."

"What else could I have done with Dave, Mr. Sexton?" says Professor Herbert. "The boys didn't have any business all climbing that cherry tree after one lizard. One boy could have gone up in the tree and got it. The farmer charged us six dollars. It was a little steep I think but we had it to pay. Must I make five boys pay and let your boy off? He said he didn't have the dollar and couldn't get it. So I put it in for him. I'm letting him work it out. He's not working for me. He's working for the school!"

"I jist don't know what you could a-done with 'im," says Pa, "only a-larruped 'im with a withe! That's what he needed!"

"He's too big to whip," says Professor Herbert pointing at me. "He's a man in size."

"He's not too big fer me to whip," says Pa. "They ain't too big until they're over twenty-one! It jist didn't look fair to me! Work one and let th' rest out because they got th' money. I don't see what bugs has got to do with a high school! It don't look good to me nohow!"

Pa picked up his gun and put it back in its holster. The red color left Professor Herbert's face. He talked more to Pa. Pa softened a little. It looked funny to see Pa in the high school building. It was the first time he'd ever been there.

"We were not only hunting snakes, toads, flowers, butterflies, lizards," says Professor Herbert, "but, Mr. Sexton, I was hunting dry timothy grass to put in an incubator and raise some protozoa."

"I don't know what that is," says Pa. "Th' incubator is th' new-fangled way o' cheatin' th' hens and raisin' chickens. I ain't so sure about th' breed o' chickens you mentioned."

"You've heard of germs, Mr. Sexton, haven't you," says Professor Herbert.

"Jist call me Luster if you don't mind," says Pa, very casual like.

"All right, Luster, you've heard of germs, haven't you?"

"Yes," says Pa, "but I don't believe in germs. I'm sixty-five years old and I ain't seen one yet!"

"You can't see them with your naked eye," says Professor Herbert. "Just keep that gun in the holster and stay with me in the high school today. I have a few things I want to show you. That scum on your teeth has germs in it."

"What," says Pa, "you mean to tell me I've got germs on my teeth!"

"Yes," says Professor Herbert. "The same kind as we might be able to find in a living black snake if we dissect it!"

"I don't mean to dispute your word," says Pa, "but I jist don't believe it. I don't believe I have germs on my teeth!"

"Stay with me today and I'll show you. I want to take you through the school anyway! School has changed a lot in the hills since you went to school. I don't guess we had high schools in this county when you went to school!"

"No," says Pa, "jist readin', writin', and cipherin'.[3] We didn't have all this bug larnin', frog larnin', and findin' germs on your teeth and in the middle o' black snakes! Th' world's changin'."

"It is," says Professor Herbert, "and we hope all for the better. Boys like your own there are going to help change it. He's your boy. He knows all of what I've told you. You stay with me today."

"I'll shore stay with you," says Pa. "I want to see th' germs off'n my teeth. I jist want to see a germ. I've never seen one in my life. 'Seein' is believin,' Pap allus told me."

Pa walks out of the office with Professor Herbert. I just hoped Professor Herbert didn't have Pa arrested for pulling his gun. Pa's gun has always been a friend to him when he goes to settle disputes.

The bell rang. School took up. I saw the students when they marched in the schoolhouse look at Pa. They would grin and punch each other. Pa just stood and watched them pass in at the schoolhouse door. Two long lines marched in the house. The boys and girls were clean and well-dressed. Pa stood over in the school yard under a leafless elm, in his sheepskin coat, his big boots laced in front with buckskin, and his heavy socks stuck above his boot tops. Pa's overalls legs were baggy and wrinkled between his coat and boot tops. His blue work shirt showed at the collar. His big black hat showed his gray-streaked black hair. His face was hard and weather-tanned to the color of a ripe fodder blade. His hands were big and gnarled like the roots of the elm tree he stood beside.

When I went to my first class, I saw Pa and Professor Herbert going around over the schoolhouse. I was in my geometry class when Pa and Professor Herbert came in the room. We were explaining our propositions on the blackboard. Professor Herbert and Pa just quietly came in and sat down for awhile. I heard Fred Wurts whisper to Glenn Armstrong: "Who is that old man? Lord, he's a rough looking scamp." Glenn whispered back: "I think he's Dave's Pap." The students in geometry looked at Pa. They must have wondered what he was doing in school. Before the class was over, Pa and Professor Herbert got up and went out. I saw them together down on the playground. Professor Herbert was explaining to Pa. I could see the print of Pa's gun under his coat when he'd walk around.

At noon in the high-school cafeteria Pa and Professor Herbert sat together at the little table where Professor Herbert always ate by himself. They ate together. The students watched the way Pa ate. He ate with his knife instead of his fork. A lot of the students felt sorry for me after they found out he was my father. They didn't have to feel sorry for me. I wasn't ashamed of Pa after I found out he wasn't going to shoot Professor Herbert. I was glad they had made friends. I wasn't ashamed of Pa. I wouldn't be as long as he behaved. He would find out about the high school as I had found out about the Lambert boys across the hill.

In the afternoon when we went to biology Pa was in the class. He was sitting on one of the high stools beside the microscope. We went ahead with our work just as if Pa wasn't in the class. I saw Pa take his knife and scrape tartar from one of his teeth. Professor Herbert put it on the lens and adjusted the microscope for Pa. He adjusted it and worked awhile. Then he says: "Now Luster, look! Put your eye right down to the light. Squint the other eye!"

Pa put his head down and did as Professor Herbert said. "I see 'im," says Pa. "Who'd a ever thought that? Right on a body's teeth! Right in a body's mouth. You're right certain they ain't no fake to this, Professor Herbert?"

"No, Luster," says Professor Herbert. "It's there. That's the germ. Germs live in a world

---

3. ***cipherin'***, arithmetic.

we cannot see with the naked eye. We must use the microscope. There are millions of them in our bodies. Some are harmful. Others are helpful."

Pa holds his face down and looks through the microscope. We stop and watch Pa. He sits upon the tall stool. His knees are against the table. His legs are long. His coat slips up behind when he bends over. The handle of his gun shows. Professor Herbert pulls his coat down quickly.

"Oh, yes," says Pa. He gets up and pulls his coat down. Pa's face gets a little red. He knows about his gun and he knows he doesn't have any use for it in high school.

"We have a big black snake over here we caught yesterday," says Professor Herbert. "We'll chloroform him and dissect him and show you he has germs in his body too."

"Don't do it," says Pa. "I believe you. I jist don't want to see you kill the black snake. I never kill one. They are good mousers and a lot o' help to us on the farm. I like black snakes. I jist hate to see people kill 'em. I don't allow 'em killed on my place."

The students look at Pa. They seem to like him better after he said that. Pa with a gun in his pocket but a tender heart beneath his ribs for snakes, but not for man! Pa won't whip a mule at home. He won't whip his cattle.

"Man can defend hisself," says Pa, "but cattle and mules can't. We have the drop on 'em. Ain't nothin' to a man that'll beat a good pullin' mule. He ain't got th' right kind o' a heart!"

Professor Herbert took Pa through the laboratory. He showed him the different kinds of work we were doing. He showed him our equipment. They stood and talked while we worked. Then they walked out together. They talked louder when they got in the hall.

When our biology class was over I walked out of the room. It was our last class for the day. I would have to take my broom and sweep two hours to finish paying for the split cherry tree. I just wondered if Pa would want me to stay. He was standing in the hallway watching the students march out. He looked lost among us. He looked like a leaf turned brown on the tree among the treetop filled with growing leaves.

I got my broom and started to sweep. Professor Herbert walked up and says: "I'm going to let you do that some other time. You can go home with your father. He is waiting out there."

I laid my broom down, got my books, and went down the steps.

Pa says: "Ain't you got two hours o' sweepin' yet to do?"

I says: "Professor Herbert said I could do it some other time. He said for me to go home with you."

"No," says Pa. "You are goin' to do as he says. He's a good man. School has changed from my day and time. I'm a dead leaf, Dave. I'm behind. I don't belong here. If he'll let me I'll get a broom and we'll both sweep one hour. That pays your debt. I'll hep you pay it. I'll ast 'im and see if he won't let me hep you."

"I'm going to cancel the debt," says Professor Herbert. "I just wanted you to understand, Luster."

"I understand," says Pa, "and since I understand he must pay his debt fer th' tree and I'm goin' to hep 'im."

"Don't do that," says Professor Herbert. "It's all on me."

"We don't do things like that," says Pa. "We're just and honest people. We don't want somethin' fer nothin'. Professor Herbert, you're wrong now and I'm right. You'll haf to listen to me. I've larned a lot from you. My boy must go on. Th' world has left me. It changed while I've raised my family and plowed th' hills. I'm a just and honest man. I don't skip debts. I ain't larned 'em to do that. I ain't got much larnin' myself but I do know right from wrong atter I see through a thing."

Professor Herbert went home. Pa and I stayed and swept one hour. It looked funny to see Pa use a broom. He never used one at home. Mom used the broom. Pa used the plow. Pa did hard work. Pa says: "I can't sweep. Durned if I can. Look at th' streaks o' dirt I leave on th' floor! Seems like no work a-tall fer me. Brooms is too light 'r somethin'. I'll jist do th' best I can, Dave. I've been wrong about th' school."

I says: "Did you know Professor Herbert can get a warrant out for you for bringing your pistol to school and showing it in his office! They can railroad you for that!"

"That's all made right," says Pa. "I've made that right. Professor Herbert ain't goin' to take it to court. He likes me. I like 'im. We jist had to get together. He had the remedies. He showed me. You must go on to school. I am as strong a man as ever come out'n th' hills fer my years and th' hard work I've done. But I'm behind, Dave. I'm a little man. Your hands will be softer than mine. Your clothes will be better. You'll allus look cleaner than your old Pap. Jist remember, Dave, to pay your debts and be honest. Jist be kind to animals and don't bother th' snakes. That's all I got agin th' school. Puttin' black snakes to sleep and cuttin' 'em open."

It was late when we got home. Stars were in the sky. The moon was up. The ground was frozen. Pa took his time going home. I couldn't run like I did the night before. It was ten o'clock before we got the work finished, our suppers eaten. Pa sat before the fire and told Mom he was going to take her and show her a germ some time. Mom hadn't seen one either. Pa told her about the high school and the fine man Professor Herbert was. He told Mom about the strange school across the hill and how different it was from the school in their day and time.

Discussion

1. (a) From what point of view is the story told? **(b)** Which of the following words could be used to describe the narrator: likable, weak, intelligent, sensitive, cruel, loving, disloyal? Give examples from the story to support your choices.

2. (a) What incident marks the turning point of the story? **(b)** Trace the pattern of events that leads to the turning point. **(c)** How is the conflict resolved? (You may wish to review *plot* in the Handbook of Literary Terms.)

3. One reader argues that the major conflict in "Split Cherry Tree" is not between Luster Sexton and Professor Herbert or between Luster Sexton and his son Dave, but rather between the old ways represented by Luster and the new ways represented by Professor Herbert. Do you agree or disagree? Support your opinion with examples from the story.

Application

Characterization

An author may develop characters in a story by describing them directly or by revealing them through their speech, actions, and thoughts as well as through the reactions of others to them.

1. In "Split Cherry Tree" we learn about Luster from his speech and actions when he becomes angry at learning why Dave is two hours late, when he cannot understand why a field trip is part of a school day, and when he puts on his gun and accompanies Dave to school. What additional information about Luster do we get when Dave says, "Pa's gun has always been a friend to him when he goes to settle disputes"?

2. (a) How do the other students first react to Luster's presence? **(b)** What does Luster say to cause them to change their opinion of him? Find passages in the text to support your answers.

3. (a) What do we learn about Luster from the description of the way he is dressed the morning he goes to visit the school? **(b)** At the end of the story, what do you learn from the description of him as he stands watching the students leave school?

Comment: Origins

After "Split Cherry Tree" was published in the 1930s, Jesse Stuart (1907–1984) received letters by the hundreds from all over the world asking about the origins of the story. Some readers, confusing Jesse Stuart, the writer, with Dave, the narrator of the story, asked if Stuart's own father was the model for Luster Sexton.

Stuart explained that his own father had never required convincing of the importance of education; the character of Luster Sexton is based on a story Jesse Stuart heard when he himself was teaching in a one-room school in Kentucky. A textbook salesman who often called on Jesse Stuart told the story of a man in a neighboring county who, when his son was required to help pay for property destroyed during a field trip, took his gun to school to settle the issue with the son's teacher. The angry parent was mollified only when the teacher used a microscope to let him see the germs from his own teeth. Years after hearing the salesman repeat the story, Jesse Stuart wrote "Split Cherry Tree."

But Stuart does more than recount an amusing anecdote; he presents characters we can care about in a place we can—because of his skill at describing—easily imagine. In showing the hill farm lying in the cold evening as Dave hurries through his chores, in having Mrs. Sexton tell Luster not to "plague" Dave at school in front of the other students, by describing the effect of Luster's presence at school on Professor Herbert, on Dave, and on the other students, Jesse Stuart allows us to experience the feel of that particular place. In "Split Cherry Tree," as in most of his stories, essays, poems, and novels, Jesse Stuart not only tells of human conflicts but shows with loving accuracy the land and people of the Kentucky hills that were his birthplace and remained his home.

The Scarlet Ibis

James Hurst

I did not know then that pride is . . . a seed that bears two vines, life and death.

It was in the clove of seasons,[1] summer was dead but autumn had not yet been born, that the ibis[2] lit in the bleeding tree. The flower garden was stained with rotting brown magnolia petals and ironweeds grew rank amid the purple phlox. The five o'clocks by the chimney still marked time, but the oriole nest in the elm was untenanted and rocked back and forth like an empty cradle. The last graveyard flowers were blooming, and their smell drifted across the cotton field and through every room of our house, speaking softly the names of our dead.

It's strange that all this is still so clear to me,

1. ***clove of seasons,*** the interval between two seasons.
2. ***ibis*** (ī'bis).

now that that summer has long since fled and time has had its way. A grindstone stands where the bleeding tree stood, just outside the kitchen door, and now if an oriole sings in the elm, its song seems to die up in the leaves, a silvery dust. The flower garden is prim, the house a gleaming white, and the pale fence across the yard stands straight and spruce. But sometimes (like right now), as I sit in the cool, green-draped parlor, the grindstone begins to turn, and time with all its changes is ground away—and I remember Doodle.

Doodle was just about the craziest brother a boy ever had. Of course, he wasn't a crazy crazy like old Miss Leedie, who was in love with President Wilson and wrote him a letter every day, but was a nice crazy, like someone you meet in your dreams. He was born when I was six and was, from the outset, a disappointment. He seemed all head, with a tiny body which was red and shriveled like an old man's. Everybody thought he was going to die—everybody except Aunt Nicey, who had delivered him. She said he would live because he was born in a caul and cauls were made from Jesus' nightgown. Daddy had Mr. Heath, the carpenter, build a little mahogany coffin for him. But he didn't die, and when he was three months old Mama and Daddy decided they might as well name him. They named him William Armstrong, which was like tying a big tail on a small kite. Such a name sounds good only on a tombstone.

I thought myself pretty smart at many things, like holding my breath, running, jumping, or climbing the vines in Old Woman Swamp, and I wanted more than anything else someone to race to Horsehead Landing, someone to box with, and someone to perch with in the top fork of the great pine behind the barn, where across the fields and swamps you could see the sea. I wanted a brother. But Mama, crying, told me that even if William Armstrong lived, he would never do these things with me. He might not, she sobbed, even be "all there." He might, as long as he lived, lie on the rubber sheet in the center of the bed in the front bedroom where the white marquisette curtains billowed out in the afternoon sea breeze, rustling like palmetto fronds.

It was bad enough having an invalid brother, but having one who possibly was not all there was unbearable, so I began to make plans to kill him by smothering him with a pillow. However, one afternoon as I watched him, my head poked between the iron posts of the foot of the bed, he looked straight at me and grinned. I skipped through the rooms, down the echoing halls, shouting, "Mama, he smiled. He's all there! He's all there!" and he was.

When he was two, if you laid him on his stomach, he began to try to move himself, straining terribly. The doctor said that with his weak heart this strain would probably kill him, but it didn't. Trembling, he'd push himself up, turning first red, then a soft purple, and finally collapse back onto the bed like an old worn-out doll. I can still see Mama watching him, her hand pressed tight across her mouth, her eyes wide and unblinking. But he learned to crawl (it was his third winter), and we brought him out of the front bedroom, putting him on the rug before the fireplace. For the first time he became one of us.

As long as he lay all the time in bed, we called him William Armstrong, even though it was formal and sounded as if we were referring to one of our ancestors, but with his creeping around on the deerskin rug and beginning to talk, something had to be done about his name. It was I who renamed him. When he crawled, he crawled backwards, as if he were in reverse and couldn't change gears. If you called him, he'd turn around as if he were going in the other direction, then he'd back right up to you to be picked up. Crawling backward made him look like a doodlebug, so I began to call him Doodle, and in time even Mama and Daddy thought it was a better name than William Armstrong. Only Aunt Nicey disagreed. She said caul babies should be treated with special respect since they might turn out to be saints. Renaming my brother was perhaps the kindest thing I ever did for him, because nobody expects much from someone called Doodle.

Although Doodle learned to crawl, he showed no signs of walking, but he wasn't idle. He talked so much that we all quit listening to what he said. It was about this time that Daddy built him a go-cart and I had to pull him around. At first I just paraded him up and down the piazza, but then he started crying to be taken out into the yard and it ended up by my having to lug him wherever I went. If I so much as picked up my cap, he'd start crying to go with me and Mama would call from wherever she was, "Take Doodle with you."

He was a burden in many ways. The doctor had said that he mustn't get too excited, too hot, too cold, or too tired and that he must always be treated gently. A long list of don'ts went with him, all of which I ignored once we got out of the house. To discourage his coming with me, I'd run with him across the ends of the cotton rows and careen him around corners on two wheels. Sometimes I accidentally turned him over, but he never told Mama. His skin was very sensitive, and he had to wear a big straw hat whenever he went out. When the going got rough and he had to cling to the sides of the go-cart, the hat slipped all the way down over his ears. He was a sight. Finally, I could see I was licked. Doodle was my brother and he was going to cling to me forever, no matter what I did, so I dragged him across the burning cotton field to share with him the only beauty I knew, Old Woman Swamp. I pulled the go-cart through the sawtooth fern, down into the green dimness where the palmetto fronds whispered by the stream. I lifted him out and set him down in the soft rubber grass beside a tall pine. His eyes were round with wonder as he gazed about him, and his little hands began to stroke the rubber grass. Then he began to cry.

"For heaven's sake, what's the matter?" I asked, annoyed.

"It's so pretty," he said. "So pretty, pretty, pretty."

After that day Doodle and I often went down into Old Woman Swamp. I would gather wild flowers, wild violets, honeysuckle, yellow jasmine, snakeflowers, and water lilies, and with wire grass we'd weave them into necklaces and crowns. We'd bedeck ourselves with our handiwork and loll about thus beautified, beyond the touch of the everyday world. Then when the slanted rays of the sun burned orange in the tops of the pines, we'd drop our jewels into the stream and watch them float away toward the sea.

There is within me (and with sadness I have watched it in others) a knot of cruelty borne by the stream of love, much as our blood sometimes bears the seed of our destruction, and at times I was mean to Doodle. One day I took him up to the barn loft and showed him his casket, telling him how we all had believed he would die. It was covered with a film of Paris green[3] sprinkled to kill the rats, and screech owls had built a nest inside it.

Doodle studied the mahogany box for a long time, then said, "It's not mine."

"It is," I said. "And before I'll help you down from the loft, you're going to have to touch it."

"I won't touch it," he said sullenly.

"Then I'll leave you here by yourself," I threatened, and made as if I were going down.

Doodle was frightened of being left. "Don't go leave me, Brother," he cried, and he leaned toward the coffin. His hand, trembling, reached out, and when he touched the casket he screamed. A screech owl flapped out of the box into our faces, scaring us and covering us with Paris green. Doodle was paralyzed, so I put him on my shoulder and carried him down the ladder, and even when we were outside in the bright sunshine, he clung to me, crying, "Don't leave me. Don't leave me."

When Doodle was five years old, I was embarrassed at having a brother of that age who couldn't walk, so I set out to teach him. We

---

3. ***Paris green,*** a poisonous emerald-green powder used to kill insects.

were down in Old Woman Swamp and it was spring and the sick-sweet smell of bay flowers hung everywhere like a mournful song. "I'm going to teach you to walk, Doodle," I said.

He was sitting comfortably on the soft grass, leaning back against the pine. "Why?" he asked.

I hadn't expected such an answer. "So I won't have to haul you around all the time."

"I can't walk, Brother," he said.

"Who says so?" I demanded.

"Mama, the doctor—everybody."

"Oh, you can walk," I said, and I took him by the arms and stood him up. He collapsed onto the grass like a half-empty flour sack. It was as if he had no bones in his little legs.

"Don't hurt me, Brother," he warned.

"Shut up. I'm not going to hurt you. I'm going to teach you to walk." I heaved him up again, and again he collapsed.

This time he did not lift his face up out of the rubber grass. "I just can't do it. Let's make honeysuckle wreaths."

"Oh yes you can, Doodle," I said. "All you got to do is try. Now come on," and I hauled him up once more.

It seemed so hopeless from the beginning that it's a miracle I didn't give up. But all of us must have something or someone to be proud of, and Doodle had become mine. I did not know then that pride is a wonderful, terrible thing, a seed that bears two vines, life and death. Every day that summer we went to the pine beside the stream of Old Woman Swamp, and I put him on his feet at least a hundred times each afternoon. Occasionally I too became discouraged because it didn't seem as if he was trying, and I would say, "Doodle, don't you *want* to learn to walk?"

He'd nod his head, and I'd say, "Well, if you don't keep trying, you'll never learn." Then I'd paint for him a picture of us as old men, white-haired, him with a long white beard and me still pulling him around in the go-cart. This never failed to make him try again.

Finally one day, after many weeks of practicing, he stood alone for a few seconds. When he fell, I grabbed him in my arms and hugged him, our laughter pealing through the swamp like a ringing bell. Now we knew it could be done. Hope no longer hid in the dark palmetto thicket but perched like a cardinal in the lacy toothbrush tree, brilliantly visible. "Yes, yes," I cried, and he cried it too, and the grass beneath us was soft and the smell of the swamp was sweet.

With success so imminent, we decided not to tell anyone until he could actually walk. Each day, barring rain, we sneaked into Old Woman Swamp, and by cotton-picking time Doodle was ready to show what he could do. He still wasn't able to walk far, but we could wait no longer. Keeping a nice secret is very hard to do, like holding your breath. We chose to reveal all on October eighth, Doodle's sixth birthday, and for weeks ahead we mooned around the house, promising everybody a most spectacular surprise. Aunt Nicey said that, after so much talk, if we produced anything less tremendous than the Resurrection, she was going to be disappointed.

At breakfast on our chosen day, when Mama, Daddy, and Aunt Nicey were in the dining room, I brought Doodle to the door in the go-cart just as usual and had them turn their backs, making them cross their hearts and hope to die if they peeked. I helped Doodle up, and when he was standing alone I let them look. There wasn't a sound as Doodle walked slowly across the room and sat down at his place at the table. Then Mama began to cry and ran over to him, hugging him and kissing him. Daddy hugged him too, so I went to Aunt Nicey, who was thanks praying in the doorway, and began to waltz her around. We danced together quite well until she came down on my big toe with her brogans, hurting me so badly I thought I was crippled for life.

Doodle told them it was I who had taught him to walk, so everyone wanted to hug me, and I began to cry.

"What are you crying for?" asked Daddy,

but I couldn't answer. They did not know that I did it for myself; that pride, whose slave I was, spoke to me louder than all their voices; and that Doodle walked only because I was ashamed of having a crippled brother.

Within a few months Doodle had learned to walk well and his go-cart was put up in the barn loft (it's still there) beside his little mahogany coffin. Now, when we roamed off together, resting often, we never turned back until our destination had been reached, and to help pass the time, we took up lying. From the beginning Doodle was a terrible liar and he got me in the habit. Had anyone stopped to listen to us, we would have been sent off to Dix Hill.

My lies were scary, involved, and usually pointless; but Doodle's were twice as crazy. People in his stories all had wings and flew wherever they wanted to go. His favorite lie was about a boy named Peter who had a pet peacock with a ten-foot tail. Peter wore a golden robe that glittered so brightly that when he walked through the sunflowers they turned away from the sun to face him. When Peter was ready to go to sleep, the peacock spread his magnificent tail, enfolding the boy gently like a closing go-to-sleep flower, burying him in the gloriously iridescent, rustling vortex. Yes, I must admit it, Doodle could beat me lying.

Doodle and I spent lots of time thinking about our future. We decided that when we were grown we'd live in Old Woman Swamp and pick dog-tongue for a living. Beside the stream, he planned, we'd build us a house of whispering leaves and the swamp birds would be our chickens. All day long (when we weren't gathering dog-tongue) we'd swing through the cypresses on the rope vines, and if it rained we'd huddle beneath an umbrella tree and play stickfrog. Mama and Daddy could come and live with us if they wanted to. He even came up with the idea that he could marry Mama and I could marry Daddy. Of course, I was old enough to know this wouldn't work out, but the picture he painted was so beautiful and serene that all I could do was whisper Yes, yes.

Once I had succeeded in teaching Doodle to walk, I began to believe in my own infallibility and I prepared a terrific development program for him, unknown to Mama and Daddy, of course. I would teach him to run, to swim, to climb trees, and to fight. He, too, now believed in my infallibility, so we set the deadline for these accomplishments less than a year away, when, it had been decided, Doodle could start to school.

That winter we didn't make much progress, for I was in school and Doodle suffered from one bad cold after another. But when spring came, rich and warm, we raised our sights again. Success lay at the end of summer like a pot of gold, and our campaign got off to a good start. On hot days, Doodle and I went down to Horsehead Landing and I gave him swimming lessons or showed him how to row a boat. Sometimes we descended into the cool greenness of Old Woman Swamp and climbed the rope vines or boxed scientifically beneath the pine where he had learned to walk. Promise hung about us like the leaves, and wherever we looked, ferns unfurled and birds broke into song.

That summer, the summer of 1918, was blighted. In May and June there was no rain and the crops withered, curled up, then died under the thirsty sun. One morning in July a hurricane came out of the east, tipping over the oaks in the yard and splitting the limbs of the elm trees. That afternoon it roared back out of the west, blew the fallen oaks around, snapping their roots and tearing them out of the earth like a hawk at the entrails of a chicken. Cotton bolls were wrenched from the stalks and lay like green walnuts in the valleys between the rows, while the cornfield leaned over uniformly so that the tassels touched the ground. Doodle and I followed Daddy out into the cotton field, where he stood, shoulders sagging, surveying the ruin. When his chin sank down onto his chest, we were frightened, and Doodle slipped his hand into mine. Suddenly Daddy straightened his shoulders, raised a giant knuckly fist, and with a voice that seemed to rumble out of the earth itself began cursing heaven, hell, the weather, and the Republican Party. Doodle and I, prodding each other and giggling, went back to the house, knowing that everything would be all right.

And during that summer, strange names were heard through the house: Château-Thierry, Amiens, Soissons, and in her blessing at the supper table, Mama once said, "And bless the Pearsons, whose boy Joe was lost at Belleau Wood."[4]

So we came to that clove of seasons. School was only a few weeks away, and Doodle was far behind schedule. He could barely clear the ground when climbing up the rope vines and his swimming was certainly not passable. We decided to double our efforts, to make that last drive and reach our pot of gold. I made him swim until he turned blue and row until he couldn't lift an oar. Wherever we went, I purposely walked fast, and although he kept up, his face turned red and his eyes became glazed. Once, he could go no further, so he collapsed on the ground and began to cry.

"Aw, come on, Doodle," I urged. "You can do it. Do you want to be different from everybody else when you start school?"

"Does it make any difference?"

"It certainly does," I said. "Now, come on," and I helped him up.

As we slipped through dog days, Doodle began to look feverish, and Mama felt his forehead, asking him if he felt ill. At night he didn't sleep well, and sometimes he had nightmares, crying out until I touched him and said, "Wake up, Doodle. Wake up."

It was Saturday noon, just a few days before school was to start. I should have already admitted defeat, but my pride wouldn't let me. The excitement of our program had now been gone for weeks, but still we kept on with a tired doggedness. It was too late to turn back, for we had both wandered too far into a net of expectations and had left no crumbs behind.

Daddy, Mama, Doodle, and I were seated at the dining-room table having lunch. It was a hot day, with all the windows and doors open in case a breeze should come. In the kitchen Aunt Nicey was humming softly. After a long silence, Daddy spoke. "It's so calm, I wouldn't be surprised if we had a storm this afternoon."

"I haven't heard a rain frog," said Mama, who believed in signs, as she served the bread around the table.

"I did," declared Doodle. "Down in the swamp."

"He didn't," I said contrarily.

"You did, eh?" said Daddy, ignoring my denial.

"I certainly did," Doodle reiterated, scowling at me over the top of his iced-tea glass, and we were quiet again.

Suddenly, from out in the yard, came a strange croaking noise. Doodle stopped eating, with a piece of bread poised ready for his mouth, his eyes popped round like two blue buttons. "What's that?" he whispered.

I jumped up, knocking over my chair, and had reached the door when Mama called, "Pick up the chair, sit down again, and say excuse me."

By the time I had done this, Doodle had excused himself and had slipped out into the yard. He was looking up into the bleeding tree. "It's a great big red bird!" he called.

The bird croaked loudly again, and Mama and Daddy came out into the yard. We shaded our eyes with our hands against the hazy glare of the sun and peered up through the still leaves. On the topmost branch a bird the size of a chicken, with scarlet feathers and long legs, was perched precariously. Its wings hung down loosely, and as we watched, a feather dropped away and floated slowly down through the green leaves.

"It's not even frightened of us," Mama said.

"It looks tired," Daddy added. "Or maybe sick."

---

4. ***Château-Thierry*** (sha tō′tyär′i *or* shä tō tye rē′), ***Amiens*** (am′i-ənz *or* ä myaɴ′), ***Soissons*** (swä sôɴ′), ***Belleau*** (bel ō′) ***Wood,*** French locations in or near which World War I battles were fought.

Doodle's hands were clasped at his throat, and I had never seen him stand still so long. "What is it?" he asked.

Daddy shook his head. "I don't know, maybe it's——"

At that moment the bird began to flutter, but the wings were uncoordinated, and amid much flapping and a spray of flying feathers, it tumbled down, bumping through the limbs of the bleeding tree and landing at our feet with a thud. Its long, graceful neck jerked twice into an S, then straightened out, and the bird was still. A white veil came over the eyes and the long white beak unhinged. Its legs were crossed and its clawlike feet were delicately curved at rest. Even death did not mar its grace, for it lay on the earth like a broken vase of red flowers, and we stood around it, awed by its exotic beauty.

"It's dead," Mama said.

"What is it?" Doodle repeated.

"Go bring me the bird book," said Daddy.

I ran into the house and brought back the bird book. As we watched, Daddy thumbed through its pages. "It's a scarlet ibis," he said, pointing to a picture. "It lives in the tropics—South America to Florida. A storm must have brought it here."

Sadly, we all looked back at the bird. A scarlet ibis! How many miles it had traveled to die like this, in *our* yard, beneath the bleeding tree.

"Let's finish lunch," Mama said, nudging us back toward the dining room.

"I'm not hungry," said Doodle, and he knelt down beside the ibis.

"We've got peach cobbler for dessert," Mama tempted from the doorway.

Doodle remained kneeling. "I'm going to bury him."

"Don't you dare touch him," Mama warned. "There's no telling what disease he might have had."

"All right," said Doodle. "I won't."

Daddy, Mama, and I went back to the dining room table, but we watched Doodle through the open door. He took out a piece of string from his pocket and, without touching the ibis, looped one end around its neck. Slowly, while singing softly "Shall We Gather at the River," he carried the bird around to the front yard and dug a hole in the flower garden, next to the petunia bed. Now we were watching him through the front window, but he didn't know it. His awkwardness at digging a hole with a shovel whose handle was twice as long as he was made us laugh, and we covered our mouths with our hands so he wouldn't hear.

When Doodle came into the dining room, he found us seriously eating our cobbler. He was pale and lingered just inside the screen door. "Did you get the scarlet ibis buried?" asked Daddy.

Doodle didn't speak but nodded his head.

"Go wash your hands, and then you can have some peach cobbler," said Mama.

"I'm not hungry," he said.

"Dead birds is bad luck," said Aunt Nicey poking her head from the kitchen door. "Specially *red* dead birds!"

As soon as I had finished eating, Doodle and I hurried off to Horsehead Landing. Time was short, and Doodle still had a long way to go if he was going to keep up with the other boys when he started school. The sun, gilded with the yellow cast of autumn, still burned fiercely, but the dark green woods through which we passed were shady and cool. When we reached the landing, Doodle said he was too tired to swim, so we got into a skiff and floated down the creek with the tide. Far off in the marsh a rail was scolding, and over on the beach locusts were singing in the myrtle trees. Doodle did not speak and kept his head turned away, letting one hand trail limply in the water.

After we had drifted a long way, I put the oars in place and made Doodle row back against the tide. Black clouds began to gather in the southwest, and he kept watching them, trying to pull the oars a little faster. When we reached Horsehead Landing, lightning was playing across half the sky and thunder roared out, hiding even the sound of the sea. The sun disappeared and darkness descended, almost like night. Flocks of marsh crows flew by, heading inland to their roosting trees, and two egrets, squawking, arose from the oyster-rock shallows and careened away.

Doodle was both tired and frightened, and when he stepped from the skiff he collapsed onto the mud, sending an armada of fiddler crabs rustling off into the marsh grass. I helped him up, and as he wiped the mud off his trousers, he smiled at me ashamedly. He had failed and we both knew it, so we started back home, racing the storm. We never spoke (What are the words that can solder cracked pride?); but I knew he was watching me, watching for a sign of mercy. The lightning was near now, and from fear he walked so close behind me he kept stepping on my heels. The faster I walked, the faster he walked; so I began to run. The rain was coming, roaring through the pines; and then like a bursting Roman candle, a gum tree ahead of us was shattered by a bolt of lightning. When the deafening peal of thunder had died, and in the moment before the rain arrived, I heard Doodle, who had fallen behind, cry out, "Brother, Brother, don't leave me! Don't leave me!"

The knowledge that Doodle's and my plans had come to naught was bitter, and that streak of cruelty within me awakened. I ran as fast as I could, leaving him far behind with a wall of rain dividing us. The drops stung my face like nettles, and the wind flared the wet glistening leaves of the bordering trees. Soon I could hear his voice no more.

I hadn't run too far before I became tired, and the flood of childish spite evanesced as well. I stopped and waited for Doodle. The sound of rain was everywhere, but the wind had died and it fell straight down in parallel paths like ropes hanging from the sky. As I waited, I peered through the downpour, but no one came. Finally I went back and found him huddled beneath a red nightshade bush beside the road. He was sitting on the ground, his face buried in his arms, which were resting on his drawn-up knees. "Let's go, Doodle," I said.

He didn't answer, so I placed my hand on his forehead and lifted his head. Limply, he fell backwards onto the earth. He had been bleeding from the mouth, and his neck and the front of his shirt were stained a brilliant red.

"Doodle! Doodle!" I cried, shaking him; but there was no answer but the ropy rain. He lay very awkwardly, with his head thrown far back, making his vermilion neck appear unusually long and slim. His little legs, bent sharply at the knees, had never before seemed so fragile, so thin.

I began to weep, and the tear-blurred vision in red before me looked very familiar. "Doodle!" I screamed above the pounding storm and threw my body to the earth above his. For a long long time, it seemed forever, I lay there crying, sheltering my fallen scarlet ibis from the heresy of rain.

Discussion

1. (a) Outline the circumstances leading to the death of Doodle. **(b)** How much is the narrator to blame? Do you blame him or do you pity him? Explain your reactions.

2. Review the narrator's efforts to make Doodle into the kind of brother and companion he'd always wanted. **(a)** Why does he decide to teach Doodle to walk? **(b)** What is the result of his effort? **(c)** Is this really progress? Explain.

3. Describe the following incidents and explain how each helps to characterize Doodle. **(a)** Doodle's first visit to Old Woman Swamp; **(b)** Doodle's reaction when his brother announces that he is going to teach Doodle to walk; **(c)** Doodle's "lie" about the boy and his pet peacock; **(d)** Doodle's behavior from the time they first hear the cry of the ibis until the bird is buried.

4. When telling this story, the narrator—now grown up—is recounting events that occurred when he was a boy. **(a)** In what ways might his story have been different if he (like Dave in "Split Cherry Tree") were telling it close to the time it actually happened? **(b)** Does this distance between the event and the telling make you more or less sympathetic to the narrator's grief over the death of his brother? Explain.

Vocabulary

Combined Exercise

Number your paper from 1 to 10. For each item, write the letter of the correct answer after the number of the item. As you work on this exercise, consult your Glossary as often as necessary.

1. An *armada* is **(a)** a small animal with a hard shell; **(b)** a fleet of warships; **(c)** a healing liquid; **(d)** a boulder.

2. *Solder* rhymes with **(a)** folder; **(b)** fodder; **(c)** balder; **(d)** ladder.

3. The word *reiterate* has a root (the main part of the word, the part from which other words are made) that means **(a)** say; **(b)** do; **(c)** over; **(d)** again.

4. The word *reiterate* has a prefix (a group of letters added at the beginning of a root to add to or change the meaning of that root) that means **(a)** again; **(b)** over; **(c)** not; **(d)** down.

5. A *frond* is a **(a)** pal; **(b)** monster; **(c)** leaf; **(d)** fantasy.

6. Which of the following is the opposite of *infallibility?* **(a)** balance; **(b)** freedom; **(c)** unreliability; **(d)** insincerity.

7. What would most likely be *vermilion?* **(a)** eyes; **(b)** skin; **(c)** teeth; **(d)** blood.

8. What would most likely be *iridescent?* **(a)** mud; **(b)** a telephone; **(c)** a rainbow; **(d)** hair.

9. Which word is a synonym for *blight?* **(a)** hope; **(b)** disease; **(c)** despair; **(d)** joy.

10. Who would be most likely to tend *phlox?* **(a)** a shepherd; **(b)** a dog; **(c)** a gardener; **(d)** a dentist.

Composition

Think of something that has happened to you recently that you can share with your classmates and teacher. This event need not be tragic. You might choose something odd or funny—or something that taught you a lesson.

Then, devise two short compositions, each describing the same event and each written from the first person point of view with you as narrator. In the first composition, assume that the time is the present; in the second, assume that you are forty years old. (See *Prewriting,* page 663, in Composition Guide.)

Comment: Symbolism in "The Scarlet Ibis"

Symbols are found everywhere, but many times we do not recognize them as such. The cross on the top of the church spire, the silhouette of a jumping deer on a road sign, a giant hot dog outside a diner—all are symbols. We see and understand what they mean: religion, warning, food. Yet we seldom recognize them as symbols.

Symbols are also frequently found in literature, where they may be used to make a point or to create a mood. But because they have a literal as well as a symbolic meaning, it may be difficult at times to decide whether something is indeed a symbol. For example, in "The Scarlet Ibis" the ibis is first of all a bird; and—as a bird and nothing more—it serves an important function in the development of the plot. But a careful reading gives rise to questions such as, "Does the ibis represent a person?" and "Does it represent a quality such as courage or endurance or beauty?" and "Why did the author choose—over all other kinds of birds—a scarlet ibis?"

James Hurst has written, "The ancient Egyptians worshiped the ibis because, they said, it destroyed the crocodiles. In their liturgy, it took second place only to the phoenix. So I chose as my symbol a scarlet ibis, the most beautiful and rare member of the ibis family. . . .

"I wanted a bird to represent Doodle—not Doodle's physical self, but his spirit. Certainly, Doodle inside had much more to admire than his outside. . . .

"This bird must be destined to die," continues the author, "as Doodle was to die. A local bird would have to be sick. Was the ibis sick? If the ibis had been back in a mangrove swamp, would it have died? Could not perhaps Doodle in another society have survived?

"To further my symbolism, Doodle unconsciously identifies himself with the scarlet ibis and at the very end his outside comes to resemble the bird when he dies in the same position the bird died, with the front of his shirt stained with blood."

The ibis has other qualities that might be considered symbolic. The color scarlet is often associated with blood, or with tragedy. It may also stand for courage. Do any of these symbolic associations apply to Doodle? Which ones?

A work of literature may include more than one symbol. At the end of "The Scarlet Ibis," a great storm causes the death of the sick boy. He tries too hard to escape from it, and his fragile body collapses. Do you think the storm has symbolic significance? If so, what might it symbolize?

Setting may also have symbolic significance. James Hurst had a definite purpose in choosing the setting he did. He explains, "The story was set in 1918 so that World War I would loom in the background, amid other misfortunes, i.e., the drouth and the storm. A major cause of wars is the desire to transform others into one's own image, and Doodle's and his brother's struggle resembles on a minute, personal scale, the great war."

Hurst goes on to say that there are three sentences that are very important to the meaning of the story:

There is within me (and with sadness I have watched it in others) a knot of cruelty borne by the stream of love, much as our blood sometimes bears the seed of our destruction.

Pride is a wonderful, terrible thing, a seed that bears two vines, life and death.

Brother, brother, don't leave me. Don't leave me.

"This last sentence," James Hurst continues, "could almost be called Doodle's theme and I hear it as the classic cry of all mankind wishing to belong and never to be lonely."

Unit 1 Review: *The First Short Story Unit*

Content Review

1. (a) From the stories you have read in this unit, select three characters that you especially admire and explain why you find each admirable. **(b)** Which characters do you consider less than admirable? Why?

2. (a) You studied characterization in connection with "Split Cherry Tree." What other story might have been used to illustrate methods of characterization? In the story you have chosen, which methods does the author use? **(b)** Symbolism is especially important in "The Scarlet Ibis." Name another selection in which it is important. Explain your choice. **(c)** "Blues Ain't No Mockin Bird" is told from the first person point of view. Name a story in the unit that is told from the third person omniscient point of view. What are the advantages of using third person omniscient in this particular story?

3. Explain why you agree or disagree with this statement: Without learning terms such as *plot, point of view, characterization,* and *setting,* one can understand and discuss these stories just as well—and appreciate them more. Give specific examples to support your argument.

Concept Review:
Interpretation of New Material

Read the short story that follows. Then, on a separate sheet of paper, write your answers to the questions.

The Woman Who Had No Eye for Small Details

William Maxwell

Once upon a time there was a woman who had no eye for those small details and dainty effects that most women love to spend their time on—curtains and doilies, and the chairs arranged so, and the rugs so, and a small picture here, and a large mirror there. She did not bother with all this because, in the first place, she lived alone and had no one but herself to please; and, anyway, she was not interested in material objects. So her house was rather bare, and, to tell the truth, not very comfortable. She lived very much in her mind, which fed upon books: upon what Erasmus and Darwin and Gautama Buddha and Pascal and Spinoza and Nietzsche and St. Thomas Aquinas[1] had thought; and what she herself thought about what they thought. She was not a homely woman. She had good bones and beautiful heavy hair, which was very long, and which she wore in a braided crown around her head. But no man had ever courted her, and at her present age she did not expect this to happen. If some man had looked at her with interest,

---

1. ***Erasmus . . . Thomas Aquinas.*** These seven names refer to philosophers and scholars in various disciplines from diverse countries and historical periods.

she would not have noticed it; and this would, of course, have been enough to discourage further attentions.

Her house was the last house on a narrow dirt road, deep in the country, and if she heard the sound of a horse and buggy or a wagon, it was somebody coming to see her, which didn't often happen. She kept peculiar hours, and ate when she was hungry, and the mirror over the dressing table was sometimes shocked at her appearance; but since she almost never looked in it, she was not aware of the wisps of hair that needed pinning up, the eyes clouded by absent-mindedness, the sweater with a button missing, worn over a dress that belonged in the rag bag. A blind man put down in her cottage would have thought there were two people, not one, living in it, for she talked to herself a great deal.

Birds in great numbers nested in the holes of her apple trees and in the ivy that covered her stone chimney. Their cheeping, chirping sounds were the background of all that went on in her mind. Often she caught sight of them just as they were disappearing, and was not sure whether she had seen a bird or only seen its flight—so like the way certain thoughts again and again escaped her just as she reached out for them. When the ground was covered with snow, the birds closed in around the house and were at the feeding stations all day long. Even the big birds came—the lovely gentle mourning doves, and the pheasants out of the woods, and partridge, and quail. In bitter weather, when the wind was like iron, she put pans of warm water out for them, and, in a corner sheltered from the wind, kept a patch of ground swept bare, since they wouldn't use the feeders. And at times she was as occupied—or so she told herself—as if she were bringing up a large family of children, like her sister.

Her sister's children were as lively as the

birds, and even noisier; and they were a great pleasure to the woman who lived all alone, when she went to visit them. She played cards with them, and let them read to her, and listened to all that they had to say, which their mother was too busy to do. While she was there she was utterly at their disposal, so they loved her, and didn't notice the wisps of hair that needed pinning up, or that there was a button missing from her sweater, or the fact that her dress was ready for the rag bag. Looking around, she thought how, though her sister's house was small and the furniture shabby, everything her eye fell upon was there because it served some purpose or because somebody loved it. The pillows were just right against your back, the colors cheerful, the general effect of crowdedness reflected the busy life of the family. Their house was them, in a way hers was not. Her house, to be her, would have had to be made of pine boughs or have been high up in some cliff. The actual house sheltered her and that was all that could be said for it.

Her nieces and nephews would have been happy to have her stay with them forever, but she always said, "I have to get back to my little house," in a tone of voice grownups use when they don't intend to discuss something.

"Your house won't run off," her sister would say. "Why do you worry about it so? I don't see why you don't make us a real visit."

"Another time," the woman said, and went on putting her clothes in her suitcase. The real reason that she could not stay longer she did not tell them, because she knew they would not take it seriously: she could not bear the thought of the birds coming to the feeders and finding nothing but dust and chaff where they were accustomed to find food. So home she went, promising to come back soon, and never outstaying her welcome.

But no woman—no man, either—is allowed to live completely in her mind, or in books, or with only the birds for company. One day when she opened her mailbox, which was with a cluster of other mailboxes at a crossroads a quarter of a mile away, there was a letter from her sister. She put it in her pocket, thinking that she knew what was in it. Her sister's letters were, as a rule, complaining. Her life was hard. Her handsome, easygoing, no-good husband had deserted her, and she supported herself and the children by fine sewing. She worried about the children, because they were growing up without a father. And though they were not perfect, their faults loomed larger in her eyes than they perhaps needed to. In any case, she was tired and overworked and had no one else to complain to.

Hours later, the woman remembered that she had not read the letter, which turned out to be only three lines long: "I am very sick and the doctor says I must go to the hospital and there is no one to look after the children. Please come as soon as you can get here."

All the time the woman was packing, she kept thinking now about her poor sister and now about the poor birds. For it was the middle of the winter, there was deep snow on the ground, and the wind crept even into the house through the crack under the door, through closed windows. She filled the feeders to overflowing with seeds and suet, and sprinkled cracked corn on the ground, knowing that in two days' time it would all be gone. It was snowing again when she locked the door behind her and started off, with her old suitcase, to the nearest farmhouse. She would have to ask the farmer to hitch up his horse and sleigh and drive her to the station in the village, where she could take a train to the place where her sister lived. Fluffed out with cold, the birds sat and watched her go.

When she came back she was not alone. The farmer's sleigh was full of children with sober, pale faces. They climbed down without a word and stood looking at their new home. The woman had left at the beginning of February, and it was now nearly the end of March. The snow on the roof, melting, had made heavy cornices of ice along the eaves, and the ice, melting, had made long, thin icicles. The woman got down, and thanked the farmer, and stood looking around, to see if there were any birds. The trees were empty, there was no sound in the ivy, and the cold wind went right through her.

"Come, children," she said, as she searched through her purse for her door key. "Let us go in out of the cold. You can help me build a fire."

Inside it seemed even colder, but the stoves soon made a difference. She was so busy feeding the children and warming their beds that she scarcely had time to go to the door and throw out a handful of seed on the snow. No birds came. The next day, she swept a bare place in the sheltered corner, and put out corn for the pheasants and quail, and filled the feeders. But she did all this with a heavy heart, knowing that it was to no purpose. And her sister's death had been a great tragedy and she did not see how she could fill her sister's place in the children's hearts or do for them what their mother had done. The corn on the ground, the sunflower seeds in the feeders were untouched when night fell.

Inside the house there was the same unnatural quiet. The woman did not talk to herself, because she was not alone. The children said, "Yes, please," and "No, thank you," and politely looked at the books she gave them to read, and helped set the table, and brought in wood and water; but she could see that they were waiting for only one thing—to go home. And there was no home for them to go to now but here. They did not quarrel with one another, as they used to, or ask her riddles, or beg her to play Old Maid with them. In the face of disaster they were patient. They could have walked on air and passed through solid walls. They looked as if they could read her mind, but theirs were no longer open to her. Though they cried at home, they did not cry here—at least not where she could see them. In their beds in the night, she had no doubt.

The next morning, exhausted, she overslept, and when she came into the kitchen the children were crowded at the window. Something outside occupied their attention so they could hardly answer when she said good morning to them.

"Your birds have come back," the oldest nephew said.

"Oh surely not!" she cried, and hurried to the window. On the ground outside, in the midst of all the whiteness and brightness, it was like a party. The cardinals, the chickadees, the sparrows, the juncos, the nuthatches, the jays were waiting their turn at the feeders, pecking at the corn in the sheltered place, leaving hieroglyphs in the snow. Somehow, mysteriously, deep in the woods perhaps, they had managed without her help. They had survived. And were chirping and cheeping.

"We got our own breakfast," the children said. Though they didn't yet know it, they would survive also.

The tears began to flow down her cheeks, and the children came and put their arms around her. "So silly of me," she said, wiping her eyes with her handkerchief, only to have to do it again. "I thought they were all—I didn't think they'd survive the cold, with nobody to feed them, for so long." Then more tears, which kept her from going on. When she could speak, she said, "I know it's not—I know you're not happy here the way you were at home." She waited until she could speak more evenly. "The house is not very comfortable, I know. I'm different from your mother. But I loved her, and if you will let me, I will look after you the best I can. We'll look after each other."

Their faces did not change. She was not even sure that they heard what she had said. Or if they heard but didn't understand it. Together, they carried warm water in pans, they swept off a new place for the quail, they hung suet in bags from the branches of the hemlock. They got out the bird book, and from that they moved on to other tasks, and the house was never quite so sad again. Little by little it changed. It took on the look of that other house, where everywhere about you there were traces of what someone was doing, as sharp and clear and interesting as the footprints of the birds in the snow.

1. In the first sentence, the observation about women could be considered an example of **(a)** point of view; **(b)** symbol; **(c)** stereotype; **(d)** none of these.

2. The beginning paragraph serves mainly to **(a)** establish character; **(b)** advance the plot; **(c)** present a symbol; **(d)** provide setting.

3. Which of the following comparisons is *not* suggested in paragraph 3? **(a)** The birds are like the woman's thoughts; **(b)** The birds are like a family of children; **(c)** The wind is like iron; **(d)** The birds are like ivy.

4. As described in paragraph 4, the woman's relationship with her sister's children is **(a)** loving and devoted; **(b)** stern but understanding; **(c)** loyal and humorous; **(d)** casual and forgiving.

5. The woman goes home after brief visits with her sister's family because **(a)** she fears she will wear out her welcome; **(b)** the children get on her nerves; **(c)** her sister does nothing but complain; **(d)** she worries about the birds.

6. Which event is the most crucial to the development of the plot? **(a)** the woman's first visit to the sister; **(b)** the death of the sister; **(c)** the letter from the sister; **(d)** the first ride in the farmer's sleigh.

7. When the children first come to stay with the woman, they are **(a)** angry and resentful; **(b)** nasty and undisciplined; **(c)** grieving and polite; **(d)** destructive and charming.

8. The children and the birds are alike because **(a)** they are always hungry; **(b)** they are survivors; **(c)** they hate cold weather; **(d)** they make unending demands for attention.

9. The story is told from what point of view? **(a)** first person; **(b)** third person omniscient; **(c)** both first and third; **(d)** none of these.

10. Which element is most important in this story? **(a)** symbolism; **(b)** point of view; **(c)** plot; **(d)** characterization.

Composition Review

Choose *one* of the following assignments.

1. Imagine that you have been a guest for two weeks in one of the homes described in a story from this unit.

Write a letter to a friend describing this home, your reactions to the people living there, whether or not you felt comfortable, and your feelings upon leaving.

2. Several characters in stories from this unit have met with opposing forces. These characters all attempted to fight back, and their efforts met with different degrees of success. Assume that you are one of the characters listed below and that you are writing after the confrontation has occurred.

Compose a diary entry in which you describe the event and your methods of coping with it. Explain whether you feel you were successful in overcoming opposition. Perhaps now—with hindsight—you could suggest a more effective method of coping.

Rainsford ("The Most Dangerous Game")
Granddaddy ("Blues Ain't No Mockin Bird")
Luster ("Split Cherry Tree")

3. Assume that one of your classmates observed, "I never want to grow old because old people seem pathetic; they have no power and can't make decisions. Nobody even listens to old people."

Write a letter to your classmate agreeing or disagreeing with this observation. Mention details or qualities about Granny and Granddaddy ("Blues Ain't No Mockin Bird") and old Mose in "A Death in the House."

Unit 2

Modern Drama

The Miracle Worker

See **PROTAGONIST/ANTAGONIST** Handbook of Literary Terms

The Miracle Worker

William Gibson

CAST				
	A DOCTOR	MARTHA	ANAGNOS	A SERVANT
	KATE	PERCY	ANNIE SULLIVAN	OFFSTAGE VOICES
	ARTHUR KELLER	AUNT EV	VINEY	
	HELEN	JAMES	BLIND GIRLS	

Time *The 1880s*

Place *In and around the Keller homestead in Tuscumbia, Alabama; also, briefly the Perkins Institution for the Blind, in Boston.*

Act One

Scene 1

It is night over the Keller homestead. Inside, three adults in the bedroom are grouped around a crib, in lamplight. They have been through a long vigil, and it shows in their tired bearing and disarranged clothing. One is a young gentlewoman with a sweet girlish face, KATE KELLER; *the second is an elderly* DOCTOR, *stethoscope at neck, thermometer in fingers; the third is a hearty gentleman in his forties with chin whiskers,* CAPTAIN ARTHUR KELLER.

DOCTOR. She'll live.

KATE. Thank God.

(The DOCTOR *leaves them together over the crib, packs his bag.)*

DOCTOR. You're a pair of lucky parents. I can tell you now, I thought she wouldn't.

KELLER. Nonsense, the child's a Keller, she has the constitution of a goat. She'll outlive us all.

DOCTOR *(amiably).* Yes, especially if some of you Kellers don't get a night's sleep. I mean you, Mrs. Keller.

KELLER. You hear, Katie?

KATE. I hear.

KELLER *(indulgent).* I've brought up two of them, but this is my wife's first, she isn't battle-scarred yet.

KATE. Doctor, don't be merely considerate, will my girl be all right?

DOCTOR. Oh, by morning she'll be knocking down Captain Keller's fences again.

KATE. And isn't there anything we should do?

KELLER *(jovial).* Put up stronger fencing, ha?

DOCTOR. Just let her get well, she knows how to do it better than we do.

(He is packed, ready to leave.)

Main thing is the fever's gone, these things come and go in infants, never know why. Call it acute congestion of the stomach and brain.

KELLER. I'll see you to your buggy, Doctor.

DOCTOR. I've never seen a baby, more vitality, that's the truth.

(He beams a good night at the baby and KATE, *and* KELLER *leads him downstairs with*

a lamp. They go down the porch steps, and across the yard, where the DOCTOR *goes off left;* KELLER *stands with the lamp aloft.* KATE *meanwhile is bent lovingly over the crib, which emits a bleat; her finger is playful with the baby's face.)*

KATE. Hush. Don't you cry now, you've been trouble enough. Call it acute congestion, indeed. I don't see what's so cute about a congestion, just because it's yours. We'll have your father run an editorial in his paper, the wonders of modern medicine, they don't know what they're curing even when they cure it. Men, men and their battle scars, we women will have to——

(But she breaks off, puzzled, moves her finger before the baby's eyes.)

Will have to—Helen?

(Now she moves her hand, quickly.)

Helen.

(She snaps her fingers at the baby's eyes twice, and her hand falters; after a moment she calls out, loudly.)

Captain. Captain, will you come——

(But she stares at the baby, and her next call is directly at her ears.)

Captain!

(And now, still staring, KATE *screams.* KELLER *in the yard hears it, and runs with the lamp back to the house.* KATE *screams again, her look intent on the baby and terrible.* KELLER *hurries in and up.)*

KELLER. Katie? What's wrong?

KATE. Look.

(She makes a pass with her hand in the crib, at the baby's eyes.)

KELLER. What, Katie? She's well, she needs only time to——

KATE. She can't see. Look at her eyes.

(She takes the lamp from him, moves it before the child's face.)

She can't *see!*

KELLER *(hoarsely).* Helen.

KATE. Or hear. When I screamed she didn't blink. Not an eyelash——

KELLER. Helen. Helen!

KATE. She can't *hear* you!

KELLER. *Helen!*

(His face has something like fury in it, crying the child's name; KATE *almost fainting presses her knuckles to her mouth, to stop her own cry.)*

(The room dims out quickly.)

Scene 2

Time, in the form of a slow tune of distant belfry chimes which approaches in a crescendo and then fades, passes; the light comes up again on a day five years later, on three kneeling children and an old dog outside around the pump.

The dog is a setter named BELLE, *and she is sleeping. Two of the children are Negroes,* MARTHA *and* PERCY. *The third child is* HELEN, *six and a half years old, quite unkempt, in body a vivacious little person with a fine head, attractive, but noticeably blind, one eye larger and protruding; her gestures are abrupt, insistent, lacking in human restraint, and her face never smiles. She is flanked by the other two, in a litter of paper-doll cutouts, and while they speak* HELEN'*s hands thrust at their faces in turn, feeling baffledly at the movements of their lips.*

MARTHA *(snipping).* First I'm gonna cut off this doctor's legs, one, two, now then——

PERCY. Why you cuttin' off that doctor's legs?

MARTHA. I'm gonna give him a operation. Now I'm gonna cut off his arms, one, two. Now I'm gonna fix up——

(She pushes HELEN'*s hand away from her mouth.)*

You stop that.

PERCY. Cut off his stomach, that's a good operation.

MARTHA. No, I'm gonna cut off his head first, he got a bad cold.

PERCY. Ain't gonna be much of that doctor left to fix up, time you finish all them opera——

(But HELEN *is poking her fingers inside his mouth, to feel his tongue; he bites at them, annoyed, and she jerks them away.* HELEN *now fingers her own lips, moving them in imitation, but soundlessly.)*

MARTHA. What you do, bite her hand?

PERCY. That's how I do, she keep pokin' her fingers in my mouth, I just bite 'em off.

MARTHA. What she tryin' do now?

PERCY. She tryin' *talk*. She gonna get mad. Looka her tryin' talk.

(HELEN *is scowling, the lips under her fingertips moving in ghostly silence, growing more and more frantic, until in a bizarre rage she bites at her own fingers. This sends* PERCY *off into laughter, but alarms* MARTHA.)

MARTHA. Hey, you stop now.

(She pulls HELEN*'s hand down.)*

You just sit quiet and——

(But at once HELEN *topples* MARTHA *on her back, knees pinning her shoulders down, and grabs the scissors.* MARTHA *screams,* PERCY *darts to the bell string on the porch, yanks it, and the bell rings.*

Inside, the lights have been gradually coming up on the main room, where we see the family informally gathered, talking, but in pantomime: KATE *sits darning socks near a cradle, occasionally rocking it;* CAPTAIN KELLER *in spectacles is working over newspaper pages at a table; a benign visitor in a hat,* AUNT EV, *is sharing the sewing basket, putting the finishing touches on a big shapeless doll made out of towels; an indolent young man,* JAMES KELLER, *is at the window watching the children.*

With the ring of the bell, KATE *is instantly on her feet and out the door onto the porch, to take in the scene; now we see what these five years have done to her, the girlish playfulness is gone, she is a woman steeled in grief.)*

KATE *(for the thousandth time).* Helen.

(She is down the steps at once to them, seizing HELEN*'s wrists and lifting her off* MARTHA; MARTHA *runs off in tears and screams for Momma, with* PERCY *after her.)*

Let me have those scissors.

(Meanwhile the family inside is alerted, AUNT EV *joining* JAMES *at the window;* CAPTAIN KELLER *resumes work.)*

JAMES *(blandly).* She only dug Martha's eyes out. Almost dug. It's always almost, no point worrying till it happens, is there?

(They gaze out, while KATE *reaches for the scissors in* HELEN*'s hand. But* HELEN *pulls the scissors back, they struggle for them a moment, then* KATE *gives up, lets* HELEN *keep them. She tries to draw* HELEN *into the house.* HELEN *jerks away.* KATE *next goes down on her knees, takes* HELEN*'s hands gently, and using the scissors like a doll, makes* HELEN *caress and cradle them; she points* HELEN*'s finger housewards.* HELEN*'s whole body now becomes eager; she surrenders the scissors,* KATE *turns her toward the door and gives her a little push.* HELEN *scrambles up and toward the house, and* KATE *rising follows her.)*

AUNT EV. How does she stand it? Why haven't you seen this Baltimore man? It's not a thing you can let go on and on, like the weather.

JAMES. The weather here doesn't ask permission of me, Aunt Ev. Speak to my father.

AUNT EV. Arthur. Something ought to be done for that child.

KELLER. A refreshing suggestion. What?

*(*KATE *entering turns* HELEN *to* AUNT EV, *who gives her the towel doll.)*

AUNT EV. Why, this very famous oculist in Baltimore I wrote you about, what was his name?

KATE. Dr. Chisholm.[1]

AUNT EV. Yes, I heard lots of cases of blindness people thought couldn't be cured he's cured, he just does wonders. Why don't you write to him?

KELLER. I've stopped believing in wonders.

KATE *(rocks the cradle).* I think the Captain will write to him soon. Won't you, Captain?

KELLER. No.

JAMES *(lightly).* Good money after bad, or bad after good. Or bad after bad——

AUNT EV. Well, if it's just a question of money,

---

1. ***Chisholm*** (chiz′əm).

The young Helen Keller

Arthur, now you're marshal you have this Yankee money.[2] Might as well——

KELLER. Not money. The child's been to specialists all over Alabama and Tennessee, if I thought it would do good I'd have her to every fool doctor in the country.

KATE. I think the Captain will write to him soon.

KELLER. Katie. How many times can you let them break your heart?

KATE. Any number of times.

(HELEN meanwhile sits on the floor to explore the doll with her fingers, and hand pauses over the face: this is no face, a blank area of towel, and it troubles her. Her hand searches for features, and taps questioningly for eyes, but no one notices. She then yanks at her AUNT's dress, and taps again vigorously for eyes.)

AUNT EV. What, child?

(Obviously not hearing, HELEN commences to go around, from person to person, tapping for eyes, but no one attends or understands.)

KATE *(no break).* As long as there's the least chance. For her to see. Or hear, or——

KELLER. There isn't. Now I must finish here.

KATE. I think, with your permission, Captain, I'd like to write.

KELLER. I said no, Katie.

AUNT EV. Why, writing does no harm, Arthur, only a little bitty letter. To see if he can help her.

KELLER. He can't.

KATE. We won't know that to be a fact, Captain, until after you write.

KELLER *(rising, emphatic).* Katie, he can't.

(He collects his papers.)

JAMES *(facetiously).* Father stands up, that makes it a fact.

KELLER. You be quiet! I'm badgered enough here by females without your impudence.

(JAMES shuts up, makes himself scarce. HELEN now is groping among things on KELLER's

2. ***now . . . money.*** Though Keller owned property, he lacked ready cash until he was appointed federal marshal.

desk, and paws his papers to the floor. KELLER *is exasperated.)*
Katie.
*(*KATE *quickly turns* HELEN *away, and retrieves the papers.)*
I might as well try to work in a henyard as in this house——

JAMES *(placating).* You really ought to put her away, Father.

KATE *(staring up).* What?

JAMES. Some asylum. It's the kindest thing.

AUNT EV. Why, she's your sister, James, not a nobody——

JAMES. Half sister, and half—mentally defective, she can't even keep herself clean. It's not pleasant to see her about all the time.

KATE. Do you dare? Complain of what you *can* see?

KELLER *(very annoyed).* This discussion is at an end! I'll thank you not to broach it again, Ev.
(Silence descends at once. HELEN *gropes her way with the doll, and* KELLER *turns back for a final word, explosive.)*
I've done as much as I can bear, I can't give my whole life to it! The house is at sixes and sevens from morning till night over the child, it's time some attention was paid to Mildred here instead!

KATE *(gently dry).* You'll wake her up, Captain.

KELLER. I want some peace in the house, I don't care how, but one way we won't have it is by rushing up and down the country every time someone hears of a new quack. I'm as sensible to this affliction as anyone else, it hurts me to look at the girl.

KATE. It was not our affliction I meant you to write about, Captain.
*(*HELEN *is back at* AUNT EV, *fingering her dress, and yanks two buttons from it.)*

AUNT EV. Helen! My buttons.
*(*HELEN *pushes the buttons into the doll's face.* KATE *now sees, comes swiftly to kneel, lifts* HELEN'*s hand to her own eyes in question.)*

KATE. Eyes?
*(*HELEN *nods energetically.)*
She wants the doll to have eyes.
(Another kind of silence now, while KATE *takes pins and buttons from the sewing basket and attaches them to the doll as eyes.* KELLER *stands, caught, and watches morosely.* AUNT EV *blinks, and conceals her emotion by inspecting her dress.)*

AUNT EV. My goodness me, I'm not decent.

KATE. She doesn't know better, Aunt Ev. I'll sew them on again.

JAMES. Never learn with everyone letting her do anything she takes it into her mind to——

KELLER. You be quiet!

JAMES. What did I say now?

KELLER. You talk too much.

JAMES. I was agreeing with you!

KELLER. Whatever it was. Deprived child, the least she can have are the little things she wants.
*(*JAMES, *very wounded, stalks out of the room onto the porch; he remains here, sulking.)*

AUNT EV *(indulgently).* It's worth a couple of buttons, Kate, look.
*(*HELEN *now has the doll with eyes, and cannot contain herself for joy; she rocks the doll, pats it vigorously, kisses it.)*
This child has more sense than all these men Kellers, if there's ever any way to reach that mind of hers.
(But HELEN *suddenly has come upon the cradle, and unhesitatingly overturns it; the swaddled baby tumbles out, and* CAPTAIN KELLER *barely manages to dive and catch it in time.)*

KELLER. *Helen!*
(All are in commotion, the baby screams, but HELEN *unperturbed is laying her doll in its place.* KATE *on her knees pulls her hands off the cradle, wringing them;* HELEN *is bewildered.)*

KATE. Helen, Helen, you're not to do such things, how can I make you understand——

KELLER *(hoarsely).* Katie.

KATE. How can I get it into your head, my darling, my poor——

KELLER. Katie, some way of teaching her an iota of discipline has to be——

KATE *(flaring).* How can you discipline an afflicted child? Is it her fault?

(HELEN's fingers have fluttered to her mother's lips, vainly trying to comprehend their movements.)

KELLER. I didn't say it was her fault.

KATE. Then whose? I don't know what to do! How can I teach her, beat her—until she's black and blue?

KELLER. It's not safe to let her run around loose. Now there must be a way of confining her, somehow, so she can't——

KATE. Where, in a cage? She's a growing child, she has to use her limbs!

KELLER. Answer me one thing, is it fair to Mildred here?

KATE *(inexorably).* Are you willing to put her away?

(Now HELEN's face darkens in the same rage as at herself earlier, and her hand strikes at KATE's lips. KATE catches her hand again, and HELEN begins to kick, struggle, twist.)

KELLER. Now what?

KATE. She wants to talk, like—*be* like you and me.

(She holds HELEN struggling until we hear from the child her first sound so far, an inarticulate weird noise in her throat such as an animal in a trap might make; and KATE releases her. The second she is free HELEN blunders away, collides violently with a chair, falls and sits weeping. KATE comes to her, embraces, caresses, soothes her, and buries her own face in her hair, until she can control her voice.)

Every day she slips further away. And I don't know how to call her back.

AUNT EV. Oh, I've a mind to take her up to Baltimore myself. If that doctor can't help her, maybe he'll know who can.

KELLER *(presently, heavily).* I'll write the man, Katie.

(He stands with the baby in his clasp, staring at HELEN's head, hanging down on KATE's arm.

The lights dim out, except the one on KATE and HELEN. In the twilight, JAMES, AUNT EV, and KELLER move off slowly, formally, in separate directions; KATE with HELEN in her arms remains motionless in an image which overlaps into the next scene and fades only when it is well under way.)

Scene 3

Without pause, from the dark down left we hear a man's voice with a Greek accent speaking:

ANAGNOS. —who could do nothing for the girl, of course. It was Dr. Bell who thought she might somehow be taught.[3] I have written the family only that a suitable governess, Miss Annie Sullivan, has been found here in Boston—

(The lights begin to come up, down left, on a long table and chair. The table contains equipment for teaching the blind by touch—a small replica of the human skeleton, stuffed animals, models of flowers and plants, piles of books. The chair contains a girl of twenty, ANNIE SULLIVAN, with a face which in repose is grave and rather obstinate, and when active is impudent, combative, twinkling with all the life that is lacking in HELEN's, and handsome; there is a crude vitality to her. Her suitcase is at her knee. ANAGNOS, a stocky bearded man, comes into the light only toward the end of his speech.)

ANAGNOS. —and will come. It will no doubt be difficult for you there, Annie. But it has been difficult for you at our school too, hm? Gratifying, yes, when you came to us and could not spell your name, to accomplish so much here in a few years, but always an Irish battle. For independence.

(He studies ANNIE, humorously; she does not open her eyes.)

This is my last time to counsel you, Annie, and you do lack some—by some I mean *all*—

3. ***It was Dr. Bell who thought she might somehow be taught.*** Dr. Chisholm, the oculist in Baltimore, could do nothing for Helen, but he urged Captain Keller to contact Dr. Alexander Graham Bell, the inventor of the telephone. Dr. Bell, whose lifelong interest was the teaching of the deaf, advised Keller to write to Michael Anagnos, the director of the Perkins Institution for the Blind in Boston.

what, tact or talent to bend. To others. And what has saved you on more than one occasion here at Perkins is that there was nowhere to expel you to. Your eyes hurt?

ANNIE. My ears, Mr Anagnos.

(And now she has opened her eyes; they are inflamed, vague, slightly crossed, clouded by the granular growth of trachoma,[4] and she often keeps them closed to shut out the pain of light.)

ANAGNOS *(severely).* Nowhere but back to Tewksbury,[5] where children learn to be saucy. Annie, I know how dreadful it was there, but that battle is dead and done with, why not let it stay buried?

ANNIE *(cheerily).* I think God must owe me a resurrection.

ANAGNOS *(a bit shocked).* What?

ANNIE *(taps her brow).* Well, He keeps digging up that battle!

ANAGNOS. That is not a proper thing to say, Annie. It is what I mean.

ANNIE *(meekly).* Yes. But I know what I'm like, what's this child like?

ANAGNOS. Like?

ANNIE. Well—Bright or dull, to start off.

ANAGNOS. No one knows. And if she is dull, you have no patience with this?

ANNIE. Oh, in grown-ups you have to, Mr. Anagnos. I mean in children it just seems a little—precocious, can I use that word?

ANAGNOS. Only if you can spell it.

ANNIE. Premature. So I hope at least she's a bright one.

ANAGNOS. Deaf, blind, mute—who knows? She is like a little safe, locked, that no one can open. Perhaps there is a treasure inside.

ANNIE. Maybe it's empty, too?

ANAGNOS. Possible. I should warn you, she is much given to tantrums.

ANNIE. Means something is inside. Well, so am I, if I believe all I hear. Maybe you should warn *them.*

ANAGNOS *(frowns).* Annie. I wrote them no word of your history. You will find yourself among strangers now, who know nothing of it.

ANNIE. Well, we'll keep them in a state of blessed ignorance.

ANAGNOS. Perhaps *you* should tell it?

ANNIE *(bristling).* Why? I have enough trouble with people who don't know.

ANAGNOS. So they will understand. When you have trouble.

ANNIE. The only time I have trouble is when I'm right.

(But she is amused at herself, as is ANAGNOS.*)*

Is it my fault it's so often? I won't give them trouble, Mr. Anagnos, I'll be so ladylike they won't notice I've come.

ANAGNOS. Annie, be—humble. It is not as if you have so many offers to pick and choose. You will need their affection, working with this child.

ANNIE *(humorously).* I hope I won't need their pity.

ANAGNOS. Oh, we can all use some pity.

(Crisply)

So. You are no longer our pupil, we throw you into the world, a teacher. *If* the child can be taught. No one expects you to work miracles, even for twenty-five dollars a month. Now, in this envelope a loan, for the railroad, which you will repay me when you have a bank account. But in this box, a gift. With our love.

*(*ANNIE *opens the small box he extends, and sees a garnet ring. She looks up, blinking, and down.)*

I think other friends are ready to say goodbye.

(He moves as though to open doors.)

ANNIE. Mr. Anagnos.

(Her voice is trembling.)

Dear Mr. Anagnos, I——

(But she swallows over getting the ring on her finger, and cannot continue until she finds a woebegone joke.)

Well, what should I say, I'm an ignorant opin-

---

4. ***trachoma*** (trə kō′mə), a contagious inflammation of the eyelids.

5. ***Tewksbury,*** a poorhouse maintained by the state of Massachusetts.

ionated girl, and everything I am I owe to you?

ANAGNOS *(smiles)*. That is only half true, Annie.

ANNIE. Which half? I crawled in here like a drowned rat, I thought I died when Jimmie died, that I'd never again—come alive. Well, you say with love so easy, and I haven't *loved* a soul since and I never will, I suppose, but this place gave me more than my eyes back. Or taught me how to spell, which I'll never learn anyway, but with all the fights and the trouble I've been here it taught me what help is, and how to live again, and I don't want to say goodbye. Don't open the door, I'm crying.

ANAGNOS *(gently)*. They will not see.

(He moves again as though opening doors, and in comes a group of girls, eight-year-olds to seventeen-year-olds; as they walk we see they are blind. ANAGNOS *shepherds them in with a hand.)*

A CHILD. Annie?

ANNIE *(her voice cheerful)*. Here, Beatrice..

(As soon as they locate her voice they throng joyfully to her, speaking all at once; ANNIE *is down on her knees to the smallest, and the following are the more intelligible fragments in the general hubbub.)*

CHILDREN. There's a present. We brought you a going-away present, Annie!

ANNIE. Oh, now you shouldn't have——

CHILDREN. We did, we did, where's the present?

SMALLEST CHILD *(mournfully)*. Don't go, Annie, away.

CHILDREN. Alice has it. Alice! Where's Alice? Here I am! Where? Here!

(An arm is aloft out of the group, waving a present; ANNIE *reaches for it.)*

ANNIE. I have it. I have it, everybody, should I open it?

CHILDREN. Open it! Everyone be quiet! Do, Annie! She's opening it. Ssh!

(A settling of silence while ANNIE *unwraps it. The present is a pair of smoked glasses, and she stands still.)*

Is it open, Annie?

ANNIE. It's open.

CHILDREN. It's for your eyes, Annie. Put them on, Annie! 'Cause Mrs. Hopkins said your eyes hurt since the operation. And she said you're going where the sun is *fierce*.

ANNIE. I'm putting them on now.

SMALLEST CHILD *(mournfully)*. Don't go, Annie, where the sun is fierce.

CHILDREN. Do they fit all right?

ANNIE. Oh, they fit just fine.

CHILDREN. Did you put them on? Are they pretty, Annie?

ANNIE. Oh, my eyes feel hundreds of per cent better already, and pretty, why, do you know how I look in them? Splendiloquent. Like a race horse!

CHILDREN *(delighted)*. There's another present! Beatrice! We have a present for Helen, too! Give it to her, Beatrice. Here, Annie!

(This present is an elegant doll, with movable eyelids and a momma sound.)

It's for Helen. And we took up a collection to buy it. And Laura dressed it.

ANNIE. It's beautiful!

CHILDREN. So don't forget, you be sure to give it to Helen from us, Annie!

ANNIE. I promise it will be the first thing I give her. If I don't keep it for myself, that is, you know I can't be trusted with dolls!

SMALLEST CHILD *(mournfully)*. Don't go, Annie, to her.

ANNIE *(her arm around her)*. Sarah, dear. I don't *want* to go.

SMALLEST CHILD. Then why are you going.

ANNIE. *(gently)*. Because I'm a big girl now, and big girls have to earn a living. It's the only way I can. But if you don't smile for me first, what I'll just have to do is——

(She pauses, inviting it.)

SMALLEST CHILD. What?

ANNIE. Put *you* in my suitcase, instead of this doll. And take *you* to Helen in Alabama!

(This strikes the children as very funny, and they begin to laugh and tease the smallest child, who after a moment does smile for ANNIE.*)*

ANAGNOS *(then)*. Come, children. We must get

the trunk into the carriage and Annie into her train, or no one will go to Alabama. Come, come.

(He shepherds them out and ANNIE *is left alone on her knees with the doll in her lap. She reaches for her suitcase, and by a subtle change in the color of the light, we go with her thoughts into another time. We hear a boy's voice whispering; perhaps we see shadowy intimations of these speakers in the background.)*

BOY'S VOICE. Where we goin', Annie?

ANNIE *(in dread).* Jimmie.

BOY'S VOICE. Where we goin'?

ANNIE. I said—I'm takin' care of you——

BOY'S VOICE. Forever and ever?

MAN'S VOICE *(impersonal).* Annie Sullivan, aged nine, virtually blind. James Sullivan, aged seven—What's the matter with your leg, Sonny?

ANNIE. Forever and ever.

MAN'S VOICE. Can't he walk without that crutch? *(*ANNIE *shakes her head, and does not stop shaking it.)*

Girl goes to the women's ward. Boy to the men's.

BOY'S VOICE *(interior).* Annie! Annie, don't let them take me—Annie!

ANAGNOS *(offstage).* Annie! Annie?

(But this voice is real, in the present, and ANNIE *comes up out of her horror, clearing her head with a final shake; the lights begin to pick out* KATE *in the* KELLER *house, as* ANNIE *in a bright tone calls back.)*

ANNIE. Coming!

(This word catches KATE, *who stands half turned and attentive to it, almost as though hearing it. Meanwhile* ANNIE *turns and hurries out, lugging the suitcase.)*

Scene 4

The room dims out; the sound of railroad wheels begins from off left, and maintains itself in a constant rhythm underneath the following scene; the remaining lights have come up on the KELLER *homestead.* JAMES *is lounging on the porch, waiting. In the upper bedroom which is to be* ANNIE'*s,* HELEN *is alone, puzzledly exploring, fingering, and smelling things, the curtains, empty drawers in the bureau, water in the pitcher by the washbasin, fresh towels on the bedstead. Downstairs in the family room* KATE *turning to a mirror hastily adjusts her bonnet, watched by a Negro servant in an apron,* VINEY.

VINEY. Let Mr. Jimmy go by hisself, you been pokin' that garden all day, you ought to rest your feet.

KATE. I can't wait to see her, Viney.

VINEY. Maybe she ain't gone be on this train neither.

KATE. Maybe she is.

VINEY. And maybe she ain't.

KATE. And maybe she is. Where's Helen?

VINEY. She upstairs, smellin' around. She know somethin' funny's goin' on.

KATE. Let her have her supper as soon as Mildred's in bed, and tell Captain Keller when he comes that we'll be delayed tonight.

VINEY. Again.

KATE I don't think we need say *again.* Simply delayed will do.

(She runs upstairs to ANNIE'*s room,* VINEY *speaking after her.)*

VINEY. I mean that's what he gone say. "What, again?"

*(*VINEY *works at setting the table. Upstairs* KATE *stands in the doorway, watching* HELEN'*s groping explorations.)*

KATE. Yes, we're expecting someone. Someone for my Helen.

*(*HELEN *happens upon her skirt, clutches her leg;* KATE *in a tired dismay kneels to tidy her hair and soiled pinafore.)*

Oh, dear, this was clean not an hour ago. *(*HELEN *feels her bonnet, shakes her head darkly, and tugs to get it off.* KATE *retains it with one hand, diverts* HELEN *by opening her other hand under her nose.)*

Here. For while I'm gone.

*(*HELEN *sniffs, reaches, and pops something*

into her mouth, while KATE *speaks a bit guiltily.)*

I don't think one peppermint drop will spoil your supper.

(She gives HELEN *a quick kiss, evades her hands, and hurries downstairs again. Meanwhile* CAPTAIN KELLER *has entered the yard from around the rear of the house, newspaper under arm, cleaning off and munching on some radishes; he sees* JAMES *lounging at the porch post.)*

KELLER. Jimmie?

JAMES *(unmoving).* Sir?

KELLER *(eyes him).* You don't look dressed for anything useful, boy.

JAMES. I'm not. It's for Miss Sullivan.

KELLER. Needn't keep holding up that porch, we have wooden posts for that. I asked you to see that those strawberry plants were moved this evening.

JAMES. I'm moving your—Mrs. Keller, instead. To the station.

KELLER *(heavily).* Mrs. Keller. Must you always speak of her as though you haven't met the lady?

*(*KATE *comes out on the porch, and* JAMES *inclines his head.)*

JAMES *(ironic).* Mother.

(He starts off the porch, but sidesteps KELLER*'s glare like a blow.)*

I said Mother!

KATE. Captain.

KELLER. Evening, my dear.

KATE. We're off to meet the train, Captain. Supper will be a trifle delayed tonight.

KELLER. What, again?

KATE *(backing out).* With your permission, Captain?

(And they are gone. KELLER *watches them offstage, morosely.*

Upstairs HELEN *meanwhile has groped for her mother, touched her cheek in a meaningful gesture, waited, touched her cheek, waited, then found the open door, and made her way down. Now she comes into the family room, touches her cheek again;* VINEY *regards her.)*

VINEY. What you want, honey, your momma?

*(*HELEN *touches her cheek again.* VINEY *goes to the sideboard, gets a tea-cake, gives it into* HELEN*'s hand;* HELEN *pops it into her mouth.)*

Guess one little tea-cake ain't gone ruin your appetite.

(She turns HELEN *toward the door.* HELEN *wanders out onto the porch, as* KELLER *comes up the steps. Her hands encounter him, and she touches her cheek again, waits.)*

KELLER. She's gone.

(He is awkward with her; when he puts his hand on her head, she pulls away. KELLER *stands regarding her, heavily.)*

She's gone, my son and I don't get along, you don't know I'm your father, no one likes me, and supper's delayed.

*(*HELEN *touches her cheek, waits.* KELLER *fishes in his pocket.)*

Here. I brought you some stick candy, one nibble of sweets can't do any harm.

(He gives her a large stick candy; HELEN *falls to it.* VINEY *peers out the window.)*

VINEY *(reproachfully).* Cap'n Keller, now how'm I gone get her to eat her supper you fill her up with that trash?

KELLER *(roars).* Tend to your work!

*(*VINEY *beats a rapid retreat.* KELLER *thinks better of it, and tries to get the candy away from* HELEN*, but* HELEN *hangs on to it; and when* KELLER *pulls, she gives his leg a kick.* KELLER *hops about,* HELEN *takes refuge with the candy down behind the pump, and* KELLER *then irately flings his newpaper on the porch floor, stamps into the house past* VINEY *and disappears.)*

Scene 5

The lights half dim on the homestead, where VINEY *and* HELEN *going about their business soon find their way off. Meanwhile, the railroad sounds off left have mounted in a crescendo to a climax typical of a depot at arrival time, the lights come up on stage left, and we see a sug-*

gestion of a station. Here ANNIE *in her smoked glasses and disarranged by travel is waiting with her suitcase, while* JAMES *walks to meet her; she has a battered paper-bound book, which is a Perkins report,*[6] *under her arm.*

JAMES *(coolly).* Miss Sullivan?

ANNIE *(cheerily).* Here! At last, I've been on trains so many days I thought they must be backing up every time I dozed off——

JAMES. I'm James Keller.

ANNIE. James?

(The name stops her.)

I had a brother Jimmie. Are you Helen's?

JAMES. I'm only half a brother. You're to be her governess?

ANNIE *(lightly).* Well. Try!

JAMES *(eying her).* You look like half a governess.

*(*KATE *enters.* ANNIE *stands moveless, while* JAMES *takes her suitcase.* KATE*'s gaze on her is doubtful, troubled.)*

Mrs. Keller, Miss Sullivan.

*(*KATE *takes her hand.)*

KATE *(simply).* We've met every train for two days.

*(*ANNIE *looks at* KATE'S *face, and her good humor comes back.)*

ANNIE. I changed trains every time they stopped, the man who sold me that ticket ought to be tied to the tracks——

JAMES. You have a trunk, Miss Sullivan?

ANNIE. Yes. *(She passes* JAMES *a claim check, and he bears the suitcase out behind them.* ANNIE *holds the battered book.* KATE *is studying her face, and* ANNIE *returns the gaze; this a mutual appraisal, Southern gentlewoman and workingclass Irish girl, and* ANNIE *is not quite comfortable under it.)*

You didn't bring Helen, I was hoping you would.

KATE. No, she's home.

(A pause. ANNIE *tries to make ladylike small talk, though her energy now and then erupts; she catches herself up whenever she hears it.)*

ANNIE. You—live far from town, Mrs. Keller?

KATE. Only a mile.

ANNIE. Well. I suppose I can wait one more mile. But don't be suprised if I get out to push the horse!

KATE. Helen's waiting for you, too. There's been such a bustle in the house, she expects something, heaven knows what.

(Now she voices part of her doubt, not as such, but ANNIE *understands it.)*

I expected—a desiccated spinster. You're very young.

ANNIE *(resolutely).* Oh, you should have seen me when I left Boston. I got much older on this trip.

KATE. I mean, to teach anyone as difficult as Helen.

ANNIE. *I* mean to try. They can't put you in jail for trying!

KATE. Is it possible, even? To teach a deaf-blind child *half* of what an ordinary child learns—has that ever been done?

ANNIE. Half?

KATE. A tenth.

ANNIE *(reluctantly).* No.

*(*KATE*'s face loses its remaining hope, still appraising her youth.)*

Dr. Howe did wonders, but—an ordinary child? No, never. But then I thought when I was going over his reports—

(She indicates the one in her hand.)

—he never treated them like ordinary children. More like—eggs everyone was afraid would break.

KATE *(a pause).* May I ask how old you are?

ANNIE. Well, I'm not in my teens, you know! I'm twenty.

KATE. All of twenty.

*(*ANNIE *takes the bull by the horns, valiantly.)*

ANNIE. Mrs. Keller, don't lose heart just because I'm not on my last legs. I have three big advantages over Dr. Howe that money couldn't buy for you. One is his work behind me, I've

---

6. ***Perkins report,*** report written by Dr. Samuel G. Howe, the founder of the Perkins Institution. During the 1830s Dr. Howe had taught Laura Bridgman, a young woman who was both blind and deaf, to communicate. He described his teaching methods and his progress in his annual reports to the directors of the Perkins Institution.

Helen Keller and Annie Sullivan

read every word he wrote about it and he wasn't exactly what you'd call a man of few words. Another is to *be* young, why, I've got energy to do anything. The third is, I've been blind.

(But it costs her something to say this.)

KATE *(quietly).* Advantages.

ANNIE *(wry).* Well, some have the luck of the Irish, some do not.

(KATE smiles; she likes her.)

KATE. What will you try to teach her first?

ANNIE. First, last, and—in between, language.

KATE. Language.

ANNIE. Language is to the mind more than light is to the eye. Dr. Howe said that.

KATE. Language.

(She shakes her head.)

We can't get through to teach her to sit still. You *are* young, despite your years, to have such—confidence. Do you, inside?

(ANNIE studies her face; she likes her, too.)

ANNIE. No, to tell you the truth I'm as shaky inside as a baby's rattle!

(They smile at each other, and KATE pats her hand.)

KATE. Don't be.

(JAMES returns to usher them off.)

We'll do all we can to help, and to make you feel at home. Don't think of us as strangers, Miss Annie.

ANNIE *(cheerily).* Oh, strangers aren't so strange to me. I've known them all my life!

(KATE smiles again, ANNIE smiles back, and they precede JAMES offstage.)

Scene 6

The lights dim on them, having simultaneously risen full on the house; VINEY has already entered the family room, taken a water pitcher, and come out and down to the pump. She pumps real water. As she looks offstage, we hear the clop of hoofs, a carriage stopping, and voices.

VINEY. Cap'n Keller! Cap'n Keller, they comin'!

(She goes back into the house, as KELLER comes out on the porch to gaze.)

She sure 'nuff came, Cap'n.

(KELLER descends, and crosses toward the carriage; this conversation begins offstage and moves on.)

KELLER *(very courtly).* Welcome to Ivy Green, Miss Sullivan. I take it you are Miss Sullivan——

KATE. My husband, Miss Annie, Captain Keller.

ANNIE *(her best behavior).* Captain, how do you do.

KELLER. A pleasure to see you, at last. I trust you had an agreeable journey?

ANNIE. Oh, I had several! When did this country get so big?

JAMES. Where would you like the trunk, Father?

KELLER. Where Miss Sullivan can get at it, I imagine.

ANNIE. Yes, please. Where's Helen?

KELLER. In the hall, Jimmie——

KATE. We've put you in the upstairs corner room, Miss Annie, if there's any breeze at all this summer, you'll feel it——

(In the house the setter BELLE *flees into the family room, pursued by* HELEN *with groping hands; the dog doubles back out the same door, and* HELEN *still groping for her makes her way out to the porch; she is messy, her hair tumbled, her pinafore now ripped, her shoelaces untied.* KELLER *acquires the suitcase, and* ANNIE *gets her hands on it too, though still endeavoring to live up to the general air of propertied manners.*[7]*)*

KELLER. *And* the suitcase——

ANNIE *(pleasantly).* I'll take the suitcase, thanks.

KELLER. Not at all, I have it, Miss Sullivan.

ANNIE. I'd like it.

KELLER *(gallantly).* I couldn't think of it, Miss Sullivan. You'll find in the South we——

ANNIE. Let me.

KELLER. —view women as the flowers of civiliza——

ANNIE *(impatiently).* I've got something in it for Helen!

(She tugs it free; KELLER *stares.)*

Thank you. When do I see her?

KATE. There. There is Helen.

*(*ANNIE *turns, and sees* HELEN *on the porch. A moment of silence. Then Annie begins across the yard to her, lugging her suitcase.)*

KELLER *(sotto voce*[8]*).* Katie ——

*(*KATE *silences him with a hand on his arm. When* ANNIE *finally reaches the porch steps she stops, contemplating* HELEN *for a last moment before entering her world. Then she drops the suitcase on the porch with intentional heaviness,* HELEN *starts with the jar, and comes to grope over it.* ANNIE *puts forth her hand, and touches* HELEN*'s.* HELEN *at once grasps it, and commences to explore it, like reading a face. She moves her hand on to* ANNIE*'s forearm, and dress; and* ANNIE *brings her face within reach of* HELEN*'s fingers, which travel over it, quite without timidity, until they encounter and push aside the smoked glasses.* ANNIE*'s gaze is grave, unpitying, very attentive. She puts her hands on* HELEN*'s arms, but* HELEN *at once pulls away, and they confront each other with a distance between. Then* HELEN *returns to the suitcase, tries to open it, cannot.* ANNIE *points* HELEN*'s hand overhead.* HELEN *pulls away, tries to open the suitcase again;* ANNIE *points her hand overhead again. Then* HELEN *points overhead, a question, and* ANNIE, *drawing* HELEN*'s hand to her own face, nods.* HELEN *now begins tugging the suitcase toward the door; when* ANNIE *tries to take it from her, she fights her off and backs through the doorway with it.* ANNIE *stands a moment, then follows her in, and together they get the suitcase up the steps into* ANNIE*'s room.)*

KATE. Well?

KELLER. She's very rough, Katie.

KATE. I like her, Captain.

KELLER. Certainly rear a peculiar kind of young woman in the North. How old is she?

KATE *(vaguely).* Ohh—Well, she's not in her teens, you know.

KELLER. She's only a child. What's her family like, shipping her off alone this far?

KATE. I couldn't learn. She's very close-mouthed about some things.

---

7. ***general air of propertied manners,*** atmosphere of wealth and distinction.

8. ***sotto voce*** (sot′ō vō′chē), in a low tone.

KELLER. Why does she wear those glasses? I like to see a person's eyes when I talk to——

KATE. For the sun. She was blind.

KELLER. Blind.

KATE. She's had nine operations on her eyes. One just before she left.

KELLER. Blind, good heavens, do they expect one blind child to teach another? Has she experience at least, how long did she teach there?

KATE. She was a pupil.

KELLER *(heavily).* Katie, Katie. This is her first position?

KATE *(bright voice).* She was valedictorian——

KELLER. Here's a houseful of grownups can't cope with the child, how can an inexperienced half-blind Yankee schoolgirl manage her?

*(*JAMES *moves in with the trunk on his shoulder.)*

JAMES *(easily).* Great improvement. Now we have two of them to look after.

KELLER. You look after those strawberry plants!

*(*JAMES *stops with the trunk.* KELLER *turns from him without another word, and marches off.)*

JAMES. Nothing I say is right.

KATE. Why say anything?

(She calls.)

Don't be long, Captain, we'll have supper right away——

(She goes into house, and through the rear door of the family room. JAMES *trudges in with the trunk, takes it up the steps to* ANNIE*'s room, and sets it down outside the door. The lights elsewhere dim somewhat.)*

Scene 7

Meanwhile, inside, ANNIE *has given* HELEN *a key; while* ANNIE *removes her bonnet,* HELEN *unlocks and opens the suitcase. The first thing she pulls out is a voluminous shawl. She fingers it until she perceives what it is; then she wraps it around her, and acquiring* ANNIE*'s bonnet and smoked glasses as well, dons the lot: the shawl swamps her, and the bonnet settles down upon the glasses, but she stands before a mirror cocking her head to one side, then to the other, in a mockery of adult action.* ANNIE *is amused, and talks to her as one might to a kitten, with no trace of company manners.*

ANNIE. All the trouble I went to and that's how I look?

*(*HELEN *then comes back to the suitcase, gropes for more, lifts out a pair of female drawers.)*

Oh, no. Not the drawers!

(But HELEN *discarding them comes to the elegant doll. Her fingers explore its features, and when she raises it and finds its eyes open and close, she is at first startled, then delighted. She picks it up, taps its head vigorously, taps her own chest, and nods questioningly.* ANNIE *takes her finger, points it to the doll, points it to* HELEN, *and touching it to her own face, also nods.* HELEN *sits back on her heels, clasps the doll to herself, and rocks it.* ANNIE *studies her, still in bonnet and smoked glasses like a caricature of herself, and addresses her humorously.)*

All right, Miss O'Sullivan. Let's begin with doll.

(She takes HELEN*'s hand; in her palm* ANNIE*'s forefinger points, thumb holding her other fingers clenched.)*

D.

(Her thumb next holds all her fingers clenched, touching HELEN*'s palm.)*

O.

(Her thumb and forefinger extend.)

L.

(Same contact repeated.)

L.

(She puts HELEN*'s hand to the doll.)*

Doll.

JAMES. You spell pretty well.

*(*ANNIE *in one hurried move gets the drawers swiftly back into the suitcase, the lid banged shut, and her head turned, to see* JAMES *leaning in the doorway.)*

Finding out if she's ticklish? She is.

(ANNIE regards him stonily, but HELEN after a scowling moment tugs at her hand again, imperious. ANNIE repeats the letters, and HELEN interrupts her fingers in the middle, feeling each of them, puzzled. ANNIE touches HELEN's hand to the doll, and begins spelling into it again.)

JAMES. What is it, a game?

ANNIE *(curtly).* An alphabet.

JAMES. Alphabet?

ANNIE. For the deaf.

(HELEN now repeats the finger movements in air, exactly, her head cocked to her own hand, and ANNIE's eyes suddenly gleam.)

Ho. How *bright* she is!

JAMES. You think she knows what she's doing?

(He takes HELEN's hand, to throw a meaningless gesture into it; she repeats this one too.)

She imitates everything, she's a monkey.

ANNIE *(very pleased).* Yes, she's a bright little monkey, all right.

(She takes the doll from HELEN, and reaches for her hand; HELEN instantly grabs the doll back. ANNIE takes it again, and HELEN's hand next, but HELEN is incensed now; when ANNIE draws her hand to her face to shake her head no, then tries to spell to her, HELEN slaps at ANNIE's face. ANNIE grasps HELEN by both arms, and swings her into a chair, holding her pinned there, kicking, while glasses, doll, bonnet fly in various directions. JAMES laughs.)

JAMES. She wants her doll back.

ANNIE. When she spells it.

JAMES. Spell, she doesn't know the thing has a name, even.

ANNIE. Of course not, who expects her to, now? All I want is her fingers to learn the letters.

JAMES. Won't mean anything to her.

(ANNIE gives him a look. She then tries to form HELEN's fingers into the letters, but HELEN swings a haymaker instead, which ANNIE barely ducks, at once pinning her down again.)

Doesn't like that alphabet, Miss Sullivan. You invent it yourself?

(HELEN is now in a rage, fighting tooth and nail to get out of the chair, and ANNIE answers while struggling and dodging her kicks.)

ANNIE. Spanish monks under a—vow of silence. Which I wish *you'd* take!

(And suddenly releasing HELEN's hands, she comes and shuts the door in JAMES's face. HELEN drops to the floor, groping around for the doll. ANNIE looks around desperately, sees her purse on the bed, rummages in it, and comes up with a battered piece of cake wrapped in newspaper; with her foot she moves the doll deftly out of the way of HELEN's groping, and going on her knee she lets HELEN smell the cake. When HELEN grabs for it, ANNIE removes the cake and spells quickly into the reaching hand.)

Cake. From Washington up North, it's the best I can do.

(HELEN's hand waits, baffled. ANNIE repeats it.)

C, a, k, e. Do what my fingers do, never mind what it means.

(She touches the cake briefly to HELEN's nose, pats her hand, presents her own hands. HELEN spells the letters rapidly back. ANNIE pats her hand enthusiastically, and gives her the cake; HELEN crams it into her mouth with both hands. ANNIE watches her, with humor.)

Get it down fast, maybe I'll steal that back too. Now.

(She takes the doll, touches it to HELEN's nose, and spells again into her hand.)

D, o, l, l. Think it over.

(HELEN thinks it over, while ANNIE presents her own hand. Then HELEN spells three letters. ANNIE waits a second, then completes the word for HELEN in her palm.)

L.

(She hands over the doll, and HELEN gets a good grip on its leg.)

Imitate now, understand later. End of the first les——

(She never finishes, because HELEN swings the doll with a furious energy, it hits ANNIE

squarely in the face, and she falls back with a cry of pain, her knuckles up to her mouth. HELEN *waits, tensed for further combat. When* ANNIE *lowers her knuckles she looks at blood on them; she works her lips, gets to her feet, finds the mirror, and bares her teeth at herself. Now she is furious herself.)*

You little wretch, no one's taught you *any* manners? I'll——

(But rounding from the mirror she sees the door slam, HELEN *and the doll are on the outside, and* HELEN *is turning the key in the lock.* ANNIE *darts over, to pull the knob; the door is locked fast. She yanks it again.)*

Helen! Helen, let me out of——

(She bats her brow at the folly of speaking, but JAMES, *now downstairs hears her and turns to see* HELEN *with the key and doll groping her way down the steps;* JAMES *takes in the whole situation, makes a move to intercept* HELEN, *but then changes his mind, lets her pass, and amusedly follows her out onto the porch. Upstairs* ANNIE *meanwhile rattles the knob, kneels, peers through the keyhole, gets up. She goes to the window, looks down, frowns.* JAMES *from the yard sings gaily up to her:)*

JAMES. Buffalo girl, are you coming out tonight,
Coming out tonight,
Coming out——

(He drifts back into the house. ANNIE *takes a handkerchief, nurses her mouth, stands in the middle of the room, staring at door and window in turn, and so catches sight of herself in the mirror, her cheek scratched, her hair dishevelled, her handkerchief bloody, her face disgusted with herself. She addresses the mirror, with some irony.)*

ANNIE. Don't worry. They'll find you, you're not lost. Only out of place.

(But she coughs, spits something into her palm, and stares at it, outraged.)

And toothless.

(She winces.)

Oo! It hurts.

(She pours some water into the basin, dips the handkerchief, and presses it to her mouth. Standing there, bent over the basin in pain—with the rest of the set dim and unreal, and the lights upon her taking on the subtle color of the past—she hears again, as do we, the faraway voices, and slowly she lifts her head to them; the boy's voice is the same, the others are cracked old crones in a nightmare, and perhaps we see their shadows.)

BOY'S VOICE. It hurts. Annie, it hurts.

FIRST CRONE'S VOICE. Keep that brat shut up, can't you, girlie, how's a body to get any sleep in this damn ward?

BOY'S VOICE. It hurts. It hurts.

SECOND CRONE'S VOICE. Shut up, you!

BOY'S VOICE. Annie, when are we goin' home? You promised!

ANNIE. Jimmie——

BOY'S VOICE. Forever and ever, you said forever——

*(*ANNIE *drops the handkerchief, averts to the window, and is arrested there by the next cry.)*

Annie? Annie, you there? Annie! It *hurts!*

THIRD CRONE'S VOICE. Grab him, he's fallin'!

BOY'S VOICE. *Annie!*

DOCTOR'S VOICE *(a pause, slowly).* Little girl. Little girl, I must tell you your brother will be going on a——

(But ANNIE *claps her hands to her ears, to shut this out; there is instant silence.*

As the lights bring the other areas in again, JAMES *goes to the steps to listen for any sound from upstairs.* KELLER *reentering from left crosses toward the house; he passes* HELEN *en route to her retreat under the pump.* KATE *reenters the rear door of the family room, with flowers for the table.)*

KATE. Supper is ready, Jimmie, will you call your father?

JAMES. Certainly.

(But he calls up the stairs, for ANNIE*'s benefit:)*

Father! Supper!

KELLER *(at the door).* No need to shout, I've been cooling my heels for an hour. Sit down.

JAMES. Certainly.

KELLER. Viney!

(VINEY backs in with a roast, while they get settled around the table.)

VINEY. Yes, Cap'n, right here.

KATE. Mildred went directly to sleep, Viney?

VINEY. Oh yes, that babe's a angel.

KATE. And Helen had a good supper?

VINEY *(vaguely).* I dunno, Miss Kate, somehow she didn't have much of a appetite tonight—

KATE *(a bit guilty).* Oh. Dear.

KELLER *(hastily).*Well, now. Couldn't say the same for my part, I'm famished. Katie, your plate.

KATE *(looking).* But where is Miss Annie?

(A silence)

JAMES. *(pleasantly).* In her room.

KELLER. In her room? Doesn't she know hot food must be eaten hot? Go bring her down at once, Jimmie.

JAMES *(rises).* Certainly. I'll get a ladder.

KELLER *(stares).* What?

JAMES. I'll need a ladder. Shouldn't take me long.

KATE *(stares).* What shouldn't take you——

KELLER. Jimmie, do as I say! Go upstairs at once and tell Miss Sullivan supper is getting cold.

JAMES. She's locked in her room.

KELLER. Locked in her——

KATE. What on earth are you——

JAMES. Helen locked her in and made off with the key.

KATE *(rising).* And you sit here and say nothing?

JAMES. Well, everyone's been telling me not to say anything.

(He goes serenely out and across the yard, whistling. KELLER thrusting up from his chair makes for the stairs.)

KATE. Viney, look out in back for Helen. See if she has that key.

VINEY. Yes, Miss Kate.

(VINEY goes out the rear door.)

KELLER *(calling down).* She's out by the pump!

(KATE goes out on the porch after HELEN, while KELLER knocks on ANNIE's door, then rattles the knob, imperiously.)

Miss Sullivan! Are you in there?

ANNIE. Oh, I'm in here, all right.

KELLER. Is there no key on your side?

ANNIE *(with some asperity).* Well, if there was a key in here, *I* wouldn't be in here. Helen took it, the only thing on my side is me.

KELLER. Miss Sullivan. I——

(He tries, but cannot hold it back.)

Not in the house ten minutes, I don't see *how* you managed it!

(He stomps downstairs again, while ANNIE mutters to herself.)

ANNIE. And even I'm not on my side.

KELLER *(roaring).* Viney!

VINEY *(reappearing).* Yes, Cap'n?

KELLER. Put that meat back in the oven!

(VINEY bears the roast off again, while KELLER strides out onto the porch. KATE is with HELEN at the pump, opening her hands.)

KATE. She has no key.

KELLER. Nonsense, she must have the key. Have you searched in her pockets?

KATE. Yes. She doesn't have it.

KELLER. Katie, she must have the key.

KATE. Would you prefer to search her yourself, Captain?

KELLER. No, I would not prefer to search her! She almost took my kneecap off this evening, when I tried merely to——

(JAMES reappears carrying a long ladder, with PERCY running after him to be in on things.)

Take that ladder back!

JAMES. Certainly.

(He turns around with it. MARTHA comes skipping around the upstage corner of the house to be in on things, accompanied by the setter BELLE.)

KATE. She could have hidden the key.

KELLER. Where?

KATE. Anywhere. Under a stone. In the flower beds. In the grass——

KELLER. Well, I can't plow up the entire grounds to find a missing key! Jimmie!

JAMES. Sir?

KELLER. Bring me a ladder!

JAMES. Certainly.

From the Broadway production of *The Miracle Worker*

*(*VINEY *comes around the downstage side of the house to be in on things; she has* MILDRED *over her shoulder, bleating.* KELLER *places the ladder against* ANNIE'*s window and mounts.* ANNIE *meanwhile is running about making herself presentable, washing the blood off her mouth, straightening her clothes, tidying her hair. Another Negro servant enters to gaze in wonder, increasing the gathering ring of spectators.)*

KATE *(sharply)*. What is Mildred doing up?

VINEY. Cap'n woke her, ma'am, all that hollerin'.

KELLER. Miss Sullivan!

*(*ANNIE *comes to the window, with as much air of gracious normality as she can manage;* KELLER *is at the window.)*

ANNIE *(brightly)*. Yes, Captain Keller?

KELLER. Come out!

ANNIE. I don't see how I can. There isn't room.

KELLER. I intend to carry you. Climb onto my shoulder and hold tight.

ANNIE. Oh, no. It's—very chivalrous of you, but I'd really prefer to——

KELLER. Miss Sullivan, follow instructions! I will not have you also tumbling out of our windows.

*(*ANNIE *obeys, with some misgivings.)*

I hope this is not a sample of what we may expect from you. In the way of simplifying the work of looking after Helen.

ANNIE. Captain Keller. I'm perfectly able to go down a ladder under my own——

KELLER. I doubt it, Miss Sullivan. Simply hold onto my neck.

(He begins down with her, while the spectators stand in a wide and somewhat awe-stricken circle, watching. KELLER *half-misses a rung, and* ANNIE *grabs at his whiskers.)*

My *neck,* Miss Sullivan!

ANNIE. I'm sorry to inconvenience you this way—

KELLER. No inconvenience, other than having that door taken down and the lock replaced, if we fail to find that key.

ANNIE. Oh, I'll look everywhere for it.

KELLER. Thank you. Do not look in any rooms that can be locked. There.

(He stands her on the ground. JAMES *applauds.)*

ANNIE. Thank you very much.

(She smooths her skirt, looking as composed and ladylike as possible. KELLER *stares around at the spectators.)*

KELLER. Go, go, back to your work. What are you looking at here? There's nothing here to look at.

(They break up, move off.)

Now would it be possible for us to have supper, like other people?

(He marches into the house.)

KATE. Viney, serve supper. I'll put Mildred to sleep.

(They all go in. JAMES *is the last to leave, murmuring to* ANNIE *with a gesture.)*

JAMES. Might as well leave the l, a, d, d, e, r, hm?

*(*ANNIE *ignores him, looking at* HELEN; JAMES *goes in too. Imperceptibly the lights commence to narrow down.* ANNIE *and* HELEN *are now alone in the yard,* HELEN *seated at the pump, where she has been oblivious to it all, a battered little savage, playing with the doll in a picture of innocent contentment.* ANNIE *comes near, leans against the house, and taking off her smoked glasses, studies her, not without awe. Presently* HELEN *rises, gropes around to see if anyone is present;* ANNIE *evades her hand, and when* HELEN *is satisfied she is alone, the key suddenly protrudes out of her mouth. She takes it in her fingers, stands thinking, gropes to the pump, lifts a loose board, drops the key into the well, and hugs herself gleefully.* ANNIE *stares. But after a moment she shakes her head to herself, she cannot keep the smile from her lips.)*

ANNIE. You *devil.*

(Her tone is one of great respect, humor, and acceptance of challenge.)

You think I'm so easily gotten rid of? You have a thing or two to learn, first. I have nothing else to do.

(She goes up the steps to the porch, but turns for a final word, almost of warning.)

And nowhere to go.

(And presently she moves into the house to the others, as the lights dim down and out, except for the small circle upon HELEN *solitary at the pump, which ends the act.)*

Discussion

1. *The Miracle Worker* begins when Helen Keller is nineteen months old. What are some advantages of beginning the play this way? (What do you learn about Helen and about her background?)

2. (a) What does the incident with Martha and Percy tell you about Helen? **(b)** How does she react when she is frustrated?

3. The scissors incident prompts a heated discussion during the second scene. **(a)** Characterize Kate's attitude toward Helen's affliction. **(b)** To what extent does Kate's attitude bring her in conflict with Captain Keller? **(c)** What is the significance of the incident with the towel doll?

4. The third scene, which takes place at the Perkins Institution, introduces Annie Sullivan. **(a)** Cite passages to show that Annie is "obstinate," "impudent," and "combative." **(b)** What other traits does Annie reveal in this scene? **(c)** Summarize what you learn about Annie's background.

5. The fourth scene shows the members of the Keller family as they await Annie's arrival. **(a)** Does this scene suggest a reason for the strained relations between James and Captain Keller? Explain your answer. **(b)** What identical action do Kate, Viney, and Captain Keller perform in this scene? **(c)** Why is this action highly significant?

6. (a) What is Kate's first impression of Annie? **(b)** What changes this impression?

7. (a) Upon arriving at the Keller home, how does Annie manage to antagonize Captain Keller? **(b)** Why does she need her suitcase? **(c)** How does Kate react when Captain Keller and James voice their doubts about Annie?

8. Annie hopes to teach language to Helen. **(a)** How does she proceed to do so? **(b)** What is Helen's reaction? **(c)** What is James's reaction?

9. There are several incidents in which the mounting tension of Act One is relieved by humor. Cite passages that illustrate this.

10. What personality traits do Annie and Helen have in common?

Vocabulary

Context

In Act One we learn much about the main characters through Gibson's use of adjectives and adverbs. From the list below, choose a word that is a synonym for the word in parentheses in each sentence. Rewrite the sentences on your paper. You will not use all of the words on the list.

benign	impudent
vivacious	obstinate
jovial	combative
indolent	irately
morosely	valiantly
indulgent	imperious
inarticulate	oblivious

1. Aunt Ev is a _____ (kindly) person.

2. Annie behaves _____ (boldly) when faced with an extremely difficult situation.

3. Helen is _____ (haughty) in demanding her doll.

4. Captain Keller _____ (angrily) flings the newspaper.

5. James seems to be an _____ (idle) young man.

6. Captain Keller is _____ (merry) as he jests with Kate.

7. Captain Keller watches Helen _____ (sadly).

8. Annie is _____ (stubborn).

9. Helen is a _____ (lively) little girl.

10. Annie's _____ (bold) look indicates her determination.

Comment: Stage Directions

The people involved in putting on a play—actors, directors, set and costume designers, and producers—must be able to visualize in their imaginations what the playwright intends. To assist them in this process, modern dramatists often devote the same care to writing stage directions as they do to writing dialogue. They describe the stage sets, the lighting effects, the costumes. They describe the way characters speak and move as well as the changing positions of these characters on the stage as the play progresses. Because you are reading a play rather than seeing it performed, stage directions can help you visualize what the playwright intends the audience to see and hear.

Notice, for example, how Gibson describes the interior of the Keller household and the activities of some of its inhabitants (page 70, column a). If you were a set designer, where would you place the characters, and what would you have them doing? If you were an actor, what would the word *benign* tell you about Aunt Ev? What would *indolent* tell you about James Keller? Note the description of Kate on page 68, column a. Compare that description to the one on page 70, column a. If you were playing the role, how would you reveal Kate's character in each scene?

Notice, also, that Gibson uses lighting to change scenes and to convey moods. Rather than pulling the curtain at the end of each scene, he lightens or darkens parts of the stage. For example, he shifts the focus from Helen, Martha, and Percy by gradually lighting a room in the Keller house (page 70, column a). On page 73, column a, he reveals the close relationship between Kate and Helen by isolating them in light. Yet almost immediately the audience hears the voice of Mr. Anagnos, the lights rise on him, and a new scene is established. What might be Gibson's purpose in keeping Kate and Helen lighted during the opening conversation between Dr. Anagnos and Annie? On page 83, column b, Gibson slightly shifts the color of the light. What are his purposes in doing so?

Most playwrights do their best to help the reader visualize the play in performance. Careful, detailed reading can be the next best thing to watching the play from third-row center.

Act Two

Scene 1

It is evening.

The only room visible in the Keller house is ANNIE*'s, where by lamplight* ANNIE *in a shawl is at a desk writing a letter; at her bureau* HELEN *in her customary unkempt state is tucking her doll in the bottom drawer as a cradle, the contents of which she has dumped out, creating as usual a fine disorder.*

ANNIE *mutters each word as she writes her letter, slowly, her eyes close to and almost touching the page, to follow with difficulty her penwork.*

ANNIE. ". . . and, nobody, here, has, attempted, to, control, her. The, greatest, problem, I, have, is, how, to, disipline, her, without, breaking, her, spirit." *(Resolute voice)* "But, I, shall, insist, on, reasonable, obedience, from, the, start——" *(At which point* HELEN, *groping about on the desk, knocks over the inkwell.* ANNIE *jumps up, rescues her letter, rights the inkwell, grabs a towel to stem the spillage, and then wipes at* HELEN*'s hands;* HELEN *as always* *pulls free, but not until* ANNIE *first gets three letters into her palm.)*

Ink.

*(*HELEN *is enough interested in and puzzled by this spelling that she proffers her hand again; so* ANNIE *spells and impassively dunks it back in the spillage.)*

Ink. It has a name.

(She wipes the hand clean, and leads HELEN *to her bureau, where she looks for something to engage her. She finds a sewing card, with needle and thread, and going to her knees, shows* HELEN*'s hand how to connect one row of holes.)*

Down. Under. Up. And be careful of the needle——

*(*HELEN *gets it, and* ANNIE *rises.)*

Fine. You keep out of the ink and perhaps I can keep out of—the soup.

(She returns to the desk, tidies it, and resumes writing her letter, bent close to the page.)

"These, blots, are, her, handiwork, I——"

(She is interrupted by a gasp: HELEN *has stuck her finger, and sits sucking at it, darkly. Then with vengeful resolve she seizes her doll, and is about to dash its brains out on the floor when* ANNIE *diving catches it in one hand, which she at once shakes with hopping pain but otherwise ignores, patiently.)*

All right, let's try temperance.

(Taking the doll, she kneels, goes through the motion of knocking its head on the floor, spells into HELEN*'s hand:)*

Bad, girl.

(She lets HELEN *feel the grieved expression on her face.* HELEN *imitates it. Next she makes* HELEN *caress the doll and kiss the hurt spot and hold it gently in her arms, then spells into her hand:)*

Good, girl.

(She lets HELEN *feel the smile on her face.* HELEN *sits with a scowl, which suddenly clears; she pats the doll, kisses it, wreathes her face in a large artificial smile, and bears the doll to the washstand, where she carefully sits it.* ANNIE *watches, pleased.)*

Very good girl——

(Whereupon HELEN *elevates the pitcher and dashes it on the floor instead.* ANNIE *leaps to her feet, and stands inarticulate;* HELEN *calmly gropes back to sit to the sewing card and needle.*

ANNIE *manages to achieve self-control. She picks up a fragment or two of the pitcher, sees* HELEN *is puzzling over the card, and resolutely kneels to demonstrate it again. She spells in* HELEN*'s hand.*

KATE *meanwhile coming around the corner with folded sheets on her arm, halts at the doorway and watches them for a moment in silence; she is moved, but level.)*

KATE *(presently).* What are you saying to her?

*(*ANNIE *glancing up is a bit embarrassed, and rises from the spelling, to find her company manners.)*

ANNIE. Oh, I was just making conversation. Saying it was a sewing card.

KATE. But does that——

(She imitates with her fingers)

—mean that to her?

ANNIE. No. No, she won't know what spelling is till she knows what a word is.

KATE. Yet you keep spelling to her. Why?

ANNIE *(cheerily).* I like to hear myself talk!

KATE. The Captain says it's like spelling to the fence post.

ANNIE *(a pause).* Does he, now.

KATE. Is it?

ANNIE. No, it's how I watch you talk to Mildred.

KATE. Mildred.

ANNIE. Any baby. Gibberish, grown-up gibberish, baby-talk gibberish, do they understand one word of it to start? Somehow they begin to. If they hear it, I'm letting Helen hear it.

KATE. Other children are not—impaired.

ANNIE. Ho, there's nothing impaired in that head, it works like a mousetrap!

KATE *(smiles).* But after a child hears how many words, Miss Annie, a million?

ANNIE. I guess no mother's ever minded enough to count.

(She drops her eyes to spell into HELEN*'s*

hand, again indicating the card; HELEN *spells back, and* ANNIE *is amused.)*

KATE *(too quickly).* What did she spell?

ANNIE. I spelt card. She spelt cake!

(She takes in KATE*'s quickness, and shakes her head, gently.)*

No, it's only a finger-game to her, Mrs. Keller. What she has to learn first is that things have names.

KATE. And when will she learn?

ANNIE. Maybe after a million and one words.

(They hold each other's gaze; KATE *then speaks quietly.)*

KATE. I should like to learn those letters, Miss Annie.

ANNIE *(pleased).* I'll teach you tomorrow morning. That makes only half a million each!

KATE *(then).* It's her bedtime.

*(*ANNIE *reaches for the sewing card,* HELEN *objects,* ANNIE *insists, and* HELEN *gets rid of* ANNIE*'s hand by jabbing it with the needle.* ANNIE *gasps, and moves to grip* HELEN*'s wrist; but* KATE *intervenes with a proffered sweet, and* HELEN *drops the card, crams the sweet into her mouth, and scrambles up to search her mother's hands for more.* ANNIE *nurses her wound, staring after the sweet.)*

I'm sorry, Miss Annie.

ANNIE *(indignantly).* Why does she get a reward? For stabbing me?

KATE. Well——

(Then, tiredly)

We catch our flies with honey, I'm afraid. We haven't the heart for much else, and so many times she simply cannot be compelled.

ANNIE *(ominous).* Yes. I'm the same way myself.

*(*KATE *smiles, and leads* HELEN *off around the corner.* ANNIE *alone in her room picks up things and in the act of removing* HELEN*'s doll gives way to unmannerly temptation: she throttles it. She drops it on her bed, and stands pondering. Then she turns back, sits decisively, and writes again, as the lights dim on her.)*

(Grimly)

"The, more, I, think, the, more, certain, I, am, that, obedience, is, the, gateway, through, which, knowledge, enters, the, mind, of, the, child——"

Scene 2

On the word "obedience" a shaft of sunlight hits the water pump outside, while ANNIE*'s voice ends in the dark, followed by a distant cockcrow; daylight comes up over another corner of the sky, with* VINEY*'s voice heard at once.*

VINEY. Breakfast ready!

*(*VINEY *comes down into the sunlight beam, and pumps a pitcherful of water. While the pitcher is brimming we hear conversation from the dark; the light grows to the family room of the house where all are either entering or already seated at breakfast, with* KELLER *and* JAMES *arguing the war.*[1] HELEN *is wandering around the table to explore the contents of the other plates. When* ANNIE *is in her chair, she watches* HELEN. VINEY *reenters, sets the pitcher on the table;* KATE *lifts the almost empty biscuit plate with an inquiring look,* VINEY *nods and bears it off back, neither of them interrupting the men.* ANNIE *meanwhile sits with fork quiet, watching* HELEN, *who at her mother's plate pokes her hand among some scrambled eggs.* KATE *catches* ANNIE*'s eyes on her, smiles with a wry gesture.* HELEN *moves on to* JAMES*'s plate, the male talk continuing,* JAMES *deferential and* KELLER *overriding.)*

JAMES.—no, but shouldn't we give the devil his due, Father? The fact is we lost the South two years earlier when he outthought us behind Vicksburg.

KELLER. Outthought is a peculiar word for a butcher.

JAMES. Harness maker, wasn't he?

KELLER. I said butcher, his only virtue as a soldier was numbers and he led them to slaugh-

1. ***the war,*** the Civil War.

ter with no more regard than for so many sheep.

JAMES. But even if in that sense he was a butcher, the fact is he——

KELLER. And a drunken one, half the war.

JAMES. Agreed, Father. If his own people said he was I can't argue he——

KELLER. Well, what is it you find to admire in such a man, Jimmie, the butchery or the drunkenness?

JAMES. Neither, Father, only the fact that he beat us.

KELLER. He didn't.

JAMES. Is it your contention we won the war, sir?

KELLER. He didn't beat us at Vicksburg. We lost Vicksburg because Pemberton gave Bragg five thousand of his cavalry and Loring, whom I knew personally for a nincompoop before you were born, marched away from Champion's Hill with enough men to have held them, we lost Vicksburg by stupidity verging on treason.

JAMES. I would have said we lost Vicksburg because Grant was one thing no Yankee general was before him——

KELLER. Drunk? I doubt it.

JAMES. Obstinate.

KELLER. Obstinate. Could any of them compare even in that with old Stonewall?[2] If he'd been there we would still have Vicksburg.

JAMES. Well, the butcher simply wouldn't give up, he tried four ways of getting around Vicksburg and on the fifth try he got around. Anyone else would have pulled north and——

KELLER. He wouldn't have got around if we'd had a Southerner in command, instead of a half-breed Yankee traitor like Pemberton——

(While this background talk is in progress, HELEN *is working around the table, ultimately toward* ANNIE*'s plate. She messes with her hands in* JAMES*'s plate, then in* KELLER*'s, both men taking it so for granted they hardly notice. Then* HELEN *comes groping with soiled hands past her own plate, to* ANNIE*'s; her hand goes to it, and* ANNIE*, who has been waiting, deliberately lifts and removes her hand.* HELEN *gropes again,* ANNIE *firmly pins her by the wrist, and removes her hand from the table.* HELEN *thrusts her hands again,* ANNIE *catches them, and* HELEN *begins to flail and make noises; the interruption brings* KELLER*'s gaze upon them.)* What's the matter there?

KATE. Miss Annie. You see, she's accustomed to helping herself from our plates to anything she——

ANNIE *(evenly).* Yes, but *I'm* not accustomed to it.

KELLER. No, of course not. Viney!

KATE. Give her something, Jimmie, to quiet her.

JAMES *(blandly).* But her table manners are the best she has. Well.

(He pokes across with a chunk of bacon at HELEN*'s hand, which* ANNIE *releases; but* HELEN *knocks the bacon away and stubbornly thrusts at* ANNIE*'s plate,* ANNIE *grips her wrists again, the struggle mounts.)*

KELLER. Let her this time, Miss Sullivan, it's the only way we get any adult conversation. If my son's half merits that description.

(He rises.)

I'll get you another plate.

ANNIE *(gripping* HELEN*).* I have a plate, thank you.

KATE *(calling).* Viney! I'm afraid what Captain Keller says is only too true, she'll persist in this until she gets her own way.

KELLER *(at the door).* Viney, bring Miss Sullivan another plate——

ANNIE *(stonily).* I have a plate, nothing's wrong with the *plate,* I intend to keep it. *(Silence for a moment, except for* HELEN*'s noises as she struggles to get loose; the* KELLERS *are a bit nonplussed, and* ANNIE *is too darkly intent on* HELEN*'s manners to have any thoughts now of her own.)*

JAMES. Ha. You see why they took Vicksburg?

KELLER *(uncertainly).* Miss Sullivan. One plate

---

2. ***old Stonewall,*** Thomas J. "Stonewall" Jackson (1824-1863), a general in the Confederate Army.

or another is hardly a matter to struggle with a deprived child about.

ANNIE. Oh, I'd sooner have a more——

*(*HELEN *begins to kick,* ANNIE *moves her ankles to the opposite side of the chair)*

—heroic issue myself, I——

KELLER. No, I really must insist you——

*(*HELEN *bangs her toe on the chair and sinks to the floor, crying with rage and feigned injury;* ANNIE *keeps hold of her wrists, gazing down, while* KATE *rises.)*

Now she's hurt herself.

ANNIE *(grimly).* No, she hasn't.

KELLER. Will you please let her hands go?

KATE. Miss Annie, you don't know the child well enough yet, she'll keep——

ANNIE. I know an ordinary tantrum well enough, when I see one, and a badly spoiled child——

JAMES. Hear, hear.

KELLER *(very annoyed).* Miss Sullivan! You would have more understanding of your pupil if you had some pity in you. Now kindly do as I——

ANNIE. Pity?

(She releases HELEN *to turn equally annoyed on* KELLER *across the table; instantly* HELEN *scrambles up and dives at* ANNIE*'s plate. This time* ANNIE *intercepts her by pouncing on her*

wrists like a hawk, and her temper boils.)

For this *tyrant?* The whole house turns on her whims, is there anything she wants she doesn't get? I'll tell you what I pity, that the sun won't rise and set for her all her life, and every day you're telling her it will, what good will your pity do her when you're under the strawberries, Captain Keller?

KELLER *(outraged).* Kate, for the love of heaven will you——

KATE. Miss Annie, please, I don't think it serves to lose our——

ANNIE. It does you good, that's all. It's less trouble to feel sorry for her than to teach her anything better, isn't it?

KELLER. I fail to see where you have taught her anything yet, Miss Sullivan!

ANNIE. I'll begin this minute, if you'll leave the room, Captain Keller!

KELLER *(astonished).* Leave the——

ANNIE. Everyone, please.

(She struggles with HELEN, *while* KELLER *endeavors to control his voice.)*

KELLER. Miss Sullivan, you are here only as a paid teacher. Nothing more, and not to lecture——

ANNIE. I can't *un*teach her six years of pity if you can't stand up to one tantrum! Old Stonewall, indeed. Mrs. Keller, you promised me help.

KATE. Indeed I did, we truly want to——

ANNIE. Then leave me alone with her. Now!

KELLER *(in a wrath).* Katie, will you come outside with me? At once, please.

(He marches to the front door. KATE *and* JAMES *follow him. Simultaneously* ANNIE *releases* HELEN*'s wrists, and the child again sinks to the floor, kicking and crying her weird noises;* ANNIE *steps over her to meet* VINEY *coming in the rear doorway with biscuits and a clean plate, surprised at the general commotion.)*

VINEY. Heaven sakes——

ANNIE. Out, please.

(She backs VINEY *out with one hand, closes the door on her astonished mouth, locks it, and removes the key.* KELLER *meanwhile snatches his hat from a rack, and* KATE *follows him down the porch steps.* JAMES *lingers in the doorway to address* ANNIE *across the room with a bow.)*

JAMES. If it takes all summer, General.

*(*ANNIE *comes over to his door in turn, removing her glasses grimly; as* KELLER *outside begins speaking,* ANNIE *closes the door on* JAMES, *locks it, removes the key, and turns with her back against the door to stare ominously at* HELEN, *kicking on the floor.*

JAMES *takes his hat from the rack, and going down the porch steps joins* KATE *and* KELLER *talking in the yard,* KELLER *in a sputter of ire.)*

KELLER. This girl, this—cub of a girl—*presumes!* I tell you, I'm of half a mind to ship her back to Boston before the week is out. You can inform her so from me!

KATE *(eyebrows up).* I, Captain?

KELLER. She's a *hireling!* Now I want it clear, unless there's an apology and complete change of manner she goes back on the next train! Will you make that quite clear?

KATE. Where will you be, Captain, while I am making it quite——

KELLER. At the office!

(He begins off left, finds his napkin still in his irate hand, is uncertain with it, dabs his lips with dignity, gets rid of it in a toss to JAMES, *and marches off.* JAMES *turns to eye* KATE.*)*

JAMES. Will you?

*(*KATE*'s mouth is set, and* JAMES *studies it lightly.)*

I thought what she said was exceptionally intelligent. I've been saying it for years.

KATE *(not without scorn).* To his face?

(She comes to relieve him of the white napkin, but reverts again with it.)

Or will you take it, Jimmie? As a flag?

Scene 3

JAMES *stalks out, much offended, and* KATE *turning stares across the yard at the house; the lights narrowing down to the following panto-*

mime in the family room leaves her motionless in the dark.

*(*ANNIE *meanwhile has begun by slapping both keys down on a shelf out of* HELEN'S *reach; she returns to the table, upstage.* HELEN'S *kicking has subsided, and when from the floor her hand finds* ANNIE'S *chair empty she pauses.* ANNIE *clears the table of* KATE'S, JAMES'S, *and* KELLER'S *plates; she gets back to her own across the table just in time to slide it deftly away from* HELEN'S *pouncing hand. She lifts the hand and moves it to* HELEN'S *plate, and after an instant's exploration,* HELEN *sits again on the floor and drums her heels.* ANNIE *comes around the table and resumes her chair. When* HELEN *feels her skirt again, she ceases kicking, waits for whatever is to come, renews some kicking, waits again.* ANNIE *retrieving her plate takes up a forkful of food, stops it halfway to her mouth, gazes at it devoid of appetite, and half-lowers it; but after a look at* HELEN *she sighs, dips the forkful toward* HELEN *in a for-your-sake toast, and puts it in her own mouth to chew, not without an effort.*

HELEN *now gets hold of the chair leg, and half-succeeds in pulling the chair out from under her.* ANNIE *bangs it down with her rear, heavily, and sits with all her weight.* HELEN'S *next attempt to topple it is unavailing, so her fingers dive in a pinch at* ANNIE'S *flank.* ANNIE *in the middle of her mouthful almost loses it with startle, and she slaps down her fork to round on* HELEN. *The child comes up with curiosity to feel what* ANNIE *is doing, so* ANNIE *resumes eating, letting* HELEN'S *hand follow the movement of her fork to her mouth; whereupon* HELEN *at once reaches into* ANNIE'S *plate.* ANNIE *firmly removes her hand to her own plate.* HELEN *in reply pinches* ANNIE'S *thigh, a good mean pinchful that makes* ANNIE *jump.* ANNIE *sets the fork down, and sits with her mouth tight.* HELEN *digs another pinch into her thigh, and this time* ANNIE *slaps her hand smartly away;* HELEN *retaliates with a roundhouse fist that catches* ANNIE *on the ear, and* ANNIE'S *hand leaps at once in a forceful slap across* HELEN'S *cheek;* HELEN *is the startled one now.* ANNIE'S *hand in compunction falters to her own face, but when* HELEN *hits at her again,* ANNIE *deliberately slaps her again.* HELEN *lifts her fist irresolute for another roundhouse,* ANNIE *lifts her hand resolute for another slap, and they freeze in this posture, while* HELEN *mulls it over. She thinks better of it, drops her fist, and giving* ANNIE *a wide berth, gropes around to her mother's chair, to find it empty; she blunders her way along the table upstage, and encountering the empty chairs and missing plates, she looks bewildered; she gropes back to her mother's chair, again touches her cheek and indicates the chair, and waits for the world to answer.*

ANNIE *now reaches over to spell into her hand, but* HELEN *yanks it away; she gropes to the front door, tries the knob, and finds the door locked, with no key. She gropes to the rear door, and finds it locked, with no key. She commences to bang on it.* ANNIE *rises, crosses, takes her wrists, draws her resisting back to the table, seats her, and releases her hands upon her plate; as* ANNIE *herself begins to sit,* HELEN *writhes out of her chair, runs to the front door, and tugs and kicks at it.* ANNIE *rises again, crosses, draws her by one wrist back to the table, seats her, and sits;* HELEN *escapes back to the door, knocking over her mother's chair en route.* ANNIE *rises again in pursuit, and this time lifts* HELEN *bodily from behind and bears her kicking to her chair. She deposits her, and once more turns to sit.* HELEN *scrambles out, but as she passes* ANNIE *catches her up again from behind and deposits her in the chair;* HELEN *scrambles out on the other side, for the rear door, but* ANNIE *at her heels catches her up and deposits her again in the chair. She stands behind it.* HELEN *scrambles out to her right, and the instant her feet hit the floor* ANNIE *lifts and deposits her back; she scrambles out to her left, and is at once lifted and deposited back. She tries right again and is deposited back, and tries left again and is deposited back, and now feints* ANNIE *to the right but is off to her left, and is promptly deposited back. She sits a moment, and then starts straight over the tabletop, dishware notwithstanding;* ANNIE *hauls her in and deposits her back, with her plate spilling in her lap, and she melts to the floor and crawls under the table, laborious among its legs and chairs; but* ANNIE *is swift around the table and waiting on the other side when she surfaces, immediately bearing her aloft;* HELEN *clutches at* JAMES*'s chair for anchorage but it comes with her, and halfway back she abandons it to the floor.* ANNIE *deposits her in her chair, and waits.* HELEN *sits tensed motionless. Then she tentatively puts out her left foot and hand,* ANNIE *interposes her own hand, and at the contact* HELEN *jerks hers in. She tries her right foot,* ANNIE *blocks it with her own, and* HELEN *jerks hers in. Finally, leaning back, she slumps down in her chair, in a sullen biding.*

ANNIE *backs off a step, and watches;* HELEN *offers no move.* ANNIE *takes a deep breath. Both of them and the room are in considerable disorder, two chairs down and the table a mess, but* ANNIE *makes no effort to tidy it; she only sits on her own chair, and lets her energy refill. Then she takes up knife and fork, and resolutely addresses her food.* HELEN*'s hand comes out to explore, and seeing it* ANNIE *sits without moving; the child's hand goes over her hand and fork, pauses—*ANNIE *still does not move—and withdraws. Presently it moves for her own plate, slaps about for it, and stops, thwarted. At this,* ANNIE *again rises, recovers* HELEN*'s plate from the floor and a handful of scattered food from the deranged tablecloth, drops it on the plate, and pushes the plate into contact with* HELEN*'s fist. Neither of them now moves for a pregnant moment—until* HELEN *suddenly takes a grab of food and wolfs it down.* ANNIE *permits herself the humor of a minor bow and warming of her hands together; she wanders off a step or two, watching.* HELEN *cleans up the plate.*

After a glower of indecision, she holds the empty plate out for more. ANNIE *accepts it, and crossing to the removed plates, spoons food from them onto it; she stands debating the spoon, tapping it a few times on* HELEN*'s plate; and when she returns with the plate she brings the spoon, too. She puts the spoon first into* HELEN*'s hand, then sets the plate down.* HELEN *discarding the spoon reaches with her hand, and* ANNIE *stops it by the wrist; she replaces the spoon in it.* HELEN *impatiently discards it again, and again* ANNIE *stops her hand, to replace the spoon in it. This time* HELEN *throws the spoon on the floor.* ANNIE *after considering it lifts* HELEN *bodily out of the chair, and in a wrestling match on the floor closes her fingers upon the spoon, and returns her with it to the chair.* HELEN *again throws the spoon on the floor.* ANNIE *lifts her out of the chair again; but in the struggle over the spoon* HELEN *with* ANNIE *on her back sends her sliding over her head;* HELEN *flees back to her chair and scrambles into it. When* ANNIE *comes after her she clutches it for dear life;* ANNIE *pries one hand loose, then the other, then the first again, then the other again, and then lifts* HELEN *by the waist, chair and all, and shakes the chair loose.* HELEN *wrestles to get free, but* ANNIE *pins her to the floor, closes her fingers upon the spoon, and lifts her kicking under one arm; with her other hand she gets the chair in place again, and plunks* HELEN *back on it. When she releases her hand,* HELEN *throws the spoon at her.*

ANNIE *now removes the plate of food.* HELEN *grabbing finds it missing, and commences to bang with her fists on the table.* ANNIE *collects a fistful of spoons and descends with them and the plate on* HELEN*; she lets her smell the plate, at which* HELEN *ceases banging, and* ANNIE *puts the plate down and a spoon in* HELEN*'s hand.* HELEN *throws it on the floor.* ANNIE *puts another spoon in her* *hand.* HELEN *throws it on the floor.* ANNIE *puts another spoon in her hand.* HELEN *throws it on the floor. When* ANNIE *comes to her last spoon she sits next to* HELEN, *and gripping the spoon in* HELEN*'s hand compels her to take food in it up to her mouth.* HELEN *sits with lips shut.* ANNIE *waits a stolid moment, then lowers* HELEN*'s hand. She tries again;* HELEN*'s lips remain shut.* ANNIE *waits, lowers* HELEN*'s hand. She tries again; this time* HELEN *suddenly opens her mouth and accepts the food.* ANNIE *lowers the spoon with a sigh of relief, and* HELEN *spews the mouthful out at her face.* ANNIE *sits a moment with eyes closed, then takes the pitcher and dashes its water into* HELEN*'s face, who gasps astonished.* ANNIE *with* HELEN*'s hand takes up another spoonful, and shoves it into her open mouth.* HELEN *swallows involuntarily, and while she is catching her breath* ANNIE *forces her palm open, throws four swift letters into it, then another four, and bows toward her with devastating pleasantness.)*

ANNIE. Good girl.

*(*ANNIE *lifts* HELEN*'s hand to feel her face nodding;* HELEN *grabs a fistful of her hair, and yanks. The pain brings* ANNIE *to her knees, and* HELEN *pummels her; they roll under the table, and the lights commence to dim out on them.)*

Scene 4

Simultaneously the light at left has been rising slowly, so slowly that it seems at first we only imagine what is intimated in the yard: a few ghostlike figures, in silence, motionless, waiting. Now the distant belfry chimes commence to toll the hour, also very slowly, almost—it is twelve—interminably; the sense is that of a long time passing. We can identify the figures before the twelfth stroke, all facing the house in a kind of watch: KATE *is standing exactly as before, but now with the baby* MILDRED *sleeping in her arms, and placed here and there, unmoving, are* AUNT EV *in her hat with a hanky to her nose, and the two Negro children,* PERCY *and* MARTHA *with necks outstretched eagerly, and* VINEY *with a knotted kerchief on her head and a feather duster in her hand.*

The chimes cease, and there is silence. For a long moment none of the group moves.

VINEY *(presently).* What am I gone do, Miss Kate? It's noontime, dinner's comin', I didn't get them breakfast dishes out of there yet.

*(*KATE *says nothing, stares at the house.* MARTHA *shifts* HELEN*'s doll in her clutch, and it plaintively says momma.)*

KATE *(presently).* You run along, Martha.

*(*AUNT EV *blows her nose.)*

AUNT EV *(wretchedly).* I can't wait out here a minute longer, Kate, why, this could go on all afternoon, too.

KATE. I'll tell the Captain you called.

VINEY *(to the children).* You hear what Miss Kate say? Never you mind what's going on here.

(Still no one moves.)

You run along tend your own bizness.

(Finally VINEY *turns on the children with the feather duster.)*

Shoo!

(The two children divide before her. She chases them off. AUNT EV *comes to* KATE, *on her dignity.)*

AUNT EV. Say what you like, Kate, but that child is a *Keller.*

(She opens her parasol, preparatory to leaving.)

I needn't remind you that all the Kellers are cousins to General Robert E. Lee. I don't know *who* that girl is.

(She waits; but KATE *staring at the house is without response.)*

The only Sullivan I've heard of—from Boston too, and I'd think twice before locking her up with that kind—is that man John L.[3]

(And AUNT EV *departs, with head high. Pres-*

3. ***John L.,*** Aunt Ev is referring to John L. Sullivan (1858-1918), the world heavyweight boxing champion.

ently VINEY *comes to* KATE, *her arms out for the baby.)*

VINEY. You give me her, Miss Kate, I'll sneak her in back, to her crib.

(But KATE *is moveless, until* VINEY *starts to take the baby;* KATE *looks down at her before relinquishing her.)*

KATE *(slowly).* This child never gives me a minute's worry.

VINEY. Oh yes, this one's the angel of the family, no question bout *that.*

(She begins off rear with the baby, heading around the house; and KATE *now turns her back on it, her hand to her eyes. At this moment there is the slamming of a door, and when* KATE *wheels* HELEN *is blundering down the porch steps into the light, like a ruined bat out of hell.* VINEY *halts, and* KATE *runs in;* HELEN *collides with her mother's knees, and reels off and back to clutch them as her savior.* ANNIE *with smoked glasses in hand stands on the porch, also much undone, looking as though she had indeed just taken Vicksburg.* KATE *taking in* HELEN*'s ravaged state becomes steely in her gaze up at* ANNIE.*)*

KATE. What happened?

*(*ANNIE *meets* KATE*'s gaze, and gives a factual report, too exhausted for anything but a flat voice.)*

ANNIE. She ate from her own plate.

(She thinks a moment.)

She ate with a spoon. Herself.

*(*KATE *frowns, uncertain with thought, and glances down at* HELEN.*)*

And she folded her napkin.

*(*KATE*'s gaze now wavers, from* HELEN *to* ANNIE, *and back.)*

KATE *(softly).* Folded—her napkin?

ANNIE. The room's a wreck, but her napkin is folded.

(She pauses, then:)

I'll be in my room, Mrs. Keller.

(She moves to reenter the house; but she stops at VINEY*'s voice.)*

VINEY *(cheery).* Don't be long, Miss Annie. Dinner be ready right away!

*(*VINEY *carries* MILDRED *around the back of the house.* ANNIE *stands unmoving, takes a deep breath, stares over her shoulder at* KATE *and* HELEN, *then inclines her head graciously, and goes with a slight stagger into the house. The lights in her room above steal up in readiness for her.*

KATE *remains alone with* HELEN *in the yard, standing protectively over her, in a kind of wonder.)*

KATE *(slowly).* Folded her napkin.

(She contemplates the wild head in her thighs, and moves her fingertips over it, with such a tenderness, and something like a fear of its strangeness, that her own eyes close; she whispers, bending to it:)

My Helen—folded her napkin——

(And still erect, with only her head in surrender, KATE *for the first time that we see loses her protracted war with grief; but she will not let a sound escape her, only the grimace of tears comes, and sobs that shake her in a grip of silence. But* HELEN *feels them, and her head comes up in its own wondering, to interrogate her mother's face, until* KATE *buries her lips in the child's palm.)*

Scene 5

Upstairs, ANNIE *enters her room, closes the door, and stands back against it; the lights, growing on her with their special color, commence to fade on* KATE *and* HELEN. *Then* ANNIE *goes wearily to her suitcase, and lifts it to take it toward the bed. But it knocks an object to the floor, and she turns back to regard it. A new voice comes in a cultured murmur, hesitant as with the effort of remembering a text:*

MAN'S VOICE. This—soul——

*(*ANNIE *puts the suitcase down, and kneels to the object: it is the battered Perkins report, and she stands with it in her hand, letting memory try to speak:)*

This—blind, deaf, mute—woman——

*(*ANNIE *sits on her bed, opens the book, and finding the passage, brings it up an inch from*

her eyes to read, her face and lips following the overheard words, the voice quite factual now:)

Can nothing be done to disinter this human soul? The whole neighborhood would rush to save this woman if she were buried alive by the caving in of a pit, and labor with zeal until she were dug out. Now if there were one who had as much patience as zeal, he might awaken her to a consciousness of her immortal——

(When the boy's voice comes, ANNIE *closes her eyes, in pain.)*

BOY'S VOICE. Annie? Annie, you there?

ANNIE. Hush.

BOY'S VOICE. Annie, what's that noise?

*(*ANNIE *tries not to answer; her own voice is drawn out of her, unwilling.)*

ANNIE. Just a cot, Jimmie.

BOY'S VOICE. Where they pushin' it?

ANNIE. To the deadhouse.

BOY'S VOICE. Annie. Does it hurt, to be dead?

*(*ANNIE *escapes by opening her eyes, her hand works restlessly over her cheek; she retreats into the book again, but the cracked old crones interrupt, whispering.* ANNIE *slowly lowers the book.)*

FIRST CRONE'S VOICE. There is schools.

SECOND CRONE'S VOICE. There is schools outside——

THIRD CRONE'S VOICE. —schools where they teach blind ones, worse'n you——

FIRST CRONE'S VOICE. To read——

SECOND CRONE'S VOICE. To read and write——

THIRD CRONE'S VOICE. There is schools outside where they——

FIRST CRONE'S VOICE. There is schools——

(Silence. ANNIE *sits with her eyes shining, her hand almost in a caress over the book. Then:)*

BOY'S VOICE. You ain't goin' to school, are you, Annie?

ANNIE *(whispering).* When I grow up.

BOY'S VOICE. You ain't either, Annie. You're goin' to stay here take care of me.

ANNIE. I'm goin' to school when I grow up.

BOY'S VOICE. You said we'll be together, forever and ever and ever——

ANNIE *(fierce).* I'm goin' to school when I grow up!

DOCTOR'S VOICE *(slowly).* Little girl. Little girl, I must tell you. Your brother will be going on a journey, soon.

*(*ANNIE *sits rigid, in silence. Then the boy's voice pierces it, a shriek of terror.)*

BOY'S VOICE. *Annie!*

(It goes into ANNIE *like a sword, she doubles into it; the book falls to the floor. It takes her a racked moment to find herself and what she was engaged in here; when she sees the suitcase she remembers, and lifts it once again toward the bed. But the voices are with her, as she halts with suitcase in hand.)*

FIRST CRONE'S VOICE. Goodbye, Annie.

DOCTOR'S VOICE. Write me when you learn how.

SECOND CRONE'S VOICE. Don't tell anyone you came from here. Don't tell anyone——

THIRD CRONE'S VOICE. Yeah, don't tell anyone you came from——

FIRST CRONE'S VOICE. Yeah, don't tell anyone ——

SECOND CRONE'S VOICE. Don't tell any——

(The echoing voices fade. After a moment ANNIE *lays the suitcase on the bed; and the last voice comes faintly, from far away.)*

BOY'S VOICE. Annie. It hurts, to be dead. Forever.

*(*ANNIE *falls to her knees by the bed, stifling her mouth in it. When at last she rolls blindly away from it, her palm comes down on the open report; she opens her eyes, regards it dully, and then, still on her knees, takes in the print.)*

MAN'S VOICE *(factual).* —might awaken her to a consciousness of her immortal nature. The chance is small indeed; but with a smaller chance they would have dug desperately for her in the pit; and is the life of the soul of less import than that of the body?

*(*ANNIE *gets to her feet. She drops the book on the bed, and pauses over her suitcase; after a moment she unclasps and opens it. Standing before it, she comes to her decision; she at once turns to the bureau, and taking*

her things out of its drawers, commences to throw them into the open suitcase.)

Scene 6

In the darkness down left a hand strikes a match, and lights a hanging oil lamp. It is KELLER*'s hand, and his voice accompanies it, very angry; the lights rising here before they fade on* ANNIE *show* KELLER *and* KATE *inside a suggestion of a garden house, with a bay-window seat toward center and a door at back.*

KELLER. Katie, I will not *have* it! Now you did not see when that girl after supper tonight went to look for Helen in her room——

KATE. No.

KELLER. The child practically climbed out of her window to escape from her! What kind of teacher *is* she? I thought I had seen her at her worst this morning, shouting at me, but I come home to find the entire house disorganized by her—Helen won't stay one second in the same room, won't come to the table with her, won't let herself be bathed or undressed or put to bed by her, or even by Viney now, and the end result is that *you* have to do more for the child than before we hired this girl's services! From the moment she stepped off the train she's been nothing but a burden, incompetent, impertinent, ineffectual, immodest——

KATE. She folded her napkin, Captain.

KELLER. What?

KATE. Not ineffectual. Helen did fold her napkin.

KELLER. What in heaven's name is so extraordinary about folding a napkin?

KATE *(with some humor).* Well. It's more than you did, Captain.

KELLER. *Katie,* I did not bring you all the way out here to the garden house to be frivolous. Now, how does Miss Sullivan propose to teach a deaf-blind pupil who won't let her even touch her?

KATE *(a pause).* I don't know.

KELLER. The fact is, today she scuttled any chance she ever had of getting along with the child. If you can see any point or purpose to her staying on here longer, it's more than——

KATE. What do you wish me to do?

KELLER. I want you to give her notice.

KATE. I can't.

KELLER. Then if you won't, I must. I simply will not——

(He is interrupted by a knock at the back door. KELLER *after a glance at* KATE *moves to open the door;* ANNIE *in her smoked glasses is standing outside.* KELLER *contemplates her, heavily.)*

Miss Sullivan.

ANNIE. Captain Keller.

(She is nervous, keyed up to seizing the bull by the horns again, and she assumes a cheeriness which is not unshaky.)

Viney said I'd find you both over here in the garden house. I thought we should—have a talk?

KELLER *(reluctantly).* Yes, I— Well, come in.

*(*ANNIE *enters, and is interested in this room; she rounds on her heel, anxiously, studying it.* KELLER *turns the matter over to* KATE*, sotto voce.)*

Katie.

KATE *(turning it back, courteously).* Captain.

*(*KELLER *clears his throat, makes ready.)*

KELLER. I, ah—wanted first to make my position clear to Mrs. Keller, in private. I have decided I—am not satisfied—in fact, am deeply dissatisfied—with the manner in which——

ANNIE *(intent).* Excuse me, is this little house ever in use?

KELLER *(with patience).* In the hunting season. If you will give me your attention, Miss Sullivan.

*(*ANNIE *turns her smoked glasses upon him; they hold his unwilling stare.)*

I have tried to make allowances for you because you come from a part of the country where people are—women, I should say—come from who—well, for whom——

(It begins to elude him.)

—allowances must—be made. I have decided,

nevertheless, to—that is, decided I—

(Vexedly)

Miss Sullivan, I find it difficult to talk through those glasses.

ANNIE *(eagerly, removing them)*. Oh, of course.

KELLER *(dourly)*. Why do you wear them, the sun has been down for an hour.

ANNIE *(pleasantly, at the lamp)*. Any kind of light hurts my eyes.

(A silence; KELLER *ponders her, heavily.)*

KELLER. Put them on. Miss Sullivan, I have decided to—give you another chance.

ANNIE *(cheerfully)*. To do what?

KELLER. To—remain in our employ.

*(*ANNIE*'s eyes widen.)*

But on two conditions. I am not accustomed to rudeness in servants or women, and that is the first. If you are to stay, there must be a radical change of manner.

ANNIE *(a pause)*. Whose?

KELLER *(exploding)*. Yours, young lady, isn't it obvious? And the second is that you persuade me there's the slightest hope of your teaching a child who flies from you now like the plague, to anyone else she can find in this house.

ANNIE *(a pause)*. There isn't.

*(*KATE *stops sewing, and fixes her eyes upon* ANNIE.*)*

KATE. What, Miss Annie?

ANNIE. It's hopeless here. I can't teach a child who runs away.

KELLER *(nonplussed)*. Then—do I understand you—propose——

ANNIE. Well, if we all agree it's hopeless, the next question is what——

KATE. Miss Annie.

(She is leaning toward ANNIE, *in deadly earnest; it commands both* ANNIE *and* KELLER.*)*

I am not agreed. I think perhaps you—underestimate Helen.

ANNIE. I think everybody else here does.

KATE. She did fold her napkin. She learns, she learns, do you know she began talking when she was six months old? She could say "water." Not really—"wahwah." "Wahwah," but she meant water, she knew what it meant, and only six months old, I never saw a child so—bright, or outgoing——

(Her voice is unsteady, but she gets it level.)

It's still in her, somewhere, isn't it? You should have seen her before her illness, such a good-tempered child—

ANNIE *(agreeably)*. She's changed.

(A pause, KATE *not letting her eyes go; her appeal at last is unconditional, and very quiet.)*

KATE. Miss Annie, put up with it. And with us.

KELLER. Us!

KATE. Please? Like the lost lamb in the parable, I love her all the more.

ANNIE. Mrs. Keller, I don't think Helen's worst handicap is deafness or blindness. I think it's your love. And pity.

KELLER. Now what does that mean?

ANNIE. All of you here are so sorry for her you've kept her—like a pet, why, even a dog you housebreak. No wonder she won't let me come near her. It's useless for me to try to teach her language or anything else here. I might as well——

KATE *(cuts in)*. Miss Annie, before you came we spoke of putting her in an asylum.

*(*ANNIE *turns back to regard her. A pause)*

ANNIE. What kind of asylum?

KELLER. For mental defectives.

KATE. I visited there. I can't tell you what I saw, people like—animals, with *—rats,* in the halls, and——

(She shakes her head on her vision.)

What else are we to do, if you give up?

ANNIE. Give up?

KATE. You said it was hopeless.

ANNIE. Here. Give up, why, I only today saw what has to be done, to begin!

(She glances from KATE *to* KELLER, *who stare, waiting; and she makes it as plain and simple as her nervousness permits.)*

I—want complete charge of her.

KELLER. You already have that. It has resulted in——

ANNIE. No, I mean day and night. She has to be dependent on me.

KATE. For what?

ANNIE. Everything. The food she eats, the clothes she wears, fresh——

(She is amused at herself, though very serious.)

—air, yes, the air she breathes, whatever her body needs is a—primer, to teach her out of. It's the only way, the one who lets her have it should be her teacher.

(She considers them in turn; they digest it, KELLER *frowning,* KATE *perplexed.)*

Not anyone who *loves* her, you have so many feelings they fall over each other like feet, you won't use your chances and you won't let me.

KATE. But if she runs from you—*to* us——

ANNIE. Yes, that's the point. I'll have to live with her somewhere else.

KELLER. What!

ANNIE. Till she learns to depend on and listen to me.

KATE *(not without alarm).* For how long?

ANNIE. As long as it takes.

(A pause. She takes a breath.)

I packed half my things already.

KELLER. Miss Sullivan!

(But when ANNIE *attends upon him he is speechless, and she is merely earnest.)*

ANNIE. Captain Keller, it meets both your conditions. It's the one way I can get back in touch with Helen, and I don't see how I can be rude to you again if you're not around to interfere with me.

KELLER *(red-faced).* And what is your intention if I say no? Pack the other half, for home, and abandon your charge to—to——

ANNIE. The asylum?

(She waits, appraises KELLER*'s glare and* KATE*'s uncertainty, and decides to use her weapons.)*

I grew up in such an asylum. The state almshouse.

*(*KATE*'s head comes up on this, and* KELLER *stares hard;* ANNIE*'s tone is cheerful enough, albeit level as gunfire.)*

Rats—why, my brother Jimmie and I used to play with the rats because we didn't have toys. Maybe you'd like to know what Helen will find there, not on visiting days? One ward was full of the—old women, crippled, blind, most of them dying, but even if what they had was catching there was nowhere else to move them, and that's where they put us. There were younger ones across the hall with T.B. and epileptic fits and some insane. Some just had the D.T.'s. The room Jimmie and I played in was the deadhouse, where they kept the bodies till they could dig——

KATE *(closes her eyes).* Oh, my dear——

ANNIE. —the graves.

(She is immune to KATE*'s compassion.)*

No, it made me strong. But I don't think you need send Helen there. She's strong enough.

(She waits again; but when neither offers her a word, she simply concludes.)

No, I have no conditions, Captain Keller.

KATE *(not looking up).* Miss Annie.

ANNIE. Yes.

KATE *(a pause).* Where would you—take Helen?

ANNIE. Ohh——

(Brightly)

Italy?

KELLER *(wheeling).* What?

ANNIE. Can't have everything, how would this garden house do? Furnish it, bring Helen here after a long ride so she won't recognize it, and you can see her every day. If she doesn't know. Well?

KATE *(a sigh of relief).* Is that all?

ANNIE. That's all.

KATE. Captain.

*(*KELLER *turns his head; and* KATE*'s request is quiet but firm.)*

With your permission?

KELLER *(teeth in cigar).* Why must she depend on you for the food she eats?

ANNIE *(a pause).* I want control of it.

KELLER. Why?

ANNIE. It's a way to reach her.

KELLER *(stares).* You intend to *starve* her into letting you touch her?

ANNIE. She won't starve, she'll learn. All's fair in love and war, Captain Keller, you never cut supplies?

KELLER. This is hardly a war!

ANNIE. Well, it's not love. A siege is a siege.

KELLER *(heavily).* Miss Sullivan. Do you *like* the child?

ANNIE *(straight in his eyes).* Do you?

(A long pause)

KATE. You could have a servant here——

ANNIE *(amused).* I'll have enough work without looking after a servant! But that boy Percy could sleep here, run errands——

KATE *(also amused).* We can let Percy sleep here, I think, Captain?

ANNIE *(eagerly).* And some old furniture, all our own——

KATE *(also eager).* Captain? Do you think that walnut bedstead in the barn would be too——

KELLER. I have not yet consented to Percy! Or to the house, or to the proposal! Or to Miss Sullivan's—staying on when I——

(But he erupts in an irate surrender.)

Very well, I consent to everything!

(He shakes the cigar at ANNIE.*)*

For two weeks. I'll give you two weeks in this place, and it will be a miracle if you get the child to tolerate you.

KATE. Two weeks? Miss Annie, can you accomplish anything in two weeks?

KELLER. Anything or not, two weeks, then the child comes back to us. Make up your mind, Miss Sullivan, yes or no?

ANNIE. Two weeks. For only one miracle?

(She nods at him, nervously.)

I'll get her to tolerate me.

*(*KELLER *marches out, and slams the door.* KATE *on her feet regards* ANNIE, *who is facing the door.)*

KATE *(then).* You can't think as little of love as you said.

*(*ANNIE *glances questioning.)*

Or you wouldn't stay.

ANNIE *(a pause).* I didn't come here for love. I came for money!

*(*KATE *shakes her head to this, with a smile; after a moment she extends her open hand.* ANNIE *looks at it, but when she puts hers out it is not to shake hands, it is to set her fist in* KATE'*s palm.)*

KATE *(puzzled).* Hm?

ANNIE. A. It's the first of many. Twenty-six!

*(*KATE *squeezes her fist, squeezes it hard, and hastens out after* KELLER. ANNIE *stands as the door closes behind her, her manner so apprehensive that finally she slaps her brow, holds it, sighs, and, with her eyes closed, crosses herself for luck.)*

Scene 7

The lights dim into a cool silhouette scene around her, the lamp paling out, and now, in formal entrances, persons appear around ANNIE *with furniture for the room:* PERCY *crosses the stage with a rocking chair and waits;* MARTHA *from another direction bears in a stool,* VINEY *bears in a small table, and the other Negro servant rolls in a bed partway from left; and* ANNIE, *opening her eyes to put her glasses back on, sees them. She turns around in the room once, and goes into action, pointing out locations for each article; the servants place them and leave, and* ANNIE *then darts around, interchanging them. In the midst of this—while* PERCY *and* MARTHA *reappear with a tray of food and a chair, respectively—*JAMES *comes down from the house with* ANNIE'*s suitcase, and stands viewing the room and her quizzically;* ANNIE *halts abruptly under his eyes, embarrassed, then seizes the suitcase from his hand, explaining herself brightly.*

ANNIE. I always wanted to live in a doll's house!

(She sets the suitcase out of the way, and continues; VINEY *at left appears to position a rod with drapes for a doorway, and the other servant at center pushes in a wheelbarrow loaded with a couple of boxes of* HELEN'*s toys and clothes.* ANNIE *helps lift them into the room, and the servant pushes the wheelbarrow off. In none of this is any heed taken of the imaginary walls of the garden house, the*

furniture is moved in from every side and itself defines the walls.

ANNIE *now drags the box of toys into center, props up the doll conspicuously on top; with the people melted away, except for* JAMES, *all is again still. The lights turn again without pause, rising warmer.)*

JAMES. You don't let go of things easily, do you? How will you—win her hand now, in this place?

ANNIE *(curtly).* Do I know? I lost my temper, and here we are!

JAMES *(lightly).* No touching, no teaching. Of course you *are* bigger——

ANNIE. I'm not counting on force, I'm counting on her. That little imp is dying to know.

JAMES. Know what?

ANNIE. Anything. Any and every crumb in God's creation. I'll have to use that appetite too.

(She gives the room a final survey, straightens the bed, arranges the curtains.)

JAMES *(a pause).* Maybe she'll teach you.

ANNIE. Of course.

JAMES. That she isn't. That there's such a thing as—dullness of heart. Acceptance. And letting go. Sooner or later we all give up, don't we?

ANNIE. Maybe you all do. It's my idea of the original sin.

JAMES. What is?

ANNIE *(witheringly).* Giving up.

JAMES *(nettled).* You won't open her. Why can't you let her be? Have some—pity on her, for being what she is——

ANNIE. If I'd ever once thought like that, I'd be dead!

JAMES *(pleasantly).* You will be. Why trouble?

(ANNIE *turns to glare at him; he is mocking.)*

Or will you teach me?

(And with a bow, he drifts off.

Now in the distance there comes the clopping of hoofs, drawing near, and nearer, up to the door; and they halt. ANNIE *wheels to face the door. When it opens this time, the* KELLERS—KATE *in traveling bonnet,* KELLER *also hatted—are standing there with* HELEN *between them; she is in a cloak.* KATE *gently cues her into the room.* HELEN *comes in groping, baffled, but interested in the new surroundings;* ANNIE *evades her exploring hand, her gaze not leaving the child.)*

ANNIE. Does she know where she is?

KATE *(shakes her head).* We rode her out in the country for two hours.

KELLER. For all she knows, she could be in another town——

(HELEN *stumbles over the box on the floor and in it discovers her doll and other battered toys, is pleased, sits to them, then becomes puzzled and suddenly very wary. She scrambles up and back to her mother's thighs, but* ANNIE *steps in, and it is hers that* HELEN *embraces.* HELEN *recoils, gropes, and touches her cheek instantly.)*

KATE. That's her sign for me.

ANNIE. I know.

(HELEN *waits, then recommences her groping, more urgently.* KATE *stands indecisive, and takes an abrupt step toward her, but* ANNIE*'s hand is a barrier.)*

In two weeks.

KATE. Miss Annie, I—Please be good to her. These two weeks, try to be very good to her——

ANNIE. I will.

(KATE, *turning then, hurries out. The* KELLERS *cross back of the main house.*

ANNIE *closes the door.* HELEN *starts at the door jar, and rushes it.* ANNIE *holds her off.* HELEN *kicks her, breaks free, and careens around the room like an imprisoned bird, colliding with furniture, groping wildly, repeatedly touching her cheek in a growing panic. When she has covered the room, she commences her weird screaming.* ANNIE *moves to comfort her, but her touch sends* HELEN *into a paroxysm of rage; she tears away, falls over her box of toys, flings its contents in handfuls in* ANNIE*'s direction, flings the box too, reels to her feet, rips curtains from the window, bangs and kicks at the door, sweeps objects off the mantelpiece and shelf, a little tornado* *incarnate, all destruction, until she comes upon her doll and in the act of hurling it, freezes. Then she clutches it to herself, and in exhaustion sinks sobbing to the floor.* ANNIE *stands contemplating her, in some awe.)*

Two weeks.

(She shakes her head, not without a touch of disgusted bewilderment.)

What did I get into now?

(The lights have been dimming throughout, and the garden house is lit only by moonlight now, with ANNIE *lost in the patches of dark.)*

Scene 8

KATE, *now hatless and coatless, enters the family room by the rear door, carrying a lamp.* KELLER, *also hatless, wanders simultaneously around the back of the main house to where* JAMES *has been waiting, in the rising moonlight, on the porch.*

KELLER. I can't understand it. I had every intention of dismissing that girl, not setting her up like an empress.

JAMES. Yes, what's her secret, sir?

KELLER. Secret?

JAMES *(pleasantly).* That enables her to get anything she wants out of you? When I can't.

*(*JAMES *turns to go into the house, but* KELLER *grasps his wrist, twisting him half to his knees.* KATE *comes from the porch.)*

KELLER *(angrily).* She does *not* get anything she——

JAMES *(in pain).* Don't—don't——

KATE. Captain.

KELLER. He's afraid.

(He throws JAMES *away from him, with contempt.)*

What *does* he want out of me?

JAMES *(an outcry).* My God, don't you know?

(He gazes from KELLER *to* KATE.*)*

Everything you forgot, when you forgot my mother.

KELLER. What!

*(*JAMES *wheels into the house.* KELLER *takes a stride to the porch, to roar after him.)*

One thing that girl's secret is not, she doesn't fire one shot and disappear!

*(*KATE *stands rigid, and* KELLER *comes back to her.)*

Katie. Don't mind what he——

KATE. Captain, *I* am proud of you.

KELLER. For what?

KATE. For letting this girl have what she needs.

KELLER. Why can't my son be? He can't bear me, you'd think I treat him as hard as this girl does Helen——

(He breaks off, as it dawns in him.)

KATE *(gently).* Perhaps you do.

KELLER. But he has to learn some respect!

KATE *(a pause, wryly).* Do you like the child?

(She turns again to the porch, but pauses, reluctant.)

How empty the house is, tonight.

(After a moment she continues on in. KELLER *stands moveless, as the moonlight dies on him.)*

Scene 9

The distant belfry chimes toll, two o'clock, and with them, a moment later, comes the boy's voice on the wind, in a whisper:

BOY'S VOICE. Annie. Annie.

(In her patch of dark ANNIE, *now in her nightgown, hurls a cup into a corner as though it were her grief, getting rid of its taste through her teeth.)*

ANNIE. No! No pity, I won't have it.

(She comes to HELEN, *prone on the floor.)*

On either of us.

(She goes to her knees, but when she touches HELEN's *hand the child starts up awake, recoils, and scrambles away from her under the bed.* ANNIE *stares after her. She strikes her palm on the floor, with passion.)*

I *will* touch you!

(She gets to her feet, and paces in a kind of anger around the bed, her hand in her hair, and confronting HELEN *at each turn.)*

How, how? How do I——

(ANNIE stops. Then she calls out urgently, loudly.)

Percy! Percy!

(She moves swiftly to the drapes, at left.)

Percy, wake up!

(PERCY's voice comes in a thick sleepy mumble, unintelligible.)

Get out of bed and come in here, I need you.

(ANNIE darts away, finds and strikes a match, and touches it to the hanging lamp; the lights come up dimly in the room, and PERCY stands bare to the waist in torn overalls between the drapes, with eyes closed, swaying. ANNIE goes to him, pats his cheeks vigorously.)

Percy. You awake?

PERCY. No'm.

ANNIE. How would you like to play a nice game?

PERCY. Whah?

ANNIE. With Helen. She's under the bed. Touch her hand.

(She kneels PERCY down at the bed, thrusting his hand under it to contact HELEN's; HELEN emits an animal sound and crawls to the opposite side, but commences sniffing. ANNIE rounds the bed with PERCY and thrusts his hand again at HELEN; this time HELEN clutches it, sniffs in recognition, and comes scrambling out after PERCY, to hug him with delight. PERCY alarmed struggles, and HELEN's fingers go to his mouth.)

PERCY. Lemme go. Lemme go——

(HELEN fingers her own lips, as before, moving them in dumb imitation.)

She tryin' talk. She gonna hit me——

ANNIE *(grimly).* She *can* talk. If she only knew, I'll show you how. She makes letters.

(She opens PERCY's other hand, and spells into it:)

This one is C. C.

(She hits his palm with it a couple of times, her eyes upon HELEN across him; HELEN gropes to feel what PERCY's hand is doing, and when she encounters ANNIE's she falls back from them.)

She's mad at me now, though, she won't play. But she knows lots of letters. Here's another, A. C, a. C, a.

(But she is watching HELEN, who comes groping, consumed with curiosity; ANNIE makes the letters in PERCY's hand, and HELEN pokes to question what they are up to. Then HELEN snatches PERCY's other hand, and quickly spells four letters into it. ANNIE follows them aloud.)

C, a, k, e! She spells cake, she gets cake.

(She is swiftly over to the tray of food, to fetch cake and a jug of milk.)

She doesn't know yet it means this. Isn't it funny she knows how to spell it and doesn't *know* she knows?

(She breaks the cake in two pieces, and extends one to each; HELEN rolls away from her offer.)

Well, if she won't play it with me, I'll play it with you. Would you like to learn one she doesn't know?

PERCY. No'm.

(But ANNIE seizes his wrist, and spells to him.)

ANNIE. M, i, l, k. M is this. I, that's an easy one, just the little finger. L is this——

(And HELEN comes back with her hand, to feel the new word. ANNIE brushes her away, and continues spelling aloud to PERCY. HELEN's hand comes back again, and tries to get in; ANNIE brushes it away again. HELEN's hand insists, and ANNIE puts it away rudely.)

No, why should I talk to you? I'm teaching Percy a new word. L.K is this——

(HELEN now yanks their hands apart; she butts PERCY away, and thrusts her palm out insistently. ANNIE's eyes are bright, with glee.)

Ho, you're *jealous*, are you!

(HELEN's hand waits, intractably waits.)

All right.

(ANNIE spells into it, "milk"; and HELEN after a moment spells it back to ANNIE. ANNIE

takes her hand, with her whole face shining. She gives a great sigh.)

Good! So I'm finally back to where I can touch you, hm? Touch and go! No love lost, but here we go.

(She puts the jug of milk into HELEN*'s hand and squeezes* PERCY*'s shoulder.)*

You can go to bed now, you've earned your sleep. Thank you.

*(*PERCY *stumbling up weaves his way out through the drapes.* HELEN *finishes drinking, and holds the jug out, for* ANNIE; *when* ANNIE *takes it,* HELEN *crawls onto the bed, and makes for sleep.* ANNIE *stands, looks down at her.)*

Now all I have to teach you is—one word. Everything.

(She sets the jug down. On the floor now ANNIE *spies the doll, stoops to pick it up, and with it dangling in her hand, turns off the lamp. A shaft of moonlight is left on* HELEN *in the bed, and a second shaft on the rocking chair; and* ANNIE, *after putting off her smoked glasses, sits in the rocker with the doll. She is rather happy, and dangles the doll on her knee, and it makes its momma sound.* ANNIE *whispers to it in mock solicitude.)*

Hush, little baby. Don't—say a word——

(She lays it against her shoulder, and begins rocking with it, patting its diminutive behind; she talks the lullaby to it, humorously at first.)

Momma's gonna buy you—a mockingbird:
If that—mockingbird don't sing——

(The rhythm of the rocking takes her into the tune, softly, and more tenderly.)

Momma's gonna buy you a diamond ring:
If that diamond ring turns to brass——

(A third shaft of moonlight outside now rises to pick out JAMES *at the main house, with one foot on the porch step; he turns his body, as if hearing the song.)*

Momma's gonna buy you a looking glass:
If that looking glass gets broke——

(In the family room a fourth shaft picks out KELLER *seated at the table, in thought; and he, too, lifts his head, as if hearing.)*

Momma's gonna buy you a billy goat:
If that billy goat won't pull——

(The fifth shaft is upstairs in ANNIE*'s room, and picks out* KATE, *pacing there; and she halts, turning her head, too, as if hearing.)*

Momma's gonna buy you a cart and bull:
If that cart and bull turns over,
Momma's gonna buy you a dog named Rover:
If that dog named Rover won't bark——

(With the shafts of moonlight on HELEN, *and* JAMES *and* KELLER *and* KATE, *all moveless, and* ANNIE *rocking the doll, the curtain ends the act.)*

Discussion

1. The first scene of Act Two begins and ends with the contents of Annie's letter. **(a)** How does Annie propose to handle Helen? **(b)** What does Kate do and say in this scene to demonstrate a different philosophy of handling Helen?

2. Scene two takes place at the breakfast table. How is the breach between James and Captain Keller further developed in this scene?

3. During scene two, Annie's attitude toward Helen again conflicts sharply with the attitude of the Kellers. **(a)** What prompts Annie to say, "It's less trouble to feel sorry for her than to teach her anything better. . . ."? **(b)** Do you think she is justified in making this statement? Explain.

4. Discuss the Captain's attitude toward Annie.

5. **(a)** What does the battle between Annie and Helen in scene three reveal about the character of each? **(b)** What does this scene contribute to the play?

6. Why is Kate so moved emotionally when she learns that Helen folded her napkin?

7. In scene five Gibson again dramatizes incidents from Annie's past. What occurred in Annie's past that made her unusually capable of handling Helen and yet, at the same time, made her want to leave the Keller household?

8. **(a)** Why do Keller and Kate have a private talk in the garden house in scene six? **(b)** How does Kate react to her husband's statements?

9. **(a)** What conditions does Captain Keller demand that Annie fulfill if she is to continue her work? **(b)** How does Annie respond to his second condition? **(c)** Why does Kate plead with Annie to stay?

10. **(a)** What does Annie consider Helen's greatest handicap to be? **(b)** By what strategy does she hope to "reach" Helen? **(c)** What strategies does she employ to win the Kellers to her point of view?

11. What is the significance of the conversation between Annie and James in scene seven?

12. In scene eight, which takes place on the moonlit porch, how is the estrangement between James and his father explained?

13. **(a)** In scene nine, what use does Annie make of Percy? **(b)** What does Annie mean when she says, "Now all I have to teach you is—one word. Everything"?

Vocabulary

Pronunciation, Dictionary

Use your Glossary to find the proper meanings and pronunciations of the following words. Then consider each statement and indicate on your paper "T" if it is true, "F" if false.

mull	flank	dour
berth	feint	feign
wry	siege	thwart
ire	shaft	whim

1. *Dour* can be pronounced either to rhyme with *sure* or with *hour.*

2. You would "give a wide *berth*" to a good friend.

3. *Feign* and *feint* are both nouns.

4. *Ire* and *wry* contain the same vowel sound.

5. If you *thwart* people, you may incur their *ire.*

6. *Flank* is the only word listed that can refer to a bodily part.

7. If you must make a quick decision, you should *mull* it over.

8. *Wry* is an adjective which means "twisted."

9. *Whims* are long-lasting.

10. *Siege* and *feint* have the same vowel sound.

Composition

Select one of the following statements from the first two acts: **(a)** "Language is to the mind more than light is to the eye." **(b)** "The greatest problem I have is how to discipline her without breaking her spirit." **(c)** "It's less trouble to feel sorry for her than to teach her anything better, isn't it?" Write an interpretation of the statement you select by **(1)** analyzing the meaning and purpose of the statement within the play, **(2)** showing how the statement could apply to situations outside the play, and **(3)** explaining why you agree or disagree with the statement. (See *Defending Your Position,* page 672, in Composition Guide.)

Act Three

Scene 1

The stage is totally dark, until we see ANNIE *and* HELEN *silhouetted on the bed in the garden house.* ANNIE*'s voice is audible, very patient, and worn; it has been saying this for a long time.*

ANNIE. Water, Helen. This is water. W, a, t, e, r. It has a *name.*

(A silence. Then:)

Egg, e, g, g. It has a *name,* the name stands for the thing. Oh, it's so simple, simple as birth, to explain.

(The lights have commenced to rise, not on the garden house but on the homestead. Then:)

Helen, Helen, the chick *has* to come out of its shell, sometime. You come out, too.

(In the bedroom, upstairs, we see VINEY *unhurriedly washing the window, dusting, turning the mattress, readying the room for use again; then in the family room a diminished group at one end of the table—*KATE, KELLER, JAMES*—finishing up a quiet breakfast; then outside, down right, the other Negro servant on his knees, assisted by* MARTHA, *working with a trowel around a new trellis and wheelbarrow. The scene is one of everyday calm, and all are oblivious to* ANNIE*'s voice.)*

There's only one way out, for you, and it's language. To learn that your fingers can talk. And say anything, anything you can name. This is mug. Mug, m, u, g. Helen, it has a *name.* It—has—a—name——

*(*KATE *rises from the table.)*

KELLER *(gently).* You haven't eaten, Katie.

KATE *(smiles, shakes her head).* I haven't the appetite. I'm too—restless, I can't sit to it.

KELLER. You should eat, my dear. It will be a long day, waiting.

JAMES *(lightly).* But it's been a short two weeks. I never thought life could be so—noiseless, went much too quickly for me.

*(*KATE *and* KELLER *gaze at him, in silence.* JAMES *becomes uncomfortable.)*

ANNIE. C, a, r, d. Card. C, a——

JAMES. Well, the house has been practically normal, hasn't it?

KELLER *(harshly).* Jimmie.

JAMES. Is it wrong to enjoy a quiet breakfast, after five years? And you two even seem to enjoy each other——

KELLER. It could be even more noiseless, Jimmie, without your tongue running every minute. Haven't you enough feeling to imagine what Katie has been undergoing, ever since—

*(*KATE *stops him, with her hand on his arm.)*

KATE. Captain.

(To JAMES*)*

It's true. The two weeks have been normal, quiet, all you say. But not short. Interminable.

(She rises, and wanders out; she pauses on the porch steps, gazing toward the garden house.)

ANNIE *(fading)*. W, a, t, e, r. But it means *this*. W, a, t, e, r. *This*. W, a, t——

JAMES. I only meant that Miss Sullivan is a boon. Of contention, though, it seems.

KELLER *(heavily)*. If and when you're a parent, Jimmie, you will understand what separation means. A mother loses a—protector.

JAMES *(baffled)*. Hm?

KELLER. You'll learn, we don't just keep our children safe. They keep us safe.

(He rises, with his empty coffee cup and saucer.)

There are of course all kinds of separation, Katie has lived with one kind for five years. And another is disappointment. In a child.

(He goes with the cup out the rear door. JAMES *sits for a long moment of stillness. In the garden house the lights commence to come up;* ANNIE, *haggard at the table, is writing a letter, her face again almost in contact with the stationery;* HELEN, *apart on the stool, and for the first time as clean and neat as a button, is quietly crocheting an endless chain of wool, which snakes all around the room.)*

ANNIE. "I, feel, every, day, more, and, more, in——"

(She pauses, and turns the pages of a dictionary open before her; her finger descends the words to a full stop. She elevates her eyebrows, then copies the word.)

"—adequate."

(In the main house JAMES *pushes up, and goes to the front doorway, after* KATE.)

JAMES. Kate?

*(*KATE *turns her glance.* JAMES *is rather weary.)*

I'm sorry. Open my mouth, like that fairy tale, frogs jump out.

KATE. No. It has been better. For everyone.

(She starts away, up center.)

ANNIE *(writing)*. "If, only, there, were, someone, to, help, me, I, need, a, teacher, as, much, as, Helen——"

JAMES. Kate.

*(*KATE *halts, waits.)*

What does he want from me?

KATE. That's not the question. Stand up to the world, Jimmie, that comes first.

JAMES *(a pause, wryly)*. But the world is him.

KATE. Yes. And no one can do it for you.

JAMES. Kate.

(His voice is humble.)

At least we—Could you—be my friend?

KATE. I am.

*(*KATE *turns to wander, up back of the garden house.* ANNIE'*s murmur comes at once; the lights begin to die on the main house.)*

ANNIE. "—my, mind, is, undisiplined, full, of, skips, and, jumps, and——"

(She halts, rereads, frowns.)

Hm.

*(*ANNIE *puts her nose again in the dictionary, flips back to an earlier page, and fingers down the words;* KATE *presently comes down toward the bay window with a trayful of food.)*

Disinter—disinterested—disjoin—dis——

(She backtracks, indignant.)

Disinterested, disjoin—Where's disipline?

(She goes a page or two back, searching with her finger, muttering.)

What a dictionary, have to know how to spell it before you can look up how to spell it, disciple, *discipline!* Diskipline.

(She corrects the word in her letter.)

Undisciplined.

(But her eyes are bothering her, she closes them in exhaustion and gently fingers the eyelids. KATE *watches her through the window.)*

KATE. What are you doing to your eyes?

*(*ANNIE *glances around; she puts her smoked glasses on, and gets up to come over, assuming a cheerful energy.)*

ANNIE. It's worse on my vanity! I'm learning to spell. It's like a surprise party, the most unexpected characters turn up.

KATE. You're not to overwork your eyes, Miss Annie.

ANNIE. Well.

(She takes the tray, sets it on her chair, and carries chair and tray to HELEN.)

Whatever I spell to Helen I'd better spell right.

KATE *(almost wistful)*. How—serene she is.

ANNIE. She learned this stitch yesterday. Now I can't get her to stop!

(She disentangles one foot from the wool chain, and sets the chair before HELEN. HELEN *at its contact with her knee feels the plate, promptly sets her crocheting down, and tucks the napkin in at her neck, but* ANNIE *withholds the spoon; when* HELEN *finds it missing, she folds her hands in her lap, and quietly waits.* ANNIE *twinkles at* KATE *with mock devoutness.)*

Such a little lady, she'd sooner starve than eat with her fingers.

(She gives HELEN *the spoon, and* HELEN *begins to eat, neatly.)*

KATE. You've taught her so much, these two weeks. I would never have——

ANNIE. Not enough.

(She is suddenly gloomy, shakes her head.) Obedience isn't enough. Well, she learned two nouns this morning, key and water, brings her up to eighteen nouns and three verbs.

KATE *(hesitant)*. But—not——

ANNIE. No. Not that they mean things. It's still a finger-game, no meaning.

(She turns to KATE, *abruptly.)*

Mrs. Keller——

(But she defers it; she comes back, to sit in the bay and lift her hand.)

Shall we play our finger-game?

KATE. How will she learn it?

ANNIE. It will come.

(She spells a word; KATE *does not respond.)*

KATE. How?

ANNIE *(a pause)*. How does a bird learn to fly?

(She spells again.)

We're born to use words, like wings, it has to come.

KATE. How?

ANNIE *(another pause, wearily)*. All right. I don't know how.

(She pushes up her glasses, to rub her eyes.)

I've done everything I could think of. Whatever she's learned here—keeping herself clean, knitting, stringing beads, meals, setting-up exercises each morning, we climb trees, hunt eggs, yesterday a chick was born in her hands—all of it I spell, everything we do, we never stop spelling. I go to bed with—writer's cramp from talking so much!

KATE. I worry about you, Miss Annie. You must rest.

ANNIE. Now? She spells back in her *sleep,* her fingers make letters when she doesn't know! In her bones those five fingers know, that hand aches to—speak out, and something in her mind is asleep, how do I—nudge that awake? That's the one question.

KATE. With no answer.

ANNIE *(long pause)*. Except keep at it. Like this.

(She again begins spelling—"I, need"—and KATE*'s brows gather, following the words.)*

KATE. More—time?

(She glances at ANNIE, *who looks her in the eyes, silent.)*

Here?

ANNIE. Spell it.

*(*KATE *spells a word—"no"—shaking her head;* ANNIE *spells two words—"why, not" back—with an impatient question in her eyes; and* KATE *moves her head in pain to answer it.)*

KATE. Because I can't——

ANNIE. Spell it! If she ever learns, you'll have a lot to tell each other, start now.

*(*KATE *painstakingly spells in air. In the midst of this the rear door opens, and* KELLER *enters with the setter* BELLE *in tow.)*

KELLER. Miss Sullivan? On my way to the office, I brought Helen a playmate——

ANNIE. Outside please, Captain Keller.

KELLER. My dear child, the two weeks are up today, surely you don't object to——

ANNIE *(rising)*. They're not up till six o'clock.

KELLER *(indulgent)*. Oh, now. What difference can a fraction of one day——

ANNIE. An agreement is an agreement. Now you've been very good, I'm sure you can keep it up for a few more hours.

(She escorts KELLER *by the arm over the threshold; he obeys, leaving* BELLE.*)*

KELLER. Miss Sullivan, you are a tyrant.

ANNIE. Likewise, I'm sure. You can stand there, and close the door if she comes.

KATE. I don't think you know how eager we are to have her back in our arms——

ANNIE. I do know, it's my main worry.

KELLER. It's like expecting a new child in the house. Well, she *is* so—composed, so—— *(Gently)* Attractive. You've done wonders for her, Miss Sullivan.

ANNIE *(not a question).* Have I.

KELLER. If there's anything you want from us in repayment tell us, it will be a privilege to——

ANNIE. I just told Mrs. Keller. I want more time.

KATE. Miss Annie——

ANNIE. Another week.

(HELEN *lifts her head, and begins to sniff.)*

KELLER. We miss the child. *I* miss her, I'm glad to say, that's a different debt I owe you——

ANNIE. Pay it to Helen. Give *her* another week.

KATE *(gently).* Doesn't she miss us?

KELLER. Of course she does. What a wrench this unexplainable—exile must be to her, can you say it's not?

ANNIE. No. But I——

(HELEN *is off the stool, to grope about the room; when she encounters* BELLE, *she throws her arms around the dog's neck in delight.)*

KATE. Doesn't she need affection too, Miss Annie?

ANNIE *(wavering).* She—never shows me she needs it, she won't have any—caressing or——

KATE. But you're not her mother.

KELLER. And what would another week accomplish? We are more than satisfied, you've done more than we ever thought possible, taught her constructive——

ANNIE. I can't promise anything. All I can——

KELLER *(no break).* —things to do, to behave like—even look like—a human child, so manageable, contented, cleaner, more——

ANNIE *(withering).* Cleaner.

KELLER. Well. We say cleanliness is next to godliness, Miss——

ANNIE. Cleanliness is next to nothing, she has to learn that everything has its name! That words can be her *eyes,* to everything in the world outside her, and inside too, what is she without words? With them she can think, have ideas, be reached, there's not a thought or fact in the world that can't be hers. You publish a newspaper, Captain Keller, do I have to tell you what words are? And she has them already——

KELLER. Miss Sullivan.

ANNIE. —eighteen nouns and three verbs, they're in her fingers now, I need only time to push *one* of them into her mind! One, and everything under the sun will follow. Don't you see what she's learned here is only clearing the way for that? I can't risk her unlearning it, give me more time alone with her, another week to——

KELLER. Look.

(He points, and ANNIE *turns.* HELEN *is playing with* BELLE*'s claws; she makes letters with her fingers, shows them to* BELLE, *waits with her palm, then manipulates the dog's claws.)*

What is she spelling?

(A silence)

KATE. Water?

*(*ANNIE *nods.)*

KELLER. Teaching a dog to spell.

(A pause)

The dog doesn't know what she means, any more than she knows what you mean, Miss Sullivan. I think you ask too much, of her and yourself. God may not have meant Helen to have the—eyes you speak of.

ANNIE *(toneless).* I mean her to.

KELLER *(curiously).* What is it to you?

*(*ANNIE*'s head comes slowly up.)*

You make us see how we indulge her for our sake. Is the opposite true, for you?

ANNIE *(then).* Half a week?

KELLER. An agreement *is* an agreement.

ANNIE. Mrs. Keller?

KATE *(simply)*. I want her back.

(A wait; ANNIE *then lets her hands drop in surrender, and nods.)*

KELLER. I'll send Viney over to help you pack.

ANNIE. Not until six o'clock. I have her till six o'clock.

KELLER *(consenting)*. Six o'clock. Come, Katie.

*(*KATE *leaving the window joins him around back, while* KELLER *closes the door; they are shut out.*

Only the garden house is daylit now, and the light on it is narrowing down. ANNIE *stands watching* HELEN *work* BELLE*'s claws. Then she settles beside them on her knees, and stops* HELEN*'s hand.)*

ANNIE *(gently)*. No.

(She shakes her head, with HELEN*'s hand to her face, then spells.)*

Dog. D, o, g. Dog.

(She touches HELEN*'s hand to* BELLE. HELEN *dutifully pats the dog's head, and resumes spelling to its paw.)*

Not water.

*(*ANNIE *rolls to her feet, brings a tumbler of water back from the tray, and kneels with it, to seize* HELEN*'s hand and spell.)*

Here. Water. *Water.*

(She thrusts HELEN*'s hand into the tumbler.* HELEN *lifts her hand out dripping, wipes it daintily on* BELLE*'s hide, and taking the tumbler from* ANNIE, *endeavors to thrust* BELLE*'s paw into it.* ANNIE *sits watching, wearily.)*

I don't know how to tell you. Not a soul in the world knows how to tell you. Helen, Helen.

(She bends in compassion to touch her lips to HELEN*'s temple, and instantly* HELEN *pauses, her hands off the dog, her head slightly averted. The lights are still narrowing, and* BELLE *slinks off. After a moment* ANNIE *sits back.)*

Yes, what's it to me? They're satisfied. Give them back their child and dog, both housebroken, everyone's satisfied. But me, and you.

*(*HELEN*'s hand comes out into the light, groping.)*

Reach. *Reach!*

*(*ANNIE *extending her own hand grips* HELEN*'s; the two hands are clasped, tense in the light, the rest of the room changing in shadows.)*

I wanted to teach you—oh, everything the earth is full of, Helen, everything on it that's ours for a wink and it's gone, and what we are on it, the—light we bring to it and leave behind in—words, why, you can see five thousand years back in a light of words, everything we feel, think, know—and share, in words, so not a soul is in darkness, or done with, even in the grave. And I know, I *know,* one word and I can put the world in your hand—and whatever it is to me, I won't take less! How, how, how do I tell you that *this*——

(She spells.)

—means a *word,* and the word means this *thing,* wool?

(She thrusts the wool at HELEN*'s hand;* HELEN *sits, puzzled.* ANNIE *puts the crocheting aside.)*

Or this—s, t, o, o, l—means this *thing,* stool?

(She claps HELEN*'s palm to the stool.* HELEN *waits, uncomprehending.* ANNIE *snatches up her napkin, spells:)*

Napkin!

(She forces it on HELEN*'s hand, waits, discards it, lifts a fold of the child's dress, spells:)*

Dress!

(She lets it drop, spells:)

F, a, c, e, face!

(She draws HELEN*'s hand to her cheek, and pressing it there, staring into the child's responseless eyes, hears the distant belfry begin to toll, slowly: one, two, three, four, five, six.)*

Scene 2

On the third stroke the lights stealing in around the garden house show us figures waiting: VI-

Helen Keller

NEY, *the other servant,* MARTHA, PERCY *at the drapes, and* JAMES *on the dim porch.* ANNIE *and* HELEN *remain, frozen. The chimes die away. Silently* PERCY *moves the drape-rod back out of sight;* VINEY *steps into the room—not using the door—and unmakes the bed; the other servant brings the wheelbarrow over, leaves it handy, rolls the bed off;* VINEY *puts the bed linens on top of a waiting boxful of* HELEN*'s toys, and loads the box on the wheelbarrow;* MARTHA *and* PERCY *take out the chairs, with the trayful, then the table; and* JAMES, *coming down and into the room, lifts* ANNIE*'s suitcase from its corner.* VINEY *and the other servant load the remaining odds and ends on the wheelbarrow, and the servant wheels it off.* VINEY *and the children departing leave only* JAMES *in the room with* ANNIE *and* HELEN. JAMES *studies the two of them, without mockery, and then, quietly going to the door and opening it, bears the suitcase out, and housewards. He leaves the door open.*

KATE *steps into the doorway, and stands.* ANNIE *lifting her gaze from* HELEN *sees her; she takes* HELEN*'s hand from her cheek, and returns it to the child's own, stroking it there twice, in her mother-sign, before spelling slowly into it:*

M, o, t, h, e, r. Mother.

(HELEN *with her hand free strokes her cheek, suddenly forlorn.* ANNIE *takes her hand again.)*

M, o, t, h——

(But KATE *is trembling with such impatience that her voice breaks from her, harsh.)*

KATE. Let her *come!*

*(*ANNIE *lifts* HELEN *to her feet, with a turn, and gives her a little push. Now* HELEN *begins groping, sensing something, trembling herself; and* KATE *falling one step in onto her knees clasps her, kissing her.* HELEN *clutches her, tight as she can.* KATE *is inarticulate, choked, repeating* HELEN*'s name again and again. She wheels with her in her arms, to stumble away out the doorway;* ANNIE *stands unmoving, while* KATE *in a blind walk carries* HELEN *like a baby behind the main house, out of view.*

ANNIE *is now alone on the stage. She turns, gazing around at the stripped room, bidding it silently farewell, impassively, like a defeated general on the deserted battlefield. All that remains is a stand with a basin of water; and here* ANNIE *takes up an eyecup, bathes each of her eyes, empties the eyecup, drops it in her purse, and tiredly locates her smoked glasses on the floor. The lights alter subtly; in the act of putting on her glasses* ANNIE *hears something that stops her, with head lifted. We hear it too, the voices out of the past, including her own now, in a whisper:)*

BOY'S VOICE. You said we'd be together, forever—You promised, forever and—*Annie!*

ANAGNOS'S VOICE. But that battle is dead and done with, why not let it stay buried?

ANNIE'S VOICE *(whispering).* I think God must owe me a resurrection.

ANAGNOS'S VOICE. What?

(A pause, and ANNIE *answers it herself, heavily.)*

ANNIE. And I owe God one.

BOY'S VOICE. Forever and ever—

*(*ANNIE *shakes her head.)*

—forever, and ever, and—

*(*ANNIE *covers her ears.)*

—forever, and ever, and ever——

(It pursues ANNIE*; she flees to snatch up her purse, wheels to the doorway, and* KELLER *is standing in it. The lights have lost their special color.)*

KELLER. Miss—Annie.

(He has an envelope in his fingers.)

I've been waiting to give you this.

ANNIE *(after a breath).* What?

KELLER. Your first month's salary.

(He puts it in her hand.)

With many more to come, I trust. It doesn't express what we feel, it doesn't pay our debt. For what you've done.

ANNIE. What have I done?

KELLER. Taken a wild thing, and given us back a child.

ANNIE *(presently).* I taught her one thing, no. Don't do this, don't do that——

KELLER. It's more than all of us could, in all the years we——

ANNIE. I wanted to teach her what language is. I wanted to teach her yes.

KELLER. You will have time.

ANNIE. I don't know how. I know without it to do nothing but obey is—no gift, obedience without understanding is a—blindness, too. Is that all I've wished on her?

KELLER *(gently).* No, no——

ANNIE. Maybe. I don't know what else to do. Simply go on, keep doing what I've done, and have—faith that inside she's—That inside it's waiting. Like water, underground. All you can do is keep on.

KELLER. It's enough. For us.

ANNIE. You can help, Captain Keller.

KELLER. How?

ANNIE. Even learning no has been at a cost. Of much trouble and pain. Don't undo it.

KELLER. Why should we wish to——

ANNIE *(abruptly).* The world isn't an easy place for anyone, I don't want her just to obey but to let her have her way in everything is a lie, to *her,* I can't——

(Her eyes fill, it takes her by surprise, and she laughs through it.)

And I don't even love her, she's not my child! Well. You've got to stand between that lie and her.

KELLER. We'll try.

ANNIE. Because *I* will. As long as you let me stay, that's one promise I'll keep.

KELLER. Agreed. We've learned something too, I hope.

(A pause)

Won't you come now, to supper?

ANNIE. Yes.

(She wags the envelope, ruefully.)

Why doesn't God pay His debts each month?

KELLER. I beg your pardon?

ANNIE. Nothing. I used to wonder how I could—

(The lights are fading on them, simultaneously rising on the family room of the main house, where VINEY *is polishing glassware at the table set for dinner.)*

—earn a living.

KELLER. Oh, you do.

ANNIE. I really do. Now the question is, can I survive it!

*(*KELLER *smiles, offers his arm.)*

KELLER. May I?

*(*ANNIE *takes it, and the lights lose them as he escorts her out.)*

Scene 3

Now in the family room the rear door opens, and HELEN *steps in. She stands a moment, then sniffs in one deep grateful breath, and her hands go out vigorously to familiar things, over the door panels, and to the chairs around the table, and over the silverware on the table, until she meets* VINEY*; she pats her flank approvingly.*

VINEY. Oh, we glad to have you back too, prob'ly.

*(*HELEN *hurries groping to the front door, opens and closes it, removes its key, opens and closes it again to be sure it is unlocked, gropes back to the rear door and repeats the procedure, removing its key and hugging herself gleefully.*

AUNT EV *is next in by the rear door, with a relish tray; she bends to kiss* HELEN*'s cheek.* HELEN *finds* KATE *behind her, and thrusts the keys at her.)*

KATE. What? Oh.

(To EV*)*

Keys.

(She pockets them, lets HELEN *feel them.)*

Yes, I'll keep the keys. I think we've had enough of locked doors, too.

*(*JAMES, *having earlier put* ANNIE*'s suitcase inside her door upstairs and taken himself out of view around the corner, now reappears and comes down the stairs as* ANNIE *and* KELLER *mount the porch steps. Following them into the family room, he pats* ANNIE*'s hair in passing, rather to her surprise.)*

JAMES. Evening, General.

(He takes his own chair opposite.

VINEY *bears the empty water pitcher out to the porch. The remaining suggestion of garden house is gone now, and the water pump is unobstructed;* VINEY *pumps water into the pitcher.*

KATE *surveying the table breaks the silence.)*

KATE. Will you say grace, Jimmie?

(They bow their heads, except for HELEN, *who palms her empty plate and then reaches to be sure her mother is there.* JAMES *considers a moment, glances across at* ANNIE, *lowers his head again, and obliges.)*

JAMES *(lightly).* And Jacob was left alone, and wrestled with an angel until the breaking of the day; and the hollow of Jacob's thigh was out of joint, as he wrestled with him; and the angel said, Let me go, for the day breaketh. And Jacob said, I will not let thee go, except thou bless me. Amen.

*(*ANNIE *has lifted her eyes suspiciously at* JAMES, *who winks expressionlessly and inclines his head to* HELEN.*)*

Oh, you angel.

(The others lift their faces; VINEY *returns with the pitcher, setting it down near* KATE, *then goes out the rear door; and* ANNIE *puts a napkin around* HELEN.*)*

AUNT EV. That's a very strange grace, James.

KELLER. Will you start the muffins, Ev?

JAMES. It's from the Good Book, isn't it?

AUNT EV *(passing a plate)*. Well, of course it is. Didn't you know?

JAMES. Yes, I knew.

KELLER *(serving)*. Ham, Miss Annie?

ANNIE. Please.

AUNT EV. Then why ask?

JAMES. I meant it *is* from the Good Book, and therefore a fitting grace.

AUNT EV. Well, I don't know about *that.*

KATE *(with the pitcher)*. Miss Annie?

ANNIE. Thank you.

AUNT EV. There's an awful *lot* of things in the Good Book that I wouldn't care to hear just before eating.

(When ANNIE *reaches for the pitcher,* HELEN *removes her napkin and drops it to the floor.* ANNIE *is filling* HELEN*'s glass when she notices it; she considers* HELEN*'s bland expression a moment, then bends, retrieves it, and tucks it around* HELEN*'s neck again.)*

JAMES. Well, fitting in the sense that Jacob's thigh was out of joint, and so is this piggie's.

AUNT EV. I declare, James——

KATE. Pickles, Aunt Ev?

AUNT EV. Oh, I should say so, you know my opinion of your pickles——

KATE. This is the end of them, I'm afraid. I didn't put up nearly enough last summer, this year I intend to——

(She interrupts herself, seeing HELEN *deliberately lift off her napkin and drop it again to the floor. She bends to retrieve it, but* ANNIE *stops her arm.)*

KELLER *(not noticing)*. Reverend looked in at the office today to complain his hens have stopped laying. Poor fellow, *he* was out of joint, all he could——

(He stops too, to frown down the table at KATE, HELEN, *and* ANNIE *in turn, all suspended in midmotion.)*

JAMES *(not noticing)*. I've always suspected those hens.

AUNT EV. Of what?

JAMES. I think they're Papist. Has he tried——

(He stops, too, following KELLER*'s eyes.* ANNIE *now stops to pick the napkin up.)*

AUNT EV. James, now you're pulling my—lower extremity, the first thing you know we'll be—

(She stops, too, hearing herself in the silence. ANNIE, *with everyone now watching, for the third time puts the napkin on* HELEN. HELEN *yanks it off, and throws it down.* ANNIE *rises, lifts* HELEN*'s plate, and bears it away.* HELEN, *feeling it gone, slides down and commences to kick up under the table; the dishes jump.* ANNIE *contemplates this for a moment, then coming back takes* HELEN*'s wrists firmly and swings her off the chair.* HELEN *struggling gets one hand free, and catches at her mother's skirt; when* KATE *takes her by the shoulders,* HELEN *hangs quiet.)*

KATE. Miss Annie.

ANNIE. No.

KATE *(a pause). It's a very special day.*

ANNIE *(grimly)*. It will be, when I give in to that.

(She tries to disengage HELEN*'s hand;* KATE *lays hers on* ANNIE*'s.)*

KATE. Please. I've hardly had a chance to welcome her home——

ANNIE. Captain Keller.

KELLER *(embarrassed)*. Oh. Katie, we—had a little talk, Miss Annie feels that if we indulge Helen in these——

AUNT EV. But what's the child done?

ANNIE. She's learned not to throw things on the floor and kick. It took us the best part of two weeks and——

AUNT EV. But only a napkin, it's not as if it were breakable!

ANNIE. And everything she's learned *is?* Mrs. Keller, I don't think we should—play tug-of-war for her, either give her to me or you keep her from kicking.

KATE. What do you wish to do?

ANNIE. Let me take her from the table.

AUNT EV. Oh, let her stay, my goodness, she's only a child, she doesn't have to wear a napkin if she doesn't want to her first evening——

ANNIE *(level)*. And ask outsiders not to interfere.

AUNT EV *(astonished)*. Out—outsi—I'm the child's *aunt!*

KATE *(distressed)*.Will once hurt so much, Miss

Annie? I've—made all Helen's favorite foods, tonight.

(A pause)

KELLER *(gently).* It's a homecoming party, Miss Annie.

(ANNIE after a moment releases HELEN. But she cannot accept it, at her own chair she shakes her head and turns back, intent on KATE.)

ANNIE. She's testing you. You realize?

JAMES *(to ANNIE).* She's testing you.

KELLER. Jimmie, be quiet.

(JAMES sits, tense.)

Now she's home, naturally she——

ANNIE. And wants to see what will happen. At your hands. I said it was my main worry, is this what you promised me not half an hour ago?

KELLER *(reasonably).* But she's *not* kicking, now——

ANNIE. And not learning not to. Mrs. Keller, teaching her is bound to be painful, to everyone. I know it hurts to watch, but she'll live up to just what you demand of her, and no more.

JAMES *(palely).* She's testing *you.*

KELLER *(testily).* Jimmie.

JAMES. I have an opinion. I think I should——

KELLER. No one's interested in hearing your opinion.

ANNIE. *I'm* interested, of course she's testing me. Let me keep her to what she's learned and she'll go on learning from me. Take her out of my hands and it all comes apart.

(KATE closes her eyes, digesting it; ANNIE sits again, with a brief comment for her.)

Be bountiful, it's at her expense.

(She turns to JAMES, flatly.)

Please pass me more of—her favorite foods.

(Then KATE lifts HELEN's hand, and turning her toward ANNIE, surrenders her; HELEN makes for her own chair.)

KATE *(low).* Take her, Miss Annie.

ANNIE *(then).* Thank you.

(But the moment ANNIE rising reaches for her hand, HELEN begins to fight and kick, clutching to the tablecloth, and uttering laments. ANNIE again tries to loosen her hand, and KELLER rises.)

KELLER *(tolerant).* I'm afraid you're the difficulty, Miss Annie. Now I'll keep her to what she's learned, you're quite right there——

(He takes HELEN's hands from ANNIE, pats them; HELEN quiets down.)

—but I don't see that we need send her from the table, after all, she's the guest of honor. Bring her plate back.

ANNIE. If she was a seeing child, none of you would tolerate one——

KELLER. Well, she's not, I think some compromise is called for. Bring her plate, please.

(ANNIE's jaw sets, but she restores the plate, while KELLER fastens the napkin around HELEN's neck; she permits it.)

There. It's not unnatural, most of us take some aversion to our teachers, and occasionally another hand can smooth things out.

(He puts a fork in HELEN's hand; HELEN takes it. Genially:)

Now. Shall we start all over?

(He goes back around the table, and sits. ANNIE stands watching. HELEN is motionless, thinking things through, until with a wicked glee she deliberately flings the fork on the floor. After another moment she plunges her hand into her food, and crams a fistful into her mouth.)

JAMES *(wearily).* I think we've started all over—

(KELLER shoots a glare at him, as HELEN plunges her other hand into ANNIE's plate. ANNIE at once moves in, to grasp her wrist, and HELEN flinging out a hand encounters the pitcher; she swings with it at ANNIE; ANNIE falling back, blocks it with an elbow, but the water flies over her dress. ANNIE gets her breath, then snatches the pitcher away in one hand, hoists HELEN up bodily under the other arm, and starts to carry her out, kicking. KELLER stands.)

ANNIE *(savagely polite).* Don't get up!

KELLER. Where are you going?

ANNIE. Don't smooth anything else out for me,

don't interfere in any way! I treat her like a seeing child because I *ask* her to see, I *expect* her to see, don't undo what I do!

KELLER. Where are you taking her?

ANNIE. To make her fill this pitcher again!

(She thrusts out with HELEN *under her arm, but* HELEN *escapes up the stairs and* ANNIE *runs after her.* KELLER *stands rigid.* AUNT EV *is astounded.)*

AUNT EV. You let her speak to you like that, Arthur? A creature who *works* for you?

KELLER *(angrily).* No. I don't.

(He is starting after ANNIE *when* JAMES, *on his feet with shaky resolve, interposes his chair between them in* KELLER*'s path.)*

JAMES. Let her go.

KELLER. What!

JAMES *(a swallow).* I said—let her go. She's right.

*(*KELLER *glares at the chair and him.* JAMES *takes a deep breath, then headlong:)*

She's right, Kate's right, I'm right, and you're wrong. If you drive her away from here it will be over my dead—chair, has it never occurred to you that on one occasion you might be consummately wrong?

*(*KELLER*'s stare is unbelieving, even a little fascinated.* KATE *rises in trepidation, to mediate.)*

KATE. Captain.

*(*KELLER *stops her with his raised hand; his eyes stay on* JAMES*'s pale face, for a long hold. When he finally finds voice, it is gruff.)*

KELLER. Sit down, everyone.

(He sits. KATE *sits.* JAMES *holds onto his chair.* KELLER *speaks mildly.)*

Please sit down, Jimmie.

*(*JAMES *sits, and a moveless silence prevails;* KELLER*'s eyes do not leave him.*

ANNIE *has pulled* HELEN *downstairs again by one hand, the pitcher in her other hand, down the porch steps, and across the yard to the pump. She puts* HELEN*'s hand on the pump handle, grimly.)*

ANNIE. All right. Pump.

*(*HELEN *touches her cheek, waits uncertainly.)*

No, she's not here. Pump!

(She forces HELEN*'s hand to work the handle, then lets go. And* HELEN *obeys. She pumps till the water comes, then* ANNIE *puts the pitcher in her other hand and guides it under the spout, and the water tumbling half into and half around the pitcher douses* HELEN*'s hand.* ANNIE *takes over the handle to keep water coming, and does automatically what she has done so many times before, spells into* HELEN*'s free palm:)*

Water. W, a, t, e, r. *Water.* It has a—name——

(And now the miracle happens. HELEN *drops the pitcher on the slab under the spout, it shatters. She stands transfixed.* ANNIE *freezes on the pump handle: there is a change in the sundown light, and with it a change in* HELEN*'s face, some light coming into it we have never seen there, some struggle in the depths behind it; and her lips tremble, trying to remember something the muscles around them once knew, till at last it finds its way out, painfully, a baby sound buried under the debris of years of dumbness.)*

HELEN. Wah. Wah.

(And again, with great effort)

Wah. Wah.

*(*HELEN *plunges her hand into the dwindling water, spells into her own palm. Then she gropes frantically,* ANNIE *reaches for her hand, and* HELEN *spells into* ANNIE*'s hand.)*

ANNIE *(whispering).* Yes.

*(*HELEN *spells it out again.)*

Yes!

*(*HELEN *grabs at the handle, pumps for more water, plunges her hand into its spurt and grabs* ANNIE*'s to spell it again.)*

Yes! Oh, my dear——

(She falls to her knees to clasp HELEN*'s hand, but* HELEN *pulls it free, stands almost bewildered, then drops to the ground, pats it swiftly, holds up her palm, imperious.* ANNIE *spells into it:)*

Ground.

*(*HELEN *spells it back.)*

Yes!

*(*HELEN *whirls to the pump, pats it, holds up her palm, and* ANNIE *spells into it.)*

Pump.

*(*HELEN *spells it back.)*

Yes! Yes!

(Now HELEN *is in such an excitement she is possessed, wild, trembling, cannot be still, turns, runs, falls on the porch steps, claps it, reaches out her palm, and* ANNIE *is at it instantly to spell:)*

Step.

*(*HELEN *has no time to spell back now, she whirls groping, to touch anything, encounters the trellis, shakes it, thrusts out her palm, and* ANNIE *while spelling to her cries wildly at the house.)*

Trellis. Mrs. Keller! *Mrs. Keller.*

(Inside, KATE *starts to her feet.* HELEN *scrambles back onto the porch, groping, and finds the bell string, tugs it; the bell rings, the distant chimes begin tolling the hour, all the bells in town seem to break into speech while* HELEN *reaches out and* ANNIE *spells feverishly into her hand.* KATE *hurries out, with* KELLER *after her;* AUNT EV *is on her feet, to peer out the window; only* JAMES *remains at the table, and with a napkin wipes his damp brow. From up right and left the servants—*VINEY*, the two Negro children, the other servant—run in, and stand watching from a distance as* HELEN*, ringing the bell, with her other hand encounters her mother's skirt;*

when she throws a hand out, ANNIE *spells into it:)*

Mother.

*(*KELLER *now seizes* HELEN'*s hand, she touches him, gestures a hand, and* ANNIE *again spells:)*

Papa—she *knows!*

*(*KATE *and* KELLER *go to their knees, stammering, clutching* HELEN *to them, and* ANNIE *steps unsteadily back to watch the threesome,* HELEN *spelling wildly into* KATE'*s hand, then into* KELLER'*s.* KATE *spelling back into* HELEN'*s; they cannot keep their hands off her, and rock her in their clasp.*

Then HELEN *gropes, feels nothing, turns all around, pulls free, and comes with both hands groping, to find* ANNIE. *She encounters* ANNIE'*s thighs,* ANNIE *kneels to her,* HELEN'*s hand pats* ANNIE'*s cheek impatiently, points a finger, and waits; and* ANNIE *spells into it:)*

Teacher.

*(*HELEN *spells it back, slowly;* ANNIE *nods.)*

Teacher.

(She holds HELEN'*s hand to her cheek. Presently* HELEN *withdraws it, not jerkily, only with reserve, and retreats a step. She stands thinking it over, then turns again and stumbles back to her parents. They try to embrace her, but she has something else in mind, it is to get the keys, and she hits* KATE'*s pocket until* KATE *digs them out for her.*

ANNIE *with her own load of emotion has retreated, her back turned, toward the pump, to sit;* KATE *moves to* HELEN, *touches her hand questioningly, and* HELEN *spells a word to her.* KATE *comprehends it, their first act of verbal communication, and she can hardly utter the word aloud, in wonder, gratitude, and deprivation; it is a moment in which she simultaneously finds and loses a child.)*

KATE. Teacher?

*(*ANNIE *turns; and* KATE, *facing* HELEN *in her direction by the shoulders, holds her back, holds her back, and then relinquishes her.* HELEN *feels her way across the yard, rather shyly, and when her moving hands touch* ANNIE'*s skirt she stops. Then she holds out the keys and places them in* ANNIE'*s hand. For a moment neither of them moves. Then* HELEN *slides into* ANNIE'*s arms, and lifting away her smoked glasses, kisses her on the cheek.* ANNIE *gathers her in.*

KATE *torn both ways turns from this, gestures the servants off, and makes her way into the house, on* KELLER'*s arm. The servants go, in separate directions.*

The lights are half down now, except over the pump. ANNIE *and* HELEN *are here, alone in the yard.* ANNIE *has found* HELEN'*s hand, almost without knowing it, and she spells slowly into it, her voice unsteady, whispering:)*

ANNIE. I, love, Helen.

(She clutches the child to her, tight this time, not spelling, whispering into her hair.)

Forever, and——

(She stops. The lights over the pump are taking on the color of the past, and it brings ANNIE'*s head up, her eyes opening, in fear; and as slowly as though drawn she rises, to listen, with her hand on* HELEN'*s shoulders. She waits, waits, listening with ears and eyes both, slowly here, slowly there: and hears only silence. There are no voices. The color passes on, and when her eyes come back to* HELEN *she can breathe the end of her phrase without fear:)*

—ever.

(In the family room KATE *has stood over the table, staring at* HELEN'*s plate, with* KELLER *at her shoulder; now* JAMES *takes a step to move her chair in, and* KATE *sits, with head erect, and* KELLER *inclines his head to* JAMES; *so it is* AUNT EV, *hesitant, and rather humble, who moves to the door.*

Outside HELEN *tugs at* ANNIE'*s hand, and* ANNIE *comes with it.* HELEN *pulls her toward the house; and hand in hand, they cross the yard, and ascend the porch steps, in the rising lights, to where* AUNT EV *is holding the door open for them. The curtain ends the play.)*

Discussion

1. How are Annie's fatigue and desperation suggested in the first scene of Act Three?

2. What different kinds of separation is Captain Keller talking about in scene one?

3. (a) In her brief conversation with James, what advice does Kate give her stepson? **(b)** What does he request of her? **(c)** Is the advice she gives him the advice he needs? Explain why or why not.

4. Cite passages in which Annie, despite fatigue, retains **(a)** her sense of humor, and **(b)** her determination.

5. (a) What has Annie managed to teach Helen in the two weeks? **(b)** What has she been unable to teach Helen?

6. (a) Is it understandable that Kate and Keller refuse to give Annie another week with Helen? Why or why not? **(b)** Is their decision a wise one? Why or why not?

7. The second scene consists of a brief conversation between Annie and Captain Keller. What does Annie mean by these comments: **(a)** ". . . obedience without understanding is a blindness, too." **(b)** ". . . to let her (Helen) have her own way in everything is a lie, to her . . . "?

8. The concluding scene of the play begins as Annie and the members of the Keller family gather at the dinner table. **(a)** How does Helen's behavior renew the major conflict of the play? **(b)** How does each individual at the table react to Helen's behavior? **(c)** What seems to be Helen's purpose in behaving as she does?

9. How does the renewed conflict affect the relationship **(a)** between Annie and Helen, and **(b)** between James and Keller?

10. (a) At what point in the final scene does the play reach a climax, or turning point? **(b)** Has this climax been foreshadowed? Explain.

11. (a) What is the miracle that is accomplished? **(b)** How does Helen react when it is accomplished?

12. The stage direction toward the end of the play contains this statement: ". . . it is a moment in which she (Kate) simultaneously finds and loses a child." Explain the significance of this statement.

Application

Protagonist/Antagonist

1. If Annie is the chief character—the protagonist—in the play, then in what ways is Helen her antagonist? At what point is Helen no longer Annie's antagonist?

2. What other characters are Annie's antagonists? At what times in the play are they her antagonists?

3. If Helen is a protagonist, what outside forces are her antagonists? (You may wish to review the article on page 649 in the Handbook of Literary Terms.)

Composition

Assume you are one of the following: Captain Keller, Kate Keller, or James Keller. In the voice of the character you have selected, write two letters.

In the first letter, express your reaction to Annie Sullivan after she has been at the Keller household for a brief period of time. In the second letter, report your view of Annie and of Helen after you have witnessed Helen's breakthrough. Write both of your letters to the same person. (For example, you might write the two letters to Anagnos.) (See *Making Comparisons and Contrasts,* page 665.)

William Gibson 1914–

After two years of trying to adjust to the rigors of study, William Gibson dropped out of the City College of New York; he worked at various jobs, including jazz pianist in a night club and amateur actor.

In 1940, he married and moved to Topeka, Kansas, where he wrote a verse play which was produced by the local theater. In 1945, he received an award from *Poetry* magazine for several of his poems. But his first popular success came with his first novel, *The Cobweb* (1954).

Three years later, *The Miracle Worker* was presented as a play on television. It was so popular that it was rewritten for the stage (1959), and then for the movies (1962). The film, with Anne Bancroft as Annie Sullivan and Patty Duke as Helen Keller, won two Academy Awards.

Today, Gibson lives with his family in Stockbridge, Massachusetts. Two of his most recent plays are *Golda,* about Israel's Golda Meir, which premiered in 1977, and *Monday After the Miracle,* a sequel to *The Miracle Worker,* which premiered in 1982.

Comment: The Manual Alphabet

When Annie arrives at the railroad station in Tuscumbia, she astonishes Kate by saying that "first, last and—in between" she will teach language to Helen. Annie believes that the manual alphabet, or fingerspelling, long an effective method for helping to teach the deaf, will be equally effective in teaching a girl who is both deaf and blind.

As shown in the illustration on this page, the manual alphabet consists of twenty-six different finger positions—one position for each letter of the alphabet. Unlike other forms of sign language which must be seen to be taught—hand signs, facial and body gestures, and pantomime—fingerspelling may be taught by touch alone. But fingerspelling is slow, is relatively difficult for young children to learn, and strains the attention of both adults and children if used for long periods. It is used mainly to communicate the more difficult or unusual words and ideas that cannot easily be conveyed through signs and gestures.

The manual alphabet was used in France as early as the eighteenth century, but no one knows precisely who invented it—or when. Remember that in Act One of *The Miracle Worker,* James asks Annie if she invented it. Answering him, Annie refers to "Spanish monks under a—vow of silence," which she angrily wishes James would take. Annie's remark is not merely sarcastic; some scholars believe that a community of Spanish monks who had vowed silence invented the twenty-six finger positions in order to communicate with one another without speaking aloud.

"The Manual Alphabet," from *Anne Sullivan Macy: The Story Behind Helen Keller* by Nella Braddy. Copyright 1933 by Nella Braddy Henney. Reprinted by permission of Doubleday & Company, Inc.

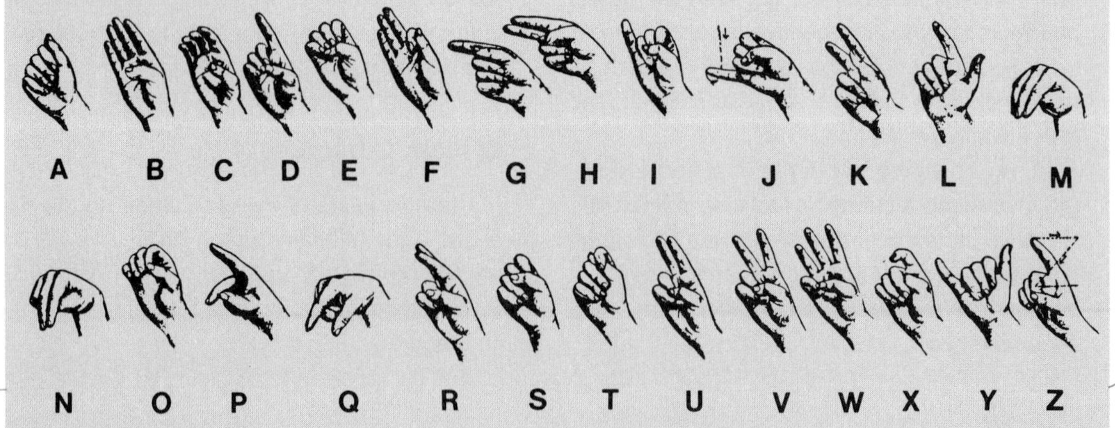

Unit 2 Review: *Modern Drama*

Content Review

1. In the first scene in which Annie appears (Act One, scene 3), she says, "I think God must owe me a resurrection." (To *resurrect* means to bring back to life again or to bring into use again.) **(a)** How does the idea of resurrection apply to the following characters: Helen, Annie, James? **(b)** In what indirect way is Jimmie Sullivan resurrected? **(c)** What correspondence is there between the idea of resurrection and the title of the play, *The Miracle Worker?* (Look up the meaning of *miracle.*)

2. Various characters within and outside the play are represented as being obstinate, some favorably, some unfavorably (refer, for example, to James and Captain Keller's argument over General Grant in Act Two, scene 2). *Obstinate* can mean not giving up, being stubborn or hard, or not easily controlled. **(a)** Explain specifically in what sense (or senses) the following characters are obstinate: Captain Keller, Helen, Annie; and tell why you regard the characteristic as a help or a hindrance to each character. **(b)** What events suggest that obştinacy, while often a virtue, needs to be tempered with love and affection to be effective?

3. (a) What is Annie's theory of teaching and learning? (Refer to her letters to Anagnos and to her treatment of Helen in your explanation.) **(b)** How do Annie's ideas about teaching and learning differ from those of Kate, Captain Keller, and James? **(c)** Which approach—Annie's or, say, Kate's—do you regard as more effective in teaching children with special problems? In teaching children without special problems? In each case, why?

4. Keys play an important part in the play. Recall the scenes in which they are used; and think about the various uses of keys: e.g., "to lock in," "to lock out," "to unlock." Write a paper in which you describe the important incidents involving the use of keys and, secondly, in which you analyze how the specific uses of keys suggest certain relationships among the characters. (For example, what is suggested by Helen's handing Annie the keys from her mother at the end of the play?)

Concept Review: Interpretation of New Material

The following is an excerpt from *The Innocents,* a dramatic adaptation of *The Turn of the Screw* by Henry James. The setting is an English country house in 1880. After the mysterious death of the previous governess, Miss Giddens comes to take care of eight-year-old Flora and her twelve-year-old brother Miles, orphans who are under the guardianship of a loveless but duty-bound uncle. The ghosts of the previous governess and a deceased male servant, whether real or imagined, are presences throughout the play, and the evil influence they exert provides the drama with its ominous atmosphere.

Read the following excerpt, which focuses on the initial meeting between Miss Giddens and Flora; then answer the questions that come after.

from The Innocents • *William Archibald*

MISS GIDDENS *(as* FLORA *curtsies to her).* How do you do, Flora? *(*FLORA *curtsies again, smiling.)* And you—you are Mrs. Grose—the housekeeper, of course?

MRS. GROSE *(curtseying).* Yes, Miss—and you must forgive me. I meant to have tea ready for you—but, now—I'll have it here if you don't mind waiting a moment— *(She goes, in confusion, to door Right, then turns, flushed and beaming.)* I'm glad you've come— *(Exits.)*

MISS GIDDENS *(to* MRS. GROSE*).* Thank you. Well, Flora—?

*(*MISS GIDDENS *and* FLORA *stand, silently for a moment, smiling at each other.)*

FLORA. Would you like to take off your hat?

MISS GIDDENS *(sitting on love seat, taking off hat).* Thank you—

FLORA *(taking hat from her).* I shall put it here— Won't you sit down? *(Puts it on desk.)*

MISS GIDDENS. Thank you. Come sit by me— *(*FLORA *goes to sit on love seat.)* We must get to know each other, you know—

FLORA. Oh, I'm sure we will. You're staying, aren't you? You told Mrs. Grose your trunk was here—

MISS GIDDENS *(laughing).* Why, of course I'm staying! I wouldn't be much of a governess if I didn't—now would I? So, I *shall*— *(Wooing her)* —if you'd like me to?

FLORA. Oh, yes—*(Pauses)* I hope you'll like your room—

MISS GIDDENS. I'm sure it's lovely—

FLORA. If you don't—you may choose another— There are thirty-five—most of them closed—and think of it! One hundred and forty windows! Shall we go into the garden and count them?

MISS GIDDENS *(charmed by the politeness).* I *would* like to—but poor Mrs. Grose would be alone with her tea—and I did say I'd like some.

FLORA. *You* didn't. *She* said she'd get it.

MISS GIDDENS *(taken aback—laughing).* Oh— It wouldn't be polite, now would it? To go walking in the garden?

FLORA. *I* often do. . . .

MRS. GROSE *(entering from Right, carrying a tray of tea things).* You're famished for a cup, I'm sure—after your long journey—so I'll set it down and leave you and the little lady to talk— *(Sets tray on desk—turns to Right.)*

MISS GIDDENS. Mrs. Grose? Won't you sit with me a while? There're things I'd like to ask you—

MRS. GROSE. Things, Miss?

MISS GIDDENS. Yes—I don't know the habits of the house—it would make it easier if you told me—

MRS. GROSE. Why, yes, if you'd like, Miss. *(Remains standing, Right of desk.)*

MISS GIDDENS *(rising).* Will you have some tea, Flora?

FLORA. No, thank you.

MISS GIDDENS *(going to desk).* Do sit down, Mrs. Grose.

MRS. GROSE *(sitting on chair at desk).* Thank you, Miss—

MISS GIDDENS *(*MISS GIDDENS *pours tea into cups—as she does this she starts to laugh softly, looking at* MRS. GROSE, *then* FLORA, *who sits quietly).* And I was so afraid!

FLORA *(wonderingly).* Afraid?

MISS GIDDENS. Timid, Flora—couldn't make up my mind for days— Should I accept this post—should I? Shouldn't I? None of my brothers or sisters could help me! I wouldn't ask advice! *(Laughs)*

FLORA *(Laughing).* I never take advice!

MRS. GROSE *(seriously).* Now, Miss Flora—

MISS GIDDENS *(as she takes a cup of tea to* MRS. GROSE, *who rises embarrassedly).* But why should one take advice, Mrs. Grose? Or give it? *(As* MRS. GROSE *remains standing—cup in hand—slightly ill-at-ease.)* Do sit down, Mrs. Grose— *(As she returns to love seat, sits.)* Of course, advice is forced upon you, in as large a family as mine was—

FLORA *(fascinated).* How large?

MISS GIDDENS. Very large. In a very small house. Secrets were difficult.

FLORA. But "possible"?

MISS GIDDENS. Not for long.

FLORA. That *must* have been annoying.

MISS GIDDENS. Well—*(Laughing)* Of course we shared our secrets when we were your age—but grown-ups never knew—

FLORA *(laughing with her).* They never do—do they?

MRS. GROSE. Now, Miss Flora—

MISS GIDDENS *(to* MRS. GROSE, *smiling).* Oh, they found out after awhile! My family believed in open doors and after-dinner conferences—

MRS. GROSE. And a very *sensible* thing, too, Miss—

FLORA *(to* MISS GIDDENS*).* Is it?

MRS. GROSE *(vexedly).* Miss *Flora*—

MISS GIDDENS *(realizing that perhaps she has been a little too free with* FLORA*).* Yes, Flora. A *very* sensible thing— *(Smiling)* Now, wouldn't you like to walk in the garden while I speak to Mrs. Grose? *(She goes with* FLORA *to window.)*

FLORA *(the perfect "obedient" child).* Why, yes, if you'd like me to, Miss Giddens.

MISS GIDDENS. And I'll come out when I've had a cup of tea— *(*FLORA *curtsies to her, goes through French window and out into garden.)* Poor little thing. She looks so lonely out there—

MRS. GROSE. Lonely, Miss? Most independent. Just as soon wander off by herself—though as easy with company as any—

MISS GIDDENS *(looking out).* She *is* lonely, though. Perhaps it's because I grew up in a large family— Well, at least she has a beautiful garden to walk in— *(Softly)* It *is* a beautiful garden—so quiet, so peaceful— The thickness of the trees seems to form a wall between one path and another. As I walked under them I had a feeling of solitude—and yet, I also felt that I was not completely alone— *(Turning to* MRS. GROSE*)* When you walked in the garden—your first day here—what did you think, Mrs. Grose?

MRS. GROSE *(softly).* I was young, Miss—I thought it was all very beautiful—

MISS GIDDENS *(moving away from window; looking about room, taking in each detail of it).* How awful if it were an ugly one! *(She laughs softly.)* How awful if this room were cold and ugly! I was almost afraid it might be! *(Returns to love seat. Sits down; takes her cup.)*

MRS. GROSE *(puzzled).* Might be, Miss?

MISS GIDDENS *(seriously).* No. I didn't think that. I suppose I knew it would be beautiful—because his house on Harley Street was— *(Pause.)* Mrs. Grose—perhaps it isn't any of my business—but he, their uncle, when I spoke to him—when he engaged me—he was so brief with me. He said he didn't want to be bothered by letters from me about the children— He said that, you know—he made it seem *the* important part of his terms. He said—under no condition was I to *bother him.* Doesn't he love them?

MRS. GROSE *(uncomfortably).* I'm sure he does—in his fashion, Miss, If you'll excuse me—

MISS GIDDENS. I don't understand how he could choose to ignore them. But I know so little— Only that their parents died soon after Miss Flora's birth and that *he* is their sole guardian—

MRS. GROSE. Yes, Miss— But you must understand, Miss— He's not a young man and he's never enjoyed good health— He was always a studious man—wrapped up in his work— He's never had any family responsibilities before— *(Gently)* But he does keep this house on—especially for them. He *is* doing all that can be expected—

MISS GIDDENS. Yes, after all, Miles and Flora aren't his children— And, he certainly *was* absorbed in his work— He could scarcely spare the time to interview me and spent most of it talking about his collection of Chinese paintings— *(Looks about the room)* I see he's got some of them here— I must admit they're rather beautiful—but I couldn't help being angry when he spoke to me about not bothering him about the children. *(Gently)* You see, I have been in the midst of my family, first as a child, then as a guardian to my younger brothers and sisters— *(Rising, moving about the room, taking in the details of it)* It isn't enough to give a child a house and garden as beautiful as these— *(Wryly)* I'm afraid I showed him how angry I was. I'm afraid *that* is why he engaged me—because I "stood up" to him. I was caught. I showed how much I loved children—and that I would do *anything* to make them happy. That was all he wanted, apparently— Someone to take the responsibility off *his* shoulders. Well, here I am. *(Gently)* And I'm embarrassing you— I don't mean to. *(Laughs)* And what an easy task it will be! An affectionate task! And all within a large roomy house surrounded by a lovely garden! *(Determinedly)* And—when he pays us a visit—

MRS. GROSE. I don't expect he will, Miss. He's been here only once or twice that I can bring to mind. Though there were times in the months just passed when—

MISS GIDDENS *(taken aback).* When *what,* Mrs. Grose?

MRS. GROSE. When *he* should have been the one to shoulder the—

MISS GIDDENS. The what, Mrs. Grose?

MRS. GROSE. Bygones is bygones.

MISS GIDDENS. Not if I'm to do my work satisfactorily—

MRS. GROSE. Pardon me, Miss. It isn't to do with you—you'd best forget I spoke—so—so out of place. *(She rises.)*

MISS GIDDENS *(stubbornly).* Mrs. Grose. What was she like?

MRS. GROSE *(uncomfortably).* Who, Miss?

MISS GIDDENS. The lady who was here before.

MRS. GROSE. The last governess? She was also young and pretty, Miss, even as you—

MISS GIDDENS *(smiling with embarrassment).* He doesn't mind them being young and pretty!

MRS. GROSE *(turning to her—vehemently).* Oh, no—it was the way he liked everyone! *(Flushing)* I mean—why should the Master mind?

MISS GIDDENS. But of whom did you speak *first?*

MRS. GROSE *(blankly).* Why, of *him.*

MISS GIDDENS. Of the Master? *(Lights dim slightly.)*

MRS. GROSE. Of who else? *(They search each other's faces.)*

MISS GIDDENS *(casually).* Mrs. Grose—was she—my predecessor—careful, particular—in her work?

MRS. GROSE *(against her will).* About some things—yes—

MISS GIDDENS. But not about all?

MRS. GROSE. Well, Miss, she's passed on. I won't tell tales.

MISS GIDDENS *(quickly).* I understand your feeling—but— Did she die here?

MRS. GROSE. No—she went away. *(FLORA appears at window.)*

MISS GIDDENS. Went *away?* To die? She was taken ill you mean—and went home?

MRS. GROSE. She was not taken ill so far as ap-

peared in this house. She—she left it to go home, she said, for a short holiday. At the very moment I was expecting her back I heard from the Master that she was dead.

MISS GIDDENS. But of what?

(The TWO WOMEN *stare at each other. Through scene, LIGHTS dim. Only from the French window comes a last ray of sunlight.)*

FLORA *(in a small, clear voice).* Miss Giddens—aren't you coming for a walk?

---

1. Mrs. Grose holds the position of **(a)** guardian; **(b)** teacher; **(c)** governess; **(d)** housekeeper.

2. When she first appears, Mrs. Grose seems **(a)** excited; **(b)** calm; **(c)** unhappy; **(d)** afraid.

3. Write two adjectives that describe Flora.

4. Cite two specific examples from this scene to explain why you chose these adjectives.

5. Using information supplied by Mrs. Grose, describe Flora and Miles's uncle.

6. When Flora agrees to go out into the garden, the italicized comment describes her as *"The perfect 'obedient' child."* The word *obedient* is put into quotation marks to indicate **(a)** Flora only appears to be obedient; **(b)** it expresses Mrs. Grose's opinion; **(c)** obedience is Flora's strong point; **(d)** Flora's obedience goes unnoticed.

7. Miss Giddens says that as she walked in the garden she had "a feeling of solitude," yet also felt that she "was not completely alone." This is an example of **(a)** foreshadowing; **(b)** stereotype; **(c)** point of view; **(d)** symbolism.

8. Of the following, what does Mrs. Grose *not* say about the children's uncle? **(a)** He is an older man. **(b)** He is in bad health. **(c)** He is studious. **(d)** He is handsome.

9. Stage directions can be useful in revealing character. With which character is each of the following associated: **(a)** Who acts "uncomfortably" and is described as "flushed and beaming"? **(b)** Who questions "wonderingly" and is "fascinated" by others? **(c)** Who speaks "determinedly," "gently," and "stubbornly"?

10. When Miss Giddens speaks of "open doors and after-dinner conferences" in her family, she is referring to **(a)** honesty; **(b)** strict rules; **(c)** eating habits; **(d)** carelessness.

Composition Review

Choose one of the following topics for your composition.

1. Assume that you know Flora well and that you have recently met Miss Giddens, whom you like. What personality traits does Flora have that may cause problems for Miss Giddens?

Write a letter to Miss Giddens, warning her of the difficulties she is likely to encounter with Flora and explaining the reason for these difficulties. Suggest methods she might use to overcome these problems. Make the tone of your letter polite but firm.

2. Assume that you can employ either Annie Sullivan or Miss Giddens to be a teacher for children and caretaker of a large house. Using information you have learned through the selections, make a list of what you consider to be the positive and negative aspects of each woman. You might think about each woman's family background, personality, and method of handling responsibilities.

Write a letter of acceptance to one and a letter of rejection to the other, explaining the reasons for your choice. Feel free to use the information you have collected.

Unit 3
Poetry

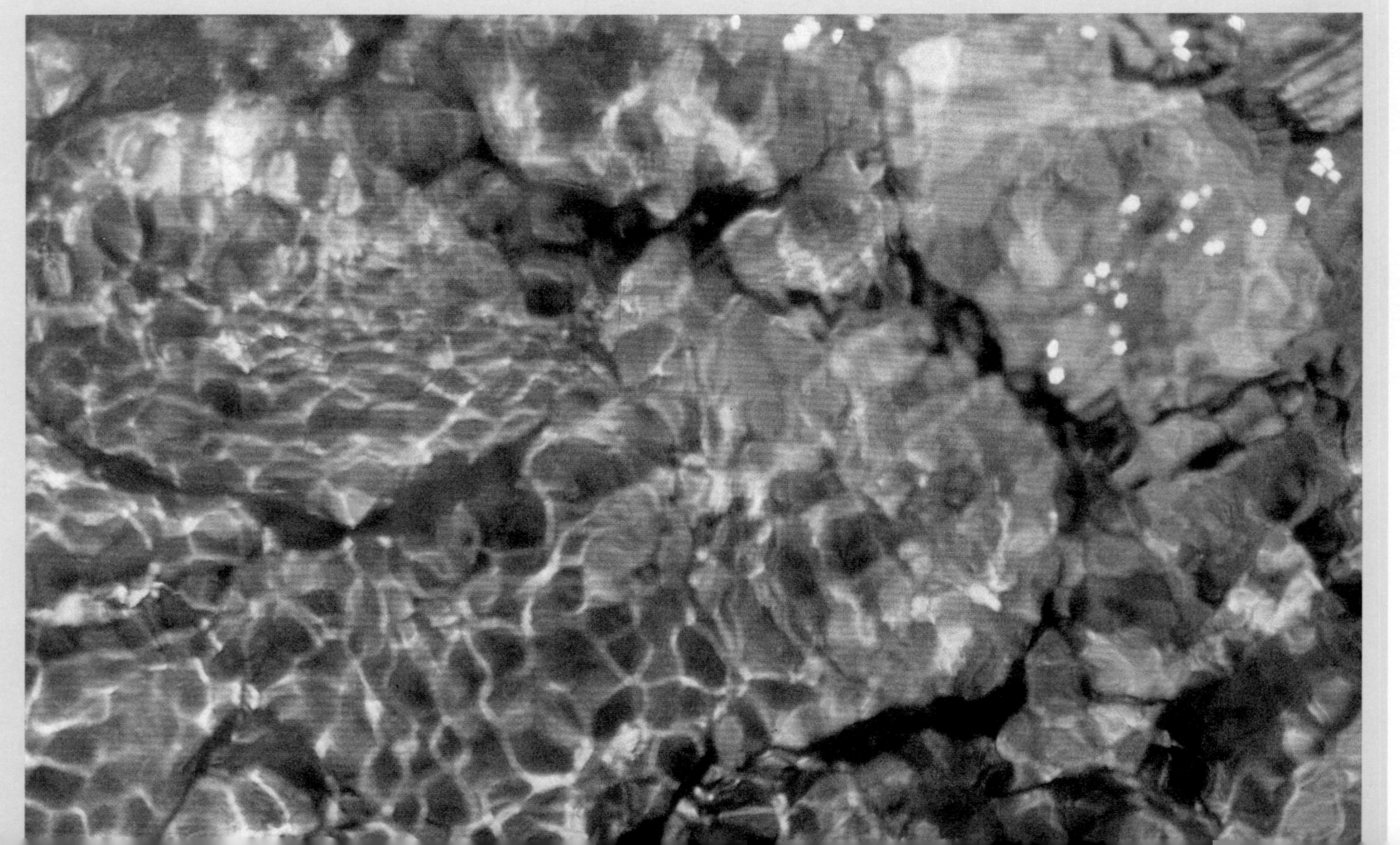

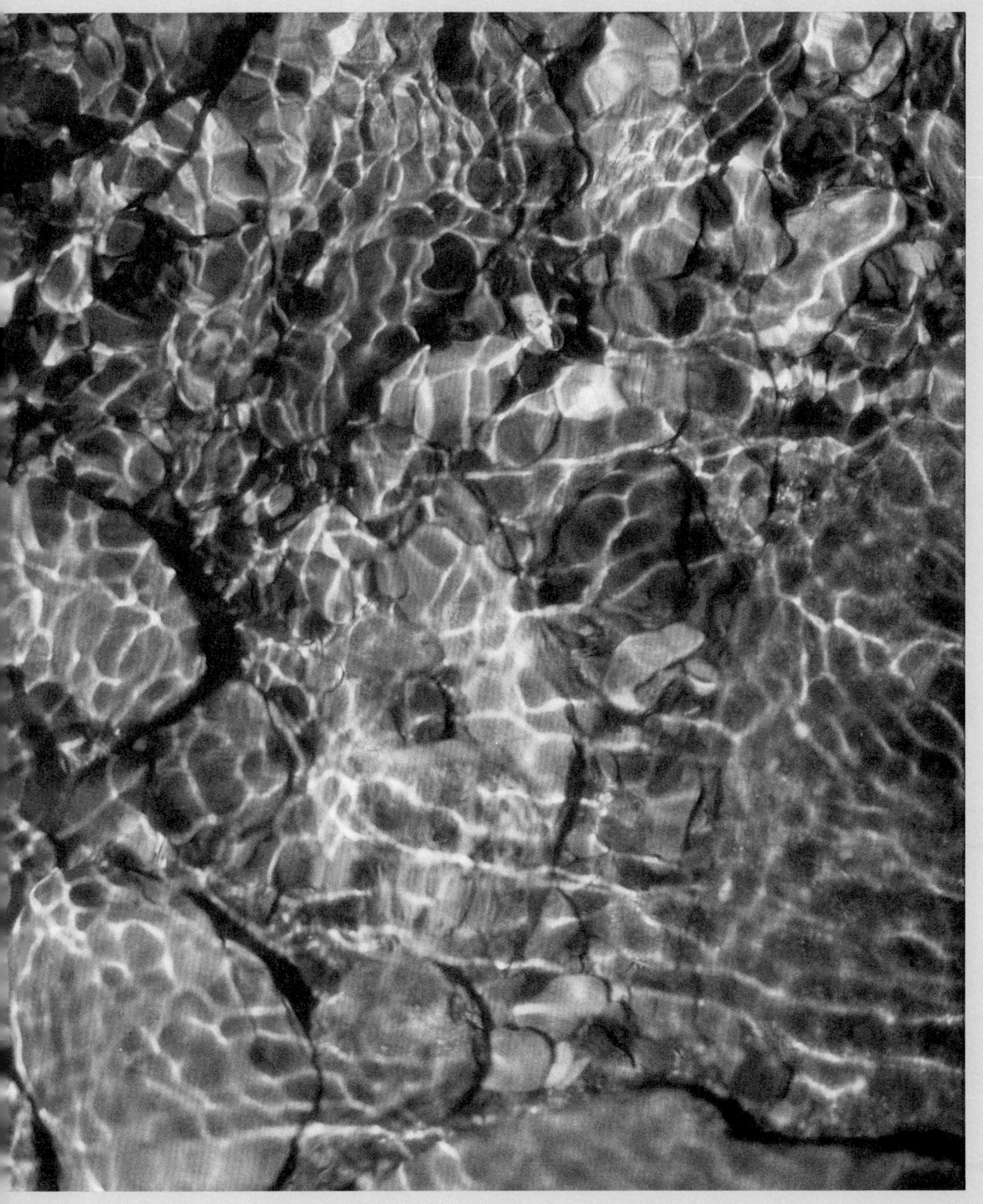

Goals and Destinations

There are as many reasons for writing poems as there are emotions. Poems in this group speak of goals (where a person wants to go) and destinations (where that person may actually end up).

Pole Vault

Grace Butcher

The miracle lies in the strange awkward run
transformed to fantastic flight.
The confrontation is between
the man and the invisible mountain.
The glass whip flares, bends in the sun,
flings him to the top of his strength
and enough beyond.
He has time to smile
during his endless fall
through the defeated air.

See **SIMILE** Handbook of Literary Terms

Daybreak in Alabama

Langston Hughes

When I get to be a composer
I'm gonna write me some music about
Daybreak in Alabama
And I'm gonna put the purtiest songs in it
Rising out of the ground like a swamp mist
And falling out of heaven like soft dew.
I'm gonna put some tall tall trees in it
And the scent of pine needles
And the smell of red clay after rain
And long red necks
And poppy colored faces
And big brown arms
And the field daisy eyes
Of black and white black white black people
And I'm gonna put white hands
And black hands and brown and yellow hands
And red clay earth hands in it
Touching everybody with kind fingers
And touching each other natural as dew
In that dawn of music when I
Get to be a composer
And write about daybreak
In Alabama.

See **SATIRE** Handbook of Literary Terms

Mr. Artesian's[1] *Conscientiousness*

Ogden Nash

Once there was a man named Mr. Artesian and his
activity was tremendous,
And he grudged every minute away from his desk be-
cause the importance of his work was so stupendous;
And he had one object all sublime,
Which was to save simply oodles of time.
He figured that sleeping eight hours a night meant that
if he lived to be seventy-five he would have spent
twenty-five years not at his desk but in bed,
So he cut his slumber to six hours which meant he only
lost eighteen years and nine months instead,
And he figured that taking ten minutes for breakfast
and twenty minutes for luncheon and half an hour
for dinner meant that he spent three years, two
months and fifteen days at the table,
So that by subsisting solely on bouillon cubes which he
swallowed at his desk to save this entire period he
was able,
And he figured that at ten minutes a day he spent a little
over six months and ten days shaving,

1. ***artesian*** (ar tē′zhən). An artesian well is a deep-drilled well, especially one from which water gushes up under its own pressure.

So he grew a beard, which gave him a considerable saving,
And you might think that now he might have been
  satisfied, but no, he wore a thoughtful frown,
Because he figured that at two minutes a day he would
  spend thirty-eight days and a few minutes in
  elevators just traveling up and down,
So as a final timesaving device he stepped out the
  window of his office, which happened to be on the
  fiftieth floor,
And one of his partners asked "Has he vertigo?"[2] and
  the other glanced out and down and said "Oh no,
  only about ten feet more."

---

2. ***vertigo*** (vėr′tə gō), dizziness.

See **METAPHOR** in Handbook of Literary Terms

O Daedalus,[1] Fly Away Home

Robert Hayden

Drifting night in the Georgia pines,
coonskin drum and jubilee banjo.
  Pretty Malinda, dance with me.

Night is juba, night is conjo,
  Pretty Malinda, dance with me.

Night is an African juju man
weaving a wish and a weariness together
  to make two wings.

  O fly away home fly away

(Continued)

---

1. ***Daedalus*** (ded′l əs), in Greek legends, a skilled workman from Athens who built the labyrinth at Crete. He and his son were then imprisoned in this maze. They escaped by flying away on wings that Daedalus made of feathers and wax.

Do you remember Africa?

O cleave the air fly away home

My gran, he flew back to Africa,
just spread his arms and
flew away home.

Drifting night in the windy pines;
night is a laughing, night is a longing.
Pretty Malinda, come to me.

Night is a mourning juju man
weaving a wish and a weariness together
to make two wings.

O fly away home fly away

Comment: On "O Daedalus, Fly Away Home"

The poem is set in Georgia, at night, among the slaves. The lines follow the rhythm of the coonskin drum and the thrum of the banjo. So strong is the beat and so musical the words that reading the poem aloud results in something very close to singing.

Night brings the slaves time for throwing off their shackles, both physical and mental, time for remembering Africa in the juba dance they have brought with them from across the ocean. Night's cloak of darkness makes it possible to conjure up memories and dreams. Night acts for them the way a juju man, a wielder of supernatural powers, would.

Lines 6 and 7 (which are repeated later in the poem as a sort of chorus) reveal the depth and the intensity of the slaves' yearning, a desire hidden beneath the nighttime jubilee, a longing "to make two wings" to use to fly away, back to their native land.

The poem is rich in references to culture and legend. The line "to make two wings" recalls an old Negro spiritual: "O Lord, I want two wings / To scale the gate / O Lord, I want two wings to fly away." In this lively song, the words *two wings* are sung on high, bright notes that leap up from the sorrowful-sounding bass of "O Lord, I want . . ."

The poet, Robert Hayden, alludes both to the Greek myth of Daedalus (see footnote 1) and to a tale of black people who could fly. According to that legend, there once was a tribe of Africans who were able to fly. When they were taken as slaves, many members of this tribe escaped their cruel bondage by flying home to Africa. The myth was kept alive in slaves' quarters and around their campfires: "My gran, he flew back . . . home" (lines 12–14).

The night moves on and the party dies down; the night is now compared to a "mourning juju man." Can he really work the magic necessary to fly his people home? The poem ends with the cry to Daedalus, the same cry used in the title and interspersed with the narrative. It is a final declaration of anguish and desire.

See **ALLUSION** Handbook of Literary Terms

Ithaca[1]

C.P. Cavafy Translated by Rae Dalven

When you start on your journey to Ithaca,
then pray that the road is long,
full of adventure, full of knowledge.
Do not fear the Lestrygonians
and the Cyclopes and the angry Poseidon.[2]
You will never meet such as these on your path,
if your thoughts remain lofty, if a fine
emotion touches your body and your spirit.
You will never meet the Lestrygonians,
the Cyclopes and the fierce Poseidon,
if you do not carry them within your soul,
if your soul does not raise them up before you.

Then pray that the road is long.
That the summer mornings are many,
that you will enter ports seen for the first time
with such pleasure, with such joy!
Stop at Phoenician[3] markets,
and purchase fine merchandise,
mother-of-pearl and corals, amber and ebony,
and pleasurable perfumes of all kinds,
buy as many pleasurable perfumes as you can;
visit hosts of Egyptian cities,
to learn and learn from those who have knowledge.

(Continued)

1. ***Ithaca*** (ith′ə kə), a small island west of Greece, the legendary home of Ulysses, hero of Greek myth.
2. ***Lestrygonians . . . Poseidon.*** The Lestrygonians (les tri gō′nē ənz) were a tribe of barbarians; the Cyclopes (sī klō′pēz) a tribe of one-eyed, man-eating giants. Both had to be overcome by Ulysses and his men on their journey home to Ithaca. Poseidon (pə sīd′n), Greek god of the sea, had been angered by Ulysses. The angry Poseidon plagued him with storm, shipwreck, and other natural disasters. These and other adventures of Ulysses during his return voyage to Ithaca are described in *The Odyssey* by the Greek poet Homer (eighth century, B.C.)
3. ***Phoenician*** (fə nish′ən), of or having to do with Phoenicia, an ancient country on the Mediterranean, famous for its traders.

Cavafy (kä vä′fē).

Always keep Ithaca fixed in your mind.
To arrive there is your ultimate goal.
But do not hurry the voyage at all.
It is better to let it last for long years;
and even to anchor at the isle when you are old,
rich with all that you have gained on the way,
not expecting that Ithaca will offer you riches.

Ithaca has given you the beautiful voyage.
Without her you would never have taken the road.
But she has nothing more to give you.

And if you find her poor, Ithaca has not defrauded you.
With the great wisdom you have gained, with so much experience,
you must surely have understood by then what Ithacas mean.

Discussion

Pole Vault

1. Contrast the description of the run (line 1) with the description of the flight (line 2).

2. (a) What is a *confrontation?* **(b)** Who is confronting what?

3. What is the "glass whip"? Do you think this is an effective description? Explain.

4. Reread the descriptions of the fall (line 9) and the air (line 10). Do you think these descriptions are, in the context of the poem, effective? Explain.

5. In this poem, what is the goal? What is the destination?

Daybreak in Alabama

1. Name some of the things that the speaker plans to put into his music.

2. "Daybreak in Alabama" was written in the first half of the twentieth century. What kind of daybreak does the speaker mean?

Mr. Artesian's Conscientiousness

1. Is this poem best described by the word *tragic, silly,* or *humorous?*

2. A *pun* is a play on words often done for humorous effect. One type of pun is the using of words alike or nearly alike in sound but different in meaning. Using footnote 2 as a guide, pronounce *vertigo.* Then, explain the pun found in the last three lines of the poem.

3. (a) Why might the poet have chosen to name his character *Mr. Artesian?* (Review footnote 1, if necessary.) **(b)** Note the punctuation in the poem, especially that in lines 7–26. What is the effect of this punctuation? (Rereading the poem aloud will be helpful to you in answering.)

O Daedalus, Fly Away Home

1. What is the cause of the weariness mentioned in lines 7 and 19?

2. In Greek legend, Daedalus fashioned wings for himself and his son from feathers and wax. In this poem, what would be used to make the wings?

Ithaca

1. (a) According to the narrator, what will the journey to Ithaca offer? **(b)** Why should the traveler "pray that the road is long" (line 2)?

2. (a) Why is there no need to fear "the Lestrygonians and the Cyclopes and the angry Poseidon"? **(b)** What might they symbolize? Explain your answer.

3. Is Ithaca more desirable as a goal or as a destination? Explain.

Application

Simile

In describing the music he plans to write, the narrator in "Daybreak in Alabama" says that it will rise from the ground "like a swamp mist" and descend from the heavens "like soft dew." Comparisons such as these, comparisons that use "like" or "as," are called *similes.*

1. What things are being compared in line 19?

2. Do you think the simile in line 19 is effective? Explain.

Satire

1. (a) In "Mr. Artesian's Conscientiousness," what is Mr. Artesian's goal? **(b)** What is his destination?

2. In this poem, who and/or what is being satirized?

Metaphor

1. "O Daedalus, Fly Away Home" contains a number of metaphors that use the word *night.* In what ways is the Georgia night like an African juju man?

2. (a) In the metaphor in line 18, what is the effect of the word *mourning?* **(b)** In what way is this metaphor different from the ones used earlier in the poem?

Allusion

By alluding to the adventures of Ulysses on his way home to Ithaca, the poet makes a comparison between that legendary journey and the journey described in the poem, "Ithaca." In what ways are these journeys alike? In what ways are they different? (You may wish to reread the footnotes provided with the poem before answering.)

Grace Butcher 1934–

A former United States track champion, Grace Butcher teaches English at Kent State University in Ohio. She is also an active runner.

Langston Hughes 1902–1967

Langston Hughes had published a poem and a play by the time he was nineteen. That poem, "The Negro Speaks of Rivers," remains a favorite today. A prolific writer of poems, plays, short stories, and history, Hughes chose to use his talents "to explain and illuminate" the condition of black people in America.

Ogden Nash 1902–1971

Ogden Nash attended Harvard University; later he moved to New York City and to the editorial staff of *The New Yorker.* A writer whose wit and gift for satire has entertained several generations of readers, Nash is also known for his ability to create unlikely and highly amusing rhymes.

Robert Hayden 1913–1980

Robert Hayden believed that "the best artists—the great artists—are always on the side of justice and truth and human freedom. . . ." Hayden's own poetry, while often speaking of the black experience in the United States, also deals with these universal and timeless qualities. Recognition of Hayden's work won him numerous honors, including the 1975 Fellowship of the Academy of American Poets and an appointment as Consultant in Poetry to the Library of Congress.

C. P. Cavafy 1863–1933

Constantine P. Cavafy, a Greek poet who spent most of his life in Alexandria, Egypt, is considered to be among the greatest poets of modern Greece.

Assertions

When we assert ourselves, we tell where we stand; we stand up to be counted; we declare that we are unique, that we are special.

See **IMAGERY** Handbook of Literary Terms

Jenny Joseph

When I am an old woman I shall wear purple
With a red hat which doesn't go, and doesn't suit me,
And I shall spend my pension on brandy and summer gloves
And satin sandals, and say we've no money for butter.
I shall sit down on the pavement when I'm tired
And gobble up samples in shops and press alarm bells
And run my stick along the public railings
And make up for the sobriety of my youth.
I shall go out in my slippers in the rain
And pick the flowers in other people's gardens
And learn to spit.

You can wear terrible shirts and grow more fat
And eat three pounds of sausages at a go
Or only bread and pickle for a week
And hoard pens and pencils and beermats and things in boxes.

But now we must have clothes that keep us dry
And pay our rent and not swear in the street
And set a good example for the children.
We will have friends to dinner and read the papers.
But maybe I ought to practise a little now?
So people who know me are not too shocked and surprised
When suddenly I am old and start to wear purple.

See **RHYME** and **RHYTHM** Handbook of Literary Terms

The Lamentation of the Old Pensioner[1]

William Butler Yeats

Although I shelter from the rain
Under a broken tree,
My chair was nearest to the fire
In every company
That talked of love or politics,
Ere Time transfigured me.

Though lads are making pikes[2] again
For some conspiracy,
And crazy rascals rage their fill
At human tyranny,
My contemplations are of Time
That has transfigured me.

There's not a woman turns her face
Upon a broken tree,
And yet the beauties that I loved
Are in my memory;
I spit into the face of Time
That has transfigured me.

---

1. ***pensioner*** (pen′shə nər), retired person living on a pension, a monthly payment from a company or the government.
2. ***pikes,*** weapons.

Yeats (yāts).

Birdfoot's Grampa

Joseph Bruchac III

The old man
must have stopped our car
two dozen times to climb out
and gather into his hands
the small toads blinded
by our lights and leaping,
live drops of rain.

The rain was falling,
a mist about his white hair
and I kept saying
you can't save them all,
accept it, get back in
we've got places to go.

But, leathery hands full
of wet brown life,
knee deep in the summer
roadside grass,
he just smiled and said
they have places to go to
too.

Bruchac (brü′chak).

Making a Fist

Naomi Shihab Nye

For the first time, on the road north of Tampico,[1]
I felt the life sliding out of me,
a drum in the desert, harder and harder to hear.
I was seven, I lay in the car
watching palm trees swirl a sickening pattern past the glass.
My stomach was a melon split wide inside my skin.

"How do you know if you are going to die?"
I begged my mother.
We had been traveling for days.
With strange confidence she answered,
"When you can no longer make a fist."

Years later I smile to think of that journey,
the borders we must cross separately,
stamped with our unanswerable woes.
I who did not die, who am still living,
still lying in the backseat behind all my questions,
clenching and opening one small hand.

---

1. ***Tampico*** (tam pē′kō), seaport in E Mexico.

Shihab (shē′hab).

A Man

Nina Cassian

Translated by
Roy MacGregor-Hastie

While fighting for his country, he lost an arm
and was suddenly afraid:
"From now on, I shall only be able to do things by halves.
I shall reap half a harvest.
I shall be able to play either the tune
or the accompaniment on the piano,
but never both parts together.
I shall be able to bang with only one fist
on doors, and worst of all
I shall only be able to half hold
my love close to me.
There will be things I cannot do at all,
applaud for example,
at shows where everyone applauds."

From that moment on, he set himself to do everything with
twice as much enthusiasm.
And where the arm had been torn away
a wing grew.

"A Man" by Nina Cassian, *Anthology of Contemporary Romanian Poetry*. Edited, translated, and with an introduction by Roy MacGregor-Hastie. Published by Peter Owen, London. Reprinted by permission.

Discussion

Warning

1. (a) What kind of woman does the speaker want to be when she grows old? **(b)** What kind of person is she now? **(c)** Why must she wait until she is old before making the change?

2. Which type person does the speaker prefer—the kind she is now or the kind she will become? How do you know?

4. In the third stanza, the speaker refers to "borders we must cross" alone and describes herself "still lying in the backseat . . . clenching and opening one small hand." **(a)** To what earlier events do these refer? **(b)** What additional significance are they given in this stanza?

The Lamentation of the Old Pensioner

1. Who is speaking in the poem?

2. (a) What does *transfigured* mean? **(b)** In what sense has the man been transfigured? **(c)** Where does he lay the blame?

3. The old man mourns the loss of a number of things. What are some of these?

4. With what emotion do you think the last two lines of the poem should be read? Why?

Birdfoot's Grampa

1. Describe the setting of the poem.

2. (a) What kind of man is Birdfoot's grampa? **(b)** In what ways is he different from the speaker?

3. (a) If you were in the car when the discussion began, with whom would you side—the speaker or Birdfoot's grampa? **(b)** Would you feel any different at the end of the poem? Explain.

Making a Fist

1. Do you think this poem ends on an optimistic or a pessimistic note? Explain.

2. (a) What event does the speaker describe in the first two stanzas? **(b)** When did it take place?

3. In the first two stanzas, what images help you to experience the child's feelings? What metaphors?

A Man

1. What is the initial reaction of the man upon losing an arm?

2. (a) Is the last line of the poem literal or metaphoric? Explain. **(b)** Is Cassian saying something about the way we should live our lives? If so, what?

3. Is the title, "A Man," a good title? Explain.

4. Do you think this man reacted the way most humans would react in similar circumstances? Explain.

Application

Imagery

Imagery is the representation in words of sense experience: what can be seen, heard, touched, tasted, smelled, as well as what can be felt internally.

1. Find several images used to describe the speaker in "Warning" as she will be when she grows old. To what senses do they appeal?

2. Find images used to describe the speaker as she is now. In what ways are these images different from those discussed in question 1?

Rhyme and Rhythm

Rhyme and rhythm are two of the most common and easily recognized elements in poetry. Rhyme is the repetition of word-ending sounds. When sounds are repeated at the ends of lines of poetry, they are arranged in a pattern within the poem called a rhyme scheme. Rhythm is the arrangement of stressed and unstressed sounds. In some poems, rhyme and rhythm fall into fairly regular patterns that are easy to identify. In others, the use that is made of the elements will be less easy to see. As you discuss the rhyme and rhythm of poems in this unit, you might occasionally review the two articles, *rhyme* and *rhythm,* in the Handbook of Literary Terms.

1. Does "The Lamentation of the Old Pensioner" have a regular pattern of end rhyme? If so, what is this rhyme scheme?

2. (a) Is the rhythm regular or irregular? Explain. **(b)** What does the rhythm of the lines suggest to you about the person who is speaking them?

Jenny Joseph 1932–

Born in England, Joseph worked as a newspaper reporter, lived in Rhodesia and South Africa, and later ran a pub. *The Unlooked for Season* is one of her poetry collections.

William Butler Yeats 1865–1939

William Butler Yeats was born in Dublin of Anglo-Irish parents. His long and productive career as writer left us with some of the best-loved poetry of modern times. Yeats was recipient of the Nobel Prize for Literature in 1923.

Joseph Bruchac III 1942–

Joseph Bruchac III is of mixed Slovak, English, and Native American (Abenaki) descent. Bruchac has taught creative writing and poetry to students of all ages; he has established creative writing programs for inmates of several prisons and has edited a compilation of their work, *The Light from Another Country.* His own poems and stories have been published in the United States and translated into numerous foreign languages. His writings include *The Poetry of Pop, Translator's Son, The Dream of Jesse Brown,* and *Other Poems.*

Naomi Shihab Nye 1952–

In reply to a letter from a reader who also "makes a fist" in order to "cross borders," Naomi Shihab Nye writes, "It is comforting to know we are never alone." She has published several books of poetry, including *Eye-to-Eye* (1978), *Different Ways to Pray* (1980), and *Hugging the Jukebox* (1982).

Nina Cassian 1924–

Nina Cassian, an artist and composer as well as a poet, was born in Galati, Romania. Since her first volume of poetry, *A One-to-One Scale,* appeared in 1948, she has published numerous books. She has also translated the works of many noted authors and received prizes for her children's books.

Tributes

Sometimes the poet must pay tribute, must tell what it is that fires the deep admiration, or keeps a memory vivid, or creates an overwhelming sense of appreciation.

See **FIGURATIVE LANGUAGE** Handbook of Literary Terms

Miss Rosie

Lucille Clifton

When I watch you
wrapped up like garbage
sitting, surrounded by the smell
of too old potato peels
or
when I watch you
in your old man's shoes
with the little toe cut out
sitting, waiting for your mind
like next week's grocery
I say
when I watch you
you wet brown bag of a woman
who used to be the best looking gal in Georgia
used to be called the Georgia Rose
I stand up
through your destruction
I stand up

See **ASSONANCE** and **CONSONANCE** Handbook of Literary Terms

The Bean Eaters

Gwendolyn Brooks

They eat beans mostly, this old yellow pair.
Dinner is a casual affair.
Plain chipware on a plain and creaking wood,
Tin flatware.

Two who are Mostly Good.
Two who have lived their day,
But keep on putting on their clothes
And putting things away.

And remembering . . .
Remembering, with twinklings and twinges,
As they lean over the beans in their rented back room that is full of beads and receipts and dolls and cloths, tobacco crumbs, vases and fringes.

See **HYPERBOLE** Handbook of Literary Terms

The Funeral

Gordon Parks

After many snows I was home again.
Time had whittled down to mere hills
The great mountains of my childhood.
Raging rivers I once swam trickled now
like gentle streams.
And the wide road curving on to China or
Kansas City or perhaps Calcutta,
Had withered to a crooked path of dust
Ending abruptly at the county burying ground.
Only the giant who was my father
remained the same.
A hundred strong men strained beneath his coffin
When they bore him to his grave.

The Courage That My Mother Had

Edna St. Vincent Millay

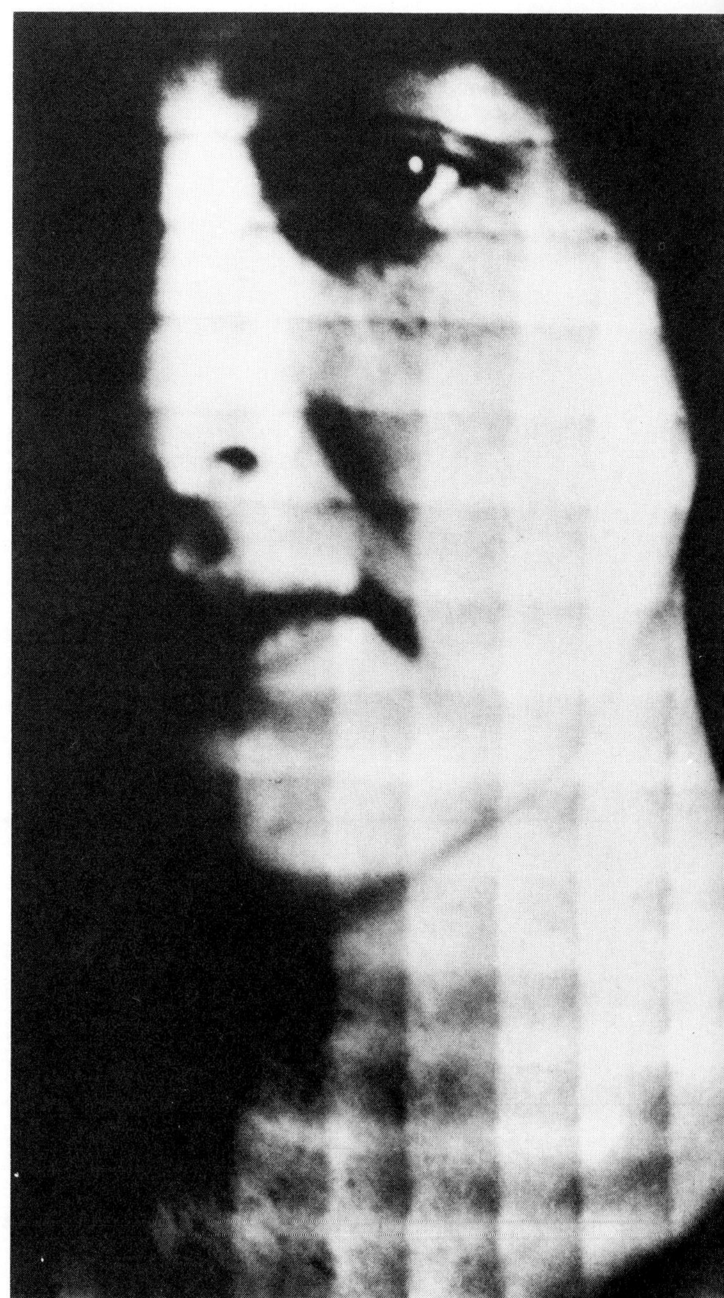

The courage that my mother had
Went with her, and is with her still:
Rock from New England quarried;
Now granite in a granite hill.

The golden brooch my mother wore
She left behind for me to wear;
I have no thing I treasure more:
Yet, it is something I could spare.

Oh, if instead she'd left to me
The thing she took into the grave!—
That courage like a rock, which she
Has no more need of, and I have.

Discussion

Miss Rosie

1. (a) What are the two similes in this poem? **(b)** Are they appropriate or inappropriate comparisons? Why?

2. What points in Miss Rosie's life do the "wet brown bag of a woman" and "the Georgia Rose" represent? What can the reader infer about the years between?

3. One can stand up *to* something or someone, stand up out of honor or respect, stand up *for* something, and stand up simply to get on with something. In what sense do you think the speaker "stands up" through Miss Rosie's destruction?

The Bean Eaters

1. What do the following details add—through what they picture and what the words suggest—to this portrait of two lives: **(a)** "They eat beans mostly"; **(b)** creaking wood, tin flatware; **(c)** rented back room; **(d)** receipts; **(e)** dolls; **(f)** tobacco crumbs?

2. (a) How might the reader's feelings toward these two have been affected if line 5 had described them as "Always Good"? **(b)** What kinds of memories does the phrase "twinklings and twinges" suggest?

The Funeral

1. (a) When the speaker returns home after many years, he finds his perception of the area where he grew up to be very different from his view of it when he was a child. In what ways has it changed? **(b)** Only one thing has not changed. What is that?

2. The speaker does not specify any of his father's characteristics, but it is possible to speculate about what the man was like. How would you describe him?

The Courage That My Mother Had

1. (a) What two of her mother's possessions does the poet mention? **(b)** What value does she place on each?

2. Edna St. Vincent Millay uses both a metaphor and a simile to describe her mother's courage. In what lines do you find these? To what does each compare the courage?

3. (a) What is the literal meaning of line 4? **(b)** In what ways is it appropriate figurative language as well?

Application

Figurative Language

1. In lines 1–4 of "Miss Rosie," to what is Miss Rosie compared?

2. What does the comparison in lines 9 and 10 indicate about Miss Rosie's state of mind and her source of food?

3. What does the comparison to "a wet brown bag" tell you about Miss Rosie? In what way does this comparison reinforce the picture presented in the first four lines?

Assonance and Consonance

1. Note that line 1 of "The Bean Eaters" contains two examples of assonance: the repetition of the *ea* sound in *eat* and *beans,* and the ō sound in *old* and *yellow.* Find other examples of assonance in the poem.

2. (a) At what point in the poem does the emphasis on assonance stop and the emphasis on consonance begin? **(b)** In what ways is this change of sound tied to a change of thought?

Hyperbole

Gordon Parks uses hyperbole, or overstatement, when he says "a hundred strong men strained beneath his coffin." Why might the poet have chosen to use hyperbole in this particular case?

Lucille Clifton 1936–

Lucille Clifton was born Thelma Lucille Sayles in Depew, a community outside Buffalo, New York. The poet Robert Hayden recognized and encouraged her talent. Clifton has written poetry, short stories, children's books, and *Generations,* an account that traces her family from the present day back to the roots of her African heritage.

Gwendolyn Brooks 1917–

Gwendolyn Brooks grew up in Chicago, where she still lives. She published her first collection of poems, *A Street in Bronzeville,* in 1945. In addition to a novel, *Maud Martha,* she has written several volumes of poetry, one of which, *Annie Allen,* earned a 1950 Pulitzer Prize. In 1968 Gwendolyn Brooks was named Poet Laureate of Illinois.

Gordon Parks 1912–

Creative in more than one area, Parks has been a photographer for *Life,* a movie producer and director, as well as a writer. His works include *The Learning Tree, A Choice of Weapons, A Poet and His Camera,* and *Moments Without Proper Names.*

Edna St. Vincent Millay 1892–1950

Edna St. Vincent Millay was born in Rockland, Maine. Her first poem, "Renascence," was published when she was only nineteen. From the 1920s until her death in 1950, she wrote many volumes of poetry and several verse plays. Her collection of poems, *The Harp-Weaver,* won the 1923 Pulitzer Prize.

Comment: Reading Poetry Aloud

The same skills you use in understanding prose apply to understanding poetry. One difference between the two forms, however, is that most poetry is intended for the ear as well as for the eye. Not until you are able to read poetry aloud and enjoy hearing it read aloud can you really appreciate all that poetry has to offer.

Characteristics of poetry such as figures of speech, sensory imagery, rhythm, and rhyme become more forceful when they are heard. This is *why* poetry should be read aloud. But *how* should it be read?

Poetry should be read aloud in a way that brings out the meaning and feeling intended by the poet. Look at the four poems in this grouping. They are different in appearance; the length of their lines varies; they have different themes; they have different rhythms. Before you can effectively read any one of these poems aloud, you must know what mood the poet intended and what the lines mean. In other words, you must have knowledge of what the poet is saying. Your voice must then reflect what is appropriate to the meaning of the words. If the meaning of one line is not completed until the next line, you would not pause at the end of the first line any more than you would say, "I am going (pause) downtown." In reading "Miss Rosie," you would not read ". . . surrounded by the smell (pause) of too old potato peels" simply because you come to the end of a line.

Now look at "The Courage That My Mother

Had." In the first two stanzas, note the formal punctuation—colons and semicolons—and the fact that each stanza is made up of a single sentence. Read these stanzas aloud, noting how the punctuation contributes to the seriousness and the formality of the tone. Then look at the last stanza—the use of the less formal dash, the emotion conveyed by combining it with the exclamation point. In what ways does this change in punctuation suggest a change in the speaker's tone?

Look back at "Mr. Artesian's Conscientiousness." Why would this poem be read very differently from "The Courage That My Mother Had"?

"The Funeral" is a good poem to practice reading aloud. The ideas are easy to follow; the emphasis falls naturally on the important words.

As you study a poem, take time to read it aloud. A careful reading, attention to details such as word choice, tone, punctuation, and a little practice will allow you to communicate the meaning.

Legacies

Legacies are both what is left to us and what we pass on to those who come after. Whether a legacy be material or spiritual, it is seldom viewed with indifference.

Legacies

Nikki Giovanni

her grandmother called her from the playground
    "yes, ma'am"
    "i want chu to learn how to make rolls," said the old
woman proudly
but the little girl didn't want
to learn how because she knew
even if she couldn't say it that
that would mean when the old one died she would be less
dependent on her spirit so
she said
    "i don't want to know how to make no rolls"
with her lips poked out
and the old woman wiped her hands on
her apron saying "lord
    these children"
and neither of them ever
said what they meant
and i guess nobody ever does

See **ALLITERATION** Handbook of Literary Terms

Puritan Sonnet[1]

Elinor Wylie

Down to the Puritan marrow of my bones
There's something in this richness that I hate.
I love the look, austere, immaculate,
Of landscapes drawn in pearly monotones.
There's something in my very blood that owns
Bare hills, cold silver on a sky of slate,
A thread of water, churned to milky spate[2]
Streaming through slanted pastures fenced with stones.

I love those skies, thin blue or snowy gray.
Those fields sparse-planted, rendering meager sheaves;
That spring, briefer than apple-blossom's breath,
Summer, so much too beautiful to stay,
Swift autumn, like a bonfire of leaves,
And sleepy winter, like the sleep of death.

---

1. ***sonnet*** (son′it), a poem having fourteen lines and a prescribed pattern of rhythm and rhyme.
2. ***spate*** (spāt), a sudden flood, an outburst.

The Mouth of the Hudson

Robert Lowell

(For Esther Brooks)

A single man stands like a bird-watcher,
and scuffles the pepper and salt snow
from a discarded, gray
Westinghouse Electric cable drum.
He cannot discover America by counting
the chains of condemned freight trains
from thirty states. They jolt and jar
and junk in the siding below him.
He has trouble with his balance.
His eyes drop,
and he drifts with the wild ice
ticking seaward down the Hudson,
like the blank sides of a jig-saw puzzle.

The ice ticks seaward like a clock.
A Negro toasts
wheat-seeds over the coke-fumes
of a punctured barrel.
Chemical air
sweeps in from New Jersey,
and smells of coffee.

Across the river,
ledges of suburban factories tan
in the sulphur-yellow sun
of the unforgivable landscape.

Comment: On "The Mouth of the Hudson"

Through the ages poets have written in celebration of the beauty of particular times, seasons, and places. On occasion, poets may also write of places considered to be spoiled. At such times they take the human race to task for destroying, or at least having little regard for, the world around them. For example, the English poet William Blake (1757–1827), who wrote countless poems in praise of the beauty of his homeland, also was known to condemn the condition—both physical and spiritual—of the city of London. More and more modern poets have found reason to add their voices to such protest. In "The Mouth of the Hudson," the American poet Robert Lowell speaks out.

This poem does not tell a story; rather, it conveys Lowell's impression of a particular place at a particular time. What does the poet see? In Lowell's bleak landscape, a lone man stands looking out over the Hudson River, where it empties itself into the sea. Mixed with soot and dirt, the fallen snow has acquired the color of "pepper and salt." On a railroad siding below him are "condemned freight trains from thirty states" that "jolt and jar and junk," going nowhere, rusting in their tracks. Note how the alliteration as well as the choppy rhythm of the one-syllable words helps to create this picture of the freight trains. The poem has no regular pattern of end rhyme or of rhythm, but it does rely on the devices of poetry in creating its images.

The reference to discovering America (line 5) might suggest several ideas to the reader. First, the Hudson River was a scene of early explorations by Europeans on the North American continent. The logs of many sailing ships referred to the beauty of this waterway. Later, after the United States was established, to "discover America" was the ambition of many young writers as they set out to explore and celebrate their country. Now, the speaker finds little there to celebrate or to inspire.

The solitary observer watches the ice move with the current as the river flows into the sea. Two similes convey the coldness and the hopelessness of the scene. In the current, chunks of ice make a ticking sound as they touch. Seen from above, the ice looks like pieces of a jigsaw puzzle, but a puzzle with the pieces lying facedown: There is no pattern in them, no sense to be found in their movement. They "tick like a clock." Might the poet be suggesting that time is running out? Such thoughts seem in keeping with the bleakness of the picture being painted.

Even the man toasting wheat seeds uses a fuel that pollutes. From across the river in New Jersey comes additional pollution. Note here the appeal to the sense of smell. Most readers familiar with the odor described will find the description surprisingly accurate.

The final image lifts readers' eyes to the New Jersey shore. The description of this view is almost spat out in a heavily accented rhythm that becomes apparent when the poem is read aloud. When the poem has ended, the reader is left with questions, questions that are all too readily answered: Who is not to be forgiven? Whom does the poet blame? How will future generations view the legacy left them at the mouth of the Hudson?

See **IRONY** Handbook of Literary Terms

My Mother, Who Came from China, Where She Never Saw Snow

Laureen Mar

In the huge, rectangular room, the ceiling
a machinery of pipes and fluorescent lights,
ten rows of women hunch over machines,
their knees pressing against pedals
and hands pushing the shiny fabric thick as tongues
through metal and thread.
My mother bends her head to one of these machines.
Her hair is coarse and wiry, black as burnt scrub.
She wears glasses to shield her intense eyes.
A cone of orange thread spins. Around her,
talk flutters harshly in Toisan wah.[1]
Chemical stings. She pushes cloth
through a pounding needle, under, around, and out,
breaks thread with a snap against fingerbone, tooth.
Sleeve after sleeve, sleeve.
It is easy. The same piece.
For eight or nine hours, sixteen bundles maybe,
250 sleeves to ski coats, all the same.
It is easy, only once she's run the needle
through her hand. She earns money
by each piece, on a good day,
thirty dollars. Twenty-four years.
It is frightening how fast she works.
She and the women who were taught sewing
terms in English as Second Language.
Dull thunder passes through their fingers.

---

1. ***Toisan wah*** (toi′sän′ wä), a Chinese dialect.

In the Plaza We Walk

Nephtalí De León

In the plaza we walk
under the Mexican moon
full of tangerine smells.

A cart pulls over
full of the fruit
full of the moon
        and the lonely star.

So we buy two
but he says "three for a peso"
        but we buy two.

Tangerines peeled
            we walk
        hand in hand
        spitting the seeds
            for future tangerines
        and more lovers to be.

In the plaza we walk
        under tangerine moons.

"In the Plaza We Walk" by Nephtalí De León in *Caracol*, June 1975. Reprinted by permission of the author.

Keeping Hair

Ramona C. Wilson

My grandmother had braids
at the thickest, pencil wide
held with bright wool
cut from her bed shawl.
No teeth left but white hair
combed and wet carefully
early each morning.
The small wild plants found among stones
on the windy and brown plateaus
revealed their secrets to her hand
and yielded to her cooking pots.
She made a sweet amber water
from willows,
boiling the life out
to pour onto her old head.
"It will keep your hair."
She bathed my head, once
rain water not sweeter.
The thought that once
when I was so very young
her work-bent hands
very gently and smoothly
washed my hair in willows
may also keep my heart.

Discussion

Legacies

1. Why do you think the grandmother speaks *proudly* (line 4)?

2. (a) How does the girl respond to the grandmother's offer? **(b)** What does this response *not* suggest about how the girl is really feeling? Before answering, read lines 5, 6, 8, 9 (skip line 7) to yourself.

3. Why might the girl want to be dependent, or closely tied to, her grandmother's spirit after the older woman has died?

4. Do you agree with the last line of the poem? Explain.

Puritan Sonnet

1. Reread lines 1–2. Is the speaker where she wishes to be? How do you know?

2. (a) What is a Puritan? **(b)** Where in the United States did most Puritans settle? **(c)** What is the speaker's legacy from Puritan ancestors?

3. (a) What images does the speaker use to describe the land that she loves? **(b)** What season does she seem to like best? Explain.

The Mouth of the Hudson

1. The word *unforgivable* ("not deserving forgiveness") is usually applied to a person's behavior. *(His not calling home all summer is unforgivable.)* As it is used in the poem, does the word apply to the landscape itself? to someone or something else? Explain your answer.

2. (a) Where is the speaker? **(b)** What time of year is it? **(c)** What is the speaker doing?

3. (a) What leads the speaker to describe the snow as "pepper and salt snow." **(b)** Find other images that describe what the speaker sees.

My Mother, Who Came from China . . .

1. Describe the mother's work. Where does she work? For how many years has she worked there?

2. How does the speaker feel about her mother and the other women? Use as many adjectives as you think necessary to describe her feelings.

In the Plaza We Walk

1. Why does the couple buy only two tangerines?

2. What images help convey the feeling of the speaker and his impression of the evening?

3. What "legacy" do the lovers leave?

Keeping Hair

1. What does the grandmother use to wash her hair? Why? (Remember that one meaning of *keep* is "to preserve.")

2. (a) According to the speaker, what does her memory of having her hair washed "in willows" do? **(b)** Is she speaking literally or figuratively? Explain.

Application

Alliteration

Alliteration is the repetition of beginning sounds of words within a poem.

1. Find examples of alliteration in "Puritan Sonnet."

2. What effect does the use of alliteration have on you as you read or hear the poem read aloud?

Irony

1. Explain the irony in lines 19–20 of "My Mother, Who Came from China . . ."

2. Now that you have read and discussed the poem, look again at the title. Why might it be considered ironic?

Composition

Suppose that you are in your ninetieth year and are drawing up your will. Because you have more time than money, you decide to leave to your one great-grandchild advice based on the wisdom gained during your long life. After some consideration, you decide on the single most important piece of advice you can offer.

Write a two-page paper to be incorporated into your will. Offer the advice, explain how you gained the knowledge that allows you to speak with authority, and tell the ways you think it will help your descendant.

Nikki Giovanni 1943–

After graduating in 1967 from Fisk University, Nikki Giovanni received a Ford Foundation Grant that enabled her to publish her first book of poetry, *Black Feeling, Black Talk.* Since that time she has published several more collections of poems, made a recording on which she reads her poems to the accompaniment of gospel music, and received numerous awards for her work.

Elinor Wylie 1885–1928

Elinor Wylie spent much of her childhood in Washington, D.C., where her father served as Assistant Attorney General under Theodore Roosevelt. As an adult, she lived in New York City. Her work is represented in most collections of twentieth-century poetry of the United States.

Robert Lowell 1917–1977

Robert Lowell was raised in Boston and educated at Harvard and at Kenyon College in Ohio. His poetry was received with praise and enthusiasm from the time he began publishing. In 1947 he received a Pulitzer Prize, in 1960 a National Book Award, and in 1962 the Bollingen Translation Prize. He also served as Consultant in Poetry to the Library of Congress.

Laureen Mar 1953–

Laureen Mar was born in Seattle. She pursued her Master of Fine Arts degree at Columbia University, where she specialized in creative writing. Her poetry has appeared in *Mademoiselle, Greenfield Review, Asian American Women Writers,* and *Intro 7.*

Nephtalí De León 1945–

Nephtalí De León was born in Laredo, Texas, and raised in various farm labor camps. He has founded a newspaper, published books of stories, poems, and plays, and written books for children. His works include *Chicanos: Our Background and Our Pride,* and *Poems with Illustrated Woodcuts.*

Ramona C. Wilson 1945–

Ramona C. Wilson, a member of the Colville tribe, was born in Washington. Her poems have been published in a number of collections, including *Voices from Wah-Kon-tah, Voices of the Rainbow,* and *American Indian Women Writers.*

Stories

Perhaps these poems are the most popular kind. After all, everybody loves a story.

See **MOOD** Handbook of Literary Terms

The Skater of Ghost Lake

William Rose Benét

Ghost Lake's a dark lake, a deep lake and cold:
Ice black as ebony, frostily scrolled;
Far in its shadows a faint sound whirrs;
Steep stand the sentineled deep, dark firs.

A brisk sound, a swift sound, a ring-tinkle-ring;
Flit-flit—a shadow, with a stoop and a swing,
Flies from a shadow through the crackling cold.
Ghost Lake's a deep lake, a dark lake and old!

Leaning and leaning, with a stride and a stride,
Hands locked behind him, scarf blowing wide,
Jeremy Randall skates, skates late,
Star for a candle, moon for a mate.

Black is the clear glass now that he glides,
Crisp is the whisper of long lean strides,
Swift is his swaying—but pricked ears hark.
None comes to Ghost Lake late after dark!

Cecily only—yes, it is she!
Stealing to Ghost Lake, tree after tree,
Kneeling in snow by the still lake side,
Rising with feet winged, gleaming, to glide.

Dust of the ice swirls. Here is his hand.
Brilliant his eyes burn. Now, as was planned,
Arm across arm twined, laced to his side,
Out on the dark lake lightly they glide.

Dance of the dim moon, a rhythmical reel,
A swaying, a swift tune—skurr of the steel;
Moon for a candle, maid for a mate,
Jeremy Randall skates, skates late.

Black as if lacquered the wide lake lies;
Breath is a frost-fume, eyes seek eyes;
Souls are a sword-edge tasting the cold.
Ghost Lake's a deep lake, a dark lake and old!

Benét (bə nā′).

Far in the shadows hear faintly begin
Like a string pluck-plucked of a violin,
Muffled in mist on the lake's far bound,
Swifter and swifter, a low singing sound!

Far in the shadows and faint on the verge
Of blue cloudy moonlight, see it emerge,
Flit-flit—a phantom, with a stoop and a
swing . . .
Ah, it's a night bird, burdened of wing!

Pressed close to Jeremy, laced to his side,
Cecily Culver, dizzy you glide.
Jeremy Randall sweepingly veers
Out on the dark ice far from the piers.

"Jeremy!" "Sweetheart?" "What do you fear?"
"Nothing, my darling—nothing is here!"
"Jeremy?" "Sweetheart?" "What do you flee?"
"Something—I know not; something I see!"

Swayed to a swift stride, brisker of pace,
Leaning and leaning, they race and they race;
Ever that whirring, that crisp sound thin
Like a string pluck-plucked of a violin;

Ever that swifter and low singing sound
Sweeping behind them, winding them round;
Gasp of their breath now that chill flakes fret:
Ice black as ebony—blacker—like jet!

Ice shooting fangs forth—sudden like spears;
Crackling of lightning—a roar in their ears!
Shadowy, a phantom swerves off from its
prey . . .
No, it's a night bird flit-flits away!

Low-winging moth-owl, home to your sleep!
Ghost Lake's a still lake, a cold lake and deep.
Faint in its shadows a far sound whirrs.
Black stand the ranks of its sentinel firs.

Mungojerrie and Rumpelteazer

T. S. Eliot

Mungojerrie and Rumpelteazer were a very notorious couple of cats.
As knockabout clowns, quick-change comedians, tight-rope walkers and acrobats
They had an extensive reputation. They made their home in Victoria Grove[1]——
That was merely their centre of operation, for they were incurably given to rove.
They were very well known in Cornwall Gardens, in Launceston Place and in Kensington Square——
They had really a little more reputation than a couple of cats can very well bear.

---

1. ***Victoria Grove.*** This and all other place names are in or around London.

If the area window was found ajar
And the basement looked like a field of war,
If a tile or two came loose on the roof,
Which presently ceased to be waterproof,
If the drawers were pulled out from the bedroom chests,
And you couldn't find one of your winter vests,
Or after supper one of the girls
Suddenly missed her Woolworth pearls:
Then the family would say: "It's that horrible cat!
It was Mungojerrie—or Rumpelteazer!"—And most of the time they left it at that.

Mungojerrie and Rumpelteazer had a very unusual gift of the gab.
They were highly efficient cat-burglars as well, and remarkably smart at a smash-and-grab.
They made their home in Victoria Grove. They had no regular occupation.
They were plausible fellows, and liked to engage a friendly policeman in conversation.

When the family assembled for Sunday dinner,
With their minds made up that they wouldn't get thinner
On Argentine joint,[2] potatoes and greens,
And the cook would appear from behind the scenes
And say in a voice that was broken with sorrow:
"I'm afraid you must wait and have dinner *tomorrow!*
For the joint has gone from the oven—like that!"
Then the family would say: "It's that horrible cat!
It was Mungojerrie—or Rumpelteazer!"—And most of the time they left it at that.

Mungojerrie and Rumpelteazer had a wonderful way of working together.
And some of the time you would say it was luck, and some of the time you would say it was weather.
They would go through the house like a hurricane, and no sober person could take his oath
Was it Mungojerrie—or Rumpelteazer? or could you have sworn that it mightn't be both?

(Continued)

2. ***Argentine joint*** (är′jən tīn), beef roast from Argentina.

And when you heard a dining-room smash
Or up from the pantry there came a loud crash
Or down from the library came a loud *ping*
From a vase which was commonly said to be Ming——
Then the family would say: "Now which was which cat?
It was Mungojerrie AND Rumpelteazer!"—And there's nothing at all to
be done about that!

Comment: Mungojerrie, Rumpelteazer, and "Old Possum"

T. S. Eliot has long been famous for complex, highly symbolic poetry concerned with the human condition in twentieth-century society. But "Mungojerrie and Rumpelteazer" shows us Eliot's lighter side. It is just one of the fifteen poems that make up *Old Possum's Book of Practical Cats,* Eliot's whimsical collection of cat characters. Eliot—known to close friends by the nickname "Old Possum"—introduces us to such memorable cats as Old Gumbie Cat, Growltiger, and Skimbleshanks, as well as to Mungojerrie and Rumpelteazer. Old Gumbie Cat, whose real name is Jennyanydots, spends her nights trying to teach good manners and household skills to mice and cockroaches, and her days simply sitting. Growltiger, on the other hand, lives the exciting life of a ship's cat, getting into hair-raising adventures everywhere he goes. And Skimbleshanks runs a passenger train practically single-handedly. Every cat in the collection has a unique personality, pursuing interests and activities very much its own.

Eliot uses a wide variety of rhyme schemes and rhythm to help convey these individual personalities. If you simply look at "Mungojerrie and Rumpelteazer," you can see that the lines of the second stanza are shorter than those of the first. In fact, the stanzas alternate in line length depending on what the cats are doing. Read the poem out loud, and notice how the longer lines (describing the two cats as they roam about town) seem more rambling and leisurely, while the shorter lines (describing the cats when they are at work) seem more businesslike. Eliot's attention to sound pattern and its ability to convey particular types of personalities and activities contributes as much as the narrative itself toward describing each cat's individuality.

Although *Old Possum's Book of Practical Cats* was published over forty years ago, its lighthearted charm and ability to delight all kinds of readers—especially cat-lovers—make it seem quite contemporary. It appealed particularly to Andrew Lloyd Webber, a musician and lyricist, and to Trevor Nunn, a director, who in 1982 turned Eliot's cats into the characters of a musical play—*Cats*—that was highly successful in London and on Broadway. The remarkable individuality of character that Eliot achieved in poetry made translation to the stage an easy matter.

See **BLANK VERSE** Handbook of Literary Terms

The Death of the Hired Man

Robert Frost

Mary sat musing on the lamp-flame at the table,
Waiting for Warren. When she heard his step,
She ran on tiptoe down the darkened passage
To meet him in the doorway with the news
And put him on his guard. "Silas is back."
She pushed him outward with her through the door
And shut it after her. "Be kind," she said.
She took the market things from Warren's arms
And set them on the porch, then drew him down
To sit beside her on the wooden steps.

"When was I ever anything but kind to him?
But I'll not have the fellow back," he said.
"I told him so last haying, didn't I?
If he left then, I said, that ended it.
What good is he? Who else will harbor him
At his age for the little he can do?
What help he is there's no depending on.
Off he goes always when I need him most.
He thinks he ought to earn a little pay,
Enough at least to buy tobacco with,
So he won't have to beg and be beholden.
'All right,' I say, 'I can't afford to pay
Any fixed wages, though I wish I could.'
'Someone else can.' 'Then someone else will have to.'
I shouldn't mind his bettering himself
If that was what it was. You can be certain,
When he begins like that, there's someone at him
Trying to coax him off with pocket money—

(Continued)

In haying time, when any help is scarce.
In winter he comes back to us. I'm done."

"Sh! not so loud: he'll hear you," Mary said.

"I want him to: he'll have to soon or late."
"He's worn out. He's asleep beside the stove.
When I came up from Rowe's I found him here,
Huddled against the barn door fast asleep,
A miserable sight, and frightening, too—
You needn't smile—I didn't recognize him—
I wasn't looking for him—and he's changed.
Wait till you see."

"Where did you say he'd been?"

"He didn't say. I dragged him to the house,
And gave him tea and tried to make him smoke.
I tried to make him talk about his travels.
Nothing would do: he just kept nodding off."

"What did he say? Did he say anything?"

"But little."

"Anything? Mary, confess
He said he'd come to ditch the meadow for me."

"Warren!"

"But did he? I just want to know."

"Of course he did. What would you have him say?
Surely you wouldn't grudge the poor old man
Some humble way to save his self-respect.
He added, if you really care to know,
He meant to clear the upper pasture, too.
That sounds like something you have heard before?
Warren, I wish you could have heard the way
He jumbled everything. I stopped to look
Two or three times—he made me feel so queer—
To see if he was talking in his sleep.
He ran on Harold Wilson—you remember—
The boy you had in haying four years since.
He's finished school, and teaching in his college.
Silas declares you'll have to get him back.

He says they two will make a team for work:
Between them they will lay this farm as smooth!
The way he mixed that in with other things.
He thinks young Wilson a likely lad, though daft
On education—you know how they fought
All through July under the blazing sun,
Silas up on the cart to build the load,
Harold along beside to pitch it on."

"Yes, I took care to keep well out of earshot."

"Well, those days trouble Silas like a dream.
You wouldn't think they would. How some things linger!
Harold's young college-boy's assurance piqued him.
After so many years he still keeps finding
Good arguments he sees he might have used.
I sympathize. I know just how it feels
To think of the right thing to say too late.
Harold's associated in his mind with Latin.
He asked me what I thought of Harold's saying
He studied Latin, like the violin,
Because he liked it—that an argument!
He said he couldn't make the boy believe
He could find water with a hazel prong—
Which showed how much good school had ever done him.
He wanted to go over that. But most of all
He thinks if he could have another chance
To teach him how to build a load of hay——"

"I know, that's Silas's one accomplishment.
He bundles every forkful in its place,
And tags and numbers it for future reference,
So he can find and easily dislodge it
In the unloading. Silas does that well.
He takes it out in bunches like big birds' nests.
You never see him standing on the hay
He's trying to lift, straining to lift himself."

"He thinks if he could teach him that, he'd be
Some good perhaps to someone in the world.
He hates to see a boy the fool of books.
Poor Silas, so concerned for other folk,
And nothing to look backward to with pride,
And nothing to look forward to with hope,
So now and never any different."

(Continued)

Part of a moon was falling down the west,
Dragging the whole sky with it to the hills.
Its light poured softly in her lap. She saw it
And spread her apron to it. She put out her hand
Among the harplike morning-glory strings,
Taut with the dew from garden bed to eaves,
As if she played unheard some tenderness
That wrought on him beside her in the night.
"Warren," she said, "he has come home to die:
You needn't be afraid he'll leave you this time."

"Home," he mocked gently.

"Yes, what else but home?

It all depends on what you mean by home.
Of course he's nothing to us, any more
Than was the hound that came a stranger to us
Out of the woods, worn out upon the trail."

"Home is the place where, when you have to go there,
They have to take you in."

"I should have called it
Something you somehow haven't to deserve."

Warren leaned out and took a step or two,
Picked up a little stick, and brought it back
And broke it in his hand and tossed it by.
"Silas has better claim on us you think
Than on his brother? Thirteen little miles
As the road winds would bring him to his door.
Silas has walked that far no doubt today.
Why doesn't he go there? His brother's rich,
A somebody—director in the bank."

"He never told us that."

"We know it, though."

"I think his brother ought to help, of course.
I'll see to that if there is need. He ought of right
To take him in, and might be willing to—
He may be better than appearances.
But have some pity on Silas. Do you think

(Continued)

If he had any pride in claiming kin
Or anything he looked for from his brother,
He'd keep so still about him all this time?"

"I wonder what's between them."

"I can tell you.
Silas is what he is—we wouldn't mind him—

But just the kind that kinsfolk can't abide.
He never did a thing so very bad.
He don't know why he isn't quite as good
As anybody. Worthless though he is,
He won't be made ashamed to please his brother."

"*I* can't think Si ever hurt anyone."

"No, but he hurt my heart the way he lay
And rolled his old head on that sharp-edged chair-back.
He wouldn't let me put him on the lounge.
You must go in and see what you can do.
I made the bed up for him there tonight.
You'll be surprised at him—how much he's broken.
His working days are done; I'm sure of it."

"I'd not be in a hurry to say that."

"I haven't been. Go, look, see for yourself.
But, Warren, please remember how it is:
He's come to help you ditch the meadow.
He has a plan. You mustn't laugh at him.
He may not speak of it, and then he may.
I'll sit and see if that small sailing cloud
Will hit or miss the moon."

It hit the moon.
Then there were three there, making a dim row,
The moon, the little silver cloud, and she.

Warren returned—too soon, it seemed to her—
Slipped to her side, caught up her hand and waited.

"Warren?" she questioned.

"Dead," was all he answered.

Discussion

The Skater of Ghost Lake

1. Several interpretations of this poem are possible. What do you think actually happens at Ghost Lake on the night the poet describes? What evidence in the poem leads you to this belief?

2. Which of the following purposes do you believe best explains Benét's main reason for writing this poem? Explain your choice. **(a)** to create a sense of fear and wonder in the reader; **(b)** to tell in poetic form the story of two people skating late at night; **(c)** to develop a mood through the use of images, rhythm, and sounds; **(d)** any combination of the above.

Mungojerrie and Rumpelteazer

1. What images illustrate the way these two cats are likely to behave?

2. (a) Chart the rhyme scheme of this poem. **(b)** Does the poem have a clearly defined pattern of rhythm?

3. In what ways do the rhythm and rhyme contribute to the overall meaning of the poem?

The Death of the Hired Man

1. (a) How does Warren feel about the hired man, Silas? **(b)** Why? What reasons does he give?

2. (a) What were the arguments between Silas and Harold Wilson about? **(b)** Why does Mary mention them to Warren?

3. (a) How does Warren define *home?* **(b)** How does Mary define *home?* **(c)** Do you agree with either? Explain.

4. What does the description of the moonlight scene (lines 103–110) contribute to the development and mood of the poem?

5. What do the brevity and manner in which Warren announces Silas's death suggest about Warren?

6. Do you think Silas was a failure? Why or why not?

Application

Mood

"The Skater of Ghost Lake" is a *narrative poem*—that is, it tells a story. Like all good ghost stories, however, Benét's narrative also establishes a mood.

1. Imagine that you were narrating to someone the mere events that occur in this poem. What brief description would you give? Then mention some words and details that you would add to your summary of events in order to convey the mood.

2. What images in the poem do you think help to create the mood of a ghost story?

Blank Verse

"The Death of the Hired Man" is written in *blank verse.* (See Handbook of Literary Terms.) Why are certain lines (39, 45, 47, 113, 119, 130, 139, 166) divided into two sections?

Vocabulary

Combined Exercise

Use your Glossary to complete the exercise that follows. Write the letter of each answer you choose on your paper.

1. Someone who has just finished a *reel* is most likely to be **(a)** from Scotland; **(b)** out of breath; **(c)** angry; **(d)** an ice skater.

2. If your bedroom is directly under the *eaves,* it is **(a)** in the basement; **(b)** on the top floor; **(c)** very large; **(d)** none of these.

3. A *plausible* story is one that **(a)** appears to be true; **(b)** is amusing; **(c)** is not true; **(d)** is told by a criminal.

4. The *au* in *plausible* is pronounced like **(a)** the *o* in *order;* **(b)** the *o* in *open;* **(c)** the *a* in *hat;* **(d)** the *a* in *age.*

5. A *sentinel* is most likely to be found near **(a)** a frozen lake; **(b)** a hockey stadium; **(c)** an army camp; **(d)** an expensive hotel.

6. In *sentinel,* the accent falls on **(a)** the first syllable; **(b)** the second syllable; **(c)** the third syllable; **(d)** the second and third syllables.

7. If you *veer* your motorbike to avoid hitting a porcupine, you are most likely to **(a)** crash; **(b)** turn; **(c)** stop; **(d)** none of these.

8. After a garden has been *ditched,* it **(a)** has a trench around it; **(b)** has been weeded; **(c)** has been sold; **(d)** has been abandoned to the weeds.

9. A fence made of *scrolls* of wrought iron would be **(a)** very high; **(b)** very low; **(c)** plain; **(d)** fancy.

10. *Scroll* rhymes with **(a)** maul; **(b)** toil; **(c)** roll; **(d)** none of these.

Composition

Suppose that a group of exchange students will be visiting your English class for a week. During one of the class periods, you and your classmates will present a poetry reading. You have been chosen to read a story poem, but it is up to you to decide which one and to convince your classmates that your choice is the best possible one. You must choose from among the three poems in this cluster.

Choose the poem that you think best suited to an audience like the group of exchange students, an audience with a good grasp of the English language but unfamiliar with poetry written in English. Then, write a short paper in which you defend your choice and attempt to convince your classmates to your way of thinking. (See *Defending Your Position,* page 672, in Composition Guide.)

William Rose Benét 1886–1950

Benét was awarded the Pulitzer Prize for Poetry in 1942. He was an Associate Editor of the *New York Post's Literary Review* and one of the founders and first editors of *The Saturday Review of Literature.*

Thomas Stearns Eliot 1888–1965

Born in St. Louis, T. S. Eliot spent most of his life in England. Known for poetry that departed in subject and tone from most poetry written up to that time, Eliot is considered one of the foremost poets and critics of this century. Another side of Eliot is shown in his poems about cats. (See Comment article in the group of poems.) Eliot was awarded the Nobel Prize for Literature in 1948.

Robert Frost 1874–1963

Frost became America's most honored poet: he received four Pulitzer Prizes and numerous other awards and honorary degrees. His eighty-eighth birthday in March, 1962, was another high point in Frost's career. On that day he published his most recent volume of poetry, *In the Clearing,* and received a Congressional Medal in ceremonies at the White House.

Unit 3 Review: *Poetry*

Content Review

1. Select a poem in this unit that has given you greater insight into your life or the world around you. Explain why it affected you as it did.

2. (a) Divide the poems in this unit into those that use end rhyme and regular meter and those that do not. **(b)** Do you prefer one set of poems over the other because of the lack of or use of rhyme and rhythm?

3. Of the many goals you read about in the first grouping, which one to you seemed worth striving for? Why?

4. Which character in the "Assertions" group did you find most admirable? least admirable? Why?

5. Suppose you know somebody who has been accused of a crime. The person is innocent, but you must find a lawyer to present the case. If the following four were available to you, tell which you would choose and why: Mr. Artesian, the old pensioner, the speaker in "Making a Fist," the speaker in "The Mouth of the Hudson."

6. If someone were to say to you, "Anybody can break up sentences on a page so that they *look* like a poem. Most of what is called poetry in this unit isn't poetry at all," how would you respond? Would you agree? disagree? What evidence would you use to support your position?

Concept Review: Interpretation of New Material

Read the following poem aloud. Then on your paper, write the answers to the questions.

Insomniac • *Patricia Y. Ikeda*

Sometimes when the moon
Looks like a slice of orange impaled on a tree fork
And the air is heavy with heat,
I die over and over in my bed
And think of that time when I will not rise,
Or whisper names into the shrill din
Of cricket voices that invades my room,
Or write poetry that must be destroyed
Because it is infected with night madness.

The Starry Night by Vincent Van Gogh, 1889. Collection, The Museum of Modern Art, New York. Acquired through the Lillie P. Bliss Bequest.

When summer is ripe and rank
With wet grass odors and berry smells,
I lie awake in the hot darkness,
The shadows sliding over my bedspread
Making dark patterns, like blood.
I raise my hands to my eyes.

When it is too hot to sleep
And my sheets will not lie unwrinkled
Under my restless body,
I sing muffled songs under the covers,
Or turn on my bed light and read
Until it is morning and my eyes burn,
Or walk in the still dark house
With the puzzled dog one clicking step behind.
We share our insomnia like a secret pact
And do not tell the others at breakfast.

1. The comparison of the moon to a slice of orange (lines 1 and 2) is a(n) **(a)** simile; **(b)** personification; **(c)** metaphor: **(d)** allusion.

2. The comparison suggested in the phrase "tree fork" is a **(a)** simile; **(b)** metaphor; **(c)** stereotype; **(d)** hyperbole.

3. Which words best describe the mood of the poem? **(a)** calm and dignified; **(b)** restless and oppressive; **(c)** joyous and exuberant; **(d)** sweet and nostalgic.

4. The title, based on the root *somnus,* refers to a person who cannot **(a)** think; **(b)** eat; **(c)** sleep; **(d)** write.

5. Judging by the evidence in the poem, what kind of person does the speaker appear to be? **(a)** calmly rational; **(b)** melancholy and sensitive; **(c)** humorous; **(d)** a nature lover.

6. When the poet mentions a "time when I will not rise," she is referring to **(a)** oversleeping; **(b)** illness; **(c)** laziness; **(d)** death.

7. Which is the most plausible setting for the poem? **(a)** an inner-city dwelling; **(b)** a suburban apartment; **(c)** a house in the country or suburbs; **(d)** a camper under the stars.

8. In stanza 2 there is an appeal to all of the senses *except* **(a)** sight; **(b)** smell; **(c)** touch; **(d)** hearing.

9. Ikeda makes a strong appeal to readers' senses in order to communicate her experience. Such an appeal and the pictures it evokes is called **(a)** imagery; **(b)** irony; **(c)** hyperbole; **(d)** simile.

10. Ikeda's tone can best be described as **(a)** nonchalant; **(b)** comical; **(c)** melancholy; **(d)** light.

Composition Review

1. Imagine that a classmate read "Insomniac" and commented: "Instead of rambling for twenty-five lines, Ikeda simply could have said, 'I can't sleep.' "

Defend the poem to your friend in a composition in which you explain the ways in which Ikeda has done more than this three-word summary does. (In developing this paper, you may want to consider such matters as the poet's use of details and figurative language and her appeal to the senses.)

2. Imagine that you are one of a group from another planet sent to Earth to study our culture. Your specific assignment is our attitude toward old people. After reading the views of the poets in this unit who write about the aged, you report your findings. Remember that because you have read only these views, you may base your findings only on these poems.

Write a composition in which you tell the ways we regard old people in our society.

3. This unit contains poems about bad cats; women doing piecework in a loft sewing factory; people walking out of windows, spitting tangerine seeds, looking at landscapes marred by pollution. In your opinion, are these suitable subjects for poems?

Write a composition in which you explain your views. (In gathering evidence to support your opinion, review the various terms from the Handbook of Literary Terms introduced in this unit.)

Unit 4

Shakespearean Drama

Romeo and Juliet

Marti Maraden as Juliet, Richard Monette as Romeo in *Romeo and Juliet,* Stratford Festival, Canada, 1977.

Introduction

The thirty-seven plays of Shakespeare remain popular after almost 300 years. Hollywood makes movies of them; television broadcasts them; actors vie to work in them; scholars study them; and audiences find them irresistible. What is it about Shakespeare's plays that commands such admiration?

All plays consist of five basic elements, elements as old as the earliest Greek drama: *plot, character, theme, language,* and *spectacle.* Some playwrights excel at one or two elements; Shakespeare excels at virtually all.

Plot

For his plots, Shakespeare draws from the history of England, from Greek and Roman stories, from medieval tales, and from the fables of his own time. Often he combines sources, juggling several plots—one major line of action and one or more minor lines.

A good plot develops because of the characters in it. In *Romeo and Juliet* the conflict grows naturally from these particular characters in this particular situation. Note how many developments are the inevitable result of this interaction between characters and events.

Characters

Great writers create characters who have two almost contradictory qualities: the unique and the universal. Unique characters have specific traits that make them stand out. However, if characters are also typical of a particular type of person, they are said to be universal.

Romeo, for example, is unique in many ways, but he is also the universal lover overcome with emotion and the thrill of being in love. As you read through the play, ask yourself if you haven't met some of these characters: the concerned parents, the life-of-the-party, the rejected suitor.

Theme

The theme (the main idea or underlying meaning) of any work grows out of the characters and their actions. Theme is not simply the "moral" or the "lesson" to be learned, but rather a statement of some insight about human nature. As you read the play, you will soon be aware of recurrent ideas: love, vengeance, fate. None of these alone is the theme of the play, but together they enable you to make a statement about the theme.

Language

Shakespeare's plays consist of three kinds of language: prose, blank verse, and rhymed couplets (two lines of verse with end rhyme). Shakespeare revels in word play, filling his drama with puns and double meanings. He is a master at creating figurative language. His lines are rich in imagery. And often he repeats important images, thus creating a pattern. For example, in *Romeo and Juliet* look for references to stars, light, and death. Then, ask why these particular images are important in understanding the theme.

Spectacle

Shakespeare did not have at his disposal the elaborate scenery that often characterizes modern theater. (See the Comment article at the end of Act One.) But the lack of scenery in no way limits the spectacle. Through Shakespeare's skill as a playwright, you will—in the first act of *Romeo and Juliet*—"see" sword fighting and dancing; you will "hear" music; and, best of all, you will experience poetry that will carry you to a sixteenth-century town and introduce you to two of the world's most famous young lovers.

See **PERSONIFICATION** in Handbook of Literary Terms

Romeo and Juliet

William Shakespeare

CHARACTERS

ESCALUS (es′kə ləs), *Prince of Verona.*
MONTAGUE (mon′tə gyü) } CAPULET (kap′yü let) } *heads of two feuding households.*
LADY MONTAGUE } LADY CAPULET } *their wives.*
ROMEO, *son of the Montagues.*
JULIET, *daughter of the Capulets.*
MERCUTIO (mėr kyü′shi ō), *kinsman of Prince Escalus and friend of Romeo.*
BENVOLIO (ben vōl′i ō), *nephew of Montague and friend of Romeo.*
TYBALT (tib′əlt), *nephew of Capulet's wife.*
PARIS, *kinsman of Prince Escalus and a suitor of Juliet.*
FRIAR LAURENCE, *counselor of Romeo.*
FRIAR JOHN, *trusted messenger of Friar Laurence.*
NURSE, *servant and friend of Juliet.*
OLD MAN, *member of the Capulet family.*
BALTHASAR (bäl′thə zär′), *servant of Romeo.*
SAMPSON } GREGORY } *servants of Capulet.*
ABRAHAM, *servant of Montague.*
PETER, *servant of Juliet's nurse.*
APOTHECARY
CHORUS
MASKERS, MUSICIANS, WATCHMEN, PAGES, OFFICERS, CITIZENS, *and* ATTENDANTS

Prologue

CHORUS° *(spoken by a single actor).* Two households, both alike in dignity,
In fair Verona, where we lay our scene,
From ancient grudge break to new mutiny,°
Where civil blood makes civil hands unclean.

chorus, the chorus summarizes the action of the play.

mutiny, rioting.

William Shakespeare, *Romeo and Juliet,* c. 1594-1596. (Abridged.)

From forth the fatal loins of these two foes
A pair of star-crossed lovers° take their life;
Whose misadventured piteous overthrows
Do with their death bury their parents' strife.
The fearful passage° of their death-marked love,
And the continuance of their parents' rage,
Which, but° their children's end, naught could remove,
Is now the two hours' traffic of our stage;
The which if you with patient ears attend,
What here shall miss, our toil shall strive to mend.[1]
(Exit.)

star-crossed, ill-fated. In Shakespeare's day it was commonly believed that the stars controlled people's lives.

fearful passage, progress that is full of fear.

but, except for.

1. Where is the setting of the play? What will happen to the characters by the end of the play? What words or phrases suggest the atmosphere of the play?

Act One

Scene 1: A public square in Verona.

Enter SAMPSON *and* GREGORY, *servants of the house of* CAPULET, *armed with swords and bucklers.°*

SAMPSON. Gregory, on my word, we'll not carry coals.°

GREGORY. No, for then we should be colliers.°

SAMPSON. I mean an° we be in choler,° we'll draw.

GREGORY. Ay, while you live, draw your neck out o' the collar.°

SAMPSON *(with mock belligerence).* I strike quickly, being moved.

GREGORY. But thou art not quickly moved to strike.

SAMPSON. A dog of the house of Montague moves me.

GREGORY. To move is to stir; and to be valiant is to stand. Therefore, if thou art moved, thou runn'st away.

SAMPSON. A dog of that house shall move me to stand. I will take the wall of° any man . . . of Montague's. . . .

GREGORY. The quarrel is between our masters and us their men.

SAMPSON. 'Tis all one. I will show myself a tyrant. . . .

GREGORY *(warningly).* Here comes two of the house of the Montagues.

bucklers, small shields.
carry coals, endure insults.
colliers, coal or charcoal dealers; persons looked down on.
an, if.
in choler, angry.
collar, a halter used by the hangman.

take the wall of, figurative for "get the better of."

(Enter ABRAHAM *and* BALTHASAR, *servants of the* MONTAGUES.*)*

SAMPSON. My naked weapon is out; quarrel, I will back thee.

GREGORY. How! Turn thy back and run?

SAMPSON. Fear me not.°

GREGORY. No, marry,° I fear thee!

SAMPSON. Let us take the law of° our sides; let *them* begin.

GREGORY. I will frown as I pass by, and let them take it as they list.°

SAMPSON. Nay, as they dare. I will bite my thumb° at them, which is a disgrace to them if they bear it.

Fear me not. Don't mistrust me.
marry, by the Virgin Mary; a mild oath.
take the law of, have the law on.

list, wish.
bite my thumb, an insulting gesture.

ABRAHAM. Do you bite your thumb at us, sir?[2]

2. How do Sampson and Gregory taunt Abraham into starting a fight?

SAMPSON. I do bite my thumb, sir.

ABRAHAM. Do you bite your thumb at *us,* sir?

SAMPSON *(aside to* GREGORY*).* Is the law of our side if I say "Ay"?

GREGORY. No.

SAMPSON *(to* ABRAHAM*).* No, sir, I do not bite my thumb at you, sir; but I bite my thumb, sir.

GREGORY *(to* ABRAHAM*).* Do you quarrel, sir?

ABRAHAM. Quarrel, sir? No, sir.

SAMPSON. If you do, sir, I am for you. I serve as good a man as you.

ABRAHAM. No better.

SAMPSON. Well, sir.

GREGORY *(aside to* SAMPSON*).* Say "better"; here comes one of my master's kinsmen.[3]

3. Both Sampson and Gregory, at heart, are cowards. What suddenly gives them the courage to draw their swords?

SAMPSON. Yes, better, sir.

ABRAHAM. You lie.

(Enter BENVOLIO, *a nephew of* MONTAGUE *and hence a first cousin of* ROMEO.*)*

SAMPSON. Draw, if you be men. Gregory, remember thy swashing° blow.

swashing, crushing.

(The four SERVANTS *fight.)*

BENVOLIO. Part, fools! . . . *(He beats down their swords.)*

(Enter TYBALT, *a hot-headed youth, nephew of* LADY CAPULET *and first cousin of* JULIET.*)*

TYBALT *(contemptuously).* What, art thou drawn among these heartless hinds?°
Turn thee, Benvolio, look upon thy death.

heartless hinds, cowardly servants.

BENVOLIO *(quietly).* I do but keep the peace. Put up thy sword,
Or manage it to part these men with me.

TYBALT *(scornfully).* What, drawn, and talk of peace? I hate the word
As I hate hell, all Montagues, and thee.[4]

4. Describe the differences between Benvolio and Tybalt.

(They fight.)
Have at thee,° coward!

Have at thee. I shall attack you; be on your guard.

(Enter several of both houses, who join the fray; then enter an OFFICER *and* CITIZENS *with clubs or other weapons.)*

FIRST CITIZEN. Clubs, bills, and partisans!° Strike! Beat them down!
Down with the Capulets! Down with the Montagues!

bills . . . partisans, long-handled spears with sharp cutting blades.

(Enter CAPULET *in his gown° and* LADY CAPULET.*)*

gown, dressing gown.

CAPULET *(who cannot resist joining in the quarrel).* What noise is this? Give me my long sword, ho!

LADY CAPULET *(scornfully)*. A crutch,° a crutch! Why call you for a
sword?
CAPULET. My sword, I say! Old Montague is come,
And flourishes his blade in spite° of me.

crutch. Lady Capulet implies that a crutch is better suited to her aged husband than is a sword.

spite, defiance.

(Enter MONTAGUE *and* LADY MONTAGUE.*)*

MONTAGUE. Thou villain Capulet! *(To his wife)* Hold me not, let me
go.
LADY MONTAGUE. Thou shalt not stir one foot to seek a foe.

(Enter PRINCE ESCALUS, *head of Verona's government, with* ATTENDANTS.*)*

ESCALUS *(sternly)*. Rebellious subjects, enemies to peace,
Profaners of this neighbor-stainèd steel—
Will they not hear?[5] What, ho! You men, you beasts,
That quench the fire of your pernicious rage
With purple fountains issuing from your veins,[6]
On pain of torture, from those bloody hands
Throw your mistempered weapons to the ground,
And hear the sentence of your movèd prince.
Three civil brawls, bred of an airy word
By thee, old Capulet, and Montague,
Have thrice disturbed the quiet of our streets. . . .
If ever you disturb our streets again,
Your lives shall pay the forfeit of the peace.[7]
For this time, all the rest depart away.
You, Capulet, shall go along with me;
And, Montague, come you this afternoon
To know our further pleasure in this case,
To old Freetown, our common judgment place.
Once more, on pain of death, all men depart.

5. Escalus breaks off his speech in line 61 to ask a question. Why do you think this is necessary?

6. What are the "purple fountains"?

forfeit of the peace, penalty for disturbing the peace.

7. What will be the penalties for any further outbreaks of fighting?

(Exeunt° all but MONTAGUE, LADY MONTAGUE, *and* BENVOLIO.*)*

MONTAGUE. Who set this ancient quarrel new abroach?°
(To BENVOLIO*)* Speak, nephew. Were you by when it began?
BENVOLIO. Here were the servants of your adversary,
And yours, close fighting ere I did approach.
I drew to part them; in the instant came
The fiery Tybalt, with his sword prepared,
Which, as he breathed defiance to my ears,
He swung about his head and cut the winds,
Who, nothing hurt withal,° hissed him in scorn.
While we were interchanging thrusts and blows,
Came more and more and fought on part and part,
Till the prince came, who parted either part.
LADY MONTAGUE. O, where is Romeo? Saw you him today?
Right glad I am he was not at this fray.

Exeunt, the plural form of *exit.*

set . . . new abroach, reopened or started again this old quarrel.

Who . . . withal, the winds, hurt not at all by Tybalt's swinging of his sword.

BENVOLIO. Madam, an hour before the worshiped sun
Peered forth the golden window of the east,
A troubled mind drave me to walk abroad;
Where, underneath the grove of sycamore
That westward rooteth from the city's side,
So early walking did I see your son.
Towards him I made, but he was ware of me
And stole into the covert of the wood.
I, measuring his affections° by my own,
Pursued my humor,° not pursuing his,
And gladly shunned who gladly fled from me.

MONTAGUE. Many a morning hath he there been seen,
With tears augmenting the fresh morning's dew,
Adding to clouds more clouds with his deep sighs.
But all so soon as the all-cheering sun
Should in the farthest east begin to draw
The shady curtains from Aurora's° bed,
Away from light steals home my heavy° son,
And private in his chamber pens himself,
Shuts up his windows, locks fair daylight out,
And makes himself an artificial night.
Black and portentous must this humor prove,
Unless good counsel may the cause remove.[8]

affections, wishes, feelings.

humor, mood, whim.

Aurora, goddess of the dawn.

heavy, sad.

8. How do Benvolio and Montague, Romeo's father, describe Romeo's behavior?

Frances-Regis Klanfer as Montague, Gregory Wanless as Benvolio, Karen Austin as Lady Montague in *Romeo and Juliet,* Stratford Festival, Canada, 1977.

BENVOLIO. My noble uncle, do you know the cause?
MONTAGUE. I neither know it nor can learn of him.
BENVOLIO. Have you importuned him by any means?
MONTAGUE. Both by myself and many other friends;
But he, his own affections' counselor,
Is to himself—I will not say how true—
But to himself so secret and so close,°
So far from sounding and discovery,°
As is the bud bit with an envious° worm
Ere he can spread his sweet leaves° to the air,
Or dedicate his beauty to the sun.
Could we but learn from whence his sorrows grow,
We would as willingly give cure as know.

(Enter ROMEO *absorbed in thought.)*
BENVOLIO. See where he comes; so please you, step aside.
I'll know his grievance or be much denied.°
MONTAGUE. I would thou wert so happy by thy stay°
To hear true shrift.° Come, madam, let's away.
(Exeunt MONTAGUE *and* LADY MONTAGUE.*)*
BENVOLIO. Good morrow, cousin.°
ROMEO. Is the day so young?
BENVOLIO. But new struck nine.
ROMEO. Ay me! Sad hours seem long.
Was that my father that went hence so fast?
BENVOLIO. It was. What sadness lengthens Romeo's hours?
ROMEO. Not having that which, having, makes them short.[9]
BENVOLIO. In love?
ROMEO. Out——
BENVOLIO. Of love?
ROMEO. Out of her favor where I am in love.
BENVOLIO. Alas, that Love, so gentle in his view,
Should be so tyrannous and rough in proof!°
ROMEO. Alas, that Love, whose view is muffled still,°
Should, without eyes, see pathways to his will!
Where shall we dine? O me! What fray was here?
Yet tell me not, for I have heard it all.
Here's much to do with hate, but more with love.
Why, then, O brawling love! O loving hate! . . .
O heavy lightness, serious vanity;°
Misshapen chaos of well-seeming forms!
Feather of lead, bright smoke, cold fire, sick health!
Still-waking° sleep, that is not what it is!
This love feel I, that feel no love in this.°
Dost thou not laugh?
BENVOLIO. No, coz,° I rather weep.

close, not inclined to talk.

sounding and discovery, responding to efforts to understand his views.
envious, malicious.

Ere . . . leaves, before the bud can open its sweet leaves.

be much denied. He will find it difficult to refuse me an answer.
happy by thy stay, fortunate in your waiting.
To hear true shrift, as to hear true confession.

Good morrow, cousin. Good morning, cousin (any relative).

9. In order to maintain the rhythm of a line, Shakespeare often omits a word or words; such an omission is called an ellipsis. As reader, you must supply the omitted words; for example, "Not having that which, if I had it, would make the hours short."

proof, experience.

view . . . still, sight is blindfolded always.

vanity, frivolity.

Still-waking, always awake.

that feel . . . in this, that cannot take any pleasure in this love.

coz, a short form of *cousin.*

ROMEO. Good heart, at what?
BENVOLIO. At thy good heart's oppression.
ROMEO. Why, such is love's transgression.
Griefs of mine own lie heavy in my breast,
Which thou wilt propagate, to have it pressed°
With more of thine; this love that thou hast shown
Doth add more grief to too much of mine own. . . .
Farewell, my coz.
BENVOLIO. Soft! I will go along;
An if you leave me so, you do me wrong.
ROMEO. Tut, I have lost myself; I am not here.
This is not Romeo; he's some otherwhere.
BENVOLIO. Tell me in sadness,° who is that you love. . . .
ROMEO. In sadness, cousin, I do love a woman.
BENVOLIO *(smiling)*. I aimed so near when I supposed you loved.
ROMEO. A right good mark-man! And she's *fair*° I love.
BENVOLIO. A right *fair*° mark, fair coz, is soonest hit.
ROMEO. Well, in that hit you miss. She'll not be hit
With Cupid's arrow. She hath Dian's wit° . . .
From Love's weak childish bow she lives unharmed.
She will not stay the siege of loving terms,°
Nor bide the encounter of assailing eyes . . .
O, she is rich in beauty, only poor
That, when she dies, with beauty dies her store.°
BENVOLIO. Then she hath sworn that she will still live chaste?
ROMEO. She hath, and in that sparing makes huge waste,
For beauty starved with her severity
Cuts beauty off from all posterity.
She is too fair, too wise, wisely too fair,
To merit bliss by making me despair.
She hath forsworn to love, and in that vow
Do I live dead that live to tell it now.
BENVOLIO. Be ruled by me: forget to think of her.
ROMEO. O, teach me how I should forget to think!
BENVOLIO. By giving liberty unto thine eyes;
Examine other beauties.
ROMEO. 'Tis the way
To call hers exquisite, in question more.°
These happy masks that kiss fair ladies' brows,
Being black, put us in mind they hide the fair.°
He that is strucken blind cannot forget
The precious treasure of his eyesight lost. . . .
Farewell. Thou canst not teach me to forget.
BENVOLIO. I'll pay that doctrine,° or else die in debt.
(Exeunt.)

pressed, oppressed.

sadness, seriousness.

fair, beautiful.

fair, clear, distinct. A play on words.

Dian's wit, the wisdom of the goddess Diana.

She will not . . . terms. She will not listen to avowals of love.

with beauty . . . store. She will die without children, and therefore her beauty will die with her.

'Tis the way . . . more. To make her beauty the subject of more discussion is only to make me more aware of how exquisite her beauty is.

These happy masks . . . fair. The black masks that women sometimes wear in public (a common practice in Shakespeare's time) remind us of the beauty they hide.

pay that doctrine, teach Romeo to forget.

Scene 2: A street in Verona.

Enter CAPULET, PARIS, *and* SERVANT.

CAPULET *(addressing* PARIS*).* But Montague is bound° as well as I,
In penalty alike; and 'tis not hard, I think,
For men so old as we to keep the peace.

PARIS. Of honorable reckoning° are you both;
And pity 'tis you lived at odds so long.
But now, my lord, what say you to my suit?

CAPULET. But saying o'er what I have said before:
My child is yet a stranger in the world;
She hath not seen the change of fourteen years.
Let two more summers wither in their pride,
Ere we may think her ripe to be a bride. . . .
The earth hath swallowed all my hopes but she;
She is the hopeful lady of my earth.°
But woo her, gentle Paris, get her heart;
My will to her consent is but a part.°
An she agree, within her scope of choice
Lies my consent and fair according voice.
This night I hold an old accustomed feast,
Whereto I have invited many a guest
Such as I love, and you, among the store,
One more, most welcome, makes my number more.
At my poor house look to behold this night
Earth-treading stars that make dark heaven light:
Such comfort as do lusty young men feel
When well-appareled April on the heel
Of limping winter treads, even such delight
Among fresh female buds shall you this night
Inherit° at my house; hear all, all see,
And like her most whose merit most shall be. . . .
Come, go with me. *(To* SERVANT, *giving him a paper)* Go, sirrah,° trudge about
Through fair Verona; find those persons out
Whose names are written there, and to them say
My house and welcome on their pleasure stay.

(Exeunt CAPULET *and* PARIS.*)*

SERVANT *(peering at the paper).* Find them out whose names are written here. It is written that the shoemaker should meddle with his yard, and the tailor with his last, the fisher with his pencil, and the painter with his nets; but I am sent to find those persons whose names are here writ, and can never find what names the writing person hath here writ. I must to the learned . . .[10]

bound, obliged to keep the peace.

reckoning, reputation.

hopeful lady of my earth, center of my existence.

My will . . . part. My wishes are of secondary importance to her consent.

Inherit, enjoy.

sirrah, customary form of address to servants.

10. In some editions of this play, this servant is called *Clown.* His confusion of the terms of various professions is another variation of word play. Can you match the proper term with its profession?

(Enter BENVOLIO *and* ROMEO.*)*

BENVOLIO. Tut, man, one fire burns out another's burning,
One pain is lessened by another's anguish. . . .
Take thou some new infection to thy eye,
And the rank poison of the old will die.

ROMEO. Your plantain leaf° is excellent for that.

plantain leaf, used as a salve for bruises.

BENVOLIO. For what, I pray thee?

ROMEO. For your broken shin.

BENVOLIO. Why, Romeo, art thou mad?

ROMEO. Not mad, but bound more than a madman is;
Shut up in prison, kept without my food,
Whipped and tormented and—God-den,° good fellow.

God-den, a greeting like "good evening"; literally, "God give you a good evening."

SERVANT. God gi' god-den. I pray, sir, can you read?

ROMEO. Ay, mine own fortune in my misery.

SERVANT. Perhaps you have learned it without book; but, I pray, can you read anything you see?

ROMEO. Ay, if I know the letters and the language.

SERVANT. Ye say honestly; rest you merry!°

rest you merry! May you continue happy.

(He thinks ROMEO *is not taking him seriously, and starts to leave.)*

ROMEO. Stay, fellow; I can read. *(He reads the paper.)*
"Signior Martino and his wife and daughters; County Anselme and his beauteous sisters; the lady widow of Vitruvio; Signior Placentio and his lovely nieces; Mercutio and his brother Valentine; mine uncle Capulet, his wife and daughters; my fair niece Rosaline; Livia; Signior Valentio and his cousin Tybalt; Lucio and the lively Helena."

(He returns the paper to the SERVANT.*)*

A fair assembly; whither should they come?

SERVANT. Up.

ROMEO. Whither?

SERVANT. To supper; to our house.

ROMEO. Whose house?

SERVANT. My master's.

ROMEO. Indeed, I should have asked you that before.

SERVANT. Now I'll tell you without asking. My master is the great rich Capulet; and if you be not of the house of Montagues, I pray come and crush a cup° of wine. Rest you merry!

crush a cup, have a drink; a slang term like "crack a bottle" today.

(Exit.)

BENVOLIO. At this same ancient° feast of Capulet's
Sups the fair Rosaline whom thou so lovest,
With all the admirèd beauties of Verona.
Go thither, and, with unattainted° eye,
Compare her face with some that I shall show,
And I will make thee think thy swan a crow. . . .

ancient, customary.

unattainted, unprejudiced, impartial.

ROMEO. One fairer than my love! The all-seeing sun
Ne'er saw her match since first the world begun.

Richard Monette as Romeo, Gregory Wanless as Benvolio in *Romeo and Juliet*, Stratford Festival, Canada, 1977.

BENVOLIO. Tut, you saw her fair, none else being by,
Herself poised with herself in either eye:
But in that crystal scales let there be weighed
Your lady's love against some other maid
That I will show you shining at this feast,
And she shall scant show well that now shows best.[11]
ROMEO. I'll go along, no such sight to be shown,
But to rejoice in splendor of mine own.°
(Exeunt.)

11. How might this chance meeting with the servant advance the plot? As you read the play, note how many examples of coincidence occur.

splendor of mine own, the beauty of the lady I love.

Scene 3: A room in Capulet's house.[12]

12. In this scene you will meet Juliet, her mother, and the nurse. Think of words that describe each person. Consider what each character says and does as well as what one character says about another.

Enter LADY CAPULET *and* NURSE.

LADY CAPULET. Nurse, where's my daughter? Call her forth to me.
NURSE. . . . I bade her come. What, lamb! What, ladybird!
God forbid! Where's this girl? What, Juliet!

(Enter JULIET.*)*

JULIET. How now! Who calls?
NURSE. Your mother.
JULIET. Madam, I am here. What is your will?
LADY CAPULET. This is the matter:—Nurse, give leave° awhile,
We must talk in secret. Nurse, come back again.
I have remembered me, thou's° hear our counsel.
Thou know'st my daughter's of a pretty age.
NURSE. Faith, I can tell her age unto an hour.
LADY CAPULET. She's not fourteen.
NURSE. I'll lay fourteen of my teeth—
And yet, to my teen° be it spoken, I have but four—
She is not fourteen. How long is it now
To Lammastide?°
LADY CAPULET. A fortnight and odd days.
NURSE. Even or odd, of all days in the year,
Come Lammas Eve at night shall she be fourteen.
Susan[13] and she—God rest all Christian souls!—
Were of an age. Well, Susan is with God;
She was too good for me. But, as I said,
On Lammas Eve at night shall she be fourteen;
That shall she, marry; I remember it well.
'Tis since the earthquake° now eleven years;
And she was weaned—I never shall forget it—
Of all the days of the year, upon that day. . . .
My lord and you were then at Mantua:—
Nay, I do bear a brain;° but, as I said. . . .
Since that time it is eleven years;
For then she could stand alone. Nay, by the rood,°
She could have run and waddled all about,
For even the day before, she broke her brow.°
And then my husband—God be with his soul!
A'° was a merry man—took up the child.
"Yea," quoth he, "dost thou fall upon thy face?
Thou wilt fall backward when thou hast more wit,
Wilt thou not, Jule?" and, by my holidame,°
The pretty wretch left crying and said "Aye."
To see, now, how a jest shall come about!
I warrant, an I should live a thousand years,

give leave, leave us alone.

thou's, thou shalt.

teen, sorrow, grief.

Lammastide, August 1.

13. Who was Susan? What has probably happened to her?

earthquake, possibly a reference to a famous earthquake in 1580.

bear a brain, have a good brain or memory.

rood, Holy Cross.

even . . . brow, just the day before she cut her forehead.

A', he.

by my holidame, a mild oath.

I never should forget it: "Wilt thou not, Jule?" quoth he;
And, pretty fool, it stinted° and said "Aye."

LADY CAPULET. Enough of this; I pray thee, hold thy peace.

NURSE. Yes, madam; yet I cannot choose but laugh
To think it should leave crying and say "Aye". . . .

JULIET. And stint thou, too, I pray thee, Nurse, say I.

NURSE. Peace, I have done. God mark thee to His grace!
Thou wast the prettiest babe that e'er I nursed;
An I might live to see thee married once,
I have my wish.

LADY CAPULET. Marry,° that "marry" is the very theme
I came to talk of. Tell me, daughter Juliet,
How stands your disposition to be married?

JULIET. It is an honor that I dream not of. . . .

LADY CAPULET. Well, think of marriage now . . . younger than you
Here in Verona, ladies of esteem,
Are already mothers; by my count,
I was your mother much upon these years°
That you are now a maid. Thus, then, in brief:
The valiant Paris seeks you for his love.

NURSE. A man, young lady! Lady, such a man
As all the world—why, he's a man of wax.°

LADY CAPULET. Verona's summer hath not such a flower.

NURSE. Nay, he's a flower; in faith, a very flower.

LADY CAPULET *(to* JULIET*).* What say you? Can you love the gentleman?
This night you shall behold him at our feast.
Read o'er the volume of young Paris' face
And find delight writ there with beauty's pen;
Examine every married lineament
And see how one another lends content
And what obscured in this fair volume lies
Find written in the margent of his eyes. . . .
Speak briefly; can you like of Paris' love?

JULIET. I'll look to like, if looking liking move.°
But no more deep will I endart mine eye
Than your consent gives strength to make it fly.

(Enter a SERVANT.*)*

SERVANT. Madam, the guests are come, supper served up, you called, my young lady asked for, the nurse cursed in the pantry, and everything in extremity. I must hence to wait; I beseech you, follow straight.°

LADY CAPULET. We follow thee. *(Exit* SERVANT.*)*
Juliet, the county stays.°

NURSE. Go girl, seek happy days.

(Exeunt.)

stinted, stopped crying.

Marry, indeed.

much upon these years, almost at the same age.

a man of wax, as handsome as if modeled in wax.

I'll look . . . move. I am ready to look on him favorably—if just looking at him can inspire liking.

straight, immediately.

the county stays. Count Paris awaits you.

Scene 4: A street in Verona that same evening.

Enter ROMEO, MERCUTIO, BENVOLIO, TORCHBEARERS, *and five or six friends, all but* MERCUTIO *are in masks.*

ROMEO. What, shall this speech be spoke for our excuse?
Or shall we on without apology?
BENVOLIO. The date is out of such prolixity°. . .
We'll measure them a measure,° and be gone.
ROMEO. Give me a torch; I am not for this ambling;°
Being but heavy, I will bear the light.
MERCUTIO. Nay, gentle Romeo, we must have you dance.
ROMEO. Not I, believe me. You have dancing shoes
With nimble soles; I have a soul[14] of lead
So stakes me to the ground I cannot move.
MERCUTIO. You are a lover; borrow Cupid's wings,
And soar with them above a common bound.°
ROMEO. I am too sore enpiercèd with his shaft
To soar with his light feathers; and so bound,
I cannot bound a pitch above dull woe.[15]
Under love's heavy burden do I sink.
MERCUTIO. And, to sink in it, should you burden love—
Too great oppression for a tender thing.
ROMEO *(sighing)*. Is love a tender thing? It is too rough.
Too rude, too boisterous, and it pricks like thorn.[16]
MERCUTIO. If love be rough with you, be rough with love. . . .
Give me a case° to put my visage in:
A visor for a visor!° *(Puts on a mask)* What care I
What curious eye doth quote° deformities? . . .
BENVOLIO. Come, knock and enter; and no sooner in
But every man betake him to his legs.
ROMEO. A torch for me. Let wantons light of heart
Tickle the senseless rushes° with their heels;
For I am proverbed with a grandsire phrase,°
I'll be a candle-holder,° and look on. . . .
MERCUTIO. . . . . Come, we burn daylight,° ho!
ROMEO. Nay, that's not so.
MERCUTIO. I mean, sir, in delay
We waste our lights in vain, like lamps by day. . . .
ROMEO. We mean well in going to this mask, sir;
But 'tis no wit to go.
MERCUTIO. Why, may one ask?
ROMEO. I dreamed a dream tonight.°
MERCUTIO. And so did I.
ROMEO. Well, what was yours?
MERCUTIO. That dreamers often lie.
ROMEO. In bed asleep while they do dream things true.

speech . . . prolixity, it was once customary for maskers to be preceded by a messenger who made an elaborate excuse for their appearance at a party. Benvolio says this is old-fashioned.
measure . . . measure, perform a dance.
ambling, dancing in an affected manner.

14. Did you catch the play on words: *Light/heavy, soul/sole?*

bound, leap, also limit, or boundary.

15. Romeo responds to Mercutio's teasing wit with some word play of his own. How many meanings of the word *bound* can you find?

16. Describe Romeo's mood in this scene.

case, mask.
A visor . . . visor, a mask for an ugly, masklike face.
quote, take notice of.

senseless rushes, unfeeling fibers used as floor coverings.
proverbed . . . phrase, taught by an old saying.
candle-holder, spectator.
burn daylight, to light a candle while the sun is shining; that is, to waste time, as Mercutio explains.

tonight, last night.

MERCUTIO. O, then, I see Queen Mab° hath been with you.
She is the fairies' midwife, and she comes
In shape no bigger than an agate stone
On the forefinger of an alderman,
Drawn with a team of little atomies°
Athwart men's noses as they lie asleep;
Her wagon spokes made of long spinners'° legs,
The cover of the wings of grasshoppers,
The traces of the smallest spider's web,
The collars of the moonshine's watery beams,
Her whip of cricket's bone, the lash of film,°
Her wagoner° a small gray-coated gnat,
Not half so big as a round little worm
Pricked from the lazy finger of a maid.°
Her chariot is an empty hazelnut
Made by the joiner squirrel or old grub,
Time out o' mind the fairies' coachmakers.
And in this state° she gallops night by night
Through lovers' brains, and then they dream of love . . .
O'er lawyers' fingers, who straight dream on fees;
O'er ladies' lips who straight on kisses dream,
Which oft the angry Mab with blisters plagues,
Because their breaths with sweetmeats tainted are.
Sometime she gallops o'er a courtier's nose,
And then dreams he of smelling out a suit° . . . .
Sometimes she driveth o'er a soldier's neck,
And then dreams he of cutting foreign throats,
Of breaches, ambuscadoes, Spanish blades,°
Of healths five-fathom deep; and then anon
Drums in his ear, at which he starts and wakes,
And being thus frighted swears a prayer or two
And sleeps again. This is that very Mab
That plaits the manes of horses in the night,
And bakes the elf locks in foul sluttish hairs,°
Which once untangled much misfortune bodes . . .
This is she——

ROMEO. Peace, peace, Mercutio, peace!
Thou talk'st of nothing.

MERCUTIO. True, I talk of dreams,
Which are the children of an idle brain,
Begot of nothing but vain fantasy,
Which is as thin of substance as the air
And more inconstant than the wind, who woos
Even now the frozen bosom of the north,
And, being angered, puffs away from thence,
Turning his face to the dew-dropping south.

Queen Mab, the fairy queen.

atomies, tiny creatures.

spinners', spiders'.

film, delicate, light thread.

wagoner, coachman.

worm . . . maid. It was popularly believed that worms breed in the fingers of the idle.

state, pomp, dignity.

smelling out a suit, seeing an opportunity to gain royal favor.

ambuscadoes, Spanish blades, surprise attacks with swords made of fine steel from Toledo, in Spain.

bakes . . . hairs, mats together and tangles the hair.

BENVOLIO. This wind you talk of blows us from ourselves;
Supper is done, and we shall come too late.
ROMEO. I fear, too early; for my mind misgives
Some consequence yet hanging in the stars°
Shall bitterly begin his fearful date°
With this night's revels and expire° the term
Of a despisèd life closed in my breast
By some vile forfeit of untimely death.
But He that hath the steerage of my course,
Direct my sail! On, lusty gentlemen. . . .
(Exeunt.)

misgives . . . stars, forbodes some future misfortune not yet determined.
his fearful date, its dreaded time.
expire, bring to an end.

Scene 5: A spacious room in Capulet's house.

. . . .

MUSICIANS *waiting. Enter* CAPULET, LADY CAPULET, *with* JULIET, *the* NURSE, TYBALT, *and others of the* CAPULET *clan, mingling with, and talking to, the* GUESTS.*)*

CAPULET. *(As he speaks, the conversation dies down.)* Welcome, gentlemen! Ladies that have their toes
Unplagued with corns will have a bout° with you.
Ah ha, my mistresses! Which of you all
Will now deny to dance? She that makes dainty,°
She, I'll swear, hath corns; am I come near ye now?°

have a bout, dance a turn.

makes dainty, affectedly hesitates to dance.
am . . . now? Have I hit home to the truth?

*(*ROMEO, BENVOLIO, *and* MERCUTIO *enter the room.)*
Welcome, gentlemen! I have seen the day
That I have worn a visor and could tell
A whispering tale in a fair lady's ear,
Such as would please. 'Tis gone, 'tis gone, 'tis gone.
You are welcome, gentlemen! Come, musicians, play.
A hall, a hall!° Give room, and foot it, girls.
(Music plays, the guests dance, and CAPULET *walks around the room.)*
(To SERVANTS*)* More light, you knaves, and turn the tables up,°
And quench the fire, the room is grown too hot. . . .
(To an elderly kinsman) Nay, sit, nay, sit, good cousin Capulet,
For you and I are past our dancing days.
How long is 't now since last yourself and I
Were in a mask?

A hall, a hall! Make room!

turn the tables up. The tables were flat leaves hinged together and placed on trestles. When they were folded, they took little space.

SECOND CAPULET. By'r lady,° thirty years.
CAPULET. What, man! 'Tis not so much, 'tis not so much.
'Tis since the nuptial of Lucentio,
Come Pentecost as quickly as it will,
Some five and twenty years, and then we masked.

By'r lady, by the Virgin Mary; a mild oath.

SECOND CAPULET. 'Tis more, 'tis more, his son is elder, sir;
His son is thirty.
CAPULET. Will you tell me that?
His son was but a ward two years ago.

(ROMEO, *who has been trying to locate* ROSALINE, *catches a fleeting glimpse of* JULIET, *whose beauty dazzles him. He halts a passing* SERVANT.)

ROMEO. What lady is that, which doth enrich the hand
Of yonder knight?
SERVANT. I know not, sir.°
ROMEO. O, she doth teach the torches to burn bright!
It seems she hangs upon the cheek of night
Like a rich jewel in an Ethiope's ear;
Beauty too rich for use, for earth too dear!°
So shows a snowy dove trooping with crows,
As yonder lady o'er her fellows shows.
The measure done, I'll watch her place of stand,
And, touching hers, make blessèd my rude hand.
Did my heart love till now? Forswear it, sight!
For I ne'er saw true beauty till this night.
TYBALT *(who has been standing near* ROMEO*).* This by his voice, should be a Montague. *(To a servant)*
Fetch me my rapier, boy. What, dares the slave
Come hither, covered with an antic face,
To fleer° and scorn at our solemnity?°
Now, by the stock and honor of my kin,
To strike him dead I hold it not a sin.
CAPULET *(overhearing* TYBALT*).* Why, how now, kinsman! Wherefore storm you so?
TYBALT. Uncle, this is a Montague, our foe,
A villain that is hither come in spite,
To scorn at our solemnity this night.
CAPULET. Young Romeo, is it?
TYBALT. 'Tis he, that villain Romeo.
CAPULET. Content thee, gentle coz, let him alone;
He bears him like a portly° gentleman;
And, to say truth, Verona brags of him
To be a virtuous and well-governed youth.
I would not for the wealth of all the town
Here in my house do him disparagement;
Therefore be patient, take no note of him.
It is my will, the which if thou respect,
Show a fair presence and put off these frowns,
An ill-beseeming semblance for a feast.
TYBALT. It fits° when such a villain is a guest;
I'll not endure him.

I know not, sir. The servant has been hired for the party and does not know Juliet.

dear, precious.

fleer, sneer.
solemnity, celebration.

portly, dignified.

It fits, a frown is fitting.

CAPULET *(sternly, while restraining* TYBALT*)*. He shall be endured.
What, goodman boy!° I say, he shall. Go to;°
Am I the master here, or you? Go to.
You'll not endure him! God shall mend my soul!°
You'll make a mutiny among my guests! . . .

goodman boy, a scornful term.
Go to, come now (a reproof).

God . . . soul! God save me!

TYBALT *(grumbling)*. Why, Uncle, 'tis a shame.

CAPULET. Go to, go to.
You are a saucy boy; is't so, indeed?
This trick may chance to scathe° you, I know what.
You must contrary me!° Marry, 'tis time.
(To GUESTS.*)* Well said, my hearts!° *(To* TYBALT*)* You are a princox;° go.
Be quiet, or—*(To* SERVANTS*)* More light, more light! *(To* TYBALT*)* For shame!
I'll make you quiet. *(To* GUESTS*)* What, cheerly, my hearts!

scathe, injure.

You must contrary me! You insist on opposing my wishes!
Well said, my hearts! You have danced well, good fellows!
princox, a saucy youngster.

TYBALT. Patience perforce° with willful choler meeting
Makes my flesh tremble in their different greeting.°
I will withdraw; but this intrusion shall,
Now seeming sweet, convert to bitter gall.
(Exit)

Patience perforce, imposed patience or restraint.
different greeting, opposition.

ROMEO *(finally reaching* JULIET *and placing his palm up as if to dance. Instead, however, he ignores the music and simply speaks)*. If I profane with my unworthiest hand
This holy shrine, the gentle fine° is this:
My lips, two blushing pilgrims, ready stand
To smooth that rough touch with a tender kiss.

gentle fine, mild penance.

JULIET. Good pilgrim,° you do wrong your hand too much,
Which mannerly devotion shows in this;
For saints have hands that pilgrims' hands do touch,
And palm to palm is holy palmers' kiss.

pilgrim. Romeo was masquerading as a palmer—a pilgrim who had visited the Holy Land.

ROMEO. Have not saints lips, and holy palmers too?
JULIET. Ay, pilgrim, lips that they must use in prayer.
ROMEO. O, then, dear saint, let lips do what hands do;
They pray, grant thou, lest faith turn to despair.
JULIET. Saints do not move, though grant for prayers' sake.
ROMEO. Then move not, while my prayer's effect I take
Thus from my lips, by yours, my sin is purged.
(His lips touch hers briefly.)
JULIET. Then have my lips the sin that they have took.
ROMEO. Sin from my lips? O trespass sweetly urged!
Give me my sin again.
(They kiss again until JULIET *breaks the spell by teasing* ROMEO.*)*
JULIET. You kiss by the book.°

by the book, according to rule.

NURSE *(who has made her way through the crowds to find* JULIET*)*.
Madam, your mother craves a word with you.
*(*JULIET *reluctantly leaves* ROMEO.*)*

ROMEO *(to the* NURSE*)*. What is her mother?
NURSE *(to* ROMEO*)*. Marry, bachelor,
Her mother is the lady of the house,
And a good lady, and a wise and virtuous.
I nursed her daughter, that you talked withal;°
I tell you, he that can lay hold of her
Shall have the chinks.°

withal, with.

chinks, money (inherited by Juliet from her father).

(NURSE *moves away from* ROMEO *and into the crowd.)*
ROMEO *(stricken)*. Is she a Capulet?
O dear° account! My life is my foe's debt.°

dear, costly.
my foe's debt, a debt due my foe, which he may or may not take, as he wishes.

BENVOLIO *(coming forward)*. Away, be gone; the sport is at the best.
ROMEO. Ay, so I fear; the more is my unrest.
CAPULET *(addressing the guests who are about to take their leave)*.
Nay, gentlemen, prepare not to be gone;
We have a trifling foolish banquet towards.°

foolish banquet towards, a simple dessert about to be served.

(BENVOLIO *says something to* CAPULET, *who laughs.)*
Is it e'en so? Why, then, I thank you all;
I thank you, honest gentlemen; good night.
(To a SERVANT*)* More torches here! Come on, then, let's to bed.
Ah, sirrah, by my fay,° it waxes late;
I'll to my rest.

fay, faith.

(BENVOLIO *and* ROMEO *join the departing guests;* NURSE *stands near* JULIET.*)*
JULIET. Come hither, Nurse. What is yond gentleman?
NURSE. The son and heir of old Tiberio.
JULIET. What's he that now is going out of door?
NURSE. Marry, that, I think, be young Petrucio.
JULIET. What's he that follows there, that would not dance?
NURSE. I know not. *(The* NURSE *does know, but tries to keep* JULIET *from learning that the man is* ROMEO*—and a Montague.)*
JULIET. Go, ask his name. If he is married,
My grave is like to be my wedding bed.
NURSE *(seeing that it is useless to hide* ROMEO*'s identity)*.
His name is Romeo, and a Montague,
The only son of your great enemy.
JULIET. My only love sprung from my only hate!
Too early seen unknown, and known too late!
Prodigious° birth of love it is to me,
That I must love a loathèd enemy.

Prodigious, suggesting bad luck.

NURSE. What's this? What's this?
JULIET. A rhyme I learned even now
Of one I danced withal.
(A call off-stage: "Juliet.")
NURSE. Anon, anon!
Come, let's away; the strangers all are gone.
(Exeunt.)

Richard Monette as Romeo, Marti Maraden as Juliet in *Romeo and Juliet,* Stratford Festival, Canada, 1977.

Discussion

Prologue and Scene 1

1. (a) Name the two feuding families. **(b)** Identify the following characters and the family with which each is associated: Tybalt, Benvolio, Romeo. **(c)** Who is Escalus and what is his power over the two families?

2. (a) How does Benvolio propose to change Romeo's mood? **(b)** What is Romeo's reaction?

3. (a) Why is it necessary for Scene 1 to take place in a public square? **(b)** The two heads of families arrive on the scene quickly. Where might a set designer place their two houses?

4. To the people of Shakespeare's time, disorder in a community threatened the authority of the ruler and the stability of the state. Find examples of this belief in Escalus's speech.

Scene 2

1. What two lines of action—one concerning Paris; the other, Romeo—are set in motion?

2. What arguments used by Benvolio persuade Romeo to attend the party?

3. Does Capulet seem sincere in his concern for his daughter's happiness in marriage? Cite lines from the play to support your opinion.

4. What other side of his character does Romeo show in his scene with the servant?

Scene 3

1. What line of action, established in Scene 2, continues in this scene?

2. The nurse is not a clown like the servants. She provides humor, but she also exhibits other qualities. Describe these, paying particular attention to her relationship with Juliet.

3. At the time in which the play is set, marriages were often arranged by parents for their children. Love was an emotion that came after marriage, if at all. What makes Juliet's parents unusual in their attitude?

Scene 4

1. Romeo and his friends plan to attend their enemy's party. What will keep them from being detected?

2. What causes Mercutio to tell Romeo about Queen Mab?

3. What does Mercutio's speech about the fairy queen tell us about his imagination? his sense of humor? his beliefs about free will and destiny (or fate)?

4. Where does this scene take place? What other people, not of Romeo's group, would you expect to be on the stage?

Scene 5

1. (a) Describe the general atmosphere as the scene opens. **(b)** How is that atmosphere affected by Tybalt's reaction to Romeo? **(c)** Describe the atmosphere as the scene ends.

2. Having fallen deeply in love, Romeo and Juliet kiss and part. Then each makes a surprising discovery. **(a)** What is that discovery? **(b)** How does the discovery affect each of them?

3. In line 36, Romeo asks, "Did my heart love till now?" **(a)** What is he implying? **(b)** How would you answer his question? Why?

Composition

It's been an eventful day for Juliet. Assume that she sits down to write an entry in her diary immediately after the Sunday evening party.

Write Juliet's entry for her. First, list the events of the day that she might consider important. Then, arrange these events in the order that Juliet might discuss them in her diary. Be sure that the tone and content of the diary entry is keeping with Juliet's personality—polite and obedient yet emotional and strong-willed.

Comment: Staging Plays in Shakespeare's Time

By modern standards, the stage of the sixteenth century was primitive and the properties, or props, (furniture and small articles such as swords) almost nonexistent. However, it is important to remember that the audience viewing the plays—unlike you and your contemporaries—had not experienced electric lighting (and the elaborate staging it allows), movies, or television. What they were seeing was the latest in stagecraft in the 1590s.

The theaters used during Shakespeare's time have been either dismantled or destroyed by fire, but drawings and descriptions from the period allow us to imagine how they looked. The illustration here is of the Globe—the playhouse most closely associated with Shakespeare and the one where many of his plays were first performed.

As you study the illustration, note that the *platform* (also called the *cockpit*) in the center jutted out into the area in front of it. (The ground in this area was paved with bricks.) The platform was about 5½ feet high. The roof, or *canopy,* was supported by two columns, and this canopy extended to cover about half of the cockpit. The rooms on the top two floors could be curtained or not, depending on the requirements of a particular play. The middle room of the top floor was used as a musicians' gallery. The three rooms above it are called *huts;* and above them was the *turret,* from which the flag was flown to indicate that a performance was to be given. Both ordinary doors and trap doors allowed characters to enter and exit various parts of the stage.

Surrounding the entire stage was a hollow, eight-sided structure three stories high. (It is not shown in the illustration.) This building formed a circle—a "wooden O," as Shakespeare calls it. While the structure itself had a roof, the area it enclosed did not. Those people who could afford only the lowest admission fee stood in the unroofed, brick-paved yard to watch the play. These people were—aptly—called *groundlings.* People who were more well-to-do paid higher admission fees to sit within the structure, where benches were placed on each of the three floors.

The actors' costumes often were used to state rank, profession, or affiliation. Escalus's crown announces that he is a ruler. A ring of keys at Lady Capulet's waist indicates her position as lady of the house. Servants' livery (uniforms) indicates loyalty—for example, servants of the Capulets might wear blue; servants of the Montagues, red.

Painted scenery was not used until very late in the sixteenth century. Shakespeare indicated the location of a scene through dialogue or props such as a stool, a rock, or an altar.

Sound effects were provided by the musicians. They accompanied songs; and, in *Romeo and Juliet,* they provided music for the ball at the Capulets's. In addition, they might have rung bells to announce the time and provided sounds such as cannon fire or thunder. In the Prologue to Shakespeare's *The Life of King Henry V* (a play having scenes set in both England and France and containing scenes of battle), the audience is asked, "Can this cockpit hold / The vasty fields of France? Or may we cram / Within this wooden O the very casques[1] / That did affright the air at Agincourt?"[2] If taken literally, both questions could only be answered, "No." But the Prologue continues by urging, "Into a thousand parts divide one man" and "Think, when we talk of horses, that you see them / Printing their proud hoofs in the receiving earth," so that the audience might indeed "see" a mighty army. Thus viewers are encouraged to allow the play to work on their imaginations. The present-day reader could do worse than follow this advice.

1. ***casque*** (kask), a helmet.
2. ***Agincourt*** (aj′in kôrt), a village in France, scene of an English victory under Henry V in 1415.

Act Two

Scene 1: A lane outside the wall of Capulet's orchard; after the party.

Enter ROMEO.

ROMEO. Can I go forward when my heart is here?
Turn back, dull earth,° and find thy center° out.
(He climbs the wall and leaps down within it.)

dull earth, Romeo himself.
thy center, Juliet.

(Enter BENVOLIO *and* MERCUTIO.*)*

BENVOLIO *(calling to the hidden* ROMEO*).* Romeo! My cousin Romeo!
MERCUTIO. He is wise,
And, on my life, hath stolen him home to bed.
BENVOLIO. He ran this way, and leaped this orchard wall.
Call, good Mercutio.
MERCUTIO *(jestingly).* Nay, I'll conjure too.
Romeo! Humors!° Madman! Passion! Lover!
Appear thou in the likeness of a sigh;
Speak but one rhyme, and I am satisfied;
Cry but "Ay me"; pronounce but "love" and "dove". . . .
(To BENVOLIO*)* He heareth not, he stirreth not, he moveth not;
The ape° is dead, and I must conjure him.
(Calls jestingly to ROMEO*)* I conjure thee by Rosaline's bright eyes,

Humors! Romantic whims.

ape, used as a term of endearment.

By her high forehead and her scarlet lip . . .
That in thy likeness thou appear to us!
BENVOLIO. An if he hear thee, thou wilt anger him.
MERCUTIO. This cannot anger him . . . my invocation
Is fair and honest,° and in his mistress' name
I conjure only but to raise up him.
BENVOLIO. Come, he hath hid himself among these trees,
To be consorted with the humorous night;°
Blind is his love and best befits the dark.
MERCUTIO. If love be blind, love cannot hit the mark. . . .
Romeo, good night. I'll to my truckle bed;°
This field bed° is too cold for me to sleep.
Come, shall we go?
BENVOLIO. Go, then; for 'tis in vain
To seek him here that means not to be found.
(Exeunt.)

honest, honorable.

consorted . . . night, associated with the moist night.

truckle bed, a small bed that can be run under a larger one.
field bed, the ground.

Scene 2: A beautiful orchard in the Capulets' grounds, with a balcony of the house prominently placed outside Juliet's bedroom.

Enter ROMEO.
ROMEO. He jests at scars that never felt a wound.°
(Catching sight of JULIET *at her dimly lighted window.)*
But soft, what light through yonder window breaks?
It is the east, and Juliet is the sun.
Arise, fair sun, and kill the envious moon,
Who is already sick and pale with grief,
That thou her maid art far more fair than she.
Be not her maid, since she is envious . . .
*(*JULIET *steps out onto the balcony.)*
It is my lady. O, it is my love!
O, that she knew she were!
She speaks, yet she says nothing. What of that?
Her eye discourses; I will answer it.
I am too bold, 'tis not to me she speaks;
Two of the fairest stars in all the heaven,
Having some business, do entreat her eyes
To twinkle in their spheres° till they return.
What if her eyes were there, they in her head?
The brightness of her cheek would shame those stars
As daylight doth a lamp; her eyes in heaven
Would through the airy region stream so bright
That birds would sing and think it were not night.
See how she leans her cheek upon her hand!

He jests . . . wound. Romeo has overheard the jests made by Mercutio, who, Romeo says, has never known the pangs of love.

spheres, the hollow, transparent globes in which, it was believed, the stars and other planets were set.

O, that I were a glove upon that hand,
That I might touch that cheek![17]

17. When Romeo speaks of and to Juliet, Shakespeare uses many images of light. What examples can you find in lines 2–20?

JULIET. Ay me!
ROMEO. She speaks.
O, speak again, bright angel, for thou art
As glorious to this night, being o'er my head,
As is a wingèd messenger of heaven
Unto the white-upturnèd wondering eyes
Of mortals that fall back to gaze on him
When he bestrides the lazy-pacing clouds
And sails upon the bosom of the air.
JULIET *(unaware that she is being overheard).* O Romeo, Romeo,
wherefore[18] art thou Romeo?

18. "Wherefore" means *why*. Juliets asks *why* he is a Montague, not where he is.

Deny thy father and refuse thy name;
Or, if thou wilt not, be but sworn my love,
And I'll no longer be a Capulet.
ROMEO *(aside).* Shall I hear more, or shall I speak at this?
JULIET. 'Tis but thy name that is my enemy;
Thou art thyself, though not a Montague.°
What's Montague? It is nor hand nor foot,

though . . . Montague, even if you were not a Montague.

Marti Maraden as Juliet in *Romeo and Juliet,* Stratford Festival, Canada, 1977.

Nor arm, nor face, nor any other part
Belonging to a man. O, be some other name!
What's in a name? That which we call a rose
By any other name would smell as sweet;
So Romeo would, were he not Romeo called,
Retain that dear perfection which he owes°
Without that title. Romeo, doff thy name,
And for that name, which is no part of thee,
Take all myself.

ROMEO *(speaking loudly enough to be heard by* JULIET*).*
I take thee at thy word.
Call me but love, and I'll be new baptized;
Henceforth I never will be Romeo.

JULIET. What man art thou that thus bescreened in night
So stumblest on my counsel?°

ROMEO. By a name
I know not how to tell thee who I am.
My name, dear saint, is hateful to myself,
Because it is an enemy to thee;
Had I it written, I would tear the word.

JULIET. My ears have not yet drunk a hundred words
Of thy tongue's utterance, yet I know the sound.
Art thou not Romeo and a Montague?

ROMEO. Neither, fair saint, if either thee dislike.

JULIET. How camest thou hither, tell me, and wherefore?
The orchard walls are high and hard to climb,
And the place death, considering who thou art,
If any of my kinsmen find thee here.

ROMEO. With love's light wings did I o'erperch° these walls;
For stony limits cannot hold love out,
And what love can do, that dares love attempt;
Therefore thy kinsmen are no let° to me.

JULIET. If they do see thee, they will murder thee.

ROMEO. Alack, there lies more peril in thine eye
Than twenty of their swords; look thou but sweet,
And I am proof° against their enmity.

JULIET. I would not for the world they saw thee here.

ROMEO. I have night's cloak to hide me from their eyes;
And but thou love me,° let them find me here.
My life were better ended by their hate
Than death prorogued,° wanting of° thy love.

JULIET. By whose direction found'st thou out this place?

ROMEO. By love, who first did prompt me to inquire;
He lent me counsel and I lent him eyes.
I am no pilot; yet, wert thou as far

owes, owns.

counsel, secret thoughts.

o'erperch, fly over and perch beyond.

let, hindrance.

proof, safeguarded by armor.

but thou love me, unless you love me.

prorogued, postponed.
wanting of, lacking.

As that vast shore washed with the farthest sea,
I would adventure for such merchandise.
JULIET. Thou know'st the mask of night is on my face,
Else would a maiden blush bepaint my cheek
For that which thou hast heard me speak tonight.
Fain° would I dwell on form,° fain, fain deny
What I have spoke; but farewell compliment!°
Dost thou love me? I know thou will say "Ay,"
And I will take thy word. Yet, if thou swear'st,
Thou mayst prove false; at lovers' perjuries,
They say, Jove° laughs. O gentle Romeo,
If thou dost love, pronounce it faithfully;
Or if thou think'st I am too quickly won,
I'll frown and be perverse and say thee nay,
So thou wilt woo; but else, not for the world.
In truth, fair Montague, I am too fond,°
And therefore thou mayst think my 'havior light.
But trust me, gentleman, I'll prove more true
Than those that have more cunning to be strange.°
I should have been more strange, I must confess,
But that thou overheard'st, ere I was ware,
My true love's passion; therefore pardon me,
And not impute this yielding to light love,
Which the dark night hath so discoverèd.°
ROMEO. Lady, by yonder blessèd moon I vow
That tips with silver all these fruit tree tops——
JULIET. O, swear not by the moon, the inconstant moon,[19]
That monthly changes in her circled orb,
Lest that thy love prove likewise variable.
ROMEO. What shall I swear by?
JULIET. Do not swear at all;
Or, if thou wilt, swear by thy gracious self,
Which is the god of my idolatry,
And I'll believe thee.
ROMEO. If my heart's dear love——
JULIET. Well, do not swear. Although I joy in thee,
I have no joy of this contract tonight;
It is too rash, too unadvised,° too sudden,
Too like the lightning, which doth cease to be
Ere one can say "It lightens." Sweet, good night!
This bud of love, by summer's ripening breath,
May prove a beauteous flower when next we meet.[20]
Good night, good night! As sweet repose and rest
Come to thy heart as that within my breast.
ROMEO. O, wilt thou leave me so unsatisfied?
JULIET. What satisfaction canst thou have tonight?

Fain, gladly.
dwell on form, stick to formalities.
compliment, ceremony, formal manners.

Jove, ruler of the gods and men.

fond, foolish.

strange, reserved, distant.

discoverèd, revealed.

19. Why does Juliet object to Romeo's vow "by the moon"?

unadvised, heedless.

20. What worries Juliet about the rapidity with which she and Romeo have fallen in love? What simile does she use to express her concern?

ROMEO. The exchange of thy love's faithful vow for mine.
JULIET. I gave thee mine before thou didst request it,
And yet I would it were to give again.
ROMEO. Wouldst thou withdraw it? For what purpose, love?
JULIET. But to be frank,° and give it thee again.
And yet I wish but for the thing I have.
My bounty is as boundless as the sea,
My love as deep; the more I give to thee,
The more I have, for both are infinite.
(NURSE *calls "Juliet" from inside the bedroom.)*
I hear some noise within; dear love, adieu![21]
Anon, good Nurse! Sweet Montague, be true.
Stay but a little, I will come again.
(JULIET *goes into her bedroom.)*
ROMEO. O blessèd, blessèd night! I am afeard.
Being in night, all this is but a dream,
Too flattering-sweet to be substantial.
(JULIET returns to the balcony.)
JULIET. Three words, dear Romeo, and good night indeed.
If that thy bent of love° be honorable,
Thy purpose marriage, send me word tomorrow,
By one that I'll procure to come to thee,
Where and what time thou wilt perform the rite;
And all my fortunes at thy foot I'll lay
And follow thee my lord throughout the world.
NURSE *(within the bedroom).* Madam!
JULIET. I come, anon.—But if thou meanest not well,
I do beseech thee——
NURSE *(within and more persistently).* Madam!
JULIET. By and by° I come—
To cease thy suit, and leave me to my grief.
Tomorrow will I send.
ROMEO. So thrive my soul——
JULIET. A thousand times good night!
(JULIET *goes inside for a few moments.)*
ROMEO. A thousand times the worse, to want thy light.
Love goes toward love as schoolboys from their books,
But love from love, toward school with heavy looks.
(ROMEO *reluctantly begins to back away when* JULIET *reappears.)*
JULIET. Hist! Romeo, hist! *(To herself)* O, for a falconer's voice,
To lure this tassel-gentle° back again!
Bondage is hoarse, and may not speak aloud;°
Else would I tear the cave where Echo° lies,
And make her airy tongue more hoarse than mine
With repetition of my Romeo's name.
ROMEO. It is my soul that calls upon my name.

frank, generous.

21. Note how many times Juliet leaves the balcony during the rest of the scene. What does each absence give Romeo the opportunity to say?

thy bent of love, the intentions of your love.

By and by, at once.

tassel-gentle, a male hawk.

Bondage . . . speak aloud. I am bound down by the necessity of not being overheard.

Echo, a nymph who pined away for a handsome youth until only her voice was left.

How silver-sweet sound lovers' tongues by night,
Like softest music to attending ears!

JULIET. Romeo!

ROMEO. My dear?

JULIET. At what o'clock tomorrow
Shall I send to thee?

ROMEO. At the hour of nine.

JULIET. I will not fail; 'tis twenty years till then.
I have forgot why I did call thee back.

ROMEO. Let me stand here till thou remember it.

JULIET. I shall forget, to have thee still stand there,
Remembering how I love thy company.

ROMEO. And I'll still stay, to have thee still forget,
Forgetting any other home but this.

JULIET. 'Tis almost morning; I would have thee gone,
And yet no further than a wanton's bird,
Who lets it hop a little from her hand,
Like a poor prisoner in his twisted gyves,
And with a silk thread plucks it back again,
So loving-jealous of his liberty.

ROMEO. I would I were thy bird.

JULIET. Sweet, so would I;
Yet I should kill thee with much cherishing.
Good night, good night! Parting is such sweet sorrow
That I shall say good night till it be morrow.

(She goes into her room.)

ROMEO. Sleep dwell upon thine eyes, peace in thy breast!
Would I were sleep and peace, so sweet to rest!
Hence will I to my ghostly° father's cell,
His help to crave, and my dear hap° to tell.

(Exit.)

ghostly, spiritual.

dear hap, good fortune.

Scene 3: Friar Laurence's cell.

Enter FRIAR LAURENCE *with a basketful of herbs believed to be health-giving.*

FRIAR LAURENCE. The gray-eyed morn smiles on the frowning night,
Check'ring the eastern clouds with streaks of light,
And fleckèd darkness like a drunkard reels
From forth day's path and Titan's° fiery wheels.
Now, ere the sun advance his burning eye,
The day to cheer and night's dank dew to dry,
I must up-fill this osier cage° of ours

Titan's. Helios, the sun god, was descended from a race of giants called Titans.

osier cage, willow basket.

With baleful weeds and precious-juicèd flowers . . .
Many for many virtues excellent,
None but for some° and yet all different.
O, mickle° is the powerful grace° that lies
In herbs, plants, stones, and their true qualities;
For naught so vile that on the earth doth live
But to the earth some special good doth give,
Nor aught so good but strained from that fair use
Revolts from true birth,° stumbling on abuse.
Virtue itself turns vice, being misapplied,
And vice sometime's by action dignified.
(ROMEO *enters and stands by the door unseen.)*
Within the infant rind of this small flower
Poison hath residence and medicine powers;
For this, being smelt, with that part cheers each part,°
Being tasted, slays all senses with the heart.°
Two such opposèd kings encamp them still
In man as well as herbs—grace and rude will;°
And where the worser is predominant,
Full soon the canker° death eats up that plant.

(ROMEO *advances and speaks.)*
ROMEO. Good morrow, Father.
FRIAR LAURENCE. Benedicite!°
What early tongue so sweet saluteth me?
Young son, it argues a distempered head
So soon to bid good morrow° to thy bed.
Care keeps his watch in every old man's eye,
And where care lodges, sleep will never lie;
But where unbruisèd youth with unstuffed brain°
Doth couch his limbs, there golden sleep doth reign.
Therefore thy earliness doth me assure
Thou art up-roused by some distemperature;
Or if not so, then here I hit it right—
Our Romeo hath not been in bed tonight.
ROMEO. That last is true; the sweeter rest was mine.
FRIAR LAURENCE. God pardon sin! Wast thou with Rosaline?
ROMEO. With Rosaline, my ghostly father? No;
I have forgot that name, and that name's woe.
FRIAR LAURENCE. That's my good son; but where hast thou been then?
ROMEO. I'll tell thee, ere thou ask it me again.
I have been feasting with mine enemy,
Where on a sudden one hath wounded me,
That's by me wounded; both our remedies

None but for some. No plant entirely lacks value.
mickle, much.
grace, virtue, worth.

Revolts . . . birth, betrays its own special purpose.

that part . . . part. Its odor refreshes all parts of the body.
with the heart, by stopping the heart.

rude will, violent, lustful disposition.

canker, cankerworm, which destroys plants.

Benedicite (ben′ə dis′ə tā). God bless us.

good morrow, farewell.

unstuffed brain, mind unoccupied with busy thoughts and cares.

Within thy help and holy physic° lies.
I bear no hatred, blessèd man, for, lo,
My intercession likewise steads° my foe.

FRIAR LAURENCE. Be plain, good son, and homely in thy drift;°
Riddling confession finds but riddling shrift.°

ROMEO. Then plainly know my heart's dear love is set
On the fair daughter of rich Capulet.
As mine on hers, so hers is set on mine,
And all combined,° save what thou must combine
By holy marriage. When and where and how
We met, we wooed, and made exchange of vow,
I'll tell thee as we pass; but this I pray,
That thou consent to marry us today.

FRIAR LAURENCE. Holy Saint Francis, what a change is here!
Is Rosaline, whom thou didst love so dear,
So soon forsaken? Young men's love then lies
Not truly in their hearts, but in their eyes.
Jesu Maria, what a deal of brine
Hath washed thy sallow cheeks for Rosaline!
How much salt water thrown away in waste,
To season love, that of it doth not taste!
The sun not yet thy sighs from heaven clears,
Thy old groans ring yet in my ancient ears;
Lo, here upon thy cheek the stain doth sit
Of an old tear that is not washed off yet:
If e'er thou wast thyself and these woes thine,
Thou and these woes were all for Rosaline.
And art thou changed? Pronounce this sentence then:
Women may fall when there's no strength in men.

ROMEO. Thou chid'st° me oft for loving Rosaline.

FRIAR LAURENCE. For doting, not for loving, pupil mine.

ROMEO. And bad'st me bury love.

FRIAR LAURENCE. Not in a grave,
To lay one in, another out to have.

ROMEO. I pray thee, chide me not; she whom I love now
Doth grace for grace and love for love allow;
The other did not so.

FRIAR LAURENCE. O, she knew well
Thy love did read by rote° and could not spell.
But come, young waverer, come, go with me,
In one respect I'll thy assistant be;
For this alliance may so happy prove
To turn your households' rancor to pure love.[22]

ROMEO. O, let us hence; I stand on° sudden haste.

FRIAR LAURENCE. Wisely and slow; they stumble that run fast.

(ROMEO and the FRIAR go out.)

physic, medicine.

steads, helps.

homely . . . drift, simple and direct.

shrift, absolution.

all combined, the arrangement is complete.

chid'st, scolded.

did read by rote, merely repeated conventional expressions of love.

22. What moves Friar Laurence to assist Romeo?

I stand on, I am in a position demanding.

Scene 4: A street in Verona on the morning after the ball.

Enter MERCUTIO *and* BENVOLIO.

MERCUTIO. Where the devil should this Romeo be?
Came he not home tonight?°

BENVOLIO. Not to his father's; I spoke with his man.

MERCUTIO. Ah, that same pale hard-hearted wench, that Rosaline,
Torments him so that he will sure run mad.

BENVOLIO. Tybalt, the kinsman of old Capulet,
Hath sent a letter to his father's house.

MERCUTIO. A challenge, on my life.

BENVOLIO. Romeo will answer it.

MERCUTIO. Any man that can write may answer a letter.

BENVOLIO. Nay, he will answer the letter's master, how he dares, being dared.°

MERCUTIO. Alas, poor Romeo! He is already dead, stabbed with a white wench's black eye, shot through the ear with a love song; the very pin of his heart cleft with the blind bow-boy's buttshaft; and is he a man to encounter Tybalt?

BENVOLIO. Why, what is Tybalt?

MERCUTIO. More than Prince of Cats,° I can tell you. O, he is the courageous captain of compliments.° He fights as you sing, keeps time, distance, and proportion;° rests me his minim rest,° one, two, and the third in your bosom; the very butcher of a silk button,° a duelist, a duelist; a gentleman of the very first house,° of the first and second cause.° Ah, the immortal passado!° the punto reverso!° the hai!° . . .

(Enter ROMEO, *who shows no sign of his former moodiness.)*

BENVOLIO. Here comes Romeo, here comes Romeo!

MERCUTIO. . . . Signior Romeo, bon jour!° There's a French salutation to your French slop.° You gave us the counterfeit° fairly last night.

ROMEO. Good morrow to you both. What counterfeit did I give you?

MERCUTIO. The slip,° sir, the slip; can you not conceive?

ROMEO. Pardon, good Mercutio, my business was great; and in such a case as mine a man may strain courtesy.

(He laughs and claps MERCUTIO *on the shoulder.)*

MERCUTIO. That's as much as to say, such a case as yours constrains a man to bow in the hams.

ROMEO. Meaning, to curtsey.

MERCUTIO. Thou hast most kindly hit it.

ROMEO. A most courteous exposition.

MERCUTIO. Nay, I am the very pink of courtesy.

tonight, last night.

dared, challenged.

Prince of Cats, a play on Tybalt's name. In a collection of fables the name of the Prince of Cats was Tibert or Tibalt.

captain of compliments, master of rules of ceremony in dueling.

time, distance, and proportion, technical fencing terms.

minim rest, a half rest in music.

butcher . . . button, one who can select and cut off any button of his adversary.

of the very first house, of first rank as a duelist.

of the first . . . cause, ready to quarrel over anything—or nothing.

passado (pə sä′dō), a step forward or aside in thrusting.

punto reverso (pun′tō ri vėr′sō), a backhanded thrust from the left side of the body.

hai (hā), a thrust that strikes the opposing duelist.

Signior (sē′nyôr) . . . **bon jour** (bôN zhür′). Sir Romeo, good day.

slop, large breeches (a French style).

gave . . . counterfeit, played us a trick.

slip, a counterfeit coin.

ROMEO. Pink for flower.

MERCUTIO. Right.

ROMEO. Why, then *(Kicking him lightly)* is my pump well-flowered.

MERCUTIO. Sure wit, follow me this jest now til thou hast worn out thy pump, that when the single sole of it is worn, the jest may remain after the wearing solely singular.

ROMEO. O single-soled jest, solely singular for the singleness.

MERCUTIO. Come between us, good Benvolio; my wits faint.

ROMEO. Swits and spurs, swits and spurs; or I'll cry a match. . . .

MERCUTIO. Why, is not this better now than groaning for love? Now art thou sociable, now art thou Romeo. Now art thou what thou art, by art as well as by nature. . . .

ROMEO. Here's goodly gear!°

gear, business.

(Enter NURSE *and* PETER, *her servant. He is carrying a large fan.)*

ROMEO. A sail, a sail!

MERCUTIO. Two, two; a shirt and a smock.°

shirt . . . smock, indicating a man and a woman.

NURSE. Peter!

PETER. Anon!

NURSE. My fan, Peter.

MERCUTIO. Good Peter, to hide her face, for her fan's the fairer face.

NURSE. God ye good morrow,° gentlemen.

God . . . morrow. God give you a good morning.

MERCUTIO. God ye good den, fair gentlewoman. . . .

NURSE. . . . Gentlemen, can any of you tell me where I may find the young Romeo?

ROMEO. I can tell you; but young Romeo will be older when you have found him than he was when you sought him. I am the youngest of that name, for fault° of a worse. . . .

fault, lack.

NURSE. If you be he, sir, I desire some confidence° with you.

confidence, the nurse's blunder for *conference.*

BENVOLIO. She will indite° him to some supper. . . .

indite. Imitating the nurse, Benvolio jokingly misuses *indite* for *invite.*

MERCUTIO. Romeo, will you come to your father's? We'll to dinner thither.

ROMEO. I will follow you.

MERCUTIO. Farewell, ancient lady; farewell. *(Singing)* "Lady, lady, lady."

(Exeunt MERCUTIO *and* BENVOLIO.*)*

NURSE. Marry, farewell! I pray you, sir, what saucy merchant° was this, that was so full of his ropery?°

merchant, fellow.

ropery, roguery.

ROMEO. A gentleman, Nurse, that loves to hear himself talk, and will speak more in a minute than he will stand to° in a month.

stand to, maintain.

NURSE. An a' speak anything against me, I'll take him down, an a' were lustier than he is, and twenty such Jacks;° and if I cannot, I'll find those that shall. Scurvy knave! I am none of his flirt-

Jacks, rascals.

gills.° *(To* PETER*)* And thou must stand by, too, and suffer every knave to use me at his pleasure?

PETER. I saw no man use you at his pleasure. If I had, my weapon should quickly have been out, I warrant you. I dare draw as soon as another man if I see occasion in a good quarrel, and the law on my side.

NURSE. Now, afore God, I am so vexed that every part about me quivers. *(Muttering to herself)* Scurvy knave! *(To* ROMEO, *after regaining her composure)* Pray you, sir, a word; and, as I told you, my young lady bade me inquire you out. What she bade me say, I will keep to myself; but first let me tell ye, if ye should lead her into a fool's paradise, as they say, it were a very gross kind of behavior, as they say. For the gentlewoman is young; and, therefore, if you should deal double with her, truly it were an ill thing to be offered to any gentlewoman, and very weak dealing.

ROMEO. Nurse, commend me to thy lady and mistress. I protest° unto thee——

NURSE. Good heart, and, i' faith, I will tell her as much. Lord, Lord, she will be a joyful woman.

ROMEO. What wilt thou tell her, Nurse? Thou dost not mark me.°

NURSE. I will tell her, sir, that you do protest; which, as I take it, is a gentlemanlike offer.

ROMEO. Bid her devise
Some means to come to shrift this afternoon;
And there she shall at Friar Laurence' cell
Be shrived and married. Here *(Offers money)* is for thy pains.

NURSE. No, truly, sir, not a penny.

ROMEO. Go to;° I say you shall.

NURSE *(taking the money and pocketing it).* This afternoon, sir? Well, she shall be there.

ROMEO. And stay, good Nurse, behind the abbey wall.
Within this hour my man shall be with thee,
And bring thee cords made like a tackled stair;°
Which to the high topgallant° of my joy
Must be my convoy° in the secret night.
Farewell; be trusty, and I'll quit° thy pains.
Farewell; commend me to thy mistress.

NURSE. Now God in heaven bless thee! *(She turns to go but stops and calls to* ROMEO.*)* Hark you, sir.

ROMEO. What say'st thou, my dear Nurse?

NURSE. Is your man secret?° Did you ne'er hear say,
Two may keep counsel, putting one away?

ROMEO. I warrant thee, my man's as true as steel.

NURSE. Well, sir, my mistress is the sweetest lady—Lord, Lord, When 'twas a little prating thing! O, there is a nobleman in

flirt-gills, flirtatious women.

protest, vow.

mark me, pay attention to what I say.

Go to, say nothing more.

tackled stair, rope ladder.

topgallant, summit, height.

convoy, means of conducting me.

quit, reward.

secret, trustworthy.

town, one Paris, that would fain lay knife aboard;° but she, good soul, had as lief see a toad, a very toad, as see him. I anger her sometimes and tell her that Paris is the properer° man; but, I'll warrant you, when I say so, she looks as pale as any clout° in the versal° world. Doth not rosemary and Romeo begin both with a letter?°

ROMEO. *(breaking out in loud laughter).* Ay, Nurse; what of that? Both with an R.

NURSE. Ah, mocker! That's the dog's name;° R is for the—No; I know it begins with some other letter; and she hath the prettiest sententious° of it, of you and rosemary, that it would do you good to hear it.

ROMEO. Commend me to thy lady.

NURSE. Ay, a thousand times. *(Exit* ROMEO.*)* Peter!

PETER. Anon!

NURSE. Peter, take my fan, and go before, and apace.

(Exeunt.)

fain . . . aboard, gladly seize, in the manner of a pirate, what he desires.

properer, handsomer.

clout, rag.
versal, universal.
a letter, the same letter.

the dog's name. The sound of the letter *R* was thought to resemble a dog's snarl.

sentențious, the nurse's error for *sentences (clever sayings).*

Scene 5: Capulet's orchard.

Enter JULIET.

JULIET *(with ever rising anxiety).* The clock struck nine when I did send the nurse;
In half an hour she promised to return.
Perchance she cannot meet him—that's not so.
O, she is lame! Love's heralds should be thoughts,
Which ten times faster glide than the sun's beams,
Driving back shadows over louring hills.
Therefore do nimble-pinioned doves draw love,°
And therefore hath the wind-swift Cupid wings.
Now is the sun upon the highmost hill
Of this day's journey, and from nine till twelve
Is three long hours, yet she is not come.
Had she affections and warm youthful blood,
She would be as swift in motion as a ball;
My words would bandy° her to my sweet love,
And his to me.
But old folks, many feign as they were dead—
Unwieldy, slow, heavy, and pale as lead.
O God, she comes![23]

(Enter NURSE *and* PETER.*)*

O honey Nurse, what news?
Hast thou met with him? Send thy man away.

nimble-pinioned . . . love. Swift-winged doves drew the chariot of Venus, goddess of love.

bandy, hurry.

23. Juliet's opening speech is a *soliloquy,* a speech representing a character's thoughts. What is Juliet's state of mind? How does she explain the nurse's long absence?

NURSE. Peter, stay at the gate.
(Exit PETER.*)*
JULIET. Now, good, sweet Nurse,—O Lord, why look'st thou sad?
Though news be sad, yet tell them° merrily;

news . . . them. *News* was often used in the plural.

If good, thou shamest the music of sweet news
By playing it to me with so sour a face.
NURSE. I am aweary; give me leave awhile.
Fie, how my bones ache! What a jaunce° have I had!

jaunce, rough jaunt.

JULIET. I would thou hadst my bones, and I thy news.
Nay, come, I pray thee, speak; good, good Nurse, speak.
NURSE. Jesu, what haste? Can you not stay awhile?
Do you not see that I am out of breath?
JULIET *(with exasperation).* How art thou out of breath when thou hast breath
To say to me that thou art out of breath?
The excuse that thou dost make in this delay
Is longer than the tale thou dost excuse.°

excuse, put off by making excuses.

Is thy news good, or bad? Answer to that;
Say either, and I'll stay the circumstance.°

stay the circumstance, await details.

Let me be satisfied is 't good or bad?
NURSE. Well, you have made a simple choice; you know not how to choose a man. Romeo? No, not he; though his face be better than any man's, yet his leg excels all men's; and for a hand, and a foot, and a body, though they be not to be talked on, yet they are past compare. He is not the flower of courtesy, but, I'll warrant him, as gentle as a lamb. Go thy ways, wench; serve God. What, have you dined at home?
JULIET. No, no. But all this did I know before.
What says he of our marriage? What of that?
NURSE. Lord, how my head aches! What a head have I!
It beats as it would fall in twenty pieces.
My back—O my back, my back!
Beshrew° your heart for sending me about

Beshrew, ill luck to.

To catch my death with jauncing up and down!
JULIET. I' faith, I am sorry that thou art not well.
(Beseechingly) Sweet, sweet, sweet Nurse, tell me, what says my love?
NURSE. Your love says, like an honest gentleman, and a courteous, and a kind, and a handsome, and I warrant, a virtuous—
Where is your mother?
JULIET *(bewildered).* Where is my mother! Why, she is within;
Where should she be? *(Angrily)* How oddly thou repliest!—
"Your love says, like an honest gentleman,
'Where is your mother?' "
NURSE. O God's lady dear!
Are you so hot? Marry, come up, I trow;°

Marry . . . I trow. Come, now; you are too impatient, I declare.

Is this the poultice for my aching bones?
Henceforward do your messages yourself.

JULIET. Here's such a coil!° Come, what says Romeo?

coil, commotion.

NURSE. Have you got leave to go to shrift today?

JULIET. I have.

NURSE. Then hie° you hence to Friar Laurence' cell;
There stays a husband to make you a wife.
Now comes the wanton blood up in your cheeks;
They'll be in scarlet straight at any news.
Hie you to church; I must another way
To fetch a ladder, by the which your love
Must climb a bird's nest soon when it is dark:
I am the drudge, and toil in your delight.
Go; I'll to dinner; hie you to the cell.

hie, hasten.

JULIET. Hie to high fortune! Honest Nurse, farewell.[24]

(They go out in opposite directions.)

24. Shakespeare often signals the end of a scene with a couplet. Why might he do this?

Scene 6: Friar Laurence's cell.

Enter FRIAR LAURENCE *and* ROMEO.

FRIAR LAURENCE. So smile the heavens upon this holy act
That after hours with sorrow chide us not!

ROMEO. Amen, amen! But come what sorrow can,
It cannot countervail° the exchange of joy
That one short minute gives me in her sight.
Do thou but close our hands with holy words,
Then love-devouring death do what he dare;
It is enough I may but call her mine.

countervail, balance, equal.

FRIAR LAURENCE. These violent delights have violent ends
And in their triumph die, like fire and powder,
Which as they kiss consume.° The sweetest honey
Is loathsome in his own deliciousness
And in the taste confounds° the appetite.
Therefore love moderately; long love doth so;
Too swift arrives as tardy as too slow.

These violent delights . . . consume. In lines 9–11 Friar Laurence expresses a premonition of evil.

confounds, destroys.

(Enter JULIET.*)*

Here comes the lady. O, so light a foot
Will ne'er wear out the everlasting flint.°
A lover may bestride the gossamer°
That idles in the wanton summer air,
And yet not fall; so light is vanity.°

wear out . . . flint. The friar is suggesting the roughness of life's journey.

gossamer, cobweb.

so light is vanity, so unsubstantial are the illusions of love.

JULIET. Good even° to my ghostly confessor.

even, evening.

FRIAR LAURENCE. Romeo shall thank thee, daughter, for us both.

JULIET. As much to him,° else is his thanks too much.
ROMEO. Ah, Juliet, if the measure of thy joy
Be heaped like mine, and that° thy skill be more
To blazon° it, then sweeten with thy breath
This neighbor air, and let rich music's tongue
Unfold the imagined happiness that both
Receive in either by this dear encounter.
JULIET. Conceit,° more rich in matter than in words,
Brags of his substance, not of ornament.
They are but beggars that can count their worth;
But my true love is grown to such excess
I cannot sum up sum of half my wealth.
FRIAR LAURENCE. Come, come with me, and we will make short work;
For, by your leaves, you shall not stay alone
Till Holy Church incorporate two in one.
(Exeunt.)

As much to him, the same greeting to him.

that, if.

blazon, proclaim.

Conceit, imagination, understanding.

Marti Maraden as Juliet, Leo Leyden as Friar Laurence, Richard Monette as Romeo in *Romeo and Juliet*, Stratford Festival, Canada, 1977.

Discussion

Scene 1

1. Why does Romeo hide from his two friends?

2. Do Benvolio and Mercutio realize that Romeo has found a new love? Cite lines to support your answer.

3. What purpose does this brief scene serve? Does it **(a)** provide background? **(b)** advance the plot? **(c)** reveal new aspects of a character? **(d)** contribute to or suggest theme?

Scene 2

1. What problems does Juliet envision growing out of her love for Romeo?

2. (a) What influence does true love have on Romeo? How has his attitude toward life changed? **(b)** How does Romeo approach love—cautiously or impulsively? **(c)** Is his approach the same as or different from Juliet's?

3. This famous scene is usually referred to as the balcony scene. In some productions, Romeo (using vines, a trellis, or a staircase) climbs up to Juliet. Do you think that, if you were watching the play, it would be more or less effective for him to do this? Give reasons for your answer.

Scene 3

1. What adjectives might be used to describe Friar Laurence? Cite lines to support your choices.

2. (a) What proposal does Romeo make to the friar? **(b)** What doubts does the friar have about this proposal? **(c)** Why does Friar Laurence finally accept Romeo's proposal? **(d)** What warning does he give Romeo?

3. Describe the relationship between Friar Laurence and Romeo. Give reasons for your opinion.

Application

Personification

Personification is a figure of speech in which human characteristics are assigned to inanimate objects. Reread Scene 3, lines 1–4. Be prepared to discuss any examples of personification you find there.

Scene 4

1. What two events that are important to Romeo's future occur in this scene?

2. Why does Romeo keep secret from his friends the reason for his dramatic change of mood?

3. Why might Shakespeare have chosen to make this a humorous scene?

4. Outline the steps the nurse is to take in carrying out Romeo's instructions.

Scenes 5 and 6

1. Are the nurse's speeches in Scene 5 consistent or inconsistent with the impression you have gained of her in earlier scenes? Explain.

2. (a) What is the attitude of Friar Laurence toward the lovers' insistence that he marry them without delay? **(b)** How soon after they meet do they marry?

Vocabulary

Combined Skills

Use your Glossary to determine the proper meanings and pronunciations of the following words. Then answer each of the statements on your paper by indicating "T" if the statement is true, "F" if false.

adieu	scurvy	beshrew
poultice	rancor	shrive
knave	intercession	
perjury	prorogued	

1. The last syllable of *adieu* rhymes with *grow.*

2. *Perjury* is a form of lying.

3. A *poultice* is a seasoning for fowl.

4. *Rancor* can by a synonym for *affection.*

5. If someone calls you a *scurvy* person, you should be flattered.

6. A *prorogued* meeting is one that is in session.

7. *Beshrews* are kept in zoos.

8. The word *shrive* is archaic.

9. The word *knave* derives from an Old English word meaning *boy.*

10. According to its Latin prefix and root, the word *intercession* means a *going-between.*

Composition

Prince Escalus has hired you, a prophet, to predict the futures of any two of the following: Mercutio, Benvolio, Tybalt, Romeo. You choose two; and, because you are a shrewd judge of character, you set out to learn as much as you can about each man. You will base your predictions on the information you gather, and you gain this information by either watching or spying on your choices during the events of the first two acts.

Now compose your report to the prince. For each of your choices, write a well-developed paragraph.

Comment: The Elizabethan[1] View of the Heavens

The influence of fate, or the heavens, is an important theme developed throughout *Romeo and Juliet.* For the people of Shakespeare's time, this theme had deep religious significance. Playgoers interpreted Shakespeare's references to stars, spheres, and the heavens as references to destiny.

The Elizabethans knew that the moon affected the tides. If the moon had such influence on earth, they reasoned, so might the other heavenly bodies of their universe. Most Elizabethans also believed that Divine Providence, or God's will, determined the outcome of men's lives. They reconciled these two ideas in their belief that the pattern of the stars foretold and also influenced events on Earth, events dictated by Divine Providence.

Elizabethans believed that the Earth was at the center of the universe. Around the Earth revolved seven spheres. These spheres each contained one "planet." Closest to Earth was the moon, followed, in order, by Mercury, Venus, the Sun, Mars, Jupiter, and Saturn. The sphere beyond Saturn contained what were called the "fixed stars." Beyond that was a ninth circle called the Primum Mobile. This "First Mover" was responsible for the motions of all the other spheres.

Astrologers predicted events and human fortunes by studying the patterns of the heavens. They also interpreted the import of such astronomical events as eclipses of the sun and moon and the appearance of comets.

In *Romeo and Juliet,* this belief in the influence of the heavens is apparent from the start. The lovers, we are told in the prologue, are "star-crossed," or destined for unhappiness because of the patterns of the heavens when each was born. Before Romeo attends the fateful party, he fears "some consequence, yet hanging in the stars." Much later, when told that Juliet is dead, Romeo responds, "I defy you, stars" and seeks to join her in death.

---

1. ***Elizabethan,*** of the time when Elizabeth I ruled England (1558–1603).

Act Three

Scene 1: A public place in Verona, immediately following the marriage of ROMEO and JULIET.

Enter MERCUTIO, BENVOLIO, PAGE, *and* SERVANTS.

BENVOLIO. I pray thee, good Mercutio, let's retire.
The day is hot, the Capulets abroad,
And, if we meet, we shall not 'scape a brawl;
For now, these hot days, is the mad blood stirring.

MERCUTIO. Thou art like one of those fellows that when he enters the confines of a tavern claps his sword upon the table and says "God send me no need of thee!" and by the operation of the second cup° draws it on the drawer,° when indeed there is no need.

by . . . the second cup, by the time the second cup of wine begins to affect him.
drawer, one who draws wine from its container.

BENVOLIO. Am I like such a fellow?

MERCUTIO. Come, come, thou art as hot a Jack° in thy mood° as any in Italy, and as soon moved to be moody, and as soon moody to be moved.

Jack, fellow.
mood, ill humor.

BENVOLIO. And what to?°

what to, moved to what.

MERCUTIO. Nay, an there were two such, we should have none shortly, for one would kill the other. Thou! Why, thou wilt quarrel with a man that hath a hair more, or a hair less, in his beard than thou hast. Thou wilt quarrel with a man for cracking nuts, having no other reason but because thou hast hazel eyes. . . . Thy head is as full of quarrels as an egg is full of meat. . . . Thou hast quarreled with a man for coughing in the street, because he hath wakened thy dog that hath lain asleep in the sun. Didst thou not fall out with a tailor for wearing his new doublet before Easter? With another for tying his new shoes with old riband? And yet thou wilt tutor me for quarreling!

BENVOLIO. An I were so apt to quarrel as thou art, any man should buy the fee-simple of my life for an hour and a quarter.

MERCUTIO. The fee-simple!° O simple!

fee-simple, absolute ownership.

(Enter TYBALT *and other* CAPULETS.*)*

BENVOLIO. By my head, here come the Capulets.

MERCUTIO. By my heel, I care not.

TYBALT *(to his kinsmen).* Follow me close, for I will speak to them.
Gentlemen, good den; a word with one of you.

MERCUTIO. And but one word with one of us? Couple it with something; make it a word and a blow.

TYBALT. You shall find me apt enough to that, sir, an you will give me occasion.

MERCUTIO. Could you not take some occasion without giving?

TYBALT. Mercutio, thou consort'st with° Romeo——

MERCUTIO. Consort! . . . 'Zounds,° consort!

consort'st with, accompany or wait upon.
'Zounds, a form of the oath "by God's wounds."

BENVOLIO. We talk here in the public haunt of men.
Either withdraw unto some private place,
And reason coldly of your grievances,
Or else depart,° here all eyes gaze on us.

depart, separate.

MERCUTIO. Men's eyes were made to look, and let them gaze;
I will not budge for no man's pleasure, I.

(Enter ROMEO.*)*

TYBALT *(to* BENVOLIO*)*. Well, peace be with you, sir. Here comes my man.°

MERCUTIO. But I'll be hanged, sir, if he wear your livery.°
Marry, go before to field, he'll be your follower;°
Your worship in that sense may call him "man."

my man. Tybalt speaks insultingly of Romeo as though Romeo were his servant.
if . . . livery, if Romeo wears the uniform (livery) of Tybalt's servants.
go . . . follower. If you went to the field of encounter, Romeo would follow you quickly enough.

TYBALT. *(confronting* ROMEO*)*. Romeo, the love I bear thee can afford
No better term than this—thou art a villain.

ROMEO. Tybalt, the reason that I have to love thee
Doth much excuse the appertaining rage
To such a greeting;° villain am I none.
Therefore, farewell; I see thou know'st me not.

appertaining rage . . . greeting, rage suitable to such a greeting.

TYBALT *(contemptuously)*. Boy, this shall not excuse the injuries
That thou hast done me; therefore turn and draw.

ROMEO. I do protest, I never injured thee,
But love thee better than thou canst devise,
Till thou shalt know the reason of my love.
And so, good Capulet—which name I tender°
As dearly as my own—be satisfied.

tender, cherish.

MERCUTIO. O calm, dishonorable, vile submission! . . .
(He draws his sword.)
Tybalt, you rat catcher,° will you walk?°

rat catcher, an allusion to Tybalt as Prince of Cats.
walk, step aside with me.

TYBALT. What wouldst thou have with me?

MERCUTIO. Good King of Cats, nothing but one of your nine lives; that I mean to make both withal,° and, as you shall use me hereafter, dry-beat the rest of the eight.° Will you pluck your sword out of his pilcher° by the ears? Make haste, lest mine be about your ears ere it be out.

that . . . withal. That one life I intend to take at once.
dry-beat . . . eight, soundly beat your other eight lives.
his pilcher, its scabbard.

TYBALT. *(drawing)*. I am for you.

ROMEO. Gentle Mercutio, put thy rapier up.

MERCUTIO. Come, sir, your passado.

(TYBALT *and* MERCUTIO *fight.)*

ROMEO. Draw, Benvolio; beat down their weapons.
Gentleman, for shame, forbear this outrage!
Tybalt, Mercutio, the prince expressly hath
Forbidden bandying in Verona streets.
Hold, Tybalt! Good Mercutio!

(TYBALT, *reaching under* ROMEO'*s arm, stabs* MERCUTIO *and flies with his followers.)*

MERCUTIO. I am hurt.
A plague o' both your houses! I am sped°. . . .

sped, done for.

BENVOLIO. What, art thou hurt?

MERCUTIO. Ay, ay, a scratch, a scratch; marry, 'tis enough.
Where is my page? Go, villain,° fetch a surgeon.

villain, a form of address to a servant.

(Exit PAGE.*)*

ROMEO. Courage, man; the hurt cannot be much.

MERCUTIO. No, 'tis not so deep as a well, nor so wide as a church door; but 'tis enough, 'twill serve. Ask for me tomorrow, and you shall find me a grave man.° I am peppered,° I warrant, for this world. A plague o' both your houses! 'Zounds, a dog, a rat, a mouse, a cat, to scratch a man to death! A braggart, a rogue, a villain, that fights by the book of arithmetic!° Why the devil came you between us? I was hurt under your arm.

a grave man. Thus Mercutio puns with his last breath.
peppered. Mercutio means that receiving the one wound is as serious as being peppered with many wounds.

book of arithmetic, a textbook on fencing.

ROMEO. I thought all for the best.

MERCUTIO. Help me into some house, Benvolio,
Or I shall faint. A plague o' both your houses!
They have made worms' meat of me; I have it,
And soundly too. Your houses!

(MERCUTIO *is helped off by* BENVOLIO *and some* SERVANTS.*)*

ROMEO. This gentleman, the prince's near ally,°
My very° friend, hath got his mortal hurt
In my behalf; my reputation stained
With Tybalt's slander—Tybalt, that an hour
Hath been my kinsman! O sweet Juliet,
Thy beauty hath made me effeminate
And in my temper softened valor's steel!

ally, kinsman.
very, true.

(Reenter BENVOLIO.*)*

BENVOLIO. O Romeo, Romeo, brave Mercutio's dead!
That gallant spirit hath aspired° the clouds,
Which too untimely here did scorn the earth.

aspired, soared to.

ROMEO. This day's black fate on moe° days doth depend;°
This but begins the woe others must end.

moe, more.
depend, hang over threateningly.

(Reenter TYBALT.*)*

BENVOLIO. Here comes the furious Tybalt back again.

ROMEO. Alive, in triumph—and Mercutio slain!
Away to heaven, respective lenity,°
And fire-eyed fury be my conduct° now!
Now, Tybalt, take the villain back again
That late thou gavest me; for Mercutio's soul
Is but a little way above our heads,
Staying for thine to keep him company:
Either thou, or I, or both, must go with him.

respective lenity, considerate mildness.
conduct, guide.

Paul Batten as Tybalt, Richard Monette as Romeo in *Romeo and Juliet,* Stratford Festival, Canada, 1977.

TYBALT. Thou wretched boy, that didst consort him here,
Shalt with him hence.
ROMEO *(drawing his sword).* This shall determine that.
(They fight. TYBALT *falls dead.)*
BENVOLIO. Romeo, away, be gone!
The citizens are up, and Tybalt slain.
Stand not amazed;° the prince will doom thee death
If thou art taken; hence, be gone, away!
ROMEO. O, I am fortune's fool!°
BENVOLIO. Why dost thou stay?
(Exit ROMEO.*)*

amazed, stupefied.

fortune's fool, the plaything or pawn of fate.

(Enter several CITIZENS.*)*[25]
FIRST CITIZEN. Which way ran he that killed Mercutio?
Tybalt, that murderer, which way ran he?
BENVOLIO. There lies that Tybalt.
FIRST CITIZEN. *(to* BENVOLIO*).* Up, sir, go with me;
I charge thee in the prince's name, obey.

25. By bringing the citizens on stage, what does Shakespeare suggest about the street brawl and its effect on the lives of people other than the participants?

(Enter PRINCE ESCALUS, *attended;* MONTAGUE, CAPULET, THEIR WIVES, *and* OTHERS.*)*
PRINCE. Where are the vile beginners of this fray?
BENVOLIO. O noble Prince, I can discover° all
The unlucky manage° of this fatal brawl.
There lies the man, slain by young Romeo,
That slew thy kinsman, brave Mercutio.
LADY CAPULET. Tybalt, my cousin! O my brother's child!
O Prince! O cousin! Husband! O, the blood is spilt
Of my dear kinsman! Prince, as thou art true,
For blood of ours shed blood of Montague.
O cousin, cousin!
PRINCE. Benvolio, who began this bloody fray?
BENVOLIO. Tybalt, here slain, whom Romeo's hand did slay;
Romeo that spoke him fair, bade him bethink
How nice° the quarrel was, and urged withal
Your high displeasure. All this, uttered
With gentle breath, calm look, knees humbly bowed,
Could not take truce° with the unruly spleen°
Of Tybalt deaf to peace, but that he tilts°
With piercing steel at bold Mercutio's breast,
Who, all as hot, turns deadly point to point,
And, with a martial scorn, with one hand beats
Cold death aside, and with the other sends
It back to Tybalt, whose dexterity
Retorts° it. Romeo he cries aloud,
"Hold, friends; friends, part," and, swifter than his tongue,

discover, reveal.

manage, conduct.

nice, trivial.

take truce, make peace.
unruly spleen, ungovernable rage.
tilts, strikes.

Retorts, returns.

His agile arm beats down their fatal points,
And 'twixt them rushes; underneath whose arm
An envious thrust from Tybalt hit the life
Of stout° Mercutio, and then Tybalt fled;
But by and by comes back to Romeo,
Who had but newly entertained° revenge,
And to 't they go like lightning, for ere I
Could draw to part them, was stout Tybalt slain,
And, as he fell, did Romeo turn and fly.
This is the truth, or let Benvolio die.

stout, brave.

entertained, harbored thoughts of.

LADY CAPULET. He is a kinsman to the Montague;
Affection makes him false; he speaks not true.
Some twenty of them fought in this black strife,
And all those twenty could but kill one life.
I beg for justice, which thou, Prince, must give.
Romeo slew Tybalt; Romeo must not live.

PRINCE. Romeo slew him, he slew Mercutio;
Who now the price of his dear blood doth owe?

MONTAGUE. Not Romeo, Prince; he was Mercutio's friend.
His fault concludes but what the law should end—
The life of Tybalt.

PRINCE. And for that offense
Immediately we do exile him hence.
I have an interest in your hate's proceeding,
My blood° for your rude brawls doth lie a-bleeding;
But I'll amerce° you with so strong a fine
That you shall all repent the loss of mine.°
(Shouting above loud outcries from MONTAGUES *and* CAPULETS.*)*
I will be deaf to pleading and excuses;
Nor tears nor prayers shall purchase out abuses.°
Therefore use none. Let Romeo hence in haste,
Else, when he's found, that hour is his last.
Bear hence this body and attend our will.
Mercy but murders, pardoning those that kill.
(Exeunt.)

My blood, the blood of my kin.

amerce, punish by fine.

mine, my blood.

purchase out abuses, exempt misdeeds from penalty.

Scene 2: Capulet's orchard.

Enter JULIET.

JULIET. Gallop apace, you fiery-footed steeds,
Toward Phoebus'° lodging; such a wagoner
As Phaëthon° would whip you to the west,
And bring in cloudy night immediately. . . .
Spread thy close curtain, love-performing night,
That runaways' eyes may wink, and Romeo

Phoebus (fē'bəs), the sun god.

Phaëthon (fā'ə thon). He was allowed to drive the chariot of the sun for a day. Too weak to control the horses, he nearly destroyed the universe.

Leap to these arms, untalked of and unseen.
Come, night; come, Romeo; come, thou day in night,
For thou wilt lie upon the wings of night
Whiter than new snow on a raven's back.
Come, gentle night, come, loving, black-browed night,
Give me my Romeo, and, when he shall die,
Take him and cut him out in little stars,
And he will make the face of heaven so fine
That all the world will be in love with night
And pay no worship to the garish sun. . . .[26]
(She looks around eagerly.) So tedious is this day
As is the night before some festival
To an impatient child that hath new robes
And may not wear them.
O, here comes my nurse,
And she brings news; and every tongue that speaks
But Romeo's name speaks heavenly eloquence.

(Enter NURSE *with the rope-ladder.)*
Now, Nurse, what news? What, hast thou there the cords
That Romeo bid thee fetch?

NURSE. Ay, ay, the cords.
(She throws down the ladder abruptly.)

JULIET. Ay me! What news? Why dost thou wring thy hands?

NURSE. Ah, well-a-day!° He's dead, he's dead, he's dead!
We are undone, lady, we are undone!
Alack the day! He's gone, he's killed, he's dead!

JULIET. Can heaven be so envious?

NURSE. Romeo can,
Though heaven cannot. O Romeo, Romeo!
Who ever would have thought it? Romeo!

JULIET. What devil art thou, that dost torment me thus?
This torture should be roared in dismal hell.
Hath Romeo slain himself? Say thou but "Ay"
And that bare vowel "I" shall poison more
Than the death-darting eye of cockatrice.°
I am not I, if there be such an I,
Or those eyes shut that make thee answer "Ay."
If he be slain, say "Ay"; or, if not, "No."
Brief sounds determine of my weal or woe.°

NURSE. I saw the wound, I saw it with mine eyes—
God save the mark!° —here on his manly breast.
A piteous corse,° a bloody piteous corse;
Pale, pale as ashes, all bedaubed in blood,
All in gore-blood;° I swounded° at the sight.

JULIET. O, break, my heart! Poor bankrupt, break at once!

26. To what is Romeo being compared in these lines?

well-a-day, alas.

cockatrice, a fabled serpent that could kill with its glance.

determine . . . woe, decide my well-being or my sorrow.

God . . . mark. God have mercy on us.

corse, corpse.

gore-blood, clotted blood.
swounded, swooned.

To prison, eyes; ne'er look on liberty!
Vile earth, to earth resign;° end motion° here;
And thou and Romeo press one heavy bier!

NURSE. O Tybalt, Tybalt, the best friend I had!
O courteous Tybalt; honest gentleman!
That ever I should live to see thee dead!

JULIET. What storm is this that blows so contrary?
Is Romeo slaughtered, and is Tybalt dead?
My dear-loved cousin, and my dearer lord?
Then, dreadful trumpet,° sound the general doom!
For who is living if those two are gone?

NURSE. Tybalt is gone, and Romeo banishèd;
Romeo that killed him, he is banishèd;

JULIET. O God! Did Romeo's hand shed Tybalt's blood?

NURSE. It did, it did; alas the day, it did!

JULIET. O serpent heart, hid with a flowering face!
Did ever dragon keep° so fair a cave? . . .
Beautiful tyrant! Fiend angelical!
Dove-feathered raven! Wolfish-ravening lamb!
Despised substance of divinest show!
Just opposite to what thou just seemest,
A damned saint, a honorable villain!
O nature, what hadst thou to do in hell,
When thou didst bower° the spirit of a fiend
In mortal paradise of such sweet flesh?
Was ever book containing such vile matter
So fairly bound? O, that deceit should dwell
In such a gorgeous palace!

NURSE. There's no trust,
No faith, no honesty in men; all perjured,
All forsworn,° all naught, all dissemblers.
Ah, where's my man? Give me some aqua vitae;°
These griefs, these woes, these sorrows make me old.
Shame come to Romeo!

JULIET. Blistered be thy tongue
For such a wish! He was not born to shame.
Upon his brow shame is ashamed to sit;
For 'tis a throne where honor may be crowned
Sole monarch of the universal earth.
O, what a beast was I to chide at him![27]

NURSE. Will you speak well of him that killed your cousin?

JULIET. Shall I speak ill of him that is my husband?
Ah, poor my lord, what tongue shall smooth thy name,
When I, thy three-hours' wife, have mangled it?
But, wherefore, villain, didst thou kill my cousin?
That villain cousin would have killed my husband.

Vile earth . . . resign. Miserable body, resign yourself to death.
motion, human activity.

dreadful trumpet, the trumpet proclaiming doomsday, or the end of the world.

keep, guard.

bower, give lodging to.

forsworn, untrue to one's sworn oath.

aqua vitae (ak′wə vī′tē), spirits to restore calmness.

27. What prompts Juliet to defend Romeo? Is this sudden change of attitude plausible?

Back, foolish tears, back to your native spring,
Your tributary drops belong to woe,
Which you, mistaking, offer up to joy.
My husband lives, that Tybalt would have slain;
And Tybalt's dead, that would have slain my husband.
All this is comfort; wherefore weep I then?
Some word there was, worser than Tybalt's death,
That murdered me. I would forget it fain;°
But, O, it presses to my memory,
Like damnèd guilty deeds to sinners' minds:
"Tybalt is dead, and Romeo—banishèd";
That "banishèd," that one word "banishèd,"
Hath slain ten thousand Tybalts. Tybalt's death
Was woe enough, if it had ended there.
Or, if sour woe delights in fellowship,
And needly° will be ranked with other griefs,
Why followed not, when she said "Tybalt's dead,"
Thy father or thy mother, nay, or both,
Which modern lamentation° might have moved?
But with a rearward° following Tybalt's death,
"Romeo is banishèd"—to speak that word
Is father, mother, Tybalt, Romeo, Juliet,
All slain, all dead. "Romeo is banishèd!"—
There is no end, no limit, measure, bound,
In that word's death; no words can that woe sound.
Where is my father, and my mother, Nurse?

NURSE. Weeping and wailing over Tybalt's corse.
Will you go to them? I will bring you thither.

JULIET. Wash they his wounds with tears? Mine shall be spent,
When theirs are dry, for Romeo's banishment.
Take up those cords. Poor ropes, you are beguiled,
Both you and I, for Romeo is exiled. . . .

NURSE. Hie to your chamber. I'll find Romeo
To comfort you. I wot° well where he is.
Hark ye, your Romeo will be here at night;
I'll to him. He is hid at Laurence' cell.

JULIET. O, find him! Give this ring to my true knight,
And bid him come to take his last farewell.

(Exeunt.)

fain, gladly.

needly, of necessity.

modern lamentation, ordinary grief.

rearward, a guard following at the rear of a group.

wot, know.

Scene 3: Friar Laurence's cell.

Enter FRIAR LAURENCE.

FRIAR LAURENCE *(calling softly)*. Romeo, come forth; come forth, thou fearful° man.

fearful, full of fear.

Affliction is enamored of thy parts°
And thou art wedded to calamity.

Affliction . . . parts. Misfortune thrives on the qualities (parts) you are showing—self-pity and despair.

(Enter ROMEO*, coming from his hiding place.)*

ROMEO. Father, what news? What is the prince's doom?°
What sorrow craves acquaintance at my hand,
That I yet know not?

doom, punishment.

FRIAR LAURENCE. Too familiar
Is my dear son with such sour company.
I bring thee tidings of the prince's doom.

ROMEO. What less than doomsday is the prince's doom?

FRIAR LAURENCE. A gentler judgment vanished° from his lips—
Not body's death, but body's banishment.

vanished, issued.

ROMEO. Ha, banishment! Be merciful, say "death";
For exile hath more terror in his look,
Much more than death. Do not say "banishment."

FRIAR LAURENCE. Hence from Verona art thou banishèd.
Be patient, for the world is broad and wide.

ROMEO. There is no world without Verona walls,
But purgatory, torture, hell itself.
Hence—banishèd is banished from the world,
And world's exile° is death. Then banishèd
Is death mistermed. Calling death "banishment,"
Thou cut'st my head off with a golden ax
And smilest upon the stroke that murders me.

world's exile, exile from the world that is everything to me—the world where Juliet dwells.

FRIAR LAURENCE. O deadly sin! O rude unthankfulness!
Thy fault our law calls death, but the kind prince,
Taking thy part, hath rushed aside° the law,
And turned that black word death to banishment.
This is dear° mercy, and thou seest it not.

rushed aside, thrust aside; dodged.

dear, rare, unusual.

ROMEO. 'Tis torture, and not mercy. Heaven is here,
Where Juliet lives; and every cat and dog
And little mouse, every unworthy thing,
Live here in heaven and may look on her. . . .
But Romeo may not; he is banishèd. . . .
Hadst thou no poison mixed, no sharp-ground knife,
No sudden mean° of death, though ne'er so mean,°
But "banishèd" to kill me?—"Banishèd"?
O Friar, the damnèd use that word in hell;
Howlings attend it. How hast thou the heart,
Being a divine, a ghostly confessor,
A sin-absolver, and my friend professed,
To mangle me with that word "banishèd"?

mean, means.
mean, base, vile.

FRIAR LAURENCE. Thou fond° mad man, hear me but speak a word.

fond, foolish.

ROMEO. O, thou wilt speak again of banishment.

FRIAR LAURENCE. I'll give thee armor to keep off that word;

Adversity's sweet milk, philosophy,
To comfort thee, though thou art banishèd.

ROMEO. Yet "banishèd"? Hang up philosophy!
Unless philosophy can make a Juliet,
Displant a town, reverse a prince's doom,
It helps not, it prevails not. Talk no more.

FRIAR LAURENCE. O, then I see that madmen have no ears.

ROMEO. How should they, when that wise men have no eyes?

FRIAR LAURENCE. Let me dispute° with thee of thy estate.°

ROMEO. Thou canst not speak of that thou dost not feel.
Wert thou as young as I, Juliet thy love,
An hour but married, Tybalt murdered,
Doting like me and like me banishèd,
Then mightst thou speak, then mightst thou tear thy hair,
And *(Flinging himself full length upon the floor and sobbing)* fall upon the ground, as I do now,
Taking the measure of an unmade grave.[28]

(The NURSE *knocks on the door.)*

FRIAR LAURENCE. Arise; one knocks. Good Romeo, hide thyself.

ROMEO. Not I; unless the breath of heart-sick groans,
Mistlike, infold me from the search of eyes.

(The NURSE *knocks again.)*

FRIAR LAURENCE. Hark, how they knock! *(In a louder tone)* Who's there? *(In an urgent whisper)* Romeo, arise;
Thou wilt be taken. *(Loudly)*—Stay awhile! Stand up.

(Louder knocking)

Run to my study.—*(Loudly)* By and by! *(To himself)* God's will,
What simpleness is this!—*(Loudly)* I come, I come!

(Knocking continues.)

Who knocks so hard? Whence come you? What is your will?

NURSE *(speaking offstage)*. Let me come in, and you shall know my errand.
I come from Lady Juliet.

FRIAR LAURENCE. Welcome, then.

(Enter NURSE, *talking as she comes into the cell.)*

NURSE. O holy Friar, O, tell me, holy Friar,
Where is my lady's lord, where's Romeo?

FRIAR LAURENCE. There on the ground, with his own tears made drunk.

NURSE. O, he is even in my mistress' case,°
Just in her case! O woeful sympathy!°
Piteous predicament! Even so lies she,
Blubbering and weeping, weeping and blubbering.
Stand up, stand up; stand, an you be a man.
For Juliet's sake, for her sake, rise and stand.
Why should you fall into so deep an O?°

dispute, reason, discuss.
estate, situation, condition.

28. Is Romeo's emotional state "in character"? What evidence exists in earlier scenes to suggest that Romeo has a tendency to be rash and overly emotional?

O, he is . . . case. Romeo is in the same state as Juliet.
woeful sympathy, sad agreement.

an O, a fit of groaning.

(ROMEO *rises.)*

ROMEO. Nurse!

NURSE. Ah sir! ah sir! Well, death's the end of all.

ROMEO. Spakest thou of Juliet? How is it with her?
Doth she not think me an old° murderer,
Now I have stained the childhood of our joy
With blood removed but little from her own?
Where is she? And how doth she? And what says
My concealed° lady to our canceled love?

NURSE. O, she says nothing, sir, but weeps and weeps,
And now falls on her bed, and then starts up,
And Tybalt calls, and then on Romeo cries,
And then down falls again.

ROMEO. As if that name,
Shot from the deadly level° of a gun,
Did murder her; as that name's cursèd hand
Murdered her kinsman. O, tell me, Friar, tell me,
In what vile part of this anatomy
Doth my name lodge? Tell me that I may sack
The hateful mansion.[29]

(ROMEO *draws his sword.)*

FRIAR LAURENCE. Hold thy desperate hand.
Art thou a man? Thy form cries out thou art;
Thy tears are womanish; thy wild acts denote
The unreasonable fury of a beast—
Unseemly woman in a seeming man,
Or ill-beseeming° beast in seeming both!
Thou hast amazed me. By my holy order,
I thought thy disposition better tempered.
Hast thou slain Tybalt? Wilt thou slay thyself?
And slay thy lady too that lives in thee,
By doing damnèd hate upon thyself?
Why rail'st thou on° thy birth, the heaven, and earth—
Since birth, and heaven, and earth, all three do meet
In thee at once, which thou at once wouldst lose? . . .
What, rouse thee, man! Thy Juliet is alive,
For whose dear sake thou wast but lately dead;
There° art thou happy. Tybalt would kill thee,
But thou slew'st Tybalt; there art thou happy too.
The law that threatened death becomes thy friend
And turns it to exile; there art thou happy. . . .
But, like a misbehaved and sullen wench,
Thou pouts upon thy fortune and thy love.
Take heed, take heed, for such die miserable.
Go, get thee to thy love, as was decreed,
Ascend her chamber, hence and comfort her.
But look thou stay not till the watch be set,°

an old, a real or actual.

concealed lady, secretly married wife.

level, line of fire.

29. Why does Romeo draw his sword?

ill-beseeming, unsuitable, inappropriate.

Why rail'st thou on, why do you compain about.

There, in this respect.

watch be set, watchmen have taken their stand at the gates of Verona.

For then thou canst not pass to Mantua,
Where thou shalt live till we can find a time
To blaze° your marriage, reconcile your friends,
Beg pardon of the prince, and call thee back
With twenty hundred thousand times more joy
Than thou went'st forth in lamentation.
Go before, Nurse. Commend me to thy lady,
And bid her hasten all the house to bed,
Which heavy sorrow makes them apt unto.°
Romeo is coming.

blaze, announce.

apt unto, inclined to.

NURSE. O Lord, I could have stayed here all the night
To hear good counsel. O, what learning is!
My lord, I'll tell my lady you will come.

ROMEO. Do so, and bid my sweet prepare to chide.

NURSE. Here is a ring she bid me give you, sir.
Hie you, make haste, for it grows very late.

(Exit NURSE.*)*

ROMEO *(regarding the ring tenderly).* How well my comfort is revived by this!

FRIAR LAURENCE *(ushering* ROMEO *to the door).* Go hence; good night; and here stands all your state—°
Either be gone before the watch be set,
Or by the break of day disguised from hence.
Sojourn in Mantua; I'll find out your man,°
And he shall signify from time to time
Every good hap° to you that chances here.
Give me thy hand; 'tis late. Farewell; good night.

here stands . . . state. Your fortune depends on acting exactly as follows.

your man, Romeo's servant, Balthasar.

hap, occurrence.

ROMEO. But that a joy past joy calls out on me,
It were a grief, so brief to part with thee.
Farewell.

(Exeunt.)

Scene 4: A room in Capulet's house.

Enter LORD *and* LADY CAPULET *and* PARIS.

CAPULET *(to* PARIS*).* Things have fallen out, sir, so unluckily
That we have had no time to move our daughter.°
Look you, she loved her kinsman Tybalt dearly,
And so did I.—Well, we were born to die.
'Tis very late, she'll not come down tonight;
I promise you, but for your company,
I would have been abed an hour ago.

move our daughter, talk to Juliet about marrying you.

PARIS. These times of woe afford no time to woo.
Madam, good night; commend me to your daughter.

LADY CAPULET. I will, and know her mind early tomorrow;
Tonight she is mewed up to her heaviness.°
CAPULET. Sir Paris, I will make a desperate tender°
Of my child's love. I think she will be ruled
In all respects by me; nay, more, I doubt it not.
Wife, go you to her ere you go to bed;
Acquaint her here of my son Paris' love,
And bid her, mark you me, on Wednesday next—
But soft! What day is this?
PARIS. Monday, my lord.
CAPULET. Monday? Ha, ha! Well, Wednesday is too soon.
O' Thursday let it be; o' Thursday, tell her,
She shall be married to this noble earl.
Will you be ready? Do you like this haste?
We'll keep no great ado—a friend or two;
For, hark you, Tybalt being slain so late,°
It may be thought we held him carelessly,°
Being our kinsman, if we revel much.
Therefore we'll have some half-a-dozen friends,
And there an end. But what say you to Thursday?
PARIS. My lord, I would that Thursday were tomorrow.
CAPULET. Well, get you gone; o' Thursday be it, then.
(To LADY CAPULET*)* Go you to Juliet ere you go to bed,
Prepare her, wife, against° this wedding day.
Farewell, my lord. Light to my chamber, ho!
Afore me,° it is so very very late
That we may call it early by-and-by.
Good night.
(Exeunt.)

mewed . . . heaviness, confined in her room with her grief.
desperate tender, rash offer.
late, recently.
held him carelessly, regarded him too lightly.
against, for.
Afore me, by my life!

Scene 5: Capulet's orchard.

Enter ROMEO *and* JULIET, *at the window of her bedroom.*
JULIET. Wilt thou be gone? It is not yet near day.
It was the nightingale, and not the lark,°
That pierced the fearful hollow of thine ear;
Nightly she sings on yond pomegranate tree.
Believe me, love, it was the nightingale.
ROMEO. It was the lark, the herald of the morn,
No nightingale. Look, love, what envious streaks
Do lace° the severing° clouds in yonder east.
Night's candles are burnt out, and jocund day
Stands tiptoe on the misty mountain tops.
I must be gone and live, or stay and die.

nightingale . . . lark. The nightingale's song is associated with the night, the lark's song with dawn.
lace, stripe, streak.
severing, scattering.

JULIET. Yond light is not daylight, I know it, I;
It is some meteor that the sun exhales,
To be to thee this night a torchbearer
And light thee on thy way to Mantua.
Therefore stay yet; thou need'st not to be gone.

ROMEO. Let me be ta'en, let me be put to death;
I am content, so thou wilt have it so. . . .
I have more care° to stay than will to go.
Come, death, and welcome! Juliet wills it so.
How is 't, my soul? Let's talk; it is not day.

care, concern, desire.

JULIET. It is, it is; hie hence, be gone, away!
It is the lark that sings so out of tune,
Straining harsh discords and unpleasing sharps°. . . .
O, now be gone; more light and light it grows.

sharps, high notes.

ROMEO. More light and light; more dark and dark our woes![30]

30. In the balcony scene, many of the images were of light. What is Shakespeare's purpose in reminding you of those same images in the opening lines of this scene? Is light still "good"?

Enter the NURSE, *to the bedchamber.*

NURSE *(urgently).* Madam!

JULIET. Nurse?

NURSE. Your lady mother is coming to your chamber.
The day is broke; be wary, look about.
(Exit.)

JULIET. Then, window, let day in and let life out.

ROMEO. Farewell, farewell! One kiss, and I'll descend.
(He starts down the ladder.)

JULIET. Art thou gone so, love, lord, ay, husband, friend?
I must hear from thee every day in the hour,
For in a minute there are many days.
O, by this count I shall be much in years
Ere I again behold my Romeo!

ROMEO. Farewell! *(Embracing her once again)*
I will omit no opportunity
That may convey my greetings, love, to thee.

JULIET. O, think'st thou we shall ever meet again?

ROMEO. I doubt it not; and all these woes shall serve
For sweet discourses in our time to come.

JULIET. O God, I have an ill-divining° soul!
Methinks I see thee, now thou art below,
As one dead in the bottom of a tomb.
Either my eyesight fails, or thou look'st pale.

ill-divining, anticipating evil.

ROMEO. And trust me, love, in my eye so do you.
Dry sorrow drinks our blood.° Adieu, adieu!
(Exit.)

Dry sorrow . . . blood. It was believed that sorrow dried up the blood.

JULIET. O fortune, fortune! All men call thee fickle;
If thou art fickle, what dost thou with him
That is renowned for faith? Be fickle, fortune,

For then I hope thou wilt not keep him long,
But send him back.

LADY CAPULET *(offstage)*. Ho, daughter! Are you up?

JULIET. Who is 't that calls? Is it my lady mother?
(To herself) Is she not down° so late, or up so early?
What unaccustomed cause procures her hither?°

(Enter LADY CAPULET.*)*

LADY CAPULET. Why, how now, Juliet!

JULIET. Madam, I am not well.

LADY CAPULET. Evermore weeping for your cousin's death?
What, wilt thou wash him from his grave with tears?
An if thou couldst, thou couldst not make him live;
Therefore, have done. Some grief shows much of love,
But much of grief shows still some want of wit.

JULIET. Yet let me weep for such a feeling loss.[31]

LADY CAPULET. So shall you feel the loss, but not the friend
Which you weep for.

JULIET. Feeling so the loss,
I cannot choose but ever weep the friend.

LADY CAPULET. Well, girl, thou weep'st not so much for his death
As that the villain lives which slaughtered him.

JULIET. What villain, madam?

LADY CAPULET. That same villain Romeo.

JULIET *(aside)*. Villain and he be many miles asunder.—
(Aloud.) God pardon him! I do, with all my heart;
And yet no man like° he doth grieve my heart.

LADY CAPULET. That is because the traitor murderer lives.

JULIET. Ay, madam, the reach of these my hands.
Would none but I might venge° my cousin's death!

LADY CAPULET. We will have vengeance for it, fear thou not;
Then weep no more. I'll send to one in Mantua,
Where that same banished runagate doth live,
Shall give him such an unaccustomed dram
That he shall soon keep Tybalt company;
And then, I hope, thou wilt be satisfied.

JULIET. Indeed, I never shall be satisfied
With Romeo till I behold him—dead°—
Is my poor heart so for a kinsman vexed.
Madam, if you could find out but a man
To bear a poison, I would temper° it,
That Romeo should, upon receipt thereof,
Soon sleep in quiet. O, how my heart abhors
To hear him named, and cannot come to him,
To wreak the love I bore my cousin
Upon his body that hath slaughtered him!

down, in bed.

procures her hither, leads her to come this way.

31. What is Lady Capulet's opinion of Juliet's behavior? What does this tell you about Lady Capulet's character?

like, so much as.

venge, avenge.

dead. Juliet arranges her words in such a way that Lady Capulet will mistakenly think that Juliet wishes to see Romeo dead.

temper, mix. Juliet continues to speak in a way that misleads her mother.

LADY CAPULET. Find thou the means, and I'll find such a man.
But now I'll tell thee joyful tidings, girl.
JULIET. And joy comes well in such a needy time;
What are they,° I beseech your ladyship?
LADY CAPULET. Well, well, thou hast a careful° father, child,
One who, to put thee from thy heaviness,
Hath sorted out° a sudden day of joy,
That thou expect'st not nor I looked not for.

they, the "joyful tidings," in line 94.

careful, taking care to ensure your well-being.

sorted out, chosen.

JULIET. Madam, in happy time, what day is that?
LADY CAPULET. Marry, my child, early next Thursday morn,
The gallant, young, and noble gentleman,
The County Paris, at Saint Peter's Church,
Shall happily make thee there a joyful bride.
JULIET *(with vigorous spirit).* Now, by Saint Peter's Church and
Peter too,
He shall *not* make me there a joyful bride.
I wonder at this haste, that I must wed[32]
Ere he that should be husband comes to woo.
I pray you, tell my lord and father, madam,
I will not marry yet, and when I do, I swear
It shall be Romeo, whom you know I hate,
Rather than Paris. These are news indeed!
LADY CAPULET *(angrily).* Here comes your father, tell him so
yourself,
And see how he will take it at your hands.

32. Do you think Lady Capulet is surprised at the tone of Juliet's refusal? Is there any evidence earlier in the play to suggest that Juliet is capable of directly defying her parents?

(Enter CAPULET *and the* NURSE.*)*

CAPULET. When the sun sets the earth doth drizzle dew;
But for the sunset of my brother's son
It rains downright.
How now, a conduit,° girl? What, still in tears?
Evermore showering? In one little body
Thou counterfeit'st a bark, a sea, a wind;
For still thy eyes, which I may call the sea,
Do ebb and flow with tears; the bark thy body is,
Sailing in this salt flood; the winds, thy sighs,
Who, raging with thy tears, and they with them,
Without a sudden calm, will overset
Thy tempest-tossèd body. How now, wife!
Have you delivered to her our decree?

conduit, fountain.

LADY CAPULET. Ay, sir, but she will none,° she gives you thanks.
I would the fool were married to her grave!
CAPULET. Soft! Take me with you,° take me with you, wife.
How! Will she none? Doth she not give us thanks?
Is she not proud? Doth she not count her blest,
Unworthy as she is, that we have wrought
So worthy a gentleman to be her bridegroom?

will none, refuses "our decree," in the preceding line.

Take me with you. Let me understand you.

JULIET. Not proud you have, but thankful that you have.
Proud can I never be of what I hate,
But thankful even for hate that is meant love.
CAPULET. How now, how now, choplogic!° What is this?
"Proud," and "I thank you," and "I thank you not";
And yet "not proud." Mistress minion,° you,
Thank me no thankings, nor proud me no prouds,
But fettle° your fine joints 'gainst° Thursday next,
To go with Paris to Saint Peter's Church,
Or I will drag thee on a hurdle° thither.
Out, you green-sickness° carrion! Out, you baggage,°
You tallow-face!
LADY CAPULET *(to* CAPULET*)*. Fie, fie! What, art you mad?
JULIET *(kneeling)*. Good father, I beseech you on my knees,
Hear me with patience but to speak a word.
CAPULET. Hang thee, young baggage, disobedient wretch!
I tell thee what: get thee to church o' Thursday
Or never after look me in the face.
*(*JULIET *starts to answer.)*
Speak not, reply not, do not answer me;
My fingers itch.° Wife, we scarce thought us blest
That God had lent us but this only child;
But now I see this one is one too much,
And that we have a curse in having her.
Out on her, hilding!°
NURSE. God in heaven, bless her!
You are to blame, my lord, to rate° her so.
CAPULET. And why, my lady wisdom? Hold your tongue,
Good prudence;° smatter° with your gossips, go.
NURSE. I speak no treason.
CAPULET *(wrathfully)*. O, God ye god-den.
NURSE. May not one speak?
CAPULET. Peace, you mumbling fool!
Utter your gravity° o'er a gossip's bowl,
For here we need it not.
LADY CAPULET. You are too hot.
CAPULET. God's bread!° It makes me mad:
Day, night, hour, tide, time, work, play,
Alone, in company—still my care hath been
To have her matched; and having now provided
A gentleman of noble parentage,
Of fair demesnes, youthful, and nobly trained,
Stuffed, as they say, with honorable parts,°
Proportioned as one's thought would wish a man—
And then to have a wretched puling fool,
A whining mammet,° in her fortune's tender,°
To answer "I'll not wed; I cannot love,

choplogic, quibbler, one who argues unfairly.

minion, darling, favored person.

fettle, make ready.
'gainst, in preparation for.

hurdle, a conveyance for transporting criminals.
green-sickness, an anemic ailment of young women.
baggage, worthless woman.

My fingers itch, that is, to choke or strike you.

hilding, good-for-nothing.

rate, berate, scold.

Good prudence, my wise one. Capulet is speaking ironically.
smatter, chatter.

gravity, wisdom.

God's bread, by the sacrament; a mild oath.

parts, qualities, abilities.

mammet, doll.
in . . . tender, offer of good fortune.

I am too young; I pray you, pardon me."
But, an you will not wed, *(Bitterly ironic)* I'll pardon you;
Graze where you will, you shall not house with me.
Look to 't, think on 't; I do not use to jest.°
Thursday is near; lay hand on heart, advise.°
An you be mine, I'll give you to my friend;
An you be not, hang, beg, starve, die in the streets,
For, by my soul, I'll ne'er acknowledge thee,
Nor what is mine shall never do thee good.
Trust to 't, bethink you; I'll not be forsworn.[33]
(Exit CAPULET.*)*

JULIET. Is there no pity sitting in the clouds,
That sees into the bottom of my grief?
O sweet my mother, cast me not away!
Delay this marriage for a month, a week;
Or, if you do not, make the bridal bed
In that dim monument where Tybalt lies.

LADY CAPULET. Talk not to me, for I'll not speak a word.
Do as thou wilt, for I have done with thee.
(Exit, leaving JULIET *and the* NURSE *alone.)*

JULIET. O God!—O Nurse, how shall this be prevented?
My husband is on earth, my faith in heaven;°
How shall that faith return again to earth
Unless that husband send it me from heaven
By leaving earth? Comfort me, counsel me.
Alack, alack, that heaven should practice stratagems°
Upon so soft a subject as myself! *(To the* NURSE*)*
What say'st thou? Hast thou not a word of joy?
Some comfort, Nurse.

NURSE. Faith, here it is.
Romeo is banished; and all the world to nothing,°
That he dares ne'er come back to challenge° you;
Or, if he do, it needs must be by stealth.
Then, since the case so stands as now it doth,
I think it best you married with the county.
O, he's a lovely gentleman!
Romeo's a dishclout to him;° an eagle, madam,
Hath not so green,° so quick, so fair an eye
As Paris hath. Beshrew° my very heart,
I think you are happy in this second match,
For it excels your first; or, if it did not,
Your first is dead, or 'twere as good he were
As living here and you no use of him.

JULIET. Speakest thou from thy heart?

NURSE. And from my soul too;
Or else beshrew them both.

I do not . . . jest. I am unaccustomed to jesting.
advise, consider carefully.

33. Are there any indications earlier in the play that Capulet is a man capable of sudden rage?

faith in heaven. Juliet refers to her marriage vows.

practice stratagems, contrive dreadful deeds.

all . . . nothing. The odds are all the world to nothing.
challenge, lay claim to.

to him, compared to him.

green. Green eyes were much admired in Shakespeare's day.
Beshrew, curse.

JULIET. Amen!
NURSE. What?
JULIET. Well, thou hast comforted me marvelous much.
Go in, and tell my lady I am gone,
Having displeased my father, to Laurence' cell,
To make confession and to be absolved.
NURSE. Marry, I will; and this is wisely done.
(Exit.)
JULIET. Ancient damnation!° O most wicked fiend!
Is it more sin to wish me thus forsworn;
Or to dispraise my lord with that same tongue
Which she hath praised him with above compare
So many thousand times? Go, counselor;
Thou and my bosom° henceforth shall be twain.
I'll to the friar to know his remedy.
If all else fail, myself have power to die.
(Exit.)

Ancient damnation, wicked old devil.

bosom, confidence.

Discussion

Scene 1

1. (a) Who renews the quarreling between the Montagues and the Capulets? **(b)** Which character attempts to serve as peacemaker? **(c)** Why does Romeo refuse Tybalt's first challenge to fight? **(d)** In their encounter with Tybalt, do Benvolio and Mercutio react "in character"; that is, does each behave as you would expect? Give reasons for your answer.

2. (a) Why does Romeo assume responsibility for avenging Mercutio's death? **(b)** Should Romeo have left Tybalt's punishment to Prince Escalus? Explain.

3. Without a curtain on his stage, Shakespeare had one practical problem: getting the dead bodies off-stage. How does he resolve it? Is the solution plausible?

Scenes 2 and 3

1. Dramatic irony occurs when the audience knows something that the characters do not. **(a)** What is Juliet's mood at the opening of Scene 2? **(b)** What do you know that Juliet does not? **(c)** Why might a playwright make use of this kind of irony? (In your answer think of its effect on you as a member of the audience.)

2. (a) What are Juliet's reactions to the news brought by the nurse? **(b)** Do you think that, despite everything, Juliet will remain true to Romeo? **(c)** Does Romeo or Juliet make the more favorable impression on you? Why?

3. According to the friar, what steps should Romeo take to safeguard himself?

Scene 4

1. Why does Capulet urge so rapid a marriage of Paris and his daughter?

2. What dramatic irony does Scene 4 contain?

Scene 5

1. Find evidence in Juliet's speech to Romeo that she is both a little girl and a maturing young woman.

2. (a) What is the nurse's advice to Juliet? **(b)** What is Juliet's reaction to that advice?

Vocabulary

Context

Using context as an aid, complete the following sentences by writing the appropriate words on your paper.

valor agile
chide abhor
herald

1. You should not ______ the children, since they are blameless.

2. You need a pencil and a mind that is ______ to solve a crossword puzzle.

3. She was brave, and her ______ was acknowledged with a medal.

4. I dislike worms, detest frogs, and ______ snakes.

5. The messenger is welcome, since he is the ______ of good news.

Composition

Assume that you, Prince Escalus, have to name the best adviser in Verona. The two finalists are the nurse and the friar. In order to accurately assess the effectiveness of these advisers, you must evaluate their advice and their actions. List both what you consider to be the appropriate and the inappropriate words and deeds of the nurse and of the friar. Use any information you can find in the first three acts. Then decide which person is the better counselor.

Prepare a short paper that you will read at the presentation of the award. When explaining the reason for your choice, use information from your lists to compare and contrast the effectiveness of the candidates.

Comment: Shakespeare's Life and Work

William Shakespeare, the foremost dramatist of his own day and one of the greatest writers of all times, was born in the town of Stratford, England, in April 1564. It is probable that he attended the town's free school where, as was the custom, he studied the Greek and Latin classics. At the age of eighteen, he married Anne Hathaway.

Several years after his marriage, Shakespeare left Stratford and went to London. There he made a name for himself as an actor. In 1594 he was listed as a member of the Lord Chamberlain's Company, a troupe of actors. Among the members of this troupe were some of the greatest actors of the time. For them, Shakespeare began writing plays. It is likely that Shakespeare, in creating various characters, took into consideration the talents of the actors who were to portray them on the stage. By the mid-1590s, Shakespeare was well established as both a playwright and an actor; his plays apparently enjoyed tremendous popularity with the theater-going public. In 1598 he was cited by a critic as the best author of both tragedy and comedy for the stage.

The Lord Chamberlain's Company continued to prosper. In 1599 the group erected the famous Globe Theater. In 1608 the company acquired control of the Blackfriars, the only theater of the time built within the city limits. Shakespeare was a stockholder in both these ventures, suggesting that he had a head for business as well as for acting and writing.

About 1612, having become a wealthy man, Shakespeare retired to Stratford where he died on April 23, 1616.

Act Four

Scene 1: Friar Laurence's cell.

Enter FRIAR LAURENCE *and* PARIS.

FRIAR LAURENCE. On Thursday, sir? The time is very short.
PARIS. My father° Capulet will have it so,
And I am nothing slow to slack his haste.°

My father, my prospective father-in-law.

nothing slow . . . haste, anxious to do nothing that might slow him down in his plans to hasten the marriage.

FRIAR LAURENCE. You say you do not know the lady's mind.
Uneven is the course; I like it not.
PARIS. Immoderately she weeps for Tybalt's death,
And therefore have I little talked of love;
For Venus smiles not in a house of tears.
Now, sir, her father counts it dangerous
That she doth give her sorrow so much sway,°
And in his wisdom hastes our marriage,
To stop the inundation of her tears;
Which, too much minded by herself alone,°
May be put from her by society.°
Now do you know the reason of this haste.

doth give . . . sway, allows her sorrow (over Tybalt's death) to control her feelings.

minded . . . alone, dwelt on by her in privacy.

May be . . . society, may be remedied if she mingles with others.

FRIAR LAURENCE *(aside).* I would I knew not why it should be slowed.
Look, sir, here comes the lady toward my cells.

(Enter JULIET.*)*

PARIS. Happily met, my lady and my wife!
JULIET. That may be, sir, when I may be a wife.
PARIS. That may be, must be, love, on Thursday next.
JULIET. What must be shall be.
FRIAR LAURENCE. That's a certain text.
PARIS. Come you to make confession to this father?
JULIET. To answer that, I should confess to you.
PARIS. Do not deny to him that you love me.
JULIET. I will confess to you that I love him.
PARIS. So will ye, I am sure, that you love me.
JULIET. If I do so, it will be of more price,
Being spoke behind your back, than to your face.
PARIS. Poor soul, thy face is much abused with tears.
JULIET. The tears have got small victory by that,
For it was bad enough before their spite.
PARIS. Thou wrong'st it, more than tears, with that report.[34]
JULIET. That is no slander, sir, which is a truth;
And what I spake, I spake it to my face.
PARIS. Thy face is mine, and thou hast slandered it.
JULIET. It may be so, for it is not mine own.

34. In this exchange between Paris and Juliet, do you learn anything new about Paris?

Are you at leisure, holy father, now,
O shall I come to you at evening mass?

FRIAR LAURENCE. My leisure serves me, pensive daughter, now.
My lord, we must entreat the time alone.°

entreat . . . alone, request that you leave Juliet and me alone.

PARIS. God shield° I should disturb devotion!
Juliet, on Thursday early will I rouse ye.
Till then, adieu; and keep this holy kiss.
(Exit.)

shield, forbid, prevent.

JULIET. O, shut the door! And when thou hast done so,
Come weep with me—past hope, past cure, past help!

FRIAR LAURENCE. Ah, Juliet, I already know thy grief;
It strains me past the compass of my wits.°
I hear thou must, and nothing may prorogue it,
On Thursday next be married to this county.

It strains . . . wits. It exceeds the limits of my wisdom.

JULIET. Tell me not, Friar, that thou hear'st of this,
Unless thou tell me how I may prevent it.
If, in thy wisdom, thou canst give no help,
Do thou but call my resolution wise,
And with this knife I'll help it presently.°
God joined my heart and Romeo's, thou our hands;
And ere this hand, by thee to Romeo sealed,
Shall be the label° to another deed,
Or my true heart with treacherous revolt
Turn to another, this shall slay them both.
Therefore, out of thy long-experienced time,
Give me some present counsel, or, behold,
'Twixt my extremes° and me this bloody knife
Shall play the umpire, arbitrating that
Which the commission° of thy years and art
Could to no issue of true honor bring.
Be not so long to speak; I long to die,
If what thou speak'st speak not of remedy.[35]

presently, at once.

label, the seal attached to a deed (a legal document) showing proof of ownership.

extremes, extreme difficulties.

commission, authority.

35. What convinces the friar to offer a solution other than death to Juliet?

FRIAR LAURENCE. Hold, daughter. I do spy a kind of hope,
Which craves as desperate an execution
As that is desperate which we would prevent.
If, rather than to marry County Paris,
Thou hast the strength of will to slay thyself,
Then is it likely thou wilt undertake
A thing like death to chide away this shame,
That copest° with death himself to 'scape from it;
And, if thou darest, I'll give thee remedy.

copest with, bargains with.

JULIET. Or, bid me leap, rather than marry Paris,
From off the battlements of yonder tower,
Or walk in thievish ways;° or bid me lurk
Where serpents are; chain me with roaring bears;
Or shut me nightly in a charnel house,°

in thievish ways, along highways where thieves hide out.

charnel house, a vault where the bodies of the dead were placed.

O'ercovered quite with dead men's rattling bones,
With reeky° shanks and yellow chapless° skulls;
Or bid me go into a new-made grave
And hide me with a dead man in his shroud—
Things that, to hear them told, have made me tremble—
And I will do it without fear or doubt,
To live an unstained wife to my sweet love.

FRIAR LAURENCE. Hold, then; go home, be merry, give consent
To marry Paris. Wednesday is tomorrow;
Tomorrow night look that thou lie alone;
Let not thy nurse lie with thee in thy chamber.
Take thou this vial, being then in bed,
And this distillèd liquor drink thou off;
When presently through all thy veins shall run
A cold and drowsy humor,° for no pulse
Shall keep his native progress, but surcease;°
No warmth, no breath, shall testify thou livest;
The roses in thy lips and cheeks shall fade
To paly ashes, thy eyes' windows fall
Like death when he shuts up the day of life.
Each part, deprived of supple government,°
Shall, stiff and stark and cold, appear like death,
And in this borrowed likeness of shrunk death
Thou shalt continue two and forty hours,
And then awake as from a pleasant sleep.[36]
Now, when the bridegroom in the morning comes
To rouse thee from thy bed, there art thou dead;
Then, as a manner of our country is,
In thy best robes uncovered° on the bier
Thou shalt be borne to that same ancient vault
Where all the kindred of the Capulets lie.
In the meantime, against thou shalt awake,°
Shall Romeo by my letters know our drift,°
And hither shall he come, and he and I
Will watch thy waking, and that very night
Shall Romeo bear thee hence to Mantua.
And this shall free thee from this present shame,
If no inconstant toy,° nor womanish fear,
Abate thy valor in the acting it.

JULIET. Give me, give me! O, tell not me of fear!

FRIAR LAURENCE. Hold! Get you gone. Be strong and prosperous
In this resolve. I'll send a friar with speed
To Mantua, with my letters to thy lord.

JULIET. Love give me strength, and strength shall help afford.
Farewell, dear father!

(Exeunt.)

reeky, foul-smelling.
chapless, with the lower jaw missing.

humor, liquid.

surcease, cease.

supple government, control over the flexibility of the body.

36. Note that the friar's hobby now becomes a critical element in the development of the plot.

uncovered, with your face uncovered.

against . . . awake, in preparation for your awakening.
drift, intentions.

inconstant toy, fickle, trifling fancy.

Scene 2: A hall in Capulet's house.

Enter CAPULET, LADY CAPULET, *the* NURSE, *and* SERVINGMEN.

CAPULET *(handing the servant a list).* So many guests invite as here are writ.

(Exit FIRST SERVANT.*)*

Sirrah, go hire me twenty cunning cooks.

SECOND SERVANT. You shall have none ill, sir; for I'll try if they can lick their fingers.

CAPULET. How canst thou try them so?

SECOND SERVANT. Marry, sir, 'tis an ill cook that cannot lick his own fingers; therefore he that cannot lick his fingers goes not with me.

CAPULET. Go, be gone.

(Exit SECOND SERVANT.*)*

We shall be much unfurnished for this time.
What, is my daughter gone to Friar Laurence?

NURSE. Ay, forsooth.

CAPULET. Well, he may chance to do some good on her. . . .

NURSE. See where she comes from shrift with merry look.

(Enter JULIET. *She is apparently in good spirits.)*

CAPULET. How now, my headstrong! Where have you been gadding?

JULIET. Where I have learned me to repent the sin
Of disobedient opposition
To you and your behests, and am enjoined
By holy Laurence to fall prostrate here
And beg your pardon. *(She kneels.)* Pardon, I beseech you!
Henceforward I am ever ruled by you.

CAPULET. Send for the county; go tell him of this.
I'll have this knot knit up tomorrow morning.

JULIET. I met the youthful lord at Laurence' cell,
And gave him what becomèd° love I might,
Not stepping o'er the bounds of modesty.

CAPULET. Why, I am glad on 't; this is well. Stand up.
This is as 't should be. Let me see the county;
Ay, marry, go, I say, and fetch him hither.
Now, afore God, this reverend holy friar,
All our whole city is much bound° to him.

JULIET. Nurse, will you go with me into my closet,°
To help me sort such needful ornaments
As you think fit to furnish° me tomorrow?

LADY CAPULET. No, not till Thursday; there is time enough.

CAPULET. Go, Nurse, go with her. We'll to church tomorrow.

(Exeunt JULIET *and* NURSE.*)*

becomèd, suitable.

bound, indebted.

closet, private room.

furnish me, fit me out.

LADY CAPULET. We shall be short in our provision;
'Tis now near night.
CAPULET. Tush, I will stir about,
And all things shall be well, I warrant thee, wife.
Go thou to Juliet, help to deck up her;
I'll not to bed tonight; let me alone;
I'll play the housewife for this once. What, ho!
They are all forth. Well, I will walk myself
To County Paris to prepare him up
Against tomorrow. My heart is wondrous light,
Since this same wayward girl is so reclaimed.
(Exeunt.)

Scene 3: Juliet's bedchamber.

Enter JULIET *and the* NURSE.
JULIET. Ay, those attires are best; but, gentle Nurse,
I pray thee, leave me to myself tonight,
For I have need of many orisons
To move the heavens to smile upon my state,
Which, well thou know'st, is cross° and full of sin.

cross, contrary.

(Enter LADY CAPULET.*)*
LADY CAPULET. What, are you busy, ho? Need you my help?
JULIET. No, madam; we have culled such necessaries
As are behoveful° for our state tomorrow.
So please you, let me now be left alone,
And let the nurse this night sit up with you,
For I am sure you have your hands full all
In this so sudden business.

behoveful, needed.

LADY CAPULET. Good night;
Get thee to bed, and rest, for thou hast need.
(Exeunt LADY CAPULET *and the* NURSE.*)*
JULIET. Farewell! God knows when we shall meet again.
I have a faint cold fear thrills through my veins,°
That almost freezes up the heat of life;
I'll call them back again to comfort me.
Nurse!—What should she do here?
My dismal scene I needs must act alone.
Come, vial.
What if this mixture do not work at all?
Shall I be married then tomorrow morning?
No, no; this shall forbid it. Lie thou there.
(She lays down her dagger.)
What if it be a poison which the friar

faint . . . veins, a feeling of coldness and faintness that courses through my veins.

Subtly hath ministered° to have me dead,
Lest in this marriage he should be dishonored
Because he married me before to Romeo?
I fear it is, and yet methinks it should not,
For he hath still been tried° a holy man.
How if, when I am laid into the tomb,
I wake before the time that Romeo
Come to redeem me?—There's a fearful point!
Shall I not then be stifled in the vault,
To whose foul mouth no healthsome air breathes in,
And there die strangled ere my Romeo comes?
Or, if I live, is it not very like°
The horrible conceit° of death and night,
Together with the terror of the place—
As° in a vault, an ancient receptacle
Where, for these many hundred years, the bones
Of all my buried ancestors are packed;
Where bloody Tybalt, yet but green in earth,°
Lies festering in his shroud; where, as they say,
At some hours in the night spirits resort;—
Alack, alack, is it not like that I,
So early waking, what with loathsome smells,
And shrieks like mandrakes'° torn out of the earth,
That living mortals, hearing them, run mad:—
O, if I wake, shall I not be distraught,
Environed with all these hideous fears,°
And madly play with my forefathers' joints,
And pluck the mangled Tybalt from his shroud,
And, in this rage,° with some great kinsman's bone,
As with a club, dash out my desperate brains?
O, look! Methinks I see my cousin's ghost
Seeking out Romeo, that did spit his body
Upon a rapier's point.—Stay, Tybalt, stay! *(Clutching the vial)*
Romeo, I come! This do I drink to thee.[37]
(She drinks and falls upon her curtained bed.)

ministered, applied or administered (something).

still been tried, always been proved to be.

like, likely.

conceit, idea.

As, namely.

green in earth, newly buried.

mandrakes, plants that resemble the human form. The mandrake was fabled to shriek and to cause madness when torn from the ground.

fears, objects of fear.

rage, madness.

37. Trace Juliet's thoughts in this soliloquy. Does she maintain her courage throughout?

Scene 4: A hall in Capulet's house.

Enter LADY CAPULET *and the* NURSE.

LADY CAPULET. Hold, take these keys, and fetch more spices, Nurse.

NURSE. They call for dates and quinces in the pastry.°

pastry, room in which pastry was made.

(Enter CAPULET.*)*

CAPULET. Come, stir, stir, stir! The second cock hath crowed,

Florence Paterson as the Nurse, Leslie Yeo as Capulet in *Romeo and Juliet,* Stratford Festival, Canada, 1977.

The curfew bell hath rung, 'tis three o'clock.
Look to the bakèd meats,° good Angelica;
Spare not for cost.

bakèd meats, pies, pastries.

NURSE. . . . Get you to bed; faith; you'll be sick tomorrow
For this night's watching.°

For . . . watching, because of lying awake tonight.

CAPULET. No, not a whit. What! I have watched ere now
All night for lesser cause, and ne'er been sick.
LADY CAPULET. Ay. . . but I'll watch you from such watching now.
(Exeunt LADY CAPULET *and* NURSE.*)*

(Enter SERVANTS *carrying baskets of food.)*
CAPULET. Now, fellow! What's there?
FIRST SERVANT. Things for the cook, sir, but I know not what.
CAPULET. Make haste, make haste.
(Exit FIRST SERVANT.*)*
(To SECOND SERVANT*)* Sirrah, fetch drier logs;
Call Peter, he will show thee where they are.
SECOND SERVANT. I have a head, sir, that will find out logs,
And never trouble Peter for the matter.
(Exit.)
CAPULET *(laughing)*. Mass,° and well said!
Thou shalt be loggerhead.° Good faith, 'tis day.
The county will be here with music straight,
For so he said he would. I hear him near.
(Music sounds offstage.)
Nurse! Wife! What, ho! What, Nurse, I say!

Mass, by the Mass.

loggerhead, blockhead.

(Enter NURSE.*)*
Go waken Juliet; go and trim her up.
I'll go and chat with Paris. Hie, make haste,
Make haste; the bridegroom he is come already;
Make haste, I say.
(Exeunt.)

Scene 5: Juliet's bedchamber. The curtains are drawn around Juliet's bed.

Enter the NURSE.

NURSE *(urgently)*. Mistress! What, mistress! Juliet! Fast,° I warrant her.
Why, lamb; why, lady! Fie, you slugabed!
Why, love, I say! *(She draws the curtains from around the bed.)* Madam! Sweetheart! Why, bride!
What, not a word? . . . How sound is she asleep! . . .
I must needs wake her. Madam, madam, madam!
What, dressed, and in your clothes, and down again!
I must needs wake you. *(Shaking her)* Lady! lady! lady!
Alas, alas! *(Running to the door)* Help, help! My lady's dead!
O well a day, that ever I was born!
Some aqua vitae, ho! My lord! My lady!

Fast, fast asleep.

(Enter LADY CAPULET.*)*

LADY CAPULET. What noise is here?
NURSE. *(Going to* LADY CAPULET*)* O lamentable day!
LADY CAPULET. What is the matter?
NURSE. Look, look! O heavy day!
LADY CAPULET. O me. O me! My child, my only life,
Revive, look up, or I will die with thee!
Help, help! Call help!

(Enter CAPULET, *still in high spirits.)*

CAPULET. For shame, bring Juliet forth; her lord is come.
NURSE. She's dead, deceased, she's dead; alack the day!
LADY CAPULET. Alack the day, she's dead, she's dead, she's dead!
CAPULET. Ha! Let me see her. Out, alas!° She's cold;
Her blood is settled,° and her joints stiff.
Life and these lips have long been separated.
Death lies on her like an untimely frost
Upon the sweetest flower of all the field. . . .

Out, alas, an exclamation of grief.

settled, thickened.

(Enter FRIAR LAURENCE *and* PARIS.*)*

FRIAR LAURENCE. Come, is the bride ready to go to church?
CAPULET *(bitterly)*. Ready to go, but never to return. . . .
Death is my son-in-law, Death is my heir;
My daughter he hath wedded. I will die
And leave him all. Life, living, all is Death's.
PARIS. Have I thought long to see this morning's face,°
And doth it give me such a sight as this?
LADY CAPULET. Accursed, unhappy, wretched, hateful day!
Most miserable hour that e'er time saw.

thought long . . . face, long looked forward to the dawn of this, my wedding day.

In lasting labor of his pilgrimage!
But° one, poor one, one poor and loving child,
But one thing to rejoice and solace in,
And cruel Death hath catched it from my sight!

NURSE. O woe! O woeful, woeful, woeful day!
Most lamentable day, most woeful day,
That ever, ever, I did yet behold!
O day! O day! O day! O hateful day!
Never was seen so black a day as this.
O woeful day, O woeful day!

PARIS. Beguiled, divorced, wronged, spited, slain!
Most detestable Death, by thee beguiled,
By cruel cruel thee quite overthrown!
O love! O life; not life, but love in death!

CAPULET. Despised, distressed, hated, martyred, killed!
Uncomfortable time, why camest thou now
To murder, murder our solemnity?
O child! O child! My soul, and not my child!
Dead art thou, dead! Alack, my child is dead,
And with my child my joys are burièd.

FRIAR LAURENCE. Peace, ho, for shame! Confusion's° cure lives not
In these confusions. Heaven and yourself
Had part in this fair maid; now heaven hath all,
And all the better is it for the maid.
Your part in her you could not keep from death,
But heaven keeps his part in eternal life.
The most you sought was her promotion;
For 'twas your heaven she should be advanced;°
And weep ye now, seeing she is advanced
Above the clouds, as high as heaven itself? . . .
Dry up your tears, and stick your rosemary°
On this fair corse; and, as the custom is,
In all her best array bear her to church. . . .

CAPULET. All things that we ordainèd festival,°
Turn from their office to black funeral—
Our instruments to melancholy bells,
Our wedding cheer to a sad burial feast,
Our solemn hymns to sullen° dirges change;
Our bridal flowers serve for a buried corse,
And all things change them to the contrary.[38]

FRIAR LAURENCE. Sir, go you in; and, madam, go with him;
And go, Sir Paris; everyone prepare
To follow this fair corse unto her grave.
The heavens do lour upon you for some ill;°
Move them no more by crossing their high will. . . .

(Exeunt CAPULET, LADY CAPULET, PARIS, *and* FRIAR.*)*

But, only.

Confusion's, destruction's.

advanced, lifted up, promoted.

rosemary, symbol of immortality and enduring love; therefore, used at both funerals and weddings.

ordainèd festival, intended to be gay and festive.

sullen, mournful.

38. Ironically, what will the wedding feast become?

ill, sin committed by you.

Discussion

Scene 1

1. (a) Why does Paris call on Friar Laurence? **(b)** What is Juliet's reason for visiting the friar? **(c)** Is it the reason she suggests to Paris? **(d)** What irony lies in the contrast between these reasons?

2. In the dialogue between Juliet and Paris, Paris makes several assertions and offers several compliments. **(a)** Does Juliet accept these? **(b)** How does Paris interpret her remarks?

3. (a) Outline, step by step, the friar's plan. **(b)** What is Juliet's reaction to that plan?

Scene 2

1. A *dilemma* is a problem with several solutions, each of which has significant drawbacks. Juliet is in a dilemma at the prospect of marriage to Paris. What solutions to her problem can you see? What are the drawbacks associated with each?

2. Capulet says, "All our whole city is much bound to him (the friar)." In what sense is the city indebted to Friar Laurence for convincing Juliet to agree to the marriage with Paris?

Scene 3

1. (a) What questions and doubts come to Juliet's mind during the famous "potion" scene? **(b)** What are your feelings toward Juliet?

2. In drinking the potion, has Juliet challenged fate or is she, too, "fortune's fool"? Explain your answer.

Scenes 4 and 5

1. Why may the hustle and bustle of preparation for the wedding feast be described as ironic?

2. What event in Scene 5 indicates that an important step in the friar's plan has worked out just as he hoped it would?

3. (a) What are your feelings toward Lord and Lady Capulet as they lament the "death" of their daughter? Explain why you feel as you do. **(b)** Why had Juliet not taken the nurse into her confidence concerning the friar's plan?

4. The four speeches that follow line 31 of Scene 5 have certain similarities. What are these?

Vocabulary

Combined Skills

Read each sentence carefully. On your paper write the letter of the choice that best completes or answers each sentence. Feel free to use your Glossary.

1. The *g* in *dirge* sounds like the *g* in **(a)** angle; **(b)** angel.

2. What would you most likely do with a *quince?* **(a)** Eat it; **(b)** Wear it; **(c)** Ride it; **(d)** Read it.

3. Which of the following is not true about the word *subtly?* **(a)** It contains a silent b; **(b)** It is an adverb; **(c)** It has three syllables; **(d)** It has a Latin root.

4. A *shroud* is a **(a)** ball gown; **(b)** burial garment; **(c)** wise person; **(d)** burrowing animal.

5. If you are *prostrate,* you are **(a)** starving; **(b)** lying down or exhausted; **(c)** unbelieving; **(d)** argumentative.

6. Which syllable in *inundation* bears the primary accent? **(a)** *in;* **(b)** *un;* **(c)** *da;* **(d)** *tion.*

7. You would most likely put *aqua vitae* in a **(a)** vile; **(b)** van; **(c)** vial; **(d)** veil.

8. Which of the following originally referred to a time for covering the fire? **(a)** solace; **(b)** dirge; **(c)** curfew; **(d)** cull.

9. A *mandrake* would be found in a(n) **(a)** zoo; **(b)** museum; **(c)** kitchen; **(d)** plant dictionary.

10. A *behest* is given by a(n) **(a)** equal; **(b)** servant; **(c)** commander; **(d)** beggar.

Act Five

Scene 1: A street in Mantua, where Romeo is living.

ROMEO *enters.*

ROMEO. If I may trust the flattering truth of sleep,
My dreams presage some joyful news at hand.
My bosom's lord sits lightly in his throne,
And all this day an unaccustomed spirit
Lifts me above the ground with cheerful thoughts.[39]
I dreamt my lady came and found me dead—
Strange dream that gives a dead man leave° to think!—
And breathed such life with kisses in my lips
That I revived and was an emperor.
Ah me, how sweet is love itself possessed,
When but love's shadows° are so rich in joy!

39. What is it that makes the exiled Romeo cheerful? Should it?

gives . . . leave, allows a dead man.

shadows, unreal images of the imagination.

(Enter BALTHASAR.*)*

News from Verona!—How now, Balthasar!
Dost thou not bring me letters from the friar?
How doth my lady? Is my father well?
How fares my Juliet? That I ask again,
For nothing can be ill if she be well.

BALTHASAR. Then she is well, and nothing can be ill.
Her body sleeps in Capel's monument,
And her immortal part with angels lives.
I saw her laid low in her kindred's vault,
And presently took post° to tell it you.
O, pardon me for bringing these ill news,
Since you did leave it for my office,° sir.

ROMEO. Is it even so? Then I defy you, stars!°
Thou know'st my lodging; get me ink and paper,
And hire post horses; I will hence tonight.

presently took post, soon set out with post horses.

office, duty.

Then . . . stars. Romeo defies the destiny that has fated him to live without Juliet.

BALTHASAR. I do beseech you, sir, have patience;
Your looks are pale and wild, and do import
Some misadventure.

ROMEO. Tush, thou are deceived.
Leave me, and do the thing I bid thee do.
Hast thou no letters to me from the friar?

BALTHASAR. No, my good lord.

ROMEO. No matter. Get thee gone,
And hire those horses; I'll be with thee straight.

(Exit BALTHASAR.*)*

Well, Juliet, I will lie with thee tonight.
Let's see for means. O mischief, thou art swift
To enter in the thoughts of desperate men!
I do remember an apothecary—

And hereabouts he dwells—which late I noted
In tattered weeds,° with overwhelming° brows,
Culling of simples.° Meager were his looks,
Sharp misery had worn him to the bones;
And in his needy shop a tortoise hung,
An alligator stuffed, and other skins
Of ill-shaped fishes; and about his shelves
A beggarly account° of empty boxes,
Green earthen pots, bladders, and musty seeds,
Remnants of packthread and old cakes of roses,°
Were thinly scattered to make up a show.
Noting this penury, to myself I said,
"An if a man did need a poison now
Whose sale is present° death in Mantua,
Here lives a caitiff° wretch would sell it him."
O, this same thought did but forerun my need,
And this same needy man must sell it me.
As I remember, this should be the house.
Being holiday, the beggar's shop is shut.
What, ho, apothecary!

weeds, clothes.
overwhelming, overhanging.
culling of simples, selecting medicinal herbs.
beggarly account, poor array.
cakes of roses, rose petals caked together for use as a perfume.
present, immediate.
caitiff, poor.

(Enter APOTHECARY.*)*

APOTHECARY. Who calls so loud?

ROMEO. Come hither, man. I see that thou art poor.
Hold, there is forty ducats; let me have
A dram of poison, such soon-speeding gear°
As will disperse itself through all the veins
That the life-weary taker may fall dead
And that the trunk° may be discharged of breath
As violently as hasty powder fired
Doth hurry from the fatal cannon's womb.

soon-speeding gear, stuff that will begin to act quickly.
trunk, body.

APOTHECARY. Such mortal drugs I have; but Mantua's law
Is death to any he that utters them.°

any . . . utters them, anyone who distributes them.

ROMEO. Art thou so bare and full of wretchedness,
And fear'st to die? Famine is in thy cheeks,
Need and oppression starveth° in thine eyes,
Contempt and beggary hangs upon thy back;
The world is not thy friend, nor the world's law;
The world affords no law to make thee rich;
Then be not poor, but break it, and take this.

starveth, show hunger.

APOTHECARY. My poverty, but not my will, consents.

ROMEO. I pay thy poverty, and not thy will.

APOTHECARY. Put this in any liquid thing you will
And drink it off; and, if you had the strength
Of twenty men, it would dispatch you straight.

ROMEO. There is thy gold, worse poison to men's souls.
Farewell. Buy food, and get thyself in flesh.
Come, cordial° and not poison, go with me
To Juliet's grave, for there must I use thee.
(Exeunt.)

cordial, a heart stimulant.

Scene 2: Friar Laurence's cell.

Enter FRIAR JOHN.

FRIAR JOHN. Holy Franciscan friar! Brother, ho!

(Enter FRIAR LAURENCE.*)*

FRIAR LAURENCE. This same should be the voice of Friar John.
Welcome from Mantua. What says Romeo?
Or, if his mind be writ,° give me his letter.

FRIAR JOHN. Going to find a barefoot brother out,
One of our order, to associate° me,
Here in this city visiting the sick,
And finding him, the searchers° of the town,
Suspecting that we both were in a house
Where the infectious pestilence did reign,
Sealed up the doors, and would not let us forth,
So that my speed to Mantua there was stayed.

FRIAR LAURENCE. Who bare my letter, then, to Romeo?

FRIAR JOHN. I could not send it—here it is again—
Nor get a messenger to bring it thee,
So fearful were they of infection.

FRIAR LAURENCE. Unhappy fortune! By my brotherhood,
The letter was not nice but full of charge
Of dear import,° and the neglecting it
May do much danger. Friar John, go hence;
Get me an iron crow,° and bring it straight
Unto my cell.

FRIAR JOHN. Brother, I'll go and bring it thee.
(Exit.)

FRIAR LAURENCE. Now must I to the monument alone.
Within this three hours will fair Juliet wake.
She will beshrew me much that Romeo
Hath had no notice of these accidents;°
But I will write again to Mantua,
And keep her at my cell till Romeo come;[40]
Poor living corse, closed in a dead man's tomb!
(Exit.)

if . . . writ, if he has sent a written message.

associate, accompany.

searchers, officials who sought out those suspected of having a highly contagious disease (the "infectious pestilence," in line 10).

Of dear import, having dreadful significance.

iron crow, crowbar.

accidents, happenings.

40. What prevented the letter from being delivered to Romeo?

Scene 3: The churchyard in Verona where the Capulets' tomb is located. It is nighttime.

Enter PARIS *and his* PAGE *bearing flowers and a torch.*

PARIS. Give me thy torch, boy; hence, and stand aloof.
Yet put it out, for I would not be seen.
(The PAGE *extinguishes the torch.)*
Under yond yew trees lay thee all along,°
Holding thine ear close to the hollow ground;
So shall no foot upon the churchyard tread
Being loose, infirm, with digging up of graves
But thou shalt hear it; whistle then to me,
As signal that thou hear'st something approach.
Give me those flowers. Do as I bid thee, go.[41]

PAGE *(speaking aside).* I am almost afraid to stand alone
Here in the churchyard; yet I will adventure. *(He retires.)*

PARIS. Sweet flower, with flowers thy bridal bed I strew.
O woe! Thy canopy is dust and stones,
Which° with sweet° water nightly I will dew,
Or, wanting° that, with tears distilled by moans.
The obsequies that I for thee will keep
Nightly shall be to strew thy grave and weep.
(The PAGE *whistles offstage.)*
The boy gives warning something doth approach.
What cursèd foot wanders this way tonight
To cross° my obsequies and true love's rite?
What, with a torch! Muffle° me, night, awhile.
(He withdraws to the shadowed side of the tomb, where he cannot be seen.)

(Enter ROMEO *and* BALTHASAR *carrying tools to open the tomb.)*

ROMEO. Give me that mattock° and the wrenching iron.
Hold, take this letter; early in the morning
See thou deliver it to my lord and father.
Give me the light. Upon thy life, I charge thee,
Whate'er thou hear'st or seest, stand all aloof,
And do not interrupt me in my course.
Why I descend into this bed of death
Is partly to behold my lady's face,
But chiefly to take thence from her dead finger
A precious ring—a ring that I must use
In dear employment. Therefore hence, be gone.
But if thou, jealous,° dost return to pry
In what I further shall intend to do,
By heaven I will tear thee joint by joint
And strew this hungry churchyard with thy limbs.

all along, at full length.

41. Has Paris been affected by Juliet's death? How do you know?

Which. The antecedent is "canopy," line 13.
sweet, perfumed.
wanting, lacking.

cross, interfere with.
Muffle, hide.

mattock, pickax.

jealous, suspicious.

The time and my intents are savage-wild,
More fierce and more inexorable far
Than empty tigers or the roaring sea.

BALTHASAR. I will be gone, sir, and not trouble you.

ROMEO. So shalt thou show me friendship. *(Offering money)* Take thou that.
Live and be prosperous, and farewell, good fellow.

BALTHASAR *(aside)*. For all this same, I'll hide me hereabout.
His looks I fear, and his intents I doubt.°

(He pretends to leave but hides nearby.)

doubt, suspect.

ROMEO. Thou detestable maw, thou womb of death,
Gorged with the dearest morsel of the earth,
Thus I enforce thy rotten jaws to open,
And, in despite,° I'll cram thee with more food!

(He succeeds in prying open the doors of the tomb.)

in despite, in defiance.

PARIS. This is that banished haughty Montague
That murdered my love's cousin, with which grief,
It is supposed, the fair creature died,
And here is come to do some villainous shame
To the dead bodies. I will apprehend him.

(He comes forward.)

Stop thy unhallowed toil, vile Montague!
Can vengeance be pursued further than death?
Condemnèd villain, I do apprehend thee;
Obey and go with me, for thou must die.

ROMEO. I must indeed; and therefore came I hither.
Good gentle youth, tempt not a desperate man;
Fly hence, and leave me. Think upon these gone;
Let them affright thee. I beseech thee, youth,
Put not another sin upon my head,
By urging me to fury. O, be gone!
By heaven, I love thee better than myself;
For I come hither armed against myself.
Stay not, be gone; live, and hereafter say
A madman's mercy bade thee run away.

PARIS. I do defy thy conjurations,° *(He draws his sword.)*
And apprehend thee for a felon here.

conjurations, solemn appeals.

ROMEO. Wilt thou provoke me? *(Drawing his own sword)* Then have at thee, boy!

PAGE. O Lord, they fight! I will go call the watch.

(Exit.)

PARIS. O, I am slain! *(He falls.)* If thou be merciful,
Open the tomb, lay me with Juliet.

(He dies.)

ROMEO. In faith, I will. Let me peruse this face.
Mercutio's kinsman, noble County Paris!

What said my man when my betossèd soul
Did not attend° him as we rode? I think
He told me Paris should have married Juliet.
Said he not so? Or did I dream it so?
Or am I mad, hearing him talk of Juliet,
To think it was so? O, give me thy hand,
One writ with me in sour misfortune's book!
I'll bury thee in a triumphant° grave.
A grave? O, no; a lantern,° slaughtered youth,
For here lies Juliet, and her beauty makes
This vault a feasting presence° full of light.
Death,° lie thou there, by a dead man interred.
(He lays PARIS *in the tomb, not far from* JULIET.*)*
How oft when men are at the point of death
Have they been merry, which their keepers call
A lightning° before death. O, how may I
Call this a lightning? O my love! my wife!
Death, that hath sucked the honey of thy breath,
Hath had no power yet upon thy beauty:
Thou art not conquered; beauty's ensign yet
Is crimson in thy lips and in thy cheeks,
And death's pale flag is not advancèd there.
Tybalt, liest thou there in thy bloody sheet?
O, what more favor can I do to thee
Than with that hand that cut thy youth in twain
To sunder his that was thine enemy?
Forgive me, cousin! *(Turning again to* JULIET*)* Ah, dear Juliet,
Why art thou yet so fair? Shall I believe
That unsubstantial death is amorous,
And that the lean abhorrèd monster keeps
Thee here in the dark to be his paramour?
For fear of that, I still will stay with thee
And never from this palace of dim night
Depart again. Here, here will I remain
With worms that are thy chambermaids. O, here
Will I set up my everlasting rest,
And shake the yoke of inauspicious stars
From this world-wearied flesh. Eyes, look your last!
Arms, take your last embrace! And, lips, O you
The doors of breath, seal with a righteous kiss
A dateless° bargain to engrossing° death!
Come, bitter conduct, come, unsavory guide!
Thou desperate pilot, now at once run on
The dashing rocks thy seasick weary bark!
Here's to my love! *(He drinks the poison.)* O true apothecary!
Thy drugs are quick. Thus with a kiss I die. *(Falls.)*[42]

triumphant, glorious, honorable.

lantern, a tower filled with many windows.

feasting presence, a splendid reception room in a regal mansion.

Death, the corpse of Paris.

lightning, a revival of spirit.

dateless, everlasting.

engrossing, all-demanding.

42. Is Romeo behaving as you would expect?

(Enter, at the other end of the churchyard, FRIAR LAURENCE, *with a lantern, crowbar, mattock, and spade.)*

FRIAR LAURENCE. Saint Francis be my speed!° How oft tonight
Have my old feet stumbled at graves!° Who's there?

BALTHASAR. Here's one, a friend, and one that knows you well.

FRIAR LAURENCE. Bliss be upon you! Tell me, good my friend,
What torch is yond that vainly lends his light
To grubs and eyeless skulls? As I discern,
It burneth in the Capels' monument.

BALTHASAR. It doth so, holy sir; and there's my master,
One that you love.

FRIAR LAURENCE. Who is it?

BALTHASAR. Romeo.

FRIAR LAURENCE. How long hath he been there?

BALTHASAR. Full half an hour.

FRIAR LAURENCE. Go with me to the vault.

BALTHASAR. I dare not, sir.
My master knows not but I am gone hence,
And fearfully did menace me with death
If I did stay to look on his intents.

FRIAR LAURENCE. Stay, then; I'll go alone. Fear comes upon me;
O, much I fear some ill unthrifty thing.

BALTHASAR. As I did sleep under this yew tree here,
I dreamt my master and another fought,
And that my master slew him.

FRIAR LAURENCE. Romeo! *(He goes forward.)*
Alack, alack, what blood is this which stains
The stony entrance of this sepulcher?
What mean these masterless and gory swords
To lie discolored by this place of peace? *(He enters the tomb.)*
Romeo! O, pale! Who else? What, Paris too?
And steeped in blood? Ah, what an unkind hour
Is guilty of this lamentable chance!
The lady stirs. *(Slowly* JULIET *comes out of her trance.)*

JULIET. O comfortable° friar! Where is my lord?
I do remember well where I should be,
And there I am. Where is my Romeo?

(Offstage noise of the WATCH *approaching.)*

FRIAR LAURENCE. I hear some noise. Lady, come from that nest
Of death, contagion, and unnatural sleep.
A greater power than we can contradict
Hath thwarted our intents. Come, come away.
Thy husband in thy bosom there lies dead;
And Paris too. Come, I'll dispose of thee
Among a sisterhood of holy nuns.
Stay not to question, for the watch is coming;

speed, protector.

stumbled at graves. This was an unlucky omen.

comfortable, comforting.

Come, go, good Juliet. I dare no longer stay.
(He leaves JULIET *in the tomb.)*
JULIET. Go, get thee hence, for I will not away.
(Exit FRIAR LAURENCE.*)*
What's here? A cup closed in my true love's hand?
Poison, I see, hath been his timeless° end.
O churl!° Drunk all, and left no friendly drop
To help me after? I will kiss thy lips;
Haply° some poison yet doth hang on them,
To make me die with a restorative.° *(Kisses him)*
Thy lips are warm.
FIRST WATCHMAN *(offstage).* Lead, boy. Which way?
JULIET. Yea, noise? Then I'll be brief. O happy° dagger
(She snatches ROMEO*'s dagger.)*
This is thy sheath *(Stabs herself)*; there rust, and let me die.
(She falls on ROMEO*'s body and dies.)*

(Enter the PAGE *of* PARIS, *followed by the first watchman.)*
PAGE. This is the place; there, where the torch doth burn.
FIRST WATCHMAN. The ground is bloody; search about the church-yard.
Go, some of you; whoe'er you find, attach.° *(He enters the tomb.)*
Pitiful sight! Here lies the county slain,
And Juliet bleeding, warm, and newly dead,
Who here hath lain these two days burièd. *(To the page)*
Go, tell the prince; run to the Capulets;
Raise up the Montagues; some others search.
We see the ground whereon these woes° do lie,
But the true ground° of all these piteous woes
We cannot without circumstance descry.°

(Enter other members of the WATCH, *with* BALTHASAR.*)*
SECOND WATCHMAN. Here's Romeo's man; we found him in the churchyard.
FIRST WATCHMAN. Hold him in safety till the prince come hither.

(Reenter FRIAR LAURENCE *and another* WATCHMAN.*)*
THIRD WATCHMAN. Here is a friar that trembles, sighs, and weeps.
We took this mattock and this spade from him
As he was coming from this churchyard side.
FIRST WATCHMAN. A great suspicion;° stay the friar too.

(Enter PRINCE ESCALUS *and* ATTENDANTS.*)*
PRINCE. What misadventure is so early up,
That calls our person from our morning's rest?

timeless, untimely.

churl, miser.

Haply, perhaps.

To make . . . restorative. The very thing (a kiss) that had been a means of renewing good cheer when Romeo was alive, may now bring about Juliet's death.

happy, timely.

whoe'er . . . attach. Arrest anyone you find.

woes, the bodies of Romeo and Juliet.

ground, cause.

circumstance descry, note the details.

A great suspicion, a most suspicious thing.

(Enter LORD *and* LADY CAPULET.*)*

CAPULET. What should it be that is so shrieked abroad?
LADY CAPULET. The people in the street cry "Romeo,"
Some "Juliet," and some "Paris"; and all run
With open outcry toward our monument.
PRINCE. What fear is this which startles in our ears?
FIRST WATCHMAN. Sovereign, here lies the County Paris slain,
And Romeo dead, and Juliet, dead before,
Warm and new killed.
PRINCE. Search, seek, and know how this foul murder comes.
FIRST WATCHMAN. Here is a friar, and slaughtered Romeo's man,
With instruments upon them fit to open
These dead men's tombs.
CAPULET. O heavens! O wife, look how our daughter bleeds!
This dagger hath mista'en°—for, lo, his house°
Is empty on the back of Montague—
And it missheathèd in my daughter's bosom!

mista'en, mistaken its right target.
his house, its scabbard.

Marti Maraden as Juliet, Richard Monette as Romeo, Leo Leyden as Friar Laurence in *Romeo and Juliet,* Stratford Festival, Canada, 1977.

LADY CAPULET. O me! This sight of death is as a bell
That warns° my old age to a sepulcher.

(Enter MONTAGUE *and* OTHERS.*)*

PRINCE. Come, Montague; for thou art early up
To see thy son and heir more early down.

MONTAGUE. Alas, my liege, my wife is dead tonight;
Grief of my son's exile hath stopped her breath.
What further woe conspires against mine age?

PRINCE. Look, and thou shalt see.

MONTAGUE. O thou untaught! What manners is in this,
To press before thy father to a grave?

PRINCE. Seal up the mouth of outrage° for a while,
Till we can clear these ambiguities
And know their spring,° their head, their true descent;
And then will I be general of your woes,
And lead you even to death. Meantime, forbear
And let mischance be slave to patience.°
Bring forth the parties of suspicion.

FRIAR LAURENCE. I am the greatest, able to do least,
Yet most suspected, as the time and place
Doth make against me, of this direful murder;
And here I stand, both to impeach and purge°
Myself condemnèd and myself excused.

PRINCE. Then say at once what thou dost know in this.

FRIAR LAURENCE. I will be brief, for my short date of breath
Is not so long as is a tedious tale.
Romeo, there dead, was husband to that Juliet,
And she, there dead, that Romeo's faithful wife.
I married them, and their stol'n marriage day
Was Tybalt's doomsday, whose untimely death
Banished the new-made bridegroom from this city,
For whom, and not for Tybalt, Juliet pined.
You, to remove that siege of grief from her,
Betrothed and would have married her perforce
To County Paris. Then comes she to me
And with wild looks bid me devise some means
To rid her from this second marriage,
Or in my cell there would she kill herself.
Then gave I her, so tutored by my art,
A sleeping potion; which so took effect
As I intended, for it wrought on her
The form of death. Meantime I writ to Romeo
That he should hither come as this° dire night,
To help to take her from her borrowed° grave,
Being the time the potion's force should cease.

warns, orders.

mouth of outrage, outcry.

spring, source.

let mischance . . . patience. Let patience control your hasty reaction to these mishaps.

impeach and purge, accuse and free from blame.

as this, this very.

borrowed, used temporarily.

But he which bore my letter, Friar John,
Was stayed by accident, and yesternight
Returned my letter back. Then all alone
At the prefixèd hour of her waking,
Came I to take her from her kindred's vault,
Meaning to keep her closely° at my cell
Till I conveniently could send to Romeo.
But when I came, some minute ere the time
Of her awaking, here untimely lay
The noble Paris and true Romeo dead.
She wakes, and I entreated her come forth
And bear this work of heaven with patience.
But then a noise did scare me from the tomb,
And she, too desperate, would not go with me,
But, as it seems, did violence on herself.
All this I know; and to the marriage
Her nurse is privy;° and, if aught in this
Miscarried by my fault, let my old life
Be sacrificed, some hour before his time,
Unto the rigor of severest law.

PRINCE. We still have known thee for a holy man.
Where's Romeo's man? What can he say in this?

BALTHASAR. I brought my master news of Juliet's death;
And then in post° he came from Mantua
To this same place, to this same monument.
This letter he early bid me give his father,
And threatened me with death going in the vault,
If I departed not and left him there.

PRINCE. Give me the letter; I will look on it.
Where is the county's page that raised the watch?
Sirrah, what made° your master in this place?

PAGE. He came with flowers to strew his lady's grave,
And bid me stand aloof, and so I did.
Anon comes one with light to ope the tomb,
And by and by my master drew on° him;
And then I ran away to call the watch.

PRINCE. This letter doth make good the friar's words,
Their course of love, the tidings of her death;
And here he writes that he did buy a poison
Of a poor 'pothecary, and therewithal
Came to this vault to die, and lie with Juliet.
Where be these enemies? Capulet! Montague!
See, what a scourge is laid upon your hate,
That heaven finds means to kill your joys° with love![43]
And I, for winking at your discords, too,
Have lost a brace of kinsmen. All are punished.

closely, secretly.

privy, sharing secret knowledge of something.

in post, with the greatest possible speed.

made, did.

drew on, approached.

your joys, your children.

43. What or whom does the prince blame for the deaths of Romeo and Juliet?

CAPULET. O brother Montague, give me thy hand.
This is my daughter's jointure,° for no more
Can I demand.

MONTAGUE. But I can give thee more;
For I will raise her statue in pure gold,
That while Verona by that name is known,
There shall no figure at such rate be set°
As that of true and faithful Juliet.

CAPULET. As rich shall Romeo's by his lady's lie,
Poor sacrifices of our enmity.

PRINCE. A glooming peace this morning with it brings;
The sun, for sorrow, will not show his head.
Go hence, to have more talk of these sad things;
Some shall be pardoned, and some punishèd,
For never was a story of more woe
Than this of Juliet and her Romeo.

(Exeunt.)

jointure, dowry.

at such . . . set, be valued so greatly.

Scene from *Romeo and Juliet.* Foreground: Leo Leyden as Friar Laurence, John Goodin as the Prince of Verona, Frances-Regis Klanfer as Montague, Stratford Festival, Canada, 1977.

Concept Review: Interpretation of New Material

One of several plots in *The Merchant of Venice* is the wooing of Portia (pôr′shə), a wealthy young woman. According to the conditions of her father's will, she can marry only the suitor who makes the correct choice from among three caskets, or boxes. The suitor who wins Portia must select from among a gold, silver, and lead casket the one containing her picture. One of her numerous suitors has already chosen the gold casket and another the silver casket—neither of which contains the picture. The following scene opens as the soldier Bassanio (bä sä′nē ō), unaware of his predecessors' choices, stands before a table containing the three caskets and prepares to select the one that will enable him to marry Portia.

Read the excerpt and answer the questions that follow.

from The Merchant of Venice • *William Shakespeare*

(*from* Act Three, Scene 2)

PORTIA. I pray you, tarry: pause a day or two
Before you hazard; for, in choosing wrong,
I lose your company: therefore forbear awhile.
There's something tells me, but it is not love,
I would not lose you; and you know yourself,
Hate counsels not in such a quality.°
But lest you should not understand me well,—
And yet a maiden hath no tongue but thought,—
I would detain you here some month or two
Before you venture for me. I could teach you
How to choose right, but I am then forsworn;°
So will I never be: so may you miss me;
But if you do, you'll make me wish a sin,
That I had been forsworn. Beshrew your eyes,
They have o'erlook'd° me and divided me;
One half of me is yours, the other half yours,
Mine own, I would say; but if mine, then yours,
And so all yours. O, these naughty° times
Put bars between the owners and their rights!
And so, though yours, not yours. Prove it so,
Let fortune go to hell for it, not I.
I speak too long; but 'tis to peize° the time,
To eke° it and to draw it out in length,
To stay you from election.

quality, manner.

forsworn, perjured.

o'erlook'd, bewitched.

naughty, wicked or worthless.

peize, retard or slow down.

eke, increase.

BASSANIO. Let me choose;
For as I am, I live upon the rack.°
PORTIA. Upon the rack, Bassanio! then confess
What treason there is mingled with your love.
BASSANIO. None but that ugly treason of mistrust,
Which makes me fear th' enjoying of my love:
There may as well be amity° and life
'Tween snow and fire, as treason and my love.
PORTIA. Ay, but I fear you speak upon the rack,
Where men enforcèd to speak anything.
BASSANIO. Promise me life, and I'll confess the truth.
PORTIA. Well then, confess and live.
BASSANIO. "Confess" and "love"
Had been the very sum of my confession:
O happy torment, when my torturer
Doth teach me answers for deliverance!
But let me to my fortune and the caskets.
PORTIA. Away, then! I am lock'd in one of them:
If you do love me, you will find me out.
Nerissa° and the rest, stand all aloof.
Let music sound while he doth make his choice;
Then, if he lose, he makes a swan-like° end,
Fading in music: that the comparison
May stand more proper, my eye shall be the stream
And wat'ry death-bed for him. He may win;
And what is music then? Then music is
Even as the flourish when true subjects bow
To a new-crowned monarch: such it is
As are those dulcet sounds in break of day
That creep into the dreaming bridegroom's ear
And summon him to marriage.

upon the rack, in torment. The rack, an instrument of torture used in cases of treason, was a large frame with rollers at the ends around which ropes were wound. Victims' hands and feet were fastened to these ropes which were pulled taut by means of levers. Thus, victims were stretched until they provided the required information.
amity, peace.

Nerissa, Portia's maid.

swan-like, a reference to the belief that swans sing only once, just before death.

---

1. Lines 1-3 reveal that Portia ______ Bassanio as a suitor. **(a)** ridicules; **(b)** rejects; **(c)** welcomes; **(d)** distrusts.

2. *Hazard* in line 2 is **(a)** a noun meaning danger; **(b)** a verb meaning risk; **(c)** an adjective meaning dangerous; **(d)** none of these definitions.

3. Portia's words to Bassanio in line 12, "so may you miss me," suggest **(a)** he may be lonesome; **(b)** he may choose the wrong casket; **(c)** she may remain single; **(d)** love is hit or miss.

4. Cite the lines that suggest that Portia can help Bassanio choose the right casket.

5. Portia's speech in lines 1–24 is intended to **(a)** reveal to Bassanio the right casket; **(b)** stall for time; **(c)** discourage Bassanio from choosing; **(d)** reveal her calmness.

6. The word *bars* in line 19 refers to **(a)** cages; **(b)** pubs; **(c)** obstacles; **(d)** a jail.

7. In the same line "owners and their rights" refers to **(a)** Portia's choice of a husband; **(b)** Nerissa and the casket; **(c)** her father's ownership of Portia; **(d)** none of these.

8. This comparison is an example of **(a)** simile; **(b)** personification; **(c)** irony; **(d)** metaphor.

9. In line 46, "My eye shall be the stream" is a comparison. What figure of speech is it? **(a)** simile; **(b)** personification; **(c)** irony; **(d)** metaphor.

10. What does Portia think would be an appropriate accompaniment to the ceremony? **(a)** a toast to Bassanio's luck; **(b)** music; **(c)** a fanfare; **(d)** silence.

Composition Review

Choose one of the following composition assignments. Make your essay no less than a page.

1. Suppose you are a drama critic for your school newspaper, and in this capacity you have been asked to write a review of *Romeo and Juliet*—one that will interest other students and encourage them to read the play.

In an effort to make your review lively and appealing, choose details that you think will interest your readers.

2. A number of accidental or chance occurrences take place that foil Friar Laurence's plan and bring about the catastrophe at the end of the play.

Imagine that you are Friar Laurence writing a letter to a friend sometime after these events have occurred. Describe these chance occurrences in chronological order, explain how each altered the course of events, and include any personal feelings or opinions that you think Friar Laurence might have had.

3. Assume that your class plans to present an updated version of one scene from *Romeo and Juliet.*

Choose a scene from the play and rewrite it in your own words. You may wish to select a scene of highly charged emotion (Act Four, Scene 3), witty banter (Act Two, Scene 5), irony (Act Three, Scene 4; Act Four, Scene 2), or dramatic discovery (Act Four, Scene 5). Try to retain the meaning and significance of Shakespeare's original.

Unit 5

The Second Short Story Unit

There are four different kinds of stories in this unit:

WESTERN

The Gift of Cochise

Louis L'Amour

The warriors had been turned back each time they attacked the cabin. Yet there was no man there—only a woman and two children.

Tense, and white to the lips, Angie Lowe stood in the door of her cabin with a double-barreled shotgun in her hands. Beside the door was a Winchester '73, and on the table inside the house were two Walker Colts.

Facing the cabin were twelve Apaches on ragged calico ponies, and one of the Indians had lifted his hand palm outward. The Apache sitting the white-splashed bay pony was Cochise.

Beside Angie were her seven-year-old son Jimmy and her five-year-old daughter Jane.

Cochise sat his pony in silence, his black, unreadable eyes studied the woman, the children, the cabin, and the small garden. He looked at the two ponies in the corral and the three cows. His eyes strayed to the small stack of hay cut from the meadow, and to the few steers farther up the canyon.

Three times the warriors of Cochise had attacked this solitary cabin and three times they had been turned back. In all, they had lost seven men, and three had been wounded. Four ponies had been killed. His braves reported that there was no man in the house, only a woman and two children, so Cochise had come to see for himself this woman who was so certain a shot with a rifle and who killed his fighting men.

These were some of the same fighting men who had outfought, outguessed, and outrun the finest American army on record, an army outnumbering the Apaches by a hundred to one. Yet a lone woman with two small children had fought them off, and the woman was scarcely more than a girl. And she was prepared to fight now. There was a glint of admiration in the old eyes that appraised her. The Apache was a fighting man, and he respected fighting blood.

"Where is your man?"

"He has gone to El Paso." Angie's voice was steady, but she was frightened as she had never been before. She recognized Cochise from descriptions, and she knew that if he decided to kill or capture her it would be done. Until now, the sporadic attacks she had fought off had been those of casual bands of warriors who raided her in passing.

"He has been gone a long time. How long?"

Angie hesitated, but it was not in her to lie. "He has been gone four months."

Cochise considered that. No one but a fool would leave such a woman, or such fine children. Only one thing could have prevented his return. "Your man is dead," he said.

Angie waited, her heart pounding with heavy, measured beats. She had guessed long ago that Ed had been killed but the way Cochise spoke did not imply that Apaches had killed him, only that he must be dead or he would have returned.

"You fight well," Cochise said. "You have killed my young men."

"Your young men attacked me." She hesitated and then added, "They stole my horses."

"Your man is gone. Why do you not leave?"

Angie looked at him with surprise. "Leave? Why, this is my home. This land is mine. This spring is mine. I shall not leave."

"This was an Apache spring," Cochise reminded her reasonably.

"The Apache lives in the mountains," Angie replied. "He does not need this spring. I have two children, and I do need it."

"But when the Apache comes this way, where shall he drink? His throat is dry and you keep him from water."

The very fact that Cochise was willing to talk raised her hopes. There had been a time when the Apache made no war on the white man. "Cochise speaks with a forked tongue," she said. "There is water yonder." She gestured toward the hills, where Ed had told her there were springs. "But if the people of Cochise come in peace they may drink at this spring."

The Apache leader smiled faintly. Such a woman would rear a nation of warriors. He nodded at Jimmy. "The small one—does he also shoot?"

"He does," Angie said proudly, "and well, too!" She pointed at an upthrust leaf of prickly pear. "Show them, Jimmy."

The prickly pear was an easy two hundred yards away, and the Winchester was long and heavy, but he lifted it eagerly and steadied it against the doorjamb as his father had taught him, held his sight an instant, then fired. The bud on top of the prickly pear disintegrated.

There were grunts of appreciation from the dark-faced warriors. Cochise chuckled.

"The little warrior shoots well. It is well you have no man. You might raise an army of little warriors to fight my people."

"I have no wish to fight your people," Angie said quietly. "Your people have your ways, and I have mine. I live in peace when I am left in peace. I did not think," she added with dignity, "that the great Cochise made war on women!"

The Apache looked at her, then turned his pony away. "My people will trouble you no longer," he said. "You are the mother of a strong son."

"What about my two ponies?" she called after him. "Your young men took them from me."

Cochise did not turn or look back, and the little cavalcade of riders followed him away. Angie stepped back into the cabin and closed the door. Then she sat down abruptly, her face white, the muscles in her legs trembling.

When morning came, she went cautiously to the spring for water. Her ponies were back in the corral. They had been returned during the night.

Slowly, the days drew on. Angie broke a small piece of the meadow and planted it. Alone, she cut hay in the meadow and built another stack. She saw Indians several times, but they did not bother her. One morning, when she opened her door, a quarter of antelope lay on the step, but no Indian was in sight. Several times, during the weeks that followed, she saw moccasin tracks near the spring.

Once, going out at daybreak, she saw an Indian girl dipping water from the spring. Angie called to her, and the girl turned quickly, facing her. Angie walked toward her, offering a bright red silk ribbon. Pleased at the gift, the Apache girl left.

And the following morning there was another quarter of antelope on her step—but she saw no Indian.

Ed Lowe had built the cabin in West Dog Canyon in the spring of 1871, but it was Angie who chose the spot, not Ed. In Santa Fe they would have told you that Ed Lowe was good-looking, shiftless, and agreeable. He was, also, unfortunately handy with a pistol.

Angie's father had come from County Mayo[1] to New York and from New York to the Mississippi, where he became a tough, brawling river boatman. In New Orleans, he met a beautiful Cajun[2] girl and married her. Together, they started west for Santa Fe, and Angie was born en route. Both parents died of cholera when Angie was fourteen. She lived with an Irish family for the following three years, then married Ed Lowe when she was seventeen.

Santa Fe was not good for Ed, and Angie kept after him until they started south. It was Apache country, but they kept on until they reached the old Spanish ruin in West Dog. Here there were grass, water, and shelter from the wind.

There was fuel, and there were pinons and game. And Angie, with an Irish eye for the land, saw that it would grow crops.

The house itself was built on the ruins of the old Spanish building, using the thick walls and the floor. The location had been admirably chosen for defense. The house was built in a corner of the cliff, under the sheltering overhang, so that approach was possible from only two directions, both covered by an easy field of fire from the door and windows.

For seven months, Ed worked hard and steadily. He put in the first crop, he built the house, and proved himself a handy man with tools. He repaired the old plow they had bought, cleaned out the spring, and paved and walled it with slabs of stone. If he was lonely for the carefree companions of Santa Fe, he gave no indication of it. Provisions were low, and when he finally started off to the south, Angie watched him go with an ache in her heart.

She did not know whether she loved Ed. The first flush of enthusiasm had passed, and Ed Lowe had proved something less than she had believed. But he had tried, she admitted. And it had not been easy for him. He was an amiable soul, given to whittling and idle talk, all of which he missed in the loneliness of the Apache country. And when he rode away, she had no idea whether she would ever see him again. She never did.

Santa Fe was far and away to the north, but the growing village of El Paso was less than a hundred miles to the west, and it was there Ed Lowe rode for supplies and seed.

He had several drinks—his first in months—in one of the saloons. As the liquor warmed his stomach, Ed Lowe looked around agreeably. For a moment, his eyes clouded with worry as he thought of his wife and children back in Apache country, but it was not in Ed Lowe to worry for long. He had another drink and leaned on the bar, talking to the bartender. All Ed had ever asked of life was enough to eat, a horse to ride, an occasional drink, and companions to talk with. Not that he had anything important to say. He just liked to talk.

Suddenly a chair grated on the floor, and Ed turned. A lean, powerful man with a shock of uncut black hair and a torn, weather-faded shirt stood at bay. Facing him across the table were three hard-faced young men, obviously brothers.

Ches Lane did not notice Ed Lowe watching from the bar. He had eyes only for the men facing him. "You done that deliberate!" The statement was a challenge.

The broad-chested man on the left grinned through broken teeth. "That's right, Ches. I done it deliberate. You killed Dan Tolliver on the Brazos."[3]

---

1. ***County Mayo,*** a county in Ireland.
2. ***Cajun*** (kā′jən), a descendant of the French who came to Louisiana from southeastern Canada.
3. ***Brazos*** (brä′zōs), a river flowing southeast from northern Texas to the gulf of Mexico.

"He made the quarrel." Comprehension came to Ches. He was boxed, and by three of the fighting, blood-hungry Tollivers.

"Don't make no difference," the broad-chested Tolliver said. " 'Who sheds a Tolliver's blood, by a Tolliver's hand must die!' "

Ed Lowe moved suddenly from the bar. "Three to one is long odds," he said, his voice low and friendly. "If the gent in the corner is willin', I'll side him."

Two Tollivers turned toward him. Ed Lowe was smiling easily, his hand hovering near his gun. "You stay out of this!" one of the brothers said harshly.

"I'm in," Ed replied. "Why don't you boys light a shuck?"

"No, by—!" The man's hand dropped for his gun, and the room thundered with sound.

Ed was smiling easily, unworried as always. His gun flashed up. He felt it leap in his hand, saw the nearest Tolliver smashed back, and he shot him again as he dropped. He had only time to see Ches Lane with two guns out and another Tolliver down when something struck him through the stomach and he stepped back against the bar, suddenly sick.

The sound stopped, and the room was quiet, and there was the acrid smell of powder smoke. Three Tollivers were down and dead, and Ed Lowe was dying. Ches Lane crossed to him.

"We got 'em," Ed said, "we sure did. But they got me."

Suddenly his face changed. "Oh Lord in heaven, what'll Angie do?" And then he crumpled over on the floor and lay still, the blood staining his shirt and mingling with the sawdust.

Stiff-faced, Ches looked up. "Who was Angie?" he asked.

"His wife," the bartender told him. "She's up northeast somewhere, in Apache country. He was tellin' me about her. Two kids, too."

Ches Lane stared down at the crumpled, used-up body of Ed Lowe. The man had saved his life.

One he could have beaten, two he might have beaten; three would have killed him. Ed Lowe, stepping in when he did, had saved the life of Ches Lane.

"He didn't say where?"

"No."

Ches Lane shoved his hat back on his head. "What's northeast of here?"

The bartender rested his hands on the bar. "Cochise," he said. . . .

For more than three months, whenever he could rustle the grub, Ches Lane quartered the country over and back. The trouble was, he had no lead to the location of Ed Lowe's homestead. An examination of Ed's horse revealed nothing. Lowe had bought seed and ammunition, and the seed indicated a good water supply, and the ammunition implied trouble. But in the country there was always trouble.

A man had died to save his life, and Ches Lane had a deep sense of obligation. Somewhere that wife waited, if she was still alive, and it was up to him to find her and look out for her. He rode northeast, cutting for sign, but found none. Sandstorms had wiped out any hope of back-trailing Lowe. Actually, West Dog Canyon was more east than north, but this he had no way of knowing.

North he went, skirting the rugged San Andreas Mountains. Heat baked him hot, dry winds parched his skin. His hair grew dry and stiff and alkali-whitened. He rode north, and soon the Apaches knew of him. He fought them at a lonely water hole, and he fought them on the run. They killed his horse, and he switched his saddle to the spare and rode on. They cornered him in the rocks, and he killed two of them and escaped by night.

They trailed him through the White Sands, and he left two more for dead. He fought fiercely and bitterly, and would not be turned from his quest. He turned east through the lava beds and still more east to the Pecos.[4] He saw only two white men, and neither knew of a white woman.

---

4. ***Pecos*** (pā′kəs), a river flowing southeast from northern New Mexico through west Texas to the Rio Grande.

The bearded man laughed harshly. "A woman alone? She wouldn't last a month! By now the Apaches got her, or she's dead. Don't be a fool! Leave this country before you die here."

Lean, wind-whipped and savage, Ches Lane pushed on. The Mescaleros[5] cornered him in Rawhide Draw and he fought them to a standstill. Grimly, the Apaches clung to his trail.

The sheer determination of the man fascinated them. Bred and born in a rugged and lonely land, the Apaches knew the difficulties of survival; they knew how a man could live, how he must live. Even as they tried to kill this man, they loved him, for he was one of their own.

Lane's jeans grew ragged. Two bullet holes were added to the old black hat. The slicker was torn; the saddle, so carefully kept until now, was scratched by gravel and brush. At night he cleaned his guns and by day he scouted the trails. Three times he found lonely ranch houses burned to the ground, the buzzard- and coyote-stripped bones of their owners lying nearby.

Once he found a covered wagon, its canvas flopping in the wind, a man lying sprawled on the seat with a pistol near his hand. He was dead and his wife was dead, and their canteens rattled like empty skulls.

Leaner every day, Ches Lane pushed on. He

---

5. ***Mescaleros*** (mes′kə ler′ōs), an Apache people of western and central Texas and eastern New Mexico.

camped one night in a canyon near some white oaks. He heard a hoof click on stone and he backed away from his tiny fire, gun in hand.

The riders were white men, and there were two of them. Joe Tompkins and Wiley Lynn were headed west, and Ches Lane could have guessed why. They were men he had known before, and he told them what he was doing.

Lynn chuckled. He was a thin-faced man with lank yellow hair and dirty fingers. "Seems a mighty strange way to get a woman. There's some as comes easier."

"This ain't for fun," Ches replied shortly. "I got to find her."

Tompkins stared at him. "Ches, you're crazy! That gent declared himself in of his own wish and desire. Far's that goes, the gal's dead. No woman could last this long in Apache country."

At daylight, the two men headed west, and Ches Lane turned south.

Antelope and deer are curious creatures, often led to their death by curiosity. The longhorn, soon going wild on the plains, acquires the same characteristic. He is essentially curious. Any new thing or strange action will bring his head up and his ears alert. Often a longhorn, like a deer, can be lured within a stone's throw by some queer antic, by a handkerchief waving, by a man under a hide, by a man on foot.

This character of the wild things holds true of the Indian. The lonely rider who fought so desperately and knew the desert so well soon became a subject of gossip among the Apaches. Over the fires of many a rancheria they discussed this strange rider who seemed to be going nowhere, but always riding, like a lean wolf dog on a trail. He rode across the mesas and down the canyons; he studied sign at every water hole; he looked long from every ridge. It was obvious to the Indians that he searched for something—but what?

Cochise had come again to the cabin in West Dog Canyon. "Little warrior too small," he said, "too small for hunt. You join my people. Take Apache for man."

"No." Angie shook her head. "Apache ways are good for the Apache, and the white man's ways are good for white men—and women."

They rode away and said no more, but that night, as she had on many other nights after the children were asleep, Angie cried. She wept silently, her head pillowed on her arms. She was as pretty as ever, but her face was thin, showing the worry and struggle of the months gone by, the weeks and months without hope.

The crops were small but good. Little Jimmy worked beside her. At night, Angie sat alone on the steps and watched the shadows gather down the long canyon, listening to the coyotes yapping from the rim of the Guadalupes, hearing the horses blowing in the corral. She watched, still hopeful, but now she knew that Cochise was right: Ed would not return.

But even if she had been ready to give up this, the first home she had known, there could be no escape. Here she was protected by Cochise. Other Apaches from other tribes would not so willingly grant her peace.

At daylight she was up. The morning air was bright and balmy, but soon it would be hot again. Jimmy went to the spring for water, and when breakfast was over, the children played while Angie sat in the shade of a huge old cottonwood and sewed. It was a Sunday, warm and lovely. From time to time, she lifted her eyes to look down the canyon, half smiling at her own foolishness.

The hard-packed earth of the yard was swept clean of dust; the pans hanging on the kitchen wall were neat and shining. The children's hair had been clipped, and there was a small bouquet on the kitchen table.

After a while, Angie put aside her sewing and changed her dress. She did her hair carefully, and then, looking in her mirror, she reflected with sudden pain that she *was* pretty, and that she was only a girl.

Resolutely, she turned from the mirror and, taking up her Bible, went back to the seat under the cottonwood. The children left their playing and came to her, for this was a Sunday ritual, their only one. Opening the Bible, she read slowly,

". . . though I walk through the valley of the shadow of death, I will fear no evil; for thou art with me; thy rod and thy staff, they comfort me. Thou preparest a table before me in the presence of mine enemies: thou . . ."

"Mommy." Jimmy tugged at her sleeve. "Look!"

Ches Lane had reached a narrow canyon by midafternoon and decided to make camp. There was small possibility he would find another such spot, and he was dead tired, his muscles sodden with fatigue. The canyon was one of those unexpected gashes in the cap rock that gave no indication of its presence until you came right on it. After some searching, Ches found a route to the bottom and made camp under a wind-hollowed overhang. There was water, and there was a small patch of grass.

After his horse had a drink and a roll on the ground, it began cropping eagerly at the rich, green grass, and Ches built a smokeless fire of some ancient driftwood in the canyon bottom. It was his first hot meal in days, and when he had finished he put out his fire, rolled a smoke, and leaned back contentedly.

Before darkness settled, he climbed to the rim and looked over the country. The sun had gone down, and the shadows were growing long. After a half hour of study, he decided there was no living thing within miles, except for the usual desert life. Returning to the bottom, he moved his horse to fresh grass, then rolled in his blanket. For the first time in a month, he slept without fear.

He woke up suddenly in the broad daylight. The horse was listening to something, his head up. Swiftly, Ches went to the horse and led it back under the overhang. Then he drew on his boots, rolled his blankets, and saddled the horse. Still he heard no sound.

Climbing the rim again, he studied the desert and found nothing. Returning to his horse, he mounted up and rode down the canyon toward the flatland beyond. Coming out of the canyon mouth, he rode right into the middle of a war party of more than twenty Apaches—invisible until suddenly they stood up behind rocks, their rifles leveled. And he didn't have a chance.

Swiftly, they bound his wrists to the saddle horn and tied his feet. Only then did he see the man who led the party. It was Cochise.

He was a lean, wiry Indian of past fifty, his black hair streaked with gray, his features strong and clean-cut. He stared at Lane, and there was nothing in his face to reveal what he might be thinking.

Several of the younger warriors pushed forward, talking excitedly and waving their arms. Ches Lane understood some of it, but he sat straight in the saddle, his head up, waiting. Then Cochise spoke and the party turned, and, leading his horse, they rode away.

The miles grew long and the sun was hot. He was offered no water and he asked for none. The Indians ignored him. Once a young brave rode near and struck him viciously. Lane made no sound, gave no indication of pain. When they finally stopped, it was beside a huge anthill swarming with big red desert ants.

Roughly, they quickly untied him and jerked him from his horse. He dug in his heels and shouted at them in Spanish: "The Apaches are women! They tie me to the ants because they are afraid to fight me!"

An Indian struck him, and Ches glared at the man. If he must die, he would show them how it should be done. Yet he knew the unpredictable nature of the Indian, of his great respect for courage.

"Give me a knife, and I'll kill any of your warriors!"

They stared at him, and one powerfully built Apache angrily ordered them to get on with it. Cochise spoke, and the big warrior replied angrily.

Ches Lane nodded at the anthill. "Is this the death for a fighting man? I have fought your strong men and beaten them. I have left no trail for them to follow, and for months I have lived among you, and now only by accident have you captured me. Give me a knife," he added grimly, "and I will fight *him!*" He indicated the big, black-faced Apache.

The warrior's cruel mouth hardened, and he struck Ches across the face.

The white man tasted blood and fury. "Woman!" Ches said. "Coyote! You are afraid!" Ches turned on Cochise, as the Indians stood irresolute. "Free my hands and let me fight!" he demanded. "If I win, let me go free."

Cochise said something to the big Indian. Instantly, there was stillness. Then an Apache sprang forward and, with a slash of his knife, freed Lane's hands. Shaking loose the thongs, Ches Lane chafed his wrists to bring back the circulation. An Indian threw a knife at his feet. It was his own bowie knife.

Ches took off his riding boots. In sock feet, his knife gripped low in his hand, its cutting edge up, he looked at the big warrior.

"I promise you nothing," Cochise said in Spanish, "but an honorable death."

The big warrior came at him on cat feet. Warily, Ches circled. He had not only to defeat this Apache but to escape. He permitted himself a side glance toward his horse. It stood alone. No Indian held it.

The Apache closed swiftly, thrusting wickedly with the knife. Ches, who had learned knife-fighting in the bayou country of Louisiana, turned his hip sharply, and the blade slid past him. He struck swiftly, but the Apache's forward movement deflected the blade, and it failed to penetrate. However, as it swept up between the Indian's body and arm, it cut a deep gash in the warrior's left armpit.

The Indian sprang again, like a clawing cat, streaming blood. Ches moved aside, but a backhand sweep nicked him, and he felt the sharp bite of the blade. Turning, he paused on the balls of his feet.

He had had no water in hours. His lips were cracked. Yet he sweated now, and the salt of it stung his eyes. He stared into the malevolent black eyes of the Apache, then moved to meet him. The Indian lunged, and Ches sidestepped like a boxer and spun on the ball of his foot.

The sudden side step threw the Indian past him, but Ches failed to drive the knife into the Apache's kidney when his foot rolled on a stone. The point left a thin red line across the Indian's back. The Indian was quick. Before Ches could recover his balance, he grasped the white man's knife wrist. Desperately, Ches grabbed for the Indian's knife hand and got the wrist, and they stood there straining, chest to chest.

Seeing his chance, Ches suddenly let his knees buckle, then brought up his knee and fell back, throwing the Apache over his head to the sand. Instantly, he whirled and was on his feet, standing over the Apache. The warrior had lost his knife, and he lay there, staring up, his eyes black with hatred.

Coolly, Ches stepped back, picked up the Indian's knife, and tossed it to him contemptuously. There was a grunt from the watching Indians, and then his antagonist rushed. But loss of blood had weakened the warrior, and Ches stepped in swiftly, struck the blade aside, then thrust the point of his blade hard against the Indian's belly.

Black eyes glared into his without yielding. A thrust, and the man would be disemboweled, but Ches stepped back. "He is a strong man," Ches said in Spanish. "It is enough that I have won."

Deliberately, he walked to his horse and swung into the saddle. He looked around, and every rifle covered him.

So he had gained nothing. He had hoped that mercy might lead to mercy, that the Apache's respect for a fighting man would win his freedom. He had failed. Again they bound him to his horse, but they did not take his knife from him.

When they camped at last, he was given food and drink. He was bound again, and a blanket was thrown over him. At daylight they were again in the saddle. In Spanish he asked where they were taking him, but they gave no indication of hearing. When they stopped again, it was beside a pole corral, near a stone cabin.

When Jimmy spoke, Angie got quickly to her feet. She recognized Cochise with a start of relief, but she saw instantly that this was a war party. And then she saw the prisoner.

Their eyes met and she felt a distinct shock. He was a white man, a big, unshaven man who badly needed both a bath and a haircut, his clothes ragged and bloody. Cochise gestured at the prisoner.

"No take Apache man, you take white man. This man good for hunt, good for fight. He strong warrior. You take 'em."

Flushed and startled, Angie stared at the prisoner and caught a faint glint of humor in his dark eyes.

"Is this here the fate worse than death I hear tell of?" he inquired gently.

"Who are you?" she asked, and was immediately conscious that it was an extremely silly question.

The Apaches had drawn back and were watching curiously. She could do nothing for the present but accept the situation. Obviously they intended to do her a kindness, and it would not do to offend them. If they had not brought this man to her, he might have been killed.

"Name's Ches Lane, ma'am," he said. "Will you untie me? I'd feel a lot safer."

"Of course." Still flustered, she went to him and untied his hands. One Indian said something, and the others chuckled; then, with a whoop, they swung their horses and galloped off down the canyon.

Their departure left her suddenly helpless, the shadowy globe of her loneliness shattered by this utterly strange man standing before her, this big, bearded man brought her out of the desert.

She smoothed her apron, suddenly pale as she realized what his delivery to her implied. What must he think of her? She turned away quickly. "There's hot water," she said hastily, to prevent his speaking. "Dinner is almost ready."

She walked quickly into the house and stopped before the stove, her mind a blank. She looked around her as if she had suddenly waked up in a strange place. She heard water being poured into the basin by the door, and heard him take Ed's razor. She had never moved the box. To have moved it would——

"Sight of work done here, ma'am."

She hesitated, then turned with determination and stepped into the doorway. "Yes, Ed——"

"You're Angie Lowe."

Surprised, she turned toward him, and recognized his own startled awareness of her. As he shaved, he told her about Ed, and what had happened that day in the saloon.

"He—Ed was like that. He never considered consequences until it was too late."

"Lucky for me he didn't."

He was younger looking with his beard gone. There was a certain quiet dignity in his face. She went back inside and began putting plates on the table. She was conscious that he had moved to the door and was watching her.

"You don't have to stay," she said. "You owe me nothing. Whatever Ed did, he did because he was that kind of person. You aren't responsible."

He did not answer, and when she turned again to the stove, she glanced swiftly at him. He was looking across the valley.

There was a studied deference about him when he moved to a place at the table. The children stared, wide-eyed and silent; it had been so long since a man sat at this table.

Angie could not remember when she had felt like this. She was awkwardly conscious of her hands, which never seemed to be in the right place or doing the right things. She scarcely tasted her food, nor did the children.

Ches Lane had no such inhibitions. For the first time, he realized how hungry he was. After the half-cooked meat of lonely, trailside fires, this was tender and flavored. Hot biscuits, desert honey . . . Suddenly he looked up, embarrassed at his appetite.

"You were really hungry," she said.

"Man can't fix much, out on the trail."

Later, after he'd got his bedroll from his saddle and unrolled it on the hay in the barn, he walked back to the house and sat on the lowest step. The sun was gone, and they watched the cliffs stretch their red shadows across the valley. A quail called plaintively, a mellow sound of twilight.

"You needn't worry about Cochise," she said. "He'll soon be crossing into Mexico."

"I wasn't thinking about Cochise."

That left her with nothing to say, and she listened again to the quail and watched a lone bright star in the sky.

"A man could get to like it here," he said quietly.

Discussion

1. (a) Why does Cochise initially decide to visit the home of Angie Lowe? **(b)** How does the Apache warrior respond to the young woman? **(c)** To what agreement do Cochise and Angie come?

2. Describe the homestead of the Lowe family.

3. (a) Under what circumstances does Ed Lowe die? **(b)** Which three of the following adjectives would apply to Ed: ambitious, headstrong, immature, foresighted, well-intentioned, devoted? Explain.

4. (a) Under what circumstances does Ches Lane encounter Cochise? **(b)** How does Ches save his own life?

5. (a) In what ways are Ches Lane and Cochise alike? **(b)** Judging by evidence in the story, do you think that marriage between Ches and Angie would be happy? Explain.

Composition

Assume that you are Angie or Ches Lane, that you have married, and that you are writing to a friend three years after the events in this story. You want to bring your friend up to date about your marriage and the happenings of the last three years.

Write a letter to this friend. In the letter you might consider mentioning the homestead, your children, Cochise and the Apaches, how you fill your days, and your hopes for the future. (See *Assuming Another Voice,* page 669, in Composition Guide.)

Louis L'Amour 1908–

The best-selling writer of westerns in the world today, with more than one hundred thirty million copies of his books sold, Louis L'Amour says he never planned to do anything else with his life but write. Even in his preschool days he had been trying to tell stories.

Before being recognized as a major author, L'Amour spent his youth as a hopper of freight trains, boxer, elephant handler, seaman, and, during World War II, officer of a tank destroyer. Now he spends much of his time at a typewriter composing at least five pages a day, thirty-five pages a week, three novels a year. The owner of more than twenty thousand books about frontier life, L'Amour researches his stories carefully. Many of his better-known novels have been made into successful films. In 1984, L'Amour was awarded a Medal of Freedom in recognition of his writing.

The Man Who Shot Liberty Valance

Dorothy M. Johnson

"He was my enemy; he was my conscience; he made me whatever I am."

Bert Barricune died in 1910. Not more than a dozen persons showed up for his funeral. Among them was an earnest young reporter who hoped for a human-interest story; there were legends that the old man had been something of a gunfighter in the early days. A few aging men tiptoed in, singly or in pairs, scowling and edgy, clutching their battered hats—men who had been Bert's companions at drinking or penny ante while the world passed them by. One woman came, wearing a heavy veil that concealed her face. White and yellow streaks showed in her black-dyed hair. The reporter made a mental note: Old friend from the old District. But no story there—can't mention that.

One by one they filed past the casket, looking into the still face of old Bert Barricune, who had been nobody. His stubbly hair was white, and his lined face was as empty in death as his life had been. But death had added dignity.

One great spray of flowers spread behind the casket. The card read, "Senator and Mrs. Ransome Foster." There were no other flowers except, almost unnoticed, a few pale, leafless, pink and yellow blossoms scattered on the carpeted step. The reporter, squinting, finally identified them: son of a gun! Blossoms of the prickly pear. Cactus flowers. Seems suitable for the old man—flowers that grow on prairie wasteland. Well, they're free if you want to pick 'em, and Barricune's friends don't look prosperous. But how come the Senator sends a bouquet?

There was a delay, and the funeral director fidgeted a little, waiting. The reporter sat up straighter when he saw the last two mourners enter.

Senator Foster—sure, there's the crippled arm—and that must be his wife. Congress is still in session; he came all the way from Washington. Why would he bother, for an old wreck like Bert Barricune?

After the funeral was decently over, the reporter asked him. The Senator almost told the truth, but he caught himself in time. He said, "Bert Barricune was my friend for more than thirty years."

He could not give the true answer: He was my enemy; he was my conscience; he made me whatever I am.

Ransome Foster had been in the territory for seven months when he ran into Liberty Valance. He had been afoot on the prairie for two days when he met Bert Barricune. Up to that

---

time, Ranse Foster had been nobody in particular—a dude from the East, quietly inquisitive, moving from one shack town to another; just another tenderfoot with his own reasons for being there and no aim in life at all.

When Barricune found him on the prairie, Foster was indeed a tenderfoot. In his boots there was a warm, damp squidging where his feet had blistered, and the blisters had broken to bleed. He was bruised, sunburned, and filthy. He had been crawling, but when he saw Barricune riding toward him, he sat up. He had no horse, no saddle and, by that time, no pride.

Barricune looked down at him, not saying anything. Finally Ranse Foster asked, "Water?"

Barricune shook his head. "I don't carry none, but we can go where it is."

He stepped down from the saddle, a casual Samaritan, and with one heave pulled Foster upright.

"Git you in the saddle, can you stay there?" he inquired.

"If I can't," Foster answered through swollen lips, "shoot me."

Bert said amiably, "All right," and pulled the horse around. By twisting its ear, he held the animal quiet long enough to help the anguished stranger to the saddle. Then, on foot—and like any cowboy Bert Barricune hated walking—he led the horse five miles to the river. He let Foster lie where he fell in the cottonwood grove and brought him a hat full of water.

After that, Foster made three attempts to stand up. After the third failure, Barricune asked, grinning, "Want me to shoot you after all?"

"No," Foster answered. "There's something I want to do first."

Barricune looked at the bruises and commented, "Well, I should think so." He got on his horse and rode away. After an hour he returned with bedding and grub and asked, "Ain't you dead yet?"

The bruised and battered man opened his uninjured eye and said, "Not yet, but soon." Bert was amused. He brought a bucket of water and set up camp—a bedroll on a tarp, an armload of wood for a fire. He crouched on his heels while the tenderfoot, with cautious movements that told of pain, got his clothes off and splashed water on his body. No gunshot wounds, Barricune observed, but marks of kicks, and a couple that must have been made with a quirt.

After a while he asked, not inquisitively, but as one who has a right to know how matters stood, "Anybody looking for you?"

Foster rubbed dust from his clothes, being too full of pain to shake them.

"No," he said. "But I'm looking for somebody."

"I ain't going to help you look," Bert informed him. "Town's over that way, two miles, when you get ready to come. Cache the stuff when you leave. I'll pick it up."

Three days later they met in the town marshal's office. They glanced at each other but did not speak. This time it was Bert Barricune who was bruised, though not much. The marshal was just letting him out of the one-cell jail when Foster limped into the office. Nobody said anything until Barricune, blinking and walking not quite steadily, had left. Foster saw him stop in front of the next building to speak to a girl. They walked away together, and it looked as if the young man were being scolded.

The marshal cleared his throat. "You wanted something, Mister?"

Foster answered, "Three men set me afoot on the prairie. Is that an offense against the law around here?"

The marshal eased himself and his stomach into a chair and frowned judiciously. "It ain't customary," he admitted. "Who was they?"

"The boss was a big man with black hair, dark eyes, and two gold teeth in front. The other two——"

"I know. Liberty Valance and a couple of his boys. Just what's your complaint, now?" Foster began to understand that no help was going to come from the marshal.

"They rob you?" the marshal asked.

"They didn't search me."

"Take your gun?"

"I didn't have one."

"Steal your horse?"

"Gave him a crack with a quirt, and he left."

"Saddle on him?"

"No. I left it out there."

The marshal shook his head. "Can't see you got any legal complaint," he said with relief. "Where was this?"

"On a road in the woods, by a creek. Two days' walk from here."

The marshal got to his feet. "You don't even know what jurisdiction it was in. They knocked you around; well, that could happen. Man gets in a fight—could happen to anybody."

Foster said dryly, "Thanks a lot."

The marshal stopped him as he reached the door. "There's a reward for Liberty Valance."

"I still haven't got a gun," Foster said. "Does he come here often?"

"Nope. Nothing he'd want in Twotrees. Hard man to find." The marshal looked Foster up and down. "He won't come after you here." It was as if he had added, *Sonny!* "Beat you up once, he won't come again for that."

And I, Foster realized, am not man enough to go after him.

"Fact is," the marshal added, "I can't think of any bait that would bring him in. Pretty quiet here. Yes sir." He put his thumbs in his galluses and looked out the window, taking credit for the quietness.

Bait, Foster thought. He went out thinking about it. For the first time in a couple of years he had an ambition—not a laudable one, but something to aim at. He was going to be the bait for Liberty Valance and, as far as he could be, the trap as well.

At the Elite Cafe he stood meekly in the doorway, hat in hand, like a man who expects and deserves to be refused anything he might ask for. Clearing his throat, he asked, "Could I work for a meal?"

The girl who was filling sugar bowls looked up and pitied him. "Why, I should think so. Mr. Anderson!" She was the girl who had walked away with Barricune, scolding him.

The proprietor came from the kitchen, and Ranse Foster repeated his question, cringing, but with a suggestion of a sneer.

"Go around back and split some wood," Anderson answered, turning back to the kitchen.

"He could just as well eat first," the waitress suggested. "I'll dish up some stew to begin with."

Ranse ate fast, as if he expected the plate to be snatched away. He knew the girl glanced at him several times, and he hated her for it. He had not counted on anyone's pitying him in his new role of sneering humility, but he knew he might as well get used to it.

When she brought his pie, she said, "If you was looking for a job . . ."

He forced himself to look at her suspiciously. "Yes?"

"You could try the Prairie Belle. I heard they needed a swamper."[1]

Bert Barricune, riding out to the river camp for his bedroll, hardly knew the man he met there. Ranse Foster was haughty, condescending, and cringing all at once. He spoke with a faint sneer, and stood as if he expected to be kicked.

"I assumed you'd be back for your belongings," he said. "I realized that you would change your mind."

Barricune, strapping up his bedroll, looked blank. "Never changed it," he disagreed. "Doing just what I planned. I never give you my bedroll."

"Of course not, of course not," the new Ranse Foster agreed with sneering humility. "It's yours. You have every right to reclaim it."

Barricune looked at him narrowly and hoisted the bedroll to sling it up behind his saddle. "I should have left you for the buzzards," he remarked.

Foster agreed, with a smile that should have

---

1. ***swamper,*** a handyman or helper who performs heavy cleaning duties.

got him a fist in the teeth. "Thank you, my friend," he said with no gratitude. "Thank you for all your kindness, which I have done nothing to deserve and shall do nothing to repay."

Barricune rode off, scowling, with the memory of his good deed irritating him like lice. The new Foster followed, far behind, on foot.

Sometimes in later life Ranse Foster thought of the several men he had been through the years. He did not admire any of them very much. He was by no means ashamed of the man he finally became, except that he owed too much to other people. One man he had been when he was young, a serious student, gullible and quick tempered. Another man had been reckless and without an aim; he went West, with two thousand dollars of his own, after a quarrel with the executor of his father's estate. That man did not last long. Liberty Valance had whipped him with a quirt and kicked him into unconsciousness, for no reason except that Liberty, meeting him and knowing him for a tenderfoot, was able to do so. That man died on the prairie. After that, there was the man who set out to be the bait that would bring Liberty Valance into Twotrees.

Ranse Foster had never hated anyone before he met Liberty Valance, but Liberty was not the last man he learned to hate. He hated the man he himself had been while he waited to meet Liberty again.

The swamper's job at the Prairie Belle was not disgraceful until Ranse Foster made it so. When he swept floors, he was so obviously contemptuous of the work and of himself for doing it that other men saw him as contemptible. He watched the customers with a curled lip as if they were beneath him. But when a poker player threw a white chip on the floor, the swamper looked at him with half-veiled hatred—and picked up the chip. They talked about him at the Prairie Belle, because he could not be ignored.

At the end of the first month, he bought a Colt .45 from a drunken cowboy who needed money worse than he needed two guns. After that, Ranse went without part of his sleep in order to walk out, seven mornings a week, to where his first camp had been and practice target shooting. And the second time he overslept from exhaustion, Joe Mosten of the Prairie Belle fired him.

"Here's your pay," Joe growled, and dropped the money on the floor.

A week passed before he got another job. He ate his meals frugally in the Elite Cafe and let himself be seen stealing scraps off plates that other diners had left. Lillian, the older of the two waitresses, yelled her disgust, but Hallie, who was young, pitied him.

"Come to the back door when it's dark," she murmured, "and I'll give you a bite. There's plenty to spare."

The second evening he went to the back door, Bert Barricune was there ahead of him. He said gently, "Hallie is my girl."

"No offense intended," Foster answered. "The young lady offered me food, and I have come to get it."

"A dog eats where it can," young Barricune drawled.

Ranse's muscles tensed and rage mounted in his throat, but he caught himself in time and shrugged. Bert said something then that scared him: "If you wanted to get talked about, it's working fine. They're talking clean over in Dunbar."

"What they do or say in Dunbar," Foster answered, "is nothing to me."

"It's where Liberty Valance hangs out," the other man said casually. "In case you care."

Ranse almost confided then, but instead said stiffly, "I do not quite appreciate your strange interest in my affairs."

Barricune pushed back his hat and scratched his head. "I don't understand it myself. But leave my girl alone."

"As charming as Miss Hallie may be," Ranse told him, "I am interested only in keeping my stomach filled."

"Then why don't you work for a living? The clerk at Dowitts's quit this afternoon."

Jake Dowitt hired him as a clerk because nobody else wanted the job.

"Read and write, do you?" Dowitt asked. "Work with figures?"

Foster drew himself up. "Sir, whatever may be said against me, I believe I may lay claim to being a scholar. That much I claim, if nothing more. I have read law."

"Maybe the job ain't good enough for you," Dowitt suggested.

Foster became humble again. "Any job is good enough for me. I will also sweep the floor."

"You will also keep up the fire in the stove," Dowitt told him. "Seven in the morning till nine at night. Got a place to live?"

"I sleep in the livery stable in return for keeping it shoveled out."

Dowitt had intended to house his clerk in a small room over the store, but he changed his mind. "Got a shed out back you can bunk in," he offered. "You'll have to clean it out first. Used to keep chickens there."

"There is one thing," Foster said. "I want two half-days off a week."

Dowitt looked over the top of his spectacles. "Now what would you do with time off? Never mind. You can have it—for less pay. I give you a discount on what you buy in the store."

The only purchase Foster made consisted of four boxes of cartridges a week.

In the store, he weighed salt pork as if it were low stuff but himself still lower, humbly measured lengths of dress goods for the women customers. He added vanity to his other unpleasantnesses and let customers discover him combing his hair admiringly before a small mirror. He let himself be seen reading a small black book, which aroused curiosity.

It was while he worked at the store that he started Twotrees' first school. Hallie was responsible for that. Handing him a plate heaped higher than other customers got at the café, she said gently, "You're a learned man, they say, Mr. Foster."

With Hallie he could no longer sneer or pretend humility, for Hallie was herself humble, as well as gentle and kind. He protected himself from her by not speaking unless he had to.

He answered, "I have had advantages, Miss Hallie, before fate brought me here."

"That book you read," she asked wistfully, "what's it about?"

"It was written by a man named Plato," Ranse told her stiffly. "It was written in Greek."

She brought him a cup of coffee, hesitated for a moment, and then asked, "You can read and write American, too, can't you?"

"English, Miss Hallie," he corrected. "English is our mother tongue. I am quite familiar with English."

She put her red hands on the café counter. "Mr. Foster," she whispered, "will you teach me to read?"

He was too startled to think of an answer she could not defeat.

"Bert wouldn't like it," he said. "You're a grown woman besides. It wouldn't look right for you to be learning to read now."

She shook her head. "I can't learn any younger." She sighed. "I always wanted to know how to read and write." She walked away toward the kitchen, and Ranse Foster was struck with an emotion he knew he could not afford. He was swept with pity. He called her back.

"Miss Hallie. Not you alone—people would talk about you. But if you brought Bert——"

"Bert can already read some. He don't care about it. But there's some kids in town." Her face was so lighted that Ranse looked away.

He still tried to escape. "Won't you be ashamed, learning with children?"

"Why, I'll be proud to learn any way at all," she said.

He had three little girls, two restless little boys, and Hallie in Twotrees' first school sessions—one hour each afternoon, in Dowitt's storeroom. Dowitt did not dock his pay for the time spent, but he puzzled a great deal. So did the children's parents. The children themselves were puzzled at some of the things he read aloud, but they were patient. After all, lessons lasted only an hour.

"When you are older, you will understand this," he promised, not looking at Hallie, and then he read Shakespeare's sonnet that begins:

> No longer mourn for me when I am dead
> Than you shall hear the surly sullen bell

and ends:

> Do not so much as my poor name rehearse,
> But let your love even with my life decay,
> Lest the wise world should look into your moan
> And mock you with me after I am gone.

Hallie understood the warning, he knew. He read another sonnet, too:

> When, in disgrace with fortune and men's eyes,
> I all alone beweep my outcast state,

and carefully did not look up at her as he finished it:

> For thy sweet love remembered such wealth brings
> That then I scorn to change my state with kings.

Her earnestness in learning was distasteful to him—the anxious way she grasped a pencil and formed letters, the little gasp with which she always began to read aloud. Twice he made her cry, but she never missed a lesson.

He wished he had a teacher for his own learning, but he could not trust anyone, and so he did his lessons alone. Bert Barricune caught him at it on one of those free afternoons when Foster, on a horse from the livery stable, had ridden miles out of town to a secluded spot.

Ranse Foster had an empty gun in his hand when Barricune stepped out from behind a sandstone column and remarked, "I've seen better."

Foster whirled, and Barricune added, "I could have been somebody else—and your gun's empty."

"When I see somebody else, it won't be," Foster promised.

"If you'd asked me," Barricune mused, "I could've helped you. But you didn't want no helping. A man shouldn't be ashamed to ask somebody that knows better than him." His gun was suddenly in his hand, and five shots cracked their echoes around the skull-white, sandstone pillars. Half an inch above each of five cards that Ranse had tacked to a dead tree, at the level of a man's waist, a splintered hole appeared in the wood. "Didn't want to spoil your targets," Barricune explained.

"I'm not ashamed to ask you," Foster told him angrily, "since you know so much. I shoot straight but slow. I'm asking you now."

Barricune, reloading his gun, shook his head. "It's kind of late for that. I come out to tell you that Liberty Valance is in town. He's interested in the dude that anybody can kick around—this here tenderfoot that boasts how he can read Greek."

"Well," said Foster softly. "Well, so the time has come."

"Don't figure you're riding into town with me," Bert warned. "You're coming all by yourself."

Ranse rode into town with his gun belt buckled on. Always before, he had carried it wrapped in a slicker. In town, he allowed himself the luxury of one last vanity. He went to the barbershop, neither sneering nor cringing, and said sharply, "Cut my hair. Short."

The barber was nervous, but he worked understandably fast.

"Thought you was partial to that long wavy hair of yourn," he remarked.

"I don't know why you thought so," Foster said coldly.

Out in the street again, he realized that he did not know how to go about the job. He did not know where Liberty Valance was, and he was determined not to be caught like a rat. He intended to look for Liberty.

Joe Mosten's right-hand man was lounging at the door of the Prairie Belle. He moved over to bar the way.

"Not in there, Foster," he said gently. It was the first time in months that Ranse Foster had heard another man address him respectfully. His presence was recognized—as a menace to the fixtures of the Prairie Belle.

When I die, sometime today, he thought, they won't say I was a coward. They may say I was a fool, but I won't care by that time.

"Where is he?" Ranse asked.

"I couldn't tell you that," the man said apologetically. "I'm young and healthy, and where he is is none of my business. Joe'd be obliged if you stay out of the bar, that's all."

Ranse looked across toward Dowitt's store. The padlock was on the door. He glanced north, toward the marshal's office.

"That's closed, too," the saloon man told him courteously. "Marshal was called out of town an hour ago."

Ranse threw back his head and laughed. The sound echoed back from the false-fronted buildings across the street. There was nobody walking in the street; there were not even any horses tied to the hitching racks.

"Send Liberty word," he ordered in the tone of one who has a right to command. "Tell him the tenderfoot wants to see him again."

The saloon man cleared his throat. "Guess it won't be necessary. That's him coming down at the end of the street, wouldn't you say?"

Ranse looked, knowing the saloon man was watching him curiously.

"I'd say it is," he agreed. "Yes, I'd say that was Liberty Valance."

"I'll be going inside now," the other man remarked apologetically. "Well, take care of yourself." He was gone without a sound.

This is the classic situation, Ranse realized. Two enemies walking to meet each other along the dusty, waiting street of a western town. What reasons other men have had, I will never know. There are so many things I have never learned! And now there is no time left.

He was an actor who knew the end of the scene but had forgotten the lines and never knew the cue for them. One of us ought to say something, he realized. I should have planned this all out in advance. But all I ever saw was the end of it.

Liberty Valance, burly and broad-shouldered, walked stiff-legged, with his elbows bent.

When he is close enough for me to see whether he is smiling, Ranse Foster thought, somebody's got to speak.

He looked into his own mind and realized, This man is afraid, this Ransome Foster. But nobody else knows it. He walks and is afraid, but he is no coward. Let them remember that. Let Hallie remember that.

Liberty Valance gave the cue. "Looking for me?" he called between his teeth. He was grinning.

Ranse was almost grateful to him; it was as if Liberty had said, The time is now!

"I owe you something," Ranse answered. "I want to pay my debt."

Liberty's hand flashed with his own. The gun in Foster's hand exploded, and so did the whole world.

Two shots to my one, he thought—his last thought for a while.

He looked up at a strange, unsteady ceiling and a face that wavered like a reflection in water. The bed beneath him swung even after he closed his eyes. Far away someone said, "Shove some more cloth in the wound. It slows the bleeding."

He knew with certain agony where the wound was—in his right shoulder. When they touched it, he heard himself cry out.

The face that wavered above him was a new one, Bert Barricune's.

"He's dead," Barricune said.

Foster answered from far away, "I am not."

Barricune said, "I didn't mean you."

Ranse turned his head away from the pain,

and the face that had shivered above him before was Hallie's, white and big-eyed. She put a hesitant hand on his, and he was annoyed to see that hers was trembling.

"Are you shaking," he asked, "because there's blood on my hands?"

"No," she answered. "It's because they might have been getting cold."

He was aware then that other people were in the room; they stirred and moved aside as the doctor entered.

"Maybe you're gonna keep that arm," the doctor told him at last. "But it's never gonna be much use to you."

The trial was held three weeks after the shooting, in the hotel room where Ranse lay in bed. The charge was disturbing the peace; he pleaded guilty and was fined ten dollars.

When the others had gone, he told Bert Barricune, "There was a reward, I heard. That would pay the doctor and the hotel."

"You ain't going to collect it," Bert informed him. "It'd make you too big for your britches." Barricune sat looking at him for a moment and then remarked, "You didn't kill Liberty."

Foster frowned. "They buried him."

"Liberty fired once. You fired once and missed. I fired once, and I don't generally miss. I ain't going to collect the reward, neither. Hallie don't hold with violence."

Foster said thoughtfully, "That was all I had to be proud of."

"You faced him," Barricune said. "You went to meet him. If you got to be proud of something, you can remember that. It's a fact you ain't got much else."

Ranse looked at him with narrowed eyes. "Bert, are you a friend of mine?"

Bert smiled without humor. "You know I ain't. I picked you up off the prairie, but I'd do that for the lowest scum that crawls. I wisht I hadn't."

"Then why——"

Bert looked at the toe of his boot. "Hallie likes you. I'm a friend of Hallie's. That's all I ever will be, long as you're around."

Ranse said, "Then I shot Liberty Valance." That was the nearest he ever dared come to saying "Thank you." And that was when Bert Barricune started being his conscience, his Nemesis,[2] his lifelong enemy and the man who made him great.

"Would she be happy living back East?" Foster asked. "There's money waiting for me there if I go back."

Bert answered, "What do you think?" He stood up and stretched. "You got quite a problem, ain't you? You could solve it easy by just going back alone. There ain't much a man can do here with a crippled arm."

He went out and shut the door behind him.

There is always a way out, Foster thought, if a man wants to take it. Bert had been his way out when he met Liberty on the street of Twotrees. To go home was the way out of this.

I learned to live without pride, he told himself. I could learn to forget about Hallie.

When she came, between the dinner dishes and setting the tables for supper at the café, he told her.

She did not cry. Sitting in the chair beside his bed, she winced and jerked one hand in protest when he said, "As soon as I can travel, I'll be going back where I came from."

She did not argue. She said only, "I wish you good luck, Ransome. Bert and me, we'll look after you long as you stay. And remember you after you're gone."

"How will you remember me?" he demanded harshly.

As his student she had been humble, but as a woman she had her pride. "Don't ask that," she said, and got up from the chair.

"Hallie, Hallie," he pleaded, "how can I stay? How could I earn a living?"

She said indignantly, as if someone else had insulted him, "Ranse Foster, I just guess you could do anything you wanted to."

"Hallie," he said gently, "sit down."

---

2. ***Nemesis*** (nem′ə sis), (in Greek myths) the goddess of vengeance; also, a person who punishes and who cannot be eluded.

He never really wanted to be outstanding. He had two aims in life: to make Hallie happy and to keep Bert Barricune out of trouble. He defended Bert on charges ranging from drunkenness to stealing cattle, and Bert served time twice.

Ranse Foster did not want to run for judge, but Bert remarked, "I think Hallie would kind of like it if you was His Honor." Hallie was pleased but not surprised when he was elected. Ranse was surprised but not pleased.

He was not eager to run for the legislature—that was after the territory became a state—but there was Bert Barricune in the background, never urging, never advising, but watching with half-closed, bloodshot eyes. Bert Barricune, who never amounted to anything, but never intruded, was a living, silent reminder of three debts: a hat full of water under the cottonwoods, gunfire in a dusty street, and Hallie, quietly sewing beside a lamp in the parlor. And the Fosters had four sons.

All the things the opposition said about Ranse Foster when he ran for the state legislature were true, except one. He had been a lowly swamper in a frontier saloon; he had been a deadbeat, accepting handouts at the alley entrance of a café; he had been despicable and despised. But the accusation that lost him the election was false. He had not killed Liberty Valance. He never served in the state legislature.

When there was talk of his running for governor, he refused. Handy Strong, who knew politics, tried to persuade him.

"That shooting, we'll get around that. 'The Honorable Ransome Foster walked down a street in broad daylight to meet an enemy of society. He shot him down in a fair fight, of necessity, the way you'd shoot a mad dog—but Liberty Valance could shoot back, and he did. Ranse Foster carries the mark of that encounter today in a crippled right arm. He is still paying the price for protecting law-abiding citizens. And he was the first teacher west of Rosy Buttes. He served without pay.' You've come a long way, Ranse, and you're going further."

"A long way," Foster agreed, "for a man who never wanted to go anywhere. I don't want to be governor."

When Handy had gone, Bert Barricune sagged in, unwashed, unshaven. He sat down stiffly. At the age of fifty, he was an old man, an unwanted relic of the frontier that was gone, a legacy to more civilized times that had no place for him. He filled his pipe deliberately. After a while he remarked, "The other side is gonna say you ain't fitten to be governor. Because your wife ain't fancy enough. They're gonna say Hallie didn't even learn to read till she was growed up."

Ranse was on his feet, white with fury. "Then I'm going to win this election if it kills me."

"I don't reckon it'll kill you," Bert drawled. "Liberty Valance couldn't."

"I could have got rid of the weight of that affair long ago," Ranse reminded him, "by telling the truth."

"You could yet," Bert answered. "Why don't you?"

Ranse said bitterly, "Because I owe you too much. . . . I don't think Hallie wants to be the governor's lady. She's shy."

"Hallie don't never want nothing for herself. She wants things for you. The way I feel, I wouldn't mourn at your funeral. But what Hallie wants, I'm gonna try to see she gets."

"So am I," Ranse promised grimly.

"Then I don't mind telling you," Bert admitted, "that it was me reminded the opposition to dig up that matter of how she couldn't read."

As the Senator and his wife rode home after old Bert Barricune's barren funeral, Hallie sighed. "Bert never had much of anything. I guess he never wanted much."

He wanted you to be happy, Ranse Foster thought, and he did the best he knew how.

"I wonder where those prickly-pear blossoms came from," he mused.

Hallie glanced up at him, smiling. "From me," she said.

Discussion

1. (a) Under what circumstances do Ransome Foster and Bert Barricune first meet? **(b)** In what ways does Barricune help Foster on this occasion? **(c)** Describe how Foster happens to have been left on the prairie.

2. At one point in the story, Ransome Foster reflects on the several men he has been during his life. **(a)** Briefly describe each of these men. **(b)** Of the men he has been, which man does Foster hate? Why? **(c)** Describe the preparations Foster makes to defeat Liberty Valance in battle.

3. (a) How does Hallie befriend Foster? **(b)** In what ways is Foster able to repay some of Hallie's kindness? **(c)** Describe Bert Barricune's attitude toward Hallie's interest in Foster.

4. (a) Why doesn't Barricune take credit for killing Liberty Valance? **(b)** What does Foster mean by saying, "Then I shot Liberty Valance"? **(c)** In what way does the public's belief that he shot Valance later work against Foster?

5. (a) What does Barricune do to goad Foster into running for governor? **(b)** Is Foster ever able to repay Barricune for his acts on Foster's behalf? Explain. **(c)** Is Foster justified in his belief that Barricune was his lifelong enemy? Explain.

6. How does Hallie feel about Barricune? How do you know?

Dorothy M. Johnson 1905–1984

Dorothy M. Johnson worked as a magazine editor, news editor, and professor of journalism. A native of Iowa and a graduate of the University of Montana, where she later taught, Johnson published numerous western novels and collections of short stories, among them, *Indian Country* (1953), *The Hanging Tree* (1957), *Flame on the Frontier* (1967), *Buffalo Woman* (1977), and *All the Buffalo Returning* (1979).

In addition to winning the Spur Award of the Western Writers of America, Dorothy Johnson was made an honorary member of the Blackfoot tribe in Montana and given the Indian name "Kills-Both-Places." The movie version of "The Man Who Shot Liberty Valance" was released in 1962.

Early Marriage

Conrad Richter

She remembered the long miles they would have in the wagon, the camps at lonely places, the ugly shadow ever hovering over . . . this frontier country.

For two days the leathery face of Asa Putman had been a document in cipher to anyone who could read the code. Since Saturday but one traveler had passed his solitary post,[1] a speck of adobe and picket corrals lost on the vast, sandy stretch of the Santa Ana[2] plain. Far as the eye could see from his doorway, the rutted El Paso trail, unfenced, gutterless, innocent of grading, gravel, culverts, or telephone poles, imprinted only by iron tires, the hoofs of horses and oxen, sheep and cattle, and the paw of the loping lobo wolf, lay with dust unraised.

Ordinarily, there were freighters with cracking whips and trailers rumbling on behind. Army trains to and from the forts set up their tents for the night beyond the springs. The private coaches of Santa Fe and Colorado merchants, of cattle kings and Government officials, stopped long enough for the Putman children to admire the ladies, the magnificent woodwork, and the luxurious cushions inside. Trail herds of gaunt red steers bawled for the water in the earthen tank, and pairs and companies of horsemen rode up and down.

But since Saturday not even a solitary buckboard from the far settlements in the Cedar country had called for supplies or letters. Only a girl from the Blue Mesa had ridden in for her and her neighbors' mail. She had eaten dinner with the Putmans, refused to stay overnight, and started her long ride home.

A stranger from the East would have spoken about the stillness, the deadly waiting, and asked uneasily why Uncle Gideon hadn't come as promised. But in the Putman household it was not mentioned.

Asa deliberately busied himself about the post, filling the bin beneath the counter with navy beans and green coffee, leafing through the packet of letters in the drawer, and making a long rite out of feeding the occupants of the picket corrals—four horses of which were fresh for the next stage.

Rife, just turned fifteen, carried water and gathered cow chips in an old hide dragged by a rope to his saddle horn. Ignacita,[3] the Mexican housekeeper, spat sharply on her heavy irons in

1. ***post,*** one of a series of fixed stations that furnished relays of horses, drivers, and riders for the carrying of letters and the transportation of travelers.
2. ***Santa Ana Plain,*** a plain southwest of Santa Fe and north of Albuquerque, New Mexico.
3. ***Ignacita*** (ēg nä sē′tä).

Richter (rik′tər).

the torrid kitchen and kept glancing over her shoulder and out of the open door and windows.

And Nancy Belle, going on seventeen, packed and repacked the high, iron-bound trunk that her father had bought for her at Santa Fe and sang softly to herself in the way that women sang fifty and sixty years ago.

Saturday she was being married at Gunstock, two hundred miles away—five days' journey in a wagon, four in a saddle or buckboard.

For six months she had thought of little else. The almanac fell apart at June as naturally as her mother's Bible did at the Twenty-third Psalm. So often had she run her finger down the page that anyone might tell from the worn line of type the very day she and Stephen Dewee would be man and wife. The Dewees lived four hundred miles west across the territory in the Beaverhead country. She and Stephen were taking a mountain ranch near his people, and for the wedding they had compromised on Gunstock, nearly equidistant from both families and convenient to friends scattered up and down the Rio Grande.

She had lighted a candle in the dusk, when a figure appeared reluctantly in her doorway. Asa Putman had never been at ease in his daughter's bedroom. A tall, rawhide man in an unbuttoned, sagging vest, he was visibly embarrassed by any furnishings that suggested refinement. Invariably he kept his hat on in the house. He had it on now, a flat top and a flat brim, not so much like the Western hats you see now. Nancy Belle knew that her mother's people had never forgiven him for bringing his young wife and their two small children to this lonely post, at the mercy of outlaws and the worse Apaches.

Tonight she could see that something bothered him. He gave her a sidewise glance, so sharp and characteristic.

"I don't expect, Nancy Belle, you could put off your weddin'?"

The girl stood quietly gazing at him with a face like the tintype of her mother. But under her sedate gray dress, with tight waist and full skirts to the instep, she had frozen. She looked much older than her years. Her air of gentlefolk and her wide-apart gray eyes came from her mother. But the chin, tipped up with resolute fearlessness, was her father's.

"No, papa!" Her two clear words held all the steady insistence of the desert.

"I figured how you'd feel," he nodded, avoiding her eyes. "I just wanted to put it up to you. I'd 'a' covered the *jornada* on foot to be on time at my own weddin', but I didn't have to count on Gideon to hold me up."

"Are you telling me, papa, that you can't go to Gunstock tomorrow?" Her voice remained quiet, but a coldness had seized her. Of all the people she had visualized at her wedding, the one next to Stephen she could least spare was the tall, grave figure of her father.

"I reckon I kind of can't, Nancy Belle," he said soberly. "Rife could tend to the stage all right and do the feedin'. But they's men come to this post no boy can handle." He shifted his position. "I figured once on closin' up the post till I got back. But the stage is comin' and the mail. And the freighters count on me for feed and grub. Then I got to protect my own property and the mail and freight for the Cedar country that's in the storage room."

"I know," Nancy Belle said steadily. "I can get to Gunstock all right."

Far back in her father's assaying eyes, she fancied she saw a glint of pride.

"You're pretty nigh a woman now, Nancy Belle. And Rife's a good slice of a man. It's a straight trail to the Rio Grande, once you turn at the old post. Both you and Rife's been over it before. Of course, I'd like to be at the weddin', but the boy can tell me about it." He went to the window. "Rife!" he called.

Nancy Belle's brother came in presently. A slight boy, with his father's blue eyes, he seldom made a fuss over anything, even when he shot a stray duck on the tank or when they braked down the last cedar hill into Santa Fe with all the open doors of the plaza shops in sight. And when his father told him now, he showed neither enthusiasm nor regret—merely straightened.

"Sure. I can take you, Nancy Belle," he said.

Something pulled under his sister's tight basque.[4] She remembered the long miles they would have in the wagon, the camps at lonely places, the ugly shadow ever hovering over the outposts of this frontier country, and the blight that, since Saturday, seemed to have fallen on the trail. Her eyes swam. Now, at the last minute, she yielded.

"If you'll let me ride, papa, I'll wait another day for Uncle Gideon," she promised.

Her father's eyes moved to the ruffled red calico curtains at the shadeless windows.

"I don't hardly count on Gideon comin' any more, Nancy Belle. Besides, it's too long in the saddle to Gunstock—especially for a girl to get married. You'd be plumb wore out, and you wouldn't have your trunk. You couldn't get dressed for your weddin'."

He turned thoughtfully and went out, Rife close behind. Nancy Belle could hear her father's tones, slow and grave, coming from near one of the picket corrals.

It was too far to catch the words; but when they came in, she saw that her brother's features looked a little pale under the tan.

"You better get some sleep, Nancy Belle," her father said. "You and Rife are startin' before daylight. If Gideon comes, I'll ride after."

They had scarcely gone from the room when Ignacita came in from the kitchen, her black eyes glittering over a pile of freshly starched white in her arms.

"Nancy Belle, *chinita!*"[5] she whispered, plucking at the girl's sleeve. "You don't say to your *papacito*[6] I talk to you! I have promise I don't scare you. But I can't see you go so far in the wildness alone, *pobrecita!*[7] Sometimes people go safe from one place to the other, oh, *si!* But sometimes, *chinita,* they don't come back! You have not the oldness like Ignacita. Ay, I tell you these old eyes have seen men and women quartered from a tree like sheep or maybe tied over a stove like I don't have the words to say to you."

Nancy Belle did not answer except to lay, one by one, the ironed pieces in her trunk—a bride's muslin underwear trimmed with red and blue feather stitching; long petticoats stiffly flounced with ruffles, and nightgowns long in the sleeve and high in the neck, with ruffles at wrist and throat. The Mexican woman went on hoarsely. The girl folded away her winter's cashmere dress, buttoned up the front and with a white fichu. She unwrapped and wrapped again in crumpled white tissue the red slippers the old gentleman on the stage had sent her as a wedding present from Philadelphia.

When Ignacita had left, she opened her keepsake box covered with colored shells. The mirror on the inside lid turned back a face as calm as the little golden clouds that hung of an evening over the east to catch the desert sunset. But after she had undressed and put on her nightdress, for a long time she was aware of the soft pound of her heart faintly swaying the bed on its rawhide springs.

At the first sound of Ignacita's hand on the kitchen stove, Nancy Belle sprang out of bed. She dressed on the brown pool of burro skin, the only carpet on her adobe floor. Through the west window she could see the morning star burning like a brilliant candle. It hung, she told herself, over Gunstock and the Beaverhead, where Stephen, at this moment, in their new log ranch house, lay thinking about her.

They ate in the kitchen by lamplight. She had never been so conscious of every detail—the great white cups and saucers, the familiar steel knives, the homey smell of the scorched paper lamp shade, the unreadable eyes of her father, Rife, and Ignacita.

Asa Putman himself carried out the trunk. There was already hay in the wagon, a gunny

---

4. ***basque*** (bask), the tight-fitting bodice of a dress.
5. ***chinita*** (chē nē′tä), a term of endearment used when talking to a little girl.
6. ***papacito*** (pä pa cē′to), an affectionate term for *father.*
7. ***pobrecita*** (po bre cē′tä), poor little girl.

sack of oats, food in a canned-tomato box and utensils in another, a water keg, bedroll tied in a wagon sheet, an ax, a bridle, and her own side-saddle, made to order over a man's tree. Her eyes caught the gleam of a rifle leaning up against the seat in the lantern light. Tethered to the rear of the wagon stood her saddle mare, Fancy, with pricked-up ears. She was going along to their new ranch home. Nancy Belle felt that she was still among intimate things, but outside the little circle of light lay darkness and the unknown.

When she said good-by to her father, he kissed her—something he had not done for years.

"You haven't changed your mind, Nancy Belle?" he asked.

She climbed quickly up over the wheel to the spring seat of the wagon before he might see that she was crying. Rife swung up like a monkey on the other side and pushed the rifle into the crevice behind the seat cushion. The lines tautened and the wagons lurched.

"*Dios*[8] go with you safe to your husband, Nancy Belle!" she heard Ignacita cry after her.

The morning star had set. They moved into a world of silent blackness. Nancy Belle could not see how the horses remained on the trail. When she looked back, the only light in all these square miles of black, unfriendly earth was the yellow window of her father's post.

It was almost a vision, golden and far away, like all beautiful things. She didn't trust herself to look again.

Two hours later the wagon was a lonely speck of boat rocking in an illimitable sage-green sea beneath the sun. The canvas wagon sheet fastened over the bows was a kind of sail, and eastward the sandy water did not stop rolling till it washed up at the foot of the faintly blue ramparts of the distant Espiritu Range.

Just before they turned west on the cross trail to the Rio Grande, a heavy wagon with a yoke of oxen in front and a cow behind toiled round the crumbling adobe walls of the old, abandoned post house. A bearded man and a thin woman with a white face sat on the seat. She held a baby in her arms, and three black-eyed children peered from under the wagon sheet.

The bearded man saluted and stopped his willing team. Rife did likewise. The woman spoke first. Her tongue was swift and slightly acid.

"You better turn around and follow us if you want to save your hair!" she called. "Yesterday a sheep-herder told us he saw——"

A sharp word from the bearded man caused her to relapse into sullen silence. He asked Rife where he might be going, then climbed down to the trail and said he wanted to talk to him a little. The boy followed reluctantly behind his wagon. Nancy Belle could hear the bearded man's tones coming slow and grave like her father's, while the woman made silent and horribly expressive lip language.

Rife came back, walking stiffly. The bearded man climbed up beside the woman.

"They got to go on," he told her in a low tone, then saluted with his whip. "Good luck, boy! And you, miss!"

Rife raised his whip in stiff acknowledgment. The wagons creaked apart. Nancy Belle saw in front of her the trail to the Rio Grande, little more than a pair of wheel tracks, that lost itself on the lonely plain. Rife seemed relieved that she did not ask what the bearded man had said. But it was enough for her not to be able to forget the woman's fearful signs and mouthings and the horror in the curious eyes of the staring children.

Sister and brother talked very little. Nancy Belle saw her brother's eyes keep sweeping the country, scanning the horizons. Bunches of bear grass that might have been feathers pinioned his blue gaze, and clumps of cane cactus that seemed to hold pointing gun barrels. At arroyos thick with chamiso and Apache plume she could see his feet tighten on the footboard. Once he

---

8. ***Dios*** (dē′os), God.

pulled out the rifle, but it was only a herd of antelopes moving across the desert page.

They camped for the night when the sun was still high. Nancy Belle asked no questions as the boy drove far off the trail into a grassy *cañada*. She sang softly to herself as she fried the salt side bacon and put the black coffeepot to boil.

Rife hobbled Anton Chico and the Bar X horse and staked out Fancy close to the wagon.

She pretended not to notice when, before dark, he poured earth on the fire till not a spark or wisp of smoke remained. Out of one eye she watched him climb the side of the *cañada* and stand long minutes sweeping the country from the ridge, a slight, tense figure against the sullen glow of the sunset.

"It's all right," he said when he came down. "You can go to bed."

"What's all right?" she asked him.

"The horses," he said, turning away, and Nancy Belle felt a stab of pain that so soon this boy must bear a man's responsibilities and tell a man's lies.

She prayed silently on her blankets spread on the hay in the wagon box, and lay down with her head on the side-saddle, her unread Testament in her hand. She heard Rife unroll his camp bed on the ground beneath the wagon. It was all very strange and hushed without her father. Just to feel the Testament in her hand helped to calm her and to remember the day at the post when she had first met Stephen.

Her father had never let her come in contact with the men of the trail. Always, at the first sign of dust cloud on the horizon, he would tell both children to heap up the chip box, fill the water buckets and carry saddles and bridles into the house. But this day Asa Putman and Rife had gone to Fort Sumner. And to Nancy Belle, Uncle Gideon could seldom say no.

It had been a very hot day. She had been sitting in the shade of the earthen bank of the tank, moving her bare feet in the cool water, watching the ripples in the hot south wind. The leaves of the cottonwoods clashed overhead, and she heard nothing until she looked up, and there was a young man on a blue-gray horse, with dust clinging to his hat brim and mustache. His eyes were direct as an eagle's. Firm lines modeled his lean face. But what she noticed most at the time was the little bow tie on his dark shirt.

Instantly she had tucked her bare, wet legs under her red dress. Her face burned with shame, but the young stranger talked to her about her father coolly, as if she, a girl of fifteen, had not been caught barefooted. Then he did what in her mind was a noble thing. When Uncle Gideon came out, he magnificently turned his back for her to run into the house and pull on shoes and stockings.

She thought of Stephen constantly next day and the next. She had grown a little used to the journey without her father now—the still, uncertain nights under the wagon sheet, sitting, lying, listening, waiting; the less uncertain days with the sun on the endless spaces; her never-quiet perch on the high spring seat under the slanted bow; the bumps, creaks, and lumberings of the wagon; the sand sifting softly over the red turning wheels; all afternoon the sun in their faces; ahead the far haze and heat waves in which were still lost Gunstock and the Rio Grande. Almost she had forgotten the bearded man with the oxen and the curious, detached horror in the eyes of his children.

Since morning of the third day their progress had been slower. The trail seemed level, except for the heavy breathing of the horses. But when Nancy Belle glanced back she could see the steady grade they had been climbing. Abruptly, in mid-afternoon, she found that the long, blue Espiritu Range had disappeared, vanished behind a high pine-clad hill which was its southernmost beginning. It was like the lizard that swallowed itself, a very real lizard. At this moment they were climbing over the lizard's tail.

"Cedars!" Rife said briefly, pointing with the whip to dark sprawling growths ahead.

"You breathe deep up here!" Nancy Belle drank in the light air.

Rife took a sniff, but his blue eyes never

ceased to scan the high, black-thatched hill under whose frowning cliff they must pass.

"Soon we can see the Gunstock Mountains," Nancy Belle said.

"And Martin Cross's cabin," Rife nodded. "It's the last water to the Rio Grande."

"He's a nice old man," Nancy Bell ventured casually. "It would be nice to camp by his cabin tonight and talk."

The boy inclined his head. After a few moments he started to whistle softly. At the first cedar Nancy Belle leaped off the moving wagon and climbed back with an evergreen branch. The twig, crushed in her hand, smelled like some store in Santa Fe.

They gained the summit. A breeze was sweeping here from the southwest, and the horses freshened. But Rife had suddenly stopped whistling and Nancy Belle's sprig of cedar lay on her lap. The frowning cliff of the pine-clad hill was still there. But Martin Cross's cabin had turned to a desolate mound of ashes. As they stared, a gust of wind sent wisps of smoke scurrying from the mound, and a red eye opened to watch them from the embers. Nancy Belle felt an uncontrollable twitching in the hair roots at the base of her scalp.

Where Martin Cross's eastbound wheel tracks met the trail, Rife reluctantly halted the horses and wet his air-dried lips.

"The water keg's dry, and the horses. If papa was here, he'd drive over."

"I'm the oldest." Nancy Belle found her voice steady. "I'll ride over. There might be something we can do."

The boy rose quickly. His eyes seemed to remember something his father had said.

"You can drive the wagon over if I wave."

He had thrown her the lines and slipped back through the canvas-covered tunnel of wagon box, picking up Fancy's bridle and the rifle. Barebacked he rode toward the smoldering ashes at the foot of that frowning hill. The chestnut mare's tail and mane streamed like something gold in the wind.

When she looked back to the trail, her eyes were pinioned by a light object in the wheel track ahead of the Bar X horse. It was a long gray feather. Instantly she told herself that it had come from some wild turkey Martin Cross had shot, and yet never had air anywhere become so suddenly horrible and choking as in this canyon.

Rife did not signal her to drive over. She saw him come riding back at full speed. The mare was snorting. As he stopped her at the wagon, her chestnut head kept turning back toward what had once been a cabin. Rife slipped the lead rope about her neck and climbed into the seat with the rifle in his hands.

"The water—you wouldn't want it!" he said thickly. His cheeks, she noticed, were the color of *yeso*.[9]

"Rife"—Nancy Belle touched his arm when she had driven down the canyon—"what did you see at the cabin?"

The boy sat deaf and rigid beside her, eyes staring straight ahead. She saw that his young hands were still tortured around the barrel of his rifle.

Far down on the pitch-dark mesa she stopped the horses in the trail and listened. There were no stars, not a sound but the flapping of the wagon sheet in the wind and the clank of coffeepot and water bucket under the wagon. Half standing on the footboard, she guided the team off the trail in the intense blackness. Her swift hands helped the trembling boy stake out the mare and hobble the team. They did not light a lantern. Rife declined to eat. Nancy Belle chewed a few dry mouthfuls.

The wind came drawing out of the blackness with a great shaft. It hissed through the grass, sucked and tore at the wagon sheet, and whistled through the spokes and brake rigging. Rife did not take his bed roll under the wagon tonight. He drew the ends of the wagon sheet together and lay down in the wagon box near his sister. For a long time they were silent. When

---

9. ***color of yeso*** (ye′sô), chalky color of plaster or gypsum.

she heard his heavy breathing, she lifted the rifle from his chest.

The storm grew. Sand began pelting against the canvas and sifted into the wagon box. An invisible cloud of choking dust found its way into eyes, mouth, ears, and lungs. Nancy Belle laid down the rifle a moment to pull a blanket over the face of the boy. He tossed and muttered pitifully, but he slept on.

Magically the rain, when it came, stopped the sand and dust. The girl drank in the clean-washed air. At daylight she slipped out to the ground. The mesa, stretching away in the early light, touched here and there with feathers of mist, would have been beautiful except for a sharp new loneliness. The horses were gone!

At her exclamation, Rife appeared from the wagon box. His shame at having slept through the night was quickly overshadowed by their misfortune.

Together they found where Fancy's stake had been pulled out and dragged. Yards farther on they could tell by Anton Chico's tracks that his hobbles had parted.

Nancy Belle made her brother come back to the wagon and stuff his pockets with cold biscuits and antelope jerky. She said she would have a hot breakfast ready when he returned. The horses, perhaps, were just down in some draw where they had drifted from the wind.

When he had gone with the rifle, she filled the coffeepot from a clearing waterhole in the nearest arroyo. She fried potatoes and onions in the long-handled skillet. And when he did not come, she set fresh biscuits in the Dutch oven. Each biscuit held a square of salt side bacon in its top, and as it baked, the fat oozed down and incased it in a kind of glazed tastiness.

At noon she thought she heard a shot. Nowhere could she see him on the endless sweep of mesa. By late afternoon she was still alone. She read her Testament and wondered how many women over the world had read it in hours like this. Sitting in the shadow of the wagon, facing the direction in which he had gone, she looked up every few minutes. But all her eyes could find were cloud shadows racing across the lonely face of the mesa. All she could hear were the desolate cries from the unseen lark sparrows.

Darkness, stillness settled down on the empty land. She climbed back into the wagon and sat on the chuck-box, hands rigid on her knees. Again and again she convinced herself that the horses could not have been driven off or she would have seen the drivers' tracks. When wild, sharp barks shattered the stillness and set wires jerking in her limbs, she talked to herself steadily, but a little meaninglessly, of the post—on and on as the darkness was filled with the ringing and counter-ringing of shrill, cracked yappings—not long tones like a dog's, but incredibly short syllables rising, rising in a mad eternal scale and discord.

"I wish papa had given me two of the chairs," she repeated. "Mamma said they were post oak from Texas. She said they had got white from scrubbing. I liked the laced rawhide seats with the hair left on. It made them soft to sit on. The seats in the parlor were black. And the ones in the kitchen were red. But I liked the brockle one in my room best."

The insane din around the wagon had become terrific. There were only two or three of the animals, Nancy Belle guessed, but they threw their voices and echoes together to make a score.

"When I was little I liked to go in the storage room," her voice went on, scarcely intelligible to her own ears. "It was dark and cool, and smelled of burlap and kerosene and whisky, and sweetish with brown sugar. I can see the fat sacks of green coffee. And the round tins of kerosene had boards on the side. The flour sacks were printed: 'Rough and Ready' in red letters. Mamma once used to make our underwear out of the sacking. I can smell the salt side bacon in the gunny sacks."

She could tell from the sounds that one of the animals was running insanely back and forth near the wagon tongue. She had never noticed before that they yelped both when breathing in and out. Suddenly came silence. It warned her. Instinctively she felt for the ax.

"Nancy Belle!" a boy's far, anxious voice called from the darkness.

She hallooed and leaned out over the tailboard. Three shadowy forms were coming across the mesa in the starlight. Never had horses looked so good.

"Were you scared?" Rife greeted. "Anything bother you?"

"Nothing," Nancy Belle said. "Just coyotes."

"I had to give Fancy her head after it got dark." He slid wearily to the ground. "She brought us straight back to the wagon."

Nancy Belle had wanted to put her arms around her brother. Now she hugged the mare instead. Rife ate fresh biscuits and a tin plate of cold potatoes. He drank several tin cups of coffee. Nancy Belle had slipped the oats-laden gunny-sack *morrals* over the horses' heads.

"I had to walk halfway to the mountain," Rife said.

"Just help hitch up; then you can sleep all night," she promised.

It rained again heavily toward midnight. Flashes of lightning lit the drenched plain. For minutes at a time, quivering fingers of blue phosphorescence stood on the ears of the toiling horses. At dawn Nancy Belle still held the reins as the mud-splashed wagon crawled through a world bathed in early purple splendor.

Four days they had been crossing a hundred and seventy miles of desolate plain. Now the end waited in sight. To the west lay a land broken and tumbled by a mighty hand. Hill shouldered hill and range peered over range, all indescribably violet except where peaks tipped by the unseen sun were far-off flaming towers of copper.

It was a new land, her promised land, Stephen's land, Nancy Belle told herself, where nobody burned cow chips, but snapping cedar and pine, where cold water ran in the wooded canyons, and the eye, weary of one flat circle the horizon round, had endless geometric designs to refresh the retina.

She sang softly as the wagon lumbered to the edge of a long, shallow valley, brown and uninhabited, running north and south, and desolate except for a winding ribbon that was white with sky and narrowly bordered with green.

"Rife!" Nancy Belle cried. "The Rio Grande!"

An hour afterwards they pulled out of the sun into the shade of the long cottonwood *bosque*. Nancy Belle wasn't singing now. Where she remembered wide sandbars glistening with sky and tracked by waterfowl, a chocolate-red flood rolled. Where had been the island, tops of tule and scrub willow swung to and fro with the current.

Anton Chico and the Bar X horse stopped of their own accord in the trail, ears pricked forward at the swirling brown wash. While Rife turned the three horses loose to graze, Nancy Belle silently fried bacon and made coffee. When she had washed skillet and tin dishes in the river, the boy had wired the wagon box to the brake rigging. Now he was tying securely one end of his rope to the center of the coupling pole under the wagon. The other end she knew he would fasten to the inadequate upper horn of the side-saddle.

"I wouldn't mind the river if I just had my own saddle," he mourned.

They hitched up the team silently. Rife cinched the side-saddle on Fancy and straddled it, the single stirrup useless to a man. Nancy Belle climbed into the wagon and picked up the lines. The other bank looked as far away as the Espiritu Range from the post. She wanted to say something to her brother—some last word, in case they didn't make it. But all she did was cluck her tongue to the horses.

Gingerly, one slow foot at a time, the team moved down the trail into the water.

"Give 'em their heads!" Rife called from the right rear.

Nancy Bell held a rein in each hand. The red channel water came to the wagon tongue, covered it, reached the horses' bellies. The team wanted to stop. Nancy Belle swung her whip, a stick tipped with a long rawhide lash. The wagon went on. The collars of both horses kept dipping, but never entirely out of sight. Still barely wading, the slow team reached the firmer footing of the island.

Two-thirds of the river still rolled in front of the wagon. The west bank did not seem to have grown much closer, but the east bank behind them had moved far away. The team had to be whipped into the violent current. The water churned white through the wagon wheels. Suddenly both horses appeared to stumble and drop out of sight. Their heads came up wildly, spray blowing from their nostrils. The muddy water hid their legs, but by their bobbing motions Nancy Belle knew that they were swimming.

"Keep 'em pointed up the river!" Rife shouted.

Already she felt the wagon floating. It swung downstream with the current; then Rife's rope from Fancy's saddle snubbed it. The team was snorting with every breath. The Bar X horse swam high in the water, his withers and part of his back out of the chocolate current. But all she could see of Anton Chico were his nose and ears.

Down between her ankles she saw water in the wagon box. She thought of the hemstitched sheets at the bottom of her trunk, the towels and pillowcases crocheted with shell lace. Her blue velvet corduroy dress was probably wet already, and all the cunning print aprons with dust caps to match. River water couldn't hurt the little yellow creamer, sugar bowl, and covered butter dish that had been her mother's. And the gingham dresses could be washed. What worried her were her wedding dress and the keepsake box, especially the tintypes, one of which was Rife in a child's suit edged with black braid, his brand-new hat on his knee.

An older Rife was shouting something behind her now. She couldn't catch the words. Then she found what it was. The neck and withers of Anton Chico raised suddenly out of the water and both horses were scrambling up the steep bank below the ford. Only quick work with the lines saved the wagon from turning over. Safe and blowing on the high bank, the dripping horses shook themselves like puppies.

Nancy Belle couldn't go on until she had opened the trunk and appraised the damage. Rife unsaddled Fancy and drove on with the refreshed team. Behind his slight back in the wagon box, the girl changed to her blue velvet corduroy, which was hardly wet at all. Then she combed her hair and rolled into a cranny of her trunk the old felt hat that had been too large for her father.

A half-dozen riders met the wagon some miles down the Gunstock Canyon. All of them, Nancy Belle noticed, carried guns. Stephen wore a new white shirt and a gray hat with curled brim she had not seen before. He stood in his stirrups and swung her down in front of him on the saddle, where he kissed her. She had never felt his lips press into such a straight line.

"Papa couldn't come," she said. "So Rife brought me."

She felt Stephen's rigid arm around her.

"We just got in from the Beaverhead ourselves."

"He means they never get any news out in the Beaverhead or he'd 'a' come further east to meet you!" Uncle Billy Williams put in. He had a lovable, squeaky voice. "The Apaches been breakin' loose again. Funny you didn't hear anything over in your country."

Nancy Belle gave him an inscrutable look with her gray eyes. Uncle Billy pulled out his bandanna and blew his nose.

"They got my old friend Judge Hower and his wife and kid in a buggy on the Upper Espiritu. The man that found what they did to 'em, they say, cried like a baby."

"That's all right, Uncle Billy," Stephen said in a gentle voice.

Nancy Belle glanced at Rife. Her brother's face looked gray, the eyes staring as when he had ridden in the late afternoon sunlight from the smoking ashes of Martin Cross's cabin.

Nearly fifty people, gathered in the big parlor upstairs at the hotel, greeted Nancy Belle. An old man whose young black eyes twinkled out of a bearded face said he was glad to see that she had her "hair on straight." Rife stopped with the trunk before driving to the livery, and Stephen's mother showed Nancy Belle to a room to dress.

The guests stopped talking when she came into the parlor in her white wedding dress. Her basque came to a point in the front and back. It fitted like a glove. The silk underskirt came to her instep, and the ruffled overskirt to her knees. She had parted her hair from side to side and brushed the bangs down on her forehead. She felt very light-headed. The wagon still seemed to be jerking under her.

She glimpsed Rife gazing at her, a rapt expression in his reticent blue eyes. She was glad to see that he had brushed his hair. The brass swinging lamp had been lighted and the dark woodwork of the parlor festooned with evergreen branches. White streamers from the wall met in a papier-mâché bell in one corner. She noticed two children peering eagerly from the dark hall.

Stephen came to her, very straight in a long coat and stand-up collar with a black tie. He led her up beneath the papier-mâché bell. In a sibilant, church-like whisper, the Gunstock preacher made sure of her full name. Then he coughed and began the ceremony. He had a deep voice, but Nancy Belle didn't hear all of the service. Her mind kept going back to a tall, grave man in a lonely adobe post on the wide Santa Ana plain. And after she had said: "I do," her lips moved, but she was not praying for Stephen, her husband.

Discussion

1. For whom is Nancy Belle praying at the end of the story? Why?

2. **(a)** For what event is Nancy Belle preparing at the beginning of the story? **(b)** Why was Gunstock chosen as the site for the ceremony? **(c)** What reasons does Nancy Belle's father give for not joining her? **(d)** Do you consider Mr. Putman's reasons to be sound? Explain.

3. **(a)** Describe Nancy Belle's and Rife's encounter with the bearded man and his family. **(b)** What precautions does Rife then take to try to ensure his and Nancy Belle's safety when they camp? **(c)** Why was Martin Cross's cabin an important goal? **(d)** Describe the condition of the cabin when Rife and Nancy Belle come upon it. **(e)** What inferences can you draw about what has happened to Martin Cross and to his homestead?

4. Describe two crises on the journey that involve Nancy Belle's and Rife's horses.

5. Even after the wedding party has assembled at Gunstock, the mood does not lighten. What events and images does the author use to sustain the mood through the end of the story?

6. Conrad Richter's daughter, Harvena, said of her father's stories, ". . . more often it is the women who dominate the stories, who are stronger than the men who seek them." Might the statement apply to the characters in "Early Marriage"? Explain.

Vocabulary

Antonyms

Antonyms are words that are opposite in meaning. Each sentence that follows contains an italicized word. On your paper, rewrite each sentence, substituting for the word in italics a word from the list that is an antonym of the italicized word.

sibilant
rapt
reticent
torrid
tauten
sedate
cipher
fichu

1. Claiming that seniors had special privileges, Anna refused to move from her comfortable first-floor room to the *frigid* attic of the dorm.

2. His time as a prisoner of war had been both terrifying and challenging, and he came home *eager* to discuss it.

3. Her *wandering* attention during my first lecture gave me a good idea of the kind of student she would be.

4. If this gadget is ever going to work—which I sincerely doubt—we must find a way to *loosen* that cable.

5. Mother and Daddy often marveled that people such as they had raised a *rowdy* child such as I.

Composition

"The Gift of Cochise," "The Man Who Shot Liberty Valance," and "Early Marriage" are all regarded as "westerns." Assume that a student from another country writes to you and asks what a western is.

Base your reply on an examination of the three stories you have just read. First, reconsider the setting of each, next the type of characters, and finally the plot. Then, write a letter to the student in which you explain what a western is.

Comment: Black Riders of the Range

Cowboys are almost synonymous with the West, but many Americans are unaware of the role that black cowboys played in that chapter of history. In the years after the Civil War (1861–1865), more than five thousand black cowboys rode cattle trails north from Texas, first into Kansas along the Chisholm Trail, then into South Dakota along the Western Trail, finally into Montana along the Goodnight-Loving Trail. Most of the black cowboys had once been slaves, brought to the West by their owners from Mississippi, Georgia, and other southern states. Freed after the war, they continued to work at the one trade they had been taught, signing on as cowboys with former owners or with other cattle ranchers.

Life on the trail was hard. A herd of steers traveled only twelve to fifteen miles a day, while a herd of cows, burdened with calves born along the way, traveled still more slowly. A drive from Texas to Kansas or Wyoming could take two to three months. Enroute, cowboys occasionally froze to death or fell victim to fights with Indians, outlaws, or resentful settlers. An additional and more frequent danger was that posed by stampeding cattle. To avert that danger, herds along the trail were usually composed of no more than twenty-five hundred cattle.

A herd of that size was normally accompanied by a crew of eleven men—a trail boss, who assumed absolute authority for all important decisions; a wrangler, who was responsible for the care of as many as sixty horses; a cook, often a black, who drove the chuck wagon and frequently acted as doctor and dentist; and eight cowboys, at least two or three of whom in a typical crew were black. Although some discrimination occurred—rarely was a black man named trail boss—life on a cattle drive was too demanding to permit many racial animosities. A cowboy's ability to do his job well was rated far more critically than his skin color. Loafers, regardless of color, soon departed.

The majority of black cowboys did routine work on ranches and trails—fighting prairie fires and storms, breaking horses, stringing fence, and driving cattle. But a number of them became famous for their specialties: Bill Pickett and Henry Beckwith as bulldoggers, men who wrestled cattle to the ground; Jesse Stahl and Frank Greenway as bronc riders; George Hooker as trick rider; Jim Simpson, as "about the best roper on the range," and Bob Lemmons, as a captor of wild mustangs.

Although many of the black cowboys became respected lawmen, a few became noted lawbreakers, among them the cattle rustlers Jim Thornbill, Isom Bart, and Ben Hodges. Probably the most villainous was Cherokee Bill, who, at age fourteen murdered his brother-in-law and then went on to become a professional killer, shooting railroad agents, storekeepers, and express agents. His life was short. Born at Fort Concho, Texas, in 1876, of parents part black, part white, and part Indian, Cherokee Bill died on the gallows only a month after his twentieth birthday. The judge who sentenced him to hang expressed regret that he could provide no harsher penalty.

Trail-driving days lasted for about twenty-five years after the Civil War. By then the lands of Kansas, Nebraska, Colorado, Wyoming, South Dakota, and Montana had been widely settled with both humans and cattle, and so provided Texas with competition in the cattle market. In addition, the expansion of the railroads made it possible to ship cattle by rail, a method that proved more economical because cows were not lost as they often were on drives and because herds shipped by rail weighed more on arrival. Though some of the old black cowboys still remained in the cattle business at the turn of the century, most had departed the range to take such jobs as rodeo performers, porters on the railway, or dirt farmers. Nevertheless, one can still encounter black cowboys herding cattle on southern ranges, particularly in Florida and Texas.

For a fuller account on the history of black cowboys and their contributions to western development, read *The Adventures of the Negro Cowboys* by Philip Durham and Everett L. Jones (Dodd, Mead, and Company, 1966; Bantam Books, 1969).

MYSTERY

Camford Cottage

Michael Gilbert

"Local people won't go into the cottage. . . . They think it's haunted."

Then I know it," said Miss Symondson, "I'm certain I know it. It's at the top of a cliff. Hardly a cliff, more a headland. It's in a little garden of its own, with fields all round it. And there's a long flight of steps leading down from it to a private landing stage."

"The same place, without doubt," said Miss Melchior.[1] "It's some distance from any village. How did you come to be familiar with it?"

"I'd hardly call it familiar, since I had tea there, once only. But it was an exceptionally fine tea. That was thirty years ago. I cannot have been more than five or six at the time."

"It must have been in the days of 'Prince' Camford, the artist. He had no use for architects, you know. The house, we were told, was built by local builders from a sketch he made on the back of a drawing pad. And very well built, too, in local brick."

"I didn't realize, of course, that he was a famous artist. To me he was just a funny man with a beard. He'd come on my older brother and sister and me, playing some game in the bushes at the top of the headland, Pirates or Indians. We were dressed in holiday rags and he got us to pose for nearly an hour while he made sketches of us. Then he took us down to the house for tea. Cornish butter and cream, on scones baked by his wife, a dumpy little woman with grey hair."

"Also an artist," said Miss Melchior. "A water-colorist. You can still see her Cornish seascapes in the galleries." Miss Melchior was a woman who knew things like that. "They are both dead now. My brother bought the cottage—it had some other name—I forget it—but he named it 'Camford Cottage' after its famous builder and owner. He and Patricia spent their honeymoon there. They were the only people who ever lived in it."

"What a tragedy," said Miss Symondson. She was not thinking of the honeymoon, but of what had happened at Camford Cottage some years later. A tragedy which had been widely reported.

Frank Melchior and his wife were keen sailors; Frank possibly a little keener than Patricia, who was apt to be sick if the sea was rough. They had set out one evening intending to sail down to the southwest, with a favoring wind, spend the night at sea, round the point of Land's End, and finish up by beating up to Fowey, where they had friends. It was a trip they had made many times before. On this occasion they ran into rougher weather than they had catered for. Their boat lost its mast, the auxiliary engine failed, and they were driven on to the Pen-Gallion Shoals. Fishermen, who had

1. ***Melchior*** (mel′kyůr).

observed their plight in the early dawn, picked up Frank; Patricia's body was never recovered.

"He shut the cottage up for years after that. No one was allowed into it. He wouldn't listen to any suggestion of selling it. Not that he had to bother about the financial side of it. Patricia was a Dupont, and her money went to him. Poor compensation for a broken heart, but on top of what he was earning already, it left him free to get on with his writing."

"I read his last one a few weeks ago, when I was in bed. The nursing home got it for me out of the public library. I can't afford to pay nearly four pounds for a detective story."

"I don't believe anyone can," said Miss Melchior. "Have you met my brother?"

"Yes, once, when he came to give a talk at the school. We were all introduced. I thought him rather formidable."

"It changed him, of course."

"Has the cottage been closed ever since—ever since it happened?"

"No. In the end I persuaded him that he was being selfish." Miss Melchior spoke with the firmness of an elder sister. "We took some of his nephews and nieces, and I went down with him. I told him, 'You'll find no ghosts in Camford Cottage. It's a happy place.' The holiday was a great success. Pol-en-Perro is a wonderful place for children."

"I certainly remember it as such," said Miss Symondson wistfully. "I suppose that development has spoilt it now."

"Not a bit. The land round the cottage is farmland, and very good farmland too, I believe. No one can touch it. And, of course, when the weather was fine the children enjoyed the tiny private beach at the bottom of the steps, and the boating. Frank was nervous about letting them use the boat at all, but I told him, 'Forget the past, live in the present.' "

It had sometimes occurred to Miss Symondson that the reason Miss Melchior, who was handsome and well endowed, was not married might be on account of her firmness with everyone. She was one of the governors of the school where Miss Symondson taught, and ruled the Chairman and other governors with a rod of iron. Nevertheless, she could be kind. She had been very kind to her, when a bout of influenza, coming on top of an exceptionally hard term's work, had nearly carried her away. It was Miss Melchior who had whisked her out of her lodgings and into a private nursing home; and it was Miss Melchior who had dragooned the doctors into taking her case seriously. Now she was proposing a further kindness.

"A week will do you all the good in the world. It will quite set you up for the coming term. I'll order a stack of logs for the sitting-room fire. The cooking is all done by bottled gas. I'll have two cylinders delivered. They'll be outside the front door. I'm afraid you'll have to do your own cleaning. Local people won't go into the cottage—not since the tragedy."

"Oh, why?"

"They think it's haunted," said Miss Melchior, in the robust voice in which commonsense people speak of ghosts. "I'm sure you're not one of these people who believes in ghosts."

"If there was one, it should be haunting the Pen-Gallion Shoals, not Camford Cottage."

"*Exactly* what I told my brother. And I can assure you that when we all went down there, there were no psychic manifestations."

"But on previous occasions," said Miss Symondson, "it's only the family who have used the cottage? Are you sure your brother won't mind? Oughtn't we to ask him?"

"To the best of my knowledge, my brother is in Tangiers, gathering material for a new book. He was uncertain of his movements, and left no address. It could take weeks to get an answer."

"If you're sure he wouldn't mind."

"I am ab-so-lutely sure."

When Miss Melchior was ab-so-lutely sure, there was nothing more to be said.

For the first six days it was as agreeable as Miss Melchior had promised. Although it was

still early April, the summer, as sometimes happens in Cornwall,[2] had seemed to come earlier than it did elsewhere. The days were warm enough for strolling over the headlands and through the deep lanes, already yellow with primrose and white mayflower. The evenings were cool enough to enjoy the fire of logs which blazed in the wide brick fireplace, set squarely in the middle of the living room wall.

The nights were a little troublesome at first. Miss Symondson put it down to sleeping in a strange bed, but she was honest enough to admit that it was more than this. She was a child of the city, born and brought up among streets of houses full of people. Holidays had been things you took, with others, in camps or hotels or hostels which were even fuller of people.

Here she was conscious of being surrounded by emptiness. On one side, the sea. On the other three sides, fields. The nearest human habitation was the farmhouse which she visited daily for milk and eggs, half a mile inland down a track which was easily negotiable at this time of year by the tradesmen's vans and by the old taxi which had brought her from Pol-en-Perro Station. It must have become difficult in winter. Her only direct connection with the world outside was a telephone line; a single umbilical cord joining her to the world of men and women.

In the times when she lay awake she comforted herself with what Miss Melchior had said. It was *not* an unhappy house. Why should it be? The tragedy had not happened here, in this snug and civilized cell, but out on the wild gray sea,

2. ***Cornwall,*** the most southwestern of the counties in England, bounded on two sides by the Atlantic Ocean, on a third by the English Channel, and on the fourth by the county of Devon.

in a driving wind, among mountainous waves. Sometimes she visualized the helpless boat, its mast gone, its engine useless, drifting on to the fangs of the Pen-Gallion rocks.

She had never herself been on the sea in anything smaller than a cross-Channel steamer, and it is possible that she exaggerated its perils. She looked down on it, timidly, from the edge of the cliffs, but had never even ventured to descend the steps down to the beach and the jetty. They seemed to her to be steep and dangerous. Adequate, no doubt, for nimble children in gym shoes, or for active men and women who took care to use the tarred-rope side rail.

It was on the evening of the sixth day, with the taxi ordered for nine o'clock the next morning, and she was standing at the top of these steps, when it happened.

The day had been the warmest so far, more of an autumn than a spring day, the heat no longer fresh, but turned damp and stale. As she looked out to sea, it was as though a veil, thin at first but thickening, was being drawn across her whole field of vision. The effect was so startling that she passed a hand across her eyes to wipe away what seemed to be a blurring of her sight. Then she realized what was happening. A white fog was rolling up towards the mouth of the Bristol Channel.

It came with astonishing speed. One moment she could see. The next she was blind. One moment she was warm. The next she was shivering with cold. Thank goodness, was her first thought, that I wasn't out on the cliffs, miles from home. I shouldn't have known what to do. She turned round, with great care, took six paces up the path which led from the stairhead, found the front gate, and was soon back inside the cottage.

She turned on the lights in the sitting room, and put a match to the fire, which was neatly laid. Warmth and light soon worked their magic. The fog was outside. She was inside, safe and sound. The next few hours were pleasantly occupied with cooking and eating supper. For this last meal of the holidays she had saved a half-bottle of red wine; and, greatly daring, she drank it all, finishing the last glass with her coffee.

As she sat, pleasantly drowsy, in front of the fire, she found her thoughts going back thirty years. How odd to think that she, the very same person that she was now, changed in body but the same in essence, had sat at almost exactly the same spot that she was sitting at now. Her brother had been on her right, at the top of the tea table, piling the delicious scones with butter and cream and honey, and stuffing them into his mouth one after another. She didn't want to think too much about him. His body was in northern France, near the spot where his fighter plane had crashed.

Her sister had been sitting beyond him, half scandalized at the amount her brother was eating, half determined not to be left behind. Married now, with children of her own.

And what of herself? If she tried hard, could she summon back the six-year-old child, with pigtails, dressed in shorts and a grubby aertex shirt, with sandals on the end of brown, scratched legs. She had always been the thoughtful one, the one who noticed things. What had she been thinking about, what had she been looking at, on that summer afternoon, thirty years ago?

There had been a tiny golden clock on the mantelshelf. That had gone, of course, and had been replaced by two vases. To the right of the fireplace, there had been bookshelves. This worried her. Because she was certain that the bookshelf had not been a detached piece of furniture. The shelves, five or six of them, had been fitted into the alcove on the right of the chimney breast. Yes. And in the corresponding alcove on the other side had stood the old grandfather clock. She could remember thinking, how unusual to have two clocks in one room. Big clock and little clock. Grandfather and grandchild.

Why in the world, she said to herself, should anyone have bricked up those two alcoves, so that the wall now stretched, level with the front of the fire, from side to side?

As she asked the question, the room seemed to change. She was looking at it as it had been. The books were back on their shelves on the right, the gold clock winked on the mantelshelf, and old grandfather swung his pendulum solemnly from the recess on the left. She knew that if she could turn her eyes she would see her brother and sister, and their kind host at the other end of the table, but her head was held, as in a vise.

Something was happening to the lights. They were dimming. And the room had grown deadly cold. But it was now, once again, the room of the present, not the past. She was looking at the blank stretch of bricks on the left of the fireplace and at the lady standing in front of them. She felt unsurprised, and unafraid. The lady was smiling. Clearly she meant her no harm. It was not Mrs. Camford. This lady was younger, slimmer, and more fashionably dressed than that gray-haired, dumpy water-colorist. Surely she knew the face? She had seen it somewhere, in a fashion magazine. Of course, it was Frank Melchior's wife, Patricia.

Who was dead.

Drowned, battered to pieces, her bones washing about on the floor of the sea, under the Pen-Gallion rocks.

What was she doing here? Why was she standing, quietly, patiently. Standing like someone who had been waiting for help, and knew that help was at hand?

All at once Miss Symondson knew the terrible answer. Moreover, she knew what she had to do, and she was locked to the chair; her body shaken with uncontrollable spasms, the sweat cold on her face.

As she struggled to move, and realized she was helpless, the spell was suddenly broken.

The telephone was ringing.

A male voice said, "Miss Symondson?"

Scarcely able to speak she gasped out something.

"I can't hear you."

"Yes. It's Miss Symondson."

"My sister told me you were using the cottage. Is something wrong?"

"No. Yes."

"What is it? You're very indistinct."

Miss Symondson said, in tones of one stating some unimportant but incontrovertible fact. "I have just seen your wife. She came out from the recess which used to be beside the fireplace in the sitting room."

During the long silence which followed, she began to realize what it was she had said. He must think her absolutely mad. Perhaps she was mad. People had sometimes told her she was psychic. Had she passed over the borderline between sanity and insanity?

"I'm sure you'll think I'm raving mad," she said, with a pathetic attempt at lightness, "perhaps it was the fog and the general atmosphere and knowing—knowing the story——"

When the man spoke again it was a surprise. Before, his voice, without being rude, had been cold and formal. Now it had reverted to a friendly, conversational level.

He said, "I was interested in something you said just now. You mentioned that this—this apparition—came from the recess which used to be beside the fireplace. How did you know that there was once a recess there?"

"I came to the cottage many years ago, when I was a child. I had tea here."

"That would have been in Prince Camford's time."

"Yes."

A further silence. Then, "I don't want to alarm you, Miss Symondson, but I think you may be in some danger. I don't think you ought to spend tonight alone in the cottage."

"But how——"

"I'm speaking from Plymouth, where I landed earlier today. Is the fog very thick?"

"Yes, very."

"It usually clears before midnight. It will only take me a couple of hours to get to you. I'll fix a room for you at Truro. Sit tight, and, Miss Symondson——''

''Yes?''

''My advice to you is, keep out of the sitting room. Light the stove in the kitchen. You should be safe there.''

He rang off.

She had noticed the old black stove in the kitchen, but had not dared to tamper with it. Now she got sticks and paper, and a shovel full of coal, opened the front, and set it going. It showed a tendency to smoke, but this soon cleared, and she was able to put on a few small logs on top of the coal and closed the front. The stove gave out a companionable roar.

To be doing something was a comfort. It helped to keep her mind off the problems of what danger could possibly be lurking in that front room. It helped to pass the time. And that needed help. Only forty minutes since the telephone call. If the mist stayed thick it might take Melchior hours to reach her. He might not be there until morning.

There was a basket full of logs in the front room. They would keep the stove going for an hour or so. The alternative was to fetch a fresh supply from the woodshed, but this would involve making her way out into the fog and crossing the back yard. Surely it could not be dangerous, simply to go back into that room, just for a moment?

When she opened the door she remembered that she had turned out the light, and the switch was on the far side of the room.

She said, out loud, ''Don't be such a goose. *There's nothing in the room that can hurt you.* Just walk across and turn on the light.''

The fire in the grate had burned low, but it gave enough light for her to see, and avoid the furniture. Her hand was on the switch when she stopped.

The sound was definite and unmistakeable.

Someone was coming up the front path.

By the crunch of the footsteps on the gravel it was a man. He was coming cautiously, but was unable to avoid making some sound.

Miss Symondson was so paralyzed with fear that she was unable even to raise her hand to the light switch. She stood in the darkness of the sitting room and watched the figure loom closer through the fog.

Now he was at the door. A hand came out to try the door. Very gently.

Thank God she had bolted it, top and bottom.

The man stood still for a moment, his head bowed as though he was listening. Then he turned and marched straight up to the window, and pressed his face against it.

Miss Symondson, cowering inside, recognized him at once.

It was Frank Melchior.

She was filled with unimaginable terror. The first words which came into her head were ''He's come back for his wife.''

Plymouth? That was nonsense. He must have lied about that, and lied quite deliberately.

Why had he told her to sit in the kitchen? Was it so that no light would shine out from the front room indicating to any chance passer-by that she was in the cottage?

The man was moving now, quietly, away from the window, on the path that would take him round the house and directly to the kitchen door.

Which, she realized with frozen horror, she had left unlocked.

She tiptoed across to the front door and, with fingers which seemed not to belong to her, slid back the top bolt, and stooped to open the bottom one.

At that moment she heard the sound of the kitchen door being opened, and a voice which said, ''Hello, Miss Symondson. Where are you hiding?''

The second bolt slid back. She straightened up and eased the front door open. Gently, gently.

Footsteps crossing the kitchen floor, and the voice again, ''Are you in there? I thought I told you not to go in there.''

Then she was stumbling down the front path.

The front door, as she let go of it, swung shut behind her. The noise must have warned the man that she was escaping. As she reached the front gate she heard heavy footsteps on the path. She stepped off the path, just inside the gate, and cowered down like a wild beast. Like a wild beast, she had the sense to realize that if she moved the man would hear her; and if he heard her, he would catch her.

The footsteps crunched past. The man was outside the gate now. His steps were moving away, casting uncertainly, to right and left; lunging into the fog at some supposed shadow.

A sudden scratching of nails, on rock. A wild scream, and a series of horrible bumping noises. Then silence.

Miss Symondson got to her feet, and edged her way out of the gate until she felt the ruts of the track which led to the road. Down it she stumbled for an eternity of time, blinded by fog, her heart hammering, choking, kept going only by fear of what might be behind her.

As she reached the main road a light showed through the mist; there was a squeal of brakes and a car slid to a halt almost on top of her. The Cornish voice of Police Constable Greig said, "Why can't you look where you're going?" And then, "Why, Miss Symondson. What's to do here?"

"A killer," said Superintendent Assher to the Chief Constable of Cornwall. "A careful killer, and a killer for money."

They were standing in bright sunshine outside the door of the cottage, watching the workmen finish the demolition of the brick wall which concealed the recess behind the fireplace; a recess from which a skeleton, already identified as Patricia Melchior, had been removed and carried to the mortuary.

"You said, a careful killer?"

"Very careful. He must have been planning it for at least a year. He built that little summerhouse with his own hands." He pointed to a neat construction, in the same brick as the house, which stood at the end of the lawn. "He ordered a few hundred more bricks than he needed. And he taught himself, carefully and slowly, how to lay them. I expect his wife watched him, and admired his increasing skill. When the time was ripe, he strangled her, put her body inside, and bricked her up. To balance things, and make the wall look natural, he bricked up the other recess as well."

"Why not just bury her somewhere outside?"

"He was a writer of detective stories, sir. He knew that digging in farmland leaves traces. And if the body was recovered from the sea, the pathologist would know she'd been strangled. Safer to keep her in the house. No one had ever used it, except the two of them. No one ventured in afterwards. Maybe he spread the story of its being haunted. Later, of course, he didn't mind family parties as long as he was there to keep an eye on things. And then, by one chance in ten million, it was let, behind his back, to a woman who'd known the place as a child."

"What do you think he'd have done to her?"

"Thrown her down the steps, no doubt. Everyone would have assumed she was out in the fog, and had slipped, and killed herself. As he did."

The Chief Constable thought about it. He said, "Did you believe what she told us?"

"Most of it," said the Superintendent cautiously.

"About Mrs. Melchior appearing to her."

"I saw no reason to disbelieve that."

"Then you believe in ghosts."

"Certainly," said the Superintendent with a smile. "Good ones and bad ones. This was a good one. She'll sleep easy now, poor soul."

He was smiling because he knew that ghosts were hard things for a stolid Devonian[3] like the Chief Constable to credit. He himself had been born and bred west of the Tamar, and like all Cornishmen knew everything there was to know about ghosts.

---

3. ***Devonian,*** a native of Devon, the county adjacent to Cornwall.

Discussion

1. **(a)** Describe Camford cottage. **(b)** Under what circumstances had Miss Symondson first become acquainted with the dwelling? **(c)** Why has she returned there to live for a week?

2. **(a)** How had Patricia Melchior supposedly died? **(b)** What had been Frank Melchior's response to her death?

3. **(a)** Why do local people refuse to go into the cottage? **(b)** How do Miss Symondson and Miss Melchior regard the local inhabitants' beliefs?

4. **(a)** Describe Miss Melchior's personality. **(b)** Which of the following adjectives best describes Miss Symondson: pushy, timid, sheltered, independent, observant, dull, young, middle-aged? Explain.

5. **(a)** Describe the circumstances in which the ghost of Patricia Melchior appears to Miss Symondson. **(b)** How does Miss Symondson respond to the ghost?

6. **(a)** What nearly fatal errors does Miss Symondson make when she answers the telephone? **(b)** What advice does Frank Melchior give her? Why? **(c)** How does Miss Symondson elude her would-be killer? **(d)** Describe how Frank Melchior meets his death.

7. **(a)** What was Frank Melchior's motive for killing his wife? **(b)** Why did he not bury her on land or at sea?

Vocabulary

Combining Forms

Prince Camford's wife painted seascapes. The *-scape* part of this word means "a scenic picture or view of." It is a *combining form,* a word part that combines with words or with other combining forms to make a new word. For example, the combining form *psycho-* and the word *therapy* together make the word *psychotherapy.* The combining form *archaeo-* and the combining form *-logy* together make the word *archaeology.* Many English words—especially scientific and technical ones—have been created by using combining forms.

Identify the five combining forms in the seven words in the list. Each combining form appears twice. On your paper, list the five forms. Then write seven sentences, using a word from the list in each sentence. Be sure your sentences indicate that you know the meanings of the words; if necessary, look up the meanings in the Glossary before you begin to write.

microcomputer
megaton
dialogue
megalith
monolith
microcosm
monologue

The Man Who Knew How

Dorothy L. Sayers

"Always the same sequence of events: the hot bath, the discovery of the corpse, the inquest."

For the twentieth time since the train had left Carlisle, Pender glanced up from *Murder at the Manse* and caught the eye of the man opposite.

He frowned a little. It was irritating to be watched so closely, and always with that faint, sardonic smile. It was still more irritating to allow oneself to be so much disturbed by the smile and the scrutiny. Pender wrenched himself back to his book with a determination to concentrate upon the problem of the minister murdered in the library.

But the story was of the academic kind that crowds all its exciting incidents into the first chapter, and proceeds thereafter by a long series of deductions to a scientific solution in the last. Twice Pender had to turn back to verify points that he had missed in reading. Then he became aware that he was not thinking about the murdered minister at all—he was becoming more and more actively conscious of the other man's face. A queer face, Pender thought.

There was nothing especially remarkable about the features in themselves; it was their expression that daunted Pender. It was a secret face, the face of one who knew a great deal to other people's disadvantage. The mouth was a little crooked and tightly tucked in at the corners, as though savoring a hidden amusement. The eyes, behind a pair of rimless pince-nez, glittered curiously; but that was possibly due to the light reflected in the glasses. Pender wondered what the man's profession might be. He was dressed in a dark lounge suit, a raincoat, and a shabby soft hat; his age was perhaps about forty.

Pender coughed unnecessarily and settled back into his corner, raising the detective story high before his face, barrier-fashion. This was worse than useless. He gained the impression that the man saw through the maneuver and was secretly entertained by it. He wanted to fidget, but felt obscurely that his doing so would in some way constitute a victory for the other man. In his self-consciousness he held himself so rigid that attention to his book became a sheer physical impossibility.

There was no stop now before Rugby, and it was unlikely that any passenger would enter from the corridor to break up this disagreeable *solitude à deux*.[1] Pender could, of course, go out into the corridor and not return, but that would be an acknowledgment of defeat. Pender lowered *Murder at the Manse* and caught the man's eye again.

"Getting tired of it?" asked the man.

"Night journeys are always a bit tedious," replied Pender, half relieved and half reluctant. "Would you like a book?"

---

1. ***solitude à deux*** (sol e tüd′ ä dœ′), the seclusion of two people. [*French*]

Dr. ALICE ROUGHTON
OF OXFORD HU
G ROND
E MOON"
EKHOV

He took *The Paper-Clip Clue* from his brief-case and held it out hopefully. The other man glanced at the title and shook his head.

"Thanks very much," he said, "but I never read detective stories. They're so—inadequate, don't you think so?"

"They are rather lacking in characterization and human interest, certainly," said Pender, "but on a railway journey——"

"I don't mean that," said the other man. "I am not concerned with humanity. But all these murderers are so incompetent—they bore me."

"Oh, I don't know," replied Pender. "At any rate they are usually a good deal more imaginative and ingenious than murderers in real life."

"Than the murderers who are found out in real life, yes," admitted the other man.

"Even some of those did pretty well before they got pinched," objected Pender. "Crippen,[2] for instance; he need never have been caught if he hadn't lost his head and run off to America. George Joseph Smith did away with at least two brides quite successfully before fate and the *News of the World* intervened."

"Yes," said the other man, "but look at the clumsiness of it all; the elaboration, the lies, the paraphernalia. Absolutely unnecessary."

"Oh, come!" said Pender. "You can't expect committing a murder and getting away with it to be as simple as shelling peas."

"Ah!" said the other man. "You think that, do you?"

Pender waited for him to elaborate this remark, but nothing came of it. The man leaned back and smiled in his secret way at the roof of the carriage; he appeared to think the conversation not worth going on with. Pender found himself noticing his companion's hands. They were white and surprisingly long in the fingers. He watched them gently tapping upon their owner's knee—then resolutely turned a page—then put the book down once more and said:

"Well, if it's so easy, how would *you* set about committing a murder?"

"I?" repeated the man. The light on his glasses made his eyes quite blank to Pender, but his voice sounded gently amused. "That's different; *I* should not have to think twice about it."

"Why not?"

"Because I happen to know how to do it."

"Do you indeed?" muttered Pender, rebelliously.

"Oh, yes; there's nothing to it."

"How can you be sure? You haven't tried, I suppose?"

"It isn't a case of trying," said the man. "There's nothing uncertain about my method. That's just the beauty of it."

"It's easy to say that," retorted Pender, "but what *is* this wonderful method?"

"You can't expect me to tell you that, can you?" said the other man, bringing his eyes back to rest on Pender's. "It might not be safe. You look harmless enough, but who could look more harmless than Crippen? Nobody is fit to be trusted with *absolute* control over other people's lives."

"Bosh!" exclaimed Pender. "I shouldn't think of murdering anybody."

"Oh yes you would," said the other man, "if you really believed it was safe. So would anybody. Why are all these tremendous artificial barriers built up around murder by the Church and the law? Just because it's everybody's crime and just as natural as breathing."

"But that's ridiculous!" cried Pender, warmly.

"You think so, do you? That's what most people would say. But I wouldn't trust 'em. Not with sulphate of thanatol to be bought for two-pence at any chemist's."

"Sulphate of what?" asked Pender sharply.

"Ah! you think I'm giving something away. Well, it's a mixture of that and one or two other things—all equally ordinary and cheap. For ninepence you could make up enough to poison the entire Cabinet. Though of course one wouldn't polish the whole lot at once; it might look funny if they all died simultaneously in their baths."

2. ***Crippen.*** Hawley Harvey Crippen (1862–1910) was hanged following a sensational murder trial where he was found guilty of poisoning his wife.

"Why in their baths?"

"That's the way it would take them. It's the action of the hot water that brings on the effect of the stuff, you see. Any time from a few hours to a few days after administration. It's quite a simple chemical reaction and it couldn't possibly be detected by analysis. It would just look like heart failure."

Pender eyed him uneasily. He did not like the smile; it was not only derisive, it was smug, it was almost gloating, triumphant! He could not quite put the right name to it.

"You know," pursued the man, pulling a pipe from his pocket and beginning to fill it, "it is very odd how often one seems to read of people being found dead in their baths. It must be a very common accident. Quite temptingly so. After all, there is a fascination about murder. The thing grows upon one—that is, I imagine it would, you know."

"Very likely," said Pender.

"I'm sure of it. No, I wouldn't trust anybody with that formula—not even a virtuous young man like yourself."

The long white fingers tamped the tobacco firmly into the bowl and struck a match.

"But how about you?" said Pender, irritated. (Nobody cares to be called a virtuous young man.) "If nobody is fit to be trusted——"

"I'm not, eh?" replied the man. "Well, that's true, but it can't be helped now, can it? I know the thing and I can't unknow it again. It's unfortunate, but there it is. At any rate you have the comfort of knowing that nothing disagreeable is likely to happen to *me*. Dear me! Rugby already. I get out here. I have a little bit of business to do at Rugby."

He rose and shook himself, buttoned his raincoat about him, and pulled the shabby hat more firmly down about his enigmatic glasses. The train slowed down and stopped. With a brief goodnight and a crooked smile, the man stepped onto the platform. Pender watched him stride quickly away into the drizzle beyond the radius of the gas light.

"Dotty or something," said Pender, oddly relieved. "Thank goodness, I seem to be going to have the compartment to myself."

He returned to *Murder at the Manse,* but his attention still kept wandering from the book he held in his hand.

"What was the name of that stuff the fellow talked about? Sulphate of what?"

For the life of him he could not remember.

It was on the following afternoon that Pender saw the news item. He had bought the *Standard* to read at lunch, and the word *Bath* caught his eye; otherwise, he would probably have missed the paragraph altogether, for it was only a short one.

Wealthy Manufacturer Dies in Bath

Wife's Tragic Discovery

A distressing discovery was made early this morning by Mrs. John Brittlesea, wife of the well-known head of Brittlesea's Engineering Works at Rugby. Finding that her husband, whom she had seen alive and well less than an hour previously, did not come down in time for his breakfast, she searched for him in the bathroom, where the engineer was found lying dead in his bath, life having been extinct, according to the medical men, for half an hour. The cause of the death is pronounced to be heart failure. The deceased manufacturer . . .

"That's an odd coincidence," said Pender. "At Rugby. I should think my unknown friend could be interested—if he is still there, doing his bit of business. I wonder what his business is, by the way."

It is a very curious thing how, when once your attention is attracted to any particular set of circumstances, that set of circumstances seems to haunt you. You get appendicitis: immediately the newspapers are filled with paragraphs about statesmen suffering from appendicitis and victims dying of it; you learn that all your acquaintances have had it, or know friends who have had it and either died of it, or recovered from it with more surprising and spectacular rapidity than yourself; you cannot open a popular magazine without seeing its cure mentioned as one of the triumphs of modern surgery, or dip into a scientific treatise without coming across a comparison of the vermiform appendix in men and monkeys. Probably these references to appendicitis are equally frequent at all times, but you only notice them when your mind is attuned to the subject. At any rate, it was in this way that Pender accounted to himself for the extraordinary frequency with which people seemed to die in their baths at this period.

The thing pursued him at every turn. Always the same sequence of events: the hot bath, the discovery of the corpse, the inquest. Always the same medical opinion: heart failure following immersion in too hot water. It began to seem to Pender that it was scarcely safe to enter a hot bath at all. He took to making his own bath cooler and cooler every day, until it almost ceased to be enjoyable.

He skimmed his paper each morning for headlines about baths before settling down to read the news; and was at once relieved and vaguely disappointed if a week passed without a hot-bath tragedy.

One of the sudden deaths that occurred in this way was that of a young and beautiful woman whose husband, an analytical chemist, had tried without success to divorce her a few months previously. The coroner displayed a tendency to suspect foul play, and put the husband through a severe cross-examination. There seemed, however, to be no getting behind the doctor's evidence. Pender, brooding over the improbable possible, wished, as he did every day of the week, that he could remember the name of that drug the man in the train had mentioned.

Then came the excitement in Pender's own neighborhood. An old Mr. Skimmings, who lived alone with a housekeeper in a street just around the corner, was found dead in his bathroom. His heart had never been strong. The housekeeper told the milkman that she had always expected something of the sort to happen, for the old gentleman would always take his bath so hot. Pender went to the inquest.

The housekeeper gave her evidence. Mr. Skimmings had been the kindest of employers, and she was heartbroken at losing him. No, she had not been aware that Mr. Skimmings had left her a large sum of money, but it was just like his goodness of heart. The verdict of course was accidental death.

Pender, that evening, went out for his usual stroll with the dog. Some feeling of curiosity moved him to go around past the late Mr. Skimmings's house. As he loitered by, glancing up at the blank windows, the garden gate opened and a man came out. In the light of a street lamp, Pender recognized him at once.

"Hullo!" he said.

"Oh, it's you, is it?" said the man. "Viewing the site of the tragedy, eh? What do *you* think about it all?"

"Oh, nothing very much," said Pender. "I didn't know him. Odd, our meeting again like this."

"Yes, isn't it? You live near here, I suppose."

"Yes," said Pender; and then wished he hadn't. "Do you live in these parts too?"

"Me?" said the man. "Oh, no. I was only here on a little matter of business."

"Last time we met," said Pender, "you had business at Rugby." They had fallen into step together, and were walking slowly down to the turning Pender had to take in order to reach his house.

"So I had," agreed the other man. "My business takes me all over the country. I never know where I may be wanted next, you see."

"It was while you were at Rugby that old Brittlesea was found dead in his bath, wasn't it?" remarked Pender carelessly.

"Yes, funny thing, coincidence." The man

glanced up at him sideways through his glittering glasses. "Left all his money to his wife, didn't he? She's a rich woman now. Good-looking girl—a lot younger than he was."

They were passing Pender's gate. "Come in and have a drink," said Pender, and again immediately regretted the impulse.

The man accepted, and they went into Pender's bachelor study.

"Remarkable lot of these bath deaths lately," observed Pender as he squirted soda into the tumblers.

"You think it's remarkable?" said the man, with his irritating trick of querying everything that was said to him. "Well, I don't know. Perhaps it is. But it's always a fairly common accident."

"I suppose I've been taking more notice on account of that conversation we had in the train." Pender laughed, a little self-consciously. "It just makes me wonder—you know how one does—whether anybody else had happened to hit on that drug you mentioned—what was its name?"

The man ignored the question.

"Oh, I shouldn't think so," he said. "I fancy I'm the only person who knows about that. I only stumbled on the thing by accident myself when I was looking for something else. I don't imagine it could have been discovered simultaneously in so many parts of the country. But all these verdicts just show, don't they, what a safe way it would be of getting rid of a person."

"You're a chemist, then?" asked Pender, catching at the one phrase which seemed to promise information.

"Oh, I'm a bit of everything. Sort of general utility man. I do a good bit of studying on my own, too. You've got one or two interesting books here, I see."

Pender was flattered. For a man in his position—he had been in a bank until he came into that little bit of money—he felt that he had improved his mind to some purpose, and he knew that his collection of modern first editions would be worth money some day. He went over to the glass-fronted bookcase and pulled out a volume or two to show his visitor.

The man displayed intelligence, and presently joined him in front of the shelves.

"These, I take it, represent your personal tastes?" He took down a volume of Henry James and glanced at the flyleaf. "That your name? E. Pender?"

Pender admitted that it was. "You have the advantage of me," he added.

"Oh— I am one of the great Smith clan," said the other with a laugh, "and work for my bread. You seem to be very nicely fixed here."

Pender explained about the clerkship and the legacy.

"Very nice, isn't it?" said Smith. "Not married? No. You're one of the lucky ones. Not likely to be needing any sulphate of . . . any useful drugs in the near future. And you never will, if you stick to what you've got and keep off women and speculation."

He smiled up sideways at Pender. Now that his hat was off, Pender saw that he had a quantity of closely curled gray hair, which made him look older than he had appeared in the railway carriage.

"No, I shan't be coming to you for assistance yet awhile," said Pender, laughing. "Besides, how should I find you if I wanted you?"

"You wouldn't have to," said Smith. "*I* should find *you*. There's never any difficulty about that." He grinned, oddly. "Well, I'd better be getting on. Thank you for your hospitality. I don't expect we shall meet again—but we may, of course. Things work out so queerly, don't they?"

When he had gone, Pender returned to his own armchair. He took up his glass of whiskey, which stood there nearly full.

"Funny!" he said to himself. "I don't remember pouring that out. I suppose I got interested and did it mechanically." He emptied his glass slowly, thinking about Smith.

What in the world was Smith doing at Skimmings's house?

And odd business altogether. If Skimmings's housekeeper had known about that money. . . . But she had not known, and if she had, how could she have found out about Smith and his sulfate of . . . the word had been on the tip of his tongue then.

"You would not need to find me. *I* should find *you*." What had the man meant by that? But this was ridiculous. Smith was not the devil, presumably. But if he really had this secret—if he liked to put a price upon it—nonsense.

"Business at Rugby—a little bit of business at Skimmings's house." Oh, absurd!

"Nobody is fit to be trusted. *Absolute* power over another man's life . . . it grows on you. That is, I imagine it would."

Lunacy! And, if there was anything in it, the man was mad to tell Pender about it. If Pender chose to speak he could get the fellow hanged. The very existence of Pender would be dangerous.

That whiskey!

More and more, thinking it over, Pender became persuaded that he had never poured it out. Smith must have done it while his back was turned. Why that sudden display of interest in the bookshelves? It had had no connection with anything that had gone before. Now Pender came to think of it, it had been a very stiff whiskey. Was it imagination, or had there been something about the flavor of it?

A cold sweat broke out on Pender's forehead.

A quarter of an hour later, after a powerful dose of mustard and water, Pender was downstairs again, very cold and shivering, huddling over the fire. He had had a narrow escape—if he had escaped. He did not know how the stuff worked, but he would not take a hot bath again for some days. One never knew.

Whether the mustard and water had done the trick in time, or whether the hot bath was an essential part of the treatment, at any rate Pender's life was saved for the time being. But he was still uneasy. He kept the front door on the chain and warned his servant to let no strangers into the house.

He ordered two more morning papers and the *News of the World* on Sundays, and kept a careful watch upon their columns. Deaths in baths became an obsession with him. He neglected his first editions and took to attending inquests.

Three weeks later he found himself at Lincoln. A man had died of heart failure in a Turkish bath—a fat man, of sedentary habits. The jury added a rider to their verdict of accidental death to the effect that the management should exercise a stricter supervision over the bathers and should never permit them to be left unattended in the hot room.

As Pender emerged from the hall he saw ahead of him a shabby hat that seemed familiar. He plunged after it, and caught Mr. Smith about to step into a taxi.

"Smith," he cried, gasping a little. He clutched him fiercely by the shoulder.

"What, you again?" said Smith. "Taking notes of the case, eh? *Can I do anything for you?*"

"You devil!" said Pender. "You're mixed up in this! You tried to kill me the other day."

"Did I? Why should I do that?"

"You'll swing for this," shouted Pender menacingly.

A policeman pushed his way through the gathering crowd.

"Here!" said he. "What's all this about?"

Smith touched his forehead significantly.

"It's all right, officer," said he. "The gentleman seems to think I'm here for no good. Here's my card. The coroner knows me. But he attacked me. You'd better keep an eye on him."

"That's right," said a bystander.

"This man tried to kill me," said Pender.

The policeman nodded.

"Don't you worry about that, sir," he said. "You think better of it. The 'eat in there has upset you a bit. All right, *all* right."

"But I want to charge him," said Pender.

"I wouldn't do that if I was you," said the policeman.

"I tell you," said Pender, "that this man Smith has been trying to poison me. He's a murderer. He's poisoned scores of people."

The policeman winked at Smith.

"Best be off, sir," he said. "I'll settle this.

Now, my lad"—he held Pender firmly by the arms—"just you keep cool and take it quiet. That gentleman's name ain't Smith or nothing like it. You've got a bit mixed up like."

"Well, what is his name?" demanded Pender.

"Never mind," replied the constable. "You leave him alone, or you'll be getting yourself into trouble."

The taxi had driven away. Pender glanced around at the circle of amused faces and gave in.

"All right, officer," he said. "I won't give you any trouble. I'll come round with you to the police station and tell you about it."

"What do you think o' that one?" asked the inspector of the sergeant when Pender had stumbled out of the station.

"Up the pole an' 'alf-way round the flag, if you ask me," replied his subordinate. "Got one o' them ideez fix[3] what they talk about."

"H'm!" replied the inspector. "Well, we've got his name and address. Better make a note of 'em. He might turn up again. Poisoning people so as they die in their baths, eh? That's a pretty good 'un. Wonderful how these barmy ones thinks it all out, isn't it?"

The spring that year was a bad one—cold and foggy. It was March when Pender went down to an inquest at Deptford, but a thick blanket of mist was hanging over the river as though it were November. The cold ate into your bones. As he sat in the dingy little court, peering through the yellow twilight of gas and fog, he could scarcely see the witnesses as they came to the table. Everybody in the place seemed to be coughing. Pender was coughing too. His bones ached, and he felt as though he were about due for a bout of influenza.

Straining his eyes, he thought he recognized a face on the other side of the room, but the smarting fog which penetrated every crack stung and blinded him. He felt in his overcoat pocket, and his hand closed comfortably on something thick and heavy. Ever since that day in Lincoln he had gone about armed for protection. Not a revolver—he was no hand with firearms. A sandbag was much better. He had bought one from an old man wheeling a pushcart. It was meant for keeping out drafts from the door—a good, old-fashioned affair.

The inevitable verdict was returned. The spectators began to push their way out. Pender had to hurry now, not to lose sight of his man. He elbowed his way along, muttering apologies. At the door he almost touched the man, but a stout woman intervened. He plunged past her, and she gave a little squeak of indignation. The man in front turned his head, and the light over the door glinted on his glasses.

Pender pulled his hat over his eyes and followed. His shoes had crepe rubber soles and made no sound on the pavement. The man went on, jogging quietly up one street and down another, and never looking back. The fog was so thick that Pender was forced to keep within a few yards of him. Where was he going? Into the lighted streets? Home by bus or train? No. He turned off to the left, down a narrow street.

The fog was thicker here. Pender could no longer see his quarry, but he heard the footsteps going on before him at the same even pace. It seemed to him that they were two alone in the world—pursued and pursuer, slayer and avenger. The street began to slope more rapidly. They must be coming out somewhere near the river.

Suddenly the dim shapes of the houses fell away on either side. There was an open space, with a lamp vaguely visible in the middle. The footsteps paused. Pender, silently hurrying after, saw the man standing close beneath the lamp, apparently consulting something in a notebook.

Four steps, and Pender was upon him. He drew the sandbag from his pocket.

The man looked up.

"I've got you this time," said Pender, and struck with all his force.

Pender had been quite right. He did get influenza. It was a week before he was out and

3. ***ideez fix.*** The man is mispronouncing the French term *idée fixe* (ē dā′ fēks′), a fixed idea, or obsession.

about again. The weather changed, and the air was fresh and sweet. In spite of the weakness left by the malady, he felt as though a heavy weight had been lifted from his shoulders. He tottered down to a favorite bookshop of his in the Strand, and picked up a D. H. Lawrence "first" at a price which he knew to be a bargain. Encouraged by this, he turned into a small chophouse chiefly frequented by newspaper men, and ordered a grilled cutlet and a half-tankard of bitter.

Two journalists were seated at the next table.

"Going to poor old Buckley's funeral?" asked one.

"Yes," said the other. "Poor devil— Fancy his getting bashed on the head like that. He must have been on his way down to interview the widow of that fellow who died in a bath. It's a rough district. Probably one of Jimmy the Card's crowd had it in for him. He was a great crime-reporter—they won't get another like Bill Buckley in a hurry."

"He was a decent sort, too. Great old sport. No end of a practical joker. Remember his great stunt sulphate of thanatol?"

Pender started. *That* was the word that had eluded him for so many months. A curious dizziness came over him.

". . . looking at you as sober as a judge," the journalist was saying. "No such stuff, of course, but he used to work off that wheeze on poor boobs in railway carriages to see how they'd take it. Would you believe that one chap actually offered him——"

"Hullo!" interrupted his friend. "That bloke over there has fainted. I thought he was looking a bit white."

Discussion

1. (a) Describe the physical appearance of Pender's companion on the train. **(b)** What are Pender's initial reactions to the man?

2. (a) Briefly describe the traveling companion's method for homicide. **(b)** Why does the companion refuse to divulge this method?

3. How does the conversation on the train affect Pender's habits?

4. (a) Under what circumstances does Pender encounter his traveling companion a second time? **(b)** Of what does Pender become convinced as a consequence of this encounter? **(c)** What happens at the third encounter between Pender and his companion? **(d)** How do the police react to Pender's accusations?

5. (a) Where, when, and how does Pender rid himself of the traveling companion? **(b)** To what extent is Buckley responsible for his own death? Explain.

6. Cite evidence in the story that supports the fact that Buckley was a crime-reporter.

7. Review definitions of verbal irony, irony of situation, and dramatic irony. Then, explain which of these three Dorothy Sayers makes use of in the climax and conclusion of "The Man Who Knew How."

Dorothy L. Sayers 1893–1957

An English novelist, essayist, playwright, poet, and theologian, Dorothy L. Sayers is best remembered as the creator of Lord Peter Wimsey, an affluent young nobleman-detective who appears in numerous novels written by Sayers in the 1920s and 1930s.

One of the first women to obtain an Oxford degree (1915), Sayers attained highest honors in medieval literature. Following graduation, she turned to writing mysteries as a source of income. Sayers also wrote religious essays and dramas and translated Dante's *Divine Comedy.*

DETECTIVE

Village Murders

Agatha Christie

What are the clues that lead Miss Marple to the solution of an ingenious crime?

Miss Politt took hold of the knocker and rapped politely on the cottage door. After a discreet interval she knocked again. The parcel under her left arm shifted a little as she did so, and she readjusted it. Inside the parcel was Mrs. Spenlow's new green winter dress, ready for fitting. From Miss Politt's left hand dangled a bag of black silk, containing a tape measure, a pincushion, and a large, practical pair of scissors.

Miss Politt was tall and gaunt, with a sharp nose, pursed lips, and meager iron-grey hair. She hesitated before using the knocker for the third time. Glancing down the street, she saw a figure rapidly approaching. Miss Hartnell, jolly, weather-beaten, fifty-five, shouted out in her usual loud bass voice, "Good afternoon, Miss Politt!"

The dressmaker answered, "Good afternoon, Miss Hartnell." Her voice was excessively thin and genteel in its accents. She had started life as a lady's maid. "Excuse me," she went on, "but do you happen to know if by any chance Mrs. Spenlow isn't at home?"

"Not the least idea," said Miss Hartnell.

"It's rather awkward, you see. I was to fit on Mrs. Spenlow's new dress this afternoon. Three-thirty, she said."

Miss Hartnell consulted her wrist watch. "It's a little past the half-hour now."

"Yes. I have knocked three times, but there doesn't seem to be any answer, so I was wondering if perhaps Mrs. Spenlow might have gone out and forgotten. She doesn't forget appointments as a rule, and she wants the dress to wear the day after tomorrow."

Miss Hartnell entered the gate and walked up the path to join Miss Politt outside the door of Laburnam Cottage.

"Why doesn't Gladys answer the door?" she demanded. "Oh, no, of course, it's Thursday—Gladys's day out. I expect Mrs. Spenlow has fallen asleep. I don't expect you've made enough noise with this thing."

Seizing the knocker, she executed a deafening *rat-a-tat-tat* and, in addition, thumped upon the panels of the door. She also called out in a stentorian voice: "What ho, within there!"

There was no response.

Miss Politt murmured, "Oh, I think Mrs. Spenlow must have forgotten and gone out. I'll call round some other time." She began edging away down the path.

"Nonsense," said Miss Hartnell firmly. "She can't have gone out. I'd have met her. I'll just take a look through the windows and see if I can find any signs of life."

She laughed in her usual hearty manner, to indicate that it was a joke, and applied a perfunctory glance to the nearest windowpane—perfunctory because she knew quite well that the front room was seldom used, Mr. and Mrs. Spenlow preferring the small back sitting room.

Perfunctory as it was, though, it succeeded in its object. Miss Hartnell, it is true, saw no

signs of life. On the contrary, she saw, through the window, Mrs. Spenlow lying on the hearth-rug—dead.

"Of course," said Miss Hartnell, telling the story afterward, "I managed to keep my head. That Politt creature wouldn't have had the least idea of what to do. 'Got to keep our heads,' I said to her. 'You stay here and I'll go for Constable Palk.' She said something about not wanting to be left, but I paid no attention at all. One has to be firm with that sort of person. I've always found they enjoy making a fuss. So I was just going off when, at that very moment, Mr. Spenlow came round the corner of the house."

Here Miss Hartnell made a significant pause. It enabled her audience to ask breathlessly, "Tell me, how did he look?" Miss Hartnell would then go on: "Frankly, I suspected something at once! He was far too calm. He didn't seem surprised in the least. And you may say what you like, it isn't natural for a man to hear that his wife is dead and display no emotion whatever."

Everybody agreed with this statement.

The police agreed with it too. So suspicious did they consider Mr. Spenlow's detachment that they lost no time in ascertaining how that gentleman was situated as a result of his wife's death. When they discovered that Mrs. Spenlow had been the moneyed partner, and that her money went to her husband under a will made soon after their marriage, they were more suspicious than ever.

Miss Marple, that sweet-faced (and some said vinegar-tongued) elderly spinster who lived in the house next to the rectory, was interviewed very early—within half an hour of the discovery of the crime. She was approached by Police Constable Palk, importantly thumbing a notebook. "If you don't mind, ma'am, I've a few questions to ask you."

...arple said, "In connection with the ...rs. Spenlow?"

... startled. "May I ask, madam, how ...now of it?"

"The fish," said Miss Marple.

The reply was perfectly intelligible to Constable Palk. He assumed correctly that the fishmonger's boy had brought it, together with Miss Marple's evening meal.

Miss Marple continued gently, "Lying on the floor in the sitting room, strangled—possibly by a very narrow belt. But whatever it was, it was taken away."

Palk's face was wrathful. "How that young Fred gets to know everything——"

Miss Marple cut him short adroitly. She said, "There's a pin in your tunic."

Constable Palk looked down, startled. He said, "They do say: 'See a pin and pick it up, all the day you'll have good luck.' "

"I hope that will come true. Now what is it you want me to tell you?"

Constable Palk cleared his throat, looked important, and consulted his notebook. "Statement was made to me by Mr. Arthur Spenlow, husband of the deceased. Mr. Spenlow says that at two-thirty, as far as he can say, he was rung up by Miss Marple and asked if he would come over at a quarter past three, as she was anxious to consult him about something. Now, ma'am, is that true?"

"Certainly not," said Miss Marple.

"You did not ring up Mr. Spenlow at two-thirty?"

"Neither at two-thirty nor any other time."

"Ah," said Constable Palk, and sucked his moustache with a good deal of satisfaction.

"What else did Mr. Spenlow say?"

"Mr. Spenlow's statement was that he came over here as requested, leaving his own house at ten minutes past three; that on arrival here he was informed by the maidservant that Miss Marple was 'not at 'ome.' "

"That part of it is true," said Miss Marple. "He did come here, but I was at a meeting at the Women's Institute."

"Ah," said Constable Palk again.

Miss Marple exclaimed, "Do tell me, Constable, do you suspect Mr. Spenlow?"

"It's not for me to say at this stage, but it

looks to me as though somebody, naming no names, had been trying to be artful."

Miss Marple said thoughtfully, "Mr. Spenlow?"

She liked Mr. Spenlow. He was a small, spare man, stiff and conventional in speech, the acme of respectability. It seemed odd that he should have come to live in the country; he had so clearly lived in towns all his life. To Miss Marple he confided the reason. He said, "I have always intended, ever since I was a small boy, to live in the country someday and have a garden of my own. I have always been very much attached to flowers. My wife, you know, kept a flower shop. That's where I saw her first."

A dry statement, but it opened up a vista of romance. A younger, prettier Mrs. Spenlow, seen against a background of flowers.

Mr. Spenlow, however, really knew nothing about flowers. He had no idea of seeds, of cuttings, of bedding out, of annuals or perennials. He had only a vision—a vision of a small cottage garden thickly planted with sweet-smelling, brightly colored blossoms. He had asked, almost pathetically, for instruction and had noted down Miss Marple's replies to questions in a little book.

He was a man of quiet method. It was, perhaps, because of this trait that the police were interested in him when his wife was found murdered. With patience and perseverance they learned a good deal about the late Mrs. Spenlow—and soon all St. Mary Mead knew it too.

The late Mrs. Spenlow had begun life as a betweenmaid[1] in a large house. She had left that position to marry the second gardener and with him had started a flower shop in London. The shop had prospered. Not so the gardener, who before long had sickened and died.

His widow had carried on the shop and enlarged it in an ambitious way. She had continued to prosper. Then she had sold the business at a handsome price and embarked upon matrimony for the second time—with Mr. Spenlow, a middle-aged jeweler who had inherited a small and struggling business. Not long afterward they had sold the business and come down to St. Mary Mead.

Mrs. Spenlow was a well-to-do woman. The profits from her florist's establishment she had invested—"under spirit guidance," as she explained to all and sundry. The spirits had advised her with unexpected acumen.

All her investments had prospered, some in quite a sensational fashion. Instead, however, of this increasing her belief in spiritualism, Mrs. Spenlow basely deserted mediums and sittings and made a brief but wholehearted plunge into an obscure religion with Indian affinities which was based on various forms of deep breathing. When, however, she arrived at St. Mary Mead, she had relapsed into a period of orthodox Church-of-England beliefs. She was a good deal at the Vicarage and attended church services with assiduity. She patronized the village shops, took an interest in the local happenings, and played village bridge.

A humdrum, everyday life. And—suddenly—murder.

Colonel Melchett, the chief constable, had summoned Inspector Slack.

Slack was a positive type of man. When he made up his mind, he was sure. He was quite sure now. "Husband did it, sir," he said.

"You think so?"

"Quite sure of it. You've only got to look at him. Never showed a sign of grief or emotion. He came back to the house knowing she was dead."

"Wouldn't he at least have tried to act the part of the distracted husband?"

"Not him, sir. Too pleased with himself. Some gentlemen can't act. Too stiff. As I see it, he was just fed up with his wife. She'd got the money and, I should say, was a trying woman to live with—always taking up some 'ism' or other. He cold-bloodedly decided to do away with her and live comfortably on his own."

---

1. ***betweenmaid,*** a maidservant whose work supplements that of cook and housemaid.

"Yes, that could be the case, I suppose."

"Depend upon it, that was it. Made his plans careful. Pretended to get a phone call——"

Melchett interrupted him: "No call been traced?"

"No, sir. That means either that he lied or that the call was put through from a public telephone booth. The only two public phones in the village are at the station and the post office. Post office it certainly wasn't. Mrs. Blade sees everyone who comes in. Station it might be. Train arrives at two twenty-seven and there's a bit of bustle then. But the main thing is he says it was Miss Marple who called him up, and that certainly isn't true. The call didn't come from her house, and she herself was away at the Institute."

"You're not overlooking the possibility that the husband was deliberately got out of the way—by someone who wanted to murder Mrs. Spenlow?"

"You're thinking of young Ted Gerard, aren't you, sir? I've been working on him—what we're up against there is lack of motive. He doesn't stand to gain anything."

"He's an undesirable character, though. Quite a pretty little spot of embezzlement to his credit."

"I'm not saying he isn't a wrong 'un. Still, he did go to his boss and own up to that embezzlement. And his employers weren't wise to it."

"An Oxford Grouper,"[2] said Melchett.

"Yes, sir. Became a convert and went off to do the straight thing and own up to having pinched money. I'm not saying, mind you, that it mayn't have been astuteness—he may have thought he was suspected and decided to gamble on honest repentance."

"You have a skeptical mind, Slack," said Colonel Melchett. "By the way, have you talked to Miss Marple at all?"

"What's she got to do with it, sir?"

"Oh, nothing. But she hears things, you know. Why don't you go and have a chat with her. She's a very sharp old lady."

Slack changed the subject. "One thing I've been meaning to ask you, sir: That domestic-service job where the deceased started her career—Sir Robert Abercrombie's place. That's where the jewel robbery was—emeralds—worth a packet. Never got them. I've been looking it up—must have happened when the Spenlow woman was there, though she'd have been quite a girl at the time. Don't think she was mixed up in it, do you, sir? Spenlow, you know, was one of those little tuppenny-ha'penny jewelers—just the chap for a fence."

Melchett shook his head. "Don't think there's anything in that. She didn't even know Spenlow at the time. I remember the case. Opinion in police circles was that a son of the house was mixed up in it—Jim Abercrombie—awful young waster. Had a pile of debts, and just after the robbery they were all paid off—some rich woman, so they said, but I don't know—old Abercrombie hedged a bit about the case—tried to call the police off."

"It was just an idea, sir," said Slack.

Miss Marple received Inspector Slack with gratification, especially when she heard that he had been sent by Colonel Melchett.

"Now, really, that is very kind of Colonel Melchett. I didn't know he remembered me."

"He remembers you, all right. Told me that what you didn't know of what goes on in St. Mary Mead isn't worth knowing."

"Too kind of him, but really I don't know anything at all. About this murder, I mean."

"You know what the talk about it is."

"Of course—but it wouldn't do, would it, to repeat just idle talk?"

Slack said, with an attempt at geniality, "This isn't an official conversation, you know. It's in confidence, so to speak."

"You mean you really want to know what people are saying? Whether there's any truth in it or not?"

"That's the idea."

---

2. ***Oxford Grouper,*** a member of the Oxford Group, a life-changing movement stressing personal and social regeneration. The movement was replaced in 1938 by Moral Re-armament.

"Well, of course, there's been a great deal of talk and speculation. And there are really two distinct camps, if you understand me. To begin with, there are the people who think that the husband did it. A husband or a wife is, in a way, the natural person to suspect, don't you think so?"

"Maybe," said the inspector cautiously.

"Such close quarters, you know. Then, so often, the money angle. I hear that it was Mrs. Spenlow who had the money and therefore Mr. Spenlow does benefit by her death. In this wicked world I'm afraid the most uncharitable assumptions are often justified."

"He comes into a tidy sum, all right."

"Just so. It would seem quite plausible, wouldn't it, for him to strangle her, leave the house by the back, come across the fields to my house, ask for me and pretend he'd had a telephone call from me, then go back and find his wife murdered in his absence—hoping, of course, that the crime would be put down to some tramp or burglar."

The inspector nodded. "What with the money angle—and if they'd been on bad terms lately——"

But Miss Marple interrupted him: "Oh, but they hadn't."

"You know that for a fact?"

"Everyone would have known if they'd quarreled! The maid, Gladys Brent—she'd have soon spread it round the village."

The inspector said feebly, "She mightn't have known," and received a pitying smile in reply.

Miss Marple went on: "And then there's the other school of thought. Ted Gerard. A good-looking young man. I'm afraid, you know, that good looks are inclined to influence one more than they should. Our last curate but one—quite a magical effect! All the girls came to church—evening service as well as morning. And many older women became unusually active in parish work—and the slippers and scarves that were made for him! Quite embarrassing for the poor young man.

"But let me see, where was I? Oh yes, this young man, Ted Gerard. Of course, there has been talk about him. He's come down to see her so often. Though Mrs. Spenlow told me herself that he was a member of what I think they call the Oxford Group. A religious movement. They are quite sincere and very earnest, I believe, and Mrs. Spenlow was impressed by it all."

Miss Marple took a breath and went on: "And I'm sure there was no reason to believe that there was anything more in it than that, but you know what people are. Quite a lot of people are convinced that Mrs. Spenlow was infatuated with the young man and that she'd lent him quite a lot of money. And it's perfectly true that he was actually seen at the station that day. In the train—the two twenty-seven down train. But of course it would be quite easy, wouldn't it, to slip out of the other side of the train and go through the cutting and over the fence and round by the hedge and never come out of the station entrance at all? So that he need not have been seen going to the cottage. And of course people do think that what Mrs. Spenlow was wearing was rather peculiar."

"Peculiar?"

"A kimono. Not a dress." Miss Marple blushed. "That sort of thing, you know, is, perhaps, rather suggestive to some people."

"You think it was suggestive?"

"Oh no, I don't think so. I think it was perfectly natural."

"You think it was natural?"

"Under the circumstances, yes." Miss Marple's glance was cool and reflective.

Inspector Slack said, "It might give us another motive for the husband. Jealousy."

"Oh no, Mr. Spenlow would never be jealous. He's not the sort of man who notices things. If his wife had gone away and left a note on the pincushion, it would be the first he'd know anything of that kind."

Inspector Slack was puzzled by the intent way she was looking at him. He had an idea that all her conversation was intended to hint at something he didn't understand. She said now, with some emphasis, "Didn't you find any clues, Inspector—on the spot?"

"People don't leave fingerprints and cigarette ash nowadays, Miss Marple."

"But this, I think," she suggested, "was an old-fashioned crime——"

Slack said sharply, "Now what do you mean by that?"

Miss Marple remarked slowly, "I think, you know, that Constable Palk could help you. He was the first person on the—on the 'scene of the crime,' as they say."

Mr. Spenlow was sitting in a deck chair. He looked bewildered. He said, in his thin, precise voice, "I may, of course, be imagining what occurred. My hearing is not as good as it was. But I distinctly think I heard a small boy call after me, 'Yah, who's a Crippen?'[3] It—it conveyed the impression to me that he was of the opinion that I had—had killed my dear wife."

Miss Marple, gently snipping off a dead rose head, said, "That was the impression he meant to convey, no doubt."

"But what could possibly have put such an idea into a child's head?"

Miss Marple coughed. "Listening, no doubt, to the opinions of his elders."

"You—you really mean that other people think that also?"

"Quite half the people in St. Mary Mead."

"But, my dear lady, what can possibly have given rise to such an idea? I was sincerely attached to my wife. She did not, alas, take to living in the country as much as I had hoped she would do, but perfect agreement on every subject is an impossible ideal. I assure you I feel her loss very keenly."

"Probably. But if you will excuse my saying so, you don't sound as though you do."

Mr. Spenlow drew his meager frame up to its full height. "My dear lady, many years ago I read of a certain Chinese philosopher who, when his dearly loved wife was taken from him, continued calmly to beat a gong in the street—a customary Chinese pastime, I presume—exactly as usual. The people of the city were much impressed by his fortitude."

"But," said Miss Marple, "the people of St. Mary Mead react rather differently. Chinese philosophy does not appeal to them."

"But you understand?"

Miss Marple nodded. "My uncle Henry," she explained, "was a man of unusual self-control. His motto was 'Never display emotion.' He, too, was very fond of flowers."

"I was thinking," said Mr. Spenlow with something like eagerness, "that I might, perhaps, have a pergola on the west side of the cottage. Pink roses and, perhaps, wisteria. And there is a white starry flower, whose name for the moment escapes me——"

In the tone in which she spoke to her grandnephew, aged three, Miss Marple said, "I have a very nice catalog here, with pictures. Perhaps you would like to look through it—I have to go up to the village."

Leaving Mr. Spenlow sitting happily in the garden with his catalog, Miss Marple went up to her room, hastily rolled up a dress in a piece of brown paper, and, leaving the house, walked briskly up to the post office. Miss Politt, the dressmaker, lived in rooms over the post office.

But Miss Marple did not at once go through the door and up the stairs. It was just two-thirty, and, a minute late, the Much Benham bus drew up outside the post-office door. It was one of the events of the day in St. Mary Mead. The postmistress hurried out with parcels, parcels connected with the shop side of her business, for the post office also dealt in sweets, cheap books, and children's toys.

For some four minutes Miss Marple was alone in the post office.

Not till the postmistress returned to her post did Miss Marple go upstairs and explain to Miss Politt that she wanted her own grey crepe altered and made more fashionable if that were possible. Miss Politt promised to see what she could do.

---

3. ***Crippen,*** notorious wife-poisoner. (See footnote 2 in "The Man Who Knew How.")

The chief constable was rather astonished when Miss Marple's name was brought to him. She came in with many apologies. "So sorry—so very sorry to disturb you. You are so busy, I know, but then you have always been so very kind, Colonel Melchett, and I felt I would rather come to you instead of to Inspector Slack. For one thing, you know, I should hate Constable Palk to get into any trouble. Strictly speaking, I suppose he shouldn't have touched anything at all."

Colonel Melchett was slightly bewildered. He said, "Palk? That's the St. Mary Mead constable, isn't it? What has he been doing?"

"He picked up a pin, you know. It was in his tunic. And it occurred to me at the time that it was quite probable he had actually picked it up in Mrs. Spenlow's house."

"Quite, quite. But, after all, you know, what's a pin? Matter of fact, he did pick the pin up just by Mrs. Spenlow's body. Came and told Slack about it yesterday—you put him up to that, I gather? Oughtn't to have touched anything, of course, but, as I said, what's a pin? It was only a common pin. Sort of thing any woman might use."

"Oh no, Colonel Melchett, that's where you're wrong. To a man's eye, perhaps, it looked like an ordinary pin, but it wasn't. It was a special pin, a very thin pin, the kind you buy by the box, the kind used mostly by dressmakers."

Melchett stared at her, a faint light of comprehension breaking in on him. Miss Marple nodded her head several times eagerly.

"Yes, of course. It seems to me so obvious.

She was in her kimono because she was going to try on her new dress, and she went into the front room, and Miss Politt just said something about measurements and put the tape measure round her neck—and then all she'd have to do was to cross it and pull—quite easy, so I've heard. And then of course she'd go outside and pull the door to and stand there knocking as though she'd just arrived. But the pin shows she'd already been in the house."

"And it was Miss Politt who telephoned to Spenlow?"

"Yes. From the post office at two-thirty—just when the bus comes and the post office would be empty."

Colonel Melchett said, "But, my dear Miss Marple, why? In heaven's name, why? You can't have a murder without a motive."

"Well, I think, you know, Colonel Melchett, from all I've heard, that the crime dates from a long time back. It reminds me, you know, of my two cousins, Antony and Gordon. Whatever Antony did always went right for him, and with poor Gordon it was just the other way about: race horses went lame, and stocks went down, and property depreciated. . . . As I see it, the two women were in it together."

"In what?"

"The robbery. Long ago. Very valuable emeralds, so I've heard. The lady's maid and the tweeny. Because one thing hasn't been explained—how, when the tweeny married the gardener, did they have enough money to set up a flower shop?

"The answer is, it was her share of the—the swag, I think is the right expression. Everything she did turned out well. Money made money. But the other one, the lady's maid, must have been unlucky. She came down to being just a village dressmaker. Then they met again. Quite all right at first, I expect, until Mr. Ted Gerard came on the scene.

"Mrs. Spenlow, you see, was already suffering from conscience and was inclined to be emotionally religious. This young man no doubt urged her to 'face up' and to 'come clean,' and I daresay she was strung up to do so. But Miss Politt didn't see it that way. All she saw was that she might go to prison for a robbery she had committed years ago. So she made up her mind to put a stop to it all. I'm afraid, you know, that she was always rather a wicked woman. I don't believe she'd have turned a hair if that nice, stupid Mr. Spenlow had been hanged."

Colonel Melchett said slowly, "We can—er—verify your theory—up to a point. The identity of the Politt woman with the lady's maid at the Abercrombies', but——"

Miss Marple reassured him.

"It will be all quite easy. She's the kind of woman who will break down at once when she's taxed with the truth. And then, you see, I've got her tape measure. I—er—abstracted it yesterday when I was trying on. When she misses it and thinks the police have got it—well, she's quite an ignorant woman and she'll think it will prove the case against her in some way."

She smiled at him encouragingly. "You'll have no trouble, I can assure you." It was the tone in which his favorite aunt had once assured him that he could not fail to pass his entrance examination into Sandhurst.

And he had passed.

Discussion

1. **(a)** What reason does Miss Politt give Miss Hartnell for being at Laburnam Cottage? **(b)** Why does the maid, Gladys Brent, fail to respond to Miss Politt's knocking?

2. **(a)** What circumstantial evidence makes Mr. Spenlow appear responsible for his wife's death? **(b)** What alibi does Mr. Spenlow provide for his innocence? **(c)** Describe how Miss Marple both supports and denies this alibi. **(d)** What remarks of Miss Marple to Inspector Slack serve to defend Mr. Spenlow?

3. **(a)** Describe the background and interests of Mr. Spenlow. **(b)** Describe the background and interests of his late wife. **(c)** Why was Mrs. Spenlow never accused of stealing emeralds from her former employer?

4. What circumstantial evidence ties Ted Gerard to Mrs. Spenlow's murder?

5. Explain the significance of each of the following in enabling Miss Marple to solve the crime: **(a)** a pin; **(b)** the post office; **(c)** Ted Gerard; **(d)** a flower shop; **(e)** a kimono.

6. What makes Miss Marple believe that Miss Politt will readily confess her guilt?

Agatha Christie 1890–1976

Dame Agatha Christie wrote approximately eighty detective novels, many of them featuring either the gentlewoman detective, Miss Marple, or the little Belgian detective, Hercule Poirot, noted for his tortured use of the English language.

Christie was born in Torquay, Devon, England. Until age sixteen, she was tutored at home by her mother, who encouraged her to write poetry and fiction. Although she later studied voice in Paris, Christie found that her creative strength lay in writing detective stories, not in singing opera. The [*London*] *Times Literary Supplement* once wrote of her, "Almost alone among nice English detective writers she has never excluded any characters from possible revelation as murderers, not the sweet young girl, the charming youth, the wise old man, not even the dear old lady."

See **INFERENCE** Handbook of Literary Terms

The Speckled Band

Arthur Conan Doyle

It swelled up louder and louder, a hoarse yell of pain and fear and anger all mingled in the one dreadful shriek.

It was early in April in the year '83 that I woke one morning to find Sherlock Holmes standing, fully dressed, by the side of my bed. He was a late riser, as a rule, and as the clock on the mantelpiece showed me that it was only a quarter past seven, I blinked up at him in some surprise, and perhaps just a little resentment, for I was myself regular in my habits.

"Very sorry to wake you up, Watson," said he, "but it's the common lot this morning. Mrs. Hudson has been awakened, she retorted upon me, and I on you."

"What is it, then—a fire?"

"No; a client. It seems that a young lady has arrived in a considerable state of excitement, who insists upon seeing me. She is waiting now in the sitting room."

I had no keener pleasure than in following Holmes in his professional investigations, and in admiring the rapid deductions, as swift as intuitions, and yet always founded on a logical basis, with which he unraveled the problems which were submitted to him. I rapidly threw on my clothes and was ready in a few minutes to accompany my friend down to the sitting room. A lady dressed in black and heavily veiled, who had been sitting in the window, rose as we entered.

"Good morning, madam," said Holmes cheerily. "My name is Sherlock Holmes. This is my intimate friend and associate, Dr. Watson, before whom you can speak as freely as before myself. Ha! I am glad to see that Mrs. Hudson has had the good sense to light the fire. Pray draw up to it, and I shall order you a cup of hot coffee, for I observe that you are shivering."

"It is not cold which makes me shiver," said the woman in a low voice, changing her seat as requested.

"What, then?"

"It is fear, Mr. Holmes. It is terror." She raised her veil as she spoke, and we could see that she was indeed in a pitiable state of agitation, her face all drawn and gray, with restless, frightened eyes, like those of some hunted animal.

"You must not fear," said he soothingly, bending forward and patting her forearm. "We shall soon set matters right, I have no doubt. You have come in by train this morning, I see."

"You know me, then?"

"No, but I observe the second half of a return ticket in the palm of your left glove. You must have started early, and yet you had a good drive in a dog cart,[1] along heavy roads, before you reached the station."

The lady gave a violent start and stared in bewilderment at my companion.

"There is no mystery, my dear madam,"

---

1. ***dog cart,*** a small, open, horse-drawn carriage with two seats that are placed back-to-back.

Arthur Conan Doyle, "The Speckled Band" from *The Adventures of Sherlock Holmes.* New York: Harper & Row, 1892. (Slightly abridged.)

said he, smiling. "The left arm of your jacket is spattered with mud in no less than seven places. The marks are perfectly fresh. There is no vehicle save a dog cart which throws up mud in that way, and then only when you sit on the left-hand side of the driver."

"Whatever your reasons may be, you are perfectly correct," said she. "I started from home before six, reached Leatherhead at twenty past, and came in by the first train to Waterloo. Sir, I can stand this strain no longer; I shall go mad if it continues. I have no one to turn to—none, save only one, who cares for me, and he, poor fellow, can be of little aid.

"I have heard of you, Mr. Holmes; I have heard of you from Mrs. Farintosh, whom you helped in the hour of her sore need."

"Farintosh," said he. "Ah yes, I recall the case; it was concerned with an opal tiara. I think it was before your time, Watson. I can only say, madam, that I shall be happy to devote the same care to your case as I did to that of your friend. As to reward, my profession is its own reward; but you are at liberty to defray whatever expenses I may be put to, at the time which suits you best. And now I beg that you will lay before us everything that may help us in forming an opinion upon the matter."

"My name is Helen Stoner, and I am living with my stepfather, who is the last survivor of one of the oldest Saxon families in England, the Roylotts of Stoke Moran, on the western border of Surrey."

Holmes nodded his head. "The name is familiar to me," said he.

"The family was at one time among the richest in England. In the last century, however, four successive heirs were of a dissolute and wasteful disposition, and the family ruin was eventually completed by a gambler in the days of the Regency. Nothing was left save a few acres of ground, and the two-hundred-year-old house, which is itself crushed under a heavy mortgage.

"The last squire dragged out his existence there, living the horrible life of an aristocratic pauper; but his only son, my stepfather, seeing that he must adapt himself to the new conditions, obtained an advance from a relative, which enabled him to take a medical degree, and went out to Calcutta, where, by his professional skill and his force of character, he established a large practice. In a fit of anger, however, caused by some robberies which had been perpetrated in the house, he beat his native butler to death and narrowly escaped a capital sentence. As it was, he suffered a long term of imprisonment and afterwards returned to England a morose and disappointed man.

"When Dr. Roylott was in India he married my mother, Mrs. Stoner, the young widow of Major-General Stoner, of the Bengal Artillery. My sister Julia and I were twins, and we were only two years old at the time of my mother's re-marriage. She had a considerable sum of money—and this she bequeathed to Dr. Roylott entirely while we resided with him, with a provision that a certain annual sum should be allowed to each of us in the event of our marriage. Shortly after our return to England my mother died—she was killed eight years ago in a railway accident near Crewe. Dr. Roylott then took us to live with him in the old ancestral house at Stoke Moran. The money which my mother had left was enough for all our wants, and there seemed to be no obstacle to our happiness.

"But a terrible change came over our stepfather about this time. Instead of making friends and exchanging visits with our neighbors, who had at first been overjoyed to see a Roylott of Stoke Moran back in the old family seat, he shut himself up in his house and seldom came out save to indulge in ferocious quarrels with whoever might cross his path.

"Violence of temper approaching to mania has been hereditary in the men of the family, and in my stepfather's case it had, I believe, been intensified by his long residence in the tropics. A series of disgraceful brawls took place, two of which ended in the police court, until at last he became the terror of the village, and the folks would fly at his approach, for he is a man of immense strength, and absolutely uncontrollable in his anger.

"He had no friends at all save the wandering gypsies, and he would give these vagabonds leave to encamp upon the few acres of bramble-covered land which represent the family estate. He has a passion also for Indian animals, which are sent over to him by a correspondent, and he has at this moment a cheetah and a baboon, which wander freely over his grounds and are feared by the villagers almost as much as is their master.

"You can imagine from what I say that my poor sister Julia and I had no great pleasure in our lives. No servant would stay with us, and for a long time we did all the work of the house. She was but thirty at the time of her death, and yet her hair had already begun to whiten, even as mine has."

"Your sister is dead, then?"

"She died just two years ago, and it is of her death that I wish to speak to you. You can understand that, living the life which I have described, we were little likely to see anyone of our own age and position. We had, however, an aunt who lives near Harrow. Julia went there at Christmas two years ago, and met there a major in the Marines, to whom she became engaged. My stepfather learned of the engagement when my sister returned and offered no objection to the marriage; but within a fortnight of the day which had been fixed for the wedding, the terrible event occurred which has deprived me of my only companion."

Sherlock Holmes had been leaning back in his chair with his eyes closed and his head sunk in a cushion, but he half opened his lids now and glanced across at his visitor. He wanted to hear everything.

"Pray be precise as to details," said he.

"It is easy for me to be so, for every event of that dreadful time is seared into my memory. The manor house is, as I have already said, very old, and only one wing is now inhabited. The bedrooms in this wing are on the ground floor, the sitting rooms being in the central block of the buildings. Of these bedrooms the first is Dr. Roylott's, the second my sister's, and the third my own. There is no communication between them, but they all open out into the same corridor. Do I make myself plain?"

"Perfectly so."

"The windows of the three rooms open out upon the lawn. That fatal night my sister came into my room because she was troubled by the smell of Dr. Roylott's cigar. She sat for some time, chatting about her approaching wedding. At eleven o'clock she rose to leave me, but she paused at the door and looked back.

" 'Tell me, Helen,' she said, 'have you ever heard anyone whistle in the dead of the night?'

" 'Never,' said I.

" 'I suppose that you could not possibly whistle, yourself, in your sleep?'

" 'Certainly not. But why?'

" 'Because during the last few nights I have always, about three in the morning, heard a low, clear whistle. I thought that I would just ask you whether you had heard it.'

" 'No, I have not. It must be those wretched gypsies.'

" 'Well, it is of no great consequence, at any rate.' She smiled back at me, closed my door, and a few moments later I heard her key turn in the lock."

"Indeed," said Holmes. "Was it your custom always to lock yourselves in at night?"

"Always."

"And why?"

"I think that I mentioned to you that the doctor kept a cheetah and a baboon. We had no feeling of security unless our doors were locked."

"Quite so. Pray proceed with your statement."

"I could not sleep that night. A vague feeling of impending misfortune impressed me. My sister and I, you will recollect, were twins, and you know how subtle are the links which bind two souls which are so closely allied. It was a wild night. The wind was howling outside, and the rain was beating and splashing against the

Tom Adams
'62

windows. Suddenly, amid all the hubbub of the gale, there burst forth the wild scream of a terrified woman. I knew that it was my sister's voice. I sprang from my bed, wrapped a shawl round me, and rushed to the door.

"As I entered the corridor, I seemed to hear a low whistle, such as my sister had described, and a few moments later a clanging sound, as if a mass of metal had fallen. As I ran down the passage, I saw that my sister's door was unlocked, and revolved slowly upon its hinges. I stared at it horror-stricken, not knowing what was about to issue from it. By the light of the corridor lamp I saw my sister appear at the opening, her face blanched with terror, her hands groping for help, her whole figure swaying to and fro like that of a drunkard.

"I ran to her and threw my arms around her, but at that moment her knees seemed to give way and she fell to the ground. She writhed as one who is in terrible pain, and her limbs were dreadfully convulsed. At first I thought that she had not recognized me, but as I bent over her she suddenly shrieked out in a voice which I shall never forget, 'Oh, Helen! It was the band! The speckled band!'

"There was something else which she would fain have said, and she stabbed with her finger into the air in the direction of the doctor's room, but a fresh convulsion seized her and choked her words. I rushed out, calling loudly for my stepfather, and I met him hastening from his room in his dressing gown. When he reached my sister's side she was unconscious, and though he poured brandy down her throat and sent for medical aid from the village, all efforts were in vain, for she slowly sank and died without having recovered her consciousness. Such was the dreadful end of my beloved sister."

"One moment," said Holmes, "are you sure about this whistle and metallic sound? Could you swear to it?"

"That was what the county coroner asked me at the inquiry. It is my strong impression that I heard it, and yet, among the crash of the gale and the creaking of an old house, I may possibly have been deceived."

"Was your sister dressed?"

"No, she was in her nightdress. In her right hand was found the charred stump of a match, and in her left a match box."

"Showing that she had struck a light and looked about her when the alarm took place. That is important. And what conclusions did the coroner come to?"

"He investigated the case with great care, for Dr. Roylott's conduct had long been notorious in the county, but he was unable to find any satisfactory cause of death. My evidence showed that the door had been fastened upon the inner side, and the windows were blocked by old-fashioned shutters with broad iron bars, which were secured every night.

"The walls were carefully sounded and were shown to be quite solid all round, and the flooring was also thoroughly examined, with the same result. The chimney is wide, but is barred up by four large staples. It is certain, therefore, that my sister was quite alone when she met her end. Besides, there were no marks of any violence upon her."

"How about poison?"

"The doctors examined her for it, but without success."

"Were there gypsies on the plantation at the time?"

"Yes, there are nearly always some there."

"Ah, and what did you gather from this allusion to a band—a speckled band?"

"Sometimes I have thought that it was merely the wild talk of delirium; sometimes that it may have referred to some band of people, perhaps to these very gypsies on the plantation. I do not know whether the spotted handkerchiefs which so many of them wear over their heads might have suggested the strange adjective which she used."

Holmes shook his head like a man who is far from being satisfied.

"These are very deep waters," said he; "pray go on with your narrative."

"Two years have passed since then, and my life has been until lately lonelier than ever. A month ago, however, a dear friend, whom I have known for many years, did me the honor to ask my hand in marriage and we are to be married in the spring.

"Two days ago some repairs were started in the west wing of the building, and my bedroom wall was pierced, so that I have had to move into the chamber in which my sister died, and to sleep in the very bed in which she slept. Imagine, then, my thrill of terror when last night, as I lay awake, thinking over her terrible fate, I suddenly heard in the silence of the night the low whistle which had been the herald of her own death. I sprang up and lit the lamp, but nothing was to be seen in the room.

"I was too shaken to go to bed again, however, so I dressed, and as soon as it was daylight I slipped out, got a dogcart at the Crown Inn, which is opposite, and drove to Leatherhead, from whence I have come on this morning with the one object of seeing you and asking your advice."

"You have done wisely," said my friend. "But have you told me all?"

"Why, what do you mean? What is it?"

For answer Holmes pushed back the frill of black lace which fringed the hand that lay upon our visitor's knee. Five little livid spots, the marks of four fingers and a thumb, were printed upon the white wrist.

"You have been cruelly used," said Holmes.

The lady colored deeply and covered over her injured wrist. "He is a hard man," she said, "and perhaps he hardly knows his own strength."

There was a long silence, during which Holmes leaned his chin upon his hands and stared into the crackling fire.

"This is a very deep business," he said at last. "There are a thousand details which I should desire to know before I decide upon our course of action. Yet we have not a moment to lose. If we were to come to Stoke Moran today, would it be possible for us to look over these rooms without the knowledge of your stepfather?"

"As it happens, he spoke of coming into town today upon some most important business. It is probable that he will be away all day."

"Excellent. You are not averse to this trip, Watson?"

"By no means."

"Then we shall both come. What are you going to do yourself?"

"I have one or two things which I would wish to do now that I am in town. But I shall return by the twelve o'clock train, so as to be there in time for your coming."

"And you may expect us early in the afternoon. I have myself some small business matters to attend to. Will you not wait and breakfast?"

"No, I must go. My heart is lightened already since I have confided my trouble to you. I shall look forward to seeing you again this afternoon." She dropped her thick black veil over her face and softly glided from the room.

"And what do you think of it all, Watson?" asked Sherlock Holmes, leaning back in his chair.

"It seems to me to be a most dark and sinister business."

"Dark enough and sinister enough."

"Yet if the lady is correct in saying that the flooring and walls are sound, and that the door, window, and chimney are impassable, then her sister must undoubtedly have been alone when she met her mysterious end."

"What becomes, then, of these nocturnal whistles, and what of the very peculiar words of the dying woman?" mused Holmes.

"I cannot think."

"When you combine the ideas of whistles at night, the presence of a band of gypsies who are on intimate terms with this old doctor, the fact that we have every reason to believe that the doctor has an interest in preventing his stepdaughter's marriage, the dying allusion to a band, and, finally, the fact that Miss Helen Stoner heard a metallic clang, which might have been caused by one of those metal bars that secured the shutters falling back into its place, I think that these factors all point to a theory that may help clear the mystery."

"But what, then, did the gypsies do?" I asked quickly.

"I cannot imagine," Holmes responded thoughtfully. "It is precisely for that reason that we are going to Stoke Moran this day. I want to see for myself whether there are any fatal objections to my theory. Only a spot investigation will tell me what I want to know— But what in the name of the devil!"

The ejaculation had been drawn from my companion by the fact that our door had been suddenly dashed open, and that a huge man had framed himself in the aperture. His costume was a peculiar mixture of the professional and of the agricultural, having a black top hat, a long frock coat, and a pair of high gaiters, with a hunting crop swinging in his hand. So tall was he that his hat actually brushed the crossbar of the doorway, and his breadth seemed to span it across from side to side. A large face, seared with a thousand wrinkles, burned yellow with the sun, and marked with every evil passion, was turned from one to the other of us, while his deep-set, bile-shot eyes, and his high, thin, fleshless nose, gave him somewhat the resemblance to a fierce old bird of prey.

"Which of you is Holmes?" asked this apparition.

"My name, sir; but you have the advantage of me," said my companion quietly.

"I am Dr. Grimesby Roylott, of Stoke Moran."

"Indeed, Doctor," said Holmes blandly. "Pray take a seat."

"I will do nothing of the kind. My stepdaughter has been here. I have traced her. What has she been saying to you?"

"It is a little cold for this time of year," said Holmes.

"What has she been saying to you?" screamed the old man furiously.

"But I have heard that the crocuses promise well," continued my companion imperturbably.

"Ha! You put me off, do you?" said our new visitor, taking a step forward and shaking his hunting crop. "I know you, you scoundrel! I have heard of you before. You are Holmes, the meddler."

My friend smiled.

"Holmes, the busybody!"

His smile broadened.

"Holmes, the Scotland Yard Jack-in-Office!"

Holmes chuckled heartily. "Your conversation is most entertaining," said he. "When you go out close the door, for there is a decided draught."

"I will go when I have said my say. Don't you dare to meddle with my affairs. I know that Miss Stoner has been here. I traced her! I am a dangerous man to fall foul of! See here." He stepped swiftly forward, seized the poker, and bent it into a curve with his huge brown hands.

"See that you keep yourself out of my grip," he snarled, and hurling the twisted poker into the fireplace he strode out of the room.

"He seems a very amiable person," said Holmes, laughing. "I am not quite so bulky, but if he had remained I might have shown him that my grip was not much more feeble than his own." As he spoke he picked up the steel poker and, with a sudden effort, straightened it out again.

"Fancy his having the insolence to confound[2] me with the official detective force! This incident gives zest to our investigation, however, and I only trust that our little friend will not suffer from her imprudence in allowing this brute to trace her. And now, Watson, we shall order breakfast, and afterwards I shall walk down to Doctors' Commons, where I hope to get some data which may help us in this matter."

It was nearly one o'clock when Sherlock Holmes returned from his excursion. He held in

---

2. ***confound . . . with,*** get me confused with.

his hand a sheet of blue paper, scrawled over with notes and figures.

"I have seen the will of the deceased wife," said he. "Each daughter can claim an income in case of marriage. It is evident, therefore, that if both girls had married, this beauty would have had a mere pittance, while even one of them would cripple him to a very serious extent. My morning's work has not been wasted, since it has proved that he has the very strongest motives for standing in the way of anything of the sort.

"And now, Watson, this is too serious for dawdling, especially as the old man is aware that we are interesting ourselves in his affairs; so if you are ready, we shall call a cab and drive to Waterloo. I should be very much obliged if you would slip your revolver into your pocket. An Eley's No. 2 is an excellent argument with gentlemen who can twist steel pokers into knots. That and a toothbrush are, I think, all that we need."

At Waterloo we were fortunate in catching a train for Leatherhead, where we hired a trap at the station inn and drove for four or five miles through the lovely Surrey lanes. It was a perfect day, with a bright sun and a few fleecy clouds in the heavens. The trees and wayside hedges were just throwing out their first green shoots, and the air was full of the pleasant smell of the moist earth. To me at least there was a strange contrast between the sweet promise of the spring and this sinister quest upon which we were engaged. My companion sat in the front of the trap, his arms folded, his hat pulled down over his eyes, and his chin sunk upon his breast, buried in the deepest thought. Suddenly, however, he started, tapped me on the shoulder, and pointed over the meadows.

"Look there!" said he.

A heavily timbered park stretched up in a gentle slope, thickening into a grove at the highest point. From amid the branches, there jutted out the gray gables and high rooftops of a very old mansion.

"Stoke Moran?" Holmes asked the driver.

"Yes, sir, that be the house of Dr. Grimesby Roylott," remarked the driver.

"There is some building going on there," said Holmes; "that is where we are going."

"There's the village," said the driver, pointing to a cluster of roofs some distance to the left; "but if you want to get to the house, you'll find it shorter to get over this stile, and go by the footpath over the fields. There it is, where the lady is walking."

"And the lady, I fancy, is Miss Stoner," observed Holmes, shading his eyes. "Yes, I think we had better do as you suggest."

We got off, paid our fare, and the trap rattled back on its way to Leatherhead.

"I thought it as well," said Holmes as we climbed the stile, "that this fellow should think we had come here as architects, or on some definite business. It may stop his gossip. Good afternoon, Miss Stoner. You see that we have been as good as our word."

Our client of the morning had hurried forward to meet us with a face which spoke her joy. "I have been waiting so eagerly for you," she cried, shaking hands with us warmly. "All has turned out splendidly. Dr. Roylott has gone to town, and it is unlikely that he will be back before evening."

"We have had the pleasure of making the doctor's acquaintance," said Holmes, and in a few words he sketched out what had occurred. Miss Stoner turned white to the lips as she listened.

"Good heavens!" she cried, "he has followed me, then."

"So it appears."

"He is so cunning that I never know when I am safe from him. What will he say when he returns?"

"He must guard himself, for he may find that there is someone more cunning than himself upon his track. You must lock yourself up from him tonight. If he is violent, we shall take you away to your aunt's at Harrow. Now, we must make the best use of our time, so kindly take us at once to the rooms which we are to examine."

The building was of gray, lichen-blotched stone, with a high central portion and two curving wings, like the claws of a crab, thrown out on each side. In one of these wings the windows were broken and blocked with wooden boards, while the roof was partly caved in, a picture of ruin. The central portion was in little better repair, but the right-hand block was comparatively modern, and the blinds in the windows, with the blue smoke curling up from the chimneys, showed that this was where the family resided. Some scaffolding had been erected against the end wall, and the stone work had been broken into, but there were no signs of any workmen at the moment of our visit. Holmes walked slowly up and down the ill-trimmed lawn and examined with deep attention the outsides of the windows.

"This, I take it, belongs to the room in which you used to sleep, the center one to your sister's, and the one next to the main building to Dr. Roylott's chamber?"

"Exactly so. But I am now sleeping in the middle one."

"Pending the alterations, as I understand. By the way, there does not seem to be any very pressing need for repairs at that end wall."

"There were none. I believe that it was an excuse to move me from my room."

"Ah! that is suggestive. Now, on the other side of this narrow wing runs the corridor from which these three rooms open. There are windows in it, of course?"

"Yes, but very small ones. Too narrow for anyone to pass through."

"As you both locked your doors at night, your rooms were unapproachable from that side. Now, would you have the kindness to go into your room and bar your shutters?"

Miss Stoner did so, and Holmes, after a careful examination through the open window, endeavoured in every way to force the shutter open, but without success. There was no slit through which a knife could be passed to raise the bar. Then with his lens he tested the hinges, but they were of solid iron, built firmly into the massive masonry. "Hum!" said he, scratching his chin in some perplexity, "my theory certainly presents some difficulties. No one could pass through these shutters if they were bolted. Well, we shall see if the inside throws any light upon the matter."

A small side door led into the whitewashed corridor from which the three bedrooms opened. Holmes refused to examine the third chamber, so we passed at once to the second, that in which Miss Stoner was now sleeping, and in which her sister had met with her fate. It was a homey little room, with a low ceiling and a gaping fireplace, after the fashion of old country houses. A brown chest of drawers stood in one corner, a narrow white-counterpaned bed in another, and a dressing table on the left-hand side of the window. These articles, with two small wickerwork chairs, made up all the furniture in the room save for a square of Wilton carpet in the center. The boards round and the paneling of the walls were of brown, worm-eaten oak, so old and discolored that it may have dated from the original building of the house. Holmes drew one of the chairs into a corner and sat silent, while his eyes traveled round and round and up and down, taking in every detail of the room.

"Where does that bell communicate with?" he asked at last, pointing to a thick bell-rope which hung down beside the bed, the tassel actually lying upon the pillow.

"It goes to the housekeeper's room."

"It looks newer than the other things?"

"Yes, it was only put there a couple of years ago."

"Your sister asked for it, I suppose?"

"No, I never heard of her using it. We used always to get what we wanted for ourselves."

"Indeed, it seemed unnecessary to put so nice a bell-pull there. You will excuse me for a few minutes while I satisfy myself as to this floor." He threw himself down upon his face with his lens in his hand and crawled swiftly backward and forward, examining minutely the cracks between the boards. Then he did the same with the woodwork with which the chamber was paneled. Finally he walked over to the bed and spent some time in staring at it and in running his eye up and down the wall. Finally he took the bell-rope in his hand and gave it a brisk tug.

"Why, it's a dummy," said he.

"Won't it ring?"

"No, it is not even attached to a wire. This is very interesting. You can see now that it is fastened to a hook just above where the little opening for the ventilator is."

"How very absurd! I never noticed that before."

"Very strange!" muttered Holmes, pulling at the rope. "There are one or two very singular points about this room. For example, what a fool a builder must be to open a ventilator into another room, when, with the same trouble, he might have placed the ventilator so as to communicate with the outside air!"

"That is also quite modern," said the lady.

"Done about the same time as the bell-rope?" remarked Holmes.

"Yes, there were several little changes carried out about that time."

"They seem to have been of a most interesting character—dummy bell-ropes, and ventilators which do not ventilate. With your permission, Miss Stoner, we shall now carry our researches into the inner apartment."

Dr. Grimesby Roylott's chamber was larger than that of his stepdaughter, but was as plainly furnished. A camp bed, a small wooden shelf full of books, mostly of a technical character, an armchair beside the bed, a plain wooden chair against the wall, a round table, and a large iron safe were the principal things which met the eye. Holmes walked slowly round and examined each of them with the keenest interest.

"What's in here?" he asked, tapping the safe.

"My stepfather's business papers."

"There isn't a cat in it, for example?"

"No. What a strange idea!"

"Well, look at this!" He took up a small saucer of milk which stood on the top of it.

"No; we don't keep a cat. But there is a cheetah and a baboon."

"Ah, yes, of course! Well, a cheetah is just a big cat, and yet a saucer of milk does not go very far in satisfying its wants, I daresay. There is one point which I should wish to determine." He squatted down in front of the wooden chair and examined the seat of it with the greatest attention.

"Thank you. That is quite settled," said he, rising and putting his lens in his pocket. "Hello! Here is something interesting!"

The object which had caught his eye was a small dog lash hung on one corner of the bed. The lash, however, was curled upon itself and tied so as to make a loop of whipcord.

"What do you make of that, Watson?"

"It's a common enough lash. But I don't know why it should be tied."

"That is not quite so common, is it? Ah, me! It's a wicked world, and when a clever man turns his brains to crime it is the worst of all. I think that I have seen enough now, Miss Stoner, and with your permission we shall walk out upon the lawn."

I had never seen my friend's face so grim or his brow so dark as it was when we turned from the scene of this investigation. We had walked several times up and down the lawn, neither Miss Stoner nor myself liking to break in upon his thoughts before he roused himself from his reverie.

"It is very essential, Miss Stoner," said he, "that you should absolutely follow my advice in every respect."

"I shall most certainly do so."

"The matter is too serious for any hesitation. Your life may depend upon your compliance."

"I assure you that I am in your hands."

"In the first place, both my friend and I must spend the night in your room."

Both Miss Stoner and I gazed at him in astonishment.

"Yes, it must be so. Let me explain. I believe that that is the village inn over there?"

"Yes, that is the Crown," answered Miss Stoner.

"Very good. Your windows would be visible from there?"

"Certainly."

"You must confine yourself to your room on pretense of a headache when your stepfather comes back. Then when you hear him retire for the night, you must open the shutters of your window, undo the hasp, put your lamp there as a signal to us, and then withdraw quietly with everything which you are likely to want into the room which you used to occupy."

"But what will you do?"

"We shall spend the night in your room, and we shall investigate the cause of this noise which has disturbed you."

"I believe, Mr. Holmes, that you have already made up your mind," said Miss Stoner, laying her hand upon my companion's sleeve.

"Perhaps I have."

"Then, for pity's sake, tell me what was the cause of my sister's death."

"I should prefer to have clearer proofs before I speak."

"You can at least tell me whether my own thought is correct, and if she died from some sudden fright."

"No, I do not think so. I think that there was probably some more tangible cause. And now, Miss Stoner, we must leave you, for if Dr. Roylott returned and saw us our journey would be in vain. Good-by, and be brave; for if you will do what I have told you, you may rest assured that we shall soon drive away the dangers that threaten you."

Sherlock Holmes and I had no difficulty in engaging a bedroom and sitting room at the Crown Inn. They were on the upper floor, and from our window we could command a view of the avenue gate, and of the inhabited wing of Stoke Moran Manor House. At dusk we saw Dr. Grimesby Roylott drive past, his huge form looming up beside the little figure of the lad who drove him. The boy had some slight difficulty in undoing the heavy iron gates, and we heard the hoarse roar of the doctor's voice and saw the fury with which he shook his clenched fists at him. The trap drove on, and a few minutes later we saw a sudden light spring up among the trees as the lamp was lit in one of the sitting rooms.

"Do you know, Watson," said Holmes as we sat together in the gathering darkness, "I have really some scruples as to taking you tonight. There is a distinct element of danger."

"Can I be of assistance?"

"Your presence might be invaluable."

"Then I shall certainly come."

"It is very kind of you."

"You speak of danger. You have evidently seen more in these rooms than was visible to me."

"No, but I fancy that I may have deduced a little more. I imagine that you saw all that I did."

"I saw nothing remarkable save the bell-rope, and what purpose that could answer I confess is more than I can imagine."

"You saw the ventilator, too?"

"Yes, but I do not think that it is such a very unusual thing to have a small opening between two rooms. It was so small that a rat could hardly pass through."

"I knew that we should find a ventilator before ever we came to Stoke Moran."

"My dear Holmes!"

"Oh, yes, I did. You remember in her statement she said that her sister could smell Dr. Roylott's cigar. Now, of course that suggested at once that there must be a communication between the two rooms. It could only be a small one, or it would have been remarked upon at the coroner's inquiry. I deduced a ventilator."

"But what harm can there be in that?"

"Well, there is at least a curious coincidence of dates. A ventilator is made, a cord is hung, and a lady who sleeps in the bed dies. Does not that strike you?"

"I cannot as yet see any connection."

"Did you observe anything very peculiar about that bed?"

"No."

"It was clamped to the floor. Did you ever see a bed fastened like that before?"

"I cannot say that I have," I acknowledged.

"The lady could not move her bed. It must always be in the same relative position to the ventilator and to the rope—for so we may call it, since it was clearly never meant for a bell-pull."

"Holmes," I cried, "I seem to see dimly what you are hinting at. We are only just in time to prevent some subtle and horrible crime."

"Subtle enough and horrible enough. When a doctor does go wrong he is the first of criminals. He has nerve and he has knowledge. Palmer and Pritchard were among the heads of their profession. This man strikes even deeper, but I think, Watson, that we shall be able to strike deeper still. But we shall have horrors enough before the night is over; for goodness' sake let us have a quiet pipe and turn our minds for a few hours to something more cheerful."

About nine o'clock the light among the trees was extinguished, and all was dark in the direction of the Manor House. Two hours passed slowly away, and then, suddenly, just at the stroke of eleven, a single bright light shone out right in front of us.

"That is our signal," said Holmes, springing to his feet; "it comes from the middle window."

As we passed out he exchanged a few words with the landlord, explaining that we were going on a late visit to an acquaintance, and that it was possible that we might spend the night there. A moment later we were out on the dark road, a chill wind blowing in our faces, and one yellow light twinkling in front of us through the gloom to guide us on our somber errand.

There was little difficulty in entering the grounds, for unrepaired breaches gaped in the old park wall. Making our way among the trees, we reached the lawn, crossed it, and were about to enter through the window when out from a clump of laurel bushes there darted what seemed to be a hideous and distorted child, who threw itself upon the grass with writhing limbs and then ran swiftly across the lawn into the darkness.

"Heavens!" I whispered; "did you see it?"

Holmes was for the moment as startled as I. His hand closed like a vise upon my wrist in his agitation. Then he broke into a low laugh and put his lips to my ear.

"It is a nice household," he murmured. "That is the baboon."

I had forgotten the strange pets which the doctor affected. There was a cheetah, too; perhaps we might find it upon our shoulders at any moment. I confess that I felt easier in my mind when, after following Holmes's example and slipping off my shoes, I found myself inside the bedroom. My companion noiselessly closed the shutters, moved the lamp onto the table, and cast his eyes round the room. All was as we had seen it in the daytime. Then creeping up to me and making a trumpet of his hand, he whispered into my ear so gently that it was all that I could do to distinguish the words, "The least sound would be fatal to our plans."

I nodded to show that I had heard.

"We must sit without light. He would see it through the ventilator."

I nodded again.

"Do not go asleep; your very life may depend upon it. Have your pistol ready in case we should need it. I will sit on the side of the bed, and you in that chair."

I took out my revolver and laid it on the table.

Holmes had brought up a long thin cane, and this he placed upon the bed beside him. By it he laid the box of matches and the stump of a candle. Then he turned down the lamp, and we were left in darkness.

How shall I ever forget that dreadful vigil? I could not hear a sound, not even the drawing of breath, and yet I knew that my companion sat open-eyed, within a few feet of me, in the same state of nervous tension in which I was myself. The shutters cut off the least ray of light, and we waited in absolute darkness. From outside came the occasional cry of a night bird, and once at our very window a long-drawn catlike whine, which told us that the cheetah was indeed at liberty. Far away we could hear the deep tones of the parish clock, which boomed out every quarter of an hour. How long they seemed, those quarters! Twelve struck, and one and two and three, and still we sat waiting silently for whatever might befall.

Suddenly there was the momentary gleam of a light up in the direction of the ventilator, which vanished immediately, but was succeeded by a strong smell of burning oil and heated metal. Someone in the next room had lit a dark-lantern. I heard a gentle sound of movement, and then all was silent once more, though the smell grew stronger. For half an hour I sat with straining ears. Then suddenly another sound became audible—a very gentle, soothing sound, like that of a small jet of steam escaping continually from a kettle. The instant that we heard it, Holmes sprang from the bed, struck a match, and lashed furiously with his cane at the bell-pull.

"You see it, Watson?" he yelled. "You see it?"

But I saw nothing. At the moment when Holmes struck the light I heard a low, clear whistle, but the sudden glare flashing into my weary eyes made it impossible for me to tell what it was at which my friend lashed so savagely. I could, however, see that his face was deadly pale and filled with horror and loathing.

He had ceased to strike and was gazing up at the ventilator when suddenly there broke from the silence of the night the most horrible cry to which I have ever listened. It swelled up louder and louder, a hoarse yell of pain and fear and anger all mingled in the one dreadful shriek. They say that way down in the village, and even in the distant parsonage, that cry raised the sleepers from their beds. It struck cold to our hearts, and I stood gazing at Holmes, and he at me, until the last echoes of it had died away into the silence from which it rose.

"What can it mean?" I gasped.

"It means that it is all over," Holmes answered. "And perhaps, after all, it is for the best. Take your pistol, and we will enter Dr. Roylott's room."

With a grave face he lit the lamp and led the way down the corridor. Twice he struck at the chamber door without any reply from within. Then he turned the handle and entered, I at his heels, with the cocked pistol in my hand.

It was a singular sight which met my eyes. On the table stood a dark-lantern with the shutter half open, throwing a brilliant beam of light upon the iron safe, the door of which was ajar. Beside this table, on the wooden chair, sat Dr. Grimesby Roylott, clad in a long gray dressing gown, his bare ankles protruding beneath, and his feet thrust into red heelless Turkish slippers. Across his lap lay the short stock with the long lash which we had noticed during the day. His chin was cocked upward and his eyes were fixed in a dreadful, rigid stare at the corner of the ceiling. Round his brow he had a peculiar yellow band, with brownish speckles, which seemed to be bound tightly round his head. As we entered he made neither sound nor motion.

"The band! The speckled band!" whispered Holmes.

I took a step forward. In an instant his strange headgear began to move, and there reared itself from his hair the squat diamond-shaped head and puffed neck of a loathsome serpent.

"It is a swamp adder!" cried Holmes, "the deadliest snake in India. He has died within ten seconds of being bitten. Violence does, in truth, recoil upon the violent, and the schemer falls into the pit which he digs for another. Let us thrust this creature back into its den, and we can then remove Miss Stoner to some place of shelter and let the county police know what has happened."

As he spoke he drew the dog whip swiftly from the dead man's lap, and throwing the noose round the reptile's neck he drew it from its horrid perch and, carrying it at arm's length, threw it into the iron safe, which he closed upon it.

Such are the true facts of the death of Dr. Grimesby Roylott, of Stoke Moran. It is not necessary that I should prolong a narrative which has already run to too great a length by telling how we broke the sad news to the terrified girl, how we conveyed her by the morning train to the care of her good aunt at Harrow, of how the slow process of official inquiry came to the conclusion that the doctor met his fate while indiscreetly playing with a dangerous pet. The little which I had yet to learn of the case was told me by Sherlock Holmes as we traveled back next day.

"I had," said he, "come to an entirely erroneous conclusion; which shows, my dear Watson, how dangerous it always is to reason from insufficient data. The presence of the gypsies, and the word *band,* used by the poor girl, no doubt to explain that which she had caught a hurried glimpse of by the light of her match, were sufficient to put me upon an entirely wrong scent. I can only claim the merit that I instantly reconsidered my position when it became clear to me that whatever danger threatened an occupant of the room could not come in from either the door or the window. I then sought other evidence.

"My attention was speedily drawn, as I have already remarked to you, to this ventilator, and to the bell-rope which hung down to the bed. The discovery that this was a dummy, and that the bed was clamped to the floor, instantly gave rise to the suspicion that the rope was there as a bridge for something passing through the hole and coming to the bed. The idea of a snake instantly occurred to me, and when I coupled it with my knowledge that the doctor was furnished with a supply of creatures from India, I felt that I was probably on the right track.

"The idea of using a form of poison which could not possibly be discovered by any chemical test was just such a one as would occur to a clever and ruthless man who had had an Eastern training. The rapidity with which such a poison would take effect would also, from his point of view, be an advantage. It would be a sharp-eyed coroner, indeed, who could distinguish the two little dark punctures which would show where the poison fangs had done their work.

"Then I thought of the whistle. Of course he must recall the snake before the morning light revealed it to the victim. He had trained it, probably by the use of the milk which we saw, to return to him when summoned. He would put it through this ventilator at the hour that he thought best, with the certainty that it would crawl down the rope and land on the bed. It might or might not bite the occupant, perhaps she might escape every night for a week, but sooner or later she must fall a victim.

"I had come to these conclusions before ever I had entered his room. An inspection of his chair showed me that he had been in the habit of standing on it, which of course would be necessary in order that he should reach the ventilator. The sight of the safe, the saucer of milk, and the loop of whipcord were enough to finally dispel any doubts which may have remained. The metallic clang heard by Miss Stoner was obviously caused by her stepfather hastily closing the door of his safe upon its terrible occupant. Having once made up my mind, you know the steps which I took in order to put the matter to the proof. I heard the creature hiss, as I have no doubt that you did also, and I instantly lit the light and attacked it."

"With the result of driving it through the ventilator."

"And also with the result of causing it to turn upon its master at the other side. Some of the blows of my cane came home and roused its snakish temper, so that it flew upon the first person it saw. In this way, I am no doubt indirectly responsible for Dr. Grimesby Roylott's death, and I cannot say that it is likely to weigh very heavily upon my conscience."

Discussion

1. (a) Who is the narrator of the story? **(b)** What is his relationship to Sherlock Holmes?

2. What changes in Helen Stoner's life took place in the month prior to her visit to Holmes?

3. (a) Why did Miss Stoner's stepfather go to India? **(b)** Why did he return?

4. (a) What were the terms of Mrs. Roylott's will? **(b)** Describe the behavior and interests of Dr. Roylott upon his return to Stoke Moran.

5. (a) Describe how Julia, Helen's twin sister, spent the last evening of her life. **(b)** With what words and gestures did the young woman die? **(c)** What was the coroner's verdict?

6. (a) How does Holmes react to Dr. Roylott's visit? **(b)** After that visit, how—and with what results—does Holmes spend the morning? **(c)** How does Holmes spend the afternoon at Stoke Moran? **(d)** What arrangement for the evening do he and Watson make with Helen Stoner?

Application

Inferences

1. Describe the series of deductions that Holmes makes about Helen Stoner's method of traveling on the morning she calls at his house.

2. Explain the significance of each of the following in Holmes's solving of the case: a bell rope, a saucer of milk, bedroom shutters, a dog lash, a ventilator, a bed, a cane, a whistle, a clanging sound.

3. (a) How had the word *band* almost led Holmes to an erroneous conclusion? **(b)** What evidence had prompted him to reconsider his position?

4. Readers often are called upon to make inferences as they read, drawing conclusions from the information presented by the author. **(a)** What can you infer about Watson's character and personality? **(b)** In what ways are he and Holmes alike? In what ways are they different?

Composition

Carefully review the plots, settings, and characters of the two mystery and two detective stories you have read in this unit.

Then write a short paper supporting one of the following statements:

1. Mystery and detective stories seem much alike.

2. Detective stories appear clearly different from mystery stories.

Sir Arthur Conan Doyle 1859–1930

Arthur Conan Doyle received his medical degree at Edinburgh University in 1881. After working for a time as a ship's doctor, he attempted to establish a private practice. While waiting for patients who never came, he started writing, combining his interests in detection and science to create Sherlock Holmes. This famous character is based on the author's memories of Dr. Joseph Bell, a surgeon noted for his diagnosis of occupation and character as well as of disease. *A Study in Scarlet* was published in 1887, followed by a series of short stories (later published as *The Adventures of Sherlock Holmes,* 1892) and, in 1890, *The Sign of Four.* Although Conan Doyle wished to be remembered principally for his political works and for his carefully researched historical novels, the Sherlock Holmes stories continue to overshadow all his other works.

Comment: The Incomparable Sherlock Holmes

Sherlock Holmes is the most famous of literary detectives, one whose followers throughout the world are legion. In the United States alone, one can find over one hundred and twenty local and regional Sherlock Holmes societies, dedicated to keeping alive the memory of the master English sleuth. Not counted among these is the Baker Street Irregulars, a national group located in New York City, with a membership of six hundred and with forty local affiliates of its own. Founded in 1934, the Baker Street Irregulars hosts an annual dinner and awards Irregular Shillings to members who, over a period of years, have shown serious interest in the many cases of their hero.

Holmes's enormous following is deserved. Based on Dr. Joseph Bell, a diagnostician who was one of Conan Doyle's instructors when the writer was a medical student, the detective is a remarkable creation. Brilliant and eccentric, he possesses encyclopedic knowledge, excellent powers of observation, and fine deductive ability, all of which in combination enable him to formulate his notable logical conclusions. Holmes became the model for the literary detective, and his cases set the pattern for the mystery story as a distinct literary form.

About the methods both he and his creation employ, Conan Doyle wrote:

People have often asked me whether I knew the end of a Holmes story before I started it. Of course I do. One could not possibly steer a course if one did not know one's destination. The first thing is to get your idea. Having got that key idea, one's next task is to conceal it and lay emphasis upon everything which can make for a different explanation. Holmes, however, can see all the fallacies of the alternatives, and arrives more or less dramatically at the true solution by steps which he can describe and justify. He shows his powers by what the South Americans now call "Sherlockholmitos," which means clever little deductions which have nothing to do with the matter on hand, but impress the reader with a general sense of powers.

Doyle confessed that he, himself, failed to utilize regularly the powers he gave so amply to Holmes: ". . . I must admit that in ordinary life I am by no means observant and that I have to throw myself into an artificial frame of mind before I can weigh evidence and anticipate the sequence of events."

Conan Doyle wrote sixty stories featuring Sherlock Holmes. But more than that number, including many parodies, have been written by other authors. Many have been the names (and guises) under which Holmes has appeared in works by others—among them, Herlock Sholmes, Holmock Shears, Picklock Holes, Shylock Homes, and Shamrock Jolnes. Moreover, Holmes has long been memoralized on film. The most beloved and enduring of all screen detectives, he has been portrayed by more actors than has any other figure from literature. In archives, one can find well over a hundred films about Holmes, including British, French, German, and American versions of his most celebrated case, *The Hound of the Baskervilles.*

The United States entered World War II in 1941. Between that time and the end of the war in 1945, Universal Studios made a number of movies featuring Sherlock Holmes in wartime settings. To justify wrenching the hero from his usual haunts and his period in history, the studio stated in the credits that "Sherlock Holmes is ageless, invincible, and unchanging. In solving problems of the present day he remains—as ever—the supreme master of deductive reasoning."

FANTASY

See **THEME** Handbook of Literary Terms

The Magic Shop

H. G. Wells

I stared round to see the door of the magic shop, and behold, it was not there!

I had seen the Magic Shop from afar several times; I had passed it once or twice, a shop window of alluring little objects, magic balls, magic hens, wonderful cones, ventriloquist dolls, the material of the basket trick, packs of cards that *looked* all right, and all that sort of thing; but never had I thought of going in until one day, almost without warning, Gip hauled me by my finger right up to the window, and so conducted himself that there was nothing for it but to take him in. I had not thought the place was there, to tell the truth—a modest-sized frontage in Regent Street, between the picture shop and the place where the chicks run about just out of patent incubators—but there it was sure enough. I had fancied it was down nearer the Circus, or round the corner in Oxford Street, or even in Holborn; always over the way and a little inaccessible it had been, with something of the mirage in its position; but here it was now quite indisputably, and the fat end of Gip's pointing finger made a noise upon the glass.

"If I was rich," said Gip, dabbing a finger at the Disappearing Egg, "I'd buy myself that. And that"—which was The Crying Baby, Very Human—"and that," which was a mystery, and called, so a neat card asserted, "Buy One and Astonish Your Friends."

"Anything," said Gip, "will disappear under one of those cones. I have read about it in a book.

"And there, dadda, is the Vanishing Halfpenny—only they've put it this way up so's we can't see how it's done."

Gip, dear boy, inherits his mother's breeding, and he did not propose to enter the shop or worry in any way; only, you know, quite unconsciously he lugged my finger doorward, and he made his interest clear.

"That," he said, and pointed to the Magic Bottle.

"If you had that?" I said; at which promising inquiry he looked up with a sudden radiance.

"I could show it to Jessie," he said, thoughtful as ever of others.

"It's less than a hundred days to your birthday, Gibbles," I said, and laid my hand on the doorhandle.

Gip made no answer, but his grip tightened on my finger, and so we came into the shop.

It was no common shop this; it was a magic shop, and all the prancing precedence Gip would have taken in the matter of mere toys was wanting. He left the burthen of the conversation to me. It was a little, narrow shop, not very well lit, and the doorbell pinged again with a plaintive note as we closed it behind us. For a moment or so we were alone and could glance about us. There was a tiger in *papier-mâché* on the glass case that covered the low counter—a

---

"The Magic Shop" from *Twelve Stories and a Dream* by H. G. Wells. Reprinted by permission of the Executors of the Estate of H. G. Wells.

grave, kind-eyed tiger that waggled his head in a methodical manner; there were several crystal spheres, a china hand holding magic cards, a stock of magic fishbowls in various sizes, and an immodest magic hat that shamelessly displayed its springs. On the floor were magic mirrors; one to draw you out long and thin, one to swell your head and vanish your legs, and one to make you short and fat like a draught; and while we were laughing at these the shopman, as I suppose, came in.

At any rate, there he was behind the counter—a curious, sallow, dark man, with one ear larger than the other and a chin like the toe-cap of a boot.

"What can we have the pleasure?" he said, spreading his long, magic fingers on the glass case; and so with a start we were aware of him.

"I want," I said, "to buy my little boy a few simple tricks."

"Legerdemain?"[1] he asked. "Mechanical? Domestic?"

"Anything amusing," said I.

"Um!" said the shopman, and scratched his head for a moment as if thinking. Then, quite distinctly, he drew from his head a glass ball. "Something in this way?" he said, and held it out.

The action was unexpected. I had seen the trick done at entertainments endless times before—it's part of the common stock of conjurers—but I had not expected it here. "That's good," I said, with a laugh.

"Isn't it?" said the shopman.

Gip stretched out his disengaged hand to take this object and found merely a blank palm.

"It's in your pocket," said the shopman, and there it was!

"How much will that be?" I asked.

"We make no charge for glass balls," said the shopman politely. "We get them"—he picked one out of his elbow as he spoke—"free." He produced another from the back of his neck, and laid it beside its predecessor on the counter. Gip regarded his glass ball sagely, then directed a look of inquiry at the two on the counter, and finally brought his round-eyed scrutiny to the shopman, who smiled. "You may have those too," said the shopman, "and, if you *don't* mind, one from my mouth. *So!*"

Gip counselled me mutely for a moment, and then in a profound silence put away the four balls, resumed my reassuring finger, and nerved himself for the next event.

"We get all our smaller tricks in that way," the shopman remarked.

I laughed in the manner of one who subscribes to a jest. "Instead of going to the wholesale shop," I said. "Of course, it's cheaper."

"In a way," the shopman said. "Though we pay in the end. But not so heavily—as people suppose. . . . Our larger tricks, and our daily provisions and all the other things we want, we get out of that hat. . . . And you know, sir, if you'll excuse my saying it, there *isn't* a wholesale shop, not for Genuine Magic goods, sir. I don't know if you noticed our inscription—the Genuine Magic Shop." He drew a business card from his cheek and handed it to me. "Genuine," he said, with his finger on the word, and added, "There is absolutely no deception, sir."

He seemed to be carrying out the joke pretty thoroughly, I thought.

He turned to Gip with a smile of remarkable affability. "You, you know, are the Right Sort of Boy."

I was surprised at his knowing that, because, in the interests of discipline, we keep it rather a secret even at home; but Gip received it in unflinching silence, keeping a steadfast eye on him.

"It's only the Right Sort of Boy gets through that doorway."

And, as if by way of illustration, there came a rattling at the door, and a squeaking little voice could be faintly heard. "Nyar! I *warn* 'a go in there, dadda, I *warn* 'a go in there. Ny-a-a-ah!" and then the accents of a downtrodden parent, urging consolations and propitiations. "It's locked, Edward," he said.

1. ***legerdemain*** (lej′ ər də mān′), sleight of hand, conjuring tricks.

"But it isn't," said I.

"It is, sir," said the shopman, "always—for that sort of child," and as he spoke we had a glimpse of the other youngster, a little, white face, pallid from sweet-eating and over-sapid[2] food, and distorted by evil passions, a ruthless little egotist, pawing at the enchanted pane. "It's no good, sir," said the shopman, as I moved, with my natural helpfulness, doorward, and presently the spoilt child was carried off howling.

"How do you manage that?" I said, breathing a little more freely.

"Magic!" said the shopman, with a careless wave of the hand, and behold! sparks of colored fire flew out of his fingers and vanished into the shadows of the shop.

"You were saying," he said, addressing himself to Gip, "before you came in, that you would like one of our 'Buy One and Astonish your Friends' boxes?"

Gip, after a gallant effort, said, "Yes."

"It's in your pocket."

And leaning over the counter—he really had an extraordinarily long body—this amazing person produced the article in the customary conjurer's manner. "Paper," he said, and took a sheet out of the empty hat with the springs; "string," and behold his mouth was a string-box, from which he drew an unending thread, which when he had tied his parcel he bit off—and, it seemed to me, swallowed the ball of string. And then he lit a candle at the nose of one of the ventriloquist's dummies, stuck one of his fingers (which had become sealing-wax red) into the flame, and so sealed the parcel. "Then there was the Disappearing Egg," he remarked, and produced one from within my coat breast and packed it, and also The Crying Baby, Very Human. I handed each parcel to Gip as it was ready, and he clasped them to his chest.

He said very little, but his eyes were eloquent; the clutch of his arms was eloquent. He was the playground of unspeakable emotions. These, you know, were *real* Magics.

Then, with a start, I discovered something moving about in my hat—something soft and jumpy. I whipped it off, and a ruffled pigeon—no doubt a confederate—dropped out and ran on the counter, and went, I fancy, into a cardboard box behind the *papier-mâché* tiger.

"Tut, tut!" said the shopman, dexterously relieving me of my headdress; "careless bird, and—as I live—nesting!"

He shook my hat, and shook out into his extended hand two or three eggs, a large marble, a watch, about a half-a-dozen of the inevitable glass balls, and then crumpled, crinkled paper, more and more and more, talking all the time of the way in which people neglect to brush their hats *inside* as well as out, politely, of course, but with a certain personal application. "All sorts of things accumulate, sir. . . . Not *you,* of course, in particular. . . . Nearly every customer. . . . Astonishing what they carry about with them. . . ." The crumpled paper rose and billowed on the counter more and more and more, until he was nearly hidden from us, until he was altogether hidden, and still his voice went on and on. "We none of us know what the fair semblance of a human being may conceal, sir. Are we all then no better than brushed exteriors, whited sepulchres——"

His voice stopped—exactly like when you hit a neighbor's gramophone with a well-aimed brick, the same instant silence, and the rustle of the paper stopped, and everything was still. . . .

"Have you done with my hat?" I said, after an interval.

There was no answer.

I stared at Gip, and Gip stared at me, and there were our distortions in the magic mirrors, looking very rum,[3] and grave, and quiet. . . .

"I think we'll go now," I said. "Will you tell me how much all this comes to? . . .

"I say," I said, on a rather louder note, "I want the bill; and my hat, please."

It might have been a sniff from behind the paper pile. . . .

"Let's look behind the counter, Gip," I said. "He's making fun of us."

---

2. ***over-sapid*** (sap′əd), highly seasoned.
3. ***rum,*** odd, strange.

I led Gip round the head-wagging tiger, and what do you think there was behind the counter? No one at all! Only my hat on the floor, and a common conjurer's lop-eared white rabbit lost in meditation, and looking as stupid and crumpled as only a conjurer's rabbit can do. I resumed my hat, and the rabbit lolloped a lollop or so out of my way.

"Dadda!" said Gip, in a guilty whisper.

"What is it, Gip?" said I.

"I *do* like this shop, dadda."

"So should I," I said to myself, "if the counter wouldn't suddenly extend itself to shut one off from the door." But I didn't call Gip's attention to that. "Pussy!" he said, with a hand out to the rabbit as it came lolloping past us; "Pussy, do Gip a magic!" and his eyes followed it as it squeezed through a door I had certainly not remarked a moment before. Then this door opened wider, and the man with one ear larger than the other appeared again. He was smiling still, but his eye met mine with something between amusement and defiance. "You'd like to see our showroom, sir," he said, with an innocent suavity. Gip tugged my finger forward. I glanced at the counter and met the shopman's eye again. I was beginning to think the magic just a little too genuine. "We haven't *very* much time," I said. But somehow we were inside the showroom before I could finish that.

"All goods of the same quality," said the shopman, rubbing his flexible hands together, "and that is the Best. Nothing in the place that isn't genuine Magic, and warranted thoroughly rum. Excuse me, sir!"

I felt him pull at something that clung to my coatsleeve, and then I saw he held a little, wriggling red demon by the tail—the little creature bit and fought and tried to get at his hand and in a moment he tossed it carelessly behind a counter. No doubt the thing was only an image of twisted India rubber, but for the moment——! And his gesture was exactly that of a man who handles some petty biting bit of vermin. I glanced at Gip, but Gip was looking at a magic rocking horse. I was glad he hadn't seen the thing. "I say," I said, in an undertone, and indicating Gip and the red demon with my eyes, "you haven't many things like *that* about, have you?"

"None of ours! Probably brought it with you," said the shopman—also in an undertone, and with a more dazzling smile than ever. "Astonishing what people *will* carry about with them unawares!" And then to Gip, "Do you see anything you fancy here?"

There were many things that Gip fancied there.

He turned to this astonishing tradesman with mingled confidence and respect. "Is that a Magic Sword?" he said.

"A Magic Toy Sword. It neither bends, breaks, nor cuts the fingers. It renders the bearer invincible in battle against anyone under eighteen. Half-a-crown to seven and sixpence, according to size. These panoplies on cards are for juvenile knights-errant and very useful—shield of safety, sandals of swiftness, helmet of invisibility."

"Oh, daddy!" gasped Gip.

I tried to find out what they cost, but the shopman did not heed me. He had got Gip now; he had got him away from my finger; he had embarked upon the exposition of all his confounded stock, and nothing was going to stop him. Presently I saw with a qualm of distrust and something very like jealousy that Gip had hold of this person's finger as usually he has hold of mine. No doubt the fellow was interesting, I thought, and had an interestingly faked lot of stuff, really *good* faked stuff, still——

I wandered after them, saying very little, but keeping an eye on this prestidigital[4] fellow. After all, Gip was enjoying it. And no doubt when the time came to go we should be able to go quite easily.

It was a long, rambling place, that show-

---

4. ***prestidigital*** (pres′ tə dij′ə təl), light-fingered, skilled at sleight of hand.

room, a gallery broken up by stands and stalls and pillars, with archways leading off to other departments, in which the queerest-looking assistants loafed and stared at one, and with perplexing mirrors and curtains. So perplexing, indeed, were these that I was presently unable to make out the door by which we had come.

The shopman showed Gip magic trains that ran without steam or clockwork, just as you set the signals, and then some very, very valuable boxes of soldiers that all came alive directly you took off the lid and said——. I myself haven't a very quick ear and it was a tongue-twisting sound, but Gip—he has his mother's ear—got it in no time. "Bravo!" said the shopman, putting the men back into the box unceremoniously and handing it to Gip. "Now," said the shopman, and in a moment Gip had made them all alive again.

"You'll take that box?" asked the shopman.

"We'll take that box," said I, "unless you charge its full value. In which case it would need a Trust Magnate——"

"Dear heart! *No!*" and the shopman swept the little men back again, shut the lid, waved the box in the air, and there it was, in brown paper, tied up and—*with Gip's full name and address on the paper!*

The shopman laughed at my amazement.

"This is the genuine magic," he said. "The real thing."

"It's a little too genuine for my taste," I said again.

After that he fell to showing Gip tricks, odd tricks, and still odder the way they were done. He explained them, he turned them inside out, and there was the dear little chap nodding his busy bit of a head in the sagest manner.

I did not attend as well as I might. "Hey, presto!" said the Magic Shopman, and then would come the clear, small "Hey, presto!" of the boy. But I was distracted by other things. It was being borne in upon me just how tremendously rum this place was; it was, so to speak, inundated by a sense of rumness. There was something a little rum about the fixtures even, about the ceiling, about the floor, about the casually distributed chairs. I had a queer feeling that whenever I wasn't looking at them straight they went askew, and moved about, and played a noiseless puss-in-the-corner[5] behind my back. And the cornice had a serpentine design with masks—masks altogether too expressive for proper plaster.

Then abruptly my attention was caught by one of the odd-looking assistants. He was some way off and evidently unaware of my presence—I saw a sort of three-quarter length of him over a pile of toys and through an arch—and, you know, he was leaning against a pillar in an idle sort of way doing the most horrid things with his features! The particular horrid thing he did was with his nose. He did it just as though he was idle and wanted to amuse himself. First of all it was a short, blobby nose, and then suddenly he shot it out like a telescope, and then out it flew and became thinner and thinner until it was like a long, red, flexible whip. Like a thing in a nightmare it was! He flourished it about and flung it forth as a fly-fisher flings his line.

My instant thought was that Gip mustn't see him. I turned about, and there was Gip quite preoccupied with the shopman, and thinking no evil. They were whispering together and looking at me. Gip was standing on a little stool, and the shopman was holding a sort of big drum in his hand.

"Hide and seek, dadda!" cried Gip. "You're He!"

And before I could do anything to prevent it, the shopman had clapped the big drum over him.

I saw what was up directly. "Take that off," I cried, "this instant! You'll frighten the boy. Take it off!'

The shopman with the unequal ears did so

---

5. ***puss-in-the-corner,*** a children's game similar to musical chairs.

without a word, and held the big cylinder towards me to show its emptiness. And the little stool was vacant! In that instant my boy had utterly disappeared. . . .

You know, perhaps, that sinister something that comes like a hand out of the unseen and grips your heart about. You know it takes your common self away and leaves you tense and deliberate, neither slow nor hasty, neither angry nor afraid. So it was with me.

I came up to this grinning shopman and kicked his stool aside.

"Stop this folly!" I said. "Where is my boy?"

"You see," he said, still displaying the drum's interior, "there is no deception——"

I put out my hand to grip him, and he eluded me by a dexterous movement. I snatched again, and he turned from me and pushed open a door to escape. "Stop!" I said, and he laughed, receding. I leapt after him—into utter darkness.

Thud!

"Lor' bless my 'eart! I didn't see you coming, sir!"

I was in Regent Street, and I had collided with a decent-looking working man; and a yard away, perhaps, and looking a little perplexed with himself, was Gip. There was some sort of apology, and then Gip had turned and come to me with a bright little smile, as though for a moment he had missed me.

And he was carrying four parcels in his arm!

He secured immediate possession of my finger.

For the second I was rather at a loss. I stared round to see the door of the magic shop, and, behold, it was not there! There was no door, no shop, nothing, only the common pilaster between the shop where they sell pictures and the window with the chicks! . . .

I did the only thing possible in that mental tumult; I walked straight to the curbstone and held up my umbrella for a cab.

"'Ansoms,"[6] said Gip, in a note of culminating exultation.

I helped him in, recalled my address with an effort, and got in also. Something unusual proclaimed itself in my tail-coat pocket, and I felt and discovered a glass ball. With a petulant expression I flung it into the street.

Gip said nothing.

For a space neither of us spoke.

"Dadda!" said Gip, at last, "that *was* a proper shop!"

I came round with that to the problem of just how the whole thing had seemed to him. He looked completely undamaged—so far, good; he was neither scared nor unhinged, he was simply tremendously satisfied with the afternoon's entertainment, and there in his arms were the four parcels.

Confound it! What could be in them?

"Um!" I said. "Little boys can't go to shops like that every day."

He received this with his usual stoicism, and for a moment I was sorry I was his father and not his mother, and so couldn't suddenly there, *coram publico,*[7] in our hansom, kiss him. After all, I thought, the thing wasn't so very bad.

But it was only when we opened the parcels that I really began to be reassured. Three of them contained boxes of soldiers, quite ordinary lead soldiers, but of so good a quality as to make Gip altogether forget that originally these parcels had been Magic Tricks of the only genuine sort, and the fourth contained a kitten, a little living white kitten, in excellent health and appetite and temper.

I saw this unpacking with a sort of provisional relief. I hung about in the nursery for quite an unconscionable time. . . .

That happened six months ago. And now I am beginning to believe it is all right. The kitten had only the magic natural to all kittens, and the

---

6. ***'ansoms.*** Gip is referring to a hansom cab, a two-wheeled vehicle for two passengers, drawn by one horse. The driver sits on a high seat up behind the cab, and the reins pass over the roof.
7. ***coram publico,*** publicly. [*Latin*]

soldiers seem as steady a company as any colonel could desire. And Gip——?

The intelligent parent will understand that I have to go cautiously with Gip. But I went so far as this one day. I said, "How would you like your soldiers to come alive, Gip, and march about by themselves?"

"Mine do," said Gip. "I just have to say a word I know before I open the lid."

"Then they march about alone?"

"Oh, *quite*, dadda. I shouldn't like them if they didn't do that."

I displayed no unbecoming surprise, and since then I have taken occasion to drop in upon him once or twice, unannounced, when the soldiers were about, but so far I have never discovered them performing in anything like a magical manner. . . .

It's so difficult to tell.

There's also a question of finance. I have an incurable habit of paying bills. I have been up and down Regent Street several times, looking for that shop. I am inclined to think, indeed, that in that matter honor is satisfied, and that, since Gip's name and address are known to them, I may very well leave it to these people, whoever they may be, to send in their bill in their own time.

Discussion

1. (a) Under what circumstances and for what purpose does the narrator enter the Magic Shop? **(b)** Is it likely that the narrator could have entered the shop if he had been by himself? Explain. **(c)** What does the shopman say about his young visitor, Gip? **(d)** What evidence is there that unwanted visitors cannot enter the shop?

2. Describe happenings in the shop that go beyond the magic that one might find in the usual magic store.

3. (a) In what way does the relationship between the shopman and Gip differ from that between the shopman and the narrator? **(b)** How does the shopman explain the presence of the little red demon on the narrator's coat sleeve?

4. (a) What is in the packages that Gip brings home from the shop? **(b)** In what way are the father and son not in agreement about the properties of some of these objects? **(c)** In your opinion, what is the basis for this difference of opinion?

5. When Gip and his father suddenly find themselves outside on Regent Street, the shop seems to have disappeared. What details in the first paragraph of the story foreshadow the magic character of the shop?

Application

Theme

Theme is the main idea or underlying meaning of a literary work. Which of the following best states the theme of "The Magic Shop"? **(1)** Because magic is often in the eye of the beholder, it is not easy to draw the line between what can be explained and what is truly magical. **(2)** If you hope to enter The Magic Shop, you had best obey your parents and behave yourself. **(3)** A father and son enter a magic shop, observe numerous wonderous events, and suddenly find themselves back on the street, with the magic shop nowhere in sight.

Composition

Imagine that recently your family took care of a young cousin while his parents visited India. The child, a little boy about Gip's age, stayed with you for a month, and you often babysat with him for your parents. During one afternoon of babysitting, you took him to a place very like the magic shop in the story and where your experiences were very similar to those of Gip and the narrator. The little boy's parents returned about a week ago and took their son home. Today, your parents received a letter from them. In this letter your aunt and uncle state that although the kitten and toy soldiers seem normal and their son seems to have suffered no harm, they deplore the fact that he was taken to such a place and blame you for bad judgment in taking him.

Your parents decide that it is up to you to answer this letter. Write a letter to your aunt and uncle in which you either defend your action or—if you have since decided that you should not have taken him to the shop—tell them that you agree with their judgment and why you have come to this conclusion. Remember that, whichever position you take, your object is to present your case in such a way that you restore peace in the family. (See *Revising,* page 664, in Composition Guide.)

H. G. Wells 1866–1946

Herbert George Wells was born near London to lower-middle-class parents. He was first apprenticed to a dealer in cloth and dry goods, but he quickly abandoned that career for one in teaching science. From teaching he turned to journalism, and from journalism to writing essays, novels, and short stories.

Wells's first novel, *The Time Machine* (1895), which told of a man who traveled into the future, was immediately successful. It was followed by a series of fantastic and imaginative romances, including *The Invisible Man* (1897), *The First Men in the Moon* (1901), and *The War in the Air* (1908). "War of the Worlds" (1898), the story of an attack upon Earth by men from Mars, is so realistic that when it was presented on radio in 1939 it caused thousands of listeners to panic.

Wells once said of his writing, "I write as I walk, because I want to get somewhere, and I write as straight as I can, just as I walk as straight as I can, because that is the best way to get there."

The Rule of Names

Ursula Le Guin

The rule is the same on every island in the world. "You never ask anybody his name. You never tell your own."

Mr. Underhill came out from under his hill, smiling and breathing hard. Each breath shot out of his nostrils as a double puff of steam, snow-white in the morning sunshine. Mr. Underhill looked up at the bright December sky and smiled wider than ever, showing snow-white teeth. Then he went down to the village.

"Morning, Mr. Underhill," said the villagers as he passed them in the narrow street between houses with conical, overhanging roofs like the fat red caps of toadstools. "Morning, morning!" he replied to each. (It was of course bad luck to wish anyone a *good* morning; a simple statement of the time of day was quite enough, in a place so permeated with Influences as Sattins Island, where a careless adjective might change the weather for a week.) All of them spoke to him, some with affection, some with affectionate disdain. He was all the little island had in the way of a wizard, and so deserved respect—but how could you respect a little fat man of fifty who waddled along with his toes turned in, breathing steam and smiling? He was no great shakes as a workman either. His fireworks were fairly elaborate but his elixirs were weak. Warts he charmed off frequently reappeared after three days; tomatoes he enchanted grew no bigger than canteloupes; and those rare times when a strange ship stopped at Sattins Harbor, Mr. Underhill always stayed under his hill—for fear, he explained, of the evil eye. He was, in other words, a wizard the way walleyed Gan was a carpenter: by default. The villagers made do with badly-hung doors and inefficient spells, for this generation, and relieved their annoyance by treating Mr. Underhill quite familiarly, as a mere fellow-villager. They even asked him to dinner. Once he asked some of them to dinner, and served a splendid repast, with silver, crystal, damask, roast goose, sparkling Andrades '639, and plum pudding with hard sauce; but he was so nervous all through the meal that it took the joy out of it, and besides, everybody was hungry again half an hour afterward. He did not like anyone to visit his cave, not even the anteroom, beyond which in fact nobody had ever got. When he saw people approaching the hill he always came trotting out to meet them. "Let's sit out here under the pine trees!" he would say, smiling and waving towards the fir grove, or if it was raining, "Let's go have a drink at the inn, eh?" though everybody knew he drank nothing stronger than well-water.

Some of the village children, teased by that locked cave, poked and pried and made raids

---

while Mr. Underhill was away; but the small door that led into the inner chamber was spell-shut, and it seemed for once to be an effective spell. Once a couple of boys, thinking the wizard was over on the West Shore curing Mrs. Ruuna's sick donkey, brought a crowbar and a hatchet up there, but at the first whack of the hatchet on the door there came a roar of wrath from inside, and a cloud of purple steam. Mr. Underhill had got home early. The boys fled. He did not come out, and the boys came to no harm, though they said you couldn't believe what a huge hooting howling hissing horrible bellow that little fat man could make unless you'd heard it.

His business in town this day was three dozen fresh eggs and a pound of liver; also a stop at Seacaptain Fogeno's cottage to renew the seeing-charm on the old man's eyes (quite useless when applied to a case of detached retina, but Mr. Underhill kept trying), and finally a chat with old Goody Guld, the concertina-maker's widow. Mr. Underhill's friends were mostly old people. He was timid with the strong young men of the village, and the girls were shy of him. "He makes me nervous, he smiles so much," they all said, pouting, twisting silky ringlets round a finger. "Nervous" was a newfangled word, and their mothers all replied grimly, "Nervous my foot, silliness is the word for it. Mr. Underhill is a very respectable wizard!"

After leaving Goody Guld, Mr. Underhill passed by the school, which was being held this day out on the common. Since no one on Sattins Island was literate, there were no books to learn to read from and no desks to carve initials on and no blackboards to erase, and in fact no schoolhouse. On rainy days the children met in the loft of the Communal Barn, and got hay in their pants; on sunny days the schoolteacher, Palani, took them anywhere she felt like. Today, surrounded by thirty interested children under twelve and forty uninterested sheep under five, she was teaching an important item on the curriculum: the Rule of Names. Mr. Underhill, smiling shyly, paused to listen and watch. Palani, a plump, pretty girl of twenty, made a charming picture there in the wintry sunlight, sheep and children around her, a leafless oak above her, and behind her the dunes and sea and clear, pale sky. She spoke earnestly, her face flushed pink by wind and words. "Now you know the Rules of Names already, children. There are two, and they're the same on every island in the world. What's one of them?"

"It ain't polite to ask anybody what his name is," shouted a fat, quick boy, interrupted by a little girl shrieking, "You can't never tell your own name to nobody my ma says!"

"Yes, Suba. Yes, Popi dear, don't screech. That's right. You never ask anybody his name. You never tell your own. Now think about that a minute and then tell me why we call our wizard Mr. Underhill." She smiled across the curly heads and the woolly backs at Mr. Underhill, who beamed, and nervously clutched his sack of eggs.

"'Cause he lives under a hill!" said half the children.

"But is it his truename?"

"No!" said the fat boy, echoed by little Popi shrieking, "No!"

"How do you know it's not?"

"'Cause he came here all alone and so there wasn't anybody knew his truename so they couldn't tell, and *he* couldn't——"

"Very good, Suba. Popi, don't shout. That's right. Even a wizard can't tell his truename. When you children are through school and go through the Passage, you'll leave your childnames behind and keep only your truenames, which you must never ask for and never give away. Why is that the rule?"

The children were silent. The sheep bleated gently. Mr. Underhill answered the question: "Because the name is the thing," he said in his shy, soft, husky voice, "and the truename is the true thing. To speak the name is to control the thing. Am I right, Schoolmistress?"

She smiled and curtseyed, evidently a little embarrassed by his participation. And he trotted off towards his hill, clutching his eggs to his bosom. Somehow the minute spent watching Palani and the children had made him very hungry. He locked his inner door behind him with a hasty incantation, but there must have been a leak or two in the spell, for soon the bare anteroom of the cave was rich with the smell of frying eggs and sizzling liver.

The wind that day was light and fresh out of the west, and on it at noon a little boat came skimming the bright waves into Sattins Harbor. Even as it rounded the point a sharp-eyed boy spotted it, and knowing, like every child on the island, every sail and spar of the forty boats of the fishing fleet, he ran down the street calling out, "A foreign boat, a foreign boat!" Very seldom was the lonely isle visited by a boat from some equally lonely isle of the East Reach, or an adventurous trader from the Archipelago. By the time the boat was at the pier half the village was there to greet it, and fishermen were following it homewards, and cowherds and clam-diggers and herb hunters were puffing up and down all the rocky hills, heading towards the harbor.

But Mr. Underhill's door stayed shut.

There was only one man aboard the boat. Old Seacaptain Fogeno, when they told him that, drew down a bristle of white brows over his unseeing eyes. "There's only one kind of man," he said, "that sails the Outer Reach alone. A wizard, or a warlock, or a Mage . . ."

So the villagers were breathless hoping to see for once in their lives a Mage, one of the mighty White Magicians of the rich, towered, crowded inner islands of the Archipelago. They were disappointed, for the voyager was quite young, a handsome black-bearded fellow who hailed them cheerfully from his boat, and leaped ashore like any sailor glad to have made port. He introduced himself at once as a sea-peddlar. But when they told Seacaptain Fogeno that he carried an oaken walking stick around with him, the old man nodded. "Two wizards in one town," he said. "Bad!" And his mouth snapped shut like an old carp's.

As the stranger could not give them his name, they gave him one right away: Blackbeard. And they gave him plenty of attention. He had a small mixed cargo of cloth and sandals and piswi feathers for trimming cloaks and cheap incense and levity stones and fine herbs and great glass beads from Venway—the usual peddlar's lot. Everyone on Sattins Island came to look, to chat with the voyager, and perhaps to buy something—"Just to remember him by!" cackled Goody Guld, who like all the women and girls of the village was smitten with Blackbeard's bold good looks. All the boys hung round him too, to hear him tell of his voyages to far, strange islands of the Reach or describe the great rich islands of the Archipelago, the Inner Lanes, the roadsteads white with ships, and the golden roofs of Havnor. The men willingly listened to his tales; but some of them wondered why a trader should sail alone, and kept their eyes thoughtfully upon his oaken staff.

But all this time Mr. Underhill stayed under his hill.

"This is the first island I've ever seen that had no wizard," said Blackbeard one evening to Goody Guld, who had invited him and her nephew and Palani in for a cup of rushwash tea. "What do you do when you get a toothache, or the cow goes dry?"

"Why, we've got Mr. Underhill!" said the old woman.

"For what that's worth," muttered her nephew Birt, and then blushed purple and spilled his tea. Birt was a fisherman, a large, brave, wordless young man. He loved the schoolmistress, but the nearest he had come to telling her of his love was to give baskets of fresh mackerel to her father's cook.

"Oh, you do have a wizard?" Blackbeard asked. "Is he invisible?"

"No, he's just very shy," said Palani. "You've only been here a week, you know, and we see so few strangers here. . . ." She also blushed a little, but did not spill her tea.

Blackbeard smiled at her. "He's a good Sattinsman, then, eh?"

"No," said Goody Guld, "no more than you are. Another cup, nevvy?[1] Keep it in the cup this time. No, my dear, he came in a little bit of a boat, four years ago was it? Just a day after the end of the shad run, I recall, for they was taking up the nets over in East Creek, and Pondi Cowherd broke his leg that very morning—five years ago it must be. No, four. No, five it is, 'twas the year the garlic didn't sprout. So he sails in on a bit of a sloop loaded full up with great chests and boxes and says to Seacaptain Fogeno, who wasn't blind then, though old enough goodness knows to be blind twice over, 'I hear tell,' he says, 'you've got no wizard nor warlock at all, might you be wanting one?' 'Indeed, if the magic's white!' says the Captain, and before you could say cuttlefish Mr. Underhill had settled down in the cave under the hill and was charming the mange off Goody Beltow's cat. Though the fur grew in grey, and 'twas an orange cat. Queer-looking thing it was after that. It died last winter in the cold spell. Goody Beltow took on so at that cat's death, poor thing, worse than when her man was drowned on the Long Banks, the year of the long herring-runs, when nevvy Birt here was but a babe in petticoats." Here Birt spilled his tea again, and Blackbeard grinned, but Goody Guld proceeded undismayed, and talked on till nightfall.

Next day Blackbeard was down at the pier, seeing after the sprung board in his boat which he seemed to take a long time fixing, and as usual drawing the taciturn Sattinsmen into talk. "Now which of these is your wizard's craft?" he asked. "Or has he got one of those the Mages fold up into a walnut shell when they're not using it?"

"Nay," said a stolid fisherman. "She's oop in his cave, under hill."

"He carried the boat he came in up to his cave?"

"Aye. Clear oop. I helped. Heavier as lead she was. Full oop with great boxes, and they full oop with books o' spells, he says. Heavier as lead she was." And the stolid fisherman turned his back, sighing stolidly. Goody Guld's nephew, mending a net nearby, looked up from his work and asked with equal stolidity, "Would ye like to meet Mr. Underhill, maybe?"

Blackbeard returned Birt's look. Clever black eyes met candid blue ones for a long moment; then Blackbeard smiled and said, "Yes. Will you take me up to the hill, Birt?"

"Aye, when I'm done with this," said the fisherman. And when the net was mended, he and the Archipelagan set off up the village street towards the high green hill above it. But as they crossed the common Blackbeard said, "Hold on a while, friend Birt. I have a tale to tell you, before we meet your wizard."

"Tell away," says Birt, sitting down in the shade of a live oak.

"It's a story that started a hundred years ago, and isn't finished yet—though it soon will be, very soon. . . . In the very heart of the Archipelago, where the islands crowd thick as flies on honey, there's a little isle called Pendor. The sealords of Pendor were mighty men, in the old days of war before the League. Loot and ransom and tribute came pouring into Pendor, and they gathered a great treasure there, long ago. Then from somewhere away out in the West Reach, where dragons breed on the lava isles, came one day a very mighty dragon. Not one of those overgrown lizards most of you Outer Reach folk call dragons, but a big, black, winged, wise, cunning monster, full of strength and subtlety, and like all dragons loving gold and precious stones above all things. He killed the Sealord and his soldiers, and the people of Pendor fled in their ships by night. They all fled away and left the dragon coiled up in Pendor Towers. And there he stayed for a hundred years, dragging his scaly belly over the emeralds and sapphires and coins of gold, coming forth only once in a year or two when he must eat.

---

1. ***nevvy,*** nephew.

He'd raid nearby islands for his food. You know what dragons eat?''

Birt nodded and said in a whisper, ''Maidens.''

''Right,'' said Blackbeard. ''Well, that couldn't be endured forever, nor the thought of his sitting on all that treasure. So after the League grew strong, and the Archipelago wasn't so busy with wars and piracy, it was decided to attack Pendor, drive out the dragon, and get the gold and jewels for the treasury of the League. They're forever wanting money, the League is. So a huge fleet gathered from fifty islands, and seven Mages stood in the prows of the seven strongest ships, and they sailed towards Pendor. . . . They got there. They landed. Nothing stirred. The houses all stood empty, the dishes on the tables full of a hundred years' dust. The bones of the old Sealord and his men lay about in the castle courts and on the stairs. And the Tower rooms reeked of dragon. But there was no dragon. And no treasure, not a diamond the size of a poppyseed, not a single silver bead . . . Knowing that he couldn't stand up to seven Mages, the dragon had skipped out. They tracked him, and found he'd flown to a deserted island up north called Udrath; they followed his trail there, and what did they find? Bones again. His bones—the dragon's. But no treasure. A wizard, some unknown wizard from somewhere, must have met him single-handed, and defeated him—and then made off with the treasure, right under the League's nose!''

The fisherman listened, attentive and expressionless.

''Now that must have been a powerful wizard and a clever one, first to kill a dragon, and second to get off without leaving a trace. The lords and Mages of the Archipelago couldn't track him at all, neither where he'd come from nor where he'd made off to. They were about to give up. That was last spring; I'd been off on a three-year voyage up in the North Reach, and got back about that time. And they asked me to help find the unknown wizard. That was clever of them. Because I'm not only a wizard myself, as I think some of the oafs here have guessed, but I am also a descendant of the Lords of Pendor. That treasure is mine. It's mine, and knows that it's mine. Those fools of the League couldn't find it, because it's not theirs. It belongs to the House of Pendor, and the great emerald, the star of the hoard, Inalkil the Greenstone, knows its master. Behold!'' Blackbeard raised his oaken staff and cried aloud, ''Inalkil!'' The tip of the staff began to glow green, a fiery green radiance, a dazzling haze the color of April grass, and at the same moment the staff tipped in the wizard's hand, leaning, slanting till it pointed straight at the side of the hill above them.

''It wasn't so bright a glow, far away in Havnor,'' Blackbeard murmured, ''but the staff pointed true. Inalkil answered when I called. The jewel knows its master. And I know the thief, and I shall conquer him. He's a mighty wizard, who could overcome a dragon. But I am mightier. Do you want to know why, oaf? Because I know his name!''

As Blackbeard's tone got more arrogant, Birt had looked duller and duller, blanker and blanker; but at this he gave a twitch, shut his mouth, and stared at the Archipelagan. ''How did you . . . learn it?'' he asked very slowly.

Blackbeard grinned, and did not answer.

''Black magic?''

''How else?''

Birt looked pale, and said nothing.

''I am the Sealord of Pendor, oaf, and I will have the gold my fathers won, and the jewels my mothers wore, and the Greenstone! For they are mine. —Now, you can tell your village boobies the whole story after I have defeated this wizard and gone. Wait here. Or you can come and watch, if you're not afraid. You'll never get the chance again to see a great wizard in all his power.'' Blackbeard turned, and without a backward glance strode off up the hill towards the entrance to the cave.

Very slowly, Birt followed. A good distance

from the cave he stopped, sat down under a hawthorn tree, and watched. The Archipelagan had stopped; a stiff, dark figure alone on the green swell of the hill before the gaping cave mouth, he stood perfectly still. All at once he swung his staff up over his head, and the emerald radiance shone about him as he shouted, "Thief, thief of the Hoard of Pendor, come forth!"

There was a crash, as of dropped crockery,

from inside the cave, and a lot of dust came spewing out. Scared, Birt ducked. When he looked again he saw Blackbeard still standing motionless, and at the mouth of the cave, dusty and dishevelled, stood Mr. Underhill. He looked small and pitiful, with his toes turned in as usual, and his little bowlegs in black tights, and no staff—he never had had one, Birt suddenly thought. Mr. Underhill spoke. "Who are you?" he said in his husky little voice.

"I am the Sealord of Pendor, thief, come to claim my treasure!"

At that, Mr. Underhill slowly turned pink, as he always did when people were rude to him. But he then turned something else. He turned yellow. His hair bristled out, he gave a coughing roar—and was a yellow lion leaping down the hill at Blackbeard, white fangs gleaming.

But Blackbeard no longer stood there. A gigantic tiger, color of night and lightning, bounded to meet the lion. . . .

The lion was gone. Below the cave all of a sudden stood a high grove of trees, black in the winter sunshine. The tiger, checking himself in mid-leap just before he entered the shadow of the trees, caught fire in the air, became a tongue of flame lashing out at the dry black branches. . . .

But where the trees had stood a sudden cataract leaped from the hillside, an arch of silvery crashing water, thundering down upon the fire. But the fire was gone. . . .

For just a moment before the fisherman's staring eyes two hills rose—the green one he knew, and a new one, a bare, brown hillock ready to drink up the rushing waterfall. That passed so quickly it made Birt blink, and after blinking he blinked again, and moaned, for what he saw now was a great deal worse. Where the cataract had been there hovered a dragon. Black wings darkened all the hill, steel claws reached groping, and from the dark, scaly, gaping lips fire and steam shot out.

Beneath the monstrous creature stood Blackbeard, laughing.

"Take any shape you please, little Mr. Underhill!" he taunted. "I can match you. But the game grows tiresome. I want to look upon my treasure, upon Inalkil. Now, big dragon, little wizard, take your true shape. I command you by the power of your true name—Yevaud!"

Birt could not move at all, not even to blink. He cowered, staring whether he would or not. He saw the black dragon hang there in the air above Blackbeard. He saw the fire lick like many tongues from the scaly mouth, the steam jet from the red nostrils. He saw Blackbeard's face grow white, white as chalk, and the beard-fringed lips trembling.

"Your name is Yevaud!"

"Yes," said a great, husky, hissing voice. "My truename is Yevaud, and my true shape is this shape."

"But the dragon was killed—they found dragonbones on Udrath Island——"

"That was another dragon," said the dragon, and then swooped like a hawk, talons outstretched. And Birt shut his eyes.

When he opened them the sky was clear, the hillside empty, except for a reddish-blackish trampled spot, and a few talon marks in the grass.

Birt the fisherman got to his feet and ran. He ran across the common, scattering sheep to right and left, and straight down the village street to Palani's father's house. Palani was out in the garden weeding the nasturtiums. "Come with me!" Birt gasped. She stared. He grabbed her wrist and dragged her with him. She screeched a little, but did not resist. He ran with her straight to the pier, pushed her into his fishing sloop the *Queenie,* untied the painter, took up the oars and set off rowing like a demon. The last that Sattins Island saw of him and Palani was the *Queenie*'s sail vanishing in the direction of the nearest island westward.

The villagers thought they would never stop talking about it, how Goody Guld's nephew Birt had lost his mind and sailed off with the schoolmistress on the very same day that the peddlar Blackbeard disappeared without a trace, leaving all his feathers and beads behind. But they did stop talking about it, three days later. They had other things to talk about, when Mr. Underhill finally came out of his cave.

Mr. Underhill had decided that since his truename was no longer a secret, he might as well drop his disguise. Walking was a lot harder than flying, and besides, it was a long, long time since he had had a real meal.

Discussion

1. (a) At the beginning of the story, what is the attitude of the islanders toward Mr. Underhill? **(b)** What reason does Mr. Underhill give for staying under his hill when a strange ship visits? **(c)** How does he behave toward persons visiting his cave? **(d)** When and with what cargo had he first come to Sattins Island?

2. (a) What does school mean on Sattins Island. **(b)** What is the Rule of Names? **(c)** Why is one not supposed to reveal his or her true name?

3. (a) On what evidence does Old Captain Fogeno infer that Blackbeard is a wizard? **(b)** What trade does Blackbeard claim to follow? **(c)** Describe the cargo of his ship.

4. (a) Summarize the story Blackbeard tells Birt. **(b)** What is Inalkil? **(c)** What makes Blackbeard confident that he can defeat the wizard who has stolen the jewels? **(d)** Describe Blackbeard's attitude toward the islanders.

5. (a) In the conflict between Blackbeard and Mr. Underhill, what forms does Mr. Underhill take? **(b)** What forms does Blackbeard take in return? **(c)** With what revelations does the battle end? **(d)** How does Birt respond?

6. (a) What decision does Mr. Underhill make at the end of the story? **(b)** What are the implications of the last line of the story? **(c)** Reread Mr. Underhill's explanation to Palani and her class of the Rule of Names. Does the conclusion of this story seem to justify the reason he gives for observing the rule? Explain.

Vocabulary

Compound Words, Context

In the fantasy world of Sattins Island, people give up their *childnames* when they come of age, and they are taught never to reveal their *truenames.* Both of these terms are *compound words;* a compound word is one made by joining two or more words. In naming newcomers to their island, residents also rely on compounds—*Mr. Underhill, Blackbeard.*

Fill each blank in the sentences that follow with a compound word from the list. Use context to help you make your choices; write your answers on your paper. (Note: Some words in the list are not compound.)

taciturn	poppyseed	cataract
schoolmistress	overgrown	overhanging
walleyed	permeate	nightfall
toothache	default	sunshine
hillside	bowlegs	
conical	concertina	

1. The addition of a ____ loaf to this meal would certainly be welcome.

2. Mr. Underhill stood on his ____, which made his toes turn in, and watched Gan, the ____ carpenter, make a bad job of hanging a door.

3. After great effort and many scratches, we fought our way through the ____ hedges, slid down the muddy ____, and found shelter under the ____ roof of the house.

4. After eight days of heavy fog, we were delighted to see the ____.

5. He left around noon, saying that the healing charm would work in fifteen minutes; it is now almost ____ and I still have my ____.

6. His interest in what the ____ was teaching made him stop outside the classroom door.

Composition

Imagine that you live on Sattins Island, that you keep a journal, and that the time is two weeks after the fight between Blackbeard and Mr. Underhill. Before writing your journal entry for the day, consider what changes have occurred in the village since that fight—how people feel about Yevaud, what they worry about, how they behave, what they plan for the future.

Now, compose your journal entry.

The Third Bank of the River

João Guimarães Rosa

Translated by William L. Grossman

"We had to get accustomed to the idea of Father's being out on the river. We had to but we couldn't, we never could."

My father was a dutiful, orderly, straightforward man. And according to several reliable people of whom I inquired, he had had these qualities since adolescence or even childhood. By my own recollection, he was neither jollier nor more melancholy than the other men we knew. Maybe a little quieter. It was Mother, not Father, who ruled the house. She scolded us daily—my sister, my brother, and me. But it happened one day that Father ordered a boat.

He was very serious about it. It was to be made specially for him, of mimosa wood. It was to be sturdy enough to last twenty or thirty years and just large enough for one person. Mother carried on plenty about it. Was her husband going to become a fisherman all of a sudden? Or a hunter? Father said nothing. Our house was less than a mile from the river, which around there was deep, quiet, and so wide you couldn't see across it.

I can never forget the day the rowboat was delivered. Father showed no joy or other emotion. He just put on his hat as he always did and said good-by to us. He took along no food or bundle of any sort. We expected Mother to rant and rave, but she didn't. She looked very pale and bit her lip, but all she said was "If you go away, stay away. Don't ever come back!"

Father made no reply. He looked gently at me and motioned me to walk along with him. I feared Mother's wrath, yet eagerly obeyed. We headed toward the river together. I felt bold and exhilarated, so much so that I said: "Father, will you take me with you in your boat?"

He just looked at me, gave me his blessing, and by a gesture, told me to go back. I made as if to do so but, when his back was turned, I ducked behind some bushes to watch him. Father got into the boat and rowed away. Its shadow slid across the water like a crocodile, long and quiet.

Father did not come back. Nor did he go anywhere, really. He just rowed and floated across and around, out there in the river. Everyone was appalled. What had never happened, what could not possibly happen, was happening. Our relatives, neighbors, and friends came over to discuss the phenomenon.

Mother was ashamed. She said little and

João Guimarães Rosa (zh'äô gē mä'resh rô'zä)

conducted herself with great composure. As a consequence, almost everyone thought (though no one said it) that Father had gone insane. A few, however, suggested that Father might be fulfilling a promise he had made to God or to a saint, or that he might have some horrible disease, maybe leprosy, and that he left for the sake of the family, at the same time wishing to remain fairly near them.

Travelers along the river and people living near the bank on one side or the other reported that Father never put foot on land, by day or night. He just moved about on the river, solitary, aimless, like a derelict. Mother and our relatives agreed that the food which he had doubtless hidden in the boat would soon give out and that then he would either leave the river and travel off somewhere (which would be at least a little more respectable) or he would repent and come home.

How far from the truth they were! Father had a secret source of provisions: me. Every day I stole food and brought it to him. The first night after he left, we all lit fires on the shore and prayed and called to him. I was deeply distressed and felt a need to do something more. The following day I went down to the river with a loaf of corn bread, a bunch of bananas, and some bricks of raw brown sugar. I waited impatiently a long, long hour. Then I saw the boat, far off, alone, gliding almost imperceptibly on the smoothness of the river. Father was sitting in the bottom of the boat. He saw me but he did not row toward me or make any gesture. I showed him the food and then I placed it in a hollow rock on the river bank; it was safe there from animals, rain, and dew. I did this day after day, on and on and on. Later I learned to my surprise, that Mother knew what I was doing and left food around where I could easily steal it. She had a lot of feelings she didn't show.

Mother sent for her brother to come and help on the farm and in business matters. She had the schoolteacher come and tutor us children at home because of the time we had lost. One day, at her request, the priest put on his vestments, went down to the shore, and tried to exorcise the devils that had got into my father. He shouted that Father had a duty to cease his unholy obstinacy. Another day she arranged to have two soldiers come and try to frighten him. All to no avail. My father went by in the distance, sometimes so far away he could barely be seen. He never replied to anyone and no one ever got close to him. When some newspapermen came in a launch to take his picture, Father headed his boat to the other side of the river and into the marshes, which he knew like the palm of his hand but in which other people quickly got lost. There in his private maze, which extended for miles, with heavy foliage overhead and rushes on all sides, he was safe.

We had to get accustomed to the idea of Father's being out on the river. We had to but we couldn't, we never could. I think I was the only one who understood to some degree what our father wanted and what he did not want. The thing I could not understand at all was how he stood the hardship. Day and night, in sun and rain, in heat and in the terrible mid-year cold spells, with his old hat on his head and very little other clothing, week after week, month after month, year after year, unheedful of the waste and emptiness in which his life was slipping by. He never set foot on earth or grass, on isle or mainland shore. No doubt he sometimes tied up the boat at a secret place, perhaps at the tip of some island, to get a little sleep. He never lit a fire or even struck a match and he had no flashlight. He took only a small part of the food that I left in the hollow rock—not enough, it seemed to me, for survival. What could his state of health have been? How about the continual drain on his energy, pulling and pushing the oars to control the boat? And how did he survive the annual floods, when the river rose and swept along with it all sorts of dangerous objects—branches of trees, dead bodies of animals—that might suddenly crash against his little boat?

He never talked to a living soul. And we never talked about him. We just thought. No, we could never put our father out of mind. If for a short time we seemed to, it was just a lull from which we would be sharply awakened by the realization of his frightening situation.

My sister got married, but Mother didn't want a wedding party. It would have been a sad affair, for we thought of him every time we ate some especially tasty food. Just as we thought of him in our cozy beds on a cold, stormy night—out there, alone and unprotected, trying to bail out the boat with only his hands and a gourd. Now and then someone would say that I was getting to look more and more like my father. But I knew that by then his hair and beard must have been shaggy and his nails long. I pictured him thin and sickly, black with hair and sunburn, and almost naked despite the articles of clothing I occasionally left for him.

He didn't seem to care about us at all. But I felt affection and respect for him, and, whenever they praised me because I had done something good, I said: "My father taught me to act that way."

It wasn't exactly accurate but it was a truthful sort of lie. As I said, Father didn't seem to care about us. But then why did he stay around there? Why didn't he go up the river or down the river, beyond the possibility of seeing us or being seen by us? He alone knew the answer.

My sister had a baby boy. She insisted on showing Father his grandson. One beautiful day we all went down to the riverbank, my sister in her white wedding dress, and she lifted the baby high. Her husband held a parasol above them. We shouted to Father and waited. He did not appear. My sister cried; we all cried in each other's arms.

My sister and her husband moved far away. My brother went to live in a city. Times changed, with their usual imperceptible rapidity. Mother finally moved too; she was old and went to live with her daughter. I remained behind, a leftover. I could never think of marrying. I just stayed there with the impedimenta of my life. Father, wandering alone and forlorn on the river, needed me. I knew he needed me, although he never even told me why he was doing it. When I put the question to people bluntly and insistently, all they told me was that they heard that Father had explained it to the man who made the boat. But now this man was dead and nobody knew or remembered anything. There was just some foolish talk, when the rains were especially severe and persistent, that my father was wise like Noah and had the boat built in anticipation of a new flood; I dimly remember people saying this. In any case, I would not condemn my father for what he was doing. My hair was beginning to turn gray.

I have only sad things to say. What bad had I done, what was my great guilt? My father always away and his absence always with me. And the river, always the river, perpetually renewing itself. The river, always. I was beginning to suffer from old age, in which life is just a sort of lingering. I had attacks of illness and of anxiety. I had a nagging rheumatism. And he? Why, why was he doing it? He must have been suffering terribly. He was so old. One day, in his failing strength, he might let the boat capsize; or he might let the current carry it downstream, on and on, until it plunged over the waterfall to the boiling turmoil below. It pressed upon my heart. He was out there and I was forever robbed of my peace. I am guilty of I know not what, and my pain is an open wound inside me. Perhaps I would know—if things were different. I began to guess what was wrong.

Out with it! Had I gone crazy? No, in our house that word was never spoken, never through all the years. No one called anybody crazy, for nobody is crazy. Or maybe everybody. All I did was go there and wave a handkerchief so he would be more likely to see me. I was in complete command of myself. I waited. Finally he appeared in the distance, there, then over there, a vague shape sitting in the back of the boat. I called to him several times. And I said what I was so eager to say, to state formally and under oath. I said it as loud as I could:

"Father, you have been out there long enough. You are old. . . . Come back, you don't have to do it anymore. . . . Come back and I'll go instead. Right now, if you want. Any time. I'll get into the boat. I'll take your place."

And when I had said this my heart beat more firmly.

He heard me. He stood up. He maneuvered with his oars and headed the boat toward me. He had accepted my offer. And suddenly I trembled, down deep. For he had raised his arm and waved—the first time in so many, so many years. And I couldn't . . . In terror, my hair on end, I ran, I fled madly. For he seemed to come from another world. And I'm begging forgiveness, begging, begging.

I experienced the dreadful sense of cold that comes from deadly fear, and I became ill. Nobody ever saw or heard about him again. Am I a man, after such a failure? I am what never should have been. I am what must be silent. I know it is too late. I must stay in the deserts and unmarked plains of my life, and I fear I shall shorten it. But when death comes I want them to take me and put me in a little boat in this perpetual water between the long shores; and I, down the river, lost in the river, inside the river . . . the river . . .

Discussion

1. Before taking to the river, what kind of man was Father?

2. (a) What assumptions did people make about the reason for Father's behavior? **(b)** Cite evidence that suggests the narrator's mother was concerned about her husband and wanted him to come home.

3. Read each of the following statements made by the narrator and consider what they tell you about him.

(a) "I think I was the only one who understood to some degree what our father wanted and what he did not want."

(b) "He didn't seem to care about us at all. But I felt affection and respect for him . . ."

(c) "I remained behind, a leftover. . . . Father, wandering alone and forlorn on the river, needed me."

(d) "What bad had I done; what was my great guilt?"

(e) "Had I gone crazy? No, in our house that word was never spoken. . . ."

4. (a) What happens when the narrator attempts to take his father's place in the boat? **(b)** In your opinion, why does the narrator then feel that he is "what never should have been"?

5. Would you call this story realistic? fantastic? both? neither? Explain.

Unit 5 Review: The Second Short Story Unit

Content Review

The following statements are about the short stories in the unit you have just completed. Number from 1 to 15 on a separate sheet of paper. After each number, write "a" if you *strongly agree* with the statement; "b" if you *agree;* "c" if you *have no opinion;* "d" if you *disagree;* "e" if you *strongly disagree* with the statement.

Whenever possible, be prepared to support each of your opinions with evidence from the selections.

1. Sherlock Holmes's deductions are simply lucky guesses.

2. If I were Asa Putman in "Early Marriage," I would not have permitted my young daughter and son to travel to Gunstock without an adult.

3. By standing up to Cochise and the Apaches, Angie Lowe unnecessarily risks the lives of her two young children.

4. If Pender had known from the outset of "The Man Who Knew How" that Bill Buckley was a journalist, the two men might have become close friends.

5. Bert Barricune in "The Man Who Shot Liberty Valance" led a more satisfying life than did Ransome Foster.

6. Without its unique setting, "Camford Cottage" would lack excitement and suspense. (If necessary, review *setting* in Handbook of Literary Terms.)

7. The character of Dr. Roylott in "The Speckled Band" is too angry and bitter to be believable.

8. If "The Magic Shop" had been told from Gip's point of view, the story would not have been nearly so interesting.

9. Like Bill Buckley in "The Man Who Knew How," I find detective stories inadequate and boring.

10. If Blackbeard and Mr. Underhill had killed each other in battle, the conclusion of "The Rule of Names" would have been just as effective.

11. A story like "The Third Bank of the River" does not belong in a ninth-grade anthology of literature.

12. "The Man Who Shot Liberty Valance" would be a more complex story if it were told from Hallie's point of view.

13. It is hard to believe that Miss Symondson in "Camford Cottage" could recall in detail the interior of a cottage she had visited thirty years earlier.

14. The plot of "Early Marriage" lacks excitement.

15. I would rather invite Sherlock Holmes to a dinner party than I would the shopman from "The Magic Shop."

Concept Review: Interpretation of New Material

Read the story; then, on your paper, answer the questions that follow.

The Good Provider • *Marion Gross*

Minnie Leggety turned up the walk of her Elm Street bungalow and saw that she faced another crisis. When Omar sat brooding like that, not smoking, not "studying," but just scrunched down inside of himself, she knew enough after forty years to realize that she was facing a crisis. As though it weren't enough just trying to get along on Omar's pension these days, without having to baby him through another one of his periods of discouragement! She forced a gaiety into her voice that she actually didn't feel.

"Why, hello there, Pa, what are you doing out here? Did you have to come up for air?" Minnie eased herself down beside Omar on the stoop and put the paper bag she had been carrying on the sidewalk. Such a little bag, but it had taken most of their week's food budget! Protein, plenty of lean, rare steaks and chops, that's what that nice man on the radio said old folks needed, but as long as he couldn't tell you how to buy it with steak at $1.23 a pound, he might just as well save his breath to cool his porridge. And so might she, for all the attention Omar was paying her. He was staring straight ahead as though he didn't even see her. This looked like one of his real bad spells. She took his gnarled hand and patted it.

"What's the matter, Pa? Struck a snag with your gadget?" The "gadget" filled three full walls of the basement and most of the floor space besides, but it was still a "gadget" to Minnie—another one of his ideas that didn't quite work.

Omar had been working on gadgets ever since they were married. When they were younger, she hotly sprang to his defense against her sisters-in-law: "Well, it's better than liquor, and it's cheaper than pinochle; at least I know where he is nights." Now that they were older, and Omar was retired from his job, his tinkering took on a new significance. It was what kept him from going to pieces like a lot of men who were retired and didn't have enough activity to fill their time and their minds.

"What's the matter, Pa?" she asked again.

The old man seemed to notice her for the first time. Sadly he shook his head. "Minnie, I'm a failure. The thing's no good; it ain't practical. After all I promised you, Minnie, and the way you stuck by me and all, it's just not going to work."

Minnie never had thought it would. It just didn't seem possible that a body could go gallivanting back and forth the way Pa had said they would if the gadget worked. She continued to pat the hand she held and told him soothingly, "I'm not sure but it's for the best, Pa. I'd sure have gotten airsick, or timesick, or whatever it was. What're you going to work on now that you're giving up the time machine?" she asked anxiously.

"You don't understand, Min," the old man said. "I'm through. I've failed. I've failed at everything I've ever tried to make. They always *almost* work, and yet there's always something I can't get just right. I never knew enough, Min, never had enough schooling, and now it's too late to get any. I'm just giving up altogether. I'm through!"

This *was* serious. Pa with nothing to tinker at down in the basement, Pa constantly underfoot, Pa with nothing to keep him from just slipping away like old Mr. Mason had, was something she didn't like to think about. "Maybe it isn't as bad as all that," she told him. "All those nice parts you put into your gadget, maybe you could make us a television or something with them. Land, a television, that would be a nice thing to have."

"Oh, I couldn't do that, Min. I wouldn't know how to make a television; besides, I told you, it almost works. It's just that it ain't practical. It ain't the way I pictured it. Come down, I'll show you." He dragged her into the house and down into the basement.

The time machine left so little free floor space, what with the furnace and coal bin and washtubs, that Minnie had to stand on the stairway while Pa explained it to her. It needed explanation. It had more colored lights than a pinball machine, more plugs than the Hillsdale telephone exchange, and more levers than one of those newfangled voting booths.

"Now see," he said, pointing to various parts of the machine, "I rigged this thing up so we could move forward or back in time and space both. I thought we could go off and visit foreign spots, and see great things happening, and have ourselves an interesting old age."

"Well, I don't rightly know if I'd have enjoyed that, Pa," Minnie interrupted. "I doubt I'd know how to get along with all them foreigners, and their strange talk and strange ways and all."

Omar shook his head in annoyance. "The Holy Land. You'd have wanted to see the Holy Land, wouldn't you? You could have sat with the crowd at Galilee and listened to the Lord's words right from His lips. You'd have enjoyed that, wouldn't you?"

"Omar, when you talk like that you make the whole thing sound sacrilegious and against the Lord's ways. Besides, I suppose the Lord would have spoke in Hebrew, and I don't know one word of that and you don't either. I don't know but what I'm glad you couldn't get the thing to work," she said righteously.

"But Min, it does work!" Omar was indignant. "But you said——"

"I never said it don't work. I said it ain't practical. It don't work good enough, and I don't know enough to make it work better."

Working on the gadget was one thing, but believing that it worked was another. Minnie began to be alarmed. Maybe folks had been right—maybe Omar had gone off his head at last. She looked at him anxiously. He seemed all right and, now that he was worked up at her, the depression seemed to have left him.

"What do you mean it works, but not good enough?" she asked him.

"Well, see here," Omar told her, pointing to an elaborate control board. "It was like I was telling you before you interrupted with your not getting along with foreigners, and your sacrilegion and all. I set this thing up to move a body in time and space any which way. There's a globe of the world worked in here, and I thought that by turning the globe and setting these time controls to whatever year you had in mind you could go wherever you had a mind to. Well, it don't work like that. I've been trying it out for a whole week and no matter how I set the globe, no matter how I set the time controls, it always comes out the same. It lands me over at Main and Center, right in front of Purdey's meat market."

"What's wrong with that?" Minnie asked. "That might be real convenient."

"You don't understand," Omar told her. "It isn't *now* when I get there, it's twenty years ago! That's the trouble, it don't take me none of the places I want to go, just Main and Center. And it don't take me none of the times I want to go, just twenty years ago, and I saw enough of the Depression[1] so I don't want to spend my old age

1. ***Depression,*** the worldwide reduction in business activity that occurred in the 1930s.

watching people sell apples. Then on top of that, this here timer don't work." He pointed to another dial. "It's supposed to set to how long you want to stay, wherever you want to go, but it don't work at all. Twenty mintues, and then woosh, you're right back here in the basement. Nothing works like I want it to."

Minnie had grown thoughtful as Omar re-

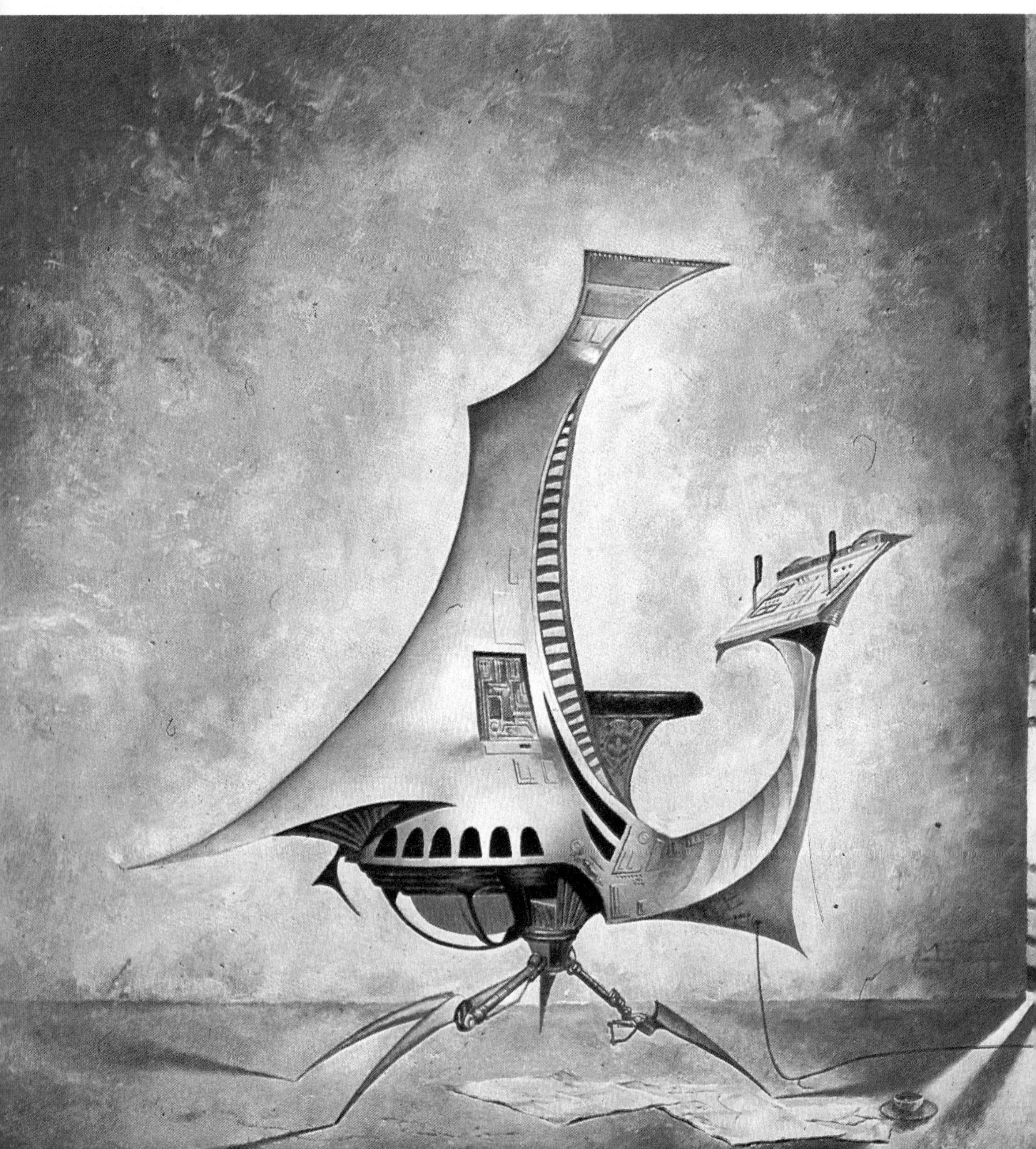

counted the faults of the machine. Wasn't it a caution the way even a smart man like Pa, a man smart enough to make a time machine, didn't have a practical ounce to his whole hundred and forty-eight pounds? She sat down heavily on the cellar steps and, emptying the contents of her purse on her broad lap, began examining the bills.

"What you looking for, Min?" Omar asked.

Minnie looked at him pityingly. Wasn't it a caution . . .

Purdey the butcher was leaning unhappily against his chopping block. The shop was clean and shining, the floor was strewn with fresh sawdust, and Purdey himself, unmindful of the expense, had for the sake of his morale donned a fresh apron. But for all that, Purdey wished that he was hanging on one of his chromium-plated meat hooks.

The sky was blue and smogless, something it never was when the shops were operating and employing the valley's five thousand breadwinners. Such potential customers as were abroad had a shabby, threadbare look to them. Over in front of the Bijou old Mr. Ryan was selling apples.

While he watched, a stout, determined-looking woman appeared at the corner of Main and Center. She glanced quickly around, brushing old Mr. Ryan and his apples with her glance, and then came briskly toward Purdey's shop. Purdey straightened up.

"Afternoon, Ma'am, what can I do for you?" He beamed as though the light bill weren't three months overdue.

"I'll have a nice porterhouse," the lady said hesitantly. "How much is porterhouse?"

"Forty-five a pound, best in the house." Purdey held up a beauty, expecting her to change her mind.

"I'll take it," the lady said. "And six lamb chops. I want a rib roast for Sunday, but I can come back for that. No use carrying too much," she explained. "Could you please hurry with that? I haven't very much time."

"New in town?" Purdey asked as he turned to ring up the sale on the cash register.

"Yes, you might say so," the woman said. By the time Purdey turned back to ask her name, she was gone. But Purdey knew she'd be back. She wanted a rib roast for Sunday. "It just goes to show you," Purdey said to himself, surveying the satisfactory tab sticking up from the register, "there still is some money around. Two dollars, and she never even batted an eyelash. It goes to show you!"

---

1. Minnie Leggety knows she faces a crisis when Omar sits **(a)** smoking; **(b)** talking; **(c)** brooding; **(d)** playing cards.

2. At the beginning of the story, Minnie has been **(a)** visiting with friends; **(b)** buying meat; **(c)** riding the bus; **(d)** phoning the doctor.

3. Omar's "gadget" occupies most of **(a)** the basement; **(b)** the attic; **(c)** the living room; **(d)** the garage.

4. Minnie **(a)** is opposed to Omar's hobby; **(b)** is in favor of his hobby; **(c)** doesn't care what her husband does; **(d)** doesn't know Omar has a hobby.

5. Omar's time machine can send a person to **(a)** the Holy Land; **(b)** Main and Center; **(c)** Ancient Rome; **(d)** Classical Greece.

6. The machine can transport a person back in time **(a)** 500 years; **(b)** 50 years; **(c)** 20 years; **(d)** 10 years.

7. Minnie uses the time machine **(a)** to travel to the Holy Land; **(b)** to visit relatives; **(c)** to shop in Paris; **(d)** to buy meat.

8. The reader can infer that the time setting at the beginning of the story is approximately **(a)** 1985; **(b)** 1955; **(c)** 1935; **(d)** 1910.

9. The story is told from **(a)** Minnie's point of view; **(b)** Omar's point of view; **(c)** the third person omniscient point of view; **(d)** the third person objective point of view.

10. "The Good Provider" fits best into which of the following categories? **(a)** western; **(b)** mystery; **(c)** detective stories; **(d)** fantasy.

Composition Review

Choose one of the following composition assignments:

1. Assume that you work for a Hollywood film studio. You have been asked to choose for possible production one of the stories in this unit. You reflect on what elements attract customers to theaters—mystery, suspense, romance, chivalry, and so forth; you weigh the costs and the difficulties of production; and you think about what stars might be featured in the film. Your purpose is to convince your supervisor that your suggestion is the one to be followed.

Then write a report to the supervisor, telling which story you've chosen and why.

2. You have been hired as a student consultant to the authors who prepared this anthology of literature. You have been asked to choose from the selections in this unit three stories to eliminate for the next edition of the book. You have also been asked to justify your choices. As you plan your assignment, you consider what elements in stories most interest students; and you reflect on the quality of each story—the presentation of setting, the construction of plot, the development of characters, the presentation of themes, and so forth.

Then, you write a report stating which three you would eliminate and why.

Unit 6

Greek Drama

Antigone

Illustrations for this play are from a production of *Antigone* at the Court Theater, Chicago, Illinois.

Introduction

The beginnings of modern drama lie in the ancient Greek celebrations in honor of Dionysus, god of wine. These celebrations, which consisted of singing, dancing, and games, were notable for the choral songs, led by a conductor. About the sixth century B.C., the conductor began joining in and adding words. Soon, actors began to perform the actions narrated in the choral song, and eventually spoken dialogue was introduced. At that point drama as we know it had come into being.

During these festivals, or celebrations, competing playwrights presented new tragedies. These tragedies were performed before the citizens of Athens in a three-day competition, and prizes were awarded to playwrights whose plays were judged the best. Sophocles, who wrote *Antigone,* was a frequent winner at the competitions.

The Theater

The Greek theater was an enormous open-air arena, usually built on the side of a hill. Its focal point was the large circular *orchestra* ("dancing-place"), which was located at the foot of the hill and had at its center an altar to Dionysus. The

chorus moved about on the orchestra; and the flute player, who provided their accompaniment, was stationed on the steps of the altar. Forming a horseshoe around the orchestra was the *theatron* ("seeing-place"), semicircular tiers of stone seats provided for the comfort of the audience. The largest of these theaters had a seating capacity of 17,000.

Slightly above the level of the orchestra was the stage on which the actors performed. It had neither a curtain nor a ceiling. Behind the stage and facing the spectators stood the *skene* (skē′nē), a three-doored building that served as a retiring place for the actors and as a background for their performance.

Because the audience sat at a distance from the stage, actions and costumes were designed for long-range, visual and auditory effect. Performers wore linen or wooden masks that displayed, with exaggeration, the most important characteristics of the various roles; for example, a wounded soldier might appear in a horribly distorted and bloody mask, an old prophet would wear an extremely wizened one. (Teiresias, the prophet who appears in *Antigone,* is old and blind; therefore, his mask would be both wrinkled and black around the eyes.) All masks were provided with huge mouth openings, so that players could project their voices to the large audience. Because most of the audience was too far away to see the performers' facial expressions, actors had to depend on voice quality and hand gestures to convey emotion. Just as the masks were exaggerated, so too were the delivery of the lines and the gestures of the actors as they spoke. The actor's height was increased by the use of tall headdresses and extremely thick-soled boots. All the players wore long, flowing robes.

The Participants

In the earliest Greek plays, the chorus was a large group of men dancing and chanting or singing in unison. Eventually the number was reduced to twelve or fifteen, and one member, the chorus leader, was given individual lines. Playwrights used the chorus to interpret and recall past events, to comment on the actions of the characters in the play, or to foretell the future. Although its role and importance varied from play to play, the chorus often expressed the emotions experienced by the audience.

Tragedy

Although the Dionysian festivals were happy affairs, from them tragedy as a form was born. Borrowing from a traditional story or legend, tragedy showed what happened when people flouted the laws of the gods. The intent of the plays was moralistic. Terrible things happened to the proud, or to those who defied the will of the gods.

Greek tragedy serves to illuminate a philosophy held by most Greeks at that time: the wrongs people do to each other will be punished by Fate; and Fate is ordained by the gods.

The Legend: A Cycle of Tragedy

Although *Antigone* is a complete play in itself, it is closely associated with two other of Sophocles' plays, *Oedipus the King* and *Oedipus at Colonus.* Oedipus, separated as a child from his parents, fulfilled a dreadful prophecy that had been made at the time of his birth: When he became an adult, he killed his father without recognizing him and later married his mother, Jocasta, whom he did not remember. When he discovered the truth, Oedipus put out his own eyes and banished himself from his kingdom of Thebes. He wandered about for many years, blind and tormented, until he finally died in Colonus, as had been prophesied.

In what seems to be the final play of the trilogy, *Antigone,* the scene is Thebes once again. The play, which takes place after the death of Oedipus, completes the cycle of tragedy that started with the birth of this great king of Thebes. Just before *Antigone* begins, the two sons of Oedipus and Jocasta have killed each other in battle. As the play opens, Antigone and Ismene, the two daughters of Oedipus and Jocasta, are talking.

Antigone

Sophocles

translated by E. F. Watling

CHARACTERS

ISMENE (is mē'nē) } *daughters of Oedipus*
ANTIGONE (an tig'ə nē) }
CREON (krē'on), *King of Thebes*
HAEMON (hē'mən), *son of Creon*
TEIRESIAS (tī rē'sē əs), *a blind prophet*
A SENTRY
A MESSENGER
EURYDICE (yü rid'i sē'), *wife of Creon*
CHORUS OF THEBAN ELDERS
KING'S ATTENDANTS
QUEEN'S ATTENDANTS
A BOY LEADING TEIRESIAS
SOLDIERS

Scene: Before the Palace at Thebes.

Enter ISMENE *from the central door of the Palace.* ANTIGONE *follows, anxious and urgent; she closes the door carefully, and comes to join her sister.*

ANTIGONE. O sister! Ismene dear, dear sister Ismene!
You know how heavy the hand of God is upon us;
How we who are left must suffer for our father, Oedipus.
There is no pain, no sorrow, no suffering, no dishonor
We have not shared together, you and I.
And now there is something more. Have you heard this order,
This latest order that the King has proclaimed to the city?
Have you heard how our dearest are being treated like enemies?
ISMENE. I have heard nothing about any of those we love,
Neither good nor evil—not, I mean, since the death
Of our two brothers, both fallen in a day.
The Argive army,[1] I hear, was withdrawn last night.
I know no more to make me sad or glad.
ANTIGONE. I thought you did not. That's why I brought you out here,
Where we shan't be heard, to tell you something alone.
ISMENE. What is it, Antigone? Black news, I can see already.
ANTIGONE. O Ismene, what do you think? Our two dear brothers . . .

1. ***Argive army*** (är'jīv *or* är'gīv), the army that attacked Thebes; from Argos (är'gos), a city in southern Greece.

Creon has given funeral honours to one,[2]
And not to the other; nothing but shame and ignominy.
Eteocles[3] has been buried, they tell me, in state,
With all honourable observances due to the dead.
But Polynices,[4] just as unhappily fallen—the order
Says he is not to be buried, not to be mourned;
To be left unburied, unwept, a feast of flesh
For keen-eyed carrion birds. The noble Creon!
It is against you and me he has made this order.
Yes, against me. And soon he will be here himself
To make it plain to those that have not heard it,
And to enforce it. This is no idle threat;
The punishment for disobedience is death by stoning.
So now you know. And now is the time to show
Whether or not you are worthy of your high blood.

ISMENE. My poor Antigone, if this is really true,
What more can I do, or undo, to help you?

ANTIGONE. *Will* you help me? Will you do something with me?
Will you?

ISMEME. Help you do what, Antigone? What do you mean?

ANTIGONE. Would you help me lift the body . . . you and me?

ISMENE. You cannot mean . . . to bury him? Against the order?

ANTIGONE. Is he not my brother, and yours, whether you like it
Or not? *I* shall never desert him, never.

ISMENE. How could you dare, when Creon has expressly forbidden
it?

ANTIGONE. He has no right to keep me from my own.

ISMENE. O sister, sister, do you forget how our father
Perished in shame and misery, his awful sin
Self-proved, blinded by his own self-mutilation?
And then his mother, his wife—for she was both—
Destroyed herself in a noose of her own making.[5]
And now our brothers, both in a single day
Fallen in an awful exaction of death for death,
Blood for blood, each slain by the other's hand.
Now we two left; and what will be the end of us,
If we transgress the law and defy our king?
O think, Antigone; we are women; it is not for us
To fight against men; our rulers are stronger than we,
And we must obey in this, or in worse than this.
May the dead forgive me, I can do no other
But as I am commanded; to do more is madness.

ANTIGONE. No; then I will not ask you for your help.
Nor would I thank you for it, if you gave it.
Go your own way; I will bury my brother;
And if I die for it, what happiness!

2. ***funeral honors to one.*** In Greek mythology, the souls of unburied human beings could not cross the River Styx to the realm of the dead but were compelled to wander forever with no permanent resting place. Consequently, burial of the dead was an important sacred duty of surviving friends and relatives.
3. ***Eteocles*** (i tē′ə klēz).
4. ***Polynices*** (pol i nī′sēz).

5. ***his mother . . . own making.*** Jocasta (jō kas′tə), realizing that she was both wife and mother to Oedipus, hanged herself.

Convicted of reverence—I shall be content
To lie beside a brother whom I love.
We have only a little time to please the living.
But all eternity to love the dead.
There I shall lie for ever. Live, if you will;
Live, and defy the holiest laws of heaven.
ISMENE. I do not defy them; but I cannot act
Against the State. I am not strong enough.
ANTIGONE. Let that be your excuse, then. I will go
And heap a mound of earth over my brother.
ISMENE. I fear for you, Antigone; I fear——
ANTIGONE. You need not fear for me. Fear for yourself.
ISMENE. At least be secret. Do not breathe a word.
I'll not betray your secret.
ANTIGONE. Publish it
To all the world! Else I shall hate you more.
ISMENE. Your heart burns! Mine is frozen at the thought.
ANTIGONE. I know my duty, where true duty lies.
ISMENE. If you can do it; but you're bound to fail.
ANTIGONE. When I have *tried* and failed, I shall have failed.
ISMENE. No sense in starting on a hopeless task.
ANTIGONE. Oh, I shall hate you if you talk like that!
And *he*[6] will hate you, rightly. Leave me alone
With my own madness. There is no punishment
Can rob me of my honorable death.
ISMENE. Go then, if you are determined, to your folly.
But remember that those who love you . . . love you still.
(ISMENE *goes into the Palace.* ANTIGONE *leaves the stage by a side exit.)*

6. ***he,*** Polynices.

(Enter the CHORUS *of Theban elders.)*
CHORUS. Hail the sun! the brightest of all that ever
Dawned on the City of Seven Gates, City of Thebes!
Hail the golden dawn over Dirce's river[7]
Rising to speed the flight of the white invaders
Homeward in full retreat!

7. ***Dirce's river.*** Dirce (dėr'sē), the wife of a previous ruler of Thebes, was brutally murdered and her corpse thrown into a stream thereafter called by her name.

The army of Polynices was gathered against us,
In angry dispute his voice was lifted against us,
Like a ravening bird of prey he swooped around us
With white wings flashing, with flying plumes,
With armed hosts ranked in thousands.

At the threshold of seven gates in a circle of blood
His swords stood round us, his jaws were opened against us;
But before he could taste our blood, or consume us with fire,

He fled, fled with the roar of the dragon behind him
    And thunder of war in his ears.

  The Father of Heaven abhors the proud tongue's boasting;
He marked the oncoming torrent, the flashing stream
Of their golden harness, the clash of their battle gear;
He heard the invader cry Victory over our ramparts,
    And smote him with fire to the ground.[8]

  Down to the ground from the crest of his hurricane onslaught
He swung, with the fiery brands of his hate brought low;
Each and all to their doom of destruction appointed
    By the god that fighteth for us.

  Seven invaders at seven gates seven defenders
Spoiled of their bronze for a tribute to Zeus;[9] save two
Luckless brothers in one fight matched together
    And in one death laid low.[10]

  Great is the victory, great be the joy
In the city of Thebes, the city of chariots.
Now is the time to fill the temples
With glad thanksgiving for warfare ended;
Shake the ground with the night-long dances,
Bacchus afoot and delight abounding.

  But see, the King comes here,
Creon, the son of Menoeceus,[11]
Whom the gods have appointed for us
In our recent change of fortune.
What matter is it, I wonder,
That has led him to call us together
By his special proclamation?

(The central door is opened, and CREON *enters.)*
CREON. My councillors: now that the gods have brought our city
Safe through a storm of trouble to tranquillity,
I have called you especially out of all my people
To conference together, knowing that you
Were loyal subjects when King Laius[12] reigned,
And when King Oedipus so wisely ruled us,
And again, upon his death, faithfully served
His sons, till they in turn fell—both slayers, both slain,
Both stained with brother-blood, dead in a day—
And I, their next of kin, inherited
The throne and kingdom which I now possess.

8. ***The Father of Heaven . . . smote him with fire to the ground.*** Zeus, who favored the Thebans in the battle, struck down the invading Argive army with thunderbolts.

9. ***Seven invaders . . . tribute to Zeus.*** Polynices and six Argive chiefs each attacked one of Thebes's seven gates, which were successfully defended by seven Theban heroes. The Theban defenders offered the armor of the slain Argive chiefs as a tribute to Zeus.

10. ***Luckless brothers . . . laid low.*** Antigone's brothers, Polynices and Eteocles, killed each other in single combat, ending the war.

11. ***Menoeceus,*** (mə nē′sē əs).

12. ***King Laius*** (lā′əs), a former king of Thebes and father of Oedipus.

No other touchstone can test the heart of a man,
The temper of his mind and spirit, till he be tried
In the practice of authority and rule.
For my part, I have always held the view,
And hold it still, that a king whose lips are sealed
By fear, unwilling to seek advice, is damned.
And no less damned is he who puts a friend
Above his country; I have no good word for him.
As God above is my witness, who sees all,
When I see any danger threatening my people,
Whatever it may be, I shall declare it.
No man who is his country's enemy
Shall call himself my friend. Of this I am sure—
Our country is our life; only when she[13]
Rides safely, have we any friends at all.
Such is my policy for our common weal.
In pursuance of this, I have made a proclamation
Concerning the sons of Oedipus, as follows:
Eteocles, who fell fighting in defence of the city,
Fighting gallantly, is to be honored with burial
And with all the rites due to the noble dead.
The other—you know whom I mean—his brother Polynices,
Who came back from exile intending to burn and destroy
His fatherland and the gods of his fatherland,
To drink the blood of his kin, to make them slaves—
He is to have no grave, no burial,
No mourning from anyone; it is forbidden.
He is to be left unburied, left to be eaten
By dogs and vultures, a horror for all to see.
I am determined that never, if I can help it,
Shall evil triumph over good. Alive
Or dead, the faithful servant of his country
Shall be rewarded.

CHORUS. Creon, son of Menoeceus,
You have given your judgment for the friend and for the enemy.
As for those that are dead, so for us who remain,
Your will is law.

CREON. See then that it be kept.

CHORUS. My lord, some younger would be fitter for that task.

CREON. Watchers are already set over the corpse.

CHORUS. What other duty then remains for us?

CREON. Not to connive at any disobedience.

CHORUS. If there were any so mad as to ask for death——

13. ***she,*** Thebes.

CREON. Ay, that is the penalty. There is always someone
Ready to be lured to ruin by hope of gain.

(He turns to go. A SENTRY *enters from the side of the stage.* CREON *pauses at the Palace door.)*

SENTRY. My lord: if I am out of breath, it is not from haste.
I have not been running. On the contrary, many a time
I stopped to think and loitered on the way,
Saying to myself "Why hurry to your doom,
Poor fool?" and then I said "Hurry, you fool.
If Creon hears this from another man,
Your head's as good as off." So here I am,
As quick as my unwilling haste could bring me;
In no great hurry, in fact. So now I am here . . .
But I'll tell my story . . . though it may be nothing after all.
And whatever I have to suffer, it can't be more
Than what God wills, so I cling to that for my comfort.
CREON. Good heavens, man, whatever is the matter?
SENTRY. To speak of myself first—I never did it, sir;
Nor saw who did; no one can punish me for that.
CREON. You tell your story with a deal of artful precaution.
It's evidently something strange.
SENTRY. It is.
So strange, it's very difficult to tell.
CREON. Well, out with it, and let's be done with you.
SENTRY. It's this, sir. The corpse . . . someone has just
Buried it and gone. Dry dust over the body
They scattered, in the manner of holy burial.
CREON. What! Who dared to do it?
SENTRY. I don't know, sir.
There was no sign of a pick, no scratch of a shovel;
The ground was hard and dry—no trace of a wheel;
Whoever it was has left no clues behind him.
When the sentry on the first watch showed it us,
We were amazed. The corpse was covered from sight—
Not with a proper grave—just a layer of earth—
As it might be, the act of some pious passer-by.
There were no tracks of an animal either, a dog
Or anything that might have come and mauled the body.
Of course we all started pitching in to each other,
Accusing each other, and might have come to blows,
With no one to stop us; for anyone might have done it,
But it couldn't be proved against him, and all denied it.
We were all ready to take hot iron in hand
And go through fire and swear by God and heaven
We hadn't done it, nor knew of anyone

That could have thought of doing it, much less done it.
  Well, we could make nothing of it. Then one of our men
Said something that made all our blood run cold—
Something we could neither refuse to do, nor do,
But at our own risk. What he said was "This
Must be reported to the King; we can't conceal it."
So it was agreed. We drew lots for it, and I,
Such is my luck, was chosen. So here I am,
As much against my will as yours, I'm sure;
A bringer of bad news expects no welcome.

CHORUS. My lord, I fear—I feared it from the first—
That this may prove to be an act of the gods.

CREON. Enough of that! Or I shall lose my patience.
Don't talk like an old fool, old though you be.
Blasphemy, to say the gods could give a thought
To carrion flesh! Held him in high esteem,
I suppose, and buried him like a benefactor—
A man who came to burn their temples down,
Ransack their holy shrines, their land, their laws?
Is that the sort of man you think gods love?
Not they. No. There's a party of malcontents
In the city, rebels against my word and law,
Shakers of heads in secret, impatient of rule;
They are the people, I see it well enough,
Who have bribed their instruments to do this thing.
Money! Money's the curse of man, none greater.
That's what wrecks cities, banishes men from home,
Tempts and deludes the most well-meaning soul,
Pointing out the way to infamy and shame.
Well, they shall pay for their success. *(To the* SENTRY*)* See to it!
See to it, you! Upon my oath, I swear,
As Zeus is my god above: either you find
The perpetrator of this burial
And bring him here into my sight, or death—
No, not your mere death shall pay the reckoning,
But, for a living lesson against such infamy,
You shall be racked and tortured till you tell
The whole truth of this outrage; so you may learn
To seek your gain where gain is yours to get,
Not try to grasp it everywhere. In wickedness
You'll find more loss than profit.

SENTRY. May I say more?

CREON. No more; each word you say but stings me more.

SENTRY. Stings in your ears, sir, or in your deeper feelings?

CREON. Don't bandy words, fellow, about my feelings.

SENTRY. Though I offend your ears, sir, it is not I
But he that's guilty that offends your soul.
CREON. Oh, born to argue, were you?
SENTRY. Maybe so;
But still not guilty in this business.
CREON. Doubly so, if you have sold your soul for money.
SENTRY. To think that thinking men should think so wrongly!
CREON. Think what you will. But if you fail to find
The doer of this deed, you'll learn one thing:
Ill-gotten gain brings no one any good.
(He goes into the Palace.)
SENTRY. Well, heaven send they find him. But whether or no,
They'll not find me again, that's sure. Once free,
Who never thought to see another day,
I'll thank my lucky stars, and keep away.
(Exit.)
CHORUS. Wonders are many on earth, and the greatest of these
Is man, who rides the ocean and takes his way
Through the deeps, through wind-swept valleys of perilous seas
That surge and sway.

He is master of ageless Earth, to his own will bending
The immortal mother of gods by the sweat of his brow,
As year succeeds to year, with toil unending
Of mule and plough.

He is lord of all things living; birds of the air,
Beasts of the field, all creatures of sea and land.
He taketh, cunning to capture and ensnare
With sleight of hand;

Hunting the savage beast from the upland rocks,
Taming the mountain monarch in his lair,
Teaching the wild horse and the roaming ox
His yoke to bear.

The use of language, the wind-swift motion of brain
He learnt; found out the laws of living together
In cities, building him shelter against the rain
And wintry weather.

There is nothing beyond his power. His subtlety
Meeteth all chance, all danger conquereth.
For every ill he hath found its remedy,
Save only death.

O wondrous subtlety of man, that draws
To good or evil ways! Great honor is given
And power to him who upholdeth his country's laws
    And the justice of heaven.

  But he that, too rashly daring, walks in sin
In solitary pride to his life's end.
At door of mine shall never enter in
    To call me friend.

(Severally,[14] *seeing some persons approach from a distance)*
O gods! A wonder to see!
Surely it cannot be——
It is no other——
Antigone!
Unhappy maid——
Unhappy Oedipus' daughter; it is she they bring.
Can she have rashly disobeyed
The order of our King?

(Enter the SENTRY, *bringing* ANTIGONE *guarded by two more soldiers.)*

SENTRY. We've got her. Here's the woman that did the deed.
We found her in the act of burying him. Where's the King?
CHORUS. He is just coming out of the palace now.

(Enter CREON.*)*

CREON. What's this? What am I just in time to see?
SENTRY. My lord, an oath's a very dangerous thing.
Second thoughts may prove us liars. Not long since
I swore I wouldn't trust myself again
To face your threats; you gave me a drubbing the first time.
But there's no pleasure like an unexpected pleasure,
Not by a long way. And so I've come again,
Though against my solemn oath. And I've brought this lady,
Who's been caught in the act of setting that grave in order.
And no casting lots for it this time—the prize is mine
And no one else's. So take her; judge and convict her.
I'm free, I hope, and quit of the horrible business.
CREON. How did you find her? Where have you brought her from?
SENTRY. She was burying the man with her own hands, and that's the truth.
CREON. Are you in your senses? Do you know what you are saying?
SENTRY. I saw her myself, burying the body of the man
Whom you said not to bury. Don't I speak plain?

14. ***Severally.*** Each of the following lines is spoken by a different member of the Chorus.

CREON. How did she come to be seen and taken in the act?
SENTRY. It was this way. After I got back to the place,
With all your threats and curses ringing in my ears,
We swept off all the earth that covered the body,
And left it a sodden naked corpse again;
Then sat up on the hill, on the windward side,
Keeping clear of the stench of him, as far as we could;
All of us keeping each other up to the mark,
With pretty sharp speaking, not to be caught napping this time.
So this went on some hours, till the flaming sun
Was high in the top of the sky, and the heat was blazing.
Suddenly a storm of dust, like a plague from heaven,
Swept over the ground, stripping the trees stark bare,
Filling the sky; you had to shut your eyes
To stand against it. When at last it stopped,
There was the girl, screaming like an angry bird,
When it finds its nest empty and little ones gone.
Just like that she screamed, seeing the body
Naked, crying and cursing the ones that had done it.
Then she picks up the dry earth in her hands,
And pouring out of a fine bronze urn she's brought
She makes her offering three times to the dead.[15]
Soon as we saw it, down we came and caught her.
She wasn't at all frightened. And so we charged her
With what she'd done before, and this. She admitted it,
I'm glad to say—though sorry too, in a way.
It's good to save your own skin, but a pity
To have to see another get into trouble,
Whom you've no grudge against. However, I can't say
I've ever valued anyone else's life
More than my own, and that's the honest truth.
CREON *(to* ANTIGONE*)*. Well, what do you say—you, hiding your head there:
Do you admit, or do you deny the deed?
ANTIGONE. I do admit it. I do not deny it.
CREON *(to the* SENTRY*)*. You—you may go. You are discharged from blame.
(Exit SENTRY.*)*
Now tell me, in as few words as you can,
Did you know the order forbidding such an act?
ANTIGONE. I knew it, naturally. It was plain enough.
CREON. And yet you dared to contravene it?
ANTIGONE. Yes.
That order did not come from God. Justice,
That dwells with the gods below, knows no such law.
I did not think your edicts strong enough

15. ***And pouring . . . to the dead,*** pouring wine or water as an offering to the gods.

To overrule the unwritten unalterable laws
Of God and heaven, you being only a man.
They are not of yesterday or today, but everlasting
Though where they came from, none of us can tell.
Guilty of their transgression before God
I cannot be, for any man on earth.
I knew that I should have to die, of course,
With or without your order. If it be soon,
So much the better. Living in daily torment
As I do, who would not be glad to die?
This punishment will not be any pain.
Only if I had let my mother's son
Lie there unburied, then I could not have borne it.
This I can bear. Does that seem foolish to you?
Or is it you that are foolish to judge me so?

CHORUS. She shows her father's stubborn spirit: foolish
Not to give way when everything's against her.

CREON. Ah, but you'll see. The over-obstinate spirit
Is soonest broken; as the strongest iron will snap
If over-tempered in the fire to brittleness.
A little halter is enough to break
The wildest horse. Proud thoughts do not sit well
Upon subordinates. This girl's proud spirit
Was first in evidence when she broke the law;
And now, to add insult to her injury,
She gloats over her deed. But, as I live,
She shall not flout my orders with impunity.
My sister's child—ay, were she even nearer,
Nearest and dearest, she should not escape
Full punishment—she, and her sister too,
Her partner, doubtless, in this burying.
Let her be fetched! She was in the house just now;
I saw her, hardly in her right mind either.
Often the thoughts of those who plan dark deeds
Betray themselves before the deed is done.
The criminal who being caught still tries
To make a fair excuse, is damned indeed.

ANTIGONE. Now you have caught, will you do more than kill me?

CREON. No, nothing more; that is all I could wish.

ANTIGONE. Why then delay? There is nothing that you can say
That I should wish to hear, as nothing I say
Can weigh with you. I have given my brother burial.
What greater honor could I wish? All these
Would say that what I did was honorable,

But fear locks up their lips. To speak and act
Just as he likes is a king's prerogative.
CREON. You are wrong. None of my subjects thinks as you do.
ANTIGONE. Yes, sir, they do; but dare not tell you so.
CREON. And you are not only alone, but unashamed.
ANTIGONE. There is no shame in honoring my brother.
CREON. Was not his enemy, who died with him, your brother?
ANTIGONE. Yes, both were brothers, both of the same parents.
CREON. You honor one, and so insult the other.
ANTIGONE. He that is dead will not accuse me of that.
CREON. He will, if you honor him no more than the traitor.
ANTIGONE. It was not a slave, but his brother that died with him.
CREON. Attacking his country, while the other defended it.
ANTIGONE. Even so, we have a duty to the dead.
CREON. Not to give equal honour to good and bad.
ANTIGONE. Who knows? In the country of the dead that may be the law.
CREON. An enemy can't be a friend, even when dead.
ANTIGONE. My way is to share my love, not share my hate.
CREON. Go then, and share your love among the dead.
We'll have no woman's law here, while I live.

(Enter ISMENE *from the Palace.)*

CHORUS. Here comes Ismene, weeping
In sisterly sorrow; a darkened brow,
Flushed face, and the fair cheek marred
With flooding rain.
CREON. You crawling viper! Lurking in my house
To suck my blood! Two traitors unbeknown
Plotting against my throne. Do you admit
To share in this burying, or deny all knowledge?
ISMENE. I did it—yes—if she will let me say so.
I am as much to blame as she is.
ANTIGONE. No.
That is not just. You would not lend a hand
And I refused your help in what I did.
ISMENE. But I am not ashamed to stand beside you
Now in your hour of trial, Antigone.
ANTIGONE. Whose was the deed, Death and the dead are witness.
I love no friend whose love is only words.
ISMENE. O sister, sister, let me share your death,
Share in the tribute of honor to him that is dead.
ANTIGONE. You shall not die with me. You shall not claim
That which you would not touch. One death is enough.
ISMENE. How can I bear to live, if you must die?

ANTIGONE. Ask Creon. Is not he the one you care for?
ISMENE. You do yourself no good to taunt me so.
ANTIGONE. Indeed no: even my jests are bitter pains.
ISMENE. But how, O tell me, how can I still help you?
ANTIGONE. Help yourself. I shall not stand in your way.
ISMENE. For pity, Antigone—can I not die with you?
ANTIGONE. You chose; life was your choice, when mine was death.
ISMENE. Although I warned you that it would be so.
ANTIGONE. Your way seemed right to some, to others mine.
ISMENE. But now both in the wrong, and both condemned.
ANTIGONE. No, no. You live. My heart was long since dead,
So it was right for me to help the dead.
CREON. I do believe the creatures both are mad;
One lately crazed, the other from her birth.
ISMENE. Is it not likely, sir? The strongest mind
Cannot but break under misfortune's blows.
CREON. Yours did, when you threw in your lot with hers.
ISMENE. How could I wish to live without my sister?
CREON. You have no sister. Count her dead already.
ISMENE. You could not take her—kill your own son's bride?
CREON. Oh, there are other fields for him to plough.
ISMENE. No truer troth was ever made than theirs.
CREON. No son of mine shall wed so vile a creature.
ANTIGONE. O Haemon, can your father spite you so?
CREON. You and your paramour, I hate you both.
CHORUS. Sir, would you take her from your own son's arms?
CREON. Not I, but death shall take her.
CHORUS. Be it so.
Her death, it seems, is certain.
CREON. Certain it is.
No more delay. Take them, and keep them within—
The proper place for women. None so brave
As not to look for some way to escape
When they see life stand face to face with death.
(The women are taken away.)
CHORUS. Happy are they who know not the taste of evil.
From a house that heaven hath shaken
The curse departs not
But falls upon all of the blood,[16]
Like the restless surge of the sea when the dark storm drives
The black sand hurled from the deeps
And the Thracian gales boom down
On the echoing shore.

In life and in death is the house of Labdacus[17] stricken.
Generation to generation,

16. ***The curse . . . upon all of the blood.*** The curse on Oedipus has passed on to his descendants.

17. ***the house of Labdacus*** (lab′də kəs), the ruling family of Thebes. Labdacus, a former king, was the grandfather of Oedipus.

With no atonement,
It is scourged by the wrath of a god.

And now for the dead dust's sake is the light of promise,
The tree's last root, crushed out
By pride of heart and the sin
Of presumptuous tongue.

For what presumption of man can match thy power,
O Zeus, that art not subject to sleep or time
Or age, living for ever in bright Olympus?
Tomorrow and for all time to come,
As in the past,
This law is immutable:
For mortals greatly to live is greatly to suffer.

Roving ambition helps many a man to good,
And many it falsely lures to light desires,
Till failure trips them unawares, and they fall
On the fire that consumes them. Well was it said,
Evil seems good
To him who is doomed to suffer;
And short is the time before that suffering comes.[18]

18. ***Evil seems good . . . suffering comes.*** Although a man may convince himself that the evil he does is good, he must eventually suffer punishment for his wrongdoing.

But here comes Haemon,
Your youngest son.
Does he come to speak his sorrow
For the doom of his promised bride,
The loss of his marriage hopes?

CREON. We shall know it soon, and need no prophet to tell us.

(Enter HAEMON.*)*

Son, you have heard, I think, our final judgment
On your late betrothed. No angry words, I hope?
Still friends, in spite of everything, my son?

HAEMON. I am your son, sir; by your wise decisions
My life is ruled, and them I shall always obey.
I cannot value any marriage tie
Above your own good guidance.

CREON. Rightly said.
Your father's will should have your heart's first place.
Only for this do fathers pray for sons
Obedient, loyal, ready to strike down
Their fathers' foes, and love their fathers' friends.
To be the father of unprofitable sons
Is to be the father of sorrows, a laughingstock
To all one's enemies. Do not be fooled, my son,

By lust and the wiles of a woman. You'll have bought
Cold comfort if your wife's a worthless one.
No wound strikes deeper than love that is turned to hate.
This girl's an enemy; away with her,
And let her go and find a mate in Hades.
Once having caught her in a flagrant act—
The one and only traitor in our State—
I cannot make myself a traitor too;
So she must die. Well may she pray to Zeus,
The god of family love. How, if I tolerate
A traitor at home, shall I rule those abroad?
He that is a righteous master of his house
Will be a righteous statesman. To transgress
Or twist the law to one's own pleasure, presume
To order where one should obey, is sinful,
And I will have none of it.
He whom the State appoints must be obeyed
To the smallest matter, be it right—or wrong.
And he that rules his household, without a doubt,
Will make the wisest king, or, for that matter,
The staunchest subject. He will be the man
You can depend on in the storm of war,
The faithfullest comrade in the day of battle.
There is no more deadly peril than disobedience;
States are devoured by it, homes laid in ruins,
Armies defeated, victory turned to rout.
While simple obedience saves the lives of hundreds
Of honest folk. Therefore, I hold to the law,
And will never betray it—least of all for a woman.
Better be beaten, if need be, by a man,
Than let a woman get the better of us.

CHORUS. To me, as far as an old man can tell,
It seems your Majesty has spoken well.

HAEMON. Father, man's wisdom is the gift of heaven,
The greatest gift of all. I neither am
Nor wish to be clever enough to prove you wrong,
Though all men might not think the same as you do.
Nevertheless, I have to be your watchdog,
To know what others say and what they do,
And what they find to praise and what to blame.
Your frown is a sufficient silencer
Of any word that is not for your ears.
But *I* hear whispers spoken in the dark;
On every side I hear voices of pity
For this poor girl, doomed to the cruellest death,
And most unjust, that ever woman suffered

For an honourable action—burying a brother
Who was killed in battle, rather than leave him naked
For dogs to maul and carrion birds to peck at.
Has she not rather earned a crown of gold?—
Such is the secret talk about the town.
Father, there is nothing I can prize above
Your happiness and well-being. What greater good
Can any son desire? Can any father
Desire more from his son? Therefore I say,
Let not your first thought be your only thought.
Think if there cannot be some other way.
Surely, to think your own the only wisdom,
And yours the only word, the only will,
Betrays a shallow spirit, an empty heart.
It is no weakness for the wisest man
To learn when he is wrong, know when to yield.
So, on the margin of a flooded river
Trees bending to the torrent live unbroken,
While those that strain against it are snapped off.
A sailor has to tack and slacken sheets
Before the gale, or find himself capsized.
So, father, pause, and put aside your anger.
I think, for what my young opinion's worth,
That, good as it is to have infallible wisdom,
Since this is rarely found, the next best thing
Is to be willing to listen to wise advice.

CHORUS. There is something to be said, my lord, for this point of view,
And for yours as well; there is much to be said on both sides.

CREON. Indeed! Am I to take lessons at my time of life
From a fellow of his age?

HAEMON. No lesson you need be ashamed of.
It isn't a question of age, but of right and wrong.

CREON. Would you call it right to admire an act of disobedience?

HAEMON. Not if the act were also dishonorable.

CREON. And was not this woman's action dishonorable?

HAEMON. The people of Thebes think not.

CREON. The people of Thebes!
Since when do I take my orders from the people of Thebes?

HAEMON. Isn't that rather a childish thing to say?

CREON. No, I am king, and responsible only to myself.

HAEMON. A one-man state? What sort of a state is that?

CREON. Why, does not every state belong to its ruler?

HAEMON. You'd be an excellent king—on a desert island.

CREON. Of course, if you're on the woman's side——

HAEMON. No, no—

Unless you're the woman. It's you I'm fighting for.
CREON. What, villain, when every word you speak is against me?
HAEMON. Only because I know you are wrong, wrong.
CREON. Wrong? To respect my own authority?
HAEMON. What sort of respect tramples on all that is holy?
CREON. Despicable coward! No more will than a woman!
HAEMON. I have nothing to be ashamed of.
CREON. Yet you plead her cause.
HAEMON. No, *yours,* and mine, and that of the gods of the dead.
CREON. You'll never marry her this side of death.
HAEMON. Then, if she dies, she does not die alone.
CREON. Is that a threat, you impudent——
HAEMON. Is it a threat
To try to argue against wrong-headedness?
CREON. You'll learn what wrong-headedness is, my friend, to your cost.
HAEMON. O father, I could call you mad, were you not my father.
CREON. Don't toady me, boy; keep that for your lady-love.
HAEMON. You mean to have the last word, then?
CREON. I do.
And what is more, by all the gods in heaven,
I'll make you sorry for your impudence.
(Calling to those within)
Bring out that she-devil, and let her die
Now, with her bridegroom by to see it done!
HAEMON. That sight I'll never see. Nor from this hour
Shall you see me again. Let those that will
Be witness of your wickedness and folly.
(Exit.)
CHORUS. He is gone, my lord, in very passionate haste.
And who shall say what a young man's wrath may do?
CREON. Let him go! Let him do! Let him rage as never man raged,
He shall not save those women from their doom.
CHORUS. You mean, then, sire, to put them both to death?
CREON. No, not the one whose hand was innocent.
CHORUS. And to what death do you condemn the other?
CREON. I'll have her taken to a desert place
Where no man ever walked, and there walled up
Inside a cave, alive, with food enough
To acquit ourselves of the blood-guiltiness
That else would lie upon our commonwealth.
There she may pray to Death, the god she loves,
And ask release from death; or learn at last
What hope there is for those who worship death.[19]
(Exit.)

19. ***I'll have her taken . . . worship death.*** If Antigone is provided with enough food to enable her to pray for her life, then whether or not she dies is up to the gods, and Creon and the state are blameless.

CHORUS. Where is the equal of Love?
Where is the battle he cannot win,
The power he cannot outmatch?
In the farthest corners of earth, in the midst of the sea,
He is there; he is here
In the bloom of a fair face
Lying in wait;
And the grip of his madness
Spares not god or man,

Marring the righteous man,
Driving his soul into mazes of sin
And strife, dividing a house.
For the light that burns in the eyes of a bride of desire
Is a fire that consumes.
At the side of the great gods
Aphrodite immortal
Works her will upon all.

(The doors are opened and ANTIGONE *enters, guarded.)*
But here is a sight beyond all bearing,
At which my eyes cannot but weep;
Antigone forth faring
To her bridal bower of endless sleep.

ANTIGONE. You see me, countrymen, on my last journey,
Taking my last leave of the light of day;
Going to my rest, where death shall take me
Alive across the silent river.[20]
No wedding day; no marriage music;
Death will be all my bridal dower.

CHORUS. But glory and praise go with you, lady,
To your resting place. You go with your beauty
Unmarred by the hand of consuming sickness,
Untouched by the sword, living and free,
As none other that ever died before you.

ANTIGONE. The daughter of Tantalus,[21] a Phrygian maid,
Was doomed to a piteous death on the rock
Of Sipylus, which embraced and imprisoned her,
Merciless as the ivy, rain and snow
Beat down upon her, mingled with her tears,
As she wasted and died. Such was her story,
And such is the sleep that I shall go to.

CHORUS. She was a goddess of immortal birth,
And we are mortals; the greater the glory,
To share the fate of a god-born maiden,
A living death, but a name undying.

20. ***silent river,*** in Greek mythology, one of the rivers that separated the land of the dead from the land of the living.

21. ***The daughter of Tantalus,*** Niobe (nī′ō bē), whose children were slain by the gods to punish her for her excessive pride. Overcome with grief, she turned into a stone from which tears continued to flow. The stone was carried by a whirlwind to Mount Sipylus (si′pi ləs) in Phrygia (frij′i ə), the kingdom of Niobe's father.

ANTIGONE. Mockery, mockery![22] By the gods of our fathers,
Must you make me a laughingstock while I yet live?
O lordly sons of my city! O Thebes!
Your valleys of rivers, your chariots and horses!
No friend to weep at my banishment
To a rock-hewn chamber of endless durance,
In a strange cold tomb alone to linger
Lost between life and death for ever.

CHORUS. My child, you have gone your way
To the outermost limit of daring
And have stumbled against Law enthroned.
This is the expiation
You must make for the sin of your father.

ANTIGONE. My father—the thought that sears my soul—
The unending burden of the house of Labdacus.
Monstrous marriage of mother and son . . .
My father . . . my parents . . . O hideous shame!
Whom now I follow, unwed, curse-ridden,
Doomed to this death by the ill-starred marriage
That marred my brother's life.

CHORUS. An act of homage is good in itself, my daughter;
But authority cannot afford to connive at disobedience.
You are the victim of your own self-will.

ANTIGONE. And must go the way that lies before me.
No funeral hymn; no marriage music;
No sun from this day forth, no light,
No friend to weep at my departing.

Enter CREON.

CREON. Weeping and wailing at the door of death!
There'd be no end of it, if it had force
To buy death off. Away with her at once.
And close her up in her rock-vaulted tomb.
Leave her and let her die, if die she must,
Or live within her dungeon. Though on earth
Her life is ended from this day, her blood
Will not be on our hands.

ANTIGONE. So to my grave,
My bridal bower, my everlasting prison,
I go, to join those many of my kinsmen
Who dwell in the mansions of Persephone,
Last and unhappiest, before my time.
Yet I believe my father will be there
To welcome me, my mother greet me gladly,
And you, my brother, gladly see me come.
Each one of you my hands have laid to rest,

22. ***mockery.*** Antigone mistakenly thinks that the Chorus, in comparing her to the gods, is making fun of her.

Pouring the due libations on your graves.
It was by this service to your dear body, Polynices,
I earned the punishment which now I suffer,
Though all good people know it was for your honor.
O but I would not have done the forbidden thing
For any husband or for any son.
For why? I could have had another husband
And by him other sons, if one were lost;
But, father and mother lost, where would I get
Another brother? For thus preferring you,
My brother, Creon condemns me and hales me away,
Never a bride, never a mother, unfriended,
Condemned alive to solitary death.
What law of heaven have I transgressed? What god
Can save me now? What help or hope have I,
In whom devotion is deemed sacrilege?
If this is God's will, I shall learn my lesson
In death; but if my enemies are wrong,
I wish them no worse punishment than mine.

CHORUS. Still the same tempest in the heart
Torments her soul with angry gusts.

CREON. The more cause then have they that guard her
To hasten their work; or they too suffer.

CHORUS. Alas, that word had the sound of death.

CREON. Indeed there is no more to hope for.

ANTIGONE. Gods of our fathers, my city, my home,
Rulers of Thebes! Time stays no longer.
Last daughter of your royal house
Go I, *his* prisoner, because I honored
Those things to which honor truly belongs.

(ANTIGONE *is led away.*)

CHORUS. So, long ago, lay Danae[23]
Entombed within her brazen bower;
Noble and beautiful was she,
On whom there fell the golden shower
Of life from Zeus. There is no tower
So high, no armory so great,
No ship so swift, as is the power
Of man's inexorable fate.

There was the proud Edonian king,
Lycurgus,[24] in rock-prison pent
For arrogantly challenging
God's laws: it was his punishment
Of that swift passion to repent

23. ***Danae*** (dan′ə ē), a maiden imprisioned in a bronze chamber by her father, who feared a prophecy that a child born to Danae would someday kill him. Zeus entered her bronze chamber as a golden rain, and from their union Perseus, who eventually did kill his grandfather, was born.

24. ***Lycurgus*** (lī kėr′gəs), a Greek king who opposed the worship of Dionysus and was punished by being imprisoned in a cave and driven insane.

In slow perception, for that he
Had braved the rule omnipotent
Of Dionysus' sovereignty.

On Phineus' wife[25] the hand of fate
Was heavy, when her children fell
Victims to a stepmother's hate,
And she endured a prison-cell
Where the North Wind stood sentinel
In caverns amid mountains wild.
Thus the grey spinners wove their spell
On her, as upon thee, my child.[26]

(Enter TEIRESIAS, *the blind prophet, led by a boy.)*

TEIRESIAS. Gentlemen of Thebes, we greet you, my companion and I,
Who share one pair of eyes on our journeys together—
For the blind man goes where his leader tells him to.

CREON. You are welcome, father Teiresias. What's your news?

TEIRESIAS. Ay, news you shall have; and advice, if you can heed it.

CREON. There was never a time when I failed to heed it, father.

TEIRESIAS. And thereby have so far steered a steady course.

CREON. And gladly acknowledge the debt we owe to you.

TEIRESIAS. Then mark me now; for you stand on a razor's edge.

CREON. Indeed? Grave words from your lips, good priest. Say on.

TEIRESIAS. I will; and show you all that my skill reveals.
At my seat of divination,[27] where I sit
These many years to read the signs of heaven,
An unfamiliar sound came to my ears
Of birds in vicious combat, savage cries
In strange outlandish language, and the whirr
Of flapping wings; from which I well could picture
The gruesome warfare of their deadly talons.
Full of foreboding then I made the test
Of sacrifice upon the altar fire.
There was no answering flame; only rank juice
Oozed from the flesh and dripped among the ashes,
Smoldering and sputtering; the gall vanished in a puff,
And the fat ran down and left the haunches bare.
Thus (through the eyes of my young acolyte,
Who sees for me, that I may see for others)
I read the signs of failure in my quest.
And why? The blight upon us is *your* doing.
The blood that stains our altars and our shrines,
The blood that dogs and vultures have licked up,

25. ***Phineus' wife*** (fin′ē əs). King Phineus imprisoned his former wife and their two sons when he believed false accusations about them made by their stepmother, Idaea (i dē′ə).

26. ***So, long ago, lay Danae . . . as upon thee, my child.*** In this speech the Chorus compares Antigone's fate to that of three other mortals who had been imprisoned.

27. ***seat of divination,*** the place where Teiresias sat to listen to the birds, which were believed to tell him the future.

It is none other than the blood of Oedipus
Spilled from the veins of his ill-fated son.
Our fires, our sacrifices, and our prayers
The gods abominate. How should the birds
Give any other than ill-omened voices,
Gorged with the dregs of blood that man has shed?
Mark this, my son: all men fall into sin.
But sinning, he is not forever lost
Hapless and helpless, who can make amends
And has not set his face against repentance.
Only a fool is governed by self-will.
  Pay to the dead his due. Wound not the fallen.
It is no glory to kill and kill again.
My words are for your good, as is my will,
And should be acceptable, being for your good.

CREON. You take me for your target, reverend sir,
Like all the rest. I know your art of old,
And how you make me your commodity
To trade and traffic in for your advancement.
Trade as you will; but all the silver of Sardis
And all the gold of India will not buy
A tomb for yonder traitor. No. Let the eagles
Carry his carcass up to the throne of Zeus;
Even that would not be sacrilege enough
To frighten me from my determination
Not to allow this burial. No man's act
Has power enough to pollute the goodness of God.
But great and terrible is the fall, Teiresias,
Of mortal men who seek their own advantage
By uttering evil in the guise of good.

TEIRESIAS. Ah, is there any wisdom in the world?

CREON. Why, what is the meaning of that wide-flung taunt?

TEIRESIAS. What prize outweighs the priceless worth of prudence?

CREON. Ay, what indeed? What mischief matches the lack of it?

TEIRESIAS. And there you speak of your own symptom, sir.

CREON. I am loth to pick a quarrel with you, priest.

TEIRESIAS. You do so, calling my divination false.

CREON. I say all prophets seek their own advantage.

TEIRESIAS. All kings, say I, seek gain unrighteously.

CREON. Do you forget to whom you say it?

TEIRESIAS. No.
Our king and benefactor, by my guidance.

CREON. Clever you may be, but not therefore honest.

TEIRESIAS. Must I reveal my yet unspoken mind?

CREON. Reveal all; but expect no gain from it.

TEIRESIAS. Does that still seem to you my motive, then?

CREON. Nor is my will for sale, sir, in your market.
TEIRESIAS. Then hear this. Ere the chariot of the sun
Has rounded once or twice his wheeling way,
You shall have given a son of your own loins
To death, in payment for death—two debts to pay:
One for the life that you have sent to death,
The life you have abominably entombed;
One for the dead still lying above ground
Unburied, unhonoured, unblest by the gods below.
You cannot alter this. The gods themselves
Cannot undo it. It follows of necessity
From what you have done. Even now the avenging Furies,
The hunters of Hell that follow and destroy,
Are lying in wait for you, and will have their prey,
When the evil you have worked for others falls on you.
Do I speak this for my gain? The time shall come,
And soon, when your house will be filled with the lamentation
Of men and of women; and every neighbouring city
Will be goaded to fury against you, for upon them
Too the pollution falls when the dogs and vultures
Bring the defilement of blood to their hearths and altars.[28]
I have done. You pricked me, and these shafts of wrath
Will find their mark in your heart. You cannot escape
The sting of their sharpness. Lead me home, my boy.
Let us leave him to vent his anger on younger ears,
Or school his mind and tongue to a milder mood
Than that which now possesses him. Lead on.
(Exit.)
CHORUS. He has gone, my lord. He has prophesied terrible things.
And for my part, I that was young and now am old
Have never known his prophecies proved false.
CREON. It is true enough; and my heart is torn in two.
It is hard to give way, and hard to stand and abide
The coming of the curse. Both ways are hard.
CHORUS. If you would be advised, my good lord Creon——
CREON. What must I do? Tell me, and I will do it.
CHORUS. Release the woman from her rocky prison.
Set up a tomb for him that lies unburied.
CREON. Is it your wish that I consent to this?
CHORUS. It is, and quickly. The gods do not delay
The stroke of their swift vengeance on the sinner.
CREON. It is hard, but I must do it. Well I know
There is no armor against necessity.
CHORUS. Go. Let your own hand do it, and no other.
CREON. I will go this instant. Slaves there! One and all.
Bring spades and mattocks out on the hill!

28. *The time shall come . . . and altars.* This prophecy by Teiresias later came true when the families of the slain Argive chiefs enlisted the aid of the Athenian king, Theseus (thē′sē əs), to obtain burial rites for their dead. The Athenian army marched against Thebes and conquered it.

My mind is made; 'twas I imprisoned her,
And I will set her free. Now I believe
It is by the laws of heaven that man must live.
(Exit.)

CHORUS. O Thou whose name is many,[29]
Son of the Thunderer, dear child of his Cadmean bride,
Whose hand is mighty
In Italia,
In the hospitable valley
Of Eleusis,
And in Thebes,
The mother-city of thy worshippers,
Where sweet Ismenus gently watereth
The soil whence sprang the harvest of the dragon's teeth,[30]

Where torches on the crested mountains gleam,
And by Castalia's stream
The nymph-train in thy dance rejoices,
When from the ivy-tangled glens
Of Nysa[31] and from vine-clad plains
Thou comest to Thebes where the immortal voices
Sing thy glad strains.

Thebes, where thou lovest most to be,
With her, thy mother, the fire-stricken one,[32]
Sickens for need of thee.
Healer of all her ills;
Come swiftly o'er the high Parnassian hills,[33]
Come o'er the sighing sea.

The stars, whose breath is fire, delight
To dance for thee; the echoing night
Shall with thy praises ring.
Zeus-born, appear! With Thyiads[34] revelling
Come, bountiful
Iacchus, King!

(Enter a MESSENGER, *from the side of the stage.)*

MESSENGER. Hear, men of Cadmus' city, hear and attend,
Men of the house of Amphion,[35] people of Thebes!
What is the life of man? A thing not fixed
For good or evil, fashioned for praise or blame.
Chance raises a man to the heights, chance casts him down,
And none can foretell what will be from what is.
Creon was once an enviable man;
He saved his country from her enemies,

29. ***Thou whose name is many.*** The Chorus invokes the god Dionysus, whose native city of Thebes was under his special protection. Bacchus, Iacchus, and God of Wine are three of his many names.

30. ***Ismenus . . . dragon's teeth.*** Cadmus, the founder of Thebes, sowed dragon's teeth in the soil from which sprang armed men who helped him build the city near the river Ismenus (is-mē′nəs).

31. ***nymph-train . . . Nysa.*** When Semele (sem′ə lē), the mother of Dionysus, died, Zeus took his infant son to the nymphs of Nysa (nī′sə), who cared for him during his childhood.

32. ***thy mother, the fire-stricken one.*** Zeus had promised Semele that he would grant her one wish. Her wish was to see him in his full splendor as the king of gods and men. Being mortal, she could not endure the sight and was consumed to ashes.

33. ***Parnassian hills.*** Parnassus (pär-nas′əs), a mountain in southern Greece, was sacred to Apollo and the Muses.

34. ***Thyiads*** (thī′yadz), women driven mad by wine and the power of Dionysus. Also called Maenads (mē′nadz).

35. ***Amphion*** (am fī′ən), a former king of Thebes.

Assumed the sovereign power, and bore it well,
The honoured father of a royal house.
Now all is lost; for life without life's joys
Is living death; and such a life is his.
Riches and rank and show of majesty
And state, where no joy is, are empty, vain
And unsubstantial shadows, of no weight
To be compared with happiness of heart.

CHORUS. What is your news? Disaster in the royal house?

MESSENGER. Death; and the guilt of it on living heads.

CHORUS. Who dead? And by what hand?

MESSENGER. Haemon is dead,
Slain by his own——

CHORUS. His father?

MESSENGER. His own hand.
His father's act it was that drove him to it.

CHORUS. Then all has happened as the prophet said.

MESSENGER. What's next to do, your worships will decide.

(The Palace door opens.)

CHORUS. Here comes the Queen, Eurydice. Poor soul,
It may be she has heard about her son.

(Enter EURYDICE, *attended by women.)*

EURYDICE. My friends, I heard something of what you were saying
As I came to the door. I was on my way to prayer
At the temple of Pallas, and had barely turned the latch
When I caught your talk of some near calamity.
I was sick with fear and reeled in the arms of my women.
But tell me what is the matter; what have you heard?
I am not unacquainted with grief,[36] and I can bear it.

MESSENGER. Madam, it was I that saw it, and will tell you all.
To try to make it any lighter now
Would be to prove myself a liar. Truth
Is always best.
It was thus. I attended your husband,
The King, to the edge of the field where lay the body
Of Polynices, in pitiable state, mauled by the dogs.
We prayed for him to the Goddess of the Roads,[37] and to Pluto,
That they might have mercy upon him. We washed the remains
In holy water, and on a fire of fresh-cut branches
We burned all that was left of him, and raised
Over his ashes a mound of his native earth.
That done, we turned toward the deep rock-chamber
Of the maid that was married with death.
Before we reached it,

36. ***I am not unacquainted with grief.*** Menoeceus, a son of Creon and Eurydice, had sacrificed himself at the beginning of the war because of a prophecy that Thebes would be saved only if he were killed.

37. ***Goddess of the Roads,*** Hecate (hek′ə tē), a goddess of the underworld who sent apparitions to frighten travelers at night.

One that stood near the accursed place had heard
Loud cries of anguish, and came to tell King Creon.
As he approached, came strange uncertain sounds
Of lamentation, and he cried aloud:
"Unhappy wretch! Is my foreboding true?
Is this the most sorrowful journey that ever I went?
My son's voice greets me. Go, some of you, quickly
Through the passage where the stones are thrown apart,
Into the mouth of the cave, and see if it be
My son, my own son Haemon that I hear.
If not, I am the sport of gods."
We went
And looked, as bidden by our anxious master.
There in the furthest corner of the cave
We saw her hanging by the neck. The rope
Was of the woven linen of her dress.
And, with his arms about her, there stood he
Lamenting his lost bride, his luckless love,
His father's cruelty.
When Creon saw them,
Into the cave he went, moaning piteously.
"O my unhappy boy," he cried again,
"What have you done? What madness brings you here
To your destruction? Come away, my son,
My son, I do beseech you, come away!"
His son looked at him with one angry stare,
Spat in his face, and then without a word
Drew sword and struck out. But his father fled
Unscathed. Whereon the poor demented boy
Leaned on his sword and thrust it deeply home
In his own side, and while his life ebbed out
Embraced the maid in loose-enfolding arms,
His spurting blood staining her pale cheeks red.

*(*EURYDICE *goes quickly back into the Palace.)*

Two bodies lie together, wedded in death,
Their bridal sleep a witness to the world
How great calamity can come to man
Through man's perversity.

CHORUS. But what is this?
The Queen has turned and gone without a word.

MESSENGER. Yes. It is strange. The best that I can hope
Is that she would not sorrow for her son
Before us all, but vents her grief in private
Among her women. She is too wise, I think,
To take a false step rashly.

CHORUS. It may be.

Yet there is danger in unnatural silence
No less than in excess of lamentation.
MESSENGER. I will go in and see, whether in truth
There is some fatal purpose in her grief.
Such silence, as you say, may well be dangerous.
(He goes in.)
(Enter Attendants preceding the King.)
CHORUS. The King comes here.
What the tongue scarce dares to tell
Must now be known
By the burden that proves too well
The guilt, no other man's
But his alone.

(Enter CREON *with the body of* HAEMON.*)*
CREON. The sin, the sin of the erring soul
Drives hard unto death.
Behold the slayer, the slain,
The father, the son.
O the curse of my stubborn will!
Son, newly cut off in the newness of youth,
Dead for my fault, not yours.
CHORUS. Alas, too late you have seen the truth.
CREON. I learn in sorrow. Upon my head
God has delivered this heavy punishment,
Has struck me down in the ways of wickedness,
And trod my gladness under foot.
Such is the bitter affliction of mortal man.

(Enter the MESSENGER *from the Palace.)*
MESSENGER. Sir, you have this and more than this to bear.
Within there's more to know, more to your pain.
CREON. What more? What pain can overtop this pain?
MESSENGER. She is dead—your wife, the mother of him that is dead—
The death wound fresh in her heart. Alas, poor lady!
CREON. Insatiable Death, wilt thou destroy me yet?
What say you, teller of evil?
I am already dead,
And is there more?
Blood upon blood?
More death? My wife?
(The central doors open, revealing the body of EURYDICE.*)*
CHORUS. Look then, and see; nothing is hidden now.
CREON. O second horror!
What fate awaits me now?

My child here in my arms . . . and there, the other . . .
The son . . . the mother . . .
MESSENGER. There at the altar with the whetted knife
She stood, and as the darkness dimmed her eyes
Called on the dead, her elder son and this,
And with her dying breath cursed you, their slayer.
CREON. O horrible . . .
Is there no sword for me.
To end this misery?
MESSENGER. Indeed you bear the burden of two deaths.
It was her dying word.
CREON. And her last act?
MESSENGER. Hearing her son was dead, with her own hand
She drove the sharp sword home into her heart.
CREON. There is no man can bear this guilt but I.
It is true, I killed him.
Lead me away, away. I live no longer.
CHORUS. 'Twere best, if anything is best in evil times.
What's soonest done, is best, when all is ill.
CREON. Come, my last hour and fairest,

My only happiness . . . come soon.
Let me not see another day.
Away . . . away . . .

CHORUS. The future is not to be known; our present care
Is with the present; the rest is in other hands.

CREON. I ask no more than I have asked.

CHORUS. Ask nothing.
What is to be, no mortal can escape.

CREON. I am nothing. I have no life.
Lead me away . . .
That have killed unwittingly
My son, my wife.
I know not where I should turn,
Where look for help.
My hands have done amiss, my head is bowed
With fate too heavy for me.

(Exit.)

CHORUS. Of happiness the crown
And chiefest part
Is wisdom, and to hold
The gods in awe.
This is the law
That, seeing the stricken heart
Of pride brought down,
We learn when we are old.

(Exeunt.)

Discussion

1. (a) Why does Creon order burial honors for Eteocles but forbid burial for Polynices? **(b)** Why does Antigone disobey?

2. What is the attitude of Ismene toward Antigone? of Antigone toward Ismene?

3. In what ways are Creon and Antigone alike?

4. (a) What does the scene between Haemon and his father reveal about the character of Haemon? of Creon? **(b)** With what arguments does Haemon try to persuade Creon to change his order?

5. (a) What similarities exist between the character and function of the Sentry in *Antigone* and the Nurse in *Romeo and Juliet*? Explain. **(b)** What other similarities are there between the two plays?

6. (a) What purpose does Teiresias serve in the play? **(b)** Teiresias says, "Only a fool is governed by self-will." Do his words apply to Creon, to Antigone, or to both?

7. On one level this play is a personal contest between a willful king and an equally willful subject over the burial of a slain soldier, but the opposition of king and subject represents several larger conflicts as well. Referring to specific lines from the play, discuss how Creon and Antigone are in basic disagreement about: **(a)** the law of the state vs. individual conscience; **(b)** youth vs. age; **(c)** man vs. woman. Which side do you favor on each issue? Why?

8. (a) At what points in the play does the chorus sympathize with Creon? with Antigone? **(b)** In each case, what causes the chorus to change its attitude?

9. (a) How long is the time span of this play? **(b)** Is the action continuous, or is it interrupted by lapses of time? **(c)** Does the action take place in more than one setting? **(d)** How does the audience find out what happens "offstage," that is, in another location?

10. Who is the protagonist in this play? the antagonist? (See *protagonist* in the Handbook of Literary Terms.) Is there a victor? Explain.

Vocabulary

Context, Dictionary

Four words are given in parentheses following each sentence. Choose the word that best completes each sentence. When you have completed both parts of this exercise, you might check your answers in the Glossary.

A. (Lines 1–533)

1. Crimes are committed with ______ when laws are not enforced. (edict, subtlety, impunity, weal)

2. You would be foolish to ______ her good advice. (weal, perpetrate, flout, rampart)

3. The king issued a(n) ______ concerning the new law. (touchstone, ignominy, edict, prerogative)

4. Because she was in charge of the class, the ______ was that she was the teacher. (impunity, presumption, prerogative, immutable)

5. Once my mother makes a decision, it is considered ______ (unalterable, ignominy, blasphemy, touchstone)

B. (Lines 534-end)

1. It is not unusual for rulers to expect their subjects to render ______ to them. (gall, defilement, homage, affliction)

2. Those who condemned Socrates wanted him to make a public apology in ______ of his errors. (defilement, durance, expiation, tempest)

3. The ______ young woman had lost all her possessions. (unscathed, rout, prudent, hapless)

4. Robbing the church was a ______. (durance, sacrilege, whet, dower)

5. It is surprising that she is so thin since she has a(n) ______ appetite. (insatiable, hapless, omnipotent, malcontent)

Composition

Assume that a classmate says, "The real hero in this play is Ismene. She's got all the virtues—honesty, loyalty, and above all, common sense."

Write a short paper to be read by your classmates and teacher in which you either agree or disagree with the statement and give reasons for your opinion.

Sophocles 495–406 B.C.

Born near Athens, Sophocles lived at a time when Greece was at its height of political power and of creation in the arts and philosophy. He was one of the most distinguished citizens of Athens—an accomplished musician and athlete as well as a successful and respected playwright. In the dramatic festivals of his age, he won the first prize twenty-four times, more than any other dramatist; but of the more than one hundred plays he wrote, only seven remain.

Unit 6 Review: Greek Drama

Content Review

1. Do you think that women in *Antigone* are portrayed in a favorable or an unfavorable light? Cite examples from the play to support your opinion.

2. A group of conservationists, concerned that a lumber company is cutting down trees in an area that could become a National Forest and Recreation Area, organizes a protest. The protesters link arms and block the entrances to the logging area. In response, the lumber company asks the police to forcefully remove the protesters. What response do you think each of the following would have to this situation? Why? **(a)** Antigone; **(b)** Creon; **(c)** Teiresias; **(d)** Haemon; **(e)** Ismene.

3. A tragic hero is usually **(a)** a noble and influential person who **(b)** meets with destruction **(c)** because of opposition from others and **(d)** because of a personal flaw in character. In the light of this definition, do you consider Antigone a tragic hero? Creon?

4. Assume you are a publicity agent for a dramatic company that is going to put on a production of *Antigone* at your school. Your job is to advertise the production and interest students (most of whom are unfamiliar with the play) in seeing the play. What topics and themes from the play would you emphasize in your advertisement?

5. The following statements offer three views of *Antigone.* Select the one that seems to you the best account for the meaning of the play. If none of the following statements satisfies you, offer your own view. In any case, support your opinion with evidence from the play.

a. The tragedy in *Antigone* results from Creon's stubbornly insisting that the law of the state be obeyed even when it conflicts with the higher moral law of the gods. Although Creon has forbidden the burial of the enemies of Thebes, Antigone is willing to sacrifice her life in order to obey the higher law, which requires that she give her brother a proper burial. When Creon cannot make Antigone bend to his will, he not only causes her death, but he also brings tragedy on himself by causing the deaths of his wife and his son.

b. The tragedy in *Antigone* results from Antigone's desire to play the role of lonely martyr. Like most people who are fanatically devoted to a cause, she has no understanding of or regard for the well-being of others. She treats even her sister cruelly when Ismene offers to share her punishment. Her blind insistence on the rightness of her action brings about not only her death but also the deaths of Haemon and Eurydice. While Creon's pride and stubbornness unquestionably contribute to the final disaster, ultimately he does try to reverse his order and release Antigone. It is not Creon, then, but Antigone, who must bear primary responsibility for the tragedy.

c. The tragedy in *Antigone* results from a conflict between the highest moral laws and the laws that govern the day-to-day affairs of a society. Neither Creon nor Antigone is "right" or "wrong," or, to put it another way, *both* Creon and Antigone are "right" *and* "wrong." We must have moral laws that provide a foundation for religion or ethics or what we call conscience, but we must also have the laws of the state that prevent the chaos that might result if everyone did what he or she thought was right. The two kinds of law are not usually in opposition, but Antigone and Creon are trapped in a situation in which the laws conflict, a situation in which neither can back down, a situation that leads to their ruin and to the deaths of innocent people. The cause of the tragedy is neither Creon nor Antigone but the situation that traps them between two irreconcilable laws.

Concept Review: Interpretation of New Material

The following is an excerpt from a Greek tragedy by Euripides (yů rip′ə dēz′), a playwright who lived in the fifth century B.C. The Greek fleet, on its way to war in Troy, has been stranded in Aulis (ô′lis), a district northwest of Athens, because there is no wind. The unfavorable weather conditions have been caused by Artemis (är′tə mis), goddess of the hunt and moon. The goddess has promised to restore the winds and assure the Greeks victory at Troy under one condition: Iphigenia (if′ə jə nī′ə), the daughter of the Greek leader Agamemnon (ag′ə mem′nän), must be sacrificed. Once Agamemnon finally agrees to this sacrifice, he sends for Iphigenia, her mother Clytemnestra (klī′təm nes′trə), and brother Orestes (ô res′tēz), under the pretext that the outstanding young warrier Achilles (ə kil′ēz) wishes to marry Iphigenia. When he finally becomes aware that the proposed marriage has been used as a trick, Achilles swears to fight for Iphigenia's life. Iphigenia, who at first pleads for mercy, eventually resolves to offer herself as sacrifice.

Read the excerpt from *Iphigenia in Aulis,* then answer the questions that follow.

from Iphigenia in Aulis • *Euripides*

translated from the Greek by F. M. Stawell

IPHIGENIA. Mother, let me speak!
This anger with my father is in vain,
Vain to use force for what we cannot win.
Thank our brave friend[1] for all his generous zeal,
But never let us broil[2] him with the host,
No gain to us, and ruin for himself.
I have been thinking, mother,—hear me now!—
I have chosen death; it is my own free choice.
I have put cowardice away from me.
Honor is mine now. O, mother, say I am right!
Our country—think, our Hellas[3]—looks to me,
On me the fleet hangs now, the doom of Troy,
Our women's honor all the years to come.
My death will save them, and my name be blest,
She who freed Hellas! Life is not so sweet
I should be craven. You who bore your child,
It was for Greece you bore her, not yourself.
Think! Thousands of our soldiers stand to arms,
Ten thousand man the ships, and all on fire
To serve their outraged country, die for Greece:
And is my one poor life to hinder all?
Could we defend that? Could we call it just?

1. ***our brave friend,*** Achilles.

2. ***broil,*** to entangle or involve in conflict.

3. ***Hellas,*** Greece.

And, mother, think! How could we let our friend
Die for a woman, fighting all his folk?
A thousand women are not worth one man!
The goddess needs my blood: can I refuse?
No: take it, conquer Troy! This shall be
My husband, and my children, and my fame.
Victory, mother, victory for the Greeks!
The foreigner must never rule this land,
Our own land! They are slaves and we are free.

LEADER OF THE CHORUS. O maiden, all is generous in your heart,
But fortune and the goddess are to blame.

ACHILLES. Agamemnon's daughter, I had been thrice blest
If you could be my bride. Hellas and you,
Ye are happy in each other! All your words
Are grandly spoken, worthy of your land.
I see your nature now, see what you are,
And thirst to win you, soul of nobleness!
Come, I would help you, serve you all I can,
And take you to my home. I count it ill,
By Thetis![4] if I may not fight the Greeks
And save you. Think; death is a fearful thing.

IPHIGENIA. I will say one word, without fear of shame.
The face of Helen has roused war enough,[5]
Battles of men and murders. O my friend,
Die not because of me, slay none for me.
Let me save Hellas if I have the power.

ACHILLES. O glorious heart! What is there I can say
Against your purpose? O, your soul is great!
Why should I not speak truth? Yet, none the less,
For it may be this thought of yours will change,
Hear what I have resolved. I will go hence,
And set my men about the altar's side,
That I may save you, and not let you die.
Even you may find a meaning in my words
When the sharp steel is close upon your neck.
Your rashness must not bring you to your death.
These men of mine shall take their stand with me
Hard by the temple, and await you there.

(ACHILLES *goes out.)*

IPHIGENIA. Mother, why are you weeping silently?

CLYTEMNESTRA. Have I not cause enough to be heartsick?

IPHIGENIA. Hush! Do not weaken me; grant what I ask.

CLYTEMNESTRA. Ask on, my child; I cannot do you wrong.

IPHIGENIA. I would not have you cut your hair for me
Nor wear black raiment——

4. ***Thetis,*** sea-goddess, mother of Achilles.

5. ***Helen . . . enough.*** Helen, the beautiful wife of the Spartan King Menelaus, eloped with Paris, a prince of Troy, thus causing the Trojan War.

CLYTEMNESTRA. What is it you say?
When you are lost——
IPHIGENIA. O, never speak like that!
I am saved, saved! You will be proud of me.
CLYTEMNESTRA. I must not mourn?
IPHIGENIA. No place for mourning here,
No tomb.
CLYTEMNESTRA. Surely the slain have burial?
IPHIGENIA. The holy altar is my monument.
CLYTEMNESTRA. I will obey you, child; your words are good.
IPHIGENIA. My lot is good, and I do good to Greece.
CLYTEMNESTRA. What shall I tell your sisters of all this?
IPHIGENIA. Ah, do not dress them, either, in black robes!
CLYTEMNESTRA. Shall I not take some message to the girls,
Some loving word from you?
IPHIGENIA. Yes, my farewell.
And Orestes—O, take care of him for me,
And bring him up to manhood.
CLYTEMNESTRA. Hold him now,
Draw him to you, look your last look on him.
IPHIGENIA (*to* ORESTES). Darling, you gave me all the help you could.
CLYTEMNESTRA. Is there no more that I can do to please you?
IPHIGENIA. O, hate him not,—my father, and your husband!
CLYTEMNESTRA. He has an evil course to run for you.
IPHIGENIA. He offers me to Greece against his will.
CLYTEMNESTRA. By treachery, unworthy of his house.
IPHIGENIA. Who will go with me, lead me to the place,
Before they drag me thither by the hair?
CLYTEMNESTRA. I will, beside you.
IPHIGENIA. No . . . it is not fit.
CLYTEMNESTRA. Clutching your garments.
IPHIGENIA. Listen, mother dear.
Stay here; that is far better for us both.
One of my father's men will go with me
To the field of Artemis, where I must die.
CLYTEMNESTRA. Child, are you going?
IPHIGENIA. Yes, I will not come back.
CLYTEMNESTRA. You leave your mother?
IPHIGENIA. Yes, not as I would.
CLYTEMNESTRA. O, leave me not!
(CLYTEMNESTRA *falls fainting and is carried into the tent.*)
IPHIGENIA. I will not shed a tear.
(She turns to the women.)
Now sing the paean[6] for my destiny!
Sing to the child of Zeus, to Artemis;

6. ***paean*** (pē′ən), a song of praise or thanksgiving.

Let the glad sound be heard by all the Greeks.
Let them lift up the baskets, light the fire,
And fling the barley; bid my father come
And touch the altar. I will bring this day
Victory and salvation unto Greece.

Follow me now, the victor,
Follow the taker of Troy!
Crown my head with a garland,
Wash my hands for the rite.
Dance!
On to the shrine of the Maiden,
Artemis the blest!
She calls me, and I,
I come as the victim, I give my blood,
Fulfil the seer's command.[7]

7. ***Fulfil . . . command.*** When his fleet was stranded in the calm seas, Agamemnon consulted Calchas, a prophet, who told him that success could be assured only if Iphigenia were sacrificed.

---

1. Which of the following is *not* given as a reason for Iphigenia's willingness to sacrifice herself? **(a)** to achieve honor; **(b)** to save her country; **(c)** to earn her father's respect; **(d)** to satisfy the goddess Artemis.

2. The lines spoken by the leader of the chorus (32 and 33) serve to **(a)** provide information previously unknown; **(b)** offer general commentary on the situation; **(c)** encourage Achilles to fall in love with Iphigenia: **(d)** change the goddess's mind.

3. When she says, "On me the fleet hangs now" (line 12), Iphigenia means that **(a)** the Greeks had better sacrifice her quickly; **(b)** her own life hangs by a thread; **(c)** the fate of the fleet depends on whether she is sacrificed; **(d)** she is now in charge of the fleet.

4. Achilles' speech in lines 34–43 expresses **(a)** admiration and warning; **(b)** self-praise; **(c)** happiness and good will; **(d)** loyalty to the Greeks.

5. According to his speeches, the quality that Archilles most admires in Iphigenia is her **(a)** beauty; **(b)** rashness; **(c)** truthfulness; **(d)** nobleness.

6. The image that appears in line 57 makes a strong appeal to the sense of **(a)** sight; **(b)** sound; **(c)** touch; **(d)** smell.

7. In lines 53–60, Achilles states his plan; he intends to **(a)** pray at the altar; **(b)** marry Iphigenia; **(c)** slay Agamemnon; **(d)** be prepared to save Iphigenia.

8. According to Iphigenia's mother, Agamemnon is granting the goddess's wish by using **(a)** treachery; **(b)** devotion; **(c)** daring; **(d)** wisdom.

9. The final five lines of this passage indicate that Iphigenia views her self-sacrifice as an act of **(a)** destruction; **(b)** cruelty; **(c)** destiny; **(d)** rashness.

10. Iphigenia believes she can not only save her country but can also restore women's honor (lines 11–13). Who does she consider responsible for originally having lost this honor? **(a)** Clytemnestra; **(b)** Agamemnon; **(c)** Artemis; **(d)** Helen.

Composition Review

Choose any *one* of the following for your composition.

1. Assume that your sister, who is in the eighth grade, is looking for a positive role model—one who is *courageous, practical,* and *effective.*

In a letter directed to this imaginary sister, explain whether or not you think Antigone and Iphigenia possess qualities that your sister might imitate. You may wish to mention the italicized qualities or to suggest other attributes you think would provide a strong model for a young girl.

2. Imagine that a classmate explains to you, "Iphigenia says, 'A thousand women are not worth one man,' and she proves it by her stupid actions. She didn't have to die, but she chooses death just to be a martyr. Achilles is willing to fight to save her, but she rejects his plan. Iphigenia, like most women, is just too emotional; men are more practical."

Write a composition, directed to your classmate, in which you defend or refute this observation, citing specific passages and situations from the excerpt you have read. Begin your paper, "I strongly (agree) (disagree) that the behavior of Iphigenia and Achilles supports the assertion that men are more practical and less emotional than women."

3. "One of the lessons in both *Antigone* and *Iphigenia* is that you can't fight power. Those adults in authority (Agamemnon and Creon) are always winners, while younger people (Iphigenia, Antigone, Haemon, Achilles) are the losers." Assume that an adult whom you know well has asked you if you think that this statement about the winners and losers in *Antigone* and *Iphigenia* is valid.

Write a composition in which you agree or disagree with this statement.

Unit 7

Prose Forms

Introduction

Dearest Diary, Today was a day for finishing projects. Not only did I complete the wire sculpture in art class, but I also . . .

Dear Fred, By the time you get this, I'll be on my way to Mexico. I think I wrote to you about the photography contest . . .

Dear Sir: Last April I purchased in your grocery store . . .

Ladies and Gentlemen, it is with distinct pleasure that I introduce to you this evening that renowned authority on hot-air balloons . . .

On the evening of October 4, 1876, at approximately 8 P.M.*, a carriage wended its way slowly over the cobblestones of New Salem.*

French rolls: Three cups of sweet milk, one cup of butter and lard mixed in equal proportions, half a cup of compressed yeast, and a tablespoonful of salt. Add enough flour . . .

Words, words, words—the means by which we communicate to ourselves, to those in our immediate environment, to those distant from us in time and place. Born into a world of language, we begin by babbling, imitating the sounds and the rhythms of the words we hear. Slowly, as we learn to associate objects with words, we commence the process of internalizing language, of trying to make sense of our universe by "talking" to ourselves. Early we perceive the importance of *I,* and we attempt through language to relate that *I* to other members of our family. As we mature, we develop the ability to see the world from the viewpoint of others as well as from our own. In addition, we learn to view our world dispassionately as well as emotionally, and we acquire the ability to shift our focus from emotions to facts. To the degree that emphasis remains upon *I* and upon emotions, we say the language employed is *subjective.* To the degree that it remains upon others and facts, we say the language is *objective.*

Many gradations are possible: a person using *I* could speak or write fairly factually about his/her experiences; a person using *he, she,* or *they* could write quite emotionally about the experiences of others.

In any case, our language, whether written or spoken, can never be totally subjective or objective. Even when describing complex feelings such as those that we experience when, for example, we fall in love, we inevitably use some language that is objective. However, we can never completely divorce our emotions from events or people we describe. Though we may place emphasis upon facts and upon others rather than upon ourselves, it is nevertheless we who select the facts, and it is we who put them in an order that best serves our purpose. In short, behind the most "objective" piece of spoken or written prose is the *I* of the speaker or writer. A good listener or reader learns to ask questions of that *I:* Who is he/she? What is he/she saying? What is he/she not saying—what facts have been left out? What does he/she want from me? Can I trust him/her?

In the unit that follows you will find nonfiction prose selections that range widely in degree of subjectivity or objectivity. In addition, you will encounter language that ranges from the intimate, *informal* speech used with friends to the more distant, *formal* prose used with strangers. As you read, consider carefully both what is being said and who is saying it. Remember that behind the prose is a real person, the writer. That person may speak either informally or formally about the subject, and may choose to use either the subjective *I,* or the more objective third person *he, she,* or *they.* The writer's particular choice can determine the effectiveness of the writing.

From the Index of American Design, National Gallery of Art

". . . The Awful Sweetness of Walking with God"

Esther Edwards

Daughter of the famous colonial preacher Jonathan Edwards, young Esther Edwards reveals in a handful of journal entries the vitality and complexity of her personality.

Northampton, Massachusetts, *February 13, 1741*. This is my ninth birthday, and Mrs. Edwards, my mother, has had me stitch these sundry sheets of paper into a book to make me a journal.

January 9, 1742. Mrs. Edwards was thirty-three years old today. That seems very old. I wonder if I shall live to be thirty-three. [She died when she was twenty-six.] Mrs. Edwards seemed very serious all the day long; as if she were inwardly praying, "Lord, so teach me to number my days that I may apply my heart unto wisdom." Indeed, this she said to us girls when we were trying to practice some birthday frolics on her. And when she came from her devotions her face actually shone, as though, like Moses, she had come down from the Mount. I do not think we girls ever will be so saintly as our mother is. At any rate, we do not begin so. I do not know as I want to be.

February 13. Have just come tripping upstairs from morning worship and the song of the service still follows me. I have been thinking what a singing family the Edwards family is. Mother's voice we have heard in psalms and hymns and spiritual songs ever since our early babyhood. She sang us on our pilgrim way when we were in our cradles. And to all the house her voice is always uplifting like the lark's, as though her soul were mounting up to heaven's shining gate on wings of song. If father ever gets low-spirited from his "humors," as he calls them, her voice is to him like medicine, as David's harp was to King Saul. And when she once begins, there is Sarah and Jerusha and myself, like the ascending heights of an organ, ready to unite in making a joyful noise to the Lord, all over the house, so that our home is more like an aviary than the dwelling of a Colonial parson.

My mother says my journal thus far is rather stilted and mature for me; though everything in the family is mature.

March 6. Have just been caring for my mockingbird, who is now rewarding me with song. The cat was lurking in the hall and I have just driven her away with a broom with which I have been sweeping the living room. Though down by the fireside, at twilight, she is my favorite too. And even father, sometimes, while with us after supper, seems to enjoy her purring as he strokes her in his lap. Though I doubt if she has much divinity about her unless it is in her sparks of electricity when she is rubbed the wrong way.

May 1. I have just come back from a wonderful ride with my honored father, Mr. Edwards, through the spring woods. He usually rides alone. But today he said he had something he wanted to show me. The forests between our house and the full-banked river were very beautiful. The wild cherry and the dogwood were in full bloom. The squirrels were leaping from tree to tree, and the birds were making a various melody. Though father is usually taciturn or preoccupied—my mother will call these large words—even when he takes one of us children with him, today he discoursed to me of the awful sweetness of walking with God in Nature. He seems to feel God in the woods, the sky, and the grand sweep of the river which winds so majestically through the woody silences here.

When we reached the "Indian's Well," I slid off and brought a birchbark cup of crystal water for father to drink. But not before I had given myself a great surprise. For, having put on my mother's hat in sport, the first reflection in the dark water seemed to be the face of my mother instead of my own!

June, 1743. My mother has just come into the house with a bunch of sweet peas and put them on the stand where my honored father is shaving, though his beard is very slight. We have abundance of flowers and a vegetable garden which is early and thrifty. My honored father, of course, has not time to give attention to the garden, and so Mrs. Edwards looks after everything there. Almost before the snow has left the hills, she has it plowed and spaded by Rose's husband, who does all the hard work there. She is our colored cook. We hire her services from one of the prominent people in Father's parish, who owns both her and her husband. That word "owns" sounds strange about people!

Discussion

1. Look up *awful* in your Glossary. Which definition fits the word as it is used in this selection?

2. Cite evidence that suggests Esther Edwards was **(a)** fun-loving; **(b)** devout; **(c)** respectful; **(d)** observant; **(e)** mature.

3. If someone were to ask you what kind of home life and family Reverend Edwards had, what might you say based upon information Esther has furnished?

4. If Esther were alive today and in your class, would she be a girl you would like for a friend? Why or why not?

Composition

Assume that you keep a diary that will be read 250 years from now.

Write an entry that communicates to future readers something interesting about you and the times in which you live. You might describe a typical day in your life or a day on which some important personal or historical event occurs. (See *Writing a Description,* page 667, in Composition Guide.)

Esther Edwards 1732–1758

At the age of twenty, Edwards married a Presbyterian clergyman, Aaron Burr, one of the founders (and later president) of Princeton University. They had two children, a son and daughter; the son, named Aaron for his father, grew up to be the third Vice-President of the United States.

Reflections of a Seventeen-Year-Old

Sylvia Plath

Seventeen-year-old Sylvia Plath, who was to become a noted American poet, records her turbulent feelings in this entry from her diary.

November 13, 1949

As of today I have decided to keep a diary again—just a place where I can write my thoughts and opinions when I have a moment. Somehow I have to keep and hold the rapture of being seventeen. Every day is so precious I feel infinitely sad at the thought of all this time melting farther and farther away from me as I grow older. *Now, now* is the perfect time of my life.

In reflecting back upon these last sixteen years, I can see tragedies and happiness, all relative—all unimportant now—fit only to smile upon a bit mistily.

I still do not know myself. Perhaps I never will. But I feel free—unbound by responsibility, I still can come up to my own private room, with my drawings hanging on the walls . . . and pictures pinned up over my bureau. It is a room suited to me—tailored, uncluttered and peaceful . . . I love the quiet lines of the furniture, the two bookcases filled with poetry books and fairy tales saved from childhood.

At the present moment I am very happy, sitting at my desk, looking out at the bare trees around the house across the street . . . Always I want to be an observer. I want to be affected by life deeply, but never so blinded that I cannot see my share of existence in a wry, humorous light and mock myself as I mock others.

I am afraid of getting older. I am afraid of getting married. Spare me from cooking three meals a day—spare me from the relentless cage of routine and rote. I want to be free—free to know people and their backgrounds—free to move to different parts of the world, so I may learn that there are other morals and standards

---

besides my own. I want, I think, to be omniscient. . . . I think I would like to call myself "The girl who wanted to be God." Yet if I were not in this body, where *would* I be? Perhaps I am *destined* to be classified and qualified. But, oh, I cry out against it. I am I—I am powerful—but to what extent? I am I.

Sometimes I try to put myself in another's place, and I am frightened when I find I am almost succeeding. How awful to be anyone but I. I have a terrible egotism. I love my flesh, my face, my limbs, with overwhelming devotion. I know that I am "too tall" and have a fat nose, and yet I pose and prink before the mirror, seeing more and more how lively I am. . . . I have erected in my mind an image of myself—idealistic and beautiful. Is not that image, free from blemish, the true self—the true perfection? Am I wrong when this image insinuates itself between me and the merciless mirror? (Oh, even now I glance back on what I have just written—how foolish it sounds, how overdramatic.)

Never, never, never will I reach the perfection I long for with all my soul—my paintings, my poems, my stories—all poor, poor reflections . . . for I have been too thoroughly conditioned to the conventional surroundings of this community . . . my vanity desires luxuries which I can never have. . . .

I am continually more aware of the power which change plays in my life. . . . There will come a time when I must face myself at last. Even now I dread the big choices which loom up in my life—what college? what career? I am afraid. I feel uncertain. What is best for me? What do I want? I do not know. I love freedom. I deplore constrictions and limitations. . . . I am not as wise as I have thought. I can see, as from a valley, the roads lying open for me, but I cannot see the end—the consequences. . . .

Oh, I love *now*, with all my fears and forebodings, for now I still am not completely molded. My life is still just beginning. I am strong. I long for a cause to devote my energies to. . . .

Discussion

1. Cite evidence that suggests Sylvia was **(a)** happy; **(b)** fearful; **(c)** vain; **(d)** humble; **(e)** dedicated.

2. What specific differences do you see between Sylvia's personality, as indicated by this entry, and Esther Edwards's, as indicated by her diary?

3. Sylvia makes a number of comments about being free or desiring freedom. **(a)** What does freedom seem to mean to her? **(b)** Do you think her notions of freedom are realistic? Explain. **(c)** Based on evidence in the two diaries, compare Sylvia's concept of freedom with Esther's.

4. Is Sylvia's diary entry predominately subjective or objective? What about Esther's? Explain.

5. Which of the two young women do you find more likeable? Explain your opinion.

Sylvia Plath 1932–1963

Sylvia Plath was born in Boston, graduated from Smith College, and attended Cambridge University in England on a Fulbright scholarship. It was there that she met her future husband, the English poet Ted Hughes. Her collections of poetry include *Ariel, The Colossus, Crossing the Water,* and *Winter Trees.* She is also the author of the novel, *The Bell Jar,* and of a children's book, *The Bed Book.* A prolific writer, she kept journals and corresponded avidly with family and friends. In 1963, Sylvia Plath took her own life.

Lincoln's Reply to His Stepbrother

Abraham Lincoln

Abraham Lincoln's stepmother, Sally Bush Lincoln, was living with her son, John D. Johnston, on a farm in Coles County, Illinois. Johnston had written to Lincoln asking for a loan.

[Dec. 24, 1848]

Dear Johnston:

Your request for eighty dollars, I do not think it best to comply with now. At the various times when I have helped you a little, you have said to me, "We can get along very well now," but in a very short time I find you in the same difficulty again. Now this can only happen by some defect in your conduct. What that defect is, I think I know. You are not *lazy,* and still you *are* an *idler*. I doubt whether since I saw you, you have done a good whole day's work, in any one day. You do not very much dislike to work, and still you do not work much, merely because it does not seem to you that you could get much for it.

This habit of uselessly wasting time is the whole difficulty; it is vastly important to you, and still more so to your children, that you should break this habit. It is more important to them, because they have longer to live, and can keep out of an idle habit before they are in it, easier than they can get out after they are in.

You are now in need of some ready money; and what I propose is, that you shall go to work, "tooth and nail," for somebody who will give you money for it.

Let father and your boys take charge of your things at home—prepare for a crop, and make the crop, and you go to work for the best money wages, or in discharge of any debt you owe, that you can get. And to secure you a fair reward for your labor, I now promise you that for every dollar you will, between this and the first of May, get for your own labor either in money or in your own indebtedness, I will then give you one other dollar.

By this, if you hire yourself at ten dollars a month, from me you will get ten more, making twenty dollars a month for your work. In this, I do not mean you shall go off to St. Louis, or the lead mines, or the gold mines in California, but I mean for you to go at it for the best wages you can get close to home—in Coles County.

"Abraham Lincoln's Reply to His Stepbrother" in *Constitutional Edition of Lincoln's Writings,* Vol. II, ed. by A. B. Lapsley. New York: G. P. Putnam's Sons, 1905.

Now if you will do this, you will soon be out of debt, and what is better, you will have a habit that will keep you from getting in debt again. But if I should now clear you out, next year you will be just as deep in as ever. You say you would almost give your place in Heaven for $70 or $80. Then you value your place in Heaven very cheaply, for I am sure you can with the offer I make you get the seventy or eighty dollars for four or five months' work. You say if I furnish you the money you will deed me the land, and if you don't pay the money back, you will deliver possession——

Nonsense! If you can't now live *with* the land, how will you then live without it? You have always been kind to me, and I do not now mean to be unkind to you. On the contrary, if you will but follow my advice, you will find it worth more than eight times eighty dollars to you.

Affectionately

Your brother

A. Lincoln

Discussion

1. (a) What proposition had Johnston first made Lincoln? **(b)** Why does Lincoln dismiss the offer?

2. (a) What counterproposal does Lincoln make his stepbrother? **(b)** Do you consider Lincoln's proposal to be fair or unfair? Explain.

3. Consider the following questions from Lincoln's point of view: **(a)** How will his stepbrother benefit from the proposal? **(b)** How might his stepbrother's children benefit?

4. (a) Is the language in Lincoln's letter to his stepbrother more objective or subjective? Explain. **(b)** If Lincoln were writing to a general about a military campaign, do you think his language would be more subjective or less subjective than that used in the letter to his stepbrother? Explain your opinion.

Composition

Assume that you are Mr. Jonathan Dole, 11 Hayes Street, Springfield, Illinois. Your daughter is seriously ill and needs an operation that will cost eighty dollars. You do not have the money.

Write a letter to President Lincoln in which you request the funds. Compose your letter in the light of what you have learned about Lincoln's character from his letter to his stepbrother. (See *Assuming Another Voice,* page 669, in Composition Guide.)

from Aunt Arie interviewed by Mike Cook and Paul Gillespie

Some might consider Aunt Arie's life unbearably harsh and unrewarding. She herself doesn't see it that way at all.

I was born an' raised on Hick'ry Knoll 'til I was eight years old. It'uz a hard livin'. I don't know how Poppy made it. Mommy never see'd a well day in her life. She was born with somethin' th' matter with her head—one side'a her head run from th' time she was born 'til she died. But I can tell y'one thing. In your life, don't never care a cent in this world t'wait on your mother, whether she's sick or not sick. When she's gone, you'll be glad y'did. Yes you will. 'Cause I've not got a thing in this world t'regret. I waited on my mother day and night—what I mean *day* and *night*. Many a night I been up waitin' on my mother when ever' body else was in th' bed asleep. I rejoice over that. God'll repay you for all that. God'll certainly bless y'fer it.

Poppy had a awful hard time, an' his daddy died a way 'fore he was born so he had a hard time t'begin with. Well, atter he's married he had a worse time *I'll* say, with all 'at sickness 'n'ever'thing on 'im. Mommy did love wheat bread, an' he worked for a peck a'corn a day so he could get Mommy bread t'eat. Why, he'uz as good t'Mommy as a baby. Now Ulysses[1] didn't believe this, an' I didn't care whether he did'r not—you know, if I tell anybody anything an' they believe it, it's all right; an' if they don't believe it, I don't care whether they do'r not—I never heard Poppy give Mommy a ill word in my life. Now we had some hogs, and one of our hogs got in a neighbor's corn patch an' eat some of his corn. And he come after Poppy an'told him t'come get his hog, an' he charged Poppy two dollers fer what it eat. Poppy's s'mad he didn't know what t'do. That'uz th' maddest I've ever seed Poppy in my life. An' Mommy—he called her Dink, that was her nickname—she said something t'Poppy. "Now," he says, "Dink, don't you say a *word* to me while I'm mad." An' that was ever'thing's ever said about that. She hushed, of course. An' he never said nary another word. That was th'illest word I ever heered Poppy tell Mommy in my life.

It's a whole lot easier today. I've hoed corn many a day fer a quarter. *Many* a day. An' we used t'pick huckleberries, me'n m'brother did, an' swap two gallons a'huckleberries fer one gallon a'syrup. Had t'do something t'make a livin'. But we always had plenty t'eat. We always had plenty a'what we had. We didn't have no great stuff that cost a lot. We never did buy that. Well, we just didn't have nothin't'pay fer't, an' we always tried t'pay as we went. You know, if y'get goin' in debt, next thing y'know you can't pay it t'save yore life. I'm scared t'death a debts. I owe fer this road now, an' it worries me t'death. Used t'be I didn't have enough money t'mail a letter with. An' you know how much candy I bought in my life 'fore I's married? I bought one nickel's worth a'candy in my life. I just didn't have nothin' t'buy *with*. Poppy hired a girl t'stay with Mommy 'til I got big enough t'do th' work, an' y'know how much he'd have t'pay? Seventy-five cents a week. They'd work all week fer seventy-five cents.

---

1. ***Ulysses,*** Aunt Arie's deceased husband.

An' picked blackberries'n'strawberries. Always had somethin' t'eat. Pickled beans'n' ever'thin'. Why, we've pickled beans in a twenty gallon barrel; but I ain't got any this year. Groundhogs eat m'beans up an' I never had nary one t'pick. I had two bushel baskets full'a cans, an' I took 'em out there an' poured 'em in th' groundhog's hole an' took a stick an' beat'em in. An' you know, that groundhog left an' never did come back. Couldn't bear them rattlin' things. Just couldn't stand 'em *(laughing).*

An' we've raised high as seventy-five bushel a'Irish 'taters over'n'at field over there. Did'ja ever put up any sweet 'taters? Well, I'm gonna tell y'how. Law, I'uz s'glad t'know how I didn't know what t'do. Dig yer sweet 'taters an' sun'em 'til they gets just th' least bit swiveled, I call it; an' put 'em in pasteboard boxes an' cover'em up. They ain't nary one a'mine rotted yet. We kep'em in th' tater house. One day that 'tater house fell down—fell out, side of it, did up there. I went t'get'taters an' they's th'biggest light in th'house, an' I said, "What in th' world's th' matter with th' tater house?" Here they was, th' side of it fell out.

Y'ever eat any lye hominy? Boys, 'at's th'best stuff ever you eat in yore life. It sure is. Boys, I've made many a pot full. And soap, law, I've made many a pot'a soap too. Had th' ash hopper, oak ashes. And bottomed chairs—I guess I bottomed 'bout ever'one a'these. He'ped to do it. I can't make th' splits. I bottom'em with white oak splits. Some people bottoms'em with bark, but I never did. Bark does easy t'what th' wood does. Course it don't last like wood. Tain't good like wood. *(We asked her to tell us more about the bark method.)* Use young poplar bark in th' spring a'th' year when th' sap rises; y'can't make it no other time. Only cut little poles certain lengths an'then peel'em an' use that while it's green. If y'wait 'til it gets all dried up, it'll break all t'pieces. An' always join th' ends under th'bottom. Never do jine'em on th'top a'th' chairs. On th'bottom so they won't bother nothin'.

An' I've made baskets. I've made lots'a baskets. I love t'fool wi'my hands. I just love t'fool with 'em. I made 'em with white oak splits, an' I've made some with willers. Willer baskets is hard 'cause y'have to'go off t'th'branch, an' we ain't got no willers grows on this place like a heap a'people has. Get'cha little willers, well, long as they grow. Ain't none of 'em big as yer finger. An' y'have t'have a big pot a'water by th'fire an' keep them willers soft in that. Didn't, they'd break all t'pieces. Put 'em in hot water an' th' bark just peels off like ever'thing. Gather 'em when th' sap first rises on 'em pretty good, an y'can skin'em pretty well without scaldin'-em; but if y'don't, y'have t'scald'em. I'd rather scald'em. They last longer I always think.

An' I've made foot mats out'a corn shucks—t'wipe yer feet on. That's easy, an' that's th' prettiest work! They make th' best foot mats. I ain't made none since m'hand's paralyzed. I reckon God just didn't intend fer me t'work my hand!

Used t'raise corn pones too. You ever eat any corn pones were raised? It's made out'a corn meal. Now hits another hard job, an' I love it better'n a cat loves sweet milk, I shore do. But I ain't raised none in a long time. Poppy always had me t'raise him a corn pone t'go t'Nantahaly. See, Poppy raised stock an'turned on Nantahaly range. Whenever th' time come, "I'm' a goin' t'Nantahaly a certain day an' you raise me some corn pones," well, 'at's what I done. I had a big oven a'purpose t'bake'em in. Have t'cook'em on th' fireplace. An' Lester Mann, he found out I could do that, an'they's'good; why he a-a-a-always, when he started t'th' mountains, he always come an' I raised him a corn pone. Hit'd be five inches thick. An' you take that corn pone an' slice it an' lay it in grease an' fry it in a pan in th' mountains, an' that was hot bread, y'see? An' law, they thought that'uz th' greatest thing in th' world. I've raised many a one that's went t'Nantahaly.

I'll tell'y', be a neighbor and you'll have neighbors. Now I've tried that by experience. I do try t'be good t'ever'body, and I try t'treat ever'body just as I'd have them treat me. I don't care th' goodness you do, you'll always get repaid for it. Double. Fourfold. You children remember that. Th' more you do for people, th' more they'll do for you. Always remember, t'have a friend, be one.

Doesn't being here alone bother you sometimes?

Well, it's mighty lonesome. When it comes storms an' things like that, it's not s'good. And still I don't mind it a bit in th' world. Ain't only one thing I'm afraid of, an'that's snakes. When 'at big'n come in that big pile here awhile back, hit scared th' life out'a me just about. I like t'never got over it. But I ain't like this pore old woman lives over here. She's afraid of a bear an'carries a'axe with her ever'time she comes over here. Tickles me. A little old hand axe. I said, "What you goin' do wi'that?" She said, "Kill a bear." I've lived here eighty years an'never see'd a bear in my life. An' I'll tell you th' truth, I'm not bothered with one single thing in this world here. That groundhog's only thing in this world that bothers me. An th' fox. They won't let me have a chicken. I had twenty hens an' two roosters, an' they catched th' last one of 'em. I wanted t'get s'more, an' Ulysses said they wadn't no use.

We made a good life here, but we put in lots'a'time. Many an'many a night I've been workin' when two o'clock come in th'mornin'—cardin'n'spinnin'n'sewin'. They want me t'sell an'move away from here, but I won't do it. It's just home—'at's all. I spent my happiest days here.

Discussion

1. (a) According to Aunt Arie, what was unusual about the relationship between her father and mother? **(b)** Why might Ulysses have doubted his wife's story?

2. Cite evidence from the interview that indicates Aunt Arie's attitudes toward **(a)** working hard; **(b)** being in debt; **(c)** taking care of one's mother; **(d)** being a good neighbor.

3. Aside from facts about her life, what information that might not be found in books did the high-school interviewers learn from Aunt Arie?

Comment: The Foxfire Books and Aunt Arie

In 1966, Eliot Wigginton, fresh out of college, began teaching English and geography in the 240-pupil Rabun Gap-Nacoochee School in Georgia. When Mr. Wigginton found that students in the school, located in the Appalachian Mountains, were not interested in traditional lessons, he asked them if they would like to produce their own magazine, one that would feature the folklore of Appalachian residents—their superstitions, old home remedies, weather signs, hunting stories, beliefs, recipes, and handicrafts. The result was *Foxfire,* a magazine (and later a bestselling series of books) that soon attracted subscribers in all fifty states and a dozen foreign countries. Run by students, *Foxfire* has been written about in magazines like *Saturday Review, New Republic, National Geographic, Scholastic Scope,* and *Whole Earth Catalogue;* and it has received grants from the National Endowment for the Humanities.

Mike Cook and Paul Gillespie were students of Wigginton; their interview with Aunt Arie appeared in the first *Foxfire Book.*

Aunt Arie Carpenter, born in 1885, died in 1978 at the age of 93. In addition to her appearance in the first *Foxfire Book,* she is the subject of *You and Aunt Arie,* by Pamela Wood (Nederland, Colorado: Institutional Development and Economic Affairs Service, Inc. [IDEA], 1975). Wood's book is intended to help students discover "Aunt Aries" within their own community and to learn how to publish a magazine like *Foxfire* about the region in which they live. In 1983, E. P. Dutton Company published *Aunt Arie: A Foxfire Portrait,* edited by Linda Garland Page and Eliot Wigginton.

See **CONNOTATION/DENOTATION** Handbook of Literary Terms

I Have a Dream . . .

Martin Luther King, Jr.

On August 28, 1963, Dr. Martin Luther King, Jr. addressed over 200,000 people who had marched on Washington, D.C., for "Jobs and Freedom."

. . . Five score years ago, a great American, in whose symbolic shadow we stand, signed the Emancipation Proclamation. This momentous decree came as a great beacon light of hope to millions of Negro slaves who had been seared in the flames of withering injustice. It came as a joyous daybreak to end the long night of captivity.

But one hundred years later, we must face the tragic fact that the Negro is still not free. One hundred years later, the life of the Negro is still sadly crippled by the manacles of segregation and the chains of discrimination. One hundred years later, the Negro lives on a lonely island of poverty in the midst of a vast ocean of material prosperity. One hundred years later, the Negro is still languished in the corners of American society and finds himself an exile in his own land. So we have come here today to dramatize an appalling condition.

In a sense we have come to our nation's Capital to cash a check. When the architects of our republic wrote the magnificent words of the Constitution and the Declaration of Independence, they were signing a promissory note to which every American was to fall heir. This note was a promise that all men would be guaranteed the unalienable rights of life, liberty, and the pursuit of happiness.

It is obvious today that America has defaulted on this promissory note insofar as her citizens of color are concerned. Instead of honoring this sacred obligation, America has given the Negro people a bad check; a check which has come back marked "insufficient funds." But we refuse to believe that the bank of justice is bankrupt. We refuse to believe that there are insufficient funds in the great vaults of opportunity of this nation. So we have come to cash this check—a check that will give us upon demand the riches of freedom and the security of justice. We have also come to this hallowed spot to remind America of the fierce urgency of *now*. This is no time to engage in the luxury of cooling off or to take the tranquilizing drug of gradualism. *Now* is the time to make real the promises of Democracy. *Now* is the time to rise from the dark and desolate valley of segregation to the

sunlit path of racial justice. *Now* is the time to open the doors of opportunity to all of God's children. *Now* is the time to lift our nation from the quicksands of racial injustice to the solid rock of brotherhood.

It would be fatal for the nation to overlook the urgency of the moment and to underestimate the determination of the Negro. This sweltering summer of the Negro's legitimate discontent will not pass until there is an invigorating autumn of freedom and equality. Nineteen sixty-three is not an end, but a beginning. Those who hope that the Negro needed to blow off steam and will now be content will have a rude awakening if the nation returns to business as usual. There will be neither rest nor tranquillity in America until the Negro is granted his citizenship rights. The whirlwinds of revolt will continue to shake the foundations of our nation until the bright day of justice emerges.

But there is something that I must say to my people who stand on the warm threshold which leads into the palace of justice. In the process of gaining our rightful place we must not be guilty of wrongful deeds. Let us not seek to satisfy our thirst for freedom by drinking from the cup of bitterness and hatred. We must forever conduct our struggle on the high plane of dignity and discipline. We must not allow our creative protest to degenerate into physical violence. Again and again we must rise to the majestic heights of meeting physical force with soul force. The marvelous new militancy which has engulfed the Negro community must not lead us to a distrust of all white people, for many of our white brothers, as evidenced by their presence here today, have come to realize that their destiny is tied up with our destiny and their freedom is inextricably bound to our freedom. We cannot walk alone.

And as we walk, we must make the pledge that we shall march ahead. We cannot turn back. There are those who are asking the devotees of civil rights, "When will you be satisfied?" We can never be satisfied as long as the Negro is the victim of the unspeakable horrors of police brutality. We can never be satisfied as long as our bodies, heavy with the fatigue of travel, cannot gain lodging in the motels of the highways and the hotels of the cities. We cannot be satisfied as long as the Negro's basic mobility is from a smaller ghetto to a larger one. . . . We can never be satisfied as long as a Negro in Mississippi cannot vote and a Negro in New York believes he has nothing for which to vote. No, no, we are not satisfied, and we will not be satisfied until justice rolls down like waters and righteousness like a mighty stream.

I am not unmindful that some of you have come here out of great trials and tribulations. Some of you have come fresh from narrow jail cells. Some of you have come from areas where your quest for freedom left you battered by the storms of persecution and staggered by the winds of police brutality. You have been the veterans of creative suffering. Continue to work with the faith that unearned suffering is redemptive.

Go back to Mississippi, go back to Alabama, go back to South Carolina, go back to Georgia, go back to Louisiana, go back to the slums and ghettos of our northern cities, knowing that somehow this situation can and will be changed. Let us not wallow in the valley of despair.

I say to you today, my friends, that in spite of the difficulties and frustrations of the moment I still have a dream. It is a dream deeply rooted in the American dream.

I have a dream that one day this nation will rise up and live out the true meaning of its creed: "We hold these truths to be self-evident; that all men are created equal."

I have a dream that one day on the red hills of Georgia the sons of former slaves and the sons of former slaveowners will be able to sit down together at the table of brotherhood.

I have a dream that one day even the state of Mississippi, a desert state sweltering with the heat of injustice and oppression, will be transformed into an oasis of freedom and justice.

I have a dream that my four little children will one day live in a nation where they will not be judged by the color of their skin but by the content of their character.

I have a dream today.

I have a dream that one day the state of Alabama, whose governor's lips are presently dripping with the words of interposition and nullification, will be transformed into a situation where little black boys and black girls will be able to join hands with little white boys and white girls and walk together as sisters and brothers.

I have a dream today.

I have a dream that one day every valley shall be exalted, every hill and mountain shall be made low, the rough places will be made plains, and the crooked places will be made straight, and the glory of the Lord shall be revealed, and all flesh shall see it together.[1]

This is our hope. This is the faith with which I return to the South. With this faith we will be able to hew out of the mountain of despair a stone of hope. With this faith we will be able to transform the jangling discords of our nation into a beautiful symphony of brotherhood. With this faith we will be able to work together, to pray together, to struggle together, to go to jail together, to stand up for freedom together, knowing that we will be free one day.

This will be the day when all of God's children will be able to sing with new meaning

My country, 'tis of thee,
Sweet land of liberty,
    Of thee I sing:
Land where my fathers died,
Land of the pilgrims' pride,
From every mountain-side
    Let freedom ring.

---

1. ***every valley . . . see it together*** (Isaiah 40:4 and 5).

And if America is to be a great nation this must become true. So let freedom ring from the prodigious hilltops of New Hampshire. Let freedom ring from the mighty mountains of New York. Let freedom ring from the heightening Alleghenies of Pennsylvania!

Let freedom ring from the snowcapped Rockies of Colorado!

Let freedom ring from the curvacious peaks of California!

But not only that; let freedom ring from Stone Mountain of Georgia!

Let freedom ring from Lookout Mountain of Tennessee!

Let freedom ring from every hill and molehill of Mississippi. From every mountainside, let freedom ring.

When we let freedom ring, when we let it ring from every village and every hamlet, from every state and every city, we will be able to speed up that day when all of God's children, black men and white men, Jews and Gentiles, Protestants and Catholics, will be able to join hands and sing in the words of the old Negro spiritual, "Free at last! free at last! thank God almighty, we are free at last!"

Discussion

1. Black people were legally emancipated one hundred years before this speech was made. Why, then, does Dr. King call for action?

2. King speaks of "meeting physical force with soul force" and of "creative suffering." **(a)** What do you think he means by each of these terms? **(b)** How might each of these be used to attain his dream?

3. Dr. King states that the marchers have come to Washington to "cash a check." **(a)** In your own words, explain the meaning of this statement. **(b)** Do you think this metaphor is well chosen? Why or why not?

4. Is Dr. King's dream a dream for blacks alone? Explain.

Application

Connotation/Denotation

The *connotation* of a word is the association surrounding the word that is not part of its *denotation,* or dictionary meaning. Look up the dictionary definitions of the following words from Dr. King's speech. Then, discuss the connotation of each word as it is used in the speech: *seared, defaulted, tranquilizing, freedom, nullification, justice.*

Vocabulary

Combined Skills

Number your paper from 1 to 10. Then choose the letter that represents the most appropriate answer to each statement. Feel free to consult your glossary.

1. *Nullification* has a primary accent on the following syllable: **(a)** nul; **(b)** fi; **(c)** ca; **(d)** tion.

2. The opposite of *degenerate* is **(a)** lessen; **(b)** improve; **(c)** demand; **(d)** question.

3. The greatest number of *sweltering* days would most likely occur in **(a)** winter; **(b)** fall; **(c)** summer; **(d)** spring.

4. An object said to have *mobility* can be easily **(a)** seen; **(b)** moved; **(c)** replaced; **(d)** purchased.

5. A word that comes from an Old English root meaning "to roll" is **(a)** seared; **(b)** oasis; **(c)** wallow; **(d)** value.

6. A person with a *"prodigious* amount of *tribulation"* would have **(a)** no appetite;

(b) great troubles; **(c)** a humorous outlook; **(d)** much common sense.

7. A synonym for *manacles* is **(a)** headgear; **(b)** baskets; **(c)** handcuffs; **(d)** hardware.

8. A *momentous* occasion is **(a)** always enjoyable; **(b)** very important; **(c)** frequently forgotten; **(d)** seldom noticed.

9. If you were lost in a desert and out of supplies, you would welcome **(a)** manacles; **(b)** an oasis; **(c)** a searing sun; **(d)** a promissory note.

10. Rights that are *unalienable* cannot be **(a)** proven; **(b)** transferred; **(c)** mentioned; **(d)** increased.

Composition

Have the lives of black people been improving since Dr. King spoke in 1963? Consult reference sources to help you determine and/or support an answer to this question. Examine areas such as income, housing, schooling, political leadership, and jobs. A librarian could help you locate sources of such information.

Then, write a well-organized composition titled "Dr. King, Your Dream [Is] [Is Not] Coming True." (See *Evaluating Your Evidence,* page 670, in Composition Guide.)

Martin Luther King, Jr. 1929–1968

A clergyman and civil rights leader, Dr. King was born in Atlanta, Georgia, and educated at Morehouse College, Crozer Theological Seminary, and Boston University. He achieved national prominence in 1955 when he led a nonviolent boycott of a bus line in Montgomery, Alabama. He founded the Southern Christian Leadership Conference and, in recognition of his efforts in defense of the rights of blacks in the United States, he was awarded the Nobel Peace Prize in 1964. While planning a Poor People's March on the nation's capital, he was assassinated in Memphis, Tennessee.

from Growing Up

Russell Baker

I did not dare tell anybody for fear of being laughed at in the schoolyard, but secretly I decided that what I'd like to be when I grew up was a writer.

I began working in journalism when I was eight years old. It was my mother's idea. She wanted me to "make something" of myself and, after a levelheaded appraisal of my strengths, decided I had better start young if I was to have any chance of keeping up with the competition.

The flaw in my character which she had already spotted was lack of "gumption." My idea of a perfect afternoon was lying in front of the radio rereading my favorite Big Little Book,[1] *Dick Tracy Meets Stooge Viller*. My mother despised inactivity. Seeing me having a good time in repose, she was powerless to hide her disgust. "You've got no more gumption than a bump on a log," she said. "Get out in the kitchen and help Doris do those dirty dishes."

My sister Doris, though two years younger than I, had enough gumption for a dozen people. She positively enjoyed washing dishes, making beds, and cleaning the house. When she was only seven she could carry a piece of short-weighted cheese back to the A & P, threaten the manager with legal action, and come back triumphantly with the full quarter-pound we'd paid for and a few ounces extra thrown in for forgiveness. Doris could have made something of herself if she hadn't been a girl. Because of this defect, however, the best she could hope for was a career as a nurse or schoolteacher, the only work that capable females were considered up to in those days.

This must have saddened my mother, this twist of fate that had allocated all the gumption to the daughter and left her with a son who was content with Dick Tracy and Stooge Viller. If disappointed, though, she wasted no energy on self-pity. She would make me make something of myself whether I wanted to or not. "The Lord helps those who help themselves," she said. That was the way her mind worked.

She was realistic about the difficulty. Having sized up the material the Lord had given her to mold, she didn't overestimate what she could do with it. She didn't insist that I grow up to be President of the United States.

Fifty years ago parents still asked boys if they wanted to grow up to be President, and asked it not jokingly but seriously. Many parents who were hardly more than paupers still believed their sons could do it. Abraham Lincoln had done it. We were only sixty-five years from Lincoln. Many a grandfather who walked among us could remember Lincoln's time. Men of grandfatherly age were the worst for asking if you wanted to grow up to be President. A surprising number of little boys said yes and meant it.

I was asked many times myself. No, I would say, I didn't want to grow up to be President. My mother was present during one of these interrogations. An elderly uncle, having posed the usual question and exposed my lack of interest

---

1. ***Big Little Book.*** First published in 1932, Big Little Books sold for ten cents, were bound in cardboard covers, and were approximately three inches by three inches. Each page of print was accompanied by a full-page illustration. Usually the books, which had wide appeal, featured the adventures of popular comic strip or movie heroes.

in the Presidency, asked, "Well, what *do* you want to be when you grow up?"

I loved to pick through trash piles and collect empty bottles, tin cans with pretty labels, and discarded magazines. The most desirable job on earth sprang instantly to mind. "I want to be a garbage man," I said.

My uncle smiled, but my mother had seen the first distressing evidence of a bump budding on a log. "Have a little gumption, Russell," she said. Her calling me Russell was a signal of unhappiness. When she approved of me I was always "Buddy."

When I turned eight years old she decided that the job of starting me on the road toward making something of myself could no longer be safely delayed. "Buddy," she said one day, "I want you to come home right after school this afternoon. Somebody's coming and I want you to meet him."

When I burst in that afternoon she was in conference in the parlor with an executive of the Curtis Publishing Company. She introduced me. He bent low from the waist and shook my hand. Was it true as my mother had told him, he asked, that I longed for the opportunity to conquer the world of business?

My mother replied that I was blessed with a rare determination to make something of myself.

"That's right," I whispered.

"But have you got the grit, the character, the never-say-quit spirit it takes to succeed in business?"

My mother said I certainly did.

"That's right," I said.

He eyed me silently for a long pause, as though weighing whether I could be trusted to keep his confidence, then spoke man-to-man. Before taking a crucial step, he said, he wanted to advise me that working for the Curtis Publishing Company placed enormous responsibility on a young man. It was one of the great companies of America. Perhaps the greatest publishing house in the world. I had heard, no doubt, of the *Saturday Evening Post?*

Heard of it? My mother said that everyone in our house had heard of the *Saturday Post* and that I, in fact, read it with religious devotion.

Then doubtless, he said, we were also familiar with those two monthly pillars of the magazine world, the *Ladies Home Journal* and the *Country Gentleman.*

Indeed we were familiar with them, said my mother.

Representing the *Saturday Evening Post* was one of the weightiest honors that could be bestowed in the world of business, he said. He was personally proud of being a part of that great corporation.

My mother said he had every right to be.

Again he studied me as though debating whether I was worthy of a knighthood. Finally: "Are you trustworthy?"

My mother said I was the soul of honesty.

"That's right," I said.

The caller smiled for the first time. He told me I was a lucky young man. He admired my spunk. Too many young men thought life was all play. Those young men would not go far in this world. Only a young man willing to work and save and keep his face washed and his hair neatly combed could hope to come out on top in a world such as ours. Did I truly and sincerely believe that I was such a young man?

"He certainly does," said my mother.

"That's right," I said.

He said he had been so impressed by what he had seen of me that he was going to make me a representative of the Curtis Publishing Company. On the following Tuesday, he said, thirty freshly printed copies of the *Saturday Evening Post* would be delivered at our door. I would place these magazines, still damp with the ink of the presses, in a handsome canvas bag, sling it over my shoulder, and set forth through the streets to bring the best in journalism, fiction, and cartoons to the American public.

He had brought the canvas bag with him. He presented it with reverence fit for a chasuble. He showed me how to drape the sling over my left shoulder and across the chest so that the

THE SATURDAY EVENING POST

A ... Y
Foun... ...nklin

Volume 205, Number 17

OCT. 22, 1932

5cts. THE COPY

10c. in Canada (INCLUDING TAX)

ROSE WILDER LANE · OWEN JOHNSON

pouch lay easily accessible to my right hand, allowing the best in journalism, fiction, and cartoons to be swiftly extracted and sold to a citizenry whose happiness and security depended upon us soldiers of the free press.

The following Tuesday I raced home from school, put the canvas bag over my shoulder, dumped the magazines in, and, tilting to the left to balance their weight on my right hip, embarked on the highway of journalism.

We lived in Belleville, New Jersey, a commuter town at the northern fringe of Newark. It was 1932, the bleakest year of the Depression. My father had died two years before, leaving us with a few pieces of Sears, Roebuck furniture and not much else, and my mother had taken Doris and me to live with one of her younger brothers. This was my Uncle Allen. Uncle Allen had made something of himself by 1932. As salesman for a soft-drink bottler in Newark, he had an income of thirty dollars a week; wore pearl-gray spats, detachable collars, and a three-piece suit; was happily married; and took in threadbare relatives.

With my load of magazines I headed toward Belleville Avenue. That's where the people were. There were two filling stations at the intersection with Union Avenue, as well as an A & P, a fruit stand, a bakery, a barber shop, Zuccarelli's drug store, and a diner shaped like a railroad car. For several hours I made myself highly visible, shifting position now and then from corner to corner, from shop window to shop window, to make sure everyone could see the heavy black lettering on the canvas bag that said THE SATURDAY EVENING POST. When the angle of the light indicated it was suppertime, I walked back to the house.

"How many did you sell, Buddy?" my mother asked.

"None."

"Where did you go?"

"The corner of Belleville and Union Avenues."

"What did you do?"

"Stood on the corner waiting for somebody to buy a *Saturday Evening Post.*"

"You just stood there?"

"Didn't sell a single one."

"For heaven's sake, Russell!"

Uncle Allen intervened. "I've been thinking about it for some time," he said, "and I've about decided to take the *Post* regularly. Put me down as a regular customer." I handed him a magazine and he paid me a nickel. It was the first nickel I earned.

Afterwards my mother instructed me in salesmanship. I would have to ring doorbells, address adults with charming self-confidence, and break down resistance with a sales talk pointing out that no one, no matter how poor, could afford to be without the *Saturday Evening Post* in the home.

I told my mother I'd changed my mind about wanting to succeed in the magazine business.

"If you think I'm going to raise a good-for-nothing," She replied, "you've got another think coming." She told me to hit the streets with the canvas bag and start ringing doorbells the instant school was out next day. When I objected that I didn't feel any aptitude for salesmanship, she asked how I'd like to lend her my leather belt so she could whack some sense into me. I bowed to superior will and entered journalism with a heavy heart.

My mother and I had fought this battle almost as long as I could remember. It probably started even before memory began, when I was a country child in northern Virginia and my mother, dissatisfied with my father's plain workman's life, determined that I would not grow up like him and his people, with calluses on their hands, overalls on their backs, and fourth-grade educations in their heads. She had fancier ideas of life's possibilities. Introducing me to the *Saturday Evening Post,* she was trying to wean me as early as possible from my father's world where men left with their lunch pails at sunup, worked with their hands until the grime ate into the pores, and died with a few sticks of mail-order furniture as their legacy. In my mother's vision of the better life there were desks and white collars, well-pressed suits, evenings of reading and lively talk, and perhaps—if a man were very, very lucky and hit the jackpot, really made something important of himself—perhaps there might be a fantastic salary of $5,000 a year to support a big house and a Buick with a rumble seat and a vacation in Atlantic City.

And so I set forth with my sack of magazines. I was afraid of the dogs that snarled behind the doors of potential buyers. I was timid about ringing the doorbells of strangers, relieved when no one came to the door, and scared when someone did. Despite my mother's instructions, I could not deliver an engaging sales pitch. When a door opened I simply asked, "Want to buy a *Saturday Evening Post?"* In Belleville few persons did. It was a town of thirty thousand people, and most weeks I rang a fair majority of its doorbells. But I rarely sold my thirty copies. Some weeks I canvassed the entire town for six days and still had four or five unsold magazines on Monday evening; then I dreaded the coming of Tuesday morning, when a batch of thirty fresh *Saturday Evening Posts* was due at the front door.

"Better get out there and sell the rest of those magazines tonight," my mother would say.

I usually posted myself then at a busy intersection where a traffic light controlled commuter flow from Newark. When the light turned red I stood on the curb and shouted my sales pitch at the motorists.

"Want to buy a *Saturday Evening Post?"*

One rainy night when car windows were sealed against me I came back soaked and with not a single sale to report. My mother beckoned to Doris.

"Go back down there with Buddy and show him how to sell these magazines," she said.

Brimming with zest, Doris, who was then seven years old, returned with me to the corner. She took a magazine from the bag, and when the light turned red she strode to the nearest car and banged her small fist against the closed window. The driver, probably startled at what he took to be a midget assaulting his car, lowered the window to stare, and Doris thrust a *Saturday Evening Post* at him.

"You need this magazine," she piped, "and it only costs a nickel."

Her salesmanship was irresistible. Before the light changed half a dozen times she disposed of the entire batch. I didn't feel humiliated. To the contrary. I was so happy I decided to give her a treat. Leading her to the vegetable store on Belleville Avenue, I bought three apples, which cost a nickel, and gave her one.

"You shouldn't waste money," she said.

"Eat your apple." I bit into mine.

"You shouldn't eat before supper," she said. "It'll spoil your appetite."

Back at the house that evening, she dutifully reported me for wasting a nickel. Instead of a scolding, I was rewarded with a pat on the back for having the good sense to buy fruit instead of candy. My mother reached into her bottomless supply of maxims and told Doris, "An apple a day keeps the doctor away."

By the time I was ten I had learned all my mother's maxims by heart. Asking to stay up past normal bedtime, I knew that a refusal would be explained with, "Early to bed and early to rise, makes a man healthy, wealthy, and wise." If I whimpered about having to get up early in the morning, I could depend on her to say, "The early bird gets the worm."

The one I most despised was, "If at first you don't succeed, try, try again." This was the battle cry with which she constantly sent me back into the hopeless struggle whenever I moaned that I had rung every doorbell in town and knew there wasn't a single potential buyer left in Belleville that week. After listening to my explanation, she handed me the canvas bag and said, "If at first you don't succeed . . ."

Three years in that job, which I would gladly have quit after the first day except for her insistence, produced at least one valuable result. My mother finally concluded that I would never make something of myself by pursuing a life in business and started considering careers that demanded less competitive zeal.

One evening when I was eleven I brought home a short "composition" on my summer vacation which the teacher had graded with an A. Reading it with her own schoolteacher's eye, my mother agreed that it was top-drawer seventh-grade prose and complimented me. Nothing more was said about it immediately, but a new idea had taken life in her mind. Halfway through supper she suddenly interrupted the conversation.

"Buddy," she said, "maybe you could be a writer."

I clasped the idea to my heart. I had never met a writer, had shown no previous urge to write, and hadn't a notion how to become a writer, but I loved stories and thought that making up stories must surely be almost as much fun as reading them. Best of all, though, and what really gladdened my heart, was the ease of the writer's life. Writers did not have to trudge through the town peddling from canvas bags, defending themselves against angry dogs, being rejected by surly strangers. Writers did not have to ring doorbells. So far as I could make out, what writers did couldn't even be classified as work.

I was enchanted. Writers didn't have to have any gumption at all. I did not dare tell anybody for fear of being laughed at in the schoolyard, but secretly I decided that what I'd like to be when I grew up was a writer.

Discussion

1. (a) What was the "flaw" Russell's mother spotted in his character? **(b)** In what ways did this trait show itself? **(c)** Did Russell's sister Doris share the trait? Explain.

2. (a) Cite evidence suggesting that the man from the Curtis Publishing Company regarded highly the company he represented. **(b)** Do you believe the man to have been sincere? Why or why not? **(c)** What did Russell's mother do to convince the representative that her son should get a job?

3. (a) Describe Russell's first day selling magazines. **(b)** Afterward, what instructions did his mother give him? **(c)** What was her purpose in doing so? **(d)** How did Russell respond to this advice?

4. (a) What finally persuaded Russell's mother that her son might become something other than a businessman? **(b)** How did Russell react to this new possibility? Why?

5. Cite passages in the selection that you find humorous.

Composition

What is the hardest, most disagreeable work you have ever done? Baby-sitting? Mowing lawns? Selling door-to-door? Doing chores around the house?

Write a brief paper describing one such job. Provide your reader with appropriate details about when and where you did the work, how you did it, for whom you worked, and why you worked. Before you begin to write, decide whether you want your account to be serious or humorous; then, carefully select events and language that will support your purpose. (See *Revising*, page 664, in Composition Guide.)

The Dog That Bit People

James Thurber

"Mother used to send a box of candy every Christmas to the people the Airedale bit. The list finally contained forty or fifty names."

Probably no one man should have as many dogs in his life as I have had, but there was more pleasure than distress in them for me except in the case of an Airedale named Muggs. He gave me more trouble than all the other fifty-four or -five put together, although my moment of keenest embarrassment was the time a Scotch terrier named Jeannie, who had just had six puppies in the clothes closet of a fourth floor apartment in New York, had the unexpected seventh and last at the corner of Eleventh Street and Fifth Avenue during a walk she had insisted on taking. Then, too, there was the prize-winning French poodle, a great big black poodle—none of your little, untroublesome white miniatures—who got sick riding in the rumble seat of a car with me on her way to the Greenwich Dog Show. She had a red rubber bib tucked around her throat and, since a rain storm came up when we were halfway through the Bronx, I had to hold over her a small green umbrella, really more of a parasol. The rain beat down fearfully, and suddenly the driver of the car drove into a big garage, filled with mechanics. It happened so quickly that I forgot to put the umbrella down and I will always remember, with sickening distress, the look of incredulity mixed with hatred that came over the face of the particular hardened garage man that came over to see what we wanted, when he took a look at me and the poodle. All garage men, and people of that intolerant stripe, hate poodles with their curious haircut, especially the pompons that you got to leave on their hips if you expect the dogs to win a prize.

But the Airedale, as I have said, was the worst of all my dogs. He really wasn't my dog, as a matter of fact: I came home from a vacation one summer to find that my brother Roy had bought him while I was away. A big, burly, choleric dog, he always acted as if he thought I wasn't one of the family. There was a slight advantage in being one of the family, for he didn't bite the family as often as he bit strangers. Still, in the years that we had him he bit everybody but mother, and he made a pass at her once but missed. That was during the month when we suddenly had mice, and Muggs refused to do anything about them. Nobody ever had mice exactly like the mice we had that month. They acted like pet mice, almost like mice somebody had trained. They were so friendly that one night when mother entertained at dinner the Friraliras, a club she and my father had belonged to for twenty years, she put down a lot of little dishes with food in them on the pantry floor so that the mice would be satisfied with that and wouldn't come into the dining room. Muggs stayed out in the pantry with the mice, lying on the floor, growling to himself—not at the mice, but about all the people in the next room that he would have liked to get at. Mother slipped out into the pantry once to see how everything was going. Everything was going fine. It made her so mad to see Muggs lying there, oblivious of the mice—they came running up to her—that she slapped him and he slashed at her, but didn't make it. He was sorry immediately, mother said. He was always sorry, she said, after he bit someone, but we could not understand how she figured this out. He didn't act sorry.

Mother used to send a box of candy every Christmas to the people the Airedale bit. The list finally contained forty or more names. Nobody could understand why we didn't get rid of the dog. I didn't understand it very well myself, but we didn't get rid of him. I think that one or two people tried to poison Muggs—he acted poisoned once in a while—and old Major Moberly fired at him once with his service revolver near the Seneca Hotel in East Broad Street—but Muggs lived to be almost eleven years old and even when he could hardly get around he bit a Congressman who had called to see my father on business. My mother had never liked the Congressman—she said the signs of his horoscope showed he couldn't be trusted (he was Saturn with the moon in Virgo)—but she sent him a box of candy that Christmas. He sent it right back, probably because he suspected it was trick candy. Mother persuaded herself it was all for the best that the dog had bitten him,

Lots of people reported our dog to the police.

even though father lost an important business association because of it. "I wouldn't be associated with such a man," mother said. "Muggs could read him like a book."

We used to take turns feeding Muggs to be on his good side, but that didn't always work. He was never in a very good humor, even after a meal. Nobody knew exactly what was the matter with him, but whatever it was it made him irascible, especially in the mornings. Roy never felt very well in the morning, either, especially before breakfast, and once when he came downstairs and found that Muggs had moodily chewed up the morning paper he hit him in the face with a grapefruit and then jumped on the dining-room table, scattering dishes and silverware and spilling the coffee. Muggs's first free leap carried him all the way across the table and into a brass fire screen in front of the gas grate but he was back on his feet in a moment and in the end he got Roy and gave him a pretty vicious bite in the leg. Then he was all over it; he never bit anyone more than once at a time. Mother always mentioned that as an argument in his favor; she said he had a quick temper but that he didn't hold a grudge. She was forever defending him. I think she liked him because he wasn't well. "He's not strong," she would say, pityingly, but that was inaccurate; he may not have been well but he was terribly strong.

One time my mother went to the Chittendon Hotel to call on a woman mental healer who was lecturing in Columbus on the subject of "Harmonious Vibrations." She wanted to find out if it was possible to get harmonious vibrations into a dog. "He's a large tan-colored Airedale," mother explained. The woman said that she had never treated a dog but she advised my mother to hold the thought that he did not bite and would not bite. Mother was holding the thought the very next morning when Muggs got the iceman, but she blamed that slip-up on the iceman. "If you didn't think he would bite you, he wouldn't," mother told him. He stomped out of the house in a terrible jangle of vibrations.

One morning when Muggs bit me slightly,

more or less in passing, I reached down and grabbed his short stumpy tail and hoisted him into the air. It was a foolhardy thing to do and the last time I saw my mother, about six months ago, she said she didn't know what possessed me. I don't either, except that I was pretty mad. As long as I held the dog off the floor by his tail he couldn't get at me, but he twisted and jerked so, snarling all the time, that I realized I couldn't hold him that way very long. I carried him to the kitchen and flung him onto the floor and shut the door on him just as he crashed against it. But I forgot about the backstairs. Muggs went up the backstairs and down the frontstairs and had me cornered in the living room. I managed to get up onto the mantelpiece above the fireplace, but it gave way and came down with a tremendous crash throwing a large marble clock, several vases, and myself heavily to the floor. Muggs was so alarmed by the racket that when I picked myself up he had disappeared. We couldn't find him anywhere, although we whistled and shouted, until old Mrs. Detweiler called after dinner that night. Muggs had bitten her once, in the leg, and she came into the living room only after we assured her that Muggs had run away. She had just seated herself when, with a great growling and scratching of claws, Muggs emerged from under a davenport where he had been quietly hiding all the time and bit her again. Mother examined the bite and put arnica[1] on it and told Mrs. Detweiler that it was only a bruise. "He just bumped you," she said. But Mrs. Detweiler left the house in a nasty state of mind.

Lots of people reported our Airedale to the police but my father held a municipal office at the time and was on friendly terms with the police. Even so, the cops had been out a couple times—once when Muggs bit Mrs. Rufus Sturtevant and again when he bit Lieutenant-Governor Malloy—but mother told them that it hadn't been Muggs's fault but the fault of the people who were bitten. "When he starts for them, they scream," she explained, "and that excites him." The cops suggested that it might be a good idea to tie the dog up, but mother said that it mortified him to be tied up and that he wouldn't eat when he was tied up.

Muggs at his meals was an unusual sight.

Muggs at his meals was an unusual sight. Because of the fact that if you reached toward the floor he would bite you, we usually put his food plate on top of an old kitchen table with a bench alongside the table. Muggs would stand on the bench and eat. I remember that my mother's Uncle Horatio, who boasted that he was the third man up Missionary Ridge,[2] was splutteringly indignant when he found out that we fed the dog on a table because we were afraid to put his plate on the floor. He said he wasn't afraid of any dog that ever lived and that he would put the dog's plate on the floor if we would give it to him. Roy said that if Uncle Horatio had fed Muggs on the ground just before the battle he would have been the first man up Missionary Ridge. Uncle Horatio was furious. "Bring him in! Bring him in now!" he shouted. "I'll feed the — on the floor!" Roy was all for giving him a chance, but my father wouldn't hear of it. He said that Muggs had already been fed. "I'll feed him again!" bawled Uncle Horatio. We had quite a time quieting him.

In his last year Muggs used to spend practically all of his time outdoors. He didn't like to stay in the house for some reason or other—per-

---

1. ***arnica*** (är′nə kə), a healing liquid applied to bruises and sprains.
2. ***Missionary Ridge,*** site of a Civil War battle.

haps it held too many unpleasant memories for him. Anyway, it was hard to get him to come in and as a result the garbage man, the iceman, and the laundryman wouldn't come near the house. We had to haul the garbage down to the corner, take the laundry out and bring it back, and meet the iceman a block from home. After this had gone on for some time we hit on an ingenious arrangement for getting the dog in the house so that we could lock him up while the gas meter was read, and so on. Muggs was afraid of only one thing, an electrical storm. Thunder and lightning frightened him out of his senses (I think he thought a storm had broken the day the mantelpiece fell). He would rush into the house and hide under a bed or in a clothes closet. So we fixed up a thunder machine out of a long narrow piece of sheet iron with a wooden handle on one end. Mother would shake this vigorously when she wanted to get Muggs into the house. It made an excellent imitation of thunder, but I suppose it was the most roundabout system for running a household that was ever devised. It took a lot out of mother.

A few months before Muggs died, he got to "seeing things." He would rise slowly from the floor, growling low, and stalk stiff-legged and menacing toward nothing at all. Sometimes the Thing would be just a little to the right or left of a visitor. Once a Fuller Brush salesman got hysterics. Muggs came wandering into the room like Hamlet following his father's ghost. His eyes were fixed on a spot just to the left of the Fuller Brush man, who stood it until Muggs was about three slow, creeping paces from him. Then he shouted. Muggs wavered on past him into the hallway grumbling to himself but the Fuller man went on shouting. I think mother had to throw a pan of cold water on him before he stopped. That was the way she used to stop us boys when we got into fights.

Muggs died quite suddenly one night. Mother wanted to bury him in the family lot under a marble stone with some such inscription as "Flights of angels sing thee to thy rest" but we persuaded her it was against the law. In the end we just put up a smooth board above his grave along a lonely road. On the board I wrote with an indelible pencil "Cave Canem."[3] Mother was quite pleased with the simple classic dignity of the old Latin epitaph.

---

3. ***"Cave Canem"*** (kä′vā kä′nem). "Beware of the dog."

Discussion

1. (a) Relate some of the excuses Mother offered for Muggs's behavior. **(b)** How did she lessen the anger of those he had bitten?

2. (a) Why did the Thurbers keep Muggs? **(b)** Why didn't they at least tie him up? **(c)** How did Muggs's decision to spend his time outdoors affect their lives?

3. What were the symptoms of Muggs's final illness?

4. Thurber creates humor in a number of ways. Select a passage or an episode that you find amusing. **(a)** Is the situation exaggerated? **(b)** Is it presented in a matter-of-fact, understated way? **(c)** Is it ironic? **(d)** Does the situation contain incongruous elements (for instance, a dog riding in a rumble seat with a parasol over him)?

James Thurber 1894–1961

Friends characterized Thurber as shy, brooding, absent-minded, and unpredictable. He said of himself that he had "never been able to maintain a consistent attitude toward life or reality, or toward anything else."

Thurber gradually "worked his way down" from managing editor of *The New Yorker* to editor of the Talk of the Town department of that magazine.

See **TONE** Handbook of Literary Terms

Ponds

Lewis Thomas

You'd think they were rats or roaches, the way people began to talk: "Get those goldfish out of that pond . . ."

Large areas of Manhattan are afloat. I remember when the new Bellevue Hospital was being built, fifteen years ago; the first stage was the most spectacular and satisfying, an enormous square lake. It was there for the two years, named Lake Bellevue, while the disconsolate Budget Bureau went looking for cash to build the next stage. It was fenced about and visible only from the upper windows of the old hospital, but pretty to look at, cool and blue in midsummer, frozen gleaming as Vermont in January. The fence, like all city fences, was always broken, and we could have gone down to the lake and used it, but it was known to be an upwelling of the East River. At Bellevue there were printed rules about the East River: if anyone fell in, it was an emergency for the Infectious-Disease Service, and the first measures, after resuscitation, were massive doses of whatever antibiotics the hospital pharmacy could provide.

But if you cleaned the East River you could have ponds all over town, up and down the East Side of Manhattan anyway. If you lifted out the Empire State Building and the high structures nearby, you would have, instantly, an inland sea. A few holes bored in the right places would let water into the subways, and you'd have lovely underground canals all across to the Hudson, uptown to the Harlem River, downtown to the Battery, a Venice underground, without pigeons.

It wouldn't work, though, unless you could find a way to keep out the fish. New Yorkers cannot put up with live fish out in the open. I cannot explain this, but it is so.

There is a new pond, much smaller than Lake Bellevue, on First Avenue between Seventieth and Seventy-first, on the east side of the street. It emerged sometime last year, soon after a row of old flats had been torn down and the hole dug for a new apartment building. By now it is about average size for Manhattan, a city block long and about forty feet across, maybe eight feet deep at the center, more or less kidney-shaped, rather like an outsized suburban swimming pool except for the things floating, and now the goldfish.

With the goldfish, it is almost detestable. There are, clearly visible from the sidewalk, hundreds of them. The neighborhood people do not walk by and stare into it through the broken fence, as would be normal for any other Manhattan pond. They tend to cross the street, looking away.

Now there are complaints against the pond, really against the goldfish. How could people do such a thing? Bad enough for pet dogs and cats to be abandoned, but who could be so unfeeling as to abandon goldfish? They must have come

down late at night, carrying their bowls, and simply dumped them in. How could they?

The ASPCA[1] was called, and came one afternoon with a rowboat. Nets were used, and fish taken away in new custodial bowls, some to Central Park, others to ASPCA headquarters, to the fish pound. But the goldfish have multiplied, or maybe those people with their bowls keep coming down late at night for their furtive, unfeeling dumping. Anyway, there are too many fish for the ASPCA, for which this seems to be a new kind of problem. An official stated for the press that the owners of the property would be asked to drain the pond by pumping, and then the ASPCA would come back with nets to catch them all.

1. ***ASPCA,*** American Society for Prevention of Cruelty to Animals.

You'd think they were rats or roaches, the way people began to talk. Get those goldfish out of that pond, I don't care how you do it. Dynamite, if necessary. But get rid of them. Winter is coming, someone said, and it is deep enough so that they'll be swimming around underneath the ice. Get them out.

It is this knowledge of the East River, deep in the minds of all Manhattan residents, more than the goldfish themselves, I think. Goldfish in a glass bowl are harmless to the human mind, maybe even helpful to minds casting about for something, anything, to think about. But goldfish let loose, propagating themselves, worst of all *surviving* in what has to be a sessile eddy of the East River, somehow threaten us all. We do not like to think that life is possible under some conditions, especially the conditions of a Manhattan pond. There are four abandoned tires, any number of broken beer bottles, fourteen shoes and a single sneaker, and a visible layer, all over the surface, of that grayish-green film that settles on all New York surfaces. The mud at the banks of the pond is not proper country mud but reconstituted Manhattan landfill, ancient garbage, fossilized coffee grounds and grapefruit rind, the defecation of a city. For goldfish to be swimming in such water, streaking back and forth mysteriously in small schools, feeding, obviously feeding, looking as healthy and well-off as goldfish in the costliest kind of window-box aquarium, means something is wrong with our standards. It is, in some deep sense beyond words, insulting.

I thought I noticed a peculiar sort of fin on the undersurface of two of the fish. Perhaps, it occurs to me now in a rush of exultation, in such a pond as this, with all its chemical possibilities, there are contained some mutagens, and soon there will be schools of mutant goldfish. Give them just a little more time, I thought. And then, with the most typically Manhattan thought I've ever thought, I thought: The ASPCA will come again, next month, with their rowboat and their nets. The proprietor will begin pumping out the pond. The nets will flail, the rowboat will settle, and then the ASPCA officials will give a sudden shout of great dismay. And with a certain amount of splashing and grayish-greenish spray, at all the edges of the pond, up all the banks of ancient New York landfill mud, crawling on their new little feet, out onto the sidewalks, up and down and across the street, into doorways and up the fire escapes, some of them with little suckers on their little feet, up the sides of buildings and into open windows, looking for something, will come the goldfish.

It won't last, of course. Nothing like this ever does. The mayor will come and condemn it in person. The Health Department will come and recommend the purchase of cats from out of town because of the constitutional boredom of city cats. The NIH[2] will send up teams of professionals from Washington with a new kind of antifish spray, which will be recalled four days later because of toxicity to cats.

After a few weeks it will be finished anyway, like a lot of New York events. The goldfish will dive deep and vanish, the pond will fill up with sneakers, workmen will come and pour concrete over everything, and by next year the new building will be up and occupied by people all unaware of their special environmental impact. But what a time it was.

---

2. ***NIH,*** National Institutes of Health.

Discussion

1. (a) What evidence does Thomas offer to support his first sentence, "Large areas of Manhattan are afloat"? **(b)** What body of water is responsible for this situation? **(c)** Describe the condition of that water.

2. (a) How do those in the neighborhood respond to the appearance of live goldfish in the pond on First Avenue between Seventieth and Seventy-first streets? **(b)** What are their apparent reasons for objecting to the appearance of the fish? **(c)** What may be their real reason?

3. (a) Describe Thomas's fantasy about "mutant goldfish." **(b)** In the fantasy, what forces will be called out against these mutants? **(c)** What eventually will happen to the fish?

4. Is Thomas's language more subjective than objective? more objective than subjective? Explain.

Application
Tone

If necessary, review the definition of *tone* in the Handbook of Literary Terms. Then, decide on three words that you feel describe the tone of "Ponds." Be prepared to cite examples of words and details from the article to support each of your choices.

Vocabulary
Context, Dictionary

Read the following sentences carefully, paying special attention to the italicized words. Then from **(a)**, **(b)**, or **(c)**, choose the sentence that most closely approximates the original meaning. Use your Glossary if necessary.

1. The *disconsolate* child required *resuscitation.* **(a)** The bored child needed to be entertained. **(b)** The extremely unhappy child needed to be revived. **(c)** The sick child had to go to the hospital.

2. Some *mutant* plants are *sessile.* **(a)** Some new varieties of plants grow from the base, instead of from a stem. **(b)** Some peculiar-looking plants can be dangerous. **(c)** Some very rare plants are quite valuable.

3. A *fossilized* organism can never be *reconstituted.* **(a)** An organism that is truly sick can never be cured. **(b)** A broken organism cannot be mended. **(c)** The hardened remains of an organism cannot be brought back to life.

4. A man can develop a *constitutional* weakness if the *toxicity* of the air he breathes is too high. **(a)** The human body can become inherently weak if the air a person breathes is badly polluted. **(b)** A man will act against the Constitution of the United States if he inhales laughing gas. **(c)** A person can be committed to an institution for not breathing enough air.

5. The burglar gave the room a *furtive* glance, and felt *exultation* when he saw the gleaming silver. **(a)** The burglar opened his eyes wide but was disappointed when he saw the silver. **(b)** The burglar quietly and quickly looked over the room, and felt a sense of triumph when he saw the silver. **(c)** The burglar could scarcely see what he was doing, so he felt very lucky to have noticed the silver.

Lewis Thomas 1913–

In 1970, the editor of the *New England Journal of Medicine* asked Dr. Lewis Thomas to begin writing a monthly essay for that journal. Collected in 1974 in a book titled *Lives of a Cell: Notes of a Biology Watcher,* the scientific essays won for Dr. Thomas the National Book Award for their elegant, poetic, and sometimes mystical observations about the place of humans in the biological world. In 1979 appeared a second collection of essays, *The Medusa and the Snail: More Notes of a Biology Watcher,* from which "Ponds" is taken. This collection was winner of an American Book Award. Dr. Thomas's autobiography, *The Youngest Science: Notes of a Medicine Watcher* was published in 1983. Also published in 1983 was the collection *Late Night Thoughts on Listening to Mahler's Ninth Symphony.*

The son of a doctor and a nurse, Dr. Thomas is former dean of the medical schools at Yale and New York Universities and former chancellor of the Memorial Sloan-Kettering Cancer Center in New York. In addition to being a renowned biologist, researcher, administrator, and essayist, he is a poet.

See **STYLE** Handbook of Literary Terms

A Lincoln Preface

Carl Sandburg

"It was a time when a man with a policy would have been fatal to the country. I never had a policy. I have simply tried to do what seemed best each day, as each day came."

In the time of the April lilacs in the year 1865, a man in the City of Washington, D.C., trusted a guard to watch at a door, and the guard was careless, left the door, and the man was shot, lingered a night, passed away, was laid in a box, and carried north and west a thousand miles; bells sobbed; cities wore crepe; people stood with hats off as the railroad burial car came past at midnight, dawn, or noon.

During the four years of time before he gave up the ghost, this man was clothed with despotic power, commanding the most powerful armies till then assembled in modern warfare, enforcing drafts of soldiers, abolishing the right of habeas corpus,[1] directing politically and spiritually the wild, massive forces loosed in civil war.

Four billion dollars' worth of property was taken from those who had been legal owners of it, confiscated, wiped out as by fire, at his instigation and executive direction; a class of chattel property[2] recognized as lawful for two hundred years went to the scrap pile.

When the woman who wrote *Uncle Tom's Cabin* came to see him in the White House, he greeted her, "So you're the little woman who wrote the book that made this great war," and as they seated themselves at a fireplace, "I do love an open fire; I always had one to home." As they were finishing their talk of the days of blood, he said, "I shan't last long after it's over."

An Illinois Congressman looked in on him as he had his face lathered for a shave in the White House, and remarked, "If anybody had told me that in a great crisis like this the people were going out to a little one-horse town and pick out a one-horse lawyer for President, I wouldn't have believed it." The answer was, "Neither would I. But it was a time when a man with a policy would have been fatal to the country. I never had a policy. I have simply tried to do what seemed best each day, as each day came."

"I don't intend precisely to throw the Constitution overboard, but I will stick it in a hole if I can," he told a Cabinet officer. The enemy was violating the Constitution to destroy the Union, he argued, and therefore, "I will violate the Constitution, if necessary, to save the

1. ***habeas corpus*** (hā′bē əs kôr′pəs), order requiring that a prisoner be brought before a judge or into court to decide whether he or she is being held lawfully. The right of habeas corpus is a protection against unjust imprisonment.
2. ***chattel property,*** property that is not real estate; slaves.

Union." He instructed a messenger to the Secretary of the Treasury, "Tell him not to bother himself about the Constitution. Say that I have that sacred instrument here at the White House, and I am guarding it with great care."

When he was renominated, it was by the device of seating delegates from Tennessee, which gave enough added votes to seat favorable delegates from Kentucky, Missouri, Louisiana, Arkansas, and from one county in Florida. Until late in that campaign of 1864, he expected to lose the November election; military victories brought the tide his way; the vote was 2,200,000 for him and 1,800,000 against him. Among those who bitterly fought him politically, and accused him of blunders or crimes, were Franklin Pierce, a former President of the United States; Horatio Seymour, the governor of New York; Samuel F. B. Morse, inventor of the telegraph; Cyrus H. McCormick, inventor of the farm reaper; General George B. McClellan, a Democrat who had commanded the Army of the Potomac; and the Chicago *Times,* a daily newspaper. In all its essential propositions the Southern Confederacy had the moral support of powerful, respectable elements throughout the North, probably more than a million voters believing in the justice of the cause of the South as compared with the North.

While propagandas raged, and the war winds howled, he sat in the White House, the Stubborn Man of History, writing that the Mississippi was one river and could not belong to two countries, that the plans for railroad connection from coast to coast must be pushed through and the Union Pacific realized.

His life, mind, and heart ran on contrasts. When his white kid gloves broke into tatters while shaking hands at a White House reception, he remarked, "This looks like a general bustification." When he talked with an Ohio friend one day during the 1864 campaign, he mentioned one public man, and murmured, "He's a thistle! I don't see why God lets him live." Of a devious senator, he said. "He's too crooked to lie still!" And of a New York editor, "In early life in the West, we used to make our shoes last a great while with much mending, and sometimes, when far gone, we found the leather so rotten the stitches would not hold. Greeley is so rotten that nothing can be done with him. He is not truthful; the stitches all tear out." As he sat in the telegraph office of the War Department, reading cipher dispatches, and came to the words, Hosanna and Husband, he would chuckle, "Jeffy D.," and at the words, Hunter and Happy, "Bobby Lee."[3]

While the luck of war wavered and broke and came again, as generals failed and campaigns were lost, he held enough forces of the Union together to raise new armies and supply them, until generals were found who made war as victorious war has always been made, with terror, frightfulness, destruction, and valor and sacrifice past words of man to tell.

A slouching, gray-headed poet, haunting the hospitals at Washington, characterized him as "the grandest figure on the crowded canvas of the drama of the nineteenth century—a Hoosier Michelangelo."

His own speeches, letters, telegrams, and official messages during that war form the most significant and enduring document from any one man on why the war began, why it went on, and the dangers beyond its end. He mentioned "the politicians," over and again "the politicians," with scorn and blame. As the platoons filed before him at a review of an army corps, he asked, "What is to become of these boys when the war is over?"

He was a chosen spokesman; yet there were times he was silent; nothing but silence could at those times have fitted a chosen spokesman; in the mixed shame and blame of the immense wrongs of two crashing civilizations, with nothing to say, he said nothing, slept not at all, and wept at those times in a way that made weeping appropriate, decent, majestic.

His hat was shot off as he rode alone one

---

3. ***"Jeffy . . . Lee."*** Jefferson Davis, president of the Confederacy, and Robert E. Lee, Confederate general.

FOUR SCORE AND SEVEN YEARS
AGO OUR FATHERS BROUGHT FORTH
ON THIS CONTINENT A NEW NATION

night in Washington; a son he loved died as he watched at the bed; his wife was accused of betraying information to the enemy, until denials from him were necessary; his best companion was a fine-hearted and brilliant son with a deformed palate and an impediment of speech; when a Pennsylvania congressman told him the enemy had declared they would break into the city and hang him to a lamp post, he said he had considered "the violent preliminaries" to such a scene; on his left thumb was a scar where an ax had nearly chopped the thumb off when he was a boy; over one eye was a scar where he had been hit with a club in the hands of a Negro trying to steal the cargo off a Mississippi River flatboat; he threw a cashiered officer out of his room in the White House, crying, "I can bear censure, but not insult. I never wish to see your face again."

As he shook hands with the correspondent of the London *Times,* he drawled, "Well, I guess the London *Times* is about the greatest power on earth—unless perhaps it is the Mississippi River." He rebuked with anger a woman who got on her knees to thank him for a pardon that saved her son from being shot at sunrise; and when an Iowa woman said she had journeyed out of her way to Washington just for a look at him, he grinned, "Well, in the matter of looking at one another, I have altogether the advantage."

He asked his Cabinet to vote on the high military command, and after the vote, told them the appointment had already been made; one Cabinet officer, who had been governor of Ohio, came away personally baffled and frustrated from an interview, to exclaim, to a private secretary, "That man is the most cunning person I ever saw in my life"; an Illinois lawyer who had been sent on errands carrying his political secrets, said, "He is a trimmer and such a trimmer as the world has never seen."

He manipulated the admission of Nevada as a state in the Union, when her votes were needed for the Emancipation Proclamation, saying, "It is easier to admit Nevada than to raise another million of soldiers." At the same time he went to the office of a former New York editor, who had become Assistant Secretary of War, and said the votes of three congressmen were wanted for the required three-quarters of votes in the House of Representatives, advising, "There are three that you can deal with better than anybody else. . . . Whatever promise you make to those men, I will perform it." And in the same week, he said to a Massachusetts politician that two votes were lacking, and, "Those two votes must be procured. I leave it to you to determine how it shall be done; but remember that I am President of the United States and clothed with immense power, and I expect you to procure those votes." And while he was thus employing every last resource and device of practical politics to constitutionally abolish slavery, the abolitionist Henry Ward Beecher attacked him with javelins of scorn and detestation in a series of editorials that brought from him the single comment, "Is thy servant a dog?"

When the King of Siam sent him a costly sword of exquisite embellishment, and two elephant tusks, along with letters and a photograph of the King, he acknowledged the gifts in a manner as lavish as the Orientals. Addressing the King of Siam as "Great and Good Friend," he wrote thanks for each of the gifts, including "also two elephants' tusks of length and magnitude such as indicate they could have belonged only to an animal which was a native of Siam." After further thanks for the tokens received, he closed the letter to the King of Siam with strange grace and humor, saying, "I appreciate most highly your Majesty's tender of good offices in forwarding to this Government a stock from which a supply of elephants might be raised on our soil. . . . Our political jurisdiction, however, does not reach a latitude so low as to favor the multiplication of the elephant, and steam on land as well as water has been our best agent of transportation. . . . Meantime, wishing for your Majesty a long and happy life, and, for the generous and emulous people of Siam, the highest possible prosperity, I commend both to the blessing of Almighty God."

He sent hundreds of telegrams, "Suspend death sentence," or "Suspend execution" of So-and-So, who was to be shot at sunrise. The telegrams varied oddly at times, as in one, "If Thomas Samplogh, of the First Delaware Regiment, has been sentenced to death, and is not yet executed, suspend and report the case to me." And another, "Is it Lieut. Samuel B. Davis whose death sentence is commuted? If not done, let it be done."

While the war drums beat, he liked best of all the stories told of him, one of two Quakeresses heard talking in a railway car. "I think that Jefferson will succeed." "Why does thee think so?" "Because Jefferson is a praying man." "And so is Abraham a praying man." "Yes, but the Lord will think Abraham is joking."

An Indiana man at the White House heard him say, "Voorhees, don't it seem strange to you that I, who could never so much as cut off the head of a chicken, should be elected, or selected, into the midst of all this blood?"

A party of American citizens, standing in the ruins of the Forum in Rome, Italy, heard there the news of the first assassination of the first American dictator, and took it as a sign of the growing up and the aging of the civilization on the North American continent. Far out in Coles County, Illinois, a beautiful, gaunt old woman in a log cabin said, "I knowed he'd never come back."

Of men taking too fat profits out of the war, he said, "Where the carcass is, there will the eagles be gathered together."

An enemy general, Longstreet, after the war, declared him to have been "the one matchless man in forty millions of people," while one of his private secretaries, Hay, declared his life to have been the most perfect in its relationships and adjustments since that of Christ.

Between the days in which he crawled as a baby on the dirt floor of a Kentucky cabin, and the time when he gave his final breath in Washington, he packed a rich life with work, thought, laughter, tears, hate, love.

With vast reservoirs of the comic and the droll, and notwithstanding a mastery of mirth and nonsense, he delivered a volume of addresses and letters of terrible and serious appeal, with import beyond his own day, shot through here and there with far, thin ironies, with paragraphs having raillery of the quality of the Book of Job, and echoes as subtle as the whispers of wind in prairie grass.

Perhaps no human clay-pot has held more laughter and tears.

The facts and myths of his life are to be an American possession, shared widely over the world, for thousands of years, as the tradition of Knute or Alfred, Lao-tse or Diogenes, Pericles or Caesar,[4] are kept. This because he was not only a genius in the science of neighborly human relationships and an artist in the personal handling of life from day to day, but a strange friend and a friendly stranger to all forms of life that he met.

He lived fifty-six years of which fifty-two were lived in the West—the prairie years.

---

4. ***Knute . . . Caesar,*** great statesmen and philosophers of ancient times.

Discussion

1. **(a)** What is a preface? **(b)** Do you think that this selection does what a preface is supposed to do? Explain your opinion.

2. In this selection, is Sandburg being objective or subjective about Lincoln? Explain.

Application

Style

1. Authors choose and arrange language and incidents to shape readers' attitudes toward their subjects. What attitudes or feelings toward Lincoln do you think Sandburg hoped to arouse with each of the following? **(a)** " . . . bells sobbed, cities wore crepe . . ." **(b)** " 'I never had a policy. I have simply tried to do what seemed best each day.' " **(c)** " 'I will violate the Constitution, if necessary, to save the Union.' " **(d)** "His life, mind, and heart ran on contrasts." **(e)** " ' . . . a Hoosier Michelangelo' " **(f)** " 'What is to become of these boys when the war is over?' " **(g)** " . . . he wept . . . in a way that made weeping appropriate, decent, majestic."

2. Look up the following words in a dictionary: *chronological, anecdotal, spatial, deductive, causal.* Which best describes the organizational pattern of Sandburg's preface?

Vocabulary

Dictionary

Number your paper from 1 to 10. Then write the word that is most nearly the same in meaning as the italicized word.

1. *despotic:* **(a)** unhappy; **(b)** unreasonable; **(c)** despairing; **(d)** tyrannical.
2. *confiscated:* **(a)** paid; **(b)** seized; **(c)** given; **(d)** hesitated.
3. *censure:* **(a)** restriction; **(b)** criticism; **(c)** approval; **(d)** debate.
4. *rebuked:* **(a)** scolded; **(b)** inquired; **(c)** confirmed; **(d)** approved.
5. *procured:* **(a)** fought; **(b)** requested; **(c)** obtained; **(d)** denied.
6. *detestation:* **(a)** pain; **(b)** hatred; **(c)** ability; **(d)** disappointment.
7. *jurisdiction:* **(a)** dread; **(b)** authority; **(c)** fantasy; **(d)** possibility.
8. *droll:* **(a)** amusing; **(b)** forceful; **(c)** serious; **(d)** dangerous.
9. *commend:* **(a)** recommend; **(b)** blame; **(c)** strengthen; **(d)** criticize.
10. *majestic:* **(a)** stately; **(b)** flat; **(c)** unusual; **(d)** calm.

Carl Sandburg 1878–1967

Upon completing in 1924 *Abraham Lincoln: The Prairie Years,* a two-volume biography of Lincoln's life before he became President, Carl Sandburg wrote a preface that "would begin at the death of Lincoln and work back to the day he left Illinois. The reader could then turn to the book and begin with the birth of Lincoln." But when Sandburg decided to write the four-volume *Abraham Lincoln: The War Years,* published in 1939 and awarded the Pulitzer Prize for history, he abandoned the early preface, which is reprinted here.

Unit 7 Review: *Prose Forms*

Content Review

The following statements are about the selections in the unit you have just completed. Number from 1 to 10 on a separate sheet of paper. After each number, write "a" if you *strongly agree* with the statement that corresponds in number; "b" if you *agree;* "c" if you *have no opinion;* "d" if you *disagree;* "e" if you *strongly disagree* with the statement.

Whenever possible, be prepared to support each of your opinions with evidence from the selections.

1. If Lincoln were President today, he would be able to resolve the nation's major problems.

2. If Aunt Arie had had a college education, her life would have been much more satisfying.

3. James Thurber and Abraham Lincoln had similar senses of humor.

4. ". . . The Awful Sweetness of Walking with God" is more subjective than is "Reflections of a Seventeen-Year-Old."

5. If I were John D. Johnston, Lincoln's letter would infuriate me.

6. Martin Luther King, Jr.'s address would have been more effective if he had not used figurative language.

7. Aunt Arie would have had more respect for Esther than for Sylvia.

8. Of all the selections in this unit, Sylvia Plath's diary entry has the most consistently objective language.

9. Lewis Thomas and James Thurber probably would have enjoyed each other's company.

10. "The Dog That Bit People" is more amusing than is the selection from *Growing Up.*

Concept Review: Interpretation of New Material

The following excerpt from Mary Hemingway's autobiography describes a canoe trip taken by the author and her father in northern Minnesota when she was twelve. Read the excerpt. Then on a separate sheet of paper answer the questions that follow.

from How It Was • *Mary Hemingway*

As we turned a bend, we came sharp upon a doe and her fawn as they stood in the shallow water, drinking. Both they and we were too surprised to move as the current carried us smoothly and silently toward them. It took us so close that I felt I could reach out and touch them, and hesitated, feeling the gesture would be presumptuous. Across the closing gap of water the doe and I looked straight into each other's eyes, her great eyes questioning, deep blue-black in the pupils, polite and interested. Then we were passing them. The mother caught our scent and soundlessly signaled to her fawn. They turned and moved without haste up the low bank and into the forest, the doe turning her head to watch us. I looked back too, saw their slim brown shanks disappear in the shadows and watched the place until the river carried us around another bend. Even though my father had forewarned me, I was unprepared for the towering excitement of

Courtesy, Mary Welsh Hemingway.

so close a meeting with a creature so beautiful, and then so quickly snatched away.

"Did you ever see anything so beautiful, Papa? And did you smell them? They smelled awfully strong to me. They smelled more like rabbits than like horses. And she didn't look frightened."

"You see now, Mary, why I do not hunt them."

I remembered my father's refusal to go deer hunting with friends. I also remembered slowly, the flavor coming strong and salty into my mouth, the taste of roasted venison, and it was like a mouthful of pebbles that had to be swallowed.

"What have we done? We've eaten them." There on the happy river I could not admit such treachery, and with female guile found a whipping boy for my conscience. "How could we? You brought the meat home. How could you?"

"Yes, I like it very much. When an Indian offers me some, I always take it."

"Gee, Papa, I am ashamed."

This was the kind of growing-up problem that my father so often helped me resolve. Now that he was a protagonist in the tangle, it seemed more grievous. From the blue canopy above us the sun was giving a joyous sheen to the traveling river and to every leaf and blade along its bank. It cheered me only a little.

A mile or two later my father said, "You must not feel too bad that you have eaten deer meat. You hadn't made their acquaintance, you know."

"But, Papa, you had."

"Yes."

"I don't know, Papa. I don't know at all." I was feeling lonely.

"You will later."

That night in a new balsam bed I kept my ears alert for the sound of a deer moving and stayed awake to look again and again to the rim of our firelight. I hoped to find a pair of bright eyes there and to apologize.

By the next afternoon our river was entering country that had been cut over by lumbermen, spoiled country compared to that we had left. We had more sky but the forests were thin and empty of their shadows and mystery. Our paddling muscles moved smoothly and comfortably, but it saddened me to be approaching civilization so soon again. "Let's turn around and go back. Let's just live on the river and in the forest," I said. There was still a sore place inside me from our perfidy to the deer, but I had a store of less painful ideas needing to be discussed. Some had come from *As You Like It.* "My age is as a lusty winter, frosty, but kindly," I had read, and "his big manly voice, turning again toward childish treble." I hadn't known any old man with a childish voice.

"You haven't changed at all since I first knew you, Papa," I said. "Have you changed?"

"You have."

"But I don't want to grow up."

"You only do it a little bit each day. The world is full of good things to learn."

"Did you want to grow up, when you were little, Papa?"

"Partly, so that I could work and buy presents for my mother."

Downriver there was a big gap in the right-bank trees, the first clearing we saw. Some outpost of civilization, and I still had the distressing problem of the deer needing to be resolved.

"I wish we could turn around and go back," I said. "Even against the current."

"Wait. We have the best part of the river ahead of us."

In the clearing the profile of a cabin roof was just visible above the grasses of the bank where we pulled ashore. This was the fellow, my father said, who could tell us what chances we had of running Dead Man Rapids which were just ahead of us. If the water was too low, we should have to portage a couple of miles around the rapids, a ponderous task. My father went to talk to the homesteader and the man returned to the riverbank with him and looked me over doubtfully.

"Water's not too low," he said, "but it's mighty fast. You got plenty boulders. A couple of fellows, river men, turned over, must be about three weeks ago."

"What do you say, Mary?" my father asked, flattering me.

I knew what he wished me to say and I said it. If grownup men stopped to consider the peril of the rapids, the possible broken bones, or cracked skulls, I thought, how satisfying it would be for us to get through.

"Keep to midstream," the homesteader advised as we shoved off.

As we turned into the current again we could feel its pace quickening. Ahead of the clearing the forest rose like the forest of our first two days but thicker and higher-walled on each bank. The water which had borne us amiably and silently for fifty miles or more now began hurrying forward, folding and sliding in deepening eddies, its voice rising to a murmur and then quickly to a rumble. My father stretched his back high in the stern of the canoe to pick a course among the rocks which we already saw were scattered recklessly everywhere between the banks, many of them looming above the surface. The more dangerous ones, I knew, were those only slightly submerged.

I was kneeling in the bow to give my paddle leverage and speed for fending us off rocks on either side, when we reached the first big boulders. Around their sides the river roared, creaming and frothing white and splashing onto us. Then we were sliding among them, dropping as fast, I thought, as a toboggan on an icy hill. We rushed close around the edge of one big stone and my straining eyes failed to see another one just below the surface and straight in our course. We brushed its top and it held us. I saw the heavy flow of water pushing almost to the top of our gunwales.

"Pull deep," my father shouted and we pulled hard to starboard and slipped off the rock. I did not take time to turn around to see if the rock had opened a hole in our canoe. If it had, I would know soon enough.

We had two miles more of foaming, runaway water to cover, with the river taking undisputed charge of our speed and my father seeking the deeper channels second by second before we were in them. Working against the nearest dangers I swung my paddle breathlessly, pushing us off rocks on one side then on the other of our fragile bow. In a short, straight, briefly uncluttered stretch, I looked up from the racing water and was frightened by the drop in our horizon.

From its stony banks to the long, dark line of treetops against the sky, our world slanted downward like an enormous ramp. My back was wet with splashings and once I noticed that my arms were growing tired and slow. But the river hurled us forward, bouncing us into the swiftest narrow channels between the boulders until ahead we saw, happily, a reach of smooth, dark, untroubled water. When we arrived there my father settled into his seat and lighted his pipe. "Take a rest," he said. "You did well."

From inside my tiredness I saw that the shadows of late afternoon were beginning to seep from the forest out over our river which was moving serenely and softly again, and we could hear birds and frogs starting their evening songs.

"You never paddled such a long and steep rapids before," my father said. "Didn't you like it?"

"It was wonderful. Isn't it wonderful to win?" The fast work had brought hunger rising in me, and with it, my problem. "And now, Papa, could you tell me, if you once decided not to hunt deer, why did you eat it?" I didn't realize I was being a nag.

"It was simple hunger, once or twice. But it's really not as easy as that. It's partly a thing called inertia. You must look that up in your dictionary. Partly something else. Call it expediency, or call it compromise. You are too young to understand these words or the ideas they stand for."

My father spoke about new concepts I would learn some day and how they would be easier for me to accept and practice after my conscience had grown older and weaker. (I understood something of my conscience. It was a part of me which was forever causing trouble, disappointing my mother who expected from it much more vigor and devotion to duty than she found.)

"I'm sorry, Papa. But I don't see yet what my conscience—or 'compromise'—has to do with eating those beautiful deer. It would be like eating one of my kittens. If it's wrong now, won't it be just as wrong when I'm older and have learned all those new ideas?"

"Perhaps. But then you may not *think* it's so wrong." There was Shakespeare again. "There is nothing either good or bad, but thinking makes it so."

"You mean that people don't grow better as they grow up, that they are just as naughty just as often?" This was dangerous territory. In northern Minnesota good children did not question aloud the precepts of their elders.

"I'll tell you a secret," my father said. "In many ways you don't grow better as you grow up. Or know better. But you keep that to yourself."

It was a lightning flash of revelation. How could an adult, even my father, smash the old rule so easily? The superiority of grownups had been an absolute, undisputed boundary of my thinking. If adults could be doubted with impunity, who were the new authorities?

Now the forest was a dark gray wall on both sides of us, with the strip of sky above and the moving silver of the river giving us the only light. I wished again we could stay there on the shining river, our world simple and sufficient unto itself and us. But I noticed that my ache about the deer had receded a little. It seemed a lifetime since we had started paddling through the wild rice.

When I was almost asleep that night a new question drifted into my head. Had my father belittled grownups, I wondered, in order to help me become one?

---

1. In her encounter with the doe and her fawn, the young narrator is left with the feeling of **(a)** dislike of their odor; **(b)** concern about their food supply; **(c)** fear for their safety; **(d)** awe and appreciation of their beauty.

2. This encounter with the doe heightens the narrator's later feelings of **(a)** guilt about having eaten venison; **(b)** childishness; **(c)** fear about the turbulent waters; **(d)** reluctance to leave the river.

3. Mary says, "I hoped to find a pair of bright eyes there and to apologize" (page 462, column b, paragraph 7). These words indicate she wished to **(a)** tell her father she regrets having angered him; **(b)** calm the muskrats for having disturbed them; **(c)** make up to nature for her invasion; **(d)** make known to the doe her mental suffering and guilt.

4. Mary, recalling the taste of venison, says it was "like a mouthful of pebbles that had to be swallowed." This figure of speech is a **(a)** metaphor; **(b)** personification; **(c)** simile; **(d)** none of the above.

5. The quotations from *As You Like It* are relevant to the narrative, especially to the discussion directly following their appearance because they deal with **(a)** death; **(b)** aging; **(c)** winter; **(d)** children.

6. Mary handles the rapids with **(a)** courage and competence; **(b)** fear and reluctance; **(c)** inexperience and inadequacy; **(d)** reckless abandon.

7. When Mary and her father approach civilization, she expresses a desire to turn around, to live on the river and in the forest. This indicates her wish to **(a)** find the doe again; **(b)** remain in a secure setting and resolve her questions; **(c)** shoot the rapids once again; **(d)** rest her weary muscles.

8. Shakespeare's words, "There is nothing either good or bad, but thinking makes it so," mean **(a)** too much thinking is dangerous; **(b)** it is necessary to use your head; **(c)** notions of right and wrong depend upon individual interpretations; **(d)** good and bad are as different as day and night.

9. Judging from this account, who would you say makes the sharpest distinction between right and wrong? **(a)** Shakespeare; **(b)** the young narrator; **(c)** her father; **(d)** the old homesteader.

10. Hemingway's account is **(a)** objective; **(b)** subjective; **(c)** neither; **(d)** both.

Composition Review

Choose one of the following assignments and write a composition.

1. The young narrator in the excerpt from *How It Was* wants to believe that the conscience of an adult is as strong as that of a child.

Assume you have a twelve-year-old brother or sister who agrees with Hemingway that adults *can* maintain a clear distinction between right and wrong. Select one adult from a selection in this unit and explain how that character serves to prove or disprove this observation about conscience. Direct your composition to your assumed (or perhaps real) younger sister or brother.

2. In one sense, Hemingway's account might be viewed as a child's initiation into the adult world.

In an essay directed to your classmates, explain how each of the following works provides a lesson to a person in the process of growing up: "Aunt Arie," the excerpt from *Growing Up.*

Unit 8 The Novel

A Tale of Two Cities

Charles Dickens

Introduction

"It was the best of times, it was the worst of times, it was the age of wisdom, it was the age of foolishness . . ."

With these statements, Charles Dickens (1812–1870) begins *A Tale of Two Cities,* his novel set in both England and France during the beginnings of the French Revolution. The statements describe a subject that Dickens was particularly well qualified to write about.

Dickens was born into a middle-class family, but his father lived so far beyond his income that he was finally imprisoned for debt. At the age of twelve, Charles was forced to quit school and take a job in a shoe-polish factory to help support the family. Dickens's five months in the factory made an impression on him that lasted through his adult life. In many of his books, his sympathies clearly lie with the underdogs of society—the working poor. He had experienced at first hand their long hours of hard labor; he had known hunger, poverty, and the humiliation of his father's imprisonment. When he set out to tell the story of the oppressed poor of France, he was able to draw on his own experience as he portrayed their lives, their longings, and their many legitimate grievances.

After his father's release from prison, Dickens received three more years of schooling. At the age of sixteen, he became a clerk in a law firm. Here he had ample opportunity to observe English lawyers and English courts, a knowledge that he used not only in *A Tale of Two Cities* but in many of his other novels. He increased his knowledge of the law when he worked as a reporter assigned to cover the Parliament.

Setting

London and Paris, the two cities of the title, are less than three hundred miles apart; but in the late eighteenth century, they were separated by more than the English Channel. Although both countries had a king, an aristocracy, a middle class and a large number of poor, England was ruled by a combination of aristocrats and commoners. In France, however, only the aristocrats ruled, and their rule was not a benevolent one. To support the lavish style of the lives led by the aristocrats, the people paid high taxes. (Ironically, some of these taxes helped the American colonists launch their own revolution against the English in 1776.) Further, the French poor were deprived of even the most basic rights. Unlike the English, they were not allowed to hold public meetings; they could not criticize the government; they had little access to their country's system of justice. In fact, a nobleman with a personal grudge could secure a *lettre de cachet,* or warrant of imprisonment, fill in the name of the person he wanted to get rid of, and have that person thrown into prison without benefit of a hearing or a trial, for an unspecified amount of time. Dickens does not hesitate to note the inequities of the British legal system, but he also makes clear that before their revolution the French citizens suffered far greater injustice.

In Paris, the symbol of injustice and oppression was the Bastille, a fourteenth-century fortress that became a prison for political offenders. On July 14, 1789, a mob of Parisians, led by a wine merchant named Cholat, stormed the Bastille and freed the seven political prisoners held there. It was an event that began a revolution. By 1793, the French king and queen, Louis XVI and Marie Antoinette, many members of the aristocracy and of the upper-middle classes, and lower-class citizens who had angered those newly come to power had been killed by the "National Razor," the guillotine.

Characters

A Tale of Two Cities is an historical novel, one that reconstructs the spirit of a time in the past. Dickens wrote it in 1859, about seventy years after the French Revolution had actually occurred. To make his novel as accurate as possible, Dickens read many accounts of the time in which the action takes place. He then peopled his novel with a variety of characters, some of whom were real historical personages. For example, in Chapter XIX, Book the Second, he refers to Foulon, a wealthy man who made a great deal of money selling supplies to the army and navy. In Chapter V, Book the Third, a woodcutter calls himself "the Samson of the firewood guillotine," a reference to a man named Samson who was the revolutionists' chief executioner. Many of the major characters, however, are fictitious.

Dickens includes representatives of each social class in his novel. The main characters include **Dr. Manette,** a middle-class Frenchman who has been unjustly imprisoned in the Bastille for eighteen years, and his daughter, **Lucie,** who has lived in England since she was taken there at the age of three; **Charles Darnay,** a Frenchman who has rejected his aristocratic past, as well as his real name, and has become an *emigré,* or immigrant, living and working in England; the **Defarges,** the owner of a wine shop and his sinister wife, who live in the poorest section of Paris; **Mr. Jarvis Lorry,** a bachelor employee of an English bank, and **Sydney Carton,** a young Englishman who has never lived up to his potential. As you read about each of these and about the other characters, ask yourself where Dickens's sympathies lie: with the Manettes, with the French aristocrats, or with the poor of France.

Theme

A Tale of Two Cities contains two major themes. One is love and resurrection; the second is injustice and revolution. The book contains many examples of love: love between a parent and child, between a faithful servant and that servant's employer, between a man and a woman. Note as you read how often the power of love results in rebirth, or the saving of a life. Against these examples of love and selflessness, Dickens opposes the awesome power of hate and selfishness. Often this hate grows out of injustice and moves people to personal and civil revolt.

The Novel

Because the book was written in serial form and released to the public one chapter at a time, Dickens often includes puzzling details and mysteries. These details, which are important in the later unfolding of the plot, were meant to hold the reader's interest until the next chapter was published. Remember the character who, in one chapter, isn't even named; keep in mind the reference to an "honest trade," a trade that is identified many chapters later; try to figure out relationships that are only hinted at. And when you finish the book, ask yourself if it ends on a note of optimism or pessimism. You may be surprised by your conclusion.

A Tale of Two Cities

Charles Dickens

In Three Books

Book the First: Recalled to Life

CHAPTER I
THE PERIOD

It was the best of times, it was the worst of times, it was the age of wisdom, it was the age of foolishness, it was the epoch of belief, it was the epoch of incredulity, it was the season of light, it was the season of darkness, it was the spring of hope, it was the winter of despair. We had everything before us, we had nothing before us, we were all going direct to heaven, we were all going direct the other way. In short, the period was so far like the present period that some of its noisiest authorities insisted on its being received, for good or for evil, in the superlative degree of comparison only.

There were a king with a large jaw and a queen with a plain face on the throne of England;[1] there were a king with a large jaw and a queen with a fair face on the throne of France.[2] In both countries it was clearer than crystal to the lords of the state preserves of loaves and fishes[3] that things in general were settled forever.

It was the year of our Lord one thousand seven hundred and seventy-five.

France rolled with exceeding smoothness downhill, making paper money and spending it. There were trees, already marked by the Woodman, Fate, to be sawed into boards, to make a certain movable framework with a sack and a knife in it, terrible in history. In the rough outhouses of the lands adjacent to Paris, there were rude carts, which the Farmer, Death, had already set apart to be his tumbrils[4] of the Revolution. But that Woodman and that Farmer, though they work unceasingly, work silently, and no one heard them as they went about with muffled tread.

In England there was scarcely an amount of order and protection to justify much national boasting. Daring burglaries by armed men and highway robberies took place in the capital itself every night; families were publicly cautioned not to go out of town without removing their furniture to upholsterers' warehouses for security; the mail was waylaid by seven robbers, and the guard shot three dead, and then got shot dead himself by the other four, "in consequence of the failure of his ammunition"; after which the mail was robbed in peace. That magnificent

1. ***king with a large jaw . . . England,*** George III and Queen Charlotte Sophia.
2. ***king with a large jaw . . . France,*** Louis XVI and Marie Antoinette (an′twə net′).
3. ***lords of . . . fishes,*** the nobility. The allusion to loaves and fishes recalls the New Testament account of Christ's feeding the multitudes.
4. ***tumbril,*** (tum′brəl), a farmers' cart used for carrying condemned persons to the guillotine (gil′ə tēn).

Charles Dickens, *A Tale of Two Cities*, 1859. (Abridged.)

potentate, the Lord Mayor of London, was made to stand and deliver on Turnham Green by one highwayman who despoiled the illustrious creature in sight of all his retinue; thieves snipped off diamond crosses from the necks of noble lords at Court drawing-rooms; musketeers went into St. Giles'[5] to search for contraband goods, and the mob fired on the musketeers, and the musketeers fired on the mob, and nobody thought any of these occurrences much out of the common way. In the midst of them, the hangman was in constant requisition; now stringing up long rows of miscellaneous criminals; now hanging a housebreaker on Saturday who had been taken on Tuesday; today taking the life of an atrocious murderer, and tomorrow of a wretched pilferer who had robbed a farmer's boy of sixpence.

All these things, and a thousand like them, came to pass in and close upon the dear old year one thousand seven hundred and seventy-five. Environed by them, while the Woodman and the Farmer worked unheeded, those two of the large jaws, and those other two of the plain and the fair faces, trod with stir enough, and carried their divine rights[6] with a high hand. Thus did the year one thousand seven hundred and seventy-five conduct their Greatnesses and myriads of small creatures—the creatures of this chronicle among the rest—along the roads that lay before them.

CHAPTER II
THE MAIL

It was the Dover road[1] that lay, on a Friday night late in November, before the first of the persons with whom this history has business. The Dover road lay, as to him, beyond the Dover mail as it lumbered up Shooter's Hill. He walked uphill in the mire by the side of the mail as the rest of the passengers did; not because they had the least relish for walking exercise, under the circumstances, but because the hill and the harness and the mud and the mail were all so heavy that the horses had three times already come to a stop. Reins and whip and coachman and guard, however, forbade the argument that some brute animals are endued with Reason; and the team had capitulated and returned to their duty.

With drooping heads and tremulous tails they mashed their way through the thick mud, floundering and stumbling between whiles, as if they were falling to pieces at the larger joints. As often as the driver rested them and brought them to a stand with a wary "Wo-ho! so-ho then!" the near leader violently shook his head and everything upon it—like an unusually emphatic horse, denying that the coach could be got up the hill. Whenever the leader made this rattle the passenger started, as a nervous passenger might, and was disturbed in mind.

There was a steaming mist in all the hollows, and it had roamed in its forlornness up the hill, like an evil spirit, seeking rest and finding none. A clammy and intensely cold mist, it made its slow way through the air in ripples that visibly followed and overspread one another, as the waves of an unwholesome sea might do. It was dense enough to shut out everything from the light of the coach lamps but these its own workings and a few yards of road; and the reek of the laboring horses steamed into it, as if they had made it all.

Two other passengers were plodding up the hill by the side of the mail. All three were wrapped to the cheekbones and over the ears, and wore jackboots.[2] Not one of the three could have said, from anything he saw, what either of the other two was like; and each was hidden under almost as many wrappers from the eyes of the mind as from the eyes of the body of his two companions. In those days travelers were very

5. ***St. Giles'***, church in the central part of London.
6. ***divine rights***, the prevailing eighteenth-century idea that a king received his royal authority from God and, therefore, was responsible only to God for his actions.

1. ***Dover Road***, highway between London and the port city of Dover, a popular departure point for France.
2. ***jackboots***, large strong boots reaching above the knees, formerly worn by cavalrymen.

shy of being confidential on a short notice, for anybody on the road might be a robber or in league with robbers. As to the latter, when every posting house and alehouse could produce somebody in "the Captain's"[3] pay, ranging from the landlord to the lowest stable nondescript, it was the likeliest thing upon the cards. So the guard of the Dover mail thought to himself, that Friday night in November one thousand seven hundred and seventy-five, lumbering up Shooter's Hill, as he stood on his own particular perch behind the mail, beating his feet, and keeping an eye and hand on the arm-chest before him, where a loaded blunderbuss lay at the top of six or eight loaded horse pistols, deposited on a substratum of cutlass.

The Dover mail was in its usual genial position that the guard suspected the passengers, the passengers suspected one another and the guard, they all suspected everybody else, and the coachman was sure of nothing but the horses, as to which cattle he could with a clear conscience have taken his oath on the two Testaments that they were not fit for the journey.

The last burst carried the mail to the summit of the hill. The horses stopped to breathe again, and the guard got down to open the coach door to let the passengers in.

"Tst! Joe!" cried the coachman in a warning voice. "I say a horse at a canter coming up, Joe."

"*I* say a horse at a gallop, Tom," returned the guard, leaving his hold of the door, and mounting nimbly to his place. "Gentlemen! In the King's name, all of you!"

With this hurried adjuration, he cocked his blunderbuss, and stood on the offensive.

The sound of a horse at a gallop came fast and furiously up the hill.

"So-ho!" the guard sang out, as loud as he could roar. "Yo there! Stand! I shall fire!"

The pace was suddenly checked, and, with much splashing and floundering, a man's voice called from the mist, "Is that the Dover mail?"

"Never you mind what it is!" the guard retorted. "What are you?"

"*Is* that the Dover mail?"

"Why do you want to know?"

"I want a passenger, if it is."

"What passenger?"

"Mr. Jarvis Lorry."

The passenger showed in a moment that it was his name. The guard, the coachman, and the two other passengers eyed him distrustfully.

"Keep where you are," the guard called to the voice in the mist, "because, if I should make a mistake, it could never be set right in your lifetime. Gentleman of the name of Lorry answer straight."

"What is the matter?" asked the passenger, then, with mildly quavering speech. "Who wants me? Is it Jerry?"

("I don't like Jerry's voice, if it is Jerry," growled the guard to himself. "He's hoarser than suits me, is Jerry.")

"Yes, Mr. Lorry."

"What is the matter?"

"A dispatch sent after you from over yonder. T. and Co."

The figures of a horse and rider came slowly through the eddying mist to the side of the mail, where the passenger stood. The rider stooped and handed the passenger a small, folded paper. The rider's horse was blown, and both horse and rider were covered with mud, from the hoofs of the horse to the hat of the man.

"Guard!" said the passenger, in a tone of quiet business confidence.

The watchful guard, with his right hand at the stock of his raised blunderbuss, his left at the barrel, and his eye on the horseman, answered curtly, "Sir."

"There is nothing to apprehend. I belong to Tellson's Bank. You must know Tellson's Bank in London. I am going to Paris on business. I may read this?"

"If so be as you're quick, sir."

He opened it in the light of the coach lamp on that side, and read—first to himself and then aloud: " 'Wait at Dover for Mam'selle.' It's not

3. ***"the Captain's,"*** the head robber's.

long, you see, guard. Jerry, say that my answer was, RECALLED TO LIFE."

Jerry started in his saddle. "That's a blazing strange answer, too," said he, at his hoarsest.

"Take that message back, and they will know that I received this, as well as if I wrote. Make the best of your way. Good night."

With those words the passenger opened the coach door and got in; not at all assisted by his fellow passengers, who had expeditiously secreted their watches and purses in their boots, and were now making a general pretense of being asleep. The coach lumbered on again, with heavier wreaths of mist closing round it as it began the descent.

Jerry, left alone in the mist and darkness, dismounted meanwhile, not only to ease his spent horse, but to wipe the mud from his face, and shake the wet out of his hat brim, which might be capable of holding about half a gallon.

"After that there gallop, old lady, I won't trust your forelegs till I get you on the level," said this hoarse messenger, glancing at his mare. " 'Recalled to life.' That's a blazing strange message. Much of that wouldn't do for you, Jerry! I say, Jerry! You'd be in a blazing bad way, if recalling to life was to come into fashion, Jerry!"

CHAPTER III
THE NIGHT SHADOWS

A wonderful fact to reflect upon, that every human creature is constituted to be that profound secret and mystery to every other. A solemn consideration, when I enter a great city by night, that every one of those darkly clustered houses encloses its own secret; that every room in every one of them encloses its own secret; that every beating heart, in the hundreds of thousands of breasts there, is, in some of its imaginings, a secret to the heart nearest it! Something of the awfulness even of Death itself is referable to this. My friend is dead, my neighbor is dead, my love, the darling of my soul, is dead; it is the inexorable consolidation and perpetuation of the secret that was always in that individuality, and which I shall carry in mine to my life's end. In any of the burial places of this city through which I pass, is there a sleeper more inscrutable than its busy inhabitants are, in their innermost personality, to me, or than I am to them?

As to this, his natural and not to be alienated inheritance, the messenger on horseback had exactly the same possessions as the King, the first Minister of State, or the richest merchant in London. So with the three passengers shut up in the narrow compass of one lumbering old mail coach; they were mysteries to one another, as complete as if each had been in his own coach and six, or his own coach and sixty, with the breadth of a county between him and the next.

The messenger rode back at an easy trot, stopping pretty often at alehouses by the way to drink, but evincing a tendency to keep his own counsel and to keep his hat cocked over his eyes. He had eyes that assorted very well with that decoration, being of a surface black, with no depth in the color or form, and much too near together—as if they were afraid of being found out in something, singly, if they kept too far apart. They had a sinister expression, under an old cocked hat and over a great muffler for the chin and throat, which descended nearly to the wearer's knees. When he stopped for drink, he moved this muffler with his left hand, only while he poured his liquor in with his right; as soon as that was done, he muffled again.

"No, Jerry, no!" said the messenger, harping on one theme as he rode. "It wouldn't do for you, Jerry. Jerry, you honest tradesman, it wouldn't suit *your* line of business! Recalled—! Bust me if I don't think he'd been a-drinking!"

His message perplexed his mind to that degree that he was fain several times to take off his hat to scratch his head. Except on the crown, which was raggedly bald, he had stiff black hair, standing jaggedly all over it and growing downhill almost to his broad, blunt nose. It was so much more like the top of a strongly spiked wall than a head of hair, that the best of players at leapfrog might have declined him, as the most dangerous man in the world to go over.

While he trotted back with the message he was to deliver to the night watchman in his box at the door of Tellson's Bank by Temple Bar,[1] who was to deliver it to greater authorities within, the shadows of the night took such shapes to him as arose out of the message, and took such shapes to the mare as arose out of *her* private topics of uneasiness. They seemed to be numerous, for she shied at every shadow on the road.

The mail coach lumbered, jolted, rattled, and bumped upon its tedious way, with its three fellow-inscrutables inside. To whom, likewise, the shadows of the night revealed themselves, in the forms their dozing eyes and wandering thoughts suggested.

Tellson's Bank had a run upon it in the mail. As the bank passenger nodded in his place with half-shut eyes, the little coach windows and the bulky bundle of opposite passenger, became the bank and did a great stroke of business. The rattle of the harness was the chink of money, and more drafts were honored in five minutes than even Tellson's, with all its foreign and home connection, ever paid in thrice the time. Then the strong rooms underground at Tellson's, with such of their valuable stores and secrets as were known to the passenger—and it was not a little that he knew about them—opened before him, and he went in among them with the great keys and the feebly burning candle, and found them safe and strong and sound and still, just as he had last seen them.

But, though the bank was almost always with him, and though the coach—in a confused way, like the presence of pain under an opiate—was always with him, there was another current of impression that never ceased to run, all through the night. He was on his way to dig someone out of a grave.

Now, which of the multitude of faces that showed themselves before him was the true face of the buried person the shadows of the night did not indicate; but they were all the faces of a man of five-and-forty by years, and they differed principally in the passions they expressed, and in the ghastliness of their worn and wasted state. Pride, contempt, defiance, stubbornness, submission, lamentation, succeeded one another; so did varieties of sunken cheek, cadaverous color, emaciated hands, and figures. But the face was in the main one face, and every head was prematurely white. A hundred times the dozing passenger inquired of this spector:

"Buried how long?"

The answer was always the same: "Almost eighteen years."

"You had abandoned all hope of being dug out?"

"Long ago."

"You know that you are recalled to life?"

"They tell me so."

"I hope you care to live?"

"I can't say."

"Shall I show her to you? Will you come and see her?"

The answers to this question were various and contradictory. Sometimes the broken reply was "Wait! It would kill me if I saw her too soon." Sometimes it was given in a tender rain of tears, and then it was "Take me to her." Sometimes it was staring and bewildered, and then it was, "I don't know her. I don't understand."

After such imaginary discourse, the passenger in his fancy would dig and dig, dig—now with a spade, now with a great key, now with his hands—to dig this wretched creature out. Got out at last, with earth hanging about his face and hair, he would suddenly fall away to dust. The passenger would then start to himself, and lower the window, to get the reality of mist and rain on his cheek.

Yet even when his eyes were opened on the

1. ***Temple Bar,*** the gate built by Christopher Wren (c. 1672) on the site of one of the entrances to the city of London; it was a gathering place for lawyers.

mist and rain, on the moving patch of light from the lamps, and the hedge at the roadside retreating by jerks, the night shadows outside the coach would fall into the train of the night shadows within. The real banking house by Temple Bar, the real business of the past day, the real strong rooms, the real express sent after him, and the real message returned, would all be there. Out of the midst of them the ghostly face would rise, and he would accost it again.

"Buried how long?"

"Almost eighteen years."

"I hope you care to live?"

"I can't say."

Dig—dig—dig—until an impatient movement from one of the two passengers would admonish him to pull up the window, draw his arm securely through the leather strap, and speculate upon the two slumbering forms, until his mind lost its hold of them, and they again slid away into the bank and the grave.

"Buried how long?"

"Almost eighteen years."

"You had abandoned all hope of being dug out?"

"Long ago."

The words were still in his hearing as just spoken—distinctly in his hearing as ever spoken words had been in his life—when the weary passenger started to the consciousness of daylight and found that the shadows of the night were gone.

He lowered the window and looked out at the rising sun. There was a ridge of plowed land, with a plow upon it where it had been left last night when the horses were unyoked; beyond, a quiet coppice wood, in which many leaves of burning red and golden yellow still remained upon the trees. Though the earth was cold and wet, the sky was clear, and the sun rose bright, placid, and beautiful.

"Eighteen years!" said the passenger, looking at the sun. "Gracious Creator of day! To be buried alive for eighteen years!"

Discussion

Chapter I

1. What examples does Dickens give to show that in 1775 conditions were bad in France? in England?

2. Who are the Woodman and the Farmer?

3. What is "a certain movable framework"?

4. What do you learn about the setting, the characters, and some of the themes to be developed in the novel? (Note especially the last paragraph.)

Chapter II

1. (a) What is the setting of this chapter? **(b)** What characters are introduced? **(c)** Why are the characters so suspicious of each other?

2. (a) Describe the mood of this scene. **(b)** In what way does the mist contribute to this mood?

3. (a) What do you think is the most important phrase in this chapter? **(b)** What makes you think it is important? **(c)** Do you have any idea at this point what it could possibly mean? **(d)** What is Jerry's reaction to the phrase?

Chapter III

1. In the first paragraph, what point about human beings does the narrator make?

2. What does the second paragraph suggest about the narrator's regard for social-class distinctions?

3. What does Mr. Lorry's dream suggest about his purpose for making the trip?

CHAPTER IV
THE PREPARATION

When the mail got successfully to Dover, in the course of the forenoon, the head drawer[1] at the Royal George Hotel opened the coach door as his custom was. He did it with some flourish of ceremony, for a mail journey from London in winter was an achievement to congratulate an adventurous traveler upon.

By that time there was only one adventurous traveler left to be congratulated, for the two others had been set down at their respective roadside destinations. The mildewy inside of the coach was rather like a larger dog kennel. Mr. Lorry, the passenger, shaking himself out of it, in a tangle of shaggy wrapper, flapping hat, and muddy legs, was rather like a larger sort of dog.

"There will be a packet to Calais[2] tomorrow, drawer?"

"Yes, sir, if the weather holds and the wind sets tolerable fair. The tide will serve pretty nicely at about two in the afternoon, sir. Bed, sir?"

"I shall not go to bed till night; but I want a bedroom and a barber."

"And then breakfast, sir? Yes, sir."

The coffee room had no other occupant, that forenoon, than the gentleman in brown. His breakfast table was drawn before the fire, and as he sat, with its light shining on him waiting for the meal, he sat so still that he might have been sitting for his portrait.

Very orderly and methodical he looked, with a hand on each knee, and a loud watch ticking a sonorous sermon under his flapped waistcoat. He had a good leg, and was a little vain of it, for his brown stockings fitted sleek and close; his shoes and buckles, too, though plain, were trim. He wore an odd little sleek crisp flaxen wig setting very close to his head; which wig, it is to be presumed, was made of hair, but which looked far more as though it was spun from filaments of silk or glass. His linen was as white as the tops of the waves that broke upon the neighboring beach or the specks of sail that glinted in the sunlight far at sea. A face habitually suppressed and quieted was still lighted up under the quaint wig by a pair of moist bright eyes that it must have cost their owner, in years gone by, some pains to drill to the composed and reserved expression of Tellson's Bank. He had a healthy color in his cheeks, and his face, though lined, bore few traces of anxiety. But perhaps the confidential bachelor clerks in Tellson's Bank were principally occupied with the cares of other people; and perhaps second-hand cares, like second-hand clothes, come easily off and on.

Completing his resemblance to a man who was sitting for his portrait, Mr. Lorry dropped off to sleep. The arrival of his breakfast roused him, and he said to the drawer, as he moved his chair to it:

"I wish accommodation prepared for a young lady who may come here at any time today. She may ask for Mr. Jarvis Lorry, or she may only ask for a gentleman from Tellson's Bank. Please to let me know."

"Yes, sir. Tellson's Bank in London, sir?"

"Yes."

"Yes, sir. We have oftentimes the honor to entertain your gentlemen in their traveling backwards and forwards betwixt London and Paris, sir. A vast deal of traveling, sir, in Tellson and Company's House."[3]

"Yes. We are quite a French House, as well as an English one."

"Yes, sir. Not much in the habit of such traveling yourself, I think, sir?"

"Not of late years. It is fifteen years since we—since I—came last from France."

"Indeed, sir? That was before my time here, sir. Before our people's time here, sir. The George was in other hands at that time, sir."

"I believe so."

---

1. ***head drawer,*** chief doorman.
2. ***packet to Calais*** (ka lā′), a boat traveling regularly to Calais, a port city on the extreme northern coast of France. A packet carries passengers, mail, and goods.
3. ***Tellson and Company's House,*** bank or banking house with its headquarters in London but also operating a flourishing branch in Paris.

"But I would hold a pretty wager, sir, that a House like Tellson and Company was flourishing, a matter of fifty, not to speak of fifteen, years ago?"

"You might treble that, and say a hundred and fifty, yet not be far from the truth."

"Indeed, sir!"

When Mr. Lorry had finished his breakfast, he went out for a stroll on the beach. The little narrow, crooked town of Dover hid itself away from the beach and ran its head into the chalk cliffs, like a marine ostrich. The beach was a desert of heaps of sea and stones tumbling wildly about, and the sea did what it liked, and what it liked was destruction. It thundered at the town, and thundered at the cliffs, and brought the coast down, madly.

As the day declined into the afternoon, and the air, which had been at intervals clear enough to allow the French coast to be seen, became again charged with mist and vapor, Mr. Lorry sat before the coffee-room fire, awaiting his dinner as he had awaited his breakfast. He had just poured out his last glassful of wine when a rattling of wheels came up the narrow street and rumbled into the inn yard.

He set down his glass untouched. "This is Mam'selle!" said he.

In a very few minutes the waiter came in to announce that Miss Manette had arrived from London, and would be happy to see the gentleman from Tellson's.

"So soon?"

Miss Manette had taken some refreshment on the road, and was extremely anxious to see the gentleman from Tellson's immediately, if it suited his convenience.

The gentleman from Tellson's had nothing left for it but to empty his glass with an air of stolid desperation, settle his odd little flaxen wig at the ears, and follow the waiter to Miss Manette's apartment. Mr. Lorry saw, standing to receive him by the table between them and the fire, a young lady of not more than seventeen, in a riding cloak, and still holding her straw traveling hat by its ribbon in her hand. As his eyes rested on a short, slight, pretty figure, a quantity of golden hair, a pair of blue eyes that met his own with an inquiring look, and a forehead with a singular capacity of lifting and knitting itself into an expression that was not quite one of perplexity, or wonder, or alarm, or merely of a bright, fixed attention, though it included all the four expressions—as his eyes rested on these things, a sudden vivid likeness passed before him, of a child whom he had held in his arms on the passage across that very Channel, one cold time, when the hail drifted heavily and the sea ran high. The likeness passed away, like a breath along the surface of the gaunt pier glass behind her, and he made his formal bow to Miss Manette.

"Pray take a seat, sir." In a very clear and pleasant young voice; a little foreign in its accent, but a very little indeed.

"I kiss your hand, miss," said Mr. Lorry, with the manners of an earlier date, as he made his formal bow again, and took his seat.

"I received a letter from the Bank, sir, yesterday, informing me that some intelligence—or discovery——"

"The word is not material, miss; either word will do."

"—respecting the small property of my poor father, whom I never saw—so long dead——"

Mr. Lorry moved in his chair.

"—rendered it necessary that I should go to Paris, there to communicate with a gentleman of the Bank, so good as to be dispatched to Paris for the purpose."

"Myself."

"As I was prepared to hear, sir."

She curtsied to him. He made her another bow.

"I replied to the Bank, sir, that as it was considered necessary, by those who know, and who are so kind as to advise me, that I should go to France, and that as I am an orphan and have no friend who could go with me, I should esteem it highly if I might be permitted to place myself, during the journey, under that worthy gentleman's protection. The gentleman had left London, but I think a messenger was sent after him to beg the favor of his waiting for me here."

"I was happy," said Mr. Lorry, " to be entrusted with the charge. I shall be more happy to execute it."

"Sir, I thank you indeed. I thank you very gratefully. It was told me by the Bank that the gentleman would explain to me the details of the business, and that I must prepare myself to find them of a surprising nature. I have done my best to prepare myself, and I naturally have a strong and eager interest to know what they are."

"Naturally," said Mr. Lorry. "Yes—I——"

After a pause, he added, again settling the crisp flaxen wig at the ears:

"It is very difficult to begin."

He did not begin, but, in his indecision, met her glance. The young forehead lifted itself into that singular expression—but it was pretty and characteristic, besides being singular—and she raised her hand, as if with an involuntary action she caught at, or stayed, some passing shadow.

"Are you quite a stranger to me, sir?"

"Am I not?" Mr. Lorry opened his hands, and extended them outwards with an argumentative smile. He went on. "In your adopted country, I presume, I cannot do better than address you as a young English lady, Miss Manette?"

"If you please, sir."

"Miss Manette, I am a man of business. I have a business charge to acquit myself of. In your reception of it don't heed me any more than if I was a speaking machine—truly, I am not much else. I will, with your leave, relate to you, miss, the story of one of our customers."

"Story!"

He seemed willfully to mistake the word she had repeated when he added, in a hurry, "Yes, customers; in the banking business we usually call our connection our customers. He was a French gentleman; a scientific gentleman; a man of great acquirements—a doctor."

"Not of Beauvais?"[4]

"Why, yes, of Beauvais. Like Monsieur Manette, your father, the gentleman was of Beauvais. Like Monsieur Manette, your father, the gentleman was of repute in Paris. I had the honor of knowing him there. Our relations were business relations, but confidential. I was at that time in our French House, and had been—oh! twenty years."

"At that time—I may ask, at what time, sir?"

"I speak, miss, of twenty years ago. He married—an English lady—and I was one of the trustees. His affairs, like the affairs of many other French gentlemen and French families, were entirely in Tellson's hands. In a similar way I am, or I have been, trustee of one kind or other for scores of our customers. These are mere business relations, miss; there is no friendship in them, no particular interest, nothing like sentiment. To go on—"

"But this is my father's story, sir; and I begin to think"—the curiously roughened forehead was very intent upon him—"that when I was left an orphan through my mother's surviving my father only two years, it was you who brought me to England. I am almost sure it was you."

Mr. Lorry took the hesitating little hand that confidingly advanced to take his, and he put it with some ceremony to his lips. He then conducted the young lady straightway to her chair again, and, holding the chair back with his left hand, and using his right by turns to rub his chin, pull his wig at the ears, or point what he said, stood looking down into her face while she sat looking up into his.

"Miss Manette, it *was* I. And you will see how truly I spoke of myself just now, in saying I had no feelings, and that all the relations I hold with my fellow creatures are mere business relations, when you reflect that I have never seen you since. No; you have been the ward of Tellson's House since, and I have been busy with the other business of Tellson's House since. Feelings! I have no time for them, no chance of them.

---

4. ***Beauvais*** (bō vā′), a city in northern France.

"So far, miss—as you have remarked—this is the story of your regretted father. Now comes the difference. If your father had not died when he did— Don't be frightened! How you start!"

She did, indeed, start. And she caught his wrist with both her hands.

"Pray," said Mr. Lorry, in a soothing tone, bringing his left hand from the back of the chair to lay it on the supplicatory fingers that clasped him in so violent a tremble, "pray control your agitation—a matter of business. As I was saying——"

Her look so discomposed him that he stopped, wandered, and began anew.

"As I was saying: if Monsieur Manette had not died; if he had suddenly and silently disappeared; if he had been spirited away; if it had not been difficult to guess to what dreadful place, though no art could trace him; if he had an enemy in some compatriot who could exercise a privilege that I in my own time have known the boldest people afraid to speak of in a whisper, across the water there; for instance, the privilege of filling up blank forms for the consignment of anyone to the oblivion of a prison for any length of time; if his wife had implored the King, the Queen, the court, the clergy, for any tidings of him, and all quite in vain—then the history of your father would have been the history of this unfortunate gentleman, the Doctor of Beauvais."

"I entreat you to tell me more, sir."

"I will. I am going to. You can bear it?"

"I can bear anything but the uncertainty you leave me in at this moment."

"You speak collectedly, and you—*are* collected. That's good!" (Though his manner was less satisfied than his words.) "A matter of business. Regard it as a matter of business—business that must be done. Now if this doctor's wife, though a lady of great courage and spirit, had suffered so intensely from this cause before her little child was born——"

"The little child was a daughter, sir?"

"A daughter. A—a—matter of business—don't be distressed. Miss, if the poor lady had suffered so intensely before her little child was born that she came to the determination of sparing the poor child the inheritance of any part of the agony she had known the pains of, by rearing her in the belief that her father was dead— No, don't kneel! In Heaven's name, why should you kneel to me!"

"For the truth. O dear, good, compassionate sir, for the truth!"

"A—a matter of business. You confuse me, and how can I transact business if I am confused? Let us be clear-headed. If you could kindly mention now, for instance, what nine times ninepence are, or how many shillings in twenty guineas,[5] it would be so encouraging. I should be so much more at my ease about your state of mind."

Without directly answering to this appeal, she sat so still when he had gently raised her, and the hands that had not ceased to clasp his wrists were so much more steady than they had been, that she communicated some reassurance to Mr. Jarvis Lorry.

"That's right, that's right. Courage! Business! You have business before you; useful business. Miss Manette, your mother took this course with you. And when she died—I believe brokenhearted—having never slackened her unavailing search for your father, she left you, at two years old, to grow to be blooming, beautiful, and happy, without the dark cloud upon you of living in uncertainty whether your father soon wore his heart out in prison, or wasted there through many lingering years."

As he said the words he looked down, with an admiring pity, on the flowing, golden hair, as if he pictured to himself that it might have been already tinged with gray.

"You know that your parents had no great possession, and that what they had was secured to your mother and to you. There has been no

---

5. ***nine times ninepence . . . guineas.*** Pence, shillings, and guineas—coins of bronze, silver, and gold, respectively—are units of English currency. Mr. Lorry makes this request to reassure himself that he has not shocked Miss Manette into a state of complete confusion.

new discovery of money or of any other property; but——''

He felt his wrist held closer, and he stopped. The expression in the forehead, which had so particularly attracted his notice, and which was now immovable, had deepened into one of pain and horror.

''But he has been—been found. He is alive. Greatly changed, it is too probable; almost a wreck, it is possible; though we will hope the best. Still, alive. Your father has been taken to the house of an old servant in Paris, and we are going there: I, to identify him if I can; you, to restore him to life, love, duty, rest, comfort.''

A shiver ran through her frame, and from it through his. She said, in a low, distinct, awe-stricken voice, as if she were saying it in a dream: ''I am going to see his ghost! It will be his ghost—not him!''

Mr. Lorry quietly chafed the hands that held his arm. ''There, there, there! See now, see now! The best and the worst are known to you, now. You are well on your way to the poor wronged gentleman, and, with a fair sea voyage, and a fair land journey, you will be soon at his dear side.''

She repeated in the same tone, sunk to a whisper, ''I have been happy, yet his ghost has never haunted me!''

''Only one thing more,'' said Mr. Lorry, laying stress upon it as a wholesome means of enforcing her attention: ''He has been found under another name; his own, long forgotten or long concealed. It would be worse than useless now to inquire which; worse than useless to seek to know whether he has been for years overlooked, or always designedly held prisoner. It would be worse than useless now to make any inquiries, because it would be dangerous. Better not to mention the subject, anywhere or in any way, and to remove him—for a while at all events—out of France. Even I, safe as an Englishman, and even Tellson's, important as they are to French credit, avoid all naming of the matter. I carry about me not a scrap of writing openly referring to it. This is a secret service altogether. My credentials, entries, and memoranda are all comprehended in the one line, 'Recalled to Life,' which may mean anything. But what is the matter! She doesn't notice a word! Miss Manette!''

Perfectly still and silent, and not even fallen back in her chair, she sat utterly insensible. So close was her hold upon his arm that he feared to detach himself lest he hurt her; therefore he called loudly for assistance without moving.

A wild-looking woman, whom even in his agitation, Mr. Lorry observed to be all of a red color, and to have red hair, and to be dressed in some extraordinary tight-fitting fashion, and to have on her head a most wonderful bonnet like a Stilton cheese,[6] came running into the room in advance of the inn servants, and settled the question of his detachment from the young lady, by laying a brawny hand upon his chest, and sending him flying back against the nearest wall.

(''I really think this must be a man!'' was Mr. Lorry's breathless reflection, simultaneously with his coming against the wall.)

''Why, look at you all!'' bawled this figure, addressing the inn servants. ''Why don't you go and fetch things? I'll let you know, if you don't bring smelling salts, cold water, and vinegar, quick, I will.''

There was an immediate dispersal for these restoratives, and she softly laid the patient on a sofa, and tended her with great skill and gentleness, calling her ''my bird!''

''And you in brown!'' she said, indignantly turning to Mr. Lorry. ''Couldn't you tell her what you had to tell her, without frightening her to death? Look at her, with her pretty pale face and her cold hands. Do you call *that* being a banker?''

Mr. Lorry was so exceedingly disconcerted by a question so hard to answer that he could only look on, at a distance.

''I hope she will do well now,'' said Mr. Lorry.

---

6. ***Stilton cheese,*** a round, rich, waxy white cheese veined with blue-green mold.

"No thanks to you in brown, if she does. My darling pretty!"

"I hope," said Mr. Lorry, after another pause of feeble sympathy and humility, "that you accompany Miss Manette to France?"

"A likely thing, too!" replied the strong woman. "If it was ever intended that I should go across salt water, do you suppose Providence would have cast my lot in an island?"

This being another question hard to answer, Mr. Jarvis Lorry withdrew to consider it.

CHAPTER V
THE WINE SHOP

A large cask of wine had been dropped and broken in the street. The accident had happened in getting it out of a cart. The cask had tumbled out with a run, the hoops had burst, and it lay on the stones just outside the door of the wine shop, shattered like a walnut shell.

All the people within reach had suspended their business, or their idleness, to run to the spot and drink the wine. Some men kneeled down, made scoops of their two hands joined, and sipped, or tried to help women, who bent over their shoulders, to sip, before the wine had all run out between their fingers. Others, men and women, dipped in the puddles with little mugs of mutilated earthenware, or even with handkerchiefs from women's heads, which were squeezed dry into infants' mouths. Others devoted themselves to the sodden and lee-dyed pieces of the cask, licking and even champing the moister wine-rotted fragments with eager relish.

A shrill sound of laughter and of amused voices—voices of men, women, and children—resounded in the street while this wine game lasted. When the wine was gone, and the places where it had been most abundant were raked into a gridiron pattern by fingers, these demonstrations ceased, as suddenly as they had broken out.

The wine was red wine, and had stained the ground of the narrow street in the suburb of Saint Antoine,[1] in Paris, where it was spilled. It had stained many hands, too, and many faces, and many naked feet, and many wooden shoes; and one tall joker, his head more out of a long squalid bag of a nightcap than in it, scrawled upon a wall with his finger dipped in muddy wine lees—BLOOD.

The time was to come when that wine, too, would be spilled on the street stones, and when the stain of it would be red upon many there.

And now that the cloud settled on Saint Antoine, which a momentary gleam had driven from his sacred countenance, the darkness of it was heavy—cold, dirt, sickness, ignorance, and want were the lords in waiting on the saintly presence—nobles of great power all of them; but, most especially the last. Samples of a people that had undergone a terrible grinding and regrinding in the mill shivered at every corner, passed in and out at every doorway, looked from every window, fluttered in every vestige of a garment that the wind shook. The mill which had worked them down was the mill that grinds young people old; the children had ancient faces and grave voices; and upon them, and upon the grown faces, and plowed into every furrow of age and coming up afresh, was the sign Hunger. It was prevalent everywhere. Hunger was pushed out of the tall houses in the wretched clothing that hung upon poles and lines; Hunger was patched into them with straw and rag and wood and paper; Hunger was repeated in every fragment of the small modicum of firewood that the man sawed off; Hunger stared down from the smokeless chimneys, and started up from the filthy street that had no offal, among its refuse, of anything to eat. Hunger was the inscription on the baker's shelves, written in every small loaf of his scanty stock of bad bread; at the sausage shop, in every dead-dog preparation that was offered for sale. Hunger rattled its dry

1. ***Saint Antoine*** (an′twän), a poor suburb of Paris at the time of the story. Now within the city limits, the Rue St. Antoine still remains one of the poorest parts of Paris.

bones among the roasting chestnuts in the turned cylinder; Hunger was shred into atomies in every farthing porringer of husky chips of potato, fried with some reluctant drops of oil.

Its abiding place was in all things fitted to it. A narrow, winding street, full of offense and stench, with other narrow, winding streets diverging, all peopled by rags and nightcaps, and all smelling of rags and nightcaps, and all visible things with a brooding look upon them that looked ill. In the hunted air of the people there was yet some wild beast thought of the possibility of turning at bay. Depressed and slinking though they were, eyes of fire were not wanting among them; nor compressed lips, white with what they suppressed; nor foreheads knitted into the likeness of the gallows rope they mused about enduring, or inflicting. The trade signs were, all, grim illustrations of Want. The butcher and the porkman painted up only the leanest scrags of meat; the baker, the coarsest of meager loaves. The people rudely pictured as drinking in the wine shops croaked over their scanty measures of thin wine and beer, and were gloweringly confidential together. Nothing was represented in a flourishing condition save tools and weapons; but the cutler's knives and axes were sharp and bright, the smith's hammers were heavy, and the gunmaker's stock was murderous. The crippling stones of the pavement, with their many little reservoirs of mud and water, had no footways, but broke off abruptly at the doors. The kennel,[2] to make amends, ran down the middle of the street—when it ran at all; which was only after heavy rains, and then it ran, by many eccentric fits, into the houses. Across the streets, at wide intervals, one clumsy lamp was slung by a rope and pulley; at night, when the lamplighter had let these down, and lighted and hoisted them again, a feeble grove of dim wicks swung in a sickly manner overhead, as if they were at sea. Indeed they were at sea, and the ship and crew were in peril of tempest.

For the time was to come when the gaunt scarecrows of that region should have watched the lamplighter, in their idleness and hunger, so long as to conceive the idea of improving on his method, and hauling up men by those ropes and pulleys, to flare upon the darkness of their condition. But the time was not come yet; and every wind that blew over France shook the rags of the scarecrows in vain, for the birds, fine in song and feather, took no warning.[3]

The wine shop was a corner shop, better than most others in its appearance and degree, and the master of the wine shop had stood outside it, in a yellow waistcoat and green breeches, looking on at the struggle for the lost wine. "It's not my affair," said he, with a final shrug of the shoulders. "The people from the market did it. Let them bring another."

This wine-shop keeper was a bull-necked, martial-looking man of thirty, and of a hot temperament, for although it was a bitter day, he wore no coat. His shirt sleeves were rolled up, too, and his brown arms were bare to the elbows. Neither did he wear anything more on his head than his own crisply curling, short dark hair. He was a dark man altogether, with good eyes and a good bold breadth between them. Good-humored looking on the whole, but implacable-looking, too; evidently a man of a strong resolution and a set purpose, a man not desirable to be met, rushing down a narrow pass with a gulf on either side, for nothing would turn the man.

Madame Defarge, his wife, sat in the shop behind the counter as he came in. Madame Defarge was a stout woman of his own age, with a watchful eye that seldom seemed to look at anything, a large hand heavily ringed, a steady face, strong features, and great composure of manner. There was a character about Madame Defarge, from which one might have predicted that she did not often make mistakes against herself in any of the reckonings over which she presided. Madame Defarge, being sensitive to cold,

---

2. ***kennel,*** a little channel; gutter.

3. ***the birds . . . warning.*** The French aristocracy, in high spirits and finely dressed, paid no attention to the suffering or to the rising discontent among the lower classes.

VINS

was wrapped in fur, and had a quantity of bright shawl twined about her head, though not to the concealment of her large earrings. Her knitting was before her, but she had laid it down to pick her teeth with a toothpick. She said nothing when her lord came in, but coughed just one grain of cough. This, in combination with the lifting of her darkly defined eyebrows over her toothpick by the breadth of a line, suggested to her husband he would do well to look round the shop, among the customers, for any new customer who had dropped in.

The wine-shop keeper accordingly rolled his eyes about until they rested upon an elderly gentleman and a young lady, who were seated in a corner. As he passed behind the counter, he took notice that the elderly gentleman said in a look to the young lady, "This is our man."

But he feigned not to notice the two strangers, and fell into discourse with the triumvirate of customers who were drinking at the counter.

"How goes it, Jacques?"[4] said one of these three to Monsieur Defarge. "Is all the spilt wine swallowed?"

"Every drop, Jacques," answered Monsieur Defarge.

When this interchange of Christian name was effected, Madame Defarge, picking her teeth with her toothpick, coughed another grain of cough, and raised her eyebrows by the breadth of another line.

"It is not often," said the second of the three, addressing Monsieur Defarge, "that many of these miserable beasts know the taste of wine, or of anything but black bread and death. Is it not so, Jacques?"

"It is so, Jacques," Monsieur Defarge returned.

The last of the three now said his say. "Ah! So much the worse! A bitter taste it is that such poor cattle always have in their mouths, and hard lives they live, Jacques. Am I right, Jacques?"

"You are right, Jacques."

This third interchange of the Christian name was completed at the moment when Madame Defarge put her toothpick by, kept her eyebrows up, and slightly rustled in her seat.

"Gentlemen," said her husband, who had kept his bright eye observantly upon her, "good day. The chamber that you wished to see is on the fifth floor. The doorway of the staircase gives on the little courtyard close to the left here. But, now that I remember, one of you has already been there and can show the way. Gentlemen, adieu!"

They paid for their wine and left the place. The eyes of Monsieur Defarge were studying his wife at her knitting, when the elderly gentleman advanced from his corner and begged the favor of a word.

"Willingly, sir,"said Monsieur Defarge.

Their conference was very short, but very decided. Almost at the first word, Monsieur Defarge started and became deeply attentive. It had not lasted a minute, when he nodded and went out. The gentleman then beckoned to the young lady, and they, too, went out. Madame Defarge knitted with nimble fingers and saw nothing.

Mr. Jarvis Lorry and Miss Manette, emerging from the wine shop thus, joined Monsieur Defarge in the doorway to which he had directed his other company just before. It opened from a stinking little black courtyard and was the general public entrance to a great pile of houses, inhabited by a great number of people. In the gloomy entry to the gloomy, tile-paved staircase, Monsieur Defarge bent on one knee to the child of his old master, and put her hand to his lips. It was a gentle action, but not at all gently done; a remarkable transformation had come over him in a few seconds. He had no good humor in his face, nor any openness of aspect left, but had become a secret, angry, dangerous man.

"It is very high; it is a little difficult. Better to begin slowly." Thus said Monsieur Defarge,

---

4. ***Jacques*** (zhäk), a French word for man or fellow; also a proper name (*James* in English). During the days preceding the revolution, this name was used as a password of the mysterious secret society, the *Jacquerie*, which some authorities believe to have planned and brought about the revolution.

in a stern voice, to Mr. Lorry as they began ascending the stairs.

"Is he alone?" the latter whispered.

"Alone! God help him, who should be with him!" said the other in the same low voice.

"Is he always alone, then?"

"Yes."

"Of his own desire?"

"Of his own necessity. As he was, when I first saw him after they found me and demanded to know if I would take him, and, at my peril be discreet—as he was then, so he is now."

"He is greatly changed?"

"Changed!"

The keeper of the wine shop stopped to strike the wall with his hand, and mutter a tremendous curse. No direct answer could have been half so forcible. Mr. Lorry's spirits grew heavier and heavier, as he and his two companions ascended higher and higher.

At last, the top of the staircase was gained. There was yet an upper staircase, of a steeper inclination and of contracted dimensions, to be ascended before the garret story was reached. The keeper of the wine shop turned himself about here, and, carefully feeling in the pockets of the coat he carried over his shoulder, took out a key.

"The door is locked then, my friend?" said Mr. Lorry, surprised.

"Aye. Yes," was the grim reply of Monsieur Defarge.

"You think it necessary to keep the unfortunate gentleman so retired?"

"I think it necessary to turn the key." Monsieur Defarge whispered it closer in his ear and frowned heavily.

"Why?"

"Why! Because he has lived so long locked up that he would be frightened—rave—die—come to I know not what harm—if this door was left open."

"Is it possible!" exclaimed Mr. Lorry.

"Is it possible?" repeated Defarge, bitterly. "Yes. And a beautiful world we live in, when it *is* possible, and when many other such things are possible, and not only possible, but done—done, see you!—under that sky there, every day. Long live the Devil. Let us go on."

They went up slowly and softly. The staircase was short, and they were soon at the top. There, as it had an abrupt turn in it, they came all at once in sight of three men, bent down close together at the side of a door, intently looking into the room to which the door belonged, through some chinks or holes in the wall. On hearing footsteps close at hand, these three turned, rose, and showed themselves to be the three of one name who had been drinking in the wine shop.

"I forgot them in the surprise of your visit," explained Monsieur Defarge. "Leave us, good boys."

The three glided by and went silently down.

There appearing to be no other door on that floor, and the keeper of the wine shop going straight to this one when they were left alone, Mr. Lorry asked in a whisper, with a little anger: "Do you make a show of Monsieur Manette?"

"I show him to a chosen few."

"Is that well?"

"*I* think it is well."

"Who are the few? How do you choose them?"

"I choose men of my name—Jacques is my name—to whom the sight is likely to do good. Enough; you are English; that is another thing. Stay there, if you please."

With an admonitory gesture to keep them back, he struck twice or thrice upon the door—evidently with no other object than to make a noise there. With the same intention, he drew the key across it three or four times before he put it clumsily into the lock, and turned it as heavily as he could.

The door slowly opened inwardly under his hand, and he looked into the room and said something. A faint voice answered something.

He looked back over his shoulder and beckoned them to enter. Mr. Lorry got his arm securely around the daughter's waist and held her, for he felt that she was sinking. Rendered in a manner desperate, by her state and by the beckoning of their conductor, he lifted her a little, and hurried her into the room. He set her down just within the door, and held her, clinging to him.

Defarge drew out the key, closed the door, locked it on the inside, took out the key again, and held it in his hand. All this he did, methodically, and with as loud and harsh an accompaniment of noise as he could make. Finally, he walked across the room with a measured tread to where the window was. He stopped there and faced round.

The garret, built to be a depository for firewood and the like, was dim and dark; for the window, of dormer shape, was in truth a door in the roof, with a little crane over it for the hoisting up of stores from the street, and closing up the middle in two pieces, like any other door of French construction. To exclude the cold, one half of this door was fast closed, and the other was opened but a very little way. It was difficult, on first coming in, to see anything, and long habit alone could have slowly formed in anyone the ability to do any work requiring nicety in such obscurity. Yet work of that kind was being done in the garret; for, with his back toward the door and his face toward the window where the keeper of the wine shop stood looking at him, a white-haired man sat on a low bench, stooping forward and very busy, making shoes.

CHAPTER VI
THE SHOEMAKER

"Good day!" said Monsieur Defarge, looking down at the white head that bent low over the shoemaking.

It was raised for a moment, and a very faint voice responded to the salutation, as if it were at a distance:

"Good day!"

"You are still hard at work, I see?"

After a long silence, the head was lifted for another moment, and the voice replied, "Yes—I am working." This time a pair of haggard eyes had looked at the questioner, before the face had dropped again.

"I want," said Defarge, who had not removed his gaze from the shoemaker, "to let in a little more light here. You can bear a little more?"

"I must bear it, if you let it in." (Laying the palest shadow of a stress upon the second word.)

The opened half-door was opened a little farther and secured at that angle for the time. A broad ray of light fell into the garret, and showed the workman with an unfinished shoe upon his lap, pausing in his labor. His few common tools and various scraps of leather were at his feet and on his bench. He had a white beard, raggedly cut but not very long, a hollow face, and exceedingly bright eyes. The hollowness and thinness of his face would have caused them to look large under his yet dark eyebrows and his confused white hair, though they had been really otherwise; but they were naturally large and looked unnaturally so. His yellow rags of shirt lay open at the throat and showed his body to be withered and worn.

He had put up a hand between his eyes and the light, and the very bones of it seemed transparent. So he sat, with a steadfastly vacant gaze, pausing in his work. He never looked at the figure before him, without first looking down on this side of himself, then on that, as if he had lost the habit of associating place with sound; he never spoke, without first wandering in this manner and forgetting to speak.

"Are you going to finish that pair of shoes today?" asked Defarge, motioning to Mr. Lorry to come forward.

"What did you say?"

"Do you mean to finish that pair of shoes today?"

"I can't say that I mean to. I suppose so. I don't know." Reminded of his work, he bent over it again.

Mr. Lorry came silently forward, leaving the daughter by the door. When he had stood for a minute or two by the side of Defarge, the shoemaker looked up. He showed no surprise at seeing another figure, but the unsteady fingers of one of his hands strayed to his lips as he looked at it (his lips and his nails were of the same pale lead-color), and then the hand dropped to his work, and he once more bent over the shoe.

"You have a visitor, you see," said Monsieur Defarge.

"What did you say?"

"Here is a visitor."

The shoemaker looked up as before, but without removing a hand from his work.

"Come!" said Defarge. "Show him that shoe you are working at."

Mr. Lorry took it in his hand.

"Tell monsieur what kind of shoe it is and the maker's name."

"It is a lady's shoe in the present mode. I never saw the mode. I have had a pattern in my hand." He glanced at the shoe with some little passing touch of pride.

"And the maker's name?" said Defarge.

"Did you ask me for my name?"

"Assuredly I did."

"One Hundred and Five, North Tower."

"Is that all?"

"One Hundred and Five, North Tower."

With a weary sound that was not a sigh nor a groan, he bent to work again until the silence was again broken.

"You are not a shoemaker by trade?" said Mr. Lorry, looking steadfastly at him.

His haggard eyes turned to Defarge as if he would have transferred the question to him; but as no help came from that quarter, they turned back on the questioner when they had sought the ground.

"I am not a shoemaker by trade? No, I was not a shoemaker by trade. I—I learned it here. I taught myself. I asked leave to——"

He lapsed away for minutes. His eyes came slowly back at last to the face from which they had wandered; when they rested on it, he started and resumed, in the manner of a sleeper that moment awake.

"I asked leave to teach myself, and I got it with much difficulty after a long while, and I have made shoes ever since."

As he held out his hand for the shoe that had been taken from him, Mr. Lorry said, still looking steadfastly in his face:

"Monsieur Manette, do you remember nothing of me?"

The shoe dropped to the ground, and he sat looking fixedly at the questioner.

"Monsieur Manette," Mr. Lorry laid his hand upon Defarge's arm, "do you remember nothing of this man? Look at him. Look at me. Is there no old banker, no old servant, no old time, rising in your mind?"

As the captive of many years sat looking fixedly, by turns, at Mr. Lorry and at Defarge, some long obliterated marks of an active intelligence in the middle of the forehead gradually forced themselves through the black mist that had fallen on him. They were overclouded again, they were fainter, they were gone; but they had been there. And so exactly was the expression repeated on the fair young face of her who had crept to a point where she could see him, that it looked as though it had passed like a moving light from him to her.

She moved from the wall of the garret, very near to the bench on which he sat. She stood like a spirit beside him, and he bent over his work.

It happened, at length, that he had occasion to change the instrument in his hand for his shoemaker's knife. He had taken it up and was stooping to work again, when his eyes caught the skirt of her dress. He raised them and saw her face. The two spectators started forward, but she stayed them with a motion of her hand. She had no fear of his striking at her with the knife, though they had.

He stared at her with a fearful look, and in the pauses of his quick and labored breathing, he was heard to say:

"What is this?"

With the tears streaming down her face, she put her two hands to her lips and kissed them to him.

"You are not the gaoler's daughter?"

She sighed, "No."

"Who are you?"

Not yet trusting of her voice, she sat down on the bench beside him; he laid the knife down softly, as he sat staring at her.

Her golden hair, which she wore in long curls, had been hurriedly pushed aside, and fell down over her neck. Advancing his hand by little and little, he took it up and looked at it. In the midst of the action he went astray, and, with another deep sigh, fell to work at his shoemaking.

But not for long. She laid her hand upon his shoulder. After looking doubtfully at it, two or three times, as if to be sure that it was really there, he laid down his work, put his hand to his neck, and took off a blackened string with a scrap of folded rag attached to it. He opened this carefully on his knee, and it contained a very little quantity of hair: not more than one or two long golden hairs, which he had, in some old day, wound off upon his finger.

He took her hair into his hand again, and looked closely at it. "It is the same. How can it be!" He turned her full to the light and looked at her.

"She had laid her head upon my shoulder that night when I was summoned out—she had a fear of my going, though I had none—and when I was brought to the North Tower they found these upon my sleeve. 'You will leave me them? They can never help me to escape in the body, though they may in spirit.' Those were the words I said."

He formed this speech with his lips many times before he could utter it. But when he did find spoken words for it, they came to him coherently, though slowly.

"How was this?— *Was it you?*"

Once more the two spectators started, as he turned upon her with a frightful suddenness. But she sat perfectly still in his grasp and only said, in a low voice, "I entreat you, good gentlemen, do not come near us!"

"Hark!" he exclaimed. "Whose voice was that?"

His hands released her as he uttered this cry, and went up to his white hair, which they tore in a frenzy. It died out, as everything but his shoemaking did die out of him, and he refolded his little packet and tried to secure it in his breast; but he still looked at her and gloomily shook his head.

"No, no, no; you are too young, too blooming. It can't be. See what the prisoner is. No, no. She was—and he was—before the slow years of the North Tower—ages ago. What is your name, my gentle angel?"

"Oh, sir, at another time you shall know my name, and who my mother was, and who my father, and how I never knew their hard, hard history. But I cannot tell you at this time.

"If you hear in my voice any resemblance to a voice that once was sweet music in your ears, weep for it! If you touch, in touching my hair, anything that recalls a beloved head that lay on your breast when you were young and free, weep for it! If I bring back the remembrance of a home long desolate, while your poor heart pined away, weep for it, weep for it!"

He had sunk in her arms, and his face dropped on her breast, a sight so touching, yet so terrible in the tremendous wrong and suffering which had gone before it, that the two beholders covered their faces.

When the quiet of the garret had been long undisturbed, they came forward to raise the father and daughter from the ground. He had gradually dropped to the floor, and lay there in a lethargy, worn out. She had nestled down with him, that his head might lie upon her arm.

"If, without disturbing him," she said, raising her hand to Mr. Lorry as he stooped over them, after repeated blowings of his nose, "all could be arranged for our leaving Paris at once, so that, from the very door, he could be taken away——"

"But, consider. Is he fit for the journey?"

"More fit for that, I think, than to remain in this city, so dreadful to him."

"It is true," said Defarge, who was kneeling to hear. "More than that; Monsieur Manette is, for all reasons, best out of France. Say, shall I hire a carriage and post horses?"

"That's business," said Mr. Lorry, "and if business is to be done, I had better do it."

"Then be so kind," urged Miss Manette, "as to leave us here. You see how composed he has become, and you cannot be afraid to leave him with me now. If you will lock the door to secure us from interruption, I will take care of him until you return, and then we will remove him straight."

Both Mr. Lorry and Defarge were rather disinclined to this course, and in favor of one of them remaining. But, as there were not only carriage and horses to be seen to, but traveling papers, and as time pressed, for the day was drawing to an end, it came at last to their hastily dividing the business that was necessary to be done, and hurrying away to do it.

Mr. Lorry and Monsieur Defarge had made all ready for the journey and had brought with them, besides traveling cloaks and wrappers, bread and meat, wine, and hot coffee. Monsieur Defarge and Mr. Lorry roused the captive and assisted him to his feet.

In the submissive way of one long accustomed to obey under coercion, he ate and drank what they gave him to eat and drink, and put on the cloak and other wrappings that they gave him to wear. He readily responded to his daughter's drawing her arm through his, and took—and kept—her hand in both his own.

They began to descend; Monsieur Defarge going first with the lamp, Mr. Lorry closing the little procession. They had not traversed many steps of the long main staircase when the prisoner stopped, and stared at the roof and round at the walls.

That he had no recollection of his having been brought from his prison to that house was apparent. They heard him mutter, "One Hundred and Five, North Tower"; and when he looked about him, it evidently was for the strong fortress walls which had long encompassed him.

No crowd was about the door; no people were at any of the windows; not even a chance passer-by was in the street. Only one soul was to be seen, Madame Defarge—who leaned against the doorpost, knitting, and saw nothing.

The prisoner had got into a coach, and his daughter had followed him, when Mr. Lorry's feet were arrested on the step by his asking, miserably, for his shoemaking tools and the unfinished shoes. Madame Defarge called to her husband that she would get them. She quickly brought them down and handed them in—and immediately afterwards leaned against the doorpost, knitting, and saw nothing.

Defarge got upon the box and gave the word "To the Barrier!"[1] The postilion cracked his whip, and they clattered away.

Under the overswinging lamps—swinging ever brighter in the better streets, and ever dimmer in the worse—and by lighted shops, gay crowds, illuminated coffee houses, and theater doors, to one of the city gates. Soldiers with lanterns, at the guardhouse there, "Your papers, travelers!" "See here then, Monsieur the Officer," said Defarge, getting down and taking him gravely apart, "these are the papers of monsieur inside, with the white head. They were consigned to me, with him, at the——." He dropped his voice, there was a flutter among the military lanterns, and one of them being handed into the coach by an arm in uniform, the eyes connected with the arm looked at monsieur with the white head. "It is well. Forward!" from the uniform. "Adieu!" from Defarge. And so, under a short grove of feebler and feebler overswinging lamps, out under the great grove of stars.

Beneath that arch of unmoved and eternal lights the shadows of the night were broad and black. All through the cold and restless interval,

1. ***the Barrier,*** the gate of Paris where travelers' identification was checked.

until dawn, they whispered in the ears of Mr. Jarvis Lorry—sitting opposite the buried man who had been dug out, and wondering what subtle powers were forever lost to him, and what were capable of restoration—the old inquiry:

"I hope you care to be recalled to life?"

And the old answer:

"I can't say."

Discussion

Chapter IV

1. (a) Describe the appearance and manner of Mr. Jarvis Lorry and of Miss Manette.

2. (a) What story does Mr. Lorry tell Miss Manette? **(b)** By what method does he relate the story? **(c)** What does his method of telling the story reveal to you about Mr. Lorry?

3. (a) What have you learned so far of the relationships of Mr. Lorry, Miss Manette, and Doctor Manette? **(b)** What is the relationship of the "wild woman" to Miss Manette?

4. How does the author lighten the serious tone of this chapter?

Chapter V

1. What might the red wine symbolize?

2. What evidence does the narrator present to show that people in Saint Antoine were living under "explosive" conditions?

3. (a) In what activity is Madame Defarge constantly engaged? **(b)** What do you infer about her from her manner?

4. What had been Monsieur Defarge's relationship to Miss Manette's father?

Chapter VI

1. (a) Describe the emotional state of the old shoemaker. **(b)** What does "One Hundred and Five, North Tower" mean to him? to the reader?

2. Why does Doctor Manette remove a bit of cloth tied around his neck and take from it two golden hairs?

3. What is the connection between Miss Manette's attempt to make her father weep and the title of Book the First?

Discussion

Book the First

1. Identify the following characters and indicate both their past and present relationships. **(a)** Mr. Lorry, **(b)** Lucie Manette, **(c)** the Defarges, **(d)** Jerry Cruncher, **(e)** Doctor Manette.

2. How is each of these characters associated with London? with Paris?

3. Remember that Dickens wrote *A Tale of Two Cities* in serial form, publishing one chapter weekly. To keep his readers interested enough to buy each installment, he incorporated some element of mystery or surprise in each chapter. Such elements create suspense, the desire to know what is going to happen next. What characters, events, and themes established in Book the First do you think will be important in the rest of the novel? What mysteries have not been solved?

Vocabulary

Root Words

Many words that seem quite different actually have developed from the same root. The English language is derived fundamentally from Anglo-Saxon but also contains words with foreign roots. For example, the Latin word *solvere,* meaning "to loosen," is the root of such different words as "dissolve" and "absolute." Similarly, the Latin word *pati,* meaning "to suffer," is the root for words like "passive" and "compassion."

Below are two word families—words that are derived from either the root *solvere* or the root *pati.* Using the context clues available in each sentence, fill in the blank with the word from the list that best completes the sentence. The word family from which you should choose is noted in parentheses at the end of each sentence. Write the appropriate word on your paper.

solvere

absolve	resolve
dissolute	resolute
insoluble	solution

pati

compatible	impatience
dispassionate	impassive
impassible	passivity

1. When the lawyer learned of Miss Fallon's imprisonment, he was determined to _______ the problem once and for all. *(solvere)*

2. Their natures were so _______ that he and his wife were very happy together. *(pati)*

3. Known as "The Hanging Judge," he was _______ in his determination to send as many people as possible to the gallows. *(solvere)*

4. Standing at the altar, the groom began to show _______ as the time slowly passed without word of his bride-to-be. *(pati)*

5. For poor Milton, the decision to take his brother's share of the money seemed the perfect _______ to all his problems. *(solvere)*

Composition

You are a reviewer for the *London Review of Books.* Your assignment is to evaluate Book the First of *A Tale of Two Cities;* the last chapter of Book the First has just been published. Remember that a book review is not just a plot summary; it is an expression of opinions and judgments about various aspects of a literary work. For example, you might want to evaluate and give your reactions to Dickens's skill at devising a plot and his ability to develop characters and suggest setting. (If necessary reread the articles on these terms in the Handbook of Literary Terms before you begin to write.)

Now, write a two- to three-page review of Book the First. You might begin by stating whether you plan to continue reading installments of the novel as they are published. (See *Defending Your Position,* page 672, in Composition Guide.)

Book the Second: The Golden Thread

CHAPTER I
FIVE YEARS LATER

Tellson's Bank by Temple Bar was an old-fashioned place, even in the year one thousand seven hundred and eighty. It was very small, very dark, very ugly, very incommodious. It was an old-fashioned place, moreover, in that the partners in the House were proud of its smallness, proud of its darkness, proud of its ugliness, proud of its incommodiousness. They were even boastful of its eminence in those particulars, and were fired by an express conviction that, if it were less objectionable, it would be less respectable. This was no passive belief, but an active weapon which they flashed at more convenient places of business. Tellson's, they said, wanted no elbow room, Tellson's wanted no light, Tellson's wanted no embellishment. Noakes and Co.'s might, or Snooks Brothers' might, but Tellson's, thank heaven!——

Any one of these partners would have disinherited his son on the question of rebuilding Tellson's. In this respect the House was much on a par with the Country, which did very often disinherit its sons for suggesting improvements in laws and customs that had long been highly objectionable but were only the more respectable.

Thus it had come to pass that Tellson's was the triumphant perfection of inconvenience. After bursting open a door of idiotic obstinacy with a weak rattle in its throat, you fell into Tellson's down two steps and came to your senses in a miserable little shop with two little counters, where the oldest of men made your check shake as if the wind rustled it, while they examined the signature by the dingiest of windows, which were always under a shower-bath of mud from Fleet Street, and which were made the dingier by their own iron bars proper, and the heavy shadow of Temple Bar. If your business necessitated your seeing "the House," you were put into a species of Condemned Hold at the back, where you meditated on a misspent life, until the House came with its hands in its pockets, and you could hardly blink at it in the dismal twilight. Your money came out of, or went into, wormy old wooden drawers, particles of which flew up your nose and down your throat when they were opened and shut. Your bank notes had a musty odor, as if they were fast decomposing into rags again. Your plate was stowed away among the neighboring cesspools, and evil communications corrupted its good polish in a day or two. Your deeds got into extemporized strong rooms made of kitchens and sculleries. Your lighter boxes of family papers went upstairs into a Barmecide room,[1] that always had a great dining table in it and never had a dinner, and where, even in the year one thousand seven hundred and eighty, the first letters written to you by your old love, or by your little children, were but newly released from the horror of being ogled through the windows, by the heads exposed on Temple Bar.[2]

But indeed, at that time, putting to death was a recipe much in vogue with all trades and professions, and not least of all with Tellson's. Death is Nature's remedy for all things, and why not Legislation's? Accordingly, the forger was put to Death; the utterer of a bad note was put to Death; the unlawful opener of a letter was put to Death; the holder of a horse at Tellson's door, who made off with it, was put to Death; the sounders of three-fourths of the notes in the whole gamut of Crime were put to Death. Not that it did the least good in the way of prevention—it might almost have been worth remarking that the fact was exactly the reverse—but, it

---

1. ***Barmecide*** (bär′mə sīd) ***room***, a room for pretended feasts with empty dishes. Barmecide was a wealthy man in *The Arabian Nights* who gave a beggar such a "feast."
2. ***heads . . . Temple Bar.*** The heads of executed criminals were displayed on the iron spikes of the gate.

cleared off—as to this world—the trouble of each particular case, and left nothing else connected with it to be looked after. Thus, Tellson's, in its day, like greater places of business, had taken so many lives that, if the heads laid low before it had been ranged on Temple Bar instead of being privately disposed of, they would probably have excluded what little light the ground floor had, in a rather significant manner.

Cramped in all kinds of dim cupboards and hutches at Tellson's, the oldest of men carried on the business gravely. When they took a young man into Tellson's London House, they hid him somewhere till he was old. They kept him in a dark place, like a cheese, until he had the full Tellson flavor and blue mold upon him. Then only was he permitted to be seen, spectacularly poring over large books.

Outside Tellson's—never by any means in it, unless called in—was an odd-job man, an occasional porter and messenger, who served as the live sign of the House. He was never absent during business hours, unless upon an errand, and then he was represented by his son, a grisly urchin of twelve, who was his express image. People understood that Tellson's, in a stately way, tolerated the odd-job man. The House had always tolerated some person in that capacity, and time and tide had drifted this person to the post. His surname was Cruncher and, on the youthful occasion of his renouncing by proxy the works of darkness, in the easterly parish church of Houndsditch, he had received the added appellation of Jerry.

The scene was Mr. Cruncher's private lodging in Hanging Sword Alley, Whitefriars,[3] the time, half-past seven of the clock on a windy March morning, Anno Domini seventeen hundred and eighty. (Mr. Cruncher himself always spoke of the year of our Lord as Anna Dominoes; apparently under the impression that the Christian era dated from the invention of a popular game, by a lady who had bestowed her name upon it.)

Mr. Cruncher's apartments were not in a savory neighborhood and were but two in number, even if a closet with a single pane of glass in it might be counted as one. But they were very decently kept. Early as it was, on the windy March morning, the room in which he lay abed was already scrubbed throughout; and between the cups and saucers arranged for breakfast, and the lumbering deal table, a very clean white cloth was spread.

Mr. Cruncher reposed under a patchwork counterpane. At first he slept heavily, but, by degrees, began to roll and surge in bed, until he rose above the surface, with his spiky hair looking as if it must tear the sheets to ribbons. At which juncture, he exclaimed, in a voice of dire exasperation:

"Bust me, if she ain't at it agin!"

A woman of orderly and industrious appearance rose from her knees in a corner, with sufficient haste and trepidation to show that she was the person referred to.

"What!" said Mr. Cruncher, looking out of bed for a boot. "You're at it agin, are you?"

After hailing the morn with this second salutation, he threw a boot at the woman as a third. It was a very muddy boot, and may introduce the odd circumstance connected with Mr. Cruncher's domestic economy, that whereas he often came home after banking hours with clean boots, he often got up next morning to find the same boots covered with clay.

"What," said Mr. Cruncher, after missing his mark, "what are you up to, Aggerawayter?"[4]

"I was only saying my prayers."

"Saying your prayers! You're a nice woman! What do you mean by flopping yourself down and praying agin me?"

"I was not praying against you; I was praying for you."

"You weren't! And if you were, I won't be took the liberty with. Here! your mother's a

3. ***Hanging Sword Alley, Whitefriars,*** name of a street and district in London, frequented by criminals and evildoers.
4. ***Aggerawayter,*** Mr. Cruncher's garbled version of aggravator, his name for his wife when she displeased him with her too careful observance of religious duties.

nice woman, young Jerry, going apraying agin your father's prosperity. You've got a dutiful mother, you have, my son. You've got a religious mother, you have, my boy; going and flopping herself down, and praying that the bread and butter may be snatched out of the mouth of her only child.

"And what do you suppose, you conceited female," said Mr. Cruncher, with unconscious inconsistency, "that the worth of *your* prayers may be?"

"They only come from the heart, Jerry. They are worth no more than that."

"Worth no more than that," repeated Mr. Cruncher. "They ain't worth much, then. Whether or no, I won't be prayed agin, I tell you. I can't afford it. I'm not a-going to be made unlucky by *your* sneaking. If you must go flopping yourself down, flop in favor of your husband and child, and not in opposition to 'em. B-u-u-ust me!" said Mr. Cruncher, who all this time had been putting on his clothes, "if I ain't, what with piety and one blowed thing and another, been choused this last week into as bad luck as ever a poor devil of a honest tradesman met with! Young Jerry, dress yourself, my boy, and while I clean my boots keep a eye upon your mother now and then, and if you see any signs of more flopping, give me a call. For, I tell you," here he addressed his wife once more, "I won't be gone agin, in this manner. I won't put up with it, Aggerawayter, and what do you say now!"

Growling, in addition, such phrases as, "Ah! yes! You're religious, too. You wouldn't put yourself in opposition to the interests of your husband and child, would you? Not you!" and throwing off other sarcastic sparks from the whirling grindstone of his indignation, Mr. Cruncher betook himself to his boot cleaning and his general preparation for business. In the meantime, his son, whose head was garnished with tenderer spikes, and whose young eyes stood close by one another, as his father's did, kept the required watch upon his mother. He greatly disturbed that poor woman at intervals, by darting out of his sleeping closet with a suppressed cry of, "You are going to flop, mother. Halloa, father!" and, after raising this fictitious alarm, darting in again with an undutiful grin.

Mr. Cruncher's temper was not at all improved when he came to his breakfast. He resented Mrs. Cruncher's saying grace with particular animosity. "Now, Aggerawayter! What are you up to? At it agin?"

His wife explained that she had merely "asked a blessing."

"Don't do it!" said Mr. Cruncher, looking about, as if he rather expected to see the loaf disappear under the efficacy of his wife's petitions. "I ain't a-going to be blest out of house and home. I won't have my wittles blest off my table. Keep still!"

Exceedingly red-eyed and grim, as if he had been up all night at a party which had taken anything but a convivial turn, Jerry Cruncher worried his breakfast rather than ate it, growling over it like any four-footed inmate of a menagerie. Toward nine o'clock he smoothed his ruffled aspect, and presenting as respectful and businesslike an exterior as he could overlay his natural self with, issued forth to the occupation of the day.

It could scarcely be called a trade, in spite of his favorite description of himself as "a honest tradesman." His stock consisted of a wooden stool, made out of a broken-backed chair cut down, which stool young Jerry, walking at his father's side, carried every morning to beneath the banking-house window that was nearest Temple Bar; where, with the addition of the first handful of straw that could be gleaned from any passing vehicle to keep the cold and wet from the odd-job man's feet, it formed the encampment for the day. On this post of his, Mr. Cruncher was as well known to Fleet Street, and the Temple, as the Bar itself—and was almost as ill-looking.

Encamped at a quarter before nine, in good time to touch his three-cornered hat to the oldest men as they passed in to Tellson's, Jerry took up his station on this windy March morning, with young Jerry standing by him. Father and son, extremely like each other, looking silently on at the morning traffic in Fleet Street, with their two heads as near to one another as the two eyes of each were, bore a considerable resemblance to a pair of monkeys.

The head of one of the regular indoor messengers attached to Tellson's establishment was put through the door, and the word was given:

"Porter wanted!"

"Hooray, father! Here's an early job to begin with!"

Having thus given his parent God speed, young Jerry seated himself on the stool and cogitated.

"Always rusty! His fingers is always rusty!" muttered young Jerry. "Where does my father get all that iron rust from? He don't get no iron rust here!"

CHAPTER II
A SIGHT

"You know the Old Bailey[1] well, no doubt?" said one of the oldest of clerks to Jerry, the messenger.

"Ye-es, sir," returned Jerry, in something of a dogged manner. "I *do* know the Bailey."

"Just so. And you know Mr. Lorry."

"I know Mr. Lorry, sir, much better than I know the Bailey. Much better," said Jerry, not unlike a reluctant witness at the establishment in question, "than I, as a honest tradesman, wish to know the Bailey."

"Very well. Find the door where the witnesses go in, and show the doorkeeper this note for Mr. Lorry. He will then let you in."

"Into the court, sir?"

"Into the court."

"Am I to wait in the court, sir?"

"I am going to tell you. The doorkeeper will pass the note to Mr. Lorry, and you make any gesture that will attract Mr. Lorry's attention and show him where you stand."

"Is that all, sir?"

"That's all. He wishes to have a messenger at hand. This is to tell him you are there."

As the ancient clerk deliberately folded and superscribed the note, Mr. Cruncher remarked:

"I suppose they'll be trying forgeries this morning?"

"Treason!"

"That's quartering," said Jerry. "Barbarous!"

"It is the law," remarked the ancient clerk, turning his surprised spectacles upon him. "It is the law."

"It's hard in the law to spile a man, I think. It's hard enough to kill him, but it's wery hard to spile him, sir."

"Not at all," returned the ancient clerk. "Speak well of the law. Take care of your chest and voice, my good friend, and leave the law to take care of itself."

"It's the damp, sir, what settles on my chest," said Jerry. "A damp way of earning a living mine is."

"Well," said the old clerk, "we all have our various ways of gaining a livelihood. Some of us have damp ways, and some of us have dry ways. Here is the letter. Go along." Jerry took the letter, and with the skill of a man accustomed to make his way quietly, found the door he sought and handed in his letter through a trap in it. After some delay and demur, the door grudgingly turned on its hinges a very little way and allowed Mr. Jerry Cruncher to squeeze himself into court.

"What's on?" he asked, in a whisper, of the man he found himself next to.

"The treason case."

"The quartering one, eh?"

"Ah!" returned the man, with a relish; "he'll be drawn on a hurdle to be half hanged, and then he'll be taken down and sliced before his own face, and then his inside will be taken out and burnt while he looks on, and then his head

1. ***Old Bailey,*** the chief court in London for trying criminal cases.

will be chopped off, and he'll be cut into quarters. That's the sentence."

"If he's found guilty, you mean to say?" Jerry added, by way of proviso.

"Oh! they'll find him guilty," said the other. "Don't you be afraid of that."

Mr. Cruncher's attention was here diverted to the doorkeeper, whom he saw making his way to Mr. Lorry, with the note in his hand. Mr. Lorry sat at a table, among the gentlemen in wigs; not far from a wigged gentleman, the prisoner's counsel, who had a great bundle of papers before him, and nearly opposite another wigged gentleman with his hands in his pockets, whose whole attention, when Mr. Cruncher looked at him then or afterwards, seemed to be concentrated on the ceiling of the court. After some gruff coughing and rubbing of his chin and signing with his hand, Jerry attracted the notice of Mr. Lorry, who had stood up to look for him, and who quietly nodded and sat down again.

The entrance of the judge, and a consequent great stir and settling down in the court, stopped the dialogue. Presently, the dock became the central point of interest. Two jailers, who had been standing there, went out, and the prisoner was brought in and put to the bar.

Everybody present, except the one wigged gentleman who looked at the ceiling, stared at him. Eager faces strained round pillars and corners to get a sight of him; spectators stood a-tiptoe, got upon ledges, stood upon next to nothing, to see every inch of him. Conspicuous among these latter, like an animated bit of the spiked wall of Newgate,[2] Jerry stood.

The object of all this staring was a young man of about five-and-twenty, well-grown and well-looking, with a sunburnt cheek and a dark eye. He was plainly dressed in black or very dark gray, and his hair, which was long and dark, was gathered in a ribbon at the back of his neck; more to be out of his way than for ornament. He was quite self-possessed, bowed to the judge, and stood quiet.

Silence in the court! Charles Darnay had yesterday pleaded Not Guilty to an indictment denouncing him—with infinite jingle and jangle—for that he was a false traitor to our serene, illustrious, excellent, and so forth, prince, our Lord the King, by reason of his having, on divers occasions, and by divers means and ways, assisted Lewis, the French King, in his wars against our said serene, illustrious, excellent, and so forth; that was to say, by coming and going, between the dominions of our said serene, illustrious, excellent, and so forth, and those of the said French Lewis, and wickedly, falsely, traitorously, and otherwise evil-adverbiously, revealing to the said French Lewis what forces our said serene, illustrious, excellent, and so forth, had in preparation to send to Canada and North America. Jerry, with his head becoming more and more spiky as the law terms bristled it, made out that the aforesaid, Charles Darnay, stood there before him; that the jury were swearing in, and that Mr. Attorney General was making ready to speak.

The accused, who was—and who knew he was—being mentally hanged, beheaded, and quartered by everybody there, neither flinched from the situation nor assumed any theatrical air in it. He was quiet and attentive; watched the opening proceedings with a grave interest; and stood with his hands resting on the slab of wood before him, so composedly that they had not displaced a leaf of the herbs with which it was strewn as a precaution against jail air and jail fever.

Over the prisoner's head there was a mirror, to throw the light down upon him. He looked up and when he saw the glass his face flushed, and his right hand pushed the herbs away.

About on a level with his eyes, there sat two persons upon whom his look immediately rested; so immediately, all the eyes that were turned upon him, turned to them.

The spectators saw in the two figures a young lady of little more than twenty and a gentleman who was evidently her father; a man of very remarkable appearance in respect of the

---

2. ***Newgate,*** a famous London prison, near the Old Bailey.

absolute whiteness of his hair, and a certain indescribable intensity of face; a handsome man, not past the prime of life.

His daughter had one of her hands drawn through his arm, as she sat by him, and the other pressed upon it. She had drawn close to him, in her dread of the scene, and in her pity for the prisoner. This had been so very noticeable, so very powerfully and naturally shown, that starers who had had no pity for him were touched by her; and the whisper went about, "Who are they?"

"Witnesses."

"For which side?"

"Against."

"Against what side?"

"The prisoner's."

The judge, whose eyes had gone in the general direction, recalled them, leaned back in his seat, and looked steadily at the man whose life was in his hand, as Mr. Attorney General rose to spin the rope, grind the ax, and hammer the nails into the scaffold.

CHAPTER III
A DISAPPOINTMENT

Mr. Attorney General had to inform the jury that the prisoner before them, though young in years, was old in the treasonable practices which claimed the forfeit of his life. That this correspondence with the public enemy was not a correspondence of today, or of yesterday, or even of last year, or of the year before. That it was certain the prisoner had, for longer than that, been in the habit of passing and repassing between France and England, on secret business of which he could give no honest account. That, if it were in the nature of traitorous ways to thrive—which happily it never was—the real wickedness and guilt of his business might have remained undiscovered. That Providence, however, had put it into the heart of a person who was beyond fear and beyond reproach to ferret out the nature of the prisoner's schemes, and, struck with horror, to disclose them to his Majesty's Chief Secretary of State and most honorable Privy Council.[1] That this patriot would be produced before them. That his position and attitude were, on the whole, sublime. That he had been the prisoner's friend, but, at once in an auspicious and an evil hour detecting his infamy, had resolved to immolate the traitor he could no longer cherish in his bosom, on the sacred altar of his country. That, if statues were decreed in Britain, as in ancient Greece and Rome, to public benefactors, this shining citizen would assuredly have had one. That, as they were not so decreed, he probably would not have one. That Virtue, as had been observed by the poets—in many passages which he well knew the jury would have at the tips of their tongues, whereat the jury's countenances displayed a guilty consciousness that they knew nothing about the passages—was in a manner contagious; more especially the bright virtue known as patriotism, or love of country. That the lofty example of this immaculate and unimpeachable witness for the Crown had communicated itself to the prisoner's servant, and engendered in him a holy determination to examine his master's table drawers and pockets, and secrete his papers. That he (Mr. Attorney General) was prepared to hear some disparagement attempted of this admirable servant; but that, in a general way, he preferred him to his (Mr. Attorney General's) brothers and sisters, and honored him more than his (Mr. Attorney General's) father and mother. That he called with confidence on the jury to come and do likewise. That the evidence of these two witnesses, coupled with the documents of their discovering that would be produced, would show the prisoner to have been furnished with lists of his Majesty's forces, and of their disposition and preparation, both by sea and land, and would leave no doubt that he had habitually conveyed such information to a hostile power. That these lists could not be proved to be in the prisoner's

1. ***Privy Council,*** a group of counselors selected by the King of England to advise him in matters of state.

handwriting; but that it was all the same; that, indeed, it was rather the better for the prosecution, as showing the prisoner to be artful in his precautions. That the proof would go back five years, and would show the prisoner already engaged in these pernicious missions, within a few weeks before the date of the very first action fought between the British troops and the Americans. That, for these reasons, the jury, being a loyal jury (as he knew they were), and being a responsible jury (as *they* knew they were), must positively find the prisoner guilty, and make an end of him, whether they liked it or not. That they never could lay their heads upon their pillows; that they never could tolerate the idea of their wives laying their heads upon their pillows; that they never could endure the notion of their children laying their heads upon their pillows: in short, that there never more could be, for them or theirs, any laying of heads upon pillows at all, unless the prisoner's head was taken off. That head Mr. Attorney General concluded by demanding of them, in the name of everything he could think of with a round turn in it, and on the faith of his solemn asseveration that he already considered the prisoner as good as dead and gone.

When the Attorney General ceased, a buzz arose in the court as if a cloud of great blueflies were swarming about the prisoner, in anticipation of what he was soon to become. When toned down again, the unimpeachable patriot appeared in the witness box.

Mr. Solicitor General then, following his leader's lead, examined the patriot, John Barsad, gentleman. The story of his pure soul was exactly what Mr. Attorney General had described it to be—perhaps, if it had a fault, a little too exactly. Having released his noble bosom of its burden, he would have modestly withdrawn himself, but that the wigged gentleman with the papers before him, sitting not far from Mr. Lorry, begged to ask him a few questions. The wigged gentleman sitting opposite, still looking at the ceiling of the court.

Had he ever been a spy himself? No, he scorned the base insinuation. What did he live upon? His property. Where was his property? He didn't precisely remember where it was. What was it? No business of anybody's. Had he inherited it? Yes, he had. From whom? Distant relation. Very distant? Rather. Ever been in prison? Certainly not. Never in a debtors' prison? Didn't see what that had to do with it. Never in a debtors' prison?—Come, once again. Never? Yes. How many times? Two or three times. Not five or six? Perhaps. Of what profession? Gentleman. Ever been kicked? Might have been. Frequently? No. Ever kicked downstairs? Decidedly not; once received a kick on the top of a staircase, and fell downstairs. Kicked on that occasion for cheating at dice? Something to that effect was said by the intoxicated liar who committed the assault, but it was not true. Swear it was not true? Positively. Ever live by cheating at play? Never. Ever live by play? Not more than other gentlemen do. Ever borrow money of the prisoner? Yes. Ever pay him? No. Was not this intimacy with the prisoner, in reality a very slight one, forced upon the prisoner in coaches, inns, and packets? No. Sure he saw the prisoner with these lists? Certain. Knew no more about the lists? No. Had not procured them himself, for instance? No. Expect to get anything by this evidence? No. Not in regular government pay and employment, to lay traps? Oh, dear no. Or to do anything? Oh, dear no. Swear that? Over and over again. No motives but motives of sheer patriotism? None whatever.

The virtuous servant, Roger Cly, swore his way through the case at a great rate. He had taken service with the prisoner four years ago. He had asked the prisoner, aboard the Calais packet, if he wanted a handy fellow, and the prisoner had engaged him. He had not asked the prisoner to take the handy fellow as an act of charity—never thought of such a thing. He began to have suspicions of the prisoner soon afterwards. In arranging his clothes he had seen similar lists to these in the prisoner's pockets, over and over again. He had taken these lists from the drawer of the prisoner's desk. He had not put them there first. He had seen the prisoner show these identical lists to French gentlemen of Calais, and similar lists to French gentlemen, both at Calais and Boulogne.[2] He loved his country, and couldn't bear it, and had given information. He had never been suspected of stealing a silver teapot; he had been maligned respecting a mustard-pot, but it turned out to be only a plated one. He had known the last witness seven or eight years; that was merely a coincidence. He didn't call it a particularly curious coincidence; most coincidences were curious. Neither did he call it a curious coincidence that true patriotism was *his* only motive too. He was a true Briton, and hoped there were many like him.

The blueflies buzzed again, and Mr. Attorney General called Mr. Jarvis Lorry.

"Mr. Jarvis Lorry, are you a clerk in Tellson's Bank?"

"I am."

"On a certain Friday night in November one thousand seven hundred and seventy-five, did business occasion you to travel between London and Dover by the mail?"

"It did."

"Were there any other passengers in the mail?"

"Two."

"Mr. Lorry, look upon the prisoner. Was he one of those two passengers?"

"I cannot undertake to say that he was."

"Does he resemble either of these two passengers?"

"Both were so wrapped up, and the night was so dark, and we were all so reserved that I cannot undertake to say even that."

"Mr. Lorry, look again upon the prisoner. Supposing him wrapped up as those two passengers were, is there anything to render it unlikely that he was one of them?"

"No."

"You will not swear, Mr. Lorry, that he was not one of them?"

"No."

"So at least you say he may have been one of them?"

"Yes. Except that I remember them both to have been—like myself—timorous of highwaymen, and the prisoner has not a timorous air."

"Did you ever see a counterfeit of timidity, Mr. Lorry?"

"I certainly have seen that."

"Mr. Lorry, look once more upon the prisoner. Have you seen him, to your certain knowledge, before?"

"I have."

"When?"

"I was returning from France a few days afterwards, and, at Calais, the prisoner came on board the packet ship in which I returned, and made the voyage with me."

"At what hour did he come on board?"

"At a little after midnight."

"In the dead of the night. Was he the only passenger who came on board at that untimely hour?"

"He happened to be the only one."

"Never mind about 'happening,' Mr. Lorry. He was the only passenger who came on board in the dead of the night?"

"He was."

"Were you traveling with any companion?"

"With two companions. A gentleman and lady. They are here."

"Had you any conversation with the prisoner?"

"Hardly any. The weather was stormy, and the passage rough, and I lay on a sofa, almost from shore to shore."

"Miss Manette!"

The young lady, to whom all eyes had turned before, and now turned again, stood up. Her father rose with her, and kept her hand drawn through his arm.

"Miss Manette, look upon the prisoner."

To be confronted with such pity, and such earnest youth and beauty, was far more trying to the accused than to be confronted with the

---

2. ***Boulogne*** (bü lōn′), a seaport in northern France.

crowd. His efforts to control and steady his breathing shook the lips from which the color rushed to his heart. The buzz of the great flies was loud again.

"Miss Manette, have you seen the prisoner before?"

"Yes, sir."

"Where?"

"On board of the packet ship just now referred to, sir, and on the same occasion."

"You are the young lady just now referred to?"

"Oh! most unhappily, I am!"

The plaintive tone of her compassion merged into the less musical voice of the judge, as he said fiercely: "Answer the questions put to you, and make no remark upon them."

"Miss Manette, had you any conversation with the prisoner on that passage across the Channel?"

"Yes, sir."

"Recall it."

In the midst of a profound stillness, she faintly began:

"When the gentleman came on board——"

"Do you mean the prisoner?" inquired the judge, knitting his brows.

"Yes, my Lord."

"Then say the prisoner."

"When the prisoner came on board, he noticed that my father," turning her eyes lovingly to him, "was in a very weak state of health. My father was so reduced that I was afraid to take him out of the air; I had made a bed for him on the deck near the cabin steps, and I sat at his side to take care of him. There were no other passengers that night but we four. The prisoner was so good as to advise me how I could shelter my father from the wind and weather, better than I had done. I had not known how to do it well, not understanding how the wind would set when we were out of the harbor. He did it for me. He expressed great gentleness and kindness for my father's state, and I am sure he felt it. That was the manner of our beginning to speak together."

"Let me interrupt you for a moment. Had he come on board alone?"

"No."

"How many were with him?"

"Two French gentlemen."

"Had they conferred together?"

"They had conferred together until it was necessary for the French gentlemen to be landed in their boat."

"Had any papers been handed about among them, similar to these lists?"

"Some papers had been handed about among them, but I don't know what papers."

"Like these in shape and size?"

"Possibly, but indeed I don't know: they stood at the top of the cabin steps to have the light of the lamp that was hanging there; it was a dull lamp, and they spoke very low, and I did not hear what they said, and saw only that they looked at papers."

"Now, to the prisoner's conversation, Miss Manette."

"The prisoner was as open in his confidence with me—which arose out of my helpless situation—as he was kind, and good, and useful to my father. I hope," bursting into tears, "I may not repay him by doing him harm today."

Buzzing from the blueflies.

"Miss Manette, if the prisoner does not perfectly understand that you give the evidence which you cannot escape giving with great unwillingness, he is the only person present in that condition. Please go on."

"He told me that he was traveling on business of a delicate and difficult nature, which might get people into trouble and that he was therefore traveling under an assumed name. He said that this business had taken him to France, and might take him backwards and forwards between France and England for a long time to come."

"Did he say anything about America, Miss Manette? Be particular."

"He tried to explain to me how that quarrel had arisen, and he said that, so far as he could judge, it was a wrong and foolish one on England's part. He added, in a jesting way, that perhaps George Washington might gain almost as great a name in history as George the Third. But there was no harm in his way of saying this; it was said laughingly and to beguile the time."

The judge looked up from his notes to glare at the tremendous heresy about George Washington. Mr. Attorney General now signified to my Lord that he deemed it necessary to call the young lady's father, Doctor Manette.

"Doctor Manette, look upon the prisoner. Have you ever seen him before?"

"Once. When he called at my lodgings in London. Some three years ago."

"Can you identify him as your fellow passenger on board the packet, or speak to his conversation with your daughter?"

"Sir, I can do neither."

"Is there any particular and special reason for your being unable to do either?"

He answered, in a low voice, "There is."

"Has it been your misfortune to undergo a long imprisonment, without trial, or even accusation, in your native country, Doctor Manette?"

He answered in a tone that went to every heart, "A long imprisonment."

"Were you newly released on the occasion in question?"

"They tell me so."

"Have you no remembrance of the occasion?"

"None. My mind is a blank, from some time—I cannot even say what time—when I employed myself, in my captivity, in making shoes, to the time when I found myself living in London with my dear daughter here. She had become familiar to me, when a gracious God restored my faculties; but, I am quite unable to say how she had become familiar. I have no remembrance of the process."

Mr. Attorney General sat down, and the father and daughter sat down together.

A singular circumstance then arose in the case. The object in hand being to show that the prisoner went down, with some fellow plotter untracked, in the Dover mail on that Friday night in November five years ago, and got out of the mail in the night, as a blind, at a place where he did not remain, but from which he traveled back some dozen miles or more, to a garrison and dockyard, and there collected information; a witness was called to identify him as having been at the precise time required, in the coffee room of an hotel in that garrison-and-dockyard town, waiting for another person. The prisoner's counsel was cross-examining this witness with no result when the wigged gentleman who had all this time been looking at the ceiling of the court, wrote a word or two on a little piece of paper, screwed it up, and tossed it to him. Opening this piece of paper in the next pause, the counsel looked with great attention and curiosity at the prisoner.

"You say again you are quite sure that it *was* the prisoner?"

The witness was quite sure.

"Did you ever see anybody very like the prisoner?"

Not so like, the witness said, as that he could be mistaken.

"Look well upon that gentleman, my learned friend there," pointing to him who had tossed the paper over, "and then look well upon the prisoner. How say you? Are they very like each other?"

Allowing for my learned friend's appearance being careless and slovenly if not debauched, they were sufficiently like each other to surprise, not only the witness, but everybody present, when they were thus brought into comparison. My Lord being prayed to bid my learned friend lay aside his wig, and giving no very gracious consent, the likeness became much more remarkable. My Lord inquired of Mr. Stryver (the prisoner's counsel) whether they were next to try Mr. Carton (name of my learned friend) for treason? But, Mr. Stryver replied to my Lord, no; but he would ask the witness to tell him whether what happened once might happen twice; whether he would have been so confident if he had seen this illustration of his rashness sooner, whether he would be so confident, having seen it, and more. The upshot of which was to smash this witness like a crockery vessel, and shiver his part of the case to useless lumber.

Mr. Stryver now fitted the prisoner's case on the jury, like a compact suit of clothes, showing them how the patriot, Barsad, was a hired spy and traitor, one of the greatest scoundrels upon earth since accursed Judas. How the virtuous servant, Cly, was his friend and partner; how the watchful eyes of those forgers and false swearers had rested on the prisoner as a victim, because some family affairs in France, he being of French extraction, did require his making those passages across the Channel—though what those affairs were, a consideration for others who were near and dear to him forbade him, even for his life, to disclose. How the evidence that had been warped and wrested from the young lady, whose anguish in giving it they had witnessed, came to nothing, involving the mere little innocent gallantries and politenesses likely to pass between any young gentleman and young lady so thrown together—with the exception of that reference to George Washington, which was altogether too extravagant and impossible to be regarded in any other light than as a monstrous joke.

Mr. Stryver then called his few witnesses, and Mr. Cruncher had next to attend while Mr. Attorney General turned the whole suit of clothes Mr. Stryver had fitted on the jury inside out; showing how Barsad and Cly were even a hundred times better than he had thought them, and the prisoner a hundred times worse. Lastly, came my Lord himself, turning the suit of clothes, now inside out, now outside in, but on the whole decidedly trimming and shaping them into grave clothes for the prisoner.

And now, the jury turned to consider, and the great flies swarmed again.

Mr. Carton, who had so long sat looking at the ceiling of the court, changed neither his place nor his attitude, even in this excitement. While his learned friend, Mr. Stryver, whispered with those who sat near, and from time to time glanced anxiously at the jury; while all the spectators moved more or less, and grouped themselves anew; while even my Lord himself arose from his seat, and slowly paced up and down his platform; this one man sat leaning back, with his torn gown half off him, his untidy wig put on just as it had happened to light on his head after its removal, his hands in his pockets, and his eyes on the ceiling as they had been all day. Something especially reckless in his demeanor not only gave him a disreputable look, but so diminished the strong resemblance he undoubtedly bore to the prisoner that many of the lookers-on, taking note of him now, said to one another they would hardly have thought the two were so alike.

Yet this Mr. Carton took in more of the details of the scene than he appeared to take in; for now, when Miss Manette's head dropped upon her father's breast, he was the first to see it, and to say audibly: "Officer! Look to that young lady. Help the gentleman to take her out. Don't you see she will fall!"

There was much commiseration for her as she was removed, and much sympathy with her father. It had evidently been a great distress to him to have the days of his imprisonment recalled. He had shown strong internal agitation when he was questioned, and that pondering or brooding look which made him old had been upon him, like a heavy cloud, ever since. As he passed out, the jury, who had turned back, spoke, through their foreman.

They were not agreed and wished to retire. My Lord—perhaps with George Washington on his mind—showed some surprise that they were not agreed, but signified his pleasure that they should retire under watch and ward, and retired himself. The trial had lasted all day, and the lamps in the court were now being lighted. It began to be rumored that the jury would be out a long while. The spectators dropped off to get refreshment, and the prisoner withdrew to the back of the dock and sat down.

Mr. Lorry, who had gone out when the young lady and her father went out, now reappeared, and beckoned to Jerry, who in the slackened interest, could easily get near him.

"Jerry, if you wish to take something to eat, you can. You will be sure to hear when the jury come in. Don't be a moment behind them, for I want you to take the verdict back to the bank. You are the quickest messenger I know, and will get to Temple Bar long before I can."

Mr. Carton came up at the moment, and touched Mr. Lorry on the arm.

"How is the young lady?"

"She is greatly distressed; but her father is comforting her, and she feels the better for being out of court."

"I'll tell the prisoner so." Mr. Carton made his way to the outside of the bar.

"Mr. Darnay!"

The prisoner came forward directly.

"You will naturally be anxious to hear of the witness, Miss Manette. She will do very well. You have seen the worst of her agitation."

"I am deeply sorry to have been the cause of it. Could you tell her so for me?"

"Yes, I could. I will, if you ask it."

"I do ask it. Accept my cordial thanks."

"What," said Carton, still only half-turned towards him, "do you expect, Mr. Darnay?"

"The worst."

"It's the wisest thing to expect, and the likeliest. But I think their withdrawing is in your favor."

An hour and a half limped heavily away. The hoarse messenger had dropped into a doze, when a loud murmur and a rapid tide of people setting up the stairs that led to the court, carried him along with them.

"Jerry! Jerry!" Mr. Lorry was already calling at the door when he got there.

"Here, sir! Here I am, sir!"

Mr. Lorry handed him a paper through the throng. "Quick! Have you got it?"

"Yes, sir."

Hastily written on the paper was the word ACQUITTED."

"If you had sent the message, 'Recalled to Life,' again," muttered Jerry as he turned, "I should have known what you meant this time."

He had no opportunity of saying, or so much as thinking, anything else, until he was clear of the Old Bailey; for the crowd came pouring out with a vehemence that nearly took him off his legs, and a loud buzz swept into the street as if the baffled blueflies were dispersing in search of other carrion.

Discussion

Chapter I

1. In what way is the narrator's description of Tellson's Bank both humorous and ironic?

2. (a) What is Jerry Cruncher's attitude toward his wife's praying? **(b)** Why might she be praying for Jerry? **(c)** What other clues arouse your suspicion about Jerry's claim to being an "honest tradesman"? (Also, review Jerry's comments to himself in Chapters II and III, Book the First.)

Chapter II

1. (a) What is the defendant's name? **(b)** What is the charge against him? **(c)** If he is found guilty, what will be his punishment?

2. In the late eighteenth century, people attended trials in the same way that we go to the movies—for entertainment. **(a)** What is the atmosphere in the courtroom? Comment on the attitudes of the spectators, the judge, and Mr. Attorney General. **(b)** Does the final sentence of the chapter make you feel optimistic or pessimistic about the defendant's chances?

Chapter III

1. (a) Who are the first two witnesses against Darnay? **(b)** Considering the testimony of these two witnesses, how strong would you judge the prosecution's case to be? **(c)** Who are the two wigged gentlemen, the one who defends the accused and the other who stares at the ceiling? **(d)** How does the defense attorney manage to discredit the two witnesses?

2. Several times throughout the description of the trial, the narrator refers to the "buzzing of blue flies." What idea does he convey with this figurative expression?

3. What coincidence saves the prisoner's life?

4. Although the prisoner is acquitted, Dickens has titled this chapter "A Disappointment." Why?

CHAPTER IV
CONGRATULATORY

From the dimly lighted passages of the court, the last sediment of the human stew that had been boiling there all day was straining off, when Doctor Manette, Lucie Manette, Mr. Lorry, the solicitor for the defense, and its counsel, Mr. Stryver, stood gathered around Mr. Charles Darnay—just released—congratulating him on his escape from death.

It would have been difficult by a far brighter light to recognize in Doctor Manette, intellectual of face and upright of bearing, the shoemaker of the garret in Paris. Yet no one could have looked at him twice without looking again, even though the opportunity of observation had not extended to the mournful cadence of his low, grave voice, and to the abstraction that overclouded him fitfully, without any apparent reason. While one external cause, and that a reference to his long lingering agony, would always—as on the trial—evoke this condition from the depths of his soul, it was also in its nature to arise of itself, and to draw a gloom over him, as incomprehensible to those unacquainted with his story as if they had seen the shadow of the actual Bastille[1] thrown upon him by a summer sun, when the substance was three hundred miles away.

Only his daughter had the power of charming this black brooding from his mind. She was the golden thread that united him to a Past beyond his misery, and to a Present beyond his misery; and the sound of her voice, the light of her face, the touch of her hand, had a strong beneficial influence with him almost always. Not absolutely always, for she could recall some occasions on which her power had failed; but they were few and slight, and she believed them over.

Mr. Darnay had kissed her hand fervently and gratefully, and had turned to Mr. Stryver, whom he warmly thanked.

Mr. Stryver, a man of little more than thirty but looking twenty years older than he was, stout, loud, red, bluff, and free from any drawback of delicacy, had a pushing way of shouldering himself, morally and physically, into companies and conversations, that argued well for his shouldering his way up in life.

He still had his wig and gown on, and he said, squaring himself at his late client to that degree that he squeezed the innocent Mr. Lorry clean out of the group: "I am glad to have

1. ***Bastille*** (ba stēl′), an old fortress in Paris used as a prison especially for political offenders. Destroyed on July 14, 1789, the beginning of the French Revolution, the word *bastille* has come to mean any prison.

brought you off with honor, Mr. Darnay. It was an infamous prosecution, grossly infamous; but not the less likely to succeed on that account."

"You have laid me under an obligation to you for life—in two senses," said his late client, taking his hand.

"I have done my best for you, Mr. Darnay; and my best is as good as another man's, I believe."

It clearly being incumbent on someone to say, "Much better," Mr. Lorry said it—perhaps not quite disinterestedly, but with the interested object of squeezing himself back again.

"You think so?" said Mr. Stryver. "Well! you have been present all day and you ought to know. You are a man of business, too."

"And as such," quoth Mr. Lorry, whom the counsel learned in the law had now shouldered back into the group, just as he had previously shouldered him out of it, "as such I will appeal to Doctor Manette, to break up this conference and order us all to our homes. Miss Lucie looks ill, Mr. Darnay has had a terrible day, we are worn out."

"Speak for yourself, Mr. Lorry," said Stryver; "I have a night's work to do yet. Speak for yourself."

"I speak for myself," answered Mr. Lorry, "and for Mr. Darnay, and for Miss Lucie, and—Miss Lucie, do you not think I may speak for us all?" He asked her the question pointedly, and with a glance at her father.

His face had become frozen, as it were, in a very curious look at Darnay; an intent look, deepening into a frown of dislike and distrust, not even unmixed with fear. With this strange expression on him his thoughts had wandered away.

"My father," said Lucie, softly laying her hand on his.

He slowly shook the shadow off, and turned to her.

"Shall we go home, my father?"

With a long breath, he answered, "Yes."

Mr. Stryver had left them in the passages, to shoulder his way back to the robing room. Another person, who had not joined the group, or interchanged a word with any one of them, but who had been leaning against the wall where its shadow was darkest, had silently strolled out after the rest, and had looked on until the coach drove away. He now stepped up to where Mr. Lorry and Mr. Darnay stood upon the pavement.

"So, Mr. Lorry! Men of business may speak to Mr. Darnay now?"

Nobody had made any acknowledgment of Mr. Carton's part in the day's proceedings; nobody had known of it. He was unrobed and was none the better for it in appearance.

"If you knew what a conflict goes on in the business mind when the business mind is divided between good-natured impulse and business appearances, you would be amused, Mr. Darnay."

Mr. Lorry reddened and said warmly, "You have mentioned that before, sir. We men of business who serve a House are not our own masters. We have to think of the House more than ourselves."

"*I* know, *I* know," rejoined Mr. Carton, carelessly. "Don't be nettled, Mr. Lorry. You are as good as another, I have no doubt; better, I dare say."

"And indeed, sir," pursued Mr. Lorry, not minding him, "I really don't know what you have to do with the matter. If you'll excuse me, as very much your elder, for saying so, I really don't know that it is your business."

"Business! Bless you, *I* have no business," said Mr. Carton.

"It is a pity you have not, sir."

"I think so, too."

"If you had," pursued Mr. Lorry, "perhaps you would attend to it."

"Lord love you, no!—I shouldn't," said Mr. Carton.

"Well, sir!" cried Mr. Lorry, thoroughly heated by his indifference, "business is a very good thing, and a very respectable thing. And, sir, if business imposes its restraints and its silences and impediments, Mr. Darnay as a young gentleman of generosity knows how to make allowance for that circumstance. Mr. Darnay, good night, God bless you, sir! I hope you have been this day preserved for a prosperous and happy life—Chair there!"

Perhaps a little angry with himself, as well as with the barrister, Mr. Lorry bustled into the chair, and was carried off to Tellson's. Carton, who smelt of port wine, and did not appear to be quite sober, laughed then, and turned to Darnay:

"This is a strange chance that throws you and me together. This must be a strange night to you, standing alone here with your counterpart on these street stones?"

"I hardly seem yet," returned Charles Darnay, "to belong to this world again."

"I don't wonder at it; it's not so long since you were pretty far advanced on your way to another. You speak faintly."

"I begin to think I *am* faint."

"Then why the devil don't you dine? I dined, myself, while those numskulls were deliberating which world you should belong to—this, or some other. Let me show you the nearest tavern to dine well at."

Drawing his arm through his own, he took him down Ludgate Hill to Fleet Street, and so, up a covered way, into a tavern. Here they were shown into a little room, where Charles Darnay was soon recruiting his strength with a good plain dinner and good wine; while Carton sat opposite to him at the same table, with his separate bottle of port before him, and his fully half-insolent manner upon him.

"Do you feel yet that you belong to this terrestrial scheme again, Mr. Darnay?"

"I am frightfully confused regarding time and place; but I am so far mended as to feel that."

"It must be an immense satisfaction!"

He said it bitterly, and filled up his glass again, which was a large one.

"As to me, the greatest desire I have is to forget that I belong to it. It has no good in it for me—except wine like this—nor I for it. So we are not much alike in that particular. Indeed, I begin to think we are not much alike in any particular, you and I."

Confused by the emotion of the day and feeling his being there with this double of coarse deportment to be like a dream, Charles Darnay was at a loss how to answer; finally, answered not at all.

"Now your dinner is done," Carton presently said, "why don't you call a health, Mr. Darnay; why don't you give your toast?"

"What health? What toast?"

"Why, it's on the tip of your tongue. It ought to be, it must be, I'll swear it's there."

"Miss Manette, then!"

Looking his companion full in the face while he drank the toast, Carton flung his glass over his shoulder against the wall, where it shivered to pieces; then rang the bell, and ordered in another.

"That's a fair young lady to hand to a coach in the dark, Mr. Darnay!" he said, filling his new goblet.

A slight frown and a laconic "Yes" were the answer.

"That's a fair young lady to be pitied by and wept for by! How does it feel? Is is worth being tried for one's life, to be the object of such sympathy and compassion, Mr. Darnay?"

Again Darnay answered not a word.

"She was mightily pleased to have your message, when I gave it her. Not that she showed she was pleased, but I suppose she was."

The allusion served as a timely reminder to Darnay that this disagreeable companion, had, of his own free will, assisted him in the strait of the day. He turned the dialogue to that point, and thanked him for it.

"I neither want any thanks, nor merit any," was the careless rejoinder. "It was nothing to do, in the first place; and I don't know why I did it, in the second. Mr. Darnay, let me ask you a question."

"Willingly, and a small return for your good offices."

"Do you think I particularly like you?"

"Really, Mr. Carton," returned the other,

oddly disconcerted, "I have not asked myself that question."

"But ask yourself the question now."

"You have acted as if you do; but I don't think you do."

"*I* don't think I do," said Carton. "I begin to have a very good opinion of your understanding."

"Nevertheless," pursued Darnay, rising to ring the bell, "there is nothing in that, I hope, to prevent my calling the reckoning, and our parting without ill-blood on either side."

Carton rejoining, "Nothing in life!" Darnay rang. "Do you call the whole reckoning?" said Carton. On his answering in the affirmative, "Then bring me another pint of wine, drawer, and wake me at ten."

The bill being paid, Charles Darnay rose and wished him good night. Without returning the wish, Carton rose too, with something of a threat of defiance in his manner, and said, "A last word, Mr. Darnay: you think I am drunk?"

"I think you have been drinking, Mr. Carton."

"Think? You know I have been drinking."

"Since I must say so, I know it."

"Then you shall likewise know why. I am a disappointed drudge, sir. I care for no man on earth, and no man on earth cares for me."

"Much to be regretted. You might have used your talents better."

"Maybe so, Mr. Darnay; maybe not. Don't let your sober face elate you, however; you don't know what it may come to. Good night!"

When he was left alone, this strange being took up a candle, went to a glass that hung against the wall, and surveyed himself minutely in it.

"Do you particularly like the man?" he muttered, at his own image; "why should you particularly like a man who resembles you? There is nothing in you to like; you know that. Ah, confound you! What a change you have made in yourself! A good reason for taking to a man, that he shows you what you have fallen away from, and what you might have been! Change places with him, and would you have been looked at by those blue eyes as he was, and commiserated by that agitated face as he was? Come on, and have it out in plain words! You hate the fellow."

He resorted to his pint of wine for consolation, drank it all in a few minutes, and fell asleep on his arms, with his hair straggling over the table, and a long winding sheet in the candle dripping down upon him.

CHAPTER V
THE JACKAL

It had once been noted at the Bar that while Mr. Stryver was a glib man, and an unscrupulous, and a ready, and a bold, he had not that faculty of extracting the essence from a heap of statements, which is among the most striking and necessary of the advocate's accomplishments. But a remarkable improvement came upon him as to this. The more business he got, the greater his power seemed to grow of getting at its pith and marrow; and however late at night he sat carousing with Sydney Carton, he always had his points at his fingers' ends in the morning.

Sydney Carton, idlest and most unpromising of men, was Stryver's great ally. Stryver never had a case in hand anywhere but Carton was there, with his hands in his pockets, staring at the ceiling of the court; they went the same Circuit, and even there they prolonged their usual orgies late into the night, and Carton was rumored to be seen at broad day, going home stealthily and unsteadily to his lodgings, like a dissipated cat. At last it began to get about, among such as were interested in the matter, that although Sydney Carton would never be a lion, he was an amazing good jackal, and that he rendered suit and service to Stryver in that humble capacity.

"Ten o'clock, sir," said the man at the tavern, whom he had charged to wake him, "ten o'clock, sir."

"*What's* the matter?"

"Ten o'clock. sir."

"What do you mean? Ten o'clock at night?"

"Yes, sir. Your honor told me to call you."

"Oh! I remember. Very well, very well."

After a few dull efforts to get to sleep again, which the man dexterously combated by stirring the fire continuously for five minutes, he got up, tossed his hat on, and walked out. He turned into the Temple,[1] and having revived himself by twice pacing the pavements of King's Bench walk, turned into the Stryver chambers.

"You are a little late, Memory," said Stryver.

"About the usual time."

They went into a dingy room lined with books and littered with papers, where there was a blazing fire. A kettle steamed upon the hob, and in the midst of the wreck of papers a table shone, with plenty of wine upon it, and brandy, and rum, and sugar, and lemons.

"That was a rare point, Sydney, that you brought to bear upon the identification. How did you come by it?"

"I thought he was rather handsome, and I should have been much the same sort of fellow, if I had had any luck."

Mr. Stryver laughed till he shook his precocious paunch.

"You and your luck, Sydney! Get to work; get to work."

Sullenly enough, the jackal loosened his dress, went into an adjoining room, and came back with a large jug of cold water, a basin, and a towel or two. Steeping the towels in the water, and partially wringing them out, he folded them on his head in a manner hideous to behold, sat down at the table, and said, "Now I am ready!"

"Not much boiling down to be done tonight, Memory," said Mr. Stryver, gaily, as he looked among his papers.

"How much?"

"Only two sets of them."

"Give me the worst first."

"There they are, Sydney. Fire away!"

The lion then composed himself on his back on a sofa on one side of the drinking table, while the jackal sat at his own paper-bestrewn table proper, on the other side of it, with the bottles and glasses ready to his hand. Two or three times the matter in hand became so knotty that the jackal found it imperative to get up and steep his towels anew.

At length the jackal had got together a compact repast for the lion, and proceeded to offer it to him. The lion took it with care and caution, made his selections from it, and his remarks upon it, and the jackal assisted both. When the repast was fully discussed, the lion put his hands in his waistband and lay down to meditate. The jackal then applied himself to the collection of a second meal; this was administered to the lion in the same manner and not disposed of until three in the morning.

"And now we have done, Sydney, fill a bumper of punch," said Mr. Stryver.

The jackal removed the towels from his head, shook himself, yawned, shivered, and complied.

"You were very sound, Sydney, in the matter of those crown witnesses today. Every question told."

"I always am sound; am I not?"

"I don't gainsay it. What has roughened your temper? Put some punch to it and smooth it again."

With a deprecatory grunt, the jackal again complied.

"The old Sydney Carton of old Shrewsbury School," said Stryver, "the old seesaw Sydney."

"Ah!" returned the other, sighing. "Yes! The same Sydney, with the same luck. Even then I did exercises for other boys, and seldom did my own."

"And why not?"

"God knows. It was my way, I suppose."

"Carton," said his friend, "your way is, and

---

1. ***Temple,*** the lodge of the Knights Templars in London. At the time of the story and at present, the site is occupied by buildings belonging to English legal societies.

always was, a lame way. You summon no energy and purpose. Look at me."

"Oh, botheration!" returned Sydney, with a lighter and more good-humored laugh, "don't *you* be moral!"

"How have I done what I have done?" said Stryver. "How do I do what I do?"

"Partly through paying me to help you, I suppose. You were always in the front rank, and I always behind."

"And whose fault was that?"

"Upon my soul, I am not sure that it was not yours. It's a gloomy thing, however, to talk about one's past, with day breaking. Turn me in some other direction."

"Well then! Pledge me to the pretty witness," said Stryver, holding up his glass.

"Pretty witness," he muttered, "who's your pretty witness?"

"The picturesque doctor's daughter, Miss Manette."

"*She* pretty?"

"Why, man alive, she was the admiration of the whole Court!"

"Rot the admiration of the whole Court! Who made the Old Bailey a judge of beauty? She was a golden-haired doll!"

"Do you know, Sydney," said Mr. Stryver, looking at him with sharp eyes, "I rather thought, at the time, that you sympathized with the golden-haired doll, and were quick to see what happened to the golden-haired doll?"

"Quick to see what happened! If a girl, doll or no doll, swoons within a yard or two of a man's nose, he can see it. I pledge you, but I deny the beauty. And now I'll have no more drink; I'll get to bed."

When his host followed him out on the staircase with a candle to light him down the stairs, the day was coldly looking in through its grimy windows, the air was cold and sad, the dull sky overcast, the river dark and dim, the whole scene like a lifeless desert.

Waste forces within him and a desert all around, this man stood still on his way across a silent terrace and saw for a moment, lying in the wilderness before him, a mirage of honorable ambition, self-denial, and perseverance. A moment, and it was gone. Climbing to a high chamber in a well of houses, he threw himself down in his clothes on a neglected bed, and its pillow was wet with wasted tears.

Sadly, sadly, the sun rose; it rose upon no sadder sight than the man of good abilities and good emotions, incapable of their directed exercise, incapable of his own help and his own happiness, sensible of the blight on him, and resigning himself to let it eat him away.

CHAPTER VI
HUNDREDS OF PEOPLE

The quiet lodgings of Doctor Manette were in a quiet street corner not far from Soho Square. On the afternoon of a certain fine Sunday, when the waves of four months had rolled over the trial for treason, Mr. Jarvis Lorry walked along the sunny streets from Clerkenwell where he lived, on his way to dine with the Doctor. After several relapses into business absorption, Mr. Lorry had become the Doctor's friend, and the quiet street corner was the sunny part of his life.

A quainter corner was not to be found in London. The front windows commanded a pleasant little vista of street that had a congenial air of retirement. It was a cool spot, a wonderful place for echoes, a very harbor from the raging streets.

The Doctor occupied two floors of a large still house and received such patients here as his old reputation, and its revival in the floating whispers of his story, brought him. His scientific knowledge and his skill in conducting ingenious experiments brought him otherwise into moderate request, and he earned as much as he wanted.

These things were within Mr. Jarvis Lorry's thoughts when he rang the doorbell on the fine Sunday afternoon.

"Doctor Manette at home?"

Expected home.

"Miss Lucie at home?"

Expected home.

"As I am at home myself, I'll go upstairs."

There were three rooms on a floor and, the doors by which they communicated being put open that the air might pass freely through them all, Mr. Lorry walked from one to another. The first was the best room and in it were Lucie's birds, flowers, books, desk, worktable, and box of water colors; the second the Doctor's consulting room, used also as the dining room; the third was the Doctor's bedroom, and there, in a corner, stood the disused shoemaker's bench and tray of tools, much as it had stood on the fifth floor of the house by the wine shop in Paris.

"I wonder," said Mr. Lorry, pausing in his looking about, "that he keeps that reminder of his sufferings about him!"

"And why wonder at that?" was the abrupt inquiry.

It proceeded from Miss Pross, the wild red woman, strong of hand, whose acquaintance he had first made at the Royal George Hotel at Dover and had since improved.

"How do you do?" inquired that lady then.

"I am pretty well, I thank you," answered Mr. Lorry, with meekness. "How are you?"

"I am very much put out about my Ladybird."

"May I ask the cause?"

"I don't want dozens of people who are not worthy of Ladybird to come looking after her," said Miss Pross.

"*Do* dozens come for that purpose?"

"Hundreds," said Miss Pross.

It was characteristic of this lady that whenever her original proposition was questioned, she exaggerated it.

"Dear me!" said Mr. Lorry.

"I have lived with the darling—or the darling has lived with me, and paid me for it; which she certainly should never have done, you may take your affidavit, if I could have afforded to keep either myself or her for nothing—since she was ten years old. And it's really very hard," said Miss Pross.

Mr. Lorry knew Miss Pross to be very jealous, but he also knew her by this time to be, beneath the surface of her eccentricity, one of those unselfish creatures much nearer to the lower Angels than many ladies better got up by Nature and Art, who had balances at Tellson's.

"There never was nor will be but one man worthy of Ladybird," said Miss Pross; "and that was my brother Solomon, if he hadn't made a mistake in life."

Here again: Mr. Lorry's inquiries into Miss Pross's personal history had established the fact that her brother Solomon was a heartless scoundrel who had stripped her of everything she possessed, as a stake to speculate with, and had abandoned her in her poverty forevermore.

"As we happen to be alone for the moment, and are both people of business," he said, when they had got back to the drawing room and had sat down there, "let me ask you—does the Doctor, in talking with Lucie, never refer to the shoemaking time, yet?"

"Never."

"Do you suppose," Mr. Lorry went on, "that Doctor Manette has any theory of his own, preserved through all those years, relative to the cause of his being so oppressed; perhaps, even to the name of his oppressor?"

"I don't suppose anything but what Ladybird tells me."

"And that is——?"

"That she thinks he has."

"Now don't be angry at my asking all these questions, but is it not remarkable that Doctor Manette, unquestionably innocent of any crime as we are all well assured he is, should never touch upon that question?"

"Well! To the best of my understanding," said Miss Pross, softened by the tone of the apology, "he is afraid of the whole subject."

"Afraid?"

"It's plain enough, I should think, why he may be. It's a dreadful remembrance. Besides that, his loss of himself grew out of it. Not knowing how he lost himself or how he recovered himself, he may never feel certain of not losing himself again."

It was a profounder remark than Mr. Lorry had looked for. "True," said he. "Yet a doubt lurks in my mind, Miss Pross, whether it is good for Doctor Manette to have that suppression always shut up within him. Indeed, it is this doubt that has led me to our present confidence."

"Can't be helped," said Miss Pross, shaking her head. "Touch that string, and he instantly changes for the worse. Better leave it alone. Sometimes he gets up in the dead of the night, and will be heard, by us overhead there, walking up and down, walking up and down, in his room. Ladybird has learned to know then that his mind is walking up and down in his old prison. She hurries to him, and they go on together, walking up and down, until her love and company have brought him to himself."

The corner has been mentioned as a wonderful corner for echoes; it had begun to echo so resoundingly to the tread of coming feet that it seemed that the very mention of that weary pacing to and fro had set it going.

"Here they are!" said Miss Pross, rising to break up the conference, "and now we shall have hundreds of people pretty soon!"

On Sundays Miss Pross dined at the Doctor's table, but on other days persisted in taking her meals at unknown periods, either in the lower regions, or in her own room. On this occasion, Miss Pross, responding to Ladybird's pleasant face and efforts to please her, unbent exceedingly; so the dinner was very pleasant, too.

It was an oppressive day, and, after dinner, Lucie proposed that the wine should be carried out under the plane tree, and they should sit there in the air. As everything revolved about her, they went out under the plane tree, and she carried the wine down for the special benefit of Mr. Lorry.

Still, the Hundreds of people did not present themselves. Mr. Darnay presented himself while they were sitting under the plane tree, but he was only One.

Doctor Manette received him kindly, and so did Lucie. But Miss Pross suddenly became afflicted with a twitching in the head and body, and retired into the house.

"Pray, Doctor Manette," said Mr. Darnay, as they sat under the plane tree—and he said it in pursuit of the topic in hand, which happened to be the old buildings of London—"have you seen much of the Tower?"[1]

"Lucie and I have been there, but only casually. We know that it teems with interest, little more."

"*I* have been there, as you remember," said Darnay, with a smile, though reddening a little angrily, "in another character, and not in a character that gives facilities for seeing much of it. They told me a curious thing when I was there."

"What was that?" Lucie asked.

"In making some alterations the workmen came upon an old dungeon, which had been for many years built up and forgotten. Upon a corner stone in an angle of the wall, one prisoner, who seemed to have gone to execution, had cut as his last work, three letters. At first they were read as D. I. C.; but, on being more carefully examined, the last letter was found to be G. There was no record or legend of any prisoner with those initials, and it was suggested that the letters were not initials, but the word *Dig*. The floor was examined very carefully under the inscription, and, in the earth beneath a stone, were found the ashes of a paper, mingled with the ashes of a small leather bag. The unknown prisoner had written something, and hidden it away to keep it from the jailer."

"My father," exclaimed Lucie, "you are ill!"

He had suddenly started up, with his hand to his head. His manner and his look quite terrified them all.

"No, my dear, not ill. There are large drops

---

1. ***Tower,*** the Tower of London, ancient palace-fortress, used at various times as palace, prison, mint, arsenal.

of rain falling, and they made me start. We had better go in."

He recovered himself almost instantly. Rain was really falling in large drops, and he showed the back of his hand with raindrops on it. But he said not a single word in reference to the discovery that had been told of, and, as they went into the house, the business eye of Mr. Lorry either detected, or fancied it detected, on his face, as it turned toward Charles Darnay, the same singular look that had been upon it when it turned toward him in the passages of the court house. He recovered himself so quickly, however, that Mr. Lorry had doubts of his business eye.

Tea time, and Miss Pross making tea, with another fit of the jerks upon her, and yet no Hundreds of people. Mr. Carton had lounged in, but he made only Two. When the tea table was done with, they all moved to one of the windows, and looked out into the heavy twilight.

"The raindrops are still falling, large, heavy, and few," said Doctor Manette. "It comes slowly."

There was a great hurry in the streets, of people speeding away to get shelter before the storm broke; the wonderful corner for echoes resounded with the echoes of footsteps coming and going, yet not a footstep was there.

"A multitude of people, and yet a solitude!" said Darnay, when they had listened for a while.

"Is it not impressive, Mr. Darnay?" asked Lucie. "Sometimes I have sat here of an evening, until I have fancied—but even the shade of a foolish fancy makes me shudder tonight when all is so black and solemn——"

"Let us shudder, too. We may know what it is."

"It will seem nothing to you. I have sometimes sat here alone of an evening, listening, until I have made the echoes out to be the echoes of all the footsteps that are coming by-and-by into our lives."

"There is a great crowd coming one day into our lives, if that be so," Sydney Carton struck in, in his moody way. "And I hear them!" he added, after a peal of thunder. "Here they come, fast, fierce, and furious!"

It was the rush and roar of rain that stopped him, for no voice could be heard in it. A memorable storm of thunder and lightning broke with that sweep of water, and there was not a moment's interval in crash, and fire, and rain, until after the moon rose at midnight.

The great bell of Saint Paul's was striking one in the cleared air when Mr. Lorry, escorted by Jerry, high-booted and bearing a lantern, set forth on his return passage to Clerkenwell. There were solitary patches of road on the way between Soho and Clerkenwell, and Mr. Lorry, mindful of footpads, always retained Jerry for this service; though it was usually performed a good two hours earlier.

"What a night it has been! Almost a night, Jerry," said Mr. Lorry, "to bring the dead out of their graves."

"I never see the night myself, master—nor yet I don't expect to—what would do that," answered Jerry.

"Good night, Mr. Carton," said the man of business. "Good night, Mr. Darnay. Shall we ever see such a night again, together!"

Perhaps. Perhaps, see the great crowd of people with its rush and roar, bearing down upon them, too.

Discussion

Chapter IV

1. Is any reason provided for Dr. Manette's reaction to Charles Darnay?

2. (a) Describe Mr. Stryver. **(b)** In what way is his name a clue to his character?

3. Why does Carton annoy Mr. Lorry?

4. (a) Why does Carton assert that he hates Darnay? **(b)** Describe Carton and Darnay.

Chapter V

1. In what ways is Sydney Carton's relationship to Mr. Stryver like that of a jackal to a lion?

2. In what ways is Sydney Carton "his own worst enemy"?

3. For which of the two characters in this chapter does Dickens create sympathy? Quote lines to support your answer.

Chapter VI

1. How long after the trial does the action of this chapter take place?

2. (a) Establish the identity of each of the following characters (all of whom you have met earlier in the novel): Dr. Manette, Mr. Lorry, Miss Pross, Lucie Manette, Charles Darnay, Sydney Carton, Jerry Cruncher. **(b)** What new character, mentioned by Miss Pross, do you hear about for the first time in this chapter?

3. (a) How does Dr. Manette react to Charles's story about the prisoner in the Tower of London? **(b)** How do you explain this reaction?

4. What purpose do you think the footsteps, the echoes, the rainstorm, and the repeated reference to many people are meant to serve?

5. What do you make of Mr. Lorry's conversation with Jerry?

CHAPTER VII
MONSEIGNEUR IN TOWN

Monseigneur,[1] one of the great lords in power at the Court, held his fortnightly reception in his grand hotel in Paris. Monseigneur was in his inner room, his sanctuary of sanctuaries, the Holiest of Holiests to the crowd of worshipers in the suite of rooms without. Monseigneur was about to take his chocolate. Monseigneur could swallow a great many things with ease, and was by some few sullen minds supposed to be rapidly swallowing France; but his morning's chocolate could not so much as get into the throat of Monseigneur, without the aid of four strong men besides the Cook.

Yes. It took four men, all four ablaze with gorgeous decoration, and the Chief of them unable to exist with fewer than two gold watches in his pocket, emulative of the noble and chaste fashion set by Monseigneur, to conduct the happy chocolate to Monseigneur's lips. One lackey carried the chocolate pot into the sacred presence; a second milled and frothed the chocolate with the little instrument he bore for that function; a third presented the favored napkin; a fourth—he of the two gold watches—poured the chocolate out. It was impossible for Monseigneur to dispense with one of these attendants on the chocolate and hold his high place under the admiring heavens. Deep would have been the blot upon his escutcheon if his chocolate had been ignobly waited on by only three men; he must have died of two.

Monseigneur, having taken his chocolate, caused the doors of the Holiest of Holiests to be thrown open, and issued forth. Then, what submission, what cringing and fawning, what servility, what abject humiliation! As to bowing down in body and spirit, nothing in that way was left for heaven—which may have been one among other reasons why the worshipers of Monseigneur never troubled it.

Bestowing a word of promise here and a smile there, a whisper on one happy slave and a wave of the hand on another, Monseigneur affably passed through his rooms. Monseigneur turned, and came back again, and so in due

1. ***Monseigneur*** (môn se nyœr′), a French title of honor given to princes, bishops, and other persons of importance and here used to personify the French aristocracy. It later refers to a specific person bearing this title.

course of time got himself shut up in his sanctuary by the chocolate sprites, and was seen no more.

The show being over, the flutter in the air became quite a little storm, and there was soon but one person left of all the crowd, and he, with his hat under his arm and his snuffbox in his hand, slowly passed among the mirrors on his way out.

"I devote you," said this person turning in the direction of the sanctuary, "to the Devil!"

With that he shook the snuff from his fingers as if he had shaken the dust from his feet, and quietly walked downstairs.

He was a man of about sixty, handsomely dressed, haughty in manner, and with a face like a fine mask. A face of a transparent paleness; every feature in it clearly defined; one set expression on it. The nose, beautifully formed otherwise, was very slightly pinched at the top of each nostril. In those two compressions, or dints, the only little change that the face ever showed, resided. They persisted in changing color sometimes, and they would be occasionally dilated and contracted by something like a faint pulsation; then they gave a look of treachery and cruelty to the whole countenance. Still, it was a handsome face, and a remarkable one.

Its owner went downstairs into the courtyard, got into his carriage, and drove away. Not many people had talked with him at the reception; he had stood in a little space apart, and Monseigneur might have been warmer in his manner. It appeared, under the circumstances, rather agreeable to him to see the common people dispersed before his horses, and often barely escaping from being run down. His man drove as if he were charging an enemy, and the furious recklessness of the man brought no check into the face, or to the lips, of the master.

With a wild rattle and clatter, the carriage dashed through streets and swept round corners, women screaming before it and men clutching children out of its way. At last, swooping at a street corner by a fountain, one of its wheels came to a sickening little jolt, there was a loud cry from a number of voices, and the horses reared and plunged.

But for the latter inconvenience, the carriage probably would not have stopped; carriages were often known to drive on and leave their wounded behind, and why not? But the frightened valet had got down in a hurry, and there were twenty hands at the horses' bridles.

"What has gone wrong?" said Monsieur, calmly looking out.

A tall man in a nightcap had caught up a bundle from among the feet of the horses, and had laid it on the basement of the fountain, and was down in the mud and wet, howling over it like a wild animal.

"Pardon, Monsieur the Marquis!" said a ragged and submissive man. "It is a child."

"Why does he make that abominable noise? Is it his child?"

"Excuse me, Monsieur the Marquis—it is a pity—yes."

The fountain was in a space some ten or twelve yards square. As the tall man suddenly got up from the ground, and came running at the carriage, Monsieur the Marquis clapped his hand for an instant on his sword hilt.

"Killed!" shrieked the man, in wild desperation, extending both arms above his head, and staring at him. "Dead!"

The people closed round. Monsieur the Marquis ran his eyes over them as if they had been rats come out of their holes.

He took out his purse.

"It is extraordinary to me," said he, "that you people cannot take care of yourselves and your children. One or the other of you is forever in the way. How do I know what injury you have done my horses? See! Give him that."

He threw a gold coin for the valet to pick up, and all the heads craned forward that all the eyes might look down at it as it fell. The tall man called out again with a most unearthly cry, "Dead!"

He was arrested by the quick arrival of another man, for whom the rest made way. On seeing him the miserable creature fell upon his

shoulder, sobbing and crying, and pointing to the fountain, where some women were stooping over the motionless bundle, and moving gently about it. They were as silent, however, as the men.

"I know all, I know all," said the last comer. "Be a brave man, my Gaspard! It is better for the poor little plaything to die so than to live. It has died in a moment without pain. Could it have lived an hour as happily?"

"You are a philosopher, you there," said the Marquis, smiling. "How do they call you?"

"They call me Defarge."

"Of what trade?"

"Monsieur the Marquis, vendor of wine."

"Pick up that, philosopher and vendor of wine," said the Marquis, throwing him another gold coin, "and spend it as you will. The horses there; are they right?"

Without deigning to look at the assemblage a second time, Monsieur the Marquis leaned back in his seat, and was just being driven away with the air of a gentleman who had accidentally broken some common thing, and had paid for it, and could afford to pay for it; when his ease was suddenly disturbed by a coin flying into his carriage, and ringing on its floor.

"Hold!" said Monsieur the Marquis. "Hold the horses! Who threw that?"

He looked to the spot where Defarge the vendor of wine had stood a moment before; but the wretched father was groveling on his face on the pavement in that spot, and the figure that stood beside him was the figure of a dark stout woman, knitting.

"You dogs!" said the Marquis, but smoothly, and with an unchanged front, except as to the spots on his nose. "I would ride over any of you very willingly, and exterminate you from the earth. If I knew which rascal threw at the carriage, and if that brigand were sufficiently near it, he should be crushed under the wheels."

So cowed was their condition and so long and hard their experience of what such a man could do to them, within the law and beyond it, that not a voice, or a hand, or even an eye was raised. Among the men, not one. But the woman who stood knitting looked up steadily, and looked the Marquis in the face. It was not for his dignity to notice it; his contemptuous eyes passed over her, and over all the other rats; and he leaned back in his seat again, and gave the word, "Go on!"

He was driven on, and other carriages came whirling by in quick succession; the Minister, the State-Projector, the Farmer General, the Doctor, the Lawyer, the Ecclesiastic, the Grand Opera, the Comedy, the whole Fancy Ball in a bright continuous flow came whirling by. The rats had crept out of their holes to look on, and they remained looking on for hours; soldiers and police often passing between them and the spectacle, and making a barrier behind which they slunk, and through which they peeped. The father had long ago taken up his bundle and hidden himself away with it when the one woman who had stood conspicuous, knitting, still knitted on with the steadfastness of Fate. The water of the fountain ran; the swift river ran; the day ran into evening; so much life in the city ran into death according to rule; time and tide waited for no man; the rats were sleeping close together in their dark holes again; the Fancy Ball was lighted up at supper; all things ran their course.

CHAPTER VIII
MONSEIGNEUR IN THE COUNTRY

A beautiful landscape with the corn bright in it, but not abundant. Patches of poor rye where corn should have been, patches of poor peas and beans, patches of most coarse vegetable substitutes for wheat. On inanimate nature, as on the men and women who cultivated it, a prevalent tendency toward an appearance of vegetating unwillingly—a dejected disposition to give up, and wither away.

Monsieur the Marquis in his traveling carriage (which might have been lighter), conducted by four post horses and two postilions, fagged up a steep hill. A blush on the countenance of Monsieur the Marquis was no impeachment of his high breeding; it was not from within; it was occasioned by an external circumstance beyond his control—the setting sun.

The sunset struck so brilliantly into the traveling carriage when it gained the hilltop that its occupant was steeped in crimson. "It will die out," said Monsieur the Marquis, glancing at his hands, "directly."

In effect, the sun was so low that it dipped at the moment. When the heavy drag had been adjusted to the wheel,[1] and the carriage slid down hill, with a cinderous smell, in a cloud of dust, the red glow departed quickly; the sun and the Marquis going down together; there was no glow left when the drag was taken off.

But there remained a broken country, bold and open, a little village at the bottom of the hill, a broad sweep and rise beyond it, a church tower, a windmill, a forest for the chase, and a crag with a fortress on it used as a prison. Round upon all these darkening objects as the night drew on, the Marquis looked, with the air of one who was coming near home.

The village had its one poor street, with its poor brewery, poor tannery, poor tavern, poor stableyard for relay of post horses, poor fountain, all usual poor appointments. It had its poor people too. All its people were poor, and many of them were sitting at their doors, shredding spare onions and the like for supper, while many were at the fountain, washing leaves, and grasses, and any such small yieldings of the earth that could be eaten. Expressive signs of what made them poor were not wanting; the tax for the state, the tax for the church, the tax for the lord, tax local and tax general, were to be paid here and to be paid there until the wonder was that there was any village left unswallowed.

Few children were to be seen, and no dogs. As to the men and women, their choice on earth was stated in the prospect— Life on the lowest terms that could sustain it, down in the little village under the mill; or captivity and Death in the dominant prison on the crag.

Heralded by a courier in advance, and by the cracking of his postilions' whips, which twined snakelike about their heads, as if he came attended by the Furies,[2] Monsieur the Marquis drew up in his traveling carriage at the posting-house gate. It was hard by the fountain, and the peasants suspended their operations to look at him. Monsieur the Marquis cast his eyes over the submissive faces that drooped before him, when a grizzled mender of the roads joined the group.

"Bring me hither that fellow!" said the Marquis.

The fellow was brought, cap in hand, and the other fellows closed round to look and to listen, in the manner of the people at the Paris fountain.

"I passed you on the road?"

"Monseigneur, it is true. I had the honor of being passed on the road."

"Coming up the hill, and at the top of the hill, both?"

"Monseigneur, it is true."

"What did you look at, so fixedly?"

"Monseigneur, I looked at the man."

He stooped a little, and with his tattered blue cap pointed under the carriage.

"What man, pig? And why look there?"

"Pardon, Monseigneur; he swung by the chain of the shoe—the drag."

"Who?" demanded the traveler.

"Monseigneur, the man."

"May the Devil carry away these idiots! How do you call the man? You know all the men of this part of the country. Who was he?"

"Your clemency, Monseigneur! He was not of this part of the country. Of all the days of my life, I never saw him."

"Swinging by the chain? To be suffocated?"

---

1. ***When the heavy drag . . . the wheel,*** a weighted obstruction placed against the wheel of a carriage to prevent the carriage from going downhill too fast.

2. ***the Furies,*** in Greek and Roman mythology, three female spirits who pursued and tormented evildoers.

"With your gracious permission, that was the wonder of it, Monseigneur. His head hanging over—like this!"

He turned himself sideways to the carriage, and leaned back, with his face thrown up to the sky, and his head hanging down; then recovered himself, fumbled with his cap, and made a bow.

"What was he like?"

"Monseigneur, he was whiter than the miller. All covered with dust, white as a specter, tall as a specter!"

The picture produced an immense sensation in the little crowd; but all eyes, without comparing notes with other eyes, looked at Monsieur the Marquis.

"Truly, you did well," said the Marquis, "to see a thief accompanying my carriages, and not open that great mouth of yours. Bah! Put him aside, Monsieur Gabelle!"

Monsieur Gabelle was the postmaster, and some other taxing functionary united; he had come out with great obsequiousness to assist at this examination, and had held the examined by his arm in an official manner.

"Bah! Go aside!" said Monsieur Gabelle.

"Lay hands on this stranger if he seeks your village tonight, and be sure his business is honest, Gabelle."

"Monseigneur, I devote myself to your orders."

"Did he run away, fellow?—where is that accursed?"

The accursed was under the carriage with some half-dozen particular friends, pointing out the chain. Some half-dozen other particular friends promptly hauled him out, and presented him breathless to Monsieur the Marquis.

"Did the man run away, dolt, when we stopped for the drag?"

"Monseigneur, he precipitated himself over the hillside, head first, as a person plunges into the river."

"See to it, Gabelle. Go on!"

The half-dozen who were peering at the chain were still among the wheels like sheep; the wheels turned so suddenly they were lucky to save their skins and bones; they had very little else to save, or they might not have been so fortunate.

The burst with which the carriage started out of the village and up the rise beyond was soon checked by the steepness of the hill. Gradually it subsided to a footpace, swinging and lumbering upward among the many sweet scents of a summer night.

The scents rose all around him, and rose on the dusty, ragged, and toil-worn group at the fountain not far away; to whom the mender of roads still enlarged upon his man like a specter as long as they could bear it. By degrees, they dropped off one by one, and lights twinkled in little casements.

The shadow of a large high-roofed house, and of many overhanging trees, was upon Monsieur the Marquis by that time; and the shadow was exchanged for the light of a flambeau, as his carriage stopped, and the great door of his château was opened to him.

"Monsieur Charles, whom I expect, is he arrived from England?"

"Monseigneur, not yet."

CHAPTER IX
THE GORGON'S HEAD

It was a heavy mass of building, that château of Monsieur the Marquis, with a large stone courtyard before it, and two stone sweeps of staircase meeting in a stone terrace before the principal door, and stone urns, and stone flowers, and stone faces of men, and stone heads of lions, in all directions. As if the Gorgon's head[1] had surveyed it, when it was finished, two centuries ago.

Up the broad flight of shallow steps, Monsieur the Marquis went from his carriage. The great door clanged behind him, and Monsieur

1. ***Gorgon's head,*** in Greek mythology, one of three sisters, with snakes for hair, whose look turned the beholder into stone. Medusa, one of the Gorgons, was slain by Perseus.

the Marquis crossed a hall grim with certain old boar spears, swords and knives of the chase; grimmer with certain heavy riding rods and riding whips, of which many a peasant, gone to his benefactor Death, had felt the weight.

Monsieur the Marquis went up the staircase to a door in a corridor. This admitted him to his own private apartment of three rooms, his bedchamber and two others. High vaulted rooms with cool uncarpeted floors, great dogs upon the hearth for the burning of wood, and all luxuries befitting the state of a marquis in a luxurious age and country.

A supper table was laid for two, in the third of the rooms; a round room, in one of the château's four extinguisher-topped towers. A small lofty room, with its window wide open, and the wooden jalousie blinds closed, so that the dark night only showed in slight horizontal lines of black, alternating with their broad lines of stone color.

"My nephew," said the Marquis, glancing at the supper preparation. "They said he was not arrived."

Nor was he; but, he had been expected with Monseigneur.

"It is not probable he will arrive tonight; nevertheless, leave the table as it is."

In a quarter of an hour Monseigneur sat down alone to his sumptuous and choice supper. His chair was opposite to the window, and he was raising his glass of Bordeaux to his lips, when he put it down.

"What is that?" he calmly asked, looking with attention at the horizontal lines of black and stone color.

"Monseigneur? That?"

"Outside the blinds. Open the blinds." It was done.

"Well?"

"Monseigneur, it is nothing. The trees and the night are all that are here." The servant had thrown the blinds wide and stood, looking round for instruction.

"Good," said the imperturbable master. "Close them again."

That was done too, and the Marquis went on with his supper. He was halfway through it, when he again stopped with his glass in his hand, hearing the sound of wheels. It came on briskly, and came up to the front of the château.

"Ask who is arrived."

It was the nephew of Monseigneur.

He was to be told, said Monseigneur, that supper awaited him then and there, and that he was prayed to come to it. In a little while he came. He had been known in England as Charles Darnay.

Monseigneur received him in a courtly manner, but they did not shake hands.

"You left Paris yesterday, sir?" he said to Monseigneur, as he took his seat at table.

"Yesterday. And you?"

"I come direct."

"From London?"

"Yes."

"You have been a long time coming," said the Marquis, with a smile.

"On the contrary; I come direct."

"Pardon me! I mean not a long time on the journey; a long time intending the journey."

"I have been detained by" —the nephew stopped a moment in his answer— "various business."

"Without doubt," said the polished uncle.

So long as a servant was present no other words passed between them. When coffee had been served and they were alone together, the nephew opened a conversation.

"I have come back, sir, as you anticipate, pursuing the object that took me away. It carried me into great and unexpected peril; but it is a sacred object, and if it had carried me to death I hope it would have sustained me."

"Not to death," said the uncle.

"I doubt, sir," returned the nephew, "whether, if it had carried me to the utmost brink of death, you would have cared to stop me there."

The uncle made a graceful gesture of protest, so clearly a form of good breeding that it was not reassuring.

"Indeed, sir," pursued the nephew, "for anything I know, you may have expressly worked to give a more suspicious appearance to the circumstances that surrounded me."

"No, no, no," said the uncle, pleasantly.

"But, however that may be," resumed the nephew, glancing at him with deep distrust, "I know you would stop me by any means and would know no scruple as to means."

"My friend, I told you so," said the uncle, with a fine pulsation in the two marks. "Do me the favor to recall that I told you so, long ago."

"I recall it."

"Thank you," said the Marquis—very sweetly indeed.

"In effect, sir," pursued the nephew, "I believe it to be at once your bad fortune, and my good fortune, that has kept me out of a prison in France here."

"I do not quite understand," returned the uncle, sipping his coffee. "Dare I ask you to explain?"

"I believe that if you were not in disgrace with the Court, a letter *de cachet*[2] would have sent me to some fortress indefinitely."

"It is possible," said the uncle, with great calmness. "For the honor of the family, I could even resolve to incommode you to that extent. These little instruments of correction, these slight favors that might so incommode you, are sought by so many and granted to so few! It used not to be so, but France in all such things is changed for the worse."

"We have so asserted our station, both in the old time and in the modern time also," said the nephew, gloomily, "that I believe our name to be more detested than any name in France."

"Let us hope so," said the uncle. "Detestation of the high is the involuntary homage of the low. Meanwhile, I will preserve the honor of the family, if you will not. But you must be fatigued. Shall we terminate our conference for the night?"

"A moment more."

"An hour, if you please."

"Sir," said the nephew, "we have done wrong and are reaping the fruits of wrong."

"*We* have done wrong?" repeated the Marquis.

"Our family, whose honor is of so much account to both of us, in such different ways. Even in my father's time, we did a world of wrong, injuring every human creature who came between us and our pleasure. Why need I speak of my father's time, when it is equally yours? Can I separate my father's twin brother from himself?"

"Death has done that!" said the Marquis.

"And has left me," answered the nephew, "bound to a system that is frightful to me; responsible for it, but powerless in it; seeking to execute the last request of my dear mother's lips, to have mercy and to redress; and tortured by seeking assistance and power in vain."

"Seeking them from me, my nephew," said the Marquis, "you will forever seek them in vain, be assured."

Every fine straight line in the clear whiteness of his face was cruelly, craftily, and closely compressed, while he stood looking quietly at his nephew, with his snuffbox in his hand. He touched him on the breast, as though his finger were the fine point of a small sword, with which, in delicate finesse, he ran him through the body, and said:

"My friend, I will die, perpetuating the system under which I have lived. Better to be a rational creature," he added, after ringing a small bell on the table, "and accept your natural destiny. But you are lost, Monsieur Charles, I see."

"This property and France are lost to me," said the nephew, sadly. "I renounce them."

"Are they yours to renounce? France may be, but the property? It is scarcely worth mentioning; but, is it yet?"

"I had no intention to claim it. If it passed to

2. ***letter de cachet,*** usually ***lettre de cachet*** (let′rə də kä shā′), a letter bearing the seal of the king of France, frequently an order for someone to be imprisoned or exiled. This royal order provided no opportunity for a hearing for its recipient, and often contained no mention of the crime of which he was accused or of a date for his release.

me from you tomorrow, I would abandon it and live elsewhere. What is it but a wilderness of misery and ruin?''

''Hah!'' said the Marquis, glancing round the luxurious room.

''To the eye it is fair enough, here; but seen by daylight, it is a crumbling tower of waste, mismanagement, extortion, debt, mortgage, oppression, hunger, nakedness, and suffering.''

''Hah!'' said the Marquis again, in a well-satisfied manner.

''If it ever becomes mine, it shall be put into some hands qualified to free it so that the miserable people who cannot leave it and who have been long wrung to the last point of endurance, may, in another generation, suffer less; but it is not for me. There is a curse on it, and on all this land.''

''And you?'' said the uncle. ''Forgive my curiosity; do you, under your new philosophy, graciously intend to live?''

''I must do, to live, what others of my countrymen even with nobility at their backs, may have to do some day—work.''

''In England, for example?''

''Yes. The family honor, sir, is safe from me in this country. The family name can suffer from me in no other, for I bear it in no other.''

The ringing of the bell had caused the adjoining bedchamber to be lighted. It now shone brightly through the door of communication. The Marquis looked that way, and listened for the retreating step of his valet.

''England is very attractive to you, seeing how indifferently you have prospered there,'' he observed then, turning his calm face to his nephew with a smile.

''I have already said that, for my prospering there, I may be indebted to you, sir. For the rest, it is my refuge.''

''They say, those boastful English, that it is the refuge of many. You know a compatriot who has found a refuge there? A doctor?''

''Yes.''

''With a daughter?''

''Yes.''

''Yes,'' repeated the Marquis. ''A doctor with a daughter. Yes. You are fatigued. I look to the pleasure of seeing you again in the morning. Good repose! Light Monsieur my nephew to his chamber there—and burn Monsieur my nephew in his bed, if you will,'' he added to himself, before he summoned his valet to his own bedroom.

The valet come and gone, Monsieur the Marquis walked to and fro in his loose chamber robe, to prepare himself gently for sleep that hot, still night.

''I am cool now,'' said Monsieur the Marquis, ''and may go to bed.''

So, leaving only one light burning, he let his thin gauze curtains fall around him, and heard the night break its silence with a long sigh as he composed himself to sleep.

The fountain in the village flowed unseen and unheard, and the fountain at the château dropped unseen and unheard through three dark hours. Then the gray water of both began to be ghostly in the light, and the eyes of the stone faces of the château were opened.

Lighter and lighter, until at last the sun touched the tops of the still trees, and poured its radiance over the hill. In the glow the water of the château fountain seemed to turn to blood, and the stone faces crimsoned. The carol of the birds was loud and high, and, on the weather-beaten sill of the great window of the bedchamber of Monsieur the Marquis, one little bird sang its sweetest song with all its might. At this the nearest stone face seemed to stare amazed, and, with open mouth and dropped underjaw, looked awe-stricken.

Now the sun was full up, and movement began in the village. Casement windows opened, doors were unbarred, and people came forth shivering—chilled, as yet, by the new sweet air. Then began the rarely lightened toil of the day among the village population. Some, to the fountain; some, to the fields; men and women here, to dig and delve; men and women there, to see to the poor livestock, and lead the bony cows out, to such pasture as could be found by the roadside. In the church and at the Cross, a kneeling figure or two.

The château awoke later, as became its quality, but awoke gradually and surely. First, the lonely boar spears and knives of the chase had been reddened as of old, then, had gleamed trenchant in the morning sunshine; now, doors and windows were thrown open, horses in their stables looked round over their shoulders at the light and freshness pouring in at doorways, leaves sparkled and rustled at iron-grated windows, dogs pulled hard at their chains, and reared impatient to be loosed.

All these trivial incidents belonged to the routine of life, and the return of morning. Surely, not so the ringing of the great bell of the château, nor the running up and down the stairs; nor the hurried figures on the terrace; nor the booting and tramping here and there and everywhere, nor the quick saddling of horses and riding away?

What winds conveyed this hurry to the grizzled mender of roads, already at work on the hilltop beyond the village, with his day's dinner—not much to carry—lying in a bundle that it was worth no crow's while to peck at, on a heap of stones? Had the birds, carrying some grains of it to a distance, dropped one over him as they sow chance seeds? Whether or no, the mender of roads ran, on the sultry morning, as if for his life, down the hill, knee-high in dust, and never stopped till he got to the fountain.

All the people of the village were at the fountain, standing about in their depressed manner, and whispering low, but showing no other emotions than grim curiosity and surprise. The led cows, hastily brought in and tethered to anything that would hold them, were looking stupidly on, or lying down chewing the cud of nothing particularly repaying their trouble. Some of the people of the château, and some of those of the posting house, and all the taxing authorities, were armed more or less and were crowded on the other side of the little street in a purposeless way, that was highly fraught with nothing.

Already the mender of roads had penetrated into the midst of a group of fifty particular friends, and was smiting himself in the breast with his blue cap. What did all this portend, and what portended the swift hoisting-up of Monsieur Gabelle behind a servant on horseback, and the conveying away of the said Gabelle—double-laden though the horse was—at a gallop.

It portended that there was one stone face too many up at the château.

The Gorgon had surveyed the building again in the night, and had added the one stone face wanting; the stone face for which it had waited through about two hundred years.

It lay back on the pillow of Monsieur the Marquis. It was like a fine mask, suddenly startled, made angry, and petrified. Driven home into the heart of the stone figure attached to it, was a knife. Round its hilt was a frill of paper, on which was scrawled:

"Drive him fast to his tomb. This, from JACQUES."

CHAPTER X
TWO PROMISES

More months, to the number of twelve, had come and gone, and Mr. Charles Darnay was established in England as a higher teacher of the French language who was conversant with French literature. In this age he would have been a professor; in that age he was a tutor. As a tutor, whose attainments made the student's way pleasant and profitable, and as an elegant translator who brought something to his work besides dictionary knowledge, young Mr. Darnay soon became known and encouraged. He was well acquainted, moreover, with the circumstances of his country, and those were of ever growing interest. So, with perseverance and untiring industry, he prospered.

A certain portion of his time was passed at Cambridge, where he read with undergraduates. The rest of his time he passed in London.

He had loved Lucie Manette from the hour

of his danger. He had never heard a sound so sweet and dear as the sound of her compassionate voice; he had never seen a face so tenderly beautiful as hers when it was confronted with his own on the edge of the grave that had been dug for him. But he had not yet spoken to her on the subject; the assassination at the deserted château far away had been done a year, and he had never yet, by so much as a single spoken word, disclosed to her the state of his heart.

It was again summer when, lately arrived in London from his college occupation, he turned into the quiet corner in Soho, bent on opening his mind to Doctor Manette.

He found the Doctor reading in his armchair. The energy which had at once supported him under his old sufferings had been gradually restored to him. He was now a very energetic man indeed, with great firmness of purpose, strength of resolution, and vigor of action. To him now entered Charles Darnay, at sight of whom he laid aside his book and held out his hand.

"Charles Darnay! I rejoice to see you. We have been counting on your return these three or four days past. Mr. Stryver and Sydney Carton were both here yesterday, and both made you out to be more than due."

"I am obliged to them for their interest in the matter," he answered. "Miss Manette——"

"Is well," said the Doctor, "and your return will delight us all. She has gone out but will soon be home."

"Doctor Manette, I knew she was from home. I took the opportunity of her being from home, to beg to speak to you."

There was a blank silence.

"Yes?" said the Doctor, with evident constraint. "Bring your chair here, and speak on."

He complied as to the chair, but appeared to find the speaking on less easy.

"I have had the happiness, Doctor Manette, of being so intimate here," he began, "for some year and a half, that I hope the topic on which I am about to touch may not——"

He was stayed by the Doctor's putting out his hand to stop him.

"Is Lucie the topic?"

"She is."

"It is hard for me to speak of her at any time. It is very hard for me to hear her spoken of in that tone of yours, Charles Darnay."

"It is a tone of fervent admiration, true homage, and deep love, Doctor Manette!" he said deferentially.

There was another blank silence before her father rejoined:

"Have you spoken to Lucie?"

"No."

"Nor written?"

"Never."

"It would be ungenerous to affect not to know that your self-denial is to be referred to your consideration for her father. Her father thanks you."

He offered his hand; but his eyes did not go with it.

"I know," said Darnay, respectfully, "how can I fail to know, Doctor Manette, I who have seen you together, that between you and Miss Manette there is an affection so unusual, so touching, that it can have few parallels, even in the tenderness between a father and child. I have known this, since I have known you."

Her father sat silent.

"Dear Doctor Manette, always knowing this, always seeing her and you with this hallowed light about you, I have forborne, and forborne, as long as it was in the nature of man to do it. I have felt, and do even now feel, that to bring my love between you, is to touch your history with something not quite so good as itself. But I love her. Heaven is my witness that I love her!"

"I believe it," answered her father, mournfully. "I have thought so before now. I believe it."

"But do not believe," said Darnay, upon whose ear the mournful voice struck with a reproachful sound, "that if my fortune were so cast as that, being one day so happy as to make her my wife, I must at any time put any separation between her and you, I could or would breathe a word of what I now say.

"No, dear Doctor Manette. Like you, a voluntary exile from France; like you, driven from it by its distractions, oppressions, and miseries; like you, striving to live away from it by my own exertions, and trusting in a happier future; I look only to sharing your fortunes, sharing your life and home, and being faithful to you to the death. Not to divide with Lucie her privilege as your child, companion, and friend; but to come in aid of it, and bind her closer to you if such a thing can be."

Her father rested his hands upon the arms of his chair, and looked up for the first time since the beginning of the conference. A struggle was evident in his face; a struggle with that occasional look which had a tendency in it to dark doubt and dread.

"You speak so feelingly and so manfully, Charles Darnay, that I thank you with all my heart, and will open all my heart—or nearly so. Have you any reason to believe that Lucie loves you?"

"None. As yet, none."

"Do you seek any promise from me?"

"I do seek that."

"What is it?"

"It is that if Miss Manette would bring to you at any time, on her part, such a confidence as I have ventured to lay before you, you will bear testimony to what I have said, and to your belief in it. I hope you may be able to think so well of me as to urge no influence against me. I say nothing more of my stake in this; this is what I ask. The condition on which I ask it, and which you have an undoubted right to require, I will observe immediately."

"I give the promise," said the Doctor, "without any condition. I believe your object to be, purely and truthfully, as you have stated it. I believe your intention is to perpetuate, and not to weaken, the ties between me and my other and far dearer self. If she should ever tell me that you are essential to her perfect happiness, I will give her to you. If there were—Charles Darnay, if there were——"

The young man had taken his hand gratefully; their hands were joined as the Doctor spoke:

"—any fancies, any reasons, any apprehensions, anything whatsoever, new or old, against the man she really loved—the direct responsibility thereof not lying on his head—they should all be obliterated for her sake. She is everything to me; more to me than suffering, more to me than wrong, more to me—Well! This is idle talk."

"Your confidence in me ought to be returned with full confidence on my part. My present name, though but slightly changed from my mother's, is not my own. I wish to tell you what that is, and why I am in England."

"Stop!" said the Doctor of Beauvais. "If your suit should prosper, if Lucie should love you, you shall tell me on your marriage morning. Do you promise?"

"Willingly."

"Give me your hand. She will be home directly. Go! God bless you!"

It was dark when Charles Darnay left him, and it was an hour later and darker when Lucie came home.

"My father!" she called to him. "Father dear!"

She heard a low hammering sound in his bedroom. She looked in at his door and came running back crying to herself, "What shall I do! What shall I do!"

Her uncertainty lasted but a moment; she hurried back, and tapped at his door, and softly called to him. The noise ceased at the sound of her voice, and he presently came out to her, and they walked up and down together for a long time.

She came down from her bed, to look at him in his sleep that night. He slept heavily, and his tray of shoemaking tools, and his old unfinished work, were all as usual.

Discussion

Chapter VII

1. (a) Why do you think the narrator describes in detail the episode of the hot chocolate? **(b)** In what ways does this scene contrast with the scene at the fountain?

2. What is the significance of the gold coin to the Marquis? to Defarge?

Chapter VIII

1. Dickens frequently presents conditions, events, or characters in such a way that readers are either sympathetic or unsympathetic to them. In Chapters VII and VIII, with what or whom are you sympathetic? unsympathetic?

2. What has the man seen under the carriage?

3. Who is "Monsieur Charles"?

4. Why has Dickens devoted two chapters to Monsieur the Marquis, a minor character?

Chapter IX

1. In what ways are Charles and his uncle different?

2. (a) In what way does the message left on the hilt of the knife provide a clue to the identity of the murderer? **(b)** In Chapters VII and VIII, you saw the conditions under which the peasants lived. How is the murder in this chapter related to those conditions?

Chapter X

1. (a) How long has it been since Darnay's return from France? **(b)** How has he been employed since his return?

2. (a) What are the "two promises" in this chapter? **(b)** What is the Doctor's reaction when Darnay tells him of his love for Lucie? **(c)** What is his reaction after Darnay has left?

CHAPTER XI
THE FELLOW OF NO DELICACY

If Sydney Carton ever shone anywhere, he certainly never shone in the house of Doctor Manette. He had been there often during a whole year, and had always been the same moody and morose lounger there. When he cared to talk, he talked well; but the cloud of caring for nothing, which overshadowed him with such a fatal darkness, was very rarely pierced by the light within him.

And yet he did care something for the streets that environed that house, and for the stones that made their pavements. Many a night he vaguely and unhappily wandered there, when wine had brought no transitory gladness to him; many a dreary daybreak revealed his solitary figure lingering there.

On a day in August, Sydney's feet still trod those stones. From being irresolute and purposeless his feet became animated by an intention, and, in the working out of that intention, they took him to the Doctor's door.

He was shown upstairs, and found Lucie at her work, alone. She had never been quite at her ease with him, and received him with some little embarrassment. But, looking up at his face in the interchange of the first few commonplaces, she observed a change in it.

"I fear you are not well, Mr. Carton!"

"No. But the life I lead, Miss Manette, is not conducive to health. What is to be expected of, or by, such profligates?"

"Is it not—forgive me—a pity to live no better life?"

"God knows it is a shame!"

"Then why not change it?"

Looking gently at him again, she was surprised and saddened to see that there were tears in his eyes. There were tears in his voice too, as he answered:

"It is too late for that. I shall never be better than I am. I shall sink lower, and be worse. I am like one who died young. All my life might have been."

"No, Mr. Carton. I am sure that the best part of it might still be; I am sure that you might be much, much worthier of yourself."

"Say of you, Miss Manette, and although I know better—although in the mystery of my own wretched heart I know better—I shall never forget it!"

She was pale and trembling. He came to her relief with a fixed despair of himself which made the interview unlike any other that could have been holden.

"If it had been possible, Miss Manette, that you could have returned the love of the man you see before you—self-flung away, wasted, drunken, poor creature of misuse as you know him to be—he would have been conscious this day and hour, in spite of his happiness, that he would bring you to misery, bring you to sorrow and repentance, blight you, disgrace you, pull you down with him. I know very well that you can have no tenderness for me; I ask for none; I am even thankful that it cannot be."

"Without it, can I not save you, Mr. Carton? Can I not recall you—forgive me again!—to a better course? Can I in no way repay your confidence? I know this is a confidence," she modestly said, after a little hesitation, and in earnest tears, "I know you would say this to no one else. Can I turn it to no good account for yourself, Mr. Carton?"

He shook his head.

"The utmost good that I am capable of now, Miss Manette, I have come here to realize. Let me carry through the rest of my misdirected life the remembrance that I opened my heart to you, last of all the world; and that there was something left in me at this time which you could pity. I distress you; I draw fast to an end. Will you let me believe that the last confidence of my life was reposed in you and will be shared by no one?"

"If that will be a consolation to you, yes."

"Not even by the dearest one ever to be known to you?"

"Mr. Carton," she answered, after an agitated pause, "the secret is yours, not mine; and I promise to respect it."

"Thank you. And again, God bless you."

He put her hand to his lips, and moved toward the door.

He was so unlike what he had ever shown himself to be, and it was so sad to think how much he had thrown away, that Lucie Manette wept mournfully for him as he stood looking back at her.

"Be comforted!" he said, "I am not worth such feeling, Miss Manette. My last supplication of all, is this; it is useless to say it, I know, but it rises out of my soul. For you, and for any dear to you, I would do anything. I would embrace any sacrifice for you and for those dear to you. The time will come, the time will not be long in coming, when new ties will be formed about you—the dearest ties that will ever grace and gladden you. O Miss Manette, when the little picture of a happy father's face looks up in yours, when you see your own bright beauty springing up anew at your feet, think now and then that there is a man who would give his life, to keep a life you love beside you!"

He said, "Farewell!" said a last, "God bless you!" and left her.

CHAPTER XII
THE HONEST TRADESMAN

To the eyes of Mr. Jeremiah Cruncher, sitting on his stool in Fleet Street with his grisly urchin beside him, a vast number and variety of objects in movement were every day presented. Time was, when a poet sat upon a stool in a public place, and mused in the sight of men. Mr. Cruncher, sitting on a stool in a public place, but not being a poet, mused as little as possible, and looked about him.

Ronald Searle

It fell out that he was thus engaged when an unusual concourse down Fleet Street westward attracted his attention. Looking that way, Mr. Cruncher made out that some kind of funeral was coming along, and that there was popular objection to this funeral, which engendered uproar.

The crowd approached; they were bawling and hissing round a dingy hearse and dingy mourning coach, in which there was only one mourner, with an increasing rabble surrounding the coach, deriding him, and incessantly calling out: "Yah! Spies! Tst! Spies!"

Funerals had at all times a remarkable attraction for Mr. Cruncher; he always pricked up his senses and became excited when a funeral passed Tellson's. Naturally, therefore, a funeral with this uncommon attendance excited him greatly, and he asked of the first man who ran against him:

"What is it, brother? What's it about?"

"*I* don't know," said the man. "Spies! Yaha! Tst! Spies!"

At length, a person better informed on the merits of the case tumbled against him, and from this person he learned that the funeral was the funeral of one Roger Cly.

"Was *he* a spy?" asked Mr. Cruncher.

"Old Bailey spy," returned his informant.

"Why, to be sure!" exclaimed Jerry, recalling the trial at which he had assisted. "I've seen him. Dead, is he?"

"Dead as mutton," returned the other, "and can't be too dead. Have 'em out, there! Spies! Pull 'em out! Spies!"

The idea was so acceptable, in the prevalent absence of any idea, that the crowd caught it up with eagerness, and loudly repeating the suggestion to have 'em out, and to pull 'em out, mobbed the two vehicles so closely that they came to a stop. On the crowd's opening the coach doors, the one mourner scuffled out and was in their hands for a moment; but he was so alert and made such good use of his time that in another moment he was scouring away up a bystreet after shedding his cloak, hat, long hatband, white pocket handkerchief, and other symbolical tears.

These the people tore to pieces and scattered far and wide with great enjoyment, while the tradesmen hurriedly shut up their shops; for a crowd in those times stopped at nothing, and was a monster much dreaded. They had already got the length of opening the hearse to take the coffin out, when some brighter genius proposed, instead, its being escorted to its destination amidst general rejoicing. Practical suggestions being much needed, this suggestion, too, was received with acclamation, and the coach was immediately filled with eight inside and a dozen out, while as many people got on the roof of the hearse as could by any exercise of ingenuity stick upon it. Among the first of these volunteers was Jerry Cruncher himself, who modestly concealed his spiky head from the observation of Tellson's, in the further corner of the mourning coach.

The officiating undertakers made some protest against these changes in the ceremonies; but, the river being alarmingly near, and several voices remarking on the efficacy of cold immersion in bringing refractory members of the profession to reason, the protest was faint and brief. The remodeled procession started, with a chimney sweep driving the hearse—advised by the regular driver, who was perched beside him under close inspection, for the purpose—and with a pieman, also attended by his cabinet minister, driving the mourning coach. A bear leader, a popular street character of the time, was impressed as an additional ornament, before the cavalcade had gone far down the Strand; and his bear, who was black and very mangy, gave quite an undertaking air to that part of the procession in which he walked.

Thus, with beer drinking, pipe smoking, song roaring, and infinite caricaturing of woe, the disorderly procession went its way, recruiting at every step, and all the shops shutting up about it. Its destination was the old church of Saint Pancras, far off in the fields. It got there in course of time; insisted on pouring into the burial ground; finally, accomplished the interment of the deceased Roger Cly in its own way, and highly to its own satisfaction.

The dead man disposed of, and the crowd being under the necessity of providing some other entertainment for itself, another brighter genius—or perhaps the same—conceived the humor of impeaching casual passers-by, as Old Bailey spies, and wreaking vengeance on them. Chase was given to some scores of inoffensive persons who had never been near the Old Bailey in their lives, in the realization of this fancy, and they were roughly hustled and maltreated. The transition to the sport of window breaking, and thence to the plundering of public houses, was easy and natural. At last, after several hours, when sundry summer houses had been pulled down, and some area railings had been torn up, a rumor got about that the Guards were coming. Before this rumor, the crowd gradually melted away, and perhaps the Guards came, and perhaps they never came; and this was the usual progress of a mob.

Mr. Cruncher did not assist at the closing sports, but had remained behind in the churchyard, to confer and condole with the undertakers. The place had a soothing influence on him. He procured a pipe from a neighboring public house and smoked it, looking in at the railings and maturely considering the spot.

"Jerry," said Mr. Cruncher, apostrophizing himself in his usual way, "you see that there Cly that day, and you see with your own eyes that he was a young 'un and a straight made 'un."

Having smoked his pipe out and ruminated a little longer, he turned himself about, and made a short call upon his medical adviser—a distinguished surgeon.

Young Jerry relieved his father with dutiful interest, and reported no job in his absence. The bank closed, the ancient clerks came out, the usual watch was set, and Mr. Cruncher and his son went home to tea.

"Now, I tell you where it is!" said Mr. Cruncher to his wife, on entering. "If, as a honest tradesman, my wentures goes wrong tonight, I shall make sure that you've been praying agin me, and I shall work you for it just the same as if I seen you do it."

The dejected Mrs. Cruncher shook her head.

"Why, you're at it afore my face!" said Mr. Cruncher, with signs of angry apprehension.

"I am saying nothing."

"Well, then; don't meditate nothing. You might as well flop as meditate. You may as well go again' me one way as another. Drop it altogether."

"You were going out tonight?" asked his decent wife.

"Yes, I am."

"May I go with you, father?" asked his son, briskly.

"No, you mayn't. I'm a-going—as your mother knows—a-fishing. That's where I'm going to. Going a-fishing."

"Your fishing rod gets raything rusty don't it, father?"

"Never you mind."

"Shall you bring any fish home, father?"

"If I don't, you'll have short commons, tomorrow," returned that gentleman; "that's questions enough for you; I ain't a-going out till you've been long abed."

He devoted himself during the remainder of the evening to keeping a vigilant watch on Mrs. Cruncher, and sullenly holding her in conversation that she might be prevented from meditating any petitions to his disadvantage. The devoutest person could have rendered no greater homage to the efficacy of an honest prayer than he did in this distrust of his wife. It was as if a professed unbeliever in ghosts should be frightened by a ghost story.

Thus the evening wore away until Young Jerry was ordered to bed, and his mother, laid under similar injunctions, obeyed them. Mr. Cruncher did not start upon his excursion until nearly one o'clock. Toward that small and ghostly hour he rose up from his chair, took a key out of his pocket, opened a locked cupboard, and brought forth a sack, a crowbar of convenient size, a rope and chain, and other fishing tackle of that nature. Disposing these articles about him, he bestowed a parting defiance on Mrs. Cruncher, extinguished the light, and went out.

Young Jerry, who had only made a feint of undressing when he went to bed, was not long after his father. Under cover of the darkness he followed out of the room, followed down the stairs, followed down the court, followed out into the streets.

Impelled by a laudable ambition to study the art and mystery of his father's honest calling, Young Jerry, keeping as close to house fronts, walls, and doorways as his eyes were close to one another, held his honored parent in view. The honored parent had not gone far when he was joined by another disciple of Izaak Walton,[1] and the two trudged on together. Within half an hour another fisherman was picked up. They turned out of the road, and up a blind lane, of which a wall—some ten feet high—formed one side. Young Jerry saw his honored parent nimbly scaling an iron gate. He was soon over, and then the second fisherman got over, and then the third.

It was now Young Jerry's turn to approach the gate; which he did, holding his breath. Crouching down in a corner there, and looking in, he made out the three fishermen creeping through some rank grass, and all the gravestones in the church—it was a large churchyard that they were in—looking on like ghosts in white. They did not creep far before they stopped; then they began to fish.

They fished with a spade at first. Presently the honored parent appeared to be adjusting some instrument like a great corkscrew. Now they seemed to have got a bite. There was a screwing and complaining sound down below, and their bent figures were strained, as if by a weight. By degrees the weight came to the surface. Young Jerry knew what it would be; but when he saw it and saw his honored parent about to wrench it open, he was so frightened that he made off and never stopped until he had run a mile or more. He had a strong idea that the coffin he had seen was running after him; so that when the boy got to his own door he had reason for being half dead. And even then it would not leave him, but followed him upstairs with a bump on every stair, scrambled into bed with him, and bumped down on his breast when he fell asleep.

From his oppressed slumber, Young Jerry in his closet was awakened after daybreak and before sunrise by the presence of his father in the family room. Something had gone wrong with him; at least, Young Jerry inferred, from the circumstance of his holding Mrs. Cruncher by the ears, and knocking the back of her head against the headboard of the bed.

"I told you I would," said Mr. Cruncher, "and I did."

"Jerry, Jerry, Jerry!" his wife implored.

"You oppose yourself to the profit of the business," said Jerry, "and me and my partners suffer. You was to honor and obey; why the devil don't you?"

"I try to be a good wife, Jerry," the poor woman protested.

"Is it being a good wife to oppose your husband's business? Is it honoring your husband to dishonor his business? Is it obeying your husband to disobey him on the wital subject of his business?"

"You hadn't taken to the dreadful business then, Jerry."

"It's enough for you," retorted Mr. Cruncher, "to be the wife of a honest tradesman, and not to occupy your female mind with calculations when he took to his trade or when he didn't. A honoring and obeying wife would let his trade alone altogether. Call yourself a religious woman? If you're a religious woman, give me a irreligious one! You have no more nat'ral sense of duty than the bed of this here Thames River has of a pile, and similarly it must be knocked into you."

---

1. ***Izaak Walton,*** English writer [1593–1683] and author of *The Compleat Angler*, a book on fishing. His name has become synonymous with *fisherman.*

The altercation terminated in the honest tradesman's kicking off his clay-soiled boots, and lying down at his length on the floor. After taking a timid peep at him lying on his back, with his rusty hands under his head for a pillow, his son lay down too, and fell asleep again.

There was no fish for breakfast, and not much of anything else. Mr. Cruncher, out of spirits, and out of temper, kept an iron potlid by him as a projectile for the correction of Mrs. Cruncher, in case he should observe any symptoms of her saying Grace. He was brushed and washed at the usual hour and set off with his son to pursue his ostensible calling.

"Father," said Young Jerry, as they walked along, taking care to keep at arm's length and to have the stool well between them; "what's a resurrection-man?"

Mr. Cruncher came to a stop on the pavement before he answered, "How should I know?"

"I thought you knowed everything, father," said the artless boy.

"Hem! Well," returned Mr. Cruncher, going on again, and lifting off his hat to give his spikes free play, "he's a tradesman."

"What's his goods, father?" asked the brisk Young Jerry.

"His goods," said Mr. Cruncher, after turning it over in his mind, "is a branch of scientific goods."

"Persons' bodies, ain't it, father?" asked the lively boy.

"I believe it is something of that sort," said Mr. Cruncher.

"Oh, father, I should so like to be a resurrection-man when I'm quite growed up!"

Mr. Cruncher was soothed, but shook his head in a dubious and moral way. "It depends upon how you dewelop your talents. Be careful to dewelop your talents, and never to say no more than you can help to nobody, and there's no telling at the present time what you may not come to be fit for." As Young Jerry, thus encouraged, went on a few yards in advance, to plant the stool in the shadow of the Bar, Mr. Cruncher added to himself: "Jerry, you honest tradesman, there's hopes wot that boy will yet be a blessing to you, and a recompense to you for his mother!"

CHAPTER XIII
KNITTING

This had been the third morning in succession on which there had been early drinking at the wine shop of Monsieur Defarge. There had been more of early brooding than drinking; for many men had listened and whispered and slunk about there from the time of the opening of the door who could not have laid a piece of money on the counter to save their souls. These were to the full as interested in the place, however, as if they could have commanded whole barrels of wine; and they glided from seat to seat, and from corner to corner, swallowing talk in lieu of drink, with greedy looks.

Notwithstanding an unusual flow of company, the master of the wine shop was not visible. He was not missed; for, nobody who crossed the threshold looked for him, nobody asked for him, nobody wondered to see only Madame Defarge in her seat, presiding over the distribution of wine, with a bowl of battered small coins before her, as much defaced and beaten out of their original impress as the small coinage of humanity from whose ragged pockets they had come.

Thus, Saint Antoine, until high noontide, when two dusty men passed through his streets, of whom one was Monsieur Defarge, the other a mender of roads in a blue cap. All adust and athirst, the two entered the wine shop. Their arrival had lighted a kind of fire in the breast of Saint Antoine, fast spreading as they came along, which stirred and flickered in flames of faces at most doors and windows. Yet no one had followed them, and no man spoke when they entered the wine shop, though the eyes of every man there were turned upon them.

"Good-day, gentlemen!" said Monsieur Defarge.

It may have been a signal for loosening the general tongue. It elicited an answering chorus of "Good-day!"

"It is bad weather, gentlemen," said Defarge, shaking his head.

Upon which every man looked at his neighbor, and then all cast down their eyes and sat silent. Except one man, who got up and went out.

"My wife," said Defarge aloud, addressing Madame Defarge, "I have traveled certain leagues with this good mender of roads, called Jacques. I met him—by accident—a day and a half's journey out of Paris. He is a good child, this Jacques. Give him to drink, my wife!"

A second man got up and went out. Madame Defarge set wine before the mender of roads called Jacques, who doffed his blue cap to the company, and drank. In the breast of his blouse he carried some coarse dark bread; he ate of this between whiles, and sat munching and drinking near Madame Defarge's counter. A third man got up and went out.

Defarge refreshed himself with a draft of wine and stood waiting until the countryman had made his breakfast. He looked at no one present, and no one now looked at him; not even Madame Defarge, who had taken up her knitting, and was at work.

"Have you finished, friend?" he asked, in due season.

"Yes, thank you."

"Come, then! You shall see the apartment that I told you you could occupy. It will suit you to a marvel."

Out of the wine shop into the street, out of the street into a courtyard, out of the courtyard up a steep staircase, out of the staircase into a garret—formerly the garret where a white-haired man sat very busy, making shoes.

No white-haired man was there now; but the three men were there who had gone out of the wine shop singly, and had once looked in at him through the chinks in the wall.

Defarge closed the door and spoke in a subdued voice:

"Jacques One, Jacques Two, Jacques Three! This is the witness encountered by appointment, by me, Jacques Four. He will tell you all. Speak, Jacques Five!"

The mender of roads, blue cap in hand, said, "Where shall I commence, monsieur?"

"Commence," was Monsieur Defarge's not unreasonable reply, "at the commencement."

"I saw him then, messieurs," began the mender of roads, "a year ago this running summer, underneath the carriage of the Marquis, hanging by the chain."

Jacques One struck in, and asked if he had ever seen the man before.

"Never," answered the mender of roads.

Jacques Three demanded how he afterwards recognized him then.

"By his tall figure," said the mender of roads. "When Monsieur the Marquis demands that evening, 'Say, what is he like?' I make response, 'Tall as a specter.'"

"You should have said, short as a dwarf," returned Jacques Two.

"But what did I know? The deed was not then accomplished. Observe! Under those circumstances even, I do not offer my testimony. Monsieur the Marquis indicates me with his finger, and says, 'To me! Bring that rascal!' My faith, messieurs, I offer nothing.'

"He is right there, Jacques," murmured Defarge, to him who had interrupted. "Go on!"

"Good!" said the mender of roads, with an air of mystery. "The tall man is lost, and he is sought—how many months? Nine, ten, eleven?"

"No matter, the number," said Defarge. "He is well hidden, but at last he is unluckily found. Go on!"

"I am again at work upon the hillside. I am collecting my tools to descend to my cottage in the village below, where it is already dark, when I raise my eyes, and see coming over the hill six soldiers. In the midst of them is a tall man with his arms bound—tied to his sides—like this!''

With the aid of his indispensable cap, he represented a man with his elbows bound fast at his hips, with cords that were knotted behind him.

''I stand aside, messieurs, to see the soldiers and their prisoner pass—for it is a solitary road, that, where any spectacle is well worth looking at—and at first, as they approach, I see no more than that they are six soldiers with a tall man bound, and that they are almost black to my sight. I see that they are covered with dust, and that the dust moves with them as they come, tramp, tramp! But when they advance quite near to me, I recognize the tall man, and he recognizes me. Ah, but he would be content to precipitate himself over the hillside once again, as on the evening he and I first encountered, close to the same spot!

''I do not show the soldiers that I recognize the tall man; he does not show the soldiers that he recognizes me; we do it with our eyes. 'Come on!' says the chief of that company, pointing to the village, 'bring him fast to his tomb!' and they bring him faster. I follow. His arms are swelled because of being bound so tight, his wooden shoes are large and clumsy, and he is lame. Because he is consequently slow, they drive him with their guns—like this!''

He imitated the action of a man's being impelled forward by the butt ends of muskets.

''As they descend the hill like madmen running a race, he falls. They laugh and pick him up again. His face is bleeding and covered with dust, but he cannot touch it; thereupon they laugh again. They bring him into the village; all the village runs to look; they take him past the mill, and up to the prison; all the village sees the prison gate open in the darkness of the night, and swallow him!

''All the village,'' pursued the mender of roads, ''whispers by the fountain; in the morning, my tools upon my shoulder, I make a circuit by the prison on my way to my work. There I see him, high up, behind the bars of a lofty iron cage, bloody and dusty as last night, looking through. He has no hand free, to wave to me; I dare not call to him; he regards me like a dead man.''

Defarge and the three glanced darkly at one another. The looks of all of them were dark, repressed, and revengeful, as they listened to the countryman's story; the manner of all of them, while it was secret, was authoritative too. They had the air of a rough tribunal; Jacques One and Two sitting on the old pallet bed, each with his chin resting on his hand, and his eyes intent on the road mender; Jacques Three equally intent, on one knee behind them, with his agitated hand always gliding over the network of fine nerves about his mouth and nose; Defarge standing between them and the narrator, whom he had stationed in the light of the window, by turns looking from him to them, and from them to him.

''Go on, Jacques,'' said Defarge.

''He remains up there in his iron cage some days. The village looks at him by stealth, for it is afraid. They whisper at the fountain that although condemned to death he will not be executed; they say that petitions have been presented in Paris, showing that he was enraged and made mad by the death of his child; they say that a petition has been presented to the King himself. What do I know? It is possible. Perhaps yes, perhaps no.''

''Listen then, Jacques,'' Number One of that name sternly interposed. ''Know that a petition was presented to the King and Queen. All here, yourself excepted, saw the King take it, in his carriage in the street, sitting beside the Queen. It is Defarge whom you see here, who, at the hazard of his life, darted out before the horses, with the petition in his hand.''

''And once again listen, Jacques!'' said the kneeling Number Three: his fingers ever wandering over and over those fine nerves, with a strikingly greedy air, as if he hungered for something—that was neither food nor drink; ''the guard horse and foot, surrounded the petitioner, and struck him blows. You hear?''

''I hear, messieurs.''

''Go on then,'' said Defarge.

"Again, on the other hand, they whisper at the fountain," resumed the countryman, "that he is brought down into our country to be executed on the spot, and that he will very certainly be executed. They even whisper that because he has slain Monseigneur, and because Monseigneur was the father of his tenants—serfs—what you will—he will be executed as a parricide.

"Well! Some whisper this, some whisper that; they speak of nothing else. At length, on Sunday night, when all the village is asleep, come soldiers, winding down from the prison. Workmen dig, workmen hammer, soldiers laugh and sing; in the morning by the fountain, there is raised a gallows forty feet high, poisoning the water."

The mender of roads pointed as if he saw the gallows somewhere in the sky.

"All work is stopped, all assemble there. At midday, the roll of drums. Soldiers have marched into the prison in the night, and he is in the midst of many soldiers. He is bound as before, and in his mouth there is a gag—tied so, with a tight string, making him look almost as if he laughed." He suggested it, by creasing his face with his two thumbs, from the corners of his mouth to his ears. "On the top of the gallows is fixed the knife, blade upwards, with its point in the air. He is hanged there forty feet high—and is left hanging, poisoning the water."

They looked at one another as he used his blue cap to wipe his face on which the perspiration had started afresh while he recalled the spectacle.

"It is frightful, messieurs. How can the women and children draw water! Who can gossip of an evening under that shadow! Under it, have I said? The shadow struck across the church, across the mill, across the prison—seemed to strike across the earth, messieurs!"

The hungry man gnawed one of his fingers as he looked at the other three, and his finger quivered with the craving that was on him.

"That's all, messieurs. I left at sunset—as I had been warned to do—and I walked on, that night and half next day, until I met—as I was warned I should—this comrade. With him, I came on through the rest of yesterday and through last night. And here you see me!"

After a gloomy silence the first Jacques said, "Good! You have acted and recounted faithfully. Will you wait for us a little, outside the door?"

"Very willingly," said the mender of roads, whom Defarge escorted to the top of the stairs and, leaving seated there, returned.

"How say you, Jacques?" demanded Number One. "To be registered?"

"To be registered as doomed to destruction," returned Defarge.

"Magnificent!" croaked the man with the craving.

"The Château and all the race?" inquired the first.

"The Château and all the race," returned Defarge. "Extermination."

The hungry man repeated, in a rapturous croak, "Magnificent!" and began gnawing another finger.

"Are you sure," asked Jacques Two, of Defarge, "that no embarrassment can arise from our manner of keeping the register? Without doubt it is safe, for no one beyond ourselves can decipher it; but shall we always be able to decipher it—or, I ought to say, will she?"

"Jacques," returned Defarge, drawing himself up, "if madame my wife undertook to keep the register in her memory alone, she would not lose a word of it—not a syllable of it. Knitted, in her own stitches and her own symbols, it will always be as plain to her as the sun. It would be easier for the weakest poltroon that lives to erase himself from existence than to erase one letter of his name or crimes from the knitted register of Madame Defarge."

There was a murmur of confidence and approval, and then the man who hungered asked: "Is this rustic to be sent back soon? I hope so. He is very simple; is he not a little dangerous?"

"He knows nothing," said Defarge; "I will

take care of him, and set him on his road. He wishes to see the Court; let him see it on Sunday."

"What?" exclaimed the hungry man, staring. "Is it a good sign that he wishes to see royalty and nobility?"

"Jacques," said Defarge; "judiciously show a cat milk, if you wish her to thirst for it. Judiciously show a dog his natural prey, if you wish him to bring it down one day."

Nothing more was said, and the mender of roads, already dozing on the topmost stair, was advised to take some rest. He needed no persuasion, and was soon asleep.

Worse quarters than Defarge's wine shop could have easily been found in Paris for a provincial slave of that degree. Saving for a mysterious dread of madame by which he was constantly haunted, his life was very new and agreeable. But madame sat all day at her counter, so expressly unconscious of him, and so particularly determined not to perceive that his being there had any connection with anything below the surface, that he shook in his wooden shoes whenever his eye lighted on her. For he contended with himself that it was impossible to foresee what the lady might pretend next; and he felt assured that if she should take it into her brightly ornamented head to pretend that she had seen him do a murder and afterwards flay the victim, she would infallibly go through with it until the play was played out.

When Sunday came, the mender of roads was not enchanted to find that madame was to accompany monsieur and himself to Versailles.[1] It was additionally disconcerting to have madame still with her knitting in her hands as the crowd waited to see the carriage of the King and Queen.

"What do you make, madame?" asked a man near her.

"Many things."

"For instance——"

"For instance," returned Madame Defarge, composedly, "shrouds."

The man moved a little farther away, as soon as he could, and the mender of roads fanned himself with his blue cap. Soon the large-faced King and the fair-faced Queen came in their golden coach, attended by a glittering multitude of laughing ladies and fine lords; the mender of roads cried, "Long live the King, Long live the Queen, Long live everybody!" until he absolutely wept with sentiment.

"Bravo!" said Defarge, clapping him on the back when it was over, "you are a good boy!"

The mender of roads was now coming to himself, and was mistrustful of having made a mistake in his late demonstrations; but no.

"You are the fellow we want," said Defarge; "you make these fools believe it will last forever. Then they are the more insolent, and it is the nearer ended."

Madame Defarge nodded in confirmation.

"As to you," said she, "you would shout and shed tears for anything, if it made a show and a noise. Say! Would you not?"

"Truly, madame, I think so. For the moment."

"If you were shown a great heap of dolls, and were set upon them to pluck them to pieces and despoil them, for your own advantage, you would pick out the richest and gayest. Say. Would you not?"

"Truly yes, madame."

"Yes. And if you were shown a flock of birds, unable to fly, and were set upon them to strip them of their feathers, for your own advantage, you would set upon the birds of the finest feathers; would you not?"

"It is true, madame."

"You have seen both dolls and birds today," said Madame Defarge. "Now go home!"

---

1. ***Versailles*** (vər sī′), a city twelve miles southwest of Paris and the seat of the principal royal dwelling, the Palace of Versailles.

Discussion

Chapter XI

1. (a) What new side of Sydney Carton's nature is revealed in this chapter? **(b)** Although both Darnay and Carton declare their devotion to Lucie, each does it in his own way. Compare the behavior of the two men.

2. Carton makes Lucie a promise. What is it?

Discussion

Chapter XII

1. (a) Where have you met "the spy" Roger Cly before? **(b)** Who do you suppose is the "one mourner" at his funeral?

2. (a) At what point in the novel did you first surmise Jerry's "trade"? **(b)** What kind of luck did Jerry have on this "fishing" trip? How do you know? **(c)** Does the explanation of his trade also explain Jerry's attitude toward prayer? Explain.

Chapter XIII

1. (a) Why do the five men meet in the garret above the wine shop? **(b)** What story does the road mender relate?

2. (a) What is Dickens's purpose in revealing in detail the execution of the Marquis's murderer? **(b)** For what does Jacques Three hunger? **(c)** What do his peculiar actions contribute to the mood of this chapter?

3. In what ways do the raising of the gallows and the hanging of the murderer poison the water in the fountain?

4. (a) After the road mender has given his testimony, what decision is reached? **(b)** Whom will it affect? **(c)** What is the purpose of the secret register and how is it kept?

5. At the end of the chapter is Madame Defarge speaking of real dolls and birds or of something else?

Comment: The National Razor

At the London trial in Book the Second, Chapter II, Jerry Cruncher speaks of "quartering" as "barbarous." Review in that chapter how an excited spectator decribes to Jerry his own version of the torture that will befall Charles Darnay if he is convicted of treason. In Paris, the death penalty would be carried out in a more humane way.

Dr. Joseph I. Guillotin, a surgeon and a member of the Revolutionary Assembly, proposed in 1789 that persons condemned to death be executed swiftly and mercifully by a beheading machine, which thereafter came to bear his name. Before the revolution, only French nobles had the privilege of being decapitated for capital crimes; common people were hanged, burned at the stake, or tortured to death.

Decapitating machines of one design or another had been known in other countries: ancient Persia, Germany and Italy during the Middle Ages, Scotland during the sixteenth and seventeenth centuries, and even France long before the revolution.

During the revolution French people called the guillotine "the national razor." It was fashionable for revolutionists to wear miniature guillotines suspended as charms from necklaces.

The machine designed by Dr. Guillotin was first used April 25, 1792. Between August 10 of that year and July 31, 1794, approximately 20,000 persons were executed. Though no longer used for political terrorism, the guillotine remains the legal method of execution in France.

CHAPTER XIV
STILL KNITTING

Madame Defarge and monsieur her husband returned amicably to the bosom of Saint Antoine, while a speck in a blue cap toiled through the darkness, and through the dust, and down the weary miles, slowly tending toward where the château of Monsieur the Marquis, now in his grave, listened to the whispering trees.

The Defarges, husband and wife, came lumbering under the starlight, in their public vehicle, to that gate of Paris whereunto their journey tended. Monsieur Defarge alighted; knowing one or two of the soldiery there, and one of the police. The latter he was intimate with, and affectionately embraced. When Saint Antoine had again enfolded the Defarges in his dusky wings, Madame Defarge spoke to her husband:

"Say then; what did Jacques of the police tell thee?"

"Very little tonight, but all he knows. There is another spy commissioned for our quarter."

"Eh, well!" said Madame Defarge. "It is necessary to register him. How do they call that man?"

"He is English."

"So much the better. His name?"

"Barsad," said Defarge. "John."

"John Barsad," repeated madame, after murmuring it once to herself. "Good. His appearance; is it known?"

"Age, about forty years; height, about five feet nine; black hair; complexion dark; generally, rather handsome visage; eyes dark, face thin, long, and sallow; nose aquiline, but not straight, having a peculiar inclination toward the left cheek; expression, therefore, sinister."

"Eh, my faith. It is a portrait!" said madame, laughing. "He shall be registered tomorrow."

They turned into the wine shop, which was closed—for it was midnight—and where Madame Defarge immediately took her post at her desk, counted the small moneys, examined the stock, went through the entries in the book, made other entries of her own, checked the serving man in every possible way, and finally dismissed him to bed.

Next noontide saw the admirable woman in her usual place in the wine shop, knitting away assiduously. A rose lay beside her, and if she now and then glanced at the flower, it was with no infraction of her usual preoccupied air. There were a few customers, drinking or not drinking, standing or seated, sprinkled about.

A figure entering at the door threw a shadow on Madame Defarge which she felt to be a new one. She laid down her knitting, and began to pin her rose in her headdress, before she looked at the figure.

It was curious. The moment Madame Defarge took up the rose the customers ceased talking, and began gradually to drop out of the wine shop.

"Good day, madame," said the newcomer.

"Good day, monsieur."

She said it aloud, but added to herself, as she resumed her knitting: "Hah! Good day, age about forty, height about five feet nine, black hair, generally rather handsome visage, complexion dark, eyes dark, thin long and sallow face, aquiline nose but not straight, having a peculiar inclination toward the left cheek which imparts a sinister expression! Good day one and all!"

"Have the goodness to give me a little glass of old cognac."

"JOHN," thought madame, checking off her work as her fingers knitted, and her eyes looked at the stranger. "Stay long enough, and I shall knit 'BARSAD' before you go."

The spy, who was there to pick up any crumbs he could find, stood with an air of gossiping gallantry, leaning his elbow on Madame Defarge's little counter.

"A bad business this, madame, of Gaspard's execution. Ah! the poor Gaspard!" With a sigh of great compassion.

"My faith!" returned madame, coolly and lightly, "if people use knives for such purposes, they have to pay for it. He knew beforehand what the price of his luxury was; he has paid the price."

"I believe," said the spy, "there is much compassion and anger in this neighborhood, touching the poor fellow?"

"Is there?" asked madame, vacantly.

"Is there not?"

"—Here is my husband!" said Madame Defarge.

As the keeper of the wine shop entered, the spy saluted him by saying, with an engaging smile, "Good day, Jacques!" Defarge stopped short and stared at him.

"Good day, Jacques!" the spy repeated; with not quite so much confidence, or quite so easy a smile under the stare.

"You deceive yourself, monsieur," returned the keeper of the wine shop. "I am Ernest Defarge."

"It is all the same," said the spy, airily, but discomfited too; "good day!"

"Good day!" answered Defarge, drily.

"The pleasure of conversing with you, Monsieur Defarge, recalls to me," pursued the spy, "that I have the honor of cherishing some interesting associations with your name."

"Indeed!" said Defarge, with much indifference.

"Yes, indeed. When Doctor Manette was released, you, his old domestic, had the charge of him, I know. You see I am informed of the circumstances?"

"Such is the fact, certainly," said Defarge. He had it conveyed to him, in an accidental touch of his wife's elbow, as she knitted and warbled, that he would do best to answer, but with brevity.

"It was to you," said the spy, "that his daughter came; and it was from your care that his daughter took him, accompanied by Monsieur Lorry—of the bank of Tellson and Company—over to England."

"Such is the fact," repeated Defarge.

"Very interesting remembrances!" said the spy. "I have known Doctor Manette and his daughter, in England."

"Yes?" said Defarge.

"You don't hear much about them now?" said the spy. "She is going to be married."

"Going?" echoed madame. "She was pretty enough to have been married long ago. You English are cold, it seems to me."

"Oh! You know I am English?"

"I perceive your tongue is," returned madame, "and what the tongue is, I suppose the man is."

He did not take the identification as a compliment; but he made the best of it, and turned it off with a laugh. After sipping his cognac to the end, he added:

"Yes, Miss Manette is going to be married. But not to an Englishman; to one who, like herself, is French by birth. And speaking of Gaspard—ah, poor Gaspard! It is a curious thing that—she is going to marry the nephew of Monsieur the Marquis, for whom Gaspard was exalted to that height of so many feet; in other words, the present Marquis. But he lives unknown in England, he is no Marquis there; he is Mr. Charles Darnay. D'Aulnais is the name of his mother's family."

Madame Defarge knitted steadily, but the intelligence had a palpable effect upon her husband. The spy would have been no spy if he had failed to see it. Having made, at least, this one hit, whatever it might prove to be worth, Mr. Barsad paid for what he had drunk, and took his leave.

"Can it be true," said Defarge, in a low voice, "what he has said of Ma'amselle Manette?"

"As he has said it," retorted madame, lifting her eyebrows a little, "it is probably false. But it may be true."

"If it is, I hope, for her sake, Destiny will keep her husband out of France."

"Her husband's destiny," said Madame Defarge, with her usual composure, "will take him where he is to go, and will lead him to the end that is to end him. That is all I know."

"But it is very strange—now, at least, is it not very strange"—said Defarge, rather pleading with his wife to induce her to admit it, "that, after all our sympathy of Monsieur her father, and herself, her husband's name should be proscribed under your hand at this moment, by the side of that infernal dog's who has just left us?"

"Stranger things than that will happen when it does come," answered madame. "I have them both here, of a certainty; and they are both here for their merits; that is enough."

She rolled up her knitting when she had said those words and presently took the rose out of the handkerchief that was wound about her head.

In the evening, Madame Defarge with her work in her hand was accustomed to pass from place to place and from group to group; a Missionary—there were many like her—such as the world will do well never to breed again.

All the women knitted. They knitted worthless things; but the mechanical work was a mechanical substitute for eating and drinking; the hands moved for the jaws and the digestive apparatus; if the bony fingers had been still, the stomachs would have been more famine-pinched.

But as the fingers went, the eyes went, and the thoughts. And as Madame Defarge moved on from group to group, all three went quicker and fiercer among every little knot of women that she had spoken with, and left behind.

Her husband smoked at his door, looking after her with admiration. "A great woman," said he, "a strong woman, a grand woman, a frightfully grand woman!"

Darkness closed around, and then came the ringing of church bells and the distant beating of the military drums in the Palace Courtyard, as the women sat knitting, knitting. Darkness encompassed them. Another darkness was closing in as surely, when the church bells, then ringing pleasant in many an airy steeple over France, should be melted into thundering cannon; when the military drums should be beating to drown a wretched voice, the voice of Power and Plenty, Freedom and Life. So much was closing in about the women who sat knitting, knitting, that they their very selves were closing in around a structure yet unbuilt, where they were to sit knitting, knitting, counting dropping heads.

CHAPTER XV
NINE DAYS

The marriage day was shining brightly, and they were ready outside the closed door of the Doctor's room, where he was speaking with Charles Darnay. They were ready to go to church; the beautiful bride, Mr. Lorry, and Miss Pross—to whom the event, through a gradual process of reconcilement to the inevitable would have been one of absolute bliss but for the yet lingering consideration that her brother Solomon should have been the bridegroom.

"And so," said Mr. Lorry, who could not sufficiently admire the bride, and who had been moving round her to take in every point of her quiet, pretty dress; "and so it was for this, my sweet Lucie, that I brought you across the Channel, such a baby! Lord bless me! How little I thought what I was doing! How lightly I valued the obligation I was conferring on my friend Mr. Charles!"

"You didn't mean it," remarked the matter-of-fact Miss Pross, "and therefore how could you know it? Nonsense!"

"Really? Well; but don't cry," said the gentle Mr. Lorry.

"I am not crying," said Miss Pross; "*you* are."

"I, my Pross?" (By this time, Mr. Lorry dared to be pleasant with her, on occasion.)

"You were, just now; I saw you do it, and I don't wonder at it. Such a present of plate as you made 'em is enough to bring tears into anybody's eyes. There's not a fork or a spoon in the collection that I didn't cry over, last night after the box came, till I couldn't see it."

"I am highly gratified," said Mr. Lorry. "Dear me! This is an occasion that makes a man speculate on all he has lost. Dear, dear, dear!

To think that there might have been a Mrs. Lorry any time these fifty years almost!"

"Not at all!" From Miss Pross.

"You think there never might have been a Mrs. Lorry?" asked the gentleman of that name.

"Pooh!" rejoined Miss Pross; "you were a bachelor in your cradle."

"Well!" observed Mr. Lorry, beamingly adjusting his little wig, "that seems probable too."

"And you were cut out for a bachelor," pursued Miss Pross, "before you were put in your cradle."

"Then, I think," said Mr. Lorry, "that I was very unhandsomely dealt with, and that I ought to have had a voice in the selection of my pattern. Enough! Now, my dear Lucie," drawing his arm soothingly round her waist, "I hear them moving in the next room, and Miss Pross and I, as two formal folks of business, are anxious not to lose the final opportunity of saying something to you that you wish to hear. You leave your good father, my dear, in hands as earnest and as loving as your own; he shall be taken every conceivable care of; during the next fortnight, while you are in Warwickshire and thereabouts, even Tellson's shall go to the wall—comparatively speaking—before him. And when, at the fortnight's end, he comes to join you and your beloved husband, on your other fortnight's trip in Wales, you shall say that we have sent him to you in the best health and in the happiest frame. Now I hear Somebody's step coming to the door. Let me kiss my dear girl with an old-fashioned bachelor blessing before Somebody comes to claim his own."

The door of the Doctor's room opened, and he came out with Charles Darnay. He was so deadly pale—which had not been the case when they went in together—that no vestige of color was in his face. But in the composure of his manner he was unaltered, except that to Mr. Lorry it disclosed some shadowy indication that the old air of avoidance and dread had lately passed over him, like a cold wind.

He gave his arm to his daughter, and took her downstairs to the chariot which Mr. Lorry had hired in honor of the day. The rest followed in another carriage, and soon, in a neighboring church, where no strange eyes looked on, Charles Darnay and Lucie Manette were happily married.

They returned home to breakfast, and all went well, and in due course the golden hair that had mingled with the poor shoemaker's white locks in the Paris garret, was mingled with them again in the morning sunlight, on the threshold of the door at parting.

It was a hard parting, though not for long. But her father said at last, gently disengaging himself from her enfolding arms, "Take her, Charles! She is yours!"

And her agitated hand waved to them from a chaise window, and she was gone.

The preparations having been very simple and few, the Doctor, Mr. Lorry, and Miss Pross, were left quite alone. It was when they returned into the welcome shade of the cool old hall that Mr. Lorry observed a great change to have come over the Doctor.

"I think," he whispered to Miss Pross, after anxious consideration, "we had best not speak to him just now, or at all disturb him. I must look in at Tellson's; so I will go there at once and come back presently. Then we will take him a ride into the country, and all will be well."

It was easier for Mr. Lorry to look in at Tellson's than to look out of Tellson's. He was detained two hours. When he came back to the Doctor's rooms, he was stopped by a low sound of knocking.

"Good God!" he said, with a start. "What's that?"

Miss Pross, with a terrified face, was at his ear. "O me! All is lost!" cried she, wringing her hands. "What is to be told to Ladybird? He is making shoes!"

Mr. Lorry said what he could to calm her, and went himself into the Doctor's room. The bench was turned toward the light, as it had been when he had seen the shoemaker at his work before, and he was very busy.

"Doctor Manette. My dear friend, Doctor Manette!"

The Doctor looked at him for a moment, half inquiringly, and bent over his work again.

He had laid aside his coat and waistcoat; his shirt was open at the throat, and even the old haggard, faded surface of face had come back to him. He worked hard—impatiently—as if in some sense of having been interrupted.

Mr. Lorry glanced at the work in his hand, and observed that it was a shoe of the old size and shape. He took up another that was lying by him, and asked what it was.

"A young lady's walking shoe," he muttered, without looking up. "It ought to have been finished long ago."

"But, Doctor Manette. Look at me."

He obeyed, in the old mechanically submissive manner.

"You know me, my dear friend? Think again. This is not your proper occupation. Think, dear friend!"

Nothing would induce him to speak more. He looked up, for an instant at a time, when he was requested to do so; but no persuasion would extract a word from him.

Two things at once impressed themselves on Mr. Lorry, as important above all others; the first, that this must be kept secret from Lucie; the second, that it must be kept secret from all who knew him. In conjunction with Miss Pross, he took immediate steps toward the latter precaution, by giving out that the Doctor was not well, and required a few days of complete rest.

In the hope of his recovery, Mr. Lorry resolved to watch him attentively, with as little appearance as possible of doing so. He therefore made arrangements to absent himself from Tellson's for the first time in his life, and took his post by the window in the same room.

He was not long in discovering that it was worse than useless to speak to him, since, on being pressed, he became worried. He abandoned that attempt on the first day, and resolved merely to keep himself always before him, as a silent protest against the delusion into which he had fallen, or was falling. He remained, therefore, in his seat near the window, reading and writing, and expressing in as many pleasant and natural ways as he could think of, that it was a free place.

Doctor Manette took what was given him to eat and drink, and worked on, that first day, until it was too dark to see. When he put his tools aside, Mr. Lorry rose and said:

"Will you go out?"

He looked down at the floor on either side of him in the old manner, looked up in the old manner, and repeated:

"Out?"

"Yes; for a walk with me. Why not?"

He made no effort to say why not, and said not a word more. But Mr. Lorry thought he saw that he was in some misty way asking himself, "Why not?" The sagacity of the man of business perceived an advantage here, and determined to hold it.

On the second day, Mr. Lorry saluted him cheerfully by his name, and spoke to him on topics that had been of late familiar to them. He returned no reply, but it was evident that he heard what was said, and that he thought about it, however confusedly. This encouraged Mr. Lorry to have Miss Pross in with her work, several times during the day; at those times, they quietly spoke of Lucie, and of her father then present, precisely in the usual manner, and as if there were nothing amiss. This was done without any demonstrative accompaniment, not long enough, or often enough to harass him; and it lightened Mr. Lorry's friendly heart to believe that he looked up oftener, and appeared to be stirred by some perception of inconsistencies surrounding him.

When it fell dark again, Mr. Lorry asked him as before.

"Dear Doctor, will you go out?"

As before, he repeated, "Out?"

"Yes; for a walk with me. Why not?"

This time Mr. Lorry feigned to go out when he could extract no answer from him, and, after remaining absent for an hour, returned. In the meanwhile, the Doctor had removed to the seat in the window, but, on Mr. Lorry's return, he slipped away to his bench.

The time went slowly on, and Mr. Lorry's hope darkened, and his heart grew heavier and heavier every day. The third day came and went, the fourth, the fifth. Five days, six days, seven days, eight days, nine days.

With a hope ever darkening, and with a heart always growing heavier and heavier, Mr. Lorry passed through this anxious time. The secret was well kept, and Lucie was unconscious and happy; but he could not fail to observe that the shoemaker, whose hand had been a little out at first, was growing dreadfully skillful, and that he had never been so intent on his work, and that his hands had never been so nimble and expert as in the dusk of the ninth evening.

CHAPTER XVI
AN OPINION

Worn out by anxious watching, Mr. Lorry fell asleep at his post. On the tenth morning of his suspense, he was startled by the shining of the sun into the room where a heavy slumber had overtaken him.

He rubbed his eyes and roused himself; but he doubted, when he had done so, whether he was not still asleep. For, going to the door of the Doctor's room and looking in, he perceived that the shoemaker's bench and tools were put aside again, and that the Doctor himself sat reading at the window. He was in his usual morning dress, and his face—which Mr. Lorry could distinctly see—though still very pale, was calmly studious and attentive.

Within a few minutes Miss Pross stood whispering at his side. If he had had any particle of doubt left, her talk would of necessity have resolved it; but he was by that time clear-headed, and had none. He advised that they should let the time go by until the regular breakfast hour, and should then meet the Doctor as if nothing unusual had occurred.

When the breakfast was done and cleared away, and he and the Doctor were left together, Mr. Lorry said, feelingly:

"My dear Manette, I am anxious to have your opinion, in confidence, on a very curious case in which I am deeply interested; that is to say, it is very curious to me; perhaps, to your better information it may be less so."

Glancing at his hands, which were discolored by his late work, the Doctor looked troubled, and listened attentively. He had already glanced at his hands more than once.

"Doctor Manette," said Mr. Lorry, touching him affectionately on the arm, "the case is the case of a particularly dear friend of mine. Pray advise me well for his sake—and above all, for his daughter's, my dear Manette."

"If I understand," said the Doctor, in a subdued tone, "some mental shock——?"

"Yes!"

"Be explicit," said the Doctor. "Spare no detail."

Mr. Lorry saw that they understood one another, and proceeded:

"My dear Manette, it is the case of an old and a prolonged shock from which the sufferer recovered, by a process that he cannot trace himself—as I once heard him publicly relate in a striking manner. But, unfortunately, there has been"—he paused and took a deep breath— "a slight relapse."

The Doctor, in a low voice, asked, "Of how long duration?"

"Nine days and nights."

"How did it show itself? I infer," glancing at his hands again, "in the resumption of some old pursuit connected with the shock?"

"That is the fact."

"Now, did you ever see him," asked the Doctor, distinctly and collectedly, though in the same low voice, "engaged in that pursuit originally?"

"Once."

"And when the relapse fell on him, was he in

most respects—or in all respects—as he was then?''

''I think in all respects.''

''Does his daughter know of the relapse?''

''No. It has been kept from her. It is known only to myself, and to one other who may be trusted.''

The Doctor grasped his hand, and murmured, ''That was very kind.'' Neither of the two spoke for a little while.

''Now,'' said Mr. Lorry, gently, ''to what would you refer this attack?''

''I believe,'' returned Doctor Manette, ''that there had been a strong revival of the train of thought and remembrance that was the first cause of the malady. Some intense associations of a most distressing nature were vividly recalled, I think. It is probable that there had long been a dread lurking in his mind that those associations would be recalled—say, under certain circumstances—say, on a particular occasion. He tried to prepare himself in vain; perhaps the effort to prepare himself made him less able to bear it.''

''Would he remember what took place in the relapse?'' asked Mr. Lorry, with natural hesitation.

The Doctor looked desolately round the room, shook his head, and answered, in a low voice, ''Not at all.''

''Now, as to the future,'' hinted Mr. Lorry.

''As to the future,'' said the Doctor, recovering firmness, ''I should have great hope. As it pleased heaven in its mercy to restore him so soon, I should have great hope. I should hope that the worst was over.''

''That's good comfort. I am thankful!'' said Mr. Lorry.

''I am thankful!'' repeated the Doctor, bending his head with reverence.

''The occupation resumed under the influence of this passing affliction so happily recovered from,'' said Mr. Lorry, clearing his throat, ''we will call—blacksmith's work. We will say, to put a case and for the sake of illustration, that he had been used, in his bad time, to work at a little forge. We will say that he was unexpectedly found at his forge again. Is it not a pity that he should keep it by him?''

The Doctor beat his foot nervously on the ground.

''He has always kept it by him,'' said Mr. Lorry, with an anxious look at his friend. ''Now, would it not be better that he should let it go?''

''You see,'' said Doctor Manette, after an uneasy pause, ''it is very hard to explain the workings of this poor man's mind. He once yearned so frightfully for that occupation, and it was so welcome when it came; no doubt it relieved his pain so much, by substituting the perplexity of the fingers for the perplexity of the brain, that he has never been able to bear the thought of putting it quite out of his reach. Even now, when he is more hopeful of himself than he has ever been, the idea that he might need that old employment, and not find it, gives him a sudden sense of terror, like that which strikes the heart of a lost child.''

He looked like his illustration, as he raised his eyes to Mr. Lorry's face.

''I would not keep it,'' said Mr. Lorry, shaking his head; for he gained in firmness as he saw the Doctor disquieted. ''I only want your authority. I am sure it does no good. Come! Give me your authority, like a dear good man. For his daughter's sake, my dear Manette!''

Very strange to see what a struggle there was within him!

''In her name, then, let it be done. But let it be removed when he is not there; let him miss his old companion after an absence.''

Mr. Lorry readily engaged for that, and the conference was ended. They passed the day in the country, and the Doctor was quite restored. On the fourteenth day he went to join Lucie and her husband, and she had no suspicions.

On the night of the day on which he left the house, Mr. Lorry went into his room with a chopper, saw, chisel, and hammer, attended by Miss Pross carrying a light. There with closed doors, and in a mysterious and guilty manner, Mr. Lorry hacked the shoemaker's bench to pieces, while Miss Pross held the candle as if she were assisting at a murder—for which, indeed, in her grimness, she was no unsuitable figure. The burning of the body—previously reduced to pieces convenient for the purpose—was commenced without delay in the kitchen fire; and the tools, shoes, and leather were buried in the garden. So wicked do destruction and secrecy appear to honest minds that Mr. Lorry and Miss Pross, while engaged in the commission of their deed and in the removal of its traces, almost felt, and almost looked, like accomplices in a horrible crime.

Discussion

Chapter XIV

1. Where has Barsad appeared before?

2. What is the significance of the rose?

3. What was the subtle contest between Madame Defarge and Barsad?

Chapter XV

1. Miss Pross's brother Solomon has been mentioned before. Why does Dickens mention him again?

2. (a) Regarding Dr. Manette's relapse, what connection do you find between this chapter and Chapter X? **(b)** What do you think really troubles him?

Chapter XVI

1. (a) How does Mr. Lorry go about presenting his problem to Dr. Manette? **(b)** Why does he use this approach?

2. (a) What purpose did the making of shoes serve for Dr. Manette, both in prison and during his relapse? **(b)** How did Mr. Lorry finally persuade Dr. Manette to give up his shoemaker's bench and tools?

CHAPTER XVII
A PLEA

When the newly married pair came home, the first person who appeared, to offer his congratulations, was Sydney Carton. They had not been at home many hours when he presented himself. He was not improved in habits, or in looks, or in manner; but there was a certain rugged air of fidelity about him, which was new to the observation of Charles Darnay.

He watched his opportunity of taking Darnay aside into a window, and of speaking to him when no one overheard.

"Mr. Darnay," said Carton, "I wish we might be friends."

"We are already friends, I hope."

"You are good enough to say so, as a fashion of speech; but, I don't mean any fashion of speech. Indeed, when I say I wish we might be friends, I scarcely mean quite that, either."

Charles Darnay—as was natural—asked him, in all good humor and good fellowship, what he did mean?

"Upon my life," said Carton, smiling, "I find that easier to comprehend in my own mind, than to convey to yours. However, let me try. You remember a certain famous occasion when I was more drunk than—than usual?"

"I remember a certain famous occasion when you forced me to confess that you had been drinking."

"I remember it too. The curse of those occasions is heavy upon me, for I always remember them. I hope it may be taken into account one day, when all days are at an end for me! Don't be alarmed; I am not going to preach."

"I am not at all alarmed. Earnestness in you is anything but alarming to me."

"Ah!" said Carton, with a careless wave of his hand, as if he waved that away. "On the drunken occasion in question—one of a large number, as you know—I was insufferable about liking you, and not liking you. I wish you would forget it."

"I forgot it long ago."

"Fashion of speech again! But, Mr. Darnay, oblivion is not so easy to me as you represent it to be to you. I have by no means forgotten it, and a light answer does not help me to forget it."

"If it was a light answer," returned Darnay, "I beg your forgiveness for it. I had no other object than to turn a slight thing, which to my surprise seems to trouble you too much, aside. I declare to you, on the faith of a gentleman, that I have long dismissed it from my mind. Good heaven, what was there to dismiss! Have I had nothing more important to remember, in the great service you rendered me that day?"

"As to the great service," said Carton, "I am bound to avow to you, when you speak of it in that way, that it was mere professional claptrap. I don't know that I cared what became of you, when I rendered it.—Mind! I say when I rendered it; I am speaking of the past."

"You make light of the obligation," returned Darnay, "but I will not quarrel with *your* light answer."

"Genuine truth, Mr. Darnay, trust me! I have gone aside from my purpose; I was speaking about our being friends. Now, you know me as a dissolute dog, who has never done any good, and never will."

"I don't know that you 'never will.' "

"But I do, and you must take my word for it. Well! If you could endure to have such a worthless fellow coming and going at odd times, I should ask that I might be permitted to come and go as a privileged person here; that I might be regarded as a useless—and I would add, if it were not for the resemblance I detected between you and me, an unornamental—piece of furniture, tolerated for its old service, and taken no notice of. I doubt if I should abuse the permission. It is a hundred to one if I should avail myself of it four times in a year. It would satisfy me, I dare say, to know that I had it."

"Will you try?"

"That is another way of saying that I may use that freedom with your name?"

They shook hands upon it, and Sydney turned away. Within a minute afterwards, he was, to all outward appearance, as unsubstantial as ever.

When he was gone, and in the course of an evening passed with Miss Pross, the Doctor, and Mr. Lorry, Charles Darnay made some mention of this conversation in general terms, and spoke of Sydney Carton as a problem of carelessness and recklessness. He spoke of him, in short, not bitterly or meaning to bear hard upon him, but as anybody might who saw him as he showed himself.

He had no idea that this could dwell in the thoughts of his fair young wife; but, when he afterwards joined her in their own rooms, he found her waiting for him with the old pretty lifting of the forehead strongly marked.

"We are thoughtful tonight!" said Darnay, drawing his arm about her.

"Yes, dearest Charles," with the inquiring and attentive expression fixed upon him, "for we have something on our mind tonight."

"What is it, my Lucie?"

"Will you promise not to press one question on me, if I beg you not to ask it?"

"Will I promise? What will I not promise to my love?"

"I think, Charles, poor Mr. Carton deserves more consideration and respect than you expressed for him tonight."

"Indeed, my own? Why so?"

"That is what you are not to ask me. But I think—I know—he does."

"If you know it, it is enough. What would you have me do, my life?"

"I would ask you, dearest, to be very generous with him always, and very lenient on his faults when he is not by. I would ask you to believe that he has a heart he very, very seldom reveals, and that there are deep wounds in it. My dear, I have seen it bleeding."

"It is a painful reflection to me," said Charles Darnay, quite astounded, "that I should have done him any wrong. I never thought this of him."

"My husband, it is so. I fear he is not to be reclaimed; there is scarcely a hope that anything in his character or fortunes is reparable now. But I am sure that he is capable of good things, gentle things, even magnanimous things."

She looked so beautiful in the purity of her faith in this lost man that her husband could have looked at her for hours.

"And, O my dearest love!" she urged, clinging nearer to him, "remember how strong we are in our happiness, and how weak he is in his misery!"

The supplication touched him home. "I will always remember it, dear heart! I will remember it as long as I live."

He bent over the golden head and put the rosy lips to his, and folded her in his arms. If one forlorn wanderer then pacing the dark streets could have heard her innocent disclosure, and could have seen the drops of pity kissed away by her husband, he might have cried to the night—and the words would not have parted from his lips for the first time—"God bless her for her sweet compassion!"

CHAPTER XVIII
ECHOING FOOTSTEPS

A wonderful corner for echoes, it has been remarked, that corner where the Doctor lived. Ever busily winding the golden thread which bound her husband, and her father, and herself, and her old companion, in a life of quiet bliss, Lucie sat in the still house in the tranquilly resounding corner, listening to the echoing footsteps of years.

At first there were times, though she was a perfectly happy young wife, when her work would slowly fall from her hands, and her eyes would be dimmed. For there was something coming in the echoes, something light, afar off, and scarcely audible yet, that stirred her heart too much. That time passed, and her little Lucie lay on her bosom. Then, among the advancing echoes, there was the tread of her tiny feet and the sound of her prattling words.

Ever winding the golden thread that bound them all together, Lucie heard in the echoes of years none but friendly and soothing sounds. Her husband's step was strong and prosperous among them; her father's firm and equal.

The echoes rarely answered to the actual tread of Sydney Carton. Some half-dozen times a year, at most, he claimed his privilege of coming in uninvited, and would sit among them through the evening. He never came there heated with wine.

These were among the echoes to which Lucie, sometimes pensive, sometimes amused and laughing, listened in the echoing corner, until her little daughter was six years old.

But other echoes, from a distance, rumbled menacingly all through this space of time. And now, about little Lucie's sixth birthday, they began to have an awful sound, as of a great storm in France with a dreadful sea rising.

On a night in mid-July, one thousand seven hundred and eighty-nine, Mr. Lorry came in late, from Tellson's, and sat himself down by Lucie and her husband. It was a hot, wild night, and they were all reminded of the Sunday night when they had looked at the lightning from the same place.

"I began to think," said Mr. Lorry, pushing his brown wig back, "that I should have to pass the night at Tellson's. We have been so full of business all day, that we have not known which way to turn. There is such an uneasiness in Paris that we have actually a run of confidence upon us! Our customers over there seem not to be able to confide their property to us fast enough. There is positively a mania among some of them for sending it to England."

"That has a bad look," said Darnay.

"A bad look, you say, my dear Darnay? Yes, but we don't know what reason there is in it. Where is Manette?"

"Here he is," said the Doctor, entering.

"I am quite glad you are at home; for these hurries and forebodings by which I have been surrounded all day long have made me nervous. You are not going out?"

"No; I am going to play backgammon with you, if you like," said the Doctor.

"I don't think I do like. I am not fit to be pitted against you tonight. Is the tea board still there, Lucie?"

"Of course; it has been kept for you."

"Thank ye, my dear. The precious child is safe in bed?"

"And sleeping soundly."

"That's right; all safe and well! I don't know why anything should be otherwise than safe and well here, thank God; but I have been so put out all day, and I am not as young as I was! My tea, my dear! Thank ye. Now, let us sit quiet, and hear the echoes."

Headlong, mad, and dangerous footsteps to force their way into anybody's life, footsteps not easily made clean again if once stained red, the footsteps raging in Saint Antoine afar off, as the little circle sat in the dark London window.

A tremendous roar arose from the throat of Saint Antoine, and a forest of naked arms struggled in the air, all the fingers convulsively clutching at every weapon or semblance of a weapon.

Who gave them out, whence they last came, no eye in the throng could have told; but muskets were being distributed—so were cartridges, powder, ball, bars of iron and wood, knives, axes, pikes, every weapon ingenuity could devise. People who could lay hold of nothing else set themselves with bleeding hands to force stones and bricks out of their places in walls. Every pulse and heart in Saint Antoine was on high fever strain and at high fever heat. Every living creature there held life as of no account, and was demented with a passionate readiness to sacrifice it.

As a whirlpool of boiling waters has a center point, so all this raging circled round Defarge's wine shop, where Defarge himself, already begrimed with gunpowder and sweat, issued orders, issued arms, thrust this man back, dragged this man forward, disarmed one to arm another, labored and strove in the thickest of the uproar.

"Keep near me, Jacques Three," cried Defarge; "Jacques One and Two, separate and put yourselves at the head of as many patriots as you can. Where is my wife?"

"Here you see me!" said madame, composed as ever, but not knitting today. Madame's resolute right hand was occupied with an ax, and in her girdle were a pistol and a cruel knife.

"Where do you go, my wife?"

"I go," said madame, "with you at present. You shall see me at the head of women, by-and-by."

"Come, then!" cried Defarge, in a resounding voice. "Patriots and friends, we are ready! The Bastille!"

With a roar that sounded as if all the breath in France had been shaped into the detested word, the living sea rose, wave on wave, depth on depth, and overflowed the city to that point. Alarm bells ringing, drums beating, the sea raging and thundering on its new beach, the attack begun.

Deep ditches, double drawbridge, massive stones walls, eight great towers, cannon, muskets, fire, and smoke. Through the fire and through the smoke—in the fire and in the smoke, for the sea cast him up against a cannon, and on the instant he became a cannonier—Defarge of the wine shop worked like a manful soldier, two fierce hours.

Deep ditch, single drawbridge, massive stone walls, eight great towers, cannon, muskets, fire, and smoke. One drawbridge down! "Work, comrades all, work! Work, Jacques One, Jacques Two, Jacques One Thousand, Jacques

Two Thousand, Jacques Five-and-Twenty Thousand; in the name of all the angels or the devils—which you prefer—work!'' Thus Defarge of the wine shop, still at his gun, which had long grown hot.

''To me, women!'' cried madame his wife. ''What! We can kill as well as the men when the place is taken!'' And to her, with a shrill, thirsty cry, trooping women variously armed, but all armed alike in hunger and revenge.

Cannon, muskets, fire and smoke; but, still the deep ditch, the single drawbridge, the massive stone walls, and the eight great towers. Slight displacements of the raging sea, made by the falling wounded. Flashing weapons, blazing torches, smoking wagonloads of wet straw, hard work at neighboring barricades in all directions, shrieks, volleys, execrations, bravery without stint, boom, smash, and rattle, and the furious sounding of the living sea; but, still the deep ditch, and the single drawbridge, and the massive stone walls, and the eight great towers, and still Defarge of the wine shop at his gun, grown doubly hot by the service of four fierce hours.

A white flag from within the fortress, and a parley—suddenly the sea rose and swept Defarge of the wine shop over the lowered drawbridge, past the massive stone outer walls, in among the eight great towers surrendered!

So resistless was the force of the ocean bearing him on that even to draw his breath or turn his head was impracticable until he was landed in the outer courtyard of the Bastille. There, against a wall, he made a struggle to look about him. Jacques Three was nearly at his side; Madame Defarge, still heading some of her women, was visible in the inner distance, her knife in her hand. Everywhere was tumult, exultation, deafening and maniacal bewilderment, astounding noise, yet furious dumb show.

''The Prisoners!''

''The Records!''

''The secret cells!''

''The instruments of torture!''

''The Prisoners!''

Of all these cries, and ten thousand incoherencies, ''The Prisoners!'' was the cry most taken up by the sea that rushed in. When the foremost billows rolled past, bearing the prison officers with them, and threatening them all with instant death if any secret nook remained undisclosed, Defarge laid his hand on the breast of one of these men—a man who had a lighted torch in his hand—and got him between himself and the wall.

''Show me the North Tower!'' said Defarge. ''Quick!''

''I will faithfully,'' replied the man, ''if you will come with me. But there is no one there.''

''What is the meaning of One Hundred and Five, North Tower?'' asked Defarge. ''Quick!''

''The meaning, monsieur?''

''Does it mean a captive, or a place of captivity? Or do you mean that I shall strike you dead?''

''Kill him!'' croaked Jacques Three, who had come close up.

''Monsieur, it is a cell.''

''Show it me!''

''Pass this way, then.''

The turnkey stopped at a low door, put a key in a clashing lock, swung the door slowly open, and said, as they all bent their heads and passed in:

''One Hundred and Five, North Tower!''

There was a small, heavily grated, unglazed window high in the wall, a stone screen before it, so that the sky could be only seen by stooping low and looking up. There was a small chimney, heavily barred across, a few feet within. There was a heap of old wood ashes on the hearth. There was a stool, and table, and a straw bed. There were the four blackened walls, a rusted iron ring in one of them.

''Pass that torch slowly along these walls, that I may see them,'' said Defarge to the turnkey.

The man obeyed, and Defarge followed the light closely with his eyes.

''Stop!—Look here, Jacques!''

Ronald Searle

"A. M.!" croaked Jacques Three, as he read greedily.

"Alexandre Manette," said Defarge in his ear, following the letters with his swart forefinger. "And here he wrote 'a poor physician.' "

"What is that in your hand? A crowbar? Give it me!"

He had his gun in his own hand. He made a sudden exchange of the two instruments, and turning on the worm-eaten stool and table, beat them to pieces in a few blows.

"Hold the light higher!" he said, wrathfully, to the turnkey. "Look among those fragments with care, Jacques. And see! Here is my knife," throwing it to him; "rip open that bed, and search the straw. Hold the light higher, you!"

With a menacing look at the turnkey, he crawled upon the hearth, and, peering up the chimney, struck and prised at its sides with the crowbar. In a few minutes some mortar and dust came dropping down, which he averted his face to avoid; and in it, and in the old wood ashes, and in a crevice in the chimney into which his weapon had slipped or wrought itself, he groped with a cautious touch.

"Nothing in the wood, and nothing in the straw, Jacques?"

"Nothing."

"Let us collect them together, in the middle of the cell. So! Light them, you!"

The turnkey fired the little pile, which blazed high and hot. Stooping again to come out at the low-arched door, they left it burning, and retraced their way to the courtyard, until they were in the raging flood once more.

They found it surging and tossing, in quest of Defarge himself. Saint Antoine was clamorous to have its wine-shop keeper foremost in the guard upon the governor who had defended the Bastille and shot the people. Otherwise the governor would escape, and the people's blood—suddenly of some value, after many years of worthlessness—be unavenged.

In the howling universe of passion and contention that seemed to encompass this grim old officer conspicuous in his gray coat and red decoration, there was but one quite steady figure, and that was a woman's. "See, there is my husband!" she cried, pointing him out. "See Defarge!" She stood immovable close to the grim old officer, and remained immovable close to him; remained immovable close to him through the streets, as Defarge and the rest bore him along; remained immovable close to him when he was near his destination, and began to be struck at from behind; remained immovable close to him when the long gathering rain of stabs and blows fell heavy; was so close to him when he dropped dead, that, suddenly animated, she put her foot upon his neck, and with her cruel knife—long ready—hewed off his head.

The hour was come when Saint Antoine was to execute his horrible idea of hoisting up men for lamps to show what he could be and do. The sea rushed on.

The sea of black and threatening waters, and of destructive upheaving of wave against wave, whose depths were yet unfathomed and whose forces were yet unknown. The remorseless sea of turbulently swaying shapes, voices of vengeance, and faces hardened in the furnaces of suffering until the touch of pity could make no mark on them.

Seven prisoners released, seven gory heads on pikes, the keys of the accursed fortress of the eight strong towers, some discovered letters and other memorials of prisoners of old time, long dead of broken hearts—such, and suchlike, the loudly echoing footsteps of Saint Antoine escort through the Paris streets in mid-July, one thousand seven hundred and eighty-nine. Now, heaven defeat the fancy of Lucie Darnay and keep these feet far out of her life! For they are headlong, mad, and dangerous; and in the years so long after the breaking of the cask at Defarge's wine-shop door, they are not easily purified when once stained red.

Discussion

Chapter XVII

1. (a) What was Sydney Carton's plea? **(b)** How do Charles and Lucie react to this plea?

2. (a) What part of Sydney Carton's nature is revealed in this chapter? **(b)** Do you think Lucie's confidence in him is justified? Explain.

Chapter XVIII

1. (a) How is the passage of time indicated? **(b)** The two scenes in this chapter are dramatically contrasted. What is that contrast and how does Dickens weave the scenes together?

2. (a) Does Dickens tell you what Defarge is searching for in the prison cell? **(b)** Does Defarge find what he is looking for?

Comment: A Lively History

Before writing *A Tale of Two Cities,* which was published in 1859, Dickens read many historical accounts of the French Revolution. In 1837, Thomas Carlyle had published a three-volume history of the revolution. Dickens incorporated into his book many of Carlyle's facts. As you read the following excerpts from Carlyle's chapters describing the storming of the Bastille, compare Carlyle's vivid and immediate style with that of Dickens in the chapter called "Echoing Footsteps."

On Monday [July 13th] the huge city has awoke, not to its weekday industry: to what a different one! The working man has become a fighting man; has one want only: that of arms. The industry of all crafts has paused:—except the smith's, fiercely hammering pikes.

Pikes are fabricated; fifty thousand of them, in six-and-thirty hours. Dig trenches, unpave the streets, cram the earth in barrel-barricades. Have scalding pitch, at least boiling water ready, ye weak old women!

Great is the moment when the long-enthralled soul from amid its chains and squalid stagnancy, arises, and swears by Him that made it, that it will be *free.* Forward, ye maddened sons of France; be it towards this destiny or towards that! Around you is but starvation, falsehood, corruption, and the calm of death.

To the living and the struggling, a new, Fourteenth morning dawns. The bustlings and preparings, the tremors and menaces; the tears that fell from old eyes. . . . By the memory of your father's wrongs, by the hope of your children's rights. . . . Help for you is none, if not in your own right hands. This day ye must do or die.

All morning, since nine, there has been a cry everywhere: To the Bastille! The multitude flows on, welling through every street: tocsin furiously pealing, all drums beating the *générale* [general alarm], the Suburb Saint Antoine rolling hitherward wholly, as one man!

Cholat the wine-merchant has become an impromptu cannoneer. Let conflagration rage. Guardrooms are burnt. Straw is burnt. Blood flows.

How the great Bastille Clock ticks in its Inner Court. It tolled One when the firing began; and is now pointing towards Five, and still firing slakes not. Far down, in their vaults, the seven prisoners hear muffled din as of earthquakes; their Turnkeys answer vaguely.

The poor Invalides [defenders of the Bastille]

have sunk under their battlements, or rise only with reversed muskets: they have made a white flag of napkins. The very Swiss [other defenders] look weary of firing; a porthole at the drawbridge is opened, as by one that would speak. See Hussier Maillard [one of the mob leaders] on his plank, swinging over the abyss of that stone Ditch; plank resting on parapet, he hovers perilous; deftly, unerring he walks with outspread palm. The Swiss holds a paper through his porthole; Terms of surrender: Pardon, immunity to all! Are they accepted? On the word of an officer, "they are." Sinks the drawbridge; rushes in the living deluge: the Bastille is fallen! "Victoire!"

CHAPTER XIX
THE SEA STILL RISES

Haggard Saint Antoine had had only one exultant week in which to soften his modicum of hard and bitter bread to such extent as he could, with the relish of fraternal embraces and congratulations, when Madame Defarge sat at her counter, as usual, presiding over the customers. Madame Defarge wore no rose in her head, for the great brotherhood of Spies had become, even in one short week, extremely chary of trusting themselves to the saint's mercies. The lamps across his streets had a portentously elastic swing with them.

Madame Defarge, with her arms folded, sat in the morning light and heat, contemplating the wine shop and the street. In both, there were several knots of loungers, squalid and miserable, but now with a manifest sense of power enthroned on their distress. The raggedest nightcap, awry on the wretchedest head, had this crooked significance in it: "I know how hard it has grown for me, the wearer of this, to support life in myself; but do you know how easy it has grown for me, the wearer of this, to destroy life in you?" Every lean bare arm, that had been without work before, had this work always ready for it now, that it could strike. The fingers of the knitting women were vicious, with the experience that they could tear. There was a change in the appearance of Saint Antoine; the image had been hammering into this for hundreds of years, and the last finishing blows had told mightily on the expression.

Madame Defarge sat observing it, with such suppressed approval as was to be desired in the leader of the Saint Antoine women. One of her sisterhood knitted beside her. The short, rather plump wife of a starved grocer, and the mother of two children withal, this lieutenant had already earned the complimentary name of The Vengeance.

"Hark!" said The Vengeance. "Listen, then! Who comes?"

As if a train of powder laid from the outermost bound of the Saint Antoine Quarter to the wine shop door, had been suddenly fired, a fast spreading murmur came rushing along.

"It is Defarge," said madame. "Silence, patriots!"

Defarge came in breathless, pulled off a red cap he wore, and looked around him! "Listen!" said madame again. "Listen to him!" Defarge stood, panting, against a background of eager eyes and open mouths, formed outside the door; all those within the wine shop had sprung to their feet.

"Say then, my husband. What is it?"

"News from the other world!"

"How, then?" cried madame, contemptuously. "The other world?"

"Does everybody here recall old Foulon, who told the famished people that they might eat grass, and who died, and went to hell?"

"Everybody!" from all throats.

"The news is of him. He is among us!"

"Among us!" from the universal throat again. "And dead?"

"Not dead! He feared us so much—and with reason—that he caused himself to be represented as dead, and had a grand mock funeral. But they have found him alive, hiding in the country, and have brought him in. I have seen him but now, on his way to the Hôtel de Ville, a prisoner. I have said that he had reason to fear us. Say all! *Had* he reason?"

Wretched old sinner of more than three score years and ten, if he had never known it yet, he would have known it in his heart of hearts if he could have heard the answering cry.

A moment of profound silence followed. Defarge and his wife looked steadfastly at one another. The Vengeance stooped, and the jar of a drum was heard as she moved it at her feet behind the counter.

"Patriots!" said Defarge, in a determined voice, "are we ready?"

Instantly Madame Defarge's knife was in her girdle; the drum was beating in the streets, as if it and a drummer had flown together by magic; and The Vengeance, uttering terrific shrieks, and flinging her arms about her head like all the forty Furies at once, was tearing from house to house, rousing the women.

The men were terrible, in the bloody minded anger with which they looked from windows, caught up what arms they had, and came pouring down into the streets; but the women were a sight to chill the boldest. From such household occupations as their bare poverty yielded, from their children, from their aged and their sick crouching on the bare ground famished and naked, they ran out with streaming hair, urging one another and themselves to madness with the wildest cries and actions. Villain Foulon taken, my sister! Old Foulon taken, my mother! Miscreant Foulon taken, my daughter! Then a score of others ran into the midst of these, beating their breasts, tearing their hair, and screaming, Foulon alive! Foulon who told the starving people they might eat grass! Foulon who told my old father he might eat grass, when I had no bread to give him! Foulon who told my baby it might suck grass, when these breasts were dry with want! O mother of God, this Foulon! O heaven, our suffering! Hear me, my dead baby and my withered father; I swear on my knees, on these stones, to avenge you on Foulon! Husbands and brothers, and young men, Give us the blood of Foulon, Give us the head of Foulon, Give us the heart of Foulon, Give us the body and soul of Foulon, Rend Foulon to pieces, and dig him into the ground, that grass may grow from him! With these cries, numbers of the women, lashed into blind frenzy, whirled about, striking and tearing at their own friends until they dropped into a passionate swoon, and were only saved by the men belonging to them from being trampled under foot.

Nevertheless, not a moment was lost; not a moment! This Foulon was at the Hôtel de Ville, and might be loosed. Never, if Saint Antoine knew his own sufferings, insults, and wrongs! Armed men and women flocked out of the Quarter so fast, and drew even these last dregs after them with such a force of suction that within a quarter of an hour there was not a human creature in Saint Antoine's bosom but a few old crones and the wailing children.

No. They were all by that time choking the Hall of Examination where this old man, ugly and wicked, was, and overflowing into the adjacent open space and streets. The Defarges, husband and wife, The Vengeance, and Jacques Three were in the first press, and at no great distance from him in the Hall.

"See!" cried madame, pointing with her knife. "See the old villain bound with ropes. That was well done to tie a bunch of grass upon his back. Ha, ha! That was well done. Let him eat it now!'' Madame put her knife under her arm, and clapped her hands as at a play.

The people immediately behind Madame Defarge, explaining the cause of her satisfaction to those behind them, and those again explaining to others, and those to others, the neighboring streets resounded with the clapping of hands. Similarly, during two or three hours of drawl, and the winnowing of many bushels of words, Madame Defarge's frequent expressions of impatience were taken up, with marvelous quickness, at a distance; the more readily, because certain men who had by some wonderful exercise of agility climbed up the external architecture to look in from the windows knew Madame Defarge well and acted as a telegraph between her and the crowd outside the building.

At length the sun rose so high that it struck a kindly ray as of hope or protection, directly down upon the old prisoner's head. The favor was too much to bear; in an instant the barrier of dust and chaff that had stood surprisingly long went to the winds, and Saint Antoine had got him!

It was known directly, to the farthest confines of the crowd. Defarge had but sprung over a railing and a table and folded the miserable wretch in a deadly embrace—Madame Defarge had but followed and turned her hand in one of the ropes with which he was tied—The Vengeance and Jacques Three were not yet up with them, and the men at the windows had not yet swooped into the Hall, like birds of prey from their high perches—when the cry seemed to go up, all over the city, ''Bring him out! Bring him to the lamp!''

Down, and up, and head foremost on the steps of the building; now, on his knees; now, on his feet; now, on his back; dragged, and struck at, and stifled by the bunches of grass and straw that were thrust into his face by hundreds of hands; torn, bruised, panting, bleeding, yet always entreating and beseeching for mercy; now full of vehement agony of action, with a small clear space about him as the people drew one another back that they might see; now a log of dead wood drawn through a forest of legs; he was hauled to the nearest street corner where one of the fatal lamps swung, and there Madame Defarge let him go—as a cat might have done to a mouse—and silently and composedly looked at him while they made ready, and while he besought her; the women passionately screeching at him all the time, and the men sternly calling out to have him killed with grass in his mouth. Once he went aloft, and the rope broke, and they caught him shrieking; twice he went aloft, and the rope broke, and they caught him shrieking; then the rope was merciful, and held him, and his head was soon upon a pike, with grass enough in the mouth for all Saint Antoine to dance at the sight of.

Nor was this the end of the day's bad work, for Saint Antoine so shouted and danced his angry blood up that it boiled again, on hearing when the day closed in that the son-in-law of the despatched, another of the people's enemies and insulters, was coming into Paris under a guard five hundred strong in cavalry alone. Saint Antoine wrote his crimes on flaring sheets of paper, seized him—would have torn him out of the breast of an army to bear Foulon company—set his head and heart on pikes, and carried the spoils of the day, in wolf procession, through the streets.

Not before dark night did the men and women come back to the children wailing and breadless. Then the miserable baker's shops were beset by long files of them, patiently waiting to buy bad bread; and while they waited with stomachs faint and empty, they beguiled the time by embracing one another on the triumphs of the day, and achieving them again in gossip. Gradually these strings of ragged people shortened and frayed away; and then poor lights began to shine in high windows, and slender fires were made in the streets, at which neighbors cooked in common, afterwards supping at their doors.

Scanty and insufficient suppers those, and

innocent of meat, as of most other sauce to wretched bread. Yet human fellowship infused some nourishment into the flinty viands, and struck some sparks of cheerfulness out of them. Fathers and mothers who had had their full share in the worst of the day played gently with their meager children; and lovers, with such a world around them and before them, loved and hoped.

It was almost morning when Defarge's wine shop parted with its last knot of customers, and Monsieur Defarge said to madame his wife while fastening the door:

"At last it is come, my dear!"

"Eh well!" returned madame. "Almost."

Saint Antoine slept, the Defarges slept; even The Vengeance slept with her starved grocer, and the drum was at rest. The drum's was the only voice in Saint Antoine that blood and hurry had not changed. The Vengeance, as custodian of the drum, could have wakened him up and had the same speech out of him as before the Bastille fell, or old Foulon was seized; not so with the hoarse tones of the men and women in Saint Antoine's bosom.

CHAPTER XX
FIRE RISES

There was a change on the village where the fountain fell, and where the mender of roads went forth daily to hammer out of the stones on the highway such morsels of bread as might serve for patches to hold his poor ignorant soul and his poor reduced body together. The prison on the crag was not so dominant as of yore; there were soldiers to guard it, but not many; there were officers to guard the soldiers, but not one of them knew what his men would do—beyond this: that it would probably not be what he was ordered.

Far and wide lay a ruined country, yielding nothing but desolation. Every green leaf, every blade of grass and blade of grain, was as shriveled and poor as the miserable people. Everything was bowed down, dejected, oppressed, and broken. Habitations, fences, domesticated animals, men, women, children, and the soil that bore them—all worn out.

In these times, as the mender of roads worked, solitary, in the dust, not often troubling himself to reflect that dust he was and to dust he must return, being for the most part too much occupied in thinking how little he had for supper and how much more he would eat if he had it—in these times as he raised his eyes from his lonely labor, and viewed the prospect, he would see some rough figure approaching on foot, the like of which was once a rarity in those parts, but was now a frequent presence. As it advanced, the mender of roads would discern, without surprise, that it was a shaggy-haired man, of almost barbarian aspect, tall, in wooden shoes that were clumsy even to the eyes of a mender of roads, grim, rough, swart, steeped in the mud and dust of many highways, dank with the marshy moisture of many low grounds, sprinkled with the thorns and leaves and moss of many byways through woods.

Such a man came upon him, like a ghost, at noon in the July weather, as he sat on his heap of stones under a bank, taking such shelter as he could get from a shower of hail.

The man looked at him, looked at the village in the hollow, at the mill, and at the prison on the crag. When he had identified these objects in what benighted mind he had, he said, in a dialect that was just intelligible:

"How goes it, Jacques?"

"All well, Jacques."

"Touch then!" They joined hands, and the man sat down on the heap of stones.

"No dinner?"

"Nothing but supper now," said the mender of roads, with a hungry face.

"It is the fashion," growled the man. "I meet no dinner anywhere."

He took out a blackened pipe, filled it, lighted it with flint and steel, pulled at it until it was in a bright glow; then, suddenly held it from him and dropped something into it from between his finger and thumb, that blazed and went out in a puff of smoke.

"Touch then." It was the turn of the mender of roads to say it this time, after observing these operations. They again joined hands. "Tonight?" said the mender of roads.

"Tonight," said the man, putting the pipe in his mouth.

"Where?"

"Here."

He and the mender of roads sat on the heap of stones looking silently at one another, with the hail driving in between them like a pigmy charge of bayonets, until the sky began to clear over the village.

"Show me!" said the traveler then, moving to the brow of the hill.

"See!" returned the mender of roads, with extended finger. "You go down here, and straight through the street, and past the fountain——"

"To the devil with all that!" interrupted the other, rolling his eye over the landscape. "*I* go through no streets and past no fountains. Well?"

"Well! About two leagues beyond the summit of that hill above the village."

"Good. When do you cease to work?"

"At sunset."

"Will you wake me, before departing? I have walked two nights without resting. Let me finish my pipe, and I shall sleep like a child. Will you wake me?"

"Surely."

The wayfarer smoked his pipe out, put it in his breast, slipped off his great wooden shoes, and lay down on his back on the heap of stones. He was fast asleep directly, indifferent to showers of hail and intervals of brightness, to sunshine on his face and shadow, to the pattering lumps of dull ice on his body and the diamonds into which the sun changed them, until the sun was low in the west, and the sky was glowing. Then the mender of roads, having got his tools together and all things ready to go down into the village, roused him.

"Good!" said the sleeper, rising on his elbow. "Two leagues beyond the summit of the hill?"

"About."

"About. Good!"

The mender of roads went home, with the dust going on before him according to the set of the wind, and was soon at the fountain, squeezing himself in among the lean kine brought there to drink, and appearing even to whisper to them in his whispering to all the village. When the village had taken its poor supper, it did not creep to bed, as it usually did, but came out of doors again, and remained there. A curious contagion of whispering was upon it, and also, when it gathered together at the fountain in the dark, another curious contagion of looking expectantly at the sky in one direction only. Monsieur Gabelle, chief functionary of the place, became uneasy; went out on his housetop alone, and looked in that direction too; glanced down from behind his chimneys at the darkening faces by the fountain below, and sent word to the sacristan who kept the keys of the church, that there might be need to ring the tocsin by-and-by.

The night deepened. The trees environing the old château, keeping its solitary state apart, moved in a rising wind, as though they threatened the pile of building, massive and dark in the gloom. Up the two terrace flights of steps the rain ran wildly, and beat at the great door, like a swift messenger rousing those within; uneasy rushes of wind went through the hall, among the old spears and knives, and passed lamenting up the stairs, and shook the curtains of the bed where the last Marquis had slept. East, west, north, and south, through the woods, four heavy-treading, unkempt figures crushed the high grass and cracked the branches, striding on cautiously to come together in the courtyard. Four lights broke out there and moved away in different directions, and all was black again.

But not for long. Presently, the château began to make itself strangely visible by some light of its own, as though it were growing luminous. Then a flickering streak played behind the architecture of the front, picking out transparent places, and showing where balustrades, arches, and windows were. Then it soared higher, and grew broader and brighter. Soon, from a score of the great windows, flames burst forth, and the stone faces, awakened, stared out of fire.

A faint murmur arose about the house from the few people who were left there, and there was a saddling of a horse and riding away. There was spurring and splashing through the darkness, and bridle was drawn in the space by the village fountain, and the horse in a foam stood at Monsieur Gabelle's door. "Help, Gabelle! Help, everyone!" The tocsin rang impatiently, but other help—if that were any—there was none. The mender of roads and two hundred and fifty particular friends stood with folded arms at the fountain, looking at the pillar of fire in the sky. "It must be forty feet high," said they grimly; and never moved.

The rider from the château and the horse in a foam clattered away through the village and galloped up the stony steep to the prison on the crag. At the gate a group of officers were looking at the fire; removed from them, a group of soldiers. "Help, gentlemen—officers! The château is on fire; valuable objects may be saved from the flames by timely aid! Help, help!" The officers looked toward the soldiers who looked at the fire; gave no orders; and answered, with shrugs and biting of lips, "It must burn."

As the rider rattled down the hill again and through the street, the village was illuminating. The mender of roads and the two hundred and fifty particular friends, inspired as one man and woman by the idea of lighting up, had darted into their houses, and were putting candles in every dull little pane of glass. The general scarcity of everything occasioned candles to be borrowed in a rather peremptory manner of Monsieur Gabelle; and in a moment of reluctance and hesitation on that functionary's part, the mender of roads, once so submissive to authority, had remarked that carriages were good to make bonfires with, and that post horses would roast.

The château was left to itself to flame and burn. In the roaring and raging of the conflagration, a red-hot wind, driving straight from the infernal regions, seemed to be blowing the edifice away. With the rising and falling of the blaze, the stone faces showed as if they were in torment. When great masses of stone and timber fell, the face with the two dints in the nose became obscured; anon struggled out of the smoke again, as if it were the face of the cruel Marquis, burning at the stake and contending with the fire.

The château burned; the nearest trees, laid hold of by the fire, scorched and shriveled; trees at a distance, fired by the four fierce figures, begirt the blazing edifice with a new forest of smoke. Molten lead and iron boiled in the marble basin of the fountain; the water ran dry; the extinguished tops of the towers vanished like ice before the heat, and trickled down into four rugged wells of flame. Great rents and splits branched out in the solid walls, like crystallization; stupefied birds wheeled about and dropped into the furnace; four fierce figures trudged away, east, west, north, and south, along the night-enshrouded roads, guided by the beacon they had lighted, toward their next destination. The illuminated village had seized hold of the tocsin, and, abolishing the lawful ringer, rang for joy.

Not only that; but the village, light-headed with famine, fire, and bell-ringing, and bethinking itself that Monsieur Gabelle had to do with the collection of rent and taxes—though it was but a small installment of taxes, and no rent at all, that Gabelle had got in those latter days—became impatient for an interview with him, and, surrounding his house, summoned him to come forth for personal conference. Whereupon, Monsieur Gabelle did heavily bar his door, and retire to hold counsel with himself. The result of that conference was that Gabelle again withdrew himself to his housetop behind his stack of chimneys; this time resolved, if his door were broken in (he was a small Southern man of retaliative temperament), to pitch himself head foremost over the parapet, and crush a man or two below.

Probably, Monsieur Gabelle passed a long night up there, with the distant château for fire and candle, and the beating at his door, combined with the joy-ringing, for music; not to mention his having an ill-omened lamp slung across the road before his posting-house gate, which the village showed a lively inclination to displace in his favor. A trying suspense, to be passing a whole summer night on the brink of the black ocean, ready to take that plunge into it upon which Monsieur Gabelle had resolved! But, the friendly dawn appearing at last, and the rush candles of the village guttering out, the people happily dispersed, and Monsieur Gabelle came down bringing his life with him for that while.

Within a hundred miles, and in the light of other fires, there were other functionaries less fortunate, that night and other nights, whom the rising sun found hanging across once peaceful streets, where they had been born and bred; also, there were other villagers and townspeople less fortunate than the mender of roads and his fellows, upon whom the functionaries and soldiery turned with success, and whom they strung up in their turn. But the fierce figures were steadily wending east, west, north, and south, be that as it would; and whosoever hung, fire burned. The altitude of the gallows that would turn to water and quench it, no functionary, by any stretch of mathematics, was able to calculate successfully.

CHAPTER XXI
DRAWN TO THE LOADSTONE ROCK

In such risings of fire and risings of sea—the firm earth shaken by the rushes of an angry ocean which had now no ebb, but was always on the flow, higher and higher, to the terror and wonder of the beholders on the shore—three years of tempest were consumed. Three more birthdays of little Lucie had been woven by the golden thread into the peaceful tissue of the life of her home.

Many a night and many a day had its inmates listened to the echoes in the corner, with hearts that failed them when they heard the thronging feet. For, the footsteps had become to their minds as the footsteps of a people, tumultuous under a red flag and with their country declared in danger, changed into wild beasts, by terrible enchantment long persisted in.

Monseigneur, as a class, had dissociated himself from the phenomenon of his not being appreciated: of his being so little wanted in France, as to incur considerable danger of receiving his dismissal from it and this life together. Like the fabled rustic who raised the devil with infinite pains, and was so terrified at the sight of him that he could ask the Enemy no question, but immediately fled; so, Monseigneur, after boldly reading the Lord's Prayer backwards for a great number of years, and performing many other potent spells for compelling the Evil One, no sooner beheld him in his terrors than he took to his noble heels.

The Court, from that exclusive inner circle to its outermost rotten ring of intrigue, corruption, and dissimulation, was all gone together. Royalty was gone; had been besieged in its Palace and "suspended" when the last tidings came over.

The August of the year one thousand seven hundred and ninety-two was come, and Monseigneur was by this time scattered far and wide.

As was natural, the headquarters and great gathering place of Monseigneur, in London, was Tellson's Bank. Spirits are supposed to haunt the places where their bodies most resorted, and Monseigneur without a guinea haunted the spot where his guineas used to be. Moreover, it was the spot to which such French intelligence as was most to be relied upon came quickest. Again: Tellson's was a munificent house, and extended great liberality to old customers who had fallen from their high estate. Again: those nobles who had seen the coming storm in time, and anticipating plunder or confiscation, had made provident remittances to Tellson's, were always to be heard of there by their needy brethren. To which it must be added that every newcomer from France reported himself and his tidings at Tellson's, almost as a matter of course. For such variety of reasons, Tellson's was at that time, as to French intelligence, a kind of High Exchange; and this was so well known to the public, and the inquiries made there were in consequence so numerous, that Tellson's sometimes wrote the latest news out in a line or so and posted it in the Bank windows, for all who ran through Temple Bar to read.

On a steaming, misty afternoon, Mr. Lorry sat at his desk, and Charles Darnay stood leaning on it, talking with him in a low voice.

"But, although you are the youngest man that ever lived," said Charles Darnay, rather hesitating, "I must still suggest to you——"

"I understand. That I am too old?" said Mr. Lorry.

"Unsettled weather, a long journey, uncertain means of traveling, a disorganized country, a city that may not be even safe for you."

"My dear Charles," said Mr. Lorry, with cheerful confidence, "you touch some of the reasons for my going; not for my staying away. It is safe enough for me; nobody will care to interfere with an old fellow of hard upon fourscore. As to its being a disorganized city, if it were not, there would be no occasion to send somebody from our House here to our House there, who knows the city and the business, of old. As to uncertain traveling, the long journey, and winter weather, if I were not prepared to submit to a few inconveniences for the sake of Tellson's, after all these years, who ought to be?"

"I wish I were going myself," said Charles Darnay, somewhat restlessly, and like one thinking aloud.

"Indeed! You wish you were going yourself? And you a Frenchman born?"

"My dear Mr. Lorry, it is because I am a Frenchman born, that the thought has passed through my mind. One cannot help thinking one might be listened to, and might have the power to persuade to some restraint. Only last night, after you left us, when I was talking to Lucie ——"

"When you were talking to Lucie," Mr. Lorry repeated. "I wonder you are not ashamed to mention Lucie! Wishing you were going to France at this time of day!"

"However, I am not going," said Charles Darnay, with a smile. "It is more to the purpose that you say you are."

"And I am, in plain reality. The truth is, my dear Charles, you can have no conception of the peril in which our books and papers over yonder are involved. The Lord above knows what the compromising consequences would be to numbers of people, if some of our documents were seized or destroyed; and they might be at any time, you know, for who can say that Paris is not set afire today, or sacked tomorrow! Now, a judicious selection from these and the burying of them, or otherwise getting of them out of harm's way, is within the power—without loss of precious time—of scarcely anyone but myself, if anyone. And shall I hang back, when Tellson's says this—Tellson's whose bread I have eaten these sixty years—because I am a little stiff about the joints? Why, I am a boy, sir, to half a dozen old codgers here!"

"How I admire the gallantry of your youthful spirit, Mr. Lorry."

"Tut! Nonsense, sir!—And, my dear Charles," said Mr. Lorry, "you are to remember that getting things out of Paris at this present time is next to an impossibility. Papers and precious matters were this very day brought to us here—I speak in strict confidence—by the strangest bearers you can imagine, every one of whom had his head hanging on by a single hair as he passed the Barriers. At another time our parcels would come and go, as easily as in businesslike Old England; but now, everything is stopped."

"And do you really go tonight?"

"I really go tonight, for the case has become too pressing to admit of delay."

"And do you take no one with you?"

"All sorts of people have been proposed to me, but I intend to take Jerry. Jerry has been my body guard on Sunday nights for a long time past, and I am used to him. Nobody will suspect Jerry of being anything but an English bulldog, or of having any design in his head but to fly at anybody who touches his master."

"I must say again that I heartily admire your gallantry and youthfulness."

"I must say again, nonsense! When I have executed this commission, I shall, perhaps, retire and live at my ease. Time enough then to think about growing old."

The House approached Mr. Lorry, and laying a soiled and unopened letter before him, asked if he had yet discovered any traces of the person to whom it was addressed. The House laid the letter down so close to Darnay that he saw the direction—the more quickly because it was his own right name. The address, turned into English, ran:

"Very pressing. To Monsieur heretofore the Marquis St. Evrémonde, of France. Confided to the care of Messrs. Tellson and Co., Bankers, London, England."

On the marriage morning, Dr. Manette had made it his one urgent and express request to Charles Darnay that the secret of his name should be kept inviolate between them. Nobody else knew it to be his name; his own wife had no suspicion of the fact; Mr. Lorry could have none.

"No," said Mr. Lorry, in reply to the House; "I have referred it, I think, to everybody now here, and no one can tell me where this gentleman is to be found."

Darnay, unable to restrain himself any longer, said: "I know the fellow."

"Will you take charge of the letter?" said Mr. Lorry. "You know where to deliver it?"

"I do."

"Will you undertake to explain that we suppose it to have been addressed here, on the chance of our knowing where to forward it, and that it has been here some time?"

"I will do so. Do you start for Paris from here?"

"From here, at eight."

"I will come back, to see you off."

Darnay made the best of his way into the quiet of the Temple, opened the letter, and read it.

"Prison of the Abbaye, Paris
"June 21, 1792

MONSIEUR HERETOFORE THE MARQUIS:

After having long been in danger of my life at the hands of the village, I have been seized, with great violence, and brought a long journey on foot to Paris. Nor is that all; my house has been destroyed—razed to the ground.

The crime for which I am imprisoned, Monsieur heretofore the Marquis, and for which I shall be summoned before the tribunal, and shall lose my life—without your so generous help—is, they tell me, treason against the majesty of the people, in that I have acted against them for an emigrant. It is in vain I represent that I have acted for them, and not against, according to your commands. It is in vain I represent that, before the sequestration of emigrant property,[1] I had remitted the imposts they had ceased to pay; that I had collected no rent. The only response is, that I have acted for an emigrant, and where is that emigrant?

Ah! most gracious Monsieur heretofore the Marquis, I send my desolate cry across the sea, hoping it may perhaps reach your ears through the great bank of Tilson.

For the love of heaven, of justice, of generosity, of the honor of your noble name, I supplicate you, Monsieur heretofore the Marquis, to succor and release me. My fault is that I have

1. ***the sequestration of emigrant property,*** the seizing and holding of property belonging to French aristocrats who left France at the beginning of the French Revolution and were, therefore, called emigrants.

been true to you. Oh, Monsieur heretofore the Marquis, I pray you be you true to me!

From this prison of horror, whence I every hour tend nearer to destruction, I send you, Monsieur heretofore the Marquis, assurance of my dolorous and unhappy service.

"Your afflicted,

"GABELLE."

The latent uneasiness in Darnay's mind was aroused to vigorous life by this letter. The peril of an old servant and a good one, whose only crime was fidelity to himself and his family, stared him so reproachfully in the face that, as he walked to and fro in the Temple considering what to do, he almost hid his face from the passers-by. He knew very well that in his love for Lucie, his renunciation of his social place had been incomplete.

But he had oppressed no man, imprisoned no man; he was so far from having exacted payment of his dues that he had relinquished them of his own will, thrown himself on a world with no favor in it, won his own private place there, and earned his own bread. Monsieur Gabelle had held the impoverished estate on written instructions to spare the people, to give them what little there was to give and no doubt he had put the fact in plea and proof, for his own safety, so that it could not but appear now.

This favored the desperate resolution Charles Darnay had begun to make, that he would go to Paris.

Yes. Like the mariner in the old story, the winds and streams had driven him within the influence of the Loadstone Rock,[2] and it was drawing him to itself, and he must go.

Yes. The Loadstone Rock was drawing him, and he must sail on, until he struck. He knew of no rock; he saw hardly any danger. The intention with which he had done what he had done presented it before him in an aspect that would be gratefully acknowledged in France on his presenting himself to assert it. Then that glorious vision of doing good, which is so often the sanguine mirage of so many good minds, arose before him, and he even saw himself with some influence to guide this raging Revolution that was running so fearfully wild.

As he walked to and fro with his resolution made, he considered that neither Lucie nor her father must know of it until he was gone. He walked to and fro, with thoughts very busy, until it was time to return to Tellson's and take leave of Mr. Lorry. As soon as he arrived in Paris he would present himself to this old friend, but he must say nothing of his intention now.

A carriage was ready at the Bank door, and Jerry was booted and equipped.

"I have delivered that letter," said Charles Darnay to Mr. Lorry. "I would not consent to your being charged with any written answer, but perhaps you will take a verbal one?"

"That I will, if it is not dangerous."

"Not at all. Though it is to a prisoner in the Abbaye."

"What is his name?" said Mr. Lorry.

"Gabelle."

"Gabelle. And what is the message?"

"Simply, that 'he has received the letter, and will come.' "

"Any time mentioned?"

"He will start tomorrow night."

"Any person mentioned?"

"No."

He helped Mr. Lorry to wrap himself in a number of coats and cloaks, and went out with him from the old Bank, into Fleet Street. "My love to Lucie, and to little Lucie," said Mr. Lorry at parting, "and take precious care of them till I come back."

That night—it was the fourteenth of August—he sat up late, and wrote two fervent letters; one was to Lucie, explaining the strong obligation he was under to go to Paris, and showing her the reasons that he had, for feeling confident that he could become involved in no personal danger there; the other was to the Doctor, confiding Lucie and their dear child to his

---

2. ***the Loadstone Rock,*** a mythical rock which drew ships to their destruction by magnetic attraction of their iron parts.

care, and dwelling on the same topics with the strongest assurance. To both he wrote that he would dispatch letters immediately after his arrival.

The unseen force was drawing him fast. He left his two letters with a trusty porter, to be delivered half an hour before midnight, and no sooner; took horse for Dover; and began his journey. "For the love of heaven, of justice, of generosity, of the honor of your noble name!" was the poor prisoner's cry with which he strengthened his sinking heart, as he left all that was dear on earth behind him, and floated away for the Loadstone Rock.

Discussion
Chapter XIX

1. The title of this chapter is a metaphor. What two things are being compared?

2. Do you think Dickens is sympathizing with or criticizing the people of Saint Antoine? Support your opinion with lines from the chapter.

Chapter XXI

1. (a) What connection has Tellson's Bank with the French aristocracy in France? in England? **(b)** What draws Mr. Lorry to Paris? **(c)** What is the irony in Mr. Lorry's confidence in Jerry's innocent simplicity?

2. (a) Why does Darnay decide to go to Paris? **(b)** Do you consider his reasons sound? **(c)** Do you think Gabelle's letter could be a deliberate trap?

Discussion
Book the Second

1. Things that happen to minor characters often affect the lives of major characters. Explain how the actions of the following minor characters affect both the plot and the lives of other, more important characters: **(a)** the Marquis; **(b)** Gaspard, the tall man; **(c)** Gabelle.

2. Dickens introduces several motifs, or patterns of images, in this second book. Explain the significance of each of the following: **(a)** echoes; **(b)** footsteps; **(c)** golden thread; **(d)** the sea; **(e)** fire; **(f)** the loadstone.

Vocabulary
Etymology

In *A Tale of Two Cities,* Dickens uses many words that were common in the nineteenth century but are used only rarely today. A study of the origins of these words will give you an opportunity to examine the kind of language that Dickens was most familiar with.

Look up the origin and definition of the following italicized words in your Glossary. Then read the sentence in which each word appears and decide whether the statement is true (T) or false (F).

1. Even a man with poor vision can use a *blunderbuss* to hunt game.

2. A *postilion* is the person who lights the street lamps at night.

3. A wounded deer can hide itself in a *coppice* and escape the hunter.

4. The local *tribunal* is published every Thursday.

5. Generations have paid *homage* to our country's great leaders.

6. A *tocsin* is a deadly form of bacteria.

7. The crippled man needed an *escutcheon* to help him walk.

8. An angry *execration* should be hospitalized.

9. *Poltroons* are delicious if baked in a 325° oven.

10. One of the *sacristan's* duties is to keep the communion cup safely locked away.

French revolutionaries storm the Bastille, symbol of official tyranny and repression.

Comment: Symbolism

Writers use symbols to convey ideas in memorable ways. A symbol is a thing that stands for or represents another thing, idea, or quality. The lion, for example, symbolizes courage; the olive branch stands for peace. A flag represents a country, and a heart can symbolize romantic love.

The titles of the three books in *A Tale of Two Cities* illustrate this principle. "Recalled to Life," the first title, suggests that prison symbolizes death. "The Golden Thread," the second title, represents the blonde Lucie who fashions the loving home that mends her father's health and that creates ties to bind Mr. Lorry, Sydney Carton, and Charles Darnay to her. What symbolism might be found in the title of the third book, "The Track of a Storm"? Places described in the novel also have symbolic meaning. To the revolutionaries, the Bastille is a particularly loathsome symbol of oppression and tyranny; when they take to the streets, it is their first objective.

Various objects and actions take on symbolic meanings within the context of the novel. In an early chapter, how does the spilled wine symbolically foreshadow the coming revolution? In the hands of a sweet grandmother, knitting is a symbol of love or industry. What does Madame Defarge's knitting represent? As you continue to read, pay special attention to actions (such as footsteps or Doctor Manette's shoemaking) that are given strong emphasis. By assigning persons, places, things, or actions both literal and figurative meanings, Dickens creates symbols that enrich his work.

Book the Third: The Track of a Storm

CHAPTER I
IN SECRET

The traveler fared slowly on his way, who fared toward Paris from England in the autumn of the year one thousand seven hundred and ninety-two.

Every towngate and village taxing house had its bank of citizen-patriots with their national muskets in a most explosive state of readiness, who stopped all comers and goers, cross-questioned them, inspected their papers, looked for their names in lists of their own, turned them back or sent them on, or stopped them and laid them in hold, as their capricious judgment or fancy deemed best for the dawning Republic One and Indivisible, of Liberty, Equality, Fraternity, or Death.

A very few French leagues of his journey were accomplished when Charles Darnay began to perceive that for him along these country roads there was no hope of return until he should have been declared a good citizen at Paris. Whatever might befall now, he must on to his journey's end. Not a mean village closed upon him, not a common barrier dropped across the road behind him, but he knew it to be another iron door, in the series that was barred between him and England. He had been days upon his journey in France alone, when he went to bed tired out, in a little town on the high road, still a long way from Paris.

Nothing but the production of the afflicted Gabelle's letter from his prison of the Abbaye would have got him on so far. His difficulty at the guardhouse in this small place had been such that he felt his journey to have come to a crisis. And he was, therefore, as little surprised as a man could be, to find himself awakened by a timid local functionary and three armed patriots in rough red caps and with pipes in their mouths.

"Emigrant," said the functionary, "I am going to send you on to Paris, under an escort."

"Citizen, I desire nothing more than to get to Paris, though I could dispense with the escort."

"Silence!" growled a red-cap, striking at the coverlet with the butt end of his musket.

"It is as the good patriot says," observed the functionary. "You must have an escort—and must pay for it."

"I have no choice," said Charles Darnay.

"Choice! Listen to him!" cried the scowling red-cap. "As if it was not a favor to be protected from the lamp-iron!"

"It is always as the good patriot says," observed the functionary. "Rise and dress yourself, emigrant."

When they came to the town of Beauvais—which they did at eventide—Darnay could not conceal from himself that the aspect of affairs was alarming. An ominous crowd gathered to see him dismount at the posting yard, and many voices called loudly, "Down with the emigrant!"

"Emigrant, my friends! Do you not see me here, in France, of my own will?"

"You are a cursed emigrant," cried a farrier, making at him, hammer in hand, "and a cursed aristocrat!"

The postmaster interposed himself between this man and the rider's bridle and soothingly said, "Let him be; let him be! He will be judged at Paris."

"Judged!" repeated the farrier. "Aye! and condemned as a traitor." The crowd roared approval. Darnay said, as soon as he could make his voice heard:

"Friends, you are deceived. I am not a traitor."

"He lies!" cried the smith. "He is a traitor since the decree. His life is forfeit to the people."

At the instant when Darnay saw a rush in the eyes of the crowd, the postmaster shut and barred the gates. The crowd groaned, but no more was done.

"What is this decree that the smith spoke

of?'' Darnay asked the postmaster, when he had thanked him.

''Truly, a decree for selling the property of emigrants.''

''When passed?''

''On the fourteenth.''

''The day I left England!''

''Everyone says it is but one of several, and that there will be others—if there are not already—banishing all emigrants, and condemning all to death who return. That is what he meant when he said your life was not your own.''

''But there are no such decrees yet?''

''What do I know!'' said the postmaster, shrugging his shoulders; ''there may be, or there will be.''

Daylight at last found them before the wall of Paris. The Barrier was closed and strongly guarded when they rode up to it.

''Where are the papers of this prisoner?'' demanded a resolute-looking man.

Naturally struck by the disagreeable word, Charles Darnay requested the speaker to take notice that he was a free traveler and French citizen, in charge of an escort which the disturbed state of the country had imposed upon him and which he had paid for.

''Where,'' repeated the same personage, without taking any heed of him whatever, ''are the papers of this prisoner?''

The drunken patriot produced them. Casting his eyes over Gabelle's letter, the same personage showed surprise, and looked at Darnay with close attention.

He left escort and escorted without saying a word, and went into the guardroom.

When he had sat in his saddle some half hour, Darnay found himself confronted by the same man in authority, who directed the guard to open the Barrier. Then he delivered to the escort a receipt for the escorted, and requested him to dismount. Darnay accompanied his conductor into a guardroom, where an officer of a coarse, dark aspect, presided.

''Citizen Defarge,'' said he to Darnay's conductor, ''is this the emigrant Evrémonde?''

''This is the man.''

''Your age, Evrémonde?''

''Thirty-seven.''

''Married, Evrémonde?''

''Yes.''

''Where is your wife, Evrémonde?''

''In England.''

''Without doubt. You are consigned, Evrémonde, to the prison of La Force.''

''Just heaven!'' exclaimed Darnay. ''Under what law and for what offense?''

The officer looked up from his slip of paper for a moment.

''We have new laws, Evrémonde, and new offenses, since you were here.'' He said it with a hard smile.

''I entreat you to observe that I have come here voluntarily, in response to that written appeal of a fellow countryman which lies before you. I demand to do so without delay. Is not that my right?''

''Emigrants have no rights, Evrémonde,'' was the stolid reply. The officer wrote until he had finished, read over to himself what he had written, sanded it, and handed it to Defarge with the words, ''In secret.''

Defarge motioned to the prisoner that he must accompany him and a guard of two armed patriots.

''Is it you,'' said Defarge, in a low voice, as they went down the guardhouse steps, ''who married the daughter of Doctor Manette, once a prisoner in the Bastille?''

''Yes,'' replied Darnay, looking at him with surprise.

''My name is Defarge, and I keep a wine shop in the Quarter Saint Antoine. Possibly you have heard of me.''

''My wife came to your house to reclaim her father? Yes!''

The word ''wife'' seemed to serve as a gloomy reminder to Defarge to say with sudden impatience, ''In the name of that sharp female La Guillotine, why did you come to France?''

''You heard me say why, a minute ago. Do you not believe it is the truth?''

"A bad truth for you," said Defarge.

"Indeed I am lost here. All is so changed. Will you render me a little help?"

"None." Defarge spoke, looking straight before him.

"Will you answer me a single question?"

"Perhaps. You can say what it is."

"In this prison that I am going to so unjustly, shall I have some free communication with the world outside?"

"You will see."

"I am not to be buried there, prejudged, and without any means of presenting my case?"

"You will see. But what then? Other people have been similarly buried in worse prisons, before now."

"But never by me, Citizen Defarge."

Defarge walked on in a steady and set silence. Darnay made haste to say:

"It is of the utmost importance to me that I communicate to Mr. Lorry of Tellson's Bank, an English gentleman now in Paris, the fact that I have been thrown into the prison of La Force. Will you cause that to be done for me?"

"I will do," Defarge doggedly rejoined, "nothing for you. My duty is to my country and the People. I am the sworn servant of both. I will do nothing for you."

Charles Darnay felt it hopeless to entreat him further. That he had fallen among far greater dangers than those which had developed when he left England he knew now. He could not but admit to himself that he might not have made this journey if he could have foreseen the events of a few days. Of unjust treatment in detention, and in cruel separation from his wife and child, he foreshadowed the likelihood; but, beyond this, he dreaded nothing distinctly. With this on his mind, he arrived at the prison of La Force.

A man with a bloated face opened the wicket to whom Defarge presented "The Emigrant Evrémond."

"In secret, too," grumbled the jailer, looking at the written paper. "As if I was not already full to bursting! Come with me, emigrant."

The wicket opened on a stone staircase, leading upward. When they had ascended forty steps the jailer opened a low door, and they passed into a solitary cell.

"Yours," said the jailer.

"Why am I confined alone?"

"How do I know!"

"I can buy pen, ink, and paper?"

"Such are not my orders. You will be visited, and can ask then. At present you may buy food, nothing more."

There were in the cell, a chair, a table, and a straw mattress. When the jailer was gone, Darnay thought, "Now am I left, as if I were dead." Stopping then, to look down at the mattress, he turned from it with a sick feeling, and thought, "And here in these crawling creatures is the first condition of the body after death."

CHAPTER II
THE GRINDSTONE

Tellson's Bank, in the Saint Germain Quarter of Paris, was in a large house, approached by a courtyard and shut off from the street by a high wall and a strong gate. The house belonged to a great nobleman who had lived in it until he made a flight from the troubles, in his own cook's dress, and got across the borders.

What money would be drawn out of Tellson's henceforth, and what would lie there, forgotten, what plate and jewels would tarnish in Tellson's hiding places, while the depositors rusted in prisons, how many accounts with Tellson's, never to be balanced in this world, must be carried over into the next, no man could have said, that night, any more than Mr. Jarvis Lorry could, though he thought heavily of these questions.

"Thank God," said Mr. Lorry, clasping his hands, "that no one near and dear to me is in this dreadful town tonight. May He have mercy on all who are in danger!"

Soon afterwards, the bell at the great gate sounded, he heard the gate clash, and all was quiet. Then his door suddenly opened, and two figures rushed in, at sight of which he fell back in amazement.

Lucie and her father! Lucie with her arms stretched out to him, and with that old look of earnestness upon her face.

"What is this?" cried Mr. Lorry, breathless and confused. "What is the matter? Lucie! Manette! What has happened? What has brought you here? What is it?"

With the look fixed upon him, in her paleness and wildness, she panted imploringly, "O my dear friend! My husband!"

"Your husband, Lucie?"

"Here."

"Here, in Paris?"

"Has been here some days—three or four—I don't know how many. An errand of generosity brought him here unknown to us; he was stopped and sent to prison."

The old man uttered an irrepressible cry. Almost at the same moment the bell of the gate rang again, and a loud noise of feet and voices came pouring into the courtyard.

"What is that noise?" said the Doctor.

"Don't look!" cried Mr. Lorry. "Don't look out! Manette, for your life, don't touch the blind!"

The Doctor turned, with his hand upon the fastening of the window, and said, with a cool, bold smile:

"My dear friend, I have a charmed life in this city. I have been a Bastille prisoner. There is no patriot in Paris—in Paris? In France—who, knowing me to have been a prisoner in the Bastille, would touch me, except to overwhelm me with embraces. My old pain has given me a power that has brought us through the Barrier, gained us news of Charles there, and brought us here. I knew it would be so; I knew I could help Charles; I told Lucie so—what is that noise?" His hand was again upon the window.

"Don't look!" cried Mr. Lorry, absolutely desperate. "No, Lucie, my dear, nor you!" He got his arm around her, and held her. "Don't be so terrified, my love. I solemnly swear to you that I know of no harm having happened to Charles. What prison is he in?"

"La Force!"

"La Force! Lucie, my child, you will compose yourself now, to do exactly as I bid you; for more depends upon it than you can think, or I can say. There is no help for you in any action on your part tonight; you cannot possibly stir out. I say this, because what I must bid you to do for Charles' sake is the hardest thing to do of all. You must instantly be obedient, still, and quiet. You must let me put you in a room at the back here. You must leave your father and me alone for two minutes, and as there are Life and Death in the world you must not delay."

"I will be submissive to you. I see in your face that you know I can do nothing else. I know you are true."

The old man kissed her, hurried her into his room, and turned the key; then came hurrying back to the Doctor, partly opened the blind, put his hand upon the Doctor's arm, and looked out with him into the courtyard.

Looked out upon a throng of men and women; not enough in number to fill the courtyard; not more than forty or fifty in all. The people in possession of the house had let them in at the gate, and they had rushed in to work at the grindstone; it had evidently been set up there for their purpose, as in a convenient and retired spot.

But, such awful workers, and such awful work! The grindstone had a double handle and turning it madly were two men whose faces, as their long hair flapped back when the whirlings of the grindstone brought their faces up, were more horrible and cruel than the visages of the wildest savages in their most barbarous disguise. False eyebrows and moustaches were stuck upon them, and their hideous countenances were all bloody and sweaty, and all awry with howling, and all staring and glaring with beastly excitement and want of sleep. As these ruffians turned and turned, their matted locks now flung over their eyes, now flung backward over their necks, some women held wine to their mouths that they might drink; and what with dropping blood, and what with dropping wine, and what with the stream of sparks struck out of the stone, all their wicked atmosphere seemed gore and fire. The eye could not detect one creature in the group free from the smear of blood. Shouldering one another to get next at the sharpening stone were men stripped to the waist, the stain all over their bodies; men in rags, with the stain upon those rags; men set off with spoils of women's lace and silk and ribbon, the stain dyeing those trifles. Hatchets, knives, bayonets, swords, brought to be sharpened, were red with it. And as the frantic wielders of these weapons snatched them from the stream of sparks and tore away into the streets, the same red hue was in their frenzied eyes—eyes which any unbrutalized beholder would have given twenty years of life to petrify with a well directed gun.

They drew back from the window, and the Doctor looked for explanation in his friend's ashy face.

"They are," Mr. Lorry whispered, glancing fearfully at the locked room, "murdering the prisoners. If you really have the power you think you have—as I believe you have—make yourself known to these devils, and get taken to La Force. It may be too late—I don't know!"

Doctor Manette pressed his hand, hastened bareheaded out of the room, and was in the courtyard when Mr. Lorry regained the blind.

His streaming white hair, his remarkable face, and the impetuous confidence of his manner, as he put the weapons aside like water, carried him in an instant to the heart of the concourse at the stone. For a few moments there was a pause, and a hurry, and a murmur, and the unintelligible sound of his voice; and then Mr. Lorry saw him, surrounded by all, and in the midst of a line of twenty men long, all linked shoulder to shoulder, and hand to shoulder, hurried out with cries of—"Live the Bastille prisoner! Help for the Bastille prisoner's kindred in La Force! Room for the Bastille prisoner in front there! Save the prisoner Evrémonde at La Force!" and a thousand answering shouts.

He closed the lattice again with a fluttering heart, closed the window and the curtain, hastened to Lucie, and told her that her father was assisted by the people, and gone in search of her husband. He found her child and Miss Pross with her; but, it never occurred to him to be surprised by their appearance until a long time afterwards, when he sat watching them in such quiet as the night knew.

Lucie had, by that time, fallen into a stupor on the floor at his feet, clinging to his hand. Miss Pross had laid the child down on his own bed, and her head had gradually fallen on the pillow beside her pretty charge. Oh, the long, long night, with the moans of the poor wife! And oh, the long, long night, with no return of her father and no tidings!

The great grindstone, Earth, had turned when Mr. Lorry looked out again, and the sun was red on the courtyard. But the lesser grindstone stood alone there in the calm morning air, with a red upon it that the sun had never given, and would never take away.

CHAPTER III
THE SHADOW

One of the first considerations which arose in the business mind of Mr. Lorry when business hours came round, was this—that he had no right to imperil Tellson's by sheltering the wife of an emigrant prisoner under the Bank roof. His own possessions, safety, life, he would have hazarded for Lucie and her child, without a moment's demur; but the great trust he held was not his own, and as to that business charge he was a strict man of business.

Noon coming, and the Doctor not returning, and every minute's delay tending to compromise Tellson's, Mr. Lorry advised with Lucie. She said that her father had spoken of hiring a lodging for a short term, in that Quarter, near the Banking house. As there was no business objection to this, and as he foresaw that even if it were all well with Charles, and he were to be released, he could not hope to leave the city,

Mr. Lorry went out in quest of such a lodging and found a suitable one, high up in a removed by-street where the closed blinds in all the other windows of a high melancholy square of buildings marked deserted homes.

To this lodging he at once removed Lucie and her child, and Miss Pross; giving them what comfort he could, and much more than he had himself. He left Jerry with them, as a figure to fill a doorway that would bear considerable knocking on the head, and returned to his occupations. A disturbed and doleful mind he brought to bear upon them, and slowly and heavily the day lagged on with him.

It wore itself out, and wore him out with it, until the Bank closed. He was again alone in his room of the previous night, considering what to do next, when he heard a foot upon the stair. In a few moments a man stood in his presence, who addressed him by his name.

"Your servant," said Mr. Lorry. "Do you know me?"

He was a strongly made man with dark curling hair, from forty-five to fifty years of age. For answer, he repeated, without any change of emphasis, the words:

"Do you know me?"

"I have seen you somewhere."

"Perhaps at my wine shop?"

"You come from Doctor Manette?"

"Yes. I come from Doctor Manette."

"And what says he? What does he send me?"

Defarge gave into his anxious hand an open scrap of paper. It bore the words in the Doctor's writing:

"Charles is safe, but I cannot safely leave this place yet. I have obtained the favor that the bearer has a short note from Charles to his wife. Let the bearer see his wife."

It was dated from La Force, within an hour.

"Will you accompany me," said Mr. Lorry, joyfully relieved, "to where his wife resides?"

"Yes," returned Defarge.

Scarcely noticing as yet in what a curiously reserved way Defarge spoke, Mr. Lorry went with him into the courtyard. There they found two women; one knitting.

"Madame Defarge!" said Mr. Lorry, who had left her in exactly the same attitude some seventeen years ago. "Does madame go with us?"

"Yes. That she may be able to recognize the faces and know the persons. It is for their safety."

Mr. Lorry led the way. Both the women followed; the second woman being The Vengeance.

They passed through the intervening streets as quickly as they might, ascended the staircase of the new domicile, were admitted by Jerry, and found Lucie weeping, alone. She was thrown into a transport by the tidings Mr. Lorry gave her of her husband, and clasped the hand that delivered his note—little thinking what it had been doing near him in the night, and might, but for a chance, have done to him.

"DEAREST—Take courage. I am well, and your father has influence around me. You cannot answer this. Kiss our child for me."

That was all the writing. It was so much, however, to her who received it, that she turned from Defarge to his wife, and kissed one of the hands that knitted. It was a loving, thankful, womanly action, but the hand made no response—dropped cold and heavy, and took to its knitting again.

There was something in its touch that gave Lucie a check. She stopped in the act of putting the note in her bosom, and looked terrified at Madame Defarge. Madame Defarge met the lifted eyebrows and forehead with a cold, impassive stare.

"Is that his child?" said Madame Defarge, stopping in her work for the first time, and pointing her knitting needle at little Lucie as if it were the finger of Fate.

"Yes, madame," answered Mr. Lorry; "this is our poor prisoner's darling daughter, and only child."

The shadow attendant on Madame Defarge

and her party seemed to fall so threatening and dark on the child that her mother instinctively kneeled on the ground beside her, and held her to her breast. The shadow attendant on Madame Defarge and her party seemed then to fall, threatening and dark, on both the mother and the child.

"What is it your husband says in that little letter?" asked Madame Defarge, with a lowering smile. "Influence; he says something touching influence?"

"That my father," said Lucie, hurriedly taking the paper from her breast, but with her alarmed eyes on her questioner and not on it, "has much influence around him."

"Surely it will release him!" said Madame Defarge. "Let it do so."

She resumed her knitting and went out. The Vengeance followed. Defarge went last and closed the door.

"Courage, my dear Lucie," said Mr. Lorry, as he raised her. "Courage, courage! So far all goes well with us—much, much better than it has of late gone with many poor souls. Cheer up, and have a thankful heart."

"I am not thankless, I hope, but that dreadful woman seems to throw a shadow on me and on all my hopes."

"Tut, tut!" said Mr. Lorry; "what is this despondency? A shadow indeed! No substance in it, Lucie."

But the shadow of the manner of these Defarges was dark, for all that, and in his secret mind it troubled him greatly.

CHAPTER IV
CALM IN STORM

Doctor Manette did not return until the morning of the fourth day of his absence. Not until long afterwards did Lucie know that eleven hundred defenseless prisoners had been killed by the populace. She only knew that there had been an attack upon the prisons, that all prisoners had been in danger, and that some had been dragged out by the crowd and murdered.

To Mr. Lorry, the Doctor communicated that the crowd had taken him through a scene of carnage to the prison of La Force. That, in the prison he had found a self-appointed Tribunal sitting, before which the prisoners were brought singly, and by which they were rapidly ordered to be put forth to be massacred, or to be released, or—in a few cases—to be sent back to their cells. That, presented by his conductors to this Tribunal, he had announced himself by name and profession as having been for eighteen years a secret and unaccused prisoner in the Bastille; that one of the body so sitting in judgment had risen and identified him, and that this man was Defarge.

That, hereupon, he had ascertained that his son-in-law was among the living prisoners, and had pleaded hard for his life and liberty. That, in the first frantic greetings lavished on himself as a notable sufferer under the overthrown system, it had been accorded to him to have Charles Darnay brought before the Court and examined. That, he seemed on the point of being at once released, when the tide in his favor met with some unexplained check—not intelligible to the Doctor—which led to a few words of secret conference. That, the man sitting as President had then informed Doctor Manette that the prisoner must remain in custody, but should, for his sake, be held in safe custody. That, immediately, the prisoner was removed to the interior of the prison again; but that he, the Doctor, had then so strongly pleaded for permission to remain and assure himself that his son-in-law was, through no malice or mischance, delivered to the concourse whose murderous yells outside the gate had often drowned the proceedings, that he had obtained the permission and had remained until the danger was over.

Greater things than the Doctor had at that time to contend with would have yielded before his persevering purpose. While he kept himself in his place, as a physician, whose business was with all degrees of mankind, he used his influence so wisely that he was soon the inspecting physician of three prisons, and among them La Force. He could now assure Lucie that her husband was no longer confined alone; he saw her husband weekly, and brought sweet messages to her, straight from his lips; sometimes her husband himself sent a letter to her—though never by the Doctor's hand—but she was not permitted to write to him; for, among the many wild suspicions of plots in the prisons, the wildest of all pointed at emigrants who were known to have made friends abroad.

But though the Doctor never ceased trying to get Charles Darnay set at liberty, or at least to get him brought to trial, the public current of the time set too strong and fast for him. The new era began; the King was tried, doomed, and beheaded; the Republic of Liberty, Equality, Fraternity, or Death, declared for victory or death against the world in arms. Above all, one hideous figure grew familiar—the figure of the sharp female, La Guillotine.

It was the popular theme for jests; it was the best cure for headache, it infallibly prevented the hair from turning gray, it imparted a peculiar delicacy to the complexion, it was the National Razor which shaved close. It was the sign of the regeneration of the human race. Models of it were worn on breasts from which the Cross was discarded, and it was bowed down to and believed in where the Cross was denied.

It sheared off heads so many that it, and the ground it polluted, were a rotten red. It hushed the eloquent, struck down the powerful, abolished the beautiful and good. Twenty-two friends of high public mark it had lopped the heads off, in one morning, in as many minutes. The name of the strong man of Old Scripture[1] had descended to the functionary who worked it; but, so armed, he was stronger than his namesake, and blinder, and tore away the gates of God's own Temple every day.

Among these terrors, the Doctor walked with a steady head; confident in his power, cautiously persistent, never doubting that he would save Lucie's husband at last. Yet the current of the time swept by, so strong and deep, and carried the time away so fiercely, that Charles had lain in prison one year and three months.

Still the Doctor walked among the terrors with a steady head. No man better known than he, in Paris at that day; no man in a stranger situation. Silent, humane, indispensable in hospital and prison, using his art equally among assassins and victims, he was a man apart. In the exercise of his skill, the appearance and the story of the Bastille Captive removed him from all other men. He was not suspected or brought in question any more than if he had indeed been recalled to life some eighteen years before, or were a Spirit moving among mortals.

1. ***the strong man of Old Scripture.*** Samson, in the Old Testament, was famous for his tremendous physical strength.

Discussion

Chapter I

1. In Chapter XXI of Book the Second, Darnay appears to be unaware of the dangers involved in his returning to Paris. Trace the events in this chapter that change his attitude.

2. (a) On what charge is Darnay arrested? **(b)** In Book the First, Doctor Manette had been unjustly arrested under the laws of the royal government. What does Darnay's arrest show about the "justice" of the new laws?

3. (a) What do you think are Defarge's real feelings toward Darnay? **(b)** Why do you think he chooses not to show his real feelings?

4. Compare Darnay's imprisonment in La Force with what you know of Doctor Manette's imprisonment in the Bastille.

Chapter II

1. (a) What effect does the arrival of Lucie and Doctor Manette have on Mr. Lorry? **(b)** Is he glad to see them? Why or why not?

2. Why is Doctor Manette so confident of his power to help Charles Darnay?

3. In his description of the grindstone and the grinders, Dickens creates a powerful symbol. **(a)** What does the grindstone symbolize? **(b)** What is its effect on the people who surround it?

Chapter III

1. (a) How does Defarge explain Madame Defarge's desire to meet Lucie? **(b)** Do you think this is the real reason? **(c)** Why might Madame's interest in little Lucie be ominous?

2. The word *shadow* is used several times in relation to Madame Defarge and her party. Supposing that this shadow is not actually cast by her body, what particular significance do you think this word has?

Chapter IV

1. In what ways is Doctor Manette able to be of help to Charles? to Lucie? to others?

2. (a) The narrator makes several religious references in the description of La Guillotine and its "functionary." What are these? **(b)** Explain the irony to be found in the description.

CHAPTER V
THE WOOD SAWYER

One year and three months. During all that time Lucie was never sure, from hour to hour, but that the Guillotine would strike off her husband's head next day. Every day, through the stony streets, the tumbrils now jolted heavily, filled with Condemned. Lovely girls; bright women, brown-haired, black-haired, and gray; youths; stalwart men and old; gentle born and peasant born; all red wine for La Guillotine, all daily brought into light from the dark cellars of the loathsome prisons, and carried to her through the street to slake her devouring thirst. Liberty, Equality, Fraternity, or Death—the last, much the easiest to bestow, O Guillotine!

As soon as they were established in their new residence, she arranged the little household as exactly as if her husband had been there. Everything had its appointed place and its appointed time. Little Lucie she taught, regularly. The belief that they would soon be reunited—the little preparations for his speedy return, the setting aside of his chair and his book—these, and the solemn prayer at night for one dear prisoner especially, among the many unhappy souls in prison—were almost the only reliefs of her heavy mind.

Sometimes, at night on kissing her father, she would burst into the grief she had repressed all day, and say that her sole reliance, under heaven, was on him. He always resolutely answered: "Nothing can happen to him without my knowledge, and I know that I can save him, Lucie."

They had not made the round of their changed life many weeks, when her father said to her, one evening:

"My dear, there is an upper window in the prison, to which Charles can sometimes gain access at three in the afternoon. When he can get to it, he might see you in the street, he thinks, if you stood in a certain place that I can show you. But you will not be able to see him, my poor child, and even if you could, it would be unsafe for you to make a sign of recognition."

"O show me the place, Father. I will go there every day."

From that time, in all weathers, she waited there two hours. As the clock struck two, she was there; at four she turned resignedly away. When it was not too inclement for her child to be with her, they went together; at other times she was alone; but she never missed a single day.

It was the dark and dirty corner of a small winding street. The hovel of a cutter of wood was the only house at that end; all else was wall. On the third day of her being there, he noticed her.

"Good day, citizeness."

"Good day, citizen."

This mode of address was now prescribed by decree. It had been established voluntarily some time ago, among the more thorough patriots; but was now law for everybody.

"Walking here again, citizeness?"

"You see me, citizen!"

The wood sawyer, who was a little man with a redundancy of gesture—he had once been a mender of roads—cast a glance at the prison, pointed at the prison, and putting his ten fingers before his face to represent bars, peeped through them jocosely.

"But it's not my business," said he. And went on sawing his wood.

Next day he was looking out for her, and accosted her the moment she appeared.

"What? Walking here again, citizeness?"

"Yes, citizen."

"Ah! A child too! Your mother, is it not, my little citizeness?"

"Do I say yes, mamma?" whispered little Lucie, drawing close to her.

"Yes, dearest."

"Yes, citizen."

"Ah! but it's not my business. My work is my business. See my saw! I call it my Little Guillotine. La, la, la; La, la, la! And off his head comes!"

The billet fell as he spoke, and he threw it into a basket.

"I call myself the Samson of the firewood guillotine. See here again! Loo, loo, loo; Loo, loo, loo! And off her head comes. All the family!"

Lucie shuddered as he threw two more billets into his basket, but it was impossible to be there while the wood sawyer was at work, and not be in his sight. Thenceforth, to secure his good will, she always spoke to him first, and often gave him drinking-money, which he readily received.

In all weathers, in the snow and frost of winter, in the bitter winds of spring, in the hot sunshine of summer, in the rains of autumn, and again in the snow and frost of winter, Lucie passed two hours of every day at this place. Her husband saw her—so she learned from her father—it might be once in five or six times; it might be twice or thrice running; it might be not for a week or a fortnight together. It was enough that he did see her when the chances served, and on that possibility she would have waited out the day, seven days a week. On a lightly snowing afternoon she arrived at the usual corner. It was a day of wild rejoicing, and festival. She had seen the houses, as she came along, decorated with little pikes, with little red caps stuck upon them; with tricolored ribbons; also, with the standard inscription Republic One and Indivisible. Liberty, Equality, Fraternity, or Death!

Presently she heard a troubled movement and a shouting coming along, which filled her with fear. A moment afterwards a throng of people came pouring around the corner by the prison wall. Five hundred people were dancing like five thousand demons. There was no other music than their own singing. They danced to the popular Revolution song, keeping a ferocious time that was like a gnashing of teeth in unison. Men and women danced together, women danced together, men danced together.

They advanced, retreated, struck at one another's hands, clutched at one another's heads, spun round alone, caught one another and spun round in pairs, until many of them dropped. While those were down, the rest linked hand in hand, and all spun round together; then the ring broke, and in separate rings of two and four they turned and turned until they all stopped at once, began again, struck, clutched, and tore, and then reversed the spin, and all spun round another way. Suddenly they stopped again, paused, struck out the time afresh, formed into lines the width of the public way, and, with their heads low down and their hands high up, swooped screaming off. No fight could have been half so terrible as this dance. It was so emphatically a fallen sport—a healthy pastime changed into a means of angering the blood, bewildering the senses, and steeling the heart. Such grace as was in it made it the uglier, showing how warped and perverted all things good by nature were become.

This was the Carmagnole.[1] As it passed, leaving Lucie frightened and bewildered in the doorway of the wood-sawyer's house, the feathery snow fell as quietly and lay as white and soft as if it had never been.

"O my father!" for he stood before her when she lifted up her eyes, "such a cruel, bad sight."

"I know, my dear, I know. I have seen it many times. Don't be frightened! Not one of them would harm you."

"I am not frightened for myself, my father. But when I think of my husband, and the mercies of these people——"

"We will set him above their mercies soon. I left him climbing to the window. There is no one here to see. You may kiss your hand toward that highest shelving roof."

"I do so, father, and I send him my soul with it!"

A footstep in the snow. Madame Defarge.

"I salute you, citizeness," from the Doctor.

"I salute you, citizen." Madame gone, like a shadow over the white road.

"Give me your arm, my love, with an air of cheerfulness for his sake. Charles is summoned for tomorrow."

"For tomorrow!"

"I am prepared, but there are precautions to be taken, that could not be taken until he was actually summoned. You are not afraid?"

She could scarcely answer, "I trust in you."

"Do so, implicitly. Your suspense is nearly ended, my darling; he shall be restored to you within a few hours; I have encompassed him with every protection. I must see Lorry.

"I must see Lorry," the Doctor repeated, turning her another way.

A murky red and yellow sky, and a rising mist from the Seine,[2] denoted the approach of darkness. It was almost dark when they arrived at the Bank.

Who could that be with Mr. Lorry—the owner of the ridingcoat upon the chair—who must not be seen? From whom, newly arrived, did Mr. Lorry come out, agitated and surprised, to take his favorite in his arms? To whom did he repeat her faltering words, when, raising his voice and turning his head toward the door of the room from which he had issued, he said: "Removed to the Conciergerie[3] and summoned for tomorrow?"

CHAPTER VI
TRIUMPH

The dread Tribunal of five Judges, Public Prosecutor, and determined Jury, sat every day. Their lists went forth every evening, and were read out by jailers of various prisons to their prisoners. The standard jailer joke was, "Come and listen to the Evening Paper, you inside there!"

"Charles Evrémonde, called Darnay!"

So at last began the Evening Paper at La Force.

When a name was called, its owner stepped into a spot reserved for those announced as being thus fatally recorded. Charles Evré-

---

1. ***The Carmagnole,*** a bizarre dance and song popular among the French Revolutionists. The term was also used for the popular costume the Revolutionists wore—a jacket with a wide collar and metal buttons; a blue, white, and red waistcoat; and a red cap.
2. ***Seine*** (sān), the river that flows through the city of Paris.
3. ***Conciergerie*** (kōN syerzh′ərē), a prison where prisoners awaited trial.

monde, called Darnay, had reason to know the usage; he had seen hundreds pass away so.

The passage to the Conciergerie was short and dark; the night in its vermin-haunted cells was long and cold. Next day fifteen prisoners were put to the bar before Charles Darnay's name was called. All the fifteen were condemned, and the trials of the whole occupied an hour and a half.

"Charles Evrémonde, called Darnay," was at length arraigned.

His Judges sat upon the Bench in feathered hats; but the rough red cap and tricolored cockade was the headdress otherwise prevailing. Looking at the Jury and the turbulent audience, he might have thought that the usual order of things was reversed, and that the felons were trying the honest men. The lowest, cruelest, and worst populace of a city were the directing spirits of the scene: noisily commenting, applauding, disapproving, anticipating, and precipitating the result, without a check.

Under the President sat Doctor Manette, in his usual quiet dress. As well as the prisoner could see, he and Mr. Lorry were the only men there, unconnected with the Tribunal, who wore their usual clothes, and had not assumed the coarse garb of the Carmagnole.

Charles Evrémonde, called Darnay, was accused by the public prosecutor as an emigrant, whose life was forfeit under the decree which banished all emigrants on pain of death. It was nothing that the decree bore date since his return to France. There he was, and there the decree; he had been taken in France, and his head was demanded.

"Take off his head!" cried the audience. "An enemy to the Republic!"

The President rang his bell to silence those cries and asked the prisoner whether it was not true that he had lived many years in England?

Undoubtedly it was

Was he not an emigrant then? What did he call himself?

Not an emigrant, he hoped, within the spirit of the law.

Why not? the President desired to know.

Because he had voluntarily relinquished a title that was distasteful to him, and had left his country—before the word emigrant in the present acceptation by the Tribunal was in use—to live by his own industry in England, rather than on the industry of the overladen people of France.

What proof had he of this?

He handed in the names of two witnesses: Théophile Gabelle, and Alexandre Manette.

But he had married in England?

True, but not an English woman.

A citizeness of France?

Yes. By birth.

Her name and family?

"Lucie Manette, only daughter of Doctor Manette, the good physician who sits there."

This answer had a happy effect upon the audience. Cries in exaltation of the well-known good physician rent the hall. So capriciously were the people moved that tears immediately rolled down several ferocious countenances which had been glaring at the prisoner a moment before, as if with impatience to pluck him out into the streets and kill him.

The President asked why had he returned to France when he did, and not sooner?

He had not returned sooner because he had no means of living in France save those he had resigned; whereas, in England, he lived by giving instruction in the French language and literature. He had returned when he did, on the written entreaty of a French citizen, who represented that his life was endangered by his absence. He had come back to save a citizen's life and to bear his testimony, at whatever personal hazard. Was that criminal in the eyes of the Republic?

The populace cried enthusiastically, "No!" and the President rang his bell to quiet them. Which it did not, for they continued to cry "No!" until they left off, of their own will.

The President required the name of that citizen. The accused explained that the citizen was his first witness. He also referred with confidence to the citizen's letter, which he did not doubt would be found among the papers then before the President.

The Doctor had taken care that it should be there—had assured him that it would be there—and at this stage of the proceedings it was produced and read.

Doctor Manette was next questioned. His high personal popularity, and the clearness of his answers, made a great impression; but as he proceeded, as he showed that the accused was his first friend on his release from his long imprisonment; that the accused had remained in England, always faithful and devoted to his daughter and himself in their exile; that, far from being in favor with the Aristocrat government there, he had actually been tried for his life by it, as the foe of England and friend of the United States—as he brought these circumstances into view, with the greatest discretion and with the straightforward force of truth and earnestness, the Jury and the populace became one. At last, when he appealed by name to Monsieur Lorry, an English gentleman then and there present, who, like himself, had been a witness on that English trial and could corroborate his account of it, the Jury declared that they had heard enough, and that they were ready with their votes if the President were content to receive them.

At every vote—the Jurymen voted aloud and individually—the populace set up a shout of applause. All the voices were in the prisoner's favor, and the President declared him free. No sooner was the acquittal pronounced than tears were shed, and such fraternal embraces were bestowed upon the prisoner that after his long and unwholesome confinement he was in danger of fainting from exhaustion.

His removal, to make way for other accused persons who were to be tried, rescued him from these caresses for the moment. Five were to be tried together, next, as enemies of the Republic. So quick was the Tribunal to compensate itself and the nation for a chance lost that these five came down to him before he left the place, condemned to die within twenty-four hours. The first of them told him so, with the customary prison sign of Death—a raised finger—and they all added in words, "Long live the Republic!"

The five had had, it is true, no audience to lengthen their proceedings, for when Darnay and Doctor Manette emerged from the gate, there was a great crowd about it. They put him into a great chair over which they had thrown a red flag, and to the back of it had bound a pike with a red cap on top. In this car of triumph, not even the Doctor's entreaties could prevent his being carried to his home on men's shoulders, with a confused sea of red caps heaving about him, and casting up to sight such wrecks of faces that he more than once misdoubted his mind being in confusion, and that he was in the tumbril on his way to the Guillotine.

In wild procession, they carried him thus into the courtyard of the building where he lived. Lucie's father had gone before to prepare her, and when her husband stood upon his feet, she dropped insensible in his arms.

As he held her to his heart, a few of the people fell to dancing. Instantly all the rest fell to dancing, and the courtyard overflowed with the Carmagnole. Then the Carmagnole absorbed them and whirled them away.

After grasping the Doctor's hand, as he stood victorious and proud before him; after grasping the hand of Mr. Lorry, who came in breathless from his struggle against the waterspout of the Carmagnole; after kissing little Lucie, who was lifted up to clasp her arms round his neck; and after embracing the ever zealous and faithful Pross; Charles took his wife in his arms.

"Lucie! My own! I am safe."

"O dearest Charles, let me thank God for this on my knees."

They all reverently bowed their heads and hearts. When she was again in his arms, he said to her:

"Now speak to your father, dearest. No other man in all France could have done what he has done for me."

She laid her head upon her father's breast, as she had laid his poor head on her breast, long, long ago. He was happy in the return he had made her, he was recompensed for his suffering, he was proud of his strength. "My darling," he remonstrated, "don't tremble so. I have saved him."

CHAPTER VII
A KNOCK AT THE DOOR

"I have saved him." It was not another of the dreams in which he had often come back; he was really here. And yet his wife trembled, and a vague fear was upon her.

Her father, cheering her, showed a compassionate superiority to this woman's weakness. No One Hundred and Five, North Tower, now! He had accomplished the task he had set himself, his promise was redeemed, he had saved Charles.

Their housekeeping was of a very frugal kind; not only because that was the safest way of life, but because they were not rich. Charles, throughout his imprisonment, had had to pay heavily for his bad food, and for his guard, and toward the living of the poorer prisoners. Partly on this account, and partly to avoid a domestic spy, they kept no servant; and Jerry—almost wholly transferred to them by Mr. Lorry—had become their daily retainer.

For some months, Miss Pross and Mr. Cruncher had discharged the office of purveyors; the former carrying the money; the latter, the basket. Every afternoon they fared forth, and made and brought home such purchases as were needful.

"There's all manner of things wanted," said Miss Pross, "and we shall have a time of it. We want wine, among the rest."

They went out, leaving Lucie, her husband, her father, and the child, by a bright fire. Mr. Lorry was expected presently. Miss Pross had lighted the lamp, but had put it aside in a corner, that they might enjoy the firelight. All was quiet, and Lucie was more at ease than she had been.

"What is that?" she cried, all at once.

"My dear!" said her father, "command yourself. What a disordered state you are in! The least thing—nothing—startles you! *You,* your father's daughter!"

"I thought," said Lucie, with a pale face and in a faltering voice, "that I heard strange feet upon the stairs."

"My love, the staircase is as still as death."

As he said the word, a blow was struck upon the door.

"Oh father, father. What can this be! Hide Charles. Save him!"

"My child," said the Doctor, rising, and laying his hand upon her shoulder, "I *have* saved him. What weakness is this, my dear! Let me go to the door."

He took the lamp in his hand, crossed the two intervening outer rooms, and opened it. Four rough men in red caps, armed with sabers and pistols, entered the room.

"The Citizen Evrémonde, called Darnay," said the first.

"Who seeks him?" answered Darnay.

"I seek him. We seek him. I know you, Evrémonde. I saw you before the Tribunal today. You are again the prisoner of the Republic."

The four surrounded him where he stood with his wife and child clinging to him.

"Tell me how and why am I again a prisoner?"

"It is enough that you return to the Conciergerie, and will know tomorrow. You are summoned for tomorrow."

Dr. Manette, who stood with the lamp in his hand, as if he were a statue made to hold it, put the lamp down, and, taking the speaker, not ungently, by the front of his red woolen shirt, said:

"You know him, you have said. Do you know me?"

"Yes, I know you, Citizen Doctor."

"We all know you, Citizen Doctor," said the other three.

He looked abstractedly from one to another, and said:

"Will you answer me then? How does this happen?"

"Citizen Doctor," said the first, reluctantly, "he has been denounced to the Section of Saint Antoine. This citizen," pointing out the second, "is from Saint Antoine."

"He is accused by Saint Antoine."

"Of what?" asked the Doctor.

"Citizen Doctor," said the first with his former reluctance, "ask no more. If the Republic demands sacrifices from you, without doubt you as a good patriot will be happy to make them. The Republic goes before all. The People is supreme. Evrémonde, we are pressed."

"One word," the Doctor entreated. "Will you tell me who denounced him?"

"It is against rule," answered the first; "but you can ask him of Saint Antoine here."

The Doctor turned his eyes upon that man, who moved uneasily on his feet, and at length said:

"Truly it is against rule. But he is denounced by the Citizen and Citizeness Defarge. And by one other."

"What other?"

"Do *you* ask, Citizen Doctor?"

"Yes."

"Then," said he of Saint Antoine, with a strange look, "you will be answered tomorrow. Now, I am dumb!"

CHAPTER VIII
A HAND OF CARDS

Happily unconscious of the new calamity at home, Miss Pross threaded her way along the narrow streets, and crossed the river by the bridge of the Pont-Neuf, reckoning in her mind the number of indispensable purchases she had to make. Mr. Cruncher, with the basket, walked at her side. They both looked to the right and to the left into most of the shops they passed, had a wary eye for all gregarious assemblages of people, and turned out of their road to avoid any very excited group of talkers. It was a raw evening, and the misty river showed where the barges were stationed in which the smiths worked, making guns for the Army of the Republic.

Having purchased a few small articles of grocery, and a measure of oil for the lamp, Miss Pross bethought herself of the wine they wanted. After peeping into several wine shops, she stopped at the sign of The Good Republican Brutus of Antiquity, where the aspect of things rather took her fancy.

As their wine was measuring out, a man parted from another man in a corner, and rose to depart. In going, he had to face Miss Pross. No sooner did he face her than Miss Pross uttered a scream and clapped her hands.

In a moment the whole company were on their feet. That somebody was assassinated by somebody vindicating a difference of opinion was the likeliest occurrence. Everybody looked to see somebody fall, but only saw a man and a woman standing staring at each other; the man with all the outward aspect of a Frenchman and a thorough Republican; the woman, evidently English.

"What is the matter?" said the man who had caused Miss Pross to scream; speaking in a vexed, abrupt voice—though in a low tone—and in English.

"Oh, Solomon, dear Solomon!" cried Miss Pross. "After not hearing of you for so long I find you here!"

"Don't call me Solomon. Do you want to be the death of me?" asked the man, in a furtive, frightened way.

Miss Pross burst into tears. "Have I ever been so hard with you that you ask me such a cruel question?"

"Then," said Solomon, "come out, if you want to speak to me. Pay for your wine, and come out. Who's this man?"

Miss Pross said through her tears, "Mr. Cruncher."

"Let him come out too," said Solomon. "Does he think me a ghost?"

Apparently, Mr. Cruncher did, to judge from his looks. He said not a word, however, and Miss Pross, exploring the depths of her reticule through her tears, paid for her wine. As she did so, Solomon turned to the followers of The Good Republican Brutus and offered a few words of explanation in French which caused them all to relapse into their former pursuits.

"Now," said Solomon, stopping at the dark street corner, "what do you want?"

"How dreadfully unkind in a brother nothing has ever turned my love away from!" cried Miss Pross, "to give me such a greeting, and show me no affection."

"There. Con-found it!" said Solomon, making a dab at Miss Pross's lips. "Now are you content?"

Miss Pross only shook her head and wept in silence.

"If you expect me to be surprised,"said her brother Solomon, "I am not; I knew you were here; if you really don't want to endanger my existence—I half believe you do—go as soon as possible. I am busy. I am an official."

Mr. Cruncher, touching him on the shoulder, hoarsely and unexpectedly interposed with the following singular question:

"I say! Might I ask the favor? As to whether your name is John Solomon or Solomon John?"

The official turned toward him with sudden distrust.

"Come!" said Mr. Cruncher. "John Solomon or Solomon John? And regarding that name of Pross, likewise. That warn't your name over the water."

"What do you mean?"

"Well, I don't know all I mean, for I can't call to mind what your name was, over the water."

"No?"

"No. But I know you. You was a spy-witness at the Bailey. What was you called at that time?"

"Barsad," said another voice, striking in.

"That's the name for a thousand pound!" cried Jerry.

The speaker who struck in was Sydney Carton. He had his hands behind him under the skirts of his riding coat, and he stood at Mr. Cruncher's elbow as negligently as he might have stood at the Old Bailey itself.

"Don't be alarmed, my dear Miss Pross. I arrived at Mr. Lorry's, to his surprise, yesterday evening. I present myself here, to beg a little talk with your brother. I wish for your sake Mr. Barsad was not a Sheep of the Prisons."

Sheep was a cant word of the time for a spy. The spy asked him how he dared——

"I'll tell you," said Sydney. "I lighted on you, Mr. Barsad, coming out of the Conciergerie an hour or more ago. You have a face to be remembered, and I remember faces well. Made curious by seeing you, and having a reason for associating you with the misfortunes of a friend, I walked into the wine shop here, close after you, and sat near you. I had no difficulty in deducing from your unreserved conversation, and the rumor openly going about, the nature of your calling. And gradually, what I had done at random seemed to shape into a purpose, Mr. Barsad."

"What purpose?" the spy asked.

"It might be dangerous to explain in the street. Could you favor me with some minutes of your company—at the office of Tellson's Bank?"

"Under a threat?"

"Oh! Did I say that?"

"Then why should I go there?"

"Really, Mr. Barsad, I can't say, if you can't."

Carton's negligent recklessness of manner came powerfully in aid of his quickness and skill, in such a business as he had in his secret mind, and with such a man as he had to do with. His practiced eye saw it, and made the most of it.

"Now," said the spy, casting a reproachful look at his sister; "if any trouble comes of this, it's your doing."

"Come, come, Mr. Barsad!" exclaimed Sydney. "Don't be ungrateful. But for my great respect for your sister, I might not have led up so pleasantly to a little proposal that I wish to make. Do you go with me to the Bank?"

"I'll hear what you have to say. Yes, I'll go."

"I propose that we first conduct your sister safely to the corner of her own street. Let me take your arm, Miss Pross. This is not a good city, at this time, for you to be out in, unprotected; and as your escort knows Mr. Barsad, I will invite him to Mr. Lorry's with us. Are we ready? Come then!"

Miss Pross to the end of her life remembered, that as she pressed her hands on Sydney's arm and looked up in his face, imploring him to do no hurt to Solomon, there was a braced purpose in the arm and a kind of inspiration in the eyes, which not only contradicted his light manner, but changed and raised the man. They left her at the corner of the street, and Carton led the way to Mr. Lorry's, which was within a few minutes' walk. John Barsad, or Solomon Pross, walked at his side.

Mr. Lorry had just finished his dinner. He turned his head as they entered and showed the surprise with which he saw a stranger.

"Miss Pross' brother, sir," said Sydney, "Mr. Barsad."

"Barsad?" repeated the old gentleman, "Barsad? I have an association with the name—and with the face."

"I told you you had a remarkable face, Mr. Barsad," observed Carton, coolly. "Pray sit down."

As he took a chair himself, he supplied the link that Mr. Lorry wanted, by saying to him, "Witness at that trial." Mr. Lorry immediately remembered, and regarded his new visitor with an undisguised look of abhorrence.

"Mr. Barsad has been recognized by Miss Pross as the affectionate brother you have heard of," said Sydney. "I pass to worse news. Darnay has been arrested again."

Struck with consternation, the old gentleman exclaimed, "What do you tell me! I left him safe and free within these two hours."

"Arrested for all that. When was it done, Mr. Barsad?"

"Just now, if at all."

"Mr. Barsad is the best authority possible, sir," said Sydney, "and I have it from Mr. Barsad's communication to a friend and brother Sheep over a bottle of wine that the arrest has taken place. There is no earthly doubt that he is retaken."

Mr. Lorry's business eye read in the speaker's face that it was loss of time to dwell upon the point. Confused, but sensible that something might depend upon his presence of mind, he commanded himself and was silently attentive.

"I trust," said Sydney, "the influence of Doctor Manette may stand him in as good stead tomorrow—you said he would be before the Tribunal tomorrow, Mr. Barsad?——"

"Yes; I believe so."

"—In as good stead tomorrow as today. But it may not be so. I own to you, I am shaken, Mr. Lorry, by Doctor Manette's not having had the power to prevent this arrest."

"He may not have known of it."

"But that very circumstance would be alarming, when we remember how identified he is with his son-in-law."

"That's true," Mr. Lorry acknowledged.

"In short," said Sydney, "this is a desperate time, when desperate games are played for desperate stakes. Let the Doctor play the winning game; I will play the losing one. Now, the stake I have resolved to play for, in case of the worst, is a friend in the Conciergerie. And the friend I purpose to win is Mr. Barsad."

"You need have good cards, sir," said the spy.

"I'll run them over. I'll see what I hold—Mr. Lorry, I wish you'd give me a little brandy."

It was put before him, and he drank off a glassful. "Mr. Barsad," he went on, in the tone of one who really was looking over a hand at cards: "Sheep of the prisons, now turnkey, now prisoner, always spy and secret informer, represents himself to his employers under a false name. That's a very good card. Mr. Barsad, now in the employ of the republican French government, was formerly in the employ of the aristocratic English government, the enemy of France and freedom. That's an excellent card. Inference clear as day that Mr. Barsad, still in the pay of the English government, is the spy of Pitt,[1] the treacherous foe of the Republic crouching in its bosom, the English traitor. That's a card not to be beaten. Have you followed my hand, Mr. Barsad?"

"Not to understand your play," returned the spy.

"I play my Ace, Denunciation of Mr. Barsad to the nearest Section Committee. Look over your hand, Mr. Barsad, and see what you have. Don't hurry."

It was a poorer hand than he suspected. Mr. Barsad saw losing cards in it that Sydney Carton knew nothing of. Thrown out of his honorable employment in England, he had crossed the Channel, and accepted service in France: first, as a tempter and an eavesdropper among his own countrymen there; gradually, as a tempter and an eavesdropper among the natives. He knew that under the overthrown government he had been a spy upon Saint Antoine and Defarge's wine shop; had received from the police such information concerning Doctor Manette's imprisonment, release, and history as should serve him for an introduction to conversation with the Defarges; and tried them on Madame Defarge, and had broken down with them signally. He always remembered with fear and trembling that that terrible woman had knitted when he talked with her, and had looked ominously at him as her fingers moved. He had since seen her, in the Section of Saint Antoine, over and over again produce her knitted registers, and denounce people whose lives the guillotine then surely swallowed up. Once denounced, and on such grave grounds as had just now been suggested, he foresaw that the dreadful woman would produce against him that fatal register, and would quash his last chance of life. Besides that all secret men are men soon terrified, here were surely cards enough of one black suit, to justify the holder in growing livid as he turned them over.

"You scarcely seem to like your hand," said Sydney, with the greatest composure. "Do you play?"

"I think, sir," said the spy, as he turned to Mr. Lorry, "I may appeal to a gentleman of your years and benevolence to put it to this other gentleman, so much your junior, whether he can reconcile it to his station to play that Ace of which he has spoken. I admit that *I* am a spy, and that it is considered a discreditable station—though it must be filled by somebody—but this gentleman is no spy, and why should he so demean himself as to make himself one?"

"I play my Ace, Mr. Barsad," said Carton, "without any scruple, in a very few minutes."

"I should have hoped, gentlemen both," said the spy, "that your respect for my sister——"

"I could not better testify my respect for your sister than by finally relieving her of her brother," said Sydney Carton.

"You think not, sir?"

"I have thoroughly made up my mind about it."

The smooth manner of the spy received such a check from the inscrutability of Carton—who was a mystery to wiser and honester men than he—that it faltered here. While he was at a loss, Carton said, resuming his former air of contemplating cards:

"And indeed, now I think again, I have a strong impression that I have another good card here, not yet enumerated. That friend and fellow Sheep, who spoke of himself as pasturing in the country prisons; who was he?"

"French. You don't know him," said the spy, quickly.

"French, eh?" repeated Carton. "Well; he may be."

"Is," said the spy; "though it's not important."

"Though it's not important," repeated Car-

1. ***Pitt.*** William Pitt was prime minister of England from 1783–1801.

ton, in the same mechanical way—"No. Yet I know the face."

"I think not. I am sure not. It can't be," said the spy.

"It—can't—be," muttered Sydney Carton, retrospectively. "Can't—be. Spoke good French. Yet like a foreigner?"

"Provincial," said the spy.

"No. Foreign!" cried Carton, striking his open hand on the table, as a light broke clearly on his mind. "Cly! Disguised, but the same man—at the Old Bailey."

"Now, you are hasty, sir," said Barsad, with a smile.

"Cly—who I will admit was a partner of mine—has been dead several years. He was buried in London, at the church of Saint Pancras-in-the-Fields. His unpopularity with the blackguard multitude prevented my following his remains, but I helped to lay him in his coffin."

Here Mr. Lorry became aware of a remarkable goblin shadow on the wall. He discovered it to be caused by a rising and stiffening of all the hair on Mr. Cruncher's head.

"Let us be reasonable," said the spy, "and let us be fair. To show you how mistaken you are, I will lay before you a certificate of Cly's burial which I happen to have carried in my pocket," with a hurried hand he produced and opened it, "ever since. There it is. Look at it, look at it. You may take it in your hand; it's no forgery."

Here Mr. Lorry perceived the reflection on the wall to elongate and Mr. Cruncher rose and stepped forward. Unseen by the spy, Mr. Cruncher stood at his side, and touched him on the shoulder like a ghostly bailiff.

"That there Roger Cly, master," said Mr. Cruncher, "so *you* put him in his coffin?"

"I did."

"Who took him out of it?"

Barsad leaned back and stammered, "What do you mean?"

"I mean," said Mr. Cruncher, "that he warn't never in it. I'll have my head took off, if he was ever in it."

The spy looked round at the two gentlemen; they both looked in unspeakable astonishment at Jerry.

"I tell you," said Jerry, "that you buried paving stones and earth in that there coffin. Don't go and tell *me* that you buried Cly. It was a take in. Me and two more knows it."

"How do you know it?"

"What's that to you?" growled Mr. Cruncher, "it's you I have got a old grudge again, is it, with your shameful impositions upon tradesmen! I'd catch hold of your throat and choke you for half a guinea."

Sydney Carton, who, with Mr. Lorry, had been lost in amazement at this turn of the business, here requested Mr. Cruncher to explain himself.

"At another time, sir," he returned, evasively, "the present time is ill-conwenient for explainin'. What I stand to is that he knows well wot that there Cly was never in that there coffin. Let him say he was and I'll catch hold of his throat and choke him for half a guinea or I'll out and announce him."

"I see one thing," said Carton. "I hold another card, Mr. Barsad. Impossible for you to outlive denunciation, when you are in communication with another aristocratic spy who has feigned death and come to life again! A plot of the foreigner against the Republic. A strong card—a certain Guillotine card! Do you play?"

"No!" returned the spy. "I throw up. I confess that we were so unpopular with the mob that I got away from England at the risk of death, and that Cly never would have got away but for that sham. Though how this man knows it was a sham is a wonder of wonders to me."

"Never you trouble your head about this man," retorted the contentious Mr. Cruncher; "you'll have trouble enough with giving your attention to that gentleman."

The Sheep of the prisons turned from him to Sydney Carton, and said, with more decision, "You told me you had a proposal; what is it? Now, it is of no use asking too much of me. Remember! I may denounce you if I think proper, and I can swear my way through stone walls. What do you want with me?''

''Not very much. You are a turnkey at the Conciergerie?''

''I tell you once for all, there is no such thing as an escape possible,'' said the spy, firmly.

''Why need you tell me what I have not asked? You are a turnkey at the Conciergerie?''

''I am sometimes.''

''You can be when you choose.''

''I can pass in and out when I choose.''

Sydney Carton filled another glass with brandy, poured it slowly out upon the hearth, and watched it as it dropped. It being all spent, he said, rising:

''So far, we have spoken before these two, because it was as well that the merits of the cards should not rest solely between you and me. Let us have one final word alone.''

CHAPTER IX
THE GAME MADE

While Sydney Carton and the sheep of the prisons were in the adjoining dark room, Mr. Lorry looked at Jerry in considerable doubt and mistrust. That honest tradesman's manner of receiving the look did not inspire confidence; he changed the leg on which he rested as often as if he had fifty of those limbs and were trying them all; he examined his fingernails with a very questionable closeness of attention; and whenever Mr. Lorry's eye caught his, he was taken with that peculiar kind of short cough requiring the hollow of a hand before it, which is seldom, if ever, known to be an infirmity attendant on perfect openness of character.

''Jerry,'' said Mr. Lorry. ''Come here.''

Mr. Cruncher came forward sideways, with one of his shoulders in advance of him.

''What have you been, besides a messenger?''

After some cogitation, accompanied with an intent look at his patron, Mr. Cruncher conceived the idea of replying, ''Agricultooral character.''

''My mind misgives me much,'' said Mr. Lorry, ''that you have used the great house of Tellson's as a blind, and that you have had an unlawful occupation of an infamous description. If you have, don't expect me to keep your secret. Tellson's shall not be imposed upon.''

''I hope, sir,'' pleaded the abashed Mr. Cruncher, ''that a gentleman like yourself wot I've had the honor of odd jobbing till I'm gray at it, would think twice about harming of me, even if it wos so—I don't say it is, but even if it wos. And which it is to be took into account that if it wos, it wouldn't, even then, be all o' one side. There'd be two sides to it. There might be medical doctors at the present hour a-banking away like smoke at Tellson's, and a-cocking their medical eyes at that tradesman on the sly. Well, that 'ud be imposing, too, on Tellson's. For you cannot sarse the goose and not the gander. Then, wot with undertakers, and wot with parish clerks, and wot with sextons, and wot with private watchmen—all awaricious and all in it—a man wouldn't get much by it, even if it wos so. And wot little a man did get would never prosper with him, Mr. Lorry. He'd never have no good of it; he'd want all along to be out of the line, if he could see his way out, being once in—even if it wos so.''

''Ugh!'' cried Mr. Lorry, rather relenting, nevertheless. ''I am shocked at the sight of you.''

''Now, what I would humbly offer to you, sir,'' pursued Mr. Cruncher, ''even if it wos so, which I don't say it is——''

''Don't prevaricate,'' said Mr. Lorry.

''No, I will *not,* sir,'' returned Mr. Cruncher, as if nothing were further from his thoughts or practice—''which I don't say it is—wot I would humbly offer to you, sir, would be this. A man don't see all this a-goin' on dreadful round him in the way of subjects without heads, without havin' his serious thoughts. And these here would be mine, that wot I said just now, I up and said in the good cause when I might have kep' it back.''

''That at least is true,'' said Mr. Lorry. ''It

may be that I shall yet stand your friend, if you deserve it, and repent in action—not in words. I want no more words."

Mr. Cruncher knuckled his forehead, as Sydney Carton and the spy returned. "Adieu, Mr. Barsad," said the former; "you have nothing to fear from me."

He sat down in a chair on the hearth. When they were alone, Mr. Lorry asked what he had done.

"Not much. If it should go ill with the prisoner, I have insured access to him, once."

Mr. Lorry's countenance fell.

"It is all I could do," said Carton. "To propose too much, would be to put this man's head under the ax, and, as he himself said, nothing worse could happen to him if he were denounced."

"But access to him," said Mr. Lorry, "if it should go ill before the Tribunal, will not save him."

"I never said it would."

Mr. Lorry's eyes sought the fire; he was an old man now, overborne with anxiety of late, and his tears fell.

"You are a good man and a true friend," said Carton, in an altered voice. "Forgive me if I notice that you are affected. I could not see my father weep, and sit by, careless. And I could not respect your sorrow more, if you were my father. You are free from that misfortune, however.

"To return to poor Darnay," said Carton. "Don't tell her of this interview, or this arrangement. It would not enable her to go to see him. She might think it was contrived, in case of the worst, to convey to him the means of anticipating the sentence."

Mr. Lorry had not thought of that, and he looked quickly at Carton to see if it were in his mind. It seemed to be; he returned the look, and evidently understood it.

"She might think a thousand things," Carton said, "and any of them would only add to her trouble. Don't speak of me to her. I had better not see her. I can do any little helpful work for her that my hand can find to do, without that. You are going to her, I hope? She must be very desolate tonight."

"I am going now, directly."

"I am glad of that. She has such a strong attachment to you and reliance on you. How does she look?"

"Anxious and unhappy, but very beautiful."

"Ah!"

It was a long, grieving sound, like a sigh—almost like a sob. It attracted Mr. Lorry's eyes to Carton's face, which was turned to the fire. A light, or a shade—the old gentleman could not have said which—passed from it as swiftly as a change will sweep over a hillside on a wild bright day, and he lifted his foot to put back one of the little flaming logs, which was tumbling forward. He wore the white riding coat and top boots, and the light of the fire touching their light surfaces made him look very pale, with his long brown hair, all untrimmed, hanging loose about him. His indifference to fire was sufficiently remarkable to elicit a word of remonstrance from Mr. Lorry; his boot was still upon the hot embers of the flaming log, when it had broken under the weight of his boot.

"I forgot it," he said.

Mr. Lorry's eyes were again attracted to his face. Taking note of the wasted air which clouded the naturally handsome features, and having the expression of prisoners' faces fresh in his mind, he was strongly reminded of that expression.

"And your duties here have drawn to an end, sir?" said Carton, turning to him.

"Yes. As I was telling you last night when Lucie came in so unexpectedly, I have at length done all that I can do here. I hoped to have left them in perfect safety, and then to have quitted Paris. I have my Leave to Pass. I was ready to go."

Carton terminated the conversation here, by rising to help him on with his outer coat. "I'll walk with you to her gate. You know my vagabond habits. If I should prowl about the streets a long time, don't be uneasy; I shall reappear in the morning. You go to the Court tomorrow?"

"Yes, unhappily."

"I shall be there, but only as one of the crowd. My spy will find a place for me. Take my arm, sir."

Mr. Lorry did so, and they went out in the streets. A few minutes brought them to Mr. Lorry's destination. Carton left him there; but lingered at a little distance, turned back to the gate when it was shut, and touched it. He had heard of her going to the prison every day. "She came out here," he said, looking about him, "turned this way, must have trod on these stones often. Let me follow in her steps."

Sydney had not gone far when he stopped in the middle of the street under a glimmering lamp, and wrote with his pencil on a scrap of paper. Then, traversing with the decided step of one who remembered the way well, several dark and dirty streets, he stopped at a chemist's shop. A small, dim, crooked shop, kept in a tortuous, uphill thoroughfare, by a small, dim, crooked man.

Giving this citizen good night, as he confronted him at his counter, he laid the scrap of paper before him. "Whew!" the chemist whistled softly, as he read it.

"For you, citizen?"

"For me."

"You will be careful to keep them separate, citizen? You know the consequences of mixing them?"

"Perfectly."

Certain small packets were made and given to him. He put them, one by one, in the breast of his inner coat, counted out the money for them, and deliberately left the shop.

"There is nothing more to do," said he, glancing upward at the moon, "until tomorrow. I can't sleep."

It was not a reckless manner, the manner in which he said these words. It was the settled manner of a tired man, who had wandered and got lost, but at length struck his road and saw its end.

Long ago, when he had been famous as a youth of great promise, he had followed his father to the grave. His mother had died, years before. These solemn words, which had been read at his father's grave, arose in his mind as he went down the dark streets. "I am the resurrection and the life, saith the Lord; he that believeth in me, though he were dead, yet shall he live; and whosoever liveth and believeth in me, shall never die."

In a city dominated by the ax, alone at night, with natural sorrow rising in him for the victims then awaiting their doom in the prisons, the chain of association that brought the words home might have been easily found. He did not seek it, but repeated them and went on.

Few coaches were abroad, for riders in coaches were liable to be suspected. But, the theaters were all well filled, and the people poured cheerfully out as he passed. At one of the theater doors, there was a little girl with a mother, looking for a way across the street through the mud. He carried the child over, and before the timid arm was loosed from his neck asked her for a kiss.

"I am the resurrection and the life, saith the Lord; he that believeth in me, though he were dead, yet shall he live; and whosoever liveth and believeth in me, shall never die."

Now that the night wore on, the words were in the echoes of his feet. Perfectly calm and steady, he sometimes repeated them to himself as he walked, but he heard them always.

The night wore out, and he stood upon the bridge listening to the water as it splashed the river walls of the Island of Paris. He walked by the stream and in the light and warmth of the sun fell asleep on the bank. When he awoke, he lingered yet a little longer, watching an eddy that turned and turned purposeless, until the stream absorbed it, and carried it on to the sea.— "Like me!"

A trading boat glided by him. As its silent track in the water disappeared, the prayer that had broken up out of his heart for a merciful consideration of all his poor blindnesses and errors, ended in the words, "I am the resurrection and the life."

Mr. Lorry was already out when he got back, and it was easy to surmise where the good old man was gone. Sydney Carton drank a little coffee, ate some bread, and, having washed and changed, went out to the place of trial.

The court was all astir and abuzz, when the black sheep—whom many fell away from in dread—pressed him into an obscure corner among the crowd. Mr. Lorry was there, and Doctor Manette. She was there, beside her father.

When her husband was brought in, she turned a look upon him, so sustaining, so encouraging, so full of admiring love and pitying tenderness, yet so courageous for his sake, that it called the healthy blood into his face, brightened his glance and animated his heart. If there had been any eyes to notice the influence of her look, on Sydney Carton, it would have been seen to be the same influence exactly.

Before that unjust Tribunal there was little or no order of procedure, insuring to any accused person any reasonable hearing. There could have been no such Revolution, if all laws, forms, and ceremonies had not first been so monstrously abused that the suicidal vengeance of the Revolution was to scatter them all to the winds.

Every eye was turned to the Jury. The same determined patriots and good republicans as yesterday and the day before, and tomorrow and the day after. Eager and prominent among them, one man with a craving face and his fingers perpetually hovering about his lips, whose appearance gave great satisfaction to the spectators. A life-thirsting, cannibal-looking, bloody-minded Juryman, the Jacques Three of Saint Antoine. The whole Jury, as a jury of dogs empaneled to try the deer.

Every eye then turned to the five Judges and the Public Prosecutor. No favorable leaning in that quarter today. A fell, uncompromising, murderous business-meaning there.

Charles Evrémonde, called Darnay. Released yesterday. Reaccused and retaken yesterday. Indictment delivered to him last night. Suspected and denounced enemy of the Republic, aristocrat, one of a family of tyrants, one of a race proscribed, for that they had used their abolished privileges to the infamous oppression of the people. Charles Evrémonde, called Darnay, in right of such proscription, absolutely dead in Law:

To this effect, in as few or fewer words, the Public Prosecutor.

The President asked, was the accused openly denounced or secretly?

"Openly, President."

"By whom?"

"Three voices. Ernest Defarge, wine vendor."

"Good."

"Thérèse Defarge, his wife."

"Good."

"Alexandre Manette, physician."

A great uproar took place in the court, and in the midst of it, Doctor Manette was seen, pale and trembling, standing where he had been seated.

"President, I indignantly protest that this is a forgery and a fraud. You know the accused to be the husband of my daughter. My daughter, and those dear to her, are far dearer to me than my life. Who and where is the false conspirator who says I denounce the husband of my child?"

"Citizen Manette, be tranquil. To fail in submission to the authority of the Tribunal would be to put yourself out of Law. As to what is dearer to you than life, nothing can be so dear to a good citizen as the Republic."

Loud acclamations hailed this rebuke. The President rang his bell, and with warmth resumed:

"If the Republic should demand sacrifice of your child herself, you would have no duty but to sacrifice her. Listen to what is to follow. In the meanwhile, be silent!"

Frantic acclamations were again raised. Doc-

tor Manette sat down, his lips trembling. The craving man on the jury rubbed his hands together and restored the usual hand to his mouth.

Defarge was produced, and rapidly expounded the story of the imprisonment, of his having been a mere boy in the Doctor's service, of the release, and of the state of the prisoner when released and delivered to him. This short examination followed, for the court was quick with its work.

"You did good service at the taking of the Bastille?"

"I believe so."

"Inform the Tribunal of what you did that day within the Bastille, citizen."

"I knew," said Defarge, looking down at his wife, "that this prisoner had been confined in cell One Hundred and Five, North Tower. As I serve my gun that day, I resolve when the place shall fall, to examine that cell. It falls. I mount to the cell, with a fellow citizen who is one of the Jury, directed by a jailer. I examine it very closely. In a hole in the chimney, where a stone has been worked out and replaced, I find this written paper. I confide this paper, in the writing of Doctor Manette, to the President."

"Let it be read."

In a dead silence and stillness—the prisoner under trial looking lovingly at his wife, his wife only looking from him to look with solicitude at her father, Doctor Manette keeping his eyes fixed on the reader, Madame Defarge never taking hers from the prisoner, Defarge never taking his from his wife, and all other eyes intent upon the Doctor, who saw none of them—the paper was read as follows.

Discussion

Chapter V

1. What does the narrator mean by the sentence "Liberty, Equality, Fraternity, or Death—the last, much the easiest to bestow, O Guillotine"?

2. Earlier in the book you met the wood sawyer. **(a)** What was he called? **(b)** How might his presence in Paris be a threat to Lucie?

3. What descriptive details make the Carmagnole frightening rather than joyous?

4. Who do you think is the "owner of the riding coat"? Cite reasons for your answer.

Chapter VI

1. (a) How does the mob react to the evidence and testimony presented in the trial? **(b)** In what ways has Dickens prepared you for the crowd's reaction? for Charles's release?

2. (a) Whose testimony marks the turning point in the trial? **(b)** What makes this testimony particularly effective?

3. (a) Compare this trial with Darnay's trial in Book the Second. **(b)** Which one do you consider more just? Give reasons for your answer.

Chapter VIII

1. What past incidents play a part in the surprising turn of events in this chapter?

2. What kind of "hand" does Carton hold against Solomon Pross, alias John Barsad?

3. In what way does Cruncher's information help to develop the plot? **(b)** How does Carton react to Cruncher's information?

Chapter IX

1. (a) What is the most important fact that Carton reveals to Mr. Lorry? **(b)** Why does Carton not want Lucie to know he has gained access to the prison?

2. Briefly recount the conversation between Carton and the chemist. What significance might it have?

3. (a) Cite lines that describe the atmosphere in the court. **(b)** What does this atmosphere suggest about the likelihood of a fair trial?

CHAPTER X
THE SUBSTANCE OF THE SHADOWS

"I, Alexandre Manette, unfortunate physician, native of Beauvais, and afterwards resident in Paris, write this melancholy paper in my doleful cell in the Bastille, during the last month of the year, 1767. I write it at stolen intervals under every difficulty. I design to secrete it in the wall of the chimney, where I have slowly and laboriously made a place of concealment for it. Some pitying hand may find it there, when I and my sorrows are dust.

"These words are formed by the rusty iron point with which I write with difficulty in scrapings of soot and charcoal from the chimney, mixed with blood, in the last month of the tenth year of my captivity. Hope has quite departed from my breast. I know from terrible warnings I have noted in myself that my reason will not long remain unimpaired, but I solemnly declare that I am at this time in the possession of my right mind—that my memory is exact and circumstantial—and that I write the truth as I shall answer for these my last recorded words, whether they be ever read by men or not, at the Eternal Judgment Seat.

"One cloudy moonlight night, in the third week of December in the year 1757, I was walking on a retired part of the quay by the Seine at an hour's distance from my place of residence in the Street of the School of Medicine, when a carriage came along behind me, driven very fast. As I stood aside to let that carriage pass, apprehensive that it might otherwise run me down, a head was put out at the window, and a voice called to the driver to stop.

"The carriage stopped as soon as the driver could rein his horses, and the same voice called to me by my name. I answered. The carriage was then so far in advance of me that two gentlemen had time to open the door and alight before I came up with it. I observed that they were both wrapped in cloaks, and appeared to conceal themselves. As they stood side by side near the carriage door, I also observed that they both looked of about my own age, or rather younger, and that they were greatly alike, in stature, manner, voice, and—as far as I could see—face too.

" 'You are Doctor Manette?' said one.

" 'I am.'

" 'Doctor Manette, formerly of Beauvais,' said the other; 'the young physician, originally an expert surgeon, who within the last year or two has made a rising reputation in Paris?'

" 'Gentlemen,' I returned, 'I am that Doctor Manette of whom you speak so graciously.'

" 'We have been to your residence,' said the first, 'and being informed that you were probably walking in this direction, we followed, in the hope of overtaking you. Will you please to enter the carriage?'

"The manner of both was imperious, and they both moved, as these words were spoken, so as to place me between themselves and the carriage door. They were armed. I was not.

" 'Gentlemen,' said I, 'pardon me; but I usually inquire who does me the honor to seek my assistance, and what is the nature of the case to which I am summoned.'

"The reply to this was made by him who had spoken second. 'Doctor, your clients are people of condition. As to the nature of the case, our confidence in your skill assures us that you will ascertain it for yourself better than we can describe it. Enough. Will you please to enter the carriage?'

"I could do nothing but comply. They entered after me—the last springing in, after putting up the steps. The carriage turned about, and drove on at its former speed.

"I repeat this conversation exactly as it occurred. I have no doubt that it is, word for word, the same. I describe everything exactly as it took place.

"The carriage left the streets behind, passed the North Barrier, and emerged upon the country road. At two thirds of a league from the Barrier—I did not estimate the distance at that time, but afterwards when I traversed it—it struck out of the main avenue, and presently stopped at a solitary house. We all three alighted, and walked to the door of the house. It was not opened immediately, in answer to the bell, and one of my conductors struck the man who opened it, with his heavy riding glove, across the face.

"There was nothing in this action to attract my particular attention, for I had seen common people struck more commonly than dogs. But, the other of the two struck the man in like manner; the look and bearing of the brothers were so exactly alike that I then first perceived them to be twin brothers.

"From the time of our alighting at the outer gate—which one of the brothers had opened to admit us, and had relocked—I had heard cries proceeding from an upper chamber. I was conducted to this chamber, the cries growing louder as we ascended the stairs, and I found a patient in a high fever of the brain, lying on a bed.

"The patient was a woman of great beauty, not much past twenty. Her hair was torn and ragged, and her arms were bound to her sides with sashes and handkerchiefs. I noticed that these bonds were all portions of a gentleman's dress. On one of them, a fringed scarf, I saw the armorial bearings of a noble, and the letter E.

"Her eyes were dilated and wild, and she constantly uttered piercing shrieks, and repeated the words: 'My husband, my father, and my brother!' An instant she would pause, then repeat the cry, then count up to twelve and say, 'Hush!' There was no variation in the order, or the manner.

" 'How long,' I asked, 'has this lasted?'

"To distinguish the brothers, I will call them the elder and the younger; by the elder I mean him who exercised the most authority. The elder replied, 'Since last night.'

" 'She has a husband, a father, and a brother?'

" 'A brother.'

" 'I do not address her brother?'

"He answered with great contempt, 'No.'

" 'She has some recent association with the number twelve?'

"The younger brother impatiently rejoined, 'With twelve o'clock!'

" 'See, gentlemen,' said I, 'how useless I am. If I had known what I was to see, I could have come provided. As it is, time must be lost. There are no medicines in this lonely place.'

"The younger said haughtily, 'There is a case of medicines here,' brought it from a closet, and put it on the table.

"I opened some of the bottles, smelled them, and put the stoppers to my lips. If I had wanted to use anything save narcotic medicines that were poisons in themselves, I would not have administered any of those.

" 'Do you doubt them?' asked the younger brother.

" 'You see, monsieur, I am going to use them,' I replied.

"I made the patient swallow, with great difficulty, and after many efforts, the dose that I desired to give. I then sat down by the side of the bed. There was a timid and suppressed woman in attendance—wife of the man downstairs—who had retreated into a corner.

"I had sat by the side of the bed for half an hour, with the two brothers looking on, before the elder said:

" 'There is another patient.'

"I was startled, and asked, 'Is it a pressing case?'

" 'You had better see,' he carelessly answered; and took up a light.

"The other patient lay in a back room across a second staircase, which was a species of loft over a stable. On some hay on the ground, with a cushion thrown under his head, lay a handsome peasant boy of not more than seventeen. He lay on his back, teeth set, right hand clenched on his breast, his glaring eyes looking straight upward. I could not see where his wound was, as I kneeled over him; but I could see that he was dying of a wound from a sharp point.

" 'I am a doctor,' said I. 'Let me examine it.'

" 'I do not want it examined,' he answered; 'let it be.'

"It was under his hand, and I soothed him to let me move his hand away. The wound was a sword thrust, received from twenty to twenty-four hours before, but no skill could have saved him if it had been looked to without delay. He was then dying fast. As I turned my eyes to the elder brother, I saw him looking down at this handsome boy whose life was ebbing out, as if he were a wounded bird, or a hare, or rabbit; not at all as if he were a fellow creature.

" 'How has this been done, monsieur?' said I.

" 'A crazed young common dog! A serf! Forced my brother to draw upon him, and has fallen by my brother's sword—like a gentleman.'

"There was no touch of pity, sorrow, or kindred humanity in this answer. The speaker seemed to acknowledge that it was inconvenient to have that different order of creature dying there, and that it would have been better if he had died in the usual obscure routine of his vermin kind. He was quite incapable of any compassionate feeling about the boy, or about his fate.

"The boy's eyes had slowly moved to him as he had spoken, and they now slowly moved to me.

" 'Doctor, they are very proud, these nobles; but we common dogs are proud too, sometimes. They plunder us, outrage us, beat us, kill us; but we have a little pride left, sometimes. She—have you seen her, Doctor?'

"I said, 'I have seen her.'

" 'She is my sister, Doctor. They have had their shameful rights, these nobles, in the modesty and virtue of our sisters, many years, but we have had good girls among us. She was a good girl, betrothed to a good young man. We were all tenants of his—that man's who stands there.'

"It was with greatest difficulty that the boy gathered force to speak; but his spirit spoke with dreadful emphasis.

" 'We were so robbed by that man who stands there—taxed by him without mercy, obliged to work for him without pay, to grind our corn at his mill, to feed scores of his tame birds on our wretched crops and forbidden for our lives to keep a single tame bird of our own— I say we were so robbed, and hunted, and were made so poor that our father told us it was a dreadful thing to bring a child into the world, and that what we should most pray for was that our women might be barren and our miserable race die out!'

"I had never before seen the sense of being oppressed, bursting forth like a fire until I saw it in the dying boy.

" 'Nevertheless, Doctor, my sister married. He was ailing at that time, poor fellow, and she married her lover that she might tend and comfort him in our cottage. She had not been married many weeks, when that man's brother saw her and admired her, and asked that man to lend her to him—for what are husbands among us! My sister was good and virtuous, and hated his brother with a hatred as strong as mine. What did the two then, to persuade her husband to use his influence with her, to make her willing?'

"The boy's eyes slowly turned to the looker-on, and I saw in the two faces that all he said was true. The two opposing kinds of pride confronting one another, I can see, even in this Bastille; the gentleman's, negligent indifference; the peasant's, passionate revenge.

" 'You know, Doctor, that it is among the rights of these nobles to harness us common dogs to carts, and drive us. They so harnessed and drove him. You know that it is among their rights to keep us in their grounds all night, quieting the frogs, in order that their noble sleep may not be disturbed. They kept him out in the unwholesome mists at night, and ordered him back into his harness in the day. But he was not persuaded. No! Taken out of harness one day at noon, to feed—if he could find food—he sobbed twelve times, once for every stroke of the bell, and died on her bosom.'

"Nothing human could have held life in the boy but his determination to tell all his wrongs. He forced back the gathering shadows of death, as he forced his clenched right hand to remain clenched, and to cover his wound.

" 'Then with that man's permission and even with his aid, his brother took her away; in spite of what I know she must have told his brother, his brother took her away—for his pleasure and diversion, for a little while. I saw her pass me on the road. When I took the tidings home, our father's heart burst. I took my young sister—for I have another—to a place beyond the reach of this man. Then I tracked the brother here, and last night climbed in—a common dog, but sword in hand——

" 'She heard me, and ran in. I told her not to come near us till he was dead. He came in and first tossed me some pieces of money; then struck at me with a whip. But I, though a common dog, so struck at him as to make him draw. Let him break into as many pieces as he will the sword that he stained with my common blood; he drew to defend himself—thrust at me with all his skill for his life.'

"My glance had fallen, but a few moments before, on the fragments of a broken sword, lying among the hay.

"That weapon was a gentleman's. In another place, lay an old sword that seemed to have been a soldier's.

" 'Now, lift me up, Doctor; lift me up. Where is he?'

" 'He is not here,' I said, supporting the boy, and thinking that he referred to the brother.

" 'He! Proud as these nobles are, he is afraid to see me. Where is the man who was here? Turn my face to him.'

"I did so, raising the boy's head against my knee.

" 'Marquis,' said the boy, turning to him with his eyes open wide, and his right hand raised, 'in the days when all these things are to be answered for, I summon you and yours, to the last of your bad race, to answer for them. I mark this cross of blood upon you, as a sign that I do it. In the days when all these things are to be answered for, I summon your brother, the worst of the bad race, to answer for them separately. I mark this cross of blood upon him, as a sign that I do it.'

"Twice, he put his hand to the wound in his breast, and with his forefinger drew a cross in the air. He stood for an instant with the finger yet raised, and, as it dropped, he dropped with it, and I laid him down dead.

"When I returned to the bedside of the young woman, I found her raving in precisely the same order and continuity. I knew that this might last for many hours, and that it would probably end in the silence of the grave.

"I repeated the medicines I had given her, and I sat at the side of the bed until the night was far advanced. She never abated the piercing quality of her shrieks, never stumbled in the distinctness or the order of her words.

"This lasted twenty-six hours from the time when I first saw her. I had come and gone twice, and was again sitting by her, when she began to falter. I did what little could be done to assist that opportunity, and by-and-by she sank into a lethargy, and lay like the dead. I called the woman to assist me to compose her figure and the dress she had torn. It was then that I knew her condition to be that of one in whom the first expectations of being a mother have arisen; it was then I lost the little hope I had had of her.

" 'Is she dead?' asked the Marquis, coming booted into the room from his horse.

" 'Not dead,' said I; 'but like to die.'

" 'What strength there is in these common bodies!' he said, looking down at her with some curiosity.

" 'There is prodigious strength,' I answered him, 'in sorrow and despair.'

"He first laughed at my words, and then frowned at them. He moved a chair with his foot near to mine, ordered the woman away, and said in a subdued voice:

" 'Doctor, finding my brother in this difficulty with these hinds, I recommended that your aid be invited. Your reputation is high, and, as a young man with your fortune to make, you are probably mindful of your interest. The things you see here, are things to be seen, and not spoken of.'

"I listened to the patient's breathing, and avoided answering. 'Do you honor me with your attention, Doctor?'

" 'Monsieur,' said I, 'in my profession, the communications of patients are always received in confidence.' I was guarded in my answer, for I was troubled in my mind with what I had heard and seen.

"Her breathing was difficult to trace. There was life, and no more. Looking round, I found both the brothers intent upon me.

"She lingered for a week. Toward the last I could understand some few syllables that she said to me, by placing my ear close to her lips. She asked me where she was, and I told her; who I was, and I told her. It was in vain that I asked her for her family name. She faintly shook her head upon the pillow, and kept her secret, as the boy had done.

"I had no opportunity of asking her any question, until I had told the brothers she could not live another day. Until then, one or other of them had always jealously sat behind the curtain at the head of the bed when I was there. But when it came to that, they seemed careless what communication I might hold with her; as if—the thought passed through my mind—I were dying too.

"I always observed that their pride bitterly resented the younger brother's having crossed swords with a peasant, and that peasant a boy. The only consideration that appeared to affect the mind of either of them was the consideration that this was highly degrading to the family.

"As often as I caught the younger brother's eyes, their expression reminded me that he disliked me deeply, for knowing what I knew from the boy. He was smoother and more polite to me than the elder; but I saw this. I also saw that I was an incumbrance in the mind of the elder, too.

"My patient died, two hours before midnight—at a time, by my watch, answering almost to the minute when I had first seen her. I was alone with her, when her forlorn young head drooped and all her earthly sorrows ended.

"The brothers were waiting in a room downstairs, impatient to ride away. I had heard them, striking their boots with their riding whips, and loitering up and down.

" 'At last she is dead?' said the elder, when I went in.

" 'She is dead,' said I.

" 'I congratulate you, my brother,' were his words as he turned round.

"He now gave me a rouleau of gold. I took it but laid it on the table. I had resolved to accept nothing.

" 'Pray excuse me,' said I. 'Under the circumstances, no.'

"They exchanged looks, but bent their heads to me as I bent mine to them, and we parted without another word.

"I am weary, weary, weary—worn down by misery. I cannot read what I have written with this gaunt hand.

"Early in the morning, the rouleau of gold was left at my door in a little box, with my name on the outside. From the first, I had anxiously considered what I ought to do. I decided, that day, to write privately to the Minister, stating the nature of the two cases to which I had been summoned, and the place to which I had gone; in effect, stating all the circumstances. I knew what the immunities of the nobles were, and I expected that the matter would never be heard of, but I wished to relieve my own mind. I had no apprehension whatever of my real danger; but I was conscious that there might be danger for others, if others were compromised by possessing the knowledge that I possessed. The letter was before me just completed, when I was told that a lady waited, who wished to see me. . . .

"I am growing more and more unequal to the task I have set myself. It is so cold, so dark, my senses are so benumbed, and the gloom upon me is so dreadful.

"The lady was young, engaging, and handsome, but not marked for long life. She was in great agitation. She presented herself to me as the wife of the Marquis St. Evrémonde. I connected the title by which the boy had addressed the elder brother, with the initial letter embroidered on the scarf, arriving at the conclusion that I had seen that nobleman very lately.

"She had in part suspected, and in part discovered, the main facts of the cruel story, of her husband's share in it, and my being resorted to. She did not know that the girl was dead. Her hope had been, she said in great distress, to show her, in secret, a woman's sympathy.

"She had reasons for believing that there was a young sister living, and her greatest desire was to help that sister. I could tell her nothing but that there was such a sister; beyond that, I knew nothing.

"She was a good, compassionate lady, and not happy in her marriage. How could she be! The brother distrusted and disliked her, and she stood in dread of him, and in dread of her husband too. When I handed her down to the door, there was a child, a pretty boy from two to three years old, in her carriage.

" 'For his sake, Doctor,' she said, pointing to him in tears, 'I would do all I can to make what poor amends I can. He will never prosper in his inheritance otherwise. I have a presentiment that if no other innocent atonement is made for this, it will one day be required of him. What I have left to call my own—it is little beyond the worth of a few jewels—I will make it the first charge of his life to bestow on this injured family, if the sister can be discovered.'

"She kissed the boy, and said, 'It is for thine own dear sake. Thou wilt be faithful, little Charles?' The child answered her bravely, 'Yes!' I kissed her hand, and she went away. I never saw her more. I sealed my letter, and delivered it myself that day.

"That night, the last night of the year, a man in a black dress demanded to see me, and softly followed my servant, Ernest Defarge, into the room where I sat with my wife—O my wife, beloved of my heart! My fair young English wife! 'An urgent case in the Rue St. Honoré,' he said. It would not detain me. He had a coach in waiting.

"When I was clear of the house, a black muffler was drawn tightly over my mouth from behind, and my arms were pinioned. The two brothers crossed the road from a dark corner, and identified me with a single gesture. The Marquis took from his pocket the letter I had written, showed it me, burned it in the light of a lantern, and extinguished the ashes with his foot. Not a word was spoken. I was brought here, to my living grave.

"If it had pleased God to put it in the hard heart of either of the brothers, in all these frightful years, to grant me any tidings of my dearest wife—so much as to let me know by a word whether alive or dead—I might have thought that He had not quite abandoned them. But now I believe that the mark of the red cross is fatal to them, and that they have no part in His mercies. And them and their descendants, to the last of their race, I, Alexandre Manette, unhappy prisoner, do this last night of the year 1767, in my unbearable agony, denounce to the times when all these things shall be answered for. I denounce them to heaven and to earth."

A terrible sound arose when the reading of this document was done. Little need to show how the Defarges had not made the paper public with the other captured Bastille memorials and had kept it, biding their time. Little need to show that this detested family name was wrought into the fatal register. The man never trod ground whose virtues and services would have sustained him in that place that day, against such denunciation.

And all the worse for the doomed man that the denouncer was a well-known citizen, his own attached friend, the father of his wife. One of the frenzied aspirations of the populace was for imitations of the questionable public virtues of antiquity, and for sacrifices and self-immolations on the people's altar. Therefore when the President said—else had his own head quivered on his shoulders—that the good physician of the Republic would deserve better still of the Republic by rooting out an obnoxious family of aristocrats, and would doubtless feel a sacred glow and joy in making his daughter a widow and her child an orphan, there was wild excitement, patriotic fervor, not a touch of human sympathy.

"Much influence around him, has that Doctor?" murmured Madame Defarge, smiling to The Vengeance. "Save him now, my Doctor, save him!"

At every Juryman's vote, there was a roar. Another and another. Roar and roar.

Unanimously voted. At heart and by descent an aristocrat, an enemy of the Republic, a notorious oppressor of the People. Back to the Conciergerie, and Death within four-and-twenty hours!

CHAPTER XI
DUSK

The wife of the innocent man thus doomed to die fell under the sentence, as if she had been mortally stricken. But so strong was the voice within her, representing that she of all the world must uphold him in his misery, and not augment it, that it quickly raised her, even from that shock.

The judges having to take part in a public demonstration out of doors, the Tribunal adjourned. The quick noise and movement of the court's emptying itself had not ceased, when Lucie stood stretching out her arms toward her husband, with nothing in her face but love and consolation.

"If I might touch him! If I might embrace him once! Oh, good citizens, if you would have so much compassion for us!"

There was but a jailer left, with two of the men who had taken him last night, and Barsad. The people had all poured out to the show in the streets. Barsad proposed, "Let her embrace him; it is but a moment." They passed her over the seats in the hall to a raised place, where he, by leaning over the dock, could fold her in his arms.

"Farewell, darling of my soul. My parting blessing on my love. We shall meet again, where the weary are at rest!"

"I can bear it, dear Charles. I am supported from above; don't suffer for me. A parting blessing for our child."

"I send it to her by you, say farewell to her by you."

Her father had followed her, and would have fallen on his knees to them, but Darnay seized him, crying:

"No, no! What have you done that you should kneel to us! We know now what a struggle you underwent when you suspected my descent, and when you knew it. We thank you with all our hearts, and all our love and duty. Heaven be with you!"

Her father's only answer was to draw his hands through his white hair, and wring them with a shriek of anguish.

"It could not be otherwise," said the prisoner. "Be comforted, and Heaven bless you!"

As he was drawn away, his wife released him, and stood looking after him with her hands touching one another in the attitude of prayer, and with a radiant look upon her face, in which there was even a comforting smile. As he went out at the prisoners' door, she turned, laid her head lovingly on her father's breast, tried to speak to him, and fell at his feet.

Then, issuing from the obscure corner from which he had never moved, Sydney Carton came and took her up. His arm trembled as it raised her, and supported her head. Yet, there was an air about him that was not all of pity—that had a flush of pride in it.

"Shall I take her to a coach? I shall never feel her weight." He carried her to the door, and laid her tenderly down in a coach. Her father and their old friend got into it, and he took his seat beside the driver.

When they arrived at the gateway where he had paused not many hours before to picture to himself on which of the rough stones of the street her feet had trod, he lifted her again, carried her up the staircase, and laid her on a couch, where her child and Miss Pross wept over her.

"Don't recall her to herself," he said softly; "she is better so. Don't revive her to consciousness; she only faints."

"Oh, Carton, Carton, dear Carton!" cried little Lucie, throwing her arms round him, in a burst of grief. "Now that you have come, I think you will do something to help mamma, something to save papa!"

He bent over, laid her blooming cheek against his and looked at her unconscious mother.

"Before I go," he said, and paused— "I may kiss her?"

It was remembered afterwards that when he bent down and touched her face with his lips, he murmured some words. The child, who was nearest to him told them afterwards, and told her grandchildren when she was a handsome old lady, that she heard him say, "A life you love."

When he had gone into the next room, he turned suddenly on Mr. Lorry and her father, and said to the latter:

"You had great influence but yesterday, Doctor Manette; let it at least be tried. These judges are very friendly to you, are they not?"

"Nothing connected with Charles was concealed from me. I had the strongest assurances that I should save him; and I did." He returned the answer in great trouble, and very slowly.

"Try them again. The hours between this and tomorrow afternoon are few and short, but try."

"I intend to try. I will not rest a moment."

"That's well. I have known such energy as yours do great things before now—though never," he added, with a smile and a sigh together, "such as this. Of little worth as life is when we misuse it, it is worth that effort. It would cost nothing to lay down if it were not."

"I will go," said Doctor Manette, "to the Prosecutor and the President straight, and to others whom it is better not to name. But stay! There is a celebration in the streets, and no one will be accessible until dark."

"Well! It is a forlorn hope at best, not much forlorner for being delayed till dark. I should like to know how you speed; though, mind! I expect nothing! When are you likely to have seen these dread powers, Doctor Manette?"

"Immediately after dark, I should hope. Within an hour or two from this."

"It will be dark soon after four. If I go to Mr. Lorry's at nine, shall I hear what you have done, either from our friend or from yourself?"

"Yes."

"May you prosper!"

Mr. Lorry followed Sydney to the outer door, and, touching him on the shoulder, caused him to turn.

"I have no hope," said Mr. Lorry, in a sorrowful whisper.

"Nor have I."

"If any one or all of these men were disposed to spare him, I doubt if they durst spare him after the demonstration in the court."

"And so do I. I heard the fall of the ax in that sound."

Mr. Lorry leaned his arm upon the doorpost, and bowed his face upon it.

"Don't despond," said Carton, very gently; "don't grieve. I encouraged Doctor Manette in this idea, because I felt that it might one day be consolatory to her. Otherwise, she might think 'his life was wantonly thrown away or wasted,' and that might trouble her."

"Yes, yes, yes," returned Mr. Lorry, drying his eyes, "you are right. But he will perish; there is no real hope."

"Yes. He will perish; there is no real hope," echoed Carton. And walked with a settled step, downstairs.

CHAPTER XII
DARKNESS

Sydney Carton paused in the street, not quite decided where to go. "At Tellson's Banking House at nine," he said, musing. "Shall I do well, in the meantime, to show myself? I think so. It is best these people should know there is such a man as I here; it is a sound precaution, may be a necessary preparation. But care! Let me think it out!"

Checking his steps, he took a turn or two in the already darkening street, and traced the thought in his mind to its possible consequences. His first impression was confirmed. "It is best," he said, finally resolved, "that these people should know there is such a man as I here." And he turned his face toward Saint Antoine.

Defarge had described himself, that day, as keeper of a wine shop in Saint Antoine. It was not difficult for one who knew the city well to find his house without asking any question. Having ascertained its situation, Carton dined at a place of refreshment and fell sound asleep after dinner. For the first time in many years he had no strong drink. Last night he had dropped the brandy slowly down on Mr. Lorry's hearth like a man who had done with it.

It was as late as seven o'clock when he awoke refreshed, and went out into the streets again. As he passed along toward Saint Antoine, he stopped at a shop window where there was a mirror, and slightly altered the disordered arrangement of his loose cravat, and his coat collar, and his wild hair. This done, he went on direct to Defarge's, and went in.

There happened to be no customer in the shop but Jacques Three of the restless fingers and the creaking voice. This man, whom he had seen upon the Jury, stood drinking at the little counter, in conversation with the Defarges, man and wife. The Vengeance assisted in the conversation, like a regular member of the establishment.

As Carton walked in, took his seat, and asked—in very indifferent French—for a small measure of wine, Madame Defarge cast a careless glance at him, and than a keener, and then a keener, and then advanced to him herself, and asked him what it was he had ordered.

He repeated what he had already said.

"English?" asked Madame Defarge, inquisitively.

After looking at her, as if the sound of even a single French word were slow to express itself to him, he answered in his former strong foreign accent, "Yes, madame, yes. I am English."

Madame Defarge returned to her counter to get the wine, and, as he took up a Jacobin journal[1] and feigned to pore over it, he heard her say, "I swear to you, like Evrémonde!"

Defarge brought him the wine, and gave him Good evening.

"How?"

"Good evening."

"Oh! Good evening, citizen," filling his glass. "Ah! and good wine. I drink to the Republic."

Defarge went back to the counter and said, "Certainly, a little like." Madame sternly retorted, "I tell you a good deal like." Jacques Three pacifically remarked, "He is so much in your mind, madame." The Vengeance added, with a laugh, "And you are looking forward with so much pleasure to seeing him once more tomorrow!"

Carton followed the lines of his paper, with a slow fore-finger, and a studious, absorbed face. They were all leaning on the counter close together, speaking low. After a silence of a few moments during which they all looked toward him without disturbing his attention, they resumed their conversation.

"It is true what madame says," observed Jacques Three. "Why stop? There is great force in that. Why stop?"

"Well, well," reasoned Defarge, "but one must stop somewhere. After all, the question is still where?"

"At extermination," said madame.

"Magnificent!" croaked Jacques Three. The Vengeance, also, highly approved.

"Extermination is good doctrine, my wife," said Defarge, rather troubled. "But this Doctor has suffered much; you observed his face when the paper was read."

1. ***Jacobin*** (jak′ə bin) ***journal,*** a periodical published by the members of the radical political club organized during the revolution.

"I observed his face!" repeated madame, contemptuously and angrily. "Yes. I observed his face to be not the face of a true friend of the Republic. Let him take care of his face."

"And you observed, my wife," said Defarge, in a deprecatory manner, "the anguish of his daughter."

"I observed his daughter," repeated madame; "yes, more times than one. I observed her today, and other days. I observed her in the court, and in the street by the prison. Let me but lift my finger——!" She seemed to raise it and let it fall as if the ax had dropped.

"The citizeness is superb!" croaked the Juryman.

"She is an angel!" said The Vengeance, and embraced her.

"As to thee," pursued madame, implacably, addressing her husband, "if it depended on thee—which, happily, it does not—thou would'st rescue this man even now."

"No!" protested Defarge. "But I would leave the matter there. I say, stop there."

"See you," said Madame Defarge, wrathfully. "For crimes as tyrants and oppressors, I have this race a long time on my register, doomed to destruction and extermination. Ask my husband, is that so."

"It is so," assented Defarge, without being asked.

"In the beginning of the great days, when the Bastille falls, he finds this paper of today, and brings it home; in the middle of the night when this place is clear and shut, we read it, here on this spot. Ask him, is that so."

"It is so," assented Defarge.

"That night I tell him, when the paper is read through and the lamp is burnt out, that I have a secret to communicate. Ask him, is that so."

"It is so," assented Defarge again.

"I tell him, Defarge, I was brought up among the fishermen of the seashore, and that peasant family so injured by the two Evrémonde brothers, as that Bastille paper describes, is my family. Defarge, that sister of the mortally wounded boy was my sister, that husband was my sister's husband, that unborn child was their child, that brother was my brother, that father was my father, and that summons to answer for those things descends to me! Ask him, is that so."

"It is so," assented Defarge once more.

"Then tell Wind and Fire where to stop," returned madame; "but don't tell me."

Customers entered, and the group was broken up. The English customer paid for what he had had, perplexedly counted his change, and asked, as a stranger, to be directed towards the National Palace. Madame Defarge took him to the door, and put her arm on his, in pointing out the road. The English customer was not without reflections then, that it might be a good deed to seize that arm, lift it, and strike under it sharp and deep.

But he went his way, and was soon swallowed up in the shadow of the prison wall. At the appointed hour he emerged from it to present himself in Mr. Lorry's room again, where he found the old gentleman walking to and fro in restless anxiety. He said he had been with Lucie until just now, and had only left her for a few minutes, to come and keep his appointment. Her father had not been seen since toward four o'clock. She had hopes that his mediation might save Charles, but they were very slight. He had been more than five hours gone; where could he be?

Mr. Lorry waited until ten; but, Doctor Manette not returning, and he being unwilling to leave Lucie any longer, it was arranged that he should go back to her, and come to the Banking house again at midnight. In the meanwhile, Carton would wait alone by the fire for the Doctor.

He waited, and the clock struck twelve; but Doctor Manette did not come. Mr. Lorry returned, found no tidings of him, and brought none. Where could he be?

They were discussing this question, when they heard him on the stairs. The instant he entered the room, it was plain that all was lost.

Whether he had really been to anyone, was never known. As he stood staring at them, they asked him no question, for his face told them everything.

"I cannot find it," said he, "and I must have it. Where is it?"

His head and throat were bare, and, as he spoke, he took his coat off, and let it drop on the floor.

"Where is my bench? I can't find it. Time presses: I must finish those shoes."

They looked at one another, and their hearts died within them.

"Come, come!" said he, in a whimpering miserable way; "let me get to work. Give me my work." Receiving no answer, he tore his hair. "Don't torture a poor forlorn wretch," he implored them, "but give me my work!"

Lost, utterly lost!

It was so clearly beyond hope to try to restore him—that—as if by agreement—they each soothed him to sit down before the fire, with a promise that he should have his work presently. He sank into the chair, and brooded. As if all that had happened since the garret were a dream, Mr. Lorry saw him shrink into the exact figure that Defarge had had in keeping.

Affected as they both were by this spectacle of ruin, it was not a time to yield to emotions. His lonely daughter, bereft of her final reliance, appealed to them both too strongly. They looked at one another with one meaning in their faces. Carton was the first to speak:

"The last chance is gone; it was not much. Yes; he had better be taken to her. But before you go, will you, for a moment, steadily attend to me? Don't ask me why I make the stipulations I am going to make, and exact the promise I am going to exact; I have a reason—a good one."

"I do not doubt it," answered Mr. Lorry. "Say on."

The figure in the chair was all the time rocking itself to and fro, and moaning. Carton stooped to pick up the coat which lay almost entangling his feet. As he did so, a small case fell on the floor. Carton took it up, and there was a folded paper in it. "We should look at this!" he said. Mr. Lorry nodded. He opened it, and exclaimed, "Thank God!"

"What is it?" asked Mr. Lorry, eagerly.

"A moment! Let me speak of it in its place. First," he put his hand in his coat, and took another paper from it, "that is the certificate which enables me to pass out of this city. You see—Sydney Carton, an Englishman?

"Keep it for me. I shall see him tomorrow, you remember, and I had better not take it into the prison."

"Why not?"

"I don't know; I prefer not to do so. Now, take this paper that Doctor Manette has carried about him. It is a similar certificate, enabling him and his daughter and her child, at any time, to pass the Barrier and the frontier. You see?"

"Yes!"

"Perhaps he obtained it as his last and utmost precaution against evil, yesterday. Put it up carefully with mine and your own. It is good, until recalled. But it may be soon recalled, and, I have reason to think, will be."

"They are not in danger?"

"They are in great danger, danger of denunciation by Madame Defarge. I know it from her own lips. Since then, I have seen the spy. He confirms me. He knows that a wood sawyer, living by the prison wall, has been rehearsed by Madame Defarge as to his having seen her"—he never mentioned Lucie's name—"making signs and signals to prisoners. It is easy to foresee that the pretense will be the common one, a prison plot, and that it will involve her life—and perhaps her child's—and perhaps her father's—for both have been seen with her at that place. Don't look so horrified. You will save them all."

"Heaven grant I may, Carton! But how?"

"I am going to tell you how. It will depend on you, and it could depend on no better man. This new denunciation will certainly not take place until after tomorrow. You know it is a capital crime to mourn for, or sympathize with, a victim of the Guillotine. She and her father would unquestionably be guilty of this crime, and this woman would wait to add that strength to her case, and make herself doubly sure. You follow me?"

"So attentively, and with so much confidence in what you say, that for the moment I lost sight," touching the back of the Doctor's chair, "even of this distress."

"Your preparations have been completed to return to England. Early tomorrow have horses ready, so that they may be in starting trim at two o'clock in the afternoon."

"It shall be done!" His manner was so fervent and inspiring that Mr. Lorry caught the flame and was as quick as youth.

"You are a noble heart. Did I say we could depend upon no better man? Tell her, tonight, what you know of her danger as involving her child and her father. Dwell upon that, for she would lay her own fair head beside her husband's cheerfully." He faltered for an instant; then went on as before. "For the sake of her child and her father, press upon her the necessity of leaving Paris, with them and you, at that hour. Tell her that it was her husband's last arrangement. Tell her that more depends upon it than she dare believe, or hope. You think that her father, even in this sad state, will submit himself to her; do you not?"

"I am sure of it."

"I thought so. Quietly and steadily have all these arrangements made in the courtyard here, even to the taking of your own seat in the carriage. The moment I come to you, take me in, and drive away."

"I understand that I wait for you under all circumstances?"

"You have my certificate in your hand and will reserve my place. Wait for nothing but to have my place occupied, and then for England!"

"Why, then," said Mr. Lorry, grasping his eager but so firm and steady hand, "it does not all depend on one old man, but I shall have a young and ardent man at my side."

"By the help of heaven you shall! Promise me solemnly that nothing will influence you to alter the course on which we now stand pledged to one another."

"Nothing, Carton."

"Remember these words tomorrow: change the course, or delay in it—for any reason—and no life can possibly be saved, and many lives must inevitably be sacrificed."

"I will remember them. I hope to do my part faithfully."

"And I hope to do mine. Now, good-by!"

Though he said it with a grave smile of earnestness, and though he even put the old man's hand to his lips, he did not part from him then. He helped him to arouse the rocking figure before the dying embers, to get a cloak and hat put upon it, and to tempt it forth to find where the bench and work were hidden that it still moaningly besought to have. He walked on the other side of it and protected it to the courtyard of the house where the afflicted heart outwatched the awful night. He entered the courtyard and remained there for a few moments alone, looking up at the light in the window of her room. Before he went away, he breathed a blessing toward it, and a farewell.

CHAPTER XIII
FIFTY-TWO

In the black prison of the Conciergerie the doomed of the day awaited their fate. They were in number as the weeks of the year. Fifty-two were to roll that afternoon to the boundless everlasting sea. Before their cells were quit of them, new occupants were appointed; before their blood ran into the blood spilled yesterday, the blood that was to mingle with theirs tomorrow was already set apart.

Two score and twelve were told off. From the Farmer-General of seventy, whose riches could not buy his life, to the seamstress of twenty, whose poverty and obscurity could not save her.

Charles Darnay, alone in a cell, had sustained himself with no flattering delusion since he came to it from the Tribunal. In every line of the narrative he had heard, he had heard his condemnation. He had fully comprehended that no personal influence could possibly save him, that he was virtually sentenced by the millions.

Nevertheless, it was not easy, with the face of his beloved wife fresh before him, to compose his mind to what it must bear. His hold on life was strong, and it was very, very hard, to loosen; by gradual efforts and degrees unclosed a little here, it clenched the tighter there; and when he brought his strength to bear on that hand and it yielded, this was closed again. But all this was at first. Next followed the thought that much of the future peace of mind enjoyable by the dear ones depended on his quiet fortitude. So by degrees he calmed into the better state, when he could raise his thoughts much higher, and draw comfort down.

Before dark on the night of his condemnation, he had traveled thus far on his last way. Being allowed to purchase the means of writing, and a light, he sat down to write until such time as the prison lamps should be extinguished.

He wrote a long letter to Lucie, showing her that he had known nothing of her father's imprisonment, until he had heard of it from herself, and that he had been as ignorant as she of his father's and uncle's responsibility for that misery, until the paper had been read. He had already explained that his concealment of the name he had relinquished was the one condition—fully intelligible now—that her father had attached to their betrothal. He besought her to console her father, by impressing him with the truth that he had done nothing for which he could justly reproach himself. Next to her preservation of his own last grateful love and blessing, and her overcoming of her sorrow, to devote herself to their dear child, he adjured her, as they would meet in heaven, to comfort her father.

To her father himself, he wrote in the same strain; but, he told her father that he expressly confided his wife and child to his care. He told him this, very strongly, with the hope of rousing him from any despondency or dangerous retrospect toward which he foresaw he might be tending.

To Mr. Lorry, he commended them all, and explained his worldly affairs. That done, with many added sentences of grateful friendship and warm attachment, all was done. He never thought of Carton. His mind was so full of the others, that he never once thought of him.

He had time to finish these letters before the lights were put out. When he lay down on his straw bed, he thought he had done with this world. He awoke in the somber morning, unconscious where he was or what had happened, until it flashed upon his mind, "This is the day of my death!"

Thus had he come through the hours, to the day when the fifty-two heads were to fall. And now, while he was composed, and hoped that he could meet the end with quiet heroism, a new action began in his waking thoughts, which was very difficult to master.

He had never seen the instrument that was to terminate his life. How high it was from the ground, how many steps it had, where he would be stood, how he would be touched, whether the touching hands would be dyed red, which way his face would be turned, whether he would be the first, or might be the last; these and many similar questions, in no wise directed by his will, obtruded themselves over and over again. Neither were they connected with fear; he was conscious of no fear. Rather, they originated in a strange besetting desire to know what to do when the time came; a desire gigantically disproportionate to the few swift moments to which it referred.

The hours went on as he walked to and fro, and the clocks struck the numbers he would never hear again. Nine gone forever, ten gone forever, eleven gone forever, twelve coming on to pass away. Twelve gone forever.

He had been apprized that the final hour was Three, and he knew he would be summoned some time earlier, as the tumbrils jolted slowly through the streets. He resolved to keep Two before his mind, as the hour, and so to strengthen himself that he might be able to strengthen others.

Walking regularly to and fro with his arms folded on his breast, he heard One struck away from him, without surprise. Devoutly thankful to heaven for his recovered self-possession, he thought, "There is but another now," and turned to walk again.

Footsteps in the stone passage outside the door. He stopped. The lock turned. Before the door opened, a man said in a low voice in English: "Go in alone; I wait near. Lose no time!"

The door was quickly opened and closed, and there stood before him quiet, with the light of a smile on his features, and a cautionary finger on his lip, Sydney Carton.

There was something so bright and remarkable in his look that, for the first moment, the prisoner misdoubted him to be an apparition. But he spoke, and it was his voice; he took the prisoner's hand, and it was his real grasp.

"Of all the people upon earth, you least expected to see me?" he said.

"I could not believe it to be you. I can scarcely believe it now. You are not—a prisoner?"

"No. I am accidentally possessed of a power over one of the keepers here, and in virtue of it I stand before you. I come from her—your wife, dear Darnay."

The prisoner wrung his hand.

"I bring you a request from her."

"What is it?"

"A most earnest, pressing, and emphatic entreaty, to you in the voice so dear to you."

The prisoner turned his face partly aside.

"You have no time to ask me why I bring it, or what it means; I have no time to tell you. You must comply with it—take off those boots you wear, and draw on these of mine."

There was a chair against the wall of the cell, behind the prisoner. Carton had already, with the speed of lightning, got him down into it and stood over him, barefoot.

"Draw on these boots of mine. Quick!"

"Carton, there is no escaping from this place; it never can be done. You will only die with me. It is madness."

"It would be madness if I asked you to escape; but do I? Change that cravat for this of mine, that coat for this of mine. While you do it, let me take this ribbon from your hair, and shake out your hair like this of mine!"

With a strength both of will and action, that appeared quite supernatural, he forced all these changes upon him. The prisoner was like a young child in his hands.

"Carton! Dear Carton! It is madness. It cannot be accomplished, it has been attempted, and has always failed. I implore you not to add your death to the bitterness of mine."

"Do I ask you, my dear Darnay, to pass the door? When I ask that, refuse. There are pen and ink and paper on this table. Is your hand steady enough to write?"

"It was when you came in."

"Steady it again and write what I shall dictate. Quick, friend, quick!"

Bewildered, Darnay sat down at the table. Carton, with his right hand in his breast, stood close beside him.

"Write exactly as I speak."

"To whom do I address it?"

"To no one." Carton still had his hand in his breast.

"Do I date it?"

"No."

The prisoner looked up, at each question. Carton, standing over him with his hand in his breast, looked down.

" 'If you remember,' " said Carton, dictating, " 'the words that passed between us, long ago, you will readily comprehend this when you see it. You do remember them, I know.' "

He was drawing his hand from his breast; the prisoner chancing to look up in his hurried wonder as he wrote, the hand stopped, closing upon something.

"Have you written 'forget them'?" Carton asked?

"I have. Is that a weapon in your hand?"

"No; I am not armed."

"What is it in your hand?"

"You shall know directly. Write on; there

Ronald Searle

are but a few words more." He dictated again. " 'I am thankful that the time has come, when I can prove them.' " As he said these words with his eyes fixed on the writer, his hand slowly and softly moved down close to the writer's face.

The pen dropped from Darnay's fingers on the table, and he looked about him vacantly.

"What vapor is that?" he asked.

"Vapor?"

"Something that crossed me?"

"I am conscious of nothing; there can be nothing here. Take up the pen and finish. Hurry, hurry!"

As if his memory were impaired, or his faculties disordered, the prisoner made an effort to rally his attention. As he looked at Carton with clouded eyes and with an altered manner of breathing, Carton looked steadily at him.

"Hurry, hurry!"

The prisoner bent over the paper once more.

" 'If it had been otherwise' "; Carton's hand was again watchfully and softly stealing down; " 'If it had been otherwise' "; the hand was at the prisoner's face; " 'I should but have had so much the more to answer for.' " Carton saw the pen trailing off into unintelligible signs. Carton's hand moved back to his breast no more. The prisoner sprang up with a reproachful look, but Carton's hand was firm at his nostrils. For a few seconds he struggled with the man who had come to lay down his life for him; but, within a minute or so, he was stretched insensible on the ground.

Quickly, Carton dressed himself in the clothes the prisoner had laid aside, combed back his hair, and tied it with the ribbon the prisoner had worn. Then, he softly called, "Come in!" and the spy presented himself.

"You see?" said Carton, as he kneeled beside the insensible figure, putting the paper in the breast; "is your hazard very great?"

"Mr. Carton," the spy answered, with a timid snap of his fingers, "my hazard is not *that,* if you are true to the whole of your bargain."

"Don't fear me. I will be true to the death."

"You must be, Mr. Carton, if the tale of fifty-two is to be right. Being made right by you in that dress, I shall have no fear."

"Have no fear! I shall soon be out of the way of harming you, and the rest will soon be far from here, please God! Now, get assistance and take me to the coach."

"You?" said the spy nervously.

"Him, man, with whom I have exchanged. You go out at the gate by which you brought me in?"

"Of course."

"I was weak and faint when you brought me in; I am fainter now you take me out. The parting interview has overpowered me. Such a thing has happened here, often. Quick! Call assistance!"

"You swear not to betray me?" said the trembling spy.

"Man, man!" returned Carton, stamping his foot. "You waste precious moments now? Take him yourself to the courtyard you know of, place him in the carriage, show him yourself to Mr. Lorry, tell him yourself to give him no restorative but air, and to remember my words and his promise of last night, and drive away!"

The spy withdrew, and Carton seated himself at the table, resting his forehead on his hands. The spy returned immediately, with two men.

"How, then?" said one of them, contemplating the fallen figure. "So afflicted to find that his friend has drawn a prize in the lottery of Sainte Guillotine?"

"A good patriot," said the other, "could hardly have been more afflicted if the aristocrat had drawn a blank."

They raised the unconscious figure, placed it on a litter they had brought to the door, and bent to carry it away.

"The time is short, Evrémonde," said the spy, in a warning voice.

"I know it well," answered Carton. "Be careful of my friend, I entreat you, and leave me."

"Come, then, my children," said Barsad. "Lift him, and come away!"

The door closed, and Carton was left alone. Straining, he listened for any sound that might denote suspicion or alarm. There was none. Keys turned, doors clashed, footsteps passed along distant passages; no cry was raised, or hurry made that seemed unusual. Breathing more freely in a little while, he sat down at the table, and listened until the clock struck Two.

Sounds that he was not afraid of, for he divined their meaning, then began to be audible. Several doors were opened in succession, and finally his own. A jailer, with a list in his hand, looked in, merely saying, "Follow me, Evrémonde!" and he followed into a large dark room. He could but dimly discern the others who were brought there to have their arms bound. Some were lamenting, but these were few. The great majority were silent and still, looking fixedly at the ground.

As he stood by the wall in a dim corner, while some of the fifty-two were brought in after him, a young woman, with large patient eyes, rose from the seat where he had observed her sitting, and came to speak to him.

"Citizen Evrémonde," she said, "I am a poor little seamstress, who was with you in La Force."

He murmured for answer: "True. I forget what you were accused of?"

"Plots. Though the just heaven knows I am innocent of any. Is it likely? A poor weak creature like me?"

The forlorn smile with which she said it so touched him that tears started from his eyes.

"I am not afraid to die, but I have done nothing. I am not unwilling to die, if the Republic which is to do so much good to us poor will profit by my death; but I do not know how that can be, Citizen Evrémonde."

As the last thing on earth that his heart was to warm and soften to, it warmed and softened to this pitiable girl.

"I heard you were released, Citizen Evrémonde. I hoped it was true?"

"It was. But I was again taken and condemned."

"If I may ride with you, Citizen Evrémonde, will you let me hold your hand? I am not afraid, but I am little and weak, and it will give me more courage."

As the patient eyes were lifted to his face, he saw a sudden doubt in them, and then astonishment. He pressed the work-worn young fingers, and touched his lips.

"Are you dying for him?" she whispered.

"And his wife and child. Hush! Yes."

"Oh, you will let me hold your brave hand, stranger?"

"Hush! Yes, my poor sister; to the last."

The same shadows that are falling on the prison are falling in that same hour of the early afternoon, on the Barrier with the crowd about it, when a coach going out of Paris drives up to be examined.

"Who goes here? Whom have we within? Papers!"

The papers are handed out and read.

"Alexandre Manette. Physician. French. Which is he?"

This is he; this helpless, inarticulately murmuring, wandering old man pointed out.

"Apparently the Citizen-Doctor is not in his right mind? The Revolution-fever has been too much for him?"

Greatly too much for him.

"Hah! Many suffer with it. Lucie. His daughter. French. Which is she?"

This is she.

"Apparently. Lucie, wife of Evrémonde; is it not?"

It is.

"Hah! Evrémonde has an assignation elsewhere. Lucie, her child. English. This is she?"

She and no other.

"Kiss me, child of Evrémonde. Now, thou hast kissed a good Republican; something new in thy family; remember it! Sydney Carton. Advocate. English. Which is he?"

He lies here in this corner of the carriage.

"Apparently the English advocate is in a swoon?"

It is hoped he will recover in the fresher air.

He is not in strong health, and has separated sadly from a friend who is under the displeasure of the Republic.

"Is that all? Jarvis Lorry. Banker. English. Which is he?"

"I am he."

It is Jarvis Lorry who has replied to all the previous questions. It is Jarvis Lorry who has alighted and stands with his hand on the coach door, replying to a group of officials. They leisurely walk around the carriage and leisurely mount the box, to look at what little luggage it carries on the roof; the country people press nearer to the coach doors and greedily stare in; a little child, carried by its mother, has its arm held out that it may touch the wife of an aristocrat who has gone to the Guillotine.

"Behold your papers, Jarvis Lorry, countersigned."

"One can depart, citizen?"

"One can depart. Forward, postilions!"

"I salute you, citizens. —And the first danger passed!"

These are again the words of Jarvis Lorry, as he clasps his hands and looks upward. There is terror in the carriage; there is the heavy breathing of the insensible traveler.

"Are we not going too slowly? Can they not be induced to go faster?" asks Lucie, clinging to the old man.

"It would seem like flight, my darling. I must not urge them too much; it would rouse suspicion."

"Look back, and see if we are pursued!"

"The road is clear. So far, we are not pursued."

Out of the open country, in again among dye works, tanneries, and the like. Have these men deceived us, and taken us back by another road? Is not this the same place twice over? Thank heaven, no. A village. Look back, and see if we are pursued! Hush! the posting house.

Leisurely, our four horses are taken out; leisurely, the coach stands in the little street; leisurely, the new horses come; leisurely, the new postilions follow. All the time, our overfraught hearts are beating at a rate that would far outstrip the fastest gallop of the fastest horses ever foaled.

At length the new postilions are in their saddles. We are through the village. Suddenly the horses are pulled up, almost on their haunches. We are pursued?

"Ho! Within the carriage there. Speak then!"

"What is it?" asks Mr. Lorry, looking out at window.

"How many did they say?"

"I do not understand you."

"—At the last post. How many to the Guillotine today?"

"Fifty-two."

"I said so! A brave number! My fellow citizen here would have it forty-two. Hi forward! Whoop!"

The night comes on. He moves; he is beginning to revive; he thinks they are still together; he asks him, by his name, what he has in his hand. O pity us, kind heaven, and help us! Look out, look out, and see if we are pursued.

The wind is rushing after us, the clouds are flying after us, and the whole wild night is in pursuit of us; but, so far, we are pursued by nothing else.

CHAPTER XIV
THE KNITTING DONE

In that same juncture of time when the fifty-two awaited their fate, Madame Defarge held darkly ominous council with The Vengeance and Jacques Three. Not in the wine shop did Madame Defarge confer with these ministers, but in the shed of the wood sawyer, erst a mender of roads.

"But our Defarge," said Jacques Three, "is undoubtedly a good Republican? Eh?"

"My husband, fellow citizen, is a good Republican and a bold man. But my husband is so weak as to relent toward this Doctor."

"It is a great pity," croaked Jacques Three.

"See you," said madame, "I care nothing for this Doctor, I. He may wear his head or lose it.

But, the Evrémonde people are to be exterminated, and the wife and child must follow the husband and father."

"The child also," observed Jacques Three, with a meditative enjoyment of his words, "has golden hair and blue eyes. And we seldom have a child there. It is a pretty sight!"

"In a word," said Madame Defarge, "I cannot trust my husband in this matter. I feel, since last night, that I dare not confide to him the details of my projects; if I delay, there is danger of his giving warning, and then they might escape."

"That must never be," croaked Jacques Three.

"In a word," Madame went on, "my husband has not my reason for pursuing this family to annihilation; I have not his reason for regarding this Doctor with sensibility. I must act for myself, therefore. Come hither, citizen."

The wood sawyer, who held her in mortal fear, advanced with his hand to his red cap.

"Touching those signals, little citizen," said Madame Defarge, sternly, "that she made to the prisoners; you are ready to bear witness to them this very day?"

"Aye, aye," cried the sawyer. "Every day, in all weathers, from two to four, always signaling, sometimes with the little one, sometimes without."

"Clearly plots," said Jacques Three. "Transparently!"

"There is no doubt of the Jury?" inquired Madame Defarge, letting her eyes turn to him with a gloomy smile.

"Rely upon the patriotic Jury, dear citizeness. I answer for my fellow Jurymen."

"Now, let me see," said Madame Defarge, pondering again. "Can I spare this Doctor to my husband?"

"He would count as one head," observed Jacques Three. "We really have not heads enough; it would be a pity."

"He was signaling with her when I saw her," argued Madame Defarge; "I cannot speak of one without the other; and I must not be silent, and trust the case wholly to him, this little citizen here. For I am not a bad witness."

The Vengeance and Jacques Three vied with each other in protestations that she was the most admirable and marvelous of witnesses.

"He must take his chance," said Madame Defarge. "No, I cannot spare him! You are engaged at three o'clock; you are going to see the batch of today executed—— You?"

The question was addressed to the wood sawyer, who hurriedly replied in the affirmative.

"I," said madame, "am equally engaged at the same place. After it is over—say at eight tonight—come to me, and we will give information against these people."

The wood sawyer said he would be proud to attend the citizeness. Madame Defarge beckoned the Juryman and The Vengeance and expounded her further views.

"She will now be at home, awaiting the moment of his death. She will be mourning and grieving. She will be in a state of mind to impeach the justice of the Republic. She will be full of sympathy with its enemies. I will go to her."

"What an admirable woman!" exclaimed Jacques Three, rapturously. "Ah, my cherished!" cried The Vengeance.

"Take my knitting," said Madame Defarge, "and have it ready for me in my usual seat. Keep me my usual chair. Go there, straight; there will be a greater concourse than usual today."

"I willingly obey the orders of my Chief," said The Vengeance, kissing her cheek. "You will not be late?"

"I shall be there before the commencement."

"And before the tumbrils arrive. Be sure you are there, my soul," said The Vengeance, calling after her, for she had already turned into the street, "before the tumbrils arrive!"

Madame Defarge slightly waved her hand, to imply that she heard, and might be relied upon to arrive in good time, and so went round the corner of the prison wall.

There were many women at that time, upon whom the time laid a dreadfully disfiguring hand; but there was not one among them more to be dreaded than this ruthless woman, now taking her way along the streets. Imbued from her childhood with a brooding sense of wrong, and an inveterate hatred of a class, opportunity had developed her into a tigress. She was absolutely without pity.

It was nothing to her that an innocent man was to die for the sins of his forefathers; she saw, not him, but them. It was nothing to her that his wife was to be made a widow and his daughter an orphan; that was insufficient punishment, because they were her natural enemies and her prey, and as such had no right to live. To appeal to her was made hopeless by her having no sense of pity, even for herself.

Such a heart Madame Defarge carried under her rough robe. Lying hidden in her bosom was a loaded pistol. Lying hidden at her waist was a sharpened dagger. Thus accoutered, and walking with confident tread, Madame Defarge took her way along the streets.

When the journey of the traveling coach had been planned out last night, the difficulty of taking Miss Pross in it had engaged Mr. Lorry's attention. It was not merely desirable to avoid overloading the coach, but it was of the highest importance that the time occupied in examining it and its passengers, should be reduced to the utmost; since their escape might depend on the saving of only a few seconds. Finally, he had proposed, after anxious consideration, that Miss Pross and Jerry, who were at liberty to leave the city, would leave at three o'clock in the lightest wheeled conveyance known to that period. Unencumbered with luggage, they would soon overtake the coach, and, passing it and preceding it on the road, would order its horses in advance, and greatly facilitate its progress during the precious hours of the night when delay was most to be dreaded.

Seeing in this arrangement the hope of rendering service in that pressing emergency, Miss Pross hailed it with joy. She and Jerry had beheld the coach start, had known who it was that Solomon brought, had passed some ten minutes in tortures of suspense, and were concluding their arrangements to follow the coach, even as Madame Defarge, taking her way through the streets, drew nearer and nearer to the lodging in which they held their consultation.

"What do you think, Mr. Cruncher," said Miss Pross, "of our not starting from this courtyard? Another carriage having already gone from here today, it might awaken suspicion."

"My opinion, miss," returned Mr. Cruncher, "is as you're right. Likewise would you do me the favor, miss, to take notice o' two promises and wows wot it is my wishes fur to record in this here crisis? First," said Mr. Cruncher, who was all in a tremble, "them poor things well out o' this, never no more will I do it, never no more!"

"I am quite sure, Mr. Cruncher," returned Miss Pross, "that you never will do it again, whatever it is, and I beg you not to think it necessary to mention more particularly what it is."

"No, miss," returned Jerry, "it shall not be named to you. Second: them poor things well out o' this, never no more will I interfere with Mrs. Cruncher's flopping!"

"Whatever housekeeping arrangement that may be," said Miss Pross, striving to dry her eyes and compose herself, "I have no doubt it is best that Mrs. Cruncher should have it entirely under her superintendence."

"I go so far as to say, Miss, moreover," proceeded Mr. Cruncher, with a most alarming tendency to hold forth as from a pulpit—"and let my words be took down and took to Mrs. Cruncher through yourself—that wot my opinions respectin' flopping has undergone a change, and that wot I only hope with all my heart as Mrs. Cruncher may be a-flopping at the present time."

"If we ever get back to our native land," said Miss Pross, "you may rely upon my telling Mrs. Cruncher as much as I may be able to remember and understand of what you have so impressively said. Now, pray let us think! My esteemed Mr. Cruncher, let us think!"

Still Madame Defarge came nearer and nearer.

"If you were to go before, " said Miss Pross, "stop the vehicle, and wait somewhere for me; wouldn't that be best?" Mr. Cruncher thought it might be.

"By the cathedral door," said Miss Pross. "Would it be much out of the way, to take me in, near the great cathedral door between the two towers?"

"No, miss," answered Mr. Cruncher.

"Then, like the best of men," said Miss Pross, "go to the posting house straight, and make that change."

"I am doubtful," said Mr. Cruncher, hesitating, "about leaving of you, you see."

"Have no fear for me. Take me in at the cathedral, at three o'clock, or as near it as you can, and I am sure it will be better than our going from here. Bless you, Mr. Cruncher! Think—not of me, but of the lives that may depend on us!"

This exordium, and Miss Pross's two hands in quite agonized entreaty clasping his, decided Mr. Cruncher. With an encouraging nod or two, he went out to alter the arrangements, and left her to follow as she had proposed.

Miss Pross got a basin of cold water and began laving her eyes, which were swollen and red. Haunted by feverish apprehensions, she constantly looked round to see that there was no one watching her. In one of those pauses she recoiled for she saw a figure standing in the room.

The basin fell to the ground broken, and the water flowed to the feet of Madame Defarge.

"Madame Defarge looked coldly at her and said, "The wife of Evrémonde; where is she?"

It flashed upon Miss Pross's mind that the doors were all standing open, and would suggest the flight. Her first act was to shut them. There were four in the room and she shut them all. She then placed herself before the door of the chamber which Lucie had occupied.

Madame Defarge's eyes followed her through this rapid movement. Miss Pross too was a determined woman and she measured Madame Defarge with her eyes.

"You might, from your appearance, be the wife of Lucifer," said Miss Pross. "Nevertheless, you shall not get the better of me. I am an Englishwoman."

Madame Defarge looked at her scornfully, but still with something of Miss Pross's own perception that they two were at bay. She saw a tight, hard, wiry woman before her. She knew full well that Miss Pross was the family's devoted friend; Miss Pross knew full well that Madame Defarge was the family's malevolent enemy.

"On my way yonder," said Madame Defarge, "where they reserve my chair and my knitting for me, I am come to make my compliments to her in passing. I wish to see her."

"I know your intentions are evil," said Miss Pross, "and depend upon it, I'll hold my own against them."

Each spoke in her own language; neither understood the other's words; both were very watchful, and intent to deduce from look and manner, what the unintelligible words meant.

"It will do her no good to keep herself concealed from me at this moment," said Madame Defarge. "Good patriots will know what that means. Let me see her. Do you hear?"

"No, you wicked foreign woman."

"Woman imbecile and piglike!" said Madame Defarge, frowning. "I demand to see her. Stand out of the way and let me go to her!"

"I little thought," said Miss Pross, "that I should ever want to understand your nonsensical language; but I would give all I have to know whether you suspect the truth."

Neither of them for a single moment released the other's eyes. Madame Defarge now advanced one step.

"I am a Briton," said Miss Pross, "I am desperate. The longer I keep you here, the greater hope there is for my Ladybird. I'll not leave a handful of that dark hair upon your head, if you lay a finger on me!''

Her courage brought the irrepressible tears into her eyes. This was a courage that Madame Defarge so little comprehended as to mistake for weakness. ''Ha, ha!'' she laughed, ''you poor wretch! I address myself to that Doctor.'' Then she called out, ''Citizen Doctor! Wife of Evrémonde! Child of Evrémonde!''

Perhaps the following silence, perhaps some latent disclosure in the expression of Miss Pross's face, whispered to Madame Defarge that they were gone. Three of the doors she opened swiftly, and looked in.

''Those rooms are all in disorder, there has been hurried packing, there are odds and ends upon the ground. There is no one in that room behind you! Let me look.''

''Never!'' said Miss Pross, who understood the request as perfectly as Madame Defarge understood the answer.

Madame Defarge made at the door. Miss Pross, on the instinct of the moment, seized her round the waist in both her arms, and held her tight. It was in vain for Madame Defarge to struggle and to strike; Miss Pross, with the vigorous tenacity of love, always so much stronger than hate, clasped her tight, and even lifted her from the floor in the struggle. The two hands of Madame Defarge buffeted and tore her face; but, Miss Pross, with her head down, held her round the waist, and clung to her with more than the hold of a drowning woman.

Soon Madame Defarge's hands ceased to strike, and felt at her encircled waist. ''It is under my arm,'' said Miss Pross, in smothered tones, ''you shall not draw it. I am stronger than you, I bless heaven for it. I'll hold you till one or other of us faints or dies!''

Madame Defarge's hands were at her bosom. Miss Pross looked up, saw what it was, struck at it, struck out a flash and a crash, and stood alone—blinded with smoke.

All this was in a second. As the smoke cleared, leaving an awful stillness, it passed out on the air, like the soul of the furious woman whose body lay lifeless on the ground.

In the first fright and horror of her situation, Miss Pross passed the body and ran down the stairs to call for help. Happily, she bethought herself of the consequences in time to check herself and go back. It was dreadful to go in again; but she did go in, to get the bonnet and other things she must wear. These she put on, out on the staircase, first shutting and locking the door and taking the key. She sat down on the stairs to breathe and to cry, then got up and hurried away.

By good fortune she had a veil on her bonnet, or she could hardly have gone along the streets without being stopped. By good fortune, too, she was naturally so peculiar in appearance as not to show disfigurement like any other woman. She needed both advantages, for the marks of gripping fingers were deep in her face, her hair was torn, and her dress was clutched and dragged a hundred ways. Crossing the bridge, she dropped the door key in the river.

Arriving at the cathedral, she thought, what if she were stopped at the gate, sent to prison, and charged with murder! In the midst of these fluttering thoughts, the escort appeared, took her in, and took her away.

''Is there any noise in the streets?'' she asked him.

''The usual noises,'' Mr. Cruncher replied, surprised by the question and by her aspect.

''I don't hear you,'' said Miss Pross. ''What do you say?''

''I'll nod my head,'' thought Mr. Cruncher, amazed, ''at all events she'll see that.'' And she did.

''I feel,'' said Miss Pross, ''as if there had been a flash and a crash, and that crash was the last thing I should ever hear in this life.''

''Blest if she ain't in a queer condition!'' said Mr. Cruncher, more and more disturbed. ''Wot can she have been a-takin', to keep her courage up? Hark! There's the roll of them dreadful carts! You can hear that, miss?"

"I can hear," said Miss Pross, seeing that he spoke to her, "nothing. Oh, my good man, there was first a great crash, and then a great stillness, and that stillness seems to be fixed and unchangeable, never to be broken any more as long as my life lasts."

"If she don't hear the roll of those dreadful carts, now very nigh their journey's end," said Mr. Cruncher, glancing over his shoulder, "it's my opinion that indeed she never will hear anything else in this world."

And indeed she never did.

CHAPTER XV
THE FOOTSTEPS DIE OUT FOREVER

Along the Paris streets the death carts rumble, hollow and harsh. Six tumbrils carry the day's wine to La Guillotine.

Of the riders in the tumbrils, some observe all things on their last roadside, with an impassive stare; others, with a lingering interest in the ways of life and men. Some, seated with drooping heads, are sunk in silent despair. Several close their eyes, and think. Only one, a miserable creature, of a crazed aspect, is so made drunk by horror that he sings and tries to dance. Not one appeals by look or gesture to the pity of the people.

A guard of horsemen riding abreast of the tumbrils are asked some question. It would seem to be always the same question, for it is always followed by a press of people toward the third cart. The horsemen abreast of that cart frequently point out one man in it with their swords. He stands at the back of the tumbril with his head bent down, to converse with a mere girl who sits on the side of the cart, and holds his hand. Here and there in the long street of St. Honoré cries are raised against him. If they move him at all, it is only to a quiet smile, as he shakes his hair a little more loosely about his face. He cannot easily touch his face, his arms being bound.

On the steps of a church, awaiting the coming up of the tumbrils, stands the spy. He looks into the first of them; not there. He looks into the second; not there. He asks himself, "Has he sacrificed me?" His face clears as he looks into the third.

"Which is Evrémonde?" says a man behind him.

"That. At the back there."

The man cries, "Down, Evrémonde! To the Guillotine all aristocrats! Down, Evrémonde!"

"Hush, hush!" the spy entreats him, timidly.

"And why not, citizen?"

"He is going to pay the forfeit; it will be paid in five minutes more. Let him be at peace."

But the man continuing to exclaim, "Down, Evrémonde!" Evrémonde for a moment turns toward him. Evrémonde sees the spy, looks attentively at him, and goes his way.

The clocks are on the stroke of three. Seated, as in a garden of public diversion, are a number of women, busily knitting. On one of the foremost chairs, stands The Vengeance, looking about for her friend. "Thérèse!" she cried, "Who has seen her? Thérèse Defarge! Bad Fortune!" cries The Vengeance, stamping her foot in the chair, "and here are the tumbrils! Evrémonde will be dispatched in a wink, and she not here!"

The tumbrils begin to discharge their loads. Crash—A head is held up, and the knitting women who scarcely lifted their eyes to look at it a moment ago when it could think and speak, count One.

The second tumbril empties and moves on; the third comes up. Crash!—And the knitting women, never faltering or pausing in their work, count Two.

The supposed Evrémonde descends, and the seamstress is lifted out next after him. He has not relinquished her patient hand in getting out, but still holds it as he promised. He gently places her with her back to the crashing engine that constantly whirs up and falls, and she looks into his face and thanks him.

"But for you, dear stranger, I should not be so composed, for I am naturally a poor thing, faint of heart; nor should I have been able to raise my thoughts to Him who was put to death, that we might have hope and comfort here today. I think you were sent to me by heaven."

"Or you to me," said Sydney Carton. "Keep your eyes upon me, dear child, and mind no other object."

"I mind nothing while I hold your hand. I shall mind nothing when I let it go, if they are rapid."

"They will be rapid. Fear not!"

"You comfort me so much! I am so ignorant. Am I to kiss you now? Is the moment come?"

"Yes."

She kisses his lips; he kisses hers; they solemnly bless each other. The spare hand does not tremble as he releases it. She goes next before him—is gone; the knitting women count Twenty-two.

"I am the Resurrection and the Life, saith the Lord; he that believeth in me, though he were dead, yet shall he live; and whosoever liveth and believeth in me shall never die."

The murmuring of many voices, the upturning of many faces, the pressing on of many footsteps in the outskirts of the crowd, so that is swells forward in a mass, like one great heave of water, all flashes away. Twenty-three.

They said of him, about the city that night, that it was the peacefullest man's face ever beheld there. Many added that he looked sublime and prophetic.

One of the most remarkable sufferers by the same ax—a woman—had asked at the foot of the same scaffold, not long before, to be allowed to write down the thoughts that were inspiring her. If he had given an utterance to his, and they were prophetic, they would have been these:

"I see Barsad and Cly, Defarge, The Vengeance, the Juryman, the Judge, long ranks of the new oppressors who have risen on the destruction of the old, perishing by this retributive instrument. I see a beautiful city and a brilliant people rising from this abyss, and, in their struggles to be truly free, in their triumphs and defeats, through long long years to come, I see the evil of this time and of the previous time of which this is the natural birth, gradually making expiation for itself and wearing out.

"I see the lives for which I lay down my life, peaceful, useful, prosperous, and happy, in that England which I shall see no more. I see her with a child upon her bosom, who bears my name. I see her father, aged and bent, but otherwise restored, and faithful to all men in his healing office, and at peace. I see the good old man, so long their friend, in ten years' time enriching them with all he has, and passing tranquilly to his reward.

"I see that I hold a sanctuary in their hearts, and in the hearts of their descendants, generations hence. I see her, an old woman, weeping for me on the anniversary of this day. I see her and her husband, their course done, lying side by side in their last earthly bed, and I know that each was not more honored in the other's soul than I was in the souls of both.

"I see that child who bore my name, a man winning his way up in that path of life which once was mine. I see him winning it so well that my name is made illustrious by the light of his. I see the blots I threw upon it faded away. I see him, foremost of just judges and honored men, bringing a boy of my name, with a forehead that I know and golden hair, to this place—then fair to look upon, with not a trace of this day's disfigurement—and I hear him tell the child my story, with a tender and a faltering voice.

"It is a far, far better thing that I do than I have ever done; it is a far, far better rest that I go to than I have ever known."

Ronald Searle

Discussion
Chapter X

1. **(a)** Who were the twin brothers? **(b)** Which one have you met earlier in the novel? **(c)** What do they expect Doctor Manette to do?

2. **(a)** What comments do the brothers make that are especially cruel and insensitive? **(b)** Are the brothers equally cruel?

3. **(a)** What story does the raving woman's brother tell the doctor? **(b)** In what ways is the sad story of this family related to the major themes of the book: love and resurrection; injustice and revolution?

4. The wife of the Marquis mentions a sister of the dead girl. Which character in the novel might this sister be?

5. What particular incident led to Doctor Manette's long imprisonment?

6. What is the significance of the chapter's title?

Chapter XII

1. **(a)** What is Sydney Carton's object in going to the wine shop? **(b)** What are the Defarges discussing when Carton enters the wine shop? **(c)** Explain why Defarge and his wife have different opinions on what should happen to Darnay's family.

2. What effect does his unsuccessful attempt to help Charles have on Doctor Manette?

3. **(a)** What directions did Sydney Carton give Mr. Lorry? **(b)** What do you think Sydney Carton plans to do?

Chapter XIV

1. Why does Madame Defarge decide to visit Lucie on the day of the execution?

2. What do the events of this chapter reveal about Miss Pross's character?

3. What hope do we have that Jerry has undergone a change in his ways?

Chapter XV

1. **(a)** What is Barsad's reaction to the citizen who cries, "Down Evrémonde"? **(b)** What could have prompted his reaction?

2. **(a)** What do you think prompts Carton to sacrifice himself so that Darnay might live? **(b)** How does Carton's sacrifice enable him at last to find fulfillment? What sentences provide the best evidence?

Discussion
Book the Third

1. What conflicts are resolved in Book the Third? (Focus on those associated with Charles, Barsad, Doctor Manette, and Madame Defarge.)

2. Jerry, Miss Pross, the Wood Sawyer, and Barsad are all minor characters. In your opinion, which one of them most strongly influences events in Book the Third?

3. Do you find the conclusion satisfying? believable? Does it grow naturally from the events that preceded it? Explain your opinions.

4. Can you think of another conclusion that would have been more satisfying and still met the criteria for a well-constructed plot?

Vocabulary
Affixes

Many words that we use every day are derivatives—words formed by combining root words and affixes. A root is the main part of a word. The term *affix* is used to refer to both prefixes and suffixes. A *prefix* is added at the beginning of a root; a *suffix* is added at the end. Just by recognizing and knowing the meaning of prefixes and suffixes, you can expand your vocabulary.

A. Verbs that end in *-ate* can often be changed into nouns by dropping *e* and adding the suffix *-ion,* which means "in the state or condition of." For example, *perpetuate* means "to keep from being forgotten," and *perpetuation* means "in the state of being perpetuated." (The monument was built in perpetuation of his many contributions to medical science.)

On a separate piece of paper, complete the directions in **(1)** and **(2)** for each of the following words:

dissipate	obliterate
commiserate	emulate
supplicate	confiscate

(1) Change the verb into a noun by dropping the final *e* and adding the suffix *-ion.* Write the noun on your paper.

(2) Using your Glossary if necessary, use either the noun or the verb form of the word in a sentence that shows you understand the meaning of the word. Underline the word in each sentence you write, and be prepared to read your sentence aloud.

B. On your paper, write each word and underline the suffix. Then copy the sentence that follows that word, filling in the blank with the root.

1. *disparagement:* To avoid disparagement, a person should never ______ others.

2. *cogitation:* The writer wished to work in complete quiet so he could read and ______ undisturbed.

3. *redundancy:* Homer used so many words that his teacher suggested he remove the ones that were ______.

4. *compassionate:* The neighbors showed genuine ______ when they helped the family whose house had burned down.

5. *avaricious:* The wealthy Marquis never shared his money with the villagers, who grew to hate him for his ______.

Composition

You are Lucie Manette, and you decide to get a job. You become a travel reporter for the *London Family Guide.* This magazine publishes informal, first-person essays. Your first assignment is to write a brief (one- to two-page) description of eighteenth-century Paris. You are told to cover at least three of the following topics: hospitality, justice, social classes, wine shops, influential women, transportation, the condition of the poor.

In planning the article, first list the topics that you will cover. Then, find at least three details from the novel that describe each topic. (See *Assuming Another Voice,* page 669, in Composition Guide.)

Unit 8 Review: The Novel

Content Review

1. The plot of *A Tale of Two Cities* contains three strands: the Manettes, the Evrémondes, and the revolutionists. At what point in the novel do these strands become most critically entangled?

2. *A Tale of Two Cities* contains several mob scenes both in England and in France. **(a)** What does Dickens imply about mob behavior? **(b)** What scenes best illustrate this behavior?

3. No author can be completely objective about the characters and events he or she creates. **(a)** To what extent does Dickens "take sides" in this novel? **(b)** How would you describe his attitude toward revolution in general? **(c)** Does his attitude seem to undergo any significant change during the course of the book?

4. **(a)** Do you find Lucie Manette to be a believable character? **(b)** If she can be said to represent an ideal, what characteristics does Dickens suggest a woman should have? **(c)** In your opinion does Lucie or Sydney Carton contribute more to Dickens's theme of love and resurrection? Give reasons for your answer.

5. What are some of Dickens's most striking contrasts in this novel? Consider contrasts of character, setting, idea, and mood.

Concept Review: Interpretation of New Material

The following excerpt is from Charles Dickens's novel *Hard Times,* first published in 1854. In *Hard Times,* Dickens criticizes many of the institutions of the England of his day, including factories and schools. Read the excerpt and answer the questions that follow.

from Hard Times • *Charles Dickens*

Book the First—Sowing

CHAPTER I
THE ONE THING NEEDFUL

"Now, what I want is, Facts. Teach these boys and girls nothing but Facts. Facts alone are wanted in life. Plant nothing else, and root out everything else. This is the principle on which I bring up my own children, and this is the principle on which I bring up these children. Stick to Facts, sir!"

The scene was a plain, bare, monotonous vault of a schoolroom, and the speaker's square forefinger emphasized his observations by underscoring every sentence with a line on the schoolmaster's sleeve. The emphasis was helped by the speaker's square wall of a forehead, which had

From *Hard Times* by Charles Dickens, 1854.

his eyebrows for its base, while his eyes found commodious cellarage in two dark caves, overshadowed by the wall. The emphasis was helped by the speaker's mouth, which was wide, thin, and hard set. The emphasis was helped by the speaker's voice, which was inflexible, dry, and dictatorial. The emphasis was helped by the speaker's hair, which bristled on the skirts of his bald head, a plantation of firs to keep the wind from its shining surface, all covered with knobs, like the crust of a plum pie, as if the head had scarcely warehouse-room for the hard facts stored inside. The speaker's obstinate carriage, square coat, square legs, square shoulders—nay, his very neckcloth, trained to take him by the throat with an unaccommodating grasp, like a stubborn fact—all helped the emphasis.

"In this life, we want nothing but Facts, sir; nothing but Facts!"

The speaker, and the schoolmaster, and the third grown person present, all backed a little, and swept with their eyes the inclined plane of little vessels then and there arranged in order, ready to have gallons of facts poured into them until they were full to the brim. . . .

CHAPTER II
MURDERING THE INNOCENTS

Thomas Gradgrind, sir. A man of realities. A man of facts and calculations. A man who proceeds upon the principle that two and two are four, and nothing over, and who is not to be talked into allowing for anything over. With a rule and a pair of scales, and the multiplication table always in his pocket, sir, ready to weigh and measure any parcel of human nature, and tell you exactly what it comes to. It is a mere question of figures, a case of simple arithmetic.

In such terms Mr. Gradgrind always mentally introduced himself, whether to his private circle of acquaintance or to the public in general. In such terms, no doubt, substituting the words "boys and girls" for "sir," Thomas Gradgrind now presented Thomas Gradgrind to the little pitchers before him, who were to be filled so full of facts.

Indeed, he seemed a kind of cannon loaded to the muzzle with facts, and prepared to blow them clean out of the regions of childhood at one discharge.

"Girl number twenty," said Mr. Gradgrind, squarely pointing with his square forefinger, "I don't know that girl. Who is that girl?"

"Sissy Jupe, sir," explained number twenty, blushing, standing up, and curtsying.

"Sissy is not a name," said Mr. Gradgrind. "Don't call yourself Sissy. Call yourself Cecilia."

"It's father as calls me Sissy, sir," returned the young girl in a trembling voice.

"Then he has no business to do it," said Mr. Gradgrind. "Tell him he mustn't. Cecilia Jupe. What is your father?"

"He belongs to the horse-riding, if you please, sir."

Mr. Gradgrind frowned, and waved off the objectionable calling with his hand.

"You mustn't tell us about that here. Your father breaks horses, don't he?"

"If you please, sir, when they can get any to break, they do break horses in the ring, sir."

"You mustn't tell us about the ring here. Describe your father as a horsebreaker. He doctors sick horses, I dare say?"

"Oh, yes, sir."

"Very well, then. He is a veterinary surgeon, a farrier, and horsebreaker. Give me your definition of a horse."

(Sissy Jupe thrown into the greatest alarm by this demand.)

"Girl number twenty unable to define a horse!" said Mr. Gradgrind. "Girl number twenty possessed of no facts in reference to one of the commonest of animals! Some boy's definition of a horse. Bitzer, yours."

The square finger, moving here and there, lighted suddenly on Bitzer, perhaps because he chanced to sit in the same ray of sunlight which, darting in at one of the bare windows of the intensely whitewashed room, irradiated Sissy. The boys and girls sat on the face of the inclined plane in two compact bodies, divided up the center by a narrow interval; and Sissy, being at the corner of a row on the sunny side, came in for the beginning of a sunbeam, of which Bitzer, being at the corner of a row on the other side, caught the end. But, whereas the girl was so dark-eyed and dark-haired that she seemed to receive a deeper and more lustrous color from the sun, the boy was so light-eyed and light-haired that the same rays appeared to draw out of him what little color he ever possessed. His cold eyes would hardly have been eyes, but for the short ends of lashes which, by bringing them into immediate contrast with something paler than themselves, expressed their form. His short-cropped hair might have been a mere continuation of the sandy freckles on his forehead and face. His skin was so unwholesomely deficient in the natural tinge, that he looked as though, if he were cut, he would bleed white.

"Bitzer," said Thomas Gradgrind. "Your definition of a horse."

"Quadruped. Graminivorous. Forty teeth, namely twenty-four grinders, four eye-teeth, and twelve incisive. Sheds coat in the spring; in marshy countries, sheds hoofs too. Hoofs hard, but requiring to be shod with iron. Age known by marks in mouth." Thus (and much more) Bitzer.

"Now, girl number twenty," said Mr. Gradgrind, "you know what a horse is."

---

1. The second paragraph contains many examples of **(a)** repetition; **(b)** simile; **(c)** consonance; **(d)** allusion.

2. In this selection, children are compared to **(a)** cannons; **(b)** pitchers; **(c)** horses; **(d)** plum pies.

3. This comparison is an example of **(a)** simile; **(b)** metaphor; **(c)** allusion; **(d)** alliteration.

4. The "little pitchers" are to be filled with **(a)** water; **(b)** creativity; **(c)** facts; **(d)** ideas.

5. The title of Chapter II implies that Dickens sympathizes with **(a)** Gradgrind; **(b)** Bitzer; **(c)** the children; **(d)** horses.

6. Bitzer's definition of a horse is **(a)** factual; **(b)** imaginative; **(c)** both; **(d)** neither.

7. A farrier is most likely one who works with **(a)** children; **(b)** horses; **(c)** education; **(d)** Bitzer.

8. In his pocket, Gradgrind carries a **(a)** yoyo; **(b)** strap; **(c)** multiplication table; **(d)** dictionary.

9. Sissy's father works with horses in a circus. Gradgrind, upon learning this, **(a)** states his own fondness for horses; **(b)** says he loves going to the circus; **(c)** neither of these; **(d)** both of these.

10. In the remainder of *Hard Times,* Dickens develops a contrast between the life of the circus and the life of Gradgrind's classroom. In the rest of the novel, is Dickens most likely to **(a)** show the life of the circus to be more attractive; **(b)** show the life of the classroom to be more attractive; **(c)** describe conditions in French schools and circuses; **(d)** predict the defeat of British forces in India?

Composition Review

1. Assume that a classmate has said, "Lucie Manette is far too perfect to be a believable character, and Sydney Carton is a very foolish man to give up his life as he does."

In a paper directed to your classmates and teacher, tell whether you agree or disagree with the statement. Cite examples from the text to support your position.

2. One adult reader, upon finishing *A Tale of Two Cities,* quoted the old saying, "The more things change, the more they stay the same."

In a paper directed to this adult, tell whether you agree or disagree with his opinion. Cite evidence to support your own opinion. (You might begin your paper by explaining the meaning of the saying.)

Handbook of Literary Terms

TUTOR TWO TUTORS TO TOOT

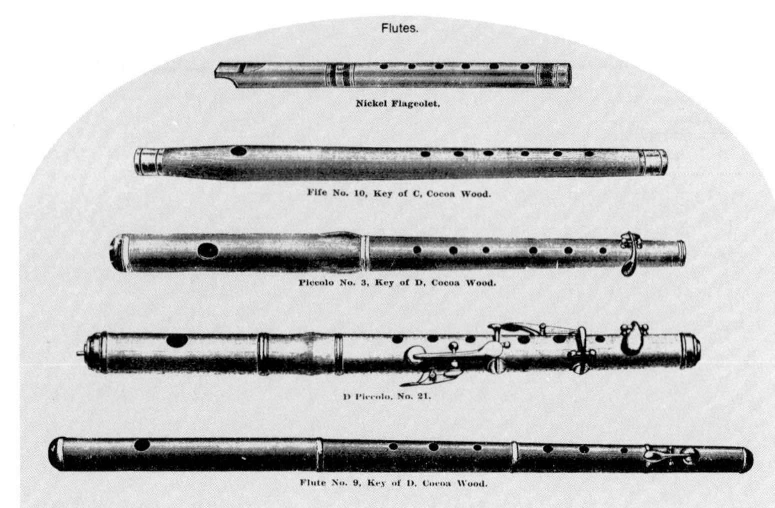

A tutor who tooted a flute
Tried to tutor two tutors to toot.
Said the two to the tutor,
"Is it harder to toot or
To tutor two tutors to toot?"

Anonymous

Tongue twisters are common to many languages. The fun of a twister is the repetition of initial consonant or vowel sounds: "As the roaring rocket rose, the restless roosters rollicked," or "Far and fast the falcon flew." When that repetition occurs on stressed syllables, the result is a pattern of sound called *alliteration.*

Alliteration is popular in our language (safe and sound, rough and ready, through thick or thin) because it gives pleasure in itself. But it is also used where possible to echo the sense and to provide emphasis. In the first five lines of his poem "Spring," Gerard Manley Hopkins uses alliteration extensively. Read the lines aloud carefully, listening for examples of alliteration.

Spring

Nothing is so beautiful as spring—
When weeds, in wheels, shoot long and lovely and lush;
Thrush's eggs look little low heavens, and thrush
Through the echoing timber does so rinse and wring
The ear, it strikes like lightnings to hear him sing;

1. In line 2, what examples of alliteration can you find? Alliteration invariably links certain words through the common sound. Why does Hopkins link the words *long, lovely,* and *lush?* Think of the sense of each of these three words—what each word means—and consider how the sound of the word echoes its sense.

2. In line 4, Hopkins creates alliteration with the words *rinse* and *wring*. Can you think of some ways in which these words are associated with the song of the thrush?

alliteration (ə lit′ə rā′ shən)

The repetition of initial and stressed sounds at the beginnings of words or in accented syllables. Alliteration is used to create melody, establish mood, call attention to certain words, and point up similarities and contrasts.

From *Poems of Gerard Manley Hopkins,* 4th ed., edited by W. H. Gardner and N. H. Mackenzie. New York: Oxford University Press, 1967.

Apply to **"Puritan Sonnet"** on page 154

allusion

Have you ever heard the expression "sour grapes"? This expression refers to a fable by Aesop in which a fox who could not reach a bunch of grapes said that they were probably sour anyway. So people said to have a sour grapes attitude condemn something because they know they cannot attain it. A reference to literature such as this one is called an *allusion*. Not confined to literature, allusions may refer to a character, thing, event, or situation—either fictional or actual. Allusions appear fairly often in daily speech. You may, for example, call someone a Romeo or attribute to someone the patience of Job without actually being aware that you are alluding, in one case, to dramatic literature and, in the other, to the Bible.

Allusions may draw on literature (Frankenstein's monster—a reference to Mary Shelley's novel *Frankenstein*), history (to meet one's Waterloo—a reference to Napoleon's decisive defeat in 1815), the Bible (to be a scapegoat—a reference to the goat mentioned in Leviticus who bore the sins of the Israelites), myth (to have an Achilles heel—a reference to the Greek hero's only vulnerable spot), or any aspect of ancient or modern society or culture (to call the mid-1950s the Sputnik era—a reference to the name of the satellite that the Soviet Union placed in orbit in 1957).

Allusions are a means of achieving conciseness or vividness. In *Romeo and Juliet,* for example, Romeo says of Rosaline: "She'll not be hit with Cupid's arrow. She hath Dian's wit." A reader who recognizes these mythological allusions will know that Romeo is bemoaning the fact that because Rosaline is as wise as Diana, the goddess of hunting, she will not fall in love.

Recognizing allusions adds to readers' enjoyment and understanding of works by enriching for them surface meanings. Someone with no knowledge of mythology might enjoy "Ithaca" (page 135), but the poem cannot be fully appreciated unless a reader recognizes that in Greek mythology Ithaca was the home of Ulysses, as well as the place where—after his many adventures—he hoped to spend his old age.

The following cartoon is humorous only to a reader familiar with the mythological King Neptune, Roman god of the waters, who is often pictured holding a three-pronged spear or trident to symbolize his mastery over the sea.

"He came with the pool."

allusion (ə lü′zhən)

A reference to a person, thing, event, situation, or aspect of culture, real or fictional, past or present. An allusion may draw from literature, myth, history, or the Bible.

Apply to **"Ithaca"** on page 135

assonance

Song

Morning opened
Like a rose,
And the snow on the roof
Rose-color took
Oh, how the street
Toward light did leap!
And the lamps went out.
Brightness fell down
From the steeple clock
To the row of shops
And rippled the bricks
Like the scales of a fish,
And all that day
Was a fairy tale
Told once in a while
To a good child.

Donald Justice

Although the final words in each pair of lines in "Song" do not rhyme, they share a common sound. What is the common sound in *opened/rose? out/down? street/leap?* What are the common sound pairs in the remaining lines of the poem? Are these sound pairs vowels or consonants?

Poets use sound patterns to achieve various effects—to please the ear, for example, or to stir an emotional response in the reader, or to lend a sense of unity to certain ideas within the poem. One of the easiest sound devices to detect is rhyme. Instead of using rhyme in his poem *(pose/rose; roof/hoof),* however, Justice chose word pairs with a common vowel sound followed by different consonant sounds *(opened/rose; roof/took)*. The use of words with identical vowel sounds followed by different consonant sounds is called *assonance (clock/shops)*.

Now read the first five lines in the poem "Song" aloud. Where else do you find the long *o* sound in *opened* and *rose* repeated? Justice has used assonance in words such as *snow, Rose-color,* and *Oh* to achieve various effects. For example, when you say the *o* sound, your mouth must open—just as morning light spreads or a rose unfolds. The word *Oh* in line 5 expresses wonder at this scene of color and beauty. The entire poem is an expression of the poet's awe. In this sense, the repeated *o* sound indicates the poet's emotion and is designed to stir an emotional response in the reader. In addition, the sound *o,* because it is a long vowel sound, cannot be said quickly; it is a slow sound that suggests the way the morning slowly unfolds in the poem. The use of assonance, then, is intended to appeal not only to emotions but also to the ear. Still another effect of assonance in this poem is to connect or unify words and ideas (morning is compared to an *o*pening r*o*se; sunshine makes the br*i*cks r*i*pple like f*i*sh; and the entire d*a*y is a fairy t*a*le).

Find examples of assonance in the following lines. Note whether assonance occurs in stressed or unstressed words or syllables.

I sift the snow on the mountains below
And their great pines groan aghast. . . .

Shelley, "The Cloud"

On either side the river lie
Long fields of barley and of rye, . . .

Tennyson, "The Lady of Shalott"

Tiger! Tiger! burning bright . . .

Blake, "The Tiger"

assonance (as′n əns)

Repetition of vowel sounds followed by different consonant sounds in stressed words or syllables.

Apply to **"The Bean Eaters"** on page 147

blank verse

I know not how to tell thee who I am.
My name, dear saint, is hateful to myself,
Because it is an enemy to thee;
Had I it written, I would tear the word.

1. Do the preceding lines, spoken by Romeo, rhyme?

2. Read these lines aloud. What words would you stress in the first line?

3. The rhythm of the first line can be indicated as follows. (Stress is indicated by the symbol ´, lack of stress by the symbol ˘.)

Ĭ knów nŏt hów tŏ téll thĕe whó Ĭ ám.

Do the other lines follow this same pattern of rhythm?

Unrhymed lines that move along in this manner—ta DUM ta DUM ta DUM ta DUM ta DUM—are called *blank verse*. The rhythms of blank verse echo the beat often found in our ordinary conversation (I'd LIKE to TELL you WHY you've MADE me MAD/but I'M aFRAID you'd NEVer UNderSTAND), and for this reason poets such as Shakespeare have used it in their works.

Read the following examples aloud to determine whether or not they are written in blank verse. (At first, you may wish to overemphasize the stressed words or syllables in determining rhythm.) Remember that a blank-verse line contains five beats, each one preceded by an unaccented word or syllable.

And, with this basket on his arm, the lad
Went up to London, found a master there,
Who, out of many, chose the trusty boy
To go and overlook his merchandise
Beyond the seas; where he grew wondrous
rich, . . .

Wordsworth, "Michael"

Of each tree in the garden we may eat,
But of the fruit of this fair tree amidst
The garden, God hath said, "Ye shall not eat
Thereof, nor shall ye touch it, lest ye die."

Milton, *Paradise Lost*

Words are like leaves; and where they most
abound,
Much fruit of sense beneath is rarely found.

Pope, *Essay on Criticism*

"Father! father! where are you going?
O do not walk so fast.
Speak father, speak to your little boy,
Or else I shall be lost."

Blake, "The Little Boy Lost"

The first two examples, by Wordsworth and Milton, are written in blank verse. The last two examples are not written in blank verse—the Pope because it rhymes and the Blake because it does not follow a blank-verse rhythm.

A skillful poet can achieve a great variety of dramatic effects and prevent monotonous rhythm by making some adjustments in blank-verse lines. While, for example, blank verse is the predominant rhythm in Shakespeare's dramas, many lines depart from the strict pattern of ten syllables with five accents. If you examine the following lines, spoken by Romeo, you will notice that they are written in blank verse, although the rhythm in some lines departs from a strict blank-verse pattern.

She speaks, yet she says nothing. What of that?
Her eye discourses; I will answer it.
I am too bold, 'tis not to me she speaks:
Two of the fairest stars in all the heaven,
Having some business, do entreat her eyes
To twinkle in their spheres till they return.

Lines 4 and 5 make a slight departure from the blank-verse pattern; their rhythm can be indicated thus:

Twó ŏf thĕ faírĕst stárs ĭn áll thĕ héavĕn,
Háving sŏme búsinĕss, dó ĕntréat hĕr éyes

Although blank verse was used more frequently by poets of the sixteenth and seventeenth centuries, it still appears in some contemporary poems. The following poem, by a twentieth-century Australian writer, is about an itinerant worker whose belongings are carried in a swag, or bundle. Note how Cato has varied the blank-verse pattern in some of the lines.

The Dead Swagman

His rusted billy left beside the tree;
Under a root, most carefully tucked away,
His steel-rimmed glasses folded in their case
Of mildewed purple velvet; there he lies
In the sunny afternoon and takes his ease,
Curled like a possum within the hollow trunk.

He came one winter evening when the tree
Hunched its broad back against the rain, and made
His camp, and slept, and did not wake again.
Now white ants make a home within his skull:
His old friend Fire has walked across the hill
And blackened the old tree and the old man
And buried him half in ashes, where he lay.

It might be called a lonely death. The tree
Had its own alien life beneath the sun,
Yet both belong to the Bush, and now are one:
The roots and bones lie close among the soil,
And he ascends in leaves towards the sky.

Nancy Cato

blank verse

Unrhymed lines, each with a pattern of five unstressed words or syllables alternating with five stressed ones. The beat of a blank-verse line can be indicated as follows: ta DUM ta DUM ta DUM ta DUM ta DUM. Poets who write in blank verse may vary the beat within this basic structure.

Apply to **"The Death of the Hired Man"** on page 167

characterization

Our interest in reading stories is primarily an interest in finding out about people, about what happens to them and why they act as they do. Sometimes a character in a story helps us understand ourselves, why we did or did not act the same way in a similar situation. More often, the characters created by writers reveal to us the variety of human responses to the hopes, cares, and confusions common to us all.

To characterize the people in a story, to reveal how and why they act as they do, an author may use a number of methods. The following scene from Guy de Maupassant's story "The Necklace" illustrates the principal methods of characterization.

She had no dresses, no jewels, nothing; and she loved only that, she felt made for that. She was filled with a desire to please, to be envied, to be bewitching and sought after. She had a rich friend, a former schoolmate at the convent, whom she no longer wished to visit because she suffered so much when she came home. For whole days at a time she wept without ceasing in bitterness and hopeless misery.

Now, one evening her husband came home with a triumphant air, holding in his hand a large envelope.

"There," said he, "there is something for you."

She quickly tore open the paper and drew out a printed card, bearing these words:

"The Minister of Public Instruction and Mme. Georges Rampouneau request the honor of M. and Mme. Loisel's company at the palace of the Ministry, Monday evening, January 18th."

Instead of being overcome with delight, as her husband expected, she threw the invitation on the table with disdain, murmuring:

"What do you wish me to do with that?"

"Why, my dear, I thought you would be pleased. You never go out, and it is such a fine opportunity, this! I had awful trouble getting it. Everyone wants to go; it is very select, and they are not giving many invitations to clerks. You will see the whole official world."

She looked at him with irritation, and said, impatiently:

"What do you wish me to put on my back if I go?"

He had not thought of that. He stammered:

"Why, the dress you go to the theatre in. It seems all right to me."

He stopped, stupefied, distracted, on seeing that his wife was crying. Two great tears descended slowly from the corners of her eyes toward the corners of her mouth. He stuttered:

"What's the matter? What's the matter?"

By a violent effort she subdued her feelings and replied in a calm voice, as she wiped her wet cheeks.

"Nothing. Only I have no dress and consequently I cannot go to this ball. Give your invitation to some friend whose wife is better equipped than I."

He was in despair. He replied:

"Let us see, Mathilde. How much would it cost, a suitable dress, which you could wear again on future occasions, something very simple?"

She reflected for some seconds, computing the cost, and also wondering what sum she could ask without bringing down upon herself an immediate refusal and an astonished exclamation from the economical clerk.

At last she answered hesitatingly:

"I don't know exactly, but it seems to me that with four hundred francs I could manage."

He turned a trifle pale, for he had been saving just that sum to buy a gun and treat himself to a little hunting the following summer, in the country near Nanterre, with a few friends who went there to shoot larks of a Sunday.

However, he said:

"Well, I think I can give you four hundred francs. But see that you have a pretty dress."

The day of the ball drew near, and Madame Loisel seemed sad, unhappy, anxious. Her dress was ready, however. Her husband said to her one evening:

"What is the matter? Come, you've been looking queer these last three days."

And she replied:

"It worries me that I have no jewels, not a single stone, nothing to put on. I shall look wretched enough. I would almost rather not go to the party."

He answered:

"You might wear natural flowers. They are very fashionable this season. For ten francs you can get two or three magnificent roses."

She was not convinced.

"No; there is nothing more humiliating than to look poor among women who are rich."

But her husband cried:

"How stupid of you! Go and find your friend Madame Forestier and ask her to lend you some jewels. You are intimate enough with her for that."

She uttered a cry of joy.

"Of course. I had not thought of that."

The next day she went to her friend's house and told her distress. Madame Forestier went to her handsome wardrobe, took out a large casket, brought it back, opened it, and said to Madame Loisel:

"Choose, my dear."

She saw first of all some bracelets, then a Venetian cross, gold and precious stones of wonderful workmanship. She tried on the ornaments before the glass, hesitated, could not make up her mind to part with them, to give them back. She kept asking:

"Have you nothing else?"

"Why, yes. See, I do not know what will please you."

All at once she discovered, in a black satin box, a splendid diamond necklace, and her heart began to beat with immoderate desire. Her hands trembled as she took it. She fastened it around her throat, over her high-necked dress, and stood lost in ectasy as she looked at herself.

"Would you lend me that,—only that?"

"Why, yes certainly."

She sprang upon the neck of her friend, embraced her rapturously, then fled with her treasure.

1. What was it that Madame Loisel "loved only"? What did she feel made for?

2. Why did she no longer wish to visit her rich friend?

3. As the day of the ball drew near, was Madame Loisel happy? frightened? sad and anxious?

The reader learns of Madame Loisel's longings, her vanity, her acute discontent, her lack of pleasure in her possessions, directly from the author. *An author may directly describe characters or explain their actions.*

4. What did Madame Loisel do with the invitation after she had read it?

5. How did she react to her husband's suggestion that she wear her theater dress to the ball?

6. What does her hesitation while trying on the jewelry tell us about her?

Madame Loisel's actions complement her personality as directly described by the author. She is disdainful of what she has, with no thought for her husband. *An author may reveal characters through their actions.*

7. Why was Madame Loisel not delighted with the invitation to the ball?

8. What reasons did she give for rejecting her husband's suggestion that she wear flowers on her dress?

What Madame Loisel says makes evident her vanity, her concern for her appearance, her acute sense of what is appropriate. *An author may reveal characters through their speech.*

9. How did Madame Loisel arrive at the figure of four hundred francs for the dress?

Through her reflecting, the reader sees that Madame Loisel is thinking not only of the cost of the dress but also of how much she can get out of her husband. *An author may reveal characters through their thoughts.*

10. What effect did Monsieur Loisel hope the invitation would have on his wife?

11. What made him despair?

12. What had he intended to do with the four hundred francs?

The reactions of Monsieur Loisel to his wife's behavior reinforce the reader's impression that she is difficult to please and thinks only of herself. Although his reasons for wanting the four hundred francs may be as selfish as hers, it is clear that Madame Loisel expects her husband to make the sacrifices necessary for domestic harmony. *An author may reveal characters through the reactions of other characters.*

characterization

The methods an author uses to develop the qualities and personalities of persons in a story. An author may describe characters directly or reveal them through their actions, speech, and thoughts, as well as through the reactions of others.

Apply to **"Split Cherry Tree"** on page 41

connotation / denotation

Horse: "Quadruped. Graminivorous. Forty teeth, namely, twenty-four grinders, four eye-teeth, and twelve incisive. Sheds coat in the spring; in marshy countries, sheds hoofs, too. Hoofs hard, but requiring to be shod with iron. Age known by marks in mouth."

Dickens, *Hard Times*

The preceding description of a horse is provided by Bitzer, a student of Thomas Gradgrind, a schoolmaster concerned only with *facts*. This description resembles the factual definition of the word *horse* that can be found in most dictionaries. Asked to describe a horse, however, few people would give so factual or literal a description. A small child, for example, might describe a horse as a wooden toy that rocks back and forth, or as a soft, stuffed animal jumbled in a box with other toys. A jockey, on the other hand, would probably think of a horse in terms of a "mount" or "winner," while a farmer might associate a horse with a plow or a bag of oats. To an older person, *horse* might conjure up memories of the buggies or carriages of a bygone era. While all of these associations are generally associated with Gradgrind's quadruped, each one is colored by a person's own experience. A writer draws upon these various associations in choosing words that have both dictionary meanings, or *denotations,* and a wealth of suggested emotional implications, or *connotations,* that would not be found in a literal dictionary definition.

By selecting words according to both their literal meanings and their connotative, or nonliteral, meanings, writers can make them serve double duty. Suppose a poet were to use a word such as *steed* or *charger* rather than *horse*. What connotations do the words *steed* or *charger* have that *horse* does not? What associations do you have with each of the following: *nag, bronco, prancer, thoroughbred?* Anyone familiar with Greek mythology would have special associations with the word *Pegasus,* the

winged horse of Greek fable, and any writer who mentioned Pegasus would build upon these connotations. Although a poet chooses single words specifically for their connotations, these words must appear with other words in a particular arrangement. The word *horse*—or *dove,* or *home,* or *telephone,* or *cake*—appears in a specific surrounding called *context.* It is not only words considered singly, but the company they keep, which establish connotations.

What connotations does the term "wild West" have for you? To what degree are your associations based on "moving-picture dreams"? Note how Boylan in the following poem uses words, images, and historical references to communicate special meanings associated with the wild West.

Wild West

Now let us speak of cowboys who on swift
White horses over blue-black deserts sped,
Their pistols blazing and their proud blood shed
In paint-flecked shanties on the haunted cliffs
Or in the bars of ghost towns. Let us tell
The legends of fierce heroes, motherless,
Not Indians, not Easterners, whose quests
And daring deeds inscribed their names in hell.
Bravely they shot it out, did Wyatt Earp,
Billy the Kid, Bill Hickok, Jesse James.
Now what remains but moving-picture dreams
Of all that fury and fast villainy?
Lone cactuses where bullets split and ripped
The courage of the eyelid from the eye?
A rusting stirrup and a rowel thrust
Up from the calcifying sun-baked dust
Where some unknown avenger fell to sleep?
A wind-blown piece of buckskin that looked grand
When it was stretched upon the living hip
Of him who lies now six feet under ground?
Cowboys were not immortal. All they did,
Guzzling and gunning, ended when they died.

Robert G. Boylan

1. In choosing to write about the wild West, Boylan has selected a subject that has numerous associations for most readers. He has strengthened these associations by conjuring up images with phrases such as the following: "paint-flecked shanties," "bars of ghost towns," "Lone cactuses," "sun-baked dust," "Guzzling and gunning." What aspect of the wild West does each of the preceding phrases suggest?

2. What connotations about the wild West are reinforced by the mentioning of historical figures?

3. The "swift white horses" mentioned in the first two lines give way in line 15 to a "rusting stirrup." What does this change imply about the wild West? In what way did horses contribute to the "fury and fast villainy" of the wild West?

connotation/denotation

The associations surrounding a word that are not part of its literal dictionary meaning or denotation. A cake, according to its denotation, is a baked mixture consisting of flour, sugar, and eggs; according to its connotation, however, a cake may suggest a birthday, a holiday, or a wedding.

"Wild West" by Robert G. Boylan, *Saturday Review,* September 21, 1957. Reprinted by permission of the author.

Apply to **"I Have A Dream"** on page 436

consonance

around/head
crumb/home
seam/swim

A Bird

A Bird came down the Walk—
He did not know I saw—
He bit an angleworm in halves
And ate the fellow, raw,

And then he drank a Dew
From a convenient Grass—
And then hopped sidewise to the Wall
To let a Beetle pass—

He glanced with rapid eyes
That hurried all around—
They looked like frightened Beads, I thought—
He stirred his Velvet Head

Like one in danger, Cautious,
I offered him a Crumb
And he unrolled his feathers
And rowed him softer home—

Than Oars divide the Ocean,
Too silver for a seam—
Or Butterflies, off Banks of Noon
Leap, plashless as they swim.

Emily Dickinson

The second and fourth lines in the first two stanzas end with rhyming words. In stanzas 3, 4, and 5, however, there are no rhyming combinations. In these stanzas, although the word pairs *(around/Head, Crumb/home, seam/swim)* do not rhyme, they share a common sound. In all three pairs, is this common sound at the beginning, middle, or end? Are the vowel sounds that precede each similar consonant sound alike or different?

The use of words with identical consonant sounds preceded by different vowel sounds is called *consonance.* Consonance may occur within a line (I me*t* a ca*t* with fee*t* of whi*t*e) as well as at the end of lines. Dickinson is one of many poets who recognized that consonance can serve to lend variety to a rhyme pattern. Skillful use of consonance should not be confused with the amateur poet's inability to find exact rhymes.

consonance (kon′sə nəns)

The repetition of identical consonant sounds that are preceded by different vowel sounds.

Apply to "**The Bean Eaters**" on page 147

figurative language

Big George by Virgil Partch. © Field Enterprises, Inc., 1977. Courtesy of Field Newspaper Syndicate.

"It doesn't pay to take the law in your own hands."

Chances are, you have heard of people who attempt to "take the law in their own hands." How would you interpret this expression? In what way does the cartoonist's interpretation differ from yours?

The cartoon derives its humor from the fact that it presents a very literal interpretation. Our language is full of expressions that should not be taken literally. Consider, for example, how a literal-minded person who has no knowledge of baseball would interpret the newspaper headlines "Red Sox Sweep a Doubleheader" and "Speedster Safe at Home on a Suicide Squeeze." In daily conversation we use phrases such as "shake a leg," "bring down the house," "bark up the wrong tree," or "I've lost my head" without considering the humor or misunderstanding that could result if these expressions were taken literally.

Poets, more than other people, use words apart from their literal meanings to achieve conciseness, clarity, power, and vividness. Such nonliteral use of words is called *figurative language*. Note how Eve Merriam uses figurative language in the poem that follows.

Ways of Composing

typewriter:
a mouthful of teeth chattering
afraid to be quiet

a pencil can lie down and dream
dark and silver silences

Eve Merriam

1. What two things is Merriam comparing?

2. To which sense(s) other than sight does she appeal in this comparison?

3. In what way does the typewriter resemble a mouthful of teeth?

4. In what way does the pencil appear to be human?

5. A literal-minded person would claim that silence has no color. Why do you think the poet has chosen the words "dark and silver" to describe the way in which a pencil is used to compose?

6. What, according to the poet, is the difference between composing by typewriter and by pencil?

7. Explain how Merriam has used words and sounds to stress the different ways of composing (for instance, the sound of the line "a mouthful of teeth chattering" versus the last two lines with their repeated *d* and *s* sounds).

8. Imagine that instead of her poem, Merriam had chosen to say, "When I compose at the typewriter, it is a quick, noisy process, while with a pencil it is a slower, quieter, more thoughtful attempt." Explain the effect of her use of figurative language when compared to this literal rephrasing of the poem.

Although figurative language is sometimes considered the special tool of poets, prose writers also use it to enhance their works. Flannery O'Connor begins her short story "The Displaced Person" with the following paragraph.

> The peacock was following Mrs. Shortley up the road to the hill where she meant to stand. Moving one behind the other, they looked like a complete procession. Her arms were folded and as she mounted the prominence, she might have been the giant wife of the countryside, come out at some sign of danger to see what the trouble was. She stood on two tremendous legs, with the grand self-confidence of a mountain, and rose, up narrowing bulges of granite, to two icy blue points of light that pierced forward, surveying everything. She ignored the white afternoon sun which was creeping behind a ragged wall of cloud as if it pretended to be an intruder and cast her gaze down the red clay road that turned off from the highway.

1. What would you gather about a party of two who seemed to constitute "a complete procession"? Is it their size, their appearance, their assurance, their flamboyance, what?

2. What kind of a woman would be described as "the giant wife of the countryside, come out at some sign of danger to see what the trouble was"?

3. What similarities does Mrs. Shortley bear to a mountain?

4. In what ways is the sun described as if it were human?

While *figurative language* is a general term for imaginative, nonliteral language, the specific devices for achieving figurative language are called *figures of speech*. Some of the most common figures of speech are metaphor, simile, personification, and hyperbole. Discussions can be found under separate entries for these words in this Handbook.

Cite at least two figures of speech in the following poem and explain how they contribute to a unique portrayal of horses.

The Horses

It has turned to snow in the night.
The horses have put on
their long fur stockings
and they are wearing
fur capes with high necks
out of which the device
of their ears makes four statues.
Their tails have caught flecks
of snow and hang down
loose as bedsheets.
They stand nose to nose
in the blue light that coats
the field before sunup
and rub dry their old kisses.

Maxine Kumin

figurative language

Language expanded beyond its usual literal meaning to achieve emphasis or to express a fitting relationship between things essentially unlike. A figurative expression usually contains a stated or implied comparison. Among the more common figures of speech are simile, metaphor, personification, and hyperbole. An effective figure of speech is brief and forceful, surprising but appropriate.

Apply to **"Miss Rosie"** on page 146

hyperbole

"I'm so hungry, I could eat a bear!"

When people say they are so hungry they could eat a bear, one can assume they are exaggerating in order to make a point. Likewise, people who have "cried their eyes out" or "given their hearts away" (medical science notwithstanding) undoubtedly still possess these organs. The use of exaggeration for effect is called *hyperbole*. In *Romeo and Juliet,* Juliet tells her departing lover, "in a minute there are many days." She might simply have said, "I'll miss you when you're gone." What does the use of hyperbole add to her statement? Romeo says of Juliet, "Two of the fairest stars in all the heaven,/Having some business, do entreat her eyes/To twinkle in their spheres till they return." Instead, Romeo might have said of Juliet, "She is fair and bright-eyed." What does the use of hyperbole add to this literal statement? An author may use hyperbole to emphasize emotion, such as Shakespeare does in the two preceding quotations. Hyperbole also may be used to achieve other effects, among them satire, humor, and sentimentality. What effect does hyperbole have in the following poem?

Two-Volume Novel

The sun's gone dim, and
  The moon's turned black;
For I loved him, and
  He didn't love back.

Dorothy Parker

hyperbole (hī pėr′bə lē)

The use of exaggeration for effect.

Apply to **"The Funeral"** on page 148

imagery

The world in all its variety comes to you through your five senses. If you are sitting in your bedroom at this moment, you might *see* a bed, a chest of drawers, perhaps a desk, some posters on a wall, a lamp; you might *hear* a radio, voices elsewhere in the house, cars, a dog barking; you *feel* the pressure of one leg against the other, a pencil or a book in your hand, even the subtle and almost unconscious feel of the fit of your shoes or the belt around your waist; you might *smell* the odor of a meal being cooked, freshly washed clothes and (if you have the windows open) the scent of autumn leaves or spring flowers; and you *taste* the candy bar you shouldn't be nibbling or the milk you've been sipping. It is through your senses that you discover your world.

A writer who presents what can be seen, heard, touched, smelled, or tasted, as well as what can be felt inside (for instance, hunger, pain, joy) creates images—collectively *imagery*. The writer of imaginative literature attempts to communicate experience—to make us hear, feel, see—rather than to dispassionately impart facts. To achieve this aim, to make it possible for the reader to participate in the experience being communicated, a writer appeals to the senses, directly through the sounds and rhythms of the words used and indirectly through the *images* presented to the reader.

In the cartoon that follows, which of the senses is the man at the typewriter stressing? Why might he be doing this?

Writers of both poetry and prose rely on images to re-create experience in such a way that readers can share that experience. In the following passage, an old woman lies ill, waiting for an ambulance to take her to the hospital.

"The face of the pear-shaped man reminded me of the mashed turnips that Aunt Mildred used to serve alongside the Thanksgiving turkey. As he got out of the strawberry-hued car, his immense fists looked like two slabs of slightly gnawed ham. He waddled over to the counter and snarled at me under his lasagna-laden breath, 'Something, my little bonbon, is fishy in Denmark.' Slowly, I lowered my grilled cheese sandwich . . ."

It was such a relief to drift, finally. Why had she spent so long learning how? The traffic sounds—horns and bells and rags of music—flowed around the voices in her room. She kept mislaying her place in time, but it made no difference; all she remembered was equally pleasant. She remembered the feel of wind on summer nights—how it billows through the house and wafts the curtains and smells of tar and roses. How a sleeping baby weighs so heavily on your shoulder, like ripe fruit. What privacy it is to walk in the rain beneath the drip and crackle of your own umbrella. She remembered a country auction she'd attended forty years ago, where they'd offered up an antique brass bed complete with all its bedclothes—sheets and blankets, pillow in a linen case embroidered with forget-me-nots. Two men wheeled it onto the platform, and its ruffled coverlet stirred like a young girl's petticoats. Behind her eyelids, Pearl Tull climbed in and laid her head on the pillow and was borne away to the beach, where three small children ran toward her, laughing, across the sunlit sand.

Anne Tyler,
Dinner at the Homesick Restaurant

1. What images of sight does the author present? Are these images general or specific? (Does she, for example, simply mention a bed or does she add words that help you to visualize that bed?)

2. What images of sound does she mention?

3. Which of the five senses are not referred to in this short passage?

4. What images reinforce the idea of drifting?

imagery

The representation in language of sense experience: what can be seen, heard, touched, tasted, smelled, as well as what can be felt internally. Images appeal to the senses of the reader, help re-create the experience being communicated, and suggest the emotional response appropriate to the experience.

Apply to "**Warning**" on page 139

inference

Read the following excerpt from "The Adventure of the Solitary Cyclist" by Sir Arthur Conan Doyle.

. . . With a resigned air and a somewhat weary smile, Holmes begged the beautiful intruder to take a seat, and to inform us what it was that was troubling her.

"At least it cannot be your health," said he, as his keen eyes darted over her; "so ardent a bicyclist must be full of energy."

She glanced down in surprise at her own feet, and I observed the slight roughening of the side of the sole caused by the friction of the edge of the pedal.

"Yes, I bicycle a good deal, Mr. Holmes. . . ."

My friend took the lady's ungloved hand, and examined it with as close an attention and as little sentiment as a scientist would show to a specimen.

"You will excuse me, I am sure. It is my business," said he, as he dropped it. "I nearly fell into the error of supposing you were typewriting. Of course, it is obvious that it is music. You observe the spatulate finger-ends, Watson, which is common to both professions? There is a spirituality about the face, however"—she gently turned it towards the light—"which the typewriter does not generate. This lady is a musician."

Arthur Conan Doyle, "The Adventure of the Solitary Cyclist" in *The Return of Sherlock Holmes.* New York: Schocken Books, 1975, pp. 48–49.

"Yes, Mr. Holmes, I teach music."

"In the country, I presume, from your complexion."

"Yes, sir, near Farnham, on the borders of Surrey."

1. How does Sherlock Holmes come to the conclusion that the woman is an ardent bicyclist?

2. What do the woman's finger-ends tell Holmes? Why does he decide she is not a typist?

3. How does he know that she lives in the country rather than the city?

From a few hints and bits of evidence—a slight roughening in a telltale place on the woman's shoes, wide fingertips, a "spiritual" face, and a healthy complexion—Sherlock Holmes determines a good deal about the woman before him. He illustrates the process of making *inferences,* drawing conclusions from limited information.

Like Holmes, the reader of fiction must make inferences about the personalities of characters and the meaning of happenings, for often the author presents characters and events directly without telling the reader about them, without explaining what kind of people the characters are or what the events illustrate. Instead, an author relies on the reader's ability to make reasonable inferences from what has been presented.

inference

A reasonable conclusion about a character or an event drawn from the limited information presented by the author.

Apply to **"The Speckled Band"** on page 332

irony

Verbal Irony

You have probably heard the expression "Thanks a lot" used sarcastically, spoken in a way to mean, "Thanks—for nothing." You might come inside from a blizzard and say to a friend, "Nice day, huh?" or call a very tall pal "Shorty." In each case you are saying one thing while meaning another, often emphasizing that meaning by your tone of voice or stress on certain words. The use of words that imply the opposite of what they literally mean is called *verbal irony.*

Irony of Situation

An aviator was sent on a mission to a distant part of the globe. When he returned to his base, he noticed it was strangely quiet. Everything was in perfect order, but there wasn't a sign of life in the place. He wandered through town in growing astonishment. Human beings and animals simply had vanished from the scene.

He tore back to the airport, filled his plane with high octane gas, and flew terrified, to New York, London, Moscow, Shanghai. While he had been on his mission, every living creature apparently had disappeared. He was the only man alive in the world! He weighed the situation carefully and found it intolerable. Suicide seemed the only solution. He swallowed a vial of deadly poison and calmly waited for it to take effect. Just as the drug reached his brain, and the room started swimming before his eyes, he heard a familiar sound.

It was the telephone ringing.

Bennett Cerf

1. What does the final sentence indicate? What do you think went through the aviator's mind when he heard the telephone ringing?

2. Is there anything he can do about this unexpected event?

This little story derives its impact from the fact that the outcome contrasts with what is ex-

Penn's Treaty by Edward Hicks
Thomas Gilcrease Institute, Tulsa, Oklahoma

pected to happen. Such a reversal of events is called *irony of situation.*

Dramatic Irony

Still another kind of irony occurs in fiction or drama when the reader or spectator knows more about the true state of affairs than the characters do. In *Romeo and Juliet,* for example, only the Nurse, Friar Laurence, and we as readers know the secret of Romeo and Juliet's marriage.

In all irony, there is the element of contrast—between what is said and what is meant (verbal), between what is expected or intended and what actually occurs (situation), or between what the reader or spectator knows and what the characters know (dramatic). Use of irony extends the meaning in a literary work through investing words and events with a double significance.

All three kinds of irony occur in *Romeo and Juliet.* Mercutio, fighting in support of Romeo, is slain under the arm of Romeo while the latter is interceding to establish peace—an example of irony of situation. In Act Three, Scene 5, there are many examples of verbal irony in Juliet's conversation with Lady Capulet. Dramatic irony occurs at the end of the play when Romeo, believing Juliet to be dead, kills himself, while the reader knows she is merely in a kind of coma.

Read the following poem and decide whether it contains verbal irony, irony of situation, dramatic irony, or all of these. Discuss the way in which the title contributes to the irony.

Immigrants

"These foreigners with strange and avid faces
Crowding our shores, marring our pleasant
places,
They must be curbed. . . ." So mused King
Powhatan,[1]
Hundred per cent, red-blood American.

Nancy Byrd Turner

1. ***King Powhatan*** (pou′ə tan′), (1550?–1618), Indian ruler in what is now Virginia during the time the early British colonists attempted to settle there.

irony

In general, a contrast between what appears to be and what really is. Verbal irony occurs when the surface meaning of what one says or writes is the opposite of the intended meaning. Irony of situation exists when what is expected or intended contrasts with what occurs. Dramatic irony occurs in fiction or drama when the reader or spectator knows more about the true state of affairs than the characters do.

Apply to **"My Mother, Who Came from China . . ."** on page 157

metaphor

The Skaters

Black swallows swooping or gliding
In a flurry of entangled loops and curves;
The skaters skim over the frozen river.
And the grinding click of their skates as
they impinge upon the surface,
Is like the brushing together of thin
wing-tips of silver.

John Gould Fletcher

1. Who are the "black swallows"?

2. What different movements of the skaters are described by "swooping or gliding"?

3. In what way are the movements of the skaters and those of swallows alike? (Note that the comparison is not only visual.)

Fletcher has compared the silhouettes of a group of graceful skaters to a flock of black swallows. This or any similar implied comparison between two things essentially unlike is called a *metaphor*. Metaphor—saying one thing in terms of another—is a basic element in poetry. But metaphor is not confined to poetry: it occurs even in daily conversation. For example, you may refer to a studious classmate as a *bookworm* or call someone with an exceptional mathematical memory a *computer*. Someone who has discovered a small part of a large problem may say, "I've uncovered the tip of the iceberg," and someone who is speechless may be called "tongue-tied." In all these metaphors there is an appropriateness between things compared (though the appropriateness may have been dulled in time through overuse of the metaphors). For instance, an iceberg, like a large problem, can be disastrous, especially when both are submerged and difficult to detect.

Like any figurative language, metaphor appeals to our imagination by making ideas more vivid. Through comparison with something else, it highlights for us particular aspects of a thing. Finally, metaphor, like figurative language in general, appeals to our emotions and senses. When the title character in the poem "Miss Rosie" (page 146) is referred to as a "wet brown bag of a woman" we see her as a destroyed, wrinkled, dark old woman. A metaphor should not be evaluated in isolation but in light of its contribution to the total mood and tone of the poem. The comparison between Miss Rosie and a wet brown bag is especially effective, since the poet has stated earlier that Rosie sits "wrapped up like garbage" and surrounded by the smell of kitchen scraps.

From the Japanese

The summer night
is a dark blue hammock
slung between the white pillars of day.

I lie there
cooling myself
with the straw-colored
flat round fan
of the full moon.

Eve Merriam

1. What associations does the word *hammock* have that make it a suitable metaphor for night? Why do you suppose Merriam chose to compare the summer night to a dark blue hammock rather than a white feather bed?

2. To what is the moon compared in the second stanza? What is the similarity in shape and color between these objects?

3. Lying in the summer night/hammock, cooling oneself with the moon/fan. What mood does this setting evoke?

Occasionally, an entire poem may rely on a single, prolonged comparison.

---

mood

Central Park Tourney

Mildred Weston

Cars
In the Park
With long spear lights
Ride at each other
Like armored knights;
Rush,
Miss the mark,
Pierce the dark,
Dash by!
Another two
Try.

Staged
In the Park
From dusk
To dawn,
The tourney goes on:
Rush,
Miss the mark,
Pierce the dark,
Dash by!
Another two
Try.

1. The central comparison or metaphor of the poem is expressed in the title and repeated in line 16. The cars approaching one another with their lights on are equated with what?

The entire poem is used to develop a basic metaphor—the comparison between onrushing cars and combatants in a tourney. This type of sustained comparison is called an *extended metaphor.*

2. In what way is the light of an oncoming car like a spear? Given this comparison, is the phrase in lines 8 and 19 appropriate?

metaphor

An implied comparison between things essentially unlike.

Apply to **"O Daedalus, Fly Away Home"** on page 133

8 A.M.

Bringing dimension to the terrace window,
the harbor, a piece of driftwood
floats like an abandoned row boat
among the logs and planks
brought in by the winter tide.

Rain, dotting the sky with the sea,
dissolves in a roll
the wake of diminished debris.

A police patrol boat glides past
like a computerized shark.
Its turn breaks against December wood;
marks the cold with a dull thud.
A thin film of paint from a discarded can

colors the fall of the next wave.
Surfacing through white crystals, a mud hen
splatters white dots across the water.
As if the day was keeping a promise,
the Elk's Club sea-wall begins to collapse,

wipe the pier clean of ads.

Duane Niatum

1. At what time of year does the poem take place? What are the weather conditions?

2. What objects are described in the poem?

3. Examine the poet's choice of adjectives—*abandoned, cold, dull, thin,* and *empty.* What feeling do these words create?

The floating driftwood, the debris, the empty pier—all are objects that combine to create a *mood* of lonely isolation. The only sign of human life is suggested by the police patrol boat, but it is ominous—like a shark. A certain aimlessness and futility are suggested by the floating refuse that rolls with the tide; the oncoming winter season suits the chill atmosphere.

4. How important do you think the setting is in this poem? For example, could the same effect and mood have been achieved if the scene had taken place on a sunny afternoon in June? if the pier had been crowded with swimmers?

5. How important in establishing the mood of the poem are the particular objects mentioned? Imagine, for example, that there were swimming ducks rather than floating driftwood; that the tide carried water lilies instead of debris; that a swan appeared rather than a mud hen.

The poet has chosen a specific setting, particular objects, and certain words and images to convey the desired mood—one of lonely isolation. Another writer may choose to create a mood that is somber or joyous, calm or turbulent, and in each case will select words, details, and a setting that combine to establish that mood.

Prose writers likewise rely heavily on words, details, and setting to convey a particular mood or atmosphere. Note how time (autumn, evening), circumstance (the narrator is alone), and use of detail ("vacant eye-like windows," "decayed trees") are carefully chosen by Edgar Allan Poe to convey a particular mood in the following passage from the beginning of his short story "The Fall of the House of Usher."

> During the whole of a dull, dark, and soundless day in the autumn of the year, when the clouds hung oppressively low in the heavens, I had been passing alone, on horseback, through a singularly dreary tract of country; and at length found myself, as the shades of the evening drew on, within view of the melancholy House of Usher. I know not how it was—but, with the first glimpse of the building, a sense of insufferable gloom pervaded my spirit. . . . I looked upon the scene before me—upon the mere house, and the simple landscape features of the domain—upon the bleak walls—upon the vacant eye-like windows—upon a few rank sedges—and upon a few white trunks of decayed trees—with an utter depression of soul.

mood

The climate of feeling in a literary work. The author's choice of setting, objects, details, images, and words all contribute in creating a specific mood.

Apply to **"The Skater of Ghost Lake"** on page 163

personification

a great mosquito dance

i look down from the high bank
eaten with dirt caves below
close to the crumbling edges
and see that the talking river
is brown and angry and has risen
above the beaver dam and roars
with a low grumbling and eats
great mouthfuls of mud

and skimming sliding over his back
a great cloud of swallows
white and green are dancing
a great mosquito dance
their flying is so swift and true
the air may hold them tightly
and as i look down on them
they become a single great bird.

Norman H. Russell

The poet describes a river that has flooded. With its high water level and fierce current, the river seems to have taken on a life of its own.

1. What human characteristics does the poet give to the river?

2. In the second stanza, does the phrase "the air may hold them tightly" influence your mental picture of the swallows flying above the river in any way? If so, how?

In his portrayal of natural forces—the river and the air—as having a will and life of their own, Russell makes use of a figure of speech called *personification.* Through the use of personification, nonhuman things, inanimate objects, or abstractions are given human characteristics. We assign human attributes to nonhuman things in our daily speech when we refer to the hands of a clock, a weeping willow tree, or fickle fortune. Personification is an effective device in poetry, for it enables the poet to present abstract qualities, emotions, events, or objects in human terms, thus making them more vivid and understandable. Shakespeare speaks of "the furious winter's rages," Ben Jon-

"a great mosquito dance" from *Indian Thoughts: The Children of God* by Norman H. Russell. Reprinted by permission of the author.

son mentions the sun being "laid to sleep," and Milton calls time "a maniac scattering dust." To what is each thing compared in these personifications? Is the comparison appropriate in each case? Explain.

At times life, but not necessarily human life, may be attributed to an idea or object. For example, we may speak of the purr of a car's engine or say that love is blind. In the following poem, inanimate objects are invested with life. What qualities are attributed to the wind? Cite other instances of personification in the poem and explain their effect.

My One Small Light

The whole earth lies defenseless
before you, wind.
You roar through mountain gorges—
Like a famished wolf tear up trees
roil sunset waters
shake the iron moon into hiding
her face in racing clouds
You shatter rooftiles
and blow campfires
into giant conflagrations
Faster than a ghostship
you rage around the globe—
The whole earth crouches flat
before your ravaging power.

Why, when alone I sheltered
in an alien cave,
did you blow out
my one small light?

Maria Berl Lee

personification (pər son′ə fə kā′shən)

A figure of speech in which human characteristics are assigned to nonhuman things, or life is attributed to inanimate objects.

Apply to **Romeo and Juliet** on page 181

plot

Feud

John Lampson and Dave Rivers had been friends when they were boys and young men, but they got into a fight, and then later John Lampson died. Dave was ashamed because after the fight he had with John, he didn't go to him and try to make it up. A long time afterward, and just because he was ashamed, he took it out on John's son.

There were really two fights between John and Dave. When they were both young men, they went out of the hill country of eastern Tennessee to work together in the West Virginia coal mines.

They both had the same thing in mind. They didn't want to be coal miners. What they wanted was to make enough money in the mines to come back into the hills and buy farms. A good many hillmen do that. When they are young, they go off to the mines or to a factory town. They work hard and save money, and then they come back. A hillman is a hillman. He doesn't want to live his life away from the hills.

You may know how miners work. Two men work together in a little room far down under the ground. It is dangerous work, and a man must have faith in his partner. Any little slip, a moment of carelessness on the part of one man, and both he and his partner may be killed.

So there are these friendships that spring up between miners. "Here I am, working with you, day after day. I am going around with your life held in the hollow of my hand." Such an experience makes two men feel close. Dave and John, both powerful men and both unmarried, had such a friendship.

And then John and Dave fought. They fought over a woman they met in a West Virginia town, and I don't know much of that side of their story. They fought once underground and once on the main street of a mining town. As it happened neither man got the woman. She married another miner and left the town in which they were working.

They fought twice, and Dave Rivers won both fights, and then they quit working together, but both stayed on in the same town.

I think later that when both men got home to the hills and each man got his own little farm in the same neighborhood and had married—it happened that they married second cousins—I think that both men wanted to make it up, but that neither man

would make the first move. "He began it," Dave Rivers said to himself. "Well, he licked me," John Lampson said. The result was a growing resentment. The two wives kept at them and both men were stubborn. . . .

But this story is not concerned primarily with two men. It concerns John Lampson's son, Jim, and Dave Rivers's daughter, Elvira.

In the hill country girls often get married at sixteen, and at that age young men push out into the world. Jim Lampson is a sensitive, rather slender man and he began paying court to Dave's daughter, Elvira.

It happens that I know about the courtship, for two reasons. I am fond of taking long walks alone in the hills, and one night I saw the two walking together hand in hand on a mountain road. And then young Jim sometimes talks to me. He is ambitious. He wants an education, and sometimes comes to me to borrow books. It was young Jim who told me what had happened between himself and Dave Rivers. His voice shook when he told me the story.

Jim is in love with Elvira and he got bold. It was Sunday, and he went to Dave Rivers's house, and there was Dave all dressed up and sitting on the porch.

"What do you want?" Dave asked gruffly, addressing young Jim.

Jim said that Dave didn't even let him come into the yard. He stood at the gate. It had been only a year since Jim's father died. A wild colt he was trying to break bolted with him.

Young Jim stood in the road and told Dave Rivers that he wanted to come into the house and call on his daughter Elvira; and Elvira, a slim, lovely mountain girl, was standing in the house doorway back of her father. She stood listening. Dave got suddenly furious. He was, I am pretty sure now, really furious that he hadn't made it up with Jim's father before his old coal-mining partner got killed. He was furious at himself, and he took it out on young Jim.

He began to rave and swear at Jim. Then he ran into the house and got his gun. He waved it about and kept on cursing: "You get out of here! You are the son of that skunk. You get out of here!"

It was all very absurd. I am sure that Dave Rivers's gun wasn't loaded.

But when he talked to me, young Jim was furious. Jim isn't one of the noisy sort. That day, after standing for a moment in the road and listening to Dave Rivers curse him and his father, Jim went white and, turning, walked trembling away.

This happened late of a Sunday afternoon in the fall, and it also happened that on that same evening I went for a walk. It might have been ten at night, and there was a moon. I went along up hill and down. It was a fine night. I was listening to the night sounds, getting the night smell. Dave Rivers's house is just at the foot of a sharp hill, and there is a wood above the house along the road. The edge of the wood is not more than a hundred yards from the house. Dave was sitting in the open doorway.

I moved into the wood by the fence and stood thinking of what Jim Lampson had told me that afternoon. "I'll go down and talk to him," I thought. I do not know Dave Rivers as I do young Jim, but Dave had said things about Jim's father I know he couldn't mean, and I had said so to young Jim. I had tried to quiet Jim, "I'll go talk to Dave Rivers tomorrow," I had said to Jim; but, "I had better do it right now," I told myself as I stood that night above the house. I hesitated. There was a lamp burning in the room at Dave Rivers's back. The man was doing what I had been doing, enjoying the night. Was he thinking of what he had done to young Jim's father and of what he had on that day done to young Jim?

I stood hesitant. There is a man's natural inclination not to interfere in other men's quarrels. "I'm going to do it," I said to myself; and then it was too late. It may be that I heard a little sound or that some instinct told me to turn my head.

In the road, twenty feet away, was young Jim, who had come silently up, and he had a gun in his hands, and it was aimed at Dave Rivers. Dave was a fair target, down there in the light from the lamp.

It was a thing to give you the shivers down to your toes. Why I didn't shout or run to young Jim I don't know. I stood frozen and silent. Of what does a man think at such moments? Did I see all that was about to happen—Dave Rivers shot by young Jim—my own position, a witness—Jim, a boy I liked—myself running afterwards to report it all to the sheriff? And then later the trial in the courtroom in town—my words sending young Jim to his death on the gallows.

But, thank heaven, it did not happen. Young Jim stood like that, his hand on the trigger of his gun, myself hidden from sight in the shadow of a tree, Dave Rivers sitting down there, smoking his pipe and unaware of it all. And then young Jim lowered his gun. After standing for a moment he turned and walked away. . . .

And so that happened, and you can see how I felt. "I'll go down to Dave Rivers and talk to him now," I told myself.

"No, I won't do that. I'll go back up the road to young Jim."

Jim lives with his mother on a farm three miles back in the hills. He is his mother's only child, but Dave Rivers has the daughter Elvira and two younger sons.

And so I stood in the road, hesitating again; and, as is usual with me, again I did nothing.

"Tomorrow," I said to myself. I went on home, but I did not sleep, and on the next day I went to Dave's house.

I went to the house in the late afternoon of a fall day, and there was Dave at work in the barnyard back of the house.

It was time for the fall pig-killing, and Dave was at it alone.

It had turned cold during the night and there was a promise of snow in the air. There was a creek near the barn, and along it red sumac grew. Dave's wife, his daughter Elvira, and the two younger children were standing and watching. Dave looked up and grunted at me.

There was a fire still blazing under a kettle but Dave had the hog in the scalding barrel filled with the boiling water. I remember the hill beyond where Dave stood, the fall colors of the trees, the bare black trunks of trees beginning to show through, the two children dancing about. And Elvira, and her slim girlishness.

"It will snow before the day is over," I thought.

How was I to begin on Dave? What would he think of my trying to interfere in one of his quarrels? Dave is a gruff one. He isn't easy to handle.

"Hello," he said, looking up and growling at me. He had the hog by the legs and was turning it about in the barrel of hot water. A hog, when ready for killing, is heavy. . . .

And then . . . it happened again.

Young Jim came from among the sumac bushes with his gun in his hand. He had come up along the creek, beyond the barn, and he walked directly to Dave. His face was white. He had made up his mind to kill Dave openly there in the daytime.

He went directly to Dave, and Dave stood for a moment, staring at him. I saw Elvira put her two hands over her eyes, and a little cry came from her lips. The wife ran toward Dave. Jim brought the gun to his shoulder.

"Now! *Now!*" I said to myself. It was a kind of inner cry. I did not speak. The hands of Death were gripping my throat.

But Death didn't get Dave. I saw his big shoulders heave, and, with a quick movement of his arms, he had the hog out of the barrel, but in doing so he fell. He and the hog were in a sprawling heap on the ground.

So there he was. In falling he had upset the barrel of boiling water, and it came flooding over his body. He was on the ground, writhing in pain.

All of this had happened more quickly than thought. The wife had been running toward her husband. She was still running. I saw Elvira take her hands from her eyes. Young Jim had thrown his gun to one side and had got his knife out of his pocket. I still stood helpless.

"No, no," I said to myself. For just a moment I thought, "He is going to kill the man with the knife," but in the next moment I saw my mistake.

Jim was on his knees beside Dave and was working furiously. He was cutting Dave's clothes away; and Dave, who had been rolling on the ground and crying with pain, was now very quiet. I saw his eyes as they were watching the boy.

And so Dave let the boy handle him like a child; and when we had got him into the house, I rode Dave's horse off to town for a doctor. I yelled with delight. I was beating the horse over the flanks with my hat. I had seen the look in Dave's eyes as he lay on the ground, letting young Jim cut his clothing away, and I knew that the feud that had begun between Dave and Jim's father and that Jim had taken up in his turn, was over at last.

Sherwood Anderson

Conflict

1. What has originally caused the feud? In what way has the feud come to involve others beside Dave Rivers and John Lampson?

2. Judging from his first encounter with Dave, how serious a problem do you think young Jim Lampson faces? Explain.

3. Does this problem involve physical or emotional barriers—or both? Explain.

In every story there is a *conflict* of opposing forces, a struggle, a problem to be resolved. This struggle or conflict may be physical or emotional; often it is both. In this story, for example, the feud, an emotional conflict, appears to require some kind of a physical solution.

Conflicts that pit a main character against an outside factor—another character or thing, the forces of nature, the power of society, etc.—are called *external conflicts*. Conflicts that occur within the main character—struggles of emotion or conscience—are called *internal conflicts*. Seldom is the conflict in a story exclusively external or internal.

The *plot* of a story refers to the related events that present and eventually resolve some problem or conflict.

Pattern of Events/Complications

Once the conflict is established, the author presents events that are related to it—details and incidents that clarify or intensify the conflict, or that work toward its resolution.

1. Why, according to the narrator, does Dave transfer his grudge from John Lampson to his son Jim?

2. What does Jim's second "visit" to Dave reveal about the method Jim has chosen to resolve the problem posed in the story?

3. Why do you think Jim does not act in this situation?

4. What factors prevent the narrator from acting once he has decided to negotiate between Dave and Jim?

The narrator in "Feud" serves to organize the story by relating the events in the order in which they have occurred. The narrator likewise exposes and intensifies the complications of the story both by revealing his own indecisions and fears and by providing us with opinions about Jim.

Climax and Conclusion

The *climax* of a story occurs when one of the main characters takes a decisive action to end the conflict or when the situation is such that the problem must be resolved in some way or another. (Occasionally, no decisive action is taken or the problem is left unresolved.)

1. What is the decisive action or climax in "Feud"?

2. What particular words and actions does the author use to lend impact and drama to the climax?

The *conclusion* of a story includes the resolving of the conflict and any events following it. Sometimes the conclusion contains a direct or an indirect comment on the significance of the conflict.

1. What is ironic about the fact that Dave is ultimately saved by Jim's knife?

2. In what way does the narrator reveal his feelings at the end of the story?

plot

A series of related events selected by the author to present and bring about the resolution of some conflict or problem. In a strongly plotted story, the events usually follow this pattern: the conflict or problem is established; complications arise from the conflict; a main character takes decisive action, or the situation itself brings about a climax; the conflict is resolved.

Apply to **"The Most Dangerous Game"** on page 20

point of view

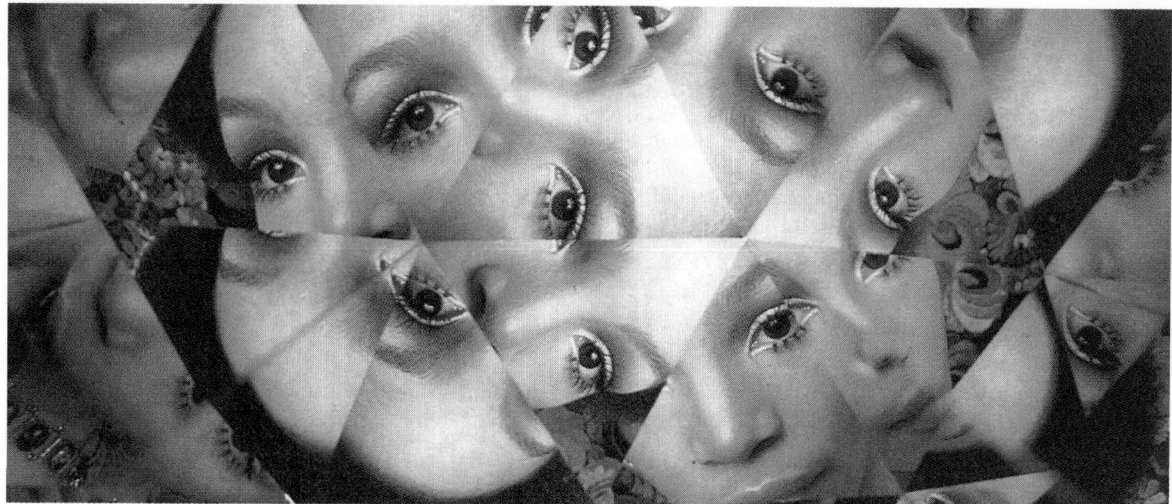

All literature must be narrated or recorded by someone, and an author must decide who that someone will be. The decision is an important one, since the selection of narrator determines the angle, or *point of view,* from which the story will be told, as well as the amount and kind of information a reader will be given. The following story derives its impact from the fact that it is told from two different points of view.

The Big Trip

This was the part of the day that Theresa liked best. Dishes done, place straightened, time to rest in bed, sip a cup of tea, watch television and have a cigarette. Being alone wasn't such a bad thing, she'd come to think. No man to order her around, no children to cause her grief, to stick her with babysitting the grandchildren when they wanted to go out on the town. Just two aloof cats, a small apartment, and her TV. The last of life for which the first was made. She was alone the first part, she'd be alone in the last part. And that was fine with her. As the years had worn on, she'd needed companionship less and less. One thing she'd come to treasure above all else—her independence. Her freedom to do as she pleased. Other women her age had ties. Not Theresa. Her life was her own, every minute of it, and that was exactly the way she wanted it.

Carefully, frugally, all these years she had saved her money for The Big Trip to Europe. It had become a joke at the office, the extent to which Theresa would go to hang onto her money. Once she had heard one of the young girls say, "If old Theresa can't take it with her, then she's not going!"

Let them laugh, she thought. When they were old, living on a pension, they would remember her—Theresa and her Big Trip Around the World. Yes, let them laugh, they who had no thought for the future, who lived from day to day, spending their money as fast as they got it.

Now she was having the joy of planning the trip, going to travel bureaus on her lunch hour, deciding on the clothes she'd buy. Oh, the countries she'd see! Switzerland, for sure. And Spain, the Netherlands, England, Italy—the world would be hers!

Retirement in two short months—and then the fun would begin! The money was ready, safely tucked away in her mattress, hundreds and hundreds of dollar bills. Just two months to wait! She shut her eyes, smiling, thinking of the moment she'd get on the airplane, when The Big Trip would finally begin. . . .

"What's she blabbering about *now?*"

The other woman shrugged. "Same old thing, how she's going to go to Europe and see everything. I kinda feel sorry for her, you know?"

"Uh, uh. Don't go feeling sorry for them, Wanda. You gotta harden your heart or you'll go crazy working here, you should excuse the expression!"

The other woman laughed at this witty remark. "Yeh. Anyway, I guess she's happy enough. I mean, look at her, off in her dream world all the time."

"Funny about her," the first woman mused. "I was here when they admitted her, ten years ago.

Seems she was a fine, normal woman, until one night she fell asleep smoking in bed. Neighbors got her out okay. She wasn't burned much, but by the time the firemen got there, her furniture was ruined, every bit of furniture burned to a cinder. You wouldn't think that would make someone go insane, would you?"

Elsin Ann Gardner

1. From whose point of view is the first set of facts presented?

2. From whose point of view is the second set of facts presented?

3. What is the basic difference between the events in the story as Theresa sees them and as the women who work in the institution see them?

first person

Imagine that Gardner had chosen to tell the story directly from Theresa's point of view, so that the opening sentence read, "This was the part of day that I liked best." This kind of narration, told by a character in the story, is called *first person* point of view. Theresa's own narration would be personal because we would be presented with information and events according to the way she sees them. Since Theresa is unaware of the full meaning of events, the information she communicates would be limited.

third person

Sometimes an author chooses not to tell a story through one of the characters, selecting instead an anonymous person outside the story as narrator. In "The Big Trip" the narrator is an outsider who speaks for the characters in the story, entering their minds to tell us what they think and how they feel. Such a narrator is called *third person*. The following are two main kinds of third person narrator.

third person omniscient

When a narrator is an outsider or third person who knows everything about the characters and can enter their minds and comment on their thoughts, actions, and feelings, that narrator is called *third person omniscient*. Such a narrator is not restricted by time, place, and character and frequently provides commentary that will enable a reader to understand the story.

third person objective

The author of "The Big Trip" might have given a purely factual account, presenting a story that could be summarized in a newspaper headline: "Woman, insane for ten years and unaware that she is institutionalized, makes European travel plans." Such an account would still be in the third person, but the outside narrator would merely relate facts without recording the thoughts and feelings of characters. This viewpoint is called *third person objective*.

Gardner's viewpoint is actually somewhere between third person omniscient and third person objective. While she faithfully portrays the thoughts, feelings, and actions of both Theresa and the women who work in the institution, she does not supply any outside commentary. Gardner's narrator leaves it to us as readers to determine that the fire has destroyed Theresa's money, her dreams, and hence her mind.

point of view

The author's choice of narrator for a story. This choice determines the amount of information a reader will be given, as well as the angle from which this information will be presented. The major points of view are *first person* and *third person*. The first person narrator is a character in the story who can reveal only his or her feelings and thoughts, or information that has been directly received from other characters. The third person narrator, an outsider, can present an omniscient or all-knowing point of view, an objective, factual point of view, or a point of view that is somewhere in the middle.

Apply to **"A Death in the House"** on page 2

protagonist/ antagonist

The chief character in a story, play, or novel is called a *protagonist*. Often, a rival or adversary called an *antagonist* attempts to thwart the protagonist. In "The Most Dangerous Game" (page 20), for example, the main conflict is provided by the rivalry between the antagonist Zaroff and the protagonist Rainsford. In the case of *Romeo and Juliet,* the roles of protagonist and antagonist are more complex. It could be argued that both the title characters are protagonists. While both Tybalt and Paris could be considered antagonists, it is mainly outside forces, rather than characters, that operate against the lovers and provide conflict in the play. The family feud, fate, chance, and bad timing all combine to thwart the lovers, and these forces help supply the dramatic conflict. Often, the antagonist can be both a single character and an outside force, as in *Antigone* (page 378). It is not only Creon but also the laws of the state, which he stubbornly enforces, that serve as antagonistic features. In "Split Cherry Tree," (page 41), is the antagonist a particular person, an outside force or forces, or both? Explain.

protagonist/antagonist

protagonist (prō tag′ə nist); antagonist (an-tag′ə nist)

The chief character in a story, play, or novel. The rival or adversary that attempts to thwart the protagonist is called an antagonist. An antagonist may be a character, an outside force or forces, or both factors working against the protagonist.

Apply to **The Miracle Worker** on page 68

rhyme

I was slifting on the soffles with a lovely liffy list,
When a tiny tiddle told me, "You had better bift
and bist."
And before I'd time to turndle, a zoot zarkle
kanked my kork.
Then jank! My jardles splastered and my gaddle
gave a gork.

One reader of this nonsense poem analyzed it this way: "I'm not really sure what has happened, but things were pleasant for the speaker until there came a warning; suddenly something bad or harsh occurred." What "words" (besides *lovely*) in the first line suggest something pleasant? This little nonsense jingle illustrates that sounds, even in nonsense "words" that have no meaning in themselves, have the power to convey certain impressions to the reader.

One of the pleasures to be derived from poetry is auditory, a pleasure in the *sound* of the words in a poem. One of the poems in the poetry unit that strikingly emphasizes sound qualities is "The Skater of Ghost Lake" (page 163). Notice, for example, the many sound repetitions in the first stanza.

Ghost Lake's a dark lake, a deep lake and cold:
Ice black as ebony, frostily scrolled;
Far in its shadows a faint sound whirrs;
Steep stand the sentineled deep, dark firs.

1. Which words are repeated in the four lines?

2. Which sounds are repeated at the ends of lines?

3. In the first line, aside from the *l* in *lake,* what beginning sound of a word is repeated?

One obvious way to emphasize certain sounds is to repeat whole words, as occurs with the repeating of *lake, dark,* and *deep* in this stanza. (The words are not repeated for their sounds alone, of course; they are obviously repeated to emphasize their sense, what they stand for, as well.) But repetition of sound would become monotonous if it were limited to this method.

A second method is rhyming. Repeating sounds (the accented vowel plus succeeding sounds) at the end of lines is called *end rhyme.* The *-old* sound of *cold* is repeated at the end of the second line, and the *-irrs* sound of *whirrs* is repeated at the end of the fourth line. (Notice that rhyming has nothing to do with spelling.) Some poets may even force rhyme to achieve a humorous effect, as Lord Byron does in "Don Juan," Canto I, lines 175–176.

But—Oh! ye lords of ladies intellectual,
Inform us truly, have they not hen-pecked you all?

If one were to chart the pattern of rhyming in a poem, one would represent the first rhyming sound as *a,* and the second rhyming sound as *b.* Thus, the pattern of rhyme, or the rhyme scheme, of the preceding stanza from "The Skater of Ghost Lake" would be expressed as *a a b b.*

Internal Rhyme

It is possible to have rhyming sounds within a line of poetry, as in the fourth line in the preceding stanza from "The Skater of Ghost Lake":

St*ee*p stand the sentineled d*eep,* dark firs.

This form of rhyme is referred to as *internal rhyme.* It is used sparingly, especially when end rhyme is employed, because it tends to create a sing-song effect.

4. In the fourth line, which beginning sounds of words are repeated? What accented vowel sound is repeated?

5. Pronounce the last word in the third line aloud slowly. What sense do you get from the sound itself?

Onomatopoeia (on′ə mat′ə pē′ə)

When the sound of a word illustrates or echoes its sense, we have an instance of *onomatopoeia.* Common examples are *buzz, ouch, murmur, gurgle,* and *purr.* This is yet another device used by poets to help achieve harmony between sound and sense. The word at the end of the third line, *whirrs,* is onomatopoetic; the sound of the word itself suggests the sound that the word stands for.

rhyme

The repetition of word-ending sounds; specifically, the repetition of accented vowel sounds plus any succeeding sounds *(first-burst, delightful-spiteful).* When sounds are repeated at the ends of lines (end rhymes), they are arranged in a pattern within the poem called a rhyme scheme. One may describe a rhyme scheme by representing sounds at ends of lines with letters of the alphabet. A rhyme occurring within a line is called an internal rhyme. Onomatopoeia is the correspondence of sound and sense in a word; the sound of the word suggests what the word stands for.

Apply to **"The Lamentation of the Old Pensioner"** page 140

rhythm

The arrangement of stressed and unstressed sounds in speech or writing is called *rhythm.* The rhythm in some pieces of writing has a definite pattern or cadence; in others it is irregular. Read the following limerick aloud several times.

> There was a young lady from Austin,
> Who started to cycle to Boston.
>   By Platte she was cross-eyed
>   From too much monoxide,
> Said she, "This is very exhaustin'."

Did you find yourself naturally stressing certain words or syllables after the first few readings? The limerick is a poetic form with a fairly definite structure. For example, the first line usually starts with "There was a . . ."; the first, second, and last lines rhyme. The reading of any limerick tends to fall into a cadence, as in this instance (capital letters indicate stressed words or syllables).

> There WAS a young LAdy from AUStin,
> Who STARted to CYcle to BOSton.
>   By PLATTE she was CROSS-eyed
>   From TOO much moNOXide,
> Said SHE, "This is VERy exHAUSTin'."

Another way of indicating stress is with the symbol ´ and lack of stress with the symbol ˘ :

Thĕre wás ă yŏung lády̆ frŏm Áustĭn

While there is some slight variation in the number of unstressed syllables preceding stressed syllables, this limerick exhibits a patterned rhythm: three stresses in the first, second, and last lines; two stresses in the third and fourth lines. This sort of regular rhythm is suitable for short, humorous verse; but in more serious poetry, writers often vary the beat to achieve emphasis and to avoid monotony.

Because the beat, or rhythm, of a work is related to its sound, rhythm is also influenced by devices such as alliteration, assonance, onomatopoeia, and rhyme. Just as poets accommodate these devices of sound to serve their individual purposes, they may choose to use—or not to use—a regular rhythm in a particular work. For example, the following lines from Gray's "Elegy Written in a Country Churchyard" portray the tired journey home of the cattle and plowman after a long day—both by the regular, dull rhythm and through the repeated long *o* sound and alliterative heavy sounds (*plowman-plods, weary-way*).

> The lowing herd wind slowly o'er the lea.
> The plowman homeward plods his weary way, . . .

Many poems, especially modern ones, do not have the marked pattern of rhythm exhibited by limericks and Gray's poem. Rather than using a regular beat, a poet may choose to employ irregular rhythms, similar to those of speech, or to vary the rhythm widely to suit the different situations in the poem. How would you describe the rhythm in the following lines by Walt Whitman?

> Afoot and light-hearted I take to the open road,
> Healthy, free, the world before me,
> The long brown path before me leading wherever
>   I choose.
>
> Henceforth I ask not good-fortune, I myself am
>   good-fortune,
> Henceforth I whimper no more, postpone no
>   more, need nothing.
> Done with indoor complaints, libraries, querulous
>   criticisms,
> Strong and content I travel the open road.

While there is rhythm in the poem, of course, it is the casual, irregular rhythm of speech rather than the measured rhythm of a regular beat. The poem's irregular pattern of sound echoes the poet's exuberance and gives his words a spontaneous quality; in addition, it helps the reader focus on the poet's thoughts more than on the rhythm of the words.

Rhythm in poetry and in prose can be used simply for enjoyment in the sound. We take pleasure in nursery rhymes and nonsensical schoolyard chants because we enjoy the cadences of such expressions. We can experience this kind of pleasure in the following lines from an old folk song:

Eyes like the morning star,
Cheeks like a rose,
Annie was a pretty girl,
God Almighty knows,
Weep all you little rains,
Wail, winds, wail—
All along, along, along,
The Colorado Trail.

or in this old nursery rhyme:

Doctor Bell fell down the well
And broke his collar-bone.
Doctors should attend the sick
And leave the well alone.

Rhythm can also serve to echo the sense, as in the following drowsy lines by Robert Burns which aptly describe a flowing river.

Flow gently, sweet Afton! among thy green braes.
Flow gently, I'll sing thee a song in thy praise;
My Mary's asleep by thy murmuring stream,
Flow gently, sweet Afton, disturb not her dream.

Another function of rhythm can be to achieve dramatic effect. This opening line of a poem by John Donne immediately attracts the reader's attention, partly because of its irregular meter and its many stressed beats.

Busy old fool, unruly sun, . . .

Finally, rhythm can be used to emphasize important words. In "Miss Rosie" (page 146), the words "I stand up" in the final line are all stressed and embody a significant statement by the poet. In the following lines from "The Rime of the Ancient Mariner," the word *ice* is emphasized by being in the stressed position each time it is used.

The ice was here, the ice was there,
The ice was all around; . . .

One additional thing to notice about rhythm is that certain lines have a definite pause at their ends, while other lines flow one into the other. A line of verse in which there is a definite pause at the end (usually indicated by punctuation) is called *end-stopped,* while a line that overflows into the next is called *run-on.* Examine each of the following poems.

I eat my peas with honey—
I've done it all my life.
It makes the peas taste funny,
But it keeps 'em on the knife!

Anonymous

Afternoon

with just enough of a breeze for him to ride it
lazily, a hawk
sails still-winged
up the slope of a stubble-covered hill,
so low
he nearly
touches his shadow.

Robert Sund

1. Which poem has only lines that are end-stopped?

2. Which poem is generally composed of run-on lines?

3. How would you describe the tone and purpose of the first poem? In what way are end-stopped lines suitable for expressing this poem?

4. In what way do run-on lines in the second poem suit Sund's subject?

rhythm

The arrangement of stressed and unstressed sounds in speech and writing. The rhythm in a poem may have a single, dominant beat; it may be varied within the poem to fit different situations and moods; or it may be casual and irregular like speech.

Apply to **"The Lamentation of the Old Pensioner"** page 140

satire

Deepest Sympathy

Your life, once filled with rays of light,
  Is now a darkened tomb;
No gleam of hope or happiness
  Can pierce the dismal gloom;
And so you sit, a saddened soul,
  Bereft and all alone,
Because you've learned to your despair
  Your picture tube has blown.

Frank Jacob

1. What is being made fun of in this poem?

2. The poem is written in the form of a sympathy card. In what way does this form heighten the ridicule? Do terms such as "darkened tomb" and "bereft and all alone" seem appropriate phrases in making fun of the subject? Why or why not?

The art of ridiculing an aspect of human nature or life in general is called *satire*. Satire may be gentle and humorous, as in the preceding poem directed to a television addict, or it may be fierce and scornful. Although primarily designed to expose, instruct, and thereby correct human foibles and institutional evils, satire can also serve to entertain and amuse. Satirists may make their points through various techniques such as sarcasm, exaggeration, humor, and absurdity. The satirist's tone may range from playfulness to scorn to outrage. The topics of satire are limitless: current clothing fads, television, government, vegetarianism, greed, commercialism, and smoking, to mention a few. A satirical remark may be merely a personal barb, as in the case of a critic's observation that a particular actress's dramatic skills ran the emotional gamut from A to B. On the other hand, the focus of satire may be much broader in scope. In the following excerpt from *Scoop* by Evelyn Waugh, we learn about the phenomenal newspaper reporter Wenlock Jakes.

". . . syndicated all over America. Gets a thousand dollars a week. When he turns up in a place you can bet your life that as long as he's there it'll be the news center of the world.

"Why, once Jakes went out to cover a revolution in one of the Balkan capitals. He overslept in his carriage, woke up at the wrong station, didn't know any different, got out, went straight to an hotel, and cabled off a thousand-word story about barricades in the streets, flaming churches, machine-guns answering the rattle of his typewriter as he wrote, a dead child, like a broken doll, spread-eagled in the deserted roadway below his window—*you* know.

"Well they were pretty surprised at his office, getting a story like that from the wrong country, but they trusted Jakes and splashed it in six national newspapers. That day every special in Europe got orders to rush to the new revolution. They arrived in shoals. Everything seemed quiet enough, but it was as much as their jobs were worth to say so, with Jakes filing a thousand words of blood and thunder a day. So they chimed in too. Government stocks dropped, financial panic, state of emergency declared, army mobilized, famine, mutiny and in less than a week there *was* an honest to God revolution under way, just as Jakes had said. There's the power of the press for you.

"They gave Jakes the Nobel Peace Prize for his harrowing descriptions of the carnage. . . ."

What is being satirized in this excerpt? Explain why the last sentence is ironic. (See the entry for Irony in this Handbook.)

Waugh has satirized the power of the press, its ability to produce news that precedes (and causes) events. Waugh's satire is aimed at those who report and publish the news, and, to a lesser degree, at those who award the Nobel Peace Prize.

satire

The art of criticizing a subject by ridiculing it and evoking toward it an attitude of amusement, contempt, or scorn. Much satire has as its central purpose the reform of persons and institutions.

Apply to "**Mr. Artesian's Conscientiousness**" on page 132

setting

The following passage appears in the early pages of Harriette Arnow's novel *The Dollmaker*. It is a description of the Kentucky land and house that Gertie Nevels, the novel's hero, plans to purchase.

Past the beehives and the orchard, sheltered by the curve of the ridge side, and on a southern slope where the early sun struck fully, lay the flattish bench of ungullied land that held the house and yard and barns and garden spot. She smiled on the shake-covered roof of the old log house; the white oak shakes, weathered to a soft gray brownness, must have been rived in the wrong time of the moon, for they had curled in places, and in some of the little cup-like hollows moss had grown. Now in the yellow sun the moss shone more gold than green, and over all the roof there was from the quickly melting frost a faint steam rising, so that the dark curled shakes, the spots of moss, the great stone chimney, all seemed bathed in a golden halo and Cassie called that the house had golden windows.

Some of the golden light seemed caught in Gertie's eyes as she walked down and around and at last stood by the yard gate.

1. What time of day is it? How do you know?

2. Is the scene a rural, urban, or suburban one?

From *The Dollmaker* by Harriette Simpson Arnow. Published by The Macmillan Company, 1954.

3. The yellow sun bathes the moss in a light of gold, while the word *golden* is repeated throughout the passage. What feeling does this color convey?

This description helps the reader locate the story in time and place by presenting a rural, early-morning scene of autumn. The picture of nature, bathed in golden sunlight, is a warm, appealing one. Such information helps to provide a *setting* for the novel. One of the main functions of setting is to provide the atmosphere in which action and conflict develop.

Another function of setting is to reveal character. The preceding scene is viewed through Gertie's eyes. If you read the passage carefully, you noticed that words such as *smiled* and *sheltered* suggest that Gertie finds the setting pleasing and secure.

Gertie never moves into her dream house, however, since her husband Clovis finds work in a plant in Detroit, and she and the children must join him. The time is the early 1940s, and the move is necessary because Clovis, too old and father of too many children to serve on active duty, is sent by the government to aid the war effort by working in a factory. Thus we see that setting can also provide conditions and surroundings that make the situation in a story and the actions of the characters necessary and believable.

As Gertie and her children approach the city, we learn of her first impression.

> It seemed suddenly to Gertie as if all the things she had seen—the blurred buildings, the smokestacks, the monstrous pipes wandering high above her, even the trucks, and the trains—as if all these were alive and breathing smoke and steam as in other places under a sky with sun or stars the breath of warm and living people made white clouds in the cold. Here there seemed to be no people, even the cars with their rolled-up windows, frosted over like those of the cab, seemed empty of people, driving themselves through a world not meant for people.

What is her initial view of Detroit? She observes that the smoking, steaming machines appear to have replaced real, breathing people. In what way does this image convey her impression of a strange, large industrial city?

The family's first glimpse of the housing project where they will live is seen from a cab.

> A few feet farther on, the car stopped, but Gertie, thinking the driver was still searching, did not move. She stared straight ahead past the dirty alley snow, littered with blowing bits of paper, tin cans, trampled banana skins, and orange peels, at a high board fence. Past the fence she saw what looked to be an empty, brush-grown field; but while she looked a train rushed past. Everything was blotted out in the waves of smoke and steam that blew down; tiny cinders whirled with the snow against the windshield, and the smell and taste of smoke choked her. The noise subsided enough that she could hear the driver say, "Well, this is it."

In the preceding descriptions Arnow has presented two contrasting settings—the rural versus the urban. Setting is an important element in *The Dollmaker,* since a dominant theme in this novel is the painful adjustment a family undergoes when uprooted from the Kentucky hills to a Detroit ghetto.

---

setting

The time and place in which the events of a narrative occur. The setting may be described specifically by the narrator or one of the characters, or it may be suggested through dialogue and action.

Apply to **"The Man to Send Rain Clouds"** on page 15

simile

May Song

Pushing up their heads
Proudly

Like
Golden nuggets
On green velvet

But
Lawn owners don't love them

Carlos Cortez

1. What are the "Golden nuggets"? What is the "green velvet"?

2. Although the poet does not actually name his subject, he provides clues. In what way do the title and last line of the poem lead you to determine the subject of the poem?

The poet indicates a similarity between dandelions and golden nuggets. What single word in the poem implies that there is a relationship between these two objects?

A directly expressed comparison between two things that are actually unlike, usually indicated by the words *like* or *as,* is called a *simile.* A simile is a type of figurative language, and as such it involves a comparison between things that have something in common but are literally unlike. "He looked like an irritated man" is not a simile, while "He looked like a horse with a burr under its saddle" is a simile because it suggests a comparison between two essentially unlike things.

As in all figurative language, the comparison in a simile should provide a new way of looking at things by appealing to the imagination and senses. Many of the authors appearing in this book use similes to provide fresh insights for a reader.

A simile differs from a metaphor in that the comparison made in a metaphor is implied (he was starry-eyed), while the comparison is directly stated in a simile (his eyes were like stars).

The following examples include various similes from "The Rime of the Ancient Mariner." In each instance, name the two things being compared. Are the comparisons appropriate? Explain. In one case, there is no simile, since the two things related by the words *like* or *as* are not essentially unlike. Locate the example that is not a simile.

The water, like a witch's oils,
  Burnt green, and blue, and white.

And every soul, it passed me by,
  Like the whizz of my crossbow!

The other was a softer voice,
  As soft as honeydew;

The ship went down like lead.

He went like one that hath been stunned, . . .

If you understand that a simile involves a comparison between two basically unlike things, you will have determined that the last of the preceding examples is not a simile—no more than is the phrase "You look like you are surprised." Although similes are indicated by the words *like* or *as,* and, less frequently, *appears, seems,* and *than,* these words frequently occur where there is no simile.

simile (sim′ə lē)

A figure of speech in which two essentially unlike things are directly compared, usually with the words *like* or *as.*

Apply to **"Daybreak in Alabama"** on page 131

stereotype

1.

Drawing by Starke; © 1950, 1978 The New York Magazine, Inc.

2. Man works from sun to sun
But woman's work is never done.

3. Standup comic relates the following:
"I told my mother-in-law to make my house her home. She did. She sold it the following week."

4. The French—they are always romantic.
Italians are gluttons for foods.
The Scottish are tight with a penny,
And Spaniards have deep, pensive moods.
Americans all drive huge autos.
The Germans are somber and stout.
And if you agree with these statements,
You've judged before trying to find out.

Each of the examples above illustrates at least one broad generalization about a particular group.

1. What generalization does the cartoon make about women? about men?

2. An old proverb is cited in the second example. The proverb views men's work as an outside job. What, are we to infer, is women's work?

3. Example 3 is one of an endless supply of mother-in-law jokes. What generalization does it make about mothers-in-law?

4. The poem in example 4 deals with national stereotypes. How do you think, for example, the stereotype of the rich American driving the big car came about?

Broad generalizations like these about particular nationalities or sexes, or about those in a specialized situation such as mothers-in-law, politicians, teenagers, librarians, and artists, are called *stereotypes*. When individuals or groups are viewed according to their stereotypes, they are denied their full range of qualities and characteristics: they are viewed as types rather than as unique persons. Because they are built on preconceived notions, stereotypes can be dangerous in real life.

When stereotyped people or situations occur in written works, they should be recognized as such. When we recognize stereotypes, we can determine if the writer has used them purposely for their associations.

Stereotypes may also serve other purposes in literature. Because stereotyped characters and situations are quickly and easily recognizable, they can function in a limited amount of space to establish a point of view, a character, or a general climate.

Minor characters are often stereotyped, since one-dimensional figures can serve as effective contrasts or foils for main characters, who are more fully portrayed. For example, in *Romeo and Juliet,* the rash young bully Tybalt serves as a foil to Romeo.

Certain plots occur with enough frequency that they seem to follow a formula, with a predictable, recurring pattern of events. The Cinderella plot—with a poor, virtuous girl who wins a hero from evil rivals—is a common theme in literature. Other recurring themes are those of the love triangle, the fated lovers, or mistaken identity. After thousands of years of literature, there are no new plots, since all stories can be reduced to some basically recognizable pattern of events. "The Speckled Band," for example, follows in the tradition of the whodunit plot. Yet Doyle has avoided triteness by introducing false clues, and unique characters such as Dr. Roylott. In the same sense, all skillful writers add new dimensions to basic story lines by introducing minor plots, three-dimensional characters, and an innovative choice of details.

stereotype (ster′ē ə tīp′)

Fixed, generalized ideas about characters and situations. Stereotyped literary characters include the hard-boiled detective, the rags-to-riches hero, and the naïve orphan who is thrust into the cruel world. Stereotyped plots in literature include those that are based on an ancestral curse or on the love triangle. An experienced reader should be able to distinguish between hack writing in which stereotypes denote a lack of skill or inventiveness, and well-wrought literature in which stereotypes are skillfully used for a purpose.

Apply to **"Blues Ain't No Mockin Bird"** on page 35

style

Hal Borland, in a collection titled *Seasonal Editorials,* describes August in this way.

August is ripe chokecherries, and flutters of jays and robins at them, scolding, quarreling over seedy fruit too puckery for any human use except in jelly. It is elderberries so heavy with their dark fruit the bushes are bowed liked hunched old women in coarse purple shawls. It is chicory in bloom, a weed in the field, an herb in the kitchen, sky blue on sunny days but sulking and refusing to reveal its face to the clouds.

August is grasshoppers, their wings rattling when they fly, seeming to know that no summer lasts forever and now they must hurry somewhere. It is the grasshopper cousins, the katydids, starting to scratch the night, to file and rasp the evening to fit the shortening days. Foretellers of first frost, some say; and often it is true.

August is crickets, too. Tree crickets, which fiddle monotonously every evening, and field crickets that trill without pause every hot afternoon, so synchronized that when you drive along a rural road it seems that the same cricket accompanies you for mile after country mile.

August is algae in the scummy waters of the pond. It is the fat thumbs of new cattail heads in the mucky margin. It is joe-pye weed purpling into blossom, and ironweed turning magenta at its floral tips. It is vervain, blue and purple, in the damp lowland.

August gives the lie to the boast that man possesses the earth. Life is the possessor, not man, an infinity of life that will outlast all winters. August and summer are the glory, the achievement that soars beyond all human dreams.

A travel brochure describes August in the following manner.

What better place to be in August than Wisconsin! The tourist who looks for excitement will delight in the Annual August Aqua Festival—a colorful panorama of fireworks, boat races, and water ballets. For those sports-minded travelers there is the luxurious Lakeside Resort, complete with a yacht club, boat rentals, swimming pool, water skiing, an eighteen-hole golf course, horseback riding, air-conditioned indoor tennis courts, and a lake teeming with bass. Travelers who want to relax and enjoy nature will revel in the spectacular scenery, placid lakes, colorful wildlife, and breathtaking masses of flowers. And those intent on simply soaking up the August sun can choose from several convenient, insect-free beach areas. August is the highlight of glorious Wisconsin summers. Come and see!

Every serious writer has a purpose for writing, and chooses and arranges words, images, and details to serve that purpose. The travel brochure is devised to promote tourism, while Borland's writing is designed to entertain and to evoke feeling. Accordingly, the writers of both pieces have created a tone through images, words, information, and sentence rhythms that suits their individual purposes. The manner in which writers shape words and ideas to purposes is called *style.* Skillful writing is a matter of adapting one's language to one's ideas and purpose—in the words of Jonathan Swift, putting "proper words in proper places." To achieve an appropriate style, a writer must remain conscious of the subject, the audience, and the occasion. Styles may range from casual to formal, serious to comic, simple to complex, dull to lively. There is great variation even within these stylistic labels; for example, two authors, both writing formal, factual prose, may still have very different styles.

Words

1. Why are words such as *insect-free* and *air-conditioned* used in the travel brochure?

2. Explain why these words would be unsuitable in Borland's account.

3. Why do words such as *puckery* and *mucky* suit Borland's description, while they might be inappropriate in the brochure?

4. Why do you think words such as *breathtaking* and *spectacular* appear so often on postcards and in travel advertisements?

The choice of words and the manner in which they are combined and arranged help to determine style. Borland carefully builds his sentences, often balancing phrases within a sentence (paragraph 1, sentence 3). For variation, he sometimes places a very short sentence next to a long one (paragraph 3). The writer of the travel piece appears more concerned with words themselves—*excitement, delight, luxurious, spectacular, glorious,* etc., than with their arrangement. Unlike Borland who expects nothing from a reader save the reader's attention, the writer of the travel piece wants the reader to spend money in Wisconsin. The travel piece, then, is designed to be appealing and brief enough to catch the eye of potential customers.

In choosing words, a writer also considers their rhythms and sounds. Borland makes ample use of alliteration in phrases such as "bushes are bowed," "foretellers of first frost," and "mucky margin." When you examine paragraph 3, sentence 2, you find that a phrase such as "fiddle monotonously" and the long, final, unpunctuated clause beginning "so synchronized" and ending with the words "for mile after country mile" suggest the dull endless drone of crickets.

Images and Figurative Language

Borland's writing is designed to evoke feeling. To this end, he has made a strong appeal to the senses of taste, sight, and sound.

1. Cite one example of appeal to each of these senses.

In addition, Borland has made frequent use of figurative language. (See the entry for *figurative language* in this Handbook.) The entire piece can be regarded as a series of metaphors that begin with "August is . . ."

2. What simile do you find in the first paragraph?

Tone

1. Would you describe Borland's tone (see the entry for *tone* in this Handbook) with any of the following words: *comic, serious, formal, simple, thoughtful, dull, satiric?* If so, which ones? If not, use a word of your own.

2. In the final paragraph Borland's tone becomes philosophical. Why, according to him, is it nature rather than human beings that "will outlast all winters"?

3. Why would a travel advertisement adopt a cheerful, light tone and emphasize human pleasures rather than remind people that nature will outlast them?

Choose any selection—prose or poetry—in this book and analyze its style. Some guidelines that should help you in your appraisal are

1. *Words* Are the words simple or ornate? conversational or formal? Are most of the words in the vocabulary of average ninth-graders, or does the author assume great experience and a vast reading knowledge on the part of the reader?

2. *Sounds* Does the writer rely heavily on techniques of sound? Is there an attempt to adjust the sounds in the work to the ideas they express? (For example, use the *s* sound in describing a snake to suggest a hissing noise.)

3. *Rhythms* Do the rhythms (or lack of rhythms) in a work suit the ideas expressed? Are the rhythms mechanical and consistent, are they nearly unpredictable, or do they shift to accommodate meaning?

4. *Imagery* Does the writer make use of imagery or figurative language?

5. *Tone* What is the author's tone?

style

The manner in which a writer makes words fit ideas in accordance with audience and purpose. The manner in which a writer uses language involves many choices: which words to use and how to arrange them; whether or not to use techniques of sound, rhythmic patterns, imagery, and figurative language; what tone to create.

Apply to "**A Lincoln Preface**" on page 455

theme

If You Hear That a Thousand People Love You

IF you hear that a thousand people love you
remember . . . saavedra is among them.

IF you hear that a hundred people love you
remember . . . saavedra is either in the first
or very last row

IF you hear that seven people love you
remember . . . saavedra is among them,
like a wednesday in the middle of the week

IF you hear that two people love you
remember . . . one of them is saavedra

IF you hear that only one person loves you
remember he is saavedra

AND when you see no one else around you,
and you find out
that no one loves you anymore,
then you will know for certain
that . . . saavedra is dead

Guadalupe de Saavedra

1. The poet narrows his focus from a potential cast of a thousand lovers to none. What does he mean when he says that if "a hundred people love you . . . last row" (lines 3 and 4)? when he says that among seven lovers he is "like a wednesday . . . week" (line 7)?

2. The poet might have concluded the poem by stating "I will always love you." In what way does the conclusion he makes in the final stanza cause his statement to be more emphatic?

3. Does the poet's use of repetition add to his message? Explain.

4. Assume that you must send a telegram of not more than ten words. What words would you use in an attempt to express the same message as emphatically as Saavedra does?

5. Which of the following statements best expresses the main idea of this poem? **(a)** Love is an amazing quality; (**b**) I could die for love of you; (**c**) I'll love you first, last, and always, until I die.

The theme of a work of literature is the main idea with which the selection deals. The main idea of Saavedra's poem is expressed in statement (**c**), since it most fully embodies the poet's sentiments. Any such paraphrase of the poem, of course, lacks the personal commitment and emphasis that the actual poem conveys through use of repetition, figurative language, and the cumulative effect that the poet achieves in counting himself among a potentially narrowing number of lovers.

While the *subject* of a work is the topic on which an author has chosen to write, the theme makes some statement or expresses an opinion about that topic. For example, the topic of "If You Hear That a Thousand People Love You" is love; the theme is the poet's limitless, unwavering love for his beloved, unaffected by any number of others who might also be counted as lovers.

Some literary works do not have a specific theme. Works written purely for entertainment or escape (a fantasy or a mystery story) or those calculated to evoke an emotion (a lyric) may not have themes. A work also may embody several themes. And while *Romeo and Juliet,* for example, portrays two young lovers fated to die, it would be an injustice to reduce the work to any of the following statements: "Young love is too intense to last," or "The course of true love ne'er runs smooth," or "Love is often the victim of fate or chance."

theme

The main idea or underlying meaning of a literary work. A theme may be directly stated, but more often it is implied.

Apply to "**The Magic Shop**" on page 348

tone

The following is a sketch by Kay Boyle written in response to a newspaper headline which read: "Deserted Wife Tells Court of Hardships Endured on Pittance of $1000 a Month." As you read it, decide how the author feels about her subject.

"I'm a poor woman now," said Mrs. Liggett, taking the stand with her lipstick putting in a word for itself every now and then. "I can't entertain any more the way I used to, I can't have a box at the opera. I can't go to a play every week the way I once did. I can't pay two hundred dollars for a dress. I can't even go to church," said Mrs. Liggett. "I can't afford to pay for a sitting as I've always done."

There were sounds of smothered weeping in the courtroom, and even the judge was seen to take out his handkerchief and blow his nose with suspicious vigor.

"Go on," said her husband's lawyer. "Go on, Mrs. Liggett," and in his gruff voice there was a noticeable quaver.

"I'm four thousand dollars in debt," said Mrs. Liggett with a dazzling smile at the jurors. "I'm way behind on my dry-cleaner's bill. We used to have the bridal suite every time we went to Europe, and now Mr. Liggett pretends he can't even let me have the thousand dollars monthly he settled on me when he deserted me three years ago!"

"It's an outrage!" cried a hysterical voice in the crowded courtroom, and a fainting woman was helped by attendants out the door.

"I've tried and tried to economize," said Mrs. Liggett. "You've no idea. I cut out olives and celery and salted nuts. Once," she said, "the children went without dessert, and I didn't have a cake or candles or anything on my birthday."

"It's terrible," said one of the jurors, his throat working.

"American womanhood," said Mrs. Liggett's attorney, his voice unsteady, "has suffered more in these last years, gentlemen of the jury, than it is possible for us to understand. . . ."

Suddenly Mr. Liggett leaped to his feet. "Listen," he cried out. "I live in one room, I walk to work every morning. . . ."

"I think he's awfully silly not to come home and use the car," said Mrs. Liggett with a lovely smile.

1. What are some of the examples Mrs. Liggett cites to prove she is now a poor woman? Do you think these details provide proof of her poverty?

2. How do the judge and members of the court react to her story?

3. What do Mrs. Liggett's final suggestion and "lovely smile" reveal about her sincerity and motives?

By now you should be able to determine the author's attitude toward her subject. Which of the following would describe this attitude: *bitter, satiric, earnest, indignant, objective, humorous, sympathetic?*

The attitude an author expresses toward a given subject is called *tone.* Unlike a speaker who can express tone through emphasis or inflection (rising and falling of the voice), a writer cannot use an actual, audible voice. Instead, writers must rely on techniques such as word choice, presentation of characters and events, and choice of details to convey their tone. Boyle informs the reader that Mrs. Liggett's lipstick puts "in a word for itself every now and then"—suggesting her lipstick is bright or heavily applied. In what way does this detail establish the author's attitude toward her subject? By the end of the passage, what is your opinion of Mrs. Liggett? What additional details helped shape that opinion?

The author uses words such as *outrage, smothered weeping,* and *noticeable quaver* which, in themselves, suggest deep emotion. In context, however, these words suggest unrealistic reactions to Mrs. Liggett's plight. In addition, the judge blows his nose "with suspicious vigor," an hysterical voice cries, "It's an outrage," and a woman faints. Mrs. Liggett's attorney finally equates the exaggerated suffering of his client with the lot of "American womanhood." In what way do these details serve to reinforce the author's tone?

Through careful selection of words and details and through exaggeration, Boyle has presented her subject humorously. But the humor has a satiric bite.

tone

The author's attitude, stated or implied, toward a subject. Words to describe attitudes include these: *serious, bitter, humorous, sympathetic, indignant, whimsical, joyous, mocking, cynical,* and *ironic.* An author's tone can be revealed through choice of words and details. Tone should not be confused with *mood,* which is the climate of feeling within a literary work; for example, an author may create a mood of quietude around a subject such as love, but treat the subject in an ironic tone.

Apply to "**Ponds**" on page 451

Composition Guide

It takes practice to become a good writer. It also takes the awareness that writing as a process begins long before you first put pen to paper, and that it does not end until you have revised, edited, and proofread your work. This Guide offers practical advice for writing many of the composition assignments in this book. Although the techniques described apply directly to the kinds of assignments that accompany selections in this text, you will find them useful in other kinds of writing as well.

This Guide includes the following articles:

Prewriting

Do you have trouble getting started when you write? Do you often find yourself staring at a blank sheet of paper, wondering how to begin? Remind yourself that a good composition does not just happen. You create it, and you do not do so all at once. Be patient and take your assignment one step at a time.

First of all, whenever you are given a composition assignment, you spend some time in preparing yourself to write. This *prewriting* can take a few minutes or several hours, but you can make the best use of the time you spend by planning your prewriting activities. Here are some suggestions:

1. Understand the assignment. You can write well only when you clearly understand what you are supposed to be writing about. Ask questions if you don't. If there are several parts to the assignment, make sure you take all the parts into account.

2. Think it over. Most of your writing assignments will be based on something you have read. Reread that selection carefully, and reread it again if necessary. The more familiar you are with a selection, the clearer it will be in your mind and the easier it will be to write about. Don't put it off—start thinking as soon as you know your assignment. Jot down all the ideas that come to your mind. Don't try for any sort of order in these notes; just be sure you can understand later what you had in mind.

3. Talk it over. Class discussions are an invaluable source of ideas. You might also try discussing the selection—and your reactions to it—with your friends. Often a friendly disagreement can result in new ideas and insights. Jot down also any ideas that come from these discussions.

4. Plan ahead. When you travel, you may take one route or another, but you must always be aware of where you're coming from and where you're going. An outline, like a road map, can help keep you from getting lost between the beginning and the end of your composition. It does not have to be formal, with Roman numerals and capital letters. For many compositions, a list of three or four points you want to cover may be just enough. All that's important is that whatever notations you make for a plan mean something to *you*.

5. Consider your audience and your purpose. Actually, you do this unconsciously before any kind of communication, written or oral. You do not, for example, talk in exactly the same way to your classmates as you do to your teacher. Similarly, you do not write in the same way for different types of readers. Since the whole point of any writing is to communicate your thoughts in the most effective way possible, consider seriously: Who is your audience? What is your purpose?

6. Write a rough draft. Promise yourself that you will *not* hand in your first version. Therefore, you do not need to worry about neatness, correctness, or penmanship. Concentrate instead on getting your ideas down on paper. Write as quickly as you can in order to keep a flow of words going. Refer to your plan from time to time to be sure you are covering all the important points. Since no one will see your first draft but you, feel free to start a sentence over, to insert things or move things around, even to write notes to yourself on how you will fix things later.

Revising

Revising is rewriting until you are convinced that your composition is as good as you can make it. This is an essential part of the writing process, but it should be done only after you have given your first draft a rest—at least overnight. This lets you look at your work in a fresh light, and you can catch errors that you might not have noticed earlier and make changes that you might have hesitated to make before.

Like prewriting, revising is best done in stages:

1. Examine your first draft. Ask yourself the following questions:

- Is the main idea of the paper clearly stated (probably in the first paragraph)?
- Does the paper convey a clear sense of progression, a steady movement from one important idea to the next? Have you used transition words *(first, next, on the other hand, as a result)* to show how your ideas are related?
- Has each paragraph been developed in sufficient detail? A short paragraph may occasionally be used for dramatic effect, but otherwise paragraphs should be equally well developed.
- Are the opening and closing paragraphs forceful and interesting? Does the last paragraph deliver what the first paragraph promises?
- Are your examples and details clear? Do they all relate directly to your purpose? Is each one necessary?
- Does the paper sound good when read aloud? Where could *and*'s be eliminated and sentences combined? Are there any monotonously repeated sentence patterns?
- Is each sentence clear and complete? Will every phrase and word be understandable to your readers?
- Have you used strong verbs and precise nouns wherever possible?
- Have you used the appropriate tone (humorous, serious, and so on) and level of formality (formal or informal) to reach your intended audience?
- Does your composition completely fulfill the assignment? (Reread your original assignment.)

2. Edit. Before typing or copying your paper in its final form, check carefully for errors in grammar, mechanics, and usage:

- Are all words spelled correctly? (Use a dictionary if you're not sure.)
- Is your punctuation logical? Is it helpful in making meaning clear?
- Have you used capitals, italics, numerals, and abbreviations correctly?
- Are quotations worded exactly as the originals? Have you used quotation marks correctly?
- Have you checked pronouns and verbs for common errors such as faulty agreement, incorrect pronoun form or reference, incorrect form of the verb?
- Can you spot any errors in word choice or usage?

3. Proofread. After you have copied or typed your final version (the one you will hand in), set the copy aside for a time (again, overnight if possible) so you can read with fresh eyes. Now proofread to make sure that you actually wrote what you meant to write. Read slowly, word by word. You may find it helpful to use a ruler or a card with a narrow slot cut in it to help you focus on only one line or a few words at a time. Watch for these common copying errors:

- The omitted word (''France rolled with exceeding downhill'').
- The doubled word (''making paper money and and spending it'').

Making Comparisons and Contrasts

''Both Romeo and Paris are compulsive and inexperienced, and they are both in love with Juliet.'' ''In *A Tale of Two Cities* the sacrifice of Sydney Carton seems even more heroic when contrasted with his earlier actions.'' Authors frequently make use of both similarities and differences to generate the conflicts that provide the plots of most stories, novels, and plays. Focusing on such similarities (making comparisons) or on such differences (making contrasts) can be an effective way of understanding the natures of two or more characters, places, situations, etc. When you write about literature, you may be able to understand a selection better if you understand the similarities and differences that are part of its structure. Here are some suggestions:

1. Find a focus. Examine your assignment to be sure you understand what is being called for. Writing assignments may be general (''Compare Antigone with her sister Ismene''), or they may be more specific (''Compare Antigone and Ismene in terms of the way each sister perceives her duty and does it''). An assignment may ask you to discuss only likenesses, or only differences—or both likenesses and differences. Your composition should fulfill the assignment exactly; it should include the similarities and/or differences called for and no others.

2. Determine points of comparison. If your parents were buying a new car, they might go from one car dealer to another, looking at various makes and models. Mentally—or perhaps even on paper—they might compare one car with another on the basis of *cost, appearance, mileage, comfort,* and *upkeep.* Each of these five categories is a point of comparison.

Sometimes a writing assignment will include points of comparison for you to consider. If it does not, you must come up with your own. You will have to decide which are important and which are not. In comparing Antigone and Ismene, for example, physical characteristics might not be important, but their background might be, since these two daughters of a former king have developed different personalities in spite of their having had the same upbringing. After some consideration, you might come up with points of comparison like these:

- Feelings for other characters
- Attitude toward authority
- Reaction to current situation
- Courage
- Actions

If the assignment were to compare two other characters, you would probably start with a totally different list. You may find later that you must drop some points of comparison and add others, but for now your list will help you get organized and keep you from comparing your subjects in unrelated categories.

3. Collect details. Use your list of points of comparison as heads for separate columns. Then go back through the selection carefully, listing in their appropriate columns whatever details you think might be useful. Include actions, speeches, descriptions, etc. For Antigone and Ismene, a partial list of one of the points of comparison might look like this:

ANTIGONE	ISMENE
Attitude toward authority	
• Defiant of Creon	• Respects the law
• Has her father's "stubborn spirit" (Chorus)	• "I can do no other/But as I am commanded"
• Honors "Those things to which honor truly belongs"	• Does not defy laws of heaven, but afraid to act against Creon
• Creon's laws not strong enough to "overrule the unwritten unalterable laws of God and heaven"	• "Our rulers are stronger than we, and we must obey them in this"
• Claims others feel the same but dare not say so	• Not ashamed to stand beside Antigone in her "hour of trial"

Strive to collect equivalent information (not similar, but parallel). That is, if you write something under Antigone's name, try to add a statement on the same topic under Ismene's. It may not be possible to make the columns equal line-for-line, but if you find that the information in a category is too skimpy or too lopsided, you may have to abandon that category and find another.

4. Choose an organizational pattern. There are a number of ways to organize a paper of comparison and contrast. You can first completely discuss one of your subjects and then turn to the other subject. For each subject, discuss the same points of comparison in exactly the same order. Be sure to give your subjects "equal time" (that is, use about the same amount of space and say approximately the same *number* of things about each).

A second method is to compare the subjects point by point, writing a sentence or two for each point. For example: "Ismene claims that 'Our rulers are stronger than we, and we must obey in this.' Antigone, on the other hand, feels that Creon and his laws are not strong enough to 'overrule the unwritten unalterable laws of God and heaven.' "

A third method is to discuss all the similarities of your subjects in one part of your paper and all the differences in another. No matter which pattern you choose, be aware that the material coming last in your paper will seem to have the greatest emphasis. Therefore, if you feel that Antigone's and Ismene's actions are more important than their attitudes or feelings for others, discuss actions last.

5. Make your comparisons and contrasts easy to spot. As you write your paper, direct your reader's attention to whatever point you're making by using words that signal the similarities and differences. Here are some words you can use:

- Similarity: *likewise, the same as, too, also, similarly, compared to.*
- Difference: *but, yet, however, on the other hand, unlike, conversely.*

Such words used at the beginning or end of every sentence can draw undue attention to themselves, however. You can avoid monotony by occasionally inserting them in the middle of a sentence. Sometimes sentence structure in itself can signal the comparison. For example: "Antigone wants her deed made known 'to all the world'; Ismene cautions secrecy." Or, "Antigone wants her deed made known 'to all the world.' Ismene wants her not to breathe a word about it."

At the same time, try to show the *significance* of the similarity or difference. For example: "In cautioning Antigone to 'at least be secret,' Ismene further demonstrates her fear of Creon."

6. Add a conclusion. The conclusion of your paper should remind your reader of the purpose for which you have made your comparisons and contrasts, with perhaps a brief summary of the points of comparison that have fulfilled that purpose. This may be the place, also, to state your own opinion or tell what you have learned.

Writing a Description

In "The Most Dangerous Game" General Zaroff is introduced in this way: "He was a tall man past middle age, for his hair was a vivid white; but his thick eyebrows and pointed military mustache were as black as the night from which Rainsford had come. His eyes, too, were black and very bright. He had high cheekbones, a sharp-cut nose, a spare, dark face, the face of a man used to giving orders, the face of an aristocrat. . . . his smile showed red lips and pointed teeth." Thus, through a series of details and images, the reader is able to visualize General Zaroff and even begin to sense what kind of person he is.

People create descriptions of many things for many reasons: a new dress, the location of a particularly good fishing spot, what happens when one chemical is added to another. But whether you are describing a person, a place, an action, or an object, the process is basically the same:

1. Form a picture. You can best create a picture for someone else only after you have fully developed that picture yourself. If you're describing a real person or place, observe carefully, looking for distinguishing characteristics. If you're describing an imaginary place, try to visualize it in every detail. What is in the foreground? the background? What colors dominate? Are there sounds? smells? Make notes of such details. (It may help to draw a rough sketch.) Try also to visualize an imaginary person performing some sort of action. How do you react to this person? How does he or she react to you?

2. Find a purpose. A good description often conveys one dominant impression. How do you feel about your subject? What mood, feeling, idea, or opinion do you want your reader to have about your subject?

No matter what your subject is, you cannot

include every detail in your composition. Your purpose will help you decide which details to emphasize and which to omit. Look again at the description of General Zaroff. Which details give you the impression that he is a sharp man? a man of contrasts? a potentially dangerous man?

From your notes choose those details that will most effectively create the dominant impression that you wish your reader to have.

3. Arrange the details. You might present your details in space order, showing where things are in terms of foreground, middle ground, and background; of left and right; or of north and south: "On my left was an immense mural depicting the Battle of Bull Run." You might present your details in the order that they impressed you: "The first thing I noticed about the car was its many dents and rust spots." Or you might arrange details in order of increasing importance: "But the most striking thing about her were her eyes."

Whichever order you choose, be consistent. Don't start with one organizational approach and suddenly shift to another.

4. Show; don't tell. You are telling when you say, "My brother is fun to be with." You are showing when you provide an anecdote, narrate an incident, or quote some conversation that demonstrates he is fun to be with. You are telling when you say, "I play softball very well." You are showing when you say, "I hit three home runs in one game, played first base for two years, and pitched several winning games." The second statement allows the reader to understand not only that you are good at softball, but *how* good you are.

5. Choose your words carefully. Strong verbs, exact nouns, and precise adjectives and adverbs help make your descriptions more effective. Verbs such as *is, am, are, was,* and *were* may be weak when they do not help a reader visualize what is happening. For a common verb such as *walk,* try substituting more precise verbs such as *stalk, march, prowl, shuffle, strut, plod, stroll,* or *saunter.*

If you have written, "Around the corner of the building came a ferocious dog," add details that will allow the reader to see that dog. What kind is it—terrier? poodle? mutt? What color is it? Is it walking? trotting? running? Are its ears lying close to its head? Is it growling? Are its fangs bared?

Use adjectives and adverbs sparingly. If you find yourself using a whole string of modifiers to describe a word ("He was a dirty, ragged, unshaven, mussed-up, lousy bum"), you may not have found the best modifier ("He was a mangy-looking bum").

6. Apply "technique." As you write your description, make use of the literary techniques you've observed in your reading:

- *Imagery.* Use words that appeal to the senses of sight, hearing, touch, smell, and taste, as is done in this example from "The Scarlet Ibis": "The flower garden was stained with rotting brown magnolia petals, and ironweeds grew rank amid the purple phlox. The five o'clocks by the chimney still marked time, but the oriole nest in the elm was untenanted and rocked back and forth like an empty cradle. The last graveyard flowers were blooming, and their smell drifted across the cotton field and through every room of our house, speaking softly the names of our dead." What sensory experiences are conveyed by this description? What can you see? hear? smell?
- *Similes and metaphors.* Figurative comparisons can make details clearer or more vivid: "His linen was as white as the tops of the waves that broke upon the neighboring beach or the specks of sail that glinted in the sunlight far at sea." Try to use fresh and original comparisons and to make them appropriate to the subject. (In the example from "The Scarlet Ibis," what is particularly appropriate about the untenanted oriole nest rocking back and forth "like an empty cradle"?)

• *Personification.* Giving objects human characteristics will enliven your description; for example: "Hunger stared down from the smokeless chimneys . . ." emphasizes the desperate lives of the poor in *A Tale of Two Cities.*

7. Don't just stop—finish. A short description does not have to be summarized. However, some sort of conclusion will help fix in your reader's mind the dominant impression you've been building. Which of the following final sentences is more effective?

• "After cleaning my room, I finally went to bed pleased with myself."

• "In the closet, the shoes were lined up, pair by pair; on the desk, the papers were straightened, the half-eaten peanut butter sandwich was gone, and the pencils were sharpened; clean sheets invited me to bed, and smiling, I climbed in and turned out the light."

Assuming Another Voice

From time to time you are asked to pretend to be someone else and to write as if you were that person—to assume that person's voice. But how *do* you go about being someone else in writing? To take on another personality—and do it convincingly—involves making an effort to put yourself in that character's place. You must think, react, and speak as that character would. Here are some suggestions on how to do it:

1. Put yourself in someone's place. The more you know about someone, the easier it is to understand how that person thinks and reacts to situations—and to predict how that person would react in a new situation. This also holds true for fictional characters. If, for example, your assignment is to write as Charles Darnay in *A Tale of Two Cities,* you first have to learn all you can about his background—his age, education, family, and so on. Make a list of the things you know about him.

Next, consider what makes Darnay "tick": What motivates him? What makes him do what he does? Clearly, in Darnay's case, much of what he does is determined by forces beyond his control and stronger than he is (the French Revolution and all that led to it). But much of what he does is also directed by his personal desires and beliefs. Analyze his behavior in various situations and add to your list brief descriptions of reasons for this behavior.

Finally, consider the situation Darnay is in *at this moment* (the situation specified in your assignment). People express themselves differently in different situations. For example, if you were Darnay, how would you feel while you were on trial for your life, accused of treason? How would you feel later, when you were safely home, relaxing with Lucie and Dr. Manette? Consider the circumstances surrounding the character you are to become, and add this information to your list.

2. Plan what you will say. This, of course, depends upon whether your assignment is specific ("Assume that you are Charles Darnay, writing a letter from a French prison to Lucie Manette in England, telling her about your arrest and imprisonment") or whether you are given free choice in what you say ("What do you think Lucie and Dr. Manette would say when they learn that Charles has been arrested? Assume that you are Lucie or Dr. Manette . . ."). If the assignment is specific, reread the relevant parts of the selection and make notes on exactly what does happen. In an assignment that gives you some choice, you will have to make up the incidents and speeches. But be sure that what you make up fits the characters and the situations. Lucie and

Dr. Manette, for example, would not be likely in this circumstance to hold a conversation about the latest book or play.

3. Plan how you will say it. Here's where your knowledge of the character's background comes into play. People from different backgrounds say things in different ways. Study some speeches your character has in the selection. Does the character use a large vocabulary in long sentences, or few words in simple sentences? Does the character speak standard English or a dialect like Aunt Arie? Do you notice any peculiar speech patterns or unusual words? Does the character tend to express emotions while speaking (like Darnay) or hide them (like Monsieur the Marquis)?

Again, consider the situation your character is in. Is the atmosphere tense and threatening, happy and relaxed, or something else? Try to picture yourself in the same situation and see how it makes you feel. This imaginative identification will help you speak more convincingly for your character.

4. Compare with the original. After you have completed your composition, read aloud at least part of the selection in which your character appears, and then read aloud what you have written. Ask yourself these questions:

- Do your words echo the original in feeling and tone?
- Do the words you have given your character sound appropriate to that character?
- Are the ideas or emotions that you have given your character consistent with his or her personality?
- Do they seem reasonable in the specific situation?

Evaluating Your Evidence

Suppose your composition assignment asks: "Does Doodle's brother in 'The Scarlet Ibis' teach him to walk because he cares strongly about him, or does he act selfishly in doing so because he is embarrassed to have a brother who cannot walk?" You could write, "Doodle's brother really cares about him and wants him to walk." Or, you could write, "Doodle's brother has a more selfish motive than a loving one." Either way, however, you can't expect your reader simply to take your word for it. You must plan on proving your point. (See "Defending Your Position" in this Guide for help with this part of the process.)

But before you can prove anything, you will need evidence with which to construct a convincing case. (It's no accident that certain terms used with this type of writing are the same terms used in a court of law.) In composition, such evidence is made up of facts, details, quotations, reasons—even inferences and opinions, if they are well-supported. To construct the most convincing case possible, you must evaluate these pieces of evidence carefully:

1. Factual evidence. The strongest evidence is facts about which there can be little or no disagreement. "The first skirmish of the Civil War was the firing on Fort Sumter on April 12, 1861" is an historical fact. In literature, a fact is something that is stated by the author; for example: "In the beginning of 'A Death in the House' Mose finds a strange creature." Generally speaking, we simply accept what the author or narrator tells us as fact.

Important issues in a work of literature are seldom resolved by simply reciting facts, however. If this were so, there would be no differences of opinion. In literature as in life, it is often how facts are interpreted that provides much of the interest and richness.

2. Inferential evidence. This kind of evidence is based on factual detail, but goes beyond such detail and into interpretation. An inference is a reasonable conclusion or generalization drawn from hints or clues of various sorts. To reach such a conclusion, you must apply logic and common sense to whatever facts are available. For example: "Toward the conclusion of 'The Most Dangerous Game' General Zaroff says, 'One of us is to furnish a repast for the hounds. The other will sleep in this very excellent bed. On guard, Rainsford.' The story then concludes, 'He had never slept in a better bed, Rainsford decided.' Rainsford has obviously won their 'game' by killing General Zaroff." Such an inference is reasonable because Zaroff leaves Rainsford no other choice. (You might consider whether it would be reasonable to infer that Rainsford actually feeds Zaroff to the hounds, whether such an act would be consistent with his character.)

Successful use of inferential evidence is a real test of your abilities as a careful reader and a persuasive writer. An inference does not carry the weight of fact, but it is valid evidence, and a combination of well-founded inferences can provide firm support for your position. It is wise to use some qualifying words such as *perhaps, probably, seems,* or *suggests* to show that you are aware of the inferential nature of your evidence and that you are deliberately evaluating it. But take care that you do not use so many qualifying words that you create an impression of weakness or uncertainty.

3. Outside evidence. At times, for specific reasons, you may find it helpful to use evidence drawn from outside the selection you're writing about. Here are two examples: "The method Annie Sullivan uses to teach language to Helen Keller in *The Miracle Worker* was invented by Dr. Samuel G. Howe in the 1830s, but Annie develops her own version of it through trial and error." "The phrase 'I have a dream' that Dr. Martin Luther King, Jr., repeats so often in his speech was to become a kind of rallying cry for the Civil Rights Movement." When you use outside evidence, make sure that it meets these qualifications:

- It is accurately quoted and comes from a reliable source. (Be sure to identify the source.)
- It is clearly related to your argument.
- It is presented as directly and concretely as possible.

4. Personal opinions and sweeping generalizations. Your opinion has a place in your writing, of course—many assignments even call for one. But when used as evidence, an unsupported opinion is weak. Unless you can make clear to your reader *why* you think a certain way, you risk losing that reader's attention (and losing your "case"). Beware of writing in circles and saying in effect nothing more than, "I believe this is true because this is what I believe is true."

A sweeping generalization is like an inference carried too far; for example: "Airdales, like Muggs in 'The Dog That Bit People' are dangerous dogs." When you find yourself using words like *always, every, never, none, nobody,* and so on, stop and think again. You may need to rephrase your statement. Unsupported sweeping generalizations are not evidence, and in most cases they should be avoided in writing.

5. Fair and unfair evidence. A quotation from a selection must not only be exactly worded, it must be true to the original tone and intention of the selection. A statement like "Amelia had no formal education past the eighth grade" may take on an entirely different meaning when seen in its original context: "Amelia had no formal education past the eighth grade, but she had read everything in the family library and could talk knowledgeably about a wide range of subjects." Using a partial and misleading quotation in this way is called quoting *out of context*.

But material need not be quoted in order to be out of context; for example, mentioning that Doodle's brother in "The Scarlet Ibis" cruelly abandons him during the storm—without adding that the brother soon goes back to find him and then weeps for a long time over Doodle's body—is also using material out of context. Any event in a literary selection must be considered as part of the whole.

Such unfair use of evidence is not always deliberate; it may be just careless. But if you read the selection closely, think about it seriously, and choose your position carefully, you will be on your way to making the best use of the best evidence available.

Defending Your Position

In a literature course, you are often asked to express and defend an opinion. Consider the following composition assignment: "Who or what actually causes the deaths of Romeo and Juliet? Is it the feud between their two families? Friar Laurence's bad planning? Or are they 'star-crossed' from the very beginning? Support your opinion with specific references to the play." In order to complete this assignment successfully, you must do two things: come to your own conclusion about the issue, and convince your readers to agree with you. Here are some guidelines:

1. Go to the source. Before you form a conclusion, reread the selection and consider it carefully. What is your general impression? What position do you think you can support most effectively, based on your understanding of the selection? Often you can make use of words or phrases in the assignment itself to put your conclusion into sentence form. State your opinion clearly and forcefully: "Romeo and Juliet die because the feud between the two families is more powerful than their love." (Not: "It seems to me maybe Romeo and Juliet die because . . .") This statement may eventually be your topic sentence, but for now it will help you focus your evidence.

2. List your evidence. Think through once more your reasons for the position you took. Write them all down as they occur to you. (Don't worry about organizing them at this point.) Include everything that supports, or "proves," your statement—facts, details, reasons, inferences, opinions—and then skim through the selection again for additional details you may have overlooked.

3. Select your evidence. Now go through your notes and choose the items that will most convincingly support your position. (See "Evaluating Your Evidence" in this Guide for help with this part of the process.)

4. Consider the other side. There are always two sides to a question—and often more. At this point stop and ask yourself, "What's the best evidence *against* my position? Why doesn't this evidence change my mind?" If in fact you *do* change your mind, it's best to do so now; change the wording of your topic sentence to reflect your new opinion. But if your position survives these two questions, plan to include a brief discussion of the opposing evidence early in your own argument. By doing so, you demonstrate to your reader that you can see other sides to an issue, and that you are intelligent enough and fair enough to consider them.

5. Arrange your evidence. Instead of simply presenting detail after detail or quote after quote, you will find it more effective to group them. A statement that summarizes a number of such details can then serve as the topic sentence of one of your paragraphs, and a number of such statements (no more than three or four) can serve as your main points of support for your topic sentence.

Generally speaking, plan to save your most convincing argument for last. That way your argument builds up force as it moves along, and your conclusion will have greater impact.

6. Explain your evidence. What may seem obvious to you may not be so obvious to your reader. When you mention a piece of evidence, make sure that your reader can understand how that evidence relates to your point. For example, suppose you mention that in *Romeo and Juliet* the friar's messenger is quarantined just as he is about to leave for Mantua, with the result that Friar Laurence arrives at the tomb only minutes too late to save the lives of both Paris and Romeo. You might introduce such a piece of evidence (or explain it afterwards) with a comment like this: "Once again, chance—or their unlucky stars—work against the lovers by providing a complication that no one is responsible for and that no one could have forseen."

A demanding and useful question to ask yourself each time you bring up a supporting detail is "So what?" It will help you decide what is really important to your argument and also what isn't.

7. Finish with authority. You have made your point and presented evidence to back it up. Now summarize that evidence and restate your conclusion in different words. But keep this part brief.

This may be the place to add also your own reaction to the selection: "I feel they were bound to die because Juliet was too trusting and Romeo always acted too hastily." Or, "If I found myself in Romeo's or Juliet's situation, I would try first to discuss it with my parents." This is not the place, however, to introduce a last-minute bit of evidence or to make a new point. Leave your reader with a sense of completeness and finality and with confidence in your ability to make a well-founded judgment.

Glossary

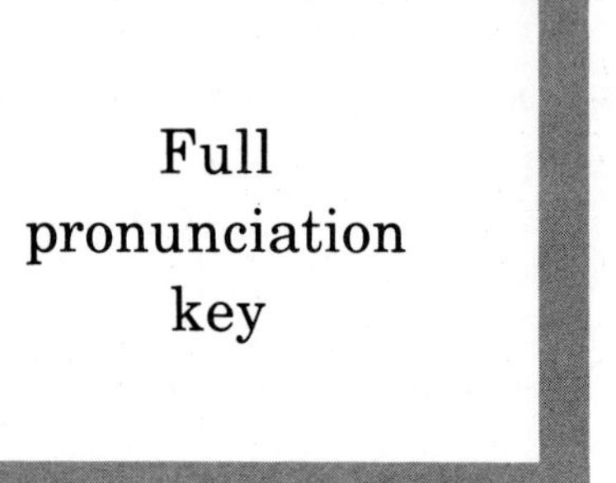

The pronunciation of each word is shown just after the word, in this way: **ab bre vi ate** (ə brē′vē āt). The letters and signs used are pronounced as in the words below. The mark ′ is placed after a syllable with primary or heavy accent, as in the example above. The mark ′ after a syllable shows a secondary or lighter accent, as in **ab bre vi a tion** (ə brē′vē ā′shən).

Some words, taken from foreign languages, are spoken with sounds that do not otherwise occur in English. Symbols for these sounds are given in the key as "foreign sounds."

a	hat, cap	j	jam, enjoy	u	cup, butter
ā	age, face	k	kind, seek	u̇	full, put
ä	father, far	l	land, coal	ü	rule, move
		m	me, am		
b	bad, rob	n	no, in	v	very, save
ch	child, much	ng	long, bring	w	will, woman
d	did, red			y	young, yet
		o	hot, rock	z	zero, breeze
e	let, best	ō	open, go	zh	measure, seizure
ē	equal, be	ô	order, all		
ėr	term, learn	oi	oil, voice	ə	represents:
		ou	house, out		a in about
f	fat, if				e in taken
g	go, bag	p	paper, cup		i in pencil
h	he, how	r	run, try		o in lemon
		s	say, yes		u in circus
i	it, pin	sh	she, rush		
ī	ice, five	t	tell, it		
		th	thin, both		
		ŦH	then, smooth		

foreign sounds

Y as in French *du.* Pronounce (ē) with the lips rounded as for (ü).

à as in French *ami.* Pronounce (ä) with the lips spread and held tense.

œ as in French *peu.* Pronounce (ā) with the lips rounded as for (ō).

N as in French *bon.* The N is not pronounced, but shows that the vowel before it is nasal.

H as in German *ach.* Pronounce (k) without closing the breath passage.

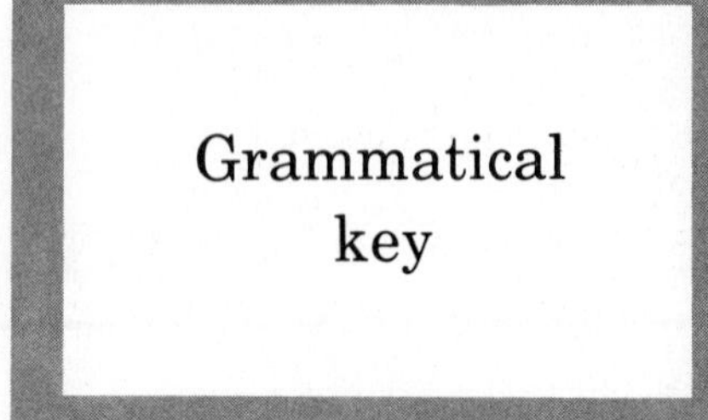

adj.	adjective	*prep.*	preposition
adv.	adverb	*pron.*	pronoun
conj.	conjunction	*v.*	verb
interj.	interjection	*v.i.*	intransitive verb
n.	noun	*v.t.*	transitive verb
sing.	singular	*pl.*	plural

a hat	**i** it	**oi** oil	**ch** child	ə = a in about
ā age	**ī** ice	**ou** out	**ng** long	e in taken
ä far	**o** hot	**u** cup	**sh** she	i in pencil
e let	**ō** open	**u̇** put	**th** thin	o in lemon
ē equal	**ô** order	**ü** rule	**ᴛʜ** then	u in circus
ėr term			**zh** measure	< = derived from

ab hor (ab hôr′), *v.t.,* **-horred, -hor ring.** regard with horror or disgust; hate completely; detest; loathe. [< Latin *abhorrere* < *ab-* from + *horrere* to shudder, shrink]

a bom i na ble (ə bom′ə nə bəl), *adj.* **1** arousing disgust and hatred; detestable; loathsome: *Kidnapping is an abominable crime.* **2** very unpleasant; disagreeable: *abominable manners.* **—a bom′i na bly,** *adv.*

ab solve (ab solv′, ab zolv′), *v.t.,* **-solved, -solv ing. 1** pronounce or set (a person) free from sin, guilt, blame, or their penalties or consequences. **2** set free (*from* a promise, obligation, or duty); release. [< Latin *absolvere* < *ab-* from + *solvere* loosen]

a dieu (ə dü′, ə dyü′), *interj., n., pl.* **a dieus** or **a dieux** (ə düz′ə dyüz′). good-by. [< Middle French < *à Dieu* to God]

ad ju ra tion (aj′ə rā′shən), *n.* an earnest or solemn appeal.

ad mon i to ry (ad mon′ə tôr′ē, ad mon′ə tōr′ē), *adj.* admonishing; warning.

af fa ble (af′ə bəl), *adj.* **1** courteous and pleasant in receiving and responding to the conversation or approaches of others. **2** gracious: *an affable smile.* [< Latin *affabilis* easy to speak to < *affari* speak to < *ad-* to + *fari* speak] **—af′fa ble ness,** *n.* **—af′fa bly,** *adv.*

af flic tion (ə flik′shən), *n.* **1** condition of continued pain or distress; misery. **2** cause of continued pain or distress; misfortune.

af ter deck (af′tər dek′), *n.* part of a deck toward or at the stern of a ship.

ag ile (aj′əl), *adj.* **1** moving with speed, ease, and elegance; lively; nimble: *as agile as a kitten.* **2** mentally alert; quick-witted. [< Latin *agilis* < *agere* to move] **—ag′ile ly,** *adv.* **—ag′ile ness,** *n.*

al ter ca tion (ôl′tər kā′shən, al′tər kā′shən), *n.* an angry dispute; noisy quarrel; wrangle.

am ber (am′bər), *n.* **1** a hard, translucent, yellow or yellowish-brown fossil resin, easily polished and used for jewelry, in making pipe stems, etc. **2** the color of amber; yellow or yellowish brown. *—adj.* **1** made of amber. **2** yellow or yellowish-brown. [< Old French *ambre* < *Arabic 'anbar* ambergris]

an a lyt ical (an′l it′ə kəl), *adj.* **1** having to do with breaking up of anything complex into its various simple elements. **2** based on the method of studying the nature of a thing or of determining its essential elements.

an i mos i ty (an′ə mos′ə tē), *n., pl.* **-ties.** keen hostile feelings; active dislike or enmity; ill will.

an ni hi la tion (ə nī′ə lā′shən), *n.* complete destruction.

Apache plume, a low shrub of southwestern United States and Mexico, having white flowers and plumelike fruiting clusters.

a pos tro phize (ə pos′trə fīz), *v.,* **-phized, -phiz ing.** *—v.i.* stop in a speech, poem, etc., and address some absent person as if he or she were present or a thing or idea as if it could appreciate what is said. *—v.t.* address an apostrophe to.

a poth e car y (ə poth′ə ker′ē), *n., pl.* **-car ies.** druggist; pharmacist. [< Late Latin *apothecarius* shopkeeper < Latin *apotheca* storehouse < Greek *apothēkē* < *apo-* + *tithenai* put]

ap pa ri tion (ap′ə rish′ən), *n.* **1** a supernatural sight or thing; ghost or phantom. **2** the appearance of something strange, remarkable, or unexpected. [< Late Latin *apparitionem*]

ap pel la tion (ap′ə lā′shən), *n.* **1** name or title describing or identifying someone. In "John the Baptist," the appellation of *John* is *the Baptist.* **2** act of calling by a name.

ap pre hen sive (ap′ri hen′siv), *adj.* afraid that some misfortune is about to occur; anxious about the future; fearful. **—ap′pre hen′sive ly,** *adv.* **—ap′pre hen′sive ness,** *n.*

ar chae ol o gist (är′kē ol′ə jist), *n.* an expert in archaeology. Also, **archeologist.**

ar chae ol o gy (är′kē ol′ə jē), *n.* the scientific study of the people, customs, and life of ancient times, antedating the keeping of historic records. Through excavation, identification, and study of the remains of ancient cities and of tools, pottery, monuments, or any other remains, archaeology is able to reconstruct a picture of life in the past. Also, **archeology.**

ar dent (ärd′nt), *adj.* **1** glowing with passion; passionate; impassioned: *ardent love.* **2** very enthusiastic; eager: *an ardent believer in the benefits of health foods.* **3** burning; fiery; hot: *an ardent fever.* **4** glowing. [< Latin *ardentem* burning] **—ar′dent ly,** *adv.*

ar ma da (är mä′də), *n.* **1** a large fleet of warships. **2** any large group of military vehicles. [< Spanish < Medieval Latin *armata* armed force.]

as sev e rate (ə sev′ə rāt′), *v.t.* **-rat ed, -rat ing.** declare solemnly; state positively. [< Latin *asseveratum* declared solemnly < *ad-* + *severus* serious] **—as sev′e ra′tion,** *n.*

as sid u ous (ə sij′ü əs), *adj.* careful and attentive; diligent. [< Latin *assiduus* < *assidere* sit by.] **—as sid′u ous ly,** *adv.* **—as sid′u ous ness,** *n.*

as sig na tion (as′ig nā′shən), *n.* **1** a secret meeting of lovers. **2** the appointment of a time and place for such a meeting. **3** an allotting; apportionment.

a tone ment (ə tōn′mənt), *n.* a giving of satisfaction for a wrong or injury; amends.

aug ment (ôg ment′), *v.t., v.i.* make or become greater in size, number, amount, or degree; increase or enlarge. [< Late Latin *augmentare* < *augmentum* an increase < Latin *augere* to increase] **—aug ment′a ble,** *adj.* **—aug ment′er,** *n.*

aus tere (ô stir′), *adj.* **1** stern in manner or appearance; harsh: *a silent, austere man.* **2** severe in self-discipline; strict in morals: *The Puritans were austere.* **3** severely simple: *The tall, plain columns stood against the sky in austere beauty.* **4** grave; somber; serious. [< Greek *austēros* < *auos* dry] **—aus tere′ly,** *adv.* **—aus tere′ness,** *n.*

a vi ar y (ā′vē er′ē), *n., pl.* **-ar ies.** house, enclosure, or large cage in which many birds, especially wild birds, are kept; bird-house. [< Latin *aviarium* < *avis* bird]

aw ful (ô′fəl), *adj.* **1** causing fear; dreadful; terrible: *an awful storm.* **2** deserving great respect and reverence; *the awful power of God.* **3** filling with awe; impressive; imposing: *The mountains rose to awful heights.*

be deck (bi dek′), *v.t.* deck out; adorn.

be hest (bi hest′), *n.* command; order. [Old English *behǣs* promise]

be night ed (bi nī′tid), *adj.* **1** not knowing right from wrong; ignorant. **2** ARCHAIC. overtaken by darkness. [< obsolete verb *benight* < *be-* + *night*]

be nign (bi nīn′), *adj.* **1** kindly in feeling; benevolent; gracious: *a benign old woman.* **2** showing a kindly feeling; gentle: *a benign countenance.* **3** favorable; propitious. **4** mild: *a benign climate.* **5** not dangerous to health; not malignant: *a benign tumor.* [< Latin *benignus* < *bene* well + *-gnus* born] **—be nign′ly,** *adv.*

be reave (bi rēv′), *v.t.,* **-reaved** or **-reft, -reav ing. 1** leave desolate and alone: *The family was bereaved by the death of the father.* **2** deprive ruthlessly; rob: *bereaved of hope.* [Old English *berēafian* < *be-* away + *rēafian* rob]

be reft (bi reft′), *adj.* bereaved: *Bereft of hope and friends, the old man led a lonely life.*

berth (bėrth), *n.* **1** place to sleep on a ship, train, or airplane. **2** a ship's place at anchor or at a wharf. **3** the space necessary for safety or convenience between a ship and other ships or the shore, rocks, etc. **4 give a wide berth to,** keep well away from.

blas phe my (blas′fə mē), *n., pl.* **-mies.** abuse or contempt for God or sacred things; profanity.

blight (blīt), *n.* **1** anything that withers hope or causes destruction or ruin. **2** decay; deterioration. *—v.t.* **1** cause to wither and die: *Mildew blighted the June roses.* **2** destroy; ruin: *The letter of rejection blighted all my hopes.* *—v.i.* be blighted; suffer from blight. [origin uncertain]

blun der buss (blun′dər bus), *n.* **1** a short gun with a wide muzzle and large bore, formerly used to shoot balls or slugs a very short distance without exact aim. **2** a blundering person. [alteration of Dutch *donderbus* thunder box]

boll (bōl), *n.* the rounded seed pod or capsule of a plant, especially that of cotton or flax. [Old English *bolla* round vessel]

bouil lon (bül′yon, bül′yən), *n.* **1** a clear, thin soup or broth. **2** a liquid, nutritive medium used for growing cultures of bacteria. [< French < *bouillir* to boil]

bri er (brī′ər), *n.* **1** a white heath tree found in southern Europe. **2** a tobacco pipe made of brierwood. Also, **briar.** [< French *bruyère* heath]

buf fet (buf′it), *n.* **1** a blow of the hand or fist. **2** a knock, stroke, or hurt. *—v.t.* **1** strike with the hand or fist. **2** knock about; strike repeatedly; beat back: *The waves buffeted me.* 3 fight or struggle against: *The boat buffeted the heavy waves caused by the storm.* —*v.i.* deal blows; struggle; contend. [< Old French, diminutive of *buffe* blow] **—buf′fet er,** *n.*

bur geon (bėr′jən), *v.i.* 1 grow or shoot forth; bud; sprout. 2 grow or develop rapidly; flourish: *Suburbs have burgeoned near the city.* —*n.* a bud; sprout. [< Old French *burjon* a bud]

bush ing (bu̇sh′ing), *n.* 1 a removable metal lining used to protect parts of machinery from wear. 2 a metal lining inserted in a hole, pipe, etc., to reduce its size. 3 a lining for a hole, to insulate one or more wires or other electrical conductors passing through. [< *bush* bushing < Middle Dutch *busse* box]

ca dav er ous (kə dav′ər əs), *adj.* 1 pale and ghastly. 2 thin and worn. 3 of or like a cadaver. **—ca dav′er ous ly,** *adv.*

cal a bash (kal′ə bash), *n.* 1 a gourdlike fruit whose dried shell is used to make bottles, bowls, drums, pipes, and rattles. 2 the tropical tree of the same family as the bignonia that it grows on. 3 bottle, bowl, drum, pipe, or rattle made from such a dried shell. [< Middle French *calabasse*]

can vass (kan′vəs), *v.t.* go through (a city, district, etc.) asking for votes, orders, donations, etc.: *Salesmen canvassed the whole city for subscriptions to magazines.*

ca pri cious (kə prish′əs, kə prē′shəs), *adj.* likely to change suddenly without reason; changeable; fickle: *capricious weather.* **—ca pri′cious ly,** *adv.* **—ca pri′cious ness,** *n.*

cap tiv i ty (kap tiv′ə tē), *n., pl.* **-ties.** 1 condition of being in prison. 2 condition of being held against one's will: *Some animals cannot bear captivity, and die after a few weeks in a cage.*

car i ca ture (kar′ə kə chu̇r, kar′ə kə-chər), *n., v.,* **-tured, -tur ing.** —*n.* 1 picture, cartoon, or description that exaggerates the peculiarities of a person or the defects of a thing. 2 imitation or rendering of something by ridiculous exaggeration of flaws in the original. —*v.t.* make a caricature of. [< French < Italian *caricatura* < *caricare* overload, exaggerate < Late Latin *carricare* to load < Latin *carrus* wagon] **—car′i ca tur′a ble,** *adj.*

caricature (def. 1) caricature of Abraham Lincoln

car nage (kär′nij), *n.* slaughter of a great number of people. [< Middle French < Italian *carnaggio,* ultimately < Latin *carnem* flesh]

cash ier (ka shir′), *v.t.* dismiss from service for some dishonorable act; discharge in disgrace. [< Dutch *casseren* < Old French *casser* or *quasser* < Latin *quassare* to break]

cat a ract (kat′ə rakt′), *n.* 1 a large, steep waterfall. 2 a violent rush or downpour of water; flood. [< Latin *cataracta* < Greek *kataraktēs* < *kata-* down + *arassein* to dash]

caul (kôl), *n.* a portion of the membrane enclosing a child in the womb that is sometimes found clinging to the head at birth. It was supposed to bring good luck and to safeguard against drowning. [Old English *cawl* basket, net]

cen sure (sen′shər), *n., v.,* **-sured, -sur ing.** —*n.* 1 expression of disapproval; unfavorable opinion; criticism. 2 penalty, as a public rebuke or suspension from office. —*v.t.* express disapproval of; find fault with; criticize. [< Latin *censura* < *censere* appraise] **—cen′sur er,** *n.*

chas u ble (chaz′yə bəl, chas′yə bəl), *n.* a sleeveless outer vestment worn by the priest at Mass. [< Old French < Late Latin *casubula* < Latin *casa* house]

châ teau (sha tō′), *n., pl.* **-teaux** (-tōz′). 1 a large country house in France or elsewhere in Europe. 2 a French castle. [< French < Latin *castellum* castle.]

chide (chīd), *v.,* **chid ed, chid, chid ing.** —*v.t.* find fault with; reproach or blame; scold: *She chided the little girl for soiling her dress.* —*v.i.* find fault; speak in rebuke: *The head nurse was always scolding and chiding.* [Old English *cīdan*] **—chid′er,** *n.* **—chid′ing ly,** *adv.*

chipyard, an area or enclosure where wood is cut up for fuel.

chol er ic (kol′ər ik), *adj.* 1 having an irritable disposition; easily made angry. 2 enraged; angry; wrathful: *a choleric outburst of temper.*

ci pher (sī′fər), *n.* 1 secret writing; code: *Part of the letter is in cipher.* 2 something in secret writing or code.

co er cion (kō ėr′shən, kō ėr′zhən), *n.* use of force; compulsion; constraint.

cog i tate (koj′ə tāt), *v.i., v.t.,* **-tat ed, -tat ing.** think over; consider with care; meditate; ponder. [< Latin *cogitatum* tossed around < *co-* (intensive) + *agitare* agitate] **—cog′i ta′tion,** *n.* **—cog′i ta′tor,** *n.*

co her ent (kō hir′ənt), *adj.* 1 logically connected; consistent: *A sentence that is not coherent is hard to understand.* 2 sticking together; holding together.

com bat ive (kəm bat′iv, kom′bə tiv), *adj.* ready to fight or oppose; fond of fighting; pugnacious. **—com bat′ive ly,** *adv.* **—com bat′ive ness,** *n.*

com mend (kə mend′), *v.t.* 1 speak well of; praise. 2 recommend. 3 hand over for safekeeping; entrust: *She commended the child to his care.* [< Latin *commendare* < *com-* + *mandare* commit, command]

com mis e rate (kə miz′ə rāt′), *v.t., v.i.,* **-rat ed, -rat ing.** feel or express sorrow for another's suffering or trouble; sympathize with; pity. [< Latin *commiseratum* pitied < *com-* + *miser* wretched] **—com mis′e ra′tion,** *n.*

com pas sion ate (kəm pash′ə nit), *adj.* desiring to relieve another's suffering; sympathetic; pitying. **—com pas′sion ate ly,** *adv.*

com pat i ble (kəm pat′ə bəl), *adj.* 1 able to exist or get on well together; agreeing; in harmony. 2 able to be combined without loss of effectiveness or danger to health: *compatible chemicals, compatible tissues.* [< Medieval Latin *compatibilem* < Latin *compati* suffer with] **—com pat′i bil′i ty,** *n.* **—com pat′i bly,** *adv.*

com ply (kəm plī′), *v.i.,* **-plied, -ply ing.** act in agreement with a request or command: *I will comply with the doctor's request.* [< Italian *complire* < Spanish *cumplir* < Latin *complere* fulfill, complete] **—com pli′er,** *n.*

con cer ti na (kon′sər tē′nə), *n.* a small musical instrument somewhat like an accordion.

con du cive (kən dü′siv, kən dyü′siv), *adj.* favorable; helpful: *Exercise is conducive to health.* **—con du′cive ness,** *n.*

con fis cate (kon′fə skāt), *v.t.,* **-cat ed, -cat ing.** 1 seize for the public treasury: *The new government confiscated the property of all the deposed leaders.* 2 seize by authority: *The teacher confiscated my comic book.* [< Latin *confiscatum* laid away in a chest < *com-* + *fiscus* chest, public treasury] **—con′fis ca′tor,** *n.*

con fis ca tion (kon′fə skā′shən), *n.* a confiscating or a being confiscated.

con front (kən frunt′), *v.t.* 1 meet face to face; stand facing. 2 face boldly; oppose. 3 bring face to face; place before: *The prosecuting attorney confronted the accused with the forged check.* [< Old French *confronter* < Medieval Latin *confrontare* < Latin *com-* together + *frontem* forehead] **—con′fron ta′tion,** *n.*

con i cal (kon′ə kəl), *adj.* 1 shaped like a cone: *conical mountains.* 2 of a cone. **—con′i cal ly,** *adv.*

con junc tion (kən jungk′shən), *n.* 1 a joining together; union; combination: *Rain in conjunction with hot weather helped the crops grow.* 2 a coming together, especially of events or circumstances. 3 the apparent nearness of two or more heavenly bodies to each other.

con sign ment (kən sīn′mənt), *n.* 1 act of consigning. 2 something consigned, especially a shipment sent to a person or company for safekeeping or sale. 3 **on consignment,** consigned to a person or company with the understanding that the goods will not be paid for until sold.

con sol a to ry (kən sol′ə tôr′ē, kən sol′ə tōr′ē), *adj.* consoling; comforting.

con sti tu tion al (kon′sta tü′she nel, kon′stə tyü′shə nəl), *adj.* of or in the constitution of a person or thing; inherent: *A constitutional weakness makes him subject to colds.*

con ten tious (kən ten′shəs), *adj.* 1 fond of arguing; given to disputing; quarrelsome. 2 characterized by contention: *a contentious campaign.* **—con ten′tious ly,** *adv.* **—con ten′tious ness,** *n.*

con ven tion al (kən ven′shə nəl), *adj.* 1 depending on conventions; customary: *"Good morning" is a conventional greeting.* 2 acting or behaving according to commonly accepted and approved ways.

con viv i al (kən viv′ē əl), *adj.* 1 fond of eating and drinking with friends; jovial; sociable. 2 of or suitable for a feast or banquet; festive. [< Latin *convivium* feast < *com-* with + *vivere* to live] **—con viv′i al ly,** *adv.*

a hat	**i** it	**oi** oil	**ch** child	a in about
ā age	**ī** ice	**ou** out	**ng** long	e in taken
ä far	**o** hot	**u** cup	**sh** she	**ə** = i in pencil
e let	**ō** open	**ů** put	**th** thin	o in lemon
ē equal	**ô** order	**ü** rule	**ᴛʜ** then	u in circus
ėr term			**zh** measure	**<** = derived from

cop pice (kop′is), *n.* copse.
copse (kops), *n.* thicket of small trees, bushes, shrubs, etc.; coppice. [< Old French *coupeïz* a cut-over forest < *couper* to cut]
cor rob o rate (kə rob′ə rāt′), *v.t.,* **-rat ed, -rat ing.** make more certain; confirm; support: *Eyewitnesses corroborated my testimony in court.* [< Latin *corroboratum* strengthened < *com-* + *roborem* oak, strength] **—cor rob′o ra′tor,** *n.*
coun te nance (koun′tə nəns), *n.* 1 expression of the face: *an angry countenance.* 2 face; features: *a noble countenance.*
crepe or **crêpe** (krāp), *n.* 1 a thin, light silk, cotton, rayon, or woolen cloth with a finely crinkled surface; crape. 2 crepe paper.
cul ti vat ed (kul′tə vā′tid), *adj.* 1 prepared and used to raise crops: *A field of wheat is cultivated land; a pasture is not.* 2 produced by cultivation; not wild: *Prize roses are cultivated flowers.* 3 improved or developed. 4 cultured; refined.
cur few (kėr′fyü), *n.* 1 rule requiring certain persons to be off the streets or at home before a fixed time: *There is a 10 p.m. curfew for children in our city.* 2 the ringing of a bell at a fixed time every evening as a signal. In the Middle Ages, it was a signal to put out lights and cover fires. 3 bell ringing such a signal: *Every night at nine the curfew rang.* 4 time when a curfew begins. [< Old French *covrefeu* < *covrir* to cover + *feu* fire]
cus to di al (ku stō′dē əl), *adj.* having to do with custody or custodians.

de face (di fās′), *v.t.,* **-faced, -fac ing.** spoil the appearance of; mar.[< Old French *defacer* < *de-* + *face* face] **—de face′a ble,** *adj.* **—de face′ment,** *n.* **—de fac′er,** *n.*
de fault (di fôlt′), *n.* 1 failure to do something or to appear somewhere when due; neglect. If, in any contest, one side does not appear, it loses by default. 2 **in default of,** in the absence of; having no; lacking: *In default of evidence, the case was dismissed.*
de file (di fīl′), *v.t.,* **-filed, -fil ing.** 1 make filthy or dirty; make disgusting in any way. 2 destroy the purity or cleanness of (anything sacred); desecrate. 3 stain; dishonor. 4 ARCHAIC. ravish.[< Old French *defouler* trample down or violate] **—de file′ment,** *n.* **—de fil′er,** *n.*
de fraud (di frôd′), *v.t.* take money, rights, etc., away from by fraud; cheat. **—de′frau da′tion,** *n.* **—de fraud′er,** *n.*
de gen e rate (di jen′ə rāt′), *v.i.* 1 grow worse; decline in physical, mental, or moral qualities. 2 (in biology) sink to a lower type; lose the normal or more highly developed characteristics of one's race or kind.
de mean or (di mē′nər), *n.* way a person looks and acts; behavior; manner.
dep re ca to ry (dep′rə kə tôr′ē, dep′rə kə tōr′ē), *adj.* 1 deprecating. 2 apologetic.
des pot ic (des pot′ik), *adj.* of a despot; having unlimited power; tyrannical. **—des pot′i cal ly,** *adv.*
de tes ta tion (dē′tes′tā′shən), *n.* 1 an intense dislike; hatred. 2 a detested person or thing.
de vi ous (dē′vē əs), *adj.* 1 out of the direct way; winding; roundabout: *We took a devious route through side streets and alleys to avoid the crowded main street.* 2 straying from the right course; not straightforward: *a devious scheme, a devious nature.*[< Latin *devius* turning aside < *de-* out of + *via* way] **—de′vi ous ly,** *adv.* **—de′vi ous ness,** *n.*
dex ter ous (dek′stər əs), *adj.* 1 skillful in using the hands or body. 2 having or showing skill in using the mind; clever. Also, **dextrous. —dex′ter ous ly,** *adv.* **—dex′ter ous ness,** *n.*
di a logue (dī′ə lôg, dī′ ə log), *n.,v.,* **-logued, -logu ing.** *—n.* 1 conversation between two or more persons. 2 conversation in a play, novel, story, etc. 3 airing of views; discussion. *—v.t.* put into dialogue. *—v.i.* hold a dialogue; converse.[< Greek *dialogos* < *dia-* between + *logos* speech]
di late (dī lāt′, də lāt′), *v.,* **-lat ed, -lat ing.** *—v.t.* make larger or wider: *When you take a deep breath, you dilate your nostrils.* *—v.i.* 1 become larger or wider: *The pupil of the eye dilates when the light gets dim.*
dirge (dėrj), *n.* a funeral song or tune. [contraction of Latin *dirige* direct! (first word in office for the dead)] **—dirge′like′,** *adj.*
dis- , *prefix.* 1 opposite of; lack of; not: *Dishonest = not honest; opposite of honest. Discomfort = lack of comfort.* 2 do the opposite of: *disentangle = do the opposite of entangle.* 3 apart; away, as in *dispel.*[< Latin]
dis com fit (dis kum′fit), *v.t.* 1 defeat the plans or hopes of; frustrate. 2 embarrass; confuse; disconcert. 3 ARCHAIC. defeat completely; rout.[< Old French *desconfit* discomfited < *des-* dis + *confire* make, accomplish]
dis con cert (dis′kən sėrt′), *v.t.* 1 disturb the self-possession of; embarrass greatly; confuse: *I was disconcerted to find that I was wearing two different shoes.* 2 upset or frustrate (plans, etc.). **—dis′con cert′ing ly,** *adv.*
dis con so late (dis kon′sə lit), *adj.* 1 without hope; forlorn; unhappy: *disconsolate over the death of a friend.* 2 causing discomfort; cheerless: *a long, disconsolate day.*[< Medieval Latin *disconsolatus* <*Latin dis-* + *consolari* to console] **—dis con′so late ly,** *adv.* **—dis con′so late ness,** *n.*
dis course (*n.* dis′kôrs, dis′kōrs; *v.* dis kôrs′, dis kōrs′), *n.,v.,* **-coursed, -cours ing.** *—n.* 1 a formal or extensive speech or writing: *Lectures and sermons are discourses.* 2 talk; conversation. *—v.i.* 1 speak or write formally or at length on some subject. 2 talk; converse.[< Latin *discursus* a running about < *dis-* + *cursus* a running]
dis cre tion (dis kresh′ən), *n.* 1 quality of being discreet; great carefulness in speech or action; good judgment; wise caution: *Use your own discretion.* 2 freedom to decide or choose: *It is within the principal's discretion to punish a pupil.*
dis par age (dis par′ij), *v.t.,* **-aged, -ag ing.** 1 speak slightingly of; belittle. 2 lower the reputation of; discredit.[< Old French *desparagier* match unequally < *des-* dis- + *parage* rank, lineage < *par* peer] **—dis par′age ment,** *n.* **—dis par′ag er,** *n.* **—dis par′ag ing ly,** *adv.*
dis pas sion ate (dis pash′ə nit), *adj.* free from emotion or prejudice; calm and impartial. **—dis pas′sion ate ly,** *adv.* **—dis pas′sion ate ness,** *n.*
dis po si tion (dis′pə zish′ən), *n.* 1 one's habitual ways of acting toward others or of thinking about things; nature: *a cheerful disposition.* 2 tendency; inclination: *a disposition to argue.*
dis sim u late (di sim′yə lāt), *v.,* **-lat ed, -lat ing.** *—v.t.* disguise or hide under a pretense; dissemble. *—v.i.* hide the truth; dissemble. **—dis sim′u la′tion,** *n.* **—dis sim′u la′tor,** *n.*
dis si pat ed (dis′ə pā′tid), *adj.* 1 indulging excessively in sensual or foolish pleasures; dissolute. 2 wasted. **—dis′si pat′ed ly,** *adv.* **—dis′si pat′ed ness,** *n.*
dis so lute (dis′ə lüt), *adj.* living an immoral life; loose in morals; licentious; dissipated.[< Latin *dissolutum* loosened, loose < *dis-* apart + *solvere* to loosen] **—dis′so lute′ly,** *adv.* **—dis′so lute′ness,** *n.*
ditch (dich), *n.* a long, narrow place dug in the earth, usually for carrying off water. *—v.t.* 1 dig a ditch in or around. 2 drive or throw into a ditch: *The careless driver ditched the car.* 3 crash-land (an airplane) in water. 4 INFORMAL. get rid of. *—v.i.* crash-land a plane in water. [Old English *dīc*] **—ditch′er,** *n.*
dog ged (dô′gid, dog′id), *adj.* not giving up; stubborn: *dogged determination.*[< *dog*] **—dog′ged ly,** *adv.* **—dog′ged ness,** *n.*
dol or ous (dol′ər əs, dō′ lər əs), *adj.* 1 full of or expressing sorrow; mournful. 2 causing or giving rise to sorrow; grievous; painful. **—dol′or ous ly,** *adv.* **—dol′or ous ness,** *n.*
doo dle bug (dü′dl bug′), *n.* larva of the ant lion, an insect that feeds on ants.
dour (důr, dour), *adj.* 1 gloomy or sullen: *a dour silence.* 2 stern; severe. [< Latin *durus* hard, stern] **—dour′ly,** *adv.* **—dour′ness,** *n.*
dow er (dou′ər), *n.* 1 a widow's share for life of her dead husband's property. 2 dowry. *—v.t.* provide with a dower; endow.[< Old French douaire < Medieval Latin *dotarium* < Latin *dotare* endow < *dotem* dowry]
droll (drōl), *adj.* odd and amusing; quaint and laughable: *a monkey's droll tricks.*[< French *drôle*] **—droll′ness,** *n.*
du bi ous (dü′bē əs, dyü′bē əs), *adj.* 1 filled with or being in doubt; doubtful; uncertain: *a dubious compliment.* 2 feeling doubt; wavering or hesitating.[< Latin *dubiosus* < *dubius* doubtful] **—du′bi ous ly,** *adv.* **— du′bi ous ness,** *n.*
dur ance (důr′əns, dyůr′əns), *n.* imprisonment.[< Old French, duration]

eaves (ēvz), *n. pl.* the lower edge of a roof that projects over the side of a building.[Old English *efes* edge]
ec cen tric i ty (ek′sen tris′ə tē), *n., pl.* **-ties** something strange or out of the ordinary; oddity; peculiarity.
ed dy (ed′ē), *n.* 1 water, air, smoke, etc., moving against the main current, especially when having a whirling motion; small whirlpool or whirlwind. 2 any similar current of fog or dust.
e dict (ē′dikt), *n.* 1 decree or law proclaimed by a king or other ruler on his or her sole authority. 2 any similar order or command.[< Latin *edictum* < *edicere* proclaim < *ex-* out + dicere say]
ef fi ca cy (ef′ə kə sē), *n.,pl.* **-cies.** power to produce the effect wanted; effectiveness: *The efficacy of aspirin in relieving headaches is well known.*[< Latin *efficacia <efficere accomplish < ex- + facere* do, make]
e ma ci ate (i mā′shē āt), *v.t.,* **-at ed, -at ing.** make unnaturally thin; cause to lose flesh or waste away: *A long illness had emaciated the patient.*[< Latin *emaciatum* made lean < *ex-* + *macies* leanness] **—e ma′ci a′tion,** *n.*
em bel lish (em bel′ish), *v.t.* 1 add beauty to; decorate; adorn; ornament. 2 make more interesting by adding real or imaginary details; elaborate: *embellish a story.* [< Old French *embelliss-,* a form of *embellir* embellish < *en-* in + *bel* handsome] **—em bel′lish ment,** *n.*
em pan el (em pan′l), *v.t.,* **-eled, el ing** or **elled, -el ling.** impanel.
em phat ic (em fat′ik), *adj.* 1 said or done with force or stress; strongly expressed: *Her answer was an emphatic "No!"* 2 speaking with force or stress; expressing oneself strongly: *The emphatic speaker often pounded the table and shouted.*
em u la tive (em′yə la′tiv), *adj.* trying to equal or excel.
em u lous (em′yə ləs), *adj.* wishing to equal or excel. **—em′u lous ly,** *adv.* **—em′u lous ness,** *n.*
en com pass (en kum′pəs), *v.t.* 1 surround completely; encircle. 2 include; contain. **—en com′pass ment,** *n.*
en cum brance (en kum′brəns), *n.* 1 something useless or in the way; hindrance; burden. 2 claim, mortgage, etc., on property. Also, **incumbrance.**
e nu me rate (i nü′mə rāt′, i nyü′mə rāt′), *v.t.,* **-rat ed, -rat ing.** 1 name one by one; list: *He enumerated the capitals of the 50 states.* 2 find out the number of; count.[< Latin *enumeratum* counted < *ex-* out + *numerous* number] **—e nu′me ra′tion,** *n.* **—e nu′me ra′tor,** *n.*
es cutch eon (e skuch′ən), *n.* shield or shield-shaped surface on which a coat of arms is put.[< Old French *escuchon* < Popular Latin *scutionem* < Latin *scutum* shield]
ev a nesce (ev′ə nes′), *v.i.,* **-nesced, -nesc ing.** disappear gradually; fade away; vanish.[< Latin *evanescere < ex- out + vanus* insubstantial]
ex alt (eg zôlt′), *v.t.* 1 make high in rank, honor, power, character, or quality; elevate. 2 fill with pride, joy, or noble feeling. 3 praise; honor; glorify.[< Latin *exaltare* < *ex-* up + *altus* high]
ex e cra tion (ek′sə krā′shən), *n.* 1 act of execrating. 2 a curse: *The mob shouted angry execrations at the assassin.* 3 person or thing execrated.
ex ile (eg′zīl, ek′sīl), *n.* 1 person who is exiled. 2 condition of being exiled; banishment. 3 any prolonged absence from one's own country. [< Old French *exilier* < Latin *exiliare* < *exilium* period or place of exile]
ex pe di tous (ek′spə dish′əs), *adj.* efficient and prompt. **—ex′pe di′tious ly,** *adv.* **—ex′pe di′tious ness,** *n.*
ex pi a tion (ek′spē ā′shən), *n.* 1 a making amends for a wrong, sin, etc.; atonement. 2 means of atonement; amends.
ex pire (ek spīr′), *v.,* **-pired, -pir ing.** *—v.i.* 1 come to an end: *You must obtain a new automobile license when your old one expires.* 2 die. 3 breathe out; exhale. *—v.t.* breathe out (air); exhale. [< Latin *exspirare* < *ex-* out + *spirare* breathe] **—ex pir′er,** *n.*
ex pound (ek spound′), *v.t.* 1 make clear; explain, interpret, etc. 2 set forth or state in detail. [< Old French *espondre* < *Latin exponere* < *ex- forth* + *ponere* put] **—ex pound′er,** *n.*
ex tem po rize (ek stem′pə riz′), *v.i., v.t.,* **-rized, -riz ing.** 1 speak, play, sing, or dance, composing as one goes along; improvise: *The pianist was extemporizing.* 2 prepare offhand; make for the occasion: *The campers extemporized a shelter for the night.* **—ex tem′por i za′tion,** *n.* **—ex tem′po riz′er,** *n.*
ex tract (ek strakt′), *v.t.* 1 pull out or draw out, usually with some effort: *extract a tooth, extract iron from the earth.* 2 obtain by pressing, squeezing, etc.: *extract oil from olives.* 3 deduce; infer: *extract a principle from a collection of facts.* 4 derive; obtain: *extract pleasure from a party.* 5 take out (a passage) from a book, speech, etc.
ex ult ant (eg zult′nt), *adj.* rejoicing greatly; exulting; triumphant: *an exultant shout.* **—ex ult′ant ly,** *adv.*
ex ul ta tion (eg′zul tā′shən, ek′sul tā′shən), *n.* an exulting; great rejoicing; triumph.

fas tid i ous (fa stid′ē əs), *adj.* hard to please; dainty in taste; easily disgusted. [< Latin *fastidiosus* < *fastidium* loathing] **—fas tid′i ous ly,** *adv.* **—fas tid′i ous ness,** *n.*
feign (fān), *v.t.* 1 put on a false appearance of; make believe; pretend: *Some animals feign death when in danger.* 2 make up to deceive; invent falsely: *feign an excuse.* *—v.i.* make oneself appear; pretend (to be): *You aren't sick; you are only feigning.* [< Old French *feign-,* a form of *feindre feign < Latin fingere* to form] **—feign′er,** *n.*
feint (fānt), *n.* 1 a false appearance; pretense: *She made a feint of studying, though actually she was listening to the radio.* 2 movement intended to deceive; sham attack; pretended blow. *—v.i.* make a feint: *The fighter feinted with his right hand and struck with his left.* [< French *feinte* < *feindre* feign]
fel on (fel′ən), *n.* a person who has committed a felony; criminal. Murderers and thieves are felons. *—adj.* wicked; cruel. [< Old French < Popular Latin *fellonem*]
fich u (fish′ü), *n.* a triangular piece of muslin, lace, etc., worn by women as a covering for the neck, throat, and shoulders. [< French]
fi nesse (fə nes′), *n.,v.,* **-nessed, -ness ing.** *—n.* 1 delicacy of execution; subtlety of craftsmanship; refined and graceful skill: *the finesse of a great violinist.* 2 the skillful handling of a delicate situation to one's advantage; subtle or tactful strategy: *A successful diplomat must be a master of finesse.* *—v.i.* 1 use finesse. 2 make a finesse in card playing. *—v.t.* 1 bring or change by finesse. 2 make or attempt a finesse with (a card). [< French < *fin* fine]
fin ick y (fin′ə kē), *adj.* too dainty or particular; too precise; fussy. **—fin′ick i ness,** *n.*
fla grant (flā′grənt), *adj.* 1 glaringly offensive; notorious; outrageous; scandalous: *a flagrant crime.* 2 glaring: *a flagrant error.* [< Latin *flagrantem* burning, blazing] **—fla′grant ly,** *adv.*
flank (flangk), *n.* 1 the fleshy or muscular part of the side of an animal or person between the ribs and the hip.
flour ish (flėr′ish), *v.i.* 1 grow or develop with vigor; do well; thrive. 2 be in the best time of life or activity: *Our business is flourishing.* 3 make a showy display. *—v.t.* wave in the air; brandish: *He flourished the letter when he saw us.*
flout (flout), *v.t.* treat with contempt or scorn; scoff at; mock: *You are foolish to flout such good advice.* *—v.i.* show contempt or scorn; scoff. *—n.* a contemptuous speech or act; mockery; scoffing. [variant of *flute,* verb] **—flout′er,** *n.* **—flout′ing ly,** *adv.*
fod der (fod′ər), *n.* coarse food for horses, cattle, etc. Hay and cornstalks with their leaves are fodder. *—v.t.* give fodder to. [Old English *fōdor* < *fōda food*]
fore bod ing (fôr bō′ding, fōr bō′ding), *n.* 1 prediction; warning. 2 a feeling that something bad is going to happen; presentiment. *—adj.* that forebodes, especially evil; warning; threatening. **—fore bod′ing ly,** *adv.*
forge (fôrj, fōrj), *n.* 1 an open fireplace or hearth with a bellows attached, used for heating metal very hot to be hammered into shape. 2 a blacksmith's shop; smithy. 3 place where wrought iron is made directly from the ore.
fort night (fôrt′nīt, fôrt′nit), *n.* two weeks. [Middle English *fourtenight* fourteen nights]
fos sil ize (fos′ə līz), *v.t., v.i.,* **-ized, -iz ing.** 1 change into a fossil. 2 make or become antiquated, set, stiff, or rigid. **—fos′sil i za′tion,** *n.*
frol ic (frol′ik), *n.,v.,* **-icked, -ick ing.** *—n.* 1 a merry prank; play; fun. 2 a joyous game or party. *—v.i.* play about joyously; have fun together; make merry: *The children frolicked with the puppy.* [originally adjective < Dutch *vrolijk* gay < Middle Dutch *vro* glad] **—frol′ick er,** *n.*
frond (frond), *n.* 1 the leaf of a fern, palm, or cycad. 2 a leaflike part which includes both stem and foliage, as the thallus of a lichen. [< Latin *frondem* leaf]

a hat	**i** it	**oi** oil	**ch** child	ə = a in about
ā age	**ī** ice	**ou** out	**ng** long	e in taken
ä far	**o** hot	**u** cup	**sh** she	i in pencil
e let	**ō** open	**ů** put	**th** thin	o in lemon
ē equal	**ô** order	**ü** rule	**ŦH** then	u in circus
ėr term			**zh** measure	**<** = derived from

fru gal (frü′gəl), *adj.* 1 avoiding waste; tending to avoid unnecessary spending; thrifty: *a frugal shopper.* 2 costing little; barely sufficient: *He ate a frugal supper.* [< Latin *frugalis* <*frugi* temperate, useful, ultimately < *fructus* fruit, produce.] **—fru′gal ly,** *adv.*

func tion ar y (fungk′shə ner′ē), *n.,pl.* **-ar ies.** an official.

fur tive (fėr′tiv), *adj.* 1 done quickly and with stealth to avoid being noticed; secret: *a furtive glance into the forbidden room.* 2 sly; stealthy: *a furtive manner.* [< Latin *furtivus* < *furtum* theft < *fur* thief] **—fur′tive ly,** *adv.* **—fur′tive ness,** *n.*

gall (gôl), *n.* 1 bile. 2 anything very bitter or harsh. 3 bitterness; hate. 4 INFORMAL. too great boldness; impudence. [Old English *gealla*]

gallus (gal′ əs), *n.,pl.* **-lus es.** Chiefly dialect. a pair of suspenders for trousers. Often, **galluses.**

gar goyle (gär′goil), *n.* figure in the shape of a grotesque animal or human being, often for draining water from the gutter of a building. [< Middle French *gargouille* throat, waterspout]

gargoyle

gran ite (gran′it), *n.* a hard, igneous rock made of grains of other rocks, chiefly quartz and feldspar, much used for buildings and monuments. [< Italian *granito* grained < *grano* grain < Latin *granum*] **—gran′ite like′,** *adj.*

gre gar i ous (grə ger′ē əs, grə - gar′ē əs), *adj.* 1 fond of being with others: *Hermits are not gregarious.* 2 living in flocks, herds, or other groups: *Sheep are gregarious, raccoons are not.* 3 of or having to do with a flock or crowd. [< Latin *gregarius* < *gregem* flock] **—gre gar′i ous ly,** *adv.* **—gregar′i ous ness,** *n.*

grind stone (grīnd′stōn′), *n.* a flat, round stone set in a frame and turned by hand, foot, or a motor. It is used to sharpen tools, such as axes and knives, or to smooth and polish things.

hal lowed (hal′ōd; *in church use, often* hal′ō id), *adj.* 1 made holy; sacred; consecrated: *A churchyard is hallowed ground.* 2 honored or observed as holy.

hap less (hap′lis), *adj.* unlucky; unfortunate. **—hap′less ly,** *adv.* **—hap′less ness,** *n.*

her ald (her′əld), *n.* 1 (formerly) an official who carried messages, made announcements, arranged and supervised tournaments and other public ceremonies, and regulated the use of armorial bearings. 2 person who carries messages and makes announcements; messenger. 3 forerunner: *Dawn is the herald of day.*

her e sy (her′ə sē), *n., pl.* **-sies.** 1 a religious doctrine or opinion rejected by the authorities of a church as contrary to the established beliefs of that church. 2 opinion or doctrine opposed to what is generally accepted as authoritative. 3 the holding of such an opinion or doctrine. [< Old French *heresie* < *Latin haeresis* < *Greek hairesis* a taking, choosing < *hairein* choose, take]

hom age (hom′ij, om′ij), *n.* 1 dutiful respect; reverence: *Everyone paid homage to the great leader.* 2 (in the Middle Ages) a pledge of loyalty and service by a vassal to a lord. 3 thing done or given to show such acknowledgment. [< Old French < Medieval Latin *hominaticum* < Latin *hominem* human being, man]

hu mor (hyü′mər, yü′mər), *n.* 1 state of mind; disposition; temper: *in good humor.* 2 fancy; whim. 3 any of four body fluids formerly supposed to deterrmine a person's health and disposition. The four humors were blood, phlegm, yellow bile, and black bile. 4 **out of humor,** in a bad mood; angry or displeased; cross.

i dle (ī′dl), *adj.,* **i dler, i dlest.** 1 doing nothing; not busy; not working: *idle hands.* 2 fond of doing nothing; not willing to work; lazy. 3 useless; worthless: *He wasted his time in idle pleasures.* 4 without any good reason, or foundation: *idle fears, idle rumors.*

i dler (ī′dlər) *n.* a lazy person.

ig no ble (ig nō′bəl), *adj.* 1 without honor; disgraceful; base: *To betray a friend is ignoble.* 2 not of noble birth or position; humble. [< Latin *ignobilis* < *in-* not + *nobilis* noble] **—ig no′ble ness,** *n.* **—ig no′bly,** *adv.*

ig no min y (ig′nə min′ē), *n., pl.* **-min ies.** 1 public shame and disgrace; dishonor 2 shameful action or conduct. [< Latin *ignominia* < *in-* not + *nominis* name]

im bue (im byü′), *v.t.,* **-bued, -bu ing.** 1 fill the mind of; inspire: *The parents imbued their children with the ambition to succeed.* 2 permeate; fill: *a mystery imbued with drama and surprise.* [< Latin *imbuere*]

im mac u late (i mak′yə lit), *adj.* 1 without a spot or stain; absolutely clean. 2 without fault or errors. 3 without sin; pure. [< Latin *immaculatus* < *in-* not + *macula* spot] **—im mac′u late ly,** *adv.* **—im mac′u late ness,** *n.*

im mi nent (im′ə nənt), *adj.* likely to happen soon; about to occur: *Black clouds show rain is imminent.* [< Latin *imminentem* overhanging, threatening] **—im′mi nent ly,** *adv.*

im mo late (im′ə lāt), *v.t.,* **-lat ed, -lat ing.** 1 kill as a sacrifice. 2 offer in sacrifice; sacrifice. [< Latin *immolatum* sacrifice, (originally) sprinkled with sacrificial meal < *in-* on + *mola* sacrificial meal] **—im′mo la′tion,** *n.* **—im′mo la′tor,** *n.*

im mu ta ble (i myü′tə bəl), *adj.* never changing; unchangeable. **—im mu′ta ble ness,** *n.* **—im mu′ta bly,** *adv.*

im pan el (im pan′l), *v.t.,* **-eled, -el ing** or **-elled, -el ling.** 1 put on a list for duty on a jury. 2 select (a jury) from such a list. Also, **empanel.**

im pas si ble (im pas′ə bəl), *adj.* 1 unable to suffer or feel pain. 2 that cannot be harmed. 3 without feeling or emotion; impassive. [< Latin *impassibilis,* ultimately < *in-* not + *pati* suffer] **—im pas′si bly,** *adv.*

im pas sive (im pas′iv), *adj.* 1 without feeling or emotion; unmoved: *Her face was impassive when we told her the news.* 2 not feeling pain or injury; insensible. **—im pas′sive ly,** *adv.* **—im pas′sive ness,** *n.*

im pa tient (im pā′shənt), *adj.* 1 not patient; not willing to put up with delay, opposition, pain, bother, etc.: *She is impatient with her little sister.* 2 uneasy and eager; restless: *The horses are impatient to start the race.* 3 showing lack of patience; cross: *an impatient answer.*

im ped i ment (im ped′ə mənt), *n.* 1 hindrance; obstruction. 2 some physical defect, especially a defect in speech.

im per i ous (im pir′ē əs), *adj.* 1 haughty or arrogant; domineering; overbearing. 2 not to be avoided; necessary; urgent. **—im per′i ous ly,** *adv.* **—im per′i ous ness,** *n.*

im pru dent (im prüd′nt), *adj.* not prudent; rash; unwise. **—im pru′dent ly,** *adv.* **—im pru′dent ness,** *n.*

im pu dent (im′pyə dənt), *adj.* shamelessly bold; very rude and insolent. [< Latin *impudentem* < *in-* not + *pudere* be modest] **—im′pu dent ly,** *adv.*

im pu ni ty (im pyü′nə tē), *n.* freedom from punishment, injury, or other bad consequences: *If laws are not enforced, crimes are committed with impunity.* [< Latin *impunitatem,* ultimately < *in-* without + *poena* punishment]

in-, *prefix.* not; the opposite of; the absence of: *Inexpensive* = not expensive. *Inattention* = the absence of attention. [< Latin]

in an i mate (in an′ə mit), *adj.* 1 not living or alive; lifeless: *Stones are inanimate objects.* 2 without liveliness or spirit; dull. **—in an′i mate ly,** *adv.* **—in an′i mate ness,** *n.*

in ar tic u late (in′ar tik′yə lit), *adj.* 1 not uttered in distinct syllables or words: *an inarticulate mutter.* 2 unable to speak in words; dumb: *inarticulate with grief. Cats and dogs are inarticulate.* 3 not able to put one's thoughts or feelings into words easily and clearly. **—in′ar tic′u late ly,** *adv.* **— in′ar tic′u late ness,** *n.*

in aus pi cious (in′ô spish′əs), *adj.* with signs of failure; unfavorable; unlucky. **—in′aus pi′cious ly,** *adv.* **—in′aus pi′cious ness,** *n.*

in clem ent (in klem′ənt), *adj.* 1 rough or stormy. 2 not merciful or kindly; severe; harsh: *an inclement ruler.* **—in clem′ent ly,** *adv.*

in com mo di ous (in′kə mō′dē əs), *adj.* 1 not roomy enough. 2 inconvenient; uncomfortable. **—in′com mo′di ous ly,** *adv.* **—in′com mo′di ous ness,** *n.*

in cre du li ty (in′krə dü′lə tē, in′krə dyü′lə tē), *n.* lack of belief; doubt.

in cum bent (in kum′bənt), *adj.* 1 lying, leaning, or pressing on something. 2 resting on a person as a duty or obligation: *She felt it incumbent upon her to answer the letter at once.* 3 currently holding an office, position, etc.: *the incumbent governor.* —*n.* person holding an office, position, etc. [< Latin *incumbentem* < *in-* on + *-cumbere* lie down] **—in cum′bent ly,** *adv.*

in cum brance (in kum′brəns), *n.* encumbrance.

in do lent (in′dl ənt), *adj.* disliking work; lazy; idle: *an indolent person who dislikes any kind of exertion.* **—in′do lent ly,** *adv.*

in dul gent (in dul′jənt), *adj.* 1 giving in to another's wishes or whims; too kind or agreeable. 2 making allowances; not critical; lenient. **—in dul′gent ly,** *adv.*

in ex or a ble (in ek′sər ə bəl), *adj.* not influenced by pleading or entreaties; relentless; unyielding: *The forces of nature are inexorable.* [< Latin *inexorabilis* < *in-* not + *exorare* prevail upon, pray earnestly < *ex-* out + *orare* pray, entreat] **—in ex′or a ble ness,** *n.* **—in ex′or a bly,** *adv.*

in ex tri ca ble (in ek′strə kə bəl), *adj.* 1 that one cannot get out of. 2 that cannot be disentangled or solved. **—in ex′tri ca bil′i ty,** *n.* **—in ex′tri ca bly,** *adv.*

in fal li bil i ty (in fal′ə bil′ə tē), *n.* 1 freedom from error; inability to be mistaken. 2 absolute reliability; sureness.

in fal li ble (in fal′ə bəl), *adj.* 1 free from error; that cannot be mistaken: *an infallible rule.* 2 absolutely reliable; sure: *infallible obedience, an infallible remedy.* 3 (in the Roman Catholic Church) incapable or error in the exposition of doctrine on faith and morals (said of the pope as head of the church). **—in fal′li bly,** *adv.*

in fa mous (in′fə məs), *adj.* 1 deserving or causing a very bad reputation; shamefully bad; disgraceful: *an infamous deed.* 2 having a very bad reputation; in public disgrace: *an infamous traitor.* [< Medieval Latin *infamosus* < Latin *infamis*] **—in′fa mous ly,** *adv.*

in firm (in fėrm′), *adj.* 1 lacking strength or health; physically weak or feeble, especially through age. 2 without a firm purpose; not steadfast; faltering. 3 not firm, solid, or strong. **—in firm′ly,** *adv.* **—in firm′ness,** *n.*

in junc tion (in jungk′shən), *n.* 1 a formal order from a court of law ordering a person or group to do, or refrain from doing, something. 2 an authoritative or emphatic order; command: *Injunctions of secrecy did not prevent the news from leaking out.* 3 act of commanding or authoritatively directing. [< Late Latin *injunctionem* < Latin *injungere* enjoin < *in-* in + *jungere* join]

in sa tia ble (in sā′shə bəl), *adj.* that cannot be satisfied; extremely greedy: *an insatiable appetite.* **—in sa′tia ble ness,** *n.* **—in sa′tia bly,** *adv.*

in scru ta ble (in skrü′tə bəl), *adj.* that cannot be understood; so mysterious or obscure that one cannot make out its meaning; incomprehensible. [< Late Latin *inscrutabilis* < Latin *in-* not + *scrutari* examine, ransack < *scruta* trash] **—in scru′ta ble ness,** *n.* **—in scru′ta bly,** *adv.*

in sol u ble (in sol′yə bəl), *adj.* 1 that cannot be dissolved; not soluble: *Fats are insoluble in water.* 2 that cannot be solved; unsolvable. **—in sol′u ble ness,** *n.* **—in sol′u bly,** *adv.*

in sti gate (in′stə gāt), *v.t.,* **-gat ed, -gat ing.** urge on; stir up: *instigate a quarrel.* [< Latin *instigatum* incited, urged on] **—in′sti gat′ing ly,** *adv.* **—in′sti ga′tion,** *n.* **—in′sti ga′tor,** *n.*

in ter (in tėr′), *v.t.,* **-terred, -ter ring.** put (a dead body) into a grave or tomb; bury. [< Medieval Latin *interrare* < Latin *in-* in + *terra* earth]

in ter ces sion (in′tər sesh′ən), *n.* 1 act or fact of interceding. 2 prayer pleading for others. [< Latin *intercessionem* < *intercedere*]

in ter ment (in tėr′mənt), *n.* act of interring; burial.

in ter pose (in′tər pōz′), *v.,* **-posed, -pos ing.** —*v.t.* 1 put between; insert. 2 put forward; break in with: *She interposed an objection at this point.* —*v.i.* 1 come or be between other things. 2 interrupt. 3 interfere in order to help; intervene. [< Middle French *interposer* < *inter-* between + *poser* to place] **—in′ter pos′a ble,** *adj.* **—in′ter pos′er,** *n.* **—in′ter pos′ing ly,** *adv.*

in ter po si tion (in′tər pə zish′ən), *n.* 1 an interposing. 2 something interposed.

in ter ro ga tion (in ter′ə gā′shən), *n.* 1 an interrogating. The formal examination of a witness by asking questions is an interrogation. 2 a question. **—in ter′ro ga′tion al,** *adj.*

in un da tion (in′un dā′shən), *n.* an inundating; flood.

in va lid (in′və lid), *n.* person who is weak because of sickness or injury; infirm or sickly person. —*adj.* 1 weak and sick; not well. 2 for the use of invalids: *an invalid chair.* —*v.t.* 1 make weak or sick; disable. 2 remove from active service because of sickness or injury: *The wounded soldier was invalided and sent home.* [< French *invalide* < Latin *invalidus* not strong.]

in vet er ate (in vet′ər it), *adj.* 1 confirmed in a habit, practice, feeling, etc.; habitual: *an inveterate smoker.* 2 long and firmly established; deeply rooted: *Cats have an inveterate dislike of dogs.* [< Latin *inveteratum* grown old, long established < *in-* in + *vetus, veteris* old] **—in vet′er ate ly,** *adv.*

in vi o late (in vī′ə lit, in vī′ə lāt), *adj.* not violated; uninjured; unbroken: *an inviolate promise.* **—in vi′o late ly,** *adv.* **—in vi′o late ness,** *n.*

ir-[1], *prefix.* the form of **in-**[1] before *r,* as in *irrational, irregular.*

ir-[2], *prefix.* the form of **in-**[2] before *r,* as in *irrigate.*

i ras ci ble (i ras′ə bəl), *adj.* 1 easily made angry; with a quick temper; irritable. 2 showing anger. [< Late Latin *irascibilis* < Latin *irasci* grow angry < *ira* anger] **—i ras′ci ble ness,** *n.* **—i ras′ci bly,** *adv.*

i rate (ī′rāt, ī rāt′), *adj.* angry; enraged. **—i′rate ly,** *adv.* **—i′rate ness,** *n.*

ire (īr), *n.* anger; wrath. [< Old French < Latin *ira*]

ir i des cent (ir′ə des′nt), *adj.* displaying changing colors; changing color when moved or turned. [< Latin *iris, iridis* rainbow] **—ir′i des′cent ly,** *adv.*

ir re press i ble (ir′i pres′ə bəl), *adj.* that cannot be repressed or restrained; uncontrollable: *irrepressible laughter.* **—ir′re press′i ble ness,** *n.* **—ir′re press′i bly,** *adv.*

jave lin (jav′lən, jav′ə lin), *n.* 1 a light spear thrown by hand. 2 a wooden or metal spear, thrown for distance in athletic contests. [< Middle French *javeline*]

jo cose (jō kōs′), *adj.* full of jokes; given to joking; jesting; humorous. [< Latin *jocosus* < *jocus* jest] **—jo cose′ly,** *adv.* **—jo cose′ness,** *n.*

jo vi al (jō′vē əl), *adj.* good-hearted and full of fun; good-humored and merry. [< Latin *Jovialis* of the planet Jupiter (those born under the planet's sign being supposedly cheerful) < *Jovis* Jove] **—jo′vi al ly,** *adv.* **—jo′vi al ness,** *n.*

ju di cious (jü dish′əs), *adj.* having, using, or showing good judgment; wise; sensible: *A judicious historian selects and weighs facts carefully and critically.* **—ju di′cious ly,** *adv.* **—ju di′cious ness,** *n.*

junc ture (jungk′chər), *n.* 1 point or line where two things join; joint. 2 point of time, especially a critical time or state of affairs: *At this juncture we must decide what move to make next.* 3 a joining. [< Latin *junctura* a joining < *jungere* to join]

jur is dic tion (jůr′is dik′shən), *n.* 1 right, power, or authority to administer justice or exercise judicial functions. 2 authority; power; control. 3 extent of authority: *The case was not within the city's jurisdiction.* 4 the things over which authority extends. 5 territory over which authority extends. [< Latin *jurisdictionem* < *jus, juris* law + *dicere* say] **—jur′is dic′tion al,** *adj.*

keen (kēn), *n.* a wailing lament for the dead. —*v.i.* wail; lament. [< Irish *caoine*] **—keen′er,** *n.*

knave (nāv), *n.* 1 a tricky, dishonest man; rogue; rascal. 2 jack. 3 ARCHAIC. a male servant or any man of humble birth or position. [Old English *cnafa* boy]

la con ic (lə kon′ik), *adj.* using few words; brief in speech or expression; concise; terse. [< Latin *Laconicus* Spartan < Greek *Lakōnikos;* Spartans were noted for pithy speech] **—la con′i cal ly,** *adv.*

lan guish (lang′gwish), *v.i.* 1 become weak or weary; lose energy; droop: *The flowers languished from lack of water.* 2 suffer under any unfavorable conditions: *He languished in prison for* *twenty years.* 3 grow dull, slack, or less intense: *Their vigilance never languished.* [< Old French *languiss-,* a form of *languir* < Latin *languere*] **—lan′guish er,** *n.* **—lan′guish ment,** *n.*

la tent (lāt′nt), *adj.* present but not active; hidden; concealed: *He carried the latent germs of the disease for years. She did not realize her latent creative ability until late in life.* [< Latin *latentem* lying hidden] **—la′tent ly,** *adv.*

leg a cy (leg′ə sē), *n., pl.* **-cies.** 1 money or other property left to a person by the will of someone who has died; bequest. 2 something that has been handed down from an ancestor or predecessor: *the legacy of freedom.* [< Medieval Latin *legatia* < Latin *legatum* bequest < *legare* bequeath.]

leth ar gy (leth′ər jē), *n., pl.* **-gies.** 1 drowsy dullness; lack of energy; sluggish inactivity. 2 (in medicine) a state of prolonged unconsciousness resembling deep sleep, from which the person can be roused but immediately loses consciousness again. [< Greek *lēthargia* < *lēthē* forgetfulness + *argos* lazy < *a-* not + *ergon* work]

load stone (lōd′stōn′), *n.* lodestone.

lode stone (lōd′stōn′), *n.* 1 piece of magnetite that attracts iron and steel. 2 something that attracts: *Gold was the lodestone that drew people to Alaska.* Also, **loadstone.**

lye hominy (lī hom′ə nē), *n.* hominy prepared from kernels of grain that have been soaked in lye to remove the hulls.

mag nan i mous (mag nan′ə məs), *adj.* 1 noble in soul or mind; generous in forgiving; free from mean or petty feelings or acts; unselfish. 2 showing or arising from a generous spirit: *a magnanimous attitude toward a conquered enemy.* [< Latin *magnanimus* < *magnus* great + *animus* spirit] **—mag nan′i mous ly,** *adv.*

ma jes tic (mə jes′tik), *adj.* of or having majesty; grand; noble; dignified; stately. **—ma jes′ti cal ly,** *adv.*

mal con tent (mal′kən tent′), *adj.* discontented; rebellious. *—n.* a discontented, rebellious person.

man a cle (man′ə kəl), *n., v.,* **-cled, -cling.** *—n.* 1 Usually, **manacles,** *pl.* fetter for the hands; handcuff. 2 anything that fetters; restraint. *—v.t.* 1 put manacles on: *manacle a prisoner.* 2 restrain; hamper. [< Old French *manicle* < Latin *manicula,* diminutive of *manus* hand]

mat tock (mat′ək), *n.* a large tool with a steel head like a pickax, but having a flat blade on one side or flat blades on both sides, used for loosening soil and cutting roots. [Old English *mattuc*]

mattock

mea ger or **mea gre** (mē′gər), *adj.* 1 lacking fullness or richness; poor or scanty; sparse: *a meager meal.* 2 thin; lean: *a meager face.* [< Old French *maigre* < Latin *macer*]

meg a lith (meg′ə lith), *n.* stone of great size, especially in ancient constructive work or in monuments left by people of prehistoric times.

meg a ton (meg′ə tun′), *n.* 1 unit of weight equal to one million tons. 2 unit of atomic power equivalent to the energy released by one million tons of TNT.

men ace (men′is), *n., v.,* **-aced, -ac ing.** *—n.* something that threatens; threat: *In dry weather forest fires are a menace.* *—v.t.* offer a menace to; threaten: *Floods menaced the valley towns with destruction.* *—v.i.* be threatening. [< Middle French < Latin *minaciae* (plural), ultimately < *minae* projecting points, threats] **—men′ac ing ly,** *adv.*

me nag er ie (mə naj′ər ē, mə nazh′ər ē), *n.* 1 collection of wild or strange animals kept in cages of enclosures, especially for exhibition, as in a zoo or a circus. 2 place where such animals are kept. [< French *ménagerie,* literally, management of a household]

mi cro com pu ter (mī′krō kəm pyü′tər), *n.* computer that contains a microprocessor and hence is either very small or much smaller than computers made from components.

mi cro cosm (mī′krō koz′əm), *n.* 1 community, etc., regarded as an epitome of the world; a little world; universe in miniature. 2 person or thing thought of as a miniature representation of the universe. [< Late Greek *mikros kosmos* little world]

mi rage (mə räzh′), *n.* 1 an optical illusion, usually in the desert, at sea, or over a hot paved road. Travelers on the desert may see a

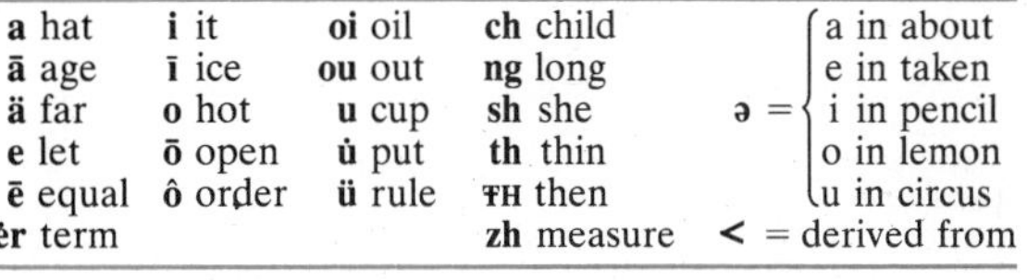

a hat	**i** it	**oi** oil	**ch** child	ə = a in about
ā age	**ī** ice	**ou** out	**ng** long	e in taken
ä far	**o** hot	**u** cup	**sh** she	i in pencil
e let	**ō** open	**ů** put	**th** thin	o in lemon
ē equal	**ô** order	**ü** rule	**ᴛʜ** then	u in circus
ėr term			**zh** measure	**<** = derived from

mirage of palm trees and water. 2 anything that does not exist; illusion. [< French < *mirer* look at]

mo bil i ty (mō bil′ə tē), *n.* a being mobile; ability or readiness to move or be moved.

mod i cum (mod′ə kəm), *n.* a small or moderate quantity. [< Latin, moderate < *modus* measure]

mo men tous (mō men′təs), *adj.* very important; of great consequence; weighty: *Choosing between peace and war is a momentous decision.* **—mo men′tous ly,** *adv.* **—mo men′tous ness,** *n.*

mon o lith (mon′l ith), *n.* 1 a single large block of stone. 2 monument, column, statue, etc., formed of a single large block of stone. 3 nation, political party, etc., that in its rigid and unyielding attitudes and policies suggests a massive block of stone. [< Greek *monolithos* < *mono-* + *lithos* stone]

mon o logue (mon′l ôg, mon′l og), *n.* 1 a long speech by one person in a group; speech that monopolizes conversation. 2 entertainment by a single speaker. 3 a play for a single actor. Also, **monolog.** [< French < *mono-* + *(dia)logue*]

mon o tone (mon′ə tōn), *n.* 1 sameness of tone, style of writing, color, etc. 2 manner of speaking, singing, etc., without change of pitch; unvaried sound or repetition of sounds: *Don't speak in a monotone; use expression.*

mo rose (mə rōs′), *adj.* gloomy; sullen; ill-humored: *a morose person.* [< Latin *morosus,* originally, set in one's ways < *morem* custom, habit] **—mo rose′ly,** *adv.* **—mo rose′ness,** *n.*

mor ti fy (môr′tə fī), *v.t.,* **-fied, -fy ing.** wound the feelings of; make feel humbled and ashamed; humiliate: *Their bad behavior mortified their parents.* [< Old French *mortifier* < Latin *mortificare* to kill < *mortem* death + *facere* to make] **—mor′ti fi′er,** *n.*

mull (mul), *v.t., v.i.* think (about) without making much progress; ponder: *mull over a problem.* [origin uncertain]

mu nif i cent (myü nif′ə sənt), *adj.* extremely generous; bountiful; bounteous. **—mu nif′i cent ly,** *adv.*

mu ta gen (myü′tə jən), *n.* agent that causes mutation in an organism. **—mu′ta gen′ic,** *adj.*

mu tant (myüt′nt), *n.* a new variety of living organism resulting from mutation. *—adj.* that is the result of mutation: *a mutant species.*

mys ti fy (mis′tə fī), *v.t.,* **-fied, -fy ing.** 1 bewilder purposely; puzzle; perplex: *The magician's tricks mystified the audience.* 2 make mysterious; involve in mystery.

nape (nāp, nap), *n.* back of the neck. [Middle English]

naught (nôt), *n.* 1 nothing. 2 zero; 0. Also, **nought.** [Old English *nāwiht* < *nā* no + *wiht* thing]

non-, *prefix.* not; not a; opposite of; lack of; failure of: *Nonessential = not essential. Nonresident = not a resident. Nonconformity = lack of conformity.* [< Latin < *non* not]

non de script (non′də skript), *adj.* not easily classified; not of any one particular kind: *We drove past a block of nondescript houses.* *—n.* a nondescript person or thing. [< *non-* + Latin *descriptum* (to be) described]

nul li fi ca tion (nul′ə fə kā′shən), *n.* 1 a making null. 2 a being nullified. 3 Often, **Nullification.** action taken by a state to nullify or declare unconstitutional a federal law or judicial decision and prevent its enforcement within the state's boundaries.

o a sis (ō ā′sis, ō′ə sis), *n., pl.* **-ses** (-sēz′). 1 a fertile spot in the desert where there is water and some vegetation. 2 any fertile spot in a barren land; any pleasant place in a desolate region. [< Late Latin < Greek]

o blit e rate (ə blit′ə rāt′), *v.t.,* **-rat ed, -rat ing.** 1 remove all traces of; blot out; efface: *The heavy rain obliterated the footprints.* 2 blot out so as to leave no distinct traces; make unrecognizable. [< Latin *obliteratum* struck out < *ob literas (scribere)* (draw) through the letters, strike out] **—o blit′e ra′tion,** *n.* **—o blit′e ra′tor,** *n.*

o bliv i on (ə bliv′ē ən), *n.* 1 condition of being entirely forgotten: *Many ancient cities have long since passed into oblivion.* 2 fact of forgetting; forgetfulness. [< Latin *oblivionem* < *oblivisci* forget]

o bliv i ous (ə bliv′ē əs), *adj.* 1 not mindful; forgetful: *The book was so interesting that I was oblivious of my surroundings.* 2 bringing or causing forgetfulness. **—o bliv′i ous ly,** *adv.* **—o bliv′i ous ness,** *n.*

ob se qui ous (əb sē′kwē əs), *adj.* polite or obedient from hope of gain or from fear; servile; fawning: *Obsequious courtiers greeted the royal couple.* [< Latin *obsequiosus* < *obsequium* dutiful service < *ob-* after + *sequi* follow] **—ob se′qui ous ly,** *adv.* **—ob se′qui ous ness,** *n.*

ob sti nate (ob′stə nit), *adj.* 1 not giving in; stubborn. 2 hard to control, treat, or remove; persistent: *an obstinate cough.* [< Latin *obstinatum* determined < *ob-* by + *stare* to stand] **—ob′sti nate ly,** *adv.* **—ob′sti nate ness,** *n.*

ob trude (əb trüd′), *v.,* **-trud ed, -trud ing.** *—v.t.* 1 put forward unasked and unwanted; force: *Don't obtrude your opinions on others.* 2 push out; thrust forward: *A turtle obtrudes its head from its shell.* *—v.i.* come unasked and unwanted; force oneself; intrude. [< Latin *obtrudere* < *ob-* toward + *trudere* to thrust] **—ob trud′er,** *n.*

of fal (ô′fəl, of′əl), *n.* 1 the waste parts of an animal killed for food. 2 garbage; refuse. 3 waste produced by any of various industrial processes as chips in milling wood, scraps of leather in trimming hides, etc. [< *off* + *fall*]

om nip o tent (om nip′ə tənt), *adj.* 1 having all power; almighty. 2 having very great power or influence. *—n.* **the Omnipotent,** God. **—om nip′o tent ly,** *adv.*

om nis cient (om nish′ənt), *adj.* knowing everything; having complete or infinite knowledge. **—om nis′cient ly,** *adv.*

o pi ate (ō′pē it, ō′pē āt), *n.* 1 any medical preparation containing opium or a derivative of opium and used especially to dull pain or bring sleep. 2 anything that quiets, soothes, etc. *—adj.* 1 containing opium. 2 bringing sleep or ease.

pal ate (pal′it), *n.* roof of the mouth. The bony part in front is the hard palate, and the fleshy part in back is the soft palate. [< Latin *palatum*] **—pal′ate less,** *adj.*

pa la tial (pə lā′shəl), *adj.* of, like, or fit for a palace; magnificent. **—pa la′tial ly,** *adv.* **—pa la′tial ness,** *n.*

pal met to (pal met′ō), *n., pl.* **-tos** or **-toes.** any of a genus of relatively small palms with fan-shaped leaves, abundant on the southeastern coast of the United States. [< Spanish *palmito,* diminutive of *palma* palm < Latin]

par ri cide (par′ə sīd), *n.* 1 act of killing one's parent or parents. 2 person who kills his parent or parents. [< Latin *parricidium*]

pas siv i ty (pa siv′ə tē), *n.* a being passive; lack of action or resistance.

per jur y (pėr′jər ē), *n., pl.* **-jur ies.** act or crime of willfully giving false testimony or withholding evidence while under oath; a swearing falsely.

per me ate (pėr′mē āt), *v.t.,* **-at ed, -at ing.** 1 spread through the whole of; pass through; pervade: *Smoke permeated the house.* 2 penetrate through pores or openings; soak through. [< Latin *permeatum* passed through < *per-* through + *meare* to pass]

per ni cious (pər nish′əs), *adj.* 1 that will destroy or ruin; causing great harm or damage; very injurious: *a pernicious habit.* 2 fatal; deadly. [< Latin *perniciosus,* ultimately < *per-* completely + *necis* death] **—per ni′cious ly,** *adv.* **—per ni′cious ness,** *n.*

per pe trate (pėr′pə trāt), *v.t.,* **-trat ed, -trat ing.** do or commit (a crime, fraud, trick, or anything bad or foolish). [< Latin *perpetratum* perpetrated < *per-* thoroughly + *patrare* perform] **—per′pe tra′tion,** *n.* **—per′pe tra′tor,** *n.*

per pet u ate (pər pech′ü āt), *v.t.,* **-at ed, -at ing.** make perpetual; keep from being forgotten: *a monument built to perpetuate the memory of a famous person.* **—per pet′u a′tion,** *n.* **—per pet′u a′tor,** *n.*

per vert (pər vėrt′), *v.t.* 1 lead or turn from what is true, desirable, good, or morally right; corrupt: *pervert the cause of justice.* 2 give a wrong meaning to; distort: *pervert a friendly remark and make it into an insult.* [< Latin *pervertere* < *per-* to destruction + *vertere* to turn] **—per vert′ed ly,** *adv.* **—per vert′er,** *n.*

phlox (floks), *n.* 1 any of a genus of common garden plants with clusters of showy flowers in various colors. 2 the flower of any of these plants. [< Greek, a kind of plant, literally, flame < *phlegein* burn]

pil lage (pil′ij), *v.,* **-laged, -lag ing,** *n.* *—v.t.* rob with violence; plunder: *Pirates pillaged the towns along the coast.* *—v.i.* take booty; plunder. *—n.* act of plundering or taking as spoil; plunder, especially as practiced in war. [< Old French < *piller* to plunder]

pin ion (pin′yən), *v.t.* 1 cut off or tie the pinions of (a bird) to prevent flying. 2 bind the arms of; bind (to something); bind: *pinion a person's arms.* [< Middle French *pignon* < Popular Latin *pinnionem* < Latin *penna* feather and *pinna* wing]

plague (plāg), *v.t.* 1 cause to suffer from a plague. 2 vex; annoy; bother. [< Late Latin *plaga* pestilence < Latin, blow, wound] **—pla′guer,** *n.*

pla toon (plə tün′), *n.* a military unit made up of two or more squads, usually commanded by a lieutenant. Several platoons make up a company. [< French *peloton,* diminutive of *pelote* pellet]

plau si ble (plô′zə bəl), *adj.* 1 appearing true, reasonable, or fair. 2 apparently worthy of confidence but often not really so: *a plausible liar.* [< Latin *plausibilis* deserving applause, pleasing < *plaudere* applaud] **—plau′si bil′i ty,** *n.* **—plau′si bly,** *adv.*

pol lute (pə lüt′), *v.t.,* **-lut ed, -lut ing.** make impure, foul, or dirty; contaminate: *The water at the bathing beach was polluted by refuse from the factory.* [< Latin *pollutum* soiled, defiled]

pol troon (pol trün′), *n.* a wretched coward. *—adj.* base; cowardly; contemptible. [< Middle French *poltrôn* < Italian *poltrone* < *poltro* lazy]

pon der (pon′dər), *v.t.* consider carefully; think over. [< Latin *ponderare* weigh < *pondus* weight] **—pon′der er,** *n.*

pos ter i ty (po ster′ə tē), *n.* 1 generations of the future: *Posterity may travel to distant planets.* 2 all of a person's descendants. [< Latin *posteritatem* < *posterus* coming after]

pos til ion or **pos til lion** (pō stil′yən, po stil′yən), *n.* person who guides a team of horses drawing a carriage or post chaise by riding the left-hand horse when one pair is used, or the left-hand horse of the leading pair when two or more pairs are used. [< French *postillon*]

poul tice (pōl′tis), *n., v.,* **-ticed, -tic ing.** *—n.* a soft, moist mass of mustard, herbs, etc., applied to the body as a medicine. *—v.t.* put a poultice on. [< Latin *pultes,* plural of *puls* mush]

pre car i ous (pri ker′ē əs, pri kar′ē əs), *adj.* 1 not safe or secure; uncertain; dangerous; risky: *Soldiers on the battlefield lead a precarious life.* 2 dependent on chance or circumstance. 3 poorly founded; doubtful. [< Latin *precarius* obtainable by prayer, uncertain < *precem* prayer] **—pre car′i ous ly,** *adv.* **—pre car′i ous ness,** *n.*

pre co cious (pri kō′shəs), *adj.* 1 developed earlier than usual in knowledge, skill, etc.: *This very precocious child could read well at the age of four.* 2 developed too early; occurring before the natural time. [< Latin *praecocem* < *praecoquere* to mature or ripen early < *prae-* pre + *coquere* ripen] **—pre co′cious ly,** *adv.* **—pre co′cious ness,** *n.*

pref ace (pref′is), *n., v.,* **-aced, -ac ing.** *—n.* 1 introduction to a book, writing, or speech. 2 something preliminary or introductory. *—v.t.* introduce by written or spoken remarks; give a preface to. [< Old French < Latin *praefationem* < *praefari* speak beforehand < *prae-* pre- + *fari* speak]

pre rog a tive (pri rog′ə tiv), *n.* 1 right or privilege that nobody else has: *The government has the prerogative of coining money.* 2 special superiority of right or privilege, such as may derive from an offical position, office, etc. [< Latin *praerogativa* allotted to vote first < *praerogare* ask for a vote first < *prae-* pre- + *rogare* ask]

pre sen ti ment (pri zen′tə mənt), *n.* a feeling or impression that something, especially something evil, is about to happen; vague sense of approaching misfortune; foreboding.

pre sump tion (pri zump′shən), *n.* 1 unpleasant boldness: *It is presumption to go to a party when one has not been invited.* 2 thing taken for granted; assumption; supposition: *Since he had the stolen jewels, the presumption was that he was the thief.* 3 cause or reason for presuming; probability. 4 act of presuming.

pre var i cate (pri var′ə kāt), *v.i.,* **-cat ed, -cat ing.** turn aside from the truth in speech or action; lie. [< Latin *praevaricatum* deviated < *prae-* pre- + *varicus* straddling < *varus* crooked] **—pre var′i ca′tor,** *n.*

pro cure (prə kyůr′), *v.t.,* **-cured, -cur ing. 1** obtain by care or effort; secure: *procure a job.* **2** bring about; cause: *procure a person's death.* [< Latin *procurare* manage < *pro-* before + *cura* care] **—pro cur′a ble,** *adj.* **—pro cure′ment,** *n.*

pro di gious (prə dij′əs), *adj.* **1** very great; huge; vast: *The ocean contains a prodigious amount of water.* **2** wonderful; marvelous. [< Latin *prodigiosus* < *prodigium* prodigy, omen] **—pro di′gious ly,** *adv.* **—pro di′gious ness,** *n.*

prof li gate (prof′lə git), *adj.* **1** very wicked; shamelessly bad. **2** recklessly extravagant. *—n.* person who is very wicked or extravagant. [< Latin *profligatum* ruined < *pro-* forth + *fligere* to strike, dash] **—prof′li gate ly,** *adv.*

pro jec tile (prə jek′təl), *n.* any object that is thrown, hurled, or shot, such as a stone or bullet.

pro logue or **pro log** (prō′lôg, prō′log), *n.* **1** introduction to a novel, poem, or other literary work. **2** speech or poem addressed to the audience by one of the actors at the beginning of a play. [< Greek *prologos* < *pro-* before + *logos* speech]

promissory note, a written promise to pay a stated sum of money to a certain person at a certain time.

prop a gate (prop′ə gāt), *v.,* **-gat ed, -gat ing.** *—v.i.* produce offspring; reproduce: *Pigions propagate at a fast rate.* *—v.t.* **1** increase in number or intensity; multiply: *Trees propagate themselves by seeds.* **2** cause to increase in number by the production of young: *Cows and sheep are propagated on farms.* **3** spread (news, knowledge, etc.); extend: *Scientists are propagating new theories regarding space travel.* **4** pass on; send further: *Sound is propagated by vibrations.* [< Latin *propagatum* propagated, originally (of plants) multiplied by slips or layering < *pro-* forth + *pagare, pangere* fasten, plant with] **—prop′a ga′tor,** *n.*

pro rogue (prō rōg′), *v.t.,* **-rogued, -rogu ing.** discontinue the regular meetings of (a lawmaking body) for a time. [< Latin *prorogare* defer < *pro-* forward + *rogare* ask for]

pro scribe (prō skrīb′), *v.t.,* **-scribed, -scrib ing. 1** prohibit as wrong or dangerous; condemn: *a religion that proscribes drinking alcohol.* **2** put outside of the protection of the law; outlaw. [< Latin *proscribere* < *pro-* forth + *scribere* write] **—pro scrib′a ble,** *adj.*

pros trate (pros′trāt), *v.,* **-trat ed, -trat ing,** *adj.* *—v.t.* lay down flat; cast down: *The captives prostrated themselves before the conqueror.* *—adj.* **1** lying flat with face downward: *She was humbly prostrate in prayer.* **2** lying flat: *I stumbled and fell prostrate on the floor.* [< Latin *prostratum* thrown down flat < *pro-* forth + *sternere* spread out]

pro vi so (prə vī′zō), *n., pl.* **-sos** or **-soes. 1** clause or article in a contract, treaty, etc., that states a condition. **2** any provision or stipulation: *She was admitted to the eighth grade with the proviso that she was to be put back if she failed any subject.* [< Latin, it being provided < *providere* provide]

pru dence (prüd′ns), *n.* **1** wise thought before acting; good judgment. **2** good management; economy.

psalm (säm, sälm), *n.* **1** a sacred song or poem. **2 Psalm,** any of the 150 sacred songs or hymns that together form a book of the Old Testament. [Old English *psealm* < Late Latin *psalmus* < Greek *psalmos,* originally, performance on a stringed instrument < *psallein* to pluck]

psy cho ther a py (sī′kō ther′ə pē), *n.* treatment of mental or emotional disorders by psychological means. **—psy′cho ther′a pist,** *n.*

quar ter (kwô′tər), *—v.t.* **1** divide into quarters. **2** divide into parts: *quarter a chicken for frying.* **3** give a place to live in; station; lodge. **4** cut the body of (a person) into quarters, as a sign of disgrace after hanging. **5** place or bear (coat of arms, etc.) in quarters of a shield. **6** range over (ground) in every direction in search of game. *—v.i.* **1** live or stay in a place. **2** (of the wind) blow on a ship's quarter. **3** range in every direction.

quince (kwins), *n.* **1** the hard, yellowish, acid, pear-shaped fruit of a small Asiatic tree of the rose family, used for preserves and jelly. **2** tree it grows on [originally plural of Middle English *quyne* < Old French *cooin* < Latin *cotoneum*]

quirt (kwėrt), *n.* a riding whip with a short, stout handle and a lash of braided leather. [< Mexican Spanish *cuarta,* ultimately < Latin *quartus* fourth]

a hat	**i** it	**oi** oil	**ch** child	a in about
ā age	**ī** ice	**ou** out	**ng** long	e in taken
ä far	**o** hot	**u** cup	**sh** she	ə = i in pencil
e let	**ō** open	**ů** put	**th** thin	o in lemon
ē equal	**ô** order	**ü** rule	**ᴛʜ** then	u in circus
ėr term			**zh** measure	< = derived from

rail ler y (rā′lər ē), *n., pl.* **-ler ies. 1** good-humored ridicule; joking; teasing. **2** a bantering remark. [< French *raillerie* < Middle French *railler.*]

ram part (ram′pärt), *n.* **1** a wide bank of earth, often with a wall on top as a fortification, built around a fort to help defend it. **2** anything that defends; defense; protection. [< Middle French *rempart* < *remparer* fortify]

ran cor (rang′kər), *n.* bitter resentment or ill will; extreme hatred or spite. [< Late Latin, rankness < Latin *rancere* be rank]

rank (rangk), *adj.* **1** growing in a thick, coarse way: *a rank growth of weeds.* **2** producing a dense but coarse growth: *rank swampland.* **3** having a strong, bad smell or taste: *rank meat, rank tobacco.*

rapt (rapt), *adj.* **1** lost in delight. **2** so busy thinking of or enjoying one thing that one does not know what else is happening. [< Latin *raptum* seized] **—rapt′ly,** *adv.* **—rapt′ness,** *n.*

re buke (ri byük′), *v.,* **-buked, -buk ing,** *n.* *—v.t.* express disapproval of; reprove. *—n.* expression of disapproval; scolding. [< Anglo-French *rebuker* < Old French *rebuchier* < *re-* back + *buchier* to strike]

rec om pense (rek′əm pens), *v.,* **-pensed, -pens ing,** *n.* *—v.t.* **1** pay (a person); pay back; reward. **2** make a fair return for (an action, anything lost, damage done, or hurt received). *—n.* **1** payment; reward. **2** return; amends. [< Late Latin *recompensare* < Latin *re-* back + *compensare* compensate]

re con sti tute (rē kon′stə tüt, rē kon′stə tyüt), *v.t.,* **-tut ed, -tut ing.** form again; bring back to its original form or consistency: *reconstitute frozen orange juice by adding water.*

re demp tive (ri demp′tiv), *adj.* serving to redeem, make good, or fulfill.

re dun dan cy (ri dun′dən sē), *n., pl.* **-cies. 1** more than is needed. **2** the use of too many words for the same idea; wordiness.

reel rēl), *v.i.* **1** sway, swing, or rock under a blow, shock, etc. **2** sway in standing or walking. **3** be in a whirl; be dizzy. **4** go with swaying or staggering movements.

re frac tor y (ri frak′tər ē), *adj.* **1** hard to manage; stubborn; obstinate: *Mules are refractory.* **2** not yielding readily to treatment: *a refractory cough.*

re it e rate (rē it′ə rāt′), *v.t.,* **-rat ed, -rat ing.** say or do several times; repeat (an action, demand, etc.) again and again: *reiterate a command.* **—re it′e ra′tion,** *n.*

re join der (ri join′dər), *n.* an answer to a reply; response.

re mon strance (ri mon′strəns), *n.* act of remonstrating; protest; complaint.

re past (ri past′), *n.* meal; food. [< Old French, ultimately < Latin *re-* again + *pascere* to feed]

re port (ri pôrt′, ri pōrt′), *n.* **1** account of something seen, heard, read, done, or considered. **2** an account officially or formally expressed, generally in writing. **3** the sound of a shot or an explosion: *the report of a gun.* **4** common talk; rumor: *Report has it that our neighbors are leaving town.* **5** reputation.

re pose (ri pōz′), *n., v.,* **-posed, -pos ing.** *—n.* **1** rest or sleep: *Do not disturb her repose.* **2** quietness; ease: *repose of manner.* **3** peace; calmness. *—v.i.* lie at rest: *The cat reposed upon the cushion.*

res o lute (rez′ə lüt), *adj.* **1** having a fixed resolve; determined; firm. **2** constant in pursuing a purpose; bold. [< Latin *resolutum* resolved] **—res′o lute′ly,** *adv.* **—res′o lute′ness,** *n.*

re solve (ri zolv′), *v.t.,* **-solved, -solv ing.** make up one's mind; determine; decide: *resolve to do better work in the future.*

re stor a tive (ri stôr′ə tiv, ri stōr′ə tiv), *adj.* having to do with or capable of restoring; tending to restore health or strength. *—n.* something that restores health, or consciousness. **—re stor′a tive ly,** *adv.*

re sus ci tate (ri sus′ə tāt), *v.,* **-tat ed, -tat ing.** *—v.t.* **1** bring back to life or consciousness; revive. **2** renew or restore (a thing). *—v.i.* come to life or consciousness again. [< Latin *resuscitare* < *re-* again + *sub-* up + *citare* rouse] **—re sus′ci ta′tion,** *n.*

re tal i a tive (ri tal′ē ā′tiv), *adj.* disposed to retaliate or to strike back.

ret i cent (ret′ə sənt), *adj.* disposed to keep silent or say little; not speaking freely; reserved in speech. [< Latin *reticentem* < *re-* back + *tacere* be silent] **—ret′i cent ly,** *adv.*

ret i cule (ret′ə kyül), *n.* a woman's small handbag, especially one with a drawstring. [< French *réticule*]

ret ro spec tive (ret′rə spek′tiv), *adj.* 1 looking back on things past; surveying past events or experiences. 2 applying to the past; retroactive. **—ret′ro spec′tive ly,** *adv.*

rig or (rig′ər), *n.* 1 strictness; severity: *The new recruits were trained with great rigor.* 2 harshness: *the rigor of a long, cold winter.* 3 chill caused by illness. 4 logical exactness: *the rigor of scientific method.* [< Latin < *rigere* be stiff]

rout (rout), *n.* 1 flight of a defeated army in disorder. 2 a complete defeat. 3 a noisy, disorderly crowd; mob; rabble. [< Middle French, detachment < Popular Latin *rupta* dispersed soldiers, ultimately < Latin *rumpere* to break]

rude (rüd), *adj.*, **rud er, rud est.** 1 not courteous; impolite: *It is rude to stare at people.* 2 roughly made or done; without finish or polish; coarse; crude: *rude tools, a rude sketch.* [< Latin *rudis*] **—rude′ly,** *adv.* **—rude′ness,** *n.*

ru mi nate (rü′mə nāt), *v.*, **-nat ed, -nat ing.** —*v.i.* 1 chew the cud. 2 think or ponder; meditate; reflect: *I ruminated on the strange events of the past week.* —*v.t.* 1 chew again (food which has been previously chewed and swallowed). 2 turn over in the mind; meditate on. **—ru′mi na′tor,** *n.*

sac ri lege (sak′rə lij), *n.* an intentional injury to anything sacred; disrespectful treatment of anyone or anything sacred: *Robbing the church was a sacrilege.* [< Latin *sacrilegium* temple robbery < *sacrum* sacred object + *legere* pick up, gather]

sac ris tan (sak′ri stən), *n.* person in charge of the sacred vessels, robes, etc., of a church. [< Medieval Latin *sacristanus,* ultimately < Latin *sacer* holy.]

sa gac i ty (sə gas′ə tē), *n.* keen, sound judgment; mental acuteness; shrewdness.

san guine (sang′gwən), *adj.* 1 naturally cheerful and hopeful: *a sanguine disposition.* 2 confident; hopeful: *sanguine of success.* [< Latin *sanguineus* < *sanguinem* blood] **—san′guine ly,** *adv.*

scroll (skrōl), *n.* 1 roll of parchment or paper, especially one with writing on it. 2 ornament resembling a partly unrolled sheet of paper, or having a spiral of coiled form. [alteration (influenced by *roll*) of Middle English, *scrow,* ultimately < Old French *escroe* scrap; of Germanic origin] **—scroll′-like′,** *adj.*

scur vy (skėr′vē), *adj.* mean; contemptible; base: *a scurvy fellow, a scurvy trick.* [< scurf] **—scur′vi ly,** *adv.*

sear (sir), *v.t.* 1 burn or char the surface of: *sear a roast.* 2 make hard or unfeeling: *A cruel person must have a seared conscience.* 3 dry up; wither: *The sun seared the grain.* —*v.i.* become dry, burned, or hard. [< Old English *sēarian* < *sēar,* adjective]

se date (si dāt′), *adj.* quiet; serious: *a sedate child who preferred reading to playing.* [< Latin *sedatum,* related to *sedere* sit]

sem blance (sem′bləns), *n.* 1 outward appearance: *Their story had the semblance of truth, but was really false.* 2 likeness: *These clouds have the semblance of a huge head.* [< Old French < *sembler* seem < Latin *similare* make similar < *similis* similar]

sen su ous (sen′shü əs), *adj.* 1 of or derived from the senses; having an effect on the senses; perceived by the senses: *a sensuous love of color.* 2 enjoying the pleasures of the senses.

sen ti nel (sen′tə nəl), *n.* 1 person stationed to keep watch and guard against surprise attacks. 2 **stand sentinel,** act as a sentinel; keep watch. [< Middle French *sentinelle* < Italian *sentinella* <Late Latin *sentinare* avoid danger wisely < Latin *sentire* to feel]

se ques tra tion (sē′kwə strā′shən, si kwes′trā′shən), *n.* 1 the seizing and holding of property until legal claims are satisfied. 2 forcible or authorized seizure; confiscation.

ses sile (ses′əl), *adj.* 1 (in botany) attached by the base instead of by a stem. 2 (in zoology) sedentary; fixed to one spot. Some barnacles are sessile [< Latin *sessilis* sitting < *sedere* sit]

shaft (shaft), *n.* 1 the long, slender stem of an arrow, spear, etc. 2 arrow or spear. 3 something aimed at a person like an arrow or spear: *shafts of ridicule.* 4 ray or beam of light.

sheaf (shēf), *n.*, *pl.* **sheaves,** *v.* —*n.* 1 one of the bundles in which grain is bound after reaping. 2 bundle of things of the same sort bound together or so arranged that they can be bound together: *a sheaf of arrows, a sheaf of papers.* —*v.t.* sheave¹. [Old English *scēaf*] **—sheaf′-like′,** *adj.*

shoat (shōt), *n.* a young pig that no longer suckles.

short shrift, 1 little or no consideration, mercy, or delay: *Violators of these new regulations will get short shrift.*

shrive (shrīv), *v.*, **shrove** or **shrived, shriv en** or **shrived, shriv ing.** ARCHAIC. —*v.t.* 1 hear the confession of and grant forgiveness to. 2 **shrive oneself,** confess one's sins to a priest and receive forgiveness. —*v.i.* 1 make confession. 2 hear confessions. [< Old English *scrīfan* < Latin *scribere* write]

shroud (shroud), *n.* cloth or garment in which a dead person is wrapped or dressed for burial.

sib i lant (sib′ə lənt), *adj.* 1 hissing. 2 produced by forcing the breath stream through a very narrow passage. [< Latin *sibilantem*] **—sib′i lant ly,** *adv.*

siege (sēj), *n.* 1 the surrounding of a fortified place by enemy forces trying to capture it; besieging or a being besieged: *The Japanese laid siege to Corregidor.* 2 any long or persistent effort to overcome resistance; any long-continued attack: *a siege of illness.* [< Old French, seat, siege, ultimately < Latin *sedere* sit]

sol der (sod′ər), *n.* 1 metal or alloy that can be melted and used for joining or mending metal surfaces, parts, etc. 2 anything that unites firmly or joins closely. —*v.t.* 1 fasten, mend, or join with solder. 2 unite firmly; join closely. [< Old French *soldure* < *solder* solidify < Latin *solidare* < *solidus* solid]

so lic i tous (sə lis′ə təs), *adj.* showing care or concern; anxious; concerned: *Parents are solicitous for their children's progress in school* [< Latin *sollicitus* < *sollus* all + *ciere* arouse] **—so lic′i tous ly,** *adv.*

so lu tion (sə lü′shən), *n.* 1 the solving of a problem: *That problem was hard; its solution required many hours.* 2 explanation or answer: *The police are seeking a solution of the crime.*

so no rous (sə nôr′əs, sə nōr′əs), *adj.* 1 giving out or having a deep, loud sound. 2 full and rich in sound. [< Latin *sonorus* < *sonare* to sound < *sonus* sound] **—so no′rous ly,** *adv.* **—so no′rous ness,** *n.*

stealth (stelth), *n.* secret or sly action: *She obtained the letter by stealth, taking it while nobody was in the room.* [< Middle English *stelthe.*]

stilt ed (stil′tid), *adj.* 1 stiffly dignified or formal: *stilted conversation.* 2 raised on or as if on stilts. **—stilt′ed ly,** *adv.*

stone boat *n.* A flat sledge or drag for transporting stones and other heavy articles or when weighted for smoothing tilled soil or breaking clods.

sub-, *prefix.* 1 under; below: *Subnormal = below normal.* 2 down; further; again: *Subdivide = divide again.* 3 near; nearly: *Subtropical =nearly tropical.*

sub mis sive (səb mis′iv), *adj.* yielding to the power, control, or authority of another; obedient; humble. **—sub mis′sive ly,** *adv.* **—sub mis′sive ness,** *n.*

sub stra tum (sub strā′təm, sub strat′əm), *n.*, *pl.* **-ta** or **-tums.** 1 layer lying under another. 2 layer of earth lying just under the surface soil; subsoil. 3 basis; foundation: *The story has a substratum of truth.*

sub tle (sut′l), *adj.*, **-tler, -tlest.** 1 delicate; thin; fine: *a subtle odor of perfume.* 2 so fine or delicate as to elude observation or analysis: *subtle distinctions.* 3 faint; mysterious: *a subtle smile.* 4 discerning; acute: *a subtle mind, subtle reasoning.* 5 sly; crafty; tricky: *a subtle scheme to get some money.* 6 skillful; clever; expert. 7 working unnoticeably or secretly; insidious: *a subtle poison.* Also, **subtile.** [< Old French *soutil* < Latin *subtilis,* originally, woven underneath] **—sub′tle ness,** *n.* **—sub tly** (sut′lē, sut′l ē), *adv.*

sub tle ty (sut′l tē), *n.*, *pl.* **-ties.** 1 subtle quality. 2 something subtle. Also, **subtility** or **subtilty.**

suc cor (suk′ər), *v.t.* help, assist, or aid (a person, etc.). [< Old French *sucurs,* ultimately < Latin *succurrere* run to help < *sub-* up to + *currere* to run] **—suc′cor er,** *n.*

sun der (sun′dər), *v.t.*, *v.i.* put asunder; separate; sever; split. —*n.* **in sunder,** apart. [Old English *sundrian* < *sundor* apart]

sun dry (sun′drē), *adj.* several; various: *From sundry hints, I guessed his age.* [Old English *syndrig* separate < *sundor* apart]

sup pli ca tion (sup′lə kā′shən), *n.* 1 a supplicating. 2 Usually, **supplications,** *pl.* a humble prayer addressed to God or a deity.

swel ter ing (swel′tər ing), *adj.* extremely and unpleasantly hot. **—swel′ter ing ly,** *adv.*

a hat	**i** it	**oi** oil	**ch** child	ə = a in about, e in taken, i in pencil, o in lemon, u in circus
ā age	**ī** ice	**ou** out	**ng** long	
ä far	**o** hot	**u** cup	**sh** she	
e let	**ō** open	**ů** put	**th** thin	
ē equal	**ô** order	**ü** rule	**ᴛʜ** then	
ėr term			**zh** measure	< = derived from

tac i turn (tas′ə tern′), *adj.* speaking very little; not fond of talking. [< Latin *taciturnus* < *tacitum* unspoken, tacit] **—tac′i turn′ly,** *adv.*

tan gi ble (tan′jə bəl), *adj.* 1 that can be touched or felt by touch: *A chair is a tangible object.* 2 real; actual; definite: *a tangible improvement, tangible evidence.* [< Late Latin *tangibilis* < *tangere* to touch] **—tan′gi bil′i ty,** *n.* **—tan′gi ble ness,** *n.*

taut (tôt), *adj.* 1 tightly drawn; tense: *a taut rope.* 2 in neat condition; tidy: *a taut ship.* [Middle English *tought*] **—taut′ly,** *adv.* **—taut′ness.** *n.*

taut en (tôt′n), *v.t., v.i.* make or become taut; tighten.

tem pest (tem′pist), *n.* 1 a violent windstorm, usually accompanied by rain, hail, or snow. 2 a violent disturbance. [< Latin *tempestas* < *tempus* time, season]

te nac i ty (ti nas′ə tē), *n.* 1 firmness in holding fast. 2 stubbornness; persistence.

thwart (thwôrt), *v.t.* prevent from doing something, particularly by blocking the way; oppose and defeat: *Lack of money thwarted the boy's plans for college.*

toad y (tō′dē), *v.,* **toad ied, toad y ing.** *—v.i.* act like a toady. *—v.t.* fawn upon; flatter. [perhaps short for *toadeater*]

toc sin (tok′sən), *n.* 1 alarm sounded on a bell; warning signal. 2 bell used to sound an alarm. [< Middle French < Provençal *tocasenh* < *tocar* strike, touch + *senh* bell]

tor rid (tôr′id, tor′id), *adj.* 1 very hot; burning; scorching: *torrid weather.* 2 exposed or subject to great heat: *torrid deserts.* [< Latin *torridus* < *torrere* to parch] **—tor′rid ly,** *adv.* **—tor′rid ness,** *n.*

touch stone (tuch′stōn′), *n.* 1 a black stone used to test the purity of gold or silver by the color of the streak made on the stone by rubbing it with the metal. 2 any means of testing; a test.

tox ic i ty (tok sis′ə tē), *n., pl.* **-ties.** toxic or poisonous quality.

tran quil ize (trang′kwə līz), *v.,* **-ized, -iz ing.** *—v.t.* make calm, peaceful, or quiet; make tranquil; calm; soothe. *—v.i.* become tranquil. **—tran′quil i za′tion,** *n.*

tran quil li ty or **tran quil i ty** (trang kwil′ə tē), *n.* tranquil condition; calmness; peacefulness; quiet.

trans gress (trans gres′, tranz gres′), *v.i.* break a law, command, etc.; sin. *—v.t.* 1 go contrary to; sin against. 2 go beyond (a limit or bound): *transgress the bounds of good taste.* [< Latin *transgressum* gone beyond < *trans-* + *gradi* to step] **—trans gres′sor,** *n.*

tra verse (*v.* trə vėrs′, trav′ərs), *v.,* **-versed, -vers ing.** *—v.t.* 1 pass across, over, or through: *We traversed the desert.* 2 go to and fro over or along (a place, etc.); cross.

trep i da tion (trep′ə dā′shən), *n.* 1 nervous dread; fear; fright. 2 a trembling. [< Latin *trepidationem* < *trepidare* to tremble < *trepidus* alarmed]

trib u la tion (trib′yə lā′shən), *n.* great trouble; severe trial; affliction. [< Late Latin *tribulationem* < *tribulare* oppress, press < Latin *tribulum* threshing sledge]

tri bu nal (tri byü′nl, trī byü′nl), *n.* 1 court of justice; place of judgment. 2 place where judges sit in a court of law. [< Latin *tribunus.*]

un-, *prefix.* not___; the opposite of___: *Unequal = not equal; the opposite of equal. Unchanged = not changed. Unjust = not just.* [Old English]

un al ien a ble (un ā′lyə nə bəl), *adj.* inalienable; that cannot be given or taken away.

un al ter a ble (un ôl′tər ə bəl), *adj.* that cannot be altered; not changeable; permanent. **—un al′ter a ble ness,** *n.* **—un al′ter a bly,** *adv.*

un can ny (un kan′ē), *adj.* 1 strange and mysterious; weird: *The trees took uncanny shapes in the darkness.* 2 so far beyond what is normal or expected as to have some special power: *an uncanny knack for solving riddles.* **—un can′ni ly,** *adv.* **—un can′ni ness,** *n.*

un fore seen (un′fôr sēn′, un′fōr sēn′), *adj.* not known beforehand; unexpected.

un sa vor y (un sā′vər ē), *adj.* 1 tasteless. 2 unpleasant in taste or smell; distasteful: *an unsavory medicine.* 3 morally unpleasant; offensive: *an unsavory reputation.*

un scathed (un skāᴛʜd′), *adj.* not harmed; uninjured.

un scru pu lous (un skrü′pyə ləs), *adj.* not careful about right or wrong; without principles or conscience.

val iant (val′yənt), *adj.* having or showing courage; brave; courageous: *a valiant soldier, a valiant deed.* [< Old French *vaillant,* present participle of *valoir* be strong < Latin *valere*] **—val′iant ly,** *adv.*

val or (val′ər), *n.* bravery; courage. [< Late Latin < Latin *valere* be strong]

veer (vir), *v.i.* change in direction; shift; turn: *The wind veered to the south. The talk veered to ghosts.* *—v.t.* change the direction of: *We veered our boat.* *—n.* a change of direction; shift; turn. [< Middle French *virer*] **—veer′ing** ly, *adv.*

ver mil ion or **ver mil lion** (vər mil′yən), *adj.* bright-red. [< Old French *vermillon* < *vermeil*]

ves tige (ves′tij), *n.* 1 a slight remnant; trace; mark: *Ghost stories are vestiges of a former widespread belief in ghosts.*

vin di cate (vin′də kāt), *v.t.,* **-cat ed, -cat ing.** 1 clear from suspicion, dishonor, a hint or charge of wrongdoing, etc.: *The verdict of "Not guilty" vindicated him.* 2 defend successfully against opposition; uphold; justify: *The heir vindicated his claim to the fortune.* 3 assert a claim to; establish possession of.

vis age (viz′ij), *n.* 1 face. 2 appearance or aspect. [< Old French < *vis* face < Latin *visus* sight < *videre* to see]

vi va cious (vī vā′shəs, vi vā′shəs), *adj.* lively; sprightly; animated; gay. **—vi va′cious ly,** *adv.* **—vi va′cious ness,** *n.*

wall eyed (wôl′īd′), *adj.* 1 having eyes that show much white and little color. 2 having one or both eyes turned away from the nose, so as to show much white. 3 having large, staring eyes, as a fish. [< Scandinavian (Old Icelandic) *vagl-eygr* < *vagl* speck in the eye + *auga* eye]

wal low (wol′ō), *v.i.* roll about; flounder: *The pigs wallowed in the mud. The boat wallowed helplessly in the stormy sea.* [Old English *wealwian* to roll] **—wal′low er,** *n.*

weal (wēl), *n.* well-being; prosperity: *Good citizens act for the public weal.* [Old English *wela* wealth, welfare]

whet (hwet), *v.,* **whet ted, whet ting,** *n.* *—v.t.* 1 sharpen by rubbing: *whet a knife.* 2 make keen or eager; stimulate: *The smell of food whetted my appetite.* *—n.* 1 act of whetting. 2 something that whets. 3 appetizer. [Old English *hwettan*] **—whet′ter,** *n.*

whim (hwim), *n.* a sudden fancy or notion; freakish or capricious idea or desire: *My cousin has a whim for gardening, but it won't last long.* [perhaps < Scandinavian (Old Icelandic) *hvim* unsteady look]

withe (wīᴛʜ, with, wiᴛʜ), *n.* 1 a willow twig. 2 any tough, easily bent twig suitable for binding or tying things together. [Old English *withthe*]

wry (rī), *adj.,* **wri er, wri est.** 1 turned to one side; twisted: *She made a wry face to show her disgust.* 2 ironic: *wry humor.* [ultimately < Old English *wrīgian* to turn] **—wry′ly,** *adv.*

Index of Reading and Literature Skills

Index of Vocabulary Exercises

Combined skills exercises

Index of Composition Assignments

Personal

Explanatory

Creative

Critical

Index of Authors and Titles

Illustration Acknowledgments

Illustration not credited is from Scott, Foresman.

Unit 1

1—Valerie Jaudon / Courtesy Sidney Janis Gallery, NYC; **3**—Tony Pupkewitz; **17**—Franz Altschuler; **21, 33**—Tom Adams; **37**—*The American Country Woman* by Dorthea Lange / Courtesy Amon Carter Museum, Ft. Worth, Texas; **43**—William A. Bake; **51**—Dr. M. D. Constable; **62**—Tom Heflin.

Unit 2

66, 67—Harriet Kittay / Courtesy The Sutton Gallery, 29 W. 57th St., NYC; **71**—Courtesy American Foundation for the Blind; **79**—Brown Brothers; **85, 92**—Arthur Kantor; **113**—Photograph by George Grantham Bain. Courtesy *Vanity Fair.* Copyright © 1919 (renewed 1947) by The Condé Nast Publications, Inc.; **119**—Arthur Kantor; **125**—From *In Ruins* by Duncan McLaren, Copyright © 1980 Duncan McLaren, Photographs Copyright © 1980 Simon Marsden. A Borzoi Book published by Alfred A. Knopf, Inc. Reproduced by permission.

Unit 3

128, 129—Mike Cauthen; **130**—Peter Read Miller / Focus West; **132**—Chicago Tribune; **136**—Dr. Robert G. Thompson; **141**—Robert Amft; **143**—Gjon Mili, *Life* Magazine © 1980 Time, Inc.; **147**—Tom Heflin, Rockford, IL; **149**—Man Ray; *Face, 1920* / Vera and Arturo Schwarz Collection, Milan, photographed by S. A. D. E. (Surrealism & Dada, Even) Archives, Milan; **152**—James A. Warner from *The Darker Brother;* **154**—Jerry Uelsmann; **158**—Franz Altschuler; **163**—Dan Morrill; **164**—From *Old Possum's Book of Practical Cats,* copyright 1939 by T. S. Eliot, copyright renewed © 1967 by Esme Valerie Eliot. Illustrations copyright © 1982 by Edward Gorey. Reprinted by permission of Harcourt Brace Jovanovich; **170**—Tony Kelly.

Unit 4

All photographs by Robert C. Ragsdale, A. R. P. S., from Stratford Festival, Canada, 1977.

Unit 5

268, 269—Valerie Jaudon / Courtesy Sidney Janis Gallery NYC; **274**—© Frank C. McCarthy; **281**—© Tjelda Michas 1983; **292**—Lee Boltin; **303**—Library of Congress; **307**—Dan Morrill; **314**—Photo by Ernst Haas; **323, 329**—Courtesy Hallmark, Inc.; **335**—Tom Adams; **349**—© Adolahe / Southern Light; **362, 363**—Illustration of dragon from p. 88, 89 by Wayne Anderson in *The Flight of Dragons* by Peter Dickinson. Illustration copyright © 1979 by Wayne Anderson. Reprinted by permission of Harper & Row, Publishers, Inc.; **367**—William A. Bake; **374, 375**—From *Alien Landscapes* by Malcolm Edwards and Robert Holdstock. Copyright (text) 1979 by Malcolm Edwards and Robert Holdstock. Copyright (Illustrations) 1979 by Young Artists. Published by Mayflower Books, Inc. Reproduced by permission.

Unit 6

All photographs of *Antigone* by Jennifer Girard; **380**—Photograph from The Guthrie Theatre Company's production of *The House of Atreus,* directed by Sir Tyrone Guthrie, designed by Tanya Moiseiwitsch. Courtesy The Guthrie Theatre, Minneapolis / St. Paul.

Unit 7

422, 423—Robert Amft; **425**—From *Treasury of American Design, National Gallery of Art;* **433**—Photograph by John T. Hill; **437**—Robert Amft; **443**—Reprinted from *The Saturday Evening Post* © 1932 The Curtis Publishing Company; **452**—© *Beeldrecht,* Amsterdam / V. A. G. A. , New York, Collection Haags Gemeentemusem—The Hague, 1981; **457**—© Robert Llewellyn; **462**—Courtesy Mary Welsh Hemingway.

Unit 8

All illustrations for *A Tale of Two Cities* by Ronald Searle; p. 565, Rizzoli Editore, Milan.

Handbook

637—From *Sherlock Holmes Investigates, Stories by Sir Arthur Conan Doyle,* selected and introduced by Michael and Mollie Hardwick, with Sidney Paget illustrations. Published by Lothrop, Lee & Shepard Co., Inc. Reproduced by permission; **647**—Don Carroll; **654**—© Michael de Camp; **661**—Tom Adams.